CBR Computer Book Review (1984)
CBRS Children's Book Review Service (1979)
CC Christian Century
CCB-B Center for Children's Books. Bulletin
CE Childhood Education
CF Canadian Forum
CG Canadian Geographic (Formerly Canadian Geographical Journal)
CGJ Canadian Geographical Journal
CH Church History
CHE Chronicle of Higher Education (1977)
CLS Comparative Literature Studies (1976)
CLW Catholic Library World
CM Carleton Miscellany
CP Contemporary Psychology (1975)
CR Contemporary Review
CRL College and Research Libraries
CS Contemporary Sociology (1976)
CSM Christian Science Monitor
CT Children Today (Formerly Children)
CW Classical World
Can Child Lit Canadian Children's Literature (1980)
Cath W Catholic World (1969-1971)
Cha Ti Changing Times (1977)
Child Lit Children's Literature (1981)
Choice Choice
Class Out Classical Outlook (1981)
Cng Change (1978)
Col Lit College Literature (1980)
Comp L Comparative Literature
Comt Commentary
Comw Commonweal
Conn Connoisseur
Cont Ed Contemporary Education (1976)
Cr Crafts Creative Crafts and Miniatures
Cr H Craft Horizons
Cres Cresset
Crit Critic
Critm Criticism
Critiq Critique
Cu H Current History (1977)
Cur R Curriculum Review
DN Dance News (1975)
Daedalus Daedalus (1976)
Dance Dancemagazine
Des Design (1975)
Dis Dissent
Dr Drama: the Quarterly Theatre Review
EHR English Historical Review
EJ English Journal
EL Educational Leadership
ES Educational Studies (1977)
Earth S Earth Science (1978)
Econ Economist
Econ. Survey Economist. Survey
Edu D Educational Digest (Canada 1977)
Emerg Lib Emergency Librarian (1981)
Enc Encounter

Esq [illegible]
Essence Essence [illegible]
Ethics Ethics (1977)
FC Film Comment (1977)
FQ Film Quarterly
FR French Review (1975)
Fant R Fantasy Review (1984)
Fine Pt Fine Print (1981)
Fly Flying
Fut Futurist (1978)
GJ Geographical Journal
GP Growing Point (1975)
GT Grade Teacher
GW Guardian Weekly
Ga R Georgia Review
Ger Q German Quarterly (1975)
HAHR Hispanic American Historical Review (1975)
HB Horn Book Magazine
H Beh Human Behavior (1976)
HE Human Events (1977)
HER Harvard Educational Review
HLR Harvard Law Review
HM Harper's Magazine
HR Hudson Review
HRNB History: Reviews of New Books (1975)
HT History Today
Har Bus R Harvard Business Review (1978)
Hi Lo High/Low Report (1980-1983)
Hisp Hispania
Historian Historian (1980)
Hob Hobbies
Hort Horticulture
Hum Humanist
ILN Illustrated London News (1977)
ILR International Labour Review
ILRR Industrial and Labor Relations Review
In Rev In Review: Canadian Books For Young People (1980)
Indexer The Indexer (1980)
Inst Instructor
Inter BC Interracial Books for Children Bulletin (1979)
JAF Journal of American Folklore
JAH Journal of American History
JAL Journal of Academic Librarianship (1975)
JAS Journal of Asian Studies
J Am St Journal of American Studies (1982)
JB Junior Bookshelf (1975)
JBL Journal of Biblical Literature (1977)
JC Journal of Communication (1980)
JE Journal of Education (1977)
JEGP Journal of English and Germanic Philology
JEH Journal of Economic History
JGE Journal of General Education
J Geront Journal of Gerontology (1984)
JHI Journal of the History of Ideas
J Ho E Journal of Home Economics
JLD Journal of Learning Disabilities (1975)

(Continued on back endsheets)

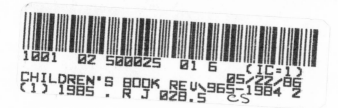

Children's Book Review Index

Master Cumulation 1965-1984

Related Gale titles include

Book Review Index series:

Periodical issues. Six bimonthly issues (February, April, June, August, October, December) with every other issue cumulating the previous issue. Annual subscription.

Annual hardbound cumulations. Each cumulation contains in a single alphabet all citations from the previous year's periodical issues.

1965-1984 Cumulation. Ten volumes present more than 1,605,000 review citations in a single alphabet. Includes Title Index.

Children's Book Review Index series:

Annual hardbound volumes. *CBRI* indexes all reviews of children's books appearing in the periodicals indexed by *BRI*.

ISSN 0147-5681

Children's Book Review Index

Master Cumulation 1965-1984

A Cumulated Index to More Than 200,000 Reviews of Approximately 55,000 Titles

In Five Volumes

Volume 2: E-K

Gary C. Tarbert
and
Barbara Beach
Editors

GALE RESEARCH COMPANY • BOOK TOWER • DETROIT, MICHIGAN 48226

Library of Congress Catalog Card Number 75-27408
ISBN 0-8103-2046-0
ISSN 0147-5681

Computerized photocomposition by
Computer Composition Corporation
Madison Heights, Michigan

Printed in the United States of America

Contents

Children's Book Review Index

E

EADINGTON, Joan
The Adventures Of Jonny Briggs
ILN-v267-D '79-p141
JB-v44-F '80-p20
Lis-v102-N 8 '79-p644
Jonny Briggs And The Galloping Wedding
GP-v22-My '83-p4088
Jonny Briggs And The Ghost
GP-v17-S '78-p3394
Jonny Briggs And The Giant Cave
GP-v21-My '82-p3887
Jonny Briggs And The Whitby Weekend
B&B-v24-Je '79-p60
GP-v18-Jl '79-p3539

* * *

EAGAN, Andrea Boroff
Why Am I So Miserable If These Are The Best Years Of My Life?
BL-v72-Ap 1 '76-p1102
BL-v76-D 15 '79-p604
EJ-v67-Ja '78-p91
EJ-v69-Ja '80-p79
HB-v52-Ag '76-p410
KR-v44-My 1 '76-p543
Kliatt-v11-Spring '77-p24
PW-v209-Je 21 '76-p91
SLJ-v23-S '76-p132
WLB-v54-Ja '80-p327

* * *

EAGAR, Frances
Midnight Patrol
GP-v13-Mr '75-p2578
Time Tangle
CCB-B-v31-N '77-p45
CLW-v49-D '77-p234
GP-v15-My '76-p2880
KR-v45-My 15 '77-p539
LA-v55-Mr '78-p371
SLJ-v24-O '77-p88

* * *

EAGER, Edward
Half Magic
CSM-v67-Je 10 '75-p16
Knight's Castle
CSM-v67-Je 10 '75-p16
Magic Or Not
BW-Jl 8 '79-pE2

* * *

EAGER, Fred
Italic Handwriting For Young People
Teacher-v96-My '79-p127

* * *

EAGLES
TES-O 1 '82-p47

* * *

EAMES, K
Whatever Comes To Mind
TES-F 4 '83-p28

* * *

EARLE, Alice Morse
Home And Child Life In Colonial Days
BL-v65-Jl 15 '69-p1278
KR-v37-Ap 15 '69-p464
LJ-v95-Ja 15 '70-p248
NYTBR-Jl 6 '69-p16
RT-v32-Ja '79-p446

* * *

EARLE, Olive L
Animals And Their Ears
ACSB-v8-Fall '75-p9
KR-v42-Mr 15 '74-p305
LJ-v99-S 15 '74-p2266
SB-v10-D '74-p256
Nuts
ACSB-v8-Fall '75-p9
BL-v71-Mr 15 '75-p749
CCB-B-v29-O '75-p26
KR-v43-Mr 1 '75-p241
SLJ-v21-My '75-p54
Pond And Marsh Plants
BL-v68-My 15 '72-p820
CCB-B-v26-N '72-p41
CLW-v43-My '72-p535
KR-v40-F 1 '72-p138
LJ-v97-S 15 '72-p2948
SB-v8-S '72-p142
Praying Mantis
BL-v65-Ap 15 '69-p959
CCB-B-v23-Ja '70-p79
CE-v46-F '70-p267
CLW-v41-My '70-p592
KR-v37-F 1 '69-p102
LJ-v94-Ap 15 '69-p1767
NYTBR, pt.2-My 4 '69-p48
SB-v5-My '69-p55
The Rose Family
BL-v66-My 1 '70-p1098
CCB-B-v24-Jl '70-p175
KR-v38-F 1 '70-p106
SB-v6-My '70-p69
SR-v53-My 9 '70-p45
Scavengers
CCB-B-v26-My '73-p136
KR-v41-Ja 1 '73-p8
LJ-v98-Jl '73-p2192
PW-v203-F 19 '73-p79
Strange Companions In Nature
BL-v62-Ap 15 '66-p830
CCB-B-v20-S '66-p7
CE-v43-Ap '67-p480
KR-v34-Ja 1 '66-p8
LJ-v91-Mr 15 '66-p1698
SB-v2-My '66-p41

* * *

EARLE, Sylvia A
Exploring The Deep Frontier
ASBYP-v14-Fall '81-p17
BL-v77-O 1 '80-p195
CCB-B-v34-Je '81-p191

EARLE, Sylvia A (continued)
LJ-v105-S 1 '80-p1743
SB-v16-My '81-p271
SLJ-v27-F '81-p83

* * *

EARLE, Vana
The Big League Book Of Baseball Fun
PW-v221-Mr 26 '82-p74
SLJ-v28-My '82-p88

* * *

EARLY Career Books
Cur R-v23-Ap '84-p21

* * *

EARLY Learning Foundation
TES-Ag 8 '80-p30

* * *

EARLY Man (Piccolo Factbooks)
TES-Ap 16 '82-p24

* * *

EARN, Josephine
Looking At Canada
BL-v73-My 1 '77-p1349
SLJ-v24-D '77-p48

* * *

EARNSHAW, Brian
Dragonfall 5 And The Empty Planet
BL-v72-My 15 '76-p1335
KR-v44-Mr 15 '76-p321
SLJ-v23-S '76-p115
TLS-Je 15 '73-p687
TLS-N 20 '81-p1361
Dragonfall 5 And The Haunted World
JB-v43-O '79-p270
Sch Lib-v27-D '79-p370
Dragonfall 5 And The Hijackers
B&B-v20-My '75-p81
Dragonfall 5 And The Master-Mind
GP-v14-Mr '76-p2819
TES-Jl 22 '83-p21
TLS-S 19 '75-p1058
Dragonfall 5 And The Royal Beast
KR-v43-N 1 '75-p1228
SLJ-v22-F '76-p44
Dragonfall 5 And The Space Cowboys
JB-v39-F '75-p37
KR-v43-F 1 '75-p121
PW-v207-F 24 '75-p116
SLJ-v21-My '75-p54
SLJ-v23-D '76-p30
TLS-N 20 '81-p1361
Dragonfall 5 And The Super Horse
GP-v16-D '77-p3225

* * *

EARTH (Look It Up)
JB-v44-Je '80-p129
Sch Lib-v28-Mr '80-p49

* * *

EARTH: The Weather
Sch Lib-v31-D '83-p367

* * *

EARTHWORM
TES-N 16 '79-p30

* * *

EAST, Ben
Danger In The Air
SLJ-v26-Ap '80-p108
Desperate Search
BL-v77-Ap 15 '81-p1142
SLJ-v26-Ap '80-p108
Forty Days Lost
BL-v77-O 15 '80-p309
SLJ-v26-Ap '80-p108
Found Alive
CCB-B-v33-My '80-p170
SLJ-v26-Ap '80-p108
Grizzly!
SLJ-v26-Ap '80-p108
Mistaken Journey
SLJ-v26-Ap '80-p108
Survival
BL-v64-D 1 '67-p415
Cur R-v19-N '80-p443
LJ-v92-O 15 '67-p3874
Trapped In Devil's Hole
BL-v77-O 15 '80-p309
SLJ-v26-Ap '80-p108

* * *

EAST, Helen
Henry's House
Sch Lib-v30-Mr '82-p31
Louisa's Garden
GP-v20-N '81-p3981
Sch Lib-v30-Mr '82-p31
Maria Goes To Work
Sch Lib-v30-Mr '82-p31
Michael Goes Shopping
GP-v20-N '81-p3981
Sch Lib-v30-Mr '82-p31
Sara By The Seashore
Sch Lib-v30-Mr '82-p31

* * *

EAST, Katherine
A King's Treasure
Brit Bk N C-Autumn '82-p28
JB-v46-Ag '82-p141
TES-D 24 '82-p25
The Sutton Hoo Ship Burial
TES-N 5 '82-p22

* * *

EASTMAN, David
The Adventure Of The Empty House
SLJ-v29-N '82-p81
The Adventure Of The Speckled Band
SLJ-v29-N '82-p81
The Final Problem
SLJ-v29-N '82-p81
The Red-Headed League
SLJ-v29-N '82-p81
Sherlock Holmes: The Adventure Of The Empty House
RT-v36-Mr '83-p700
Sherlock Holmes: The Adventure Of The Speckled Band
RT-v36-Mr '83-p700
Sherlock Holmes: The Final Problem
RT-v36-Mr '83-p700
Sherlock Holmes: The Red-Headed League
RT-v36-Mr '83-p700
Story Of Dinosaurs
ASBYP-v15-Fall '82-p57
BL-v78-Je 1 '82-p1311
SLJ-v28-Ap '82-p57
What Is A Fish
ASBYP-v15-Fall '82-p57
BL-v78-Je 1 '82-p1311
SLJ-v28-Ag '82-p95

* * *

EASTMAN, P D
Are You My Mother?
ASBYP-v17-Spring '84-p6
SLJ-v25-My '79-p38
SR-v55-D 9 '72-p76
Sch Lib-v30-D '82-p324
The Best Nest
CSM-v60-N 7 '68-pB5
LJ-v93-N 15 '68-p4425
Learning-v12-Ap '84-p50

EASTMAN, P D (continued)
TLS-D 4 '69-p1396
The Cat In The Hat Beginner Book Dictionary In French
CSM-v57-N 4 '65-pB5
LJ-v90-O 15 '65-p4612
The Cat In The Hat Beginner Dictionary
NYTBR, pt.2-My 6 '73-p37
Cat In The Hat Dictionary In French
Punch-v253-N 29 '67-p835
Everything Happens To Aaron
Inst-v87-N '77-p152
Flap Your Wings
PW-v225-Mr 30 '84-p57
SLJ-v30-Ag '84-p37
Go, Dog, Go!
SLJ-v28-F '82-p37
Sch Lib-v30-D '82-p324
TLS-Je 17 '65-p507
Perro Grande...Perro Pequeno/Big Dog...Little Dog
BL-v78-Jl '82-p1438
SLJ-v29-S '82-p103
SLJ-v29-Mr '83-p91

* * *

EASTMAN, Patricia
Sometimes Things Change
BL-v80-F 15 '84-p862
SLJ-v30-Mr '84-p142

* * *

EASTON, Lois B
Expressways
Cur R-v20-Ap '81-p164

* * *

EASTWICK, Ivy O
Seven Little Popovers
CCB-B-v33-Ap '80-p150

* * *

EASY Learning
TES-Mr 16 '84-p31

* * *

EATON, Elizabeth
Cook And Bake
GP-v14-N '75-p2746

* * *

EATON, Jeanette
Gandhi: Fighter Without A Sword
TN-v35-Summer '79-p403

* * *

EATON, Seymour
The Roosevelt Bears
NYTBR-Ja 6 '80-p31
The Roosevelt Bears Go To Washington
PW-v220-N 27 '81-p88

* * *

EATON, Su
Punch And Judy In The Rain
TES-Jl 27 '84-p21

* * *

EBERLE, Bob
Chip In
Cur R-v22-F '83-p23

* * *

EBERLE, Irmengarde
Pandas Live Here
BL-v69-Je 15 '73-p988
CCB-B-v26-Je '73-p152
KR-v41-Ap 1 '73-p389
LJ-v98-Jl '73-p2192
NYTBR-Jl 1 '73-p8
Penguins Live Here
ACSB-v8-Fall '75-p10
BL-v71-D 15 '74-p423
CCB-B-v28-D '74-p60
Inst-v84-My '75-p97
KR-v43-Ja 1 '75-p20
NYTBR-My 4 '75-p45
SB-v11-My '75-p37
SLJ-v21-Mr '75-p94
Prairie Dogs In Prairie Dog Town
ACSB-v8-Winter '75-p14
CCB-B-v28-Mr '75-p111
KR-v42-Mr 1 '74-p247
SB-v10-Mr '75-p340

* * *

EBERTS, Marjorie
Word Wise
Cur R-v21-F '82-p53

* * *

EBONY Jr!
BL-v79-F 1 '83-p729
BW-My 1 '77-pE4
CE-v59-My '83-p369
Mag Lib- '82-p216

* * *

EBY, Cecil
Siege Of The Alcazar
BL-v62-D 15 '65-p393
KR-v33-S 1 '65-p973
LJ-v90-D 1 '65-p5270

* * *

ECHEVERRIA, Eugenia
Las Frutas
BL-v79-F 15 '83-p783

* * *

ECKE, W
The Face At The Window
JB-v43-F '79-p49

* * *

ECKE, Wolfgang
The Bank Holdup
BL-v78-Ag '82-p1524
SLJ-v29-S '82-p119
The Invisible Witness
CBRS-v9-Je '81-p96
CCB-B-v35-S '81-p8
EJ-v72-F '83-p99
RT-v36-O '82-p76
SLJ-v28-S '81-p124
VOYA-v5-Ap '82-p33
The Magnet Detective Book
GP-v18-N '79-p3602
The Stolen Paintings
CBRS-v10-Ja '82-p47
CCB-B-v35-Mr '82-p126
CLW-v53-Ap '82-p401
SLJ-v28-D '81-p81

* * *

ECKER, B A
Independence Day
BL-v79-My 15 '83-p1196
Inter BC-v14-#7 '83-p36
SLJ-v30-S '83-p132
VOYA-v6-O '83-p200

* * *

ECKERT, Allan W
Blue Jacket
BL-v65-Ap 15 '69-p960
HB-v45-Ap '69-p193
KR-v37-Ap 15 '69-p460
LJ-v94-S 15 '69-p3216
NYTBR-S 21 '69-p30
PW-v195-Mr 10 '69-p74
TN-v25-Je '69-p433
The Dark Green Tunnel
BL-v80-Ap 1 '84-p1114
BW-v14-N 11 '84-p14
CCB-B-v37-Je '84-p185
PW-v225-Je 15 '84-p83
SLJ-v30-Ag '84-p72
Incident At Hawk's Hill
A Lib-v3-Ap '72-p419
B&B-v18-F '73-p120

ECKERT, Allan W (continued)
BL-v67-Jl 15 '71-p930
BL-v68-Ap 1 '72-p669
BS-v31-Jl 15 '71-p191
CCB-B-v25-Ap '72-p121
CE-v48-My '72-p421
CSM-v64-My 2 '72-p4
Cur R-v22-F '83-p83
GT-v89-My '72-p57
Inst-v82-N '72-p136
KR-v39-Mr 1 '71-p252
LJ-v96-Je 15 '71-p2105
Lis-v88-N 9 '72-p644
NS-v84-N 10 '72-p694
NYTBR-My 23 '71-p47
Obs-D 3 '72-p38
PW-v199-F 8 '71-p79
TLS-N 3 '72-p1322
Teacher-v90-Ja '73-p90
Song Of The Wild
BL-v77-O 1 '80-p205
BW-v11-Mr 8 '81-p11
CCB-B-v34-D '80-p69
KR-v48-S 1 '80-p1175
LJ-v105-N 15 '80-p2431
PW-v218-O 3 '80-p56
SLJ-v27-Mr '81-p156

* * *

ECKERT, Horst
Animal Antics
GP-v21-Mr '83-p4032
JB-v47-F '83-p26
The Big Janosch Book Of Fun And Verse
GP-v19-Ja '81-p3822
JB-v45-F '81-p20
Obs-D 7 '80-p31
Obs-Jl 19 '81-p29
Crafty Caspar And His Good Old Granny
JB-v44-O '80-p232
The Cricket And The Mole
Obs-My 8 '83-p31
Hey Presto! You're A Bear!
BL-v77-S 15 '80-p115
JB-v42-F '78-p17
KR-v48-N 1 '80-p1392
PW-v218-Jl 18 '80-p62
SLJ-v27-F '81-p57
Spec-v239-D 10 '77-p25
TES-N 18 '77-p39
Komm, Wir Finden Einen Schatz
TLS-Mr 28 '80-p358
A Letter For Tiger
GP-v20-My '81-p3893
JB-v45-D '81-p243
The Magic Auto
CCB-B-v25-F '72-p93
KR-v40-Ja 1 '72-p1
LJ-v97-My 15 '72-p1903
PW-v200-D 6 '71-p53
The Mole And The Cricket
Can Child Lit-#26 '82-p92
Emerg Lib-v9-My '82-p28
Not Quite As Grimm
B&B-v20-F '75-p79
GP-v13-Ja '75-p2552
JB-v39-F '75-p40
Obs-D 1 '74-p35
The Rain Car
GP-v17-N '78-p3426
JB-v43-F '79-p19
Rate Mal Wer Suchen Muss
BL-v75-D 1 '78-p622
Schlafe, Lieber Hampelmann
BL-v75-D 1 '78-p622
The Treasure-Hunting Trip
GP-v19-My '80-p3710
Obs-Ap 6 '80-p39
The Trip To Panama
CBRS-v10-Jl '81-p112
JB-v42-O '78-p251
Obs-Jl 16 '78-p26
RT-v36-O '82-p66
SLJ-v28-O '81-p130
Zampano's Performing Bear
JB-v40-O '76-p263

* * *

ECKSTEIN, Gustav
The Body Has A Head
BL-v66-My 15 '70-p1127
BL-v66-Je 1 '70-p1206
BS-v29-Mr 1 '70-p441
BW-v4-Mr 22 '70-p14
Cath W-v211-Jl '70-p184
Choice-v7-Je '70-p567
HB-v46-O '70-p501
KR-v37-N 15 '69-p1234
LJ-v95-F 1 '70-p504
Life-v68-F 20 '70-p12
NW-v75-Mr 2 '70-p88
NYTBR-v85-Jl 27 '80-p27
Obs-S 12 '71-p29
PW-v196-N 24 '69-p42
SB-v6-S '70-p153
WSJ-v175-Mr 31 '70-p20
Everyday Miracle
BL-v61-Jl 1 '65-p1028
CCB-B-v19-My '66-p148
KR-v33-Mr 1 '65-p247
LJ-v90-Ap 15 '65-p2030
NH-v74-N '65-p15
NYTBR-v70-My 9 '65-p36
Lives
GP-v21-Ja '83-p4025

* * *

ECKSTEIN, Joan
Fun With Growing Things
CE-v52-Mr '76-p272
PW-v208-Ag 4 '75-p57
SLJ-v22-N '75-p74

* * *

ECONOMAKIS, Olga
Oasis Of The Stars
CCB-B-v19-D '65-p61
CE-v43-N '66-p166
Comw-v83-N 5 '65-p155
HB-v41-O '65-p493
KR-v33-Ag 1 '65-p747
LJ-v90-D 15 '65-p5500
NYTBR-v70-N 7 '65-p63

* * *

EDAD Antigua
BL-v72-My 15 '76-p1342

* * *

EDDERSHAW, David
Homes
TES-O 21 '77-p18

* * *

EDDISON, Jill
The World Of The Changing Coastline
GP-v18-S '79-p3575
JB-v43-D '79-p333
Sch Lib-v28-Mr '80-p71

* * *

EDELMAN, Elaine
Boom-De-Boom
BL-v77-O 1 '80-p208
CBRS-v8-Ag '80-p131
NW-v96-D 1 '80-p103
PW-v218-O 3 '80-p66
RT-v34-Ap '81-p854
RT-v37-Ap '84-p702
SLJ-v27-F '81-p56
I Love My Baby Sister: Most Of The Time
BL-v81-S 1 '84-p63
CBRS-v13-O '84-p13
HB-v60-S '84-p579

* * *

EDELSON, Edward
Great Animals Of The Movies
BL-v77-S 15 '80-p114

EDELSON, Edward
(continued)
RT-v34-Mr '81-p736
SLJ-v27-Ag '81-p64
Great Kids Of The Movies
CCB-B-v33-O '79-p26
KR-v47-Ag 1 '79-p856
SLJ-v26-S '79-p134
Great Monsters Of The Movies
HB-v49-Je '73-p279
Inst-v82-My '73-p69
KR-v41-Je 1 '73-p602
LJ-v98-O 15 '73-p3144
PT-v8-F '75-p21
Great Movie Spectaculars
BL-v73-Ap 1 '77-p1165
SLJ-v23-Ja '77-p100
Great Science Fiction From The Movies
Teacher-v93-Ap '76-p125
Visions Of Tomorrow
BL-v71-My 1 '75-p912
KR-v43-Ja 15 '75-p72
PW-v207-Mr 31 '75-p50
SLJ-v21-Ap '75-p63
Teacher-v93-Ap '76-p40

* * *

EDEN, M
Soils And Plants
TES-N 16 '84-p27

* * *

EDEN, Michael
Islands
JB-v47-D '83-p243
SLJ-v30-Ag '84-p72
Sch Lib-v31-D '83-p369
TES-D 2 '83-p40
Rain-Forests
GP-v21-My '82-p3903
JB-v46-Je '82-p97
TES-Mr 12 '82-p36
Rivers
GP-v21-My '82-p3903
JB-v46-Je '82-p97
Sch Lib-v30-Mr '82-p40
TES-Mr 12 '82-p36
Weather
TES-N 5 '82-p22
TES-D 17 '82-p28

* * *

EDENS, Cooper
Caretakers Of Wonder
CBRS-v9-Winter '81-p41
CSM-v74-O 8 '82-pB6
PW-v218-N 28 '80-p51
VLS-O '82-p7
If You're Afraid Of The Dark, Remember The Night Rainbow
NW-v102-D 5 '83-p111
PW-v215-My 21 '79-p70
SLJ-v26-O '79-p138
The Star Cleaner Reunion
CSM-v74-O 8 '82-pB6
NW-v102-D 5 '83-p111
SLJ-v26-N '79-p64
VLS-O '82-p7
With Secret Friends
SLJ-v28-Ag '82-p114

* * *

EDET, Edna Smith
The Griot Sings
Inter BC-v10-My 50 '79-p21
LJ-v104-D 15 '79-p2627

* * *

EDEY, Maitland A
The Sea Traders
SB-v11-My '75-p40

* * *

EDGAR, Frank
Hausa Tales And Traditions
Choice-v15-Ap '78-p241
J Read-v25-Mr '82-p519
Hausa Tales And Traditions. Vol. 1
A Anth-v75-Ag '73-p1046
JAF-v84-Ap '71-p249

* * *

EDGAR, Marriot
Albert Comes Back
Brit Bk N C-Spring '81-p18
GP-v19-Ja '81-p3822
JB-v45-Je '81-p113
The Lion And Albert
GP-v17-Ja '79-p3448
JB-v42-Ap '78-p87
JB-v43-F '79-p16
Spec-v239-Jl 16 '77-p23
TLS-D 1 '78-p1397

* * *

EDINBURGH
FC-v15-Ja '79-p69
TES-Ag 20 '82-p21

* * *

EDLER, Tim
Maurice The Snake And Gaston The Near-Sighted Turtle
RT-v36-D '82-p265

* * *

EDLIN, Herbert L
Atlas Of Plant Life
B&B-v20-Ja '75-p80
BL-v70-Ja 1 '74-p488
CCB-B-v27-Mr '74-p109
Inst-v83-N '73-p127
LJ-v98-D 1 '73-p3569
LJ-v99-Ap 15 '74-p1099
RSR-v2-Ja '74-p14
TLS-D 7 '73-p1521

* * *

EDMOND, Doreen
Frog's Wooing
Brit Bk N C-Autumn '81-p16
TES-F 26 '82-p26

* * *

EDMONDS, I G
Allah's Oil
BL-v73-N 1 '76-p400
BL-v73-N 1 '76-p407
BS-v37-Jl '77-p126
LJ-v101-D 15 '76-p2583
SB-v13-D '77-p133
SLJ-v24-Ja '78-p94
Buddhism
BL-v74-Ap 1 '78-p1254
JB-v42-D '78-p309
SLJ-v25-S '78-p135
Ethiopia
BL-v72-Ap 1 '76-p1112
KR-v43-O 15 '75-p1197
SLJ-v22-Ja '76-p52
The Girls Who Talked To Ghosts
BL-v75-Jl 15 '79-p1625
CCB-B-v33-S '79-p5
EJ-v68-N '79-p76
SLJ-v26-S '79-p135
Hinduism
BL-v76-N 1 '79-p445
CLW-v52-S '80-p91
SLJ-v26-D '79-p83
Islam
BL-v74-Ja 15 '78-p811
GP-v17-My '78-p3335
JB-v43-F '79-p50
SLJ-v24-S '77-p126

EDMONDS, I G (continued)
Joel Of The Hanging Gardens
CCB-B-v20-F '67-p87
LJ-v91-Ap 15 '66-p2218
The Magic Dog
BL-v79-O 15 '82-p311
CBRS-v10-Jl '82-p127
PW-v222-S 17 '82-p115
RT-v36-F '83-p594
SLJ-v29-Ja '83-p74
The Magic Makers
BL-v73-S 1 '76-p29
BL-v73-S 1 '76-p37
BS-v36-D '76-p310
EJ-v67-S '78-p79
KR-v44-My 1 '76-p543
SE-v41-Ap '77-p348
SLJ-v22-Ap '76-p85
SLJ-v25-O '78-p121
The Mysteries Of Homer's Greeks
BL-v77-Ja 1 '81-p618
CCB-B-v34-Je '81-p192
CE-v58-Ja '82-p183
J Read-v25-Mr '82-p613
KR-v49-Mr 1 '81-p289
LA-v59-F '82-p157
SLJ-v27-My '81-p91
Other Lives
BL-v76-D 15 '79-p604
CCB-B-v33-Mr '80-p131
PW-v216-Ag 20 '79-p82
SLJ-v26-Mr '80-p139
Pakistan
KR-v43-My 15 '75-p577
SLJ-v22-D '75-p51
Roller Skating
SLJ-v26-My '80-p66
The United Nations
SLJ-v21-Ap '75-p51

* * *

EDMONDS, Walter D
Beaver Valley
BL-v67-My 15 '71-p797
BW-v5-My 9 '71-p5
HB-v47-Je '71-p286
KR-v39-Ap 15 '71-p432
LJ-v96-Jl '71-p2363
PW-v199-Mr 8 '71-p71
SB-v7-Mr '72-p316
Bert Breen's Barn
A Lib-v8-My '77-p270
BL-v72-S 1 '75-p39
BS-v35-S '75-p169
CCB-B-v29-Ja '76-p76
Comw-v102-N 21 '75-p569
HB-v51-O '75-p469
KR-v43-My 15 '75-p575
NYT-v125-D 20 '75-p25
NYTBR-Jl 20 '75-p8
NYTBR-N 16 '75-p54
NYTBR-D 7 '75-p66
PW-v207-Ap 7 '75-p81
SE-v44-O '80-p479
SLJ-v22-N '75-p74
The Night Raider
BL-v77-N 1 '80-p400
CCB-B-v34-Ap '81-p150
HB-v56-D '80-p648
NYTBR-v85-N 9 '80-p54
PW-v218-Jl 11 '80-p91
SLJ-v27-O '80-p154
VOYA-v3-F '81-p29
The Story Of Richard Storm
BL-v70-Je 1 '74-p1104
CCB-B-v28-S '74-p5
LJ-v99-S 15 '74-p2244
PW-v205-Je 3 '74-p158
Time To Go House
BL-v66-O 15 '69-p296
Comw-v91-N 21 '69-p256
HB-v45-O '69-p535
KR-v37-Ag 1 '69-p776
LJ-v94-N 15 '69-p4284
NO-v8-N 3 '69-p21
NYTBR, pt.2-N 9 '69-p30
PW-v196-Ag 11 '69-p43
Wolf Hunt
BL-v67-D 15 '70-p341
BW-v4-N 8 '70-p26
Comw-v93-N 20 '70-p201
HB-v46-D '70-p617
LJ-v96-Ja 15 '71-p267
NYTBR, pt.2-N 8 '70-p28
Spectr-v47-Mr '71-p46

* * *

EDMONDS, William
The Iguanodon Mystery
TES-N 23 '79-p36
TES-O 24 '80-p21

* * *

EDMONDSON, Madeleine
Anna Witch
BL-v79-Ja 1 '83-p608
CBRS-v11-O '82-p14
CCB-B-v36-O '82-p24
JB-v47-O '83-p206
PW-v222-O 8 '82-p62
SLJ-v29-D '82-p64

* * *

EDMONTON. Public Library
75 And Growing
In Rev-v15-Ag '81-p58

* * *

EDMUNDS, Alice
Who Puts The Blue In The Jeans?
BL-v73-Jl 1 '77-p1649
SB-v14-S '78-p109
Teacher-v95-O '77-p171
Who Puts The Grooves In The Records?
BL-v73-Jl 1 '77-p1649
BW-Jl 10 '77-pH10
SB-v14-S '78-p109
Teacher-v95-O '77-p171
Who Puts The Ice In The Cream?
Cur R-v16-My '77-p94

* * *

EDSALL, Marian S
Battle On The Rosebush
BL-v69-O 15 '72-p200
HB-v48-D '72-p612

* * *

EDUCATION Research Council Of America
Lands Of Latin America
Inter BC-v13-#2 '82-p10

* * *

EDUCATIONAL Challenges, Inc.
Spotlight On Vocabulary
Cur R-v22-Ag '83-p41
RT-v37-Ja '84-p444

* * *

EDWARDES, Dorothy
Listen With Mother Stories
TES-D 14 '79-p21

* * *

EDWARDS, A
Fishing For Beginners
JB-v43-Je '79-p166

* * *

EDWARDS, Amelia B
The Phantom Coach
B Rpt-v1-Ja '83-p43

* * *

EDWARDS, Anne
Bible For Young Readers
NYTBR-v73-S 1 '68-p17
PW-v194-Jl 8 '68-p166

EDWARDS, Anne (continued)
A Child's Bible-The Old Testament
B&B-v19-N '73-p137
Spec-v231-O 20 '73-pR20
The Great Houdini
KR-v44-D 15 '76-p1308
SLJ-v23-Mr '77-p144
P.T. Barnum
BL-v74-D 15 '77-p682
CE-v55-O '78-p41
CLW-v49-D '77-p234
KR-v45-O 1 '77-p1046
SLJ-v24-D '77-p58

* * *

EDWARDS, Audrey
The Picture Life Of Bobby Orr
BL-v73-N 15 '76-p472
CCB-B-v30-F '77-p89
SLJ-v23-D '76-p71
The Picture Life Of Muhammad Ali
Cur R-v15-D '76-p315
SLJ-v23-D '76-p72
Teacher-v96-O '78-p174
The Picture Life Of Stevie Wonder
BL-v73-Ap 15 '77-p1265
SLJ-v23-Ap '77-p65
Teacher-v96-O '78-p174

* * *

EDWARDS, Bruce
Kangaroos And Wallabies
CCB-B-v28-N '74-p41

* * *

EDWARDS, David L
The Children's Bible
SLJ-v25-Mr '79-p138
Today's Story Of Jesus
CC-v94-Jl 20 '77-p664
JB-v41-F '77-p31
PW-v211-Ap 18 '77-p62

* * *

EDWARDS, Dorothy
Crash!!
Sch Lib-v29-Je '81-p126
Dad's New Car
GP-v15-Mr '77-p3072
Ghosts And Shadows
Brit Bk N C-Spring '81-p18
GP-v19-Ja '81-p3825
GP-v20-Ja '82-p3992
JB-v45-Ap '81-p78
Sch Lib-v30-D '82-p330
Here's Sam
Brit Bk N-Je '80-p331
GP-v19-My '80-p3694
Sch Lib-v29-Je '81-p131
TES-Je 20 '80-p44
TES-My 15 '81-p29
Joe And Timothy Together
NS-v82-N 12 '71-p662
TES-N 2 '84-p26
A Look, See And Touch Book
TLS-Ap 2 '76-p389
Mark The Drummer Boy
JB-v48-Ap '84-p68
NS-v106-D 2 '83-p25
Sch Lib-v32-Mr '84-p36
TES-Je 15 '84-p36
Mists And Magic
JB-v47-D '83-p242
Sch Lib-v31-D '83-p354
TES-O 7 '83-p29
My Naughty Little Sister
TES-Jl 23 '82-p24
My Naughty Little Sister And Bad Harry
Spec-v323-My 4 '74-p552
TLS-Jl 5 '74-p722
My Naughty Little Sister And Bad Harry's Rabbit
CBRS-v9-Ag '81-p121
CCB-B-v35-F '82-p105
HB-v57-D '81-p658
JB-v42-Ap '78-p79
KR-v49-Jl 15 '81-p869
PW-v219-Je 26 '81-p60
SLJ-v28-O '81-p127
TLS-Ap 7 '78-p378
VV-v26-D 9 '81-p56
My Naughty Little Sister At The Fair
JB-v44-Je '80-p126
TES-Jl 22 '83-p21
My Naughty Little Sister Goes Fishing
B&B-v22-D '76-p76
JB-v41-F '77-p14
The Old Man Who Sneezed
GP-v22-S '83-p4140
JB-v47-D '83-p242
TES-Ag 26 '83-p20
Once, Twice, Thrice And Then Again
GP-v15-Ap '77-p3092
Obs-D 5 '76-p32
Once, Twice, Thrice Upon A Time
GP-v15-Ap '77-p3092
JB-v41-Ap '77-p91
Obs-D 5 '76-p32
The Read-Me-Another-Story Book
B&B-v22-N '76-p80
JB-v41-F '77-p20
Lis-v96-N 11 '76-p626
The Read-To-Me Story Book
TLS-S 20 '74-p1013
A Strong And Willing Girl
Brit Bk N C-Spring '81-p22
GP-v21-N '82-p3976
JB-v44-D '80-p305
NS-v100-N 14 '80-p21
Obs-Ag 24 '80-p27
Sch Lib-v29-Mr '81-p29
TES-Ja 16 '81-p34
TES-D 10 '82-p34
A Walk Your Fingers Story
TLS-Ap 2 '76-p389
A Wet Monday
GP-v14-Ja '76-p2808
HB-v53-F '77-p43
Inst-v86-N '76-p158
KR-v44-Jl 15 '76-p790
PW-v210-Ag 2 '76-p114
SLJ-v23-D '76-p65
TLS-S 19 '75-p1054
The Witches And The Grinnygog
BL-v79-Jl '83-p1400
Brit Bk N C-Spring '82-p10
CBRS-v11-Jl '83-p136
CCB-B-v37-N '83-p47
JB-v46-F '82-p32
KR-v51-Ja 1 '83-p4
SLJ-v30-S '83-p132
Sch Lib-v29-D '81-p326
TES-N 11 '83-p25

* * *

EDWARDS, E Hartley
Lucinda Prior-Palmer
Brit Bk N C-Autumn '82-p28
GP-v21-My '82-p3900
SLJ-v29-O '82-p151

* * *

EDWARDS, Elwyn H
Know Your Horses
Brit Bk N-D '80-p715

EDWARDS, Monica
(continued)
Obs-Jl 3 '66-p18

* * *

EDWARDS, Page
Scarface Joe
BL-v81-O 1 '84-p245
CBRS-v13-S '84-p8
CCB-B-v37-Jl '84-p204
KR-v52-S 1 '84-pJ79
SLJ-v31-O '84-p166

* * *

EDWARDS, Paula
Child To Child Readers
TES-Mr 9 '84-p52
Down With Fever
TES-S 21 '84-p35

* * *

EDWARDS, Peter
Simply Salt
JB-v42-O '78-p249
TES-Je 30 '78-p22
Simply Sell
JB-v42-O '78-p249
TES-Je 30 '78-p22
Simply Size
JB-v42-O '78-p249
TES-Je 30 '78-p22
TLS-S 29 '78-p1087
Simply Song
JB-v42-O '78-p249
TES-Je 30 '78-p22
Simply Soup
JB-v42-O '78-p249
TES-Je 30 '78-p22
Simply Stones
JB-v42-O '78-p249
TES-Je 30 '78-p22

* * *

EDWARDS, Phil
You Should Have Been Here An Hour Ago
CCB-B-v21-N '67-p40
KR-v35-Ap 1 '67-p458
LJ-v92-S 15 '67-p3212
PW-v191-Ap 10 '67-p79
SR-v50-Ag 19 '67-p35
Trav-v24-Ja '68-p225

* * *

EDWARDS, Sally
Isaac And Snow
BL-v70-F 15 '74-p655
HB-v50-Ap '74-p147
KR-v42-Ja 1 '74-p5
LJ-v99-F 15 '74-p571
The Man Who Said No
BS-v30-Ja 15 '71-p451
CCB-B-v24-Je '71-p155
KR-v38-O 1 '70-p1110
LJ-v95-N 15 '70-p4052
NYTBR-D 13 '70-p26

* * *

EDWARDS, Tudor
Discovering Britain: Yorkshire
JB-v42-Ag '78-p201
TES-S 22 '78-p26

* * *

EDWARDS, Victor
SOS Wildlife
Obs-Jl 27 '75-p21

* * *

EDWINA
Tippie And His Friends
SR-v3-N 29 '75-p32

* * *

EELS (Young Naturalist)
TES-N 16 '79-p29

* * *

EFRON, Marshall
Bible Stories You Can't Forget
CC-v94-My 4 '77-p436
CCB-B-v30-Mr '77-p105
CLW-v48-My '77-p443
EJ-v67-Mr '78-p92
KR-v44-O 15 '76-p1140
NYT-v126-D 21 '76-p31
NYTBR-N 14 '76-p30
NYTBR-N 14 '76-p52
NYTBR-Ag 12 '79-p27
PW-v210-D 13 '76-p62
SLJ-v23-Ja '77-p90

* * *

EGAN, E W
Ceylon: In Pictures
CSM-v59-N 2 '67-pB8
KR-v35-Ja 15 '67-p67
France: In Pictures
LJ-v91-My 15 '66-p2699
SLJ-v27-N '80-p73
SS-v57-N '66-p282

* * *

EGAN, Pamela
All This Fuss About Andy
TES-N 5 '82-p32
Don And Di-Next-Door
TES-N 5 '82-p32
Kevin's Good Day
TES-N 5 '82-p32
Must Simon Come Too?
TES-N 5 '82-p32
Sleep Well, James
TES-N 5 '82-p32
Wake Up, Judy!
TES-N 5 '82-p32

* * *

EGER, F H
Eskimo Inuit Games
In Rev-v15-Ap '81-p35

* * *

EGERTON, M
Willingly To School
JB-v39-Ap '75-p142

* * *

EGGERS, John R
Will You Help Me Create The Future Today?
Cur R-v22-O '83-p26

* * *

EGGS, C
Step By Step Recipes
TES-My 2 '80-p26

* * *

EGGS (Leprechaun Library)
Punch-v279-S 24 '80-p520

* * *

EGOFF, Sheila
One Ocean Touching
A Lib-v10-S '79-p501
Can Child Lit-#18 '80-p140
In Rev-v14-Ap '80-p29
LQ-v50-Ap '80-p268
SLJ-v26-S '79-p47
TN-v36-Fall '79-p130
Only Connect
CE-v47-O '70-p46
CSM-v69-N 2 '77-pB1
Can Child Lit-#23 '81-p81
Choice-v18-N '80-p389
Econ-v277-D 27 '80-p73
HB-v46-Ap '70-p179
In Rev-v14-D '80-p32
NS-v80-N 6 '70-p607
SR-v53-Mr 21 '70-p38
TLS-Jl 2 '70-p724
TN-v27-N '70-p98
Republic Of Childhood
Atl Pro Bk R-v10-N '83-p2

EGOFF, Sheila (continued)
Choice-v5-O '68-p932
HB-v44-Je '68-p337
JB-v40-Ap '76-p78
TN-v32-Je '76-p379

* * *

EGOFF, Sheila A
Thursday's Child
ARBA-v14-'83-p537
BL-v78-D 1 '81-p504
CE-v58-My '82-p332
Choice-v19-Mr '82-p914
Cur R-v21-Ag '82-p293
Emerg Lib-v9-My '82-p22
HB-v58-Ap '82-p184
In Rev-v16-Ap '82-p34
JAL-v8-Mr '82-p43
JLH-v18-Spring '83-p215
LQ-v52-Jl '82-p260
SLJ-v29-F '83-p38
SLMQ-v10-Summer '82-p307
TN-v39-Fall '82-p91
VOYA-v5-Je '82-p51

* * *

EGYPT, Ophelia Settle
James Weldon Johnson
BL-v70-My 15 '74-p1055
BW-My 19 '74-p4
CCB-B-v28-O '74-p27
CE-v51-N '74-p95
Choice-v12-N '75-p1132
KR-v42-Mr 1 '74-p248
LJ-v99-O 15 '74-p2739
SE-v39-Mr '75-p173
WLB-v48-Je '74-p789

* * *

EHRENSTRALE, Kristina
The Fifth Corner
GP-v23-Jl '84-p4274
JB-v48-Je '84-p137
Obs-Ap 22 '84-p23

* * *

EHRLICH, Amy
Annie
BL-v79-S 1 '82-p41
CCB-B-v35-Je '82-p186
SLJ-v29-Ja '83-p58
The Everyday Train
BB-v5-Ja '78-p1
BL-v74-S 15 '77-p192
CCB-B-v31-N '77-p45
HB-v53-O '77-p523
KR-v45-Jl 1 '77-p665
PW-v212-Ag 1 '77-p115
SLJ-v24-O '77-p100
Leo, Zack, And Emmie
BL-v78-F 15 '82-p760
CBRS-v10-N '81-p25
CCB-B-v35-O '81-p27
HB-v58-F '82-p39
KR-v50-Ja 1 '82-p5
PW-v220-O 30 '81-p66
SLJ-v28-D '81-p74
The Snow Queen
BL-v79-Ja 15 '83-p672
BL-v79-Je 1 '83-p1281
BW-v13-My 8 '83-p13
CBRS-v11-Ja '83-p41
CCB-B-v36-Mr '83-p121
CE-v59-My '83-p354
CSM-v75-D 3 '82-pB8
LATBR-D 5 '82-p10
NYTBR-v87-N 14 '82-p52
PW-v222-N 5 '82-p70
SLJ-v29-Mr '83-p154
Thumbelina
BL-v76-D 1 '79-p554
BW-v9-D 2 '79-p4
CBRS-v8-D '79-p31
CCB-B-v33-Ap '80-p145
CE-v57-S '80-p42
HM-v259-D '79-p76
KR-v48-F 15 '80-p209
LA-v57-My '80-p554
NYTBR-N 11 '79-p58
PW-v216-S 3 '79-p96
RT-v33-My '80-p971
RT-v34-O '80-p52
RT-v34-O '80-p102
SLJ-v26-Ja '80-p53
WLB-v54-Mr '80-p455
The Wild Swans
B&B-Jl '82-p35
BL-v78-Ja 15 '82-p646
CBRS-v10-D '81-p31
CCB-B-v35-F '82-p102
CLW-v53-Mr '82-p355
Inst-v91-Ap '82-p22
JB-v46-Ag '82-p132
LA-v59-Ap '82-p369
NW-v98-D 7 '81-p99
NYTBR-v86-N 15 '81-p66
PW-v220-N 13 '81-p88
SLJ-v28-Ja '82-p58
TES-Ag 13 '82-p20
TLS-Jl 23 '82-p792
Wounded Knee
BB-v3-Ap '75-p3
BL-v71-F 1 '75-p561
Inst-v84-My '75-p100
NY-v50-D 2 '74-p192
Zeek Silver Moon
BL-v69-O 1 '72-p147
CCB-B-v26-Ja '73-p75
HB-v48-Ag '72-p361
KR-v40-My 1 '72-p533
KR-v40-D 15 '72-p1408
LJ-v97-S 15 '72-p2932
LJ-v97-D 15 '72-p4056
NYTBR-Je 4 '72-p28
NYTBR-Ag 6 '72-p8
NYTBR-D 3 '72-p82
NYTBR-N 13 '77-p62
NYTBR, pt.2-N 5 '72-p30
PW-v201-Je 26 '72-p62
Teacher-v90-N '72-p69

* * *

EICHELBERGER, Rosa
Bronko
RT-v33-Ap '80-p808

* * *

EICHELBERGER, Rosa Kohler
Big Fire In Baltimore
CBRS-v7-Jl '79-p126
SLJ-v26-S '79-p135

* * *

EICHENBERG, Fritz
Ape In A Cape
Teacher-v91-S '73-p152
VLS-My '82-p12
Dancing In The Moon
CE-v61-S '84-p33
LJ-v96-Mr 15 '71-p1084
NY-v51-D 1 '75-p181
Teacher-v93-Ap '76-p123
Poor Troll
BW-v14-F 12 '84-p11

* * *

EICHLER, Margrit
Martin's Father
Lib Brow-v2-Spring '82-p5

* * *

EICHNER, James A
The First Book Of Local Government
BL-v61-Ap 15 '65-p802
BL-v73-S 15 '76-p173
SLJ-v23-My '77-p67
Teacher-v94-O '76-p22
Local Government
BL-v80-Ja 1 '84-p679
SLJ-v30-F '84-p68

* * *

EICHOLZ, R
Extending The Ideas
Cur R-v20-S '81-p376

* * *

EICHOLZ, ROBERT E
Mathematics In Our World
Cur R-v20-Je '81-p262
Mathematics In Our World. Bks. K-6
Cur R-v17-F '78-p51
Inst-v87-Ap '78-p165

* * *

EICKE, Edna
The Children Who Got Married
CCB-B-v23-F '70-p95
CSM-v61-N 6 '69-pB8
LJ-v95-Ja 15 '70-p232
What's Your Name?
CCB-B-v22-Ap '69-p124
HB-v45-Ap '69-p161
KR-v36-S 15 '68-p1041
LJ-v94-F 15 '69-p860
NYTBR-v73-O 20 '68-p38
PW-v194-O 7 '68-p55

* * *

EIGE, Lillian
The Kidnapping Of Mister Huey
B Rpt-v2-Ja '84-p32
CBRS-v11-Jl '83-p136
CCB-B-v36-Ap '83-p147
J Read-v27-Ap '84-p661
KR-v51-My 1 '83-p523
PW-v223-My 27 '83-p67
SLJ-v29-My '83-p81
VOYA-v6-Ag '83-p145

* * *

EIMERL, Sarel
Gulls
CCB-B-v24-S '70-p6
KR-v37-N 15 '69-p1198
LJ-v95-My 15 '70-p1928
SB-v5-Mr '70-p332
TLS-Ap 28 '72-p490

* * *

EINSEL, Walter
Did You Ever See?
SLJ-v25-My '79-p38

* * *

EINSTEIN, Albert
Albert Einstein: The Human Side
BAS-v36-Mr '80-p53
BS-v39-Jl '79-p127
BW-Mr 25 '79-pC1
CSM-v71-Ap 9 '79-pB3
Choice-v16-Jl '79-p688
Cng-v11-S '79-p60
KR-v47-F 1 '79-p164
LJ-v104-Mr 15 '79-p721
NYTBR-N 25 '79-p15
NYTBR-v86-My 24 '81-p19
PW-v215-Ja 29 '79-p107
PW-v219-Ja 30 '81-p74
SA-v240-Je '79-p52
SB-v15-Mr '80-p225
Sci-v216-My 21 '82-p847
WSJ-v193-Mr 19 '79-p24

* * *

EISEMAN, Alberta
Candido
CCB-B-v20-S '66-p8
HB-v42-F '66-p46
KR-v33-O 15 '65-p1076
LJ-v90-N 15 '65-p5072
SR-v49-Ja 22 '66-p45
From Many Lands
BL-v67-Ap 1 '71-p662
CCB-B-v24-F '71-p89
Comw-v93-N 20 '70-p204
KR-v38-O 15 '70-p1166
LJ-v95-D 15 '70-p4361
Gift From A Sheep
ACSB-v13-Spring '80-p28
BL-v76-S 15 '79-p120
CE-v57-S '80-p43
HB-v55-D '79-p675
KR-v47-N 1 '79-p1263
SLJ-v26-D '79-p83
Manana Is Now
BL-v69-Jl 15 '73-p1072
CCB-B-v27-S '73-p6
Inter BC-v14-#1 '83-p16
KR-v41-Ap 1 '73-p399
LJ-v98-My 15 '73-p1654
LJ-v98-My 15 '73-p1687
RR-v33-Ja '74-p224
Rebels And Reformers
BL-v73-S 1 '76-p37
KR-v44-My 15 '76-p603
Prog-v40-O '76-p60
SLJ-v23-S '76-p115
The Sunday Whirligig
BB-v6-My '78-p3
KR-v45-Jl 15 '77-p728
LA-v55-My '78-p621
PW-v212-Ag 1 '77-p116
SLJ-v24-N '77-p55
SR-v5-N 26 '77-p41

* * *

EISENBERG, Azriel
Worlds Lost And Found: Biblical Archeology
CCB-B-v18-My '65-p127
TLS-v17-Je '65-p515

* * *

EISENBERG, Eleanor
The Pretty House That Found Happiness
CCB-B-v18-Je '65-p146
LJ-v90-Ja 15 '65-p374

* * *

EISENBERG, Phyllis R
Don't Tell Me A Ghost Story
CBRS-v11-F '83-p66
SLJ-v29-Ja '83-p58
WCRB-v9-Ja '83-p46

* * *

EISENBERG, Phyllis Rose
A Mitzvah Is Something Special
BL-v75-O 1 '78-p291
CCB-B-v32-Ja '79-p79
KR-v46-N 1 '78-p1184
LA-v56-My '79-p545
PW-v214-N 27 '78-p61
SLJ-v25-O '78-p132
TES-Je 8 '84-p50
Teacher-v96-My '79-p114
WCRB-v5-Ja '79-p54

* * *

EISENHOWER, Julie N
Julie Eisenhower's Cookbook For Children
CSM-v70-Mr 6 '78-p26
KR-v43-Ag 15 '75-p921
NYTBR-N 16 '75-p34
SLJ-v22-N '75-p75

* * *

EISNER, Herbert
The Monster Plant
GP-v16-S '77-p3176

* * *

EISNER, Vivienne
A Boat, A Bat, And A Beanie
BB-v5-Ag '77-p2
KR-v45-Ap 15 '77-p430

EISNER, Vivienne (continued)
SLJ-v24-S '77-p126
The Newspaper Everything Book
CSM-v68-Ap 28 '76-p22
JB-v41-D '77-p350
TES-O 21 '77-p24
Quick And Easy Holiday Costumes
Comw-v105-N 10 '78-p735
KR-v45-D 15 '77-p1323
SLJ-v24-Mr '78-p117

* * *

EITZEN, Ruth
Ti Jacques
BL-v69-F 1 '73-p527
CCB-B-v26-F '73-p88
KR-v40-S 15 '72-p1098
LJ-v98-Ja 15 '73-p252

* * *

EKOOMIAK, Norman
An Arctic Childhood
In Rev-v15-Ap '81-p35

* * *

EKWALL, Eldon E
Diagnostic-Prescriptive Phonics Lessons
Cur R-v20-N '81-p455

* * *

EKWENSI, Cyprian
An African Night's Entertainment
BL-v73-Jl 15 '77-p1734
RT-v37-Mr '84-p596
Coal Camp Boy
J Read-v25-Mr '82-p522
The Great Elephant Bird And Other Stories
J Read-v25-Mr '82-p519
The Passport Of Malam
J Read-v25-Mr '82-p522
Samankwe In The Strange Forest
J Read-v25-Mr '82-p520

* * *

EL-SHAMY, Hasan M
Folktales Of Egypt
CCB-B-v33-Jl '80-p211
JAF-v96-Ja '83-p70
LJ-v107-Mr 15 '80-p735
MEJ-v35-Winter '81-p68

* * *

ELBERT, Virginie Fowler
Easy Enameling on Metal
BL-v72-N 15 '75-p452
KR-v43-N 1 '75-p1233
SLJ-v22-Ja '76-p45
Folk Toys Around The World And How To Make Them
HB-v60-S '84-p606
SLJ-v31-O '84-p166
Grow A Plant Pet
BL-v74-D 15 '77-p687
KR-v45-D 1 '77-p1267
SB-v14-D '78-p185
SLJ-v24-N '77-p69
Potterymaking
BL-v71-N 1 '74-p288
Des-v77-MW '76-p33
HB-v51-Ap '75-p156
SLJ-v21-Ja '75-p44

* * *

ELBORN, Andrew
Bird Adalbert
CBRS-v12-Mr '84-p80
PW-v224-D 16 '83-p71
SLJ-v30-Mr '84-p142
WLB-v58-Mr '84-p501
Noah & The Ark & The Animals
PW-v226-O 5 '84-p92

* * *

ELBOW, Meg
The Rootomom Tree
KR-v46-Ap 1 '78-p373
LA-v55-N '78-p987
SLJ-v24-Ap '78-p68

* * *

ELCOME, D
Birds
JB-v47-F '83-p23

* * *

ELCOME, David
Bird Life
Brit Bk N C-Spring '81-p29

* * *

ELDER, Bruce
Let's Go To Malaysia
TES-Mr 9 '84-p53
Let's Go To Singapore
TES-Mr 9 '84-p53

* * *

ELDER, Lauren
And I Alone Survived
BL-v74-Jl 15 '78-p1726
BS-v38-Ag '78-p159
HB-v55-O '78-p546
KR-v46-F 15 '78-p215
LJ-v103-Je 1 '78-p1166
PW-v213-F 27 '78-p149
SLJ-v25-S '78-p171

* * *

ELDIN, Peter
Hey Presto!
TES-F 27 '81-p39

* * *

ELDRED, Patricia Mulrooney
Barbra Streisand
SLJ-v23-S '76-p114
Boxing's World Champion, Muhammad Ali
BL-v73-My 15 '77-p1423
SLJ-v23-My '77-p81
Diana Ross
SLJ-v23-S '76-p114
Donny & Marie
SLJ-v25-S '78-p130
Football's Great Quarterback, Joe Namath
BL-v73-My 15 '77-p1423
SLJ-v23-My '77-p81
Kathy Whitworth
BL-v72-O 15 '75-p307
SLJ-v22-D '75-p69
Rose Kennedy, An Energizing Spirit
BL-v72-O 15 '75-p307
SLJ-v22-N '75-p75

* * *

ELDRIDGE, David
Flying Dragons
ASBYP-v14-Winter '81-p24
SLJ-v26-F '80-p53
The Giant Dinosaurs
ASBYP-v14-Winter '81-p24
SLJ-v26-F '80-p53
Last Of The Dinosaurs
ASBYP-v14-Winter '81-p24
SLJ-v26-F '80-p53
Sea Monsters
ASBYP-v14-Winter '81-p24
SLJ-v26-F '80-p53

* * *

ELDRIDGE, Roger
The Shadow Of The Gloom-World
HB-v54-Ag '78-p401
JB-v41-D '77-p350
LA-v55-S '78-p740
SLJ-v24-My '78-p76
TLS-O 21 '77-p1246

* * *

ELECTRIC Company
BW-My 1 '77-pE4

* * *

ELECTRIC Company Magazine
BL-v79-F 1 '83-p729
Cha Ti-v37-Ag '83-p47
Mag Lib- '82-p216

* * *

ELEGANT, Robert S
Mao vs. Chiang
BS-v32-F 15 '73-p529
CCB-B-v26-Mr '73-p104
KR-v40-Jl 1 '72-p731
LJ-v98-Ap 15 '73-p1394

* * *

ELEMENTARY Language Skills
Cur R-v19-S '80-p324

* * *

ELGIN, Kathleen
The Episcopalians
BL-v67-Ap 1 '71-p663
CCB-B-v24-Mr '71-p105
Comw-v93-N 20 '70-p199
LJ-v96-Ap 15 '71-p1522
The Fall Down, Break A Bone, Skin Your Knee Book
CCB-B-v29-N '75-p42
KR-v43-Mr 15 '75-p312
SLJ-v22-S '75-p101
The Human Body
BL-v65-O 15 '68-p247
BL-v68-F 1 '72-p465
BL-v70-O 15 '73-p232
CCB-B-v22-O '68-p25
CCB-B-v26-S '72-p5
CLW-v42-My '71-p568
GT-v89-Mr '72-p112
KR-v36-Je 15 '68-p646
KR-v41-O 1 '73-p1099
LJ-v93-O 15 '68-p3968
LJ-v96-My 15 '71-p1826
LJ-v96-D 15 '71-p4183
NS-v80-N 6 '70-p614
SB-v7-D '71-p254
SB-v8-My '72-p68
The Human Body: The Brain
Lis-v84-N 12 '70-p671
Spec-v226-My 29 '71-p756
The Human Body: The Digestive System
LJ-v99-F 15 '74-p571
The Human Body: The Ear
Lis-v84-N 12 '70-p671
Spec-v226-My 29 '71-p756
The Human Body: The Eye
Lis-v84-N 12 '70-p671
Spec-v226-My 29 '71-p756
The Human Body: The Female Reproductive System
CCB-B-v23-N '69-p43
KR-v37-S 1 '69-p932
LJ-v94-D 15 '69-p4602
SB-v5-S '69-p165
SR-v52-O 18 '69-p56
TES-My 26 '78-p52
The Human Body: The Glands
KR-v39-Mr 1 '71-p239
The Human Body: The Hand
Spec-v226-My 29 '71-p756
The Human Body: The Heart
HB-v46-D '70-p630
LR-v22-Winter '70-p435
Lis-v84-N 12 '70-p671
Spec-v226-My 29 '71-p756
The Human Body: The Male Reproductive System
CCB-B-v23-N '69-p43
KR-v37-S 1 '69-p932
LJ-v94-D 15 '69-p4602
SB-v5-S '69-p165
SR-v52-O 18 '69-p56
TES-My 26 '78-p52
The Human Body: The Muscles
CCB-B-v27-N '73-p41
LJ-v99-S 15 '74-p2266
SB-v9-Mr '74-p334
The Human Body: The Respiratory System
LJ-v95-Je 15 '70-p2317
Lis-v84-N 12 '70-p671
SB-v6-D '70-p249
The Human Body: The Skin
CCB-B-v24-D '70-p57
HB-v46-D '70-p630
LJ-v95-Je 15 '70-p2301
Lis-v84-N 12 '70-p671
SB-v6-S '70-p154
The Mormons
BL-v66-D 1 '69-p456
CC-v86-D 10 '69-p1584
CCB-B-v23-Ja '70-p79
LJ-v95-My 15 '70-p1952
NYTBR, pt.2-N 9 '69-p53
The Quakers
CCB-B-v22-Ja '69-p76
KR-v36-Jl 15 '68-p763
LJ-v93-O 15 '68-p3979
NYTBR-v73-N 3 '68-p42
PW-v194-Ag 12 '68-p56
SR-v51-N 9 '68-p68
Read About The Ear
CCB-B-v20-Jl '67-p169
CE-v44-Ja '68-p328
KR-v35-F 15 '67-p203
LJ-v92-Ap 15 '67-p1723
Read About The Eye
CCB-B-v21-Ja '68-p77
KR-v35-F 15 '67-p203
LJ-v92-Ap 15 '67-p1733
SB-v3-My '67-p64
Twenty-Eight Days
BL-v70-F 1 '74-p599
CCB-B-v27-Ap '74-p127
KR-v41-Je 1 '73-p608
The Unitarians
CCB-B-v25-Ja '72-p73
LJ-v97-F 15 '72-p772

* * *

ELIAS, David
Short Stories From Wales
TES-D 21 '79-p20

* * *

ELIAS, Horace J
The Wizard Of Oz
SLJ-v23-N '76-p56

* * *

ELIOT, T S
Old Possum's Book Of Practical Cats
Atl-v250-O '82-p105
B&B-D '82-p23
BL-v79-O 1 '82-p184
JB-v47-F '83-p23
Quill & Q-v49-My '83-p36
SLJ-v29-Ap '83-p34
SLMQ-v11-Spring '83-p173

* * *

ELISOFON, Eliot
A Week In Leonora's World
BL-v69-Ja 15 '73-p477
CCB-B-v25-My '72-p138

ELISOFON, Eliot (continued)
KR-v39-Jl 15 '71-p741
LJ-v96-O 15 '71-p3458
Zaire
BL-v70-S 1 '73-p50
CCB-B-v27-S '73-p6
CE-v50-F '74-p232
Inst-v82-My '73-p71
KR-v41-F 1 '73-p119
LJ-v98-Jl '73-p2185

* * *

ELKIN, Benjamin
How The Tsar Drinks Tea
BL-v68-S 15 '71-p108
CCB-B-v25-S '71-p4
GT-v89-F '72-p78
LJ-v97-Ap 15 '72-p1594
RT-v35-D '81-p331
The King Who Could Not Sleep
BL-v72-Ja 1 '76-p624
CSM-v68-My 12 '76-p24
KR-v43-N 1 '75-p1223
SLJ-v22-Ja '76-p36
Money
BL-v80-F 15 '84-p854
SLJ-v30-Mr '84-p142
Such Is The Way Of The World
BW-v2-N 3 '68-p28
CCB-B-v22-Ap '69-p124
LJ-v94-Ja 15 '69-p286
NYTBR-Ja 5 '69-p22
PW-v194-S 9 '68-p64
Why The Sun Was Late
BL-v63-N 15 '66-p376
CCB-B-v20-N '66-p40
CE-v43-My '67-p540
GT-v84-D '66-p90
HB-v43-F '67-p57
KR-v34-S 1 '66-p897
LJ-v91-O 15 '66-p5216
NYTBR-v71-N 6 '66-p71
Par-v42-F '67-p22
SR-v49-N 12 '66-p46
The Wisest Man In The World
BL-v65-Ja 15 '69-p545
CCB-B-v22-My '69-p141
KR-v36-O 15 '68-p1156
LJ-v93-N 15 '68-p4402
Obs-Ag 1 '71-p25
TLS-Jl 2 '71-p776

* * *

ELKIN, Judith
Books For The Multi-Racial Classroom
Brit Bk N C-Spring '81-p11
JB-v41-F '77-p11
The New Golden Land Anthology
GP-v22-Mr '84-p4225
JB-v48-Ap '84-p68
Sch Lib-v32-Mr '84-p76
TES-F 10 '84-p29

* * *

ELLENBY, Jean
How Does Your Garden Grow?
Sch Lib-v28-Je '80-p162

* * *

ELLENBY, Joan
The Stuart Household
TES-O 9 '81-p29

* * *

ELLENTUCK, Shan
My Brother Bernard
CCB-B-v22-Jl '69-p173
KR-v36-O 15 '68-p1156
LJ-v94-Ja 15 '69-p286
PW-v194-N 4 '68-p50
TLS-Ap 3 '69-p359
Sunflower As Big As The Sun
BL-v64-My 1 '68-p1041
BW-v2-My 5 '68-p4
CCB-B-v21-Je '68-p158
CSM-v60-My 2 '68-pB2
HB-v44-Je '68-p315
KR-v36-F 1 '68-p109
LJ-v93-Ap 15 '68-p1783
NYTBR-v73-Jl 21 '68-p22
RT-v35-Ja '82-p468
SR-v51-My 11 '68-p36
Yankel The Fool
BL-v69-Je 15 '73-p988
CCB-B-v26-Je '73-p152
KR-v41-My 1 '73-p517
LJ-v98-Jl '73-p2193
PW-v203-Ap 16 '73-p55

* * *

ELLERBY, Leona
King Tut's Game Board
CBRS-v8-Ap '80-p87
LA-v57-S '80-p652
SLJ-v26-Ag '80-p76

* * *

ELLIOT, Geraldine
The Hunter's Cave
GP-v20-Ja '82-p3996
TES-F 26 '82-p23
Long Grass Whispers
BS-v28-N 1 '68-p324
Choice-v6-Ap '69-p222
PW-v194-O 28 '68-p61
YR-v5-N '68-p15
The Long Grass Whispers
GP-v20-Ja '82-p3996
TES-F 26 '82-p23
The Singing Chameleon
GP-v20-Ja '82-p3996
TES-F 26 '82-p23
When The Leopard Passes
GP-v20-Ja '82-p3996
TES-F 26 '82-p23
Where The Leopard Passes
BS-v28-N 1 '68-p323
Choice-v6-Ap '69-p222
PW-v194-O 28 '68-p61
YR-v5-N '68-p15

* * *

ELLIOT, M
The Corn Dolly
JB-v40-Ag '76-p224
When The Night Crow Flies
JB-v42-F '78-p25

* * *

ELLIOT, Margaret
To Trick A Witch
Brit Bk N C-Autumn '81-p21

* * *

ELLIOTT, Alan C
On Sunday The Wind Came
CBRS-v8-Mr '80-p72
CCB-B-v33-My '80-p170
CLW-v52-N '80-p185
KR-v48-My 1 '80-p575
LA-v57-O '80-p789
PW-v217-Ja 25 '80-p340
SLJ-v26-Ap '80-p92

* * *

ELLIOTT, Dan
Ernie's Little Lie
SLJ-v30-S '83-p104
Grover Goes To School
RT-v37-O '83-p54
My Doll Is Lost!
CCB-B-v37-Ap '84-p145
SLJ-v30-My '84-p96

ELLIOTT, Dan (continued)
Oscar's Rotten Birthday
SLJ-v28-D '81-p76
A Visit To The Sesame Street Firehouse
CCB-B-v37-F '84-p106
SLJ-v30-Ap '84-p100

* * *

ELLIOTT, Donald
Alligators And Music
CCB-B-v30-F '77-p89
Cur R-v17-F '78-p81
PW-v210-O 4 '76-p74
PW-v226-Ag 17 '84-p58
SLJ-v23-O '76-p114
Time-v108-D 13 '76-p76
Frogs And The Ballet
BL-v75-My 1 '79-p1333
BW-My 13 '79-pK2
Dance-v53-Jl '79-p94
Dance-v54-N '80-p92
M Ed J-v66-Ja '80-p165
NY-v55-D 3 '79-p217
SLJ-v26-N '79-p76
Time-v114-D 3 '79-p100
Lambs' Tales From Great Operas
SLJ-v29-Mr '83-p174

* * *

ELLIOTT, Gordon
Oxford New Geography Series. Bks. 1-3
TES-Je 19 '81-p28

* * *

ELLIOTT, Harley
The Tiger's Spots
PW-v211-Ap 18 '77-p61
SLJ-v24-S '77-p106

* * *

ELLIOTT, Ingrid G
Hospital Roadmap
SLJ-v29-My '83-p60

* * *

ELLIOTT, J W
Nursery Rhymes And Nursery Songs
BL-v73-Jl 15 '77-p1729

* * *

ELLIOTT, Janice
The Incompetent Dragon
GP-v21-Mr '83-p4032

* * *

ELLIOTT, Paul Michael
Eskimos Of The World
BL-v73-Mr 1 '77-p1012
Cur R-v17-Ag '78-p185
KR-v44-O 1 '76-p1097
SE-v41-Ap '77-p349
SLJ-v23-Ja '77-p90

* * *

ELLIOTT, Roberta
Kirsti And Ruski
GP-v17-Ja '79-p3461
LR-v20-Summer '65-p132
Obs-Ap 18 '65-p26
Punch-v248-Ap 21 '65-p603
TLS-Je 17 '65-p514

* * *

ELLIOTT, Sarah M
Our Dirty Air
BL-v68-Ja 1 '72-p393
CCB-B-v25-D '71-p56
CLW-v43-My '72-p536
KR-v39-S 15 '71-p1017
LJ-v96-D 15 '71-p4184
SB-v7-Mr '72-p301
SR-v54-D 11 '71-p46
Our Dirty Land
ACSB-v10-Winter '77-p15
Cur R-v16-O '77-p253
KR-v44-My 1 '76-p537
SB-v12-Mr '77-p208
SLJ-v23-S '76-p132

* * *

ELLIS, Amabel W
Tu Cuerpo
BL-v78-F 1 '82-p704

* * *

ELLIS, Anne L
Dabble Duck
CBRS-v13-O '84-p13
KR-v52-S 1 '84-pJ60

* * *

ELLIS, C
Famous Ships Of World War II
JB-v41-Ag '77-p218

* * *

ELLIS, Ella T
Hugo And The Princess Nena
BL-v79-Mr 15 '83-p965
B Rpt-v2-N '83-p33
CBRS-v11-Je '83-p113
J Read-v27-D '83-p281
KR-v51-F 15 '83-p184
SLJ-v30-O '83-p166
WCRB-v9-Jl '83-p39
Sleepwalker's Moon
BL-v76-Ap 15 '80-p1202
CBRS-v8-Spring '80-p116
CCB-B-v34-S '80-p7
J Read-v24-D '80-p271
KR-v48-Mr 15 '80-p370
SLJ-v26-Ap '80-p123

* * *

ELLIS, Ella Thorp
Celebrate The Morning
BL-v69-N 15 '72-p300
CCB-B-v26-Je '73-p153
Comw-v97-N 17 '72-p157
EJ-v62-F '73-p308
HB-v48-D '72-p599
KR-v40-O 15 '72-p1200
LJ-v97-D 15 '72-p4077
Hallelujah
CCB-B-v30-Ja '77-p74
KR-v44-S 15 '76-p1039
SLJ-v23-O '76-p116
Riptide
CCB-B-v23-Je '70-p157
CSM-v61-N 6 '69-pB9
KR-v37-Ag 15 '69-p860
LJ-v94-N 15 '69-p4295
NYTBR, pt.2-N 9 '69-p48
Roam The Wild Country
BL-v64-F 1 '68-p636
BW-v2-Ja 28 '68-p12
CCB-B-v21-Ap '68-p124
CLW-v39-My '68-p665
HB-v43-O '67-p592
KR-v35-Jl 1 '67-p739
LJ-v92-N 15 '67-p4250
PW-v192-O 16 '67-p58
Where The Road Ends
BL-v70-My 1 '74-p1001
EJ-v64-Ap '75-p90
HB-v50-Ag '74-p384
KR-v42-Ap 1 '74-p371
LJ-v99-S 15 '74-p2288

* * *

ELLIS, Harry B
Ideals And Ideologies
BL-v65-S 1 '68-p53
CCB-B-v22-My '69-p141
KR-v36-F 15 '68-p192
NYTBR-v73-Je 30 '68-p26
PW-v203-Mr 12 '73-p64
SE-v33-My '69-p562
YR-v5-S '68-p3

ELLIS, Harry B (continued)
Israel
BL-v68-Je 15 '72-p903
CCB-B-v25-Jl '72-p168
CE-v49-Ja '73-p206
CSM-v64-My 4 '72-pB6
KR-v40-Ap 15 '72-p488
LJ-v98-Ap 15 '73-p1394
NYTBR-O 15 '72-p8
SLJ-v25-S '78-p156
Ironhead
BL-v65-Ja 15 '69-p546
EJ-v61-S '72-p937
HB-v45-Ap '69-p176
KR-v36-N 1 '68-p1225
NYTBR-v73-N 3 '68-p40
PW-v198-Jl 13 '70-p166
No Man For Murder
Am-v129-D 1 '73-p430
BL-v70-N 15 '73-p338
BS-v33-Ag 15 '73-p232
BW-v7-S 16 '73-p10
CCB-B-v27-Mr '74-p109
Comw-v99-N 23 '73-p216
HB-v50-F '74-p55
KR-v41-Je 1 '73-p607
LJ-v98-D 15 '73-p3719
PW-v204-Ag 6 '73-p65
Sidewalk Indian
CCB-B-v28-N '74-p41
KR-v42-My 1 '74-p488
LJ-v99-S 15 '74-p2288
NYTBR-Ag 25 '74-p8
This Mysterious River
BW-v6-My 21 '72-p5
EJ-v63-Mr '74-p104
HB-v48-Ag '72-p375
KR-v40-F 15 '72-p217
LJ-v97-Je 15 '72-p2245
NYTBR-Jl 23 '72-p8
NYTBR, pt.2-N 5 '72-p26
The Wild Horse Killers
BB-v4-My '76-p4
BL-v72-Mr 1 '76-p974
BS-v36-O '76-p239
BW-Ap 11 '76-p4
CSM-v68-My 12 '76-p28
KR-v44-F 1 '76-p134
Kliatt-v15-Fall '81-p9
LA-v54-Ja '77-p85
PW-v209-Ja 26 '76-p287
SLJ-v22-Ap '76-p85
Windows
GP-v14-N '75-p2740

* * *

ELLIS, John M
One Fairy Story Too Many
AB-v72-N 14 '83-p3346
ABC-v5-Ja '84-p56
Atl-v252-D '83-p116
BL-v80-O 1 '83-p211
BS-v43-D '83-p339
Choice-v21-F '84-p826
LJ-v108-S 15 '83-p1805
LQ-v54-O '84-p424
Parabola-v9-Ja '84-p124
TLS-Mr 30 '84-p343

* * *

ELLIS, L Ethan
40 Million Schoolbooks Can't Be Wrong
CE-v53-N '76-p99
Inst-v86-O '76-p198
KR-v43-N 1 '75-p1241
SLJ-v22-N '75-p88

* * *

ELLIS, Malcolm
Builders
Brit Bk N-Je '80-p330
JB-v44-Je '80-p129
TES-Ja 25 '80-p26
Hunters
Brit Bk N-Je '80-p330
JB-v44-Je '80-p130
TES-Ja 25 '80-p26
Migrants
Brit Bk N-Je '80-p330
Sch Lib-v28-Je '80-p162
TES-Ja 25 '80-p26
Nocturnals
Brit Bk N-Je '80-p330
Lis-v104-N 6 '80-p626
TES-Ja 25 '80-p26

* * *

ELLIS, Mel
An Eagle To The Wind
BB-v6-Ag '78-p4
BL-v74-Jl 15 '78-p1732
KR-v46-Ap 1 '78-p380

* * *

ELLIS, R
Trees For Use And Delight
JB-v41-Ag '77-p219

* * *

ELLIS, Rosemary
Papermaking
GP-v15-Mr '77-p3067
JB-v41-Je '77-p161
Pipes And Wires
GP-v14-N '75-p2740

* * *

ELLIS, V R
Menace At Oyster Bay
JB-v41-Ag '77-p219
The Tribe With No Feet
JB-v43-F '79-p29

* * *

ELLISON, Lucile W
Butter On Both Sides
CBRS-v8-F '80-p53
CCB-B-v33-Mr '80-p131
HB-v56-Ap '80-p171
KR-v48-Ja 15 '80-p66
RT-v34-N '80-p237
SLJ-v26-Mr '80-p130
The Tie That Binds
CLW-v53-N '81-p189
KR-v49-Ag 1 '81-p935
PW-v219-Je 5 '81-p83
SLJ-v27-Ag '81-p64
A Window To Look Through
HB-v58-Ag '82-p400
PW-v221-Ap 16 '82-p70
SLJ-v28-Ag '82-p96

* * *

ELLISON, Virginia H
The Pooh Cook Book
ABC-v26-My '76-p4
BL-v66-D 15 '69-p516
BW-v3-N 23 '69-p14
CE-v47-Ja '71-p211
Comw-v91-N 21 '69-p261
KR-v37-S 15 '69-p1004
LJ-v95-Mr 15 '70-p1194
NY-v45-D 13 '69-p212
NYTBR, pt.2-N 9 '69-p42
PW-v196-O 27 '69-p60
Spec-v323-My 4 '74-p552
Teacher-v91-N '73-p131
Teacher-v95-Ja '78-p42
The Pooh Get-Well Book
ABC-v26-My '76-p4
BL-v70-F 1 '74-p599
HB-v50-Ap '74-p163
KR-v41-N 15 '73-p1268
LJ-v99-S 15 '74-p2244
Teacher-v94-N '76-p38
The Pooh Party Book
ABC-v26-My '76-p4
BL-v68-F 1 '72-p465
HB-v48-F '72-p65
KR-v39-N 1 '71-p1159
LJ-v96-D 15 '71-p4178

* * *

ELMER, Irene
Anthony's Father
CCB-B-v26-D '72-p55
Inst-v82-N '72-p122
KR-v40-Ag 1 '72-p860
LJ-v97-N 15 '72-p3795
A Lodestone And A Toadstone
CCB-B-v23-Je '70-p157
KR-v37-O 1 '69-p1057
LJ-v95-F 15 '70-p769
NYTBR, pt.2-N 9 '69-p56
Nat-v209-D 15 '69-p671
Mandragora's Dragon
B&B-v11-D '65-p75
CCB-B-v18-Ja '65-p72

* * *

ELMORE, Patricia
Susannah And The Blue House Mystery
BL-v77-N 15 '80-p458
CBRS-v8-Ag '80-p137
CCB-B-v34-Mr '81-p131
CE-v58-S '81-p48
KR-v49-F 15 '81-p212
SLJ-v27-D '80-p73
Susannah And The Poison Green Halloween
BL-v79-O 1 '82-p244
CBRS-v11-O '82-p17
SLJ-v29-D '82-p82

* * *

ELPHICK, Judith
Fast And Slow
GP-v14-Mr '76-p2812
Noisy And Quiet
GP-v14-Mr '76-p2812
Old And New
GP-v14-Mr '76-p2812

* * *

ELSEY, Neil
Golf
JB-v45-Je '81-p122
TES-Mr 6 '81-p29

* * *

ELSON, Diane
A Christmas Book
B Rpt-v2-N '83-p45
CCB-B-v37-N '83-p47
SLJ-v30-O '83-p178
A Country Book
CCB-B-v37-S '83-p5
GP-v20-Ja '82-p4005
SLJ-v30-N '83-p91
Sch Lib-v30-Mr '82-p40
The First Day Of Spring
JB-v43-Ap '79-p94
If You Should Meet A Crocodile
GP-v18-Ja '80-p3634
JB-v44-Ap '80-p67
TES-N 23 '79-p34
TLS-D 14 '79-p128
A New Hat For Grace
GP-v15-Jl '76-p2921

* * *

ELSON, Peggy D
All Write
Cur R-v20-S '81-p360

* * *

ELTING, Mary
The Answer Book About You
ASBYP-v14-Fall '81-p18
CBRS-v9-N '80-p27
SB-v16-My '81-p277
Helicopters At Work
CCB-B-v27-O '73-p26
LJ-v98-Mr 15 '73-p1001
SB-v8-Mr '73-p349
If You Lived In The Days Of The Wild Mammoth Hunters
CCB-B-v23-Je '70-p157
SB-v5-Mr '70-p353
SR-v52-N 8 '69-p64
A Mongo Homecoming
CCB-B-v24-O '70-p24
KR-v37-D 1 '69-p1261
LJ-v95-Mr 15 '70-p1194
Mysterious Seas
ASBYP-v17-Spring '84-p18
BL-v80-N 1 '83-p406
SB-v20-S '84-p32
SLJ-v30-D '83-p65
A New Answer Book
JB-v43-Ap '79-p105
Par-v53-My '78-p25
Q Is For Duck
CBRS-v9-O '80-p11
CCB-B-v34-D '80-p69
Cur R-v20-Je '81-p244
EJ-v73-F '84-p103
HB-v57-F '81-p40
Inst-v90-N '80-p156
KR-v48-O 15 '80-p1351
PW-v218-Ag 15 '80-p55
RT-v35-O '81-p55
SLJ-v27-D '80-p67

* * *

ELWART, Joan P
Daisy Tells
CE-v43-N '66-p162
CLW-v37-Ap '66-p549
Right Foot Wrong Foot
CCB-B-v22-Ja '69-p77
LJ-v93-N 15 '68-p4394

* * *

ELWELL, Clarence
Two Color Phonics Workbooks
Cur R-v20-N '81-p454

* * *

ELWELL, Jerry MacElroy
Cuddles
SR-v2-My 31 '75-p34

* * *

ELWELL, Peter
The King Of The Pipers
BL-v80-Ap 15 '84-p1188
NYTBR-v89-My 27 '84-p21
PW-v225-Ap 6 '84-p75
SLJ-v30-Ag '84-p72

* * *

ELWOOD, Ann
Macmillan Illustrated Almanac For Kids
CCB-B-v35-Mr '82-p127
Kliatt-v18-Fall '84-p75
NYTBR-v87-Ja 17 '82-p30
RT-v38-D '84-p339
SLJ-v28-Ja '82-p76
Our American Minorities
BL-v80-Ja 15 '84-p719
Cur R-v18-F '79-p74
Windows In Space
ASBYP-v16-Fall '83-p22
CBRS-v10-Ag '82-p137
KR-v50-Je 15 '82-p679
SB-v18-Ja '83-p145
SLJ-v29-S '82-p119

* * *

ELWOOD, Roger
Future Kin
BL-v71-S 1 '74-p39
CSM-v67-Je 30 '75-p23
KR-v42-Ag 1 '74-p804
LJ-v99-O 15 '74-p2746
Horror Tales
PW-v207-Ja 6 '75-p58
The Many Worlds Of Andre Norton
BL-v71-N 1 '74-p283

ELWOOD, Roger (continued)
BL-v71-N 1 '74-p288
KR-v42-Jl 15 '74-p748
More Science Fiction Tales
KR-v42-D 15 '74-p1310
The Other Side Of Tomorrow
BL-v70-Ja 15 '74-p544
BS-v33-F 15 '74-p512
CCB-B-v27-My '74-p141
KR-v41-S 15 '73-p1043
LJ-v98-D 15 '73-p3710
NYTBR-F 24 '74-p8
PW-v204-S 17 '73-p56
TN-v39-Fall '82-p70
The 50-Meter Monsters And Other Horrors
Inst-v86-N '76-p159

* * *

ELY, Jean
The Inflated Dormouse
CCB-B-v24-Je '71-p156
PW-v198-S 28 '70-p79

* * *

EMANUAL, Walter
A Dog Day
TES-O 9 '81-p29

* * *

EMBERLEY, Barbara
Drummer Hoff
BL-v64-Ja 15 '68-p592
BL-v80-S 1 '83-p93
BW-v2-F 4 '68-p22
CCB-B-v21-Ja '68-p77
Emerg Lib-v11-Ja '84-p19
HB-v44-F '68-p53
KR-v35-O 15 '67-p1264
LJ-v92-D 15 '67-p4602
NO-v7-F 26 '68-p21
NS-v79-My 15 '70-p708
NYTBR-v72-N 5 '67-p67
NYTBR-v72-N 5 '67-p71
PW-v192-O 2 '67-p56
Par-v43-Je '68-p68
RT-v31-Ja '78-p426
RT-v32-N '78-p148
SR-v50-D 16 '67-p35
Spec-v224-My 9 '70-p620
TLS-Ap 16 '70-p419
Trav-v24-Ap '68-p323
One Wide River To Cross
Am-v115-N 5 '66-p551
BL-v63-N 1 '66-p327
CCB-B-v20-D '66-p56
CE-v43-My '67-p537
CSM-v58-N 3 '66-pB3
Comw-v85-N 11 '66-p181
GT-v84-My '67-p32
HB-v42-O '66-p559
KR-v34-Jl 15 '66-p683
LA-v56-Ap '79-p401
LJ-v91-Jl '66-p3528
LJ-v96-Mr 15 '71-p1087
NYTBR-v71-O 16 '66-p38
NYTBR, pt.2-F 15 '70-p24
PW-v190-D 26 '66-p99
Spec-v222-My 16 '69-p656
TLS-Je 26 '69-p695
TN-v35-Summer '79-p401
TN-v40-Fall '83-p58
Trav-v23-Ja '67-p195

* * *

EMBERLEY, Ed
A Birthday Wish
BW-D 11 '77-pE4
CCB-B-v31-F '78-p94
CSM-v69-N 2 '77-pB8
KR-v45-Jl 1 '77-p666
NYTBR-N 13 '77-p56
PW-v212-Jl 18 '77-p137
RT-v32-O '78-p32
SLJ-v24-N '77-p46
Time-v110-N 21 '77-p66
WLB-v52-N '77-p256
Ed Emberley's A B C
BL-v74-Je 15 '78-p1616
CCB-B-v32-S '78-p7
CLW-v50-O '78-p108
GP-v18-Mr '80-p3663
HB-v54-Ag '78-p385
JB-v43-D '79-p316
KR-v46-Je 1 '78-p593
NYTBR-Jl 2 '78-p11
PW-v213-Ap 10 '78-p72
RT-v33-O '79-p39
SLJ-v25-S '78-p107
VLS-My '82-p12
VV-v23-D 25 '78-p99
Ed Emberley's Amazing Look Through Book
BL-v75-My 15 '79-p1438
CCB-B-v33-O '79-p26
KR-v47-My 1 '79-p513
PW-v215-My 7 '79-p83
SLJ-v26-S '79-p109
WCRB-v5-Jl '79-p62
Ed Emberley's Big Green Drawing Book
BL-v76-S 1 '79-p42
KR-v48-F 1 '80-p129
PW-v216-D 10 '79-p70
SLJ-v26-N '79-p64
Ed Emberley's Big Orange Drawing Book
BL-v77-Ja 1 '81-p624
KR-v48-N 1 '80-p1390
NYTBR-v85-O 26 '80-p26
PW-v218-Ag 29 '80-p366
SLJ-v27-F '81-p56
Ed Emberley's Big Purple Drawing Book
BL-v78-Ja 1 '82-p596
KR-v49-N 1 '81-p1338
SLJ-v28-D '81-p51
Ed Emberley's Crazy Mixed-Up Face Game
BL-v77-Ap 15 '81-p1152
KR-v49-Ap 1 '81-p426
PW-v219-Mr 13 '81-p88
SLJ-v27-Ag '81-p54
Ed Emberley's Drawing Book
BL-v68-Je 15 '72-p908
BW-v6-My 7 '72-p14
CCB-B-v25-Je '72-p154
HB-v48-Ap '72-p164
KR-v40-Ja 15 '72-p65
PW-v201-F 28 '72-p72
Ed Emberley's Drawing Book Of Animals
BL-v66-My 15 '70-p1158
BW-v4-My 17 '70-p12
CCB-B-v24-S '70-p6
CLW-v42-O '70-p135
CSM-v62-My 7 '70-pB1
Inst-v79-Je '70-p105
JB-v42-Ap '78-p87
KR-v38-Ap 15 '70-p459
LJ-v95-My 15 '70-p1928
PW-v197-F 2 '70-p91
Time-v96-D 21 '70-p68
Ed Emberley's Drawing Book Of Faces
JB-v42-Ap '78-p87
KR-v43-My 1 '75-p509
PW-v207-My 26 '75-p60
SLJ-v22-O '75-p98
Ed Emberley's Great Thumbprint Drawing Book
BL-v73-My 15 '77-p1419
CCB-B-v31-S '77-p14
PW-v211-Mr 14 '77-p95
RT-v32-O '78-p30
RT-v32-My '79-p942
RT-v32-My '79-p945
SLJ-v24-S '77-p106
WCRB-v4-Ja '78-p67

EMBERLEY, Ed (continued)
Ed Emberley's Little Drawing Books
NYTBR-N 4 '73-p30
PW-v214-Ag 14 '78-p70
Ed Emberley's Science Flip Books
CCB-B-v36-Ap '83-p148
Inst-v92-Ap '83-p20
SA-v249-D '83-p41
Green Says Go
BL-v65-S 15 '68-p122
CCB-B-v22-S '68-p6
CSM-v60-N 7 '68-pB4
KR-v36-Jl 1 '68-p686
LJ-v93-N 15 '68-p4394
PW-v194-N 4 '68-p50
SR-v51-N 9 '68-p46
Klippity Klop
BL-v71-O 15 '74-p242
CCB-B-v28-Mr '75-p111
CE-v52-O '75-p31
EJ-v73-F '84-p104
KR-v42-S 15 '74-p1004
KR-v43-Ja 1 '75-p2
LJ-v99-D 15 '74-p3262
NYTBR-N 3 '74-p57
PW-v206-S 23 '74-p156
WLB-v49-O '74-p139
London Bridge Is Falling Down
BL-v64-D 1 '67-p448
BW-v1-N 5 '67-p2
CCB-B-v21-Ja '68-p80
CLW-v39-D '67-p299
CSM-v59-N 2 '67-pB3
HB-v43-D '67-p743
KR-v35-S 1 '67-p1039
LJ-v92-N 15 '67-p4244
NYTBR-v72-O 29 '67-p42
PW-v192-S 11 '67-p68
Trav-v24-Ap '68-p324
Rosebud
KR-v34-Ja 15 '66-p53
LJ-v91-Mr 15 '66-p1690
NO-v5-Jl 4 '66-p17
NYTBR-v71-My 22 '66-p26
PW-v189-Ap 4 '66-p62
Wing On A Flea
LJ-v96-Mr 15 '71-p1084
The Wizard Of Op
Am-v133-D 6 '75-p404
BL-v72-Ja 1 '76-p624
Cur R-v16-F '77-p62
JB-v41-O '77-p275
KR-v43-O 15 '75-p1174
Lis-v98-N 10 '77-p626
NYTBR-N 16 '75-p58
PW-v208-N 24 '75-p52
SLJ-v22-F '76-p38
Teacher-v93-Ap '76-p34
Time-v106-D 8 '75-p88

* * *

EMBERLEY, Edward
Punch And Judy: A Play For Puppets
BL-v61-Jl 15 '65-p1064
CLW-v37-O '65-p144
Comw-v83-N 5 '65-p155
HB-v41-Je '65-p295
KR-v33-Mr 1 '65-p240
LJ-v90-Ap 15 '65-p2010
NYTBR-v70-Je 6 '65-p26
SR-v48-Je 19 '65-p41

* * *

EMBERLEY, Michael
Dinosaurs!
BL-v76-Mr 15 '80-p1055
KR-v48-My 1 '80-p576
PW-v217-Ja 25 '80-p341
SLJ-v26-My '80-p54
More Dinosaurs!
BW-v14-F 12 '84-p11
PW-v224-N 11 '83-p48
SLJ-v30-F '84-p68
The Sports Equipment Book
BL-v79-O 1 '82-p251
Inst-v92-Ap '83-p20
SLJ-v29-D '82-p85

* * *

EMBERLEY, Rebecca
Drawing With Numbers And Letters
BL-v77-Jl 1 '81-p1394
KR-v49-Je 15 '81-p735
PW-v219-My 22 '81-p76
SLJ-v28-N '81-p74

* * *

EMBLETON, G A
Passenger Aircraft
TES-N 11 '83-p27
Warfare In History
TES-N 30 '84-p28

* * *

EMBRY, Margaret
The Blue-Nosed Witch
PW-v224-Jl 8 '83-p66
My Name Is Lion
BL-v67-Ja 15 '71-p419
CCB-B-v24-Mr '71-p106
KR-v38-O 15 '70-p1146
Peg-Leg Willy
CCB-B-v20-Ap '67-p119
KR-v34-O 15 '66-p1100
LJ-v91-N 15 '66-p5747
PW-v190-O 24 '66-p51
Shadi
BL-v68-S 15 '71-p108
BL-v69-O 15 '72-p178
BW-v5-My 9 '71-p17
CCB-B-v24-Je '71-p156
LJ-v97-Ap 15 '72-p1615
SR-v54-Je 19 '71-p27

* * *

EMECHETA, Buchi
The Moonlight Bride
HB-v59-O '83-p572
KR-v50-D 15 '82-p1337
TES-My 15 '81-p29
Nowhere To Play
BW-v11-Ap 12 '81-p9
Brit Bk N C-Spring '81-p22
JB-v45-Ap '81-p70
NS-v100-N 14 '80-p20
PW-v219-Mr 13 '81-p89
SLJ-v27-Mr '81-p131
Sch Lib-v29-Je '81-p132
TES-D 5 '80-p23
Titch The Cat
Brit Bk N C-Spring '81-p11
JB-v43-D '79-p324
Obs-F 11 '79-p36
Sch Lib-v27-Je '79-p135
TES-Jl 15 '83-p18

* * *

EMERSON, Anne
Peter Rabbit's Cookery Book
GP-v19-N '80-p3795
JB-v44-D '80-p289

* * *

EMERSON, Donald
Span Across A River
BS-v26-Je 1 '66-p100
CCB-B-v19-My '66-p148
CSM-v58-S 22 '66-p10
KR-v34-F 15 '66-p186
LJ-v91-My 15 '66-p2704
NYTBR-v71-Ap 24 '66-p26

* * *

EMERT, Phyllis R
Jane Frederick: Pentathlon Champion
BL-v78-F 1 '82-p710

* * *

EMERY, Anne
American Friend: Herbert Hoover
BL-v64-O 15 '67-p272
BS-v27-Jl 1 '67-p144
CCB-B-v21-Ap '68-p125
EJ-v56-N '67-p1222
EL-v88-F '68-p231
KR-v35-Ja 15 '67-p65
LJ-v92-Ap 15 '67-p1747
Danger In A Smiling Mask
CCB-B-v22-Je '69-p157
CSM-v60-N 7 '68-pB14
KR-v36-O 1 '68-p1120
LJ-v94-My 15 '69-p2123
Dinny Gordon, Senior
CCB-B-v19-D '65-p61
KR-v33-Ag 1 '65-p763
LJ-v90-S 15 '65-p3813
Jenny Lee, Patriot
CCB-B-v20-My '67-p138
KR-v34-O 1 '66-p1055
LJ-v91-D 15 '66-p6191
The Losing Game
BS-v24-Mr 15 '65-p493
CCB-B-v18-Ap '65-p116
KR-v33-Ja 15 '65-p64
LJ-v90-Mr 15 '65-p1557
NYTBR-v70-My 9 '65-p26
Mystery Of The Opal Ring
CCB-B-v21-N '67-p40
CLW-v39-F '68-p437
EJ-v57-My '68-p759
KR-v35-Ag 15 '67-p966
LJ-v92-N 15 '67-p4271
The Sky Is Falling
BS-v30-F 15 '71-p506
CCB-B-v24-F '71-p89
KR-v38-O 1 '70-p1105
LJ-v95-D 15 '70-p4362
Stepfamily
CCB-B-v34-N '80-p51
SLJ-v26-Ap '80-p123

* * *

EMIL, Jane
All About Rivers
ASBYP-v17-Spring '84-p55
SB-v20-N '84-p93

* * *

EMMENS, Carol A
An Album Of Television
SLJ-v27-S '80-p69
WLB-v57-Je '83-p870

* * *

EMMERSON, Anne
The History Of The Tale Of Peter Rabbit
B&B-v22-N '76-p76
BL-v73-My 1 '77-p1358
HB-v53-O '77-p550
SLJ-v23-My '77-p40

* * *

EMMET, E R
Mind Tickling Brainteasers
CCB-B-v31-Je '78-p158
The Puffin Book Of Brainteasers
Obs-Ja 2 '77-p27

* * *

EMMETT, Bruce
Rooftop Wizard
CCB-B-v28-My '75-p144
KR-v42-D 15 '74-p1298

* * *

EMRICH, Duncan
An Almanac Of American Folklore
HB-v49-Ap '73-p153
The Book Of Wishes And Wishmaking
BL-v67-Ap 15 '71-p700
HB-v47-Ag '71-p394
LJ-v96-Ap 15 '71-p1491
NY-v47-D 4 '71-p184
The Hodgepodge Book
BL-v69-Ap 1 '73-p763
CCB-B-v26-Jl '73-p170
Comw-v99-N 23 '73-p214
JAF-v86-O '73-p410
KR-v40-N 15 '72-p1308
KR-v40-D 15 '72-p1415
LJ-v98-Mr 15 '73-p1002
NYTBR-N 19 '72-p8
NYTBR, pt.2-N 5 '72-p29
TN-v29-Je '73-p356
The Nonsense Book
BL-v67-S 1 '70-p56
Comw-v93-N 20 '70-p206
HB-v46-O '70-p486
KR-v38-Je 15 '70-p640
LJ-v95-S 15 '70-p3046
LJ-v95-D 15 '70-p4325
NYTBR, pt.2-N 8 '70-p7
PW-v197-Je 15 '70-p66
The Nonsense Book Of Riddles, Rhymes, Tongue Twisters, Puzzles And Jokes From American Folklore
BL-v67-Ap 1 '71-p659
CCB-B-v24-Je '71-p156
JAF-v84-Jl '71-p357
TN-v27-Ja '71-p208
The Whim-Wham Book
BL-F 1 '76-p792
BS-v36-Ap '76-p28
CCB-B-v29-My '76-p142
HB-v52-Je '76-p305
KR-v43-O 15 '75-p1188
NYTBR-F 15 '76-p14
SLJ-v22-D '75-p51
Teacher-v93-Mr '76-p18

* * *

ENCHANTED Pig
BW-v14-Jl 8 '84-p8

* * *

ENCHANTMENT Of The World
Cur R-v22-O '83-p91

* * *

ENCINAS, Lydia
A Beginner's Book Of Sewing
BL-v73-Jl 15 '77-p1722
BL-v73-Jl 15 '77-p1728
PW-v211-My 23 '77-p246
SLJ-v24-S '77-p142
Raggedy Ann And Andy's Sewing Book
PW-v212-N 28 '77-p51
SLJ-v24-Ap '78-p84

* * *

ENCORE Readers
RT-v34-N '80-p223

* * *

ENCYCLOPEDIA Galactica
SLJ-v26-Ja '80-p68

* * *

ENCYCLOPEDIA Of Africa
ARBA-v8-'77-p160
BL-v73-Ap 1 '77-p1196
SE-v41-Ap '77-p349
SLJ-v23-N '76-p68

* * *

ENDE, Michael
The Dream-Eater
GP-v17-Mr '79-p3476
JB-v43-Ap '79-p94

ENDE, Michael (continued)
The Grey Gentlemen
GP-v14-Jl '75-p2656
JB-v39-Je '75-p197
Obs-N 30 '75-p27
TLS-Jl 11 '75-p767
The Neverending Story
Analog-v104-F '84-p163
B&B-D '83-p31
BL-v80-N 15 '83-p488
BS-v43-F '84-p397
BW-v13-O 16 '83-p11
BW-v14-Jl 22 '84-p12
CSM-v75-N 9 '83-p26
Econ-v289-N 26 '83-p96
Fant R-v7-My '84-p29
Fant R-v7-My '84-p30
GP-v22-Ja '84-p4192
HB-v60-Ap '84-p228
JB-v48-Ap '84-p81
KR-v51-Ag 1 '83-p844
LJ-v108-O 15 '83-p1975
NW-v102-N 14 '83-p112
NYTBR-v88-N 6 '83-p14
Obs-D 4 '83-p32
PW-v224-Ag 19 '83-p70
PW-v225-Je 8 '84-p63
TES-Ja 6 '84-p21
WSJ-v203-F 14 '84-p30
Das Schnupsenbuch
BL-v77-O 1 '80-p262

* * *

ENDERLE, Judith A
Good Junk
CBRS-v9-Ap '81-p71
PW-v219-F 27 '81-p149
SLJ-v28-Ja '82-p62

* * *

ENDERSBY, Clive
Read All About It!
Can Child Lit-#26 '82-p64

* * *

ENDICOTT, Marion
Emily Carr: The Story Of An Artist
BIC-v10-D '81-p8
Can Child Lit-#27 '82-p183
In Rev-v15-O '81-p34
Quill & Q-v48-Ja '82-p35
Quill & Q-v48-Je '82-p4

* * *

ENERGY
Cur R-v22-F '83-p80
Har Bus R-v58-Ja '80-p38
Har Bus R-v58-Ja '80-p42

* * *

ENERGY Crisis (Structural Readers)
TES-Ja 1 '82-p17

* * *

ENGDAHL, Sylvia Louise
Anywhere, Anywhen
BB-v5-My '77-p3
BL-v73-S 15 '76-p131
BL-v73-S 15 '76-p140
CE-v53-F '77-p213
KR-v44-S 15 '76-p1039
SLJ-v23-O '76-p116
Beyond The Tomorrow Mountains
BL-v69-Je 1 '73-p943
BL-v69-Je 1 '73-p946
CCB-B-v26-Je '73-p153
HB-v49-Je '73-p276
KR-v41-F 15 '73-p193
LJ-v98-S 15 '73-p2663
PT-v7-Ag '73-p90
The Doors Of The Universe
BL-v77-Ap 1 '81-p1084
BS-v41-My '81-p78
CCB-B-v34-Je '81-p192
J Read-v25-N '81-p179
SLJ-v27-Ap '81-p138
VOYA-v4-Je '81-p37
Heritage Of The Star
B&B-v19-O '73-p138
GP-v14-Mr '76-p2820
Journey Between Worlds
CCB-B-v24-Ja '71-p72
CLW-v42-Ap '71-p522
CLW-v43-O '71-p116
CSM-v62-N 12 '70-pB4
HB-v46-O '70-p479
Inst-v83-Ag '73-p74
KR-v38-Ag 15 '70-p885
LJ-v95-O 15 '70-p3636
TN-v34-Spring '78-p265
Our World Is Earth
CBRS-v8-16 '80-p67
CE-v57-S '80-p44
KR-v48-F 1 '80-p120
NYTBR-F 17 '80-p24
SB-v16-S '80-p31
SLJ-v26-F '80-p44
The Planet-Girded Suns
ACSB-v8-Spring '75-p18
BL-v71-Ja 15 '75-p501
BS-v34-F 15 '75-p518
HB-v51-F '75-p74
KR-v42-D 1 '74-p1260
KR-v43-Ja 1 '75-p12
SB-v11-My '75-p20
SLJ-v21-Mr '75-p105
The Subnuclear Zoo
BL-v74-Ja 1 '78-p746
CCB-B-v31-Ap '78-p125
KR-v45-N 1 '77-p1150
SB-v14-S '78-p111
SLJ-v24-O '77-p123
This Star Shall Abide
BL-v68-My 15 '72-p820
CCB-B-v26-F '73-p89
CLW-v54-Ap '83-p369
CSM-v64-My 4 '72-pB5
HB-v48-Je '72-p274
Inst-v83-Ag '73-p74
KR-v40-Mr 15 '72-p335
LJ-v97-My 15 '72-p1921
TN-v29-Ja '73-p167
Tool For Tomorrow
ACSB-v13-Winter '80-p17
CCB-B-v33-N '79-p45
KR-v47-Mr 15 '79-p333
SB-v15-Mr '80-p209
SLJ-v26-S '79-p135
Universe Ahead
BB-v4-Mr '76-p4
BL-v72-N 1 '75-p360
BS-v35-D '75-p270
CE-v53-O '76-p33
KR-v43-O 15 '75-p1193
SLJ-v22-N '75-p88

* * *

ENGEBRECHT, P A
Under The Haystack
BL-v69-Jl 1 '73-p1020
BS-v33-My 15 '73-p97
BW-v7-My 13 '73-p2
CCB-B-v27-S '73-p7
EJ-v63-Mr '74-p105
KR-v41-Ja 15 '73-p64
KR-v41-D 15 '73-p1356
LJ-v98-Mr 15 '73-p1002
LJ-v98-My 15 '73-p1654
NYTBR-Ag 12 '73-p8

* * *

ENGEBRECHT, Pat
The Promise Of Moonstone
CBRS-v11-Jl '83-p136
KR-v51-Je 15 '83-p663
Kliatt-v18-Fall '84-p8
SLJ-v30-O '83-p166

* * *

ENGEL, Beth B
Big Words
BL-v79-Mr 1 '83-p904
CBRS-v11-F '83-p69
CCB-B-v36-Mr '83-p125
J Read-v27-D '83-p280
KR-v50-N 15 '82-p1240
SLJ-v29-F '83-p88

* * *

ENGEL, Beth Bland
Ride The Pine Sapling
BB-v7-Je '79-p3
BL-v74-Jl 15 '78-p1732
CCB-B-v32-Ap '79-p134
Inter BC-v10-Ap 40 '79-p18
KR-v46-N 15 '78-p1247
PW-v214-Ag 28 '78-p394
SLJ-v25-O '78-p154

* * *

ENGEL, Marian
Adventure At Moon Bay Towers
BF-v4-Spring '78-p55
My Name Is Not Odessa Yarker
Can Child Lit-#21 '81-p80

* * *

ENGELMANN, Siegfried
Corrective Mathematics
Cur R-v21-F '82-p71

* * *

ENGEMAN, Jack
Doctor: His Training And Practice
CCB-B-v18-F '65-p85
CLW-v36-Mr '65-p475
Comw-v82-My 28 '65-p332
LJ-v90-F 15 '65-p969

* * *

ENGEN, Gavin M
Kit Cars
SLJ-v24-F '78-p56

* * *

ENGEN, Rodney
Kate Greenaway
BL-v72-Jl 15 '76-p1562
BL-v72-Jl 15 '76-p1595
Randolph Caldecott: 'Lord Of The Nursery'
Choice-v14-F '78-p1632
HB-v53-D '77-p676
Obs-D 5 '76-p31
SLJ-v24-O '77-p92

* * *

ENGLANDER, Alice
The Amazing Professor And His Travels In Time
JB-v47-D '83-p242

* * *

ENGLANDER, Roger
Opera
BL-v79-Ag '83-p1452
CCB-B-v37-N '83-p47
HB-v59-D '83-p723
SLJ-v30-D '83-p73
VOYA-v6-F '84-p345

* * *

ENGLE, Eloise
The Finns In America
BL-v74-My 1 '78-p1428
CE-v55-O '78-p40
SLJ-v25-S '78-p129

* * *

ENGLE, Joanna
Cap'n Kid Goes To The South Pole
PW-v223-Ap 15 '83-p51
SLJ-v30-N '83-p62

* * *

ENGLEBARDT, Leland S
You Have A Right
BL-v75-Jl 15 '79-p1625
CBRS-v7-Ag '79-p136
CCB-B-v33-Ap '80-p150
KR-v47-Je 1 '79-p643
SLJ-v26-S '79-p156
SLJ-v27-D '80-p20

* * *

ENGLEBARDT, Stanley L
Careers In Data Processing
BL-v66-D 1 '69-p449
BS-v29-O 1 '69-p254
CCB-B-v23-Mr '70-p110
CLW-v41-Mr '70-p477
KR-v37-Ag 15 '69-p862
LJ-v95-Ja 15 '70-p251
How To Get In Shape For Sports
BL-v73-N 15 '76-p472
KR-v44-O 1 '76-p1098
SLJ-v23-D '76-p72
Kids And Alcohol
BL-v72-Ja 1 '76-p625
CLW-v49-D '77-p230
KR-v43-N 1 '75-p1242
NYTBR-Ja 18 '76-p12
SB-v12-My '76-p10
SLJ-v22-F '76-p45
Miracle Chip
ACSB-v13-Spring '80-p25
BL-v76-Ja 1 '80-p666
RT-v36-Mr '83-p631
SB-v16-S '80-p1
SLJ-v26-Mr '80-p130

* * *

ENGLEBERT, Victor
Camera On Africa
BL-v67-Je 1 '71-p833
SLJ-v28-S '81-p41
Camera On The Sahara
BL-v68-Ap 15 '72-p722
CCB-B-v25-Mr '72-p105
LJ-v97-Jl '72-p2477
The Goats Of Agadez
BL-v70-S 15 '73-p118
CCB-B-v27-D '73-p62
KR-v41-Ap 15 '73-p459
LJ-v98-S 15 '73-p2638

* * *

ENGLISH, Betty L
You Can't Be Timid With A Trumpet
BL-v77-D 1 '80-p512
CCB-B-v34-F '81-p110
CE-v57-My '81-p302
KR-v49-F 15 '81-p217
ON-v45-Mr 14 '81-p43
PW-v218-N 28 '80-p50
SLJ-v27-Ja '81-p58

* * *

ENGLISH, Betty Lou
Women At Their Work
BB-v5-Ja '78-p2
BL-v73-Jl 15 '77-p1728
CCB-B-v31-N '77-p45
KR-v45-Je 1 '77-p577
PW-v211-Je 27 '77-p111
SB-v14-My '78-p36
SE-v42-Ap '78-p321
SLJ-v24-S '77-p126
Teacher-v96-My '79-p27

* * *

ENGLISH, Peter
Panama And The Canal Zone In Pictures
Inter BC-v13-#2 '82-p10

* * *

ENGLISH For Primary Schools
TES-Jl 11 '80-p29

* * *

ENGLISH For The Middle Years
TES-Jl 11 '80-p29

* * *

ENGLISH Work Books
TES-Jl 11 '80-p29

* * *

ENGVICK, William
Lullabies And Night Songs
Atl-v216-D '65-p152
BL-v62-D 1 '65-p366
CE-v43-O '66-p94
CSM-v57-N 4 '65-pB3
HB-v42-F '66-p61
LJ-v90-D 15 '65-p5500
NYRB-v5-D 9 '65-p37
NYTBR-v70-N 7 '65-p51
Nat R-v17-D 14 '65-p1165
Par-v41-Jl '66-p98
SR-v48-N 13 '65-p56
TLS-O 16 '69-p1200
Teacher-v94-Mr '77-p26

* * *

ENRIGHT, D J
Beyond Land's End
Brit Bk N-Ja '80-p16
GP-v18-Mr '80-p3673
JB-v44-Ap '80-p81
Lis-v102-N 8 '79-p643
Sch Lib-v27-D '79-p373
The Joke Shop
B&B-v22-Ja '77-p61
JB-v41-Ap '77-p108
Lis-v96-N 11 '76-p623
NS-v92-N 5 '76-p645
PW-v212-D 26 '77-p68
SLJ-v24-Mr '78-p127
Spec-v237-D 11 '76-p24
TLS-D 10 '76-p1547
Rhyme Times Rhyme
Lis-v92-N 7 '74-p617
NS-v87-My 24 '74-p742
Obs-Je 2 '74-p33
TLS-Jl 5 '74-p717
Wild Ghost Chase
JB-v42-Ag '78-p202
Lis-v100-N 9 '78-p623
NS-v95-My 19 '78-p683
Obs-Mr 26 '78-p25
Spec-v240-Ap 29 '78-p25
TES-Je 16 '78-p48
TLS-Ap 7 '78-p377

* * *

ENRIGHT, Elizabeth
Four-Story Mistake
PW-v191-Ja 23 '67-p262
TES-N 27 '81-p23
Gone-Away Lake
HB-v60-S '84-p622
NYTBR-v71-Je 5 '66-p43
The Saturdays
HB-v60-Ag '84-p499
PW-v190-Ag 29 '66-p351
TES-N 27 '81-p23
Thimble Summer
CLW-v38-Mr '67-p471
Teacher-v94-Ja '77-p134
Zeee
CCB-B-v18-My '65-p127
Comw-v82-My 28 '65-p328
HB-v41-Je '65-p276
KR-v33-Mr 15 '65-p309
LJ-v90-Je 15 '65-p2883
NYTBR-v70-Je 13 '65-p24
SR-v48-Ap 24 '65-p45

* * *

ENRIGHT, Madeline
Nature Alive
GP-v19-S '80-p3748
Obs-Ap 6 '80-p39

* * *

ENSIGN, Georgianne
The Hunt For The Mastodon
CCB-B-v26-D '72-p55
LJ-v97-Ja 15 '72-p280
SB-v8-My '72-p41

* * *

ENSOR, Wendy-Ann
Heroes And Heroines In Music
TES-Jl 23 '82-p24

* * *

ENTER
BL-v80-Je 15 '84-p1476
Inst-v93-Ja '84-p135
Mag YA- '84-p101
SLJ-v30-My '84-p39

* * *

ENTRIKEN, William
Song Of The Three Young Men
SLJ-v28-Mr '82-p151

* * *

ENVIRONMENTAL Action Coalition
It's Your Environment
ACSB-v10-Fall '77-p23
HB-v53-Je '77-p324
KR-v44-D 1 '76-p1266
SLJ-v23-Mr '77-p144

* * *

ENZENSBERGER, Hans Magnus
Allerleirauh
BL-v75-D 1 '78-p621

* * *

EPHRON, Delia
Santa And Alex
CBRS-v12-F '84-p69
NYTBR-v88-N 13 '83-p44
PW-v224-N 4 '83-p65
SLJ-v30-O '83-p176
Teenage Romance
BL-v77-My 15 '81-p1214
BS-v41-N '81-p315
BW-v12-Ag 22 '82-p12
CCB-B-v35-D '81-p67
EJ-v72-Ja '83-p78
Kliatt-v17-Winter '83-p78
LJ-v106-S 1 '81-p1631
NYTBR-v86-O 11 '81-p14
Nat-v233-N 21 '81-p547
PW-v220-Jl 31 '81-p52
PW-v222-Jl 16 '82-p77
SLJ-v28-D '81-p90
VOYA-v4-F '82-p41

* * *

EPPLE, Anne Orth
The Beginning Knowledge Book Of Fossils
CCB-B-v24-S '70-p6
KR-v37-N 1 '69-p1151
LJ-v95-S 15 '70-p3046
SB-v5-Mr '70-p322
The Lookalikes
HB-v47-O '71-p504
KR-v39-Je 15 '71-p643
LJ-v96-O 15 '71-p3466
PW-v199-Je 21 '71-p71

* * *

EPPS, Peter
Sense Or Nonsense?
TES-Mr 6 '81-p31

* * *

EPSTEIN, Anne Merrick
Good Stones
BL-v74-S 1 '77-p39
CLW-v49-O '77-p142
CSM-v69-N 2 '77-pB8
Comw-v104-N 11 '77-p731
Cur R-v17-Ag '78-p182
HB-v53-Ag '77-p439
KR-v45-Ap 1 '77-p350
LA-v55-Ap '78-p524
SLJ-v24-S '77-p143

* * *

EPSTEIN, Beryl
Lucky, Lucky White Horse
CCB-B-v19-S '65-p7
CE-v42-Ja '66-p314
HB-v41-Ap '65-p166
KR-v33-Ja 1 '65-p5
LJ-v90-F 15 '65-p960
Two Sisters And Some Hornets
CCB-B-v26-Ja '73-p75
KR-v40-S 1 '72-p1020
LJ-v98-F 15 '73-p633
Who Says You Can't?
BL-v65-Jl 1 '69-p1220
BS-v29-My 1 '69-p56
CCB-B-v23-Ja '70-p79
Comw-v90-My 23 '69-p299
KR-v37-Ja 15 '69-p59
LJ-v94-Ap 15 '69-p1794
LJ-v96-O 15 '71-p3437
NYTBR, pt.2-My 4 '69-p5
PW-v195-Mr 24 '69-p55
SR-v52-My 10 '69-p61

* * *

EPSTEIN, Edna
The First Book Of The U.N.
Cur R-v18-My '79-p153

* * *

EPSTEIN, Jean Gay
Louis Armstrong: Ambassador Satchmo
Inst-v82-N '72-p127
JLD-v11-Ap '78-p44
Teacher-v93-Ap '76-p120

* * *

EPSTEIN, June
Big Dipper
SLJ-v28-Ja '82-p63
A Swag Of Songs
CAY-v5-Fall '84-p4
JB-v48-Je '84-p125

* * *

EPSTEIN, Sam
Baseball: Hall Of Fame, Stories Of Champions
LJ-v90-Ap 15 '65-p2019
LJ-v93-My 15 '68-p2128
Dr. Beaumont And The Man With The Hole In His Stomach
BB-v6-Je '78-p2
BL-v74-My 1 '78-p1430
CCB-B-v31-Jl '78-p174
CE-v55-N '78-p104
CLW-v50-S '78-p91
Comw-v105-N 10 '78-p733
KR-v46-Mr 15 '78-p308
SB-v14-Mr '79-p232
SE-v43-Ap '79-p299
SLJ-v24-My '78-p36
SLJ-v24-My '78-p65
Teacher-v96-O '78-p162
The First Book Of Electricity
SB-v14-My '78-p38
SLJ-v23-My '77-p60
The First Book Of Italy
BL-v69-My 1 '73-p863
LJ-v98-Mr 15 '73-p1002
First Book Of Mexico
KR-v34-D 15 '66-p1286
LJ-v92-Ja 15 '67-p334
The First Book Of News
BL-v62-Mr 1 '66-p662
LJ-v90-D 15 '65-p5512
NYTBR-v71-Ja 30 '66-p22
The First Book Of Printing
BL-v72-N 15 '75-p452
SLJ-v22-O '75-p98
The First Book Of Switzerland
GJ-v132-Mr '66-p149
TLS-D 9 '65-p1157
The Game Of Baseball
CCB-B-v18-My '65-p127
LJ-v90-Ap 15 '65-p2020
George Washington Carver: Negro Scientist
JNE-v38-Fall '69-p420
Grandpa's Wonderful Glass
RT-v35-My '82-p901
Harriet Tubman
BL-v65-F 1 '69-p586
CLW-v41-O '69-p138
LJ-v94-F 15 '69-p871
Teacher-v93-Ap '76-p120
Henry Aaron: Home-Run King
BL-v72-D 15 '75-p577
Comw-v102-N 21 '75-p571
SLJ-v22-D '75-p68
Hold Everything
CCB-B-v27-O '73-p26
KR-v41-F 1 '73-p119
PW-v203-F 5 '73-p90
Jackie Robinson: Baseball's Gallant Fighter
SLJ-v21-Ap '75-p52
Kids In Court
BL-v78-Jl '82-p1433
CCB-B-v36-O '82-p25
KR-v50-My 1 '82-p561
SE-v47-Ap '83-p249
SLJ-v28-Ag '82-p124
VOYA-v5-O '82-p53
Look In The Mirror
CCB-B-v27-Ap '74-p127
KR-v41-O 15 '73-p1164
LJ-v98-D 15 '73-p3700
PW-v204-N 12 '73-p36
SB-v9-Mr '74-p326
Mexico
BL-v79-My 15 '83-p1215
Cur R-v22-O '83-p91
SLJ-v29-Mr '83-p174
SLJ-v30-N '83-p39
Michael Faraday
LJ-v96-N 15 '71-p3899
SB-v7-S '71-p110
Mister Peale's Mammoth
BL-v73-Jl 1 '77-p1651
CE-v54-N '77-p88
Comw-v104-N 11 '77-p732
HB-v53-O '77-p530
KR-v45-My 1 '77-p488
SLJ-v24-S '77-p126
More Stories Of Baseball Champions
LJ-v99-Mr 15 '74-p888
Pick It Up
BL-v68-D 15 '71-p366
KR-v39-S 1 '71-p948
LJ-v97-F 15 '72-p763
The Picture Life Of Franklin Delano Roosevelt
KR-v37-Ja 1 '69-p5
Sacramento
CE-v45-O '68-p90
LJ-v93-Ap 15 '68-p1798
Saving Electricity
SB-v13-Mr '78-p224
SLJ-v24-F '78-p46

EPSTEIN, Sam (continued)
Secret In A Sealed Bottle
ACSB-v13-Spring '80-p26
BL-v75-Ap 15 '79-p1294
CCB-B-v32-Jl '79-p189
HB-v55-Je '79-p340
KR-v47-Mr 1 '79-p264
SB-v15-Mr '80-p225
SLJ-v25-Ap '79-p54
She Never Looked Back
CCB-B-v33-My '80-p170
Cur R-v21-My '82-p225
Inter BC-v12-#4 '81-p35
KR-v48-Mr 1 '80-p290
SB-v16-Mr '81-p217
SLJ-v26-My '80-p66
Take This Hammer
LJ-v94-Jl '69-p2671
SB-v5-S '69-p123
Washington, DC
BL-v77-My 15 '81-p1252
SLJ-v28-D '81-p62
Who Needs Holes?
BW-v4-N 8 '70-p4
CCB-B-v24-Ja '71-p72
KR-v38-Ap 1 '70-p386
LJ-v96-Ap 15 '71-p1522
SB-v6-S '70-p93
Willie Mays: Baseball Superstar
SLJ-v22-S '75-p101
A Year Of Japanese Festivals
SLJ-v21-Mr '75-p95
Young Paul Revere's Boston
CCB-B-v20-Ap '67-p119
CE-v44-S '67-p54
LJ-v92-Ja 15 '67-p334

* * *

EPSTEIN, Vivian S
History Of Women For Children
Inter BC-v15-#5 '84-p18

* * *

EQUIPO, Plantel
Como Puede Ser La Democracia
BL-v79-Ap 1 '83-p1024

* * *

ERDMAN, Loula Grace
Save Weeping For The Night
CCB-B-v29-S '75-p7
KR-v43-Ap 15 '75-p460
SLJ-v21-My '75-p63

* * *

ERDOES, Richard
The Native Americans: Navajos
BL-v75-Mr 1 '79-p1087
CBRS-v7-Je '79-p106
CCB-B-v32-Jl '79-p190
SLJ-v26-O '79-p148
Sch Lib-v28-Je '80-p187
Native Americans: The Pueblos
BL-v80-Ap 1 '84-p1115
SLJ-v30-Ag '84-p72
Native Americans: The Sioux
BL-v79-F 1 '83-p723
B Rpt-v1-Ja '83-p50
CBRS-v11-S '82-p8
CLW-v54-My '83-p424
SLJ-v29-Ja '83-p74
Picture History Of Ancient Rome
CCB-B-v21-S '67-p4
CSM-v59-N 2 '67-pB9
CW-v61-F '68-p220
HB-v43-Ag '67-p479
Inst-v77-O '67-p175
KR-v35-Ap 15 '67-p502
LJ-v92-Jl '67-p2648
NYTBR-v72-My 7 '67-p41
Obs-D 3 '67-p26
SR-v50-Je 17 '67-p36
TLS-N 30 '67-p1162
The Rain Dance People
BL-v73-S 1 '76-p37
BS-v36-Ag '76-p173
KR-v44-Ap 15 '76-p486
SB-v12-D '76-p129
SLJ-v23-S '76-p132
The Sound Of Flutes
BL-v73-Ja 1 '77-p664
CCB-B-v30-Mr '77-p105
HB-v53-F '77-p47
KR-v44-O 15 '76-p1141
SE-v41-Ap '77-p349
SLJ-v26-N '79-p43
The Sun Dance People
BL-v69-O 1 '72-p147
BW-v6-Jl 16 '72-p7
CCB-B-v26-S '72-p5
CCB-B-v30-S '76-p9
KR-v40-Ap 15 '72-p488
LJ-v97-O 15 '72-p3459
NYTBR-Ag 13 '72-p8
PW-v202-Jl 31 '72-p71
SA-v229-D '73-p136

* * *

ERHLICH, Amy
Thumbelina
GP-v19-Mr '81-p3855

* * *

ERICKSON, Helen
A Young Person's Guide To The Opera
BL-v77-Ja 1 '81-p618
Brit Bk N C-Autumn '80-p27
CLW-v52-Ap '81-p406
Inst-v90-F '81-p24
SLJ-v27-Ag '81-p64
TES-Je 20 '80-p21
TLS-Jl 18 '80-p811

* * *

ERICKSON, Russell E
The Snow Of Ohreeganu
CLW-v46-F '75-p315
KR-v42-Ja 1 '74-p2
LJ-v99-Ap 15 '74-p1211
PW-v205-Ap 8 '74-p83
A Toad For Tuesday
BB-v3-Ap '75-p2
B&B-v24-Je '79-p56
BL-v71-S 15 '74-p98
BL-v71-Mr 15 '75-p766
BW-D 8 '74-p7
CCB-B-v28-Ja '75-p76
CE-v52-O '75-p32
CSM-v66-N 6 '74-p9
Choice-v12-N '75-p1132
GP-v18-Mr '80-p3656
HB-v51-F '75-p48
KR-v42-Jl 1 '74-p681
LJ-v99-S 15 '74-p2244
LJ-v99-D 15 '74-p3246
NYTBR-S 29 '74-p8
NYTBR-N 3 '74-p55
SR/W-v2-N 30 '74-p28
TES-S 19 '80-p30
Teacher-v92-My '75-p91
Warton And Morton
BL-v73-S 15 '76-p173
CCB-B-v30-Ja '77-p74
CSM-v68-N 3 '76-p26
GP-v18-Mr '80-p3656
HB-v52-D '76-p619
KR-v44-Jl 1 '76-p732
RT-v31-O '77-p17
SLJ-v23-S '76-p98
Teacher-v94-Ja '77-p130
Warton And The Castaways
BL-v78-Ap 15 '82-p1094
CE-v59-N '82-p132

ERICKSON, Russell E
(continued)
HB-v58-Ag '82-p401
JB-v46-O '82-p188
NYTBR-v87-Ap 25 '82-p45
SLJ-v28-Ap '82-p68
TES-Je 3 '83-p38
Warton And The King Of The Skies
BL-v75-N 15 '78-p545
BL-v78-F 15 '82-p761
HB-v55-F '79-p57
JB-v45-F '81-p17
KR-v46-O 1 '78-p1071
NS-v100-N 21 '80-p19
SLJ-v25-N '78-p60
TES-Mr 4 '83-p32
Warton And The Traders
BL-v75-Je 1 '79-p1490
HB-v55-Je '79-p296
JB-v45-O '81-p195
KR-v47-Je 15 '79-p686
RT-v33-Ja '80-p483
SLJ-v26-O '79-p138
TES-Ja 29 '82-p30
Warton's Christmas Eve Adventure
Am-v137-D 3 '77-p405
BB-v7-D '79-p2
BL-v74-D 15 '77-p682
HB-v54-Ap '78-p159
JB-v44-Ag '80-p175
KR-v45-N 1 '77-p1144
SLJ-v24-O '77-p88

* * *

ERICSON, Stig
Dan Henry In The Wild West
BL-v73-N 1 '76-p407
CCB-B-v30-N '76-p41
KR-v44-S 15 '76-p1043
SLJ-v23-N '76-p56

* * *

ERIKSEN, Aase
Students, Structures, Spaces
Cur R-v22-D '83-p87

* * *

ERIKSSON, Eva
Hocus Pocus
GP-v18-Ja '80-p3640
JB-v44-Je '80-p130
Sch Lib-v28-Mr '80-p31
Sometime Never
GP-v18-Ja '80-p3640
Sch Lib-v28-Mr '80-p31

* * *

ERNO, Richard B
Billy Lightfoot
CCB-B-v23-My '70-p142
CLW-v42-O '70-p138
KR-v37-O 15 '69-p1111
LJ-v95-My 15 '70-p1940

* * *

ERNST, John
Escape King
BL-v72-D 1 '75-p514
KR-v43-N 15 '75-p1290
SLJ-v22-Ja '76-p45
Teacher-v93-Mr '76-p24
Favorite Sleuths
CCB-B-v19-S '65-p7
KR-v33-Je 1 '65-p533
LJ-v90-O 15 '65-p4627
NYTBR-v70-N 7 '65-p60

* * *

ERNST, Kathryn
Charlie's Pets
BL-v74-My 15 '78-p1491
CCB-B-v32-D '78-p60
KR-v46-Je 15 '78-p634
LA-v55-S '78-p737
PW-v213-Ap 17 '78-p76
Par-v53-S '78-p32
SLJ-v25-S '78-p107
Danny And His Thumb
CCB-B-v26-Ap '73-p123
KR-v41-F 15 '73-p185
LJ-v98-Ap 15 '73-p1373
The First Americans
CBRS-v7-My '79-p95
Indians
SLJ-v26-F '80-p44
Mr. Tamarin's Trees
BL-v73-S 15 '76-p173
CCB-B-v30-F '77-p89
Inst-v86-N '76-p145
KR-v44-Je 15 '76-p680
SLJ-v23-N '76-p45
Owl's New Cards
BB-v5-Ja '78-p1
BL-v74-S 15 '77-p192
KR-v45-Jl 15 '77-p724
PW-v212-Jl 18 '77-p137
RT-v32-O '78-p36
SLJ-v24-O '77-p100

* * *

ERNST, Kathryn F
ESP McGee And The Mysterious Magician
SLJ-v30-D '83-p82

* * *

ERNST, Lisa C
The Prize Pig Surprise
CBRS-v13-O '84-p17
KR-v52-S 1 '84-pJ60
PW-v226-S 21 '84-p96
SLJ-v31-S '84-p102
Sam Johnson And The Blue Ribbon Quilt
CBRS-v12-N '83-p24
KR-v51-S 1 '83-pJ147
LA-v61-F '84-p178
Ms-v12-D '83-p70
NYTBR-v88-N 13 '83-p55
PW-v224-Ag 12 '83-p67
RT-v37-Mr '84-p647
SLJ-v30-D '83-p54

* * *

ERNST, Morris L
Lawyers And What They Do
BL-v61-Mr 15 '65-p700
BS-v25-Ap 15 '65-p51
CCB-B-v18-Je '65-p146
LJ-v90-Mr 15 '65-p1557

* * *

ERON, Judy
Charlie Rich
SLJ-v23-S '76-p114

* * *

ERSKINE, Jim
Bedtime Story
BL-v78-Je 15 '82-p1367
CBRS-v10-Ap '82-p82
CCB-B-v35-Mr '82-p127
Inst-v91-My '82-p104
LA-v59-O '82-p747
PW-v221-Mr 5 '82-p70
SLJ-v29-S '82-p108
Bert And Susie's Messy Tale
BL-v75-Jl 15 '79-p1626
CBRS-v7-Jl '79-p122
KR-v47-Ag 1 '79-p851
PW-v216-Jl 2 '79-p106
SLJ-v26-S '79-p109
The Snowman
BB-v6-D '78-p2
HB-v54-D '78-p630
KR-v46-S 1 '78-p946
PW-v214-Jl 24 '78-p100
SLJ-v25-D '78-p43

* * *

ERUP, Birgit
Susanne's Parents Get Divorced
GP-v18-My '79-p3529

* * *

ERVIN, Jane
Early Reading Comprehension In Varied Subject Matter
Cur R-v22-D '83-p19

* * *

ERWIN, Betty
The Summer Sleigh Ride
CCB-B-v20-My '67-p138

* * *

ERWIN, Betty K
Behind The Magic Line
CCB-B-v23-Ja '70-p79
Comw-v90-My 23 '69-p298
HB-v45-Ag '69-p410
KR-v37-My 15 '69-p559
LJ-v94-O 15 '69-p3820
Go To The Room Of The Eyes
Am-v121-D 13 '69-p594
BL-v66-N 1 '69-p345
CCB-B-v23-F '70-p95
Comw-v91-N 21 '69-p256
KR-v37-Ag 15 '69-p854
LJ-v94-D 15 '69-p4617
NY-v45-D 13 '69-p203
PW-v196-Ag 11 '69-p43
SLJ-v24-F '78-p35

* * *

ERWIN, John
Mrs. Fox
CCB-B-v23-S '69-p6
CSM-v61-My 8 '69-p13
KR-v37-F 1 '69-p99
LJ-v94-Ap 15 '69-p1780
NYTBR-Ap 6 '69-p20
PW-v195-My 5 '69-p52

* * *

ESBENSEN, Barbara J
Cold Stars And Fireflies
SLJ-v31-O '84-p156

* * *

ESBENSEN, Thorwald
Windows To Reading
Cur R-v17-D '78-p396
Inst-v88-F '79-p190

* * *

ESCOFET, Cristina
Llueve En La Ciudad
BL-v79-Jl '83-p1406

* * *

ESCOTT, J
The Stand-Ins
JB-v45-Ap '81-p78

* * *

ESCOTT, John
Alarm Bells
TES-Mr 19 '82-p28
TES-Mr 9 '84-p50
Bell Rescue
JB-v47-Ag '83-p161
TES-Mr 9 '84-p50
Burglar Bells
JB-v48-Ap '84-p69
TES-Mr 9 '84-p50
High Climb
JB-v42-D '78-p299
Naked Nancy And Other Stories
GP-v17-Mr '79-p3484
JB-v43-Ap '79-p114
Oddments Corner
Spec-v236-Ap 10 '76-p25
TLS-Ap 2 '76-p376
Radio Alert
GP-My '84-p4264
JB-v48-Je '84-p126
Sch Lib-v32-S '84-p233
TLS-Mr 30 '84-p337
A Walk Down The Pier
GP-v15-Mr '77-p3059
JB-v41-Je '77-p161
The Young Reporters
GP-v14-O '75-p2721
TLS-S 19 '75-p1058

* * *

ESCURY, Jenny C D'
The Wild Boar
RT-v33-Ja '80-p483

* * *

ESHMEYER, R E
Ask Any Vegetable
CLW-v47-D '75-p233
Comw-v102-N 21 '75-p571
KR-v43-Jl 15 '75-p779
PW-v208-Ag 11 '75-p118
SLJ-v22-N '75-p75

* * *

ESKENAZI, Gerald
Hockey
BL-v66-My 15 '70-p1130
BL-v70-Ja 15 '74-p535
BL-v70-Ja 15 '74-p541
BW-v4-Mr 1 '70-p3
CCB-B-v27-F '74-p93
CLW-v45-F '74-p344
Choice-v7-Jl '70-p712
Comw-v99-N 23 '73-p220
LJ-v95-Mr 1 '70-p910
LJ-v95-My 15 '70-p1965
LJ-v98-D 15 '73-p3720
NYTBR-D 7 '69-p62

* * *

ESLEY, Joan
The Visit
CBRS-v9-O '80-p11
CCB-B-v34-N '80-p51
PW-v218-Ag 15 '80-p55
SLJ-v27-N '80-p45

* * *

ESOPO
El Zorro Que Perdio La Cola
BL-v79-Jl '83-p1406

* * *

ESPELAND, Pamela
The Story Of Arachne
CBRS-v9-F '81-p53
SLJ-v27-Ap '81-p126
The Story Of Baucis And Philemon
CCB-B-v35-S '81-p8
SLJ-v28-F '82-p66
TES-Je 4 '82-p27
The Story Of Cadmus
CBRS-v9-F '81-p53
SLJ-v27-Ap '81-p126
The Story Of King Midas
SLJ-v27-Ap '81-p126
TES-Je 4 '82-p27
The Story Of Pygmalion
CBRS-v9-Spring '81-p104
CCB-B-v35-S '81-p8
LA-v58-N '81-p951
SLJ-v28-F '82-p66
TES-Je 4 '82-p27
Theseus And The Road To Athens
CBRS-v9-Spring '81-p104
SLJ-v28-F '82-p66
TES-Je 4 '82-p27
Why Do We Eat?
ASBYP-v15-Fall '82-p56

ESPELAND, Pamela
(continued)
SLJ-v28-Ag '82-p92

* * *

ESPY, Willard R
A Children's Almanac Of Words At Play
BL-v79-Ap 1 '83-p1032
BW-v13-Ja 9 '83-p12
CCB-B-v36-Mr '83-p125
CE-v59-My '83-p356
Kliatt-v17-Fall '83-p26
LATBR-Ja 16 '83-p4
NYTBR-v88-F 6 '83-p33
PW-v222-D 24 '82-p65
RT-v36-Ja '83-p469
SLJ-v29-Ag '83-p64
WSJ-v200-D 7 '82-p32

* * *

ESTEBAN, Angel
Imagen Y Sonido
BL-v78-Mr 15 '82-p967

* * *

ESTERER, Arnulf K
Saying It Without Words
BL-v76-Je 1 '80-p1422
Cur R-v20-Je '81-p245
SLJ-v27-S '80-p69

* * *

ESTES, Eleanor
The Alley
BL-v61-Ja 1 '65-p434
CLW-v36-Ja '65-p337
CSM-v57-Ja 28 '65-p5
HB-v41-F '65-p50
Inst-v74-F '65-p18
SLJ-v24-F '78-p35
The Coat-Hanger Christmas Tree
Am-v129-D 1 '73-p428
BL-v70-N 15 '73-p338
CCB-B-v27-N '73-p41
CLW-v45-D '73-p242
CSM-v65-N 7 '73-pB3
CSM-v66-D 5 '73-pB12
Comw-v99-N 23 '73-p212
GP-v15-Ap '77-p3085
HB-v49-D '73-p583
JB-v41-Ag '77-p219
KR-v41-Jl 15 '73-p754
LJ-v98-O 15 '73-p3127
PW-v204-Jl 16 '73-p111
The Hundred Dresses
RT-v33-Ap '80-p808
RT-v36-Ap '83-p802
SLJ-v25-D '78-p33
Teacher-v92-D '74-p79
Teacher-v97-S '79-p38
Lollipop Princess
BW-v2-F 25 '68-p16
CCB-B-v21-D '67-p58
CLW-v39-D '67-p295
HB-v43-D '67-p760
KR-v35-O 15 '67-p1269
LJ-v92-D 15 '67-p4602
SR-v50-N 11 '67-p45
The Lost Umbrella Of Kim Chu
BW-N 12 '78-pE4
CBRS-v7-Ja '79-p43
CCB-B-v32-Mr '79-p113
CE-v55-F '79-p223
HB-v55-F '79-p60
KR-v46-N 1 '78-p1189
PW-v214-N 27 '78-p60
SLJ-v25-Ja '79-p41
Sch Lib-v29-S '81-p234
TES-Ag 22 '80-p20
TLS-S 19 '80-p1026
Miranda The Great
BL-v63-My 1 '67-p948
CCB-B-v20-Ap '67-p120
CLW-v39-N '67-p240
HB-v43-Ap '67-p201
KR-v35-F 1 '67-p130
LJ-v92-Mr 15 '67-p1315
SR-v50-Mr 18 '67-p36
The Moffat Museum
BL-v80-O 15 '83-p358
CBRS-v12-Mr '84-p83
CCB-B-v37-N '83-p48
HB-v59-D '83-p707
KR-v51-N 1 '83-pJ191
SLJ-v30-Ja '84-p74
Moffats
BL-v80-Jl '84-p1555
PW-v193-F 26 '68-p179
The Moffats
BL-v75-Jl 15 '79-p1634
The Tunnel Of Hugsy Goode
CCB-B-v25-Ap '72-p121
CSM-v64-My 4 '72-pB6
HB-v48-Ap '72-p143
KR-v39-D 1 '71-p1256
LJ-v97-My 15 '72-p1928
NYTBR-Ap 23 '72-p8
PW-v201-Ja 17 '72-p59
SR-v55-Mr 25 '72-p110
The Witch Family
GP-v14-S '75-p2684

* * *

ESTES, Rose
Indiana Jones And The Lost Treasure Of Sheba
SLJ-v31-S '84-p139

* * *

ESTORIL, Jean
We Danced In Bloomsbury Square
CCB-B-v24-N '70-p41
CSM-v62-O 31 '70-p11
Dance-v46-Jl '72-p90
GT-v89-S '71-p155
LJ-v95-O 15 '70-p3636
LJ-v98-O 15 '73-p3123

* * *

ESTRADA, Doris
Periwinkle Jones
CCB-B-v19-S '65-p7
CE-v42-My '66-p566
KR-v33-Ag 15 '65-p820
LJ-v90-S 15 '65-p3788

* * *

ETCHEMENDY, Nancy
Stranger From The Stars
SLJ-v30-Ap '84-p113

* * *

ETCHISON, Birdie L
Me And Greenley
SLJ-v28-D '81-p62
Strawberry Mountain
SLJ-v29-S '82-p119

* * *

ETHELBERG, J
Food Chains
JB-v40-D '76-p324
The Garden Spider
GP-v15-S '76-p2950
JB-v40-O '76-p268
The Life Of The Butterfly
GP-v15-S '76-p2950
JB-v40-D '76-p324
Newts
JB-v40-D '76-p325

* * *

ETHELBERG, Jan
Tree In A Wood
Brit Bk N C-Autumn '80-p28
JB-v44-D '80-p290
TES-Je 20 '80-p25

* * *

ETHERINGTON, Frank
The General
BIC-v12-D '83-p16
Emerg Lib-v11-Ja '84-p40
Quill & Q-v50-F '84-p39
The Spaghetti Word Race
BIC-v10-O '81-p33
Can Child Lit-#25 '82-p70
Emerg Lib-v9-N '81-p35
Quill & Q-v47-Ag '81-p29
SLJ-v29-O '82-p140
Those Words
BIC-v11-Ag '82-p39
Can Child Lit-#30 '83-p84
Quill & Q-v48-Ag '82-p28

* * *

ETKIN, Ruth
Playing And Composing On The Recorder
Cur R-v17-F '78-p81
Inst-v85-N '75-p156
M Ed J-v62-F '76-p124
SLJ-v22-S '75-p101
The Rhythm Band Book
BL-v75-Ja 15 '79-p808
CBRS-v7-Je '79-p106
M Ed J-v66-F '80-p89
SLJ-v25-F '79-p54

* * *

ETS, Marie Hall
Bad Boy, Good Boy
BL-v64-Mr 1 '68-p783
BW-v1-N 5 '67-p47
CCB-B-v21-F '68-p93
KR-v35-S 15 '67-p1130
LJ-v92-N 15 '67-p4242
NYTBR-v72-N 5 '67-p63
SR-v50-N 11 '67-p42
Elephant In A Well
BL-v68-Je 15 '72-p908
CCB-B-v26-S '72-p6
CSM-v64-My 4 '72-pB2
KR-v40-F 1 '72-p130
LJ-v97-Je 15 '72-p2230
PW-v201-Mr 6 '72-p63
Gilberto And The Wind
BL-v68-Je 15 '72-p893
Nat-v209-D 15 '69-p672
SLJ-v27-Ja '81-p33
In The Forest
Teacher-v94-My '77-p110
Jay Bird
CCB-B-v28-S '74-p6
KR-v42-My 1 '74-p474
LJ-v99-S 15 '74-p2244
PW-v205-My 6 '74-p69
Just Me
B&B-v12-D '66-p68
BL-v61-My 1 '65-p872
CCB-B-v18-My '65-p128
CE-v42-D '65-p258
CLW-v37-Mr '66-p478
CSM-v57-My 6 '65-p2B
Comw-v82-My 28 '65-p327
GT-v83-Ap '66-p24
HB-v41-Ag '65-p382
Inst-v75-S '65-p166
KR-v33-Mr 15 '65-p308
LJ-v90-Ap 15 '65-p2010
Par-v41-Ag '66-p70
TLS-N 24 '66-p1083
Nine Days To Christmas
CLW-v45-N '73-p171
Teacher-v92-D '74-p14
The Story Of A Baby
CLW-v42-My '71-p568
SB-v5-S '69-p165
TN-v34-Winter '78-p161
Talking Without Words
BW-v2-N 3 '68-p5
CCB-B-v22-F '69-p91
KR-v36-Ag 15 '68-p891
LJ-v93-O 15 '68-p3956
NYTBR-v73-N 3 '68-p69
PW-v194-Ag 5 '68-p56
SR-v51-N 9 '68-p46
TN-v25-Ap '69-p309

* * *

ETTER, Les
The Game Of Hockey
SLJ-v24-D '77-p64
Get Those Rebounds!
CCB-B-v31-Jl '78-p175
CLW-v50-D '78-p238
SLJ-v24-My '78-p87
Hockey's Masked Men
SLJ-v23-Ja '77-p90
Vince Lombardi: Football Legend
SLJ-v22-S '75-p101

* * *

ETTLINGER, John R T
Choosing Books For Young People
ARBA-v15-'84-p61
Emerg Lib-v10-N '82-p29
JB-v47-Ap '83-p65
RQ-v22-Spring '83-p302
SLJ-v29-My '83-p36
VOYA-v6-Je '83-p109

* * *

EUGENE, Toni
Koalas And Kangaroos
BL-v78-My 15 '82-p1252
SB-v18-Ja '83-p146
Strange Animals Of Australia
ASBYP-v15-Fall '82-p55
Cur R-v21-My '82-p214

* * *

EUNSON, Dale
The Day They Gave Babies Away
CCB-B-v24-N '70-p41
Comw-v93-N 20 '70-p200
KR-v38-N 1 '70-p1191
LJ-v95-D 15 '70-p4348
PW-v198-Ag 31 '70-p279

* * *

EUNSON, Roby
The Soong Sisters
BL-v72-Ja 1 '76-p625
BS-v35-D '75-p295
KR-v43-O 15 '75-p1197
SLJ-v22-O '75-p106
SLJ-v22-Ja '76-p25

* * *

EVANS, Alan
Escape At The Devil's Gate
JB-v43-Ag '79-p217
Kidnap!
B&B-v22-D '76-p75
JB-v41-Ap '77-p108
Running Scared
TLS-Jl 11 '75-p763

* * *

EVANS, Arthur J
More Writing About Pictures
Cur R-v22-Ag '83-p22
Reading And Thinking
Cur R-v19-N '80-p414
Writing About Pictures
Cur R-v22-Ag '83-p22
LA-v60-Ap '83-p513

* * *

EVANS, Byron
Benny
Brit Bk N C-Spring '80-p17
JB-v44-Je '80-p130

* * *

EVANS, Chris
Baked Beans
GP-v14-N '75-p2746

EVANS, Mari (continued)
JD
BW-v7-N 11 '73-p7C
BW-S 14 '75-p4
CCB-B-v27-S '73-p7
KR-v41-Jl 1 '73-p684
LJ-v98-N 15 '73-p3451
PW-v204-Ag 6 '73-p65
Teacher-v93-Ap '76-p124
Jim Flying High
CCB-B-v33-D '79-p69
HB-v56-F '80-p43
KR-v48-Ja 1 '80-p2
NY-v55-D 3 '79-p202

* * *

EVANS, Mark
Scott Joplin And The Ragtime Years
BL-v72-Jl 15 '76-p1595
BS-v36-S '76-p195
Comw-v103-N 19 '76-p763
Inst-v85-My '76-p113
KR-v44-Mr 1 '76-p264
PW-v209-My 24 '76-p60
SE-v41-Ap '77-p348
SLJ-v22-Ap '76-p72

* * *

EVANS, R E
The American War Of Independence
SLJ-v24-Ap '78-p82

* * *

EVANS, Richard
Socialism
B&B-v23-Ja '78-p63
JB-v41-O '77-p301
TLS-D 2 '77-p1418

* * *

EVANS, Roberta
Alcohol And Alcoholism
Cur R-v16-Ag '77-p176
SLJ-v23-N '76-p56

* * *

EVANSEN, Virginia B
The Flea Market Mystery
CCB-B-v32-S '78-p7
Par-v53-S '78-p32
SLJ-v24-My '78-p84

* * *

EVARTS, Hal G
Bigfoot
BL-v70-D 1 '73-p380
BL-v70-D 1 '73-p385
BL-v73-D 15 '76-p615
KR-v41-S 1 '73-p972
LJ-v98-D 15 '73-p3719
PW-v204-D 10 '73-p37
Jay-Jay And The Peking Monster
BL-v74-My 15 '78-p1492
HB-v54-Ag '78-p401
KR-v46-My 1 '78-p500
NYTBR-Ap 30 '78-p44
SLJ-v24-My '78-p86
The Pegleg Mystery
BS-v31-Mr 15 '72-p566
CLW-v44-O '72-p193
EJ-v61-S '72-p938
HB-v48-Je '72-p274
KR-v40-F 15 '72-p201
LJ-v97-My 15 '72-p1929
The Purple Eagle Mystery
BS-v36-My '76-p62
CCB-B-v29-Jl '76-p173
CSM-v68-My 12 '76-p28
KR-v44-Mr 1 '76-p260
SLJ-v22-My '76-p78

* * *

EVE, Esme
Trees
BL-v73-Je 15 '77-p1579
SLJ-v24-S '77-p100

* * *

EVENHUIS, Gertie
The School At Schellebelle
GP-v14-S '75-p2690
What About Me?
CCB-B-v30-My '77-p140
Emerg Lib-v11-N '83-p20
HB-v53-Ap '77-p159
KR-v44-O 1 '76-p1092
NS-v87-My 24 '74-p738
Obs-Ap 14 '74-p31
SLJ-v23-O '76-p116
TLS-Jl 5 '74-p715

* * *

EVERAERE, M
Animal Friends
JB-v40-D '76-p343

* * *

EVERTON, Macduff
El Circo Magico Modelo/ Finding The Magic Circus
CBRS-v8-Ja '80-p43
CCB-B-v33-Ap '80-p150
Inter BC-v11-Ja 10 '80-p28
J Read-v24-Ja '81-p297
PW-v217-Ja 18 '80-p140
SLJ-v26-Ap '80-p92

* * *

EVERYDAY Life
Cur R-v24-N '84-p97

* * *

EVSLIN, Bernard
Greeks Bearing Gifts
BL-v73-F 1 '77-p832
CCB-B-v30-Mr '77-p106
KR-v44-N 15 '76-p1230
SLJ-v23-Ja '77-p100
The Green Hero
BL-v71-Jl 15 '75-p1190
BS-v35-S '75-p169
CCB-B-v29-O '75-p26
CE-v52-Mr '76-p268
HB-v51-Ag '75-p376
KR-v43-Ap 15 '75-p468
LJ-v100-My 15 '75-p1000
PW-v207-Mr 10 '75-p57
SLJ-v22-S '75-p118
SLJ-v26-N '79-p43
Heraclea
BB-v7-Je '79-p4
BL-v75-S 1 '78-p37
CCB-B-v32-O '78-p27
KR-v46-My 15 '78-p553
SLJ-v24-Mr '78-p136
WLB-v53-O '78-p180
Hercules
BL-v80-Jl '84-p1548
CCB-B-v37-Je '84-p185
EJ-v73-S '84-p102
HB-v60-Ag '84-p482
LA-v61-O '84-p634
SLJ-v30-My '84-p78
VOYA-v7-Ag '84-p143
Signs & Wonders
BL-v78-My 1 '82-p1151
CBRS-v10-Mr '82-p76
HB-v58-Ap '82-p178
KR-v50-F 15 '82-p210
Kliatt-v14-Winter '80-p38
LJ-v104-N 15 '79-p2473
SLJ-v28-Mr '82-p156
VOYA-v5-Ag '82-p44

* * *

EWALD, Carl
The Battle Of The Bees And Other Stories
GP-v17-S '78-p3382
SLJ-v24-Mr '78-p127
TES-Je 30 '78-p22

EWALD, Carl (continued)
The Spider
KR-v49-Mr 15 '81-p357
PW-v218-Jl 25 '80-p158
SLJ-v27-O '80-p145

* * *

EWART, Gavin
Light Verse For Children
TES-N 24 '78-p42

* * *

EWEN, David
Opera
BS-v32-O 15 '72-p338
CCB-B-v27-S '73-p7
LJ-v98-Mr 15 '73-p1011
M Ed J-v59-Ja '73-p87
Notes-v30-S '73-p58
Orchestral Music
BS-v33-D 15 '73-p428
CCB-B-v27-My '74-p141
LJ-v99-Mr 15 '74-p901
Solo Instrumental And Chamber Music. Vol. 3
BL-v71-D 1 '74-p374
CCB-B-v28-My '75-p145
JB-v39-Ap '75-p142
SLJ-v21-Ja '75-p53
Vocal Music
BL-v72-D 15 '75-p572
BL-v72-D 15 '75-p577
BS-v35-D '75-p296
CCB-B-v29-F '76-p95
CLW-v47-Ap '76-p409
JB-v41-D '77-p351
KR-v43-O 1 '75-p1140
PW-v208-O 6 '75-p85
SLJ-v22-N '75-p89

* * *

EWEN, Doris
An ABC Of Children's Names
NYTBR-v88-O 9 '83-p39
PW-v223-My 27 '83-p68
TES-N 21 '80-p35

* * *

EWEN, Robert B
Getting It Together
BL-v72-Ap 15 '76-p1178
BL-v72-Ap 15 '76-p1185
BS-v36-Je '76-p103
CP-v21-Jl '76-p507
KR-v44-F 15 '76-p206
NO-v15-Ag 21 '76-p17
SB-v13-My '77-p31
SLJ-v23-F '77-p71

* * *

EWING, Kathryn
A Private Matter
BL-v71-My 15 '75-p964
CCB-B-v29-S '75-p7
CE-v60-My '84-p308
KR-v43-Ap 1 '75-p373
NYTBR-N 16 '75-p52
PW-v207-Je 2 '75-p52
SLJ-v21-My '75-p54
Teacher-v95-O '77-p165
Things Won't Be The Same
BL-v77-D 1 '80-p512
CBRS-v9-Ja '81-p37
CCB-B-v34-Mr '81-p131
CE-v60-My '84-p308
HB-v57-F '81-p50
Inter BC-v13-#1 '82-p17
KR-v49-F 1 '81-p140
PW-v218-Ag 29 '80-p365
RT-v34-My '81-p967
RT-v35-O '81-p67
SLJ-v27-Ja '81-p59

* * *

EXLEY, Helen
What It's Like To Be Me
Econ-v281-D 26 '81-p107
Sch Lib-v30-Mr '82-p42

* * *

EXLEY, Richard
Dear World
SLJ-v26-N '79-p76

* * *

EXPECTATIONS 1975
NYTBR-Mr 28 '76-p16

* * *

EXPECTATIONS 1981
SLJ-v28-N '81-p43

* * *

EXPECTATIONS 1982
SLJ-v29-Ja '83-p34

* * *

EXPLORATIONS. Grades 2-3
Quill & Q-v50-My '84-p15

* * *

EXPLORER Guides
Cur R-v21-F '82-p104

* * *

EXPLORERS Ltd. Source Book
AF-v80-Mr '74-p36
ARBA-v9-'78-p322
BL-v74-Je 1 '78-p1574
Cha Ti-v31-O '77-p15
Choice-v11-My '74-p411
Choice-v14-Ja '78-p1478
Comw-v104-N 11 '77-p726
HB-v50-Je '74-p305
Kliatt-v11-Fall '77-p50
LJ-v99-Ja 15 '74-p228
LJ-v99-F 1 '74-p350
LJ-v99-My 15 '74-p1452
WLB-v52-N '77-p267

* * *

EXPLORING
CE-v59-My '83-p369

* * *

EXPLORING Animal Homes
Obs-Jl 23 '78-p21

* * *

EXPLORING Animal Journeys
Obs-Jl 23 '78-p21

* * *

EXPLORING (Practical Puffin)
NS-v96-N 3 '78-p594
TLS-D 1 '78-p1399

* * *

EXPLORING Primary Science 7-11. Unit 2
TES-Ap 1 '83-p37

* * *

EXPLORING Science
Cur R-v19-Je '80-p268

* * *

EYERLY, Jeannette
Escape From Nowhere
BW-v3-My 4 '69-p32
CCB-B-v23-S '69-p6
Comw-v90-My 23 '69-p300
GT-v88-Ja '71-p117
HB-v45-Ap '69-p195
KR-v37-F 15 '69-p184
LJ-v94-Ap 15 '69-p1794
NYTBR-Je 8 '69-p44
NYTBR, pt.2-My 4 '69-p10
NYTBR, pt.2-N 9 '69-p60
PW-v195-My 12 '69-p58
Girl Inside
CCB-B-v22-O '68-p25
EJ-v58-My '69-p778
HB-v44-Ag '68-p428
KR-v36-Mr 1 '68-p271
LJ-v93-Ap 15 '68-p1810

EYERLY, Jeannette
(continued)
NYTBR-v73-Ap 21 '68-p34
YR-v4-My '68-p14
Girl Like Me
Am-v115-N 5 '66-p554
BL-v63-D 15 '66-p446
CCB-B-v20-Ja '67-p73
CSM-v58-N 3 '66-pB1
Comw-v85-N 11 '66-p176
EJ-v56-F '67-p316
KR-v34-Ag 15 '66-p841
LJ-v91-S 15 '66-p4349
NYTBR-v71-N 6 '66-p16
Good-Bye To Budapest
BS-v34-O 15 '74-p329
CCB-B-v28-F '75-p92
KR-v42-Jl 15 '74-p749
LJ-v99-D 15 '74-p3277
PW-v206-Ag 26 '74-p306
He's My Baby, Now
BL-v73-Ap 15 '77-p1265
CCB-B-v31-S '77-p14
EJ-v66-S '77-p77
KR-v65-My 1 '77-p492
NYTBR-My 1 '77-p46
SLJ-v23-My '77-p69
If I Loved You Wednesday
BL-v77-O 1 '80-p205
BS-v40-Ja '81-p352
CBRS-v9-N '80-p27
CCB-B-v34-D '80-p70
J Read-v24-Ap '81-p647
KR-v49-Ja 15 '81-p79
SLJ-v27-O '80-p154
The Leonardo Touch
BB-v4-Ja '77-p2
BL-v73-O 1 '76-p243
BL-v73-O 1 '76-p251
BS-v36-Ja '77-p323
CCB-B-v30-Ja '77-p75
KR-v44-Ag 15 '76-p909
SLJ-v23-D '76-p69
The Phaedra Complex
BL-v68-N 15 '71-p286
CCB-B-v25-F '72-p90
CSM-v63-N 11 '71-pB1
EJ-v61-Ap '72-p603
GT-v89-Ja '72-p91
KR-v39-Jl 1 '71-p682
LJ-v96-O 15 '71-p3475
SR-v54-N 13 '71-p62
Radigan Cares
BS-v30-N 15 '70-p361
CCB-B-v24-D '70-p58
EJ-v60-My '71-p667
KR-v38-Jl 15 '70-p748
LJ-v96-Ja 15 '71-p275
The Seeing Summer
BL-v78-N 15 '81-p437
CBRS-v10-S '81-p7
CCB-B-v35-N '81-p45
CE-v58-Mr '82-p257
CLW-v53-Mr '82-p356
Inter BC-v13-#4 '82-p13
KR-v50-Ja 1 '82-p6
PW-v220-O 23 '81-p62
SLJ-v28-Ag '82-p115
Seth And Me And Rebel Makes Three
B Rpt-v2-Ja '84-p33
BS-v43-Je '83-p109
CBRS-v11-Jl '83-p137
CCB-B-v37-S '83-p5
KR-v51-My 15 '83-p583
SLJ-v30-S '83-p132
VOYA-v6-O '83-p200
WCRB-v9-S '83-p67
The World Of Ellen March
CCB-B-v18-Ja '65-p72
J Read-v26-F '83-p411
LJ-v90-Ja 15 '65-p387

* * *

EYRE, Frank
British Children's Books In The Twentieth Century
B&B-v17-Ap '72-p87
Econ-v241-D 18 '71-p67
HB-v48-D '72-p607
KR-v40-D 15 '72-p1435
LR-v23-Spring '72-p213
SMQ-v2-Winter '74-p152
TLS-Ap 28 '72-p473
TN-v30-Ja '74-p207

* * *

EYTON, Wendy
The Ghost Of Christmas Present And Other Stories
GP-v19-Ja '81-p3825
Sch Lib-v29-Mr '81-p29
TLS-N 21 '80-p1330

* * *

EZO
Avril
KR-v35-S 1 '67-p1046
LJ-v92-D 15 '67-p4612
LR-v25-Summer '75-p81

* * *

EZZELL, Marilyn
The Mystery At Hollowhearth House
CBRS-v10-Ag '82-p137
PW-v222-Jl 30 '82-p77
SLJ-v28-My '82-p83

F

FABE, Maxene
Beauty Millionaire
BL-v69-F 1 '73-p523
CCB-B-v26-F '73-p89
KR-v40-O 15 '72-p1205
LJ-v98-Mr 15 '73-p1011
SE-v37-D '73-p788

* * *

FABER, Doris
Bella Abzug
BL-v73-D 15 '76-p606
CCB-B-v30-D '76-p56
CE-v53-F '77-p214
KR-v44-S 1 '76-p984
SE-v48-N '84-p556
SLJ-v23-N '76-p57
Clarence Darrow: Defender Of The People
CC-v82-Je 30 '65-p838
CCB-B-v18-Je '65-p146
CSM-v57-My 6 '65-p8B
KR-v33-Ja 15 '65-p61
LJ-v90-My 15 '65-p2404
NYTBR-v70-Jl 25 '65-p20
Dwight Eisenhower
BL-v73-Jl 1 '77-p1652
SLJ-v23-Ap '77-p66
Franklin D. Roosevelt
KR-v42-D 15 '74-p1307
PW-v206-O 7 '74-p63
SLJ-v21-Mr '75-p95
Harry Truman
BL-v70-S 15 '73-p118
CCB-B-v26-My '73-p136
CLW-v45-F '74-p346
KR-v41-Mr 1 '73-p257
LJ-v98-S 15 '73-p2649
PW-v203-Ap 2 '73-p65
Love And Rivalry
BL-v80-N 1 '83-p400
B Rpt-v2-Ja '84-p41
BS-v43-Ja '84-p388
CBRS-v12-Mr '84-p83
CCB-B-v37-F '84-p106
HB-v60-F '84-p72
KR-v51-N 1 '83-pJ211
SLJ-v30-Ja '84-p85
Lucretia Mott
BL-v68-F 15 '72-p506
CCB-B-v25-Ja '72-p73
LJ-v96-D 15 '71-p4197
NHB-v34-D '71-p191
Oh, Lizzie
Am-v127-D 2 '72-p480
BL-v68-My 1 '72-p765
BL-v68-My 1 '72-p769
BW-v6-My 7 '72-p5
CCB-B-v25-My '72-p138
HB-v48-Ag '72-p386
Inter BC-v13-#1 '82-p5
KR-v40-Ja 1 '72-p9
KR-v40-D 15 '72-p1423
LJ-v97-Jl '72-p2483
NYTBR, pt.2-My 7 '72-p24
Teacher-v90-O '72-p115
Petticoat Politics
BL-v64-F 15 '68-p698
HB-v44-Ap '68-p192
Inter BC-v13-#1 '82-p4
KR-v35-O 15 '67-p1286
LJ-v93-F 15 '68-p880
Wall Street
BB-v7-D '79-p3
BL-v75-Ap 15 '79-p1287
KR-v47-My 15 '79-p581
SLJ-v25-My '79-p71

* * *

FABER Book Of Animal Stories
GP-v17-N '78-p3422
Inst-v88-My '79-p115
JB-v42-D '78-p317
LJ-v103-N 1 '78-p2250
Sch Lib-v27-Mr '79-p39
TLS-S 29 '78-p1088

* * *

FABER Book Of Carols And Christmas Songs
GP-v22-N '83-p4174

* * *

FABER Book Of Children's Songs
Obs-D 6 '70-p27
Spec-v225-D 5 '70-pR20
TLS-O 30 '70-p1268

* * *

FABER Book Of Modern Fairy Tales
Brit Bk N C-Spring '82-p5
CCB-B-v36-S '82-p6
GP-v20-Ja '82-p3996
JB-v45-D '81-p246
TES-Ja 15 '82-p36
TLS-N 20 '81-p1356

* * *

FABER Book Of North American Legends
JB-v43-O '79-p273
TES-N 11 '83-p25

* * *

FABER Book Of Northern Folk-Tales
HB-v57-Je '81-p315
JB-v45-Ap '81-p76
Obs-N 30 '80-p36
SLJ-v28-My '82-p60
TES-N 21 '80-p30
TES-N 11 '83-p25
TLS-N 21 '80-p1326

* * *

FABER Book Of Northern Legends
JB-v42-Ap '78-p100
Obs-D 11 '77-p31
TES-D 23 '77-p15
TES-N 11 '83-p25
TLS-D 2 '77-p1410

* * *

FABER Book Of Nursery Verse
Emerg Lib-v11-Ja '84-p40
TES-S 30 '83-p47

* * *

FACCI, Frances
Mister Mizu
In Rev-v15-Je '81-p36

* * *

FACE-OFF '74-'75
NYTBR-Mr 23 '75-p37
Teacher-v92-Ja '75-p112

* * *

FACES, Feats, And Figures
RT-v37-N '83-p221

* * *

FACKLAM, Margery
The Brain
ASBYP-v16-Spring '83-p21
BL-v78-Ag '82-p1524
CCB-B-v36-S '82-p8
SB-v18-Ja '83-p137
SLJ-v29-Ja '83-p84
VOYA-v5-D '82-p41
From Cell To Clone
ACSB-v13-Mr '80-p20
BB-v7-D '79-p3
BL-v76-N 1 '79-p447
BS-v39-F '80-p407
CBRS-v8-F '80-p56
CCB-B-v33-Mr '80-p131
Choice-v18-Jl '81-p1521
HB-v56-F '80-p86
KR-v47-N 15 '79-p1332
SLJ-v26-F '80-p65
Sch Lib-v30-Je '82-p179
Frozen Snakes And Dinosaur Bones
ACSB-v10-Winter '77-p16
BL-v72-Ap 15 '76-p1185
CCB-B-v30-D '76-p56
CE-v53-Mr '77-p260
Comw-v103-N 19 '76-p764
HB-v52-O '76-p527
KR-v44-Ap 1 '76-p396
SB-v12-Mr '77-p209
SE-v41-Ap '77-p348
SLJ-v22-Ap '76-p72
Wild Animals, Gentle Women
BL-v75-S 1 '78-p48
BS-v38-D '78-p290
CCB-B-v32-Ja '79-p79
CE-v56-O '79-p47
EJ-v68-F '79-p103
HB-v54-Je '78-p306
KR-v46-Jl 1 '78-p697
LA-v56-F '79-p189
SLJ-v25-Mr '79-p138
Teacher-v96-Mr '79-p32

* * *

FACTFINDERS
Brit Bk N C-Autumn '80-p7

* * *

FADER, Shirley Sloan
The Princess Who Grew Down
CCB-B-v22-Ap '69-p124
LJ-v94-Ap 15 '69-p1768

* * *

FADIMAN, Clifton
Wally The Wordworm
CBRS-v12-Ap '84-p90
CLW-v36-Mr '65-p480
PW-v224-N 25 '83-p65
SLJ-v30-Mr '84-p158
The World Treasury Of Children's Literature. Bks. 1-2
BS-v44-D '84-p358
BW-v14-N 11 '84-p11
KR-v52-S 15 '84-p913
PW-v226-O 5 '84-p92

* * *

FAGERSTROM, Grethe
Our New Baby
CCB-B-v36-S '82-p8
GP-v18-Mr '80-p3661
TES-D 21 '79-p20
TES-N 11 '83-p28

* * *

FAGG, Christopher
Ancient Greece
BL-v76-D 1 '79-p554
GP-v17-Mr '79-p3479
SLJ-v26-Ja '80-p68
TES-D 1 '78-p25
How They Built Long Ago
ASBYP-v15-Fall '82-p22
BL-v78-N 15 '81-p437
CCB-B-v35-F '82-p105
CE-v58-Mr '82-p260
SB-v17-My '82-p273
SLJ-v29-S '82-p120
Lost Cities
Econ-v277-D 27 '80-p77

* * *

FAHEY, William A
F. Scott Fitzgerald And The American Dream
CCB-B-v27-D '73-p63
KR-v41-Ag 1 '73-p821
PW-v204-Jl 23 '73-p70

* * *

FAHS, Sophia B L
Old Tales For A New Day
CCB-B-v34-My '81-p169

* * *

FAIN, James W
Rodeos
BL-v79-Ag '83-p1462
SLJ-v30-O '83-p146

* * *

FAIR, Sylvia
The Bedspread
BW-v12-F 14 '82-p11
CBRS-v10-Mr '82-p72
CCB-B-v35-Ap '82-p146
GP-v21-Mr '83-p4046
JB-v47-Je '83-p108
NYTBR-v87-Ap 25 '82-p38
PW-v221-Ja 15 '82-p99
SLJ-v28-Mr '82-p131
Sch Lib-v31-Je '83-p128
The Ivory Anvil
B&B-v20-Ja '75-p74
Obs-Ag 4 '74-p28
Obs-My 1 '77-p23
TLS-D 6 '74-p1380
The Penny Tin Whistler
JB-v41-F '77-p31
TLS-O 1 '76-p1247

* * *

FAIRCLOUGH, Chris
Let's Go To Holland
JB-v46-Je '82-p97
Bathtime
TLS-N 26 '82-p1304
A Busy Day
TLS-N 26 '82-p1304
A Day With A Traindriver
TES-Ap 6 '84-p29
In The Park
TLS-N 26 '82-p1304
Let's Go Cycling
Sch Lib-v29-S '81-p245
Let's Go To England
GP-v21-S '82-p3960
TES-N 5 '82-p22
TES-N 5 '82-p27

FAIRCLOUGH, Chris
(continued)
Let's Go To Holland
GP-v21-S '82-p3960
TES-N 5 '82-p27
Playtime
TLS-N 26 '82-p1304
Take A Trip To England
BL-v78-Jl '82-p1443
SLJ-v29-F '83-p65
Take A Trip To Holland
BL-v78-Jl '82-p1443
CE-v59-N '82-p138
SLJ-v29-F '83-p65
Take A Trip To Italy
BL-v78-N 15 '81-p437
Cur R-v21-Ag '82-p339
SLJ-v28-Mr '82-p131
Take A Trip To West Germany
BL-v78-N 15 '81-p437
Cur R-v21-Ag '82-p339
SLJ-v28-Mr '82-p131
We Live In Britain
BL-v80-Je 15 '84-p1480
SLJ-v31-S '84-p112

* * *

FAIRFAX-LUCY, Brian
Children Of The House
BW-v2-N 3 '68-p14
CCB-B-v22-Mr '69-p110
CSM-v60-My 2 '68-pB10
Econ-v237-D 26 '70-p41
KR-v36-S 1 '68-p977
LJ-v93-N 15 '68-p4402
NS-v75-My 24 '68-p694
NYTBR-v73-N 3 '68-p38
Obs-Ag 4 '68-p22
Obs-D 6 '70-p23
SR-v51-N 9 '68-p68
TLS-Je 6 '68-p579

* * *

FAIRFIELD, Lesley
Let's Eat!/Allons Manger!
BIC-v11-D '82-p8
Emerg Lib-v10-My '83-p29
SLJ-v29-Ag '83-p50
Let's Go!/Allons-Y!
BIC-v13-Ja '84-p27
Quill & Q-v50-Ja '84-p28
SLJ-v30-My '84-p64
What's The Word?/Cherchez Le Mot?
BIC-v11-D '82-p8

* * *

FAIRHOLME, Elisabeth
The Seals Of Park Lane Seek A Beau For Elaine
TLS-D 1 '78-p1397

* * *

FAIRHURST, Peter
Making A Doll's House And Its Furniture
GP-v15-O '76-p2977
Making Model Transport Vehicles
GP-v16-Ap '78-p3300
Making Model Wartime Vehicles
TES-F 27 '81-p39
Toys To Make
GP-v15-Jl '76-p2916

* * *

FAIRLESS, Caroline
Hambone
BL-v77-Mr 1 '81-p926
CBRS-v9-Winter '81-p43
CCB-B-v34-Je '81-p192
NYTBR-v85-N 9 '80-p71
PW-v218-N 21 '80-p58
SLJ-v27-Ja '81-p59

* * *

FAIRLEY, G
The Observer's Book Of Small Craft
JB-v41-Ap '77-p109

* * *

FAIRLEY, Sylvia
Frogs On The Moon
Sch Lib-v32-Je '84-p131

* * *

FAIRMAN, Paul W
Five Knucklebones
CCB-B-v26-Mr '73-p104
KR-v40-O 15 '72-p1200
LJ-v97-N 15 '72-p3805
NYTBR-N 26 '72-p8
The Forgetful Robot
B&B-v15-My '70-p44
CCB-B-v22-Ap '69-p125
CSM-v61-My 1 '69-pB5
HB-v45-F '69-p53
KR-v36-O 1 '68-p1176
LJ-v93-N 15 '68-p4403

* * *

FAIRY Poems For The Very Young
SLJ-v29-Ja '83-p58

* * *

FAIRY Tale Cookbook
HE-v42-S 4 '82-p17

* * *

FAISON, Eleanora
Becoming
SB-v13-D '77-p168
SLJ-v28-My '82-p51

* * *

FAITH In Action Series
TLS-Mr 28 '80-p364

* * *

FALARDEAU, Louise
The Care And Feeding Of Parents
BIC-v11-Mr '82-p26
In Rev-v16-Ap '82-p45

* * *

FALBO, Graciela
Papelito Violeta
TN-v40-Winter '84-p185

* * *

FALCON Comics
TES-Ja 1 '82-p17

* * *

FALK, Ann Mari
A Place Of Her Own
CCB-B-v18-Ja '65-p72
EJ-v54-My '65-p459
HB-v41-F '65-p59

* * *

FALK, Bisse
Barnens Flora 1-2
BL-v81-S 1 '84-p75
Barnens Tradbok
BL-v81-S 1 '84-p75

* * *

FALK, John R
The Young Sportsman's Guide To Dogs
CCB-B-v19-O '65-p31

* * *

FALKNER, J Meade
Moonfleet
BW-v14-S 16 '84-p12
GP-v14-Jl '75-p2678
GP-v22-My '83-p4071
TES-Mr 4 '83-p32

FALKNER, J Meade
(continued)
TES-Ja 13 '84-p22

* * *

FALKNER, Leonard
For Jefferson And Liberty
BL-v69-D 1 '72-p350
BL-v69-D 1 '72-p355
CCB-B-v27-S '73-p8
KR-v40-O 1 '72-p1156
NYTBR-Ja 7 '73-p8
NYTBR, pt.2-N 5 '72-p28

* * *

FALL, Thomas
Dandy's Mountain
BL-v64-O 1 '67-p200
BW-v1-S 24 '67-p22
CCB-B-v21-O '67-p26
HB-v43-Ag '67-p469
KR-v35-My 1 '67-p560
LJ-v92-O 15 '67-p3862
SR-v50-Jl 22 '67-p43
Goat Boy Of Brooklyn
HB-v45-Ap '69-p171
KR-v36-O 15 '68-p1162
YR-v5-N '68-p14
Wild Boy
CCB-B-v18-Jl '65-p160
KR-v33-Ap 15 '65-p434
LJ-v90-Je 15 '65-p2884
NYTBR-v70-My 9 '65-p18

* * *

FALLADA, Hans
That Rascal, Fridolin
GP-v19-N '80-p3801

* * *

FALLING Star
TES-N 19 '82-p36

* * *

FALLS, Gregory A
Homer's The Odyssey
Dr-#2 '81-p56
The Pushcart War
Emerg Lib-v11-Ja '84-p22
RT-v37-Ap '84-p714

* * *

FAMILIES
Choice-v21-My '84-p1384
JMF-v46-My '84-p501
NMR-v3-N '81-p1
TES-N 13 '81-p24

* * *

FAMILIES In Other Places
TES-Ap 18 '80-p20

* * *

FAMILY Books
Cur R-v23-Ap '84-p96

* * *

FAMILY In Australia
TES-N 16 '84-p43

* * *

FAMILY In Ireland
TES-N 16 '84-p43

* * *

FAMILY In Japan
TES-N 16 '84-p43

* * *

FAMOUS People Stories
Inst-v90-Ap '81-p115

* * *

FANNIE Farmer Junior Cookbook
NYTBR-v70-N 7 '65-p57
PW-v189-Je 13 '66-p132

* * *

FANNING, Peter
Nobody's Hero
Brit Bk N C-Autumn '81-p24
JB-v45-O '81-p209
Sch Lib-v29-S '81-p252
TES-Je 5 '81-p39

* * *

FANNING, Robbie
100 Butterflies
CBRS-v8-F '80-p56
SLJ-v26-D '79-p84

* * *

FANOUS Al Sihri. Balit Al Fidiyae
BL-v75-O 15 '78-p392

* * *

FANSHAWE, Elizabeth
Rachel
BB-v5-S '77-p2
BL-v73-Je 15 '77-p1575
Brit Bk N-Ap '84-p203
CCB-B-v30-Jl '77-p174
Econ-v257-D 20 '75-p103
KR-v45-Mr 15 '77-p280
SLJ-v24-S '77-p106
TLS-D 5 '75-p1453

* * *

FANTAISIES
In Rev-v14-Je '80-p37

* * *

FARA, Patricia
Computers
JB-v47-F '83-p40
SLJ-v30-My '84-p88
Sch Lib-v31-Je '83-p174

* * *

FARADAY, Joy
The Secret Garden
Sch Lib-v28-S '80-p262

* * *

FARALLA, Dana
Swanhilda-Of-The-Swans
CCB-B-v19-O '65-p31
The Wonderful Flying-Go-Round
BL-v62-F 1 '66-p528
CCB-B-v20-O '66-p24
GT-v83-N '65-p107
HB-v42-F '66-p52
KR-v33-S 1 '65-p905
LJ-v90-N 15 '65-p5076
NYTBR-v71-Ja 2 '66-p18
TLS-N 24 '66-p1087

* * *

FARANDOLES
In Rev-v14-Je '80-p38

* * *

FARB, Peter
Land, Wildlife, And Peoples Of The Bible
BL-v64-D 15 '67-p500
BW-v1-D 17 '67-p12
CC-v84-D 13 '67-p1601
CCB-B-v21-Jl '68-p173
CLW-v39-D '67-p296
CSM-v59-N 2 '67-pB7
Comw-v89-F 21 '69-p646
HB-v44-Ap '68-p192
KR-v35-S 1 '67-p1061
LJ-v93-Ja 15 '68-p303
NYTBR-v72-N 5 '67-p40

* * *

FARBER, Norma
As I Was Crossing Boston Common
BB-v3-N '75-p2
BL-v72-D 1 '75-p514
BW-v12-Mr 14 '82-p16
CCB-B-v29-F '76-p95

FARBER, Norma (continued)
CE-v52-Ap '76-p318
CLW-v47-F '76-p309
CSM-v67-N 5 '75-pB6
HB-v52-F '76-p40
KR-v43-O 1 '75-p1120
LA-v53-My '76-p501
LA-v58-Ap '81-p485
LATBR-Je 13 '82-p8
NW-v86-D 15 '75-p89
NYTBR-N 16 '75-p57
NYTBR-v87-Mr 28 '82-p35
PW-v208-D 8 '75-p50
RT-v36-Mr '83-p648
SLJ-v22-D '75-p42
VLS-My '82-p12
WLB-v50-D '75-p316
How Does It Feel To Be Old?
Art T-v10-Fall '80-p31
BL-v76-N 15 '79-p501
CBRS-v8-O '79-p15
CCB-B-v33-F '80-p108
CE-v57-S '80-p43
CSM-v72-F 11 '80-pB15
CT-v11-Jl '82-p36
HB-v56-F '80-p43
Inter BC-v11-Mr 30 '80-p24
KR-v47-N 15 '79-p1324
LA-v58-Ap '81-p485
Ms-v9-Ag '80-p92
NYTBR-N 11 '79-p53
NYTBR-v86-N 8 '81-p51
RT-v33-Mr '80-p730
SLJ-v26-D '79-p84
How The Hibernators Came To Bethlehem
BL-v77-O 15 '80-p325
CBRS-v9-D '80-p21
CCB-B-v34-N '80-p51
CE-v57-My '81-p302
CSM-v73-D 10 '80-p15
HB-v56-D '80-p625
LA-v58-Ap '81-p485
NYTBR-v85-D 14 '80-p37
PW-v218-Jl 18 '80-p61
SLJ-v27-O '80-p161
How The Left-Behind Beasts Built Ararat
CCB-B-v32-O '78-p27
CE-v55-Ja '79-p168
CSM-v70-S 18 '78-pB14
Comw-v105-N 10 '78-p729
HB-v55-O '78-p506
KR-v46-Jl 1 '78-p687
LA-v58-Ap '81-p485
NYTBR-F 18 '79-p20
PW-v213-Je 19 '78-p101
SLJ-v25-S '78-p107
TN-v40-Fall '83-p58
WLB-v53-O '78-p178
WLB-v55-O '80-p132
How To Ride A Tiger
CCB-B-v37-O '83-p25
PW-v224-D 16 '83-p71
SLJ-v30-Ja '84-p64
I Found Them In The Yellow Pages
KR-v41-Ap 15 '73-p451
LA-v58-Ap '81-p485
LJ-v98-N 15 '73-p3438
PW-v203-Ap 30 '73-p55
Teacher-v93-Ja '76-p34
Mercy Short
CBRS-v11-D '82-p36
CCB-B-v36-Ja '83-p87
HB-v58-D '82-p655
KR-v50-N 1 '82-p1195
LA-v60-My '83-p648
SLJ-v29-O '82-p160
Never Say Ugh To A Bug
KR-v47-My 1 '79-p513
NYTBR-Ap 29 '79-p25
SLJ-v25-My '79-p50
A Ship In A Storm On The Way To Tarshish
BB-v6-Ap '78-p1
CCB-B-v31-My '78-p140
HB-v54-F '78-p34
KR-v45-N 1 '77-p1141
LA-v55-Ap '78-p517
NYTBR-Ja 1 '78-p20
SLJ-v24-O '77-p100
Six Impossible Things Before Breakfast
CCB-B-v30-Ap '77-p123
CSM-v69-My 4 '77-pB3
HB-v53-Je '77-p307
LA-v58-Ap '81-p485
PW-v211-F 14 '77-p83
RT-v31-F '78-p576
SLJ-v23-Ap '77-p66
WCRB-v3-My '77-p39
Small Wonders
BL-v76-O 1 '79-p274
HB-v55-D '79-p673
Inst-v89-N '79-p142
KR-v47-N 15 '79-p1328
NYTBR-N 11 '79-p53
SLJ-v26-N '79-p64
There Goes Feathertop!
CSM-v71-My 14 '79-pB7
HB-v55-Ag '79-p432
KR-v47-My 15 '79-p573
LA-v56-O '79-p819
LA-v58-Ap '81-p485
NYTBR-Ap 29 '79-p25
PW-v215-Je 11 '79-p103
SLJ-v26-O '79-p138
There Once Was A Woman Who Married A Man
CE-v55-Ap '79-p295
KR-v46-O 1 '78-p1066
LA-v58-Ap '81-p485
PW-v214-Ag 14 '78-p69
SLJ-v25-N '78-p60
This Is The Ambulance Leaving The Zoo
CCB-B-v28-Jl '75-p175
KR-v43-My 15 '75-p562
SLJ-v22-S '75-p79
Three Wanderers From Wapping
BL-v74-Ap 15 '78-p1347
CCB-B-v31-Je '78-p158
KR-v46-Ap 1 '78-p373
LA-v58-Ap '81-p486
NYTBR-Ap 30 '78-p52
PW-v213-Ap 24 '78-p84
RT-v32-F '79-p606
SE-v43-Ap '79-p300
SLJ-v24-My '78-p66
Up The Down Elevator
CBRS-v8-Ja '80-p41
KR-v47-O 15 '79-p1206
NYTBR-N 11 '79-p53
PW-v216-Ag 27 '79-p385
SLJ-v26-F '80-p44
Where's Gomer?
BL-v71-N 1 '74-p290
BW-D 8 '74-p7
CCB-B-v28-D '74-p61
Choice-v12-N '75-p1132
HB-v50-D '74-p682
KR-v42-S 1 '74-p942
KR-v43-Ja 1 '75-p4
LJ-v99-N 15 '74-p3037
PW-v206-O 7 '74-p64
TN-v40-Fall '83-p58

* * *

FARIAS, Juan
Los Anos Dificiles
BL-v80-Ag '84-p1633

* * *

FARJEON, Annabel
The Book Of Ballet Stories
GP-v20-Ja '82-p4003
Sch Lib-v30-Je '82-p152

* * *

FARM Animals
CSM-v67-S 22 '75-p22

* * *

FARM House (Chubby Shape Bks.)
SLJ-v29-Ag '83-p50

* * *

FARMER, Derek
Thin King
Sch Lib-v30-D '82-p327

* * *

FARMER, Paul
A Handbook Of Composer's And Their Music
TES-Jl 8 '83-p40
Instruments Of The Orchestra
TES-Jl 8 '83-p40

* * *

FARMER, Penelope
August The Fourth
BL-v72-Je 1 '76-p1404
HB-v52-Ag '76-p395
NS-v91-My 21 '76-p686
Obs-Jl 20 '75-p23
SLJ-v23-S '76-p132
TLS-D 5 '75-p1450
Beginnings
BL-v75-My 1 '79-p1354
BW-My 13 '79-pK2
CCB-B-v33-N '79-p46
CLW-v52-My '81-p417
GP-v18-My '79-p3507
HB-v55-Je '79-p314
JB-v43-F '79-p50
KR-v47-My 1 '79-p524
LA-v57-Mr '80-p321
Obs-D 3 '78-p36
SLJ-v25-Ap '79-p67
Sch Lib-v27-Mr '79-p82
TLS-D 1 '78-p1398
A Castle Of Bone
B&B-v18-F '73-p82
B&B-v20-My '75-p66
BL-v69-F 15 '73-p572
CCB-B-v26-Je '73-p153
HB-v49-F '73-p51
KR-v40-O 15 '72-p1201
LJ-v98-F 15 '73-p652
LR-v23-Autumn '72-p299
Lis-v87-Je 29 '72-p874
NS-v84-N 10 '72-p692
NYRB-v19-D 14 '72-p41
NYT-v122-D 13 '72-p67
NYTBR-Ja 21 '73-p8
Obs-Jl 30 '72-p32
PW-v202-D 4 '72-p62
Spec-v229-N 11 '72-p755
TLS-Jl 14 '72-p802
TN-v29-Je '73-p356
Charlotte Sometimes
Am-v121-D 13 '69-p595
BL-v66-D 1 '69-p457
CCB-B-v23-Je '70-p158
CSM-v61-N 6 '69-pB5
GT-v88-S '70-p162
HB-v45-D '69-p675
HB-v60-Ap '84-p223
KR-v37-O 15 '69-p1121
LJ-v94-D 15 '69-p4604
NO-v8-N 3 '69-p20
NS-v78-O 31 '69-p622
Obs-N 30 '69-p35
SR-v53-Ja 24 '70-p37
Spec-v223-N 1 '69-p608
TLS-O 16 '69-p1190
TN-v26-Je '70-p425
The Coal Train
GP-v16-Mr '78-p3265
JB-v42-Je '78-p141
NS-v95-My 19 '78-p680
Heracles
GP-v13-Ap '75-p2611
JB-v39-Je '75-p173
Spec-v234-Ap 12 '75-p443
TLS-Ap 4 '75-p366
The Runaway Train
Brit Bk N C-Autumn '80-p20
JB-v44-D '80-p290
TES-Ag 22 '80-p20
Sea Gull
BL-v62-Je 1 '66-p959
CCB-B-v20-S '66-p8
KR-v34-Ja 1 '66-p4
LJ-v91-Ap 15 '66-p2209
NYTBR-v71-My 1 '66-p30
Obs-Jl 13 '80-p29
TLS-My 19 '66-p447
The Serpent's Teeth
CCB-B-v25-Mr '72-p105
GW-v104-Je 5 '71-p19
KR-v40-F 1 '72-p138
LJ-v97-S 15 '72-p2948
NS-v81-Mr 5 '71-p315
NYTBR-Ag 27 '72-p24
Par-v47-My '72-p40
Spec-v226-My 29 '71-p757
TLS-Ap 2 '71-p388
The Story Of Persephone
BL-v70-Mr 1 '74-p740
CCB-B-v27-Jl '74-p175
KR-v41-O 1 '73-p1099
LJ-v99-Ap 15 '74-p1218
TLS-N 3 '72-p1322
William And Mary
BB-v3-F '75-p3
BL-v71-O 1 '74-p168
CCB-B-v28-F '75-p93
CE-v51-Mr '75-p273
Comw-v101-N 22 '74-p194
GP-v13-Ja '75-p2555
HB-v50-D '74-p690
KR-v42-N 1 '74-p1160
LA-v52-S '75-p857
LJ-v99-N 15 '74-p3052
LR-v24-Winter '75-p366
NS-v88-N 8 '74-p662
Obs-D 1 '74-p35
Obs-Je 26 '77-p29
Obs-Ag 28 '77-p26
PW-v206-Ag 26 '74-p306
TLS-D 6 '74-p1380
Year King
CCB-B-v31-Ap '78-p125
GP-v16-Mr '78-p3277
HB-v54-F '78-p76
JB-v42-F '78-p54
KR-v45-N 15 '77-p1205
Lis-v98-N 10 '77-p623
Obs-D 11 '77-p31
PW-v212-O 31 '77-p59
SLJ-v24-Ja '78-p94
Sch Lib-v32-S '84-p209
TES-N 18 '77-p34
TLS-O 21 '77-p1246

* * *

FARMING And The Countryside (Place And People)
TES-N 25 '77-p25

* * *

FARNAY, Josie
Egypt: Activities & Projects In Color
SLJ-v26-O '79-p148

* * *

FARNWORTH, Warren
Approaches To Collage
BL-v73-O 15 '76-p298
Cur R-v17-F '78-p81
PW-v210-Jl 12 '76-p72
Folk Toys And How To Make Them
GP-v13-Mr '75-p2588
LR-v24-Autumn '74-p320

FARNWORTH, Warren (continued)
Industry
JB-v42-F '78-p37
TES-N 18 '77-p37

* * *

FARRAR, Richard
The Birds' Woodland
ACSB-v10-Fall '77-p16
BL-v73-S 15 '76-p173
CCB-B-v30-F '77-p90
CE-v53-O '76-p37
HB-v52-O '76-p513
KR-v44-Je 1 '76-p635
SB-v12-Mr '77-p211
SLJ-v23-O '76-p106
The Hungry Snowbird
ACSB-v9-Spring '76-p17
BL-v71-Ap 1 '75-p816
CCB-B-v29-S '75-p7
KR-v43-Mr 1 '75-p241
NYTBR-My 4 '75-p22
SLJ-v21-My '75-p68

* * *

FARRAR, Susan Clement
Samantha On Stage
BL-v75-Ap 15 '79-p1294
CBRS-v7-Spring '79-p117
CCB-B-v33-S '79-p6
CLW-v51-N '79-p182
CSM-v71-O 15 '79-pB9
KR-v47-Jl 15 '79-p793
LA-v57-Ja '80-p84
NY-v55-D 3 '79-p211
PW-v215-Ap 16 '79-p76
RT-v33-Ap '80-p862
RT-v34-O '80-p50
SLJ-v25-Ap '79-p54
TES-Ag 1 '80-p28

* * *

FARRELL, Alan
Winston Churchill
CCB-B-v19-O '65-p31
LJ-v90-F 15 '65-p960

* * *

FARRELL, Anne
Shadow Summer
GP-v17-Mr '79-p3485
JB-v43-Ag '79-p217

* * *

FARRELL, Diane
What Is A City?
HB-v46-Ap '70-p182

* * *

FARRELL, S
Her Kingdom For A Pony
JB-v42-Ap '78-p102

* * *

FARRIMOND, John
The Hills Of Heaven
GP-v17-Ja '79-p3454
The Weather Makers
JB-v45-F '81-p17

* * *

FARRIMOND, Rosalind
Seeing And Doing
GP-v22-Mr '84-p4226
TES-N 18 '83-p27

* * *

FARRINGTON, Benjamin
Aristotle
BL-v65-My 1 '69-p1003
BS-v28-Mr 1 '69-p490
Choice-v6-Je '69-p522
HB-v45-Ap '69-p183
KR-v37-F 1 '69-p111
LJ-v95-N 15 '70-p4062
TLS-My 19 '66-p452
Francis Bacon
BL-v66-Je 1 '70-p1206
BS-v29-Ja 1 '70-p388
HB-v46-F '70-p48
SB-v6-My '70-p12

* * *

FARRINGTON, Robert
Tudor Agent
B&B-v19-Jl '74-p111
GP-v17-My '78-p3345
LJ-v99-Jl '74-p1847
Obs-F 3 '74-p31

* * *

FARRIS, David
The Beaver Book Of Famous Mazes
Obs-Jl 22 '79-p37

* * *

FARRIS, Stella
The Magic Blanket
BB-v7-Ja '80-p1
GP-v18-Ja '80-p3638
NYTBR-N 11 '79-p71
PW-v216-O 8 '79-p70
RT-v37-My '84-p856
The Magic Bubble-Pipe
BW-O 8 '78-pE8
CBRS-v7-Winter '79-p51
GP-v18-My '79-p3518
KR-v46-S 15 '78-p1014
NS-v96-N 3 '78-p593
RT-v37-My '84-p856
TES-N 24 '78-p50
TLS-D 1 '78-p1397
The Magic Castle
BW-O 8 '78-pE8
CBRS-v7-Winter '79-p51
GP-v18-My '79-p3518
NS-v96-N 3 '78-p593
TES-N 24 '78-p50
TLS-D 1 '78-p1397
The Magic Teddy Bear
BB-v7-Ja '80-p1
GP-v18-Ja '80-p3638
NYTBR-N 11 '79-p71
PW-v216-O 8 '79-p70

* * *

FARROW, Rachi
Charlie's Dream
CCB-B-v31-Je '78-p158
KR-v46-Ap 1 '78-p367
PW-v213-Ja 16 '78-p100
SLJ-v24-Mr '78-p117

* * *

FARTHING, A
The Gauntlet Fair
JB-v39-F '75-p37

* * *

FARTHING, Alison
The Mystical Beast
CCB-B-v32-N '78-p42
JB-v40-O '76-p268
LA-v55-N '78-p986
LR-v25-Spring '76-p226
SLJ-v25-O '78-p144
TLS-Jl 16 '76-p882

* * *

FASS, David E
The Shofar That Lost Its Voice
SLJ-v29-Mr '83-p161

* * *

FASSI, Carlo
Figure Skating With Carlo Fassi
BL-v77-F 15 '81-p789
CCB-B-v34-Mr '81-p131
LJ-v106-Ja 15 '81-p162
SLJ-v27-Ap '81-p148
VOYA-v4-Ag '81-p35

* * *

FASSLER, Joan
Don't Worry, Dear
CCB-B-v26-S '72-p6
LJ-v97-My 15 '72-p1900
SB-v8-My '72-p4
Howie Helps Himself
BL-v71-F 1 '75-p561
CCB-B-v28-My '75-p145
CE-v52-N '75-p89
Choice-v14-N '77-p1178
Inst-v84-My '75-p104
LA-v52-S '75-p854
RT-v29-Ap '76-p719
RT-v31-Ap '78-p802
SLJ-v21-Mr '75-p87
SMQ-v8-Fall '79-p23
Teacher-v93-N '75-p111

* * *

FAST, Howard
The Hessian
Am-v127-N 18 '72-p422
B&B-v19-N '73-p99
BL-v69-S 1 '72-p27
BL-v69-S 15 '72-p85
BS-v32-S 15 '72-p277
CSM-v64-Ag 23 '72-p11
EJ-v62-Ja '73-p144
HB-v49-Je '73-p296
KR-v40-Jl 1 '72-p741
KR-v40-Jl 15 '72-p811
LJ-v97-Ag '72-p2642
LJ-v97-O 15 '72-p3473
NYTBR-S 10 '72-p41
PW-v201-Je 26 '72-p57
SR-v1-Ag 29 '72-p70
TN-v29-Ap '73-p257

* * *

FATCHEN, Max
Chase Through The Night
GP-v16-O '77-p3184
JB-v42-F '78-p37
TLS-D 2 '77-p1412
Songs For My Dog And Other People
Brit Bk N C-Autumn '80-p17
JB-v44-D '80-p290
Sch Lib-v29-Je '81-p143
TES-My 21 '82-p31
The Time Wave
JB-v43-F '79-p50
Obs-D 24 '78-p23
Sch Lib-v27-Mr '79-p54
Wry Rhymes For Troublesome Times
JB-v47-O '83-p207
Lis-v110-N 3 '83-p31
Sch Lib-v32-Mr '84-p61
TES-Jl 15 '83-p22

* * *

FATIGATI, Evelyn
Bzzz
ACSB-v10-Fall '77-p17
CSM-v68-N 3 '76-p24
SB-v13-My '77-p45
Garden On Greenway Street
SLJ-v24-S '77-p127

* * *

FATIO, Louise
The Happy Lion
B&B-v14-F '69-p57
Emerg Lib-v11-Ja '84-p19
The Happy Lion And The Bear
Spec-Je 4 '65-p732
TLS-Je 17 '65-p506
The Happy Lion's Rabbits
BL-v71-F 1 '75-p570
CCB-B-v28-My '75-p145
GP-v14-O '75-p2712
KR-v42-D 15 '74-p1298
Teacher-v92-My '75-p28
The Happy Lion's Treasure
BL-v67-Mr 15 '71-p618
CCB-B-v24-Ap '71-p122
Inst-v130-Ap '71-p134
LJ-v96-Ja 15 '71-p257
NYTBR, pt.2-N 8 '70-p53
SR-v54-F 20 '71-p30
TLS-Jl 2 '71-p776
Happy Lion's Vacation
BL-v64-O 15 '67-p273
BW-v1-O 1 '67-p24
CCB-B-v21-D '67-p58
KR-v35-Jl 15 '67-p802
LJ-v92-D 15 '67-p4635
NYTBR-v73-Ja 21 '68-p26
PW-v192-Jl 17 '67-p70
SR-v50-Ag 19 '67-p34
Hector And Christina
BL-v74-N 1 '77-p475
JB-v43-F '79-p16
PW-v212-S 12 '77-p132
RT-v32-O '78-p34
SLJ-v24-Ap '78-p68
Hector Penguin
CCB-B-v27-Ap '74-p127
Inst-v83-N '73-p120
LJ-v98-N 15 '73-p3439
NY-v49-D 3 '73-p204
PW-v204-S 3 '73-p54
TLS-Mr 29 '74-p331
Marc And Pixie And The Walls In Mrs. Jones's Garden
BL-v72-D 15 '75-p577
GP-v16-D '77-p3223
HB-v52-F '76-p41
KR-v43-O 15 '75-p1174
PW-v208-N 10 '75-p55
SLJ-v22-D '75-p42
The Three Happy Lions
Econ-v241-D 18 '71-p70

* * *

FATIO, Luisa
Dos Leones Felices
BL-v72-My 15 '76-p1343
El Leon Feliz
BL-v72-My 15 '76-p1343

* * *

FAULHABER, Martha
Music
Inst-v84-My '75-p96
SLJ-v21-Ap '75-p44
Teacher-v94-Mr '77-p20

* * *

FAULKNER, Keith
First Questions About Animals
GP-v22-Mr '84-p4222
JB-v48-Je '84-p126

* * *

FAULKNER, Margaret
I Skate!
BL-v76-D 1 '79-p554
CCB-B-v33-F '80-p108
HB-v56-F '80-p72
KR-v48-Ja 15 '80-p68
NYTBR-F 17 '80-p24
SLJ-v26-D '79-p101

* * *

FAULKNER, Nancy
Journey Into Danger
CCB-B-v20-My '67-p139
KR-v34-Je 1 '66-p541
LJ-v91-S 15 '66-p4350
The Secret Of The Simple Code
CCB-B-v19-F '66-p97
KR-v33-Jl 15 '65-p683
LJ-v90-N 12 '65-p5105
NYTBR-v70-N 7 '65-p59

FECHTER, Alyce S
(continued)
KR-v33-Ja 15 '65-p59
LJ-v90-Ap 15 '65-p2020
NYTBR-v70-My 23 '65-p30

* * *

FEDER, Carol
The Candlemaking Design Book
BL-v70-Je 1 '74-p1075
BL-v70-Je 1 '74-p1099
CCB-B-v27-Jl '74-p175
KR-v42-Mr 1 '74-p254
LJ-v99-S 15 '74-p2288

* * *

FEDER, Jan
Animal Lives
Cur R-v22-My '83-p173
The Life Of A Cat
ASBYP-v16-Fall '83-p23
GP-v21-My '82-p3903
JB-v46-Ag '82-p141
SB-v19-S '83-p32
TES-Mr 12 '82-p41
TLS-Jl 23 '82-p796
The Life Of A Dog
ASBYP-v16-Fall '83-p23
GP-v21-My '82-p3903
SB-v19-S '83-p32
TES-Mr 12 '82-p41
TLS-Jl 23 '82-p796
The Life Of A Hamster
ASBYP-v16-Fall '83-p23
SB-v19-S '83-p32
TES-Mr 12 '82-p41
TLS-Jl 23 '82-p796
The Life Of A Rabbit
ASBYP-v16-Fall '83-p23
BL-v79-F 15 '83-p776
JB-v46-Ag '82-p141
SB-v19-S '83-p32
TES-Mr 12 '82-p41
TLS-Jl 23 '82-p796

* * *

FEDER, Jane
Beany
BB-v7-N '79-p2
BL-v75-Ap 15 '79-p1294
BW-Ap 8 '79-pL5
CBRS-v7-Ap '79-p82
CLW-v51-F '80-p309
HB-v55-Ag '79-p406
Inst-v88-My '79-p106
JB-v44-Je '80-p116
KR-v47-Mr 1 '79-p258
NYTBR-Ap 29 '79-p26
Par-v54-D '79-p64
RT-v34-O '80-p41
SLJ-v25-My '79-p50
WCRB-v5-Jl '79-p62
The Night-Light
BL-v77-O 15 '80-p325
CBRS-v8-Ag '80-p131
KR-v48-Ag 15 '80-p1080
PW-v218-Jl 11 '80-p91

* * *

FEDER, Paula K
Where Does The Teacher Live?
BL-v75-My 15 '79-p1445
CBRS-v7-My '79-p95
CCB-B-v33-S '79-p6
CE-v56-Ja '80-p168
CLW-v51-F '80-p309
HB-v55-Ap '79-p186
KR-v47-Mr 1 '79-p261
LA-v56-O '79-p820
RT-v33-Ja '80-p485
RT-v34-O '80-p41
SLJ-v25-My '79-p79
SR-v6-My 26 '79-p64
WCRB-v5-S '79-p84

* * *

FEDOR, Peter
The Bird Of Happiness
Econ-v257-D 20 '75-p102
Spec-v235-D 6 '75-p734

* * *

FEEHAN, Mary
The Book Of Irish Children's Jokes
CAY-v4-Summer '83-p5

* * *

FEELINGS, Muriel L
Jambo Means Hello
BL-v70-Je 1 '74-p1104
BL-v71-Mr 15 '75-p766
BW-D 8 '74-p7
CCB-B-v28-S '74-p6
CLW-v46-My '75-p453
Choice-v12-N '75-p1132
Comw-v101-N 22 '74-p193
HB-v50-Ag '74-p367
Inst-v84-N '74-p132
KR-v42-Ap 15 '74-p418
KR-v43-Ja 1 '75-p2
LJ-v99-My 15 '74-p1451
LJ-v99-My 15 '74-p1465
LJ-v99-D 15 '74-p3247
PT-v8-S '74-p132
SMQ-v7-Spring '79-p171
Teacher-v92-N '74-p106
Teacher-v92-My '75-p91
Moja Means One
A Lib-v3-Ap '72-p419
Am-v125-D 4 '71-p486
BL-v68-Ja 1 '72-p393
BL-v68-Ap 1 '72-p669
BL-v69-My 1 '73-p836
CCB-B-v25-Je '72-p155
CE-v48-F '72-p260
CE-v61-S '84-p33
CLW-v52-Ap '81-p388
CSM-v64-Ap 4 '72-p6
GT-v89-My '72-p56
HB-v48-F '72-p40
Inter BC-v14-#7 '83-p28
KR-v39-O 15 '71-p1112
LJ-v96-D 15 '71-p4158
LJ-v96-D 15 '71-p4178
PW-v200-O 4 '71-p60
SR-v55-Ja 15 '72-p46
Zamani Goes To Market
Am-v123-D 5 '70-p494
BL-v66-Je 1 '70-p1210
CCB-B-v24-S '70-p6
HB-v46-Ag '70-p381
KR-v38-Mr 15 '70-p321
LJ-v95-N 15 '70-p4034
PW-v197-F 9 '70-p83
Spectr-v47-Mr '71-p43

* * *

FEELINGS, Tom
Black Pilgrimage
BL-v68-Je 15 '72-p903
BL-v69-My 1 '73-p837
BW-v6-My 7 '72-p13
Bl W-v22-N '72-p91
CCB-B-v26-S '72-p6
EJ-v63-Ja '74-p67
HB-v48-Ag '72-p380
KR-v40-Ap 15 '72-p489
LJ-v98-Ja 15 '73-p267
NYTBR, pt.2-My 7 '72-p30
SR-v55-My 20 '72-p82
Day Dreamers
LA-v59-My '82-p482
Something On My Mind
CE-v60-My '84-p344
CLW-v50-O '78-p111
LA-v56-Ja '79-p48
RT-v32-My '79-p974

* * *

FEENEY, Stephanie
A Is For Aloha
CCB-B-v34-Ja '81-p92
CT-v11-Ja '82-p36
Inst-v90-N '80-p50

* * *

FEERICK, John D
The First Book Of Vice-Presidents Of The United States
ARBA-v14- '83-p190
SLJ-v24-Ja '78-p87

* * *

FEGELY, Thomas D
Wonders Of Geese And Swans
ACSB-v10-Winter '77-p17
BL-v73-S 1 '76-p37
KR-v44-Je 1 '76-p636
PW-v210-Jl 19 '76-p133
SB-v12-Mr '77-p211
SLJ-v23-O '76-p116
Wonders Of Wild Ducks
ACSB-v9-Spring '76-p17
BL-v72-Ja 1 '76-p625
CCB-B-v29-Mr '76-p109
SB-v12-S '76-p104
SLJ-v22-Ja '76-p45
The World Of Freshwater Fish
ACSB-v12-Spring '79-p17
BL-v75-S 1 '78-p48
CCB-B-v32-N '78-p43
Comw-v105-N 10 '78-p734
KR-v46-Ag 1 '78-p809
SB-v15-D '79-p151
SLJ-v25-N '78-p61
The World Of The Woodlot
ACSB-v9-Spring '76-p18
BL-v71-My 1 '75-p913
HB-v51-Ag '75-p397
KR-v43-Ap 1 '75-p379
SLJ-v22-N '75-p76

* * *

FEHR, Brbara
Yankee Denim Dandies
WLB-v49-D '74-p273

* * *

FEHRENBACH, T R
The United Nations In War And Peace
BL-v65-Ja 1 '69-p494
CCB-B-v22-F '69-p92
KR-v36-S 1 '68-p989
LJ-v93-N 15 '68-p4413
LJ-v95-O 15 '70-p3603
SE-v33-My '69-p562
SR-v52-Ja 18 '69-p41

* * *

FEIG, Barbara Krane
Now You're Cooking
BS-v35-D '75-p296
NYTBR-N 16 '75-p34

* * *

FEIL, Hila
The Ghost Garden
GP-v16-My '77-p3119
HB-v52-Ag '76-p396
JB-v41-Ag '77-p233
KR-v44-F 15 '76-p200
SLJ-v22-Ap '76-p73
TLS-Mr 25 '77-p358
WCRB-v3-S '77-p58

* * *

FEILEN, John
Dirt Track Speedsters
SLJ-v23-D '76-p72
Racing On The Water
SLJ-v23-D '76-p72
Winter Sports
SLJ-v23-D '76-p72

* * *

FEINBERG, Barbara S
Franklin D. Roosevelt: Gallant President
BL-v77-Je 15 '81-p1344
KR-v49-Je 1 '81-p681
LA-v59-Mr '82-p270
PW-v219-My 8 '81-p255
SLJ-v28-D '81-p62

* * *

FEININGER, Andreas
Shells
BL-v69-Mr 1 '73-p610
Choice-v10-S '73-p1011
LJ-v97-D 15 '72-p3983
SA-v251-D '84-p30

* * *

FEINMAN, Jeffrey
The Catalog Of Free Things
ARBA-v8-'77-p58
BL-v73-Mr 1 '77-p988
BL-v73-Mr 1 '77-p1012
SLJ-v23-F '77-p78
Freebies For Kids
ARBA-v11-'80-p367
BL-v75-Jl 15 '79-p1626
BL-v80-Ja 1 '84-p679
PW-v215-Je 18 '79-p93
SLJ-v26-F '80-p35
SLJ-v26-F '80-p53
SLJ-v30-F '84-p69
Magic
CBRS-v8-Ap '80-p87
Kliatt-v14-Spring '80-p55
PW-v217-F 29 '80-p136
SLJ-v26-Ag '80-p63

* * *

FEINSON, Keith
Voyage En Aquitaine
TES-Ap 21 '78-p23

* * *

FEINSTEIN, Joe
A Silly Little Kid
CCB-B-v24-S '70-p7
LJ-v95-Ap 15 '70-p1626

* * *

FELDER, Eleanor
Careers In Publishing And Printing
BL-v73-O 15 '76-p321
Cur R-v16-My '77-p94
SLJ-v23-Ja '77-p91

* * *

FELDMAN, Anne
Firefighters
ACSB-v13-Spring '80-p27
BL-v75-Je 15 '79-p1534
SLJ-v26-N '79-p76
The Inflated Dormouse And Other Ways Of Life In The Animal World
BL-v67-Ja 1 '71-p372
BW-v4-N 8 '70-p4
HB-v46-D '70-p630
KR-v38-Ag 15 '70-p878
LJ-v95-O 15 '70-p3626
SA-v223-D '70-p134
SB-v6-D '70-p233

* * *

FELDMAN, Shirley C
Learning Ways To Read Words
Cur R-v17-D '78-p398

* * *

FELDSTEIN, Albert B
Mad For Kicks
SLJ-v27-N '80-p73
Pumping Mad
SLJ-v28-S '81-p119

* * *

FELICIANO MENDOZA, Ester
Nanas
HB-v54-D '78-p655

* * *

FELIX, Jiri
The Hamlyn Animal Encyclopedia
B&B-v21-F '76-p63
GP-v14-My '75-p2649

* * *

FELIX, Monique
Cookery
JB-v46-O '82-p188
Sch Lib-v31-Mr '83-p42
The Further Adventures Of The Little Mouse Trapped In A Book
BL-v80-Ap 1 '84-p1115
BW-v14-F 12 '84-p11
Stories With Or Without Words
Obs-N 28 '82-p31
The Story Of A Little Mouse Trapped In A Book
Inst-v91-S '81-p30
SLJ-v28-S '81-p106
Yum Yum!
CSM-v75-Ap 18 '83-p17
SLJ-v29-Ap '83-p113

* * *

FELL, Alison
The Grey Dancer
Brit Bk N C-Autumn '81-p24
Brit Bk N C-Autumn '82-p8
GP-v20-My '81-p3880
JB-v45-Ag '81-p158
TES-Je 5 '81-p37
TLS-Jl 23 '82-p797

* * *

FELLINI, Federico
Fellini On Fellini
BL-v72-Je 15 '76-p1441
CM-v17-Spring '79-p194
Choice-v13-O '76-p993
FQ-v30-Summer '77-p60
HB-v53-F '77-p80
Kliatt-v11-Fall '77-p42
LJ-v101-Jl '76-p1552

* * *

FELLOWS, Lawrence
A Gentle War
BL-v76-D 1 '79-p556
CE-v56-Ap '80-p308
KR-v48-Ja 15 '80-p68
SLJ-v26-F '80-p54

* * *

FELLY, David
The Facts About A Pop Group
GP-v15-Mr '77-p3070

* * *

FELSEN, Henry Gregor
Living With Your First Motorcycle
BL-v72-My 15 '76-p1330
BL-v72-My 15 '76-p1335
KR-v44-My 1 '76-p544
Kliatt-v11-Spring '77-p24
SLJ-v23-S '76-p132

* * *

FELT, Sue
Rosa-Too-Little
Inst-v74-Ja '65-p38
SLJ-v27-Ja '81-p33

* * *

FELTON, Harold W
Deborah Sampson: Soldier Of The Revolution
KR-v44-S 1 '76-p976
RT-v31-O '77-p19
SE-v41-Ap '77-p351
SLJ-v23-N '76-p57
Ely S. Parker
CSM-v65-N 7 '73-pB6
Inst-v82-My '73-p69
KR-v41-Jl 1 '73-p687
LJ-v98-N 15 '73-p3462
SE-v39-Mr '75-p173
James Weldon Johnson
BL-v67-Jl 1 '71-p907
CCB-B-v24-Jl '71-p169
Comw-v97-F 23 '73-p473
LJ-v96-N 15 '71-p3900
NYTBR, pt.2-My 2 '71-p43
PW-v199-My 10 '71-p43
Jim Beckwourth: Negro Mountain Man
BL-v63-F 15 '67-p624
CCB-B-v20-F '67-p88
LJ-v91-S 15 '66-p4330
NYTBR-v71-N 6 '66-p38
John Henry And His Hammer
SE-v44-O '80-p481
Mumbet
BL-v66-Jl 15 '70-p1407
CCB-B-v24-S '70-p7
CSM-v62-My 7 '70-pB1
HB-v46-Ag '70-p399
KR-v38-My 1 '70-p509
PW-v197-Mr 30 '70-p65
SR-v53-Je 27 '70-p39
Nancy Ward, Cherokee
CCB-B-v29-N '75-p43
KR-v43-Ja 15 '75-p72
SLJ-v21-My '75-p63
Nat Love
BL-v66-S 1 '69-p54
CCB-B-v22-Jl '69-p173
KR-v37-Ap 15 '69-p444
LJ-v95-D 15 '70-p4382
Pecos Bill And The Mustang
CCB-B-v20-D '66-p57
CE-v43-N '66-p160
CSM-v57-N 4 '65-pB5
KR-v33-Ag 1 '65-p748
LJ-v90-O 15 '65-p4615
Uriah Phillips Levy
BL-v75-Mr 1 '79-p1087
KR-v47-Mr 1 '79-p265
LA-v56-My '79-p545
SLJ-v25-D '78-p60

* * *

FENBY, Terry P
The Piper Of Dreams
GP-v21-N '82-p3972

* * *

FENDER, Kay
Odette
BL-v74-Je 15 '78-p1616
CSM-v70-S 18 '78-pB14
GP-v17-Jl '78-p3370
JB-v42-Je '78-p135
KR-v46-Je 1 '78-p593
NS-v95-My 19 '78-p682
Par-v53-Jl '78-p18
SLJ-v25-S '78-p107
TES-N 17 '78-p45
TLS-Jl 24 '81-p843
A Springtime In Paris
TLS-Ap 7 '78-p385

* * *

FENDERSON, Lewis H
Daniel Hale Williams
CCB-B-v26-S '72-p6
KR-v40-Ap 1 '72-p413
LJ-v97-S 15 '72-p2948

* * *

FENISONG, Ruth
Boy Wanted
CSM-v57-F 4 '65-p11
HB-v41-F '65-p52

FENISONG, Ruth (continued)
SLJ-v30-F '84-p31

* * *

FENNELL, Ian
Robottom The Robot
Brit Bk N C-Spring '81-p19
Sch Lib-v29-Je '81-p126
TLS-Mr 27 '81-p340

* * *

FENNEMA, Ilona
Dirk's Wooden Clogs
TLS-D 4 '69-p1392
Dirk's Wooden Shoes
BW-v4-My 17 '70-p8
CCB-B-v24-Jl '70-p175
KR-v38-Mr 1 '70-p238
LJ-v95-S 15 '70-p3038
SR-v53-My 9 '70-p42

* * *

FENNER, Carol
Christmas Tree On The Mountain
Atl-v218-D '66-p156
BL-v63-N 15 '66-p376
CCB-B-v20-N '66-p41
Comw-v85-N 11 '66-p172
HB-v42-D '66-p701
KR-v34-Ag 1 '66-p750
LJ-v91-O 15 '66-p5136
NYTBR-v71-D 4 '66-p68
SR-v49-D 10 '66-p56
Gorilla Gorilla
ACSB-v15-Winter '82-p9
BL-v69-Jl 1 '73-p1021
BL-v70-Mr 15 '74-p827
BW-v7-N 11 '73-p3C
CCB-B-v26-My '73-p136
CSM-v65-My 2 '73-pB4
Choice-v12-N '75-p1132
HB-v49-Ag '73-p392
KR-v41-F 15 '73-p190
KR-v41-D 15 '73-p1352
NYTBR-My 27 '73-p8
PW-v203-F 5 '73-p89
SB-v9-Mr '74-p333
TN-v30-N '73-p81
Lagalag, The Wanderer
CCB-B-v21-Jl '68-p173
KR-v36-Ja 1 '68-p1
LJ-v93-F 15 '68-p858
The Skates Of Uncle Richard
BL-v75-D 15 '78-p685
CBRS-v7-Winter '79-p54
CCB-B-v32-Mr '79-p113
HB-v55-Ap '79-p191
KR-v47-Ja 15 '79-p65
LA-v56-My '79-p546

* * *

FENNER, Phyllis R
Full Forty Fathoms
BL-v72-O 15 '75-p293
KR-v43-Ag 1 '75-p848
SLJ-v22-D '75-p58
Keeping Christmas
BL-v76-O 1 '79-p278
CCB-B-v33-N '79-p46
KR-v47-S 15 '79-p1074
SLJ-v26-O '79-p119
Lift Line
CSM-v68-N 3 '76-p20
KR-v44-Jl 15 '76-p799
SLJ-v23-D '76-p71

* * *

FENNER, Sal
Sea Machines
ASBYP-v14-Fall '81-p29
SB-v17-S '81-p34

* * *

FENTEN, Barbara
Careers In The Sports Industry
Inst-v86-My '77-p126
SLJ-v23-My '77-p80
Teacher-v95-Ja '78-p118
The Team Behind The Great Parades
BL-v78-F 15 '82-p756
PW-v220-N 20 '81-p54
SLJ-v28-F '82-p75

* * *

FENTEN, D X
Gardening...Naturally
CCB-B-v27-Mr '74-p109
KR-v41-S 15 '73-p1045
LJ-v98-N 15 '73-p3462
PW-v204-D 31 '73-p27
Indoor Gardening
ACSB-v8-Spring '75-p18
CCB-B-v28-F '75-p93
KR-v42-Ag 15 '74-p883
SB-v11-My '75-p39
SLJ-v21-Mr '75-p95
Ms.-M.D.
BL-v70-S 15 '73-p111
CCB-B-v27-S '73-p8
Inst-v82-My '73-p70
KR-v41-Ap 1 '73-p400
NYTBR-Jl 15 '73-p8
PT-v7-O '73-p138
PW-v203-My 14 '73-p47
SB-v10-My '74-p44
Plants For Pots
BL-v65-Je 15 '69-p1174
CCB-B-v23-Ja '70-p80
LJ-v94-O 15 '69-p3820
NYTBR, pt.2-My 4 '69-p49
SR-v52-My 10 '69-p58
SR-v52-N 8 '69-p68
Teacher-v94-F '77-p40
Strange Differences
ACSB-v9-Spring '76-p19
KR-v43-Je 15 '75-p664
SB-v11-Mr '76-p210
SLJ-v22-S '75-p102
TV And Radio Careers
BL-v72-My 15 '76-p1335
Cur R-v16-My '77-p95
KR-v44-Mr 1 '76-p263
SLJ-v23-O '76-p106

* * *

FENTEN, Don
Behind The Scenes Series
Cur R-v20-Ja '81-p22

* * *

FENTON, B
Looking At Maps
JB-v43-F '79-p30

* * *

FENTON, Edward
Big Yellow Balloon
BL-v64-N 1 '67-p330
BW-v1-N 5 '67-p6
CLW-v39-D '67-p299
HB-v43-D '67-p741
HB-v60-Je '84-p365
KR-v35-Ag 15 '67-p952
LJ-v93-F 15 '68-p859
NYTBR-v72-N 5 '67-p71
PW-v192-S 4 '67-p57
Duffy's Rocks
BL-v70-Jl 1 '74-p1199
BL-v71-Mr 15 '75-p766
CCB-B-v27-Jl '74-p175
GP-v14-Ja '76-p2810
GP-v16-Ap '78-p3282
HB-v50-Je '74-p285
KR-v42-F 1 '74-p120
KR-v43-Ja 1 '75-p9
LJ-v99-My 15 '74-p1482
Lis-v92-N 7 '74-p613
NS-v88-N 8 '74-p663
NYTBR-My 19 '74-p8
NYTBR-Je 2 '74-p38
NYTBR-N 3 '74-p52

FENTON, Edward (continued)
Obs-D 8 '74-p30
PW-v205-Mr 4 '74-p76
TLS-D 6 '74-p1375
Teacher-v92-S '74-p129
Matter Of Miracles
Am-v117-N 4 '67-p518
BL-v64-O 15 '67-p273
BW-v1-S 10 '67-p36
CCB-B-v21-D '67-p58
CE-v44-Ap '68-p501
HB-v43-O '67-p592
KR-v35-Je 1 '67-p645
LJ-v92-S 15 '67-p3185
NYTBR-v72-Ag 6 '67-p26
NYTBR-v72-N 5 '67-p66
PW-v192-N 27 '67-p43
Penny Candy
BL-v67-S 15 '70-p105
CCB-B-v24-N '70-p41
CE-v47-F '71-p265
KR-v38-My 1 '70-p506
LJ-v95-Jl '70-p2527
PW-v197-Ap 20 '70-p62
SR-v53-Ag 22 '70-p52
Teacher-v90-F '73-p125
The Refugee Summer
BL-v78-Ap 15 '82-p1095
CCB-B-v35-Ap '82-p147
CLW-v54-S '82-p84
GP-v22-S '83-p4137
HB-v58-Je '82-p286
KR-v50-Mr 1 '82-p275
LA-v59-N '82-p869
NYTBR-v87-Ap 25 '82-p34
Obs-Ag 7 '83-p25
SLJ-v28-Ap '82-p80
VOYA-v5-Ag '82-p30

* * *

FENTON, Ian
Looking At Creativity
GP-v16-Mr '78-p3272
JB-v42-Je '78-p152
TES-O 20 '78-p41
Looking At Music
GP-v16-Mr '78-p3272
JB-v42-Ag '78-p202
TES-O 20 '78-p41

* * *

FENTON, Robert S
Chess For You
JB-v39-F '75-p61
KR-v41-Je 15 '73-p646
LJ-v98-O 15 '73-p3144
TLS-D 6 '74-p1385

* * *

FENTON, Sophia Harvati
Ancient Egypt
CCB-B-v25-My '72-p138
KR-v39-My 15 '71-p555
SB-v7-D '71-p268
SLJ-v25-S '78-p42
Greece
CCB-B-v23-F '70-p95
KR-v37-N 1 '69-p1151
LJ-v95-Ja 15 '70-p232
SB-v5-Mr '70-p351

* * *

FERGUS, Andrew
A First Sentence Dictionary
TES-Mr 7 '80-p40

* * *

FERGUSON, Diana
Ants
SLJ-v24-S '77-p100
Beetles
BL-v73-Je 15 '77-p1579
SLJ-v24-S '77-p100
TLS-Jl 5 '74-p724
Horses
SLJ-v24-S '77-p100
Rocks
SLJ-v24-S '77-p100

* * *

FERGUSON, Dorothy
Black Duck
BL-v74-Mr 1 '78-p1102
CCB-B-v31-My '78-p141
CSM-v70-My 3 '78-pB5
Inst-v87-My '78-p113
KR-v46-Ja 15 '78-p49
SB-v14-D '78-p182
SLJ-v24-My '78-p54
WCRB-v4-Mr '78-p41

* * *

FERGUSON, Jane
A Book Of Disasters
TLS-Mr 26 '82-p343

* * *

FERGUSON, Linda
Canada
BL-v76-Ja 15 '80-p712
HB-v56-Ap '80-p183
In Rev-v14-Ap '80-p41
KR-v47-D 1 '79-p1381
SLJ-v26-F '80-p65

* * *

FERGUSON, Max
Has Anybody Seen My Umbrella?
Quill & Q-v49-N '83-p25

* * *

FERGUSON, Robert
How To Make Movies
CCB-B-v23-S '69-p7
CLW-v41-O '69-p133
LJ-v94-Jl '69-p2687
LJ-v94-S 1 '69-p2950
WLB-v47-Ja '73-p444

* * *

FERGUSON, Sheila
Village And Town Life
CCB-B-v36-Jl '83-p208
SLJ-v30-O '83-p166
TES-My 6 '83-p29

* * *

FERMAN, Edward L
Graven Images
CCB-B-v31-Ap '78-p125
LJ-v102-D 15 '77-p2515
Twenty Years Of The Magazine Of Fantasy And Science Fiction
CCB-B-v24-Ja '71-p73
LJ-v95-Je 15 '70-p2284

* * *

FERN, Eugene
Birthday Presents
CCB-B-v20-Je '67-p151
CLW-v39-O '67-p157
KR-v35-Mr 15 '67-p334
LJ-v92-Ap 15 '67-p1724

* * *

FERNANDES, Eugenie
A Difficult Day
Emerg Lib-v11-Ja '84-p40
Quill & Q-v50-Mr '84-p72
SLJ-v30-My '84-p64
The Little Boy Who Cried Himself To Sea
BIC-v11-D '82-p8
Emerg Lib-v10-My '83-p29

* * *

FERRA-MIKURA, Vera
Twelve People Are Not A Dozen
CCB-B-v19-D '65-p61
HB-v41-O '65-p502
KR-v33-My 15 '65-p498

FERRA-MIKURA, Vera
(continued)
Spec-N 11 '66-p626
TLS-N 24 '66-p1074

* * *

FERRAN, Jaime
Tarde De Circo
BL-v80-N 1 '83-p425

* * *

FERRETTI, Fred
The Great American Book Of Sidewalk, Stoop, Dirt, Curb, And Alley Games
HB-v52-Ap '76-p177
SLJ-v22-Mr '76-p102
Teacher-v93-Ap '76-p121

* * *

FERRIER, Lucy
Diving The Great Barrier Reef
SLJ-v23-S '76-p107

* * *

FERRIER, Shannon
The Kids Food Cookbook
BIC-v11-D '82-p9
Quill & Q-v49-Ja '83-p30
More Kids In The Kitchen
In Rev-v15-F '81-p36

* * *

FERRIS, Jean
Amen, Moses Gardenia
BL-v80-O 1 '83-p233
CBRS-v12-D '83-p41
CCB-B-v37-Ja '84-p85
J Read-v27-Ap '84-p661
KR-v51-S 1 '83-pJ174
SLJ-v30-N '83-p91
VOYA-v7-Ap '84-p29

* * *

FERRO, Beatriz
Caught In The Rain
BL-v76-Jl 15 '80-p1674
CBRS-v8-Ag '80-p131
LA-v57-S '80-p646
PW-v217-Ap 18 '80-p90
RT-v34-Mr '81-p733
SLJ-v27-S '80-p58
Umbrellas!
JB-v44-D '80-p282

* * *

FERRON, Yseult
Bilijoux
BL-v80-Ja 15 '84-p758

* * *

FERRY, Charles
O Zebron Falls!
BB-v6-Je '78-p4
BL-v74-N 1 '77-p475
BS-v37-D '77-p293
CCB-B-v31-Mr '78-p111
EJ-v67-F '78-p100
HB-v53-O '77-p539
KR-v45-N 1 '77-p1148
NYTBR-Mr 5 '78-p26
SLJ-v24-O '77-p123
Up In Sister Bay
CSM-v67-N 5 '75-pB11
HB-v51-D '75-p601
KR-v43-Ag 15 '75-p924
NYTBR-N 2 '75-p10
PW-v208-Ag 11 '75-p117
SLJ-v22-D '75-p59

* * *

FETTIG, Art
The Three Robots
SLJ-v27-Ag '81-p54

* * *

FEUERLICHT, Roberta Strauss
America's Reign Of Terror
CCB-B-v25-My '72-p138
LJ-v97-My 15 '72-p1921
Spec-v226-My 29 '71-p1025
Zhivko Of Yugoslavia
CCB-B-v25-Je '72-p155
KR-v39-Ag 1 '71-p809
LJ-v96-O 15 '71-p3466

* * *

FEUERSTEIN, Reuven
Instrumental Enrichment
AJMD-v85-Mr '81-p561
EL-v42-S '84-p48

* * *

FEY, James T
Long, Short, High, Low, Thin, Wide
BL-v68-Ap 15 '72-p723
CCB-B-v25-Ja '72-p73
CE-v49-O '72-p32
LJ-v97-S 15 '72-p2932
SB-v8-My '72-p10

* * *

FEYDY, Anne Lindbergh
Osprey Island
CCB-B-v28-Ap '75-p128
HB-v51-Ap '75-p146
KR-v42-N 15 '74-p1201
LA-v52-S '75-p856
LJ-v99-N 15 '74-p3045
PW-v206-N 25 '74-p46

* * *

FIAROTTA, Phyllis
Be What You Want To Be!
BL-v74-F 15 '78-p1001
Cur R-v17-My '78-p103
SLJ-v24-F '78-p46
Confetti
BL-v75-Mr 1 '79-p1087
SLJ-v25-My '79-p60
Pin It, Tack It, Hang It
CSM-v68-Ja 19 '76-p14
SLJ-v23-F '77-p63
Snips & Snails & Walnut Whales
BL-v72-S 1 '75-p39
BW-Je 8 '75-p4
CSM-v67-Jl 7 '75-p27
PW-v207-Je 9 '75-p63
SLJ-v22-N '75-p76
Sticks & Stones & Ice Cream Cones
BL-v70-My 1 '74-p1001
BW-Je 8 '75-p4
CE-v51-O '74-p36
HM-v248-F '74-p98
NYT-v123-Ja 9 '74-p40
The You And Me Heritage Tree
CSM-v68-O 27 '76-p24
Inst-v88-S '78-p214
SLJ-v23-D '76-p54
Zippers, Snaps, And Flaps
BL-v79-Je 15 '83-p1319

* * *

FICHTER, George S
American Indian Music And Musical Instruments
SLJ-v25-Ap '79-p54
Bicycles And Bicycling
SLJ-v24-My '78-p66
TES-O 20 '78-p39
Birds Of North America
ARBA-v15-'84-p657
ASBYP-v16-Winter '83-p58
BL-v79-O 15 '82-p311
SLJ-v29-N '82-p82
Cats
ACSB-v8-Winter '75-p15
RSR-v2-O '74-p22
SB-v10-D '74-p260
Teacher-v91-N '73-p130

FICHTER, George S
(continued)
Comets And Meteors
ASBYP-v16-Winter '83-p22
BL-v78-Jl '82-p1440
CBRS-v10-Jl '82-p127
SB-v18-Mr '83-p207
SLJ-v29-O '82-p147
Florida In Pictures
BL-v75-Jl 15 '79-p1626
SLJ-v26-O '79-p149
How The Plains Indians Lived
BL-v76-Jl 15 '80-p1675
CBRS-v8-Ap '80-p87
CE-v57-Mr '81-p236
SLJ-v27-Mr '81-p143
How To Build An Indian Canoe
BL-v73-Ap 1 '77-p1156
BL-v73-Ap 1 '77-p1166
KR-v45-F 1 '77-p100
SLJ-v23-Ap '77-p76
The Human Body
ACSB-v12-Winter '79-p10
SLJ-v25-S '78-p135
Insects
SLJ-v22-N '75-p76
Iraq
BL-v75-N 1 '78-p473
SLJ-v25-D '78-p51
SLJ-v30-N '83-p39
Karts And Karting
BL-v78-Jl '82-p1450
SLJ-v28-My '82-p88
Keeping Amphibians And Reptiles As Pets
SLJ-v26-F '80-p54
Poisonous Snakes
BL-v78-Jl '82-p1443
Cur R-v22-Ag '83-p49
SB-v18-My '83-p274
SLJ-v29-F '83-p75
Racquetball
BL-v76-Ja 1 '80-p670
SLJ-v26-D '79-p102
Reptiles & Amphibians Of North America
ARBA-v15-'84-p670
ASBYP-v16-Winter '83-p58
BL-v79-O 15 '82-p311
SLJ-v29-N '82-p82
Rocks & Minerals
ASBYP-v16-Winter '83-p58
BL-v79-O 15 '82-p311
SLJ-v29-N '82-p82
Snakes Around The World
ASBYP-v14-Winter '81-p24
ASBYP-v16-Fall '83-p26
SB-v16-Ja '81-p156
SLJ-v26-My '80-p82
Wildflowers Of North America
ARBA-v15-'84-p646
ASBYP-v16-Winter '83-p58
BL-v79-O 15 '82-p311
Inst-v92-Ap '83-p20
SLJ-v29-N '82-p82
Working Dogs
BL-v75-Ap 15 '79-p1294
SLJ-v26-O '79-p149

* * *

FICOWSKI, Jerzy
Sister Of The Birds And Other Gypsy Tales
BB-v5-Ap '77-p4
BL-v73-N 15 '76-p472
PW-v210-O 4 '76-p74
SLJ-v23-Mr '77-p144

* * *

FIDLER, Kathleen
The Boy With The Bronze Axe
GP-v20-Mr '82-p4030
TES-Ap 2 '82-p27
TLS-Je 6 '68-p581
The Desperate Journey
In Rev-v16-F '82-p24
The Ghosts Of Sandeel Bay
Brit Bk N C-Autumn '81-p21
JB-v45-Ag '81-p158
Sch Lib-v29-D '81-p326
The Lost Cave
JB-v42-O '78-p265
TES-Jl 21 '78-p20
Pablos And The Bull
Brit Bk N-Je '80-p331
GP-v19-Jl '80-p3720
JB-v44-D '80-p291
TES-Ja 18 '80-p41
The Railway Runaways
JB-v41-O '77-p286
Seal Story
GP-v18-Jl '79-p3558
JB-v43-D '79-p334
Turk The Border Collie
GP-v14-Ja '76-p2789
JB-v40-F '76-p42
Obs-D 7 '75-p32
Wrecks, Wreckers, And Rescuers
JB-v42-F '78-p38

* * *

FIEDEL, Roslyn
Wild Flowers
CLW-v44-N '72-p248
Dance-v46-Jl '72-p90
HB-v48-O '72-p482
KR-v40-Mr 15 '72-p328
LJ-v97-Jl '72-p2483
LJ-v98-O 15 '73-p3123

* * *

FIEDLER, Jean
In Any Spring
BL-v65-Jl 1 '69-p1220
BS-v29-Ap 1 '69-p21
CCB-B-v22-Ap '69-p125
Comw-v90-My 23 '69-p300
KR-v37-F 15 '69-p184
LJ-v94-Ap 15 '69-p1794
A Yardstick For Jessica
CCB-B-v18-Je '65-p146
The Year The World Was Out Of Step With Jancy Fried
BL-v78-Ja 15 '82-p648
CBRS-v10-Mr '82-p76
CCB-B-v35-Ja '82-p84
SLJ-v28-N '81-p90
TES-N 19 '82-p36
VOYA-v5-Ap '82-p33

* * *

FIEG, V P
Why There Aren't Many Witches
CBRS-v8-Je '80-p107
CCB-B-v33-Je '80-p188
KR-v48-Mr 15 '80-p365
SLJ-v27-O '80-p145

* * *

FIELD, C
Fiction In The Middle School
GP-v14-S '75-p2704
TLS-Ja 31 '75-p103

* * *

FIELD, Carolyn W
Subject Collections In Children's Literature
BL-v65-Jl 1 '69-p1190
BSA-P-v66-Ja '72-p91
CE-v47-D '70-p163
HB-v45-Ag '69-p425
TN-v26-Ap '70-p313
WLB-v43-Je '69-p1019

FIFE, Dale (continued)
J Read-v22-Mr '79-p561
KR-v46-Je 15 '78-p636
LA-v56-My '79-p548
NYTBR-Ap 30 '78-p32
SE-v43-Ap '79-p300
SLJ-v24-My '78-p66
Teacher-v96-O '78-p167
Ride The Crooked Wind
A Lib-v6-Mr '75-p166
BL-v70-O 1 '73-p170
KR-v41-My 1 '73-p515
LJ-v98-S 15 '73-p2650
The Sesame Seed Snatchers
BL-v80-F 1 '84-p813
CBRS-v12-Ap '84-p95
CCB-B-v37-F '84-p106
SLJ-v30-D '83-p82
Walk A Narrow Bridge
BS-v26-Ja 1 '67-p367
CCB-B-v21-D '67-p59
HB-v43-Ap '67-p212
KR-v34-O 1 '66-p1051
LJ-v91-D 15 '66-p6200
What's New, Lincoln?
BL-v66-Je 1 '70-p1212
CCB-B-v24-Jl '70-p175
GT-v88-D '70-p82
KR-v38-Mr 15 '70-p322
LJ-v95-My 15 '70-p1941
PW-v197-Mr 30 '70-p64
What's The Prize, Lincoln
BL-v68-D 15 '71-p366
CCB-B-v25-Ja '72-p73
CE-v48-My '72-p421
CLW-v45-Mr '74-p398
KR-v39-O 15 '71-p1120
LJ-v97-F 15 '72-p763
PW-v200-N 1 '71-p55
SR-v54-O 16 '71-p57
Who Goes There, Lincoln?
BL-v71-Mr 15 '75-p749
CCB-B-v28-Jl '75-p175
CE-v52-N '75-p89
KR-v43-F 1 '75-p122
LJ-v99-D 15 '74-p3266
RT-v29-Ap '76-p723
Who'll Vote For Lincoln?
CCB-B-v31-N '77-p45
KR-v45-Je 1 '77-p575
SLJ-v24-O '77-p110
Who's In Charge Of Lincoln?
BL-v61-Jl 15 '65-p1063
CCB-B-v18-Jl '65-p160
Inst-v75-S '65-p166
KR-v33-Ap 15 '65-p433
LJ-v90-Je 15 '65-p2884
NYTBR-v70-S 5 '65-p20
SR-v48-Je 19 '65-p41

* * *

FIFTY Creative Ways To Use Paperbacks In The Middle Grades
LA-v58-S '81-p735
RT-v34-Ap '81-p837
SLJ-v27-My '81-p31

* * *

FIFTY Creative Ways To Use Paperbacks In The Primary Grades
LA-v58-S '81-p735
RT-v34-Ap '81-p837
SLJ-v27-My '81-p31

* * *

FIGHTING Ships (Battlegame Books)
Obs-D 11 '77-p31

* * *

FIL De Fer
Can Child Lit-#14 '79-p50

* * *

FILLMORE, Parker
The Laughing Prince
RT-v33-F '80-p561
The Shepherd's Nosegay
RT-v33-Mr '80-p688

* * *

FILSTRUP, Chris
China: From Emperors To Communes
BL-v79-Jl '83-p1399
B Rpt-v2-N '83-p52
CBRS-v11-Spring '83-p123
SLJ-v30-S '83-p122

* * *

FINCH, Christopher
Norman Rockwell's America
BS-v36-Ap '76-p8
LJ-v101-Ja 15 '76-p330
NYTBR-D 7 '75-p86
PW-v208-N 3 '75-p66
PW-v208-D 8 '75-p50
Time-v106-D 22 '75-p67

* * *

FINCH, Irene
Science Workshop
Sch Lib-v29-D '81-p330
TES-N 5 '82-p22
Science Workshop 2
TES-Mr 11 '83-p43

* * *

FINCH, Roger
From Viking Ship To Victory
TES-O 21 '77-p20

* * *

FINCHAM, P
Discovering Britain
JB-v40-Je '76-p161

* * *

FINCHAM, Paul
At The Time Of Winston Churchill
TES-N 3 '78-p23
East Anglia
TLS-O 1 '76-p1250

* * *

FINCHER, Ernest B
The American Legal System
BL-v76-My 1 '80-p1290
SLJ-v28-S '81-p124
The Bill Of Rights
BL-v74-My 1 '78-p1430
CLW-v50-D '78-p234
Cur R-v18-My '79-p162
SLJ-v24-Ap '78-p92

* * *

FINE, Anne
The Granny Project
BL-v80-S 1 '83-p83
CCB-B-v37-O '83-p25
GP-v22-Ja '84-p4186
HB-v59-O '83-p573
JB-v48-Ap '84-p81
KR-v51-S 1 '83-pJ174
NS-v106-D 2 '83-p26
SE-v48-My '84-p377
SLJ-v30-O '83-p157
Sch Lib-v32-Mr '84-p67
TES-N 30 '84-p28
The Other Darker Ned
JB-v43-O '79-p277
Round Behind The Ice-House
Brit Bk N C-Autumn '82-p8
GP-v20-Ja '82-p4010
JB-v46-Ap '82-p71
TLS-N 20 '81-p1355
The Stone Menagerie
Brit Bk N C-Autumn '82-p8
GP-v19-S '80-p3756
JB-v44-O '80-p245
Sch Lib-v28-D '80-p393
TES-S 26 '80-p24

FINE, Anne (continued)
The Summer-House Loon
BS-v39-My '79-p72
Brit Bk N C-Spring '81-p14
CCB-B-v33-S '79-p6
EJ-v68-N '79-p75
HB-v55-Ag '79-p422
JB-v42-Ag '78-p202
KR-v47-Ap 1 '79-p392
SLJ-v25-My '79-p60
TES-Ag 25 '78-p14
TLS-Jl 7 '78-p767

* * *

FINE, Diane
The Cookie Bookie
Quill & Q-v49-N '83-p24

* * *

FINE, Joan
I Carve Stone
BL-v76-F 1 '80-p768
BW-v10-Ja 13 '80-p11
CCB-B-v33-Mr '80-p132
CE-v57-S '80-p46
HB-v56-Ap '80-p183
SLJ-v26-Mr '80-p130

* * *

FINES, John
Tudor People
JB-v42-F '78-p38
TES-O 21 '77-p20
TES-Ap 21 '78-p24

* * *

FINIFTER, Germaine
Tell Me About My Body And How It Works
Sch Lib-v32-Je '84-p143
TES-N 11 '83-p28

* * *

FINK, Dale B
Mr. Silver And Mrs. Gold
SLJ-v27-Ag '81-p54

* * *

FINKEL, George
Loyal Virginian
BS-v28-O 1 '68-p276
CSM-v60-N 7 '68-pB10
GP-v15-Mr '77-p3062
KR-v36-Ag 15 '68-p907
NYTBR-F 9 '69-p26
YR-v5-N '68
Matthew Finders
Indexer-v12-Ap '80-p30
New South Wales
Indexer-v12-Ap '80-p30
The Peace Seekers
GP-v21-Jl '82-p3941
Watch Fires To The North
BL-v64-Je 1 '68-p1133
BS-v28-My 1 '68-p64
CCB-B-v22-O '68-p26
CLW-v39-F '68-p438
CSM-v60-My 2 '68-pB8
KR-v35-S 1 '67-p1055
KR-v36-Mr 15 '68-p343
LJ-v93-Je 15 '68-p2546
NYTBR-v73-Ap 14 '68-p20
SR-v51-Jl 20 '68-p31
YR-v4-My '68-p2

* * *

FINKEL, Lawrence S
Developing Reading Comprehension Skills
Cur R-v20-Je '81-p241

* * *

FINLAY, Ian Hamilton
Poems To Hear And See
CCB-B-v25-N '71-p42
CF-v51-N '71-p53
CSM-v63-My 6 '71-pB3
KR-v39-Ja 15 '71-p53
LJ-v96-My 15 '71-p1802
NYTBR-Ap 11 '71-p22
PS-v48-Spring '74-p81
PW-v199-Ap 5 '71-p55
Poet-v121-N '72-p105
Spec-v231-O 20 '73-pR25

* * *

FINLAY, W
Spies And Secret Agents
JB-v41-Ag '77-p233

* * *

FINLAY, Winifred
Beadbonny Ash
KR-v43-S 1 '75-p1004
LR-v24-Winter '74-p185
NS-v86-N 9 '73-p703
Obs-N 25 '73-p39
SLJ-v22-N '75-p76
TLS-N 23 '73-p1435
Cap O'Rushes
CE-v52-Mr '76-p268
Obs-Ag 25 '74-p24
SLJ-v21-Mr '75-p95
Spec-v233-D 7 '74-p735
TLS-Jl 5 '74-p722
Clever And Courageous Dogs
GP-v17-N '78-p3421
JB-v42-O '78-p265
Danger At Black Dyke
B&B-v13-S '68-p46
HB-v45-Ap '69-p177
LJ-v94-F 15 '69-p883
TLS-Je 6 '68-p585
Famous Flights Of Airships And Balloons
JB-v43-D '79-p334
Ghosts, Ghouls And Spectres
GP-v15-N '76-p3003
JB-v41-Ap '77-p109
Obs-D 5 '76-p32
Secret Rooms And Hiding Places
GP-v21-N '82-p3976
Sch Lib-v31-Je '83-p140
Tales From The Borders
Brit Bk N-Je '80-p332
GP-v18-Mr '80-p3647
TES-Ja 18 '80-p38
Tales From The Hebrides And Highlands
Brit Bk N C-Autumn '80-p3
GP-v17-Ja '79-p3458
JB-v43-O '79-p270
TES-Ja 18 '80-p38
Tales Of Fantasy And Fear
Brit Bk N C-Autumn '81-p17
JB-v46-Ap '82-p72
Tales Of Sorcery And Witchcraft
JB-v44-O '80-p246
TES-F 20 '81-p27
TLS-S 19 '80-p1027
Tattercoats
BL-v74-S 1 '77-p39
GP-v15-O '76-p2960
JB-v40-D '76-p343
Obs-Jl 11 '76-p23
SLJ-v24-N '77-p56
TLS-O 1 '76-p1252
Treasure Hunters
JB-v42-O '78-p266
Vampires, Werewolves And Phantoms Of The Night
GP-v23-S '84-p4323
JB-v48-F '84-p31
TES-F 17 '84-p28

* * *

FINLAYSON, Ann
Colonial Maryland
BL-v71-D 15 '74-p418
SLJ-v21-Ja '75-p44

FINLAYSON, Ann (continued)
Greenhorn On The Frontier
BL-v70-Jl 15 '74-p1252
CCB-B-v28-O '74-p27
CE-v51-Ap '75-p326
KR-v42-Je 1 '74-p587
LJ-v99-S 15 '74-p2266
SE-v44-O '80-p479
House Cat
CCB-B-v28-D '74-p61
CLW-v46-F '75-p315
KR-v42-Ap 15 '74-p424
LJ-v99-S 15 '74-p2266
PW-v205-Je 24 '74-p60
Rebecca's War
BL-v69-S 15 '72-p99
CCB-B-v26-Mr '73-p105
KR-v40-My 15 '72-p580
LJ-v98-F 15 '73-p643
Redcoat In Boston
BS-v31-Jl 15 '71-p191
JB-v43-Ag '79-p218
LJ-v96-O 15 '71-p3475
PW-v199-My 10 '71-p43

* * *

FINLEY, D
The Rhine
JB-v40-Ap '76-p90

* * *

FINLEY, Diana
Maps Of Many Lands
GP-v13-Ap '75-p2608

* * *

FINN, Daniel M
MathComp
Cur R-v18-D '79-p422

* * *

FINN, F E S
Voices Of Today
TES-F 6 '81-p28

* * *

FINNEY, Gertrude E
Yes, A Homestead
CCB-B-v18-Ja '65-p73

* * *

FINNEY, Jack
Time And Again
BL-v67-S 1 '70-p36
BL-v67-S 15 '70-p95
BL-v67-Ap 1 '71-p654
BS-v30-Jl 15 '70-p151
BW-v4-Je 28 '70-p6
EJ-v68-F '79-p45
HB-v46-O '70-p502
KR-v38-Mr 1 '70-p272
KR-v38-Ap 15 '70-p473
LJ-v95-O 1 '70-p3304
LJ-v95-O 15 '70-p3649
Lis-v103-Ap 3 '80-p450
NO-v9-S 28 '70-p21
NYT-v119-Jl 25 '70-p21
NYTBR-Ag 2 '70-p24
Obs-Je 15 '80-p28
PW-v197-Mr 9 '70-p81
PW-v199-My 31 '71-p136
SR-v54-O 23 '71-p86
SR-v54-N 27 '71-p48
TN-v27-Ap '71-p308
Time-v96-Jl 20 '70-p76

* * *

FINNEY, Shan
Basketball
SLJ-v29-O '82-p140
Cheerleading And Baton Twirling
SLJ-v29-O '82-p151
Dance
CBRS-v11-My '83-p100
SLJ-v29-Ag '83-p64

* * *

FINNIGAN, Joan
Giants Of Canada's Ottawa Valley
Can Child Lit-#33 '84-p87
In Rev-v16-Ap '82-p46
Quill & Q-v48-My '82-p38
Look! The Land Is Growing Giants
BIC-v13-Ja '84-p26
Quill & Q-v49-N '83-p25

* * *

FINSAND, Mary J
The Town That Moved
BL-v79-Ap 15 '83-p1099
CE-v60-N '83-p140
SE-v48-My '84-p371
SLJ-v29-My '83-p90

* * *

FINZGAR, Franc S
Iz Mladih Dni
BL-v79-D 15 '82-p570

* * *

FIOR, Jane
ABC
GP-v20-Jl '81-p3919
1 2 3
GP-v20-Jl '81-p3919

* * *

FIORE, Evelyn
Mystery At Lane's End
CCB-B-v22-Jl '69-p174
CSM-v61-Je 26 '69-p7
KR-v37-Mr 1 '69-p246
LJ-v94-My 15 '69-p2124
PW-v195-Ap 7 '69-p56

* * *

FIREBIRD
B&B-v21-N '75-p60
CSM-v62-My 2 '70-p17
TLS-Ap 6 '73-p384

* * *

FIREHOUSE (Chubby Shape Bks.)
SLJ-v29-Ag '83-p50

* * *

FIRER, Benzion
Saadiah Weissman
SLJ-v30-S '83-p122

* * *

FIRGAU, Susanne
Benjamins Marchenbuch
TLS-Ap 2 '76-p390

* * *

FIRMIN, Catherine
Knitting
JB-v45-F '81-p18
TES-Ag 22 '80-p20

* * *

FIRMIN, Charlotte
Claire's Secret Ambition
GP-v18-Ja '80-p3640
NS-v98-N 9 '79-p732
Spec-v243-D 15 '79-p23
Hannah's Great Decision
GP-v17-Jl '78-p3370
JB-v42-Ag '78-p188
NS-v95-My 19 '78-p682
Spec-v240-Ap 29 '78-p24
TES-Ap 14 '78-p28
TLS-Jl 7 '78-p763

* * *

FIRMIN, Joe
Garden Birds
TES-O 21 '77-p18

* * *

FIRMIN, Peter
Basil Brush And A Dragon
BL-v74-Jl 15 '78-p1738
KR-v46-Jl 1 '78-p688
Obs-Jl 27 '75-p21

FIRMIN, Peter (continued)
SLJ-v25-S '78-p107
TLS-D 3 '71-p1517
Basil Brush And The Windmills
BL-v77-S 15 '80-p125
KR-v48-Jl 15 '80-p908
SLJ-v27-S '80-p58
Basil Brush At The Beach
BL-v72-Je 15 '76-p1470
KR-v44-Ap 15 '76-p467
PW-v209-Ap 26 '76-p59
SLJ-v23-O '76-p97
Basil Brush At The Seaside
TLS-Ap 2 '71-p389
Basil Brush Builds A House
BL-v73-Je 15 '77-p1579
KR-v45-Ap 15 '77-p425
SLJ-v24-S '77-p106
TLS-S 28 '73-p1127
Basil Brush Finds Treasure
BL-v75-Ap 15 '79-p1301
KR-v47-F 15 '79-p192
Obs-Jl 27 '75-p21
SLJ-v25-My '79-p79
TLS-D 3 '71-p1517
Basil Brush Gets A Medal
BL-v75-N 15 '78-p552
CCB-B-v32-Ja '79-p79
KR-v46-N 15 '78-p1244
TLS-S 28 '73-p1127
Basil Brush Goes Boating
BL-v73-N 15 '76-p479
KR-v44-O 1 '76-p1091
Basil Brush Goes Flying
BL-v74-D 15 '77-p687
KR-v45-N 1 '77-p1143
SLJ-v24-Ja '78-p78
Basil Brush In The Jungle
BL-v76-D 15 '79-p618
KR-v48-Ja 1 '80-p4
Obs-Jl 27 '75-p21
SLJ-v26-D '79-p94
TLS-Ap 2 '71-p389
Basil Brush On The Trail
BL-v77-My 15 '81-p1258
KR-v49-F 15 '81-p211
Chicken Stew
B&B-F '83-p29
GP-v21-Mr '83-p4046
JB-v47-F '83-p11
SLJ-v29-Ag '83-p50
TES-F 4 '83-p28
The Midsummer Notebook Of A Country Rat
GP-v22-Mr '84-p4212
Tricks And Tales
GP-v21-Mr '83-p4050
Obs-F 20 '83-p33
The Winter Diary Of A Country Rat
Brit Bk N C-Spring '82-p7
GP-v20-Ja '82-p4005
SLJ-v30-O '83-p158

* * *

FIRST, Julia
Amy
KR-v43-S 1 '75-p998
SLJ-v22-N '75-p76
Everybody But Me
BL-v72-Jl 15 '76-p1595
Cur R-v16-Ag '77-p206
KR-v44-My 15 '76-p591
SLJ-v23-S '76-p115
Flat On My Face
KR-v42-My 1 '74-p478
LJ-v99-O 15 '74-p2739
Teacher-v93-S '75-p50
Getting Smarter
KR-v42-D 15 '74-p1304
I, Rebekah, Take You, The Lawrences
BL-v77-Jl 15 '81-p1447
CBRS-v9-Je '81-p96
CCB-B-v35-O '81-p28
Cur R-v21-F '82-p35
SLJ-v27-Ag '81-p65
Look Who's Beautiful
CBRS-v8-Spring '80-p116
KR-v48-Ag 1 '80-p980
SLJ-v26-My '80-p66
Move Over, Beethoven
BB-v6-Ag '78-p3
CCB-B-v31-Ap '78-p126
SLJ-v24-Mr '78-p127
Teacher-v96-O '78-p167

* * *

FIRST Book
SLJ-v29-Ap '83-p104

* * *

FIRST Book Of Nature
TES-O 24 '80-p20

* * *

FIRST Book Series: Africa
Cur R-v20-N '81-p534

* * *

FIRST Contact
TES-Mr 10 '78-p52

* * *

FIRST Fairy Tales
TES-D 9 '83-p35

* * *

FIRST Little Golden Books
Cha Ti-v36-Jl '82-p66

* * *

FIRST Nursery Rhymes
TES-N 18 '77-p32

* * *

FIRST Prayers (Magagna)
SLJ-v29-Ap '83-p100

* * *

FIRST Prayers (Tudor)
SLJ-v29-Ap '83-p100

* * *

FIRST Steps To Language
TES-Jl 11 '80-p29

* * *

FIRST Words
TES-D 9 '83-p35

* * *

FIRTH, Lesley
Have Fun With Nature
GP-v15-S '76-p2950
Obs-Ag 22 '76-p21
Where Is It?
TES-N 16 '84-p23

* * *

FISCHER, Hans
The Birthday
HB-v56-Je '80-p278
LR-v23-Autumn '72-p299
TLS-N 3 '72-p1333
Pitschi
HB-v56-Je '80-p278
LR-v23-Autumn '72-p299
Puss In Boots
HB-v56-Je '80-p282
The Traveling Musicians
HB-v56-Je '80-p282

* * *

FISCHER, Robert
Hot Dog!
BL-v76-Jl 1 '80-p1606
RT-v34-Mr '81-p736
SLJ-v27-S '80-p70

* * *

FISCHER, Vera
One Way Is Down
CCB-B-v22-S '68-p7
CLW-v39-D '67-p297

FISCHER, Vera (continued)
HB-v44-Ap '68-p203
LJ-v92-N 15 '67-p4242
SB-v3-Mr '68-p299

* * *

FISCHER-NAGEL, Andreas
Birth Of A Kitten
GP-v21-Mr '83-p4043
JB-v47-F '83-p24
Lis-v108-N 4 '82-p26
Life Of A Butterfly
GP-v22-Mr '84-p4223
Lis-v110-N 3 '83-p31
TES-Je 29 '84-p32
Life Of The Honeybee
JB-v46-O '82-p188
Life Of The Ladybird
JB-v46-Ap '82-p66
NS-v102-D 4 '81-p17

* * *

FISCHER-NAGEL, Heiderose
A Kitten Is Born
BL-v80-O 1 '83-p261
CCB-B-v37-Mr '84-p125
HB-v60-F '84-p73
Inst-v93-N '83-p147
KR-v51-S 1 '83-pJ168
SLJ-v30-N '83-p62

* * *

FISCHLER, Stan
Getting Into Pro Soccer
BL-v75-Jl 1 '79-p1583
SLJ-v26-F '80-p54
Kings Of The Rink
BL-v75-Mr 1 '79-p1048
CCB-B-v32-Ap '79-p134
SLJ-v25-Mr '79-p147
Stan Mikita
BL-v66-F 1 '70-p639
BW-v4-Mr 1 '70-p3
CCB-B-v23-Ap '70-p127
CSM-v62-N 28 '69-pB6
LJ-v95-F 15 '70-p795
LJ-v95-My 15 '70-p1965
PW-v196-N 3 '69-p49

* * *

FISH, Nicholas
Leadfoot
TES-O 1 '82-p31

* * *

FISHER, Aileen
Anybody Home?
BL-v77-N 15 '80-p458
BOT-v4-F '81-p70
HB-v56-D '80-p632
Inst-v90-N '80-p156
KR-v48-N 15 '80-p1460
RT-v35-O '81-p57
SLJ-v27-N '80-p60
Arbor Day
BL-v61-Jl 1 '65-p1028
CCB-B-v18-Jl '65-p160
KR-v33-Ap 1 '65-p376
LJ-v90-My 15 '65-p2394
SR-v48-My 15 '65-p45
Best Little House
BL-v62-My 1 '66-p875
CCB-B-v20-N '66-p41
CE-v43-D '66-p236
HB-v42-Je '66-p299
KR-v34-Mr 1 '66-p239
LJ-v91-Je 15 '66-p3249
NYTBR-v71-My 8 '66-p43
Bicentennial Plays And Programs
CCB-B-v29-N '75-p43
PW-v207-Je 9 '75-p62
But Ostriches...
BL-v67-O 1 '70-p144
CCB-B-v24-D '70-p58
CSM-v62-O 17 '70-p13
HB-v46-O '70-p470
KR-v38-Jl 15 '70-p741
LJ-v95-N 15 '70-p4034
PW-v198-Jl 27 '70-p74
SR-v53-S 19 '70-p35
Clean As A Whistle
CSM-v61-N 6 '69-pB3
HB-v46-F '70-p31
KR-v37-S 1 '69-p924
Do Bears Have Mothers, Too
CCB-B-v27-My '74-p142
LJ-v99-F 15 '74-p561
NYTBR-N 4 '73-p61
PW-v204-D 17 '73-p38
Easter
BL-v64-Ap 15 '68-p988
CCB-B-v21-Ap '68-p125
KR-v36-Mr 15 '68-p339
LJ-v93-Ap 15 '68-p1788
Feathered Ones And Furry
BL-v68-O 1 '71-p150
CCB-B-v25-N '71-p42
CSM-v63-N 11 '71-pB2
HB-v47-O '71-p473
KR-v39-Jl 15 '71-p742
Going Barefoot
WLB-v55-O '80-p116
Holiday Programs For Boys And Girls
SLJ-v27-Ja '81-p60
Human Rights Day
BL-v63-Ap 1 '67-p856
CCB-B-v20-D '66-p57
LJ-v91-O 15 '66-p5260
I Like Weather
WLB-v55-O '80-p116
I Stood Upon A Mountain
CBRS-v8-F '80-p51
CCB-B-v33-My '80-p171
HB-v56-Ap '80-p163
KR-v48-Mr 1 '80-p282
PW-v217-Ja 11 '80-p88
SLJ-v26-Ap '80-p92
In The Middle Of The Night
BL-v61-Je 15 '65-p996
CCB-B-v18-My '65-p128
CE-v42-S '65-p54
CSM-v57-My 6 '65-p2B
Comw-v82-My 28 '65-p334
GT-v83-S '65-p14
HB-v41-Je '65-p268
KR-v33-Mr 15 '65-p309
LJ-v90-Ap 15 '65-p2010
NYTBR-v70-My 9 '65-p4
SR-v48-Ap 24 '65-p45
WLB-v55-O '80-p116
In The Woods, In The Meadow, In The Sky: Poems
BL-v62-Ja 1 '66-p450
CCB-B-v19-Jl '66-p177
CE-v42-Ap '66-p505
CLW-v37-F '66-p375
CSM-v57-N 4 '65-pB4
Comw-v83-N 5 '65-p156
HB-v41-D '65-p640
Inst-v75-Ap '66-p108
KR-v33-S 1 '65-p900
LJ-v90-O 15 '65-p4605
NYTBR-v70-N 7 '65-p6
SR-v49-My 14 '66-p39
Jeanne D'Arc
BL-v66-My 1 '70-p1098
CCB-B-v24-O '70-p24
Comw-v92-My 22 '70-p245
HB-v46-Je '70-p304
KR-v38-F 1 '70-p106
LJ-v95-My 15 '70-p1941
NYTBR, pt.2-My 24 '70-p30
PW-v197-Mr 2 '70-p82
SR-v53-Je 27 '70-p39
Listen, Rabbit
CE-v41-My '65-p490
WLB-v55-O '80-p116

FISHER, Aileen (continued)
My Cat Has Eyes Of Sapphire Blue
BL-v70-Ja 15 '74-p541
HB-v50-F '74-p59
LJ-v99-F 15 '74-p561
Teacher-v91-Mr '74-p108
My Mother And I
BL-v63-My 15 '67-p991
CCB-B-v20-Je '67-p152
HB-v43-Ag '67-p459
KR-v35-Ap 1 '67-p406
LJ-v92-Ap 15 '67-p1724
NYTBR-v72-My 7 '67-p45
PW-v191-Ap 3 '67-p56
SR-v50-My 13 '67-p50
Once We Went On A Picnic
ACSB-v9-Spring '76-p19
BL-v72-Ja 15 '76-p684
KR-v43-N 1 '75-p1224
LA-v53-My '76-p500
SB-v12-My '76-p39
SLJ-v22-F '76-p38
SLMQ-v12-Summer '84-p326
Out In The Dark And Daylight
BL-v76-Jl 1 '80-p1606
CCB-B-v33-Jl '80-p211
Inst-v90-F '81-p24
KR-v48-Ag 1 '80-p981
LA-v58-Ap '81-p479
NYTBR-v85-Ap 27 '80-p47
SLJ-v27-S '80-p58
Rabbits, Rabbits
BL-v80-N 15 '83-p496
CCB-B-v37-N '83-p48
HB-v59-D '83-p720
Inst-v93-N '83-p147
PW-v224-S 16 '83-p125
SLJ-v30-F '84-p57
SLMQ-v12-Spring '84-p188
Sing, Little Mouse
BL-v65-Jl 15 '69-p1274
CSM-v61-My 1 '69-pB4
KR-v37-My 15 '69-p556
LJ-v94-D 15 '69-p4595
PW-v195-Ap 28 '69-p88
Skip Around The Year
CCB-B-v21-Mr '68-p108
KR-v35-O 15 '67-p1277
LJ-v92-N 15 '67-p4242
NYTBR-v72-N 5 '67-p61
Teacher-v92-D '74-p15
Up, Up The Mountain
BL-v64-My 1 '68-p1042
CE-v45-S '68-p37
KR-v36-Mr 1 '68-p254
LJ-v93-Je 15 '68-p2538
Valley Of The Smallest: The Life Story Of A Shrew
BL-v63-D 1 '66-p416
CCB-B-v20-D '66-p57
CSM-v58-N 3 '66-pB11
Comw-v85-N 11 '66-p179
HB-v42-D '66-p728
KR-v34-O 1 '66-p1050
LJ-v92-F 15 '67-p878
NYTBR-v71-N 6 '66-p58
SB-v2-D '66-p214
We Alcotts
BL-v65-N 1 '68-p308
BW-v2-N 3 '68-p1
CLW-v41-O '69-p139
HB-v44-O '68-p540
Inst-v78-N '68-p156
KR-v36-Ag 15 '68-p910
NO-v7-N 4 '68-p22
NYTBR-v73-S 29 '68-p46
PW-v194-S 16 '68-p71
RR-v28-Ja '69-p169
SE-v33-My '69-p562
SR-v51-N 9 '68-p69
YR-v5-N '68-p5
We Dickinsons
Am-v113-N 20 '65-p646
Atl-v216-D '65-p158
CCB-B-v19-N '65-p43
CLW-v37-D '65-p272
Comw-v83-N 5 '65-p160
EJ-v55-My '66-p613
HB-v41-D '65-p642
KR-v33-Ag 15 '65-p825
LJ-v90-S 15 '65-p3804
NYTBR-v71-Ja 16 '66-p36
We Went Looking
BL-v65-N 1 '68-p308
BW-v2-N 3 '68-p4
CCB-B-v22-Ja '69-p77
KR-v36-Jl 1 '68-p686
LJ-v93-S 15 '68-p3290
NY-v44-D 14 '68-p213
NYTBR-v73-S 15 '68-p30
PW-v194-Jl 29 '68-p65

* * *

FISHER, David E
The Creation Of Atoms And Stars
ACSB-v13-Mr '80-p21
CBRS-v8-F '80-p56
EJ-v69-My '80-p75
HB-v55-D '79-p687
SB-v16-N '80-p91
SLJ-v26-F '80-p65
The Creation Of The Universe
BL-v74-N 1 '77-p468
HB-v54-Ag '78-p426
KR-v45-D 15 '77-p1325
Kliatt-v12-Winter '78-p53
SB-v14-S '78-p86
SLJ-v25-S '78-p156
The Ideas Of Einstein
ACSB-v15-Winter '82-p25
BL-v77-F 1 '81-p752
SB-v16-Mr '81-p218
SLJ-v27-F '81-p64

* * *

FISHER, Dorothy Canfield
Understood Betsy
BL-v68-My 15 '72-p823
BS-v31-Mr 15 '72-p566
CE-v49-D '72-p145
HB-v55-O '79-p558
LJ-v97-Mr 15 '72-p1169
NY-v48-D 2 '72-p205
PW-v201-Ja 17 '72-p59
TLS-Ap 6 '73-p381
Teacher-v90-O '72-p115

* * *

FISHER, Edward E
Factories
SE-v44-O '80-p481

* * *

FISHER, Harvey I
Wonders Of The World Of The Albatross
BL-v70-Je 15 '74-p1153
CCB-B-v28-S '74-p6
GP-v14-Ap '76-p2853
JB-v40-Ag '76-p224
LJ-v99-S 15 '74-p2266
Obs-Ap 4 '76-p27
SB-v10-D '74-p258
TLS-Ap 2 '76-p394

* * *

FISHER, Kathleen Dunning
Cook-In
BL-v66-My 1 '70-p1098
CCB-B-v24-Jl '70-p176
NYTBR, pt.2-N 9 '69-p42

* * *

FISHER, Laura
You Were Princess Last Time
CCB-B-v19-Ap '66-p129
CSM-v58-Ap 14 '66-p13
HB-v41-D '65-p632
KR-v33-O 15 '65-p1078

* * *

FISHER, Laura H

Amy And The Sorrel Summer
CCB-B-v18-Ja '65-p73

Charlie Dick
CCB-B-v25-Mr '72-p106
KR-v39-N 15 '71-p1212
LJ-v97-Je 15 '72-p2237
NYTBR-Mr 19 '72-p8
PW-v201-Ja 17 '72-p59

* * *

FISHER, Leonard E

Boxes! Boxes!
BL-v80-My 1 '84-p1245
BW-v14-Jl 8 '84-p8
CBRS-v12-Je '84-p111
CCB-B-v37-Ap '84-p146
HB-v60-Je '84-p319
NYTBR-v89-Je 17 '84-p25
PW-v225-Je 8 '84-p64
SLJ-v30-My '84-p64

The Death Of The Evening Star
BL-v69-O 15 '72-p201
CCB-B-v26-Je '73-p153
EJ-v62-Ja '73-p146
HB-v48-D '72-p595
KR-v40-Ag 15 '72-p939
LA-v58-Ap '81-p455
LJ-v98-Ja 15 '73-p259
NYTBR-N 26 '72-p10
PW-v202-S 25 '72-p60
SE-v47-Ap '83-p288

The Factories
BHR-v54-Winter '80-p533
CCB-B-v33-Ja '80-p93
HB-v55-D '79-p675
KR-v47-D 15 '79-p1431
RT-v33-My '80-p975
SLJ-v26-N '79-p76

The Hospitals
BL-v76-My 15 '80-p1363
CCB-B-v33-Je '80-p188
SB-v16-Ja '81-p153
SLJ-v27-F '81-p74

The Newspapers
BL-v77-My 1 '81-p1196
CCB-B-v35-O '81-p28
Inst-v90-My '81-p62
J Read-v25-Ja '82-p390
KR-v49-Jl 15 '81-p873
LA-v59-F '82-p158
PW-v219-Ap 10 '81-p70
SLJ-v27-Ag '81-p65

Number Art
BL-v79-Ja 1 '83-p617
BL-v79-Je 1 '83-p1282
B Rpt-v2-N '83-p39
CCB-B-v36-Ja '83-p88
HB-v59-F '83-p60
PW-v222-N 12 '82-p67
RT-v36-Ja '83-p469
SLJ-v29-D '82-p64

The Olympians
BL-v81-O 1 '84-p246

The Railroads
BHR-v54-Winter '80-p533
CCB-B-v33-Ja '80-p93
HB-v55-D '79-p675
KR-v47-D 15 '79-p1432
RT-v33-My '80-p975
SLJ-v26-N '79-p76

A Russian Farewell
BL-v77-F 15 '81-p808
CBRS-v9-N '80-p27
CCB-B-v34-My '81-p169
J Read-v25-Ja '82-p353
KR-v49-F 15 '81-p213
NYTBR-v86-Ja 18 '81-p31
RT-v35-Mr '82-p719
SLJ-v27-Ja '81-p60

The Schools
BL-v80-S 1 '83-p83
CCB-B-v37-S '83-p5
CE-v60-N '83-p140
HB-v59-O '83-p590
SLJ-v29-Ag '83-p64

The Seven Days Of Creation
BL-v78-O 15 '81-p300
CBRS-v10-N '81-p22
CCB-B-v35-S '81-p5
CE-v58-My '82-p329
LA-v59-Ap '82-p369
PW-v220-Ag 28 '81-p394
SLJ-v28-F '82-p66

The Sports
BL-v77-Ja 15 '81-p701
CCB-B-v34-F '81-p110
CE-v57-Mr '81-p236
Inst-v90-N '80-p160
LA-v58-Mr '81-p344
PW-v218-D 19 '80-p51
SLJ-v27-D '80-p77

Star Signs
CBRS-v12-Ja '84-p51
CCB-B-v37-N '83-p48
CE-v60-Mr '84-p290
PW-v224-Ag 19 '83-p78
RT-v37-Ap '84-p778
SLJ-v30-Ja '84-p74

Storm At The Jetty
BL-v77-Je 15 '81-p1345
CBRS-v9-Spring '81-p104
CCB-B-v34-Jl '81-p211
KR-v49-Je 15 '81-p735
LA-v58-S '81-p699
PW-v219-My 1 '81-p67
RT-v35-O '81-p113
SLJ-v28-O '81-p128

The Unions
BL-v78-Je 1 '82-p1311
CCB-B-v35-Jl '82-p205
CE-v59-N '82-p138
PW-v221-Je 11 '82-p62
SLJ-v29-Ja '83-p74

* * *

FISHER, Leonard Everett

Across The Sea From Galway
BL-v72-F 15 '76-p854
KR-v43-Ag 1 '75-p848
PW-v208-S 22 '75-p132
SLJ-v22-Ja '76-p52

Alphabet Art
BL-v75-Mr 1 '79-p1088
CCB-B-v32-Ap '79-p134
HB-v55-Ap '79-p206
KR-v47-Ja 15 '79-p68
SLJ-v25-My '79-p60

The Architects
CCB-B-v24-Je '71-p157
LJ-v95-S 15 '70-p3047

The Art Experience
BS-v33-D 15 '73-p428
HB-v50-F '74-p61
KR-v41-O 15 '73-p1171
LJ-v99-F 15 '74-p580

The Blacksmiths
BL-v72-Mr 15 '76-p1041
CCB-B-v29-Jl '76-p173
HB-v52-Je '76-p305
KR-v44-Mr 1 '76-p258
SLJ-v22-Ap '76-p73

The Cabinetmakers
BL-v62-Je 15 '66-p999
CCB-B-v20-S '66-p8
GT-v84-O '66-p62
LJ-v91-N 15 '66-p5777
SB-v2-S '66-p150

The Doctors
BL-v65-O 1 '68-p186
CCB-B-v22-O '68-p26
LJ-v93-O 15 '68-p3968
SB-v4-Mr '69-p305
Teacher-v86-F '69-p171

The Factories
BL-v76-N 1 '79-p447
HB-v55-D '79-p675
Inst-v89-N '79-p143

FISHER, Leonard Everett
(continued)
KR-v47-D 15 '79-p1431
SLJ-v26-N '79-p76
The Glassmakers
BL-v61-F 15 '65-p566
CCB-B-v18-My '65-p128
The Hatters
BL-v62-O 15 '65-p218
CCB-B-v19-F '66-p97
CSM-v57-N 4 '65-pB7
LJ-v91-F 15 '66-p1079
The Homemakers
CCB-B-v27-Ap '74-p128
KR-v41-O 1 '73-p1100
LJ-v99-F 15 '74-p572
Leonard Everett Fisher's Liberty Book
BL-v72-F 15 '76-p855
CCB-B-v29-My '76-p143
Comw-v103-N 19 '76-p758
KR-v44-Ja 15 '76-p75
LA-v54-F '77-p207
PW-v209-F 9 '76-p96
SLJ-v22-Mr '76-p102
Letters From Italy
BB-v5-Je '77-p3
BL-v74-S 1 '77-p40
KR-v45-F 1 '77-p98
PW-v211-Ap 25 '77-p75
SLJ-v23-Mr '77-p151
The Limners
LJ-v95-Ap 15 '70-p1648
NYTBR, pt.2-N 9 '69-p53
Noonan
BL-v74-Jl 15 '78-p1733
CCB-B-v32-D '78-p60
KR-v46-Jl 15 '78-p749
LA-v56-Ap '79-p445
SLJ-v24-My '78-p87
The Papermakers
BL-v61-Ap 15 '65-p802
CCB-B-v19-N '65-p43
CSM-v57-S 16 '65-p7
GT-v83-N '65-p123
LJ-v90-Ap 15 '65-p2020
PW-v187-My 3 '65-p116
SA-v213-D '65-p116
Peddlers
BL-v64-Mr 15 '68-p867
HB-v44-F '68-p78
KR-v35-D 1 '67-p1421
LJ-v93-Ja 15 '68-p290
NYTBR-v73-My 5 '68-p51
Teacher-v86-F '69-p171
Picture Book Of Revolutionary War Heroes
LJ-v96-F 15 '71-p724
NYTBR, pt.2-My 2 '71-p16
PW-v198-N 9 '70-p61
SR-v54-Ap 17 '71-p39
The Potters
BL-v65-Ap 15 '69-p960
CCB-B-v23-N '69-p43
CSM-v61-My 1 '69-pB8
KR-v37-Ja 15 '69-p56
LJ-v94-Ap 15 '69-p1781
SB-v5-Mr '70-p349
The Printers
BL-v61-Ap 15 '65-p802
CCB-B-v18-Je '65-p146
CSM-v57-S 16 '65-p7
GT-v83-N '65-p123
LJ-v90-My 15 '65-p2405
NYTBR-v70-My 9 '65-p20
PW-v187-My 3 '65-p116
SA-v213-D '65-p116
The Railroads
BL-v76-N 1 '79-p447
HB-v55-D '79-p675
KR-v47-D 15 '79-p1432
PW-v216-N 12 '79-p59
SLJ-v26-N '79-p76
Schoolmasters
BL-v64-D 15 '67-p501
CCB-B-v21-N '67-p40
CCB-B-v21-Ja '68-p77
CE-v44-Ap '68-p502
CSM-v59-N 2 '67-pB10
HB-v44-F '68-p78
KR-v35-Jl 1 '67-p742
LJ-v92-S 15 '67-p3186
The Shipbuilders
BL-v68-N 15 '71-p291
LJ-v97-Mr 15 '72-p1169
Shoemakers
BL-v63-Mr 15 '67-p795
HB-v43-Je '67-p362
LJ-v92-Ap 15 '67-p1733
The Silversmiths
BL-v61-F 15 '65-p578
HB-v41-F '65-p64
Sweeney's Ghost
CCB-B-v29-S '75-p8
KR-v43-My 15 '75-p567
SLJ-v22-S '75-p102
Tanners
BL-v63-N 1 '66-p322
CSM-v58-N 3 '66-pB8
SB-v2-D '66-p231
Two If By Sea
BS-v30-F 15 '71-p506
CCB-B-v25-S '71-p5
CE-v47-My '71-p438
KR-v38-O 15 '70-p1152
LJ-v95-N 15 '70-p4053
NYTBR, pt.2-N 8 '70-p3
NYTBR, pt.2-N 8 '70-p40
PW-v198-N 9 '70-p61
The Warlock Of Westfall
BL-v70-Ap 15 '74-p940
CCB-B-v27-Jl '74-p176
HB-v50-Je '74-p282
Inst-v84-N '74-p135
KR-v42-F 1 '74-p110
PW-v205-Mr 4 '74-p75
The Weavers
BL-v62-Je 15 '66-p1000
CCB-B-v19-Jl '66-p178
HB-v42-Ag '66-p446
LJ-v91-N 15 '66-p5777
NYTBR-v71-My 15 '66-p26
SB-v2-S '66-p150
The Wigmakers
BL-v62-O 15 '65-p218
CCB-B-v19-F '66-p97
CSM-v57-N 4 '65-pB7
LJ-v91-F 15 '66-p1079

* * *

FISHER, Lois I
Puffy P. Pushycat, Problem Solver
CBRS-v11-Je '83-p113
SLJ-v29-My '83-p92
Rachel Vellars, How Could You?
BL-v80-My 15 '84-p1342
B Rpt-v3-S '84-p32
CCB-B-v38-S '84-p4
SLJ-v30-Ap '84-p113
Sarah Dunes, Weird Person
CCB-B-v34-Je '81-p192
KR-v49-My 15 '81-p633
SLJ-v27-My '81-p86
VOYA-v4-Ag '81-p26
Wretched Robert
BL-v78-Je 1 '82-p1312
CCB-B-v35-Jl '82-p205
CLW-v54-Ap '83-p379
KR-v50-My 1 '82-p554
SLJ-v29-N '82-p82

* * *

FISHER, Lucretia
Two Monsters
BW-S 19 '76-pH4

FISHER, Lucretia (continued)
SLJ-v23-F '77-p56

* * *

FISHER, Paul R
The Ash Staff
BL-v76-N 1 '79-p448
CBRS-v8-Ja '80-p46
CCB-B-v33-Ap '80-p151
KR-v47-S 15 '79-p1067
SLJ-v26-Ja '80-p68
The Hawks Of Fellheath
BL-v76-Je 15 '80-p1530
BS-v40-Je '80-p116
CBRS-v8-Jl '80-p126
CCB-B-v34-N '80-p51
Cur R-v19-S '80-p336
RT-v34-Ja '81-p484
SLJ-v26-Ap '80-p109
Mont Cant Gold
BL-v77-My 1 '81-p1191
BS-v41-My '81-p79
CSM-v73-Jl 1 '81-p18
J Read-v25-Mr '82-p613
SLJ-v27-Ap '81-p126

* * *

FISHER, Robert
Amazing Monsters
Brit Bk N C-Autumn '82-p16
Econ-v285-D 25 '82-p105
GP-v21-S '82-p3958
JB-v46-Ag '82-p142
Obs-Ag 1 '82-p30
SLJ-v28-Ag '82-p115
Sch Lib-v30-Je '82-p147
Spec-v249-D 4 '82-p24
TES-Je 11 '82-p38
Ghosts Galore
BL-v80-F 15 '84-p856
JB-v48-F '84-p21
RT-v37-My '84-p889
SLJ-v30-F '84-p70
TES-S 30 '83-p47
Together Today
Sch Lib-v30-Mr '82-p91
TES-Mr 12 '82-p34

* * *

FISHER, Ronald M
A Day In The Woods
ACSB-v9-Fall '76-p16
BL-v72-F 15 '76-p852
Par-v51-Ap '76-p60

* * *

FISHER, S H
Table Top Science
HB-v48-Ag '72-p391
KR-v39-N 15 '71-p1215
LJ-v97-S 15 '72-p2948
SB-v8-My '72-p28

* * *

FISHER, Sally
The Tale Of The Shining Princess
Atl-v247-F '81-p96
BIC-v10-D '81-p29
BW-v11-Ap 12 '81-p8
LA-v58-My '81-p595
LJ-v105-D 15 '80-p2584

* * *

FISHER, Timothy
Hammocks, Hassocks And Hideaways
CCB-B-v34-Mr '81-p132
HB-v57-F '81-p66
SLJ-v27-My '81-p63
Huts, Hovels And Houses
ACSB-v13-Spring '80-p28
BL-v74-N 15 '77-p549
CCB-B-v31-F '78-p91
KR-v45-O 1 '77-p1051
NYTBR-N 13 '77-p58
PW-v212-S 12 '77-p132
SA-v237-D '77-p36
SLJ-v24-F '78-p56

* * *

FISHER, W B
The Oil States
SLJ-v28-S '81-p124
TES-Ja 9 '81-p23

* * *

FISHER, William W
Geo-Cepts
Inst-v88-S '78-p220

* * *

FISHING (Scatterbox Series)
B&B-v23-Ja '78-p63

* * *

FISHLOCK, T
Discovering Britain: Wales
JB-v44-Ap '80-p81

* * *

FISHWICK, Marshall W
Jamestown: First English Colony
BL-v62-Ja 1 '66-p450
BS-v25-N 1 '65-p312
CCB-B-v19-Jl '66-p173
CE-v42-F '66-p376
CSM-v57-N 4 '65-pB7
Comw-v83-N 5 '65-p161
GT-v83-Ja '66-p24
HB-v42-F '66-p74
KR-v33-O 1 '65-p1048
LJ-v90-D 15 '65-p5521
NYTBR-v70-N 7 '65-p30
SR-v48-N 13 '65-p62

* * *

FISK, Nicholas
Antigrav
JB-v42-O '78-p266
Sch Lib-v27-Je '79-p156
TES-N 24 '78-p50
TLS-Jl 7 '78-p764
Escape From Splatterbang
BL-v75-Mr 15 '79-p1156
CBRS-v7-Spring '79-p117
CCB-B-v33-Ja '80-p94
JB-v42-O '78-p266
KR-v47-S 15 '79-p1071
SLJ-v25-Mr '79-p138
TES-Ag 18 '78-p17
Evil Eye
TES-D 10 '82-p34
Grinny
B&B-v18-My '73-pR8
BL-v71-Mr 1 '75-p690
CCB-B-v28-Mr '75-p112
KR-v42-Ag 1 '74-p804
LJ-v99-O 15 '74-p2740
Lis-v90-N 8 '73-p642
NS-v85-My 25 '73-p779
TES-Je 29 '84-p32
TLS-Ap 6 '73-p380
Leadfoot
GP-v19-N '80-p3781
JB-v44-D '80-p305
Little Green Spacemen
JB-v39-F '75-p38
Monster Maker
BL-v76-Je 15 '80-p1530
CBRS-v8-My '80-p98
CE-v57-Ja '81-p171
JB-v43-O '79-p277
KR-v48-My 15 '80-p644
Obs-D 2 '79-p39
SLJ-v26-Mr '80-p139
Sch Lib-v27-Je '79-p153
VOYA-v3-F '81-p29
On The Flip Side
GP-v22-My '83-p4077
JB-v47-Je '83-p122

* * *

FITZGERALD, Maria
Pottery
Brit Bk N C-Spring '80-p20
JB-v44-Je '80-p130
NS-v98-N 9 '79-p733

* * *

FITZGERALD, Maureen
A Trog Christmas Story
Quill & Q-v47-Ap '81-p34
The Trog Family Of The Sixteen Mile Creek
In Rev-v15-Ap '81-p36
Quill & Q-v47-Ap '81-p34

* * *

FITZGERALD, Paul
Tom The Ferryman
Lis-v94-N 6 '75-p625

* * *

FITZ GIBBON, Constantine
Teddy In The Tree
SLJ-v24-S '77-p127

* * *

FITZGIBBON, Dan
All About Your Money
RT-v38-N '84-p227
SLJ-v30-Ap '84-p123
VOYA-v7-Ag '84-p150

* * *

FITZHUGH, Louise
Bang, Bang, You're Dead
BW-v3-Jl 13 '69-p16
CCB-B-v22-Jl '69-p174
KR-v37-Ap 15 '69-p434
LJ-v94-Je 15 '69-p2496
LJ-v95-O 15 '70-p3602
NYTBR, pt.2-My 4 '69-p53
Nat-v209-D 15 '69-p671
PW-v195-Mr 31 '69-p57
SMQ-v8-Fall '79-p26
Teacher-v96-Ja '79-p65
Harriet The Spy
BL-v80-S 1 '83-p95
BW-v11-My 10 '81-p14
CE-v42-S '65-p52
CLW-v36-Ja '65-p337
CSM-v57-F 25 '65-p7
Emerg Lib-v11-Ja '84-p21
HB-v41-F '65-p74
HB-v56-Ag '80-p442
NYTBR-v72-N 5 '67-p54
NYTBR-v73-F 25 '68-p18
NYTBR, pt.2-F 13 '72-p12
Obs-Ag 4 '74-p28
PW-v192-Jl 31 '67-p56
SR-v48-Ja 23 '65-p52
TCR-v68-F '67-p450
TLS-Jl 5 '74-p715
I Am Five
BB-v7-My '79-p2
CBRS-v7-Ja '79-p42
CCB-B-v32-F '79-p98
Inst-v88-My '79-p106
KR-v46-N 1 '78-p1184
PW-v214-O 30 '78-p51
SLJ-v25-Ja '79-p41
I Am Three
CCB-B-v35-My '82-p167
SLJ-v29-S '82-p108
The Long Secret
BS-v25-D 1 '65-p356
CCB-B-v19-Ja '66-p81
CE-v42-Ap '66-p506
CLW-v37-Ap '66-p548
Choice-v14-N '77-p1178
KR-v33-O 1 '65-p1045
LJ-v90-D 15 '65-p5513
NS-v91-My 21 '76-p687
NY-v41-D 4 '65-p218
NYTBR-v70-N 21 '65-p56
PW-v192-D 11 '67-p49
SR-v48-D 11 '65-p45
TCR-v68-F '67-p450
TLS-S 19 '75-p1051
Nobody's Family Is Going To Change
B&B-v23-Jl '78-p58
BL-v71-F 1 '75-p570
BL-v71-Mr 15 '75-p766
BL-v73-Mr 15 '77-p1100
BW-F 9 '75-p4
CCB-B-v28-My '75-p146
CE-v52-O '75-p32
CSM-v67-Je 10 '75-p16
Choice-v14-N '77-p1178
Comw-v102-N 21 '75-p566
EJ-v64-D '75-p80
GP-v15-My '76-p2890
HB-v51-Ap '75-p146
JB-v40-Je '76-p162
J Read-v19-Ja '76-p330
KR-v42-D 1 '74-p1252
LA-v52-N '75-p1169
Lis-v96-N 11 '76-p623
NYTBR-D 1 '74-p8
Obs-Ap 11 '76-p33
PT-v8-Ap '75-p108
PW-v206-N 4 '74-p68
Par-v50-O '75-p28
SLJ-v21-Ja '75-p53
TES-Jl 7 '78-p30
TES-Mr 26 '82-p29
TES-Jl 15 '83-p18
TLS-Ap 2 '76-p375
Sport
BL-v75-My 15 '79-p1438
BS-v39-N '79-p289
BW-My 13 '79-pK2
CBRS-v7-Je '79-p107
CCB-B-v32-Jl '79-p191
CE-v56-Ja '80-p169
CLW-v51-D '79-p233
HB-v55-Ag '79-p413
KR-v47-Jl 15 '79-p793
LA-v57-Ja '80-p85
NY-v55-D 3 '79-p212
NYTBR-Je 3 '79-p44
PW-v215-Je 25 '79-p123
RT-v33-Ja '80-p482
SLJ-v25-My '79-p61
SLJ-v27-Mr '81-p108
WCRB-v5-S '79-p83

* * *

FITZPATRICK, Jim
The Book Of Conquests
TES-N 24 '78-p40

* * *

FITZPATRICK, Percy
Jock Of The Bushveld
B&B-v22-Je '77-p66
TLS-D 10 '76-p1555

* * *

FITZSIMONS, Raymund
Garish Lights
BL-v67-Mr 1 '71-p541
Choice-v8-Ap '71-p246
HB-v47-F '71-p72
LJ-v96-Mr 1 '71-p836

* * *

FIX, P
Popcorn, The Hippoporhino
JB-v41-Je '77-p153

* * *

FIX, Philippe
The Kangaroo With A Hole In Her Pocket
GP-v15-Ap '77-p3083
Tim And Tilly And The Time Machine
GP-v16-Ja '78-p3252

* * *

FLEISCHHAUER-HARDT, Helga

Show Me!

BL-v71-Jl 15 '75-p1147
BL-v71-Jl 15 '75-p1190
BW-My 4 '75-p1
CCB-B-v29-O '75-p26
KR-v43-Ap 1 '75-p442
KR-v43-My 1 '75-p527
SLJ-v21-Ap '75-p51
SLJ-v22-S '75-p80
SR-v2-My 31 '75-p31
VV-v20-Je 30 '75-p41
WLB-v50-N '75-p192

* * *

FLEISCHMAN, H Samuel

Gang Girl

CCB-B-v21-S '67-p5
EJ-v57-My '68-p759

* * *

FLEISCHMAN, Paul

The Animal Hedge

CBRS-v11-Mr '83-p78
CE-v60-S '83-p52
HB-v59-Je '83-p289
KR-v51-F 15 '83-p180
PW-v223-F 25 '83-p88
SLJ-v29-Ag '83-p50

The Birthday Tree

BL-v75-Je 15 '79-p1535
CBRS-v7-Spring '79-p112
CLW-v51-F '80-p309
KR-v47-My 15 '79-p573
SLJ-v26-S '79-p110

Finzel The Farsighted

BL-v80-N 1 '83-p407
CCB-B-v37-Ja '84-p86
CE-v60-My '84-p362
KR-v51-S 1 '83-pJ147
NYTBR-v89-Mr 4 '84-p31
PW-v224-Ag 26 '83-p385
SLJ-v30-D '83-p65

Graven Images

BL-v79-N 1 '82-p368
BW-v13-F 13 '83-p9
CCB-B-v36-Mr '83-p125
HB-v58-D '82-p656
J Read-v26-My '83-p741
KR-v50-Ag 15 '82-p937
LATBR-O 17 '82-p6
NYTBR-v87-N 28 '82-p24
PW-v223-Ja 14 '83-p76
RT-v36-My '83-p944
SLJ-v29-S '82-p137

The Half-A-Moon Inn

BL-v76-Je 15 '80-p1531
BL-v78-N 1 '81-p395
BOT-v4-F '81-p78
CBRS-v8-Spring '80-p117
CE-v57-Mr '81-p207
CSM-v72-My 12 '80-pB10
HB-v56-Je '80-p294
KR-v48-Ap 15 '80-p513
LA-v58-My '81-p596
NYTBR-v85-Ap 27 '80-p45
PW-v217-Mr 7 '80-p90
SLJ-v27-O '80-p145

Path Of The Pale Horse

BL-v79-Ap 1 '83-p1032
B Rpt-v2-N '83-p33
BW-v13-My 8 '83-p15
CCB-B-v36-My '83-p165
CE-v60-N '83-p137
EJ-v73-Ja '84-p88
HB-v59-Ap '83-p170
KR-v51-Ap 1 '83-p375
LA-v60-S '83-p771
LA-v61-Ap '84-p421
NYTBR-v88-My 15 '83-p26
PW-v223-Ap 8 '83-p58
SLJ-v30-S '83-p133
VOYA-v6-O '83-p200

Phoebe Danger, Detective, In The Case Of The Two-Minute Cough

BL-v79-Je 1 '83-p1275
CBRS-v11-Jl '83-p133
KR-v51-Ap 1 '83-p376
SLJ-v29-My '83-p92

* * *

FLEISCHMAN, Sid

The Bloodhound Gang In The Case Of Princess Tomorrow

BL-v77-Ap 15 '81-p1159
CBRS-v9-Mr '81-p64
CCB-B-v34-Ap '81-p150
KR-v49-Jl 1 '81-p800
NYTBR-v86-Ap 26 '81-p62
SLJ-v27-My '81-p84

The Bloodhound Gang In The Case Of The Cackling Ghost

BL-v77-Ap 15 '81-p1159
CBRS-v9-Mr '81-p64
KR-v49-Jl 1 '81-p800
NYTBR-v86-Ap 26 '81-p62
PW-v219-F 27 '81-p150
SLJ-v27-My '81-p84

The Bloodhound Gang In The Case Of The Flying Clock

BL-v78-D 15 '81-p553
CCB-B-v35-Je '82-p187
KR-v49-O 1 '81-p1235
SLJ-v28-D '81-p81

The Bloodhound Gang In The Case Of The Secret Message

BL-v78-D 15 '81-p553
KR-v49-O 1 '81-p1235
SLJ-v28-D '81-p81

The Bloodhound Gang In The Case Of The 264-Pound Burglar

BL-v78-Je 15 '82-p1371
CCB-B-v36-O '82-p25
CSM-v74-O 8 '82-pB8
SLJ-v28-My '82-p83

By The Great Horn Spoon!

LA-v59-O '82-p759
NS-v69-My 28 '65-p848
Obs-Ap 18 '65-p26
Punch-v248-Je 16 '65-p905
TLS-Je 17 '65-p505

Chancy And The Grand Rascal

Am-v115-N 5 '66-p553
BL-v63-S 15 '66-p119
CCB-B-v20-N '66-p41
CE-v44-S '67-p50
CSM-v58-N 3 '66-pB6
GT-v84-F '67-p42
HB-v42-O '66-p569
KR-v34-Jl 1 '66-p625
LJ-v91-O 15 '66-p5226
NYTBR-v71-N 6 '66-p40
NYTBR-v71-D 4 '66-p66
PW-v190-Ag 15 '66-p64
SR-v49-D 10 '66-p57
TLS-N 30 '67-p1145
Trav-v23-Ap '67-p291

The Ghost In The Noonday Sun

Am-v113-N 20 '65-p640
BL-v62-S 1 '65-p54
CCB-B-v19-N '65-p43
HB-v41-O '65-p490
KR-v33-Mr 1 '65-p245
KR-v33-My 1 '65-p472
LJ-v90-S 15 '65-p3790
NYTBR-v70-O 24 '65-p34
Obs-N 27 '66-p28
TLS-N 24 '66-p1069

The Ghost On Saturday Night

BL-v70-Jl 15 '74-p1252
CCB-B-v28-D '74-p61
HB-v50-Ag '74-p379

FLEISCHMAN, Sid
(continued)
KR-v45-Ja 15 '77-p46
NYTBR-S 11 '77-p32
PW-v211-My 16 '77-p63
SLJ-v23-My '77-p61
Mr. Mysterious's Secrets Of Magic
BL-v72-S 1 '75-p39
HB-v51-O '75-p477
KR-v43-My 15 '75-p575
SLJ-v22-N '75-p77
TLS-D 24 '76-p1598
Secrets Of Magic
B&B-v22-Ja '77-p61
JB-v41-Ap '77-p92
LR-v25-Autumn '76-p278

* * *

FLEISCHMANN, Peter
Alexander And The Car With A Missing Headlight
CCB-B-v21-Ap '68-p125
LJ-v93-Ja 15 '68-p282
NYTBR-v73-F 18 '68-p30
YR-v4-Mr '68-p8

* * *

FLEISHER, Robbin
Quilts In The Attic
KR-v46-Ag 15 '78-p876
PW-v214-Jl 31 '78-p98
SLJ-v25-Mr '79-p121

* * *

FLEISHMAN, Seymour
Printcrafts For Fun And Profit
BL-v73-Ap 15 '77-p1265
SLJ-v23-My '77-p69
Too Hot In Potzburg
BL-v78-Mr 15 '82-p957
CBRS-v10-Mr '82-p74
PW-v220-N 27 '81-p87
SLJ-v28-Ap '82-p58

* * *

FLEMING, Alice
Alcohol
BL-v71-Jl 15 '75-p1185
BL-v71-Jl 15 '75-p1190
Cur R-v16-Ag '77-p176
KR-v43-Je 1 '75-p614
Kliatt-v13-Spring '79-p36
NYTBR-Ja 18 '76-p12
PW-v208-S 1 '75-p69
SB-v11-Mr '76-p185
SLJ-v22-S '75-p102
America Is Not All Traffic Lights
BL-v72-Je 15 '76-p1464
CCB-B-v30-S '76-p9
HB-v52-Ag '76-p416
KR-v44-Mr 1 '76-p264
NYTBR-My 2 '76-p42
PW-v209-Ap 12 '76-p65
SE-v41-Ap '77-p346
SLJ-v22-My '76-p69
Contraception, Abortion, Pregnancy
ACSB-v8-Fall '75-p10
BL-v71-Mr 15 '75-p742
CCB-B-v29-F '76-p95
KR-v42-O 15 '74-p1113
NYTBR-My 4 '75-p25
SLJ-v21-Mr '75-p105
Great Women Teachers
BL-v62-S 1 '65-p55
CCB-B-v18-Je '65-p147
KR-v33-Mr 1 '65-p248
LJ-v90-Ap 15 '65-p2032
Hosannah The Home Run
BL-v69-N 1 '72-p243
CCB-B-v26-Ja '73-p75
KR-v40-Ap 15 '72-p489
LJ-v97-N 15 '72-p3812
Teacher-v92-Mr '75-p41
Ida Tarbell
BL-v68-D 15 '71-p366
CCB-B-v26-S '72-p7
CLW-v44-N '72-p249
Comw-v95-N 19 '71-p189
EJ-v61-F '72-p303
KR-v39-Ag 15 '71-p885
LJ-v96-O 15 '71-p3475
The Senator From Maine
BL-v66-N 1 '69-p345
CCB-B-v23-Je '70-p158
KR-v37-My 15 '69-p567
LJ-v94-D 15 '69-p4604
SS-v73-Jl '82-p177
Something For Nothing
BL-v74-Jl 15 '78-p1733
Comw-v105-N 10 '78-p735
EJ-v67-N '78-p83
HB-v54-Je '78-p291
KR-v46-Je 15 '78-p641
SLJ-v25-S '78-p157
Trials That Made Headlines
BL-v71-Ap 1 '75-p809
CCB-B-v28-Je '75-p160
KR-v43-Ja 15 '75-p76

* * *

FLEMING, Ian
Chitty-Chitty-Bang-Bang: The Magical Car
BL-v61-Ja 1 '65-p435
CCB-B-v22-Ja '69-p77
NS-v82-N 12 '71-p662
PW-v194-O 14 '68-p68
Chitty-Chitty-Bang-Bang: The Magical Car
CCB-B-v18-Ja '65-p73
CE-v42-Ja '66-p316
GT-v82-Mr '65-p23
HB-v41-Ap '65-p167
Inst-v74-Ap '65-p19
TLS-Je 17 '65-p511

* * *

FLEMING, Susan
Countdown At 37 Pinecrest Drive
CBRS-v11-Ap '83-p92
SLJ-v29-D '82-p82
WCRB-v9-Ja '83-p46
The Pig At 37 Pinecrest Drive
PW-v219-Je 5 '81-p83
SLJ-v28-Ja '82-p76
Trapped On The Golden Flyer
BB-v7-F '79-p3
CCB-B-v32-N '78-p42
NYTBR-Ap 30 '78-p32
SLJ-v24-F '78-p56

* * *

FLEMING, Thomas
Benjamin Franklin
BL-v69-My 15 '73-p901
BL-v69-My 15 '73-p907
CCB-B-v27-D '73-p63
CE-v50-Mr '74-p296
KR-v40-N 1 '72-p1248
First In Their Hearts
BL-v64-Je 1 '68-p1140
CCB-B-v22-S '68-p7
LJ-v93-My 15 '68-p2120
NYTBR-v73-F 18 '68-p30
Teacher-v86-F '69-p171
The Golden Door
CCB-B-v24-F '71-p90
KR-v38-Ap 1 '70-p393
KR-v38-O 15 '70-p1166
LJ-v96-Je 15 '71-p2137

* * *

FLETCHER, Alan Mark
Fishes And Their Young
PW-v206-O 7 '74-p63
SLJ-v21-Ja '75-p44

* * *

FLETCHER, Christine
100 Key Names Across The Land
RT-v32-Ja '79-p444

* * *

FLETCHER, Elizabeth
The Little Goat
Obs-S 19 '71-p26
SLJ-v24-Mr '78-p114
What Am I?
SLJ-v24-Mr '78-p114

* * *

FLETCHER, Harold
Mathematics For Schools
Inst-v80-Ja '71-p133
TES-O 1 '82-p41

* * *

FLETCHER, Helen J
Secret Codes
SLJ-v27-Ag '81-p54

* * *

FLETCHER, Helen Jill
Put On Your Thinking Cap
BL-v65-My 1 '69-p1015
CCB-B-v22-Jl '69-p174
KR-v37-Ja 1 '69-p12
LA-v55-N '78-p960
LJ-v94-Mr 15 '69-p1325
NYTBR, pt.2-My 4 '69-p55
PW-v195-Je 2 '69-p136
String Projects
JB-v41-Ag '77-p220
KR-v42-S 1 '74-p946
SLJ-v21-Ap '75-p52

* * *

FLETCHER, J
Speed And Power Land
JB-v44-Je '80-p130

* * *

FLETCHER, John
Cars And Trucks
SLJ-v30-Mr '84-p158

* * *

FLETCHER, Sarah
Bible Story Book: New Testament
SLJ-v30-My '84-p78
Bible Story Book: Old Testament
SLJ-v30-D '83-p65

* * *

FLEXER, George
Snorkel
BB-v3-Ag '75-p3
CCB-B-v29-D '75-p62
KR-v43-Ja 15 '75-p71
PW-v207-F 3 '75-p75
SLJ-v21-Ap '75-p44

* * *

FLEXNER, Eleanor
Century Of Struggle
CC-v92-O 22 '75-p949
Choice-v12-Ja '76-p1496
Dis-v23-Spring '76-p218
Inter BC-v13-#1 '82-p4
JHI-v45-O '84-p619
Kliatt-v11-Winter '77-p24
LJ-v96-S 1 '71-p2589
NEQ-v49-Je '76-p297
NYTBR, pt.2-F 21 '71-p27

* * *

FLEXNER, James Thomas
The Double Adventure Of John Singleton Copley
Am-v121-D 13 '69-p598
HB-v45-D '69-p682
LJ-v94-N 15 '69-p4295

* * *

FLICK, Pauline
Christmas Cats
Punch-v281-D 2 '81-p1024
TES-N 20 '81-p33

* * *

FLIGHTPATH To Reading
TES-Jl 11 '80-p38

* * *

FLINDERS, Matthew
Trim
GP-v17-Jl '78-p3359
JB-v42-Ag '78-p190
Obs-Mr 26 '78-p25

* * *

FLINT, Joanne
The Mennonite Canadians
BIC-v9-Ag '80-p25
In Rev-v14-D '80-p38

* * *

FLIP Flops
Quill & Q-v50-F '84-p11

* * *

FLOETHE, Louise Lee
Bittersweet Summer
CCB-B-v18-Je '65-p147
EJ-v54-My '65-p460
Floating Market
CCB-B-v22-My '69-p141
CSM-v61-My 1 '69-pB3
LJ-v94-My 15 '69-p2099
Houses Around The World
CCB-B-v27-Mr '74-p109
KR-v41-Ag 15 '73-p884
LJ-v98-N 15 '73-p3451

* * *

FLOOD, James
Comprehension Plus Series
Cur R-v21-D '82-p487
Inst-v92-F '83-p164
RT-v37-N '83-p219

* * *

FLORA, James
The Day The Cow Sneezed
NY-v51-D 1 '75-p182
Fishing With Dad
CSM-v59-N 2 '67-pB6
Comw-v87-N 10 '67-p176
KR-v35-O 15 '67-p1264
LJ-v92-O 15 '67-p3839
NYTBR-v72-N 5 '67-p63
Grandpa's Farm: 4 Tall Tales
Atl-v216-D '65-p154
BL-v62-S 15 '65-p94
GT-v83-N '65-p106
HB-v41-O '65-p498
KR-v33-Jl 1 '65-p621
LJ-v90-S 15 '65-p3779
NYTBR-v70-N 7 '65-p55
SR-v48-N 13 '65-p57
Grandpa's Ghost Stories
BL-v75-S 15 '78-p216
CLW-v51-S '79-p92
HB-v55-O '78-p510
KR-v46-O 1 '78-p1066
RT-v33-O '79-p46
RT-v33-O '79-p95
SLJ-v25-O '78-p132
SLJ-v28-Ap '82-p31
Grandpa's Witched-Up Christmas
CCB-B-v36-S '82-p8
KR-v50-S 1 '82-p994
PW-v222-D 17 '82-p74
SLJ-v29-O '82-p168
The Great Green Turkey Creek Monster
BL-v73-N 1 '76-p408
CSM-v68-N 3 '76-p22

FLORA, James (continued)
HB-v52-D '76-p621
KR-v44-Jl 1 '76-p725
PW-v210-Ag 9 '76-p79
SLJ-v23-O '76-p97
SR-v4-N 27 '76-p36
Joking Man
CCB-B-v22-O '68-p26
HB-v44-O '68-p556
KR-v36-Jl 1 '68-p687
NYTBR-v73-N 3 '68-p67
Kangaroo For Christmas
SLMQ-v12-Summer '84-p326
Little Hatchy Hen
A Lib-v1-Ap '70-p385
BL-v66-S 15 '69-p129
CLW-v41-F '70-p384
Comw-v91-N 21 '69-p254
HB-v45-O '69-p530
KR-v37-Ag 15 '69-p849
NY-v45-D 13 '69-p192
NYTBR, pt.2-N 9 '69-p56
My Friend Charlie
BL-v61-F 15 '65-p578
CCB-B-v18-Ja '65-p73
HB-v41-F '65-p46
Pishtosh, Bullwash & Wimple
HB-v48-O '72-p461
KR-v40-Jl 1 '72-p720
LJ-v97-N 15 '72-p3796
PW-v202-Ag 7 '72-p50
Stewed Goose
BL-v70-N 15 '73-p338
CCB-B-v27-Ja '74-p78
HB-v50-F '74-p41
KR-v41-Ag 1 '73-p809
LJ-v98-N 15 '73-p3439
NY-v49-D 3 '73-p204
PW-v204-S 3 '73-p54
Wanda And The Bumbly Wizard
BL-v76-Mr 15 '80-p1055
CE-v57-Ja '81-p171
CLW-v52-N '80-p185
KR-v48-Ap 15 '80-p511
LA-v57-O '80-p794
PW-v217-F 1 '80-p108
SLJ-v26-Mr '80-p120

* * *

FLORIAN, Douglas
Airplane Ride
BL-v80-Ap 15 '84-p1188
CBRS-v12-My '84-p100
Inst-v93-My '84-p87
KR-v52-Mr 1 '84-pJ4
NYTBR-Ap 15 '84-p33
PW-v225-Ja 27 '84-p76
SLJ-v30-Ag '84-p58
A Bird Can Fly
BL-v76-Jl 15 '80-p1675
CBRS-v8-Ag '80-p132
HB-v56-D '80-p632
KR-v48-S 15 '80-p1227
RT-v34-Ap '81-p854
SB-v16-My '81-p276
SLJ-v26-Ag '80-p50
The City
BW-v12-My 9 '82-p17
CBRS-v10-My '82-p91
CCB-B-v36-N '82-p46
Inst-v91-My '82-p104
KR-v50-Mr 1 '82-p270
NYTBR-v87-Mr 7 '82-p18
PW-v221-F 12 '82-p99
SLJ-v28-Ag '82-p96
People Working
BW-v13-My 8 '83-p16
Inter BC-v15-#4 '84-p19
KR-v51-Mr 1 '83-p242
NYTBR-v88-Ap 24 '83-p24
PW-v223-Ap 1 '83-p60
SLJ-v30-S '83-p105
WCRB-v9-Jl '83-p39

* * *

FLORY, Jane
The Bear On The Doorstep
B&B-Jl '82-p35
BL-v77-S 15 '80-p114
CBRS-v9-N '80-p22
HB-v56-D '80-p633
JB-v46-O '82-p180
KR-v48-N 15 '80-p1460
NS-v104-D 3 '82-p22
PW-v218-O 31 '80-p85
RT-v35-O '81-p57
SLJ-v27-Mr '81-p131
Faraway Dream
BL-v65-Ja 1 '69-p494
CCB-B-v22-Ja '69-p77
CE-v45-Ap '69-p461
KR-v36-O 1 '68-p1114
LJ-v94-F 15 '69-p871
The Golden Venture
BL-v72-Je 1 '76-p1405
BW-Je 13 '76-pM2
CCB-B-v30-O '76-p24
CE-v53-F '77-p213
CLW-v48-Ap '77-p406
Cur R-v17-F '78-p76
HB-v52-O '76-p499
KR-v44-My 1 '76-p534
SE-v41-Ap '77-p347
SLJ-v22-My '76-p58
The Great Bamboozlement
BL-v78-My 15 '82-p1256
CBRS-v10-Spring '82-p113
HB-v58-Ag '82-p401
SLJ-v28-My '82-p60
It Was A Pretty Good Year
BL-v74-F 15 '78-p1001
CCB-B-v31-F '78-p91
KR-v45-S 1 '77-p932
SLJ-v24-O '77-p110
The Liberation Of Clementine Tipton
BB-v3-F '75-p3
B&B-v21-Je '76-p64
BL-v71-Ja 1 '75-p460
GP-v15-D '76-p3019
HB-v50-D '74-p691
JB-v40-Ag '76-p225
KR-v42-N 1 '74-p1150
LA-v52-S '75-p857
PW-v207-Ja 6 '75-p58
SLJ-v21-Mr '75-p95
The Lost And Found Princess
BL-v75-Mr 15 '79-p1156
CBRS-v7-Jl '79-p124
KR-v47-My 1 '79-p518
PW-v215-My 21 '79-p69
SLJ-v25-Ap '79-p42
Miss Plunkett To The Rescue
BL-v79-Je 1 '83-p1275
CBRS-v11-Ag '83-p143
CCB-B-v37-S '83-p6
KR-v51-Mr 1 '83-p246
PW-v223-Mr 4 '83-p99
SLJ-v29-Ag '83-p64
Mist On The Mountain
BL-v62-Je 15 '66-p1000
CCB-B-v19-Je '66-p163
CE-v43-D '66-p232
CLW-v39-N '67-p240
HB-v42-Ag '66-p435
KR-v34-Mr 15 '66-p302
LJ-v91-My 15 '66-p2689
Ramshackle Roost
BL-v69-S 15 '72-p99
CE-v49-D '72-p145
HB-v48-Ag '72-p370
KR-v40-My 1 '72-p537
LJ-v97-S 15 '72-p2949
The Unexpected Grandchildren
BB-v5-Ja '78-p1
CCB-B-v31-D '77-p59
CSM-v69-N 2 '77-pB2
Inst-v87-N '77-p154

FLORY, Jane (continued)
KR-v45-S 15 '77-p985
PW-v212-Ag 22 '77-p66
RT-v32-O '78-p38
SLJ-v24-N '77-p46
We'll Have A Friend For Lunch
A Lib-v5-S '74-p423
BL-v70-My 15 '74-p1055
CCB-B-v27-Jl '74-p176
KR-v42-Mr 15 '74-p293
LJ-v99-S 15 '74-p2245
PT-v8-Je '74-p112
PW-v205-F 25 '74-p113
Teacher-v92-F '75-p111
WLB-v48-Je '74-p801

* * *

FLOT, Jeannette B
Rosetto
TES-N 4 '83-p24

* * *

FLOURNOY, Valerie
The Best Time Of Day
CBRS-v8-S '79-p2
Inter BC-v11-Ja 10 '80-p28
PW-v216-Ag 27 '79-p386
SLJ-v26-N '79-p64
The Twins Strike Back
B Ent-v12-D '81-p22
BW-v10-Je 8 '80-p11
CBRS-v8-My '80-p95
CCB-B-v33-My '80-p171
Inter BC-v12-#1 '81-p18
KR-v48-Ag 1 '80-p977
PW-v217-Ap 18 '80-p89
SLJ-v26-Ag '80-p50

* * *

FLOWER, Phyllis
Barn Owl
ACSB-v12-Winter '79-p10
BL-v74-Mr 15 '78-p1198
CE-v55-N '78-p106
Cha Ti-v32-N '78-p23
GP-v18-Ja '80-p3628
JB-v44-Je '80-p131
KR-v46-Mr 1 '78-p242
NYTBR-Ap 30 '78-p31
RT-v33-O '79-p50
SB-v15-My '79-p41
SLJ-v24-My '78-p83
SR-v5-My 27 '78-p58
WLB-v53-Je '79-p709

* * *

FLOWERDEW, Phyllis
Goodbye Candlelight
Obs-Mr 30 '75-p24
Reading To Some Purpose
TES-Jl 16 '82-p22
Wide Range Readers (Red Book 7)
TES-Jl 16 '82-p22
Wide Range Reading
TES-Jl 14 '78-p21

* * *

FLOYD, Lucy
Agatha's Alphabet
BL-v72-N 15 '75-p452

* * *

FLYING Carpets
Lis-v110-N 3 '83-p29

* * *

FLYNN, Frank
Bernie's Bird
JB-v47-Ag '83-p161
Sch Lib-v31-Je '83-p143

* * *

FOBBESTER, J
Paper
JB-v45-Je '81-p122

* * *

FODEN, Ken
Hexagone
TES-Ap 22 '83-p29

* * *

FODOR, John T
Good Health For You
Cur R-v22-My '83-p175

* * *

FODOR, R V
Angry Waters
ACSB-v13-Mr '80-p22
BL-v76-Je 1 '80-p1423
CCB-B-v34-N '80-p52
KR-v48-My 1 '80-p587
SB-v16-Ja '81-p153
SLJ-v27-N '80-p85
Chiseling The Earth
BL-v80-S 1 '83-p84
B Rpt-v2-Ja '84-p52
CCB-B-v37-D '83-p66
HB-v59-D '83-p736
SB-v19-N '83-p77
SLJ-v30-N '83-p92
VOYA-v6-O '83-p224
Earth Afire!
ASBYP-v15-Spring '82-p34
BL-v78-F 15 '82-p756
HB-v58-Ap '82-p194
KR-v50-F 15 '82-p203
SB-v17-My '82-p255
Earth In Motion
ACSB-v12-Winter '79-p10
BB-v6-Ag '78-p3
BL-v74-Jl 1 '78-p1678
EJ-v67-O '78-p79
HB-v54-D '78-p666
KR-v46-Je 15 '78-p638
SB-v15-My '79-p40
SLJ-v25-O '78-p144
Meteorites
BL-v73-Ap 1 '77-p1166
KR-v44-D 15 '76-p1308
SB-v13-D '77-p163
SLJ-v23-Mr '77-p144
Nickels, Dimes, And Dollars
BL-v76-Ap 1 '80-p1126
CCB-B-v33-Jl '80-p212
SLJ-v27-S '80-p70
What Does A Geologist Do?
BL-v74-F 1 '78-p924
Earth S-v31-Ja '78-p39
J Read-v22-Mr '79-p563
KR-v46-Ja 15 '78-p49
SB-v14-D '78-p180
SLJ-v24-F '78-p56
What To Eat And Why
ACSB-v13-Spring '80-p29
CCB-B-v32-Ap '79-p135
Cur R-v19-Ap '80-p125
KR-v47-Mr 1 '79-p265
SB-v15-My '80-p281
SLJ-v26-F '80-p54

* * *

FODOROVA, Anna
Carlo The Crocodile
GP-v18-N '79-p3610

* * *

FOGEL, Julianna A
Wesley Paul: Marathon Runner
BL-v76-D 15 '79-p610
CCB-B-v33-Mr '80-p132
KR-v48-F 1 '80-p129
RT-v34-O '80-p56
SLJ-v26-Ja '80-p55

* * *

FOLEY, Bernice W
The Gazelle And The Hunter
Cur R-v20-Ap '81-p171

FOLEY, Bernice W (continued)
SLJ-v26-Ag '80-p50
Spaceships Of The Ancients
SLJ-v25-Ap '79-p55
A Walk Among Clouds
Cur R-v20-Ap '81-p170
SLJ-v26-Ag '80-p50

* * *

FOLEY, June
It's No Crush, I'm In Love!
BL-v78-Je 15 '82-p1367
BS-v42-Je '82-p119
CBRS-v10-My '82-p97
CCB-B-v35-My '82-p167
HB-v58-Ag '82-p411
J Read-v26-N '82-p185
Kliatt-v17-Fall '83-p8
LA-v59-N '82-p868
SLJ-v28-Ag '82-p125
VOYA-v5-Ag '82-p30
Love By Any Other Name
BL-v79-Mr 15 '83-p966
BS-v43-My '83-p73
CBRS-v11-Ap '83-p93
CCB-B-v36-My '83-p166
CLW-v55-D '83-p239
EJ-v72-O '83-p85
J Read-v27-F '84-p467
Kliatt-v17-Fall '83-p8
SLJ-v30-S '83-p134
VOYA-v6-O '83-p200

* * *

FOLEY, Louise M
The Lost Tribe
SLJ-v30-D '83-p82
The Mystery Of The Highland Crest
SLJ-v31-S '84-p139
The Sinister Studios Of KESP-TV
SLJ-v30-Mr '84-p158
VOYA-v7-Je '84-p94
Somebody Stole Second
CCB-B-v26-O '72-p24
KR-v40-Mr 1 '72-p254
LJ-v97-My 15 '72-p1929
Teacher-v94-My '77-p114
Tackle 22
BL-v75-F 15 '79-p932
CBRS-v7-F '79-p64
CCB-B-v32-Ap '79-p135
SLJ-v25-Mr '79-p121

* * *

FOLK Tales From Asia For Children Everywhere. Book 1
GP-v13-Ap '75-p2609

* * *

FOLKER, A
Children Talking
TES-F 4 '83-p28

* * *

FOLLETT, K
The Secret Of Kellerman's Studio
JB-v40-Ag '76-p198
LR-v25-Spring '76-p226

* * *

FOLLETT Social Studies
Cur R-v19-Je '80-p285

* * *

FOLLETT Social Studies 1977
Cur R-v16-O '77-p304

* * *

FOLLETT Spelling
Cur R-v19-S '80-p325

* * *

FOLSOM, Franklin
Red Power On The Rio Grande
ABC-v24-Mr '74-p35
A Lib-v6-Mr '75-p166
BL-v70-S 15 '73-p118
BS-v33-Ag 15 '73-p233
CCB-B-v27-O '73-p27
LJ-v98-N 15 '73-p3451
NY-v49-D 3 '73-p218
PW-v203-My 14 '73-p47

* * *

FOLTZ, Mary Jane
Awani
CCB-B-v18-F '65-p85

* * *

FONS, Benny
Look Out Michael
GP-v14-O '75-p2724

* * *

FONTAINE, Jan
The Spaghetti Tree
SLJ-v27-N '80-p60

* * *

FONTANE, Theodor
Sir Ribbeck Of Ribbeck Of Havelland
A Lib-v1-Ap '70-p385
BL-v65-Jl 15 '69-p1274
HB-v45-Ag '69-p396
KR-v37-Ap 15 '69-p437
LJ-v94-Jl '69-p2671
NO-v8-N 3 '69-p21
NYTBR, pt.2-My 4 '69-p53
PW-v195-Ap 14 '69-p97

* * *

FONTENOT, Mary A
Clovis And E. Escargot
RT-v36-D '82-p265
Clovis Crawfish And His Friends
RT-v36-D '82-p265
Clovis Crawfish And Michelle Mantis
RT-v36-D '82-p265
Clovis Crawfish And The Orphan Zo-Zo
SLJ-v30-D '83-p54
Clovis Crawfish And The Singing Cigales
PW-v221-Ja 1 '82-p51
SLJ-v28-Ag '82-p96
WCRB-v8-My '82-p43

* * *

FOOD
TES-N 13 '81-p24

* * *

FOOD For Thought
TES-N 5 '82-p23

* * *

FOONER, Michael
Inside Interpol
BL-v72-F 1 '76-p760
BL-v72-F 1 '76-p787
KR-v43-D 15 '75-p1382
SLJ-v22-F '76-p45
Women In Policing
BL-v73-D 1 '76-p538
KR-v44-O 15 '76-p1141
RT-v31-Mr '78-p708
SLJ-v23-Ja '77-p91

* * *

FOORD, Isabelle
The Beast In The Bag. Wild West Circus
Can Child Lit-#21 '81-p76

FORD, Barbara (continued)
CBRS-v8-Spring '80-p117
KR-v48-My 15 '80-p646
SB-v16-Ja '81-p156
SLJ-v27-Mr '81-p144

* * *

FORD, Brian J
101 Questions About Science
JB-v47-D '83-p256

* * *

FORD, Doug
Start Golf Young
BL-v75-O 1 '78-p303
SLJ-v25-D '78-p70

* * *

FORD, George
Baby's First Picture Book
SLJ-v29-Mr '83-p121

* * *

FORD, Joan E
Skate Like The Wind
Emerg Lib-v11-N '83-p37
Quill & Q-v49-N '83-p25

* * *

FORD, Lee
Water Boatman's Journey
CCB-B-v23-S '69-p7
KR-v37-Ap 15 '69-p434
LJ-v94-Jl '69-p2672

* * *

FORD, Marianne
Copycats
GP-v22-Ja '84-p4197
JB-v48-Ap '84-p81
Sch Lib-v32-Mr '84-p76
TES-N 16 '84-p23

* * *

FORDHAM, Derek
Eskimos
TES-Ja 25 '80-p26

* * *

FOREMAN, Dale I
Reading Skills For Social Studies
Cur R-v21-Ag '82-p259
Inst-v90-Mr '81-p124
Reading Skills For Social Studies Concepts
Inst-v90-Mr '81-p124
Scoring High In Math
Cur R-v18-D '79-p425

* * *

FOREMAN, Michael
All The King's Horses
CLW-v49-Ap '78-p403
GP-v15-N '76-p2992
KR-v45-Jl 1 '77-p666
LA-v55-Mr '78-p364
PW-v212-Jl 18 '77-p137
SLJ-v24-S '77-p127
SR-v5-N 26 '77-p42
Dinosaurs And All That Rubbish
BW-v7-Jl 8 '73-p13
CSM-v65-My 2 '73-pB2
GW-v107-D 16 '72-p24
KR-v41-Ap 15 '73-p452
LJ-v98-My 15 '73-p1672
Lis-v88-N 9 '72-p646
Obs-N 26 '72-p37
PW-v203-Ap 9 '73-p65
RT-v32-My '79-p918
Spec-v229-N 11 '72-p762
TLS-D 8 '72-p1495
Teacher-v92-F '75-p37
Land Of Dreams
CBRS-v11-F '83-p64
JB-v46-D '82-p219
Obs-D 5 '82-p33
RT-v36-Ap '83-p852
SLJ-v29-F '83-p66
Sch Lib-v31-Je '83-p128
TLS-N 26 '82-p1305
WLB-v57-Ap '83-p690
Monkey And The Three Wizards
GP-v15-N '76-p2992
Spec-v237-D 11 '76-p22
Panda And The Odd Lion
JB-v46-F '82-p14
Sch Lib-v30-Je '82-p119
TLS-N 20 '81-p1359
Panda's Puzzle And His Voyage Of Discovery
BB-v6-Ja '79-p1
BL-v74-My 1 '78-p1430
ILN-v265-D '77-p109
JB-v42-F '78-p16
KR-v46-Ap 1 '78-p367
LA-v56-Mr '79-p288
NYTBR-Ap 23 '78-p32
PW-v213-F 20 '78-p127
SLJ-v25-S '78-p108
TES-N 18 '77-p38
TLS-D 2 '77-p1411
Perfect Present
B&B-v13-D '67-p46
B&B-v14-Ag '69-p48
CCB-B-v21-N '67-p41
KR-v35-S 1 '67-p1040
Punch-v253-S 27 '67-p485
TLS-N 30 '67-p1149
Trick A Tracker
Brit Bk N C-Autumn '81-p14
CBRS-v10-S '81-p2
JB-v45-D '81-p242
KR-v49-S 15 '81-p1156
LA-v59-Mr '82-p267
PW-v220-Ag 28 '81-p394
SLJ-v28-N '81-p91
Two Giants
BW-v1-N 12 '67-p26
CCB-B-v21-Ap '68-p125
Comw-v87-N 10 '67-p178
KR-v35-S 15 '67-p1130
LJ-v92-D 15 '67-p4602
LJ-v95-O 15 '70-p3602
NYTBR-v72-O 1 '67-p34
Spec-v219-N 3 '67-p543
War And Peas
B&B-v21-N '75-p60
BL-v71-Ja 15 '75-p507
CCB-B-v28-My '75-p146
GP-v13-Mr '75-p2585
JB-v39-F '75-p20
KR-v42-N 15 '74-p1199
Lis-v92-N 7 '74-p617
NYTBR-Ja 12 '75-p8
Obs-D 1 '74-p35
PW-v206-N 25 '74-p44
SLJ-v21-Mr '75-p87
Winter's Tales
BB-v7-D '79-p1
BL-v76-O 15 '79-p351
CBRS-v8-Ja '80-p41
CCB-B-v33-Mr '80-p132
ILN-v267-D '79-p141
JB-v44-Ap '80-p62
KR-v47-D 15 '79-p1428
PW-v216-S 17 '79-p145
RT-v33-My '80-p971
SLJ-v26-O '79-p119

* * *

FOREST, Antonia
The Attic Term
GP-v15-Ja '77-p3041
JB-v41-F '77-p32
Obs-N 28 '76-p31
TLS-O 1 '76-p1243
The Cricket Term
GP-v14-S '75-p2690
GP-v21-My '82-p3913
JB-v39-F '75-p62

FOREST, Antonia (continued)
Spec-v233-D 7 '74-p740
Falconer's Lure
GP-v16-O '77-p3196
The Ready-Made Family
Brit Bk N C-Autumn '82-p8
Obs-D 3 '67-p26
SLJ-v27-Mr '81-p156
TES-O 31 '80-p24
TLS-N 30 '67-p1150
Run Away Home
Brit Bk N C-Autumn '82-p8
GP-v21-Jl '82-p3924
JB-v46-Je '82-p104
SLJ-v29-O '82-p168
Sch Lib-v30-Je '82-p152
TES-O 8 '82-p31

* * *

FOREST, Chantal
J'Etais A Babylone
Can Child Lit-#23 '81-p91

* * *

FORESTS
TES-N 18 '77-p37

* * *

FORGAN, Harry W
Read All About It
Teacher-v97-S '79-p132
Reading Skillbuilder Series
Cur R-v22-F '83-p42

* * *

FORMAN, Brenda
America's Place In The World Economy
BL-v66-O 15 '69-p266
CCB-B-v23-O '69-p24
KR-v37-My 15 '69-p568
LJ-v95-Ja 15 '70-p252
SR-v52-Ag 16 '69-p59

* * *

FORMAN, J
The Romans
LR-v25-Winter '77-p334

* * *

FORMAN, James
A Ballad For Hogskin Hill
CBRS-v8-D '79-p37
CCB-B-v33-Ap '80-p151
KR-v47-D 15 '79-p1434
NYTBR-Ja 13 '80-p26
SLJ-v26-Ja '80-p78
Ceremony Of Innocence
BL-v67-D 15 '70-p336
BL-v67-D 15 '70-p341
CCB-B-v24-Ja '71-p73
Cur R-v17-O '78-p343
EJ-v60-My '71-p668
EJ-v69-O '80-p16
Inter BC-v13-#6 '82-p19
KR-v38-Ag 1 '70-p805
Kliatt-v11-Spring '77-p5
LJ-v95-N 15 '70-p4053
LJ-v95-D 15 '70-p4325
NYTBR-Ja 10 '71-p26
SR-v53-N 14 '70-p39
The Cow Neck Rebels
BL-v66-D 15 '69-p516
BS-v29-N 1 '69-p306
CSM-v61-N 6 '69-pB9
HB-v46-F '70-p44
KR-v37-O 15 '69-p1122
LJ-v95-Je 15 '70-p2312
NY-v45-D 13 '69-p200
NYTBR-N 30 '69-p44
A Fine, Soft Day
BB-v7-Ap '79-p4
BL-v75-D 15 '78-p678
BS-v39-Ag '79-p167
CBRS-v7-Ja '79-p47
CCB-B-v32-My '79-p153
CE-v56-N '79-p111
Comw-v107-F 29 '80-p113
KR-v47-Ja 15 '79-p70
PW-v215-Ja 1 '79-p58
SLJ-v25-Ja '79-p60
Follow The River
BL-v72-S 1 '75-p34
HB-v51-O '75-p469
KR-v43-My 15 '75-p575
SLJ-v21-My '75-p64
Horses Of Anger
BL-v64-S 1 '67-p54
BS-v27-My 1 '67-p64
CCB-B-v21-My '68-p140
HB-v43-Je '67-p352
KR-v35-Mr 1 '67-p278
LJ-v92-My 15 '67-p2027
LJ-v95-O 15 '70-p3610
NYTBR-v72-My 7 '67-p2
Trav-v24-N '67-p99
The Life And Death Of Yellow Bird
A Lib-v6-Mr '75-p166
BL-v70-F 15 '74-p649
BL-v70-F 15 '74-p656
HB-v50-F '74-p55
KR-v41-N 15 '73-p1272
LJ-v99-S 15 '74-p2289
My Enemy, My Brother
BL-v66-S 1 '69-p44
BS-v29-Jl 1 '69-p149
BW-v3-My 4 '69-p3
CCB-B-v22-Jl '69-p174
HB-v45-Je '69-p328
KR-v37-Ap 15 '69-p452
LJ-v94-My 15 '69-p2112
LJ-v95-F 15 '70-p742
NYTBR-My 25 '69-p32
PW-v195-My 19 '69-p70
SR-v52-Je 28 '69-p39
People Of The Dream
BL-v68-Jl 15 '72-p997
BL-v68-Jl 15 '72-p1004
BW-v6-Jl 16 '72-p7
CE-v49-F '73-p257
KR-v40-My 15 '72-p589
LJ-v97-N 15 '72-p3813
NYTBR, pt.2-N 5 '72-p14
Teacher-v92-Ap '75-p113
The Pumpkin Shell
BL-v78-O 1 '81-p186
CBRS-v10-Ja '82-p47
KR-v50-Ja 1 '82-p11
Kliatt-v18-Winter '84-p8
SLJ-v28-O '81-p149
VOYA-v4-F '82-p30
Ring The Judas Bell
BL-v61-Je 15 '65-p993
BS-v25-Ap 15 '65-p51
CCB-B-v18-Jl '65-p160
CLW-v36-Ap '65-p573
CSM-v57-My 6 '65-p6B
Comw-v82-My 28 '65-p329
HB-v41-Je '65-p284
Inter BC-v13-#6 '82-p20
KR-v33-Ja 1 '65-p11
LJ-v90-Mr 15 '65-p1558
NYTBR-v70-Ap 4 '65-p22
SR-v48-Je 19 '65-p41
The Shield Of Achilles
BL-v62-Jl 1 '66-p1039
CCB-B-v20-My '67-p139
CLW-v38-N '66-p214
HB-v42-Je '66-p315
KR-v34-Ap 1 '66-p377
LJ-v91-Je 15 '66-p3264
NO-v5-Ag 1 '66-p18
NYTBR-v71-My 8 '66-p10
NYTBR-v71-D 4 '66-p66
Song Of Jubilee
BS-v31-Jl 15 '71-p191
CLW-v43-Ap '72-p481
HB-v47-Ag '71-p388
KR-v39-Ap 15 '71-p441

FORMAN, James (continued)
LJ-v96-Je 15 '71-p2137
NYTBR, pt.2-My 2 '71-p18
PW-v199-My 10 '71-p42
The Survivor
BL-v72-My 1 '76-p1263
BL-v81-O 1 '84-p214
CCB-B-v30-S '76-p9
Emerg Lib-v10-S '82-p29
KR-v44-Ap 15 '76-p482
SE-v41-Ap '77-p350
SLJ-v22-Ap '76-p86
The Traitors
BS-v28-N 1 '68-p324
BW-v3-Mr 30 '69-p16
CCB-B-v22-F '69-p92
KR-v36-S 15 '68-p1058
LJ-v95-F 15 '70-p742
NO-v8-Je 9 '69-p23
NYTBR-v73-N 3 '68-p18
SE-v33-My '69-p557
YR-v5-N '68-p1
The White Crow
CCB-B-v30-My '77-p140
KR-v44-D 1 '76-p1268
SLJ-v23-F '77-p71

* * *

FORMAN, James D
Call Back Yesterday
BL-v78-D 15 '81-p545
BS-v41-F '82-p440
CBRS-v10-F '82-p66
CCB-B-v35-Mr '82-p127
Cur R-v21-O '82-p409
HB-v58-Ap '82-p172
KR-v50-Ja 15 '82-p71
SLJ-v28-Ja '82-p86
VOYA-v5-Je '82-p32
Freedom's Blood
CBRS-v7-Ap '79-p87
CCB-B-v33-S '79-p6
SLJ-v26-S '79-p156
Inflation
BL-v74-S 1 '77-p40
SLJ-v24-O '77-p110
SS-v69-Mr '78-p85
Nazism
BL-v74-F 1 '78-p902
HB-v54-Je '78-p286
SLJ-v25-F '79-p63

* * *

FORMAN, Joan
Romanos
HB-v56-D '80-p665

* * *

FORMAN, Leona Shluger
Bico
BL-v65-Je 15 '69-p1174
CCB-B-v23-Je '70-p158
CE-v46-My '70-p434
KR-v37-Mr 15 '69-p308
LJ-v94-S 15 '69-p3204
SR-v52-My 10 '69-p56

* * *

FORRAI, Maria S
A Look At Birth
BL-v74-F 15 '78-p1004

* * *

FORREST, Antonia
Autumn Term
TES-D 9 '77-p21
End Of Term
TES-S 22 '78-p23

* * *

FORRESTER, Helen
Minerva's Stepchild
JB-v43-O '79-p287
NS-v98-Jl 6 '79-p24
Obs-Ja 13 '80-p38
SLJ-v30-Ja '84-p42

* * *

FORRESTER, Victoria
Bears & Theirs
CBRS-v10-Jl '82-p124
PW-v221-Ap 16 '82-p71
SLJ-v28-Ag '82-p115
The Candlemaker
CBRS-v13-S '84-p8
PW-v225-Je 15 '84-p83
SLJ-v31-S '84-p116
The Magnificent Moo
CBRS-v11-Spring '83-p118
KR-v51-Ja 1 '83-p1
PW-v223-Ja 7 '83-p73
SLJ-v29-Ap '83-p100
Oddward
BL-v78-My 15 '82-p1256
CBRS-v10-Jl '82-p124
PW-v221-Ap 23 '82-p92
SLJ-v28-Ag '82-p97
The Touch Said Hello
Cur R-v22-D '83-p45
Inst-v92-N '82-p150
PW-v222-Jl 23 '82-p132
SLJ-v29-O '82-p140
Words To Keep Against The Night
PW-v224-S 16 '83-p126
SLJ-v30-Ap '84-p101
SLMQ-v12-Spring '84-p188

* * *

FORSBERG, Vera
Gennet Lives In Ethiopia
BL-v65-O 1 '68-p191
CCB-B-v22-O '68-p27
LJ-v93-S 15 '68-p3301

* * *

FORSEE, Aylesa
Men Of Modern Architecture
BL-v62-My 15 '66-p912
BS-v26-My 1 '66-p57
CCB-B-v19-My '66-p148
KR-v33-O 1 '65-p1053
LJ-v91-Mr 15 '66-p1718
Pablo Casals: Cellist For Freedom
BL-v61-Jl 1 '65-p1028
CCB-B-v18-Jl '65-p161
HB-v41-Ag '65-p404
KR-v33-Ap 1 '65-p382
NYTBR-v70-Je 27 '65-p26
William Henry Jackson: Pioneer Photographer Of The West
CC-v82-Je 30 '65-p838
CCB-B-v18-F '65-p85
NYTBR-v70-Ja 3 '65-p18

* * *

FORSMAN, Bettie
From Lupita's Hill
CCB-B-v27-N '73-p42
KR-v41-Ap 1 '73-p396
LJ-v98-Jl '73-p2193

* * *

FORST, S
Pipkin
CLW-v42-My '71-p580
HB-v46-O '70-p476
LJ-v96-Mr 15 '71-p1107

* * *

FORSTER, Eric
The Pit War
JB-v42-Ap '78-p102
TES-Je 30 '78-p19

* * *

FORSYTH, A
The Money Makers
JB-v48-Je '84-p126

* * *

FORSYTH, Anne
Baxter The Travelling Cat
Brit Bk N C-Autumn '81-p20
Sch Lib-v29-S '81-p229
Sam's Wonderful Shell
Brit Bk N C-Spring '82-p12
TES-Mr 19 '82-p28

* * *

FORT, John
June The Tiger
BL-v72-F 15 '76-p855
CCB-B-v29-My '76-p143
HB-v52-F '76-p48
KR-v43-D 15 '75-p1379
SLJ-v22-Mr '76-p102

* * *

FORTE, Imogene
The Yellow Pages For Students And Teachers
Inst-v91-N '81-p78

* * *

FORTMAN, Jan
Creatures Of Mystery
Cur R-v17-Ag '78-p228
SLJ-v24-My '78-p63
Teacher-v96-S '78-p183
Houdini And Other Masters Of Magic
SLJ-v24-My '78-p64

* * *

FORTUNE, J J
Duel For The Samurai Sword
SLJ-v30-My '84-p101
VOYA-v7-O '84-p199
Evil In Paradise
SLJ-v31-S '84-p139

* * *

FOSS, Christopher F
Armoured Fighting Vehicles Of The World
ARBA-v9-'78-p786
BL-v72-Ja 1 '76-p651
BL-v75-N 15 '78-p568
WLB-v52-Ap '78-p652

* * *

FOSS, M
Traditional Nursery Rhymes And Children's Verse
JB-v41-Ap '77-p93

* * *

FOSS, Michael
The Children's Song Book
GP-v18-Mr '80-p3667
JB-v44-Ag '80-p175
TLS-Mr 28 '80-p363

* * *

FORTNUM, Peggy
Running Wild
GP-v14-Mr '76-p2832
JB-v40-F '76-p10
LR-v25-Autumn '75-p164
Obs-D 7 '75-p32

* * *

FORTS And Castles (Standard Facts)
TES-Jl 3 '81-p25

* * *

FORTUNATO, Pat
A Colonial Williamsburg Activities Book
PW-v222-S 17 '82-p115
Dino-Mite Foozles
EJ-v69-Ja '80-p77
Foozles
PW-v215-Ja 22 '79-p370
When We Were Young
CCB-B-v33-Mr '80-p132
Hi Lo-v1-F '80-p3
SLJ-v26-F '80-p54
Your Questions Answered
Emerg Lib-v10-N '82-p31

FOSS, Michael (continued)
Folk Tales Of The British Isles
Lis-v98-N 10 '77-p624
Obs-D 11 '77-p31

* * *

FOSSEY, Koen
The Mysterious Railway
TES-Ja 15 '82-p35
TLS-N 20 '81-p1358

* * *

FOSTER, Alan Dean
Star Trek Log Four
EJ-v64-N '75-p80
Teacher-v93-N '75-p118

* * *

FOSTER, Ed
Tejanos
EJ-v61-N '72-p1263
NYTBR-Ja 3 '71-p12
RT-v36-D '82-p277

* * *

FOSTER, G Allen
Sunday In Centreville
BL-v68-S 1 '71-p52
CCB-B-v24-My '71-p134
LJ-v96-Je 15 '71-p2137
SR-v54-Mr 20 '71-p31
Votes For Women
BL-v63-Ja 15 '67-p529
Inter BC-v13-#1 '82-p4
KR-v34-S 15 '66-p985
LJ-v91-N 15 '66-p5759
NYTBR-v72-Ja 8 '67-p30

* * *

FOSTER, Genevieve
Child Care Work With Emotionally Disturbed Children
CT-v1-Jl '72-p29
Choice-v9-Je '72-p579
The World Of Columbus And Sons
BL-v61-Jl 15 '65-p1064
BS-v25-Je 15 '65-p145
CCB-B-v19-S '65-p8
CSM-v57-N 4 '65-pB10
Comw-v82-My 28 '65-p331
GT-v83-N '65-p78
HB-v41-Ag '65-p400
Inst-v75-S '65-p166
KR-v33-Ap 1 '65-p386
LJ-v90-Jl '65-p3125
NYTBR-v70-Je 27 '65-p26
SA-v213-D '65-p119
SR-v48-My 15 '65-p56
The World Of William Penn
BL-v70-S 1 '73-p50
CCB-B-v27-N '73-p42
HB-v49-Ag '73-p389
KR-v41-Ap 1 '73-p389
LJ-v98-Jl '73-p2193
Year Of Columbus 1492
BL-v66-F 1 '70-p669
CLW-v43-O '71-p116
Comw-v92-My 22 '70-p251
GT-v88-F '71-p139
HB-v46-F '70-p50
KR-v37-N 15 '69-p1198
LJ-v95-Mr 15 '70-p1186
PW-v196-D 8 '69-p48
SE-v44-O '80-p479
Year Of Independence 1776
BL-v66-My 15 '70-p1160
Comw-v92-My 22 '70-p251
GT-v88-F '71-p139
HB-v46-O '70-p492
KR-v38-Mr 15 '70-p324
PW-v197-Mr 30 '70-p65
Year Of Lincoln 1861
BL-v67-N 15 '70-p267
CCB-B-v25-N '71-p42
GT-v88-F '71-p139
HB-v47-Je '71-p299
KR-v38-O 15 '70-p1153
LJ-v95-D 15 '70-p4383
The Year Of The Flying Machine 1903
KR-v45-S 15 '77-p992
RT-v32-D '78-p364
SLJ-v24-Mr '78-p136
The Year Of The Horseless Carriage 1801
CCB-B-v29-N '75-p43
Inst-v85-O '75-p192
KR-v43-My 15 '75-p570
LA-v53-My '76-p514
SLJ-v22-Mr '76-p102
Year Of The Pilgrims 1620
BL-v66-F 1 '70-p669
Comw-v92-My 22 '70-p251
GT-v88-F '71-p139
HB-v46-F '70-p50
KR-v37-N 15 '69-p1198
LJ-v95-My 15 '70-p1942
PW-v196-D 8 '69-p48

* * *

FOSTER, Hal
The Minks' Cry
SLJ-v29-N '82-p83
Prince Valiant. Vol. 2
BW-v14-O 14 '84-p11

* * *

FOSTER, Janet
A Cabin Full Of Mice
BIC-v9-D '80-p18
Brit Bk N C-Autumn '81-p29
Can Child Lit-#21 '81-p86
In Rev-v15-Ap '81-p36
Quill & Q-v47-F '81-p46
The Wilds Of Whip-Poor-Will Farm
BIC-v11-D '82-p10
Can Child Lit-#33 '84-p57
Quill & Q-v49-Mr '83-p65

* * *

FOSTER, Joanna
Pete's Puddle
BL-v65-My 1 '69-p1021
CCB-B-v22-Je '69-p157
CLW-v41-D '69-p258
CSM-v61-My 1 '69-pB4
HB-v45-Ap '69-p161
KR-v37-F 15 '69-p169
LJ-v94-Mr 15 '69-p1318
PW-v195-F 24 '69-p65

* * *

FOSTER, John
The Experience Of Sport
GP-v14-Ap '76-p2856
Fairs And Circuses
TES-O 21 '77-p24
Families And Friends
TES-O 21 '77-p24
First Love
JB-v42-Je '78-p166
A First Poetry Book
BL-v76-My 15 '80-p1362
BW-v10-My 11 '80-p15
Brit Bk N C-Spring '80-p2
CCB-B-v34-S '80-p7
GP-v18-S '79-p3583
JB-v44-Je '80-p131
NYTBR-v85-Ap 27 '80-p61
SLJ-v27-S '80-p70
SLJ-v29-Ag '83-p65
Sch Lib-v27-D '79-p378
TES-Mr 7 '80-p46
A Fourth Poetry Book
CCB-B-v37-S '83-p6
JB-v47-Je '83-p122
SLJ-v29-Ag '83-p65
Sch Lib-v31-Je '83-p156
TES-Mr 4 '83-p32

FOSTER, John (continued)
King Cinder
GP-v16-Ap '78-p3282
Legendary And Fantastic
TES-O 21 '77-p24
People Of The West
TES-O 21 '77-p24
A Second Poetry Book
SLJ-v29-Ag '83-p65
TES-Mr 4 '83-p32
A Third Poetry Book
CCB-B-v37-S '83-p6
JB-v47-F '83-p24
SLJ-v29-Ag '83-p65
Sch Lib-v31-Je '83-p156
TES-Mr 4 '83-p32

* * *

FOSTER, John L
Disasters
Sch Lib-v29-Je '81-p127
A Second Poetry Book
Sch Lib-v29-S '81-p246
TLS-Mr 27 '81-p344
Treasure
Sch Lib-v29-Je '81-p127

* * *

FOSTER, John T
The Flight Of The Lone Eagle
BL-v71-N 15 '74-p343
KR-v42-Ag 1 '74-p806
SLJ-v21-Ja '75-p53
The Gallant Gray Trotter
BL-v70-Je 15 '74-p1153
BS-v34-My 15 '74-p101
KR-v42-F 15 '74-p191
LJ-v99-D 15 '74-p3266
The Sea Miners
BL-v73-Jl 1 '77-p1652
CCB-B-v30-Je '77-p156
Cur R-v16-O '77-p254
SB-v13-Mr '78-p199
SLJ-v24-O '77-p123

* * *

FOSTER, Laura Louise
Keeping The Plants You Pick
BL-v67-O 15 '70-p191
BL-v67-Ap 1 '71-p660
CCB-B-v24-F '71-p90
Comw-v93-N 20 '70-p207
HB-v46-O '70-p490
KR-v38-Je 15 '70-p640
LJ-v95-S 15 '70-p3061
SB-v6-S '70-p139
TN-v27-Ap '71-p305

* * *

FOSTER, Leslie
Building Maths
TES-My 4 '84-p28
Circus Maths
TES-My 4 '84-p28
Clothes Maths
TES-My 4 '84-p28
Farm Maths
TES-My 4 '84-p28
Garage Maths
TES-My 4 '84-p28
Going Places Maths
TES-My 4 '84-p28
Kitchen Maths
TES-My 4 '84-p28
Playground Maths
TES-My 4 '84-p28
Seaside Maths
TES-My 4 '84-p28
Toyshop Maths
TES-My 4 '84-p28

* * *

FOSTER, M
Creating Patterns From Grasses, Seedheads And Cones
JB-v47-F '83-p40
Flower Preserving For Beginners
JB-v42-Je '78-p152

* * *

FOSTER, Marian Curtis
Miss Flora McFlimsey's Halloween
CCB-B-v26-O '72-p29
KR-v40-Ag 1 '72-p857
LJ-v97-N 15 '72-p3798
NYTBR-O 29 '72-p8
PW-v202-O 9 '72-p113
Miss Flora McFlimsey's May Day
CCB-B-v22-My '69-p145
CSM-v61-My 1 '69-pB2
KR-v37-F 1 '69-p95
LJ-v94-Ap 15 '69-p1772
PW-v195-Ja 27 '69-p97

* * *

FOSTER, Ruth
Knowing In My Bones
Dance-v51-S '77-p100
JB-v41-Ap '77-p124
The Stone Horsemen
CE-v42-My '66-p566
KR-v33-O 15 '65-p1076
LJ-v90-D 15 '65-p5514
RT-v35-N '81-p197

* * *

FOSTER, Sally
A Pup Grows Up
BL-v80-Je 15 '84-p1483
CCB-B-v37-Je '84-p185
SLJ-v31-O '84-p146

* * *

FOULDS, Elfrida Vipont Brown
Children Of The Mayflower
CCB-B-v24-D '70-p68
LJ-v95-Jl '70-p2537
PW-v197-My 25 '70-p57
TLS-D 4 '69-p1390
The Elephant And The Bad Baby
BL-v66-Ap 15 '70-p1044
BW-v4-My 17 '70-p4
CCB-B-v23-Ap '70-p136
HB-v46-Je '70-p287
KR-v37-D 15 '69-p1314
LJ-v95-My 15 '70-p1934
NS-v78-O 31 '69-p626
NYTBR-Mr 22 '70-p26
Obs-N 30 '69-p35
PW-v196-D 8 '69-p47
SR-v53-Mr 21 '70-p39
TLS-O 16 '69-p1196

* * *

FOULDS, Elfrida Vipont Brown
The Elephant And The Bad Baby
HB-v60-Je '84-p365

* * *

FOULDS, Elfrida Vipont Brown
Towards A High Attic
BS-v31-Ag 15 '72-p236
CCB-B-v25-S '71-p17
CLW-v43-F '72-p363
KR-v39-My 15 '71-p565
LJ-v96-S 15 '71-p2933

* * *

FOURNEL, Paul
Les Aventures Tres Douces De Timothee Le Reveur
BL-v79-Je 15 '83-p1345

* * *

FOURNIER, Andree-Paule
Skir The Fox
GP-v22-S '83-p4128

FOURNIER, Andree-Paule (continued)
JB-v47-Ag '83-p162
Obs-My 8 '83-p31

* * *

FOURTH Dimension. Book 2
Lis-v92-N 7 '74-p615
TLS-D 6 '74-p1383

* * *

FOURWAYS: The Language Project (Macmillan Education)
TES-Mr 6 '81-p31

* * *

FOWKE, Edith
Folktales Of French Canada
BIC-v9-Ap '80-p31
Can Child Lit-#18 '80-p96
In Rev-v14-Ag '80-p47
Ring Around The Moon
BL-v73-Ap 15 '77-p1268
CCB-B-v30-Je '77-p157
CE-v54-Ap '78-p307
Cur R-v18-F '79-p44
KR-v45-Mr 1 '77-p228
SLJ-v24-S '77-p106
TN-v34-Winter '78-p190
Riot Of Riddles
BIC-v11-D '82-p9
Sally Go Round The Sun
BL-v67-S 1 '70-p56
CCB-B-v24-N '70-p42
CE-v61-S '84-p42
CSM-v63-Ap 24 '71-p17
Comw-v93-N 20 '70-p206
KR-v38-S 15 '70-p1041
LJ-v96-S 15 '71-p2905
NY-v46-D 5 '70-p209
NYTBR, pt.2-N 8 '70-p54
PW-v198-N 30 '70-p42
SR-v53-S 19 '70-p34
TN-v34-Winter '78-p190

* * *

FOWLER, Carol
Daisy Hooee Nampeyo
BL-v74-O 1 '77-p288
CCB-B-v31-N '77-p46
SLJ-v24-Mr '78-p127
Dance
BL-v76-Mr 1 '80-p981
SLJ-v27-O '80-p145

* * *

FOWLER, Peter
Niagara
BIC-v10-N '81-p15
CG-v101-D '81-p86
In Rev-v15-O '81-p35

* * *

FOWLER, Richard
The Amazing Journey Of Spacecraft H-20
Brit Bk N C-Autumn '82-p5
Inspector Smart Gets The Message!
Brit Bk N C-Autumn '82-p5
PW-v225-Ja 6 '84-p85
RT-v37-My '84-p856
TLS-N 26 '82-p1304
Ted And Dolly's Magic Carpet Ride
Brit Bk N C-Autumn '82-p5

* * *

FOWLER, Sina Fay
Food For 50
J Ho E-v63-D '71-p695
SLJ-v27-N '80-p52

* * *

FOWLER, Virginie
Folk Arts Around The World And How To Make Them
CBRS-v9-Ag '81-p127
CCB-B-v35-O '81-p28
Cr Crafts-v8-F '82-p17
HB-v57-O '81-p550
SLJ-v28-Ja '82-p86
Paperworks
BL-v79-Mr 1 '83-p906
CBRS-v11-Ja '83-p49
HB-v59-F '83-p61
SLJ-v29-Mr '83-p175

* * *

FOWLER, Zinita
Monster Magic
Emerg Lib-v11-N '83-p28
TN-v40-Fall '83-p111
Those Singin', Dancin' Settlers
TN-v36-Winter '80-p205

* * *

FOWLES, John
Cinderella
GP-v13-Ja '75-p2552
JB-v39-F '75-p15
KR-v44-My 15 '76-p588
LA-v54-Ja '77-p77
LR-v25-Spring '75-p34
PW-v209-Ap 5 '76-p102
SLJ-v22-My '76-p49
Spec-v233-D 7 '74-p739
TLS-D 6 '74-p1382

* * *

FOX, Charles Philip
When Spring Comes
CCB-B-v18-F '65-p85
LJ-v90-Ja 15 '65-p376
When Summer Comes
CCB-B-v19-Jl '66-p178
LJ-v91-Jl '66-p3552

* * *

* * *

FOX, Dorothea W
Miss Twiggley's Tree
CCB-B-v20-Ja '67-p73
CSM-v58-N 3 '66-pB3
Inst-v76-F '67-p186
KR-v34-S 1 '66-p897
LJ-v92-Ja 15 '67-p328
PW-v190-Ag 29 '66-p344

* * *

FOX, Julian
A Cup Of Coffee
SLJ-v30-F '84-p70
TES-Ap 13 '84-p40
The Water From Your Tap
TES-N 5 '82-p28

* * *

FOX, Larry
Football Basics
BL-v78-Ap 1 '82-p1023

* * *

FOX, Lilla M
Costumes And Customs Of The British Isles
CCB-B-v28-Ja '75-p77
LJ-v99-N 15 '74-p3045
LR-v24-Summer '74-p274
Folk Costume From Eastern Europe
BL-v74-F 1 '78-p924
GP-v16-D '77-p3234
JB-v42-F '78-p39
JB-v42-Je '78-p152

* * *

FOX, Margaret
The Street Of The Starving Cats
Brit Bk N C-Spring '82-p10
TES-Ap 2 '82-p27

* * *

FOX, Mary V
Barbara Walters: The News Her Way
KR-v48-Jl 15 '80-p912
SLJ-v26-Ja '80-p69
SLJ-v27-N '80-p74
Jane Fonda: Something To Fight For
KR-v48-Jl 15 '80-p912
SLJ-v26-Ja '80-p69
Jane Goodall: Living Chimp Style
BL-v78-F 15 '82-p756
CCB-B-v35-F '82-p106
SLJ-v28-My '82-p61
Janet Guthrie: Foot To The Floor
BL-v78-S 15 '81-p104
SLJ-v28-F '82-p75
Justice Sandra Day O'Connor
BL-v79-Ap 1 '83-p1033
SLJ-v29-Ag '83-p65
VOYA-v6-Je '83-p102
Taking Part
Cur R-v20-N '81-p471

* * *

FOX, Mary Virginia
Belva Lockwood
Comw-v102-N 21 '75-p566
Lady For The Defense
BB-v3-Ag '75-p4
HB-v51-Ag '75-p391
KR-v43-Ap 15 '75-p461
PW-v207-F 24 '75-p116
SLJ-v22-S '75-p102

* * *

FOX, Michael
The Touchlings
SLJ-v28-N '81-p75

* * *

FOX, Michael W
Dr. Fox's Fables
SLJ-v27-My '81-p55
Ramu And Chennai
HB-v52-Ap '76-p153
KR-v43-D 1 '75-p1335
SLJ-v22-Ja '76-p45
Sundance Coyote
ACSB-v8-Fall '75-p12
BL-v70-Jl 15 '74-p1252
CCB-B-v28-D '74-p62
HB-v50-D '74-p703
KR-v42-Je 15 '74-p635
KR-v43-Ja 1 '75-p6
NYTBR-N 3 '74-p46
PW-v205-Jl 1 '74-p82
Vixie
CCB-B-v27-My '74-p142
CSM-v65-N 7 '73-pB5
HB-v50-Ap '74-p162
KR-v41-D 15 '73-p1366
The Way Of The Dolphin
BL-v78-Ap 1 '82-p1017
SB-v18-Mr '83-p210
SLJ-v29-N '82-p83
What Is Your Cat Saying?
ASBYP-v16-Winter '83-p24
BL-v78-Jl '82-p1443
KR-v50-My 1 '82-p556
SLJ-v29-O '82-p151
What Is Your Dog Saying?
BB-v6-F '78-p2
KR-v45-O 1 '77-p1051
SLJ-v24-Ja '78-p94
SR-v5-N 26 '77-p40
Teacher-v96-Mr '79-p30
Whitepaws
KR-v47-Ag 1 '79-p853
SB-v15-Mr '80-p228
SLJ-v26-S '79-p136
Wild Dogs Three
BL-v74-O 1 '77-p288
KR-v45-Ap 1 '77-p355
PW-v211-Ap 4 '77-p89
SLJ-v24-S '77-p107
The Wolf
BL-v69-Ap 15 '73-p810
BW-v7-N 11 '73-p3C
CCB-B-v26-Je '73-p154
HB-v49-Ag '73-p392
KR-v41-Ja 15 '73-p62
KR-v41-D 15 '73-p1352
LJ-v98-Ap 15 '73-p1386
NYTBR-Jl 29 '73-p8
PW-v203-Mr 12 '73-p65

* * *

FOX, N
Old Is Beautiful, Too!
J Geront-v39-My '84-p382

* * *

FOX, Paula
Blowfish Live In The Sea
BL-v67-F 15 '71-p492
BS-v30-F 15 '71-p506
CCB-B-v24-Mr '71-p106
CSM-v63-My 6 '71-pB6
HB-v46-D '70-p623
HB-v53-O '77-p517
KR-v38-N 1 '70-p1200
LJ-v96-Ja 15 '71-p275
NYRB-v18-Ap 20 '72-p13
NYTBR, pt.2-N 8 '70-p12
Obs-Ap 2 '72-p28
PW-v198-N 30 '70-p41
RT-v32-My '79-p973
SLJ-v25-F '79-p29
SR-v54-Ja 23 '71-p71
Spec-v228-Ap 22 '72-p625
TLS-Ap 28 '72-p477
Teacher-v92-My '75-p93

FOX, Paula (continued)

Good Ethan
Am-v129-D 1 '73-p426
CCB-B-v27-S '73-p8
HB-v49-Ag '73-p374
HB-v53-O '77-p517
KR-v41-Ap 1 '73-p380
PW-v203-Ap 9 '73-p66
Teacher-v91-Ap '74-p86

How Many Miles To Babylon?
Atl-v220-D '67-p136
BL-v69-My 1 '73-p837
BL-v77-S 15 '80-p114
BW-v1-O 8 '67-p24
CCB-B-v21-D '67-p59
HB-v43-O '67-p593
KR-v35-Jl 15 '67-p807
LJ-v92-D 15 '67-p4612
NYTBR-v72-S 3 '67-p24
NYTBR-v72-S 24 '67-p34
NYTBR-v72-N 5 '67-p66
NYTBR-v88-Ja 30 '83-p31
NYTBR, pt.2-N 8 '70-p30
NYTBR, pt.2-F 13 '72-p12
Obs-Ag 4 '68-p22
Obs-Ja 14 '73-p30
PW-v198-Jl 13 '70-p166
Punch-v255-Jl 3 '68-p33
SLJ-v25-F '79-p29
SR-v50-N 11 '67-p46
TLS-Je 6 '68-p583
Trav-v24-Ap '68-p323

The King's Falcon
BL-v66-S 1 '69-p54
CCB-B-v23-S '69-p8
CE-v47-O '70-p29
HB-v45-Ag '69-p410
KR-v37-My 1 '69-p502
LJ-v94-Je 15 '69-p2500
LJ-v94-D 15 '69-p4581
NYTBR-Je 8 '69-p44
NYTBR, pt.2-My 4 '69-p26
NYTBR, pt.2-N 9 '69-p61
PW-v195-My 19 '69-p70
SR-v52-Jl 19 '69-p43

Likely Place
CCB-B-v21-N '67-p41
CE-v44-Ja '68-p322
KR-v34-D 1 '66-p1222
LJ-v92-Mr 15 '67-p1315
NYTBR-v72-Mr 12 '67-p27
NYTBR-v72-N 5 '67-p66
PW-v191-Ap 3 '67-p56
SR-v50-My 13 '67-p54
TLS-O 3 '68-p1112

The Little Swineherd And Other Tales
BL-v75-O 1 '78-p292
CCB-B-v32-N '78-p43
CE-v55-Ap '79-p296
CSM-v70-O 23 '78-pB2
Comw-v105-N 10 '78-p731
GP-v18-Mr '80-p3647
HB-v55-O '78-p516
JB-v43-D '79-p324
KR-v46-O 1 '78-p1071
LA-v56-Ap '79-p442
NYTBR-v86-Mr 22 '81-p35
PW-v213-Je 19 '78-p100
RT-v32-My '79-p973
SLJ-v25-O '78-p144

Maurice's Room
Atl-v218-D '66-p154
BL-v63-N 15 '66-p376
CCB-B-v20-N '66-p42
CSM-v58-Ja 5 '67-p7
GT-v84-D '66-p122
HB-v42-O '66-p561
Inst-v76-N '66-p50
KR-v34-F 1 '66-p109
LJ-v91-S 15 '66-p4330
NYTBR-v71-N 6 '66-p44
PW-v190-Ag 8 '66-p60
SR-v49-O 22 '66-p62

A Place Apart
BL-v77-O 15 '80-p325
BOT-v4-F '81-p79
B Rpt-v1-Mr '83-p24
BS-v40-Mr '81-p448
BW-v11-F 8 '81-p7
BW-v12-F 14 '82-p12
CBRS-v9-Ja '81-p37
CCB-B-v34-N '80-p52
CSM-v72-O 14 '80-pB1
GP-v20-Ja '82-p4010
HB-v56-D '80-p648
JB-v45-O '81-p209
KR-v48-S 15 '80-p1235
Mac-v93-D 15 '80-p57
NS-v102-D 4 '81-p20
NW-v96-D 1 '80-p104
NYTBR-v85-N 9 '80-p55
NYTBR-v87-Ja 10 '82-p35
Obs-My 10 '81-p33
Obs-Jl 19 '81-p29
PW-v218-N 28 '80-p50
SLJ-v27-O '80-p155
TES-Je 5 '81-p39

Portrait Of Ivan
A Lib-v1-Ap '70-p385
BL-v66-F 1 '70-p670
BW-v4-Mr 29 '70-p12
CCB-B-v23-F '70-p96
GW-v103-D 19 '70-p21
HB-v46-Ap '70-p159
KR-v37-O 15 '69-p1112
LJ-v94-D 15 '69-p4581
LJ-v94-D 15 '69-p4604
NYTBR-D 7 '69-p68
NYTBR, pt.2-N 9 '69-p34
NYTBR, pt.2-N 9 '69-p60
PW-v196-N 24 '69-p42
SLJ-v25-F '79-p29
SR-v52-D 20 '69-p30
TLS-D 11 '70-p1451
Teacher-v91-My '74-p84

The Slave Dancer
B&B-v23-N '77-p82
BL-v70-Ja 1 '74-p484
BL-v70-Mr 15 '74-p827
BL-v80-S 1 '83-p95
BW-F 10 '74-p4
CCB-B-v27-Ja '74-p77
CE-v50-Ap '74-p335
CLW-v47-N '75-p165
EJ-v66-O '77-p58
EJ-v69-S '80-p87
Emerg Lib-v11-Ja '84-p21
HB-v49-D '73-p596
HB-v53-O '77-p515
KR-v41-O 1 '73-p1095
KR-v41-D 15 '73-p1350
LJ-v98-D 15 '73-p3689
LJ-v98-D 15 '73-p3711
Lis-v92-N 7 '74-p613
NS-v88-N 8 '74-p666
NS-v100-N 28 '80-p28
NYTBR-Ja 20 '74-p8
Obs-D 8 '74-p30
Obs-Je 26 '77-p29
PW-v204-D 10 '73-p36
RT-v32-My '79-p973
SLJ-v25-F '79-p29
TES-Je 10 '83-p22
TES-Jl 15 '83-p18
TLS-D 6 '74-p1375
TN-v30-Ap '74-p243
Teacher-v91-My '74-p79
VV-v19-D 16 '74-p52

The Stone-Faced Boy
BL-v65-Ja 15 '69-p546
BL-v65-Ap 1 '69-p900
BW-v3-Je 22 '69-p12
CCB-B-v22-F '69-p92
Choice-v14-N '77-p1178
HB-v45-F '69-p53
HB-v60-Ap '84-p219

FOX, Paula (continued)
KR-v36-O 1 '68-p1114
LJ-v94-Ap 15 '69-p1781
LJ-v94-My 15 '69-p2072
NS-v78-O 31 '69-p625
NYTBR-v73-N 3 '68-p33
Obs-N 30 '69-p35
RT-v32-My '79-p973
SE-v33-My '69-p555
SLJ-v25-D '78-p33
SLJ-v25-F '79-p29
SR-v51-N 9 '68-p66
Spec-v223-N 1 '69-p604
TLS-O 16 '69-p1198

* * *

FOX, Robert B
Walks Two Worlds
SLJ-v30-D '83-p65

* * *

FOX, Siv Cedering
The Blue Horse
BL-v75-Je 15 '79-p1535
HB-v55-O '79-p545
KR-v47-Jl 1 '79-p737
NYTBR-Ap 29 '79-p25
PW-v215-Ap 16 '79-p75
SLJ-v26-O '79-p138
SLJ-v26-Mr '80-p105

* * *

FOX, Sonia
Chicago Burns
CCB-B-v24-My '71-p134
KR-v39-Mr 1 '71-p239
LJ-v96-Ap 15 '71-p1502

* * *

FOX, Sonny
Jokes And Tips For The Joketeller
BL-v72-Mr 15 '76-p1041
KR-v44-Ja 15 '76-p75
SLJ-v22-Ap '76-p73

* * *

FOX, William W
The Amazing Bee
CCB-B-v31-N '77-p46
KR-v45-Je 1 '77-p577
SB-v14-My '78-p39
SLJ-v24-O '77-p100

* * *

FOXGLOVE, Lady
See Blue, Rose

* * *

FOZZIE'S Big Book Of Side-Splitting Jokes
SLJ-v28-S '81-p124

* * *

FRADIN, Dennis B
Alabama In Words And Pictures
SLJ-v27-Mr '81-p131
Alaska
Cur R-v17-Ag '78-p232
SLJ-v24-Ap '78-p68
Archaeology
BL-v80-F 15 '84-p854
SLJ-v30-Mr '84-p142
Arizona In Words And Pictures
BL-v76-My 15 '80-p1363
SLJ-v26-Ag '80-p50
TN-v41-Fall '84-p64
Arkansas In Words And Pictures
SLJ-v27-Mr '81-p131
Astronomy
BL-v79-Ag '83-p1462
SLJ-v30-O '83-p145
Bad Luck Tony
BL-v75-D 1 '78-p615
CCB-B-v32-D '78-p61
PW-v214-S 11 '78-p90
RT-v33-O '79-p45
SLJ-v25-Ja '79-p41
Beyond The Mountain, Beyond The Forest
Cur R-v18-O '79-p338
SLJ-v26-S '79-p136
Blizzards And Winter Weather
BL-v80-F 15 '84-p856
SLJ-v30-Mr '84-p159
California
BL-v73-My 15 '77-p1419
Cur R-v17-Ag '78-p232
SLJ-v24-S '77-p107
Cara
SLJ-v24-Ap '78-p69
Cave Painter
SLJ-v25-S '78-p108
Colorado In Words And Pictures
SLJ-v27-Mr '81-p131
Comets, Asteroids, And Meteors
BL-v80-Jl '84-p1548
Connecticut In Words And Pictures
SLJ-v26-Ag '80-p50
Delaware In Words And Pictures
SLJ-v27-Mr '81-p131
Droughts
BL-v80-F 15 '84-p856
SLJ-v30-Mr '84-p159
Earthquakes
ASBYP-v16-Fall '83-p24
SB-v18-My '83-p273
SLJ-v29-Ap '83-p113
Farming
BL-v80-F 15 '84-p854
SLJ-v30-Mr '84-p144
Fires
ASBYP-v16-Fall '83-p24
BL-v79-F 1 '83-p723
SB-v19-S '83-p31
SLJ-v29-Ap '83-p113
Floods
ASBYP-v16-Fall '83-p24
BL-v79-F 1 '83-p723
SB-v19-S '83-p31
SLJ-v29-Ap '83-p113
Florida In Words And Pictures
SLJ-v27-Mr '81-p131
Georgia In Words And Pictures
SLJ-v28-O '81-p128
Hawaii In Words And Pictures
RT-v34-D '80-p352
SLJ-v26-Ag '80-p50
Hurricanes
ASBYP-v16-Fall '83-p24
BL-v79-F 1 '83-p723
SB-v19-S '83-p31
SLJ-v29-Ap '83-p113
Idaho In Words And Pictures
SLJ-v27-Mr '81-p131
Illinois
BL-v73-D 1 '76-p538
Cur R-v17-Ag '78-p232
SLJ-v23-F '77-p56
Indiana In Words And Pictures
SLJ-v26-Ag '80-p50
Iowa In Words And Pictures
SLJ-v26-Ag '80-p50
Kansas In Words And Pictures
SLJ-v27-Mr '81-p131

FRADIN, Dennis B (continued)
Kentucky In Words And Pictures
SLJ-v28-O '81-p128
Louisiana In Words And Pictures
SLJ-v28-O '81-p128
Maine In Words And Pictures
SLJ-v26-Ag '80-p50
Maryland In Words And Pictures
SLJ-v27-Mr '81-p131
Massachusetts In Words And Pictures
SLJ-v28-O '81-p128
Michigan In Words And Pictures
SLJ-v26-Ag '80-p50
Minnesota In Words And Pictures
SLJ-v26-Ag '80-p50
Mississippi In Words And Pictures
SLJ-v27-Mr '81-p131
Missouri In Words And Pictures
SLJ-v27-Mr '81-p131
Montana In Words And Pictures
SLJ-v28-O '81-p128
Movies
BL-v80-F 15 '84-p854
SLJ-v30-Ap '84-p101
Nebraska In Words And Pictures
CCB-B-v33-Je '80-p189
SLJ-v26-Ag '80-p50
The Netherlands
BL-v79-Ag '83-p1464
SLJ-v30-S '83-p122
Nevada In Words And Pictures
SLJ-v28-O '81-p128
New Hampshire In Words And Pictures
SLJ-v28-O '81-p128
New Jersey In Words And Pictures
SLJ-v27-Mr '81-p131
New Mexico In Words And Pictures
SLJ-v28-O '81-p128
The New Spear
Cur R-v18-O '79-p338
SLJ-v26-S '79-p136
New York In Words And Pictures
SLJ-v28-O '81-p128
North Carolina In Words And Pictures
SLJ-v26-Ag '80-p50
North Dakota In Words And Pictures
SLJ-v28-O '81-p128
North Star
SLJ-v25-S '78-p108
Ohio
BL-v73-My 15 '77-p1419
Cur R-v17-Ag '78-p232
SLJ-v24-S '77-p107
Oklahoma In Words And Pictures
SLJ-v28-O '81-p128
Olympics
BL-v80-F 15 '84-p854
SLJ-v30-Mr '84-p140
Oregon In Words And Pictures
SLJ-v27-Mr '81-p131
Pennsylvania In Words And Pictures
SLJ-v26-Ag '80-p50
The Republic Of Ireland
BL-v81-S 1 '84-p63
Rhode Island In Words And Pictures
SLJ-v28-O '81-p128
Skylab
BL-v80-Jl '84-p1548
South Carolina In Words And Pictures
SLJ-v26-Ag '80-p50
South Dakota In Words And Pictures
SLJ-v28-O '81-p128
Tennessee In Words And Pictures
SLJ-v26-Ag '80-p50
Texas In Words And Pictures
SLJ-v28-O '81-p128
SLJ-v30-N '83-p39
Tornadoes
ASBYP-v16-Fall '83-p24
SB-v19-S '83-p31
SLJ-v29-Ap '83-p113
Utah In Words And Pictures
SLJ-v27-Mr '81-p131
Vermont In Words And Pictures
SLJ-v26-Ag '80-p50
Virginia
BL-v73-D 1 '76-p538
Cur R-v17-Ag '78-p232
SLJ-v23-F '77-p56
Volcanoes
ASBYP-v16-Fall '83-p24
SB-v18-My '83-p273
SLJ-v29-Ap '83-p113
Washington In Words And Pictures
SLJ-v27-Mr '81-p131
Wisconsin
Cur R-v17-Ag '78-p232
SLJ-v24-Ap '78-p68
Wyoming In Words And Pictures
SLJ-v26-Ag '80-p50
Young People's Stories Of Our States
Cur R-v19-S '80-p368

* * *

FRAME, Paul
Drawing Cats And Kittens
BL-v76-O 1 '79-p274
SLJ-v26-Mr '80-p130
Drawing Dogs And Puppies
CLW-v51-O '79-p141
SLJ-v25-N '78-p61
Drawing Sharks, Whales, Dolphins, And Seals
ASBYP-v17-Winter '84-p19
BL-v79-Jl '83-p1400
SLJ-v29-Ap '83-p113

* * *

FRAMPTON, V B
True Stories For The Junior Assembly
TES-Ap 24 '81-p22
TES-My 8 '81-p27

* * *

FRANCA, Mary
Rabo De Gato
BL-v79-Jl '83-p1406
SLJ-v30-My '84-p35

* * *

FRANCHERE, Ruth
Cesar Chavez
BL-v67-N 1 '70-p226
BL-v68-Je 15 '72-p894
BL-v70-O 15 '73-p225
CC-v87-D 16 '70-p1516
CCB-B-v24-F '71-p90
Comw-v93-N 20 '70-p203
GT-v88-F '71-p139

FRANCHERE, Ruth (continued)
Inst-v80-O '70-p142
KR-v38-Ag 15 '70-p879
LJ-v96-Mr 15 '71-p1132
NYTBR, pt.2-N 8 '70-p46
RT-v36-D '82-p277
Teacher-v91-S '73-p154
Stampede North
BL-v65-Ap 15 '69-p960
HB-v45-Ag '69-p416
KR-v37-Ja 1 '69-p9
LJ-v94-My 15 '69-p2099
Travels Of Colin O'Dae
BL-v63-Ja 1 '67-p488
CCB-B-v20-Ap '67-p120
CE-v44-N '67-p188
EL-v88-Ap '68-p352
KR-v34-O 1 '66-p1052
LJ-v92-Ja 15 '67-p334
NYTBR-v72-Ja 8 '67-p30
SR-v50-F 18 '67-p42
Westward By Canal
BL-v69-D 15 '72-p404
CCB-B-v26-F '73-p89
KR-v40-S 1 '72-p1031
LJ-v98-Ap 15 '73-p1386
SE-v37-D '73-p786
TN-v29-Ap '73-p251

* * *

FRANCIS, Anna B
Pleasant Dreams
BL-v80-O 1 '83-p261
CBRS-v12-N '83-p24
CCB-B-v37-F '84-p107
KR-v51-S 1 '83-pJ148
LA-v61-Ja '84-p65
SLJ-v30-N '83-p62

* * *

FRANCIS, Barrie
The Commonwealth
SLJ-v30-My '84-p78

* * *

FRANCIS, Dorothy B
Captain Morgana Mason
BL-v78-Jl '82-p1443
CBRS-v10-Jl '82-p127
SLJ-v29-S '82-p120
The Flint Hills Foal
BB-v5-Ap '77-p2
RT-v31-Ap '78-p841
SLJ-v23-Ja '77-p91
Run Of The Sea Witch
CSM-v70-My 3 '78-pB2
KR-v46-Mr 1 '78-p244
LA-v55-O '78-p864
Par-v53-Je '78-p40
SE-v43-Ap '79-p302
SLJ-v25-N '78-p61
Shoplifting
BL-v76-N 15 '79-p501
CCB-B-v33-My '80-p171
J Read-v24-Mr '81-p549
SLJ-v26-Ap '80-p123
Vandalism
BL-v79-Ap 1 '83-p1018
CBRS-v11-Spring '83-p123
SLJ-v30-N '83-p92

* * *

FRANCIS, F
Favourite Stories
JB-v39-F '75-p38

* * *

FRANCIS, Frank
Jack-A-Dandy
NS-v90-N 28 '75-p688
The Magic Wallpaper
CLW-v42-My '71-p580
GP-v17-S '78-p3401
HB-v46-D '70-p605
LJ-v96-Jl '71-p2357
PW-v198-S 7 '70-p61
TLS-Jl 2 '70-p717
Natasha's New Doll
LJ-v99-D 15 '74-p3262
Obs-D 5 '71-p34
SR/W-v2-N 30 '74-p28
TLS-D 3 '71-p1514
Pog
TES-Je 11 '82-p37
Silver Buckles
NS-v90-N 28 '75-p688
Tom Had A Horse
GP-v22-Ja '84-p4201
JB-v48-F '84-p12
Obs-D 4 '83-p32
TES-Ja 13 '84-p44

* * *

FRANCKE, Gunhild
Last Train West
GP-v16-Ja '78-p3245
JB-v42-Je '78-p152
TES-Ja 27 '78-p28

* * *

FRANCO, John M
American Indian Contributors To American Life
Inst-v86-F '77-p196
American Women Contributors To American Life
Cur R-v16-Ag '77-p187
Inst-v86-F '77-p196
Hispano-American Contributors To American Life
Inter BC-v14-#1 '83-p16

* * *

FRANCO, Marjorie
Love In A Different Key
BL-v80-O 1 '83-p233
B Rpt-v2-Ja '84-p33
CBRS-v12-Ap '84-p95
CCB-B-v37-Mr '84-p126
KR-v51-N 1 '83-pJ202
SLJ-v30-Ja '84-p85
VOYA-v7-Ap '84-p30
So Who Hasn't Got Problems?
BL-v75-Je 1 '79-p1491
BS-v39-Ag '79-p167
CBRS-v7-Je '79-p107
CCB-B-v33-S '79-p7
GP-v19-S '80-p3756
JB-v44-Ag '80-p188
KR-v47-Je 15 '79-p689
NS-v100-N 28 '80-p30
Obs-Ag 24 '80-p27
SLJ-v26-S '79-p136
Sch Lib-v28-D '80-p393

* * *

FRANCOIS, Andre
Les Larmes De Crocodile
BL-v74-N 1 '77-p486
You Are Ri-Di-Cu-Lous
CCB-B-v24-F '71-p91
LJ-v96-Ap 15 '71-p1492
NY-v46-D 5 '70-p215
NYTBR, pt.2-N 8 '70-p53
PW-v198-O 12 '70-p55

* * *

FRANK, Josette
More Poems To Read To The Very Young
CCB-B-v22-Ja '69-p77
CSM-v60-N 7 '68-pB3
KR-v36-Ag 1 '68-p821
LJ-v94-Ja 15 '69-p286
Poems To Read To The Very Young
BL-v79-Ja 1 '83-p620
CCB-B-v36-F '83-p106
CSM-v75-Je 29 '83-p9

FRANK, Josette (continued)
Cur R-v22-D '83-p45

* * *

FRANK, Penny
The Lion Story Bible
TES-N 16 '84-p27

* * *

FRANK, Phil
Subee Lives On A Houseboat
BL-v76-Ap 1 '80-p1126
SLJ-v27-S '80-p70

* * *

FRANKEL, Alona
The Family Of Tiny White Elephants
PW-v218-O 10 '80-p74
SLJ-v27-D '80-p42
Once Upon A Potty
Par-v58-Je '83-p64
SLJ-v27-D '80-p42

* * *

FRANKEL, Edward
DNA
BB-v7-My '79-p4
BL-v75-Je 1 '79-p1491
SB-v15-D '79-p149
SLJ-v25-Ap '79-p68
DNA Ladder Of Life
BL-v61-Ja 1 '65-p435
CCB-B-v19-D '65-p62
CLW-v36-F '65-p416
NH-v74-N '65-p17
SA-v213-D '65-p116

* * *

FRANKLAND, David
Old Macdonald Had A Farm
Inst-v90-N '80-p156

* * *

FRANKLIN, Benjamin
The Whistle
BL-v72-O 1 '75-p233
SLJ-v22-F '76-p38

* * *

FRANKLIN, Paula A
Indians Of North America
BL-v76-D 1 '79-p556
CCB-B-v33-Ap '80-p151
J Read-v23-My '80-p762
SB-v16-S '80-p5
SLJ-v26-Mr '80-p140

* * *

FRANKLIN Roosevelt: The Absorbing True-Life Story Of The President Who Defeated Depression And Dictators
SLJ-v23-Ap '77-p59

* * *

FRANKO, Ivan
Fox Mykyta
BL-v75-F 15 '79-p933
BW-D 10 '78-pE5
Can Child Lit-#17 '80-p81
HB-v55-Ap '79-p191
PW-v214-D 25 '78-p60
RT-v35-Mr '82-p720
SE-v43-Ap '79-p300

* * *

FRANKSTON, Jay
A Christmas Story
SLJ-v26-S '79-p137

* * *

FRANSELLA, Laura
Markets And Shops
TES-D 1 '78-p37

* * *

FRANZ, Barbara E
Nutritional Survival Manual For The 80s
ASBYP-v15-Fall '82-p24
BL-v77-Je 1 '81-p1294
CCB-B-v35-S '81-p8
KR-v49-Ap 15 '81-p508
SLJ-v28-Ja '82-p86

* * *

FRANZEN, Greta
The Great Ship Vasa
BL-v68-D 1 '71-p333
CCB-B-v25-F '72-p90
LJ-v96-N 15 '71-p3909
SA-v227-D '72-p121
SB-v7-Mr '72-p336
Yacht-v131-Je '72-p98

* * *

FRANZEN, Lavern G
Smile, Jesus Is Lord
Cres-v40-Ja '77-p27

* * *

FRANZEN, Nils-Olof
Agaton Sax And Lispington's Grandfather Clock
JB-v43-Ag '79-p218
SLJ-v25-My '79-p81
Spec-v241-D 16 '78-p24
Agaton Sax And The Big Rig
JB-v40-Ag '76-p225
SLJ-v27-My '81-p84
TLS-O 1 '76-p1239
Agaton Sax And The Diamond Thieves
CSM-v59-O 5 '67-p10
KR-v35-My 15 '67-p598
LA-v58-F '81-p184
LJ-v92-My 15 '67-p2037
RT-v34-N '80-p237
TLS-Je 17 '65-p505

* * *

FRASCINO, Edward
Eddie Spaghetti
BB-v6-S '78-p1
BL-v78-F 15 '82-p762
CCB-B-v32-S '78-p7
KR-v46-Mr 1 '78-p244
NYTBR-Ap 16 '78-p26
SLJ-v24-Ap '78-p84
SR-v5-My 27 '78-p59
Eddie Spaghetti On The Homefront
BL-v80-N 15 '83-p496
CBRS-v12-O '83-p19
KR-v51-S 1 '83-pJ161
SLJ-v30-N '83-p76

* * *

FRASCONI, Antonio
See Again, Say Again
CCB-B-v18-Ap '65-p117

* * *

FRASER, Antonia
Robin Hood
B&B-v17-D '71-pR11
B&B-v18-My '73-p125
GP-v16-Mr '78-p3259
KR-v40-Ap 15 '72-p480
LJ-v97-S 15 '72-p2949
Spec-v227-N 13 '71-p689
TES-F 3 '78-p42
TLS-D 3 '71-p1509

* * *

FRASER, Ian
The Stranger Warrior
JB-v44-Ag '80-p188
J Read-v24-N '80-p175
TES-Je 13 '80-p25

* * *

FRASER, Kathleen
Adam's World
CCB-B-v25-S '71-p5
KR-v39-Je 1 '71-p588

FRASER, Kathleen (continued)
LJ-v96-D 15 '71-p4197

* * *

FRASER, Murray
King For A Day
TES-Mr 12 '82-p35

* * *

FRAYNE, Trent
Famous Tennis Players
BL-v74-S 1 '77-p32
BL-v74-S 1 '77-p40
KR-v45-Je 15 '77-p653
KR-v45-Jl 1 '77-p673
SLJ-v24-D '77-p64
Famous Women Tennis Players
BL-v75-Jl 15 '79-p1618
CCB-B-v33-N '79-p46
In Rev-v14-F '80-p40
KR-v47-Ag 1 '79-p861

* * *

FRAZIER, Beverly
Small World Cook And Color Book
CSM-v70-Mr 6 '78-p26

* * *

FRAZIER, Claude A
Sniff, Sniff, Alergee
Inst-v88-N '78-p133

* * *

FRECH, Frances
Population Primer
Refl-v3-Winter '84-p3

* * *

FREDERICKSEN, Hazel
He-Who-Runs-Far
BL-v67-F 15 '71-p492
BL-v69-O 15 '72-p177
CCB-B-v24-Ap '71-p123
CE-v47-Mr '71-p315
KR-v38-Ag 15 '70-p873
LJ-v96-Mr 15 '71-p1115

* * *

FREDERIKSEN, Thomas
Eskimo Diary
BIC-v10-N '81-p15
GP-v20-My '81-p3899
JB-v45-O '81-p222
Quill & Q-v48-Ja '82-p35
Sch Lib-v29-S '81-p265

* * *

FREDRICKS, P C
Battle At The Blue Line
Inter BC-v13-#4 '82-p8

* * *

FREE, John B
Honeybees
GP-v17-Ja '79-p3445
JB-v43-Ap '79-p105
NS-v96-N 3 '78-p595
TES-O 27 '78-p24
TES-N 3 '78-p23
TLS-S 29 '78-p1091
Insects We Need
Brit Bk N C-Autumn '80-p28
TES-Je 20 '80-p25
TES-O 24 '80-p20
Life Under Stones
GP-v20-N '81-p3977
JB-v45-D '81-p246
SLJ-v28-Mr '82-p129

* * *

FREE Stuff For Kids
BL-v80-F 1 '84-p813
Inst-v91-O '81-p30
NYTBR-v86-Je 14 '81-p35
Obs-N 7 '82-p25
Sch Lib-v31-Mr '83-p42

* * *

FREED, Alvyn M
TA For Tots. Vol. 2
SLJ-v27-D '80-p43
TA For Tots And Other Prinzes
SB-v10-D '74-p245

* * *

FREEDGOOD, Lillian
An Enduring Image
BL-v67-Ap 15 '71-p697
BS-v30-F 1 '71-p461
CCB-B-v24-My '71-p135
CLW-v43-N '71-p172
HB-v47-F '71-p63
KR-v38-O 1 '70-p1111
LJ-v96-Mr 15 '71-p1125
NYTBR-D 20 '70-p15
PW-v198-O 19 '70-p53

* * *

FREEDMAN, Florence B
Two Tickets To Freedom
BL-v68-Ja 15 '72-p433
CCB-B-v26-S '72-p7
CSM-v63-N 11 '71-pB6
KR-v39-O 1 '71-p1075
LJ-v97-Ap 15 '72-p1604
PW-v200-N 15 '71-p72

* * *

FREEDMAN, Russell
Animal Fathers
ACSB-v9-Fall '76-p17
BB-v4-S '76-p2
BL-v72-My 1 '76-p1263
KR-v44-Ap 15 '76-p475
SB-v12-D '76-p160
SLJ-v23-S '76-p115
Teacher-v94-N '76-p130
Animal Games
ACSB-v10-Spring '77-p21
CCB-B-v30-Mr '77-p106
KR-v44-O 1 '76-p1098
LA-v54-My '77-p577
SB-v13-My '77-p43
SLJ-v23-D '76-p48
Animal Instincts
BL-v66-Jl 15 '70-p1407
BS-v30-My 1 '70-p60
KR-v38-My 1 '70-p518
LJ-v96-Je 15 '71-p2130
SB-v6-My '70-p2
Animal Superstars
BL-v78-Mr 15 '82-p957
CLW-v53-My '82-p448
SLJ-v29-N '82-p83
The Brains Of Animals And Man
BL-v69-O 15 '72-p201
CCB-B-v26-Mr '73-p105
HB-v48-O '72-p492
KR-v40-My 15 '72-p583
KR-v40-D 15 '72-p1423
LJ-v97-O 15 '72-p3460
LJ-v97-D 15 '72-p4056
SB-v8-S '72-p163
Can Bears Predict Earthquakes?
BL-v79-Mr 15 '83-p966
KR-v50-N 15 '82-p1237
SLJ-v29-F '83-p76
VOYA-v6-Ap '83-p49
Children Of The Wild West
CCB-B-v37-Ap '84-p146
CE-v61-S '84-p67
HB-v60-F '84-p74
J Read-v27-Mr '84-p563
KR-v51-N 1 '83-pJ195
Learning-v12-Ap '84-p77
NYT-v133-D 1 '83-p23
NYTBR-v88-N 13 '83-p52
PW-v224-N 18 '83-p71
SE-v48-My '84-p369

FREEDMAN, Russell
(continued)
SLJ-v30-Ja '84-p75
Dinosaurs And Their Young
ASBYP-v17-Spring '84-p18
CE-v60-My '84-p366
NYTBR-v88-N 13 '83-p46
SB-v20-S '84-p33
SLJ-v30-F '84-p58
Farm Babies
BL-v78-Ja 1 '82-p596
CCB-B-v35-N '81-p45
KR-v50-F 1 '82-p137
SLJ-v28-Ja '82-p63
The First Days Of Life
ACSB-v8-Winter '75-p16
BL-v71-Ja 1 '75-p460
KR-v42-D 1 '74-p1255
PW-v206-D 2 '74-p63
SB-v11-My '75-p35
SLJ-v21-Mr '75-p87
Getting Born
ACSB-v12-Spring '79-p18
BL-v75-O 15 '78-p371
CCB-B-v32-Ja '79-p80
KR-v47-Ja 1 '79-p9
SB-v15-D '79-p166
SLJ-v25-N '78-p61
Growing Up Wild
ACSB-v9-Spring '76-p20
BL-v72-N 1 '75-p365
KR-v43-N 15 '75-p1290
SB-v12-My '76-p40
SLJ-v22-Ja '76-p46
Hanging On
BL-v73-Ap 15 '77-p1265
CE-v54-Mr '78-p260
KR-v45-Mr 1 '77-p226
SA-v237-D '77-p34
SB-v13-D '77-p166
SLJ-v23-My '77-p50
How Animals Defend Their Young
ACSB-v12-Spring '79-p19
BB-v7-Je '79-p3
BL-v75-Ja 15 '79-p808
KR-v47-Ja 1 '79-p9
SB-v15-Mr '80-p228
SLJ-v25-Mr '79-p138
How Animals Learn
BL-v65-Jl 1 '69-p1224
GT-v87-Mr '70-p157
HB-v46-Ag '70-p406
KR-v37-Ap 15 '69-p461
LJ-v94-Je 15 '69-p2500
SB-v5-My '69-p6
SB-v6-My '70-p2
How Birds Fly
BL-v74-D 15 '77-p682
CCB-B-v31-Mr '78-p111
CLW-v49-My '78-p453
HB-v54-F '78-p70
KR-v45-N 1 '77-p1145
SA-v239-D '78-p37
SB-v14-S '78-p113
SLJ-v24-D '77-p48
SR-v5-N 26 '77-p40
Immigrant Kids
BL-v77-O 1 '80-p208
CCB-B-v34-D '80-p70
CE-v57-Mr '81-p236
CLW-v52-F '81-p309
KR-v48-Ag 15 '80-p1082
LA-v58-Mr '81-p342
RT-v34-My '81-p967
SLJ-v27-O '80-p145
SLJ-v29-Ap '83-p31
Killer Fish
ASBYP-v16-Winter '83-p24
BL-v78-Ag '82-p1524
CCB-B-v36-S '82-p8
CE-v59-Mr '83-p281
KR-v50-My 1 '82-p556
SB-v18-Ja '83-p146
SLJ-v29-S '82-p120
Killer Snakes
ASBYP-v16-Fall '83-p25
BL-v79-Ap 1 '83-p1033
CCB-B-v36-Ap '83-p148
KR-v50-D 1 '82-p1294
SB-v19-N '83-p97
SLJ-v29-Ag '83-p50
They Lived With The Dinosaurs
ASBYP-v14-Spring '81-p16
BL-v77-D 1 '80-p513
CBRS-v9-D '80-p27
CCB-B-v34-F '81-p110
CLW-v52-My '81-p452
KR-v48-D 1 '80-p1519
SB-v16-My '81-p275
SLJ-v27-F '81-p64
Tooth And Claw
ASBYP-v14-Winter '81-p26
BL-v76-Ap 15 '80-p1202
CCB-B-v33-My '80-p172
KR-v48-Je 15 '80-p781
RT-v34-Mr '81-p736
SB-v16-N '80-p93
SLJ-v27-O '80-p134
When Winter Comes
ASBYP-v14-Fall '81-p19
BL-v77-Je 15 '81-p1350
CE-v58-Ja '82-p183
KR-v49-Je 15 '81-p738
LA-v59-Mr '82-p270
SLJ-v28-F '82-p67

* * *

FREEDMAN, Sally
Monster Birthday Party
BL-v80-Ap 15 '84-p1188
CBRS-v12-Mr '84-p80
PW-v225-Mr 2 '84-p93
SLJ-v30-My '84-p65

* * *

FREEMAN, Barbara C
Book By Georgina
BL-v64-Je 15 '68-p1184
CCB-B-v21-Je '68-p158
LJ-v93-Je 15 '68-p2538
YR-v4-Je '68-p3
A Haunting Air
Am-v137-D 3 '77-p407
BL-v74-Ja 15 '78-p811
CCB-B-v31-My '78-p141
HB-v54-Ap '78-p163
JB-v40-Ag '76-p225
KR-v45-D 1 '77-p1270
LA-v55-My '78-p623
Obs-Jl 11 '76-p23
PW-v212-N 21 '77-p64
RT-v32-F '79-p608
SLJ-v24-F '78-p57
TLS-Jl 16 '76-p885
The Other Face
BL-v73-F 1 '77-p832
CSM-v69-N 2 '77-pB2
GP-v14-Jl '75-p2660
GP-v15-My '76-p2901
KR-v44-N 1 '76-p1169
SLJ-v23-Ja '77-p91
TLS-Jl 11 '75-p773
A Pocket Of Silence
BB-v7-My '79-p3
BL-v75-Ja 15 '79-p809
CBRS-v7-F '79-p67
CE-v56-O '79-p42
HB-v55-Ap '79-p192
JB-v42-F '78-p39
KR-v47-F 1 '79-p132
LA-v56-Ap '79-p443
PW-v214-N 27 '78-p61
SLJ-v25-Ap '79-p55
TES-D 2 '77-p24
TLS-Jl 15 '77-p864
Snow In The Maze
Brit Bk N-Je '80-p331

FREEMAN, Barbara C (continued)
GP-v19-Jl '80-p3715
JB-v44-Je '80-p141
NS-v98-N 9 '79-p729
Obs-D 2 '79-p38
TLS-D 14 '79-p122
Timi
LJ-v96-Ja 15 '71-p257
SLJ-v26-F '80-p44
TES-My 2 '80-p24
Two-Thumb Thomas
Obs-Jl 22 '79-p37

* * *

FREEMAN, Bill
Cedric And The North End Kids
BIC-v8-Ag '79-p26
Can Child Lit-#18 '80-p130
First Spring On The Grand Banks
Atl Pro Bk R-v10-N '83-p17
Can Child Lit-#26 '82-p80
The Last Voyage Of The Scotian
Atl Pro Bk R-v10-N '83-p17
Quill & Q-v48-Je '82-p4
Shantyman Of Cache Creek
Atl Pro Bk R-v10-N '83-p2
Shantymen Of Cache Lake
Quill & Q-v48-Je '82-p4
SN-v91-Je '76-p71

* * *

FREEMAN, Dan
Beautiful Bodies
Lis-v110-N 3 '83-p30

* * *

FREEMAN, Don
Add-A-Line Alphabet
KR-v36-Mr 1 '68-p254
LJ-v93-Je 15 '68-p2532
Beady Bear
GT-v89-F '72-p94
Bearymore
BB-v5-Mr '77-p1
BW-F 11 '79-pF2
CCB-B-v30-My '77-p140
CLW-v48-D '76-p227
HB-v53-Ap '77-p148
Inst-v92-O '82-p24
LA-v54-My '77-p579
RT-v31-O '77-p10
SLJ-v23-D '76-p48
Teacher-v95-Ja '78-p39
WCRB-v3-Mr '77-p48
Corduroy
BL-v64-My 1 '68-p1042
BW-v2-My 5 '68-p7
CCB-B-v21-Jl '68-p173
CE-v45-Ja '69-p278
CSM-v60-My 2 '68-pB2
Comw-v88-My 24 '68-p301
GP-v17-N '78-p3403
GT-v88-Ap '71-p82
HB-v44-Je '68-p315
KR-v36-F 1 '68-p109
LJ-v93-Ap 15 '68-p1788
NYTBR-v73-My 5 '68-p54
PW-v193-Mr 4 '68-p63
SR-v51-Je 15 '68-p32
Dandelion
CCB-B-v18-F '65-p86
CLW-v36-F '65-p414
Fly High, Fly Low
Choice-v14-N '77-p1178
Guard Mouse
Am-v117-N 4 '67-p514
BL-v63-My 15 '67-p991
CCB-B-v20-My '67-p139
HB-v43-Ap '67-p195
KR-v35-F 15 '67-p193
LJ-v92-My 15 '67-p2014
NYTBR, pt.1-v72-My 7 '67-p52
PW-v191-Mr 13 '67-p61
SR-v50-Ap 22 '67-p99
Teacher-v92-F '75-p115
Norman The Doorman
CSM-v61-N 6 '69-pB10
NYTBR-v86-My 3 '81-p47
NYTBR, pt.2-F 13 '72-p10
Obs-N 26 '72-p37
TLS-N 3 '72-p1333
The Paper Party
CCB-B-v28-My '75-p146
JB-v41-O '77-p275
SR-v4-My 28 '77-p33
Teacher-v94-My '77-p110
Penguins, Of All People
BL-v67-My 15 '71-p798
CCB-B-v25-Ap '72-p121
KR-v39-Ap 1 '71-p355
LJ-v96-S 15 '71-p2905
NYTBR, pt.2-My 2 '71-p45
PW-v199-Mr 29 '71-p52
SR-v54-My 15 '71-p46
A Pocket For Corduroy
BL-v74-Je 1 '78-p1551
BW-Mr 12 '78-pE6
BW-v10-Ap 13 '80-p13
CCB-B-v32-S '78-p8
CE-v55-N '78-p102
Comw-v105-N 10 '78-p729
KR-v46-My 1 '78-p493
LA-v55-O '78-p860
NYTBR-v85-Je 22 '80-p33
PW-v213-F 27 '78-p157
SLJ-v25-S '78-p108
A Rainbow Of My Own
BL-v62-Ap 15 '66-p830
CCB-B-v20-O '66-p24
EL-v87-Ja '67-p282
HB-v42-Je '66-p299
KR-v34-F 1 '66-p105
LJ-v91-Mr 15 '66-p1690
NYTBR-v71-Jl 10 '66-p38
PW-v189-F 14 '66-p144
Par-v41-D '66-p21
SR-v49-Ap 16 '66-p49
TLS-My 25 '67-p452
The Sea Lion And The Slick
JB-v40-O '76-p261

* * *

FREEMAN, Dorothy
VIP In Food Services
SLJ-v23-S '76-p115
VIP In Maintenance Services
SLJ-v23-S '76-p115
VIP In Personal And Protective Services
SLJ-v23-S '76-p115
VIP On The Backup Team In Medical Work
LJ-v99-Ap 15 '74-p1219
SB-v10-My '74-p64
VIP On The Scene In Medical Work
LJ-v99-Ap 15 '74-p1219
SB-v10-My '74-p64
VIP Who Carry Messages
SLJ-v22-S '75-p118
VIP Who Print And Publish
SLJ-v22-S '75-p118
VIP Who Work With Cars, Buses, And Trucks
Inst-v82-My '73-p70
LJ-v99-S 15 '74-p2267
VIP Who Work With Farm And Earth-Moving Machines
Inst-v82-My '73-p70
LJ-v99-S 15 '74-p2267
VIP Who Work With Recreational Vehicles
Inst-v82-My '73-p70
LJ-v99-S 15 '74-p2267
VIP Who Work With Sight And Sound
SLJ-v22-S '75-p118

* * *

FREEMAN, Edith
Tudor Life And Dress
TES-Ag 14 '81-p30

* * *

FREEMAN, Gail
Alien Thunder
BL-v79-N 15 '82-p437
B Rpt-v1-Ja '83-p39
CBRS-v11-N '82-p28
CCB-B-v36-Ja '83-p88
EJ-v72-D '83-p69
J Read-v26-Ja '83-p375
SLJ-v29-Ja '83-p84
VOYA-v5-F '83-p44
Out From Under
BL-v78-F 1 '82-p703
CBRS-v10-Mr '82-p76
SLJ-v28-Mr '82-p157

* * *

FREEMAN, Gillian
The Schoolgirl Ethic
B&B-v22-O '76-p61
Econ-v260-Jl 10 '76-p111
GP-v15-S '76-p2954
GW-v115-Jl 4 '76-p22
JB-v40-O '76-p256
Lis-v95-Je 24 '76-p820
Obs-Je 27 '76-p23
Spec-v236-Je 26 '76-p20
TLS-Jl 16 '76-p877
VS-v22-Spring '79-p352

* * *

FREEMAN, Jean Todd
Cynthia And The Unicorn
CCB-B-v21-N '67-p41
NO-v6-D 11 '67-p19
NYTBR-v72-N 5 '67-p63
PW-v192-N 6 '67-p51

* * *

FREEMAN, Lucy
The Eleven Steps
BB-v3-Ag '75-p2
CCB-B-v28-Mr '75-p112
KR-v43-Ja 1 '75-p17
PW-v207-Ja 20 '75-p76
SLJ-v21-Ja '75-p38

* * *

FREEMAN, Mae
Book Of Real Science
BL-v630-Winter '66-p323
CCB-B-v20-D '66-p57
LJ-v91-O 15 '66-p5260
SB-v2-D '66-p186
Finding Out About Shapes
BL-v66-Mr 15 '70-p927
CCB-B-v23-Je '70-p158
CLW-v42-O '70-p134
GT-v88-N '70-p136
LJ-v95-Ap 15 '70-p1626
SB-v5-Mr '70-p306
Gravity And The Astronauts
CCB-B-v24-Jl '71-p169
LJ-v97-Ap 15 '72-p1594
The Sun, The Moon, And The Stars
ACSB-v13-Spring '80-p30
BL-v75-Je 1 '79-p1491
SB-v15-Mr '80-p225
SLJ-v26-S '79-p137
Undersea Base
ACSB-v8-Fall '75-p12
CCB-B-v28-F '75-p93
CLW-v46-My '75-p453
KR-v42-Ag 15 '74-p879
PW-v206-Ag 19 '74-p83
SB-v10-Mr '75-p334
SLJ-v21-Ja '75-p38
When Air Moves
CCB-B-v22-S '68-p7
KR-v36-My 15 '68-p551
LJ-v93-S 15 '68-p3301
SB-v4-S '68-p148
SR-v51-Jl 20 '68-p31
You Will Go To The Moon
CCB-B-v25-Ap '72-p122
KR-v39-O 15 '71-p1119
LJ-v96-D 15 '71-p4195
SB-v8-My '72-p79

* * *

FREEMAN, Mae Blacker
Stars And Stripes
CCB-B-v19-S '65-p8
Par-v40-Jl '65-p29

* * *

FREEMAN, S H
Basic Baseball Strategy
BL-v62-S 1 '65-p55
CCB-B-v18-Jl '65-p161
KR-v33-Ap 1 '65-p383
LJ-v90-My 15 '65-p2416

* * *

FREEMAN, Sarah
Piccolo Picture Cook Book
GP-v14-N '75-p2746

* * *

FREEMAN, Tony
Aircraft That Work For Us
ASBYP-v15-Spring '82-p35
SB-v18-Ja '83-p148
SLJ-v28-F '82-p75
Beginning Backpacking
SLJ-v27-D '80-p77
Beginning Surfing
BL-v76-Jl 1 '80-p1613
RT-v34-D '80-p352
SLJ-v26-My '80-p89
Blimps
BL-v75-Jl 1 '79-p1579
Cur R-v19-Ap '80-p174
SB-v15-My '80-p280
SLJ-v26-S '79-p137
Hot Air Balloons
SLJ-v30-N '83-p76
An Introduction To Radio-Controlled Sailplanes
BL-v75-Jl 1 '79-p1579
Inst-v88-My '79-p113
SLJ-v26-S '79-p137
Photography
BL-v80-F 15 '84-p854
SLJ-v30-Ap '84-p101

* * *

FREESE, Arthur S
The Bionic People Are Here
BL-v75-Jl 1 '79-p1575
CCB-B-v33-N '79-p47
SLJ-v26-Ja '80-p78

* * *

FREETH, Zahra
Rashid Of Saudi Arabia
TES-Ap 10 '81-p37

* * *

FREEZER, Cyril
Model Railways
GP-v19-N '80-p3796
Sch Lib-v29-Mr '81-p36

* * *

FREGOSI, Claudia
Almira's Violets
CCB-B-v30-Ja '77-p75
CSM-v68-N 3 '76-p28
Inst-v86-N '76-p145
KR-v44-Jl 15 '76-p790
SLJ-v23-N '76-p45
WLB-v51-N '76-p258
Are There Spooks In The Dark?
BB-v5-N '77-p1

FREGOSI, Claudia (continued)
CCB-B-v31-N '77-p46
KR-v45-Jl 15 '77-p724
PW-v212-Jl 4 '77-p77
SLJ-v24-D '77-p60
SLJ-v26-Mr '80-p105
A Gift
Cur R-v17-Ag '78-p182
KR-v44-S 1 '76-p970
SLJ-v23-N '76-p46
The Happy Horse
BB-v5-O '77-p1
HB-v53-O '77-p524
KR-v45-Jl 1 '77-p666
LA-v55-Ap '78-p518
SLJ-v24-Ap '78-p69
The Mammoth, The Owl, And The Crab
BB-v3-My '75-p1
CCB-B-v29-S '75-p8
KR-v43-Mr 1 '75-p235
LA-v53-My '76-p498
PW-v207-Mr 17 '75-p56
SLJ-v22-O '75-p90
Teacher-v93-N '75-p111
The Pumpkin Sparrow
CSM-v69-My 4 '77-pB7
KR-v45-F 1 '77-p90
SLJ-v24-S '77-p107
Snow Maiden
CBRS-v8-Ja '80-p43
KR-v48-F 15 '80-p210
PW-v216-D 3 '79-p51
RT-v35-D '81-p331
SLJ-v26-Ja '80-p56

* * *

FREMANTLE, Anne
The Island Of Cats
CCB-B-v18-Mr '65-p101

* * *

FREMLIN, Robert
Three Friends
BL-v71-My 15 '75-p965
CCB-B-v29-N '75-p44
CLW-v47-N '75-p188
KR-v43-Ap 1 '75-p374
PW-v207-Mr 31 '75-p50
SLJ-v22-O '75-p90
Teacher-v94-O '76-p146

* * *

FRENCH, Dorothy K
I Don't Belong Here
BL-v76-Jl 15 '80-p1673
CCB-B-v34-S '80-p7
Hi Lo-v2-S '80-p4
SLJ-v26-Ap '80-p124
Pioneer Saddle Mystery
SLJ-v22-Mr '76-p102
Swim To Victory
CCB-B-v23-Ja '70-p80
KR-v37-Jl 1 '69-p673
LJ-v94-S 15 '69-p3204

* * *

FRENCH, Fiona
Aio The Rainmaker
BW-N 12 '78-pE1
KR-v46-D 15 '78-p1352
NW-v92-D 18 '78-p100
PW-v214-S 18 '78-p166
TLS-Jl 11 '75-p771
The Blue Bird
BL-v69-Ja 1 '73-p448
HB-v48-O '72-p456
Inst-v82-N '72-p124
KR-v40-Jl 1 '72-p721
LJ-v97-N 15 '72-p3796
Obs-My 28 '72-p33
PW-v202-Jl 10 '72-p46
TLS-Jl 14 '72-p808
City Of Gold
BB-v3-F '75-p2
B&B-v20-Ja '75-p77
BL-v71-S 15 '74-p99
CE-v51-Ja '75-p155
Inst-v84-N '74-p132
KR-v42-S 1 '74-p939
Obs-Ag 25 '74-p24
PW-v206-Ag 12 '74-p59
SLJ-v21-Ap '75-p44
TLS-S 20 '74-p1011
Future Story
CBRS-v13-O '84-p13
JB-v48-Ap '84-p56
Obs-D 11 '83-p35
Sch Lib-v31-D '83-p342
Hunt The Thimble
AB-v62-N 13 '78-p2953
BB-v7-Ap '79-p2
CBRS-v7-F '79-p61
CCB-B-v32-My '79-p153
CLW-v55-O '83-p130
GP-v17-Jl '78-p3370
JB-v42-O '78-p250
KR-v46-D 15 '78-p1352
Obs-Jl 16 '78-p26
PW-v214-N 20 '78-p60
SLJ-v25-F '79-p40
TLS-Jl 7 '78-p763
WLB-v53-Je '79-p710
Jack Of Hearts
BL-v67-Ja 15 '71-p420
CCB-B-v24-Ap '71-p123
KR-v38-O 15 '70-p1139
LJ-v96-Mr 15 '71-p1107
NYTBR, pt.2-N 8 '70-p53
PW-v198-O 12 '70-p55
TLS-O 30 '70-p1260
John Barleycorn
GP-v21-Ja '83-p4013
JB-v47-F '83-p12
Sch Lib-v31-Mr '83-p25
Matteo
JB-v41-Ap '77-p77
KR-v46-D 15 '78-p1352
Lis-v96-N 11 '76-p626
PW-v214-N 13 '78-p63
Spec-v237-D 11 '76-p22
TLS-D 10 '76-p1551
Time-v112-D 4 '78-p101
The Princess And The Musician
Brit Bk N C-Autumn '81-p11
GP-v20-S '81-p3947
JB-v45-D '81-p242
Sch Lib-v30-S '82-p222
TES-N 20 '81-p36

* * *

FRENCH, Mary
Farms
GP-v17-Jl '78-p3351

* * *

FRENCH, Michael
Flyers
SLJ-v30-O '83-p158
Indiana Jones And The Temple Of Doom
SLJ-v31-O '84-p159
Pursuit
BL-v79-S 15 '82-p105
BS-v42-Ja '83-p404
CCB-B-v36-D '82-p65
EJ-v72-D '83-p66
HB-v58-D '82-p656
Kliatt-v18-Winter '84-p10
SLJ-v29-O '82-p160
VOYA-v6-Ap '83-p37
The Throwing Season
BL-v76-Je 1 '80-p1418
CBRS-v8-My '80-p98
CCB-B-v33-Je '80-p189
EJ-v70-F '81-p62
Inter BC-v12-#3 '81-p20
KR-v48-My 15 '80-p650
Kliatt-v18-Winter '84-p10
NYTBR-v85-Ap 27 '80-p56
NYTBR-v88-D 25 '83-p19

FRENCH, Michael (continued)
SLJ-v27-N '80-p85
VOYA-v7-Ap '84-p54

* * *

FRENCH, Peter
Counting
SLJ-v23-S '76-p99

* * *

FRENCH, Simon
Hey Phantom Singlet
GP-v17-My '78-p3324
JB-v42-Ag '78-p203
TES-S 1 '78-p15

* * *

FRENZEL, Sofie
Schlaf, Kindlein, Schlaf
BL-v75-D 1 '78-p622
Widele Wedele
BL-v75-D 1 '78-p623

* * *

FRERE, Maud
My Name Is Nicole
KR-v33-O 1 '65-p1040
LJ-v90-D 15 '65-p5500
Nicole: A Little French Schoolgirl
CCB-B-v20-Ap '67-p120
CSM-v57-N 4 '65-pB1
KR-v34-Ag 1 '66-p750
LJ-v91-N 15 '66-p5748
PW-v190-Ag 8 '66-p60
Nicole's Birthday
LJ-v92-Ap 15 '67-p1724

* * *

FRESCHET, Berniece
The Ants Go Marching
HB-v49-Je '73-p282
KR-v41-My 1 '73-p510
LJ-v98-Jl '73-p2186
PW-v203-Mr 19 '73-p71
Bear Mouse
ACSB-v13-Winter '80-p5
BL-v70-F 15 '74-p656
CCB-B-v27-D '73-p63
CSM-v65-N 7 '73-pB5
Choice-v12-N '75-p1132
GP-v14-My '75-p2649
HB-v49-O '73-p455
Inst-v83-N '73-p123
JB-v39-Ap '75-p96
KR-v41-N 1 '73-p1195
LJ-v98-N 15 '73-p3439
Obs-Ap 6 '75-p30
PW-v204-S 24 '73-p188
SR/W-v1-D 4 '73-p32
Beaver On The Sawtooth
BL-v66-N 15 '69-p407
CE-v47-N '70-p90
KR-v37-S 1 '69-p933
LJ-v95-F 15 '70-p769
PW-v196-N 17 '69-p82
SB-v5-D '69-p256
Bernard And The Catnip Caper
CBRS-v10-F '82-p62
CCB-B-v35-D '81-p68
KR-v50-F 1 '82-p132
PW-v220-O 9 '81-p66
SLJ-v28-D '81-p81
Bernard Of Scotland Yard
BL-v75-Ja 1 '79-p750
CCB-B-v32-Ap '79-p135
CE-v56-O '79-p42
KR-v47-Ja 1 '79-p3
SLJ-v25-Mr '79-p121
Bernard Sees The World
CCB-B-v30-Ja '77-p75
CSM-v68-N 3 '76-p25
KR-v44-Ag 1 '76-p842
PW-v210-Ag 9 '76-p79
SLJ-v23-O '76-p97
Biography Of A Buzzard
BL-v73-Ap 1 '77-p1166
CCB-B-v30-My '77-p141
CE-v54-N '77-p90
KR-v45-Ja 1 '77-p5
SB-v13-D '77-p166
SLJ-v24-O '77-p100
Black Bear Baby
ASBYP-v14-Fall '81-p20
BL-v77-Jl 15 '81-p1450
KR-v49-Mr 15 '81-p354
SLJ-v27-My '81-p80
Sch Lib-v30-D '82-p333
Elephant & Friends
BL-v74-Ap 15 '78-p1348
CCB-B-v31-Jl '78-p175
CLW-v50-F '79-p312
CSM-v70-My 3 '78-pB10
HB-v54-Je '78-p264
KR-v46-Mr 1 '78-p238
PW-v213-F 13 '78-p127
RT-v32-D '78-p364
SLJ-v24-My '78-p54
Five Fat Raccoons
BL-v76-Jl 15 '80-p1675
KR-v48-S 1 '80-p1158
SLJ-v27-Mr '81-p131
The Flight Of The Snow Goose
BL-v67-F 15 '71-p492
CCB-B-v24-Ap '71-p123
CLW-v42-My '71-p580
CLW-v43-N '71-p172
KR-v38-N 15 '70-p1248
LJ-v96-Mr 15 '71-p1107
SR-v53-N 14 '70-p35
Grizzly Bear
BB-v4-F '76-p3
BL-v72-O 15 '75-p298
HB-v52-Ap '76-p178
JB-v41-Je '77-p154
KR-v43-Ag 15 '75-p922
Obs-F 13 '77-p35
SLJ-v22-N '75-p61
TLS-Mr 25 '77-p355
The Happy Dromedary
BB-v5-Ag '77-p1
BL-v73-My 1 '77-p1351
BW-Je 12 '77-pE4
CE-v54-O '77-p28
HB-v53-Je '77-p299
KR-v45-Mr 1 '77-p217
LA-v55-Ja '78-p43
NYTBR-My 1 '77-p42
PW-v211-F 21 '77-p79
SLJ-v23-My '77-p50
WLB-v51-My '77-p771
Kangaroo Red
BL-v62-Je 15 '66-p1000
CCB-B-v20-F '67-p88
CLW-v38-N '66-p215
KR-v34-Mr 1 '66-p247
LJ-v91-Je 15 '66-p3257
NYTBR-v71-My 8 '66-p39
SB-v2-S '66-p133
SR-v49-My 14 '66-p41
Little Black Bear Goes For A Walk
BL-v74-O 15 '77-p381
CCB-B-v31-D '77-p59
KR-v45-Ag 15 '77-p848
PW-v212-Ag 15 '77-p69
SLJ-v24-D '77-p57
Little Woodcock
Aud-v70-Mr '68-p98
BL-v64-S 15 '67-p129
BW-v2-Ja 7 '68-p10
CCB-B-v21-Mr '68-p108
CLW-v39-D '67-p299
HB-v43-O '67-p606
KR-v35-My 1 '67-p558
LJ-v92-Je 15 '67-p2444
NYTBR, pt.1-v72-My 7 '67-p49

FRESCHET, Berniece
(continued)
PW-v191-Je 5 '67-p176
SB-v3-D '67-p242
Trav-v24-Ja '68-p223
Lizard Lying In The Sun
BL-v72-S 15 '75-p171
HB-v51-O '75-p477
KR-v43-Je 15 '75-p659
LA-v53-My '76-p505
PW-v207-Je 30 '75-p57
SLJ-v22-D '75-p66
Moose Baby
ACSB-v13-Spring '80-p30
BL-v76-Ja 15 '80-p724
CCB-B-v33-F '80-p108
HB-v56-Ap '80-p184
KR-v48-F 15 '80-p214
SB-v16-S '80-p33
SLJ-v26-D '79-p94
The Old Bullfrog
BL-v64-Je 1 '68-p1140
CCB-B-v22-Ja '69-p78
CLW-v40-O '68-p150
HB-v44-Ag '68-p408
KR-v36-Ap 1 '68-p386
LJ-v93-Je 15 '68-p2532
PW-v193-Ap 22 '68-p52
Spec-v222-My 16 '69-p656
Trav-v25-N '68-p78
The Owl And The Prairie Dog
BL-v65-Jl 1 '69-p1224
BW-v3-My 4 '69-p34
CLW-v41-N '69-p198
CSM-v61-My 1 '69-pB2
KR-v37-Ap 1 '69-p372
LJ-v94-Jl '69-p2672
PW-v195-Ap 14 '69-p97
SB-v5-D '69-p252
Porcupine Baby
ACSB-v12-Spring '79-p19
BL-v74-Mr 1 '78-p1102
CCB-B-v31-My '78-p141
CE-v55-N '78-p106
KR-v46-Ja 15 '78-p46
SLJ-v24-My '78-p83
Possum Baby
ACSB-v12-Fall '79-p21
BL-v75-S 15 '78-p228
HB-v55-F '79-p93
KR-v46-S 1 '78-p949
SLJ-v25-D '78-p64
Pronghorn On The Powder River
KR-v41-O 15 '73-p1165
LJ-v99-Ja 15 '74-p209
Raccoon Baby
BL-v81-S 15 '84-p137
Sierra-v69-N '84-p94
Skunk Baby
BL-v69-Je 1 '73-p947
CCB-B-v26-My '73-p137
CSM-v65-My 2 '73-pB4
HB-v49-Je '73-p282
KR-v41-F 15 '73-p190
LJ-v98-Jl '73-p2193
PW-v203-Ap 30 '73-p55
Turtle Pond
BL-v67-Jl 1 '71-p907
KR-v39-Ap 1 '71-p355
LJ-v96-My 15 '71-p1795
PW-v199-Mr 1 '71-p58
TLS-D 6 '74-p1384
The Watersnake
BL-v76-Ja 1 '80-p666
CCB-B-v33-My '80-p172
HB-v56-Ap '80-p168
KR-v48-F 15 '80-p210
SLJ-v26-My '80-p55
The Web In The Grass
ACSB-v13-Winter '80-p5
BL-v69-F 15 '73-p572
CCB-B-v26-F '73-p89
HB-v49-F '73-p37
KR-v40-D 1 '72-p1349
LJ-v98-Ap 15 '73-p1374
Obs-Je 2 '74-p33
RT-v35-Ap '82-p789
SA-v229-D '73-p137
SB-v9-My '73-p75
TLS-Jl 5 '74-p718
TN-v29-Ap '73-p251
Where's Henrietta's Hen?
BL-v76-Mr 1 '80-p981
CBRS-v8-Mr '80-p73
CCB-B-v33-My '80-p172
Inst-v89-My '80-p91
KR-v48-Mr 1 '80-p283
PW-v217-Ja 11 '80-p88
SLJ-v26-Ap '80-p92
Wood Duck Baby
ASBYP-v17-Winter '84-p20
BL-v79-My 15 '83-p1223
CCB-B-v36-My '83-p166
SB-v19-Mr '84-p217
SLJ-v29-My '83-p90
Sierra-v69-N '84-p94
Wufu
BL-v72-O 1 '75-p233
CE-v52-Ap '76-p322
HB-v51-D '75-p604
KR-v43-Ag 1 '75-p853
PW-v208-Ag 11 '75-p117
SLJ-v22-O '75-p98
Year On Muskrat Marsh
ACSB-v8-Winter '75-p16
ACSB-v15-Winter '82-p9
BL-v70-My 15 '74-p1055
CCB-B-v27-Jl '74-p176
CE-v51-N '74-p95
CSM-v66-My 1 '74-pF5
HB-v50-Ag '74-p391
KR-v42-Ap 15 '74-p428
KR-v43-Ja 1 '75-p7
LJ-v99-S 15 '74-p2267
PW-v205-Je 10 '74-p41
SB-v10-D '74-p256

* * *

FRETZ, Sada
Going Vegetarian
ASBYP-v17-Spring '84-p19
BL-v79-Mr 15 '83-p954
CCB-B-v36-Ap '83-p148
LA-v61-Ja '84-p65
NYTBR-v88-S 18 '83-p38
PW-v223-My 13 '83-p56
SB-v19-Ja '84-p147
SLJ-v29-Ag '83-p75

* * *

FREUD, Clement
Clicking Vicky
Brit Bk N C-Spring '81-p19
GP-v19-Ja '81-p3823
ILN-v268-D '80-p93
JB-v45-Ap '81-p61
TES-Mr 13 '81-p28
TLS-N 21 '80-p1327
Grimble And Grimble At Christmas
B&B-v20-Mr '75-p81
Teacher-v92-D '74-p79

* * *

FREUDBERG, Judy
Some, More, Most
BL-v73-Mr 15 '77-p1091
Cur R-v16-O '77-p279
SLJ-v23-Mr '77-p131
TES-Jl 7 '78-p30
WLB-v51-F '77-p488

* * *

FREUND, Gisele
The World In My Camera
HB-v51-Ap '75-p172
KR-v40-Jl 15 '72-p834
KR-v42-Jl 1 '74-p715
LJ-v100-Ja 15 '75-p117

FREUND, Gisele (continued)
PW-v202-Jl 3 '72-p35

* * *

FREVERT, Patricia D
Beatrix Potter: Children's Storyteller
BL-v78-F 15 '82-p756
SLJ-v28-Mr '82-p147
Mark Twain: An American Voice
BL-v78-F 15 '82-p756
SLJ-v28-Mr '82-p147
Pablo Picasso: Twentieth-Century Genius
BL-v78-F 15 '82-p756
SLJ-v28-Mr '82-p147
Why Does Weather Change?
ASBYP-v15-Fall '82-p56
SLJ-v28-Ag '82-p92

* * *

FREWER, Glyn
Bryn Of Brockle Hanger
Brit Bk N C-Spring '81-p19
GP-v19-Mr '81-p3850
JB-v45-Ap '81-p79
Lis-v104-N 6 '80-p624
Sch Lib-v29-Mr '81-p36
The Trackers
JB-v41-Je '77-p162
LR-v25-Winter '77-p334
TLS-Mr 25 '77-p360
Tyto
BL-v74-Mr 1 '78-p1105
CE-v54-Ap '78-p307
CLW-v49-My '78-p453
CSM-v70-My 3 '78-pB7
GP-v17-Mr '79-p3474
JB-v42-D '78-p309
J Read-v22-Mr '79-p564
KR-v45-D 1 '77-p1273
LA-v55-My '78-p625
SLJ-v24-Ja '78-p88
TLS-S 29 '78-p1088

* * *

FREY, Shaney
The Complete Beginner's Guide To Swimming
SLJ-v21-My '75-p71

* * *

FRIBOURG, Marjorie G
The Supreme Court In American History
CCB-B-v19-Je '66-p163
NYTBR, pt.2-My 4 '69-p6

* * *

FRICK, Lennart
The Threat
GP-v14-Ja '76-p2797
TLS-D 5 '75-p1448

* * *

FRICKE, Pam
Careers With An Electric Company
BL-v81-O 1 '84-p246

* * *

FRIEDBERG, Ardy
My Greatest Day In Sports
BL-v80-Ap 1 '84-p1123
SLJ-v30-D '83-p87

* * *

FRIEDBERG, M Paul
Handcrafted Playgrounds
BL-v71-Je 15 '75-p1038
BW-Jl 13 '75-p4
CE-v54-Ja '78-p149
Inst-v85-Ag '75-p206
LJ-v100-My 1 '75-p840

* * *

FRIEDLANDER, Joanne K
Stock Market ABC
CCB-B-v23-N '69-p43
CE-v46-F '70-p266
Comw-v90-My 23 '69-p303
KR-v37-My 1 '69-p509
LJ-v94-O 15 '69-p3829
NY-v45-D 13 '69-p212
PW-v195-Je 2 '69-p136
SR-v52-O 18 '69-p57

* * *

FRIEDMAN, Aileen
The Castles Of The Two Brothers
CCB-B-v26-S '72-p7
KR-v40-My 15 '72-p574
LJ-v97-S 15 '72-p2932
PW-v201-Mr 13 '72-p67

* * *

FRIEDMAN, Herbert
The Amazing Universe
ACSB-v9-Fall '76-p17
BL-v72-F 15 '76-p848
BW-Mr 21 '76-p3
S&T-v51-Ap '76-p276
S&T-v52-Ag '76-p125
SB-v12-S '76-p79

* * *

FRIEDMAN, Ina R
Black Cop
BL-v70-Jl 15 '74-p1253
CCB-B-v28-O '74-p27
KR-v42-Ap 15 '74-p435
LJ-v99-S 15 '74-p2290
PW-v205-F 18 '74-p74
Escape Or Die
BL-v78-Jl '82-p1433
CBRS-v11-S '82-p8
HB-v58-O '82-p529
KR-v50-My 15 '82-p609
SLJ-v29-O '82-p151
VOYA-v5-O '82-p53
How My Parents Learned To Eat
NYTBR-v89-O 28 '84-p37

* * *

FRIEDMAN, J
The Eels' Strange Journey
JB-v44-D '80-p291

* * *

FRIEDMAN, Joy Troth
Look Around And Listen
CE-v51-Mr '75-p273
SB-v10-Mr '75-p341
SLJ-v22-O '75-p90

* * *

FRIEDMAN, Judi
The ABC Of A Summer Pond
Teacher-v93-F '76-p116
The Biting Book
KR-v43-O 15 '75-p1175
LA-v53-My '76-p501
SLJ-v22-Ja '76-p36
The Eels' Strange Journey
ACSB-v10-Winter '77-p17
BL-v72-Jl 1 '76-p1526
The Eels' Strange Journey
HB-v52-O '76-p524
KR-v44-Ap 1 '76-p396
SB-v12-D '76-p160
SLJ-v23-S '76-p99
SR-v3-My 15 '76-p39
TES-Je 6 '80-p27
TLS-Mr 28 '80-p363
Jelly Jam, The People Preserver
SB-v19-Mr '84-p215
Noises In The Woods
ACSB-v13-Winter '80-p17
BL-v75-Je 15 '79-p1541
BW-Je 10 '79-pE3
CSM-v71-My 14 '79-pB9

FRIEDMAN, Judi (continued)
RT-v33-Ja '80-p483
SB-v15-Mr '80-p228
SLJ-v26-S '79-p110

* * *

FRIEDMAN, Sara Ann
Police!
BL-v72-F 1 '76-p760
BL-v72-F 1 '76-p787
Cur R-v16-F '77-p34
KR-v43-S 15 '75-p1092
KR-v43-D 1 '75-p1340
SLJ-v22-F '76-p52

* * *

FRIEDRICH, Priscilla
The Easter Bunny That Overslept
BL-v79-Ap 15 '83-p1094
CCB-B-v36-Ap '83-p148
KR-v51-F 15 '83-p180
NYTBR-v88-Mr 27 '83-p33

* * *

FRIEDRICHSEN, Carol S
The Pooh Craft Book
BL-v73-Ja 1 '77-p665
JB-v47-F '83-p40
KR-v44-N 1 '76-p1171
PW-v210-N 8 '76-p49
SLJ-v23-D '76-p54

* * *

FRIEND, John B
Cattle Of The World
ARBA-v11-'80-p701
LJ-v103-N 1 '78-p2252

* * *

FRIEND, Morton
The Vanishing Tungus
BL-v70-S 1 '73-p50
CCB-B-v26-Jl '73-p170
KR-v40-D 1 '72-p1361

* * *

FRIEND
Mag Lib- '82-p216
Ser R-v7-Ja '81-p29

* * *

FRIERMOOD, Elisabeth Hamilton
Doc Dudley's Daughter
BL-v62-D 1 '65-p362
CCB-B-v19-F '66-p97
HB-v41-D '65-p635
KR-v33-Jl 15 '65-p689
LJ-v90-S 15 '65-p3804
Focus The Bright Land
BS-v27-O 1 '67-p263
BW-v1-O 22 '67-p14
CCB-B-v21-Je '68-p158
CLW-v39-D '67-p298
HB-v43-D '67-p757
KR-v35-Ag 1 '67-p884
LJ-v92-N 15 '67-p4259
Par-v43-Jl '68-p81
One Of Fred's Girls
CCB-B-v24-Mr '71-p106
EJ-v60-Mr '71-p406
KR-v38-S 15 '70-p1048
LJ-v96-F 15 '71-p732
Peppers' Paradise
BS-v29-D 1 '69-p352
CCB-B-v23-Ja '70-p80
KR-v37-S 1 '69-p938
LJ-v95-Ja 15 '70-p252
Whispering Willows
BL-v61-Ja 1 '65-p435
CCB-B-v18-My '65-p128

* * *

FRIES, Chloe
No Place To Hide
Hi Lo-v1-Mr '80-p4

* * *

FRIIS-BAASTAD, Babbis
Don't Take Teddy
CCB-B-v20-Jl '67-p169
CLW-v53-Ap '82-p394
GT-v89-Ap '72-p88
KR-v35-F 1 '67-p137
LJ-v92-My 15 '67-p2020
NYTBR-v72-My 21 '67-p30
RT-v34-Mr '81-p636
RT-v37-F '84-p505
SR-v50-Ap 22 '67-p100
Wanted, A Horse
CCB-B-v25-Ap '72-p122
HB-v48-Ag '72-p370
KR-v39-D 1 '71-p1256
LJ-v97-S 15 '72-p2960
SR-v55-Ap 22 '72-p84

* * *

FRIMMER, Steven
Neverland
BL-v73-F 1 '77-p800
BL-v73-F 1 '77-p832
KR-v44-N 1 '76-p1177
PW-v210-O 4 '76-p70
SLJ-v23-N '76-p68

* * *

FRISBEE, Lucy Post
John F Kennedy: Young Statesman
CCB-B-v19-O '65-p32

* * *

FRISCH, Otto Von
Animal Camouflage
HB-v50-F '74-p74
TLS-N 23 '73-p1445

* * *

FRISCH, Ulla
Get Busy-Get Better
GP-v18-My '79-p3521
JB-v43-O '79-p271
Obs-Jl 22 '79-p37
Pictures To Play With
AB-v62-N 27 '78-p3318
BB-v7-Mr '79-p2
GP-v16-Ap '78-p3300
SLJ-v25-F '79-p55

* * *

FRISEN, Gisela
The I Was So Mad I Could Have Split Book
TLS-Ap 2 '76-p381

* * *

FRISKEY, Margaret
About Measurement
CE-v42-Mr '66-p440
LJ-v90-D 15 '65-p5535
SB-v1-Mr '66-p190
Birds We Know
BL-v78-F 15 '82-p760
SLJ-v28-Mr '82-p131
Chicken Little Count-To-Ten
CE-v61-S '84-p33
LJ-v96-Mr 15 '71-p1085
Indian Two Feet And His Eagle Feather
LJ-v92-D 15 '67-p4630
PW-v192-Ag 14 '67-p50
Indian Two Feet And His Horse
TLS-O 3 '68-p1116
Indian Two Feet And The ABC Moose Hunt
SLJ-v24-F '78-p46
Indian Two Feet And The Grizzly Bear
LJ-v99-D 15 '74-p3275

FRISKEY, Margaret (continued)
Indian Two Feet And The Wolf Cubs
LJ-v96-D 15 '71-p4197
Indian Two Feet Rides Alone
SLJ-v27-D '80-p68
John Alden And The Pilgrim Cow
Inst-v82-N '72-p124
LJ-v98-Ap 15 '73-p1386
Mystery Of The Farmer's Three Fives
TLS-D 9 '65-p1149
Mystery Of The Magic Meadow
PW-v193-My 20 '68-p62
Rackety, That Very Special Rabbit
SLJ-v22-Ja '76-p36
Seven Diving Ducks
LR-v21-Autumn '67-p153
TLS-My 25 '67-p452
Shoe For My Pony
LR-v23-Summer '72-p255
Space Shuttles
ASBYP-v16-Spring '83-p61
BL-v78-Je 15 '82-p1365
SLJ-v29-O '82-p137
Three Sides And The Round One
LJ-v98-My 15 '73-p1696
The True Book Of The Moon-Ride Rock Hunt
LJ-v98-My 15 '73-p1695
PW-v202-D 18 '72-p40
The True Book Of The Moonwalk Adventure
BL-v67-Ap 15 '71-p701
CCB-B-v25-Mr '72-p106
LJ-v96-D 15 '71-p4195
SB-v7-My '71-p80
Welcome To Austria
CCB-B-v29-D '75-p62
SLJ-v22-O '75-p90
Welcome To Canada
SLJ-v22-O '75-p90
Welcome To England
Inst-v84-N '74-p139
Welcome To Germany (Federal Republic Of Germany)
SLJ-v22-O '75-p90
Welcome To Japan
RT-v29-Ja '76-p415
SLJ-v22-O '75-p90
Welcome To Mexico
SLJ-v22-O '75-p90
Welcome To Sweden
SLJ-v22-O '75-p90
What Is The Color Of The Wide, Wide World?
Inst-v83-N '73-p120
LJ-v99-Mr 15 '74-p881
SB-v10-S '74-p166

* * *

FRITH, Michael
Big Bird's Busy Book
SLJ-v22-Mr '76-p91
I'll Teach My Dog 100 Words
KR-v41-N 1 '73-p1198
LJ-v98-D 15 '73-p3700
TES-Jl 1 '83-p44
TLS-Jl 5 '74-p723

* * *

FRITZ, Jean
And Then What Happened, Paul Revere?
BL-v70-Ja 1 '74-p488
BL-v70-Mr 15 '74-p827
BW-v7-N 11 '73-p3C
BW-v7-N 11 '73-p5C
BW-v12-F 14 '82-p12
CCB-B-v27-Mr '74-p109
CSM-v66-Ja 9 '74-pF4
Cha Ti-v32-N '78-p24
Choice-v12-N '75-p1132
HB-v50-Ap '74-p159
KR-v41-O 1 '73-p1100
KR-v41-D 15 '73-p1353
LATBR-Jl 25 '82-p9
LJ-v98-D 15 '73-p3689
LJ-v98-D 15 '73-p3700
NY-v49-D 3 '73-p218
NYTBR-N 4 '73-p57
NYTBR-N 4 '73-p59
NYTBR-v87-Ja 31 '82-p31
PW-v204-N 12 '73-p37
SE-v39-Mr '75-p172
TN-v30-Ap '74-p308
Teacher-v92-N '74-p108
Teacher-v93-N '75-p117
Teacher-v93-Ja '76-p52
Brendan The Navigator
Arch-v33-S '80-p64
CCB-B-v33-N '79-p47
CLW-v51-N '79-p182
HB-v55-Ag '79-p414
KR-v47-Jl 1 '79-p743
LA-v57-Ap '80-p437
NYTBR-Ap 29 '79-p30
PW-v215-Je 25 '79-p123
RT-v33-Ap '80-p863
SLJ-v25-My '79-p35
SLJ-v25-My '79-p61
Can't You Make Them Behave, King George?
BL-v74-O 1 '77-p288
BW-v12-F 14 '82-p12
CCB-B-v31-Ja '78-p77
HB-v54-Ap '78-p174
KR-v45-Ag 15 '77-p854
LA-v60-Mr '83-p369
LATBR-Jl 25 '82-p9
NYTBR-N 6 '77-p22
NYTBR-v87-Ja 31 '82-p31
PW-v212-Ag 15 '77-p69
RT-v32-O '78-p44
RT-v32-D '78-p363
SE-v42-Ap '78-p318
SLJ-v24-N '77-p56
The Double Life Of Pocahontas
BL-v80-N 1 '83-p407
B Rpt-v2-Mr '84-p42
CBRS-v12-N '83-p30
CCB-B-v37-Ja '84-p86
HB-v59-D '83-p724
Inst-v93-N '83-p147
Inter BC-v15-#5 '84-p16
KR-v51-S 1 '83-pJ168
LA-v61-Mr '84-p293
NY-v59-D 5 '83-p207
NYT-v133-D 1 '83-p23
NYTBR-v88-N 13 '83-p41
PW-v224-S 23 '83-p73
RT-v37-Mr '84-p646
SE-v48-My '84-p372
SLJ-v30-D '83-p66
Early Thunder
BL-v64-D 1 '67-p446
BS-v27-O 1 '67-p263
BW-v1-O 1 '67-p24
CCB-B-v21-F '68-p93
CLW-v39-F '68-p438
Can Child Lit-#23 '81-p58
Comw-v87-N 10 '67-p180
HB-v43-D '67-p757
Inst-v77-F '68-p190
KR-v35-O 1 '67-p1218
LJ-v92-N 15 '67-p4260
NS-v77-My 16 '69-p700
NYTBR-v72-O 22 '67-p62
SR-v50-N 11 '67-p48
TLS-Ap 3 '69-p350
Trav-v24-Ja '68-p223

FRITZ, Jean (continued)
George Washington's Breakfast
BL-v65-Je 15 '69-p1174
BW-v3-Je 22 '69-p12
CCB-B-v22-My '69-p141
KR-v37-Ja 15 '69-p54
LJ-v94-Mr 15 '69-p1326
PW-v195-Mr 10 '69-p73
SR-v52-Ap 19 '69-p38
The Good Giants And The Bad Pukwudgies
BL-v78-Jl '82-p1444
CBRS-v10-Je '82-p103
CCB-B-v35-Je '82-p187
HB-v58-Ag '82-p391
NYTBR-v87-Ag 29 '82-p12
PW-v221-Ap 16 '82-p70
SLJ-v28-My '82-p52
Homesick
BL-v79-S 1 '82-p42
BW-v12-N 7 '82-p13
CBRS-v11-O '82-p18
CCB-B-v35-Jl '82-p206
CE-v59-Mr '83-p277
HB-v58-D '82-p649
HB-v60-Ag '84-p493
Inst-v92-N '82-p151
J Read-v26-Ap '83-p653
KR-v50-S 1 '82-p1002
LA-v60-Mr '83-p369
LA-v60-My '83-p646
LA-v61-Ap '84-p421
NY-v58-D 6 '82-p192
NYT-v132-N 30 '82-p23
NYTBR-v87-N 14 '82-p41
PW-v222-D 3 '82-p59
PW-v225-Je 1 '84-p65
SLJ-v29-S '82-p120
Jean Fritz History Paperback Set
Cur R-v22-F '83-p93
Magic To Burn
BL-v61-Mr 15 '65-p711
CCB-B-v18-Ja '65-p74
GT-v82-Mr '65-p23
Inst-v74-F '65-p18
The Man Who Loved Books
ABC-v2-N '81-p60
BL-v77-Mr 15 '81-p1027
CBRS-v9-Mr '81-p64
CCB-B-v34-Mr '81-p132
HB-v57-Je '81-p317
KR-v49-Mr 1 '81-p286
NYTBR-v86-Mr 1 '81-p24
PW-v219-Ja 9 '81-p76
SLJ-v27-Ap '81-p111
Stonewall
BL-v76-N 15 '79-p501
BOT-v2-D '79-p601
BS-v39-N '79-p289
BW-v9-Ag 12 '79-p9
CBRS-v8-S '79-p7
CCB-B-v33-O '79-p27
CE-v56-Ap '80-p308
HB-v55-O '79-p548
KR-v47-O 1 '79-p1147
LA-v57-Ap '80-p438
NYTBR-N 11 '79-p57
NYTBR-N 25 '79-p26
Nat R-v31-D 21 '79-p1638
PW-v216-Ag 27 '79-p385
SE-v44-O '80-p481
SLJ-v26-N '79-p76
Traitor
AB-v68-N 16 '81-p3446
BL-v78-D 15 '81-p547
BS-v41-Ja '82-p402
CBRS-v10-O '81-p18
CCB-B-v35-F '82-p106
CE-v59-S '82-p59
HB-v57-D '81-p676
KR-v49-N 1 '81-p1347
LA-v59-S '82-p605
NYTBR-v86-N 22 '81-p46
PW-v220-Jl 3 '81-p147
SLJ-v28-S '81-p136
VOYA-v4-F '82-p30
What's The Big Idea, Ben Franklin?
BL-v73-S 15 '76-p174
BW-D 5 '76-pH5
BW-v12-F 14 '82-p12
CCB-B-v30-S '76-p10
CE-v53-Ja '77-p152
Comw-v103-N 19 '76-p758
Cur R-v16-D '77-p363
HB-v52-O '76-p507
KR-v44-Je 1 '76-p636
LA-v54-F '77-p211
LATBR-Jl 25 '82-p9
NYTBR-Jl 4 '76-p16
NYTBR-N 14 '76-p52
NYTBR-v87-Ja 31 '82-p31
PW-v209-Je 7 '76-p74
RT-v31-O '77-p18
SB-v13-My '77-p39
SE-v41-Ap '77-p347
SLJ-v23-S '76-p99
SLJ-v29-Ap '83-p107
Teacher-v94-N '76-p134
Where Do You Think You're Going, Christopher Columbus?
BL-v77-Mr 1 '81-p963
CBRS-v9-Ja '81-p34
CCB-B-v34-F '81-p110
HB-v57-F '81-p67
Inst-v91-O '81-p29
KR-v48-N 1 '80-p1397
NYTBR-v85-N 9 '80-p60
PW-v218-N 7 '80-p62
RT-v35-Ap '82-p793
SLJ-v27-D '80-p58
Where Was Patrick Henry On The 29th Of May?
BL-v71-Jl 15 '75-p1190
BW-v12-F 14 '82-p12
CCB-B-v29-N '75-p44
CE-v52-Ja '76-p156
CSM-v75-My 13 '83-pB7
Comw-v102-N 21 '75-p570
HB-v51-O '75-p475
KR-v43-Je 15 '75-p664
LATBR-Jl 25 '82-p9
NYTBR-Je 29 '75-p8
NYTBR-N 16 '75-p56
NYTBR-v87-Ja 31 '82-p31
PW-v207-My 26 '75-p60
SE-v44-O '80-p479
SLJ-v22-S '75-p81
Teacher-v93-N '75-p113
Teacher-v93-Ja '76-p52
Who's That Stepping On Plymouth Rock?
BL-v72-N 15 '75-p452
CCB-B-v29-F '76-p95
CE-v52-F '76-p208
HB-v52-F '76-p62
KR-v43-O 15 '75-p1189
NYTBR-D 21 '75-p8
PW-v208-S 15 '75-p59
SLJ-v22-N '75-p61
Teacher-v93-N '75-p112
Why Don't You Get A Horse, Sam Adams?
BB-v3-Ap '75-p3
BL-v71-D 15 '74-p423
BL-v71-Mr 15 '75-p766
BW-v12-F 14 '82-p12
CCB-B-v28-Ap '75-p129
CE-v52-O '75-p36
Choice-v12-N '75-p1132
Comw-v102-N 21 '75-p570
HB-v51-F '75-p57
KR-v43-Ja 1 '75-p20
LATBR-Jl 25 '82-p9

FRITZ, Jean (continued)
LJ-v99-D 15 '74-p3262
NYTBR-N 3 '74-p26
NYTBR-N 3 '74-p55
NYTBR-v87-Ja 31 '82-p31
Teacher-v92-Ap '75-p108
Will You Sign Here, John Hancock?
BL-v72-Jl 1 '76-p1526
BW-v12-F 14 '82-p12
CCB-B-v30-D '76-p56
CE-v53-Ja '77-p152
Comw-v103-N 19 '76-p758
Cur R-v16-D '77-p363
HB-v52-O '76-p508
KR-v44-Je 1 '76-p636
LATBR-Jl 25 '82-p9
NYTBR-My 2 '76-p27
NYTBR-v87-Ja 31 '82-p31
PW-v209-Je 28 '76-p98
RT-v31-O '77-p18
SE-v41-Ap '77-p347
SLJ-v23-S '76-p116
SR-v4-N 27 '76-p35
Teacher-v94-N '76-p134

* * *

FROEHLICH, Margaret W
Hide Crawford Quick
BL-v79-My 15 '83-p1215
CBRS-v11-Jl '83-p137
CCB-B-v37-S '83-p6
HB-v59-Ap '83-p165
Inter BC-v15-#4 '84-p19
PW-v224-Jl 1 '83-p102
SLJ-v29-Ag '83-p76

* * *

FROG He Would A-Wooing Go
Fine Pt-v8-Ap '82-p58
LJ-v93-Mr 15 '68-p1302

* * *

FROG Princess (Isaacs)
B&B-v21-N '75-p60

* * *

FROHES Singen, Frohes Klingen
BL-v75-N 15 '78-p554

* * *

FROLOV, Vadim
What It's All About
B&B-v15-My '70-p44
BL-v65-Ja 1 '69-p488
BW-v2-N 3 '68-p30
CCB-B-v22-Ja '69-p78
EJ-v58-My '69-p778
HB-v45-F '69-p77
J Read-v25-F '82-p459
KR-v36-Ag 1 '68-p824
Lis-v83-Mr 12 '70-p351
NYTBR-v73-N 3 '68-p2
Obs-Mr 29 '70-p26
PW-v194-S 2 '68-p58
SR-v51-N 9 '68-p71
TLS-Ap 16 '70-p416

* * *

FROM A Busy Hubbub
NS-v78-O 31 '69-p630

* * *

FROMAN, Elizabeth Hull
Eba, The Absent-Minded Witch
CCB-B-v20-O '66-p24
CSM-v57-O 28 '65-p5
GT-v83-O '65-p32
HB-v41-O '65-p491
KR-v33-Ag 15 '65-p824
LJ-v90-D 15 '65-p5514
TLS-Mr 14 '68-p256
Mr. Drackle And His Dragons
LJ-v96-D 15 '71-p4178

* * *

FROMAN, Robert
Angles Are Easy As Pie
ACSB-v10-Winter '77-p18
BL-v72-Ap 15 '76-p1191
CE-v53-Ja '77-p152
KR-v44-F 15 '76-p202
SB-v12-Mr '77-p209
SLJ-v22-My '76-p49
Teacher-v94-F '77-p144
Arithmetic For Human Beings
BL-v70-Ap 15 '74-p894
Baseball-Istics
KR-v35-Ap 1 '67-p427
LJ-v92-My 15 '67-p2042
SA-v217-D '67-p140
SB-v3-D '67-p207
Bigger And Smaller
BL-v68-N 1 '71-p246
CCB-B-v25-F '72-p90
LJ-v96-S 15 '71-p2904
SA-v229-D '73-p131
SB-v7-My '71-p23
TLS-N 3 '72-p1334
Teacher-v91-S '73-p152
Billions Of Years Of You
CCB-B-v20-Je '67-p152
KR-v35-Ap 1 '67-p420
LJ-v92-Je 15 '67-p2449
PW-v191-Ap 10 '67-p82
SR-v50-My 13 '67-p55
Faster And Faster
CSM-v57-My 6 '65-p2B
A Game Of Functions
HB-v51-Ap '75-p168
KR-v42-D 1 '74-p1255
SLJ-v21-My '75-p46
The Great Reaching Out
BL-v65-F 15 '69-p655
BS-v28-Ja 1 '69-p421
LJ-v94-Ja 15 '69-p309
SB-v5-My '69-p7
The Greatest Guessing Game
ACSB-v12-Spring '79-p20
CCB-B-v32-O '78-p27
CLW-v50-D '78-p235
Cur R-v17-O '78-p322
HB-v54-Ag '78-p425
KR-v46-Jl 1 '78-p691
SB-v15-My '79-p40
SLJ-v25-N '78-p61
Hot And Cold And In Between
BL-v68-F 1 '72-p466
CCB-B-v25-Mr '72-p106
Inst-v81-F '72-p139
KR-v39-O 15 '71-p1126
SR-v54-N 13 '71-p60
Less Than Nothing Is Really Something
CCB-B-v27-Ja '74-p78
CE-v50-Ap '74-p338
HB-v50-F '74-p74
Inst-v82-My '73-p73
KR-v41-Jl 1 '73-p688
LJ-v98-S 15 '73-p2639
SB-v9-Mr '74-p326
Let's Find Out About The Clinic
CCB-B-v21-Jl '68-p174
KR-v36-F 1 '68-p118
LJ-v93-My 15 '68-p2105
LJ-v98-Mr 15 '73-p1020
Many Human Senses
BL-v63-Ja 1 '67-p488
CCB-B-v21-D '67-p59
Comw-v85-N 11 '66-p179
HB-v43-F '67-p92
KR-v34-Jl 15 '66-p699
SB-v2-Mr '67-p301
The Many Human Senses
LR-v22-Fall '69-p154
Mushrooms And Molds
BL-v69-Ap 15 '73-p811
CCB-B-v26-Ap '73-p123

FROST, Kelman (continued)
SE-v39-Mr '75-p176
TLS-Ap 28 '72-p486

* * *

FROST, Robert
Stopping By Woods On A Snowy Evening
Am-v139-D 9 '78-p444
BB-v6-D '78-p1
BL-v75-Ja 15 '79-p809
BW-D 10 '78-pE5
CBRS-v7-Mr '79-p73
CCB-B-v32-Mr '79-p114
CE-v55-Ap '79-p300
CLW-v51-O '79-p141
HB-v55-Ap '79-p182
Inst-v90-D '80-p36
KR-v47-Ja 15 '79-p61
NY-v55-D 3 '79-p200
PW-v214-D 25 '78-p59
RT-v33-O '79-p52
SLJ-v25-F '79-p40
Time-v112-D 4 '78-p101
Stories For Lesley
Atl-v254-S '84-p129
NYTBR-v89-Jl 22 '84-p24
SLJ-v30-Ag '84-p72
A Swinger Of Birches
AB-v70-N 15 '82-p3405
BS-v42-D '82-p365
GP-v22-Mr '84-p4226
Inst-v92-Mr '83-p19
JB-v48-Ap '84-p82
LA-v60-Ap '83-p486
PW-v222-O 22 '82-p55
RT-v36-Ap '83-p852
RT-v37-O '83-p64
SLJ-v29-N '82-p83
Sch Lib-v32-S '84-p247
TES-Ap 27 '84-p27

* * *

FROUD, Brian
Faeries
A Art-v43-N '79-p22
B&B-v25-N '79-p50
BL-v75-Ja 15 '79-p780
BW-D 3 '78-pE10
CC-v96-Ja 31 '79-p108
CR-v234-Mr '79-p168
CSM-v71-D 4 '78-pB3
EJ-v68-D '79-p81
GP-v18-My '79-p3507
ILN-v266-D '78-p127
JB-v43-Ap '79-p90
Kliatt-v14-Winter '80-p71
LJ-v104-Ja 1 '79-p123
NW-v92-D 18 '78-p99
NYRB-v26-Mr 8 '79-p16
NYTBR-N 25 '79-p107
TES-D 21 '79-p19
Goblins
BIC-v12-D '83-p13
CBRS-v12-N '83-p26
JB-v48-Ap '84-p69
PW-v224-S 9 '83-p65
SLJ-v30-O '83-p125

* * *

FRUCHTER, Yaakov
The Best Of Olomeinu
SLJ-v29-N '82-p84

* * *

FRUIT (Wayland World Resources)
TES-Mr 6 '81-p37

* * *

FRY, Christopher
The Boat That Mooed
Atl-v216-D '65-p154
BL-v62-N 15 '65-p330
CCB-B-v19-N '65-p44
CSM-v57-N 4 '65-pB4
KR-v33-S 1 '65-p900
LJ-v90-O 15 '65-p4605
NO-v4-S 20 '65-p21
NYRB-v5-D 9 '65-p38
NYTBR-v70-N 7 '65-p62
SR-v48-N 13 '65-p55

* * *

FRY, Edward B
Reading Drills
Cur R-v22-D '83-p19
Skimming & Scanning
Cur R-v22-D '83-p19
J Read-v22-My '79-p777

* * *

FRY, Fiona S
Horses
JB-v46-F '82-p25
SLJ-v28-Ap '82-p69

* * *

FRY, John
Winners On The Ski Slopes
SLJ-v25-My '79-p85

* * *

FRY, Rosalie K
The Castle Family
BL-v62-Jl 15 '66-p1086
CCB-B-v19-My '66-p149
CSM-v57-N 4 '65-pB6
LJ-v91-My 15 '66-p2689
TLS-D 9 '65-p1131
Gypsy Princess
CCB-B-v23-F '70-p96
GP-v16-Jl '77-p3156
HB-v45-O '69-p530
KR-v37-Jl 15 '69-p718
LJ-v95-Ja 15 '70-p240
TLS-Je 26 '69-p699
Mungo
BL-v68-Jl 15 '72-p1004
HB-v48-Ag '72-p370
KR-v40-Mr 15 '72-p324
SR-v55-D 9 '72-p79
Promise Of The Rainbow
CCB-B-v18-Je '65-p147
CE-v41-My '65-p490
CLW-v36-My '65-p641
Comw-v82-My 28 '65-p328
KR-v33-F 15 '65-p179
LJ-v90-F 15 '65-p960
NYTBR-v70-Ag 15 '65-p28
September Island
CCB-B-v18-Je '65-p147
KR-v33-Mr 1 '65-p237
LJ-v90-Mr 15 '65-p1549
LR-v20-Autumn '65-p190
Snowed Up
BL-v67-D 15 '70-p341
CE-v47-Ap '71-p377
CSM-v63-Ja 2 '71-p19
CSM-v70-Ja 30 '78-p15
GP-v21-N '82-p3997
HB-v46-D '70-p619
LJ-v95-D 15 '70-p4348
TLS-Jl 2 '71-p775
Teacher-v90-F '73-p125

* * *

FRYATT, Norma R
Faneuil Hall
HB-v46-O '70-p492
LJ-v96-O 15 '71-p3476
Sarah Josepha Hale: The Life And Times Of A Nineteenth-Century Career Woman
BL-v72-Ap 1 '76-p1112
Comw-v103-N 19 '76-p763
Cur R-v16-O '77-p316
HB-v52-Je '76-p297
SLJ-v22-F '76-p52

* * *

FRYE, Burton C
A St. Nicholas Anthology
BS-v29-Ja 1 '70-p388

FRYE, Burton C (continued)
CCB-B-v23-F '70-p96
CLW-v41-F '70-p386
LJ-v95-Mr 15 '70-p1186
NY-v45-D 13 '69-p209
NYTBR-N 30 '69-p45
TES-Je 2 '78-p21
The Joker And The Lion
JB-v45-O '81-p187
Obs-My 10 '81-p33
TES-Je 5 '81-p36
A Mouse Tale A Giant Tale
Obs-Ag 26 '84-p19
TES-Je 8 '84-p51
The Wishing Hat
BL-v73-Ap 1 '77-p1167
CSM-v69-N 2 '77-pB4
KR-v45-Mr 1 '77-p218
LA-v55-Mr '78-p366
SLJ-v23-Ap '77-p54

* * *

FRYER, Mary B
Escape
Emerg Lib-v11-N '83-p37
SLJ-v27-S '80-p43

* * *

FUCHS, E
Spreading The News
JB-v40-Ap '76-p91

* * *

FUCHS, Erich
Journey To The Moon
Am-v123-D 5 '70-p495
BL-v66-Je 1 '70-p1212
BL-v67-Ap 1 '71-p660
CCB-B-v24-Jl '70-p176
CLW-v42-O '70-p133
GT-v88-N '70-p119
HB-v46-Je '70-p285
LJ-v95-My 15 '70-p1911
LJ-v95-My 15 '70-p1929
LJ-v95-D 15 '70-p4325
NYTBR-Ap 5 '70-p26
NYTBR, pt.2-N 8 '70-p42
PW-v197-Mr 23 '70-p67
Par-v45-Ag '70-p63
SB-v6-My '70-p64
TN-v27-Ja '71-p208
TN-v28-Ap '72-p300
Looking At Maps
JB-v41-Ap '77-p92
NYT-v126-D 20 '76-pC21
SA-v237-D '77-p40
SB-v13-Mr '78-p220
SLJ-v23-F '77-p56

* * *

FUCHSHUBER, A
Toribio Y Su Sombrero Magico
BL-v76-Je 15 '80-p1546

* * *

FUCHSHUBER, Annegert
From Dinosaurs To Fossils
ASBYP-v15-Spring '82-p68
BL-v78-O 15 '81-p300
SLJ-v28-Ja '82-p63
Henry And The Bombardon
JB-v42-Ap '78-p79

* * *

FUERTES, Gloria
El Dragon Tragon
RT-v37-N '83-p139
TN-v40-Winter '84-p185

* * *

FUFUKA, Karama
My Daddy Is A Cool Dude
BL-v72-D 1 '75-p514
CCB-B-v29-Ja '76-p76
J Read-v20-F '77-p432
KR-v43-S 15 '75-p1071
LA-v59-Mr '82-p283
NYTBR-F 1 '76-p14
SLJ-v22-F '76-p45

* * *

FUJA, Abayomi
Fourteen Hundred Cowries And Other African Tales
BL-v68-S 1 '71-p56
CCB-B-v25-N '71-p42
CE-v48-Ap '72-p377
HB-v47-Ag '71-p379
KR-v39-Ap 1 '71-p372
LJ-v96-D 15 '71-p4158
LJ-v96-D 15 '71-p4184

* * *

FUJIKAWA, Gyo
Babies And Baby Animals
CSM-v67-S 22 '75-p22
A Child's Book Of Poems
CCB-B-v24-S '70-p7
PW-v212-S 26 '77-p137
Come Follow Me...
NYTBR-Ag 26 '79-p34
PW-v216-Ag 20 '79-p81
SLJ-v27-N '80-p60
Come Out And Play
CBRS-v10-O '81-p12
Fairyland
CBRS-v10-O '81-p12
Faraway Friends
CBRS-v10-O '81-p12
The Flyaway Kite
CBRS-v10-S '81-p2
Fraidy Cat
RT-v37-O '83-p58
Gyo Fujikawa's A To Z Picture Book
CE-v51-F '75-p215
NYTBR-S 8 '74-p8
PW-v206-Ag 5 '74-p59
Jenny And Jupie To The Rescue
PW-v222-S 24 '82-p73
Jenny Learns A Lesson
RT-v35-O '81-p60
Let's Eat
PW-v207-Je 2 '75-p54
Let's Grow A Garden
PW-v213-My 22 '78-p232
SLJ-v25-Ja '79-p42
Let's Play
CCB-B-v29-Ja '76-p76
PW-v207-Je 2 '75-p54
Make-Believe
CBRS-v10-O '81-p12
Millie's Secret
SLJ-v25-Ja '79-p42
Mother Goose
CBRS-v10-O '81-p12
NYTBR-v73-N 3 '68-p58
PW-v194-O 28 '68-p60
My Animal Friend
CBRS-v10-O '81-p12
My Favorite Thing
SLJ-v25-Ja '79-p42
Oh, What A Busy Day!
CCB-B-v30-Mr '77-p106
NYTBR-N 14 '76-p44
SLJ-v23-Ja '77-p82
Puppies, Pussy Cats & Other Friends
PW-v207-Je 2 '75-p54
Sam's All-Wrong Day
SLJ-v29-F '83-p66
Shags Finds A Kitten
SLJ-v30-N '83-p62
Shags Has A Dream
CBRS-v10-S '81-p2
Sleepy Time
PW-v207-Je 2 '75-p54
Par-v58-O '83-p158
Surprise! Surprise!
SLJ-v25-Ja '79-p42

FUJIKAWA, Gyo (continued)
That's Not Fair!
CCB-B-v37-D '83-p66
SLJ-v30-N '83-p62
Welcome Is A Wonderful Word
PW-v218-N 28 '80-p50
RT-v35-O '81-p65

* * *

FUJITA, T
William Tell
B&B-v22-D '76-p81
LR-v25-Autumn '76-p279

* * *

FUJITA, Tamao
The Boy And The Bird
BL-v69-D 15 '72-p405
CCB-B-v25-Jl '72-p168
HB-v48-Je '72-p260
KR-v40-Mr 1 '72-p254
LJ-v97-Je 15 '72-p2230
PW-v201-Mr 6 '72-p62

* * *

FUKEI, Arlene
East To Freedom
CCB-B-v18-Mr '65-p101

* * *

FUKUDA, Hanako
Wind In My Hand
BL-v67-S 15 '70-p106
BL-v69-F 15 '73-p553
CCB-B-v24-S '70-p7
CSM-v62-My 7 '70-pB9
Comw-v92-My 22 '70-p250
HB-v46-Ag '70-p399
Inst-v79-Je '70-p105
KR-v38-Mr 1 '70-p246
LJ-v95-D 15 '70-p4349
PW-v197-Ap 20 '70-p62

* * *

FULLE, Suzanne G
Lanterns For Fiesta
CCB-B-v27-F '74-p94
LJ-v99-Ja 15 '74-p209

* * *

FULLER, Catherine L
Beasts
BL-v65-N 1 '68-p310
BW-v2-N 3 '68-p6
HB-v45-F '69-p65
Inst-v78-N '68-p152
KR-v36-S 15 '68-p1064
LJ-v93-O 15 '68-p3980
NYTBR-v73-N 3 '68-p53
PW-v194-Ag 5 '68-p56
TN-v25-Je '69-p433

* * *

FULLER, John
Come Aboard And Sail Away
Lon R Bks-v6-F 2 '84-p11
NS-v106-D 2 '83-p27
The Extraordinary Wool Mill
GP-v19-My '80-p3694
JB-v44-Ag '80-p175
Sch Lib-v29-Mr '81-p29
TES-Mr 7 '80-p44
TLS-Mr 28 '80-p361
The Last Bid
GP-v14-Jl '75-p2667
NS-v89-My 23 '75-p694
Obs-Jl 20 '75-p23
TLS-S 19 '75-p1051
Squeaking Crust
Lis-v92-N 7 '74-p617
NS-v87-My 24 '74-p742
Obs-Je 2 '74-p33
TLS-Jl 5 '74-p717

* * *

FULLER, R Buckminster
Tetrascroll
BS-v42-S '82-p248
LATBR-S 19 '82-p12
LJ-v107-Jl '82-p1328
New Age-v7-Ap '82-p71
New Age-v7-Jl '82-p58
New Age-v9-O '83-p65
PW-v221-Je 11 '82-p54
PW-v224-Jl 1 '83-p98

* * *

FULLER, Ronald
Pilgrim
CCB-B-v34-F '81-p108
GP-v20-S '81-p3932
JB-v46-Ap '82-p66
PW-v217-Je 20 '80-p87
SLJ-v27-N '80-p74
Sch Lib-v30-Je '82-p129
TES-N 20 '81-p31

* * *

FULLER, Roy
Poor Roy
B&B-v22-Ag '77-p54
GP-v16-My '77-p3126
JB-v41-Je '77-p176
TLS-Mr 25 '77-p350

* * *

FULTON, Gwen
Did You Ever?
JB-v45-D '81-p243
Sch Lib-v29-S '81-p225

* * *

FULTON, Mary J
Detective Arthur, Master Sleuth
SLJ-v21-My '75-p69
My Friend
BW-My 2 '76-pL2
Ms-v3-D '74-p78

* * *

FUN Figures (Leisure Crafts)
TES-F 3 '78-p43

* * *

FUN To Read Books
TES-Mr 10 '78-p52

* * *

FUNAI, Mamoru
Cartoons For Kids
KR-v45-My 15 '77-p542
SLJ-v24-F '78-p47

* * *

FUNAZAKI, Yasuko
Baby Owl
BL-v77-D 15 '80-p574
CBRS-v9-Ja '81-p31
CCB-B-v34-Ap '81-p151
LA-v58-My '81-p591
SLJ-v27-Mr '81-p131

* * *

FUNCKEN, Liliane
The Lace Wars
GP-v17-My '78-p3335

* * *

FUNCRAFT Books
Inst-v88-My '79-p113

* * *

FUNFACT Books
Inst-v88-My '79-p113

* * *

FUNKE, Lewis
The Curtain Rises
BL-v68-S 1 '71-p56
CCB-B-v24-Jl '71-p169

* * *

FUR And Feathers
Emerg Lib-v9-S '81-p33
Mag Lib- '82-p723

* * *

FURCHGOTT, Terry
The Great Garden Adventure
GP-v17-N '78-p3426
JB-v43-F '79-p17
Nanda In India
JB-v47-Ag '83-p153
Phoebe And The Hot Water Bottles
CBRS-v8-Winter '80-p62
GP-v16-Jl '77-p3150
JB-v41-Ag '77-p210
SLJ-v26-Ap '80-p92
TLS-Mr 25 '77-p355

* * *

FURMAN, Victoria
Five In A Tent
CCB-B-v20-S '66-p9
KR-v34-Ap 1 '66-p375
LJ-v91-My 15 '66-p2689
Par-v41-Je '66-p76

* * *

FURMINGER, J
Mrs. Boffy's Birthday
JB-v45-Ap '81-p70

* * *

FURMINGER, Jo
A Ghost For Miss Grimscuttle
Sch Lib-v32-S '84-p237

* * *

FURNAS, C C
The Engineer
TES-My 20 '83-p28

* * *

FURNISS, Tim
Shuttle To Mars
GP-v23-S '84-p4307
Space Satellites
JB-v45-F '81-p18
Space Stowaway
Sch Lib-v30-D '82-p333
Space Today
JB-v43-D '79-p334
TES-S 12 '80-p25
The Story Of The Space Shuttle
Brit Bk N C-Spring '80-p22
GP-v18-N '79-p3612
JB-v44-Ap '80-p82
Sch Lib-v28-Mr '80-p71
TES-O 24 '80-p21
TES-N 5 '82-p28

* * *

FURRER, Jurg
Die Schildkroteninsel
BL-v72-Mr 1 '76-p985
Tortoise Island
BL-v72-S 15 '75-p164
GP-v14-O '75-p2712
Inst-v85-N '75-p150
KR-v43-Ag 1 '75-p842
NO-v14-D 27 '75-p17
PW-v207-Je 30 '75-p57
SLJ-v22-S '75-p81

* * *

FURST, Ursula
The Boy, The Bird And The Tree
GP-v14-Ap '76-p2858
JB-v40-Je '76-p142
Lis-v96-N 11 '76-p626

* * *

FUSSENEGGER, Gertrud
Noah's Ark
GP-v22-My '83-p4081
JB-v47-Je '83-p108
TES-My 13 '83-p32

* * *

FYODOROV, Vadim
An Ordinary Magic Watch
KR-v46-Ja 15 '78-p47

* * *

FYSON, J G
Friend Fire And The Dark Wings
GP-v22-My '83-p4073
HB-v60-F '84-p51
JB-v47-Ag '83-p171
SLJ-v30-F '84-p70
Sch Lib-v32-Mr '84-p46
TES-S 16 '83-p24
Journey Of The Eldest Son
BL-v63-Je 1 '67-p1045
BS-v27-Ap 1 '67-p16
CCB-B-v21-N '67-p42
HB-v43-Ap '67-p212
HT-v15-D '65-p879
KR-v35-Ja 1 '67-p6
LJ-v92-Ap 15 '67-p1747
TLS-D 9 '65-p1146
Three Brothers Of Ur
BL-v63-Je 1 '67-p1045
BS-v27-Ap 1 '67-p16
CCB-B-v21-O '67-p26
CSM-v57-My 6 '65-p7B
HB-v43-F '67-p70
KR-v34-S 1 '66-p906
KR-v34-D 1 '66-p1227
LJ-v92-Mr 15 '67-p1324

* * *

FYSON, Nance
Carpenter
GP-v20-Jl '81-p3917
JB-v45-Je '81-p114
TES-Mr 6 '81-p36

* * *

FYSON, Nance L
Chun Ling In China
Brit Bk N C-Autumn '82-p28
GP-v21-S '82-p3960
JB-v46-O '82-p189
SLJ-v30-S '83-p105
Sch Lib-v31-Mr '83-p45
TES-N 5 '82-p31

* * *

FYSON, Nance Lui
Growing Up In The Eighteenth Century
JB-v42-Ap '78-p102
TES-O 21 '77-p20

G

GABB, Michael
Creatures Great And Small
CBRS-v8-Jl '80-p129
SB-v16-Mr '81-p221
SLJ-v27-S '80-p70
Everyday Science
CBRS-v8-Jl '80-p129
SB-v16-Ja '81-p154
SLJ-v27-S '80-p70

* * *

GABRIEL, Ingrid
Herb Identifier And Handbook
ACSB-v9-Fall '76-p18
ARBA-v8-'77-p654
BL-v72-S 15 '75-p106
BL-v74-Jl 1 '78-p1695
CSM-v68-F 5 '76-p23
LJ-v100-O 15 '75-p1936
PW-v208-Jl 21 '75-p69
SB-v12-My '76-p23

* * *

GACKENBACH, Dick
Annie And The Mud Monster
CBRS-v10-Ap '82-p82
PW-v221-Ja 8 '82-p83
SLJ-v28-Mr '82-p132
Arabella And Mr. Crack
BL-v78-My 15 '82-p1256
CBRS-v10-Ap '82-p82
KR-v50-Mr 1 '82-p271
LA-v59-N '82-p864
PW-v221-Ja 29 '82-p66
SLJ-v28-Ag '82-p97
A Bag Full Of Pups
CBRS-v10-N '81-p22
CLW-v53-F '82-p300
HB-v57-D '81-p659
JB-v48-Je '84-p117
KR-v49-D 1 '81-p1462
PW-v220-S 4 '81-p60
RT-v36-O '82-p67
SLJ-v28-Ja '82-p64
TES-Je 8 '84-p51
TLS-Mr 30 '84-p339
Binky Gets A Car
CBRS-v11-Je '83-p107
CCB-B-v36-Jl '83-p209
PW-v223-Je 24 '83-p57
SLJ-v29-Ag '83-p50
Claude And Pepper
BL-v72-F 15 '76-p855
KR-v44-Ja 15 '76-p67
LA-v53-S '76-p696
PW-v209-Ja 12 '76-p51
SLJ-v22-My '76-p75
WLB-v50-My '76-p694
Claude The Dog
CCB-B-v28-N '74-p42
KR-v42-Ag 1 '74-p799
LJ-v99-O 15 '74-p2721
PW-v206-O 28 '74-p48
PW-v222-O 22 '82-p56
WLB-v49-O '74-p138
Crackle Gluck And The Sleeping Toad
BB-v7-N '79-p2
CBRS-v7-My '79-p95
KR-v47-My 1 '79-p513
LA-v57-Mr '80-p321
PW-v215-F 12 '79-p127
SLJ-v25-My '79-p51
Do You Love Me?
BL-v72-N 1 '75-p365
CCB-B-v29-D '75-p62
CLW-v47-F '76-p309
CLW-v47-Ap '76-p398
Inst-v85-N '75-p150
Inst-v89-O '79-p100
KR-v43-Jl 1 '75-p708
PW-v208-Jl 7 '75-p86
SLJ-v22-N '75-p61
Teacher-v96-O '78-p172
WLB-v50-N '75-p248
The Dog And The Deep Dark Woods
CBRS-v12-Je '84-p112
HB-v60-Je '84-p324
LA-v61-O '84-p628
PW-v225-Je 1 '84-p64
SLJ-v30-Ag '84-p59
Harry And The Terrible Whatzit
BB-v5-Je '77-p1
BL-v73-My 15 '77-p1420
CCB-B-v31-S '77-p14
CE-v54-Ja '78-p138
KR-v45-F 1 '77-p90
LA-v55-My '78-p618
NYTBR-My 1 '77-p42
NYTBR-D 9 '79-p39
NYTBR-v89-My 20 '84-p29
PW-v211-Ja 31 '77-p75
PW-v216-N 26 '79-p53
RT-v32-O '78-p34
SLJ-v23-My '77-p75
WLB-v51-My '77-p770
Hattie Be Quiet, Hattie Be Good
BL-v74-S 15 '77-p201
Comw-v104-N 11 '77-p729
HB-v53-O '77-p528
KR-v45-Je 15 '77-p624
PW-v212-Ag 8 '77-p69
SLJ-v24-D '77-p57
Sch Lib-v28-S '80-p256
Hattie Rabbit
BL-v72-My 15 '76-p1340
CE-v53-N '76-p94
KR-v44-Ap 1 '76-p388
PW-v209-Mr 29 '76-p58
SLJ-v22-My '76-p74
Hattie, Tom, And The Chicken Witch
BL-v76-Mr 15 '80-p1065
HB-v59-F '83-p96
KR-v48-Mr 15 '80-p362
PW-v217-Ap 18 '80-p89
Hound And Bear
BL-v73-S 15 '76-p182
CLW-v48-F '77-p305

GACKENBACH, Dick (continued)
CSM-v68-N 3 '76-p22
HB-v53-F '77-p37
KR-v44-Jl 15 '76-p790
PW-v210-Ag 2 '76-p114
SLJ-v23-D '76-p65
Ida Fanfanny
BB-v6-S '78-p1
BL-v75-O 1 '78-p292
KR-v46-N 1 '78-p1185
SLJ-v25-Ja '79-p42
Teacher-v96-O '78-p162
WCRB-v4-N '78-p59
The Leatherman
BB-v6-F '78-p2
BL-v74-O 1 '77-p289
KR-v45-Ag 15 '77-p850
LA-v55-F '78-p211
NYTBR-O 30 '77-p36
PW-v212-Ag 29 '77-p367
SLJ-v24-N '77-p46
Little Bug
CBRS-v9-Je '81-p92
KR-v49-Ap 1 '81-p426
LA-v58-S '81-p698
PW-v219-My 15 '81-p62
SLJ-v27-My '81-p55
VV-v26-D 9 '81-p56
McGoogan Moves The Mighty Rock
BL-v77-Ap 1 '81-p1098
CBRS-v9-Mr '81-p64
CSM-v73-My 11 '81-pB4
KR-v49-Mr 15 '81-p352
LA-v59-Ja '82-p53
NYTBR-v86-F 22 '81-p31
Mr. Wink And His Shadow, Ned
BL-v79-Mr 15 '83-p967
CBRS-v11-My '83-p96
KR-v51-F 1 '83-p116
LA-v60-S '83-p771
PW-v223-Ap 15 '83-p50
SLJ-v29-Ag '83-p50
More From Hound And Bear
HB-v56-Ap '80-p168
KR-v48-Ja 15 '80-p62
PW-v216-O 1 '79-p89
SLJ-v26-D '79-p95
Mother Rabbit's Son Tom
BL-v73-F 15 '77-p901
CCB-B-v30-Jl '77-p174
CSM-v69-My 4 '77-pB6
GP-v17-N '78-p3423
Inst-v86-My '77-p118
KR-v45-Ja 15 '77-p42
NYTBR-My 1 '77-p29
RT-v32-O '78-p30
SLJ-v23-My '77-p75
WCRB-v3-My '77-p40
WLB-v51-Ap '77-p672
Pepper And All The Legs
BL-v75-O 1 '78-p293
HB-v55-F '79-p53
KR-v46-O 15 '78-p1133
PW-v214-O 30 '78-p51
RT-v33-N '79-p217
SLJ-v25-N '78-p44
The Perfect Mouse
CBRS-v13-O '84-p13
PW-v226-S 7 '84-p78
The Pig Who Saw Everything
BB-v6-S '78-p2
BL-v74-Mr 15 '78-p1186
CCB-B-v32-O '78-p28
KR-v46-F 1 '78-p102
LA-v55-S '78-p736
PW-v213-Ja 16 '78-p100
SLJ-v24-Ap '78-p69
Poppy The Panda
PW-v226-Jl 27 '84-p144
The Princess And The Pea
CBRS-v12-S '83-p3
CCB-B-v37-Ja '84-p81
SLJ-v30-O '83-p148
What's Claude Doing?
BL-v80-My 1 '84-p1246
KR-v52-Mr 1 '84-pJ4
PW-v225-Mr 23 '84-p72
SLJ-v30-Ag '84-p59

* * *

GADLER, Steve J
Sun Power
ACSB-v12-Spring '79-p20
BL-v75-F 15 '79-p933
CBRS-v7-Mr '79-p76
Cur R-v18-O '79-p295
SB-v15-D '79-p157
SLJ-v26-S '79-p137

* * *

GADSBY, David
Alleluya!
JB-v44-Ag '80-p189
Sch Lib-v29-Je '81-p143
Flying A Round
JB-v46-D '82-p223
SLJ-v29-My '83-p61
TES-D 3 '82-p25
Harlequin
NS-v102-D 4 '81-p17
Merrily To Bethlehem
GP-v17-Ja '79-p3451
JB-v43-F '79-p30
Obs-D 3 '78-p36
TLS-D 1 '78-p1399
Ta-Ra-Ra-Boom-De-Ay
GP-v16-Ja '78-p3248
JB-v42-Ap '78-p87
Obs-O 30 '77-p26
Obs-N 27 '77-p29

* * *

GADSBY, Jean
Looking At Everyday Things
GP-v19-Ja '81-p3818
Looking At Other Children
Sch Lib-v29-Je '81-p143
TES-Mr 7 '80-p47
Looking At The World
TES-My 8 '81-p26

* * *

GAEDDERT, LouAnn
All-In-All
BL-v73-O 15 '76-p313
BL-v73-O 15 '76-p322
CCB-B-v30-Mr '77-p106
HB-v52-D '76-p631
KR-v44-S 1 '76-p984
LA-v54-Ap '77-p443
SLJ-v23-Ja '77-p100
Gustav The Gourmet Giant
BB-v5-Mr '77-p1
BL-v73-O 15 '76-p322
CLW-v48-F '77-p305
KR-v44-S 15 '76-p1034
NYTBR-N 14 '76-p38
PW-v215-Ap 23 '79-p80
SLJ-v23-N '76-p46
Just Like Sisters
BL-v78-D 15 '81-p548
CBRS-v10-F '82-p66
HB-v58-F '82-p41
KR-v50-F 1 '82-p135
PW-v220-D 11 '81-p62
SLJ-v28-O '81-p141
The Kid With The Red Suspenders
BL-v79-Je 1 '83-p1275
CCB-B-v37-S '83-p7
RT-v37-O '83-p86
SLJ-v29-My '83-p70
A New England Love Story
BL-v77-S 15 '80-p109
BS-v41-Ap '81-p38
CBRS-v9-D '80-p28
CCB-B-v34-O '80-p31

GAEDDERT, LouAnn
(continued)
HB-v57-Je '81-p317
J Read-v25-O '81-p88
KR-v49-F 15 '81-p219
SLJ-v27-My '81-p72
VOYA-v4-Je '81-p56
WLB-v55-Ap '81-p612
Noisy Nancy Norris
BL-v62-S 15 '65-p94
CCB-B-v19-S '65-p8
CSM-v58-Mr 24 '66-p10
Choice-v14-N '77-p1178
KR-v33-Je 15 '65-p572
LJ-v90-Jl '65-p3120
Too Many Girls
CCB-B-v26-O '72-p25
KR-v40-Jl 15 '72-p800
LJ-v97-D 15 '72-p4082
Your Former Friend, Matthew
BL-v80-Jl '84-p1548
CBRS-v12-Spring '84-p125
HB-v60-Ap '84-p195
SLJ-v30-Ap '84-p113

* * *

GAFFNEY, Timothy R
Jerrold Petrofsky: Biomedical Pioneer
BL-v81-S 15 '84-p127
SLJ-v31-O '84-p156

* * *

GAG, Flavia
The Melon Patch Mystery
CCB-B-v18-F '65-p86

* * *

GAG, Wanda
The ABC Bunny
Teacher-v96-My '79-p116
VLS-My '82-p12
The Funny Thing
ABC-v4-S '83-p38
Gone Is Gone
ABC-v4-S '83-p40
RT-v33-Mr '80-p688
Jorinda And Joringel
BB-v7-My '79-p2
BL-v74-Jl 1 '78-p1678
HB-v55-O '78-p507
KR-v46-Jl 15 '78-p747
PW-v222-D 3 '82-p60
Teacher-v96-My '79-p113
Millions Of Cats
ABC-v4-S '83-p25
BL-v80-Jl '84-p1555
HB-v55-O '78-p536
HE-v37-N 19 '77-p13
NYTBR-S 25 '77-p49
NYTBR-N 13 '77-p40
Obs-Mr 6 '77-p22
Teacher-v95-My '78-p104
Nothing At All
ABC-v4-S '83-p39
The Six Swans
ABC-v4-Mr '83-p59
BL-v79-F 1 '83-p723
CCB-B-v36-Mr '83-p126
NYTBR-v87-N 14 '82-p50
PW-v222-D 3 '82-p60
SLJ-v29-D '82-p48
Snippy And Snappy
ABC-v4-S '83-p38
The Sorcerer's Apprentice
BB-v7-O '79-p4
BL-v75-Je 1 '79-p1491
BW-v9-D 2 '79-p17
CCB-B-v33-S '79-p7
HB-v55-Ag '79-p428
KR-v47-Je 1 '79-p633
LA-v57-Mr '80-p327
PW-v215-Ap 9 '79-p108
PW-v222-D 3 '82-p60
RT-v34-O '80-p51
SLJ-v26-O '79-p139

* * *

GAGE, Wilson
Big Blue Island
CCB-B-v18-Je '65-p148
HB-v41-F '65-p53
The Crow And Mrs. Gaddy
BL-v80-Ap 15 '84-p1196
BW-v14-Je 10 '84-p7
GP-v23-S '84-p4303
HB-v60-Je '84-p325
KR-v52-My 1 '84-pJ34
PW-v225-F 3 '84-p403
SLJ-v30-My '84-p96
TLS-Ag 24 '84-p954
Cully Cully And The Bear
CE-v60-N '83-p137
JB-v48-F '84-p17
Down In The Boondocks
BL-v74-O 15 '77-p382
BW-v10-S 21 '80-p12
CCB-B-v31-F '78-p92
CE-v55-O '78-p38
CLW-v50-O '78-p109
Comw-v104-N 11 '77-p729
HB-v54-F '78-p41
Inter BC-v11-Ja 10 '80-p21
KR-v45-Ag 15 '77-p848
NYTBR-O 16 '77-p47
SLJ-v24-D '77-p56
The Ghost Of Five Owl Farm
B&B-v12-Je '67-p39
BL-v62-Jl 1 '66-p1049
CCB-B-v20-S '66-p9
CE-v43-Mr '67-p414
HB-v42-Ag '66-p435
KR-v34-Mr 1 '66-p245
LJ-v91-My 15 '66-p2716
PW-v189-Je 6 '66-p232
TLS-N 30 '67-p1135
Mike's Toads
CCB-B-v24-F '71-p91
HB-v46-Ag '70-p388
KR-v38-Ap 15 '70-p453
LJ-v95-D 15 '70-p4349
TN-v27-Ja '71-p209
Mrs. Gaddy And The Ghost
BB-v7-O '79-p1
BL-v76-S 15 '79-p128
GP-v20-My '81-p3875
HB-v55-O '79-p528
JB-v45-O '81-p195
KR-v47-N 1 '79-p1260
PW-v216-S 17 '79-p146
RT-v33-Mr '80-p732
SLJ-v26-D '79-p94
TES-My 21 '82-p31
Squash Pie
BL-v73-S 15 '76-p182
HB-v53-F '77-p44
Inst-v86-N '76-p146
KR-v44-Jl 15 '76-p793
SLJ-v23-D '76-p64
SLJ-v28-F '82-p37
SLJ-v28-Ap '82-p31

GAGE, Wilson
See Also Steele, Mary Q

GAGG, J C
Food And Drink
GP-v17-Jl '78-p3351

* * *

GAGNON, Cecile
Alfred Dans Le Metro
BL-v80-Ja 15 '84-p758
In Rev-v15-Ap '81-p37
Les Boutons Perdus
In Rev-v14-F '80-p41
La Chemise Qui S'Ennuyait
In Rev-v14-F '80-p42
Le Parapluie Rouge
In Rev-v14-F '80-p42
Le Roi De Novilande
BL-v80-Ja 15 '84-p758

GAGNON, Cecile (continued)
In Rev-v16-F '82-p36
Snowfeather
BIC-v10-D '81-p3
In Rev-v16-F '82-p36
Quill & Q-v48-F '82-p36

* * *

GAIDIR, Arkady
A Handful Of Stars
SLJ-v31-S '84-p116

* * *

GAIL, Marsieh
La Vida En El Renacimiento
BL-v78-Mr 15 '82-p967

* * *

GAIL, Marzieh
Life In The Renaissance
BL-v66-N 15 '69-p408
BS-v29-Jl 1 '69-p149
CCB-B-v23-F '70-p97
LJ-v94-N 15 '69-p4295
PW-v195-My 26 '69-p56

* * *

GAINES, Ernest J
A Long Day In November
BL-v69-My 1 '73-p838
BW-v5-N 7 '71-p6
CCB-B-v25-F '72-p91
HB-v48-Ap '72-p153
KR-v39-Ag 1 '71-p815
LJ-v96-D 15 '71-p4158
LJ-v96-D 15 '71-p4184
NYTBR, pt.1-F 13 '72-p8
NYTBR, pt.2-My 6 '73-p28
PW-v200-Ag 23 '71-p81
Time-v98-D 27 '71-p61

* * *

GAINES, M C
Picture Stories From The Bible
SLJ-v27-S '80-p58
SLJ-v27-F '81-p56

* * *

GALACTIC War (Battlegame Books)
Obs-D 11 '77-p31

* * *

GALANOU, Irene
Theodoros Kolokotrones
BL-v74-S 15 '77-p204

* * *

GALANTER, Eugene
Kids And Computers: The Parents' Microcomputer Handbook
BW-v13-O 2 '83-p8
Quill & Q-v49-Jl '83-p62
SB-v19-My '84-p248
Sch Lib-v32-Je '84-p162
VOYA-v6-O '83-p231

* * *

GALARZA, Ernesto
Chogorrom
BL-v72-My 15 '76-p1342
La Historia Verdadera De Una Botella De Leche
BL-v72-My 15 '76-p1341
Mas Poemas Parvulos
BL-v72-My 15 '76-p1342

* * *

GALBRAITH, Catherine A
India
BL-v68-Ap 1 '72-p671
BS-v31-D 15 '71-p433
HB-v48-Ap '72-p158
LJ-v97-F 15 '72-p784
NYTBR-F 27 '72-p8
India: Now And Through Time
LA-v58-Mr '81-p342
SLJ-v27-Ja '81-p69
SLJ-v28-S '81-p41

* * *

GALBRAITH, Clare K
Victor
Am-v125-D 4 '71-p487
CSM-v63-N 11 '71-pB1
Comw-v97-F 23 '73-p474
KR-v39-Ag 15 '71-p874
LJ-v97-Jl '72-p2484
RT-v36-D '82-p277

* * *

GALBRAITH, Kathryn O
Come Spring
BL-v76-S 1 '79-p43
CBRS-v8-Winter '80-p65
CCB-B-v33-Mr '80-p133
HB-v56-F '80-p54
KR-v47-N 1 '79-p1263
SLJ-v26-N '79-p76
Katie Did!
BL-v79-F 15 '83-p776
CBRS-v11-My '83-p97
CCB-B-v36-My '83-p166
PW-v222-O 29 '82-p45
SLJ-v29-Mr '83-p161
Spots Are Special!
BL-v72-Ap 1 '76-p1112
CLW-v48-S '76-p90
KR-v44-F 15 '76-p193
LA-v53-S '76-p698
RT-v31-O '77-p13
SLJ-v23-S '76-p99

* * *

GALDONE, Joanna
Amber Day
BL-v74-Jl 15 '78-p1733
JB-v44-Je '80-p116
NYTBR-Ja 28 '79-p25
SLJ-v25-S '78-p108
Gertrude, The Goose Who Forgot
BL-v71-Ap 1 '75-p816
CCB-B-v29-S '75-p8
GP-v15-O '76-p2974
JB-v40-O '76-p261
KR-v43-Ja 1 '75-p17
PW-v207-F 10 '75-p58
The Little Girl And The Big Bear
BL-v77-O 15 '80-p325
CCB-B-v34-Ja '81-p92
KR-v48-O 1 '80-p1293
RT-v34-Ap '81-p853
SLJ-v27-N '80-p61
TLS-S 17 '82-p1003
The Tailypo
BB-v6-Je '78-p2
BL-v74-N 1 '77-p475
Comw-v104-N 11 '77-p730
HB-v54-F '78-p40
JB-v43-Ag '79-p194
KR-v45-S 15 '77-p985
NYTBR-N 27 '77-p40
PW-v212-O 17 '77-p84
RT-v32-O '78-p38
SLJ-v24-Ja '78-p78

* * *

GALDONE, Paul
The Amazing Pig
BL-v77-Ap 15 '81-p1152
CBRS-v9-Ap '81-p74
KR-v49-Mr 15 '81-p352
LA-v58-N '81-p949
NYTBR-v86-Ap 26 '81-p54
PW-v219-F 13 '81-p94
RT-v35-Ap '82-p822
SLJ-v27-Ap '81-p112

GALDONE, Paul (continued)
Androcles And The Lion
CCB-B-v24-S '70-p8
KR-v38-Ap 15 '70-p444
LJ-v95-Jl '70-p2527
NYTBR-Je 21 '70-p22
Cinderella
BB-v7-F '79-p1
BL-v75-Ja 1 '79-p750
JB-v44-D '80-p283
PW-v214-N 20 '78-p60
RT-v33-O '79-p45
SLJ-v25-Ja '79-p42
TES-Je 20 '80-p42
The Elves And The Shoemaker
BL-v80-Je 15 '84-p1483
PW-v225-Je 29 '84-p104
SLJ-v31-S '84-p102
The Frog Prince
BB-v3-Ag '75-p2
BL-v72-O 1 '75-p233
JB-v41-O '77-p276
SLJ-v22-S '75-p82
The Gingerbread Boy
Am-v133-D 6 '75-p402
BL-v71-Mr 15 '75-p760
BL-v80-N 1 '83-p423
CCB-B-v29-S '75-p8
CLW-v47-O '75-p132
GP-v15-N '76-p2991
GP-v19-Ja '81-p3829
HB-v51-Ag '75-p373
JB-v40-O '76-p261
KR-v43-F 1 '75-p119
LA-v53-F '76-p198
PW-v207-Mr 17 '75-p56
PW-v223-Je 3 '83-p73
SLJ-v21-Ap '75-p44
The Greedy Old Fat Man
BL-v80-S 1 '83-p84
SLJ-v30-N '83-p63
Hans In Luck
BL-v76-My 1 '80-p1290
CLW-v52-O '80-p133
SLJ-v26-My '80-p82
Henny Penny
CE-v45-Ap '69-p461
HB-v45-Ap '69-p161
KR-v36-O 1 '68-p1105
PW-v194-S 16 '68-p71
The History Of Little Tom Tucker
CCB-B-v25-N '71-p42
LJ-v96-Ja 15 '71-p257
PW-v198-D 7 '70-p50
The History Of Mother Twaddle And The Marvelous Achievements Of Her Son Jack
CCB-B-v28-S '74-p7
CSM-v66-My 1 '74-pF2
HB-v50-Je '74-p273
KR-v42-F 1 '74-p105
LJ-v99-S 15 '74-p2245
PW-v205-Mr 18 '74-p54
SR/W-v1-My 4 '74-p43
Teacher-v92-O '74-p110
The House That Jack Built
RT-v32-N '78-p148
SLMQ-v12-Summer '84-p326
Jack And The Beanstalk
PW-v221-Ap 23 '82-p93
King Of The Cats
BL-v76-My 15 '80-p1363
CCB-B-v34-S '80-p13
CE-v57-Ja '81-p172
Cur R-v20-Ap '81-p170
KR-v48-Je 15 '80-p775
LA-v57-N '80-p895
PW-v217-Ap 4 '80-p75
SLJ-v26-My '80-p55
SLJ-v27-O '80-p119
TES-Je 11 '82-p37
The Little Red Hen
BL-v70-O 1 '73-p170
BL-v70-Mr 15 '74-p827
BW-v7-N 11 '73-p2C
CCB-B-v27-D '73-p63
CSM-v65-N 7 '73-pB2
Comw-v99-N 23 '73-p214
GP-v14-My '75-p2647
HB-v49-D '73-p585
JB-v39-F '75-p15
KR-v41-Je 1 '73-p596
KR-v41-D 15 '73-p1347
LJ-v98-S 15 '73-p2639
LJ-v98-D 15 '73-p3689
NYTBR-Ja 6 '74-p8
PW-v203-Je 11 '73-p155
Teacher-v91-My '74-p79
Little Red Riding Hood
BL-v71-Ja 1 '75-p460
JB-v42-F '78-p16
KR-v42-N 15 '74-p1199
PW-v206-N 25 '74-p45
The Magic Porridge Pot
BL-v73-D 15 '76-p606
CCB-B-v30-Ap '77-p123
CLW-v48-F '77-p305
Comw-v103-N 19 '76-p761
JB-v43-Ap '79-p95
KR-v44-O 15 '76-p1132
RT-v31-O '77-p12
RT-v31-F '78-p577
SLJ-v23-D '76-p49
The Monkey And The Crocodile
BL-v66-N 15 '69-p408
CCB-B-v23-Ap '70-p127
HB-v45-D '69-p668
KR-v37-Ag 15 '69-p849
LJ-v95-F 15 '70-p771
Spectr-v47-Mr '71-p45
TLS-O 30 '70-p1261
The Monster And The Tailor
BL-v79-N 1 '82-p370
CCB-B-v36-D '82-p65
EJ-v73-F '84-p104
KR-v50-Ag 15 '82-p935
PW-v222-S 24 '82-p73
SLJ-v29-D '82-p48
Puss In Boots
BB-v4-Jl '76-p2
BL-v72-My 1 '76-p1263
CCB-B-v30-O '76-p29
Comw-v103-N 19 '76-p761
HB-v60-Ap '84-p215
JB-v42-O '78-p250
KR-v44-Ap 1 '76-p384
LA-v54-F '77-p207
PW-v224-O 28 '83-p70
Par-v51-N '76-p29
SLJ-v23-S '76-p100
TES-Je 2 '78-p21
The Table, The Donkey And The Stick
BL-v73-Ja 15 '77-p718
HB-v53-Ap '77-p149
NYTBR-N 14 '76-p28
SLJ-v23-D '76-p49
The Three Bears
Am-v127-D 2 '72-p475
BL-v68-Je 15 '72-p910
BW-v6-My 7 '72-p6
CCB-B-v25-Ap '72-p122
KR-v40-Ja 15 '72-p66
LJ-v97-S 15 '72-p2933
PW-v201-F 28 '72-p73
SR-v55-Ap 22 '72-p78
TLS-Ap 6 '73-p385
The Three Billy Goats Gruff
BL-v69-Mr 15 '73-p713
BL-v80-S 1 '83-p93
CSM-v65-My 2 '73-pB2
Comw-v99-N 23 '73-p214
Emerg Lib-v9-My '82-p28
Emerg Lib-v11-Ja '84-p19
KR-v41-F 1 '73-p108

GALLANT, Roy A (continued)
BL-v80-O 15 '83-p369
CCB-B-v34-My '81-p170
S&T-v61-My '81-p440
SB-v17-N '81-p92
Once Around The Galaxy
ASBYP-v17-Spring '84-p21
BL-v80-F 1 '84-p813
CBRS-v12-Mr '84-p83
SB-v20-N '84-p92
SLJ-v30-Mr '84-p172
The Planets
ASBYP-v16-Winter '83-p25
BL-v79-S 1 '82-p42
CBRS-v10-Jl '82-p127
KR-v50-Je 1 '82-p637
NYTBR-v87-Ag 1 '82-p18
SB-v18-N '82-p90
SLJ-v29-F '83-p88
VOYA-v5-O '82-p54

* * *

GALLER, Helga
Little Nerino
CBRS-v10-Spring '82-p111
JB-v46-Ag '82-p131
SLJ-v29-Ja '83-p59
WLB-v56-Je '82-p770

* * *

GALLI, L
C'Era Una Donna, Bella Come Il Sole
TLS-Ap 2 '76-p378

* * *

GALLICO, Paul
The Day Jean-Pierre Joined The Circus
CCB-B-v24-Jl '70-p176
GP-v15-O '76-p2965
LJ-v95-F 15 '70-p778
The Day Jean-Pierre Was Pignapped
CCB-B-v19-D '65-p62
KR-v33-Jl 15 '65-p672
LJ-v90-S 15 '65-p3779
NYTBR-v70-N 7 '65-p55
The House That Wouldn't Go Away
BL-v76-My 1 '80-p1290
CBRS-v8-My '80-p98
CCB-B-v33-Je '80-p189
HB-v56-Ag '80-p406
PW-v217-Ap 18 '80-p89
SLJ-v26-Ag '80-p64
Miracle In The Wilderness
BB-v3-D '75-p4
BL-v72-O 15 '75-p280
BS-v35-D '75-p298
CCB-B-v29-Mr '76-p109
KR-v43-Ag 15 '75-p933
LJ-v100-D 1 '75-p2264
PW-v208-Ag 25 '75-p285

* * *

GALLO, Donald R
Sixteen
BL-v81-S 1 '84-p60
CBRS-v13-O '84-p19
KR-v52-S 1 '84-pJ79
SLJ-v31-O '84-p166

* * *

GALLO, Giovanni
The Lazy Beaver
CBRS-v12-O '83-p12
CCB-B-v37-O '83-p26
JB-v47-D '83-p235
PW-v224-Jl 15 '83-p52
RT-v37-Ap '84-p779
SLJ-v30-N '83-p63

* * *

GALLOB, Edward
City Leaves, City Trees
BL-v68-Jl 15 '72-p1004
CE-v49-D '72-p148
CLW-v44-O '72-p191
CSM-v67-Je 10 '75-p17
CSM-v70-S 25 '78-p15
KR-v40-My 1 '72-p538
LJ-v98-Mr 15 '73-p1002
SA-v227-D '72-p115
SB-v8-S '72-p147
TN-v29-Ap '73-p253
City Rocks, City Blocks, And The Moon
BL-v70-N 15 '73-p338
CCB-B-v27-Ap '74-p128
CE-v50-Mr '74-p296
HB-v50-Ap '74-p171
KR-v41-O 15 '73-p1165
KR-v41-D 15 '73-p1353
LJ-v98-D 15 '73-p3689
LJ-v98-D 15 '73-p3706
SA-v229-D '73-p133
SB-v10-My '74-p68

* * *

GALLOWAY, Priscilla
Good Times, Bad Times
BIC-v10-Ap '81-p30
Ms-v11-D '82-p94
Good Times, Bad Times, Mummy And Me
Can Child Lit-#25 '82-p48
In Rev-v15-Ap '81-p38
When You Were Little And I Was Big
BIC-v13-My '84-p31
Quill & Q-v50-Ap '84-p16

* * *

GAMBILL, Henrietta
Self-Control
SLJ-v29-Ap '83-p100

* * *

GAMBINO, Robert
Easy To Grow Vegetables
ACSB-v8-Fall '75-p13
BB-v3-Ja '76-p3
CLW-v47-Ap '76-p409
SLJ-v22-O '75-p106

* * *

GAMBIT Book Of Children's Songs
BL-v67-Ap 1 '71-p665
CCB-B-v24-Je '71-p160

* * *

GAMERMAN, Martha
Trudy's Straw Hat
CCB-B-v30-Je '77-p157
CSM-v69-My 4 '77-pB6
Cur R-v16-My '77-p128
KR-v45-Ja 1 '77-p1
PW-v211-Ja 17 '77-p82
SLJ-v23-My '77-p50

* * *

GAMMELL, Stephen
Git Along, Old Scudder
BL-v79-Ap 1 '83-p1033
BW-v13-My 8 '83-p16
CBRS-v11-Spring '83-p118
CCB-B-v36-Jl '83-p209
CE-v61-S '84-p65
HB-v59-Ap '83-p159
KR-v51-F 15 '83-p180
NYTBR-v88-Ap 24 '83-p24
RT-v37-N '83-p193
SLJ-v29-Ag '83-p50
Once Upon MacDonald's Farm
BL-v77-My 15 '81-p1252
BL-v79-Je 1 '83-p1282
CBRS-v9-My '81-p81
HB-v57-Ag '81-p413
KR-v49-Ap 15 '81-p498
LA-v58-S '81-p698

GAMMELL, Stephen
(continued)
NYTBR-v86-Ap 26 '81-p54
PW-v219-Ap 24 '81-p75
SLJ-v27-Ag '81-p55
The Story Of Mr. And Mrs. Vinegar
CBRS-v10-Ap '82-p82
HB-v58-Je '82-p278
KR-v50-Mr 1 '82-p271
RT-v36-O '82-p117
SLJ-v28-Mr '82-p132
Wake Up, Bear...It's Christmas!
BL-v78-S 1 '81-p44
CBRS-v10-S '81-p2
CCB-B-v35-O '81-p29
HB-v57-D '81-p653
JB-v47-F '83-p12
KR-v49-O 1 '81-p1231
NS-v104-D 3 '82-p22
NY-v57-D 7 '81-p227
RT-v35-Ja '82-p498
SLJ-v28-O '81-p155
TES-D 17 '82-p28
VV-v26-D 9 '81-p58

* * *

GAMMON, David
The Secret Of Spaniards Rock
Can Child Lit-#29 '83-p65
In Rev-v15-Ag '81-p39
Quill & Q-v48-F '82-p16

* * *

GANDINI, Lella
Ambaraba
TLS-Mr 28 '80-p360
Make It With Paper And Things
GP-v14-S '75-p2695

* * *

GANDRILLE, Francoise
Campagnols Et Compagnie
BL-v79-Je 15 '83-p1345

* * *

GANE, Margaret D
Parade On An Empty Street
BIC-v8-Ap '79-p3
Can Child Lit-#25 '82-p41
KR-v47-Ag 1 '79-p873
Mac-v91-Ap 17 '78-p88

* * *

GANS, Carl
Reptiles Of The World
BB-v3-O '75-p4
PW-v208-Ag 18 '75-p68
SLJ-v22-F '76-p45

* * *

GANS, Manfred
Yeshiva Children Write Poetry
SLJ-v23-N '76-p57

* * *

GANS, Margaret
Pam And Pam
CCB-B-v23-My '70-p143
LJ-v95-My 15 '70-p1960
Three Presents For Jamie
LJ-v95-My 15 '70-p1960

* * *

GANS, Roma
Bird Talk
BL-v68-O 15 '71-p203
CCB-B-v25-O '71-p25
KR-v39-Jl 1 '71-p679
LJ-v96-D 15 '71-p4196
NY-v47-D 4 '71-p204
SB-v7-D '71-p246
Teacher-v96-Mr '79-p30
Birds At Night
CE-v45-Ap '69-p468
KR-v36-Ap 1 '68-p398
LJ-v93-Jl '68-p2729
NS-v77-My 16 '69-p706
SB-v4-My '68-p50
TLS-Je 26 '69-p704
Teacher-v86-Ja '69-p138
Teacher-v94-Ja '77-p133
Caves
ACSB-v10-Fall '77-p19
CCB-B-v30-Je '77-p157
CLW-v49-D '77-p234
Comw-v104-N 11 '77-p733
KR-v45-F 1 '77-p96
SLJ-v23-My '77-p75
Corals
TES-Je 6 '80-p27
Hummingbirds In The Garden
BL-v65-Jl 15 '69-p1274
BW-v3-My 4 '69-p34
CSM-v61-My 1 '69-pB2
HB-v45-O '69-p549
KR-v37-Ap 15 '69-p445
LJ-v94-S 15 '69-p3195
SB-v5-S '69-p158
Icebergs
SR-v48-Ja 23 '65-p52
TLS-D 9 '65-p1157
It's Nesting Time
CCB-B-v18-Ja '65-p74
Learning-v12-Ap '84-p50
Let's-Read-And-Find-Out Science Books
Inst-v78-Ja '69-p144
Millions And Millions Of Crystals
CCB-B-v27-O '73-p27
KR-v41-My 15 '73-p563
LJ-v98-O 15 '73-p3138
SB-v9-Mr '74-p327
TLS-Jl 18 '80-p811
Oil
ACSB-v9-Spring '76-p21
CCB-B-v29-D '75-p63
CE-v52-F '76-p208
Cur R-v16-F '77-p64
KR-v43-My 15 '75-p570
SLJ-v22-F '76-p38
Streamlined
TES-Je 6 '80-p27
Water For Dinosaurs And You
BL-v69-Ja 15 '73-p492
Inst-v82-N '72-p128
KR-v40-Ag 15 '72-p943
LJ-v98-My 15 '73-p1673
SB-v8-D '72-p231
TES-Je 6 '80-p27
TLS-Mr 28 '80-p363
Teacher-v91-F '74-p98
Water Plants
TES-Je 6 '80-p27
When Birds Change Their Feathers
ASBYP-v14-Winter '81-p26
CCB-B-v33-Jl '80-p212
HB-v56-Ag '80-p426
KR-v48-Ap 1 '80-p441
SB-v16-Ja '81-p156
SLJ-v26-My '80-p56
TES-Mr 6 '81-p38

* * *

GANTOS, Jack
Aunt Bernice
KR-v46-F 15 '78-p173
PW-v213-F 6 '78-p101
SLJ-v24-My '78-p54
Fair-Weather Friends
BB-v5-Ag '77-p1
BL-v73-My 15 '77-p1420
KR-v45-F 15 '77-p161
PW-v211-Mr 28 '77-p79
SLJ-v23-My '77-p51

GANTOS, Jack (continued)
Greedy Greeny
AB-v64-N 19 '79-p3445
BB-v7-O '79-p5
BL-v76-O 15 '79-p351
CBRS-v8-Ja '80-p41
Inst-v89-N '79-p138
KR-v48-F 1 '80-p120
PW-v216-S 17 '79-p146
SLJ-v26-N '79-p65
The Perfect Pal
CBRS-v8-D '79-p32
KR-v47-O 15 '79-p1206
PW-v216-N 19 '79-p78
RT-v33-Mr '80-p731
SLJ-v26-O '79-p139
Rotten Ralph
BL-v72-My 1 '76-p1264
BW-Je 13 '76-pM2
CCB-B-v29-Jl '76-p174
CLW-v48-S '76-p83
Comw-v103-N 19 '76-p760
HB-v52-Je '76-p279
KR-v44-F 1 '76-p129
LA-v54-My '77-p581
PW-v209-F 2 '76-p99
PW-v217-Ap 25 '80-p81
RT-v31-O '77-p13
SLJ-v22-My '76-p34
SLJ-v22-My '76-p50
Rotten Ralph's Rotten Christmas
CCB-B-v38-S '84-p5
KR-v52-S 1 '84-pJ60
PW-v226-Ag 10 '84-p82
SLJ-v31-O '84-p173
Sleepy Ronald
BB-v5-F '77-p1
BL-v73-O 1 '76-p251
KR-v44-Ag 15 '76-p903
New R-v175-N 27 '76-p31
PW-v210-Jl 5 '76-p91
SLJ-v23-O '76-p97
Swampy Alligator
CBRS-v8-My '80-p92
KR-v48-My 15 '80-p641
PW-v218-Jl 18 '80-p62
SLJ-v27-S '80-p58
The Werewolf Family
CBRS-v9-D '80-p24
KR-v48-O 1 '80-p1293
RT-v35-O '81-p65
SLJ-v27-O '80-p134
Willy's Raiders
KR-v48-My 15 '80-p641
SLJ-v26-My '80-p87
Worse Than Rotten, Ralph
BB-v6-Ja '79-p2
BL-v75-S 15 '78-p216
CCB-B-v32-F '79-p98
HB-v54-D '78-p630
KR-v46-S 1 '78-p946
PW-v214-Jl 17 '78-p169
PW-v222-D 24 '82-p65
SLJ-v25-O '78-p132
VV-v23-D 25 '78-p99

* * *

GANTSCHEV, Ivan
The Christmas Train
PW-v226-S 21 '84-p97
TES-N 19 '82-p32
Journey Of The Storks
CBRS-v11-Ag '83-p140
PW-v223-Mr 18 '83-p70
SLJ-v30-N '83-p63
The Moon Lake
CBRS-v10-Winter '82-p54
CSM-v73-O 13 '81-pB6
JB-v46-Je '82-p93
SLJ-v29-S '82-p108
TES-N 20 '81-p36
WLB-v56-F '82-p450
Otto The Bear
Obs-Jl 16 '78-p26
TES-Je 23 '78-p21
Rumprump
CBRS-v12-Ag '84-p145
PW-v225-Je 15 '84-p82
SLJ-v31-S '84-p102
The Volcano
CBRS-v10-Ja '82-p41
CCB-B-v35-D '81-p68
CSM-v73-O 13 '81-pB6
WLB-v56-F '82-p450
Voyage Of The Stork Family
JB-v47-Ag '83-p153

* * *

GANTZ, Charlotte Orr
Boy With Three Names
CCB-B-v26-Je '73-p154
KR-v41-F 15 '73-p187

* * *

GANTZ, David
Blipo One's Book Of Facts And Fun
CCB-B-v37-Mr '84-p126
Captain Swifty And His Happy Hearts Band
CCB-B-v37-F '84-p107
SLJ-v30-Ap '84-p101
Captain Swifty Counts To 50
CBRS-v11-Ja '83-p41
SLJ-v29-Ja '83-p59
Captain Swifty's Book Of Opposites
SLJ-v30-Ap '84-p101
The Genie Bear With The Light Brown Hair Word Book
CBRS-v11-Ja '83-p41
SLJ-v29-Mr '83-p161

* * *

GANZ, Barbara
Alberto And His Missing Sock/Albert Y El Calcetin Perdido
BL-v72-My 15 '76-p1343
SLJ-v22-My '76-p48

* * *

GANZ, Yaffa
The Adventures Of Jeremy Levi
PW-v219-Ap 24 '81-p76
Savta Simcha And The Incredible Shabbos Bag
PW-v219-Ja 30 '81-p75

* * *

GAPPER, Frances
Jane And The Kenilwood Occurrences
JB-v43-O '79-p271
SLJ-v26-Ja '80-p69
Sch Lib-v28-Je '80-p174

* * *

GARCIA, Ann O'N
Spirit On The Wall
BL-v78-Je 1 '82-p1312
BS-v42-Je '82-p119
CBRS-v10-Je '82-p106
CLW-v54-Mr '83-p334
Inst-v91-My '82-p107
J Read-v26-Ja '83-p375
PW-v221-F 12 '82-p98
RT-v36-O '82-p117
SLJ-v28-Mr '82-p147
VOYA-v5-O '82-p42

* * *

GARCIA, Claire W
The Peanut Plan
In Rev-v14-Ag '80-p48
SLJ-v27-Ja '81-p49

* * *

GARCIA, Maria
Las Aventuras De Connie Y Diego/The Adventures Of Connie And Diego
BL-v78-S 1 '81-p54

* * *

GARCIA, Richard
Los Espiritus De Mi Tia Otilia/My Aunt Otilia's Spirits
BL-v78-S 1 '81-p54
Inter BC-v14-#1 '83-p16

* * *

GARCIA ALVAREZ, Santiago
Viaje A Los Origenes De America
BL-v79-O 1 '82-p200

* * *

GARCIA CORELLA, Laura
Ellas... Y Los Ladrones
BL-v72-My 15 '76-p1343

* * *

GARCIA LORCA, Federico
The Cricket Sings
BL-v77-F 1 '81-p752
Kliatt-v15-Winter '81-p17
Parnassus-v9-Spring '81-p253
SLJ-v29-Mr '83-p91
The Lieutenant Colonel And The Gypsy
CCB-B-v25-N '71-p42
CSM-v63-N 11 '71-pB4
KR-v39-S 1 '71-p934
LJ-v96-N 15 '71-p3893

* * *

GARCIA NAREZO, Gabriel
Animales Feroces
HB-v55-Ag '79-p446
Extranos Animales Marinos
HB-v55-Ag '79-p446
Mariposas
HB-v55-Ag '79-p446
Minerales
HB-v55-Ag '79-p446
Peces
HB-v55-Ag '79-p446
Plantas Y Flores
HB-v55-Ag '79-p446

* * *

GARCIA SANCHEZ, J L
Funny Facts About The Owl
GP-v20-My '81-p3888
JB-v45-Ag '81-p152
Los Ninos De Los Cuentos
BL-v76-Je 15 '80-p1546

* * *

GARCIA SANCHEZ, Jose L
El Cocodrilo
RT-v36-N '82-p209
La Jirafa
RT-v36-N '82-p209
El Lobo
BL-v78-Je 15 '82-p1374
RT-v36-N '82-p209
El Tigre
RT-v36-N '82-p209

* * *

GARD, Joyce
The Hagwaste Donkeys
JB-v40-Ag '76-p199
Handysides Shall Not Fall
GP-v14-Jl '75-p2667
TLS-Jl 11 '75-p770
The Mermaid's Daughter
A Lib-v1-Ap '70-p385
BL-v66-Ja 1 '70-p564
CCB-B-v24-Jl '70-p176
Comw-v91-N 21 '69-p258
HB-v46-Ap '70-p166
LJ-v95-Mr 15 '70-p1202
NS-v78-O 31 '69-p624
SR-v52-N 8 '69-p70
TLS-Je 26 '69-p690
Smudge Of The Fells
BL-v62-My 15 '66-p918
CCB-B-v20-Ap '67-p121
KR-v34-F 15 '66-p185
LJ-v91-Ap 15 '66-p2218
NYTBR-v71-My 29 '66-p16
Punch-v248-Je 16 '65-p905
TLS-Je 17 '65-p497
Snow Firing
CCB-B-v21-Mr '68-p108
CE-v45-S '68-p40
KR-v36-Ja 1 '68-p12
LJ-v93-F 15 '68-p868
Lis-v77-My 18 '67-p661
NS-v73-My 26 '67-p732
SR-v51-Mr 16 '68-p39
TLS-My 25 '67-p454
YR-v4-Mr '68-p10
Talargain
BL-v61-Jl 1 '65-p1029
BS-v25-Ap 15 '65-p51
CCB-B-v19-S '65-p8
CE-v42-S '65-p54
CSM-v57-Ag 12 '65-p7
HB-v41-Ap '65-p175
Inst-v75-S '65-p166
KR-v33-Mr 1 '65-p243
LJ-v90-Mr 15 '65-p1558
NO-v5-Ja 10 '66-p27
NYTBR-v70-My 23 '65-p30

* * *

GARDAM, Jane
Bilgewater
B&B-v22-D '76-p81
BL-v74-O 15 '77-p367
BW-Ja 8 '78-pE6
Brit Bk N C-Autumn '82-p8
CCB-B-v31-F '78-p92
Comw-v104-N 11 '77-p732
GP-v15-Ja '77-p3041
HB-v54-F '78-p54
JB-v41-Ap '77-p110
KR-v45-Ag 1 '77-p789
Lis-v96-N 11 '76-p623
Obs-N 28 '76-p31
PW-v212-O 10 '77-p70
SLJ-v24-N '77-p70
Spec-v237-D 11 '76-p24
TES-D 14 '79-p21
TLS-D 10 '76-p1549
Bridget And William
Brit Bk N C-Spring '81-p17
CBRS-v9-Je '81-p93
CCB-B-v35-O '81-p29
GP-v20-Jl '81-p3908
JB-v45-Je '81-p111
SLJ-v28-Ja '82-p64
Sch Lib-v29-Je '81-p132
TES-Mr 6 '81-p29
TES-Ap 27 '84-p27
TLS-Mr 27 '81-p340
A Few Fair Days
BL-v69-O 15 '72-p201
BW-v6-N 5 '72-p8
CCB-B-v26-My '73-p137
CSM-v64-N 8 '72-pB7
Comw-v97-N 17 '72-p156
HB-v49-F '73-p47
HT-v21-D '71-p887
KR-v40-Jl 1 '72-p724
KR-v40-D 15 '72-p1413
NS-v82-N 12 '71-p664
PW-v203-Ja 22 '73-p70
TLS-O 22 '71-p1331
The Hollow Land
BL-v78-Jl '82-p1444

GARDAM, Jane (continued)
Brit Bk N C-Spring '82-p5
CCB-B-v35-My '82-p168
Econ-v281-D 26 '81-p107
GP-v20-Ja '82-p4010
HB-v58-Je '82-p297
JB-v45-D '81-p249
LA-v60-F '83-p215
Obs-N 29 '81-p27
Punch-v281-Ag 5 '81-p235
RT-v36-N '82-p242
SLJ-v28-My '82-p61
Sch Lib-v29-D '81-p343
TES-N 20 '81-p34
TES-N 11 '83-p25
TLS-S 18 '81-p1065
VOYA-v5-F '83-p35
Horse
Brit Bk N C-Autumn '82-p20
GP-v21-Jl '82-p3933
JB-v46-Je '82-p97
Sch Lib-v30-D '82-p334
TES-Mr 19 '82-p28
Kit
JB-v48-Ap '84-p64
TES-Mr 9 '84-p50
A Long Way From Verona
B&B-v19-Ja '74-p94
BL-v68-Je 1 '72-p857
BL-v68-Je 1 '72-p860
BW-v6-My 7 '72-p5
CCB-B-v26-S '72-p7
CE-v49-F '73-p257
Comw-v97-N 17 '72-p156
Emerg Lib-v11-N '83-p20
HB-v48-Ag '72-p359
KR-v40-Mr 1 '72-p266
LJ-v97-Je 15 '72-p2243
NS-v82-N 12 '71-p661
NYTBR-Ag 11 '74-p23
NYTBR, pt.2-My 7 '72-p28
NYTBR, pt.2-N 5 '72-p26
Obs-N 28 '71-p35
PW-v201-My 15 '72-p54
Punch-v284-Ap 20 '83-p80
SR-v55-Je 17 '72-p75
Spec-v227-N 13 '71-p688
TLS-D 3 '71-p1512
The Summer After The Funeral
B&B-v19-Ja '74-p93
BL-v70-F 1 '74-p592
CCB-B-v27-Ap '74-p128
Comw-v99-N 23 '73-p216
HB-v50-F '74-p55
ILN-v265-My '77-p87
KR-v41-N 1 '73-p1211
KR-v41-D 15 '73-p1356
LJ-v98-O 15 '73-p3154
Lis-v90-N 8 '73-p641
NO-v12-D 29 '73-p15
NS-v86-N 9 '73-p699
NYTBR-F 17 '74-p8
Obs-Mr 6 '77-p22
Spec-v231-D 22 '73-p822
TES-D 23 '83-p23
TLS-N 23 '73-p1429

* * *

GARDEN, Glen
Life B.C.
TES-O 24 '80-p24

* * *

GARDEN, Nancy
Annie On My Mind
BL-v78-Ag '82-p1517
CBRS-v11-O '82-p18
CCB-B-v36-D '82-p66
Inter BC-v14-#1 '83-p35
J Read-v26-F '83-p468
KR-v50-Je 1 '82-p637
Kliatt-v18-Fall '84-p8
PW-v222-S 10 '82-p75
SLJ-v28-Ag '82-p125
VOYA-v5-Ag '82-p30
Devils And Demons
BL-v72-Jl 1 '76-p1526
KR-v44-Ap 15 '76-p475
SLJ-v23-S '76-p133
Favorite Tales From Grimm
AB-v70-N 15 '82-p3401
BL-v79-Ja 1 '83-p617
CBRS-v11-D '82-p36
CE-v59-Mr '83-p281
CSM-v75-D 3 '82-pB8
LA-v60-Ap '83-p482
NYTBR-v87-N 14 '82-p50
SLJ-v29-F '83-p76
Fours Crossing
BL-v77-My 15 '81-p1252
CBRS-v9-My '81-p86
CCB-B-v34-My '81-p170
CE-v58-Mr '82-p257
HB-v57-Ag '81-p431
J Read-v25-N '81-p181
Kliatt-v17-Winter '83-p18
PW-v219-Mr 13 '81-p89
PW-v222-O 8 '82-p63
SLJ-v27-My '81-p72
The Kids' Code And Cipher Book
BL-v78-S 15 '81-p105
HB-v57-Ag '81-p457
HE-v41-F 7 '81-p14
SLJ-v28-N '81-p104
The Loners
BL-v69-F 1 '73-p524
CCB-B-v26-Ap '73-p123
KR-v40-N 1 '72-p1245
LJ-v98-Mr 15 '73-p1012
NYTBR, pt.2-N 5 '72-p2
Watersmeet
BL-v80-N 1 '83-p408
CCB-B-v37-N '83-p48
HB-v59-O '83-p580
SLJ-v30-S '83-p134
VOYA-v6-F '84-p338
What Happened In Marston
CCB-B-v25-S '71-p6
LJ-v96-S 15 '71-p2916
PW-v199-Ap 26 '71-p60
Witches
B&B-v23-D '77-p62
BL-v72-N 1 '75-p358
KR-v43-O 15 '75-p1189
SLJ-v22-O '75-p98
TES-F 3 '78-p39

* * *

GARDEN
TES-O 24 '80-p21

* * *

GARDEN Flowers (**Spotter's Guides**)
TES-Je 16 '78-p52

* * *

GARDEN Wildlife (**Nature Trail Books**)
TES-Je 20 '80-p25

* * *

GARDENING Is Easy-When You Know How
NYTBR-Mr 16 '75-p8
WLB-v49-D '74-p273

* * *

GARDINER, John R
Stone Fox
BOT-v4-F '81-p78
CCB-B-v34-N '80-p52
CE-v57-N '80-p110
HB-v56-Je '80-p294
KR-v48-My 1 '80-p584
LA-v57-O '80-p791
LATBR-Je 26 '83-p8
NW-v96-D 1 '80-p104
NY-v56-D 1 '80-p220
NYTBR-v85-Ap 27 '80-p45

GARDNER, Martin
(continued)
NYTBR, pt.2-My 4 '69-p55
NYTBR, pt.2-N 9 '69-p62
PW-v195-Je 2 '69-p136
SA-v225-D '71-p114
Space Puzzles
CLW-v43-D '71-p224
CLW-v43-My '72-p536
GT-v89-Mr '72-p113
Inst-v82-My '73-p78
JB-v39-Ap '75-p117
LJ-v96-O 15 '71-p3476
LR-v24-Winter '75-p366
SB-v7-S '71-p122
Teacher-v90-F '73-p125

* * *

GARDNER, Mercedes
Scooter And The Magic Star
SLJ-v27-N '80-p61

* * *

GARDNER, Richard A
The Boys And Girls Book About Divorce
BL-v67-Ap 1 '71-p663
CCB-B-v24-F '71-p91
Ms-v9-Ap '81-p88
NYTBR-S 3 '72-p8
Par-v57-Ag '82-p84
Par-v59-N '84-p198
The Boys And Girls Book About One-Parent Families
LJ-v103-D 15 '78-p2531
PT-v12-F '79-p109
PW-v214-O 30 '78-p44
SB-v15-Mr '80-p224
Dr. Gardner's Fairy Tales For Today's Children
CCB-B-v28-S '74-p7
CLW-v46-S '74-p89
KR-v42-Mr 15 '74-p299
LJ-v99-My 15 '74-p1465
PW-v205-My 27 '74-p64
Dr. Gardner's Modern Fairy Tales
KR-v45-Mr 15 '77-p285
NYTBR-Ap 24 '77-p22
Dr. Gardner's Stories About The Real World
CCB-B-v26-My '73-p137
KR-v40-D 1 '72-p1355
LJ-v98-Ap 15 '73-p1386

* * *

GARDNER, Richard M
The Baboon
BL-v69-N 15 '72-p293
CCB-B-v26-Jl '73-p170
KR-v40-Jl 1 '72-p732
KR-v40-D 15 '72-p1423
LJ-v98-F 15 '73-p653
NYTBR-My 27 '73-p8
SB-v8-Mr '73-p340
Make Your Own Comics For Fun And Profit
BL-v73-S 1 '76-p37
KR-v44-Je 15 '76-p692
SLJ-v23-O '76-p105

* * *

GARDNER, Robert
Kitchen Chemistry
ASBYP-v16-Fall '83-p26
BL-v79-F 1 '83-p723
SA-v249-D '83-p36
SLJ-v29-Mr '83-p175
Magic Through Science
CE-v55-Ap '79-p300
Cur R-v18-Ag '79-p237
Inst-v87-My '78-p113
KR-v46-Ja 15 '78-p51
SA-v241-D '79-p40
SB-v14-Mr '79-p228
SLJ-v24-N '77-p70
WCRB-v4-My '78-p53
Moving Right Along
ACSB-v12-Fall '79-p22
Cur R-v18-Ag '79-p237
SB-v15-D '79-p144
SLJ-v25-Ja '79-p60
Save That Energy
ACSB-v15-Winter '82-p28
BL-v77-Je 15 '81-p1339
SLJ-v28-F '82-p88
Shadow Science
ACSB-v10-Winter '77-p18
BL-v72-Jl 1 '76-p1526
HB-v52-D '76-p649
KR-v44-Ap 1 '76-p396
SB-v12-D '76-p158
SLJ-v23-N '76-p57
Teacher-v94-N '76-p131
Space
ASBYP-v14-Spring '81-p17
CBRS-v9-F '81-p56
Cur R-v20-Je '81-p267
SB-v17-S '81-p25
SLJ-v27-Mr '81-p156
This Is The Way It Works
ASBYP-v14-Winter '81-p27
CBRS-v8-Spring '80-p117
CCB-B-v34-S '80-p8
Cur R-v20-S '81-p400
HB-v56-Ag '80-p440
SLJ-v28-Ja '82-p87
VOYA-v3-F '81-p43

* * *

GARDNER, Sandra
Six Who Dared
BL-v78-Ja 15 '82-p644
CCB-B-v35-My '82-p168
Hi Lo-v3-Mr '82-p1
SLJ-v29-S '82-p121

* * *

GARDNER-LOULAN, JoAnn
Period
B Rpt-v1-Ja '83-p45
Inter BC-v11-My '80-p17
Ms-v12-Jl '83-p43
SLJ-v26-S '79-p137
VOYA-v4-O '81-p48

* * *

GARDONYI, Geza
Slave Of The Huns
BL-v66-Jl 1 '70-p1335
BS-v30-Ap 1 '70-p17
CCB-B-v23-Je '70-p159
HB-v46-Ap '70-p166
KR-v37-D 1 '69-p1265
Obs-N 30 '69-p35
RT-v35-Ap '82-p823
TLS-D 4 '69-p1390
TLS-Ap 6 '73-p381

* * *

GARELICK, May
About Owls
ACSB-v9-Winter '76-p16
BL-v71-Je 1 '75-p1010
CCB-B-v29-N '75-p44
CE-v52-Ja '76-p158
HB-v51-Ag '75-p394
KR-v43-My 1 '75-p516
NYTBR-My 4 '75-p22
New R-v173-D 6 '75-p23
SLJ-v22-S '75-p81
SR-v2-My 31 '75-p35
WLB-v49-Je '75-p705
Down To The Beach
BL-v70-O 15 '73-p232
CCB-B-v27-D '73-p64
CE-v50-Mr '74-p296
CSM-v65-N 7 '73-pB5
Comw-v99-N 23 '73-p213
HB-v49-O '73-p455

GARELICK, May (continued)
KR-v41-Ag 1 '73-p809
LJ-v98-D 15 '73-p3700
PW-v204-Ag 20 '73-p87
Teacher-v92-My '75-p26
It's About Birds
ACSB-v12-Winter '79-p11
BL-v74-My 15 '78-p1492
CLW-v51-O '79-p142
Cur R-v18-My '79-p147
HB-v54-Ag '78-p410
Inst-v88-N '78-p133
KR-v46-Jl 1 '78-p691
SB-v15-My '79-p41
SLJ-v25-S '78-p136
Teacher-v96-N '78-p134
Runaway Plane
CCB-B-v27-N '73-p42
LJ-v98-D 15 '73-p3716
The Tremendous Tree Book
ACSB-v13-Mr '80-p24
CBRS-v8-Winter '80-p65
CCB-B-v33-My '80-p172
HB-v56-Je '80-p312
KR-v48-Mr 1 '80-p283
PW-v217-Ja 11 '80-p88
RT-v34-N '80-p236
SB-v16-S '80-p32
SLJ-v26-Mr '80-p120
What Makes A Bird A Bird?
BL-v66-F 1 '70-p670
CCB-B-v23-My '70-p143
LJ-v95-Ap 15 '70-p1626
SB-v5-Mr '70-p332
Where Does The Butterfly Go When It Rains?
SLMQ-v12-Summer '84-p326
Who Likes It Hot
BL-v69-Mr 15 '73-p714
CCB-B-v26-Jl '73-p170
Inst-v82-N '72-p128
KR-v40-S 15 '72-p1092
LJ-v98-Ap 15 '73-p1374

* * *

GARFIELD, Leon
Black Jack
B&B-v16-Ag '71-pR12
B&B-v17-D '71-pR16
B&B-v24-Je '79-p56
BL-v65-My 15 '69-p1076
BW-v3-Jl 27 '69-p12
CCB-B-v22-My '69-p142
EJ-v72-S '83-p72
HB-v45-Je '69-p310
KR-v37-Mr 15 '69-p315
LJ-v94-My 15 '69-p2112
NYTBR, pt.2-My 4 '69-p12
PW-v195-My 19 '69-p70
SR-v52-Ap 19 '69-p39
TES-F 22 '80-p29
TLS-D 4 '69-p1384
The Book Lovers
B&B-v22-Ja '77-p61
BL-v75-F 1 '79-p856
JB-v41-F '77-p50
LJ-v103-N 15 '78-p2351
PW-v214-S 11 '78-p86
Bostock And Harris
B&B-v25-Je '80-p48
Brit Bk N C-Spring '80-p14
Econ-v273-D 22 '79-p86
GP-v18-N '79-p3597
JB-v44-Je '80-p141
Obs-D 2 '79-p39
TES-Ja 4 '80-p20
The Boy And The Monkey
B&B-v15-D '69-p44
CCB-B-v24-S '70-p8
GP-v15-Jl '76-p2909
LJ-v95-D 15 '70-p4349
PW-v197-My 25 '70-p57
TLS-D 4 '69-p1390
Child O'War
B&B-v17-S '72-p101
HB-v49-F '73-p53
LJ-v98-Mr 15 '73-p1012
NS-v83-Je 2 '72-p758
Spec-v229-Ag 19 '72-p289
TLS-Jl 14 '72-p807
The Cloak
JB-v41-Ap '77-p110
TES-F 3 '78-p42
The Confidence Man
BL-v75-Ap 15 '79-p1288
Brit Bk N C-Spring '80-p6
CBRS-v7-Ap '79-p88
CCB-B-v32-Mr '79-p114
GP-v18-My '79-p3525
HB-v55-Je '79-p308
JB-v43-Ap '79-p115
KR-v47-My 15 '79-p579
Obs-D 3 '78-p36
SLJ-v25-Ap '79-p68
SLJ-v25-My '79-p35
Sch Lib-v27-Je '79-p157
TES-N 24 '78-p41
TLS-D 1 '78-p1395
Devil-In-The-Fog
B&B-v12-Mr '67-p60
BL-v63-Ja 15 '67-p532
BS-v26-D 1 '66-p338
CCB-B-v20-F '67-p88
CE-v43-My '67-p537
EJ-v72-S '83-p71
HB-v43-F '67-p71
HT-v16-D '66-p865
KR-v34-O 1 '66-p1059
LJ-v92-F 15 '67-p892
NO-v6-Mr 13 '67-p21
NS-v72-N 11 '66-p708
NYTBR-v71-N 20 '66-p55
PW-v190-O 31 '66-p85
QJS-v54-O '68-p310
SR-v49-D 10 '66-p57
TLS-N 24 '66-p1078
TLS-Mr 14 '68-p258
The Drummer Boy
B&B-v15-My '70-p47
BL-v66-Jl 15 '70-p1407
CCB-B-v24-S '70-p8
CR-v217-Jl '70-p48
EJ-v72-S '83-p72
HB-v46-Ag '70-p392
KR-v38-Ap 1 '70-p390
LJ-v95-Jl '70-p2539
Lis-v84-N 12 '70-p673
NS-v79-My 15 '70-p702
NYTBR-My 17 '70-p26
NYTBR, pt.2-N 8 '70-p34
Obs-Mr 29 '70-p26
PW-v197-Ap 13 '70-p85
Spec-v224-My 9 '70-p625
TLS-Ap 16 '70-p411
The Dumb Cake
JB-v42-Je '78-p153
TLS-Jl 7 '78-p772
The Enemy
JB-v42-O '78-p261
NS-v95-My 19 '78-p680
TES-Ag 18 '78-p17
TLS-Jl 7 '78-p772
Fair's Fair
CBRS-v12-Ja '84-p48
CCB-B-v37-N '83-p49
GP-v20-N '81-p3972
HB-v60-F '84-p52
NY-v59-D 5 '83-p206
Obs-D 6 '81-p28
PW-v224-O 28 '83-p70
SLJ-v30-O '83-p176
TES-N 20 '81-p36
TLS-N 20 '81-p1358
The Filthy Beast
JB-v42-O '78-p266
NS-v95-My 19 '78-p680
TES-Ag 18 '78-p17
TLS-Jl 7 '78-p772

GARFIELD, Leon (continued)
The Fool
GP-v16-N '77-p3198
JB-v42-F '78-p25
TES-F 3 '78-p42
Footsteps
BL-v77-O 15 '80-p325
CBRS-v9-O '80-p18
CCB-B-v34-S '80-p8
CE-v58-S '81-p48
HB-v56-O '80-p525
KR-v48-D 15 '80-p1572
NY-v56-D 1 '80-p222
PW-v219-Ja 23 '81-p124
SLJ-v27-O '80-p155
The Ghost Downstairs
B&B-v17-Ag '72-p93
B&B-v20-My '75-p66
BW-v6-My 7 '72-p13
CCB-B-v25-Jl '72-p168
EJ-v72-S '83-p71
HB-v48-D '72-p599
KR-v40-Je 1 '72-p623
LJ-v97-D 15 '72-p4056
LJ-v97-D 15 '72-p4087
Lis-v88-N 9 '72-p644
NS-v83-Je 2 '72-p760
Obs-My 28 '72-p33
PW-v201-My 15 '72-p54
Spec-v229-Ag 19 '72-p289
Teacher-v90-Ja '73-p92
The God Beneath The Sea
B&B-v16-D '70-p57
B&B-v18-Ag '73-p140
BL-v68-O 1 '71-p144
BS-v31-F 15 '72-p522
CCB-B-v25-D '71-p56
CR-v218-Je '71-p332
Emerg Lib-v9-Ja '82-p13
HB-v47-O '71-p477
HT-v20-D '70-p889
LJ-v96-Je 15 '71-p2137
NS-v80-N 6 '70-p606
NYTBR, pt.2-My 2 '71-p46
SR-v54-N 13 '71-p62
Spec-v225-D 5 '70-pR7
Spec-v226-My 29 '71-p445
TLS-O 30 '70-p1254
TLS-Ap 6 '73-p381
The Golden Shadow
BL-v70-F 1 '74-p592
BS-v33-D 1 '73-p395
CCB-B-v27-Ja '74-p78
Choice-v12-N '75-p1132
Emerg Lib-v9-Ja '82-p13
HB-v50-F '74-p45
KR-v41-D 15 '73-p1370
LJ-v99-Ap 15 '74-p1226
NS-v85-My 25 '73-p782
NYTBR-F 3 '74-p8
Obs-Jl 29 '73-p32
PW-v205-Ja 7 '74-p54
TLS-Je 15 '73-p675
Guilt And Gingerbread
TLS-S 28 '84-p1106
The House Of Cards
Brit Bk N-S '82-p575
CSM-v75-F 9 '83-p15
EJ-v72-S '83-p72
GP-v21-My '82-p3911
JB-v46-O '82-p204
KR-v50-D 1 '82-p1304
KR-v50-D 15 '82-p1340
LJ-v108-Ja 15 '83-p145
Lis-v107-My 13 '82-p27
NL-v66-Ja 24 '83-p17
Obs-My 2 '82-p30
PW-v222-N 12 '82-p58
Sch Lib-v30-S '82-p280
TLS-My 21 '82-p566
WCRB-v9-Mr '83-p39
The House Of Hanover
BL-v73-Ja 1 '77-p665
CCB-B-v30-F '77-p90
Cur R-v17-F '78-p78
GP-v15-S '76-p2943
HT-v30-Mr '80-p47
JB-v40-Ag '76-p226
KR-v44-O 1 '76-p1104
SLJ-v23-N '76-p68
TLS-Jl 16 '76-p886
Jack Holborn
BL-v62-Mr 1 '66-p664
BS-v25-Ja 1 '66-p393
CCB-B-v19-My '66-p149
EJ-v72-S '83-p71
KR-v33-O 15 '65-p1082
LJ-v91-Ja 15 '66-p434
NYTBR-v70-N 7 '65-p8
John Diamond
B&B-v25-Je '80-p49
Brit Bk N C-Autumn '80-p20
GP-v19-S '80-p3742
HT-v30-D '80-p62
JB-v44-O '80-p247
Lis-v104-N 6 '80-p624
NS-v100-N 28 '80-p30
Punch-v281-D 2 '81-p1024
Sch Lib-v28-S '80-p289
TES-Je 27 '80-p24
TES-Ap 2 '82-p27
TLS-Mr 28 '80-p355
King Nimrod's Tower
CBRS-v11-S '82-p6
CCB-B-v36-N '82-p46
HB-v58-O '82-p510
JB-v46-O '82-p182
KR-v50-Jl 1 '82-p729
LA-v60-Ap '83-p480
Obs-Jl 4 '82-p28
PW-v222-Jl 30 '82-p75
RT-v36-Mr '83-p715
SLJ-v29-O '82-p140
Sch Lib-v31-Je '83-p127
TES-S 17 '82-p34
Labour In Vain
GP-v16-N '77-p3198
JB-v41-D '77-p351
Lis-v98-N 10 '77-p624
TLS-Jl 15 '77-p859
The Lamplighter's Funeral
GP-v15-Jl '76-p2909
JB-v40-Ag '76-p226
Lis-v96-N 11 '76-p623
Obs-Jl 11 '76-p23
TLS-Jl 16 '76-p880
Mirror, Mirror
GP-v15-Jl '76-p2909
JB-v40-Ag '76-p226
Lis-v96-N 11 '76-p623
TLS-Jl 16 '76-p880
Mister Corbett's Ghost
B&B-v14-My '69-p42
CCB-B-v22-F '69-p92
CE-v45-Ap '69-p462
EJ-v72-S '83-p71
HB-v44-O '68-p560
KR-v36-Ag 1 '68-p824
LJ-v93-N 15 '68-p4403
NS-v77-My 16 '69-p700
NYTBR-v73-N 3 '68-p8
Obs-Ap 6 '69-p26
PW-v194-S 2 '68-p59
SE-v33-My '69-p555
Spec-v222-My 16 '69-p657
TLS-Ap 3 '69-p350
Moss And Blister
JB-v41-Ap '77-p111
Obs-N 28 '76-p31
TES-F 3 '78-p42
TLS-D 10 '76-p1545
The Night Of The Comet
BL-v76-D 15 '79-p611
BL-v78-F 15 '82-p762
CBRS-v8-N '79-p27
CCB-B-v33-D '79-p69
EJ-v72-S '83-p71
HB-v56-F '80-p60

GARFIELD, Leon (continued)
KR-v47-N 1 '79-p1266
SLJ-v26-N '79-p87
The Pleasure Garden
BS-v36-O '76-p212
CLW-v48-S '76-p89
EJ-v72-S '83-p71
JB-v40-Ag '76-p226
KR-v44-F 1 '76-p147
LJ-v101-Ap 1 '76-p923
Lis-v96-N 11 '76-p623
PW-v209-Mr 8 '76-p58
SLJ-v23-N '76-p75
TLS-Jl 16 '76-p880
WLB-v51-O '76-p136
The Restless Ghost
BS-v29-Ja 1 '70-p388
CCB-B-v23-My '70-p143
HB-v46-F '70-p45
KR-v37-O 15 '69-p1122
LJ-v94-N 15 '69-p4295
NYTBR-N 30 '69-p42
NYTBR, pt.2-N 9 '69-p60
PW-v196-O 20 '69-p60
SR-v53-F 21 '70-p45
Rosy Starling
GP-v16-N '77-p3198
JB-v42-F '78-p39
Obs-N 27 '77-p29
TES-F 3 '78-p42
Smith
B&B-v12-Je '67-p36
B&B-v13-Ag '68-p49
BL-v64-F 1 '68-p637
BS-v27-N 1 '67-p313
BW-v1-N 5 '67-p43
CCB-B-v21-My '68-p141
Comw-v87-N 10 '67-p281
EJ-v72-S '83-p71
HB-v43-D '67-p758
KR-v35-Jl 1 '67-p746
LJ-v92-N 15 '67-p4250
LR-v21-Summer '67-p93
Lis-v77-My 18 '67-p660
NO-v7-Ja 15 '68-p20
NS-v73-My 26 '67-p732
NYTBR-v72-N 26 '67-p62
PW-v192-O 23 '67-p52
SR-v51-F 24 '68-p51
Spec-v218-Je 2 '67-p654
TLS-My 25 '67-p446
The Sound Of Coaches
A Lib-v5-My '74-p236
B&B-v20-Ja '75-p73
BL-v70-Ap 1 '74-p868
BS-v34-Ag 1 '74-p228
BW-My 19 '74-p5
CCB-B-v27-Jl '74-p176
Choice-v12-N '75-p1132
EJ-v72-S '83-p71
HB-v50-O '74-p142
KR-v42-Ap 1 '74-p371
KR-v43-Ja 1 '75-p10
LJ-v99-My 15 '74-p1451
LJ-v99-My 15 '74-p1482
LR-v24-Winter '75-p377
Lis-v92-N 7 '74-p613
NS-v87-My 24 '74-p737
NYTBR-Je 30 '74-p30
PW-v205-Mr 4 '74-p72
PW-v209-Je 14 '76-p112
TES-O 7 '77-p22
TLS-Jl 5 '74-p713
WLB-v51-O '76-p136
The Strange Affair Of Adelaide Harris
B&B-v17-F '72-p95
B&B-v20-My '75-p66
BL-v68-My 1 '72-p765
BL-v68-My 1 '72-p769
Brit Bk N C-Spring '81-p14
CCB-B-v25-Mr '72-p106
HB-v48-Ap '72-p153
KR-v39-N 15 '71-p1217
LJ-v96-N 15 '71-p3909
LJ-v96-D 15 '71-p4159
NS-v82-N 12 '71-p661
Obs-N 28 '71-p35
SR-v55-F 19 '72-p80
Spec-v227-N 13 '71-p692
TLS-D 3 '71-p1509
TN-v28-Je '72-p433
WLB-v51-O '76-p136
Strange Fish And Other Stories
KR-v42-N 15 '74-p1201
SLJ-v21-Mr '75-p105
A Swag Of Stories
JB-v42-O '78-p267
TES-Je 16 '78-p46
TLS-Jl 7 '78-p769
Tom Titmarsh's Devil
JB-v42-Je '78-p153
TLS-Jl 7 '78-p772
The Valentine
GP-v16-N '77-p3198
JB-v41-D '77-p351
Lis-v98-N 10 '77-p624
TLS-Jl 15 '77-p859
The Writing On The Wall
CBRS-v12-O '83-p16
CCB-B-v37-Ja '84-p86
JB-v47-O '83-p198
KR-v51-S 1 '83-pJ148
RT-v37-Mr '84-p646
SLJ-v30-D '83-p54
Sch Lib-v31-D '83-p342
TES-F 17 '84-p28

* * *

GARIBALDI, Gerald
He Gave Himself To The Sea
SLJ-v27-Ja '81-p57
Nightmare In A Sea Of Mud
SLJ-v27-Ja '81-p57

* * *

GARLAN, Patricia Wallace
Orange-Robed Boy
BL-v63-Je 15 '67-p1099
CCB-B-v21-N '67-p42
CLW-v43-F '72-p329
HB-v43-Ag '67-p470
LJ-v92-My 15 '67-p2020
NYTBR-v72-Je 18 '67-p30

* * *

GARLAND, Rosemary
My Bedtime Book Of Two-Minute Stories
SLJ-v23-O '76-p98

* * *

GARLAND, Sarah
Doing The Washing
JB-v47-O '83-p198
Sch Lib-v31-D '83-p343
Going Shopping
B&B-Jl '82-p36
Brit Bk N C-Autumn '82-p11
JB-v46-Ag '82-p130
Sch Lib-v30-S '82-p222
TES-Je 18 '82-p28
TLS-Jl 23 '82-p793
Having A Picnic
Obs-Ag 26 '84-p19
Henry And Fowler
JB-v40-O '76-p262
KR-v45-My 15 '77-p537
Obs-Jl 18 '76-p20
PW-v211-Je 27 '77-p110
SLJ-v24-D '77-p44
The Joss Bird
BL-v71-My 15 '75-p965
JB-v39-Je '75-p174
KR-v43-Ap 1 '75-p367
Obs-Ap 6 '75-p30
PW-v207-Mr 31 '75-p50
SLJ-v22-S '75-p81

GARLAND, Sarah (continued)
Peter Rabbit's Gardening Book
GP-v22-My '83-p4084
PW-v225-Mr 23 '84-p72
Sch Lib-v31-S '83-p258
Potter Brownware
GP-v16-Jl '77-p3150
JB-v41-O '77-p276
KR-v45-O 15 '77-p1094
SLJ-v24-F '78-p47
Rose And Her Bath
GP-v17-S '78-p3401
TLS-Jl 2 '70-p717
TLS-Ap 2 '76-p395
Rose, The Bath And The Merboy
GP-v17-S '78-p3401
TLS-D 8 '72-p1495
The Seaside Christmas Tree
Brit Bk N C-Autumn '80-p13
GP-v19-S '80-p3752
JB-v44-D '80-p282
Sch Lib-v28-D '80-p370
TLS-Jl 18 '80-p809
Tex And Bad Hank
GP-v22-Jl '83-p4109
Tex And Gloria
GP-v22-Jl '83-p4109
Tex The Champion
GP-v22-Jl '83-p4109
Tex The Cowboy
GP-v22-Jl '83-p4109
TES-My 27 '83-p29

* * *

GARNER, Alan
The Aimer Gate
B&B-v24-Je '79-p57
BL-v76-O 1 '79-p274
BW-Jl 8 '79-pE5
CCB-B-v32-Jl '79-p191
HB-v55-O '79-p533
JB-v42-D '78-p309
KR-v47-Jl 1 '79-p740
Lis-v100-N 9 '78-p623
NYTBR-Jl 22 '79-p19
Obs-D 24 '78-p23
Obs-O 7 '79-p39
RT-v33-My '80-p973
SLJ-v26-O '79-p149
TES-S 29 '78-p29
TES-Ja 18 '80-p42
TLS-S 29 '78-p1081
Alan Garner's Fairytales Of Gold
BL-v77-Mr 1 '81-p963
CCB-B-v34-Mr '81-p132
KR-v49-Mr 15 '81-p357
SLJ-v27-Mr '81-p132
The Breadhorse
GP-v14-Jl '75-p2664
Obs-Ap 6 '75-p30
Spec-v234-Ap 12 '75-p443
TLS-Jl 11 '75-p771
A Cavalcade Of Goblins
A Lib-v1-Ap '70-p385
BL-v66-S 15 '69-p129
CCB-B-v23-D '69-p58
HB-v45-O '69-p531
KR-v37-Jl 1 '69-p680
LJ-v94-D 15 '69-p4604
PW-v195-Je 30 '69-p63
SR-v52-N 8 '69-p68
TN-v26-Ap '70-p307
Elidor
BL-v76-Ja 15 '80-p718
BS-v39-Mr '80-p465
BW-v11-Jl 26 '81-p8
CSM-v57-N 4 '65-pB6
HB-v56-Je '80-p328
NS-v70-N 12 '65-p748
Obs-D 12 '65-p28
Punch-v249-D 15 '65-p897
S Fict R-v11-My '82-p50
Spec-N 12 '65-p628
TLS-D 9 '65-p1130
WLB-v54-Ap '80-p520
Fairy Tales Of Gold
Brit Bk N C-Autumn '80-p3
Inter BC-v12-#7 '81-p20
JB-v45-Je '81-p110
Sch Lib-v29-Je '81-p133
The Girl Of The Golden Gate
Emerg Lib-v9-N '81-p35
GP-v18-Mr '80-p3647
Sch Lib-v28-Je '80-p145
TES-N 23 '79-p29
The Golden Brothers
Emerg Lib-v9-N '81-p35
GP-v18-Mr '80-p3647
Sch Lib-v28-Je '80-p145
TES-N 23 '79-p29
Granny Reardun
B&B-v23-N '77-p76
B&B-v24-Je '79-p57
BL-v75-Mr 1 '79-p1088
BW-Jl 8 '79-pE5
CCB-B-v32-Mr '79-p115
CE-v56-O '79-p42
HB-v55-Ap '79-p192
JB-v42-Je '78-p153
KR-v47-Ja 15 '79-p65
NYTBR-Jl 22 '79-p19
Obs-D 11 '77-p31
Obs-D 24 '78-p23
Obs-O 7 '79-p39
RT-v33-My '80-p973
SLJ-v25-Ap '79-p55
TES-N 18 '77-p42
TLS-D 2 '77-p1413
VV-v23-D 25 '78-p98
The Guizer
BL-v73-O 15 '76-p314
BL-v73-O 15 '76-p322
Brit Bk N C-Autumn '80-p3
GP-v14-Ja '76-p2783
HB-v52-D '76-p636
JB-v40-F '76-p42
KR-v44-Je 15 '76-p693
NS-v90-N 28 '75-p688
Obs-D 7 '75-p32
Obs-Jl 13 '80-p29
PW-v210-Jl 5 '76-p90
SLJ-v23-O '76-p116
TLS-D 5 '75-p1451
The Lad Of The Gad
Brit Bk N C-Autumn '80-p3
Brit Bk N C-Spring '81-p25
GP-v19-Mr '81-p3857
HB-v58-Ap '82-p174
JB-v45-Je '81-p122
SLJ-v28-Mr '82-p157
Sch Lib-v29-Je '81-p133
TES-N 21 '80-p30
The Moon Of Gomrath
B&B-v13-D '67-p34
BL-v76-Ja 15 '80-p718
CSM-v60-My 2 '68-pB8
EJ-v69-My '80-p75
HB-v44-F '68-p58
KR-v35-S 1 '67-p1055
LJ-v92-O 15 '67-p3848
NY-v55-D 3 '79-p212
NYTBR-v72-O 22 '67-p62
S Fict R-v11-My '82-p50
VOYA-v5-O '82-p33
The Old Man Of Mow
CCB-B-v24-O '70-p25
KR-v38-S 15 '70-p1028
LJ-v95-D 15 '70-p4349
TLS-My 25 '67-p465
The Princess And The Golden Mane
Emerg Lib-v9-N '81-p35
GP-v18-Mr '80-p3647
Sch Lib-v28-Je '80-p145
TES-N 23 '79-p29

GARNER, Alan (continued)
Red Shift
B&B-v19-N '73-p129
B&B-v20-My '75-p66
BL-v70-Mr 15 '74-p801
BS-v33-D 1 '73-p387
CCB-B-v27-My '74-p142
Emerg Lib-v9-Ja '82-p13
HB-v49-D '73-p580
HT-v23-D '73-p885
KR-v41-S 1 '73-p989
Lis-v90-N 8 '73-p639
NS-v86-N 9 '73-p700
NYTBR-O 28 '73-p48
Obs-N 25 '73-p39
PW-v204-S 3 '73-p50
Spec-v231-O 20 '73-pR16
TLS-S 28 '73-p1112
VOYA-v5-Ap '82-p59
The Stone Book
B&B-v24-Je '79-p57
BL-v75-Mr 1 '79-p1088
BW-Jl 8 '79-pE5
CCB-B-v32-Mr '79-p115
CE-v56-O '79-p42
GP-v15-N '76-p2982
HB-v55-Ap '79-p192
JB-v41-Ag '77-p220
KR-v47-Ja 15 '79-p65
Lis-v96-N 11 '76-p623
NYTBR-Jl 22 '79-p19
Obs-N 28 '76-p31
Obs-D 24 '78-p23
Obs-O 7 '79-p39
RT-v33-My '80-p973
SLJ-v25-F '79-p55
TES-Ja 18 '80-p42
TLS-O 1 '76-p1241
VV-v23-D 25 '78-p98
WLB-v53-D '78-p306
The Three Golden Heads Of The Well
Emerg Lib-v9-N '81-p35
GP-v18-Mr '80-p3647
Sch Lib-v28-Je '80-p145
TES-N 23 '79-p29
Tom Fobble's Day
B&B-v24-Je '79-p57
BL-v76-O 1 '79-p275
BW-Jl 8 '79-pE5
CCB-B-v32-Je '79-p174
GP-v16-N '77-p3207
HB-v55-O '79-p533
JB-v41-Ag '77-p220
KR-v47-Jl 1 '79-p740
NYTBR-Jl 22 '79-p19
Obs-Ap 10 '77-p21
Obs-D 24 '78-p23
Obs-O 7 '79-p39
RT-v33-My '80-p973
SLJ-v26-O '79-p149
SR-v6-N 24 '79-p65
TLS-Mr 25 '77-p360
The Weirdstone Of Brisingamen
BL-v76-Ja 15 '80-p718
HB-v46-F '70-p45
KR-v37-S 1 '69-p940
LA-v57-F '80-p191
LJ-v95-F 15 '70-p786
NY-v55-D 3 '79-p212
Obs-Ag 1 '71-p21
S Fict R-v11-My '82-p50
VOYA-v5-O '82-p33

* * *

GARNETT, David
Up She Rises
B&B-v22-Jl '77-p39
GP-v16-My '77-p3131
KR-v45-D 1 '77-p1282
LJ-v103-F 1 '78-p383
Lis-v97-Mr 24 '77-p377
NS-v93-Mr 25 '77-p407
NY-v54-S 25 '78-p158
Obs-Ap 17 '77-p24
TLS-Mr 25 '77-p334

* * *

GARNETT, Emmeline
Madame Prime Minister: Story Of Indira Gandhi
BL-v64-O 1 '67-p176
CCB-B-v21-Ap '68-p126
CLW-v39-N '67-p239
CSM-v59-N 2 '67-pB12
HB-v43-Ag '67-p484
KR-v35-Mr 1 '67-p283
LJ-v92-Ap 15 '67-p1747
PW-v191-Je 5 '67-p176
Pac A-v41-Spring '68-p122
TN-v27-Ja '71-p190
Tormented Angel: John Henry Newman
Am-v115-Jl 2 '66-p16
CCB-B-v20-Ap '67-p121
CLW-v38-N '66-p213
HB-v42-Ag '66-p441
KR-v34-Ap 15 '66-p433
LJ-v91-Je 15 '66-p3266
NO-v5-Ag 29 '66-p17
NYTBR-v71-My 8 '66-p22
PW-v189-My 23 '66-p83
YR-v5-N '68-p9

* * *

GARNETT, Eve
The Family From One End Street
BW-Mr 14 '76-p8
TES-Mr 10 '78-p52
TES-Ja 18 '80-p42
To Greenland's Icy Mountains
CCB-B-v22-Ap '69-p126
LJ-v95-Mr 15 '70-p1202
TLS-Ap 3 '69-p362

* * *

GARNETT, Richard
The White Dragon
BL-v61-Je 15 '65-p996
CCB-B-v18-F '65-p86
HB-v41-Ap '65-p175
Spec-v224-My 9 '70-p623

* * *

GARRATT, Colin
Taking Photographs
Sch Lib-v29-Je '81-p146
TES-Mr 9 '84-p47

* * *

GARRATY, John A
Encyclopedia Of American Biography
AHR-v81-F '76-p200
BL-v72-Mr 15 '76-p1068
CRL-v36-Jl '75-p311
Choice-v11-F '75-p1754
HB-v51-Je '75-p297
LJ-v100-F 1 '75-p278
LJ-v100-Ap 15 '75-p732
NYT-v124-N 23 '74-p29
NYTBR-D 1 '74-p100
Prog-v39-F '75-p61
RSR-v3-Jl '75-p29
SR-v2-My 17 '75-p27
WLB-v49-D '74-p313
Theodore Roosevelt: The Strenuous Life
BL-v64-S 15 '67-p130
BS-v27-Ag 1 '67-p183
CCB-B-v21-D '67-p54
CLW-v39-Ja '68-p373
EL-v88-F '68-p273
KR-v35-Je 1 '67-p652
LJ-v92-N 15 '67-p4260
NYTBR-v72-Jl 16 '67-p20
PW-v191-Je 5 '67-p176

* * *

GARRETT, Richard
Great Air Adventures
GP-v17-N '78-p3421
Narrow Squeaks!
GP-v14-Ap '76-p2856

* * *

GARRICK, Robert W
Defending The America's Cup
PW-v196-Ag 18 '69-p74

* * *

GARRIDO, Felipe
Tajin Y Los Siete Truenos
BL-v81-O 1 '84-p256

* * *

GARRIDO DE BOGGS, Edna
Folklore Infantil De Santo Domingo
BL-v80-S 15 '83-p155

* * *

GARRIGUE, Sheila
All The Children Were Sent Away
BB-v4-N '76-p4
BL-v72-My 15 '76-p1335
CCB-B-v30-D '76-p57
CLW-v48-O '76-p138
KR-v44-My 1 '76-p534
PW-v209-Je 7 '76-p75
RT-v31-O '77-p15
SLJ-v22-My '76-p59
Between Friends
BB-v6-N '78-p4
BL-v74-Je 15 '78-p1616
BL-v78-N 1 '81-p395
CCB-B-v32-O '78-p28
CLW-v50-S '78-p92
Cur R-v17-O '78-p272
Inst-v88-N '78-p140
KR-v46-Je 15 '78-p636
LA-v56-Ja '79-p51
NYTBR-Ap 30 '78-p28
PW-v213-My 22 '78-p233
Par-v53-O '78-p40
SLJ-v24-My '78-p66
Teacher-v96-O '78-p162

* * *

GARRISON, Christian
The Dream Eater
BL-v75-F 1 '79-p865
CBRS-v7-F '79-p61
CCB-B-v32-Ap '79-p135
KR-v47-F 1 '79-p120
New R-v180-Je 23 '79-p39
PW-v215-Ja 1 '79-p58
SLJ-v25-Ap '79-p42
Flim And Flam & The Big Cheese
BB-v5-Ap '77-p1
BL-v73-D 1 '76-p538
NYTBR-N 14 '76-p38
PW-v210-O 4 '76-p75
SLJ-v23-D '76-p49
Little Pieces Of The West Wind
BL-v72-F 1 '76-p787
CCB-B-v29-My '76-p143
CLW-v47-F '76-p309
HB-v52-F '76-p42
KR-v43-N 15 '75-p1283
PW-v208-D 1 '75-p65
SLJ-v22-F '76-p38
WLB-v50-F '76-p484

* * *

GARRISON, Margaret F
Sagebrush Girl
SLJ-v28-N '81-p91

* * *

GARRISON, Webb
Why Didn't I Think Of That?
CE-v55-O '78-p42
Inst-v87-My '78-p114
KR-v46-Ja 1 '78-p5
SB-v14-D '78-p184
SLJ-v24-Mr '78-p128
Teacher-v95-Ap '78-p117

* * *

GARROD, Stan
Samuel De Champlain
In Rev-v16-Ap '82-p48
Le Travail Des Pionniers
In Rev-v15-Ag '81-p40

* * *

GARROW, Simon
The Amazing Adventure Of Dan The Pawn
PW-v223-Mr 4 '83-p100
SLJ-v29-My '83-p70
Spec-v249-O 30 '82-p36
Spec-v249-D 4 '82-p34
TES-N 5 '82-p30

* * *

GARSHIN, V M
Traveling Frog
BL-v63-Mr 15 '67-p795
CCB-B-v20-My '67-p140
CE-v44-O '67-p117
HB-v43-F '67-p63
LJ-v91-D 15 '66-p6184
NYTBR-v71-D 25 '66-p12
RT-v35-Ja '82-p469

* * *

GARSHIN, Vsevolod
Liagushka-Puteshestvennitsa
BL-v78-N 15 '81-p452

* * *

GARSON, Eugenia
The Laura Ingalls Wilder Songbook
CCB-B-v22-F '69-p93
CLW-v41-O '69-p137
LJ-v94-F 15 '69-p871

* * *

GARST, Shannon
Ernest Thompson Seton: Naturalist
In Rev-v15-Ap '81-p16

* * *

GARSTIN, Crosbie
The Owl's House
Brit Bk N-S '82-p526
GP-v14-Jl '75-p2678

* * *

GARTEN, Jan
The Alphabet Tale
CCB-B-v18-Mr '65-p102

* * *

GARTHWAITE, Marion
The Twelfth Night Santons
Am-v113-N 20 '65-p646
Atl-v216-D '65-p159
BL-v62-N 15 '65-p330
CCB-B-v19-D '65-p62
GT-v83-D '65-p20
HB-v41-D '65-p616
KR-v33-Je 15 '65-p572
LJ-v90-O 15 '65-p4530
NYTBR-v70-D 5 '65-p60

* * *

GARTLER, Marion
Phoenix Reading Series
Cur R-v19-N '80-p430

* * *

GARVER, Susan
Coming To North America From Mexico, Cuba And Puerto Rico
BL-v78-D 1 '81-p488
CCB-B-v35-Mr '82-p127
SLJ-v29-N '82-p84

GARVER, Susan (continued)
VOYA-v5-F '83-p49

* * *

GARVEY, Robert
What Feast?
SLJ-v21-Mr '75-p96

* * *

GARY, Charles L
Flower Fables
SLJ-v25-Mr '79-p139

* * *

GARY, William R
Camping Adventure
ACSB-v10-Fall '77-p19
BL-v73-Mr 15 '77-p1086
BW-Mr 20 '77-pH4
Edu D-v10-S '78-p8
Inst-v86-Jl 5 '71-p22
SB-v13-D '77-p161

* * *

GASCOIGNE, Bamber
The Christians
Am-v137-D 31 '77-p487
B&B-v22-Ag '77-p32
BL-v74-O 1 '77-p247
BS-v37-N '77-p253
BW-O 16 '77-pE4
GW-v117-Jl 31 '77-p23
JB-v42-F '78-p54
KR-v45-Jl 1 '77-p704
LJ-v102-S 15 '77-p1859
Obs-Ag 21 '77-p29
PW-v212-Jl 11 '77-p64
Spec-v239-Jl 9 '77-p20
TT-v35-Jl '78-p234
Fearless Freddy's Magic Wish
JB-v47-Ap '83-p67
Fearless Freddy's Sunken Treasure
JB-v47-F '83-p12
Why The Rope Went Tight
BL-v78-O 15 '81-p304
Brit Bk N C-Spring '82-p2
CBRS-v10-S '81-p3
KR-v49-D 1 '81-p1462
NS-v102-D 4 '81-p19
PW-v220-D 18 '81-p70
SLJ-v28-F '82-p67
TES-Ja 15 '82-p35
TLS-S 18 '81-p1066

* * *

GASCOIGNE, Christina
Garden Hide-And-Seek
GP-v22-Mr '84-p4223
JB-v47-D '83-p235
Hide-And-Seek
TES-D 9 '83-p35
TES-F 3 '84-p31
Meadow Hide-And-Seek
GP-v22-Mr '84-p4223
Obs-Ag 7 '83-p25
Pond Hide-And-Seek
GP-v22-Mr '84-p4223

* * *

GASES, Acids And The Earth
TES-Ap 1 '83-p36

* * *

GASIOROWICZ, Nina
The Mime Alphabet Book
CCB-B-v27-Jl '74-p177
CLW-v46-S '74-p89
LJ-v99-S 15 '74-p2245
NYTBR-My 5 '74-p41

* * *

GASKIN, John
Breathing
BL-v81-O 1 '84-p246
GP-v23-Jl '84-p4296
Teeth
BL-v81-O 1 '84-p246
GP-v23-Jl '84-p4296

* * *

GASPAR, Tomas R
La Aventura De Yolanda/ Yolanda's Hike
BL-v78-S 1 '81-p54

* * *

GASPERINI, Jim
Secret Of The Knights
Fant R-v7-O '84-p41
SLJ-v30-Ag '84-p69
TES-Jl 13 '84-p25
VOYA-v7-Je '84-p94

* * *

GATCH, Jean
School Makes Sense...Sometimes!
SLJ-v27-Ja '81-p49

* * *

GATES, Arthur I
Follow Directions Books
RT-v36-My '83-p952
Read And Remember Books
RT-v36-My '83-p952
Read Beyond The Lines Books
RT-v36-My '83-p952
Reading Exercises Series
Cur R-v22-D '83-p17

* * *

GATES, Barbara
Changing Learning, Changing Lives
BL-v76-Ja 15 '80-p702
HER-v50-F '80-p119
Inter BC-v10-My 50 '79-p21
JE-v163-Winter '81-p90
Kliatt-v13-Fall '79-p37
Ms-v11-O '82-p84

* * *

GATES, Doris
Apollo The Golden God
GP-My '84-p4247
Athena
BW-v13-Je 12 '83-p12
The Cat And Mrs. Cary
BL-v76-F 15 '80-p840
Elderberry Bush
BL-v64-Ja 1 '68-p544
BW-v1-N 26 '67-p16
CCB-B-v21-F '68-p94
CLW-v39-F '68-p438
HB-v44-F '68-p65
KR-v35-N 1 '67-p1318
LJ-v92-N 15 '67-p4250
SR-v51-F 24 '68-p51
Trav-v24-Je '68-p447
A Fair Wind For Troy
BL-v73-Ja 15 '77-p718
CCB-B-v30-My '77-p141
GP-v23-S '84-p4325
HB-v52-D '76-p622
KR-v44-S 1 '76-p976
SLJ-v23-N '76-p69
A Filly For Melinda
BL-v80-Ap 15 '84-p1189
B Rpt-v3-S '84-p32
LA-v61-Mr '84-p294
SLJ-v30-Ap '84-p114
Heracles Mightiest Of Mortals
GP-v23-S '84-p4325
A Horse For Melinda
TES-N 27 '81-p23
Lord Of The Sky
BL-v69-Mr 15 '73-p714
CE-v49-Mr '73-p317
HB-v49-Ap '73-p139
KR-v40-O 15 '72-p1195
LJ-v98-Ja 15 '73-p260
Mightiest Of Mortals
BL-v72-F 15 '76-p855

GATES, Doris (continued)
HB-v52-Ap '76-p178
KR-v43-N 15 '75-p1291
SLJ-v22-Ja '76-p46
A Morgan For Melinda
BL-v76-Mr 1 '80-p981
CBRS-v8-Spring '80-p117
CCB-B-v34-S '80-p8
CLW-v52-O '80-p133
KR-v48-My 15 '80-p644
LA-v57-O '80-p791
SLJ-v26-F '80-p54
Sensible Kate
GT-v88-Ja '71-p112
SLJ-v30-F '84-p31
The Warrior Goddess
BL-v69-Mr 15 '73-p714
HB-v49-Ap '73-p139
KR-v40-O 15 '72-p1195
LJ-v98-Ja 15 '73-p260
PW-v202-N 27 '72-p40
Zeus
BW-v13-Je 12 '83-p12

* * *

GATES, Frieda
Easy To Make Costumes
BB-v7-My '79-p3
SLJ-v25-Ap '79-p52
Easy To Make Monster Masks And Disguises
BB-v7-O '79-p6
SLJ-v26-F '80-p45
Easy To Make North American Indian Crafts
BL-v78-Ja 1 '82-p597
CBRS-v10-Ja '82-p47
SLJ-v28-Ap '82-p69
Easy To Make Puppets
SLJ-v23-Mr '77-p131
Glove, Mitten, And Sock Puppets
BB-v6-Ja '79-p2
Inst-v88-Ap '79-p143
SLJ-v25-F '79-p41
Monsters And Ghouls
CBRS-v9-S '80-p7
CE-v57-N '80-p114
Inst-v90-O '80-p182
NYTBR-v85-O 26 '80-p27
North American Indian Masks
CBRS-v11-D '82-p36
CCB-B-v36-F '83-p106
Cur R-v22-Ag '83-p89
SLJ-v29-Ap '83-p114

* * *

GATES, Richard
Conservation
ASBYP-v16-Spring '83-p61
BL-v78-Je 15 '82-p1365
BL-v80-My 15 '84-p1352
SLJ-v29-O '82-p137

* * *

GATEWAY Fact Books
Cur R-v22-F '83-p78

* * *

GATHJE, Curtis
The Disco Kid
BL-v76-O 15 '79-p347
CBRS-v8-D '79-p37
SLJ-v26-N '79-p77
VOYA-v4-Ag '81-p47

* * *

GATHORNE-HARDY, Jonathan
The Airship Ladyship Adventure
BB-v5-S '77-p4
BL-v77-Je 15 '81-p1352
CCB-B-v31-S '77-p15
KR-v45-Ja 15 '77-p46
SLJ-v23-Mr '77-p144
Cyril Bonhamy And The Great Drain Robbery
GP-v22-N '83-p4151
JB-v47-O '83-p207
NS-v106-D 2 '83-p25
TES-Jl 8 '83-p26
Cyril Bonhamy V. Madam Big
Brit Bk N C-Spring '82-p11
GP-v20-N '81-p3972
JB-v46-Ag '82-p140
Lis-v106-N 5 '81-p546
Sch Lib-v30-Je '82-p129
TES-Ja 29 '82-p30
TLS-N 20 '81-p1357
Jane's Adventures In A Balloon
NS-v89-My 23 '75-p693
TLS-Ap 4 '75-p360
Jane's Adventures In And Out Of The Book
SLJ-v28-D '81-p52
Operation Peeg
BL-v76-O 1 '79-p285
CCB-B-v28-Ja '75-p77
CE-v51-Mr '75-p273
HB-v51-Ap '75-p147
KR-v42-O 1 '74-p1060
KR-v43-Ja 1 '75-p6
LJ-v99-O 15 '74-p2740
NYTBR-O 13 '74-p14
The Terrible Kidnapping Of Cyril Bonhamy
JB-v43-F '79-p30
Obs-D 10 '78-p38
TES-D 1 '78-p24

* * *

GATLAND, Kenneth
Robots
SLJ-v29-D '82-p32
Star Travel
GP-v18-N '79-p3613
The Young Scientist Book Of Spaceflight
SLJ-v25-Ap '79-p56

* * *

GATTEGNO, Jean
Lewis Carroll: Fragments Of A Looking-Glass
Ant R-v35-Winter '77-p120
Atl-v237-Mr '76-p108
B&B-v23-My '78-p61
BL-v72-Mr 1 '76-p953
BS-v36-O '76-p218
CSM-v68-Mr 4 '76-p22
Choice-v13-S '76-p821
GP-v17-My '78-p3343
KR-v44-Mr 15 '76-p362
LJ-v101-Ap 1 '76-p901
Lis-v99-My 18 '78-p649
NY-v52-Ag 16 '76-p92
NYTBR-Jl 18 '76-p6
Obs-Mr 26 '78-p24
PW-v209-Mr 22 '76-p39
TES-S 1 '78-p14
VQR-v53-Summer '77-p534

* * *

GATTI, Will
Caesar's Ghost
Sch Lib-v28-S '80-p256

* * *

GAUCH, Patricia Lee
Aaron And The Green Mountain Boys
BL-v69-N 15 '72-p300
CCB-B-v25-Je '72-p155
KR-v40-My 15 '72-p579
Christina Katerina And The Box
CCB-B-v25-O '71-p25
KR-v39-Ag 1 '71-p802
LJ-v97-Ja 15 '72-p274

GAUCH, Patricia Lee
(continued)
PW-v218-D 19 '80-p52
Christina Katerina And The First Annual Grand Ballet
Inst-v83-My '74-p95
KR-v42-Ja 1 '74-p2
LJ-v99-F 15 '74-p562
SLJ-v24-D '77-p35
Fridays
BL-v76-N 15 '79-p501
CBRS-v8-N '79-p27
HB-v56-F '80-p60
KR-v47-D 1 '79-p1379
NYTBR-F 17 '80-p24
PW-v216-N 19 '79-p78
SLJ-v26-Ja '80-p78
Grandpa And Me
BW-v6-N 5 '72-p3
CCB-B-v26-My '73-p137
LJ-v98-Ap 15 '73-p1375
PW-v202-S 18 '72-p74
RT-v35-My '82-p901
SE-v44-N '80-p602
Teacher-v96-D '78-p22
The Green Of Me
BL-v75-N 15 '78-p545
CBRS-v7-Winter '79-p56
CCB-B-v32-F '79-p98
HB-v55-F '79-p68
KR-v46-O 15 '78-p1142
NYTBR-Mr 25 '79-p33
PW-v214-O 30 '78-p50
SLJ-v25-Ja '79-p60
The Impossible Major Rogers
BL-v74-D 15 '77-p682
CCB-B-v31-Je '78-p158
HB-v54-Ap '78-p174
KR-v45-N 15 '77-p1201
SLJ-v24-Ja '78-p88
Kate Alone
BL-v77-O 1 '80-p250
CBRS-v8-Ag '80-p137
CCB-B-v34-N '80-p52
HB-v56-O '80-p519
KR-v48-S 15 '80-p1236
NYTBR-v86-F 8 '81-p20
PW-v218-O 24 '80-p49
PW-v223-Ja 21 '83-p85
RT-v35-O '81-p69
SLJ-v27-O '80-p146
The Little Friar Who Flew
BL-v77-O 15 '80-p326
CBRS-v9-S '80-p2
KR-v48-S 15 '80-p1227
PW-v218-O 31 '80-p85
SLJ-v27-N '80-p61
Morelli's Game
BL-v78-Ja 15 '82-p643
CBRS-v10-Mr '82-p77
CCB-B-v35-Mr '82-p128
HB-v58-Ap '82-p172
J Read-v25-My '82-p813
KR-v50-F 15 '82-p208
SLJ-v28-Mr '82-p157
My Old Tree
CCB-B-v24-Ja '71-p73
CLW-v42-D '70-p259
KR-v38-Ag 15 '70-p867
LJ-v96-Mr 15 '71-p1107
Night Talks
BL-v79-Ap 1 '83-p1033
CBRS-v11-Je '83-p114
CCB-B-v37-S '83-p7
EJ-v73-F '84-p106
HB-v59-Je '83-p310
KR-v51-Ap 15 '83-p461
Kliatt-v18-Fall '84-p8
NYTBR-v88-S 18 '83-p38
PW-v223-Mr 4 '83-p99
SLJ-v29-Ag '83-p76
VOYA-v6-O '83-p200
On To Widecombe Fair
BL-v74-Je 1 '78-p1551
CCB-B-v32-O '78-p28
HB-v55-O '78-p506
JB-v44-F '80-p17
KR-v46-Jl 1 '78-p687
NYTBR-Jl 2 '78-p11
SLJ-v24-My '78-p54
SR-v5-My 27 '78-p59
Teacher-v96-My '79-p113
Once Upon A Dinkelsbuhl
BB-v5-N '77-p1
BL-v73-My 15 '77-p1420
CE-v54-N '77-p86
CLW-v49-O '77-p142
HB-v53-Ag '77-p434
KR-v45-Ap 1 '77-p347
LA-v55-F '78-p211
NYTBR-Je 19 '77-p28
PW-v211-Mr 28 '77-p79
SLJ-v24-S '77-p107
This Time, Tempe Wick?
BL-v71-O 1 '74-p169
BL-v73-Mr 15 '77-p1100
BW-D 8 '74-p7
CE-v51-F '75-p216
CSM-v66-N 6 '74-p10
HB-v50-O '74-p147
KR-v42-O 15 '74-p1103
LA-v52-S '75-p855
LJ-v99-O 15 '74-p2732
NYTBR-N 3 '74-p26
PW-v206-S 23 '74-p155
SLJ-v25-D '78-p33
Thunder At Gettysburg
BL-v72-D 15 '75-p578
KR-v43-D 1 '75-p1337
SLJ-v22-Ja '76-p37

* * *

GAUCHAT, Dorothy
All God's Children
BS-v36-Ap '76-p28
KR-v43-N 15 '75-p1317
LJ-v101-Ja 15 '76-p332
PW-v208-N 17 '75-p88

* * *

GAUDREALUT-LABREQUE, Madeleine
Le Mystere Du Grenier
BL-v80-Ja 15 '84-p758

* * *

GAUDREAULT-LABRECQUE, Madeleine
Vol A Bord Du Concordia
In Rev-v14-O '80-p42

* * *

GAUL, Simon
Pushkin The Polar Bear
Spec-v251-D 3 '83-p27

* * *

GAULT, Clare
The Cartoon Book Of Sports
SLJ-v24-D '77-p65
Four Stars From The World Of Sports
SLJ-v22-D '75-p70
The Harlem Globetrotters And Basketball's Funniest Games
SLJ-v24-S '77-p127
SR-v4-My 28 '77-p31
Teacher-v94-My '77-p115
The Home Run Kings
KR-v43-Je 15 '75-p664
SLJ-v22-D '75-p68
How To Be A Good Baseball Player
Teacher-v95-O '77-p163
How To Be A Good Soccer Player
SLJ-v25-Mr '79-p121
Norman Plays Basketball
SLJ-v25-F '79-p41
Teacher-v96-O '78-p170

GAULT, Clare (continued)
Norman Plays Ice Hockey
Teacher-v93-N '75-p115
Norman Plays Soccer
SLJ-v28-D '81-p85
Pele: The King Of Soccer
Cur R-v15-D '76-p315
KR-v43-O 1 '75-p1134
PW-v208-O 27 '75-p52
SLJ-v22-D '75-p69
SLJ-v22-My '76-p80
Stories From The Olympics
KR-v44-Je 15 '76-p687
SLJ-v23-D '76-p71

* * *

GAULT, William Campbell
Backfield Challenge
BL-v64-O 1 '67-p176
CCB-B-v21-S '67-p5
KR-v35-Ap 15 '67-p505
LJ-v92-My 15 '67-p2042
SR-v50-Jl 22 '67-p43
The Big Stick
BL-v72-N 1 '75-p366
KR-v43-Ag 1 '75-p856
SLJ-v22-D '75-p69
Cut-Rate Quarterback
KR-v45-Ag 15 '77-p850
SLJ-v24-D '77-p64
Showboat In The Backcourt
Am-v135-D 11 '76-p430
KR-v44-My 1 '76-p534
LA-v54-F '77-p211
RT-v31-O '77-p20
SLJ-v22-My '76-p80
Stubborn Sam
BL-v66-S 15 '69-p129
CCB-B-v23-S '69-p8
CSM-v61-My 1 '69-pB10
KR-v37-Ap 15 '69-p452
LJ-v94-My 15 '69-p2125
PW-v195-Ap 21 '69-p66
SR-v52-Je 28 '69-p38
Super Bowl Bound
BL-v77-O 15 '80-p320
BS-v40-Ja '81-p352
CCB-B-v34-Ja '81-p92
SLJ-v27-D '80-p74
VOYA-v3-F '81-p29
Thin Ice
BL-v75-N 1 '78-p478
CCB-B-v32-Ja '79-p80
KR-v46-S 1 '78-p953
SLJ-v25-D '78-p70
Trouble At Second
KR-v41-Ap 1 '73-p384
LJ-v99-Ja 15 '74-p217
SLJ-v24-My '78-p39
The Underground Skipper
BL-v71-Je 1 '75-p1011
CCB-B-v29-S '75-p8
KR-v43-Mr 15 '75-p317
SLJ-v21-My '75-p72
Wild Willie, Wide Receiver
BL-v71-D 15 '74-p425
CSM-v67-F 5 '75-p8
KR-v42-S 15 '74-p1013
LJ-v99-D 15 '74-p3280

* * *

GAUSE, Lynne
Matu And Matsue
CCB-B-v27-Jl '74-p177

* * *

GAUTHIER, Bertrand
Etoifilan
In Rev-v14-D '80-p39
Hebert Luee
In Rev-v15-O '81-p36

* * *

GAVIN, Jamila
Kamila And Kate
GP-v22-My '83-p4089
TES-Ag 26 '83-p20
The Orange Tree And Other Stories
Brit Bk N C-Spring '81-p11
GP-v18-S '79-p3578
JB-v43-O '79-p271
Sch Lib-v27-D '79-p361
TES-Ja 9 '81-p24

* * *

GAWAIN
Sir Gawain And The Green Knight (Tolkien)
GP-v15-Ja '77-p3057
KR-v43-Ag 15 '75-p988
MLR-v64-O '69-p854
RES-v20-F '69-p70
Specu-v44-Ja '69-p176

* * *

GAWITH, Gwen
Children's Paperbacks 11 To 16
GP-v17-Jl '78-p3372

* * *

GAY, Kathlyn
Be A Smart Shopper
BL-v71-D 1 '74-p378
CCB-B-v28-Ap '75-p129
KR-v42-N 1 '74-p1154
SLJ-v21-Ja '75-p44
Body Talk
BL-v71-D 1 '74-p378
CCB-B-v28-Je '75-p161
KR-v42-N 15 '74-p1204
LA-v53-Ap '76-p442
SLJ-v21-Ja '75-p44
Care And Share
BL-v73-Ap 15 '77-p1257
BL-v73-Ap 15 '77-p1266
KR-v45-F 15 '77-p170
SLJ-v24-Ap '78-p92
Get Hooked On Vegetables
ACSB-v12-Winter '79-p12
KR-v46-Je 15 '78-p641
SB-v15-My '79-p37
SLJ-v25-S '78-p157
Junkyards
BL-v79-F 15 '83-p776
SLJ-v29-F '83-p76
Money Isn't Everything
BL-v64-Ja 1 '68-p544
CCB-B-v21-N '67-p42
KR-v35-My 15 '67-p604
LJ-v92-O 15 '67-p3863
LJ-v96-O 15 '71-p3436
NYTBR-v72-Je 25 '67-p30
Where The People Are
Am-v121-D 13 '69-p596
HB-v46-F '70-p58
LJ-v94-Ap 15 '69-p1795
NYTBR, pt.2-My 4 '69-p5
TN-v27-Je '71-p417

* * *

GAY, Michel
The Christmas Wolf
CBRS-v12-N '83-p24
CCB-B-v37-N '83-p49
KR-v51-S 1 '83-pJ148
LA-v60-N '83-p1019
NYTBR-v88-N 13 '83-p44
SLJ-v30-O '83-p176

* * *

GAY-KELLY, Doreen
Bea's Best Friend
KR-v43-Mr 15 '75-p299
PW-v207-Mr 24 '75-p48
SLJ-v21-My '75-p68

* * *

GAY Way Introductory Series
TES-Mr 12 '82-p32

GEISEL, Theodor Seuss (continued)

The Foot Book
LJ-v94-My 15 '69-p2121
NS-v77-My 16 '69-p703
TES-Jl 16 '82-p22

Great Day For Up
KR-v42-S 15 '74-p1007
LJ-v99-D 15 '74-p3275
TES-Jl 16 '82-p22
TLS-S 19 '75-p1057

Hooper Humperdink...? Not Him!
KR-v44-O 15 '76-p1135
SLJ-v23-My '77-p53

Horton Hatches The Egg
CLW-v38-Mr '67-p474
NCW-v216-Mr '73-p89
RT-v32-N '78-p148

Horton Hears A Who
BL-v80-S 1 '83-p94
Emerg Lib-v11-Ja '84-p20
NCW-v216-Mr '73-p89
WPQ-v36-Je '83-p336

Hunches In Bunches
ABC-v4-Mr '83-p58
CCB-B-v36-Ja '83-p97
KR-v50-O 15 '82-p1152
New Age-v8-D '82-p68
PW-v222-O 15 '82-p65
SLJ-v29-D '82-p58
Time-v120-D 20 '82-p79

I Can Lick 30 Tigers Today!
BW-v10-O 12 '80-p8
CSM-v61-N 6 '69-pB3
GT-v87-F '70-p144
KR-v37-O 15 '69-p1109
NYTBR, pt.2-N 9 '69-p48
PW-v196-O 27 '69-p59

I Can Read With My Eyes Shut!
CCB-B-v32-F '79-p106
SLJ-v25-D '78-p66
Time-v112-D 4 '78-p100

I Had Trouble In Getting To Solla Sollew
Am-v113-N 20 '65-p637
Atl-v216-D '65-p153
BW-v10-O 12 '80-p8
KR-v33-S 1 '65-p898
NS-v74-N 3 '67-p597
NYTBR-v70-O 31 '65-p56
SR-v48-N 13 '65-p57
TLS-N 30 '67-p1149

I Wish That I Had Duck Feet
CCB-B-v19-F '66-p101
CSM-v57-N 4 '65-pB2
LJ-v90-O 15 '65-p4602
NYTBR-v70-N 7 '65-p56

If I Ran The Zoo
BW-v10-O 12 '80-p8

In A People House
KR-v40-S 1 '72-p1025
LJ-v97-D 15 '72-p4082
PW-v202-N 20 '72-p65
Spec-v231-O 20 '73-pR24
TES-Jl 16 '82-p22
TLS-Je 15 '73-p682

The King's Stilts
WPQ-v36-Je '83-p336

The Lorax
BW-v5-N 7 '71-p3
CCB-B-v26-S '72-p16
CSM-v63-N 11 '71-pB4
CSM-v64-F 24 '72-p7
Econ-v245-D 23 '72-p46
KR-v39-Ag 1 '71-p804
LJ-v96-N 15 '71-p3895
Lis-v88-N 9 '72-p648
NYRB-v17-D 2 '71-p25
NYTBR-Ja 2 '72-p8
Obs-S 24 '72-p37
TLS-N 3 '72-p1334

The Many Mice Of Mr. Brice
GP-v14-Ja '76-p2809
TES-Jl 24 '81-p26

Maybe You Should Fly A Jet! Maybe You Should Be A Vet
CCB-B-v34-F '81-p119
Cur R-v20-Ja '81-p39
JB-v45-O '81-p198
SLJ-v27-D '80-p71

McElligot's Pool
JB-v40-F '76-p18

McElligot's Pool. The Zax. The Lorax. Scrambled Eggs Super!
NS-v98-N 9 '79-p732

Oh Say Can You Say?
HM-v259-D '79-p77
NYTBR-N 11 '79-p60
Par-v54-D '79-p64
SLJ-v26-D '79-p94

Oh, The Thinks You Can Think!
BL-v72-D 15 '75-p583
KR-v43-O 1 '75-p1128
NW-v86-D 15 '75-p92
NYTBR-N 16 '75-p40
PW-v208-N 3 '75-p72
SLJ-v22-D '75-p65
TLS-Ap 2 '76-p389

On Beyond Zebra
BW-v10-O 12 '80-p8
Inst-v93-Mr '84-p100

One Fish Two Fish Red Fish Blue Fish
LJ-v96-Mr 15 '71-p1085

Please Try To Remember The First Of Octember
SLJ-v24-Mr '78-p120

Scrambled Eggs Super!
BW-v10-O 12 '80-p8

The Shape Of Me And Other Stuff
Inst-v83-N '73-p120
KR-v41-Jl 1 '73-p683
LJ-v98-D 15 '73-p3717
PW-v204-Ag 20 '73-p87
TES-Jl 16 '82-p22

The Sneetches And Other Stories
NCW-v216-Mr '73-p89

Ten Apples Up On Top
LJ-v96-Mr 15 '71-p1085

There's A Wocket In My Pocket!
KR-v42-S 15 '74-p1007
LJ-v99-D 15 '74-p3275
TLS-S 19 '75-p1057

Thidwick, The Big-Hearted Moose
BW-v10-O 12 '80-p8
TLS-O 3 '68-p1116

The Tooth Book
CCB-B-v35-O '81-p33
PW-v220-Ag 21 '81-p56
RT-v36-O '82-p65
SB-v17-Mr '82-p217
SLJ-v28-D '81-p76
Sch Lib-v30-S '82-p227

Wacky Wednesday
CLW-v55-O '83-p131
KR-v42-O 15 '74-p1102
LJ-v99-D 15 '74-p3274

Would You Rather Be A Bullfrog?
GP-v15-S '76-p2953
SLJ-v22-D '75-p65
TLS-Ap 2 '76-p389

Yertle The Turtle And Other Stories
NCW-v216-Mr '73-p89
WPQ-v36-Je '83-p336

GEISEL, Theodor Seuss (continued)
500 Hats Of Bartholomew Cubbins
NS-v72-N 11 '66-p712
The 500 Hats Of Bartholomew Cubbins
TES-F 22 '80-p29
WPQ-v36-Je '83-p336

* * *

GEISEL, Theodor Suess
I Wish That I Had Duck Feet
Lis-v77-My 18 '67-p658
TLS-My 25 '67-p453

* * *

GEISERT, Arthur
Pa's Balloon And Other Pig Tales
BL-v80-Ag '84-p1625
CBRS-v12-Ag '84-p148
HB-v60-Ag '84-p456
KR-v52-My 1 '84-pJ30
NYTBR-v89-Jl 29 '84-p29
PW-v225-Je 22 '84-p100
SLJ-v31-O '84-p146

* * *

GEISS, Tony
The Sesame Street Bedtime Storybook
SLJ-v25-F '79-p42

* * *

GELDENHUYS, Paula
Benjamin Rocking-Horse
GP-v19-Jl '80-p3733

* * *

GELINE, Robert
Forward
BL-v72-My 15 '76-p1336
SLJ-v22-My '76-p80
Trapped In The Deep
SLJ-v27-Ja '81-p57

* * *

GELMAN, Mitch
Pro Football Showdown
SLJ-v30-D '83-p87

* * *

GELMAN, Rita
Dumb Joey
CCB-B-v27-F '74-p94
Comw-v99-N 23 '73-p213
KR-v41-Ag 15 '73-p882
LJ-v98-N 15 '73-p3440
PW-v204-O 8 '73-p97
Hey, Kid!
BL-v73-Ap 15 '77-p1271
BW-N 12 '78-pE2
SLJ-v23-My '77-p76
SR-v5-N 26 '77-p42
WLB-v51-Je '77-p808
Ouch!
BB-v6-Ap '78-p2
Inst-v86-My '77-p119
KR-v45-Ap 1 '77-p355
SB-v13-Mr '78-p223
SLJ-v23-Mr '77-p132
Professor Coconut And The Thief
SLJ-v24-O '77-p102
Uncle Hugh
SLJ-v25-F '79-p42

* * *

GELMAN, Rita G
Boats That Float
BL-v78-D 15 '81-p553
SLJ-v28-D '81-p79
Great Moments In Sports
SLJ-v28-D '81-p85
UFO Encounters
SLJ-v25-Mr '79-p139
Teacher-v96-O '78-p177

* * *

GELOTTE, Ann-Madeleine
Vi Bodde I Helenelund
BL-v81-S 1 '84-p75

* * *

GEMINI: America's Historic Walk In Space
BL-v62-O 15 '65-p188
CCB-B-v19-F '66-p107
CLW-v37-Ja '66-p332

* * *

GEMME, Leila Boyle
The Basketball Hall Of Fame
SLJ-v25-D '78-p70
Hockey Is Our Game
BL-v75-Jl 15 '79-p1632
SLJ-v25-My '79-p84
King On The Court
BL-v72-Jl 15 '76-p1595
SLJ-v22-My '76-p80
Soccer Is Our Game
BL-v76-N 15 '79-p511
SLJ-v26-D '79-p100
T-Ball Is Our Game
BL-v74-Je 15 '78-p1621
SLJ-v25-S '78-p115
Ten-Speed Taylor
BL-v75-O 15 '78-p390
RT-v32-My '79-p975
SLJ-v25-D '78-p71
The True Book Of Spinoffs From Space
BL-v73-Je 15 '77-p1575
SB-v13-Mr '78-p223
SLJ-v24-S '77-p107
Teacher-v95-Ja '78-p128
The True Book Of The Mars Landing
ACSB-v12-Winter '79-p13
BL-v74-Mr 15 '78-p1187
CCB-B-v31-Jl '78-p175
SB-v14-Mr '79-p232
SLJ-v24-Ap '78-p69

* * *

GEMMELL, David
Legend
TES-Jl 6 '84-p28

* * *

GEMMING, Elizabeth
Blow Ye Winds Westerly
BL-v68-Jl 1 '72-p942
CCB-B-v26-N '72-p41
KR-v39-D 1 '71-p1262
LJ-v97-My 15 '72-p1921
NYTBR-Mr 19 '72-p8
SE-v37-D '73-p785
Born In A Barn
BL-v71-S 15 '74-p99
KR-v42-Ag 1 '74-p806
LJ-v99-N 15 '74-p3037
SB-v11-My '75-p40
The Cranberry Book
ASBYP-v17-Winter '84-p21
BL-v80-S 1 '83-p84
CCB-B-v37-O '83-p26
HB-v59-O '83-p591
KR-v51-Je 1 '83-p620
SA-v249-D '83-p41
SE-v48-My '84-p370
SLJ-v30-O '83-p158
Guckleberry Hill
BW-v2-N 3 '68-p33
CCB-B-v22-Ap '69-p126
KR-v36-S 15 '68-p1053
LJ-v93-N 15 '68-p4414
NYTBR-v73-N 3 '68-p6
PW-v194-Ag 12 '68-p56
Lost City In The Clouds
BL-v76-Je 1 '80-p1423
CCB-B-v34-S '80-p9
KR-v48-Mr 15 '80-p367

GEMMING, Elizabeth (continued)
SLJ-v26-My '80-p67
TN-v38-Fall '81-p85
Maple Harvest
ACSB-v10-Spring '77-p22
BL-v73-S 1 '76-p38
CCB-B-v30-D '76-p57
Inst-v86-N '76-p157
KR-v44-Je 1 '76-p637
SB-v12-Mr '77-p215
SLJ-v23-S '76-p116
Wool Gathering
ACSB-v13-Spring '80-p31
BL-v76-N 1 '79-p448
HB-v56-F '80-p73
KR-v47-N 1 '79-p1265
SLJ-v26-Ap '80-p109

* * *

GENDRON, Lionel
Birth
KR-v40-Mr 15 '72-p328
LJ-v98-Mr 15 '73-p1002
NYTBR, pt.2-My 7 '72-p32
SB-v8-S '72-p161
TN-v34-Winter '78-p160

* * *

GENEROWICZ, Witold
The Train
BW-v13-Jl 10 '83-p9
Brit Bk N C-Autumn '82-p5
CBRS-v11-My '83-p97
Econ-v285-D 25 '82-p104
GP-v21-N '82-p3972
HB-v59-Ag '83-p430
JB-v46-D '82-p220
LA-v60-O '83-p896
Obs-Ag 15 '82-p23
PW-v223-Ja 21 '83-p84

* * *

GENEVIEVE
Merde!
B&B-Jl '84-p4
TES-Jl 20 '84-p21

* * *

GENIN, Robert
The Black Stallion
GP-v22-Jl '83-p4112
SLJ-v30-Mr '84-p159
The Black Stallion And Satan
GP-v22-Jl '83-p4112

* * *

GENSLER, Kinereth
The Poetry Connection
CBRS-v7-Ap '79-p88
Kliatt-v14-Winter '80-p35

* * *

GENTLE, Mary
A Hawk In Silver
GP-v16-Mr '78-p3278
JB-v42-Ap '78-p102
TLS-Ap 7 '78-p376

* * *

GEOGRAPHY Now
TES-Mr 11 '83-p42

* * *

GEORGE, David L
Freddie Freightliner Goes To Kennedy Space Center
SLJ-v30-S '83-p105
Freddie Freightliner Learns To Talk!
SLJ-v30-S '83-p105
Freddie Freightliner To The Rescue
SLJ-v30-S '83-p105

* * *

GEORGE, Edith
Was Sieht Die Ringeltaube
Ger Q-v54-My '81-p398

* * *

GEORGE, J C G
The Puffin Book Of Flags
GP-v17-S '78-p3376

* * *

GEORGE, Jean Craighead
All Upon A Sidewalk
ACSB-v8-Winter '75-p17
BL-v71-N 1 '74-p290
BW-D 8 '74-p7
HB-v51-F '75-p64
KR-v42-O 1 '74-p1063
LJ-v99-D 15 '74-p3263
PW-v206-O 7 '74-p64
SB-v11-My '75-p36
WLB-v49-Ja '75-p349
All Upon A Stone
A Lib-v3-Ap '72-p420
BL-v67-My 1 '71-p747
BL-v68-Ap 1 '72-p669
BW-v5-My 9 '71-p3
CCB-B-v24-Jl '71-p169
CE-v48-O '71-p32
CLW-v43-Mr '72-p431
Comw-v94-My 21 '71-p270
HB-v47-Ap '71-p163
JLH-v199-My 17 '71-p63
KR-v39-F 1 '71-p102
LJ-v96-My 15 '71-p1795
SB-v7-S '71-p143
SR-v54-My 15 '71-p46
The American Walk Book
ARBA-v11-'80-p318
AW-v16-Jl '79-p58
BL-v75-Ja 1 '79-p732
BOT-v2-F '79-p92
HB-v55-Je '79-p342
KR-v46-D 1 '78-p1349
Kliatt-v15-Winter '81-p55
LJ-v104-Ja 1 '79-p124
SLJ-v26-S '79-p172
WLB-v53-My '79-p645
Coyote In Manhattan
BL-v64-Ap 15 '68-p994
BW-v2-My 5 '68-p35
CCB-B-v21-My '68-p141
KR-v36-Mr 1 '68-p271
NYTBR-v73-My 5 '68-p36
PW-v193-Mr 11 '68-p49
YR-v4-My '68-p13
The Cry Of The Crow
BS-v40-Jl '80-p158
CBRS-v8-Mr '80-p76
CCB-B-v33-Ap '80-p152
Inst-v89-My '80-p91
Inst-v92-N '82-p152
KR-v48-Jl 15 '80-p910
NYTBR-v85-S 28 '80-p34
PW-v217-Je 6 '80-p82
PW-v223-F 4 '83-p368
RT-v34-Ja '81-p484
SLJ-v26-My '80-p67
Going To The Sun
BS-v36-Ag '76-p149
CCB-B-v30-S '76-p10
CLW-v48-D '76-p234
EJ-v65-O '76-p87
KR-v44-Ap 1 '76-p405
NYTBR-Je 27 '76-p30
PW-v209-My 24 '76-p60
SLJ-v22-Ap '76-p73
The Grizzly Bear With The Golden Ears
CCB-B-v35-My '82-p168
CLW-v54-N '82-p181
CSM-v74-O 8 '82-pB10
LA-v59-N '82-p865
PW-v221-Ja 29 '82-p66
SLJ-v28-Ag '82-p97

* * *

GEORGE Washington: The Inspiring True-Life Story Of The First President Of The United States
SLJ-v23-Ap '77-p59

* * *

GEORGIOU, Constantine
Children And Their Literature
BL-v65-Je 15 '69-p1156
CLW-v41-N '69-p203
CLW-v41-F '70-p387
Comw-v90-My 23 '69-p303
HB-v45-O '69-p546
Inst-v78-Je '69-p118
LJ-v94-My 15 '69-p2075
Par-v45-My '70-p107
TN-v39-Fall '82-p91
WLB-v43-My '69-p907
Rani, Queen Of The Jungle
KR-v38-O 15 '70-p1139
LJ-v96-Ja 15 '71-p258
PW-v198-D 7 '70-p50
Teacher-v92-F '75-p115
Whitey And Whiskers And Food
CCB-B-v18-Jl '65-p161

* * *

GERAS, Adele
Apricots At Midnight
BL-v79-Ja 15 '83-p675
CBRS-v11-Ja '83-p45
CCB-B-v36-D '82-p66
CE-v59-Mr '83-p277
GP-v16-O '77-p3178
HB-v59-F '83-p43
JB-v41-O '77-p287
KR-v50-S 1 '82-p997
PW-v222-O 15 '82-p66
SLJ-v29-Ja '83-p75
Beyond The Cross-Stitch Mountains
GP-v16-N '77-p3198
JB-v42-F '78-p24
The Christmas Cat
TES-D 16 '83-p20
The Girls In The Velvet Frame
BL-v76-O 15 '79-p351
CBRS-v8-Ja '80-p46
CCB-B-v33-Ja '80-p94
CLW-v52-S '80-p91
GP-v17-Ja '79-p3454
HB-v55-D '79-p662
JB-v43-F '79-p50
KR-v47-N 15 '79-p1325
Obs-D 3 '78-p36
PW-v215-Je 25 '79-p123
SLJ-v26-S '79-p138
TLS-S 29 '78-p1083
The Painted Garden
TES-Ja 18 '80-p40
The Rug That Grew
GP-v20-Ja '82-p4017
JB-v45-Je '81-p114
TES-Mr 6 '81-p29
TLS-Mr 27 '81-p340
Tea At Mrs. Manderby's
GP-v15-My '76-p2887
JB-v40-D '76-p326
A Thousand Yards Of Sea
GP-v19-Jl '80-p3733
JB-v44-D '80-p282
Voyage
BL-v79-Mr 1 '83-p870
CSM-v75-My 13 '83-pB6
EJ-v73-S '84-p103
GP-v22-Jl '83-p4099
HB-v59-Ag '83-p452
Inter BC-v15-#5 '84-p20
JB-v47-O '83-p212
J Read-v27-N '83-p183
KR-v51-F 1 '83-p124
SLJ-v29-My '83-p81
Sch Lib-v31-S '83-p269
VOYA-v6-D '83-p279

* * *

GERBER, Irving
Puerto Rico: Long Ago
Inter BC-v14-#1 '83-p16

* * *

GERBER, Merrill Joan
Name A Star For Me
BL-v79-Ap 15 '83-p1094
CBRS-v11-Jl '83-p137
CCB-B-v37-S '83-p8
KR-v51-Ap 15 '83-p461
SLJ-v29-Ag '83-p76
Please Don't Kiss Me Now
BL-v77-My 1 '81-p1191
BS-v41-Ag '81-p197
CBRS-v9-Ap '81-p77
CCB-B-v34-My '81-p170
KR-v49-S 1 '81-p1086
Kliatt-v16-Fall '82-p10
SLJ-v27-My '81-p73

* * *

GEREN, Carl
Shell Hunter
SLJ-v24-S '77-p118

* * *

GERGELY, Tibor
Animals
BL-v71-Jl 1 '75-p1127
SLJ-v22-S '75-p102
Great Big Book Of Bedtime Stories
CCB-B-v21-Ap '68-p126
CLW-v39-F '68-p440
LJ-v92-D 15 '67-p4602
NYTBR-v72-D 10 '67-p38
PW-v192-D 4 '67-p44

* * *

GERGEN, Joe
World Series Heroes And Goats
BL-v79-Ja 1 '83-p622
SLJ-v29-D '82-p85

* * *

GERINGER, Laura
Seven True Bear Stories
Hi Lo-v1-F '80-p3
LA-v56-N '79-p930
PW-v215-Ap 30 '79-p114
SLJ-v25-Ap '79-p42
SR-v6-My 26 '79-p63

* * *

GERLER, William R
A Pack Of Riddles
BB-v3-N '75-p2
BL-v72-N 15 '75-p452
CE-v53-Ja '77-p154
SLJ-v22-Ja '76-p37
Riddles, Jokes And Other Funny Things
SLJ-v22-D '75-p42

* * *

GERLINGS, Charlotte
The Ghosts Of Greywethers
JB-v47-Je '83-p123
TES-Ap 1 '83-p36

* * *

GERMAN, Donald R
Money And Banks
SLJ-v26-S '79-p138

* * *

GERMAN, John W
The Money Book
SLJ-v28-Ja '82-p76

* * *

GERMAN, Tony
River Race
BIC-v9-F '80-p22

GERMAN, Tony (continued)
Can Child Lit-#29 '83-p63
In Rev-v14-Ag '80-p48
Tom Penny
Atl Pro Bk R-v10-N '83-p2
Tom Penny And The Grand Canal
BIC-v12-F '83-p33
Emerg Lib-v10-My '83-p30
Quill & Q-v49-F '83-p39
Tom Penny (Aubry)
Can Child Lit-#23 '81-p96
Tom Penny (McElroy)
Can Child Lit-#23 '81-p96
Quill & Q-v48-Je '82-p4

* * *

GERMANY, Jean
One Jump Ahead
JB-v44-Ag '80-p196

* * *

GERNHARDT, Almut
One More Makes Four
B&B-v23-Je '78-p66
GP-v17-N '78-p3427
JB-v42-O '78-p251
Obs-Jl 16 '78-p26
TES-Je 16 '78-p47
What A Day!
JB-v45-Ap '81-p61
Obs-Mr 1 '81-p33
TES-Mr 13 '81-p28

* * *

GERNHARDT, Robert
A Pig That Is Kind
Obs-D 6 '81-p28
TES-N 20 '81-p36
TLS-N 20 '81-p1359

* * *

GERNYET, N
Katya And The Crocodile
B&B-v14-Mr '69-p52
J Read-v25-F '82-p460
LJ-v94-Jl '69-p2676
NS-v77-My 16 '69-p702

* * *

GERRARD, Frank
Meat
JB-v43-D '79-p334
Sch Lib-v28-Mr '80-p43

* * *

GERRARD, Jean
Matilda Jane
BL-v78-Ap 1 '82-p1017
BL-v80-Ja 1 '84-p680
Brit Bk N C-Autumn '81-p13
CBRS-v12-F '84-p69
GP-v20-S '81-p3950
ILN-v269-D '81-p75
JB-v45-D '81-p243
LA-v61-Mr '84-p294
LATBR-D 11 '83-p10
NW-v102-D 5 '83-p110
NY-v59-D 5 '83-p204
NYTBR-v88-N 13 '83-p55
PW-v224-Ag 19 '83-p78
RT-v37-My '84-p889
SLJ-v28-Ap '82-p58

* * *

GERRARD, Roy
The Favershams
BL-v79-Jl '83-p1400
BW-v13-My 8 '83-p13
CCB-B-v37-S '83-p8
Econ-v285-D 25 '82-p105
HB-v59-O '83-p562
JB-v46-D '82-p219
KR-v51-Ap 15 '83-p456
LATBR-My 15 '83-p7
Lis-v108-N 4 '82-p27
NW-v102-D 5 '83-p110
NYT-v133-N 30 '83-p19
NYTBR-v88-Je 19 '83-p26
PW-v223-Ap 15 '83-p50
SE-v48-My '84-p375
SLJ-v30-S '83-p105
TLS-N 26 '82-p1305
WLB-v58-N '83-p211
Sir Cedric
B&B-N '84-p20
BL-v81-O 1 '84-p246
BW-v14-S 9 '84-p11
KR-v52-S 1 '84-pJ61
NY-v60-D 3 '84-p191
TLS-O 5 '84-p1139

* * *

GERSHATOR, Phillis
Honi And His Magic Circle
BL-v76-My 1 '80-p1290
CBRS-v8-Ap '80-p84
SLJ-v26-My '80-p56

* * *

GERSON, Corinne
Closed Circle
CCB-B-v22-Je '69-p157
CSM-v60-N 7 '68-pB6
KR-v36-Ag 15 '68-p898
Good Dog, Bad Dog
SLJ-v30-D '83-p55
How I Put My Mother Through College
BL-v77-Ap 1 '81-p1099
BW-v11-Ap 12 '81-p9
CBRS-v9-My '81-p86
CCB-B-v34-My '81-p171
CE-v58-Ja '82-p180
HB-v57-Ap '81-p189
Inst-v90-My '81-p59
KR-v49-My 1 '81-p574
SLJ-v28-S '81-p124
Oh, Brother!
BL-v78-My 1 '82-p1158
CBRS-v10-My '82-p97
CLW-v54-S '82-p84
HB-v58-Ap '82-p163
LA-v59-N '82-p868
SLJ-v28-Ag '82-p115
Passing Through
BL-v75-O 1 '78-p284
CBRS-v7-Ja '79-p47
CCB-B-v32-Mr '79-p115
EJ-v68-N '79-p76
EJ-v68-D '79-p78
Emerg Lib-v9-N '81-p32
Inter BC-v13-#4 '82-p15
KR-v47-Ja 15 '79-p70
SLJ-v25-O '78-p154
TN-v36-Summer '80-p366
TN-v37-Fall '80-p59
Son For A Day
BL-v76-Je 1 '80-p1423
CBRS-v8-Jl '80-p126
CCB-B-v34-S '80-p9
CE-v57-N '80-p112
HB-v56-Ag '80-p406
KR-v48-Je 1 '80-p713
RT-v34-Ja '81-p483
SLJ-v26-My '80-p67
Tread Softly
BL-v75-Je 15 '79-p1535
CBRS-v7-Spring '79-p118
CCB-B-v33-S '79-p8
KR-v47-Ag 1 '79-p853
RT-v33-Ap '80-p862
SLJ-v25-My '79-p61

* * *

GERSON, Mary-Joan
Omoteji's Baby Brother
BL-v71-S 1 '74-p40
CCB-B-v28-N '74-p42
HB-v50-D '74-p688
KR-v42-Je 15 '74-p630
LJ-v99-S 15 '74-p2245
Ms-v3-D '74-p79
PT-v8-D '74-p131

GERSON, Mary-Joan (continued)
PW-v206-Jl 8 '74-p74
SE-v39-Mr '75-p176
Why The Sky Is Far Away
BL-v70-Ap 15 '74-p940
BL-v71-Mr 15 '75-p766
BW-My 19 '74-p4
CE-v51-O '74-p33
Choice-v12-N '75-p1132
Inst-v84-N '74-p132
KR-v42-Mr 1 '74-p241
LJ-v99-S 15 '74-p2245
PT-v8-D '74-p131
PW-v205-Mr 18 '74-p53
TES-Mr 12 '82-p38

* * *

GERSON, Noel B
The Sad Swashbuckler
BL-v73-D 1 '76-p540
BS-v36-Ja '77-p323
Choice-v13-F '77-p1653
KR-v44-My 1 '76-p544
NYTBR-My 2 '76-p34
PW-v209-Mr 8 '76-p62
SLJ-v22-My '76-p69
Statue In Search Of A Pedestal
BL-v73-F 1 '77-p800
BL-v73-F 1 '77-p833
BS-v36-D '76-p294
KR-v44-Jl 15 '76-p822
LJ-v101-Ag '76-p1622
PW-v210-Jl 26 '76-p76
The Trial Of Andrew Johnson
BB-v6-Mr '78-p3
BL-v73-My 1 '77-p1338
BL-v73-My 1 '77-p1351
Choice-v14-F '78-p1704
KR-v45-Mr 1 '77-p258
LJ-v102-Ap 15 '77-p916
SLJ-v24-N '77-p81
The Velvet Glove
BL-v72-F 1 '76-p760
BL-v72-F 1 '76-p787
KR-v43-N 1 '75-p1243
SLJ-v22-N '75-p89

* * *

GERSONI-STAVN, Diane
Sexism And Youth
Choice-v11-N '74-p1272
HB-v51-Ap '75-p162
LJ-v99-S 1 '74-p2079
RSR-v2-O '74-p28
TN-v32-Ja '76-p177
Teacher-v92-O '74-p115

* * *

GERSTEIN, Mordicai
Arnold Of The Ducks
CBRS-v11-Spring '83-p120
CCB-B-v36-My '83-p166
KR-v51-F 1 '83-p116
LA-v61-Ja '84-p66
NYT-v133-D 1 '83-p23
NYTBR-v88-Ap 10 '83-p39
PW-v223-My 27 '83-p67
RT-v37-O '83-p86
SLJ-v29-My '83-p32
SLJ-v29-My '83-p61
Follow Me!
BL-v79-Mr 15 '83-p969
CBRS-v11-Ap '83-p86
KR-v51-Ja 1 '83-p1
SLJ-v29-Ap '83-p101
Prince Sparrow
BW-v14-Ag 12 '84-p5
CBRS-v13-S '84-p2
CCB-B-v38-S '84-p5
HB-v60-S '84-p579
WLB-v59-O '84-p129
Roll Over!
BL-v81-O 1 '84-p246
CBRS-v13-S '84-p2
PW-v226-Jl 20 '84-p81
The Room
CBRS-v12-My '84-p100
NYTBR-v89-Je 10 '84-p35
PW-v225-F 17 '84-p89
SLJ-v30-Ag '84-p59

* * *

GERSTEN, Irene Fandel
Ecidujerp-Prejudice
CCB-B-v28-S '74-p8
CE-v51-N '74-p95
KR-v42-Mr 1 '74-p248
LJ-v99-My 15 '74-p1472
PW-v205-Ap 1 '74-p58
SE-v39-Mr '75-p174

* * *

GERSTING, Judith L
Yes-No, Stop-Go
BB-v6-Je '78-p2
CCB-B-v31-Mr '78-p111
Cur R-v17-F '78-p57
HB-v54-Ag '78-p425
KR-v45-N 15 '77-p1201
SB-v14-Mr '79-p229
SLJ-v25-N '78-p61

* * *

GERVAIS, C H
If I Had A Birthday Every Day
BIC-v12-D '83-p14

* * *

GERVAISE, Mary
The Secret Of Pony Pass
GP-v14-Jl '75-p2669

* * *

GERZON, Mark
The Whole World Is Watching
A Lib-v1-Mr '70-p277
B&B-v18-Ag '73-p140
BL-v66-D 1 '69-p425
BL-v66-Mr 15 '70-p910
BS-v29-S 15 '69-p223
BW-v4-Ja 25 '70-p13
CSM-v61-Ag 14 '69-p11
HB-v46-F '70-p61
HER-v40-Ag '70-p491
KR-v37-My 15 '69-p585
KR-v37-Je 15 '69-p639
LJ-v94-Jl '69-p2588
LJ-v94-D 15 '69-p4584
LJ-v94-D 15 '69-p4627
NW-v74-Ag 4 '69-p84
PW-v195-My 12 '69-p56
PW-v196-N 10 '69-p51
Prog-v34-F '70-p46
RR-v29-Mr '70-p318
SR-v52-Ag 23 '69-p37

* * *

GESNER, Clark
The Ghost On The Hill
BS-v37-Je '77-p95
CCB-B-v31-O '77-p32
GP-v15-S '76-p2932
JB-v40-O '76-p274
KR-v45-Mr 15 '77-p290
Obs-Mr 6 '77-p22
PW-v211-Mr 28 '77-p79
SLJ-v23-My '77-p78
TLS-O 1 '76-p1238
The House On The Brink
Comw-v95-N 19 '71-p181
Econ-v237-D 26 '70-p38
HB-v47-O '71-p489
KR-v39-Jl 1 '71-p683
LJ-v96-D 15 '71-p4199
Obs-N 29 '70-p31
Obs-Jl 11 '76-p23
PW-v200-Ag 16 '71-p57
Spec-v225-D 5 '70-pR7

GESNER, Clark (continued)
Spec-v225-D 5 '70-pR21
TLS-O 30 '70-p1251
The Waterfall Box
GP-v17-Mr '79-p3485
JB-v43-Ap '79-p115
Sch Lib-v27-Mr '79-p54
TES-N 24 '78-p48
TLS-D 1 '78-p1395

* * *

GESS, Diane
Sunshine Porcupine
PW-v216-Jl 30 '79-p62
WCRB-v5-S '79-p83

* * *

GESSNER, Lynne
Brother To The Navajo
CBRS-v8-F '80-p56
KR-v48-Mr 1 '80-p288
PW-v217-Ja 11 '80-p88
SLJ-v26-N '79-p77
Danny
CBRS-v7-Jl '79-p126
EJ-v68-N '79-p93
SLJ-v26-N '79-p77
Sch Lib-v28-Mr '80-p55
Edge Of Darkness
BS-v40-Ap '80-p38
CBRS-v8-D '79-p37
CCB-B-v33-Ja '80-p94
HB-v56-F '80-p61
PW-v216-O 29 '79-p82
SLJ-v26-N '79-p87
Malcolm Yucca Seed
BL-v74-F 1 '78-p924
Cur R-v17-Ag '78-p182
SLJ-v24-Ja '78-p78
TES-Ap 4 '80-p29
Navajo Slave
Comw-v103-N 19 '76-p761
EJ-v65-O '76-p89
HB-v52-Ag '76-p396
Kliatt-v13-Winter '79-p7
SE-v41-Ap '77-p349
SLJ-v22-Ja '76-p46
To See A Witch
BL-v75-D 1 '78-p616
CBRS-v7-Ja '79-p47
CCB-B-v32-Mr '79-p115
LA-v56-My '79-p548
SLJ-v25-N '78-p62

* * *

GETSINGER, John
Luis
HB-v53-Ap '77-p190
Inter BC-v14-#1 '83-p15

* * *

GETTINGS, Fred
Arthur Rackham
Apo-v104-Ag '76-p144
Atl-v238-S '76-p99
BC-v25-Winter '76-p579
BL-v72-Jl 1 '76-p1502
BL-v72-Jl 1 '76-p1526
Choice-v13-D '76-p1282
HB-v52-Ag '76-p419
KR-v44-Ap 15 '76-p528
PW-v209-Mr 15 '76-p52
Spec-v235-O 25 '75-p537
Studio-v191-Ja '76-p67
The Meaning And The Wonder Of Art
BL-v61-Ap 15 '65-p794
CCB-B-v18-Je '65-p148
CLW-v36-Ja '65-p336
LJ-v90-Ja 15 '65-p388
Techniques Of Drawing
BL-v66-Je 15 '70-p1248
TES-Ja 8 '82-p22
TLS-O 9 '69-p1169

* * *

GETTIS, Arthur
Geography
Cur R-v21-F '82-p108

* * *

GETZ, Arthur
Hamilton Duck
CCB-B-v26-Ap '73-p123
CSM-v64-N 8 '72-pB3
CSM-v65-D 4 '72-p19
LJ-v97-N 15 '72-p3796
Hamilton Duck's Springtime Story
CCB-B-v28-Ja '75-p77
CSM-v66-Jl 3 '74-p7
LJ-v99-S 15 '74-p2246
Humphrey, The Dancing Pig
BL-v77-S 1 '80-p43
CBRS-v8-Jl '80-p121
HB-v56-Ag '80-p396
KR-v48-Ag 1 '80-p977
NYTBR-v85-N 9 '80-p49
PW-v217-Je 13 '80-p74
RT-v35-O '81-p53
SLJ-v27-S '80-p58
TES-D 19 '80-p21
Tar Beach
BL-v76-O 15 '79-p352
CBRS-v8-F '80-p51
CCB-B-v33-D '79-p70
Inter BC-v12-#3 '81-p21
KR-v48-F 15 '80-p211
SLJ-v26-D '79-p74
WLB-v55-O '80-p135

* * *

GETZOFF, Carole
The Natural Cook's First Book
CCB-B-v27-Ap '74-p129
LJ-v99-S 15 '74-p2267
NYTBR-N 4 '73-p32

* * *

GEVA, Tamara
Split Seconds
AB-v51-Je 4 '73-p2079
BL-v69-Ja 15 '73-p466
BL-v69-Mr 1 '73-p643
BS-v32-N 15 '72-p374
Choice-v10-My '73-p466
HB-v50-F '74-p76
KR-v40-Ag 15 '72-p989
LJ-v97-O 1 '72-p3144
PW-v202-Ag 28 '72-p255

* * *

GEVIRTZ, Eliezer
The Mystery Of The Missing Pushke
SLJ-v29-My '83-p92

* * *

GEZI, Kalil I
Beebi, The Little Blue Bell
SLJ-v22-My '76-p76
One Little White Shoe
SLJ-v22-My '76-p76

* * *

GHAYE, T
Man
TES-Ja 13 '84-p27
Resources
TES-Ja 13 '84-p27
Settlements
TES-Ja 13 '84-p27

* * *

GHINGER, Judith
New Year's To Christmas Hooray Days
SLJ-v24-Ap '78-p83

* * *

GHOSH, A K
Legends From Indian History
JB-v47-Ap '83-p61

* * *

GHOST Hunters (Counterpoint Readers)
Teacher-v96-Mr '79-p119

* * *

GHOSTS
Mag Lib- '82-p249
NS-v94-N 4 '77-p629

* * *

GIAMBARBA, Paul
The Lighthouse At Dangerfield
CLW-v41-F '70-p384
CSM-v61-N 6 '69-pB2
HB-v45-O '69-p525
KR-v37-Ag 1 '69-p772
LJ-v95-O 15 '70-p3642
PW-v196-Ag 18 '69-p74
Yacht-v126-D '69-p98

* * *

GIANNINI
Kangaroo
SLJ-v30-Ap '84-p103

* * *

GIBBARD, Vernon
Buildings And Backgrounds
GP-v18-S '79-p3580

* * *

GIBBERD, Vernon
The Garden In England
TES-O 9 '81-p29

* * *

GIBBONS, Faye
Some Glad Morning
BL-v78-Je 15 '82-p1368
CBRS-v10-Je '82-p106
CE-v59-Ja '83-p210
HB-v58-Ag '82-p402
J Read-v26-My '83-p742
LA-v60-F '83-p215
NYTBR-v87-S 19 '82-p41
SLJ-v28-Ag '82-p116

* * *

GIBBONS, Gail
Boat Book
BL-v79-Je 1 '83-p1276
BL-v80-N 1 '83-p423
CBRS-v11-My '83-p97
CCB-B-v37-O '83-p26
CE-v60-S '83-p56
HB-v59-Ag '83-p431
KR-v51-Mr 15 '83-p304
PW-v223-Mr 11 '83-p86
SLJ-v30-S '83-p105
Christmas Time
BL-v79-O 1 '82-p244
CBRS-v11-S '82-p6
CCB-B-v36-O '82-p25
PW-v222-O 22 '82-p56
SLJ-v29-O '82-p168
Clocks And How They Go
ACSB-v13-Spring '80-p31
BL-v76-N 1 '79-p448
BOT-v2-D '79-p599
HB-v55-D '79-p676
Inst-v89-N '79-p142
KR-v47-O 15 '79-p1212
NYTBR-N 18 '79-p31
SLJ-v26-Ja '80-p56
Department Store
BL-v80-Jl '84-p1548
CBRS-v12-Spring '84-p122
CCB-B-v38-S '84-p5
KR-v52-Mr 1 '84-pJ19
Learning-v12-Ap '84-p77
SLJ-v30-Ag '84-p59
Fire! Fire!
BL-v81-O 1 '84-p247
CBRS-v13-S '84-p2
KR-v52-S 1 '84-pJ75
SLJ-v31-S '84-p102
Halloween
BL-v81-S 1 '84-p64
CBRS-v13-O '84-p13
Locks & Keys
ASBYP-v14-Spring '81-p18
BL-v77-S 15 '80-p114
HB-v56-D '80-p653
KR-v48-O 1 '80-p1301
SLJ-v27-O '80-p146
The Magnificent Morris Mouse Clubhouse
CBRS-v10-Winter '82-p54
KR-v49-O 15 '81-p1295
SLJ-v28-D '81-p76
The Missing Maple Syrup Sap Mystery
BL-v76-D 15 '79-p611
KR-v48-F 1 '80-p121
PW-v216-D 24 '79-p58
SLJ-v26-F '80-p45
New Road!
BL-v80-O 15 '83-p358
CBRS-v12-S '83-p3
CE-v60-Ja '84-p213
HB-v59-D '83-p724
KR-v51-S 1 '83-pJ168
LA-v60-N '83-p1019
NYTBR-v88-N 13 '83-p48
SE-v48-My '84-p377
SLJ-v30-N '83-p63
Paper, Paper Everywhere
BL-v79-Je 15 '83-p1338
CCB-B-v37-O '83-p26
KR-v51-My 1 '83-p526
PW-v223-F 18 '83-p129
SLJ-v29-My '83-p61
The Post Office Book
BL-v79-S 1 '82-p42
CBRS-v11-O '82-p14
CCB-B-v36-F '83-p106
HB-v58-O '82-p510
Inst-v92-N '82-p151
KR-v50-Jl 1 '82-p730
NYTBR-v87-S 26 '82-p31
SLJ-v29-N '82-p67
Salvador And Mister Sam
BL-v72-D 15 '75-p578
KR-v43-N 15 '75-p1291
SLJ-v22-Ja '76-p37
Salvador Y Senor Sam
SLJ-v22-Ja '76-p37
Sun Up, Sun Down
BL-v80-Ja 1 '84-p680
CBRS-v12-Ja '84-p48
SLJ-v30-Ja '84-p64
Thanksgiving Day
BL-v80-O 15 '83-p358
CBRS-v12-O '83-p12
CCB-B-v37-O '83-p27
CE-v60-My '84-p367
Inst-v93-N '83-p146
PW-v224-S 9 '83-p65
SLJ-v30-D '83-p55
Things To Make And Do For Columbus Day
BB-v5-O '77-p2
SLJ-v24-S '77-p107
Things To Make And Do For Halloween
BL-v72-Mr 15 '76-p1052
KR-v44-F 1 '76-p129
SLJ-v22-My '76-p50
SLJ-v23-Ja '77-p82
Things To Make And Do For Your Birthday
BB-v6-Ja '79-p1
Comw-v105-N 10 '78-p735
Inst-v87-Ap '78-p169
SLJ-v25-N '78-p62
The Too-Great Bread Bake Book
KR-v48-O 1 '80-p1293
PW-v218-Ag 1 '80-p50
SLJ-v27-N '80-p61

GIBBONS, Gail (continued)
Tool Book
ASBYP-v16-Winter '83-p26
BL-v78-Ap 15 '82-p1095
CBRS-v10-My '82-p91
CE-v59-Mr '83-p281
CSM-v74-My 14 '82-pB12
HB-v58-Ap '82-p154
Inst-v91-My '82-p109
PW-v221-Ap 2 '82-p79
SB-v18-Ja '83-p149
SLJ-v28-My '82-p52
Trucks
BL-v78-O 15 '81-p304
CBRS-v10-S '81-p3
CCB-B-v35-N '81-p46
KR-v49-O 15 '81-p1291
LA-v59-F '82-p155
PW-v220-S 18 '81-p155
SLJ-v28-N '81-p75
Tunnels
BL-v80-Ap 15 '84-p1189
CBRS-v12-My '84-p101
CCB-B-v37-My '84-p164
CE-v61-S '84-p68
HB-v60-Je '84-p348
Inst-v93-My '84-p104
PW-v225-My 18 '84-p152
SLJ-v30-My '84-p65
Willy And His Wheel Wagon
KR-v43-Mr 15 '75-p300
NYTBR-My 4 '75-p43
SLJ-v22-S '75-p81

* * *

GIBBONS, Philip
Basic Math
Cur R-v18-My '79-p130

* * *

GIBBONS, Steve
Lump And The Fire
GP-v15-Mr '77-p3072
Lump The Painter
GP-v15-Mr '77-p3072

* * *

GIBBS, Alonzo
The Least Likely One
BL-v61-Mr 15 '65-p711
CCB-B-v18-Ja '65-p74
CLW-v36-Ja '65-p337
LR-v20-Autumn '66-p499
TLS-My 19 '66-p442
Man's Calling
BS-v26-D 1 '66-p339
CCB-B-v20-My '67-p140
KR-v34-O 1 '66-p1059
LJ-v91-D 15 '66-p6201
NYTBR-v72-F 5 '67-p32
One More Day
HB-v48-Ap '72-p145
KR-v39-Jl 15 '71-p746
LJ-v97-Je 15 '72-p2238
PW-v200-Jl 26 '71-p52

* * *

GIBBS, Anthony
In My Own Good Time
CSM-v62-Ag 6 '70-p11
HB-v46-Ag '70-p409
LJ-v95-Je 15 '70-p2252
PW-v197-Mr 2 '70-p78
SR-v53-My 16 '70-p32

* * *

GIBBS, Richard
Living In Johannesburg
TES-N 13 '81-p24
Rubber Tyres On Your Bike
Brit Bk N C-Autumn '82-p31
TES-N 5 '82-p28

* * *

GIBBS, Tony
Backpacking
BL-v71-My 1 '75-p907
CCB-B-v29-S '75-p9
KR-v43-F 15 '75-p187
SLJ-v21-Ap '75-p52

* * *

GIBBS-SMITH, C H
Pioneers Of The Aeroplane
ACSB-v13-Spring '80-p32

* * *

GIBEAULT, Kathi
Susan In The Driver's Seat
SLJ-v21-Mr '75-p87

* * *

GIBLIN, James
The Scarecrow Book
BL-v77-D 1 '80-p513
CBRS-v9-D '80-p24
CCB-B-v34-Mr '81-p133
HB-v57-F '81-p68
KR-v49-Ja 1 '81-p9
LA-v58-Mr '81-p344
NYTBR-v85-O 26 '80-p27
PW-v218-O 31 '80-p85
SLJ-v27-N '80-p62

* * *

GIBLIN, James C
Chimney Sweeps
BL-v79-N 15 '82-p444
BW-v12-O 10 '82-p6
CCB-B-v36-D '82-p66
CE-v59-Mr '83-p281
CLW-v55-S '83-p87
HB-v59-F '83-p62
KR-v50-S 15 '82-p1059
NYTBR-v87-N 21 '82-p43
PW-v222-S 24 '82-p72
RT-v36-Ja '83-p469
SLJ-v29-Ja '83-p75
WCRB-v9-Ja '83-p46
Fireworks, Picnics And Flags
BL-v79-Ag '83-p1464
CCB-B-v37-O '83-p27
HB-v59-Ag '83-p461
KR-v51-My 1 '83-p527
PW-v223-My 20 '83-p236
SE-v48-My '84-p370
SLJ-v30-S '83-p122
The Skyscraper Book
ASBYP-v15-Spring '82-p36
BL-v78-D 1 '81-p496
CCB-B-v35-Mr '82-p128
SB-v17-My '82-p265

* * *

GIBSON, Althea
So Much To Live For
CCB-B-v23-D '69-p59
LJ-v94-Mr 15 '69-p1339

* * *

GIBSON, Bob
From Ghetto To Glory
BL-v65-Ja 1 '69-p482
CCB-B-v22-Je '69-p157
KR-v36-S 1 '68-p996
LJ-v93-N 15 '68-p4429
LJ-v94-F 15 '69-p740
NYT-v118-O 10 '68-p45
PW-v194-Ag 19 '68-p70
PW-v195-F 24 '69-p68
SR-v52-Je 28 '69-p38

* * *

GIBSON, Enid
Night Of The Lemures
Emerg Lib-v11-S '83-p40

* * *

GIBSON, Gloria
Mouse At School
GP-v22-My '83-p4089
JB-v47-Ag '83-p171
Mouse In The Attic
JB-v45-F '81-p18
TES-D 26 '80-p17
TLS-S 19 '80-p1033

* * *

GIBSON, Josephine
Is There A Mouse In The House?
CCB-B-v19-F '66-p98
KR-v33-O 1 '65-p1036
LJ-v91-Ja 15 '66-p418
NYTBR-v70-O 31 '65-p56

* * *

GIBSON, M
Ecology The Chain Of Life
JB-v42-D '78-p310

* * *

GIBSON, Michael
The American Indian
KR-v42-Je 15 '74-p641
LR-v25-Summer '75-p80
Ancient China
JB-v47-F '83-p41
TES-N 5 '82-p31
Digging Into The Past
Sch Lib-v28-S '80-p302
TES-Je 20 '80-p43
Gods, Men And Monsters From The Greek Myths
BL-v79-S 1 '82-p38
GP-v16-Mr '78-p3259
JB-v41-D '77-p352
SLJ-v29-O '82-p157
TES-S 30 '77-p24
The Knights
BL-v76-Mr 1 '80-p982
CE-v56-Ap '80-p306
SE-v44-O '80-p534
SLJ-v27-S '80-p82
Knights And The Crusades
GP-v14-S '75-p2680
JB-v40-F '76-p23
A New Look At Mysteries Of Archaeology
SB-v17-S '81-p35
SLJ-v27-Mr '81-p144
A New Look At Treasures Of Archaeology
CCB-B-v34-Ap '81-p151
SB-v17-S '81-p35
SLJ-v27-Mr '81-p144
Vikingos
HB-v56-D '80-p665
The Vikings
BL-v69-Mr 1 '73-p643
KR-v41-Ja 15 '73-p66
NS-v92-N 5 '76-p642
Weather
JB-v44-D '80-p306

* * *

GIBSON, T A S
Moshi The Jackal
GP-v16-Ja '78-p3239
JB-v42-Ap '78-p103
TES-Ja 6 '78-p17
TLS-Ap 7 '78-p389

* * *

GIBSON, Truman
The Lord Is My Shepherd
CCB-B-v25-Ap '72-p122
LJ-v97-Mr 15 '72-p1175

* * *

GIBSON, Walter B
The Original Houdini Scrapbook
BL-v73-O 1 '76-p243
BL-v73-O 1 '76-p251
LJ-v101-Ag '76-p1652
PW-v209-Je 28 '76-p91
SLJ-v23-S '76-p145
WCRB-v3-Mr '77-p18
Rogues' Gallery
BL-v66-Ap 15 '70-p1036
BS-v29-D 1 '69-p352
CCB-B-v23-F '70-p97
KR-v37-N 15 '69-p1202
LJ-v94-D 15 '69-p4619
NY-v45-D 13 '69-p209
PW-v196-N 10 '69-p49
SR-v52-D 20 '69-p30
Walter Gibson's Big Book Of Magic For All Ages
CBRS-v9-Ja '81-p37
LJ-v106-Ja 15 '81-p162

* * *

GICORU, Nereas
Take Me Home
BL-v73-Jl 15 '77-p1732

* * *

GIDAL, Sonia
My Village In Brazil
CCB-B-v22-F '69-p93
KR-v36-Jl 1 '68-p694
NYTBR-v73-My 5 '68-p28
My Village In Finland
BL-v63-S 15 '66-p119
CCB-B-v19-Jl '66-p178
HB-v42-Je '66-p325
LJ-v91-Jl '66-p3534
My Village In France
CCB-B-v18-Jl '65-p161
CE-v43-O '66-p103
HB-v41-Ag '65-p404
LJ-v90-N 12 '65-p5108
My Village In Ghana
CCB-B-v24-Jl '70-p177
KR-v38-Mr 1 '70-p246
LJ-v95-Je 15 '70-p2308
SR-v53-Ap 18 '70-p37
My Village In Hungary
CCB-B-v28-Ap '75-p129
Inst-v84-My '75-p99
KR-v42-D 15 '74-p1308
KR-v43-Ja 1 '75-p7
SLJ-v21-Ap '75-p52
My Village In Japan
BL-v63-Ap 15 '67-p908
CCB-B-v20-F '67-p89
CLW-v39-N '67-p240
CSM-v59-My 4 '67-pB9
LJ-v92-Ja 15 '67-p350
My Village In Korea
CCB-B-v23-O '69-p24
CSM-v61-My 1 '69-pB9
My Village In Morocco
BL-v61-F 15 '65-p578
CCB-B-v18-Ja '65-p74
HB-v41-F '65-p69
My Village In Portugal
BL-v69-My 1 '73-p855
CCB-B-v26-Mr '73-p105
KR-v40-O 1 '72-p1147
SE-v37-D '73-p791
My Village In Thailand
LJ-v96-S 15 '71-p2935
My Village In Yugoslavia
RT-v33-F '80-p561

* * *

GIEGLING, John A
Black Lightning
KR-v43-Ag 1 '75-p853
SLJ-v22-N '75-p77

* * *

GIFF, Patricia R
The Almost Awful Play
BL-v80-My 15 '84-p1342
CBRS-v12-Je '84-p114
CCB-B-v37-My '84-p164
KR-v52-My 1 '84-pJ34
NYTBR-v89-S 2 '84-p12
SLJ-v30-Ag '84-p59
The Beast In Ms. Rooney's Room
LATBR-S 16 '84-p5
PW-v226-Ag 31 '84-p437
Fourth-Grade Celebrity
BL-v76-D 15 '79-p611
CBRS-v8-N '79-p27

GIFF, Patricia R (continued)
KR-v48-F 15 '80-p215
RT-v34-N '80-p237
SLJ-v27-Mr '81-p108
The Gift Of The Pirate Queen
BL-v79-O 15 '82-p311
CBRS-v11-O '82-p18
CCB-B-v36-D '82-p67
SLJ-v29-O '82-p168
The Girl Who Knew It All
BL-v76-D 15 '79-p611
CBRS-v8-N '79-p27
CSM-v71-O 15 '79-pB4
KR-v48-F 15 '80-p215
RT-v34-N '80-p237
SLJ-v26-O '79-p150
Have You Seen Hyacinth Macaw?
BL-v77-Mr 15 '81-p1027
BL-v79-Ap 1 '83-p1042
CBRS-v9-Mr '81-p67
KR-v49-S 1 '81-p1083
SLJ-v27-My '81-p84
Left-Handed Shortstop
BL-v77-S 15 '80-p114
CBRS-v9-D '80-p28
CCB-B-v34-D '80-p70
KR-v49-F 1 '81-p141
RT-v34-My '81-p967
RT-v35-O '81-p66
SLJ-v27-D '80-p74
SLJ-v27-My '81-p27
Loretta P. Sweeny, Where Are You?
B Rpt-v3-My '84-p33
CBRS-v12-Ja '84-p51
CCB-B-v37-N '83-p49
CE-v60-My '84-p362
SLJ-v30-D '83-p66
Next Year I'll Be Special
BL-v76-Je 15 '80-p1531
CBRS-v8-Je '80-p102
CCB-B-v33-Je '80-p190
HB-v56-Ag '80-p397
KR-v48-Je 1 '80-p710
PW-v217-My 16 '80-p211
RT-v35-O '81-p61
SLJ-v26-My '80-p56
Rat Teeth
BL-v80-Jl '84-p1548
CCB-B-v38-S '84-p5
SLJ-v30-My '84-p79
Suspect
BL-v78-Ag '82-p1520
CBRS-v10-Ag '82-p138
Hi Lo-v4-O '82-p8
SLJ-v29-D '82-p82
Today Was A Terrible Day
BL-v76-Mr 15 '80-p1056
CBRS-v8-Jl '80-p121
CCB-B-v34-S '80-p9
Inst-v89-My '80-p91
KR-v48-My 1 '80-p582
Obs-Jl 19 '81-p29
PW-v217-My 30 '80-p85
RT-v35-O '81-p64
SLJ-v26-My '80-p56
TES-O 9 '81-p29
The Winter Worm Business
BL-v78-O 1 '81-p235
CBRS-v10-S '81-p7
KR-v50-Ja 15 '82-p68
SLJ-v28-N '81-p92

* * *

GIFFORD, G
Because Of Blunder
JB-v41-D '77-p333

* * *

GIFFORD, Griselda
Ben's Expedition
CSM-v57-N 4 '65-pB6
TLS-D 9 '65-p1138
TLS-Mr 25 '77-p360
Cass The Brave
JB-v43-F '79-p30
TES-Jl 11 '80-p28
Earwig And Beetle
JB-v45-O '81-p196
Sch Lib-v30-Je '82-p129
TES-Ag 14 '81-p29
TES-Mr 12 '82-p38
TLS-S 18 '81-p1068
Jenny And The Sheep Thieves
GP-v14-D '75-p2755
TLS-S 19 '75-p1060
The Magic Mitre
GP-v21-S '82-p3943
JB-v46-O '82-p189
Mirabelle's Secret
GP-v15-N '76-p3006
JB-v40-O '76-p269
TLS-Jl 16 '76-p879
Pete And The Doodlebug And Other Stories
GP-v22-My '83-p4089
JB-v47-Ag '83-p162
Sch Lib-v31-D '83-p354
TES-My 13 '83-p32
Silver's Day
JB-v45-Ap '81-p70
Sch Lib-v29-Mr '81-p29
TLS-S 19 '80-p1026

* * *

GIFT From Maine
Cur R-v24-N '84-p24

* * *

GIKOW, Louise
The Legend Of The Doozer Who Didn't
BW-v14-N 11 '84-p19

* * *

GILBERT, Harriett
Running Away
BS-v39-D '79-p353
BW-v9-N 11 '79-p21
CBRS-v8-S '79-p7
CCB-B-v33-Ja '80-p95
HB-v56-F '80-p61
J Read-v23-Ap '80-p662
KR-v47-O 1 '79-p1149
SLJ-v26-O '79-p158

* * *

GILBERT, Harry
Ghosts Don't Play Games
GP-My '84-p4260
JB-v48-Je '84-p137
Sch Lib-v32-S '84-p238
Sarah's Nest
GP-v20-My '81-p3883
JB-v45-Ag '81-p158
Obs-Mr 1 '81-p33
SLJ-v28-D '81-p71
Sch Lib-v29-S '81-p253

* * *

GILBERT, John
Bobby Clarke
BL-v73-Jl 1 '77-p1650
SLJ-v23-My '77-p80
Bobby Unser
BL-v73-Jl 1 '77-p1650
SLJ-v23-My '77-p80
Checking And Defensive Play
BL-v73-D 1 '76-p538
SLJ-v23-D '76-p72
The Golden Book Of Buccaneers
SLJ-v23-Ja '77-p92
Highwaymen And Outlaws
JB-v41-D '77-p352
Knights Of The Crusades
TES-O 20 '78-p38
Prehistoric Man
B&B-v24-Je '79-p58
Scoring
BL-v73-D 1 '76-p538

GILBERT, John (continued)
SLJ-v23-D '76-p72

* * *

GILBERT, Lynn
Particular Passions
BL-v78-D 1 '81-p481
CSM-v74-F 10 '82-p19
Cha Ti-v36-O '82-p90
HB-v58-D '82-p678
Inter BC-v13-#6 '82-p41
J Read-v26-D '82-p277
KR-v49-N 1 '81-p1382
KR-v49-N 15 '81-p1417
Kliatt-v16-Fall '82-p48
LJ-v106-O 1 '81-p1940
NYT-v131-Ag 6 '82-p22
PW-v220-O 30 '81-p59
PW-v221-Mr 19 '82-p69
SFRB-v7-N '82-p24
SLJ-v28-Mr '82-p164
VOYA-v5-F '83-p49

* * *

GILBERT, Miriam
Shy Girl
SE-v48-N '84-p543

* * *

GILBERT, Nan
The Strange New World Across The Street
CCB-B-v33-Mr '80-p133
SLJ-v26-Ja '80-p69

* * *

GILBERT, Pamela
Gemma And The Witch
JB-v47-D '83-p243
Sch Lib-v31-D '83-p352

* * *

GILBERT, Sara
By Yourself
BL-v80-Mr 1 '84-p967
N Dir Wom-v13-Mr '84-p8
PW-v224-S 30 '83-p116
SLJ-v30-F '84-p81
Fat Free
BB-v3-Ag '75-p4
BL-v71-Mr 1 '75-p690
CCB-B-v29-O '75-p27
CLW-v47-N '75-p187
Comw-v102-N 21 '75-p571
KR-v43-F 1 '75-p129
NYTBR-My 4 '75-p25
PW-v207-My 26 '75-p60
Teacher-v96-Ja '79-p33
How To Live With A Single Parent
BL-v78-F 15 '82-p753
BS-v42-Ag '82-p202
CBRS-v10-Ap '82-p88
CCB-B-v35-My '82-p168
CLW-v54-D '82-p224
Kliatt-v16-Fall '82-p38
SB-v18-Mr '83-p212
SLJ-v28-My '82-p69
VOYA-v5-O '82-p54
Trouble At Home
BL-v77-My 1 '81-p1190
CBRS-v9-Je '81-p96
CCB-B-v34-My '81-p171
J Read-v25-Ja '82-p390
KR-v49-Ap 15 '81-p509
SLJ-v27-Ag '81-p74
VOYA-v4-D '81-p42
What Happens In Therapy
BL-v79-N 1 '82-p370
BS-v42-N '82-p325
CBRS-v11-O '82-p18
CCB-B-v36-F '83-p107
CLW-v55-N '83-p188
KR-v50-Jl 15 '82-p803
Kliatt-v17-Winter '83-p52
SB-v18-My '83-p262
SLJ-v29-O '82-p160
VOYA-v6-Ap '83-p49
You Are What You Eat
BL-v73-F 15 '77-p896
Cur R-v16-Ag '77-p174
EJ-v66-N '77-p82
KR-v44-D 15 '76-p1308
PW-v211-F 21 '77-p79
SLJ-v23-F '77-p71

* * *

GILBERT, W S
Gilbert Without Sullivan
BW-v11-N 8 '81-p20
Gondoliers
CCB-B-v21-Mr '68-p108
The Nightmare Song
Brit Bk N C-Autumn '81-p11
JB-v45-Ag '81-p158

* * *

GILBREATH, Alice
Antlers To Radar
ACSB-v13-Winter '80-p18
BL-v75-F 15 '79-p933
CCB-B-v32-My '79-p153
Beginning-To-Read Riddles And Jokes
LA-v55-N '78-p960
Candles For Beginners To Make
KR-v43-F 1 '75-p124
SLJ-v21-My '75-p55
Fun With Weaving
BL-v72-Je 1 '76-p1405
KR-v44-Ap 1 '76-p397
SLJ-v23-S '76-p116
Making Toys That Crawl And Slide
SLJ-v25-F '79-p42
WCRB-v5-My '79-p37
Making Toys That Swim And Float
Inst-v88-My '79-p114
SLJ-v25-F '79-p42
WCRB-v5-My '79-p37
More Beginning Crafts For Beginning Readers
BL-v72-Jl 15 '76-p1601
CCB-B-v30-O '76-p25
PW-v209-My 3 '76-p65
SLJ-v23-O '76-p98
Nature's Squirt Guns, Bubble Pipes And Fireworks
SB-v14-S '78-p111
SLJ-v24-Mr '78-p128
Nature's Underground Palaces
ACSB-v12-Spring '79-p22
SLJ-v25-S '78-p115
Simple Decoupage
BB-v6-Ag '78-p2
BL-v74-My 1 '78-p1430
Inst-v87-My '78-p114
KR-v46-Ap 1 '78-p377
SLJ-v25-S '78-p136
Slab, Coil, And Pinch
BL-v74-S 1 '77-p41
KR-v45-Ap 1 '77-p355
SLJ-v24-S '77-p127

* * *

GILCHRIST, Guy
Jim Henson's Muppets
SLJ-v31-O '84-p156

* * *

GILCHRIST, Theo E
Halfway Up The Mountain
BL-v74-Jl 15 '78-p1738
HB-v55-O '78-p510
KR-v46-O 1 '78-p1070
PW-v213-Je 12 '78-p82
SLJ-v25-D '78-p64

GILLEO, Alma (continued)
Metric Series
SLJ-v24-N '77-p31
Prince Charles: Growing Up In Buckingham Palace
Cur R-v18-F '79-p72
SLJ-v25-D '78-p52
Water Travel From The Beginning
Cur R-v16-O '77-p303
SB-v14-Mr '79-p229
SLJ-v24-Mr '78-p118

* * *

GILLESPIE, Avon
Time After Time
Inst-v90-N '80-p162

* * *

GILLESPIE, Janet
A Joyful Noise
BL-v67-My 15 '71-p758
CLW-v43-N '71-p169
HB-v47-O '71-p505
KR-v38-N 1 '70-p1224
KR-v39-Ja 1 '71-p13
LJ-v95-D 15 '70-p4251
PW-v198-O 26 '70-p53
SR-v54-Mr 20 '71-p31

* * *

GILLHAM, Bill
The Early Words Picture Book
BL-v80-N 15 '83-p496
CBRS-v12-N '83-p24
PW-v224-Ag 12 '83-p67
SLJ-v30-F '84-p58
TES-N 11 '83-p24
The First Words Picture Book
BL-v79-D 1 '82-p498
CBRS-v10-Ag '82-p133
HB-v60-S '84-p612
JB-v46-Ag '82-p132
LATBR-O 17 '82-p6
Home Before Long
BL-v80-Ag '84-p1625
GP-v22-Ja '84-p4179
HB-v60-Je '84-p327
JB-v48-Ap '84-p70
SLJ-v31-S '84-p116
Sch Lib-v32-Mr '84-p46
TES-O 5 '84-p29
Let's Look For Colours
GP-v23-S '84-p4303
TLS-Ag 24 '84-p954
Let's Look For Numbers
GP-v23-S '84-p4303
TLS-Ag 24 '84-p954
Let's Look For Opposites
GP-v23-S '84-p4303
TLS-Ag 24 '84-p954
Let's Look For Shapes
GP-v23-S '84-p4303
TLS-Ag 24 '84-p954
My Brother Barry
BL-v78-Ap 15 '82-p1095
Brit Bk N C-Spring '82-p11
CBRS-v10-Ap '82-p88
GP-v20-Ja '82-p4011
JB-v46-Ag '82-p142
SLJ-v28-My '82-p62
Sch Lib-v30-Mr '82-p36
TES-N 20 '81-p33
A Place To Hide
GP-v22-My '83-p4076
JB-v47-Ag '83-p162
SLJ-v30-N '83-p76
Sch Lib-v31-S '83-p245
Septimus Fry F.R.S.
Brit Bk N C-Spring '81-p19
CBRS-v9-Mr '81-p62
SLJ-v27-Ap '81-p112

* * *

GILLIGAN, Shannon
The Search For Champ
SLJ-v30-F '84-p58
The Three Wishes
SLJ-v31-S '84-p139

* * *

GILLILAND, Pat
Our Magnificent Earth
ACSB-v13-Mr '80-p55
ARBA-v12-'81-p273
BL-v77-S 1 '80-p71
Choice-v17-Mr '80-p50
Cur R-v19-F '80-p83
LJ-v104-D 1 '79-p2558
RQ-v19-Spring '80-p301
SB-v15-My '80-p272
SB-v16-S '80-p15
SLJ-v27-D '80-p22
WLB-v54-Ja '80-p333

* * *

GILLON, Edmund V, Jr.
Pennsylvania Dutch Farm
PW-v217-F 1 '80-p110

* * *

GILLUM, Helen L
Looking Forward To A Career: Veterinary Medicine
BL-v72-Je 1 '76-p1405
SB-v13-S '77-p89
SLJ-v23-S '76-p116

* * *

GILMAN, David
Life On The Seashore
GP-v21-My '82-p3904
TES-Ja 15 '82-p30
The Wildlife Of Farmland
TES-Mr 9 '84-p54

* * *

GILMORE, Maeve
Captain Eustace And The Magic Room
Brit Bk N C-Spring '82-p1
GP-v20-N '81-p3982
Obs-S 13 '81-p25

* * *

GILMORE, Susan
What Goes On At A Radio Station?
BL-v80-Jl '84-p1549
CCB-B-v37-My '84-p164
HB-v60-Je '84-p349
Inst-v93-My '84-p104
SLJ-v30-Ag '84-p73

* * *

GILMOUR, Ann
Understanding Your Senses
CCB-B-v18-Mr '65-p102

* * *

GILMOUR, Ian
Voyages Of Discovery
TES-D 1 '78-p34

* * *

GILROY, Beryl
Once Upon A Time
TES-Mr 12 '82-p38

* * *

GILROY, Doug
Parkland Portraits
BIC-v9-Je '80-p28
In Rev-v14-O '80-p42

* * *

GILROY, Ruth G
Little Ego
CCB-B-v24-My '71-p135
CLW-v43-D '71-p225
KR-v38-N 15 '70-p1243
LJ-v96-Ja 15 '71-p258
SR-v54-F 20 '71-p30

GINSBURG, Mirra (continued)
Obs-Jl 20 '75-p23
PW-v207-Ap 28 '75-p45
RT-v33-F '80-p561
SLJ-v21-My '75-p46
Spec-v235-Jl 26 '75-p114
How Wilka Went To Sea
BL-v71-Ap 15 '75-p865
CCB-B-v29-S '75-p9
CE-v52-O '75-p32
HB-v51-Ag '75-p377
KR-v43-Mr 15 '75-p312
PW-v207-Ap 28 '75-p45
RT-v35-N '81-p197
SLJ-v21-My '75-p55
SR-v22-My 31 '75-p34
The Kaha Bird
BL-v68-Mr 1 '72-p563
CCB-B-v25-My '72-p139
CE-v48-My '72-p424
CLW-v43-My '72-p534
HB-v47-D '71-p607
KR-v39-N 1 '71-p1160
LJ-v97-Ja 15 '72-p281
RT-v35-N '81-p198
TN-v28-Je '72-p433
Kitten From One To Ten
BL-v77-S 1 '80-p43
CBRS-v8-Jl '80-p122
KR-v48-Ag 1 '80-p977
LA-v58-Ja '81-p80
PW-v217-Je 13 '80-p74
SLJ-v27-D '80-p43
The Lazies
BL-v70-N 15 '73-p338
CCB-B-v27-Ja '74-p78
HB-v50-Ap '74-p145
KR-v41-S 15 '73-p1040
LJ-v99-F 15 '74-p573
RT-v35-D '81-p338
Little Rystu
BL-v74-Ja 15 '78-p812
CE-v55-Ja '79-p170
CE-v55-Ap '79-p261
HB-v54-Je '78-p269
JB-v42-D '78-p293
KR-v46-F 1 '78-p103
LA-v55-N '78-p984
SLJ-v24-Mr '78-p118
TLS-S 29 '78-p1087
Teacher-v96-O '78-p162
The Magic Stove
BL-v79-Je 15 '83-p1338
CBRS-v11-Jl '83-p130
CCB-B-v37-O '83-p27
KR-v51-My 1 '83-p519
SE-v48-My '84-p376
SLJ-v30-O '83-p148
The Master Of The Winds And Other Tales From Siberia
BL-v67-F 1 '71-p450
Comw-v93-N 20 '70-p200
HB-v47-Ap '71-p165
KR-v38-S 15 '70-p1042
LJ-v95-D 15 '70-p4350
RT-v35-N '81-p198
Mushroom In The Rain
BL-v70-Ap 15 '74-p941
BL-v71-Mr 15 '75-p766
BW-My 19 '74-p4
CSM-v66-My 1 '74-pF2
Choice-v12-N '75-p1132
JB-v39-F '75-p21
KR-v42-Ja 1 '74-p3
KR-v43-Ja 1 '75-p2
NY-v50-D 2 '74-p201
Obs-D 1 '74-p35
PW-v205-F 4 '74-p72
RT-v35-Ja '82-p472
Spec-v233-D 7 '74-p739
Time-v112-D 4 '78-p103
The Night It Rained Pancakes
BL-v76-F 15 '80-p838
CSM-v72-Ap 14 '80-pB7
HB-v56-Ag '80-p401
KR-v48-Ap 15 '80-p512
PW-v217-Ap 11 '80-p77
RT-v35-D '81-p332
SLJ-v26-My '80-p81
One Trick Too Many
BL-v69-Jl 1 '73-p1021
HB-v49-Ag '73-p369
KR-v41-Ap 15 '73-p454
LJ-v98-S 15 '73-p2639
RT-v35-D '81-p332
Ookie-Spooky
BB-v7-O '79-p5
CBRS-v8-Ja '80-p41
KR-v48-F 15 '80-p211
PW-v217-Ja 18 '80-p140
SLJ-v26-Mr '80-p120
Pampalche Of The Silver Teeth
BB-v4-O '76-p2
BL-v72-Mr 1 '76-p977
CCB-B-v29-My '76-p144
CLW-v47-My '76-p444
KR-v44-Ja 15 '76-p67
LA-v54-F '77-p207
NYTBR-Je 6 '76-p55
PW-v209-Mr 1 '76-p94
RT-v35-D '81-p332
SLJ-v22-Mr '76-p91
The Proud Maiden, Tungak, And The Sun
BB-v2-Ja '75-p3
BL-v71-D 1 '74-p379
BW-D 8 '74-p7
CE-v51-Ap '75-p326
HB-v51-Ap '75-p144
Inst-v84-My '75-p104
KR-v42-O 15 '74-p1101
RT-v35-N '81-p198
SLJ-v21-Ja '75-p39
Striding Slippers
BL-v74-Ap 15 '78-p1349
KR-v46-Ap 1 '78-p367
LA-v55-N '78-p985
PW-v213-Ap 3 '78-p81
RT-v35-N '81-p199
SLJ-v24-My '78-p54
The Strongest One Of All
BL-v74-O 1 '77-p289
CSM-v70-My 3 '78-pB8
HB-v53-D '77-p658
KR-v45-Ag 15 '77-p846
NYTBR-N 27 '77-p40
PW-v212-Jl 18 '77-p138
RT-v32-O '78-p37
RT-v35-N '81-p199
SLJ-v24-N '77-p47
TES-Mr 10 '78-p60
TLS-D 2 '77-p1411
The Sun's Asleep Behind The Hill
BL-v78-Ap 1 '82-p1017
BW-v12-My 9 '82-p17
CBRS-v10-My '82-p91
CCB-B-v36-S '82-p9
CE-v59-Ja '83-p210
KR-v50-Mr 15 '82-p341
LA-v59-N '82-p866
Par-v58-O '83-p158
RT-v36-D '82-p336
SLJ-v28-Mr '82-p132
VLS-O '82-p7
Three Rolls And One Doughnut
B&B-v19-O '73-p126
BL-v67-F 15 '71-p492
CCB-B-v25-O '71-p25
CLW-v42-My '71-p578
Comw-v93-N 20 '70-p200
HB-v47-Ap '71-p165
KR-v38-N 15 '70-p1251
LJ-v96-F 15 '71-p724
LJ-v96-My 15 '71-p1781
NY-v47-D 4 '71-p184

GINSBURG, Mirra (continued)
RT-v35-D '81-p332
TLS-S 28 '73-p1115
The Twelve Clever Brothers And Other Fools
BL-v76-Ja 1 '80-p666
CCB-B-v33-Ap '80-p152
KR-v48-F 15 '80-p218
RT-v34-O '80-p103
RT-v35-N '81-p199
SLJ-v26-Mr '80-p131
Two Greedy Bears
BL-v73-O 15 '76-p322
CLW-v48-Ap '77-p403
HB-v53-F '77-p37
JB-v43-F '79-p17
KR-v44-S 15 '76-p1034
NYTBR-N 14 '76-p26
PW-v210-O 18 '76-p64
RT-v31-O '77-p14
RT-v35-Ap '82-p823
SLJ-v23-D '76-p49
Sch Lib-v27-Mr '79-p27
What Kind Of Bird Is That
BL-v69-Jl 15 '73-p1072
CSM-v65-My 2 '73-pB3
HB-v49-Ag '73-p372
KR-v41-Mr 1 '73-p250
RT-v35-Ja '82-p469
Where Does The Sun Go At Night?
BL-v77-N 1 '80-p404
CBRS-v9-O '80-p11
HB-v57-F '81-p41
JB-v45-Ag '81-p144
KR-v49-Ja 1 '81-p1
RT-v35-O '81-p65
SLJ-v27-O '80-p134
TES-Je 5 '81-p36
TLS-Mr 27 '81-p342
Which Is The Best Place?
BB-v5-Ap '77-p1
BL-v72-Mr 15 '76-p1045
BW-Mr 14 '76-p8
CLW-v48-S '76-p85
HB-v52-Je '76-p279
Inst-v85-My '76-p119
KR-v44-Ja 15 '76-p67
PW-v209-Ap 12 '76-p66
RT-v35-Ja '82-p468
SLJ-v22-My '76-p50

* * *

GIOVANNETTI
Max
BL-v73-My 1 '77-p1351
CCB-B-v31-N '77-p46
CLW-v49-O '77-p142
KR-v45-F 15 '77-p161
NYTBR-My 1 '77-p44
PW-v211-F 21 '77-p78
Par-v52-S '77-p95
SLJ-v24-S '77-p128
Teacher-v96-F '79-p31

* * *

GIOVANNI, Nikki
Ego-Tripping
BL-v70-Ap 1 '74-p873
BW-My 19 '74-p4
CCB-B-v27-My '74-p142
CSM-v66-My 1 '74-pF5
KR-v42-Ja 1 '74-p11
LJ-v99-Ap 15 '74-p1240
NYTBR-My 5 '74-p38
PW-v204-D 31 '73-p27
Spin A Soft Black Song
BL-v68-My 1 '72-p770
Bl S-v12-Mr '81-p85
CCB-B-v25-F '72-p91
KR-v39-O 15 '71-p1126
LJ-v97-Je 15 '72-p2230
NYTBR-N 28 '71-p8
NYTBR, pt.2-N 7 '71-p30
Vacation Time
BW-v11-Mr 8 '81-p10
CCB-B-v34-O '80-p31
KR-v48-S 1 '80-p1165
NYTBR-v85-N 9 '80-p62
PW-v217-My 23 '80-p77

* * *

GIPSON, Fred
Curly And The Wild Boar
BB-v7-N '79-p4
CCB-B-v33-S '79-p8
CLW-v51-D '79-p233
KR-v47-Ap 1 '79-p388
SLJ-v25-My '79-p35
SLJ-v25-My '79-p61
Little Arliss
BW-Jl 9 '78-pE4
CCB-B-v32-O '78-p28
CE-v55-N '78-p102
HB-v54-Ag '78-p394
KR-v46-Je 1 '78-p595
LA-v56-Ja '79-p52
NYTBR-Ap 30 '78-p52
NYTBR-v85-Ap 27 '80-p39
SE-v43-Ap '79-p298
SLJ-v24-My '78-p66

* * *

GIPSON, Morrell
Favorite Nursery Tales
CBRS-v11-Je '83-p111
CCB-B-v36-Jl '83-p209
PW-v223-Ap 8 '83-p58
SLJ-v30-S '83-p106

* * *

GIRAFFES And The Polar Bears
Econ-v285-D 25 '82-p105

* * *

GIRARD, Linda W
You Were Born On Your Very First Birthday
BL-v79-Mr 15 '83-p969
CBRS-v11-My '83-p100
CCB-B-v36-Ap '83-p148
CE-v60-N '83-p140
SB-v19-S '83-p35
SLJ-v29-Ap '83-p101

* * *

GIRARD, Pat
Flying Machines
ASBYP-v14-Fall '81-p29
SB-v17-S '81-p34

* * *

GIRARD, Suzanne
The Primary Computer Dictionary
Edu D-v15-Jl '83-p21

* * *

GIRION, Barbara
The Boy With The Special Face
CCB-B-v32-O '78-p29
CLW-v50-F '79-p300
SLJ-v25-N '78-p44
A Handful Of Stars
BL-v78-D 1 '81-p490
BS-v41-F '82-p441
CBRS-v10-Ap '82-p88
CCB-B-v35-Mr '82-p128
CLW-v53-Ap '82-p401
Cur R-v21-F '82-p34
Cur R-v22-F '83-p60
EJ-v72-D '83-p68
HB-v58-F '82-p52
J Read-v25-My '82-p813
KR-v50-F 1 '82-p140
Kliatt-v17-Fall '83-p10
LA-v60-Ap '83-p506
PW-v220-O 23 '81-p62
SLJ-v28-Ja '82-p77

GIRION, Barbara (continued)
VOYA-v5-Ap '82-p34
Joshua, The Czar, And The Chicken Bone Wish
BL-v75-F 1 '79-p865
CBRS-v7-Winter '79-p54
CCB-B-v32-Ap '79-p136
KR-v47-Ja 1 '79-p5
SLJ-v25-Mr '79-p139
Like Everybody Else
BL-v77-F 15 '81-p809
BL-v78-Jl '82-p1453
CBRS-v9-Winter '81-p47
CCB-B-v34-Mr '81-p133
Inter BC-v13-#2 '82-p34
KR-v49-Ja 15 '81-p75
Kliatt-v16-Fall '82-p10
LATBR-Jl 25 '82-p9
RT-v35-O '81-p69
SLJ-v27-F '81-p65
Misty And Me
BL-v76-D 1 '79-p557
CBRS-v8-Winter '80-p65
CCB-B-v33-Ap '80-p152
HB-v56-Ap '80-p172
KR-v47-N 1 '79-p1263
SLJ-v26-Ja '80-p69
A Tangle Of Roots
BL-v75-My 1 '79-p1356
B Rpt-v1-Mr '83-p24
BS-v39-S '79-p228
CBRS-v7-Spring '79-p118
CCB-B-v33-N '79-p47
CSM-v71-Jl 9 '79-pB6
EJ-v68-N '79-p76
EJ-v69-N '80-p88
KR-v47-Ap 1 '79-p392
Kliatt-v15-Fall '81-p10
SLJ-v25-My '79-p71
A Very Brief Season
BL-v80-My 1 '84-p1234
BS-v44-S '84-p232
CBRS-v13-S '84-p8
CCB-B-v37-Jl '84-p204
PW-v225-My 25 '84-p59
SLJ-v31-S '84-p128

* * *

GIRL Scouts Of The U.S.A.
Girl Scout Cookbook
BL-v68-Ap 1 '72-p672
CCB-B-v25-Ap '72-p122
PW-v203-My 14 '73-p47
Teacher-v91-S '73-p154
Mundos A Explorar
TN-v39-Spring '83-p219
Worlds To Explore
TN-v39-Spring '83-p218

* * *

GIRON, Nicole
El Agua
BL-v79-F 15 '83-p783
El Mar
BL-v79-F 15 '83-p783

* * *

GITANJALI
Poems Of Gitanjali
BL-v79-Jl '83-p1395
CCB-B-v37-N '83-p49
Sch Lib-v31-Mr '83-p81

* * *

GITENSTEIN, Judy
Summer Camp
SLJ-v31-S '84-p139

* * *

GITLER, Ira
Ice Hockey A To Z
ARBA-v10-'79-p349
CCB-B-v32-S '78-p8
SLJ-v25-D '78-p70
Make The Team In Ice Hockey
CCB-B-v22-My '69-p142
LJ-v94-D 15 '69-p4621

* * *

GITTINS, Anne
Tales From The South Pacific Islands
BL-v74-F 15 '78-p1004
Cur R-v17-My '78-p150
SLJ-v24-Ap '78-p84

* * *

GIVENS, Janet E
Just Two Wings
BL-v80-Je 1 '84-p1397
SLJ-v31-S '84-p102
Something Wonderful Happened
ASBYP-v16-Winter '83-p27
PW-v221-My 7 '82-p79
SLJ-v29-D '82-p48

* * *

GJERSVIK, Maryanne
Green Fun
CE-v51-O '74-p36
CSM-v67-Je 10 '75-p17
Inst-v84-My '75-p107
LJ-v99-S 15 '74-p2267
PW-v205-My 13 '74-p59
SA-v231-D '74-p158

* * *

GLADSTONE, Josephine
Stories From Ladder Street
Brit Bk N C-Spring '80-p10
TES-Mr 7 '80-p49

* * *

GLADSTONE, Lise
The Inside Kid
PW-v211-My 9 '77-p92
SLJ-v24-S '77-p108

* * *

GLADSTONE, M J
A Carrot For A Nose
BL-v71-O 1 '74-p169
BL-v71-Mr 15 '75-p766
CCB-B-v28-Mr '75-p112
Choice-v12-N '75-p1132
HB-v51-Ap '75-p157
Hob-v79-F '75-p136
Inst-v84-N '74-p137
KR-v42-Ag 1 '74-p811
KR-v43-Ja 1 '75-p12
LJ-v99-D 15 '74-p3247
LJ-v99-D 15 '74-p3272
NY-v50-D 2 '74-p204
NYTBR-Ag 18 '74-p8
NYTBR-N 3 '74-p54
NYTBR-D 1 '74-p76
PW-v206-S 30 '74-p59
WLB-v49-D '74-p271

* * *

GLANVILLE, Brian
A Bad Lot
GP-v16-O '77-p3179
Obs-Je 5 '77-p26
Goalkeepers Are Different
BL-v69-Ap 15 '73-p807
BS-v32-N 15 '72-p394
CCB-B-v26-F '73-p90
CSM-v64-N 8 '72-pB5
KR-v40-N 1 '72-p1245
LJ-v98-Mr 15 '73-p1012
TLS-D 3 '71-p1512
Kevin Keegan
JB-v45-O '81-p198
SLJ-v28-D '81-p84
Sch Lib-v29-D '81-p354
The Puffin Book Of Football
NS-v80-N 6 '70-p616
Obs-S 27 '70-p26
Obs-N 9 '75-p25
TLS-D 8 '72-p1501

GLANVILLE, Brian (continued)
The Puffin Book Of Footballers
TES-F 3 '78-p41
The Puffin Book Of Tennis
Obs-Jl 19 '81-p29
TES-Jl 17 '81-p26

* * *

GLASER, Dianne
Amber Wellington, Daredevil
KR-v43-My 15 '75-p567
SLJ-v22-S '75-p102
Amber Wellington, Witch Watcher
KR-v44-Je 15 '76-p686
SLJ-v23-D '76-p68
Teacher-v95-My '78-p109
The Case Of The Missing Six
BL-v74-My 1 '78-p1430
BL-v79-Ap 1 '83-p1042
KR-v46-Ap 1 '78-p374
SLJ-v24-My '78-p84
The Diary Of Trilby Frost
BB-v4-N '76-p2
BL-v72-My 1 '76-p1264
HB-v52-Ag '76-p404
KR-v44-My 1 '76-p541
PW-v209-Je 28 '76-p99
SE-v41-Ap '77-p350
SLJ-v23-S '76-p133
TN-v37-Fall '80-p59
Summer Secrets
BL-v74-N 1 '77-p476
KR-v45-D 1 '77-p1270
SLJ-v24-Ja '78-p94

* * *

GLASGOW, Aline
Honschi
BL-v69-Ap 15 '73-p811
CCB-B-v26-F '73-p90
KR-v40-N 15 '72-p1301
LJ-v98-Ap 15 '73-p1375
The Pair Of Shoes
Am-v125-D 4 '71-p487
BL-v68-D 15 '71-p366
CLW-v43-Ap '72-p481
KR-v39-O 15 '71-p1113
LJ-v96-N 15 '71-p3891
RT-v33-Ap '80-p809
Time-v98-D 27 '71-p61

* * *

GLASS, Andrew
Jackson Makes His Move
BL-v79-S 1 '82-p42
BW-v12-N 7 '82-p16
KR-v50-Mr 15 '82-p342
PW-v221-Mr 5 '82-p70
RT-v37-O '83-p54
SLJ-v28-My '82-p52
VV-v27-D 14 '82-p75
My Brother Tries To Make Me Laugh
CBRS-v12-Ag '84-p145

* * *

GLASS, George
Your Book Of Judo
BL-v75-D 1 '78-p607
JB-v43-F '79-p50

* * *

GLASS, Paul
Singing Soldiers
CCB-B-v22-Jl '69-p175
CSM-v61-N 29 '68-pB8
PW-v194-O 28 '68-p57
SR-v52-Je 28 '69-p39
Songs And Stories Of Afro-Americans
AB-v48-Ag 2 '71-p250
CCB-B-v25-N '71-p43
GT-v89-F '72-p139
NYTBR, pt.2-My 2 '71-p43

* * *

GLASS, Stuart M
A Divorce Dictionary
ARBA-v12-'81-p351
BL-v76-Jl 1 '80-p1606
SB-v16-Mr '81-p217
SLJ-v27-S '80-p70

* * *

GLASS (Wayland World Resources)
TES-Mr 6 '81-p37

* * *

GLASSBOROW, Caroline
Take Me To The Supermarket
Sch Lib-v27-Je '79-p131

* * *

GLASSER, Barbara
Bongo Bradley
BL-v70-N 1 '73-p291
CCB-B-v27-Mr '74-p110
LJ-v98-N 15 '73-p3452
Leroy Oops
CCB-B-v25-N '71-p43
CSM-v63-My 6 '71-pB4
LJ-v96-Je 15 '71-p2125

* * *

GLASSMAN, Carl
Hocus Focus
BB-v5-Ap '77-p2
BL-v73-F 15 '77-p896
SLJ-v23-D '76-p60

* * *

GLASSTONE, Richard
Better Ballet
B&B-v23-Ja '78-p63
GP-v16-Mr '78-p3272
JB-v42-Je '78-p153
Kliatt-v14-Winter '80-p60
I Really Want To Dance
JB-v47-F '83-p24
Sch Lib-v31-Mr '83-p42
Male Dancing As A Career
JB-v45-Je '81-p123
TES-Ja 16 '81-p23

* * *

GLATT, Louise
What To Do Until The Music Teacher Comes
Can Child Lit-#17 '80-p56
Inst-v92-S '82-p189

* * *

GLAZER, Joan I
Introduction To Children's Literature
BL-v75-Jl 1 '79-p1584
CBRS-v7-Jl '79-p127
Cur R-v19-S '80-p330
RT-v34-O '80-p106
SLJ-v26-N '79-p45
TN-v39-Fall '82-p91

* * *

GLAZER, Lee
Cookie Becker Casts A Spell
KR-v48-Jl 15 '80-p910
PW-v217-Mr 14 '80-p75
RT-v35-O '81-p65
SLJ-v26-My '80-p57

* * *

GLAZER, Tom
All About Your Name
BB-v7-My '79-p2
All About Your Name: Anne
CCB-B-v32-Mr '79-p116
SLJ-v25-F '79-p55
All About Your Name: David
SLJ-v25-F '79-p55
All About Your Name: Elizabeth
SLJ-v25-F '79-p55

GLAZER, Tom (continued)
All About Your Name: James
SLJ-v25-F '79-p55
All About Your Name: John
SLJ-v25-F '79-p55
All About Your Name: Joseph
SLJ-v25-F '79-p55
All About Your Name: Katherine
SLJ-v25-F '79-p55
All About Your Name: Mary
SLJ-v25-F '79-p55
All About Your Name: Susan
SLJ-v25-F '79-p55
All About Your Name: William
SLJ-v25-F '79-p55
Do Your Ears Hang Low?
BL-v76-Je 1 '80-p1423
CBRS-v8-Ap '80-p87
CCB-B-v33-Jl '80-p212
CE-v57-N '80-p114
HB-v56-Ag '80-p422
Eye Winker, Tom Tinker, Chin Chopper
BB-v7-Ja '80-p1
BL-v70-Ja 15 '74-p541
CCB-B-v27-Mr '74-p110
CE-v50-Mr '74-p298
HB-v50-Ap '74-p163
LJ-v99-Mr 15 '74-p881
PW-v204-D 3 '73-p41
PW-v215-Ja 22 '79-p370
Music For Ones And Twos
BL-v80-Ja 1 '84-p686
CBRS-v12-Ja '84-p46
CCB-B-v37-F '84-p107
CE-v61-S '84-p68
On Top Of Spaghetti
CBRS-v10-Je '82-p101
LJ-v92-Ja 15 '67-p258
SLJ-v28-Ag '82-p98

* * *

GLEASE, Hannah
The Magic Tree In Winter
Obs-F 1 '81-p29
The World Of Nature
TES-D 1 '78-p25

* * *

GLEASNER, Diana C
Breakthrough: Women In Writing
BL-v76-Ap 1 '80-p1116
CBRS-v9-O '80-p18
CCB-B-v34-O '80-p31
Cur R-v21-My '82-p224
Inter BC-v13-#6 '82-p38
J Read-v24-Mr '81-p548
KR-v48-Je 15 '80-p784
SLJ-v26-Ag '80-p76
Dynamite
ASBYP-v16-Spring '83-p24
BL-v79-Mr 1 '83-p905
CCB-B-v36-F '83-p107
KR-v50-N 15 '82-p1238
SLJ-v29-Ja '83-p75
The Movies
BL-v79-My 15 '83-p1216
SLJ-v29-Mr '83-p176
Women In Sports: Swimming
Cur R-v16-O '77-p315
Inter BC-v10-Ap 40 '79-p15
SLJ-v22-Ap '76-p74
Women In Sports: Track And Field
BL-v74-O 1 '77-p302
Inter BC-v10-Ap 40 '79-p10
SLJ-v24-N '77-p56

* * *

GLEASON, Judith
Orisha
BL-v68-N 1 '71-p216
CCB-B-v25-S '71-p6
KR-v39-Mr 15 '71-p296
LJ-v96-My 15 '71-p1811
NYTBR, pt.2-My 2 '71-p43
PW-v199-My 3 '71-p57

* * *

GLENDINNING, Richard
Gargantua
SLJ-v21-Mr '75-p96
Stubby
RT-v33-O '79-p95
SLJ-v25-F '79-p54

* * *

GLENDINNING, Sally
Jimmy And Joe Catch An Elephant
LJ-v95-My 15 '70-p1959
Jimmy And Joe Find A Ghost
CCB-B-v23-F '70-p97
LJ-v95-My 15 '70-p1959
Jimmy And Joe Fly A Kite
LJ-v95-D 15 '70-p4371
Jimmy And Joe Get A Hens' Surprise
LJ-v95-D 15 '70-p4371
Jimmy And Joe Go To The Fair
LJ-v96-D 15 '71-p4197
Jimmy And Joe Look For A Bear
LJ-v95-D 15 '70-p4371
Jimmy And Joe Meet A Witch
LJ-v96-D 15 '71-p4197
Jimmy And Joe Save A Christmas Deer
LJ-v98-O 15 '73-p3127

* * *

GLENDINNING, Sally P
Doll
ASBYP-v14-Spring '81-p18
SB-v16-My '81-p276
Emperor Penguin
ASBYP-v14-Spring '81-p18
Little Blue And Rusty
ASBYP-v14-Spring '81-p18
SB-v16-My '81-p276
Pen
SB-v16-My '81-p276

* * *

GLENN, Mel
Class Dismissed!
BL-v78-Je 15 '82-p1361
BL-v80-O 15 '82-p352
BL-v81-S 15 '84-p123
B Rpt-v2-S '83-p40
CBRS-v10-Jl '82-p127
CCB-B-v36-S '82-p9
SLJ-v29-O '82-p160
VOYA-v5-Ag '82-p44

* * *

GLES, Margaret
Come Play Hide And Seek
SLJ-v22-D '75-p65

* * *

GLEZOS, Petros
To Spiti Me Ta Peristeria Kai Alla Diegemata
BL-v74-S 15 '77-p204

* * *

GLICKMAN, Paul
Magic Tricks
BL-v77-Ja 15 '81-p705
SLJ-v27-Ag '81-p55

* * *

GLICKMAN, William G
Winners On The Tennis Court
BL-v74-Ap 15 '78-p1357

* * *

GLIDEWELL, Peter
Schoolgirl Chums
TES-F 24 '84-p29

* * *

GLOVACH, Linda
Let's Make A Deal
CCB-B-v29-N '75-p45
KR-v43-Mr 15 '75-p304
PW-v207-Mr 17 '75-p56
SLJ-v22-S '75-p81
The Little Witch Presents A Monster Joke Book
KR-v44-O 15 '76-p1142
SLJ-v23-Ja '77-p82
The Little Witch's Birthday Book
KR-v49-Ag 1 '81-p937
RT-v35-D '81-p366
SLJ-v28-N '81-p75
The Little Witch's Black Magic Book Of Disguises
CLW-v45-Mr '74-p398
Comw-v99-N 23 '73-p212
KR-v41-Ag 1 '73-p815
LJ-v98-D 15 '73-p3700
PW-v204-Ag 27 '73-p282
The Little Witch's Black Magic Book Of Games
CLW-v46-F '75-p315
Inst-v83-My '74-p90
KR-v42-F 1 '74-p113
PW-v205-F 25 '74-p114
SR/W-v1-My 4 '74-p43
The Little Witch's Black Magic Cookbook
KR-v40-O 15 '72-p1184
NYTBR, pt.2-N 5 '72-p10
The Little Witch's Book Of Yoga
KR-v48-F 1 '80-p130
SLJ-v26-Ja '80-p56
The Little Witch's Christmas Book
CCB-B-v28-D '74-p62
KR-v42-O 1 '74-p1057
LJ-v99-O 15 '74-p2721
PW-v206-O 28 '74-p49
The Little Witch's Halloween Book
KR-v43-N 1 '75-p1224
SLJ-v22-Ja '76-p37
The Little Witch's Spring Holiday Book
BL-v79-Ag '83-p1464
SLJ-v30-O '83-p149
The Little Witch's Thanksgiving Book
KR-v44-O 15 '76-p1141
SLJ-v23-F '77-p64
The Little Witch's Valentine Book
SLJ-v30-Ag '84-p59
Potions, Lotions, Tonics And Teas
KR-v45-Jl 15 '77-p729
SLJ-v24-D '77-p48

* * *

GLOVER, Brian
Death Angel
Brit Bk N C-Autumn '82-p24
TES-My 28 '82-p30
TLS-Mr 26 '82-p352

* * *

GLOVER, Harry
The Book Of Dogs
CCB-B-v25-S '71-p7

* * *

GLUBOK, Shirley
Art And Archaeology
BL-v62-Jl 15 '66-p1086
CCB-B-v20-S '66-p9
CSM-v58-N 3 '66-pB5
KR-v34-My 1 '66-p476
LJ-v91-Je 15 '66-p3258
NYTBR-v71-My 8 '66-p34
PW-v189-My 30 '66-p89
SB-v2-D '66-p198
SR-v49-My 14 '66-p42
The Art Of Africa
BL-v62-D 1 '65-p362
CCB-B-v19-F '66-p98
HB-v42-F '66-p74
LJ-v90-D 15 '65-p5514
SR-v48-N 13 '65-p60
The Art Of America From Jackson To Lincoln
CCB-B-v27-Ap '74-p129
CSM-v66-My 1 '74-pF3
Comw-v99-N 23 '73-p220
HB-v50-Ap '74-p166
KR-v41-N 1 '73-p1206
LJ-v99-Ja 15 '74-p209
The Art Of America In The Early Twentieth Century
BL-v71-D 1 '74-p379
CCB-B-v28-Ap '75-p129
LJ-v99-D 15 '74-p3267
The Art Of America In The Gilded Age
CCB-B-v28-S '74-p8
CSM-v66-My 1 '74-pF3
KR-v42-Ap 1 '74-p365
LJ-v99-S 15 '74-p2267
NYTBR-Je 2 '74-p8
PW-v205-My 6 '74-p69
The Art Of America Since World War II
BB-v4-Ag '76-p4
BL-v72-Je 1 '76-p1406
KR-v44-Ap 1 '76-p397
SLJ-v23-S '76-p116
SR-v3-My 15 '76-p36
The Art Of Ancient Egypt
RT-v35-Ap '82-p793
SLJ-v25-S '78-p43
The Art Of Ancient Greece
RT-v35-Ap '82-p793
Art Of Ancient Mexico
BL-v64-My 15 '68-p1094
BW-v2-Ag 25 '68-p16
CCB-B-v22-O '68-p27
CE-v45-Ap '69-p464
KR-v36-My 1 '68-p514
LJ-v93-Je 15 '68-p2538
PW-v193-My 13 '68-p59
Par-v43-S '68-p84
SR-v51-Ag 24 '68-p43
The Art Of Ancient Mexico
RT-v35-Ap '82-p793
Art Of Ancient Peru
BL-v63-D 1 '66-p416
CCB-B-v20-Ja '67-p73
CLW-v38-Ja '67-p336
HB-v43-F '67-p87
NH-v76-N '67-p29
NYT-v116-F 2 '67-p26
SR-v49-N 12 '66-p50
The Art Of Ancient Rome
BL-v61-My 15 '65-p922
CC-v82-Je 30 '65-p838
CCB-B-v18-Je '65-p148
CE-v42-Ja '66-p318
CW-v59-N '65-p77
Comw-v82-My 28 '65-p333
GT-v83-N '65-p123
HB-v41-Ag '65-p404
KR-v33-Ap 1 '65-p378
LJ-v90-My 15 '65-p2405
NO-v4-Jl 12 '65-p21
The Art Of China
BL-v69-Jl 1 '73-p1021
CCB-B-v27-S '73-p8
CE-v50-Ja '74-p168
Choice-v12-N '75-p1132
Comw-v99-N 23 '73-p220
HB-v49-Ag '73-p390
Inst-v82-My '73-p73
KR-v41-Ap 15 '73-p459
LJ-v98-S 15 '73-p2650
TLS-S 28 '73-p1125

GLUBOK, Shirley (continued)
The Art Of Colonial America
BL-v67-N 15 '70-p268
CE-v47-F '71-p266
CLW-v42-D '70-p257
Comw-v93-N 20 '70-p206
HB-v47-Je '71-p299
KR-v38-Jl 15 '70-p745
LJ-v95-O 15 '70-p3626
NYTBR, pt.2-N 8 '70-p3
PW-v198-O 19 '70-p53
The Art Of Egypt
TES-O 24 '80-p24
The Art Of Egypt Under The Pharaohs
BL-v76-Je 15 '80-p1532
CCB-B-v33-Je '80-p190
LA-v58-Mr '81-p341
RT-v34-Mr '81-p736
SLJ-v27-S '80-p70
The Art Of India
BL-v66-N 15 '69-p408
CCB-B-v23-D '69-p59
Comw-v91-N 21 '69-p262
GT-v87-Ap '70-p108
HB-v46-F '70-p52
KR-v37-O 1 '69-p1067
LJ-v94-D 15 '69-p4604
NYTBR, pt.2-N 9 '69-p52
SR-v52-N 8 '69-p68
TN-v27-Ja '71-p190
The Art Of Japan
BL-v67-S 1 '70-p57
BL-v69-F 15 '73-p553
CCB-B-v24-D '70-p58
Comw-v92-My 22 '70-p253
KR-v38-Ap 1 '70-p386
LJ-v95-Je 15 '70-p2308
NYTBR, pt.2-My 24 '70-p5
PW-v197-Ap 6 '70-p61
The Art Of Photography
AB-v61-Ja 23 '78-p485
BL-v74-O 15 '77-p375
CCB-B-v31-F '78-p94
Comw-v104-N 11 '77-p734
EJ-v67-F '78-p98
HB-v53-D '77-p674
KR-v45-O 15 '77-p1099
LA-v55-Ap '78-p519
M Photo-v42-O '78-p88
PW-v212-Ag 15 '77-p69
SLJ-v24-Ja '78-p88
SR-v5-N 26 '77-p40
Teacher-v96-My '79-p26
The Art Of The Comic Strip
BL-v75-Je 1 '79-p1492
CCB-B-v33-O '79-p27
HB-v55-Ag '79-p435
KR-v47-My 15 '79-p577
RT-v33-Ja '80-p482
SE-v44-O '80-p479
SLJ-v26-S '79-p138
The Art Of The Eskimo
CE-v42-N '65-p180
HB-v41-F '65-p64
SR-v48-Mr 27 '65-p33
Art Of The Etruscans
BL-v64-N 1 '67-p330
BW-v2-Ap 7 '68-p14
CCB-B-v21-O '67-p27
CLW-v39-D '67-p297
CSM-v59-N 2 '67-pB12
EJ-v56-N '67-p1221
HB-v44-F '68-p78
KR-v35-Ag 15 '67-p962
LJ-v92-O 15 '67-p3863
NYTBR-v73-Ja 21 '68-p26
PW-v192-D 11 '67-p46
The Art Of The New American Nation
BL-v68-Jl 1 '72-p942
CCB-B-v26-N '72-p42
HB-v48-Ag '72-p386
KR-v40-My 1 '72-p538
NYTBR-Jl 2 '72-p8
PW-v201-My 15 '72-p54
The Art Of The North American Indian
BL-v69-O 15 '72-p177
CLW-v41-Ja '70-p322
The Art Of The Northwest Coast Indians
BL-v71-Jl 1 '75-p1127
CE-v52-Ap '76-p322
KR-v43-Ap 15 '75-p461
SLJ-v22-O '75-p98
The Art Of The Old West
BL-v68-N 1 '71-p246
BW-v5-N 7 '71-p12
CCB-B-v25-F '72-p91
CE-v48-Mr '72-p312
GT-v89-Ap '72-p88
HB-v48-Ap '72-p164
KR-v39-Ag 1 '71-p810
LJ-v97-Ja 15 '72-p281
NYTBR-N 21 '71-p8
The Art Of The Plains Indians
BL-v72-F 15 '76-p855
CCB-B-v29-My '76-p144
CSM-v68-My 12 '76-p26
HB-v52-Ap '76-p178
KR-v44-F 1 '76-p137
PW-v209-Ja 5 '76-p65
SLJ-v22-My '76-p59
The Art Of The Southeastern Indians
BL-v74-Je 15 '78-p1617
CCB-B-v32-O '78-p29
CSM-v70-O 23 '78-pB6
Inst-v88-N '78-p133
KR-v46-My 1 '78-p499
LA-v56-F '79-p183
NYTBR-Ap 30 '78-p42
SE-v43-Ap '79-p300
SLJ-v25-S '78-p136
The Art Of The Southwest Indians
BL-v67-Je 1 '71-p834
CCB-B-v25-S '71-p7
CE-v48-N '71-p104
CLW-v43-N '71-p172
CSM-v63-Ag 21 '71-p13
JLD-v11-F '78-p40
KR-v39-Ap 1 '71-p372
LJ-v96-N 15 '71-p3900
PW-v200-Jl 5 '71-p50
SR-v54-Ag 21 '71-p27
The Art Of The Spanish In The United States And Puerto Rico
BL-v69-Ja 1 '73-p448
BL-v69-Ja 15 '73-p479
CC-v89-N 29 '72-p1218
CCB-B-v26-Mr '73-p106
CE-v49-Ap '73-p378
HB-v49-F '73-p64
Inst-v82-N '72-p132
KR-v40-O 1 '72-p1147
LJ-v98-Mr 15 '73-p1002
PW-v203-Ja 15 '73-p65
The Art Of The Vikings
BL-v75-Ja 15 '79-p809
CCB-B-v32-Ap '79-p136
CE-v55-Ap '79-p300
HB-v55-F '79-p77
KR-v46-O 15 '78-p1141
SE-v43-Ap '79-p300
SLJ-v25-F '79-p55
The Art Of The Woodland Indians
BL-v73-Ja 15 '77-p718
CCB-B-v30-My '77-p141
KR-v44-N 15 '76-p1224
SE-v41-Ap '77-p349
SLJ-v23-F '77-p64
Digging In Assyria
BL-v67-Ja 1 '71-p367
HB-v47-Je '71-p299

GLUBOK, Shirley (continued)
KR-v38-O 15 '70-p1167
LJ-v95-D 15 '70-p4362
SB-v6-Mr '71-p344
Discovering The Royal Tombs At Ur
BL-v66-Ja 15 '70-p615
CCB-B-v24-Jl '70-p177
Comw-v91-N 21 '69-p262
HB-v46-F '70-p51
KR-v37-O 15 '69-p1125
NYTBR, pt.2-N 9 '69-p28
Discovering Tut-Ankh-Amen's Tomb
BL-v64-Jl 1 '68-p1234
BL-v65-Ap 1 '69-p900
Comw-v105-N 10 '78-p728
KR-v36-Ap 1 '68-p407
LA-v55-O '78-p865
LJ-v93-S 15 '68-p3304
NYTBR-v73-My 5 '68-p24
NYTBR-Ap 9 '78-p20
SE-v33-My '69-p563
SLJ-v25-S '78-p43
Teacher-v96-O '78-p178
Dolls, Dolls, Dolls
BB-v3-My '75-p3
BL-v71-Je 15 '75-p1074
CCB-B-v28-Jl '75-p176
KR-v43-My 1 '75-p516
PW-v207-Ap 28 '75-p44
SLJ-v22-S '75-p102
Teacher-v93-Ap '76-p119
Fall Of The Incas
BL-v64-F 15 '68-p698
CCB-B-v21-Mr '68-p109
HB-v44-Ap '68-p193
KR-v35-N 1 '67-p1326
LJ-v93-Ja 15 '68-p291
NYTBR-v72-N 5 '67-p52
SR-v51-F 24 '68-p51
Knights In Armor
BL-v65-My 1 '69-p1015
BW-v3-My 4 '69-p22
CCB-B-v22-Je '69-p158
CE-v46-F '70-p266
HB-v45-Je '69-p316
KR-v37-Mr 15 '69-p309
LJ-v94-N 15 '69-p4286
NYTBR-Ap 6 '69-p18
PW-v195-Mr 31 '69-p57
SR-v52-My 10 '69-p56
The Mummy Of Ramose
Arch-v33-S '80-p60
BB-v6-Je '78-p6
BL-v74-Ap 15 '78-p1349
CCB-B-v32-S '78-p8
CE-v55-N '78-p106
CLW-v50-N '78-p179
Comw-v105-N 10 '78-p728
Cur R-v18-O '79-p338
HB-v54-Je '78-p286
JB-v43-F '79-p51
KR-v46-My 15 '78-p548
LA-v55-O '78-p865
NYTBR-My 14 '78-p44
SB-v15-My '79-p44
SE-v43-Ap '79-p300
SLJ-v24-My '78-p67
SLJ-v25-S '78-p43
Sch Lib-v27-Mr '79-p64
Olympic Games In Ancient Greece
BL-v73-D 15 '76-p606
CCB-B-v30-Ja '77-p75
CSM-v76-Jl 6 '84-pB5
Comw-v103-N 19 '76-p764
GP-v17-My '78-p3336
HB-v52-D '76-p634
JB-v42-O '78-p267
KR-v44-Jl 1 '76-p736
Kliatt-v18-Fall '84-p73
LA-v54-Ap '77-p439
SE-v41-Ap '77-p348
SLJ-v23-D '76-p71

* * *

GLUCK, Herb
Baseball's Great Moments
PW-v207-Ap 21 '75-p46
SLJ-v22-S '75-p120

* * *

GLUE, David
The Garden Bird Book
Nature-v300-D 9 '82-p557
TES-Ag 19 '83-p19

* * *

GLYDAL, Monica
When Olly Moved House
TES-S 30 '77-p24
When Olly Saw An Accident
TES-S 30 '77-p24

* * *

GOAMAN, Karen
Mysteries & Marvels Of The Animal World
SLJ-v30-Ag '84-p70

* * *

GOBHAI, Mehlli
Lakshmi, The Water Buffalo Who Wouldn't
BL-v66-Ja 1 '70-p564
CCB-B-v24-Jl '70-p177
CLW-v41-Ap '70-p537
GT-v87-F '70-p144
KR-v37-N 15 '69-p1191
SR-v52-N 8 '69-p64
TN-v26-Ja '70-p207
The Legend Of The Orange Princess
BL-v68-My 1 '72-p770
BW-v5-N 7 '71-p4
CCB-B-v25-Ap '72-p123
HB-v48-F '72-p45
KR-v39-S 15 '71-p1009
LJ-v97-Ap 15 '72-p1596
TN-v28-Ja '72-p203
To Your Good Health
CCB-B-v27-My '74-p143
Usha The Mouse-Maiden
BL-v65-Je 15 '69-p1174
BW-v3-My 4 '69-p7
CCB-B-v23-D '69-p59
CLW-v41-D '69-p256
HB-v45-Ag '69-p400
LJ-v94-Ap 15 '69-p1768
PW-v195-Mr 17 '69-p57

* * *

GOBLE, Paul
Brave Eagle's Account Of The Fetterman Fight
BL-v69-Ja 15 '73-p493
CCB-B-v26-Ja '73-p76
CSM-v64-N 8 '72-pB3
HB-v48-D '72-p605
Inst-v82-N '72-p132
KR-v40-Ag 15 '72-p943
KR-v40-D 15 '72-p1416
LJ-v97-D 15 '72-p4056
LJ-v97-D 15 '72-p4072
NYTBR-S 24 '72-p8
NYTBR, pt.2-N 5 '72-p29
PW-v202-S 11 '72-p58
SE-v37-D '73-p788
SR-v55-D 9 '72-p79
TN-v29-Ap '73-p253
Buffalo Woman
BL-v80-Ap 15 '84-p1189
CBRS-v12-Spring '84-p125
CCB-B-v37-My '84-p165
CE-v61-S '84-p68
HB-v60-Ag '84-p457
NYTBR-v89-Jl 1 '84-p23

GOBLE, Paul (continued)
PW-v225-Mr 23 '84-p71
Par-v59-N '84-p53
SLJ-v30-Ag '84-p59
The Friendly Wolf
BB-v4-F '76-p2
BL-v72-F 1 '76-p787
CCB-B-v29-My '76-p144
CE-v53-O '76-p33
CLW-v47-My '76-p451
CSM-v68-My 12 '76-p26
JB-v39-F '75-p38
KR-v43-D 15 '75-p1377
SE-v42-My '78-p383
SLJ-v22-F '76-p38
TLS-D 6 '74-p1382
The Gift Of The Sacred Dog
AW-v18-Mr '81-p62
BL-v77-D 15 '80-p574
CBRS-v9-D '80-p24
CCB-B-v34-Mr '81-p133
CLW-v52-Ap '81-p404
HB-v57-F '81-p42
JB-v46-Ap '82-p61
KR-v49-Ja 1 '81-p2
NW-v96-D 1 '80-p103
NYTBR-v85-N 9 '80-p64
PW-v218-D 5 '80-p53
RT-v35-O '81-p113
RT-v35-My '82-p915
SLJ-v27-D '80-p43
Sch Arts-v80-My '81-p61
The Girl Who Loved Wild Horses
BB-v7-Ap '79-p2
BL-v75-O 15 '78-p380
CCB-B-v32-Mr '79-p116
CE-v55-Ap '79-p296
Econ-v273-D 22 '79-p84
HB-v54-D '78-p631
JB-v44-F '80-p17
KR-v46-S 15 '78-p1014
LA-v56-My '79-p541
NY-v55-D 3 '79-p190
Obs-F 3 '80-p39
PW-v214-D 11 '78-p70
RT-v33-O '79-p46
SE-v43-Ap '79-p301
SE-v44-Mr '80-p246
SLJ-v25-D '78-p43
TES-Ja 18 '80-p37
TLS-D 14 '79-p127
Teacher-v96-My '79-p108
WCRB-v5-Ja '79-p55
Lone Bull's Horse Raid
BL-v70-Ja 15 '74-p541
CCB-B-v27-My '74-p143
CSM-v66-My 1 '74-pF2
Choice-v12-N '75-p1132
HB-v50-Ap '74-p158
KR-v41-N 15 '73-p1268
LJ-v99-F 15 '74-p573
NYTBR-N 4 '73-p57
NYTBR-N 11 '73-p8
PW-v204-N 12 '73-p37
TLS-N 23 '73-p1445
TN-v30-Je '74-p433
Red Hawk's Account Of Custer's Last Battle
BL-v67-D 15 '70-p341
BL-v67-Ap 1 '71-p660
BL-v69-O 15 '72-p177
CCB-B-v24-F '71-p91
HB-v47-F '71-p60
KR-v38-Ag 15 '70-p879
LJ-v95-D 15 '70-p4350
NYTBR-D 6 '70-p58
NYTBR, pt.2-N 8 '70-p22
NYTBR, pt.2-N 8 '70-p38
PW-v198-Ag 10 '70-p56
SR-v53-D 19 '70-p32
TN-v27-Ap '71-p305
Star Boy
BL-v79-Je 1 '83-p1282
CBRS-v11-My '83-p100
CCB-B-v36-Ap '83-p149
CE-v60-S '83-p56
CSM-v75-My 13 '83-pB5
HB-v59-Ag '83-p431
Inst-v92-My '83-p92
Inter BC-v15-Ja # '84-p38
LA-v60-N '83-p1027
PW-v223-F 18 '83-p130
RT-v37-Ja '84-p427
SLJ-v29-Ag '83-p51

* * *

GODDARD, Anthea
The Aztec Skull
GP-v22-N '83-p4177
JB-v41-Ap '77-p111
SLJ-v24-O '77-p111
TLS-D 10 '76-p1544

* * *

GODDARD, Carrie Lou
Isn't It A Wonder!
CLW-v48-D '76-p234
Jesus
PW-v214-Ag 7 '78-p82

* * *

GODDEN, Rumer
Candy Floss And Impunity Jane
Obs-S 28 '75-p22
The Dark Horse
Atl-v249-F '82-p87
BL-v78-O 15 '81-p266
BS-v41-Mr '82-p450
CR-v240-Ja '82-p45
GP-v20-N '81-p3987
HB-v58-Ap '82-p197
KR-v49-N 1 '81-p1358
LJ-v106-D 1 '81-p2331
Lis-v106-S 24 '81-p348
New R-v186-Je 23 '82-p39
Obs-Ja 17 '82-p31
PW-v220-N 20 '81-p44
SLJ-v28-Mr '82-p163
SLJ-v28-Ag '82-p125
Spec-v247-O 17 '81-p27
The Diddakoi
BL-v69-N 15 '72-p274
BS-v32-O 15 '72-p338
CCB-B-v26-F '73-p90
CE-v49-Ja '73-p202
CLW-v44-D '72-p312
CSM-v65-D 4 '72-p20
Comw-v97-N 17 '72-p158
HB-v48-D '72-p595
KR-v40-S 15 '72-p1098
LJ-v97-D 1 '72-p3930
LJ-v98-Ap 15 '73-p1386
NS-v84-N 10 '72-p692
PW-v202-Jl 31 '72-p67
Spec-v229-N 11 '72-p752
TES-D 10 '82-p34
TLS-N 3 '72-p1330
The Dragon Of Og
BL-v78-F 1 '82-p706
Brit Bk N C-Spring '82-p5
CBRS-v10-Mr '82-p77
CCB-B-v35-F '82-p106
CE-v59-S '82-p60
JB-v46-Ap '82-p66
LA-v59-Ap '82-p371
PW-v220-N 27 '81-p87
RT-v35-My '82-p975
SLJ-v28-N '81-p75
Sch Lib-v31-Je '83-p143
TES-Ja 15 '82-p35
TES-Ap 27 '84-p27
Four Dolls
GP-v22-Ja '84-p4190
HB-v60-S '84-p615
JB-v48-F '84-p21

GODDEN, Rumer (continued)
Home Is The Sailor
BL-v61-Mr 1 '65-p656
CCB-B-v18-F '65-p86
CE-v42-O '65-p112
CSM-v57-F 25 '65-p7
GT-v82-Ap '65-p111
HB-v41-F '65-p56
Inst-v74-Ap '65-p19
LJ-v90-F 15 '65-p960
NYTBR-v70-F 7 '65-p26
A Kindle Of Kittens
BL-v75-Ap 15 '79-p1294
CBRS-v7-Ap '79-p82
CCB-B-v32-Jl '79-p191
CLW-v51-F '80-p309
CSM-v71-My 14 '79-pB6
JB-v43-Ap '79-p95
KR-v47-Ap 1 '79-p385
NYTBR-Ap 29 '79-p26
SLJ-v25-Ap '79-p43
Sch Lib-v27-Je '79-p127
Kitchen Madonna
B&B-v13-D '67-p44
BL-v64-F 1 '68-p623
BS-v27-D 15 '67-p367
CE-v45-Ja '69-p278
GP-v16-N '77-p3216
HB-v44-Ap '68-p176
KR-v35-O 1 '67-p1230
LJ-v92-N 1 '67-p4027
NYTBR-v73-Ja 7 '68-p38
PW-v192-O 2 '67-p49
PW-v192-N 27 '67-p43
RT-v35-Mr '82-p720
Spec-v219-N 3 '67-p541
TLS-N 30 '67-p1158
Trav-v24-Ap '68-p323
Little Plum
Obs-S 28 '75-p22
Mr. McFadden's Hallowe'en
BL-v72-D 1 '75-p515
CCB-B-v29-Mr '76-p110
Econ-v257-D 20 '75-p103
GP-v14-Ja '76-p2797
HB-v51-O '75-p452
JB-v40-F '76-p23
KR-v43-Ag 1 '75-p848
Obs-D 7 '75-p32
PW-v208-Jl 28 '75-p122
SLJ-v22-Ja '76-p46
Spec-v235-D 6 '75-p732
TLS-D 5 '75-p1448
Mouse Time
TES-S 21 '84-p37
The Mousewife
BL-v76-F 15 '80-p840
BL-v79-F 15 '83-p777
BW-v12-O 10 '82-p6
CCB-B-v36-N '82-p46
CE-v59-My '83-p354
JB-v47-Ag '83-p162
NW-v100-D 6 '82-p130
PW-v222-O 15 '82-p66
RT-v36-F '83-p594
The Old Woman Who Lived In A Vinegar Bottle
BL-v69-O 15 '72-p203
BW-v6-My 7 '72-p10
CCB-B-v26-S '72-p8
CE-v49-N '72-p85
CLW-v44-O '72-p191
CSM-v65-D 4 '72-p20
CSM-v66-My 1 '74-pF5
HB-v48-Ag '72-p367
KR-v40-Mr 15 '72-p319
LJ-v97-S 15 '72-p2950
LR-v23-Autumn '72-p300
NS-v83-Je 2 '72-p763
NY-v48-D 2 '72-p205
NYTBR-Je 4 '72-p28
NYTBR, pt.2-My 7 '72-p36
NYTBR, pt.2-N 5 '72-p30
Obs-My 28 '72-p33
PW-v201-Je 12 '72-p63
SR-v55-Je 17 '72-p72
TES-Jl 23 '82-p24
TLS-Jl 14 '72-p808
TN-v29-Ja '73-p167
Teacher-v90-O '72-p115
Teacher-v92-O '74-p109
Operation Sippacik
B&B-v17-D '71-pR16
BW-v3-Jl 20 '69-p12
CCB-B-v23-N '69-p43
CSM-v61-My 1 '69-pB7
HB-v45-Je '69-p305
KR-v37-Ap 15 '69-p440
LJ-v94-My 15 '69-p2100
LR-v22-Summer '69-p95
NYTBR-Je 1 '69-p20
PW-v195-My 19 '69-p71
TLS-Ap 3 '69-p360
The Rocking Horse Secret
BL-v74-Jl 1 '78-p1678
CCB-B-v32-S '78-p8
CE-v55-Ap '79-p262
Comw-v105-N 10 '78-p731
GP-v16-Mr '78-p3274
JB-v42-Je '78-p153
KR-v46-Ap 1 '78-p374
LA-v55-O '78-p863
NS-v95-My 19 '78-p683
PW-v213-Ap 3 '78-p81
SLJ-v25-S '78-p136
TES-Ap 21 '78-p21
The Tale Of The Tales
BL-v68-Mr 1 '72-p545
BL-v68-Mr 15 '72-p611
HB-v48-F '72-p66
LJ-v97-Mr 1 '72-p897
NYTBR-Ap 9 '72-p34
Spec-v227-N 13 '71-p690
TLS-My 12 '72-p557
The Valiant Chatti-Maker
BL-v80-O 1 '83-p294
CBRS-v12-F '84-p73
CCB-B-v37-Mr '84-p126
CE-v60-Mr '84-p286
Econ-v289-N 26 '83-p97
HB-v60-F '84-p67
JB-v48-F '84-p22
NS-v106-D 2 '83-p25
SLJ-v30-F '84-p70

* * *

GODFREY, Bob
The Holiday
TES-N 11 '83-p25
The Whale
TES-N 11 '83-p25

* * *

GODFREY, Martyn
The Vandarian Incident
Can Child Lit-#26 '82-p64
In Rev-v15-Ag '81-p40
Quill & Q-v47-Je '81-p33

* * *

GODOY ALCAYAGA, Lucila
Crickets And Frogs
BL-v69-Mr 1 '73-p646
BW-v6-N 5 '72-p3
CCB-B-v26-Mr '73-p110
CE-v49-My '73-p422
HB-v48-O '72-p461
KR-v40-S 1 '72-p1022
LJ-v98-Ja 15 '73-p255
NYTBR, pt.2-N 5 '72-p47
PW-v202-D 11 '72-p35
The Elephant And His Secret
HB-v50-Ag '74-p371
PW-v205-Mr 18 '74-p52

* * *

GOELLER, Lee
How To Make An Adding Machine That Even Adds Roman Numerals
ACSB-v13-Mr '80-p25
BL-v76-D 15 '79-p611
Cur R-v19-Je '80-p257
HB-v56-Ap '80-p193
SB-v16-N '80-p90
SLJ-v26-F '80-p55

* * *

GOETZ, Delia
Islands Of The Ocean
CCB-B-v18-Je '65-p148
Lakes
BL-v70-O 1 '73-p170
CCB-B-v27-Ja '74-p78
CE-v50-Ja '74-p168
KR-v41-Ap 1 '73-p389
LJ-v98-O 15 '73-p3145
Valleys
ACSB-v9-Fall '76-p19
BL-v72-My 15 '76-p1336
KR-v44-Ap 1 '76-p397
SB-v12-D '76-p158
SLJ-v23-S '76-p116

* * *

GOFF, Beth
Where Is Daddy?
CCB-B-v23-D '69-p59
JMF-v36-F '74-p204
Ms-v12-N '83-p76
SR-v52-N 8 '69-p62
Spectr-v47-Mr '71-p46

* * *

GOFFE, Toni
A Book Of Sounds
Cur R-v18-O '79-p306
Los Deportes
BL-v78-F 1 '82-p704
Los Instrumentos Musicales
BL-v78-F 1 '82-p704
El Mundo De Los Perros
BL-v78-F 1 '82-p704
Toby's Animal Rescue Service
SLJ-v29-S '82-p108
The XYZ Of Sport
Obs-Mr 6 '77-p22

* * *

GOFFSTEIN, M B
Across The Sea
BW-v3-Mr 16 '69-p12
HB-v59-F '83-p88
KR-v36-O 1 '68-p1105
LJ-v94-F 15 '69-p861
NYTBR-v73-N 17 '68-p62
PW-v194-S 9 '68-p64
An Artist
BW-v10-N 9 '80-p14
CBRS-v9-O '80-p12
HB-v56-D '80-p633
KR-v48-S 15 '80-p1228
NYTBR-v86-Ja 11 '81-p28
PW-v218-Jl 25 '80-p157
SLJ-v27-O '80-p146
Time-v116-D 29 '80-p65
Brookie And Her Lamb
BL-v78-S 15 '81-p105
CSM-v59-N 2 '67-pB5
Inst-v92-Ap '83-p20
KR-v35-Ag 1 '67-p872
LA-v59-Mr '82-p266
LJ-v92-S 15 '67-p3177
PW-v192-Ag 28 '67-p277
Daisy Summerfield's Style
BS-v35-D '75-p300
BW-F 11 '79-pF2
CCB-B-v29-F '76-p96
HB-v52-F '76-p56
HB-v59-F '83-p90
J Read-v20-O '76-p80
KR-v43-O 1 '75-p1137
PW-v208-S 8 '75-p60
SLJ-v22-N '75-p89
Family Scrapbook
BL-v75-S 15 '78-p217
BW-D 3 '78-pE4
CCB-B-v32-D '78-p61
CE-v56-N '79-p111
CLW-v50-O '78-p109
Comw-v105-N 10 '78-p731
HB-v55-O '78-p516
KR-v46-Jl 15 '78-p747
LA-v56-Mr '79-p289
PW-v213-Je 19 '78-p100
SLJ-v25-O '78-p132
VV-v23-N 13 '78-p121
The First Books
HM-v259-D '79-p74
NYTBR-N 11 '79-p43
PW-v216-D 24 '79-p59
SLJ-v27-S '80-p58
Fish For Supper
BB-v4-My '76-p2
BL-v72-Mr 15 '76-p1045
CCB-B-v29-Jl '76-p174
HB-v52-Je '76-p279
Inter BC-v14-#7 '83-p28
KR-v44-Ap 1 '76-p385
NYTBR-My 2 '76-p46
PW-v209-Mr 8 '76-p65
SE-v44-N '80-p602
SLJ-v22-Ap '76-p60
Teacher-v94-My '77-p106
Goldie The Dollmaker
Am-v121-D 13 '69-p593
CCB-B-v23-F '70-p97
HB-v46-F '70-p41
HB-v59-F '83-p88
KR-v37-S 15 '69-p995
LJ-v94-D 15 '69-p4606
NO-v8-D 29 '69-p17
NYTBR-O 19 '69-p34
NYTBR-D 7 '69-p68
NYTBR, pt.2-N 9 '69-p63
Nat-v209-D 15 '69-p671
PW-v196-D 8 '69-p47
SR-v52-N 8 '69-p67
Sch Arts-v81-Mr '82-p40
TLS-Mr 26 '82-p347
Teacher-v96-Mr '79-p109
Laughing Latkes
BL-v77-F 15 '81-p809
CBRS-v9-N '80-p22
CCB-B-v34-Ja '81-p92
KR-v48-D 1 '80-p1514
NYTBR-v86-Ja 11 '81-p28
PW-v218-S 12 '80-p66
SLJ-v27-D '80-p44
A Little Schubert
BW-v14-N 11 '84-p21
CCB-B-v26-F '73-p90
CE-v49-Mr '73-p323
HB-v48-D '72-p582
Inst-v83-Ag '73-p194
KR-v40-N 15 '72-p1302
LJ-v98-My 15 '73-p1673
M Ed J-v60-S '73-p86
PW-v202-O 23 '72-p46
SR-v55-N 11 '72-p79
SR-v55-D 9 '72-p79
Lives Of The Artists
BL-v78-Mr 15 '82-p957
BL-v79-Je 1 '83-p1282
BW-v12-My 9 '82-p15
CBRS-v10-My '82-p97
CCB-B-v35-F '82-p107
KR-v50-Mr 1 '82-p277
NYTBR-v87-Ap 18 '82-p38
PW-v220-D 18 '81-p71
SE-v47-Ap '83-p245
SLJ-v28-Mr '82-p157
M.B. Goffstein/The First Books
PW-v216-D 24 '79-p59

GOLD, Sharlya (continued)
CLW-v48-Mr '77-p358
Inst-v86-N '76-p146
KR-v44-O 1 '76-p1093
SLJ-v23-Ja '77-p92

* * *

GOLD Dust Books
Cur R-v18-Ag '79-p211

* * *

GOLDBERG, Lazer
Learning To Choose
ACSB-v10-Fall '77-p4
BL-v73-Mr 1 '77-p1019
Inst-v87-Ja '78-p146
KR-v44-My 15 '76-p621

* * *

GOLDBERG, Moses
The Men's Cottage
Dr-#2 '81-p56

* * *

GOLDBERG, Rube
The Best Of Rube Goldberg
BL-v76-Mr 15 '80-p1017
BW-v10-Ja 6 '80-p15
CCB-B-v33-Ap '80-p154
HB-v56-Ap '80-p186
PW-v217-Ap 18 '80-p90
SLJ-v26-Ap '80-p112

* * *

GOLDBERGER, Judith M
The Looking Glass Factor
CCB-B-v33-F '80-p108
HB-v56-F '80-p54
KR-v48-F 15 '80-p216
NYTBR-D 30 '79-p19
SLJ-v26-D '79-p84

* * *

GOLDEN, Flora
Women In Sports: Horseback Riding
BL-v75-Jl 1 '79-p1583
Inter BC-v10-Ap 40 '07-p910
SLJ-v26-O '79-p150

* * *

GOLDEN, Frederic
Colonies In Space
BB-v5-S '77-p4
BL-v73-Jl 15 '77-p1728
CLW-v49-N '77-p190
HB-v53-Ag '77-p461
KR-v45-My 15 '77-p544
PW-v211-My 30 '77-p44
SB-v14-S '78-p104
SLJ-v23-My '77-p69
The Moving Continents
BL-v68-Mr 1 '72-p560
BS-v31-F 15 '72-p522
CLW-v43-My '72-p535
HB-v48-Je '72-p291
Inst-v81-Ap '72-p144
KR-v40-Ja 1 '72-p10
KR-v40-D 15 '72-p1423
LJ-v97-Jl '72-p2488
SB-v8-My '72-p38
The Trembling Earth
B Rpt-v2-Ja '84-p52
CCB-B-v37-Ja '84-p87
HB-v59-D '83-p736
LJ-v109-Mr 1 '84-p431
SB-v19-My '84-p281
SLJ-v30-O '83-p167
VOYA-v7-Ap '84-p46

* * *

GOLDEN Board Book Farm Animals
BW-My 2 '76-pL2

* * *

GOLDEN Happy Birthday Book
SLJ-v23-F '77-p56

* * *

GOLDFEDER, Cheryl
The Girl Who Wouldn't Talk
Inter BC-v11-Ja 10 '80-p20
Robin Sees A Song
Inter BC-v11-Ja 10 '80-p20

* * *

GOLDILOCKS And The Three Bears (Mahan)
SLJ-v29-O '82-p136

* * *

GOLDIN, Augusta
Geothermal Energy
ASBYP-v15-Spring '82-p37
BL-v77-Jl 15 '81-p1447
BS-v41-O '81-p277
CBRS-v10-S '81-p8
Cur R-v22-My '83-p136
KR-v49-Je 15 '81-p747
SLJ-v28-F '82-p88
Grass
BL-v74-D 1 '77-p612
KR-v45-Mr 15 '77-p292
SB-v14-S '78-p94
SLJ-v23-Ap '77-p76
Let's Go To Build A Skyscraper
BL-v70-Ap 1 '74-p873
KR-v42-F 1 '74-p114
LJ-v99-Ap 15 '74-p1219
SB-v10-Mr '75-p332
The Shape Of Water
ACSB-v12-Spring '79-p24
BL-v75-Ap 15 '79-p1295
CCB-B-v32-Je '79-p174
LA-v56-N '79-p931
SB-v15-Mr '80-p226
SLJ-v25-Ap '79-p43

* * *

GOLDIN, Augusta R
Bottom Of The Sea
BL-v63-My 15 '67-p995
CCB-B-v21-S '67-p6
KR-v35-Mr 1 '67-p273
LJ-v92-My 15 '67-p2014
NYTBR-v72-Jl 2 '67-p16
SB-v3-My '67-p39
SR-v50-My 13 '67-p53
Ducks Don't Get Wet
B&B-v13-My '68-p44
CCB-B-v19-F '66-p98
CSM-v57-My 6 '65-p2B
LJ-v90-Mr 15 '65-p1542
NYTBR-v70-My 9 '65-p30
Spider Silk
TLS-Mr 14 '68-p267
Teacher-v94-Ja '77-p133
Straight Hair, Curly Hair
CCB-B-v20-D '66-p58
GT-v84-Ja '67-p56
LJ-v91-O 15 '66-p5216
NY-v43-D 16 '67-p160
SA-v215-D '66-p143
SB-v2-D '66-p216
TLS-Mr 14 '68-p267
Teacher-v94-N '76-p34
Where Does Your Garden Grow?
BW-v1-N 26 '67-p16
CCB-B-v21-F '68-p94
CSM-v60-D 21 '67-p11
KR-v35-O 15 '67-p1278
NS-v77-My 16 '69-p706
SB-v3-D '67-p263
TLS-Je 26 '69-p704

* * *

GOLDING, Morton J
A Short History Of Puerto Rico
Choice-v12-D '75-p1275

GOLDING, Morton J
(continued)
Inter BC-v14-#1 '83-p16

* * *

GOLDMAN, Hersh
Step-By-Step To Jerusalem
PW-v214-Jl 10 '78-p136

* * *

GOLDMAN, Katie
In The Wings
BL-v79-D 15 '82-p563
BS-v42-Ja '83-p405
CBRS-v11-N '82-p28
CCB-B-v36-S '82-p9
KR-v50-O 15 '82-p1157
SLJ-v29-N '82-p99
VOYA-v6-O '83-p201
WLB-v57-Ja '83-p419

* * *

GOLDMAN, Peter
Civil Rights: The Challenge Of The 14th Amendment
BL-v62-F 1 '66-p528
CCB-B-v19-Ja '66-p82
CE-v43-O '66-p103
CLW-v37-Ja '66-p332
LJ-v91-Ja 15 '66-p435

* * *

GOLDMAN, Susan
Cousins Are Special
BL-v75-Mr 1 '79-p1089
CBRS-v7-Ap '79-p83
CCB-B-v32-My '79-p153
Cur R-v19-F '80-p51
SLJ-v25-Ap '79-p43
Grandma Is Somebody Special
BL-v73-D 1 '76-p540
Cur R-v19-F '80-p51
Inst-v86-N '76-p145
RT-v35-My '82-p901
SLJ-v23-D '76-p65
Grandpa And Me Together
CBRS-v8-My '80-p95
SLJ-v26-My '80-p82
I Hate It
Cur R-v19-F '80-p51
In The Morning Mist
Cur R-v19-F '80-p51

* * *

GOLDMAN, William
Wigger
BL-v70-Jl 15 '74-p1253
BL-v71-S 1 '74-p48
CCB-B-v28-Ja '75-p77
KR-v42-O 1 '74-p1060
LJ-v99-O 15 '74-p2721
PW-v206-Ag 19 '74-p83
Teacher-v95-O '77-p164

* * *

GOLDNER, Kathryn A
Why Mount St. Helens Blew Its Top
ASBYP-v15-Spring '82-p38
BL-v78-Mr 1 '82-p897
CBRS-v10-Mr '82-p77
CCB-B-v35-F '82-p107
Cur R-v21-D '82-p552
SB-v18-S '82-p32

* * *

GOLDNER, Nancy
Coppelia
NBR-v4-Ap '79-p14

* * *

GOLDREICH, Gloria
Lori
BL-v75-My 15 '79-p1432
CCB-B-v33-S '79-p8
EJ-v68-N '79-p77
KR-v47-My 1 '79-p522
SLJ-v25-My '79-p72
Season Of Discovery
BL-v73-F 15 '77-p896
CCB-B-v30-My '77-p141
KR-v44-O 1 '76-p1093
PW-v211-F 14 '77-p83
RT-v31-Ap '78-p839
SLJ-v23-D '76-p54
A Treasury Of Jewish Literature
BL-v78-Mr 15 '82-p949
CCB-B-v35-My '82-p169
NYTBR-v87-Ap 25 '82-p36
PW-v221-Ja 15 '82-p99
SE-v47-Ap '83-p244
SLJ-v29-S '82-p137
What Can She Be? A Computer Scientist
ACSB-v13-Spring '80-p33
BL-v75-My 15 '79-p1438
CCB-B-v33-N '79-p48
CLW-v51-Ap '80-p414
KR-v47-Je 15 '79-p687
SB-v15-Mr '80-p196
SLJ-v26-S '79-p110
What Can She Be? A Farmer
BB-v5-F '77-p2
BL-v73-O 1 '76-p251
KR-v44-Ag 15 '76-p907
SB-v13-S '77-p99
SLJ-v23-N '76-p58
What Can She Be? A Film Producer
BL-v74-D 15 '77-p682
CCB-B-v31-My '78-p141
KR-v45-O 15 '77-p1100
SB-v14-Mr '79-p228
SLJ-v24-Ja '78-p89
What Can She Be? A Geologist
BB-v5-F '77-p2
BL-v73-O 1 '76-p251
CCB-B-v30-Ja '77-p76
Inst-v86-N '76-p150
KR-v44-Ag 15 '76-p907
LA-v54-Ap '77-p439
SB-v13-D '77-p164
SLJ-v23-N '76-p58
What Can She Be? A Lawyer
CCB-B-v27-D '73-p64
CLW-v45-N '73-p190
CSM-v67-Ja 22 '75-p8
KR-v41-Ap 15 '73-p460
LJ-v98-O 15 '73-p3138
SE-v39-Mr '75-p175
What Can She Be? A Legislator
BB-v7-Ap '79-p3
BL-v75-N 15 '78-p546
Comw-v105-N 10 '78-p734
KR-v46-O 15 '78-p1141
SLJ-v25-Ap '79-p56
What Can She Be? A Musician
BB-v3-Ag '75-p2
BL-v71-Je 1 '75-p1012
CCB-B-v28-Jl '75-p176
KR-v43-My 1 '75-p516
RT-v29-F '76-p512
SLJ-v22-S '75-p102
What Can She Be? A Newscaster
BL-v70-F 1 '74-p599
CCB-B-v27-Je '74-p156
Choice-v12-N '75-p1132
KR-v41-O 1 '73-p1100
LJ-v99-Ja 15 '74-p199
SE-v39-Mr '75-p175
What Can She Be? A Police Officer
BL-v72-N 15 '75-p452
CCB-B-v29-Mr '76-p110
KR-v43-O 15 '75-p1189
SLJ-v22-F '76-p46

GOLDREICH, Gloria
(continued)
What Can She Be? A Scientist
ASBYP-v14-Fall '81-p21
BL-v77-Ap 1 '81-p1099
CCB-B-v34-Jl '81-p211
KR-v49-Ap 15 '81-p506
SB-v17-N '81-p91
SLJ-v28-D '81-p52
What Can She Be? A Veterinarian
BL-v69-N 15 '72-p300
CCB-B-v25-Jl '72-p168
KR-v40-Ap 15 '72-p481
NYTBR, pt.2-My 7 '72-p24
SB-v8-S '72-p174
What Can She Be? An Architect
BL-v70-Je 15 '74-p1153
CCB-B-v28-S '74-p8
KR-v42-Ap 15 '74-p428
LJ-v99-S 15 '74-p2268
SB-v10-D '74-p248
SE-v39-Mr '75-p175

* * *

GOLDSBOROUGH, June
The Real Book Of First Stories
LJ-v99-Mr 15 '74-p884
What's In The Woods?
KR-v44-Ag 15 '76-p903
SLJ-v23-N '76-p46

* * *

GOLDSMITH, Howard
Friends And Neighbors
Inter BC-v15-Ja # '84-p36
Invasion 2200 A.D.
CBRS-v8-D '79-p37
Cur R-v19-S '80-p336
J Read-v23-Ap '80-p662
SLJ-v26-N '79-p77
Toto The Timid Turtle
SLJ-v28-Ja '82-p64
What Makes A Grumble Smile?
SLJ-v24-S '77-p105
The Whispering Sea
BS-v37-My '77-p44
CCB-B-v30-My '77-p142
SLJ-v24-O '77-p123

* * *

GOLDSMITH, Ilse
Why You Get Sick And How You Get Well
CCB-B-v24-Jl '71-p170
Inst-v130-My '71-p79
LJ-v96-Ap 15 '71-p1502
SB-v7-My '71-p67

* * *

GOLDSMITH, John
Mrs. Babcary Goes To Sea
Brit Bk N C-Autumn '80-p13
GP-v19-Jl '80-p3734
JB-v44-D '80-p283
TES-Jl 11 '80-p38
Mrs. Babcary Goes To Town
Brit Bk N C-Autumn '80-p13
GP-v19-Jl '80-p3734
TES-Jl 11 '80-p38
Mrs. Babcary Goes West
Brit Bk N C-Autumn '80-p13
GP-v19-Jl '80-p3734
TES-Jl 11 '80-p38
Oliver And The Magic Hat
TES-S 30 '83-p42
The Rajah Of Bong And Other Owls
Brit Bk N C-Autumn '81-p27
GP-v20-My '81-p3890
JB-v45-O '81-p209
TES-Ja 15 '82-p30
Tarkina The Otter
Brit Bk N C-Autumn '81-p27
GP-v20-My '81-p3890
JB-v45-O '81-p210
TES-Ja 15 '82-p30

* * *

GOLDSMITH, M
Sooner Round The Corner
JB-v43-D '79-p325

* * *

GOLDSMITH, Ruth M
Phoebe Takes Charge
BL-v79-Ap 1 '83-p1033
CBRS-v12-S '83-p8
CCB-B-v36-Ap '83-p149
KR-v51-Ja 1 '83-p4
SLJ-v30-Ap '84-p124
VOYA-v6-O '83-p201

* * *

GOLDSTEIN, Eleanor C
SIRS Digest: Alcohol
LL-v6-N '82-p17
SIRS Digest: Family
LL-v6-N '82-p17
SIRS Digest: Food
LL-v6-N '82-p17
SIRS Digest: Population
LL-v6-N '82-p17

* * *

GOLDSTEIN, Ernest
Edward Hicks: The Peaceable Kingdom
Cur R-v22-F '83-p27
Inst-v92-S '82-p190
SLJ-v29-N '82-p84
Sch Arts-v82-D '82-p35
Emanuel Leutze: Washington Crossing The Delaware
RT-v37-D '83-p309
SLJ-v29-Ag '83-p76
Sch Arts-v82-My '83-p34
Winslow Homer: The Gulf Stream
BL-v78-My 15 '82-p1257
Cur R-v22-F '83-p27
SLJ-v29-N '82-p84
Sch Arts-v82-D '82-p35

* * *

GOLDSTEIN, Frances
Karate For Kids
SLJ-v24-D '77-p64

* * *

GOLDSTEIN, Kenneth K
New Frontiers Of Medicine
ACSB-v8-Fall '75-p14
BS-v34-Ja 15 '75-p457
CLW-v46-My '75-p452
KR-v42-D 1 '74-p1260
SB-v11-My '75-p24
SLJ-v21-Ap '75-p64

* * *

GOLDSTEIN, Philip
Animals And Plants That Trap
BL-v71-S 1 '74-p41
LJ-v99-S 15 '74-p2268
PW-v206-Jl 15 '74-p115
SB-v10-Mr '75-p336
How Parasites Live
ACSB-v9-Fall '76-p19
BL-v73-S 1 '76-p38
BS-v36-Ag '76-p149
HB-v52-O '76-p527
KR-v44-Ap 15 '76-p476
SB-v12-S '76-p103

* * *

GOLDSTEIN-JACKSON, Kevin
Activities With Everyday Objects
JB-v44-D '80-p291

GOLDSTEIN-JACKSON, Kevin (continued)
Experiments With Everyday Objects
BL-v74-My 1 '78-p1430
JB-v41-Ag '77-p221
LR-v25-Winter '77-p334
NS-v93-My 20 '77-p686
SB-v14-Mr '79-p229
Magic With Everyday Objects
GP-v18-My '79-p3521
JB-v43-O '79-p272
Things To Make With Everyday Objects
CBRS-v8-Jl '80-p126
GP-v17-S '78-p3391
JB-v42-O '78-p254
SLJ-v27-S '80-p71
TES-Jl 11 '80-p28

* * *

GOLDSTON, Robert
The American Nightmare
BL-v70-Mr 15 '74-p801
HB-v49-O '73-p475
KR-v41-D 15 '73-p1371
LJ-v99-Ap 15 '74-p1227
PW-v204-O 15 '73-p55
The American War Of National Liberation 1763-1783
BL-v73-Ap 1 '77-p1167
KR-v44-N 1 '76-p1177
SLJ-v23-F '77-p71
Barcelona
BL-v65-Jl 15 '69-p1270
HB-v45-Je '69-p314
KR-v37-Mr 15 '69-p319
LJ-v95-Ja 15 '70-p252
The Great Depression
BL-v65-F 1 '69-p582
BS-v28-Ja 1 '69-p421
BW-v3-My 4 '69-p22
CCB-B-v22-F '69-p93
CSM-v62-Ap 16 '70-p7
LJ-v94-Je 15 '69-p2509
LJ-v94-D 15 '69-p4581
NYTBR-Mr 23 '69-p26
London
BL-v65-Jl 15 '69-p1270
HB-v45-Je '69-p315
KR-v37-Mr 15 '69-p320
LJ-v94-Je 15 '69-p2509
The Long March 1934-1935
BL-v68-Ap 15 '72-p724
BS-v31-D 15 '71-p434
CCB-B-v25-Jl '72-p169
LJ-v97-Ja 15 '72-p282
New York
HB-v46-O '70-p492
KR-v38-Mr 1 '70-p251
Next Year In Jerusalem
BL-v74-F 1 '78-p902
BS-v38-O '78-p230
CCB-B-v32-O '78-p29
Comw-v107-F 29 '80-p114
HB-v54-Ag '78-p410
KR-v46-Jl 1 '78-p697
Kliatt-v14-Winter '80-p49
SE-v43-Ap '79-p300
SLJ-v25-F '79-p63
The Road Between The Wars 1918-1941
BL-v75-Ja 1 '79-p744
CBRS-v7-Ja '79-p47
CCB-B-v32-My '79-p154
HB-v55-Ap '79-p206
KR-v47-F 1 '79-p132
Kliatt-v14-Fall '80-p48
Sinister Touches
BL-v78-My 1 '82-p1151
BS-v42-O '82-p285
CCB-B-v35-Jl '82-p206
HB-v58-Je '82-p306
KR-v50-My 15 '82-p610
SLJ-v28-Ap '82-p81
VOYA-v5-D '82-p42
Suburbia
BL-v67-S 15 '70-p96
HB-v46-Ag '70-p402
KR-v38-Mr 1 '70-p252
LJ-v95-Ap 15 '70-p1496
The Sword Of The Prophet
BL-v76-N 15 '79-p493
BS-v40-Ap '80-p38
CCB-B-v33-F '80-p109
HB-v55-O '79-p548
KR-v48-Mr 1 '80-p294
SLJ-v26-S '79-p157
The Vietnamese Revolution
BL-v68-Jl 15 '72-p998
BL-v68-Jl 15 '72-p1004
BS-v32-Jl 15 '72-p184
CCB-B-v26-Mr '73-p106
KR-v40-F 15 '72-p205
LJ-v97-S 15 '72-p2960
LJ-v97-D 15 '72-p4056
PW-v202-Jl 31 '72-p71

* * *

GOLDSTON, Robert C
Civil War In Spain
BL-v63-Ap 15 '67-p902
CCB-B-v20-Mr '67-p107
CCB-B-v22-S '68-p7
HB-v42-D '66-p723
HB-v44-Ap '68-p193
KR-v34-N 1 '66-p1145
LJ-v92-Ja 15 '67-p342
NYTBR-v71-N 6 '66-p24
NYTBR-v71-D 4 '66-p66
PW-v190-N 28 '66-p61
SR-v50-Mr 18 '67-p36
TLS-Mr 14 '68-p251
Life And Death Of Nazi Germany
BL-v64-O 1 '67-p176
BS-v27-Jl 1 '67-p144
CCB-B-v21-S '67-p6
HB-v43-O '67-p604
KR-v35-Je 1 '67-p652
LJ-v92-Ap 15 '67-p1748
NYTBR-v72-My 7 '67-p2
NYTBR-v72-N 5 '67-p65
PW-v191-Je 5 '67-p177
TLS-Ja 30 '69-p105
Negro Revolution
BL-v64-Je 15 '68-p1180
BL-v65-Ap 1 '69-p900
BL-v69-My 1 '73-p838
BW-v2-Ag 25 '68-p16
CCB-B-v22-S '68-p7
CSM-v61-My 1 '69-pB7
Comw-v91-F 27 '70-p584
HB-v44-Ag '68-p438
KR-v36-Ap 15 '68-p471
LJ-v93-My 15 '68-p2120
NO-v7-N 4 '68-p23
NYTBR-v73-My 5 '68-p5
PW-v193-My 6 '68-p46
PW-v195-Je 16 '69-p79
SE-v33-My '69-p563
SR-v51-Ag 24 '68-p43
SR-v51-N 9 '68-p72
TN-v25-Ja '69-p205
YR-v5-S '68-p13
Rise Of Red China
BL-v64-Ja 1 '68-p538
BS-v27-Ja 1 '68-p392
BW-v2-Ag 4 '68-p13
CCB-B-v21-Ja '68-p77
HB-v43-D '67-p762
KR-v35-N 15 '67-p1372
LJ-v92-S 15 '67-p3198
LJ-v93-Ja 1 '68-p72
NYTBR-v72-N 5 '67-p32
PW-v195-Ja 6 '69-p55
Pac A-v43-Spring '70-p92
SR-v50-N 11 '67-p50

GOLDSTON, Robert C (continued)
Russian Revolution
BL-v63-Ap 1 '67-p844
BS-v26-D 1 '66-p339
CCB-B-v20-F '67-p89
HB-v43-F '67-p82
KR-v34-Je 1 '66-p543
LJ-v91-My 15 '66-p2704
NYTBR-v71-N 6 '66-p32
NYTBR-v71-D 4 '66-p66
SR-v50-F 18 '67-p42
TLS-N 2 '67-p1027

* * *

GOLDTHWAITE, John
Roll Call
PW-v215-F 26 '79-p184
SLJ-v26-S '79-p138

* * *

GOLDWATER, Daniel
Bridges And How They Are Built
BL-v62-Ja 15 '66-p486
CCB-B-v19-Ap '66-p129
Comw-v83-N 5 '65-p161
HB-v41-D '65-p646
KR-v33-Ag 15 '65-p825
LJ-v90-N 15 '65-p5090
NYTBR-v70-N 28 '65-p46
SB-v2-My '66-p56

* * *

GOLOMBEK, Harry
Beginning Chess
Brit Bk N-O '81-p624
ILN-v269-O '81-p106
LJ-v106-D 15 '81-p2405
Spec-v247-Jl 25 '81-p29

* * *

GOLTZ, Edna J
Indy, Son Of Cloud
Can Child Lit-#33 '84-p57

* * *

GOMEZ, Victoria
Scream Cheese And Jelly!
SLJ-v26-N '79-p60
Wags To Witches
NYTBR-v86-Ap 26 '81-p51
PW-v219-Ap 3 '81-p74
RT-v36-O '82-p79
SLJ-v28-D '81-p52

* * *

GOMI, Taro
Coco Can't Wait
BL-v80-Ap 1 '84-p1115
CBRS-v12-Ap '84-p90
NYTBR-v89-My 13 '84-p20
PW-v225-My 4 '84-p59
Par-v59-N '84-p48
SLJ-v30-My '84-p65
WCRB-v10-My '84-p46
Tabeta No Dare
BL-v79-O 15 '82-p320

* * *

GONEN, Rivka
Pottery In Ancient Times
SLJ-v23-Mr '77-p140
Weapons And Warfare In Ancient Times
SLJ-v23-Mr '77-p141

* * *

GONZALES-HABA, Manuela
Agenor, El Robot
BL-v78-N 1 '81-p380

* * *

GONZALEZ, Gloria
Gaucho
BL-v74-O 1 '77-p289
CLW-v49-Mr '78-p356
HB-v54-Ap '78-p164
Inter BC-v14-#1 '83-p16
KR-v45-Ag 1 '77-p784
SLJ-v24-N '77-p70
The Glad Man
CCB-B-v29-Je '76-p156
KR-v43-S 15 '75-p1066
Kliatt-v13-Fall '79-p7
PW-v208-Ag 25 '75-p293
SLJ-v22-O '75-p98

* * *

GONZALEZ-MENA, Janet
English Experiences
LA-v53-Ap '76-p444

* * *

GOOD, Merle
Nicole Visits An Amish Farm
BL-v79-S 15 '82-p119
CCB-B-v36-O '82-p26
CLW-v54-My '83-p424
Inst-v92-S '82-p20
KR-v50-Je 15 '82-p679
SE-v47-Ap '83-p243
SLJ-v29-Ja '83-p59

* * *

GOOD English Program
Inst-v89-S '79-p232

* * *

GOOD Housekeeping
Cooking Is Fun
Punch-v276-Ap 18 '79-p688

* * *

GOOD Idea Books
Inst-v89-Mr '80-p155

* * *

GOODACRE, E
The Word Finder Picture Book
JB-v48-F '84-p22

* * *

GOODACRE, Elizabeth
Looking For Baby Roo
B&B-v20-My '75-p79
Three Cheers For The Fliporwig
B&B-v20-My '75-p79
Words About Animals
B&B-v20-My '75-p79

* * *

GOODALL, Daphne Machin
Horses Of The World
B&B-v19-O '73-p33
BL-v62-Ap 1 '66-p741
LJ-v91-Mr 15 '66-p1435
RSR-v2-Ap '74-p38
SB-v10-Mr '75-p340
How To Ride
GP-v19-S '80-p3769
JB-v45-F '81-p28
Sch Lib-v28-D '80-p419
Zebras
ASBYP-v16-Fall '83-p22
SB-v15-My '79-p41
SLJ-v25-O '78-p132
TES-S 1 '78-p15

* * *

GOODALL, John S
Above And Below Stairs
CCB-B-v37-Ja '84-p87
SLJ-v30-O '83-p158
The Adventures Of Paddy Pork
BL-v65-Ap 1 '69-p900
BW-v2-O 20 '68-p14
CCB-B-v22-F '69-p93
KR-v36-O 15 '68-p1156
LJ-v94-F 15 '69-p861

GOODALL, John S (continued)
LJ-v94-My 15 '69-p2073
NYTBR-v73-N 3 '68-p69
PW-v194-O 28 '68-p59
Spec-v245-D 6 '80-p25
Teacher-v86-Ap '69-p184
The Ballooning Adventures Of Paddy Pork
BL-v66-N 15 '69-p408
CCB-B-v23-Mr '70-p111
CE-v46-Mr '70-p319
CSM-v61-N 6 '69-pB11
HB-v45-D '69-p663
LJ-v95-Mr 15 '70-p1186
NYTBR-O 26 '69-p44
PW-v196-S 29 '69-p58
Spec-v245-D 6 '80-p25
TLS-Ap 16 '70-p418
Before The War 1908-1939
PW-v220-Jl 17 '81-p95
SLJ-v28-S '81-p106
Creepy Castle
CCB-B-v29-Mr '76-p110
CSM-v67-N 5 '75-pB4
HB-v52-F '76-p42
KR-v43-O 1 '75-p1120
New R-v173-D 6 '75-p22
PW-v208-Jl 28 '75-p123
RT-v32-My '79-p944
RT-v34-Ja '81-p418
SLJ-v22-S '75-p81
TES-D 10 '82-p34
An Edwardian Christmas
BL-v75-S 1 '78-p48
BW-D 10 '78-pE5
CCB-B-v32-D '78-p61
CSM-v71-D 4 '78-pB20
KR-v46-D 15 '78-p1352
PW-v214-Jl 10 '78-p136
RT-v35-My '82-p932
SE-v43-Ap '79-p300
SLJ-v25-O '78-p112
Edwardian Entertainments
PW-v221-Ap 23 '82-p92
SLJ-v29-S '82-p121
An Edwardian Holiday
BL-v76-S 1 '79-p43
CCB-B-v33-Ap '80-p152
KR-v47-S 1 '79-p997
NS-v96-N 3 '78-p593
PW-v216-O 1 '79-p89
SLJ-v26-F '80-p45
An Edwardian Season
KR-v49-Ja 1 '81-p2
PW-v218-Jl 25 '80-p157
RT-v35-My '82-p933
SLJ-v27-N '80-p62
An Edwardian Summer
BL-v73-D 15 '76-p606
CCB-B-v30-Ap '77-p123
GW-v115-D 5 '76-p22
HB-v52-O '76-p490
KR-v44-S 15 '76-p1035
PW-v209-Je 28 '76-p99
RT-v35-My '82-p933
SLJ-v23-O '76-p106
Escapade
JB-v44-D '80-p283
Jacko
BL-v69-Ja 1 '73-p449
CCB-B-v26-D '72-p56
CE-v49-F '73-p257
HB-v49-Ap '73-p131
KR-v40-N 1 '72-p1232
PW-v203-F 5 '73-p89
PW-v226-S 7 '84-p79
TLS-D 3 '71-p1514
Teacher-v90-My '73-p73
John S. Goodall's Theatre: The Sleeping Beauty
CCB-B-v34-Ja '81-p92
NYTBR-v85-My 11 '80-p24
PW-v217-Je 13 '80-p74
Lavinia's Cottage
Brit Bk N C-Autumn '82-p5
JB-v47-Ap '83-p67
NYTBR-v88-Ap 24 '83-p24
PW-v223-F 4 '83-p368
TES-N 19 '82-p36
The Midnight Adventures Of Kelly, Dot, And Esmeralda
BL-v69-Jl 1 '73-p1021
CCB-B-v26-My '73-p138
CE-v50-Ja '74-p166
CLW-v45-N '73-p190
CSM-v65-My 2 '73-pB2
HB-v49-Je '73-p258
KR-v41-F 1 '73-p108
LJ-v98-Ap 15 '73-p1375
LJ-v98-My 15 '73-p1655
PW-v203-F 26 '73-p124
Par-v48-Jl '73-p71
Naughty Nancy
BB-v3-S '75-p2
CCB-B-v28-Jl '75-p176
CE-v52-N '75-p90
CLW-v47-S '75-p93
CSM-v67-My 7 '75-pB4
HB-v51-O '75-p453
JB-v39-Je '75-p174
KR-v43-Ap 15 '75-p444
PW-v207-Ap 28 '75-p45
RT-v29-My '76-p829
SLJ-v22-S '75-p81
TLS-Ap 4 '75-p366
Paddy Finds A Job
BL-v78-Ja 1 '82-p600
BW-v12-Ja 10 '82-p10
Brit Bk N C-Spring '82-p3
ILN-v269-D '81-p75
JB-v46-Ap '82-p61
RT-v37-My '84-p857
Sch Lib-v30-Mr '82-p25
Paddy Goes Traveling
ABC-v4-Mr '83-p59
BL-v79-N 15 '82-p445
CLW-v55-O '83-p140
NY-v58-D 6 '82-p186
PW-v222-N 19 '82-p76
RT-v37-O '83-p60
SLJ-v29-N '82-p67
Paddy Goes Travelling
JB-v47-F '83-p12
Paddy Pork
SLJ-v30-Ja '84-p64
Paddy Pork-Odd Jobs
JB-v48-Ap '84-p60
KR-v51-N 1 '83-pJ185
NYTBR-v88-N 13 '83-p45
PW-v224-D 2 '83-p89
Punch-v285-N 16 '83-p60
RT-v37-My '84-p889
Paddy Pork's Holiday
BL-v73-O 1 '76-p251
CCB-B-v30-O '76-p25
CE-v53-Ja '77-p147
GP-v15-O '76-p2974
JB-v40-O '76-p262
KR-v44-S 15 '76-p1035
NYTBR-N 14 '76-p39
New R-v175-N 27 '76-p31
PW-v210-O 4 '76-p75
Par-v51-N '76-p28
RT-v31-O '77-p13
RT-v34-Ja '81-p419
SLJ-v23-O '76-p98
Spec-v237-Jl 17 '76-p24
Paddy Underwater
BL-v81-O 1 '84-p248
NY-v60-D 3 '84-p191
PW-v226-Ag 10 '84-p82
Paddy's Evening Out
BL-v70-Ja 15 '74-p542
CCB-B-v27-Ap '74-p129
HB-v50-Ap '74-p139
LJ-v99-F 15 '74-p562
Spec-v231-D 22 '73-p823
TES-S 21 '84-p37

GOODALL, John S (continued)
TLS-Mr 29 '74-p331
Paddy's New Hat
BL-v77-O 15 '80-p326
CCB-B-v34-D '80-p71
CE-v57-My '81-p297
CLW-v52-Ap '81-p404
HB-v56-D '80-p633
JB-v45-Je '81-p106
KR-v49-Ja 15 '81-p72
NS-v100-N 21 '80-p19
NY-v56-D 1 '80-p218
NYTBR-v85-N 9 '80-p49
PW-v218-S 12 '80-p66
SLJ-v27-N '80-p62
Spec-v245-D 6 '80-p25
Shrewbettina Goes To Work
BL-v78-Ja 1 '82-p600
BW-v12-Ja 10 '82-p10
Brit Bk N C-Spring '82-p3
ILN-v269-D '81-p75
JB-v46-Je '82-p93
PW-v220-Ag 21 '81-p56
Shrewbettina's Birthday
BL-v67-Ap 15 '71-p701
BW-v5-My 9 '71-p6
CCB-B-v24-Jl '71-p170
CE-v48-N '71-p98
Comw-v94-My 21 '71-p266
GT-v89-S '71-p156
HB-v47-Je '71-p278
KR-v39-Ap 1 '71-p356
LJ-v96-Ap 15 '71-p1493
LJ-v96-My 15 '71-p1781
LJ-v96-D 15 '71-p4159
Life-v71-D 17 '71-p44
NS-v81-Mr 5 '71-p314
NYT-v121-D 14 '71-p43
NYTBR-Ap 4 '71-p38
PW-v199-Mr 1 '71-p58
PW-v226-S 14 '84-p143
SR-v54-Ap 17 '71-p44
TES-D 10 '82-p34
The Story Of An English Village
AB-v64-N 19 '79-p3446
BB-v7-N '79-p2
BL-v75-Mr 1 '79-p1089
BL-v79-Je 1 '83-p1282
CCB-B-v32-My '79-p154
CLW-v51-N '79-p182
EJ-v68-N '79-p72
GP-v17-S '78-p3376
HB-v55-Je '79-p292
JB-v42-D '78-p294
KR-v47-Mr 1 '79-p258
LA-v56-O '79-p823
NS-v96-N 3 '78-p593
NY-v55-D 3 '79-p217
PW-v215-Ja 8 '79-p74
SLJ-v25-Mr '79-p121
Sch Lib-v27-Je '79-p147
TES-N 3 '78-p23
TN-v37-Fall '80-p46
Teacher-v96-My '79-p115
Time-v114-D 3 '79-p99
WCRB-v5-Jl '79-p63
The Surprise Picnic
BL-v73-Mr 15 '77-p1092
BW-Jl 10 '77-pH10
CCB-B-v31-O '77-p31
HB-v53-Je '77-p299
JB-v41-O '77-p277
KR-v45-Ap 15 '77-p422
NW-v90-D 19 '77-p82
NYTBR-F 26 '78-p27
New R-v177-D 3 '77-p26
PW-v211-Ja 31 '77-p75
RT-v35-My '82-p933
SLJ-v23-Mr '77-p132
Spec-v239-Jl 16 '77-p23
Victorians Abroad
CCB-B-v35-Ap '82-p147
KR-v49-Jl 1 '81-p797
PW-v219-Ja 9 '81-p73
SLJ-v27-Ap '81-p112

* * *

GOODBODY, Slim
The Force Inside You
BL-v80-N 1 '83-p408
CBRS-v12-O '83-p19
SLJ-v30-N '83-p77
Healthy Days Diary
WCRB-v9-S '83-p67
The Healthy Habits Handbook
CBRS-v12-F '84-p73
SLJ-v30-F '84-p58

GOODBODY, Slim
See Also Burstein, John

GOODE, Clancy
The World Of Kindergarten
CCB-B-v24-My '71-p135

GOODE, Diane
My Little Library Of Christmas Classics
CCB-B-v37-N '83-p50
NYTBR-v88-D 4 '83-p79
PW-v224-S 2 '83-p80

* * *

GOODE, Ruth
Hands Up!
HB-v60-Ap '84-p209
SLJ-v30-My '84-p79
WCRB-v10-S '84-p61
People Of The First Cities
BL-v74-F 15 '78-p1004
CCB-B-v31-My '78-p142
KR-v45-N 15 '77-p1208
SB-v14-D '78-p185
SLJ-v24-F '78-p57

* * *

GOODE, Stephen
The National Defense System
BL-v73-Jl 1 '77-p1652
SLJ-v24-S '77-p143
The Prophet And The Revolutionary
BL-v72-N 15 '75-p443
BL-v72-N 15 '75-p452
KR-v43-O 15 '75-p1197
SLJ-v22-F '76-p52
Violence In America
BL-v80-F 15 '84-p850
CCB-B-v37-Je '84-p185
SLJ-v30-My '84-p88

* * *

GOODEN, Rumer
The Rocking Horse Secret
BL-v79-Ap 1 '83-p1042

* * *

GOODENOUGH, Simon
The Renaissance
BL-v76-Mr 1 '80-p982
CE-v56-Ap '80-p306
SE-v44-O '80-p534
SLJ-v27-S '80-p82

* * *

GOODENOW, Earle
Last Camel
CE-v46-S '69-p35
KR-v36-Ag 15 '68-p891
LJ-v93-O 15 '68-p3956
YR-v5-N '68-p8
The Owl Who Hated The Dark
CCB-B-v22-Je '69-p158
CSM-v61-My 1 '69-pB4
KR-v37-F 15 '69-p169
LJ-v94-My 15 '69-p2089
PW-v195-Ap 14 '69-p97

GOODWIN, Godfrey
(continued)
Sch Lib-v27-Mr '79-p54
TES-O 27 '78-p24
TLS-S 29 '78-p1082

* * *

GOODWIN, Harold
Magic Number
BL-v66-O 1 '69-p206
CCB-B-v23-S '69-p8
KR-v37-My 15 '69-p559
LJ-v94-S 15 '69-p3204
LJ-v95-O 15 '70-p3603
NYTBR, pt.2-N 9 '69-p30
Top Secret: Alligators!
BL-v72-O 1 '75-p233
Comw-v102-N 21 '75-p568
KR-v43-Jl 1 '75-p711
NYTBR-Ag 10 '75-p8
SLJ-v22-N '75-p77

* * *

GOODWIN, Mary T
Creative Food Experiences For Children
CT-v4-Mr '75-p37
Cha Ti-v36-N '82-p66
NYTBR-N 16 '75-p34
SS-v71-My '80-p120

* * *

GOODWIN, T
The Ring Of Spears
JB-v43-Ag '79-p219

* * *

GOODWIN, Tim
Saturday Went Wrong
JB-v47-D '83-p243

* * *

GOOLE, Paul
The Girl Who Loved Horses
TES-F 5 '82-p28

* * *

GOOR, Ron
All Kinds Of Feet
BL-v80-Ag '84-p1625
CCB-B-v37-Jl '84-p204
HB-v60-Ag '84-p484
Inst-v93-My '84-p102
SB-v20-N '84-p96
SLJ-v31-S '84-p102
In The Driver's Seat
BL-v79-D 15 '82-p563
CCB-B-v36-Mr '83-p126
KR-v50-Jl 15 '82-p800
NYT-v132-N 30 '82-p23
NYTBR-v87-N 14 '82-p60
SLJ-v29-N '82-p68
Shadows
BL-v78-D 15 '81-p548
CBRS-v10-S '81-p5
CCB-B-v35-Ap '82-p147
CE-v58-My '82-p329
HB-v58-F '82-p63
KR-v49-N 1 '81-p1338
LA-v59-F '82-p155
SA-v245-D '81-p38
SB-v17-Mr '82-p213
SLJ-v28-S '81-p107
Signs
BL-v80-N 1 '83-p408
CBRS-v12-S '83-p3
CCB-B-v37-Ja '84-p87
CE-v60-Mr '84-p290
HB-v59-D '83-p700
SLJ-v30-F '84-p58

* * *

GOPAL, Sarvepalli
Jawaharlal Nehru: A Biography. Vol. 2
Brit Bk N-Mr '82-p138
Choice-v18-S '80-p146
Econ-v274-F 2 '80-p95
HRNB-v8-Ag '80-p208
JAS-v40-Ag '81-p821
LJ-v105-My 15 '80-p1155
Lis-v103-Ja 24 '80-p122
Obs-Mr 2 '80-p39
TES-F 1 '80-p24

* * *

GORDE, Monique
Les Jureaux Se Deguisent
BL-v77-Mr 1 '81-p969

* * *

GORDON, Delma
Amy Loves Goodbyes
CCB-B-v20-Mr '67-p107
LJ-v91-S 15 '66-p4314

* * *

GORDON, Esther S
If An Auk Could Talk
BL-v74-S 1 '77-p41
KR-v45-Je 1 '77-p578
PW-v211-My 30 '77-p44
SLJ-v24-S '77-p108
Teacher-v95-D '77-p90
Once There Was A Giant Sea Cow
Cur R-v17-My '78-p141
Once There Was A Passenger Pigeon
ACSB-v10-Spring '77-p22
BL-v73-S 15 '76-p174
KR-v44-Je 15 '76-p688
PW-v209-Je 14 '76-p114
SB-v12-Mr '77-p212
SLJ-v23-O '76-p106
There Really Was A Dodo
ACSB-v8-Winter '75-p17
BL-v70-My 15 '74-p1055
CCB-B-v28-N '74-p42
KR-v42-My 1 '74-p484
LJ-v99-S 15 '74-p2246
PT-v8-D '74-p131
PW-v205-My 27 '74-p65
SB-v10-D '74-p259

* * *

GORDON, Ethel Edison
The Birdwatcher
BL-v70-Je 1 '74-p1081
BL-v70-Je 1 '74-p1099
BS-v34-Je 15 '74-p151
CCB-B-v28-D '74-p62
KR-v42-Mr 15 '74-p323
LJ-v99-My 1 '74-p1330
PW-v205-Mr 25 '74-p50
So Far From Home
BL-v65-My 1 '69-p1004
CCB-B-v22-Mr '69-p110
CSM-v61-Je 26 '69-p7
EJ-v58-My '69-p776
LJ-v94-F 15 '69-p883
Where Does The Summer Go?
BW-v1-O 22 '67-p14
CCB-B-v21-Ja '68-p78
CSM-v59-N 2 '67-pB11
EJ-v60-S '71-p828
KR-v35-Je 1 '67-p648
LJ-v92-O 15 '67-p3863
SR-v50-Ag 19 '67-p35

* * *

GORDON, Eugene
Saudi Arabia In Pictures
LJ-v99-F 15 '74-p573
SLJ-v27-F '81-p65

* * *

GORDON, George N
Your Career In Film Making
BL-v66-Mr 15 '70-p910
BS-v29-D 1 '69-p352
CCB-B-v23-Mr '70-p111
KR-v37-N 15 '69-p1207
NYTBR-N 23 '69-p44

GORDON, George N (continued)
Your Career In TV And Radio
BL-v62-Je 15 '66-p996
BS-v26-Jl 1 '66-p141
CCB-B-v20-S '66-p10

* * *

GORDON, Giles
Walter And The Balloon
JB-v39-F '75-p39
TLS-D 6 '74-p1378

* * *

GORDON, John
Catch Your Death
JB-v48-Je '84-p138
TES-Je 22 '84-p28
TLS-Mr 30 '84-p335
The Edge Of The World
CBRS-v12-Ap '84-p96
Fant R-v7-Ag '84-p46
GP-v22-Jl '83-p4115
HB-v59-O '83-p581
JB-v47-Je '83-p124
KR-v51-S 1 '83-pJ175
Punch-v284-Je 8 '83-p57
SLJ-v30-Ja '84-p75
Sch Lib-v32-Mr '84-p67
TES-Jl 15 '83-p22
VOYA-v6-F '84-p343
The House On The Brink
GP-v21-My '82-p3893
JB-v47-O '83-p213
TES-My 21 '82-p31
TES-Jl 15 '83-p22
The Spitfire Grave And Other Stories
Brit Bk N C-Spring '80-p16
JB-v44-Je '80-p142
Obs-D 2 '79-p38
Sch Lib-v28-Mr '80-p55
TES-Ja 18 '80-p38

* * *

GORDON, Margaret
A Paper Of Pins
CLW-v47-O '75-p132
GP-v13-Mr '75-p2584
JB-v39-Je '75-p175
KR-v43-My 15 '75-p562
Obs-Ap 6 '75-p30
SLJ-v22-S '75-p82
Spec-v235-Jl 26 '75-p114
TLS-Ap 4 '75-p366
The Supermarket Mice
CBRS-v13-O '84-p14
Sch Lib-v32-S '84-p224
TES-Je 8 '84-p51
TLS-S 28 '84-p1106
Wilberforce Goes On A Picnic
B&B-Jl '82-p35
BL-v79-S 15 '82-p113
Brit Bk N C-Autumn '82-p14
CBRS-v10-Ag '82-p133
CCB-B-v36-Ja '83-p88
JB-v46-O '82-p181
KR-v50-Jl 15 '82-p794
SLJ-v29-O '82-p141
Sch Lib-v30-S '82-p224
TES-Jl 13 '84-p25
Wilberforce Goes Shopping
GP-v22-My '83-p4081
JB-v47-Je '83-p108

* * *

GORDON, Patricia
The Boy Jones
Rp B Bk R-v26-#1 '81-p18

* * *

GORDON, Patrick
The Unfolding Past
GP-v14-S '75-p2681

* * *

GORDON, S
Picture The World Of Horses
JB-v48-Je '84-p126

* * *

GORDON, Sally
About Ponies
GP-v22-Jl '83-p4112
JB-v47-D '83-p243

* * *

GORDON, Sharon
Christmas Surprise
RT-v34-My '81-p953
SLJ-v27-O '80-p161
Dinosaur In Trouble
SLJ-v27-S '80-p59
Drip Drop
SLJ-v29-S '82-p102
Easter Bunny's Lost Egg
SLJ-v27-S '80-p59
First Day Of Spring
SLJ-v29-S '82-p102
Friendly Snowman
RT-v34-My '81-p953
SLJ-v27-S '80-p59
Maxwell Mouse
SLJ-v29-S '82-p102
Pete The Parakeet
SLJ-v27-O '80-p135
Play Ball, Kate!
CCB-B-v35-My '82-p169
SLJ-v28-Mr '82-p132
Sam The Scarecrow
BL-v77-O 15 '80-p332
SLJ-v27-O '80-p135
The Spelling Bee
SLJ-v29-S '82-p102
Three Little Witches
BL-v77-O 15 '80-p332
SLJ-v27-O '80-p135
Tick Tock Clock
ASBYP-v15-Fall '82-p57
SLJ-v28-Ag '82-p95
Trees
ASBYP-v17-Spring '84-p54
SLJ-v30-D '83-p56
What A Dog!
BL-v77-O 15 '80-p332
SLJ-v27-O '80-p135

* * *

GORDON, Sheila
A Monster In The Mailbox
BL-v75-Ja 15 '79-p809
CCB-B-v32-Ap '79-p136
CE-v55-Ap '79-p296
HB-v54-D '78-p635
KR-v47-F 1 '79-p125
SLJ-v25-N '78-p44

* * *

GORDON, Shirley
The Boy Who Wanted A Family
BL-v76-Je 1 '80-p1424
CBRS-v8-Mr '80-p73
CCB-B-v33-Jl '80-p213
KR-v48-My 1 '80-p584
SLJ-v26-Ap '80-p93
Crystal Is My Friend
BL-v74-Mr 15 '78-p1187
CCB-B-v31-Jl '78-p176
Comw-v105-N 10 '78-p730
KR-v46-Mr 1 '78-p238
SLJ-v24-Mr '78-p118
WCRB-v4-Jl '78-p46
Crystal Is The New Girl
BB-v4-My '76-p3
BL-v72-Ap 1 '76-p1113
CCB-B-v29-Je '76-p157
KR-v44-F 15 '76-p193
PW-v209-Mr 1 '76-p94
RT-v31-O '77-p10
SLJ-v22-Ap '76-p60
Grandma Zoo
CBRS-v7-Ja '79-p42

GORDON, Shirley (continued)
KR-v46-D 1 '78-p1305
PW-v214-Ag 28 '78-p395
SLJ-v25-Ja '79-p42
The Green Hornet Lunchbox
BW-v4-N 8 '70-p2
CCB-B-v24-Ap '71-p123
CLW-v42-Mr '71-p458
LJ-v96-F 15 '71-p714
Teacher-v91-S '73-p154
Happy Birthday, Crystal
BL-v78-N 15 '81-p438
CCB-B-v35-Ja '82-p85
KR-v49-N 1 '81-p1343
RT-v36-O '82-p63
SLJ-v28-F '82-p67
Me And The Bad Guys
CBRS-v9-S '80-p4
KR-v48-O 1 '80-p1299
SLJ-v27-Ja '81-p60

* * *

GORDON, Sol
Did The Sun Shine Before You Were Born?
BL-v71-F 15 '75-p618
BW-My 4 '75-p1
PW-v207-Mr 10 '75-p57
SR-v2-My 31 '75-p35
Facts About Sex
BL-v67-D 1 '70-p303
HB-v47-F '71-p65
LJ-v95-N 15 '70-p4044
NYTBR-Ag 2 '70-p18
SB-v6-S '70-p156
Facts About Sex For Today's Youth
BL-v70-O 15 '73-p221
BL-v70-O 15 '73-p232
KR-v41-Ap 15 '73-p467
LJ-v98-S 15 '73-p2664
Ms-v12-Jl '83-p43
PGJ-v48-Mr '70-p597
Par-v54-Ap '79-p24
WLB-v53-Je '79-p712
Girls Are Girls And Boys Are Boys
CCB-B-v28-Mr '75-p113
Inter BC-v11-Ja 10 '80-p26
KR-v42-N 1 '74-p1154
Ms-v9-Je '81-p70
SLJ-v21-Ap '75-p45
Signs Of Our Times 3
Hi Lo-v2-S '80-p6

* * *

GORDON, Stephen F
Making Picture-Books
HB-v46-O '70-p490
LJ-v95-D 1 '70-p4163

* * *

GORDY, Berry
Movin' Up
BL-v76-D 15 '79-p612
BW-v10-Ja 13 '80-p10
Bl S-v11-My '80-p86
CBRS-v8-Winter '80-p67
CCB-B-v33-Mr '80-p133
Inter BC-v13-#1 '82-p18
KR-v48-F 1 '80-p138
PW-v216-O 29 '79-p83
SLJ-v26-D '79-p84

* * *

GORE, Harriet Margolis
What To Do When There's No One But You
ACSB-v8-Spring '75-p20
CCB-B-v28-F '75-p93
LJ-v99-S 15 '74-p2246
SB-v10-D '74-p262
Teacher-v94-N '76-p34

* * *

GORE, Margaret
Play It Cool!
JB-v40-Ag '76-p227
TLS-Jl 16 '76-p884

* * *

GORESHT, Anne
Charlie Choppers Grows And Grows
In Rev-v14-Ap '80-p42
Inst-v90-F '81-p186

* * *

GOREY, Edward
Dracula
PW-v216-D 3 '79-p52
The Dwindling Party
ABC-v4-Mr '83-p59
B&B-F '83-p29
BL-v79-D 15 '82-p564
Brit Bk N C-Autumn '82-p5
CCB-B-v36-F '83-p108
GP-v21-N '82-p3972
LA-v60-Mr '83-p358
LATBR-O 17 '82-p6
Obs-N 28 '82-p31
PW-v222-O 15 '82-p66
RT-v37-My '84-p857
Sch Lib-v31-Je '83-p129
Spec-v249-D 4 '82-p25
TES-N 19 '82-p36
TLS-N 26 '82-p1304
Time-v120-D 20 '82-p79
The Gashleycrumb Tinies
VLS-My '82-p12
The Glorious Nosebleed
BW-Ap 6 '75-p4
VV-v20-Ap 21 '75-p40
The Loathsome Couple
New R-v176-My 28 '77-p41
Sam And Emma
Obs-D 1 '74-p35
The Tunnel Calamity
PW-v225-Je 8 '84-p64

* * *

GORHAM, Charles
Lion Of Judah: Haile Selassie I, Emperor Of Ethiopia
Am-v115-Jl 2 '66-p16
BL-v62-Je 1 '66-p959
BS-v26-Ap 1 '66-p18
CCB-B-v20-S '66-p10
KR-v34-Ja 15 '66-p66
LJ-v91-My 15 '66-p2706
NYTBR-v71-Ap 17 '66-p30
NYTBR-v71-D 4 '66-p66
SR-v49-My 14 '66-p42

* * *

GORILLA Games And Monkey Madness
LA-v55-N '78-p960

* * *

GORMLEY, Beatrice
Best Friend Insurance
BL-v80-F 1 '84-p813
CBRS-v12-O '83-p16
CCB-B-v37-Ja '84-p87
SLJ-v30-F '84-p70
Fifth Grade Magic
BL-v79-D 15 '82-p564
CBRS-v11-O '82-p18
CE-v60-S '83-p52
HB-v58-O '82-p516
LA-v60-Mr '83-p362
RT-v36-F '83-p594
SLJ-v29-O '82-p152
Mail-Order Wings
BL-v78-O 1 '81-p235
CBRS-v10-O '81-p18
CCB-B-v35-F '82-p107
LA-v59-My '82-p487
PW-v220-Jl 17 '81-p94
PW-v225-Ap 13 '84-p72
SLJ-v28-D '81-p62

* * *

GORODETZKY, Charles W
What You Should Know About Drugs
BL-v67-D 15 '70-p341
BL-v67-Ap 1 '71-p660
CCB-B-v24-F '71-p91
CE-v48-O '71-p29
CLW-v42-My '71-p578
Comw-v93-N 20 '70-p205
GT-v88-Ap '71-p69
HB-v47-Ap '71-p181
KR-v38-O 15 '70-p1154
LJ-v95-D 15 '70-p4350
NYTBR-F 7 '71-p33
NYTBR, pt.2-N 8 '70-p36
PW-v198-N 16 '70-p77
SB-v6-D '70-p251
TN-v27-Ap '71-p305

* * *

GOROG, Judith
Caught In The Turtle
CBRS-v12-F '84-p73
SLJ-v30-D '83-p82

* * *

GOROSTIZA, Carlos
El Barquito Viajero
BL-v78-Je 15 '82-p1373
RT-v36-N '82-p209
Los Dias De Fiesta
BL-v78-Je 15 '82-p1373
RT-v36-N '82-p209
Todos Al Zoologico!
BL-v78-Je 15 '82-p1373
RT-v36-N '82-p209

* * *

GORSLINE, Douglas
Nursery Rhymes
NYTBR-N 13 '77-p31
PW-v212-S 12 '77-p132
SLJ-v24-Ja '78-p80

* * *

GORSLINE, Marie
Cowboys
BL-v76-Ap 15 '80-p1204
PW-v217-F 29 '80-p136
North American Indians
SLJ-v25-S '78-p115
The Pioneers
CCB-B-v36-N '82-p47

* * *

GOSCINNY, Rene
Asterix
VV-v25-Ja 7 '80-p31
Asterix And Caesar's Gift
TES-Jl 23 '82-p24
Asterix And The Banquet
GP-v18-My '79-p3503
NS-v98-N 9 '79-p732
Asterix And The Cauldron
B&B-v22-D '76-p75
NS-v95-My 19 '78-p681
Asterix And The Chieftain's Shield
TLS-Mr 25 '77-p365
Asterix And The Great Crossing
BW-v13-Jl 10 '83-p9
GP-v14-Ap '76-p2849
Asterix And The Laurel Wreath
GP-v14-Ap '76-p2849
TLS-S 20 '74-p1001
Asterix And The Normans
Econ-v273-D 22 '79-p86
TES-Jl 23 '82-p24
Asterix At The Olympic Games
BW-v14-Ag 12 '84-p4
TLS-Jl 14 '72-p812
Asterix In Britain
Obs-O 3 '76-p22
TLS-Ap 16 '70-p417
Asterix The Gaul
Am-v122-My 30 '70-p597
BL-v66-Je 15 '70-p1248
BW-v4-Mr 8 '70-p8
BW-v4-Jl 19 '70-p7
CSM-v62-My 28 '70-p11
Lis-v81-Mr 6 '69-p316
NS-v77-Ap 25 '69-p591
Obs-Ap 6 '69-p26
PW-v197-Ap 6 '70-p61
Punch-v286-Mr 21 '84-p16
TLS-Ap 3 '69-p348
Lucky Luke
Obs-D 12 '76-p23
Nicholas And The Gang
JB-v43-Je '79-p157
TES-N 24 '78-p47
TLS-S 29 '78-p1085
Nicholas And The Gang Again
GP-v16-S '77-p3163
JB-v41-D '77-p333
Nicholas And The Gang At School
JB-v41-O '77-p287
Nicholas At Large
JB-v43-D '79-p325
Nicholas On Holiday
B&B-v23-Je '78-p66
GP-v17-S '78-p3395
JB-v42-O '78-p255
TES-S 1 '78-p15
TLS-Jl 7 '78-p771
Le Petit Nicolas
BL-v74-N 1 '77-p487
BL-v79-Je 15 '83-p1345
FR-v56-Mr '83-p599
FR-v56-Mr '83-p607
The Twelve Tasks Of Asterix
GP-v17-Jl '78-p3347
NS-v95-My 19 '78-p681

* * *

GOSFIELD, Frank
Korea
BL-v66-N 1 '69-p338
CCB-B-v23-N '69-p44
CSM-v61-My 1 '69-pB9
KR-v37-Mr 15 '69-p320
LJ-v94-S 15 '69-p3217
LJ-v94-D 15 '69-p4582
NYTBR-Mr 16 '69-p56
SR-v52-My 10 '69-p61

* * *

GOSHORN, Elizabeth
Shoestrings
KR-v43-Ag 1 '75-p843
SLJ-v22-D '75-p42

* * *

GOSNIK-GODEC, Ancka
Jancek Jezek
BL-v80-Je 1 '84-p1402

* * *

GOTTLIEB, Gerald
Early Children's Books And Their Illustration
A Art-v40-D '76-p25
ABC-v26-Jl '76-p7
ARBA-v8-'77-p38
BL-v72-Ja 1 '76-p598
BL-v72-Ja 1 '76-p625
Choice-v12-N '75-p1121
Choice-v13-My '76-p360
Comw-v104-F 18 '77-p125
HB-v52-Ap '76-p145
JAL-v2-S '76-p198
LJ-v101-Ap 1 '76-p883
LQ-v46-Jl '76-p317
NY-v51-D 29 '75-p56
NYTBR-Ja 18 '76-p8
PW-v208-O 27 '75-p52
PW-v208-N 3 '75-p48

GOTTLIEB, Gerald
(continued)
RT-v30-Mr '77-p699
SLJ-v22-F '76-p28
Sch Lib-v28-S '80-p232
TLS-Ap 2 '76-p380
TN-v32-Je '76-p380
VV-v20-D 15 '75-p74
The Story Of Masada
HB-v45-Ag '69-p421
SB-v5-S '69-p186

* * *

GOTTLIEB, Leonard
Factory Made
BL-v75-D 15 '78-p679
BW-F 11 '79-pF4
Comw-v105-N 10 '78-p735
KR-v47-Ja 1 '79-p14
SB-v15-S '79-p104
SLJ-v25-F '79-p63

* * *

GOTTLIEB, Robin
Mystery Of The Silent Friends
CCB-B-v18-F '65-p86
Secret Of The Unicom
CCB-B-v19-S '65-p9
LJ-v90-My 15 '65-p2427
NYTBR-v70-Je 6 '65-p26

* * *

GOTTLIEB, William P
Science Facts You Won't Believe
B Rpt-v2-N '83-p51
CBRS-v11-Spring '83-p123
SB-v19-Mr '84-p194
SLJ-v29-Ag '83-p65

* * *

GOTTSCHALK, Elin Toona
In Search Of Coffee Mountains
BL-v74-Ja 1 '78-p747
GP-v18-S '79-p3566
HB-v54-Ap '78-p164
JB-v43-Je '79-p166
KR-v46-Ja 1 '78-p7
Lis-v102-N 8 '79-p643
NYTBR-N 13 '77-p39
SLJ-v24-Mr '78-p137
TES-N 30 '79-p23

* * *

GOUDEY, Alice E
The Day We Saw The Sun Come Up
ACSB-v13-Winter '80-p2
NCW-v216-Mr '73-p90
Red Legs: The Story Of A Grasshopper
BL-v62-My 15 '66-p918
CCB-B-v20-F '67-p89
HB-v42-Je '66-p320
KR-v34-Mr 1 '66-p242
LJ-v91-My 15 '66-p2682
NYTBR-v71-My 8 '66-p43
SB-v2-S '66-p130

* * *

GOUDGE, Elizabeth
I Saw Three Ships
BW-v3-D 21 '69-p8
CCB-B-v23-N '69-p44
CLW-v41-N '69-p198
CSM-v61-N 6 '69-pB8
Comw-v91-N 21 '69-p252
HB-v45-D '69-p661
KR-v37-O 1 '69-p1063
LJ-v94-O 15 '69-p3851
PW-v196-S 22 '69-p85
SR-v52-D 20 '69-p29
Spec-v223-N 1 '69-p606
TES-D 14 '79-p21
TLS-D 4 '69-p1389
The Joy Of The Snow
BL-v70-Je 1 '74-p1076
BL-v70-Je 1 '74-p1099
BS-v34-Jl 15 '74-p185
HB-v50-D '74-p710
KR-v42-My 1 '74-p516
LJ-v99-Jl '74-p1802
NS-v88-S 27 '74-p429
Obs-S 8 '74-p26
PW-v205-Ap 29 '74-p47
Linnets And Valerians
BL-v61-F 15 '65-p578
CCB-B-v18-Ja '65-p74
CLW-v36-Ja '65-p337
GT-v82-Ap '65-p20
NYTBR-v70-Ja 31 '65-p26
Par-v41-F '66-p123
Rp B Bk R-v27-#1 '82-p21
SR-v48-Ja 23 '65-p52
TLS-Ap 6 '73-p381

* * *

GOUGH, Irene
The Golden Lamb
CCB-B-v22-F '69-p94
TLS-N 24 '66-p1091

* * *

GOULD, Ann
The Young Visitor's V & A
Brit Bk N-Ja '80-p8
Brit Bk N C-Autumn '82-p10
TES-S 22 '78-p94

* * *

GOULD, Gill
Animals In Danger
JB-v45-Je '81-p114
Animals In Danger: Asia
BL-v79-Ja 15 '83-p672
Animals In Danger: Europe
BL-v79-Ja 15 '83-p672
Animals In Danger: Forests Of Africa
BL-v79-Ja 15 '83-p672
Animals In Danger: North America
BL-v79-Ja 15 '83-p672
Animals In Danger: The Seas
BL-v79-Ja 15 '83-p672

* * *

GOULD, Joan
Otherborn
CBRS-v9-O '80-p18
CCB-B-v34-N '80-p53
HB-v57-Ap '81-p190
S Fict R-v10-Ag '81-p49
SLJ-v27-S '80-p71

* * *

GOULD, Laurence J
Think About It
HB-v46-Ag '70-p406
LJ-v93-N 15 '68-p4404
PW-v194-Jl 1 '68-p55
Teacher-v86-Ja '69-p138

* * *

GOULD, Lilian
Jeremy And The Gorillas
BB-v5-Ag '77-p3
KR-v45-Mr 1 '77-p223
LA-v55-Ja '78-p48
SLJ-v23-My '77-p61
Our Living Past
CCB-B-v22-Je '69-p158
KR-v37-Ap 15 '69-p461
LJ-v95-Ja 15 '70-p252
SB-v5-S '69-p146

* * *

GOULD, Marilyn
Golden Daffodils
BL-v79-Mr 15 '83-p969
SLJ-v29-Ap '83-p114
Playground Sports
BL-v75-Ap 1 '79-p1223
KR-v47-Ja 15 '79-p68
SLJ-v25-Mr '79-p139
Skateboards, Scooterboards, And Seatboards You Can Make
BL-v73-Je 15 '77-p1575
KR-v45-Ap 15 '77-p430
SLJ-v24-S '77-p128

* * *

GOULD, Toni
Spotlight On Phonics
Cur R-v21-F '82-p47

* * *

GOULDEN, Shirley
The Royal Book Of Ballet
AB-v54-N 18 '74-p2168
CCB-B-v18-Jl '65-p161
Comw-v82-My 28 '65-p333
LJ-v98-O 15 '73-p3123
NYTBR-v70-My 9 '65-p36
Teacher-v95-D '77-p29

* * *

GOUNAUD, Karen J
A Very Mice Joke Book
BL-v77-Ap 1 '81-p1099
HB-v57-Ag '81-p445
KR-v49-My 1 '81-p573
NYTBR-v86-Ap 26 '81-p51
PW-v219-Ap 10 '81-p71
RT-v36-O '82-p79
SLJ-v27-Ap '81-p112

* * *

GOURDIE, Tom
Handwriting
GP-v16-N '77-p3212

* * *

GOVAN, Christine
Phinny's Fine Summer
CLW-v40-Ap '69-p526
HB-v45-Ap '69-p171
LJ-v94-F 15 '69-p872

* * *

GOVERN, Elaine
Ice Cream Next Summer
CCB-B-v27-Ja '74-p79
LJ-v99-Mr 15 '74-p881
NYTBR-D 9 '73-p8
PW-v204-S 24 '73-p188

* * *

GOWANS, Elizabeth
The Stravaigers
Obs-Ag 26 '84-p19

* * *

GOWAR, Mick
Swings And Roundabouts
JB-v45-O '81-p196
Punch-v281-D 2 '81-p1024
Sch Lib-v29-S '81-p246
TES-Je 5 '81-p35

* * *

GOYDER, Alice
Christmas In Catland
BW-v9-D 2 '79-p17
CBRS-v8-O '79-p11
CCB-B-v33-D '79-p70
JB-v42-D '78-p294
Obs-D 3 '78-p36
SLJ-v26-O '79-p117
TLS-D 1 '78-p1397
Holiday In Catland
BW-v9-D 2 '79-p17
CBRS-v8-O '79-p11
Obs-D 3 '78-p36
SLJ-v26-N '79-p65
TLS-D 1 '78-p1397
Party In Catland
BW-v9-D 2 '79-p17
CBRS-v8-O '79-p11
Obs-D 3 '78-p36
SLJ-v26-N '79-p65
TLS-D 1 '78-p1397

* * *

GOYTISOLO, Jose A
El Lobito Bueno
SLJ-v30-My '84-p35

* * *

GRABER, Richard
Black Cow Summer
BL-v77-S 1 '80-p40
BS-v40-Ja '81-p352
CCB-B-v34-Ja '81-p93
EJ-v70-Ap '81-p78
KR-v48-O 15 '80-p1359
NYTBR-v86-F 22 '81-p31
SLJ-v27-Ja '81-p69
A Little Breathing Room
BB-v6-O '78-p4
BL-v74-Ap 15 '78-p1349
CCB-B-v32-N '78-p43
HB-v54-Je '78-p283
KR-v46-Je 1 '78-p598
SLJ-v25-S '78-p157
Pay Your Respects
BS-v39-D '79-p353
CBRS-v8-S '79-p7
CCB-B-v33-F '80-p109
HB-v56-F '80-p62
KR-v47-O 1 '79-p1150
NYTBR-v86-Ag 30 '81-p27
SLJ-v26-Ja '80-p78
VOYA-v4-Je '81-p50

* * *

GRABIANSKI, Janusz
Androcles And The Lion
BL-v67-S 15 '70-p99
CCB-B-v24-S '70-p8
CSM-v62-Jl 18 '70-p13
LJ-v95-Jl '70-p2527
NYTBR-Je 21 '70-p22
PW-v197-Mr 30 '70-p64
Grabianski's Birds
BL-v65-O 1 '68-p186
CCB-B-v22-O '68-p27
KR-v36-Ag 1 '68-p812
LJ-v93-O 15 '68-p3970
PW-v194-Ag 5 '68-p56

* * *

GRACE, Fran
Branigan's Dog
BL-v78-D 15 '81-p545
CBRS-v10-D '81-p38
CCB-B-v35-Mr '82-p128
SLJ-v28-Ja '82-p87
VOYA-v4-F '82-p32
A Very Private Performance
BL-v80-N 1 '83-p403
B Rpt-v2-Ja '84-p34
CBRS-v12-D '83-p41
CCB-B-v37-F '84-p108
SLJ-v30-F '84-p81
VOYA-v6-F '84-p338

* * *

GRACE, Patricia
The Kuia And The Spider
RT-v36-Ja '83-p469
Sch Lib-v31-D '83-p343
TES-My 27 '83-p29

* * *

GRAEBER, Charlotte
Mustard
BL-v78-Jl '82-p1444
CBRS-v10-Spring '82-p113
HB-v58-Ag '82-p402
HB-v60-F '84-p83

GRAEBER, Charlotte
(continued)
LA-v60-Ap '83-p503
PW-v221-Ap 16 '82-p70
SLJ-v28-Ag '82-p116

* * *

GRAEBER, Charlotte T
Grey Cloud
BB-v7-D '79-p4
BL-v76-D 1 '79-p557
KR-v48-F 15 '80-p216
RT-v33-My '80-p974
SLJ-v26-Ja '80-p70

* * *

GRAESCH, Heinz
Wooden Toys
BL-v80-Ja 15 '84-p710
B Rpt-v3-S '84-p40

* * *

GRAF, Rudolf F
How It Works
BL-v70-Jl 15 '74-p1220
JB-v40-F '76-p43

* * *

GRAFENAUER, Niko
Lokomotiva, Lokomotiva
BL-v79-D 15 '82-p570

* * *

GRAFF, Stewart
The Story Of World War II
BL-v74-My 15 '78-p1492
CE-v55-Ap '79-p300
Comw-v105-N 10 '78-p734
KR-v46-Ja 15 '78-p49
SLJ-v24-Mr '78-p128

* * *

GRAFTON, Carol Belanger
Optical Designs In Motion
SA-v235-D '76-p142
VV-v21-D 13 '76-p78

* * *

GRAHAM, Ada
Alligators
ACSB-v13-Mr '80-p25
BL-v76-O 1 '79-p275
KR-v48-Ja 1 '80-p7
SB-v16-N '80-p94
Audubon Readers
Par-v53-S '78-p32
Birds In Our World
BL-v71-F 15 '75-p618
Birds Of The Northern Seas
Inst-v91-Ap '82-p22
SB-v17-S '81-p33
SLJ-v27-Mr '81-p144
Bug Hunters
ACSB-v12-Fall '79-p24
BL-v74-Jl 15 '78-p1733
CSM-v70-N 13 '78-pB11
KR-v46-Jl 1 '78-p692
LA-v56-F '79-p188
SB-v15-S '79-p101
SLJ-v25-Ja '79-p53
WLB-v53-F '79-p464
Busy Bugs
ASBYP-v16-Fall '83-p27
BL-v79-Je 15 '83-p1338
CCB-B-v36-My '83-p167
Inst-v92-My '83-p93
NY-v59-D 5 '83-p206
RT-v37-D '83-p308
SB-v19-S '83-p33
SLJ-v29-My '83-p71
Careers In Conservation
BL-v76-My 15 '80-p1364
BS-v40-Je '80-p117
CCB-B-v34-S '80-p9
Cur R-v20-Ja '81-p28
J Read-v24-D '80-p273
KR-v48-Ap 1 '80-p444
SB-v16-Ja '81-p124
SLJ-v27-N '80-p74
The Careless Animal
ACSB-v10-Fall '77-p3
CCB-B-v28-Jl '75-p176
KR-v43-Mr 1 '75-p242
SLJ-v22-S '75-p102
Teacher-v92-My '75-p28
Changes Everywhere
BL-v71-F 15 '75-p618
The Changing Desert
ASBYP-v15-Spring '82-p38
BL-v78-F 1 '82-p706
BL-v80-My 15 '84-p1352
CBRS-v10-Mr '82-p77
CCB-B-v35-Je '82-p188
CE-v58-My '82-p330
CSM-v74-D 14 '81-pB11
Cur R-v22-F '83-p91
HB-v58-F '82-p78
KR-v50-Ja 15 '82-p69
SB-v17-My '82-p269
SLJ-v28-Ap '82-p81
Coyote Song
ACSB-v12-Fall '79-p24
BL-v75-Ja 1 '79-p750
CSM-v70-N 13 '78-pB11
KR-v47-Ja 15 '79-p69
SB-v15-Mr '80-p226
SLJ-v25-Ap '79-p56
WLB-v53-F '79-p464
Dooryard Garden
BL-v70-Jl 1 '74-p1199
BW-Je 9 '74-p4
CCB-B-v28-O '74-p27
CE-v51-Ja '75-p159
CSM-v66-Jl 3 '74-p7
KR-v42-Je 1 '74-p583
LJ-v99-N 15 '74-p3045
PW-v205-Je 17 '74-p69
SB-v10-D '74-p254
Falcon Flight
ACSB-v12-Fall '79-p25
BL-v75-Ja 1 '79-p750
CSM-v70-N 13 '78-pB11
Inst-v88-My '79-p114
KR-v47-Ja 15 '79-p69
SB-v15-Mr '80-p226
SLJ-v25-Ap '79-p56
WLB-v53-F '79-p464
The Floor Of The Forest
BL-v71-F 15 '75-p618
Foxtails, Ferns, And Fish Scales
BB-v5-Mr '77-p3
HB-v53-Ap '77-p172
Inst-v86-My '77-p122
KR-v44-N 1 '76-p1171
SLJ-v23-O '76-p106
The Great American Shopping Cart
CCB-B-v23-S '69-p9
KR-v37-Je 1 '69-p597
LJ-v94-N 15 '69-p4286
LJ-v96-O 15 '71-p3435
Jacob And Owl
BL-v78-Mr 15 '82-p957
CCB-B-v35-My '82-p169
CLW-v54-D '82-p224
HB-v58-Ap '82-p163
LA-v60-F '83-p214
PW-v220-N 27 '81-p87
SLJ-v28-Mr '82-p147
Let's Discover Birds In Our World
SB-v11-My '75-p34
SLJ-v21-Mr '75-p87
Let's Discover Changes Everywhere
SB-v11-My '75-p34
SLJ-v21-Mr '75-p87
Let's Discover The Floor Of The Forest
SB-v11-My '75-p34
SLJ-v21-Mr '75-p87

GRAHAM, Ada (continued)
Let's Discover Winter Woods
BL-v71-F 15 '75-p618
SB-v11-My '75-p34
SLJ-v21-Mr '75-p87
The Milkweed And Its World Of Animals
ACSB-v10-Winter '77-p19
BL-v73-N 1 '76-p408
CCB-B-v30-N '76-p41
KR-v44-Je 1 '76-p637
LA-v54-Ap '77-p436
SA-v235-D '76-p139
SLJ-v22-Ap '76-p86
Six Little Chickadees
ASBYP-v16-Fall '83-p28
Inst-v92-Mr '83-p19
KR-v50-N 15 '82-p1238
SLJ-v29-F '83-p76
Three Million Mice
BL-v78-Mr 1 '82-p897
CCB-B-v35-Ap '82-p148
CE-v59-Mr '83-p281
Cur R-v22-O '83-p22
SB-v18-S '82-p34
Whale Watch
ACSB-v12-Spring '79-p24
BL-v74-Jl 15 '78-p1733
CCB-B-v32-O '78-p30
CSM-v70-N 13 '78-pB11
EJ-v67-N '78-p83
KR-v46-Jl 1 '78-p692
Par-v53-S '78-p32
SB-v15-D '79-p166
SLJ-v25-Ja '79-p53
WLB-v53-F '79-p464

* * *

GRAHAM, Bob
Here Comes John
GP-v23-Jl '84-p4293
TES-My 25 '84-p27
TLS-Mr 30 '84-p338
Here Comes Theo
GP-v23-Jl '84-p4293
TES-My 25 '84-p27
TLS-Mr 30 '84-p338
Pearl's Place
GP-v22-Ja '84-p4201
Pete And Roland
Obs-Ap 11 '82-p31

* * *

GRAHAM, Brenda K
The Pattersons And The Mysterious Airplane
SLJ-v27-My '81-p84
The Pattersons At Turkey Hill House
SLJ-v26-Ap '80-p109

* * *

GRAHAM, Carolyn
The Electric Elephant And Other Stories
TES-S 30 '83-p29

* * *

GRAHAM, Gail
Cross-Fire
BL-v68-My 15 '72-p816
BW-v6-Ag 6 '72-p2
CCB-B-v25-My '72-p139
CSM-v64-My 4 '72-pB5
EJ-v63-Mr '74-p105
HB-v49-F '73-p55
Inter BC-v13-#6 '82-p19
KR-v40-Mr 1 '72-p266
KR-v40-D 15 '72-p1419
LJ-v97-My 15 '72-p1884
LJ-v97-My 15 '72-p1922
LJ-v97-D 15 '72-p4056
NYTBR-My 21 '72-p8
NYTBR, pt.2-N 5 '72-p26
PW-v201-Ap 17 '72-p59
SE-v37-D '73-p791
SR-v55-Ap 22 '72-p86
Teacher-v96-Ja '79-p64

* * *

GRAHAM, Gail B
The Beggar In The Blanket And Other Vietnamese Tales
BW-v4-My 17 '70-p14
CCB-B-v24-Ja '71-p73
CE-v47-Ja '71-p211
CLW-v42-O '70-p133
CSM-v62-My 7 '70-pB4
GT-v88-O '70-p22
KR-v38-My 1 '70-p510
LJ-v95-Jl '70-p2533
NYTBR-Je 14 '70-p22
NYTBR, pt.2-N 8 '70-p36
PW-v197-My 18 '70-p39

* * *

GRAHAM, Harriet
The Ring Of Zoraya
BL-v78-Jl '82-p1444
CCB-B-v36-N '82-p47
CSM-v74-O 8 '82-pB12
HB-v58-Je '82-p287
JB-v44-D '80-p306
Obs-N 30 '80-p36
RT-v36-D '82-p337
Sch Lib-v29-Mr '81-p50
Spec-v245-D 6 '80-p26
TLS-S 19 '80-p1025
Shiva's Pearls
GP-v15-D '76-p3019
JB-v41-F '77-p33
NS-v92-N 5 '76-p644
Obs-N 28 '76-p31
TLS-D 10 '76-p1552
The Street That Disappeared
JB-v41-F '77-p33
TLS-Mr 25 '77-p361
Thomas And The Rag Man's Coat
GP-v14-S '75-p2685
GP-v21-Mr '83-p4053

* * *

GRAHAM, Ian
Computer
BL-v80-Ja 1 '84-p681
BL-v80-F 1 '84-p813
Cur R-v24-N '84-p79
SLJ-v30-Ja '84-p76
Sch Lib-v31-D '83-p367
TES-N 11 '83-p26

* * *

GRAHAM, John
I Love You, Mouse
BL-v73-N 15 '76-p472
CCB-B-v30-Je '77-p158
CSM-v70-O 23 '78-pB2
GP-v16-Jl '77-p3150
HB-v53-F '77-p44
KR-v44-S 15 '76-p1035
PW-v210-Ag 23 '76-p75
SLJ-v23-N '76-p46
WCRB-v3-Mr '77-p47

* * *

GRAHAM, Lorenz
David He No Fear
BL-v68-D 15 '71-p366
CCB-B-v25-D '71-p56
CE-v48-Ja '72-p205
Comw-v95-N 19 '71-p185
HB-v47-D '71-p603
KR-v39-S 1 '71-p941
LA-v57-Ap '80-p416
LJ-v96-N 15 '71-p3900
Life-v71-D 17 '71-p50
PW-v200-N 8 '71-p49
Every Man Heart Lay Down
BL-v67-N 1 '70-p227
BW-v4-D 20 '70-p8
CCB-B-v24-N '70-p42
CE-v48-O '71-p29

GRAHAM, Lorenz (continued)
CLW-v42-D '70-p256
Comw-v93-N 20 '70-p198
GT-v88-D '70-p82
HB-v46-D '70-p603
LA-v57-Ap '80-p416
LJ-v95-O 15 '70-p3647
PW-v198-Ag 24 '70-p64
SR-v53-D 19 '70-p31
God Wash The World And Start Again
BL-v67-Je 15 '71-p871
CE-v48-O '71-p29
CSM-v63-My 6 '71-pB4
Comw-v94-My 21 '71-p264
KR-v39-Ap 15 '71-p431
LA-v57-Ap '80-p416
LJ-v96-Jl '71-p2374
PW-v199-My 3 '71-p56
TN-v35-Summer '79-p401
TN-v40-Fall '83-p58
Hongry Catch The Foolish Boy
BL-v69-Jl 15 '73-p1073
CCB-B-v26-My '73-p138
Comw-v99-N 23 '73-p212
HB-v49-Ag '73-p369
Inst-v82-My '73-p75
KR-v41-F 15 '73-p185
LJ-v98-S 15 '73-p2639
PW-v203-Mr 19 '73-p72
I, Momolu
BL-v63-N 15 '66-p376
CCB-B-v21-S '67-p6
EJ-v56-F '67-p314
HB-v43-F '67-p71
KR-v34-Ag 15 '66-p834
LJ-v91-O 15 '66-p5229
John Brown: A Cry For Freedom
BL-v77-F 15 '81-p809
BS-v40-F '81-p415
Inter BC-v12-#3 '81-p18
KR-v48-N 15 '80-p1470
LA-v58-My '81-p594
SLJ-v27-Ja '81-p60
North Town
BL-v61-My 15 '65-p914
BS-v25-My 15 '65-p98
CCB-B-v18-My '65-p129
CSM-v57-My 6 '65-p6B
KR-v33-Mr 1 '65-p249
Kliatt-v12-Winter '78-p7
LJ-v90-My 15 '65-p2418
NYTBR-v70-Ap 4 '65-p22
Return To South Town
BB-v4-Ja '77-p2
BL-v73-Mr 1 '77-p1013
CCB-B-v30-N '76-p42
KR-v44-Jl 1 '76-p738
PW-v209-Je 28 '76-p99
SLJ-v23-S '76-p133
A Road Down In The Sea
BL-v67-Ap 1 '71-p663
BW-v5-My 9 '71-p6
CCB-B-v24-My '71-p135
CE-v48-O '71-p29
Comw-v94-My 21 '71-p264
HB-v47-Ap '71-p160
KR-v39-Ja 15 '71-p50
LA-v57-Ap '80-p416
LJ-v96-Ap 15 '71-p1493
NY-v47-D 4 '71-p188
NYTBR-Ag 22 '71-p8
PW-v199-Ja 25 '71-p261
SR-v54-Mr 20 '71-p30
Song Of The Boat
BL-v72-O 15 '75-p302
CCB-B-v29-My '76-p144
CE-v53-N '76-p96
CSM-v67-N 5 '75-pB5
HB-v51-D '75-p584
KR-v43-O 15 '75-p1179
SLJ-v22-N '75-p62
Whose Town?
BL-v65-Jl 1 '69-p1226
BW-v3-My 4 '69-p3
CCB-B-v22-Je '69-p158
HB-v45-Ag '69-p416
KR-v37-Ap 15 '69-p452
LJ-v94-Je 15 '69-p2509
SR-v52-My 10 '69-p59

* * *

GRAHAM, Margaret Bloy
Be Nice To Spiders
BL-v64-O 1 '67-p197
BW-v1-N 5 '67-p7
CCB-B-v21-Mr '68-p109
CLW-v39-F '68-p440
CSM-v59-N 2 '67-pB4
HB-v43-O '67-p581
KR-v35-Jl 1 '67-p734
LJ-v92-D 15 '67-p4602
NYTBR-v72-N 5 '67-p70
SB-v3-Mr '68-p320
Teacher-v94-My '77-p110
Benjy And The Barking Bird
BL-v67-Je 1 '71-p834
CCB-B-v24-Jl '71-p170
CSM-v63-My 6 '71-pB3
HB-v47-Ap '71-p157
KR-v39-Mr 1 '71-p230
LJ-v96-My 15 '71-p1796
SR-v54-Ap 17 '71-p44
TLS-Jl 14 '72-p808
Benjy's Boat Trip
BL-v74-N 1 '77-p476
CCB-B-v31-Ap '78-p126
CLW-v49-Ap '78-p403
Comw-v104-N 11 '77-p728
HB-v54-F '78-p34
KR-v45-S 15 '77-p985
PW-v212-O 10 '77-p71
SLJ-v24-N '77-p47
Benjy's Dog House
BL-v70-D 1 '73-p386
CCB-B-v27-F '74-p94
HB-v49-D '73-p586
KR-v41-S 1 '73-p962
LJ-v99-F 15 '74-p562
PW-v204-S 3 '73-p53
SR/W-v1-D 4 '73-p30
TLS-Jl 5 '74-p718

* * *

GRAHAM, Robin Lee
The Boy Who Sailed Around The World Alone
CCB-B-v27-Je '74-p156
CSM-v65-N 7 '73-pB7
CSM-v67-Je 10 '75-p16
KR-v41-D 15 '70-p1366
LJ-v99-S 15 '74-p2268
PW-v205-Ja 28 '74-p301

* * *

GRAHAM, Shirley
Julius K. Nyerere, Teacher Of Africa
BS-v35-My '75-p51
SLJ-v22-S '75-p120

* * *

GRAHAM, Tony
The Giraffe
SLJ-v30-Mr '84-p138
The Zebra
SLJ-v30-Mr '84-p138

* * *

GRAHAM, Violet
The Ecology Of Rain Forests
GP-v15-S '76-p2950
JB-v40-Ag '76-p199
TES-F 10 '78-p25

* * *

GRAHAM, Winston
Walking Stick
B&B-v12-My '67-p32

GRAHAME, Kenneth (continued)
NY-v56-D 1 '80-p214
PW-v218-Ag 15 '80-p55
SLJ-v27-N '80-p74
Sch Lib-v29-Je '81-p133
Spec-v245-D 6 '80-p26
TES-Ja 14 '83-p30
The Wind In The Willows (Hargreaves)
GP-v21-Ja '83-p4000
JB-v47-Je '83-p114
Punch-v284-Ja 19 '83-p59
TES-Ja 14 '83-p30
The Wind In The Willows (Mendoza)
JB-v47-Ap '83-p74
Sch Lib-v31-Je '83-p146
TES-Ja 14 '83-p30
The Wind In The Willows (Shepard)
BL-v80-Ja 1 '84-p680
BW-v13-O 9 '83-p10
NY-v59-D 5 '83-p201
NYTBR-v88-N 13 '83-p41
Punch-v286-Mr 21 '84-p16
TES-Ja 14 '83-p30
The Wind In The Willows (Shephard)
TES-N 20 '81-p32
The Wind In The Willows (Worlds Classics)
BW-v13-Ap 10 '83-p12
TES-Ja 14 '83-p30
TLS-N 26 '82-p1299

* * *

GRAICHEN, Ingrid
Struppi
SLJ-v30-My '84-p62

* * *

GRAINGER, Sylvia
Leatherwork
BB-v5-F '77-p4
BL-v73-N 15 '76-p466
BL-v73-N 15 '76-p472
Des-v78-Winter '76-p29
JB-v43-Je '79-p166
SLJ-v23-D '76-p60

* * *

GRAMATKY, Hardie
Happy's Christmas
CCB-B-v24-N '70-p42
CLW-v42-O '70-p136
CSM-v63-D 12 '70-p17
Comw-v93-N 20 '70-p198
KR-v38-Ag 15 '70-p867
LJ-v95-O 15 '70-p3644
PW-v198-Ag 24 '70-p63
SR-v53-D 19 '70-p31
Hercules
Inst-v90-Ja '81-p109
NYTBR-v85-Ap 6 '80-p27
Little Toot
Teacher-v96-My '79-p117
Little Toot On The Mississippi
CCB-B-v27-D '73-p64
CLW-v45-Ap '74-p457
CSM-v66-My 1 '74-pF2
HB-v49-O '73-p456
Inst-v83-My '74-p94
JB-v39-F '75-p21
KR-v41-Jl 1 '73-p681
LJ-v98-O 15 '73-p3138
NYTBR-N 4 '73-p60
PW-v203-Je 11 '73-p153
Little Toot Through The Golden Gate
CE-v52-Mr '76-p268
JB-v41-Je '77-p154
JB-v41-O '77-p277
KR-v43-S 1 '75-p993
PW-v208-S 8 '75-p60
SLJ-v22-O '75-p90

* * *

GRAMET, Charles
Sound And Hearing
BL-v62-N 15 '65-p330
CCB-B-v19-N '65-p44
KR-v33-Ap 15 '65-p439
LJ-v90-S 15 '65-p3804

* * *

GRAN Libro De Los Animales
BL-v78-S 1 '81-p39

* * *

GRANBERG, W J
The World Of Joseph Pulitzer
BS-v25-Ag 15 '65-p215
CCB-B-v19-N '65-p44
KR-v33-Ap 15 '65-p437
LJ-v90-O 15 '65-p4629

* * *

GRANDES Rios De Africa
BL-v72-My 15 '76-p1343

* * *

GRANGER, Colin
Play Games With English. Bk. 1
TES-N 21 '80-p37
Play Games With English. Bk. 2
TES-Ag 14 '81-p22

* * *

GRANGER, Judith
Amazing World Of Dinosaurs
ASBYP-v15-Fall '82-p59
BL-v78-Jl '82-p1441
SLJ-v29-O '82-p137

* * *

GRANJA Del Abuelo
BL-v79-O 1 '82-p200

* * *

GRANNAN, Mary E
More Just Mary Stories
Atl Pro Bk R-v10-N '83-p19
Quill & Q-v47-N '81-p26

* * *

GRANT, Anne
Danbury's Burning!
BL-v73-F 15 '77-p896
CCB-B-v30-Ap '77-p123
KR-v44-N 15 '76-p1219
RT-v31-O '77-p15
SLJ-v23-Mr '77-p132

* * *

GRANT, Cynthia D
Big Time
BL-v78-Ap 1 '82-p1018
CBRS-v10-Jl '82-p127
SLJ-v28-Ap '82-p82
Hard Love
BL-v79-Ag '83-p1457
CBRS-v12-Ja '84-p52
CCB-B-v37-D '83-p67
SLJ-v30-O '83-p168
Joshua Fortune
BL-v77-Ja 1 '81-p624
CBRS-v9-Ja '81-p37
CCB-B-v34-Ja '81-p93
HB-v56-D '80-p641
KR-v48-O 1 '80-p1302
SLJ-v27-N '80-p85
VOYA-v4-Ap '81-p34
Summer Home
BL-v78-O 1 '81-p236
CBRS-v10-Mr '82-p77
CCB-B-v35-Ap '82-p148
SLJ-v28-S '81-p125
VOYA-v5-Ap '82-p34

* * *

GRAVES, Charles
Eleanor Roosevelt: First Lady Of The Land
SE-v48-N '84-p543
Eleanor Roosevelt: First Lady Of The World
CCB-B-v20-S '66-p10

* * *

GRAVES, Charles P
Matthew A. Henson
CCB-B-v25-F '72-p91
Comw-v94-My 21 '71-p267
KR-v39-Ap 1 '71-p372
LJ-v96-My 15 '71-p1819

* * *

GRAVES, Clay
Hurry Up, Christmas!
SLJ-v23-O '76-p87

* * *

GRAVES, Eleanor
The Cats
SB-v12-D '76-p161
TES-F 29 '80-p27

* * *

GRAVES, Jack A
What Is A California Sea Otter?
RT-v34-N '80-p236

* * *

GRAVES, Richard
The Victorian Christmas Song
Spec-v245-D 6 '80-p26

* * *

GRAVES, Robert
An Ancient Castle
BL-v78-Ag '82-p1524
BS-v41-F '82-p441
Brit Bk N C-Spring '81-p23
CCB-B-v36-S '82-p9
Econ-v277-D 27 '80-p77
JB-v45-Je '81-p114
KR-v50-My 15 '82-p604
Lis-v104-N 6 '80-p625
PW-v221-My 21 '82-p77
SLJ-v29-S '82-p121
TES-N 21 '80-p32
TLS-N 21 '80-p1326
Ann At Highwood Hall: Poems For Children
CCB-B-v20-S '66-p10
HB-v42-Je '66-p319
LJ-v91-Ap 15 '66-p2210
NO-v5-Jl 4 '66-p17
NY-v42-D 17 '66-p233
NYTBR-v71-My 8 '66-p36
TCR-v67-My '66-p640
The Big Green Book
CE-v45-Mr '69-p410
JB-v43-O '79-p272
NS-v95-My 19 '78-p682
Obs-Jl 23 '78-p21
Greek Gods And Heroes
BW-v10-F 3 '80-p13
Two Wise Children
CCB-B-v20-Ap '67-p121
LJ-v92-Ja 15 '67-p328
Lis-v78-N 16 '67-p643
NYRB-v7-D 15 '66-p28
Punch-v253-N 29 '67-p834
TLS-D 14 '67-p1225

* * *

GRAY, Bettyanne
Manya's Story
BS-v38-Jl '78-p117
LA-v55-S '78-p738
PW-v213-Mr 6 '78-p96
SLJ-v25-N '78-p73

* * *

GRAY, Catherine
Tammy And The Gigantic Fish
BL-v79-Mr 15 '83-p970
CBRS-v11-Je '83-p108
CCB-B-v36-Jl '83-p210
KR-v51-F 1 '83-p117
LATBR-Ap 3 '83-p8
SLJ-v29-Ap '83-p101

* * *

GRAY, Chris
Countryside In Danger
GP-v21-Mr '83-p4044
JB-v47-F '83-p25
TES-N 5 '82-p30

* * *

GRAY, Dulcie
Butterflies On My Mind
Obs-D 3 '78-p36
TES-O 20 '78-p37
TES-N 3 '78-p22

* * *

GRAY, Genevieve
Alaska Woman
SLJ-v24-My '78-p67
Blessingway
Cur R-v15-D '76-p310
The Dark Side Of Nowhere
Inter BC-v13-#4 '82-p28
Inter BC-v14-#1 '83-p16
SLJ-v24-My '78-p67
Ghost Story
BL-v71-Mr 1 '75-p690
CCB-B-v28-Jl '75-p177
KR-v43-F 1 '75-p122
NYTBR-My 4 '75-p41
SLJ-v21-Ap '75-p52
Has Anyone Seen Buddy Bascom?
SLJ-v24-My '78-p67
How Far, Felipe?
CCB-B-v31-Jl '78-p176
CLW-v50-F '79-p312
J Read-v24-Ja '81-p297
KR-v46-Mr 1 '78-p242
LA-v56-Ja '79-p49
NYTBR-Ap 30 '78-p38
SLJ-v24-My '78-p80
Keep An Eye On Kevin
CCB-B-v27-N '73-p43
KR-v41-Ja 15 '73-p58
LJ-v98-Ap 15 '73-p1375
PW-v203-F 19 '73-p79
A Kite For Bennie
BW-v6-My 7 '72-p10
CCB-B-v25-Jl '72-p169
KR-v40-Je 1 '72-p619
LJ-v97-S 15 '72-p2950
The Magic Bears
BL-v72-Je 15 '76-p1470
SLJ-v23-S '76-p116
The Secret Of The Mask
BL-v72-Je 15 '76-p1470
SLJ-v23-S '76-p116
Send Wendell
CCB-B-v28-S '74-p8
CSM-v67-Je 30 '75-p23
HB-v50-O '74-p129
KR-v42-My 1 '74-p474
LA-v52-S '75-p854
LJ-v99-S 15 '74-p2247
PW-v205-Ap 8 '74-p83
The Seven Wishes Of Joanna Peabody
BL-v69-Ja 15 '73-p493
CCB-B-v26-Je '73-p154
KR-v40-Ag 15 '72-p939
LJ-v97-N 15 '72-p3806
NYTBR, pt.2-N 5 '72-p16
PW-v202-S 4 '72-p50
Sore Loser
CCB-B-v28-Ja '75-p78
CE-v51-F '75-p216

GRAY, Genevieve (continued)
CE-v51-Mr '75-p274
CSM-v66-N 6 '74-p10
HB-v50-D '74-p692
KR-v42-My 15 '74-p535
LJ-v99-S 15 '74-p2268
The Spiderweb Stone
BL-v72-Je 15 '76-p1470
SLJ-v23-S '76-p116
Tall Singer
BL-v72-Je 15 '76-p1470
SLJ-v23-S '76-p116
Two Tickets To Memphis
SLJ-v24-My '78-p67
Varnell Roberts, Super-Pigeon
Cur R-v16-My '77-p125
KR-v43-Ag 15 '75-p916
SLJ-v22-Ja '76-p46

* * *

GRAY, J E B
Indian Tales And Legends
Sch Lib-v27-D '79-p370

* * *

GRAY, J M L
My Melody's Good-Night Book
PW-v222-Jl 30 '82-p77
SLJ-v29-Mr '83-p165

* * *

GRAY, James H
Boomtime
BIC-v9-F '80-p22
In Rev-v14-Ap '80-p42

* * *

GRAY, Jennifer
Better Diving
JB-v46-Ap '82-p72

* * *

GRAY, Lee Learner
How We Choose A President
BL-v69-S 1 '72-p46
BL-v69-S 15 '72-p86
BL-v73-Je 1 '77-p1496
BL-v77-N 1 '80-p404
CCB-B-v21-My '68-p141
CE-v45-My '69-p534
CLW-v40-O '68-p145
CSM-v60-My 2 '68-pB6
Kliatt-v11-Winter '77-p19
LJ-v93-My 15 '68-p2130
LJ-v97-O 15 '72-p3460
NYTBR-v73-My 5 '68-p4
SR-v51-Ap 20 '68-p41

* * *

GRAY, Martin
For Those I Loved
Am-v127-O 7 '72-p267
Am-v128-F 10 '73-p122
Atl-v231-Ja '73-p99
B&B-v19-Ap '74-p96
BL-v69-Ap 1 '73-p739
BL-v69-Ap 15 '73-p807
BS-v32-D 15 '72-p430
BW-v6-N 12 '72-p9
GW-v108-Ap 7 '73-p24
HB-v49-Ap '73-p169
KR-v40-S 1 '72-p1062
LJ-v97-N 1 '72-p3577
Lis-v89-My 3 '73-p590
NS-v98-N 2 '79-p673
NY-v48-D 30 '72-p72
PW-v202-O 16 '72-p47
SR-v1-N 21 '72-p62
SR-v55-D 2 '72-p79
SR-v55-D 23 '72-p69
TLS-Ap 13 '73-p417

* * *

GRAY, Mary A
The Truth About Fathers
BL-v79-S 15 '82-p113
CBRS-v10-Ag '82-p138
CCB-B-v36-D '82-p67
EJ-v71-D '82-p66
New Age-v8-D '82-p68
PW-v221-Je 18 '82-p74
SLJ-v29-O '82-p160
VOYA-v5-O '82-p42

* * *

GRAY, Nicholas Stuart
The Apple Stone
BL-v66-N 15 '69-p408
BS-v29-O 1 '69-p254
CCB-B-v23-Ap '70-p128
CSM-v61-N 6 '69-pB5
KR-v37-Ag 1 '69-p777
LJ-v94-D 15 '69-p4582
LJ-v94-D 15 '69-p4606
NO-v8-N 3 '69-p20
Obs-D 12 '65-p28
TLS-D 9 '65-p1130
The Edge Of Evening
GP-v15-My '76-p2896
JB-v40-Je '76-p152
Obs-Jl 11 '76-p23
TLS-Ap 2 '76-p383
Grimbold's Other World
BL-v64-Je 15 '68-p1185
BW-Mr 11 '79-pF2
KR-v36-F 1 '68-p114
Obs-D 10 '78-p38
Mainly In Moonlight
B&B-v25-N '79-p58
BS-v27-Je 1 '67-p105
HB-v43-Ag '67-p462
KR-v35-F 15 '67-p207
LJ-v92-Je 15 '67-p2449
LR-v20-Winter '65-p270
NS-v70-N 12 '65-p748
Obs-Jl 13 '80-p29
SLJ-v26-F '80-p55
TES-My 2 '80-p24
TLS-D 9 '65-p1130
The Wardens Of The Weir
JB-v43-Ap '79-p116
Obs-D 10 '78-p38
A Wind From Nowhere
HB-v56-F '80-p55
JB-v42-D '78-p311
Obs-Jl 23 '78-p21
SLJ-v26-D '79-p85
TES-N 3 '78-p25
TLS-Jl 7 '78-p769

* * *

GRAY, Nigel
The Deserter
AB-v60-N 14 '77-p2820
BL-v74-Ja 1 '78-p747
CCB-B-v31-F '78-p92
CE-v54-Mr '78-p258
JB-v43-O '79-p278
KR-v45-O 1 '77-p1049
SLJ-v24-O '77-p111
It'll All Come Out In The Wash
CBRS-v8-S '79-p2
CCB-B-v33-F '80-p109
KR-v47-O 1 '79-p1141
SLJ-v26-O '79-p140

* * *

GRAY, Noel
Looking At China
GP-v13-Ap '75-p2608
SLJ-v21-Ap '75-p52
SLJ-v22-Ja '76-p24

* * *

GRAY, Patricia
Come Back, Stork!
GP-v19-Jl '80-p3737
Creatures That Help Each Other
GP-v14-My '75-p2650
Creatures With Pockets
JB-v43-Ap '79-p106

GRAY, Patricia (continued)
Flightless Birds
JB-v41-Ap '77-p93
Georgie, The Gadabout Gorilla
BL-v73-Jl 15 '77-p1732
Kwamla And The Sacred Crocodiles
BL-v73-Jl 15 '77-p1733
Swimming Mammals
GP-v14-Ap '76-p2854
JB-v40-Je '76-p152
Thatch Cat
GP-v14-Ja '76-p2789
JB-v40-F '76-p23
Two Monkey Tales
Brit Bk N C-Autumn '80-p15
Upside-Down Creatures
GP-v17-My '78-p3320

* * *

GRAY, Patsey
Barefoot A Thousand Miles
BL-v80-Mr 1 '84-p967
CBRS-v12-Mr '84-p83
CCB-B-v37-My '84-p165
SLJ-v30-My '84-p88
VOYA-v7-O '84-p196

* * *

GRAY, Peter
Plague And Fire
CCB-B-v22-Je '69-p158
KR-v36-N 1 '68-p1230
LJ-v94-Mr 15 '69-p1340
TLS-Mr 14 '68-p266

* * *

GRAY, Robert
Elephants
ACSB-v8-Spring '75-p21
The Great Apes
BL-v66-S 15 '69-p137
CCB-B-v23-S '69-p9
CLW-v41-D '69-p261
KR-v37-My 15 '69-p569
LJ-v94-N 15 '69-p4286
NYTBR-S 14 '69-p30
SB-v5-D '69-p259

* * *

GRAYSON, Fred N
Oysters
KR-v44-S 1 '76-p976
SB-v13-S '77-p96
SLJ-v23-N '76-p58

* * *

GRAYSON, Marion F
Let's Count And Count Out
SLJ-v22-F '76-p39

* * *

GREAT Americans Library For Grades 4-6
LA-v53-Ap '76-p441

* * *

GREAT Big Golden Make It & Do It Book
Cur R-v20-Ap '81-p133

* * *

GREAT Big Present Book
JB-v47-D '83-p241

* * *

GREAT Escapes
TES-Jl 16 '82-p22

* * *

GREAT Medici
Clowning Aroundfi
TES-Ap 2 '82-p27

* * *

GREAT Unsolved Mysteries
RT-v32-N '78-p229

* * *

GREAT Unsolved Mysteries Library
Cur R-v22-D '83-p20

* * *

GREAVES, Griselda
The Burning Thorn
BL-v68-Mr 15 '72-p612
CCB-B-v25-F '72-p91
KR-v39-S 15 '71-p1026
LJ-v96-D 15 '71-p4189
SR-v55-Ja 15 '72-p47
TLS-Jl 2 '71-p773

* * *

GREAVES, Jeanne R
Mr. Clutterbuck Jones
JB-v47-F '83-p25

* * *

GREAVES, Margaret
The Abbotsbury Ring
GP-v18-Jl '79-p3542
JB-v43-Ag '79-p219
Sch Lib-v27-D '79-p370
Cat's Magic
BL-v77-Mr 15 '81-p1028
Brit Bk N C-Autumn '80-p21
CBRS-v9-Mr '81-p68
CCB-B-v35-S '81-p9
CE-v58-S '81-p48
GP-v19-Jl '80-p3715
JB-v44-Ag '80-p190
KR-v49-My 15 '81-p633
LA-v59-Ja '82-p58
SLJ-v27-Ap '81-p127
TLS-Mr 28 '80-p360
VOYA-v4-Je '81-p38
Charlie, Emma And Alberic
Brit Bk N C-Autumn '80-p17
JB-v44-Ag '80-p176
Sch Lib-v28-D '80-p378
TES-Ap 27 '84-p27
TLS-Mr 28 '80-p361
Charlie, Emma And The Dragon Family
Brit Bk N C-Autumn '82-p18
GP-v21-S '82-p3965
JB-v46-Je '82-p97
Sch Lib-v30-D '82-p334
Charlie, Emma And The School Dragon
GP-My '84-p4260
JB-v48-Je '84-p127
TLS-Mr 30 '84-p337
Curfew
GP-v14-Jl '75-p2678
NS-v89-My 23 '75-p698
Obs-Mr 30 '75-p24
TLS-Ap 4 '75-p369
The Dagger And The Bird
BB-v3-N '75-p3
B&B-v17-O '71-p66
BL-v71-F 15 '75-p618
CLW-v47-D '75-p234
Econ-v241-D 18 '71-p70
HB-v51-Ap '75-p147
KR-v43-Ap 1 '75-p374
NYTBR-My 4 '75-p26
Obs-Ag 1 '71-p25
PW-v207-Ap 28 '75-p45
SLJ-v21-My '75-p70
Spec-v227-N 13 '71-p702
TLS-O 22 '71-p1320
A Net To Catch The Wind
BL-v75-My 15 '79-p1438
CBRS-v7-Ap '79-p84
CLW-v51-F '80-p309
Inst-v88-My '79-p106
KR-v47-Ap 15 '79-p451
LA-v56-O '79-p821
NYTBR-Ap 8 '79-p32
RT-v33-D '79-p358
SLJ-v26-S '79-p110

GREAVES, Margaret (continued)
The Night Of The Goat
GP-v15-N '76-p3006
JB-v41-F '77-p21
Nothing Ever Happens On Sundays
GP-v15-D '76-p3016
Stone Of Terror
BL-v71-O 1 '74-p155
BS-v34-N 15 '74-p378
CCB-B-v28-Ap '75-p130
Comw-v101-N 22 '74-p194
HB-v50-O '74-p142
KR-v42-Jl 1 '74-p687
LJ-v99-D 15 '74-p3277
NYTBR-N 10 '74-p10
PW-v206-O 14 '74-p57

* * *

GREE, Alain
Beebo And The Fizzimen
JB-v39-Je '75-p170
Beebo And The Funny Machine
JB-v39-Je '75-p170
Little Tom And Some Animal Friends
TES-Je 30 '78-p23
Little Tom Finds Out About Bees
LR-v24-Autumn '73-p126
TLS-S 28 '73-p1128
Little Tom Learns About The Environment
TES-Je 30 '78-p23
Little Tom Learns About Time
TES-Je 30 '78-p23

* * *

GREEDY, Jean
The Social Context Of Art
SF-v52-D '73-p309

* * *

GREEKS
TES-Ap 2 '82-p26

* * *

GREELEY, Andrew M
Nora Maeve And Sebi
BS-v37-My '77-p44
Crit-v35-Spring '77-p90

* * *

GREELEY, Valerie
Farm Animals
BL-v81-S 1 '84-p64
TLS-Jl 24 '81-p840
Field Animals
BL-v81-S 1 '84-p64
JB-v45-O '81-p186
TLS-Jl 24 '81-p840
Pets
BL-v81-S 1 '84-p64
PW-v226-Jl 6 '84-p64
TLS-Jl 24 '81-p840
Zoo Animals
BL-v81-S 1 '84-p64
TLS-Jl 24 '81-p840

* * *

GREEN, Alexander
Scarlet Sails
BL-v64-N 1 '67-p330
CCB-B-v22-O '68-p27
EJ-v57-My '68-p758
HB-v43-O '67-p600
KR-v35-Ap 15 '67-p506
LJ-v92-S 15 '67-p3198
NYTBR-v72-N 5 '67-p64

* * *

GREEN, Allen V
Simple Tricks
LA-v55-N '78-p960

* * *

GREEN, Andrew
The Ghostly Army
Sch Lib-v28-S '80-p256

* * *

GREEN, Anne M
Good-by, Gray Lady
CCB-B-v18-Je '65-p148
NYTBR-v70-Ja 3 '65-p18

* * *

GREEN, C
Beetle Boy
JB-v41-Je '77-p162
Polar Lands
TES-N 16 '84-p27

* * *

GREEN, Carl R
The Rattlesnake
BL-v80-Ag '84-p1622
CBRS-v12-Ag '84-p149

* * *

GREEN, Christina
The Logan Stone
GP-v17-Jl '78-p3366
The Mermaid Of Zennor
JB-v44-Je '80-p131
TES-Ja 18 '80-p40

* * *

GREEN, Christopher
Deserts
JB-v47-D '83-p243
SLJ-v30-Ag '84-p72
TES-D 2 '83-p40
Making Maps
GP-v21-N '82-p3980
JB-v47-F '83-p25
Sch Lib-v31-Je '83-p152
TES-N 5 '82-p22
TES-D 17 '82-p28

* * *

GREEN, David
Chorus
GP-v16-Ja '78-p3248
Obs-Je 26 '77-p29

* * *

GREEN, Diana H
Lonely War Of William Pinto
BL-v65-O 1 '68-p186
BS-v28-S 1 '68-p226
CCB-B-v22-S '68-p7
CSM-v60-N 7 '68-pB10
HB-v45-F '69-p59
KR-v36-Je 15 '68-p649
LJ-v93-O 15 '68-p3981
LJ-v95-O 15 '70-p3610

* * *

GREEN, Janet
The Six
GP-v15-My '76-p2890
JB-v40-D '76-p357
TLS-Jl 16 '76-p884

* * *

GREEN, Kathleen
Philip And The Pooka And Other Irish Fairy Tales
BL-v62-Ap 15 '66-p831
CCB-B-v20-O '66-p25
HB-v42-Je '66-p305
LJ-v91-Ap 15 '66-p2210
NYTBR-v71-My 8 '66-p41
PW-v189-F 28 '66-p93
SR-v49-My 14 '66-p41

* * *

GREEN, Lorne E
Sandford Fleming
In Rev-v15-Ap '81-p39

* * *

GREEN, Marion
The Last Surviving Dragon
GP-v17-Ja '79-p3436

GREEN, Marion (continued)
JB-v43-F '79-p30
The Magician Who Lived On The Mountain
CBRS-v7-Ja '79-p44
SLJ-v25-Ja '79-p42

* * *

GREEN, Mary McBurney
Whose Little Red Jacket?
CCB-B-v18-Mr '65-p102
LJ-v90-Mr 15 '65-p1542
NYTBR-v70-Mr 14 '65-p30

* * *

GREEN, Melinda
Bembelman's Bakery
BL-v74-My 15 '78-p1494
CCB-B-v31-Jl '78-p177
KR-v46-Mr 1 '78-p238
Par-v53-S '78-p32
SLJ-v25-S '78-p115
Rachel's Recital
KR-v48-Ja 15 '80-p62
PW-v216-N 19 '79-p79
SLJ-v26-D '79-p74

* * *

GREEN, Miranda
Roman Archaeology
Sch Lib-v32-Je '84-p143

* * *

GREEN, Norah
Haunting At Hampton Court
Sch Lib-v28-S '80-p256

* * *

GREEN, Norma
The Hole In The Dike
BL-v71-Mr 1 '75-p690
CCB-B-v29-S '75-p9
CE-v52-F '76-p204
CSM-v67-My 7 '75-pB4
HB-v51-Ag '75-p368
KR-v43-F 1 '75-p117
SLJ-v21-Ap '75-p45

* * *

GREEN, Phyllis
Bagdad Ate It
BL-v77-Ja 15 '81-p705
SLJ-v27-D '80-p68
Eating Ice Cream With A Werewolf
BL-v79-Ag '83-p1465
CBRS-v11-Spring '83-p124
HB-v59-Je '83-p302
SLJ-v29-Ag '83-p65
The Empty Seat
CBRS-v8-Winter '80-p68
CCB-B-v33-Je '80-p190
KR-v48-Mr 1 '80-p288
RT-v34-N '80-p237
SLJ-v26-Ja '80-p70
Gloomy Louie
CBRS-v9-Ja '81-p34
SLJ-v27-Mr '81-p144
Grandmother Orphan
CCB-B-v31-Mr '78-p111
KR-v43-Je 1 '75-p603
PW-v212-Ag 22 '77-p66
SLJ-v24-F '78-p57
Ice River
CCB-B-v29-Ja '76-p77
KR-v43-Ag 15 '75-p917
SLJ-v22-S '75-p82
Mildred Murphy, How Does Your Garden Grow?
CCB-B-v30-Je '77-p158
SLJ-v23-Ap '77-p66
Nantucket Summer
BL-v71-Mr 15 '75-p760
BW-F 9 '75-p4
CCB-B-v28-My '75-p147
KR-v42-Ag 1 '74-p809
PW-v207-Ja 20 '75-p76
SLJ-v21-Ja '75-p54
A New Mother For Martha
Inter BC-v10-Mr 30 '79-p11
SLJ-v25-F '79-p56
Nicky's Lopsided, Lumpy, But Delicious Orange
CCB-B-v32-Mr '79-p116
KR-v46-N 15 '78-p1247
SLJ-v25-N '78-p62
Uncle Roland, The Perfect Guest
CBRS-v12-N '83-p27
CSM-v76-D 5 '83-p80
KR-v51-S 1 '83-pJ148
PW-v224-O 7 '83-p94
SLJ-v30-Ap '84-p101
Walkie-Talkie
CCB-B-v31-Je '78-p159
J Read-v24-Mr '81-p522
KR-v46-Ap 15 '78-p436
SLJ-v24-My '78-p76
TN-v36-Summer '80-p365
WCRB-v4-My '78-p54
Wild Violets
KR-v45-Ap 1 '77-p350
PW-v211-My 2 '77-p70
SLJ-v23-F '77-p64

* * *

GREEN, Roger Lancelyn
C.S. Lewis: A Biography
BL-v71-Ja 1 '75-p439
BS-v36-Je '76-p80
CC-v92-Je 4 '75-p579
CSM-v67-N 26 '74-p9
Choice-v11-F '75-p1776
Choice-v12-N '75-p1121
Esq-v83-Ja '75-p22
HB-v52-O '76-p520
LJ-v100-F 1 '75-p286
Nat R-v27-Mr 14 '75-p294
New R-v171-D 21 '74-p17
Sew R-v89-Ap '81-p281
A Cavalcade Of Dragons
BL-v68-S 15 '71-p108
CSM-v63-My 6 '71-pB5
HB-v47-Je '71-p283
KR-v39-Mr 15 '71-p297
LJ-v96-Je 15 '71-p2130
PW-v199-My 3 '71-p57
A Cavalcade Of Magicians
BL-v70-N 1 '73-p291
HB-v49-O '73-p461
KR-v41-Je 15 '73-p645
LJ-v98-S 15 '73-p2664
PW-v204-Jl 23 '73-p69
Heroes Of Greece And Troy
GP-v19-My '80-p3707
TES-My 9 '80-p28
TLS-F 1 '74-p117
TLS-Jl 18 '80-p797
Old Greek Fairy Tales
LJ-v95-N 15 '70-p4044
Sch Lib-v27-Mr '79-p36
The Tale Of Thebes
B&B-v23-Ja '78-p66
Class Out-v58-D '80-p58
GP-v16-Mr '78-p3259
HB-v53-D '77-p673
JAF-v92-Jl '79-p356
JB-v41-D '77-p352
TLS-Jl 15 '77-p859

* * *

GREEN, Wendy
The Steel Band
Brit Bk N C-Autumn '82-p20
GP-v21-My '82-p3888
JB-v46-Je '82-p98
TES-O 1 '82-p47
TES-Jl 15 '83-p18

GREEN, Wendy (continued)
TES-Ap 27 '84-p27

* * *

GREEN Tiger's Caravan
PW-v223-Ja 7 '83-p74

* * *

GREEN Vale School. Ninth Grade English Class, 1973
Bulldozers, Loaders, And Spreaders
CCB-B-v28-O '74-p28
KR-v42-Ag 1 '74-p797
NYTBR-Ja 19 '75-p8
SA-v231-D '74-p144
Teacher-v92-N '74-p34

* * *

GREENAWAY, Kate
A Apple Pie
NW-v86-D 15 '75-p92
The Illuminated Language Of Flowers
BL-v75-F 1 '79-p851
HB-v55-Ag '79-p442
LJ-v103-D 15 '78-p2507
The Kate Greenaway Treasury
BL-v64-F 1 '68-p618
CCB-B-v21-Ap '68-p126
HB-v44-Ap '68-p199
LA-v56-S '79-p687
LJ-v93-F 15 '68-p847
NO-v7-Mr 18 '68-p23
NYTBR-v73-Mr 10 '68-p22
PW-v192-D 11 '67-p46
Sch Lib-v27-Mr '79-p70
Kate Greenaway Wall Frieze
NS-v92-N 5 '76-p646
Kate Greenaway's Book Of Games
BL-v73-Mr 1 '77-p1019
Choice-v14-Je '77-p517
Comw-v103-N 19 '76-p764
Econ-v261-D 25 '76-p89
JB-v41-F '77-p34
NS-v92-N 5 '76-p643
Obs-D 5 '76-p32
SLJ-v23-F '77-p65
Kate Greenaway's Original Drawings For The Snow Queen
NYTBR-v86-N 15 '81-p66
The Language Of Flowers
JB-v41-O '77-p277
Obs-Je 12 '77-p25

* * *

GREENAWAY, Shirley
The Guinness Book Of Most And Least
Sch Lib-v28-S '80-p275
The Happy Prince
Sch Lib-v31-S '83-p238
Thumbelina
Sch Lib-v31-S '83-p238

* * *

GREENBANK, Anthony
Camping For Young People
GP-v18-My '79-p3522
JB-v43-Ag '79-p219
TES-N 23 '79-p36
Climbing For Young People
Brit Bk N-S '82-p532
JB-v41-D '77-p353
Coming Out Alive
Inst-v86-N '76-p159
Survival For Young People
GP-v13-Mr '75-p2576
The Survival Sourcebook
BL-v72-Mr 1 '76-p977
KR-v44-My 15 '76-p603

* * *

GREENBERG, Barbara
The Bravest Babysitter
BL-v74-D 15 '77-p683
CCB-B-v31-Je '78-p159
KR-v45-Ag 15 '77-p846
PW-v212-Ag 29 '77-p366
RT-v32-O '78-p32
SLJ-v24-D '77-p44

* * *

GREENBERG, David
Slugs
Emerg Lib-v11-N '83-p37
HB-v59-Je '83-p289
KR-v51-Mr 1 '83-p242
LATBR-Jl 17 '83-p8
LATBR-Ag 7 '83-p6
NYTBR-v88-My 15 '83-p26
PW-v223-My 27 '83-p68
Punch-v285-N 16 '83-p60
RS-Jl 21 '83-p119
SLJ-v29-Ag '83-p51

* * *

GREENBERG, Dorothy
Siege Hero
CCB-B-v20-S '66-p11
KR-v33-Ja 15 '65-p63
LJ-v90-Jl '65-p3125

* * *

GREENBERG, Jan
The Iceberg And Its Shadow
BL-v77-Ja 15 '81-p701
CBRS-v9-F '81-p56
CCB-B-v34-Ap '81-p151
KR-v49-F 15 '81-p213
Kliatt-v16-Fall '82-p10
SLJ-v27-Ja '81-p60
VOYA-v4-Ap '81-p34
No Dragons To Slay
BL-v80-N 15 '83-p489
BS-v43-Mr '84-p463
CBRS-v12-Mr '84-p84
CCB-B-v37-Mr '84-p127
Inter BC-v15-#4 '84-p17
J Read-v27-My '84-p743
SLJ-v30-D '83-p74
VOYA-v7-Je '84-p95
The Pig-Out Blues
BL-v78-Jl '82-p1437
BS-v42-O '82-p286
CBRS-v10-Ag '82-p138
CCB-B-v36-O '82-p26
J Read-v26-N '82-p185
KR-v50-My 15 '82-p608
PW-v221-My 7 '82-p80
SLJ-v29-S '82-p138
VOYA-v5-F '83-p35
A Season In-Between
BL-v76-F 1 '80-p768
BW-v10-F 10 '80-p8
CBRS-v8-F '80-p57
CCB-B-v33-Mr '80-p134
HB-v56-Ap '80-p172
KR-v48-F 1 '80-p133
Kliatt-v16-Winter '82-p8
SLJ-v26-F '80-p55

* * *

GREENBERG, Jan W
Theater Careers
BL-v79-Ag '83-p1437
B Rpt-v2-Ja '84-p43
BS-v43-O '83-p272
CCB-B-v37-D '83-p67
LATBR-N 20 '83-p18
SLJ-v30-F '84-p81
Theat J-v36-Mr '84-p146
VOYA-v6-F '84-p346

* * *

GREENBERG, Joanne
Founder's Praise
BL-v73-S 15 '76-p121
BS-v37-Ap '77-p2
CSM-v69-Mr 16 '77-p23

GREENBERG, Joanne (continued)
Choice-v14-Mr '77-p62
HB-v53-Je '77-p341
KR-v44-Ag 15 '76-p917
Kliatt-v12-Winter '78-p7
LJ-v101-O 1 '76-p2086
NYTBR-O 31 '76-p28
NYTBR-N 20 '77-p69
Obs-Ja 22 '78-p24
PW-v210-Ag 16 '76-p119
PW-v212-S 19 '77-p145
TLS-My 19 '78-p564

* * *

GREENBERG, Martin Harry
Run To Starlight
BL-v72-N 1 '75-p360
CCB-B-v29-Ja '76-p77
KR-v43-N 15 '75-p1296
NYTBR-N 16 '75-p54
NYTBR-Ja 25 '76-p10
SLJ-v22-D '75-p68
SLJ-v24-My '78-p39

* * *

GREENBERG, Polly
Birds Of The World
CBRS-v12-Mr '84-p80
SLJ-v30-Ap '84-p114
I Know I'm Myself Because...
SLJ-v28-Ag '82-p98
Oh Lord, I Wish I Was A Buzzard
BL-v65-Ja 1 '69-p496
BW-v2-N 3 '68-p4
CCB-B-v22-F '69-p94
CE-v45-Ap '69-p461
CSM-v60-N 7 '68-pB2
KR-v36-O 1 '68-p1106
NYTBR-v73-N 3 '68-p71
PW-v194-S 16 '68-p71

* * *

GREENE, Alma
Tales Of The Mohawks
Can Child Lit-#31 '83-p134

* * *

GREENE, Bette
Get On Out Of Here, Philip Hall
BL-v78-S 15 '81-p105
BW-v11-My 10 '81-p15
CBRS-v9-Je '81-p97
CCB-B-v35-O '81-p29
CLW-v53-N '81-p189
HB-v57-O '81-p534
Inter BC-v12-#6 '81-p19
JB-v47-F '83-p50
KR-v49-S 1 '81-p1083
LA-v59-Ap '82-p369
Lis-v108-N 4 '82-p24
NYTBR-v87-F 21 '82-p35
PW-v219-My 22 '81-p76
PW-v225-Ap 13 '84-p72
SLJ-v27-My '81-p64
Sch Lib-v31-Mr '83-p57
TES-Ja 21 '83-p34
TES-Jl 15 '83-p18
VOYA-v4-D '81-p29
Morning Is A Long Time Coming
BL-v74-Mr 1 '78-p1093
BS-v38-D '78-p291
CCB-B-v31-Ap '78-p127
EJ-v68-F '79-p101
EJ-v68-D '79-p78
HB-v54-Ag '78-p402
JB-v43-F '79-p66
KR-v46-F 15 '78-p183
Kliatt-v13-Fall '79-p7
NYTBR-Ap 30 '78-p30
NYTBR-Ap 22 '79-p39
PW-v213-Ja 16 '78-p99
SLJ-v24-Ap '78-p93
SLJ-v28-Ap '82-p28
Sch Lib-v27-Mr '79-p57
TES-N 24 '78-p48
TLS-D 1 '78-p1394
TN-v37-Fall '80-p60
Philip Hall Likes Me, I Reckon Maybe
BB-v2-Ja '75-p4
B&B-v22-N '76-p78
BL-v71-Mr 15 '75-p760
BL-v71-Mr 15 '75-p766
BS-v35-O '75-p228
BW-N 10 '74-p5
CCB-B-v28-Ap '75-p130
CE-v51-Ap '75-p326
CLW-v47-D '75-p208
CSM-v66-N 6 '74-p12
CSM-v76-Jl 6 '84-pB5
Choice-v12-N '75-p1132
EJ-v64-D '75-p80
HB-v51-Ap '75-p149
JB-v41-F '77-p34
KR-v42-O 15 '74-p1102
KR-v43-Ja 1 '75-p6
LA-v57-Ap '80-p417
NS-v92-N 5 '76-p644
NYTBR-N 3 '74-p53
NYTBR-D 1 '74-p76
NYTBR-D 8 '74-p8
PT-v8-Mr '75-p94
PW-v206-Ag 12 '74-p58
TLS-O 1 '76-p1247
Teacher-v92-D '74-p77
Teacher-v92-My '75-p90
Summer Of My German Soldier
BL-v70-N 15 '73-p334
BL-v70-N 15 '73-p339
BL-v70-Mr 15 '74-p827
BL-v80-S 1 '83-p95
BS-v33-D 15 '73-p428
BS-v34-D 15 '74-p428
CCB-B-v27-F '74-p94
CLW-v47-N '75-p166
Child Lit-v9-'81-p203
Choice-v12-N '75-p1132
EJ-v64-O '75-p92
EJ-v66-O '77-p58
EJ-v69-S '80-p87
EJ-v69-O '80-p16
EJ-v72-D '83-p37
Emerg Lib-v11-N '83-p21
Emerg Lib-v11-Ja '84-p21
GP-v13-Ja '75-p2557
HB-v50-F '74-p56
Inter BC-v13-#6 '82-p19
JB-v39-F '75-p62
J Read-v22-N '78-p126
KR-v41-O 15 '73-p1170
LJ-v98-O 15 '73-p3154
NYTBR-N 4 '73-p29
NYTBR-N 4 '73-p52
NYTBR-D 2 '73-p79
NYTBR-N 10 '74-p44
Obs-D 8 '74-p30
PW-v204-Ag 27 '73-p280
SE-v47-Ap '83-p289
TES-D 9 '77-p21
Them That Glitter And Them That Don't
BL-v79-Mr 1 '83-p870
BS-v43-Je '83-p109
BW-v13-My 8 '83-p14
CBRS-v11-Ap '83-p93
CCB-B-v36-My '83-p167
HB-v59-Ag '83-p453
J Read-v27-N '83-p183
KR-v51-Ap 1 '83-p379
Kliatt-v18-Spring '84-p8
PW-v223-Mr 11 '83-p87
RT-v37-O '83-p86
SLJ-v29-Ap '83-p122
VOYA-v6-O '83-p201

* * *

GREENE, Carla
Animal Doctors: What Do They Do?
BL-v64-Ja 1 '68-p544
CCB-B-v21-Mr '68-p109
KR-v35-S 1 '67-p1045
LJ-v92-D 15 '67-p4630
NYTBR-v72-N 5 '67-p60
SB-v3-D '67-p264
TLS-Ap 3 '69-p365
Los Camioneros Que Hacen?
HB-v55-Je '79-p330
Man & Ancient Civilizations
BL-v74-D 1 '77-p612
CCB-B-v31-Ja '78-p77
CE-v54-F '78-p198
KR-v45-S 15 '77-p993
SLJ-v24-O '77-p112
Moses, The Great Law-Giver
CCB-B-v22-Mr '69-p110
LJ-v94-Mr 15 '69-p1326
Our Living Earth
SLJ-v21-Mr '75-p96
Policemen And Firemen
SLJ-v28-D '81-p78

* * *

GREENE, Carol
Astronauts
BL-v80-Jl '84-p1548
A Computer Went A-Courting
SLJ-v30-Mr '84-p144
England
BL-v79-Ap 1 '83-p1031
CCB-B-v36-Mr '83-p126
SLJ-v29-Ap '83-p111
Hi, Clouds
BL-v79-Ag '83-p1470
SLJ-v30-N '83-p63
Hinny Winny Bunco
BL-v78-Ap 15 '82-p1096
CBRS-v10-My '82-p92
KR-v50-Mr 1 '82-p271
LA-v59-N '82-p865
NYTBR-v87-Ap 25 '82-p42
PW-v221-Ap 16 '82-p70
RT-v36-F '83-p594
RT-v37-Ap '84-p702
SLJ-v28-Ap '82-p58
Holidays Around The World
BL-v79-Mr 1 '83-p902
Ice Is...Whee!
BL-v79-Ag '83-p1470
SLJ-v30-N '83-p63
Japan
BL-v80-Mr 15 '84-p1058
SLJ-v30-My '84-p79
Language
BL-v80-F 15 '84-p854
SLJ-v30-Mr '84-p140
Marie Curie: Pioneer Physicist
BL-v81-S 1 '84-p64
SLJ-v31-O '84-p157
Mother Teresa: Friend Of The Friendless
BL-v80-Ja 15 '84-p748
SLJ-v30-Ap '84-p102
Music
BL-v80-F 15 '84-p854
SLJ-v30-Mr '84-p142
Please, Wind?
SLJ-v29-Ag '83-p48
Poland
BL-v79-Ag '83-p1464
SLJ-v30-S '83-p122
Rain! Rain!
SLJ-v29-Ag '83-p48
Robots
BL-v79-Ag '83-p1462
SLJ-v30-O '83-p149
Sandra Day O'Connor: First Woman On The Supreme Court
SLJ-v29-F '83-p66
Seven Baths For Naaman
SLJ-v24-D '77-p59
Shine, Sun!
BL-v79-Ag '83-p1470
SLJ-v30-N '83-p63
Snow Joe
SLJ-v29-Ag '83-p48
The Super Snoops And The Missing Sleepers
SLJ-v23-S '76-p100
The Thirteen Days Of Halloween
BL-v80-Ja 15 '84-p748
SLJ-v30-Mr '84-p144
United Nations
BL-v80-F 15 '84-p854
SLJ-v30-Mr '84-p142
Yugoslavia
BL-v81-S 1 '84-p63
SLJ-v31-O '84-p157

* * *

GREENE, Constance C
Al(exandra) The Great
BL-v78-My 1 '82-p1159
CCB-B-v35-Jl '82-p206
CE-v59-N '82-p132
HB-v58-Ag '82-p402
J Read-v26-O '82-p88
KR-v50-My 1 '82-p554
PW-v221-My 7 '82-p80
SLJ-v28-My '82-p62
Ask Anybody
BL-v79-Ap 1 '83-p1034
CBRS-v11-Jl '83-p137
CCB-B-v36-Ap '83-p149
HB-v59-Je '83-p302
KR-v51-Ap 1 '83-p376
PW-v223-Ja 28 '83-p86
PW-v225-Je 8 '84-p64
SLJ-v29-Ag '83-p65
Beat The Turtle Drum
BL-v73-N 15 '76-p472
BW-N 7 '76-pG8
CCB-B-v30-Ap '77-p124
Choice-v14-N '77-p1178
Comw-v103-N 19 '76-p762
Emerg Lib-v11-Ja '84-p21
HB-v52-D '76-p624
KR-v44-Ag 1 '76-p845
LA-v54-Ap '77-p441
NYTBR-N 14 '76-p52
NYTBR-N 21 '76-p62
NYTBR-Ja 27 '80-p35
PW-v210-Ag 9 '76-p78
RT-v31-O '77-p15
SLJ-v23-F '77-p64
SLJ-v25-D '78-p33
Teacher-v94-My '77-p109
Dotty's Suitcase
BL-v77-O 1 '80-p250
CBRS-v9-N '80-p27
CCB-B-v34-Ja '81-p93
KR-v48-S 15 '80-p1232
NYTBR-v86-F 15 '81-p22
PW-v218-O 10 '80-p74
PW-v221-Je 25 '82-p118
SLJ-v27-O '80-p146
Double-Dare O'Toole
BL-v78-S 15 '81-p105
CBRS-v10-D '81-p38
CCB-B-v35-My '82-p170
HB-v57-D '81-p663
KR-v49-O 15 '81-p1296
PW-v220-Jl 17 '81-p95
SLJ-v28-O '81-p141
The Ears Of Louis
BL-v71-D 15 '74-p425
CCB-B-v28-Ap '75-p130
HB-v51-Ap '75-p149
KR-v42-N 1 '74-p1151
PW-v206-N 11 '74-p49

GREENE, Constance C (continued)
RT-v29-Ja '76-p421
SLJ-v25-D '78-p33
Teacher-v95-My '78-p106
Getting Nowhere
BL-v74-O 1 '77-p290
BS-v37-F '78-p367
CCB-B-v31-Mr '78-p112
HB-v53-D '77-p662
KR-v45-Ag 1 '77-p789
PW-v212-Jl 4 '77-p77
SLJ-v24-O '77-p124
A Girl Called Al
A Lib-v1-Ap '70-p385
BL-v65-Jl 15 '69-p1274
BL-v75-Jl 15 '79-p1634
BW-v3-My 4 '69-p4
CCB-B-v23-S '69-p9
CE-v46-Ja '70-p213
Choice-v14-N '77-p1178
GT-v88-Ap '71-p84
HB-v45-Ag '69-p411
KR-v37-Ap 15 '69-p441
LJ-v94-My 15 '69-p2113
NYTBR-My 25 '69-p32
PW-v195-My 12 '69-p58
SR-v52-Ap 19 '69-p38
I And Sproggy
BL-v75-S 1 '78-p48
CCB-B-v32-Ja '79-p81
Emerg Lib-v9-My '82-p30
HB-v55-O '78-p516
KR-v46-S 1 '78-p950
PW-v214-Jl 10 '78-p136
SLJ-v25-S '78-p136
I Know You, Al
BL-v72-O 1 '75-p235
CCB-B-v29-F '76-p96
CE-v52-Ap '76-p318
Choice-v14-N '77-p1178
Comw-v102-N 21 '75-p569
HB-v51-D '75-p591
JB-v42-F '78-p55
KR-v43-Jl 15 '75-p776
LA-v53-My '76-p519
NY-v51-D 1 '75-p167
NYTBR-N 16 '75-p52
PW-v208-Ag 18 '75-p68
SLJ-v22-O '75-p98
TES-N 18 '77-p41
TLS-O 28 '77-p1274
Teacher-v93-Ap '76-p116
Isabelle Shows Her Stuff
BL-v81-S 15 '84-p127
CBRS-v13-O '84-p20
KR-v52-S 1 '84-pJ70
PW-v226-S 28 '84-p112
Isabelle The Itch
BL-v70-D 1 '73-p386
BL-v75-Jl 15 '79-p1634
CCB-B-v27-F '74-p95
Comw-v99-N 23 '73-p215
KR-v41-O 1 '73-p1095
LJ-v98-N 15 '73-p3452
NYTBR-N 4 '73-p42
PW-v204-N 19 '73-p60
Teacher-v92-Ap '75-p111
Leo The Lioness
BL-v67-Ja 1 '71-p372
CCB-B-v24-Ap '71-p124
Comw-v93-N 20 '70-p202
GT-v88-Ap '71-p28
HB-v47-F '71-p50
Inst-v130-Ap '71-p134
KR-v38-N 1 '70-p1201
LJ-v95-D 15 '70-p4350
NYTBR, pt.2-N 8 '70-p14
SR-v53-N 14 '70-p37
The Unmaking Of Rabbit
BL-v69-Ja 1 '73-p449
CCB-B-v26-My '73-p138
CE-v49-Mr '73-p318
HB-v49-Ap '73-p143
KR-v40-N 1 '72-p1239
NYTBR-Ja 21 '73-p8
PW-v202-N 13 '72-p45
Your Old Pal, Al
BL-v76-S 1 '79-p43
BL-v78-F 15 '82-p762
CBRS-v8-Ja '80-p46
HB-v55-O '79-p534
KR-v47-O 1 '79-p1145
PW-v216-O 29 '79-p82
SLJ-v26-O '79-p150

* * *

GREENE, Ellin
Clever Cooks
BL-v70-S 15 '73-p120
CCB-B-v27-Mr '74-p110
CSM-v65-Je 6 '73-p14
CSM-v66-D 5 '73-pB12
HB-v49-O '73-p461
KR-v41-My 15 '73-p563
KR-v41-D 15 '73-p1353
LJ-v98-S 15 '73-p2639
NYTBR-N 4 '73-p32
TN-v30-Ap '74-p308
Teacher-v91-My '74-p80
Teacher-v96-N '78-p24
Midsummer Magic
BL-v74-Ja 15 '78-p812
CE-v55-O '78-p38
Comw-v105-N 10 '78-p731
HB-v54-Ap '78-p177
KR-v45-O 15 '77-p1100
SLJ-v24-D '77-p47
Teacher-v96-N '78-p24

* * *

GREENE, Graham
The Little Fire Engine
B&B-v19-D '73-p104
BL-v71-S 1 '74-p41
CSM-v66-Jl 3 '74-p7
Econ-v249-D 29 '73-p62
HB-v50-O '74-p132
KR-v42-Je 15 '74-p630
LJ-v99-S 15 '74-p2247
Lis-v90-N 8 '73-p644
NS-v86-N 9 '73-p698
SLJ-v25-F '79-p28
Spec-v231-O 20 '73-pR14
TLS-N 23 '73-p1437
Time-v104-D 23 '74-p71
The Little Horse Bus
KR-v43-Ag 1 '75-p843
Lis-v92-N 7 '74-p617
SLJ-v22-N '75-p62
SLJ-v25-F '79-p28
TLS-D 6 '74-p1378
The Little Steamroller
KR-v43-Ag 1 '75-p843
Lis-v92-N 7 '74-p617
NYTBR-N 16 '75-p56
NYTBR-N 16 '75-p58
SLJ-v22-O '75-p81
SLJ-v25-F '79-p28
TLS-D 6 '74-p1378
The Little Train
B&B-v19-D '73-p104
BL-v71-S 1 '74-p41
CCB-B-v28-Ja '75-p78
CE-v51-N '74-p91
CSM-v66-Jl 3 '74-p7
Econ-v249-D 29 '73-p62
HB-v50-O '74-p132
KR-v42-Je 15 '74-p630
LJ-v99-S 15 '74-p2247
Lis-v90-N 8 '73-p644
NS-v86-N 9 '73-p698
PW-v205-Je 17 '74-p68
SLJ-v25-F '79-p28
Spec-v231-O 20 '73-pR14
TLS-N 23 '73-p1437
Time-v104-D 23 '74-p71
El Pequeno Tren
BL-v79-D 1 '82-p494

GREENE, Graham (continued)
Travels With My Aunt
Am-v122-Ap 4 '70-p373
Am-v122-My 2 '70-p478
Atl-v225-Ap '70-p109
B&B-v17-Mr '72-pR8
BL-v66-Ap 1 '70-p954
BS-v29-F 1 '70-p413
BS-v30-Mr 1 '71-p531
BW-v4-F 8 '70-p3
CSM-v62-F 12 '70-p11
Choice-v7-S '70-p842
Comw-v92-My 8 '70-p200
Crit-v28-Ja '70-p84
EJ-v71-F '82-p78
GW-v101-N 29 '69-p18
GW-v101-D 20 '69-p19
GW-v123-O 12 '80-p21
HB-v46-Ap '70-p187
HM-v240-Mr '70-p108
HR-v23-Spring '70-p162
KR-v37-N 15 '69-p1222
LJ-v95-Ja 1 '70-p83
LJ-v95-Ap 15 '70-p1660
Lis-v82-N 20 '69-p708
NL-v53-F 2 '70-p20
NO-v9-F 2 '70-p19
NS-v78-N 21 '69-p733
NW-v75-Ja 26 '70-p80
NY-v46-F 28 '70-p110
NYRB-v14-Mr 12 '70-p25
NYT-v119-Ja 19 '70-p45
NYTBR-Ja 25 '70-p4
NYTBR-Je 7 '70-p2
NYTBR-D 6 '70-p102
Nat R-v22-Mr 24 '70-p314
New R-v162-F 14 '70-p26
Obs-N 16 '69-p31
Obs-D 21 '69-p17
PW-v196-N 10 '69-p43
PW-v199-Ja 4 '71-p58
Punch-v257-D 17 '69-p1017
SR-v53-Ja 24 '70-p38
SR-v54-Mr 27 '71-p42
Sew R-v78-O '70-p654
Spec-v223-N 22 '69-p717
TLS-D 20 '69-p1329
Time-v95-Ja 19 '70-p68
WSJ-v175-F 5 '70-p10

* * *

GREENE, Sir Hugh
The Pirate Of The Round Pond
GP-v16-O '77-p3179
JB-v41-D '77-p355
Obs-Ap 10 '77-p21
TLS-Jl 15 '77-p861

* * *

GREENE, Jacqueline D
The Leveller
BL-v80-Jl '84-p1549
B Rpt-v3-S '84-p32
CBRS-v12-My '84-p108
CCB-B-v37-Ap '84-p146
HB-v60-Ag '84-p474
SLJ-v30-Ap '84-p114

* * *

GREENE, Laura
Careers In The Computer Industry
ASBYP-v17-Spring '84-p50
BL-v80-N 15 '83-p490
BL-v80-Ja 1 '84-p681
CBRS-v12-D '83-p40
Cur R-v23-Ap '84-p33
SB-v20-N '84-p64
SLJ-v30-Ja '84-p70
Change
SLJ-v28-Ja '82-p64
Help
PW-v220-D 18 '81-p70
SLJ-v28-F '82-p67
I Am An Orthodox Jew
CBRS-v7-Jl '79-p124
CCB-B-v33-N '79-p48
KR-v47-Ag 1 '79-p856
SLJ-v26-S '79-p110
Sign Language
BL-v77-My 15 '81-p1253
SLJ-v27-Ag '81-p65

* * *

GREENE, Liz
Looking At Astrology
PW-v213-Mr 27 '78-p72
SLJ-v25-S '78-p137
TES-O 20 '78-p41
Looking At The Mind
JB-v42-Je '78-p154
TES-O 20 '78-p41

* * *

GREENE, Richard C
The King Of Instruments
BL-v79-D 1 '82-p498
CCB-B-v36-N '82-p47

* * *

GREENE, Shep
The Boy Who Drank Too Much
BL-v75-My 1 '79-p1356
CBRS-v7-Je '79-p107
CCB-B-v33-S '79-p9
HB-v55-Ap '79-p198
KR-v47-Je 1 '79-p641
PW-v215-My 21 '79-p69
SLJ-v25-My '79-p84
SLJ-v29-D '82-p28
WLB-v54-N '79-p184

* * *

GREENE, Vivian
Chip, Oh Brother!
SLJ-v26-Ja '80-p56
Cleveland, The Disco King
SLJ-v26-Ja '80-p56
Oops! Odessa
CBRS-v8-N '79-p21
SLJ-v26-Ja '80-p56
Rotunda Ate A Cookie
SLJ-v26-Ja '80-p56

* * *

GREENFELD, Howard
Bar Mitzvah
BL-v78-N 1 '81-p388
CE-v58-Mr '82-p260
KR-v50-Ja 1 '82-p8
LA-v59-F '82-p155
PW-v220-S 11 '81-p72
SLJ-v28-Ja '82-p77
Books
AB-v60-N 14 '77-p2818
ARBA-v8-'77-p28
BL-v73-Ja 1 '77-p666
BS-v36-Mr '77-p386
CCB-B-v30-Ap '77-p124
Comw-v104-N 11 '77-p734
EJ-v66-S '77-p84
HB-v53-Ap '77-p174
JQ-v56-Spring '79-p185
KR-v44-N 1 '76-p1178
SLJ-v23-N '76-p69
SLMQ-v12-Summer '84-p263
TN-v38-Spring '82-p257
Chanukah
CCB-B-v30-D '76-p57
KR-v44-N 15 '76-p1224
PW-v210-D 6 '76-p63
SLJ-v23-Ja '77-p100
F. Scott Fitzgerald
BL-v71-D 15 '74-p419
CCB-B-v28-Mr '75-p113
KR-v42-O 15 '74-p1113
LJ-v99-D 15 '74-p3247
LJ-v99-D 15 '74-p3272
PW-v206-S 23 '74-p155
Gertrude Stein
BL-v70-O 1 '73-p162

GREENFELD, Howard (continued)
BW-v7-Je 10 '73-p12
BW-v7-N 11 '73-p3C
CCB-B-v27-N '73-p43
HB-v49-Ag '73-p389
KR-v41-Ap 15 '73-p464
KR-v41-D 15 '73-p1358
LJ-v98-Jl '73-p2200
PW-v203-Ap 23 '73-p72
Gypsies
BB-v6-Je '78-p6
BL-v74-D 15 '77-p683
BS-v37-Mr '78-p399
CCB-B-v31-Ap '78-p127
CE-v54-Ap '78-p307
CE-v55-Ap '79-p263
Comw-v105-N 10 '78-p734
HB-v54-Je '78-p295
KR-v45-N 15 '77-p1208
PW-v212-N 21 '77-p64
SE-v42-Ap '78-p319
SLJ-v24-D '77-p49
The Impressionist Revolution
BL-v69-F 1 '73-p524
CCB-B-v26-Ja '73-p76
HB-v48-O '72-p479
Marc Chagall
BL-v64-Mr 1 '68-p784
BS-v28-Ja 1 '69-p421
BW-v2-Je 2 '68-p20
CCB-B-v21-Ap '68-p126
CLW-v39-Ap '68-p608
HB-v43-D '67-p762
JPE-v75-O '67-p777
KR-v35-N 1 '67-p1327
LJ-v93-F 15 '68-p881
NO-v7-Ag 26 '68-p17
NYTBR-v73-Ap 7 '68-p26
PW-v192-D 11 '67-p46
Trav-v24-Ap '68-p323
YR-v4-Mr '68-p4
Marc Chagall: An Introduction
AB-v68-D 21 '81-p4380
BL-v77-My 1 '81-p1196
BS-v41-Ap '81-p39
PW-v219-Mr 6 '81-p95
SLJ-v27-Ag '81-p66
Pablo Picasso
BL-v67-Jl 1 '71-p905
BW-v5-My 9 '71-p12
CCB-B-v25-Mr '72-p107
Choice-v8-Je '71-p540
LJ-v97-F 15 '72-p784
PW-v200-Jl 5 '71-p50
TN-v28-Ja '72-p203
Passover
BL-v74-Je 1 '78-p1551
CCB-B-v32-S '78-p9
CE-v55-Ja '79-p170
Comw-v107-F 29 '80-p115
KR-v46-My 1 '78-p499
NYTBR-Mr 18 '79-p26
PW-v213-Mr 13 '78-p110
RT-v32-Ja '79-p488
Teacher-v96-My '79-p115
Purim
KR-v51-F 1 '83-p122
PW-v223-Mr 11 '83-p86
SLJ-v29-My '83-p71
Rosh Hashanah And Yom Kippur
BL-v76-D 1 '79-p557
CCB-B-v33-Ja '80-p95
KR-v47-D 15 '79-p1432
PW-v216-S 17 '79-p146
SLJ-v26-F '80-p55
Sumer Is Icumen In
BL-v75-N 1 '78-p478
CBRS-v7-Ja '79-p47
CCB-B-v32-D '78-p62
HB-v55-F '79-p77
KR-v46-D 15 '78-p1364
LA-v56-F '79-p189
PW-v214-Ag 28 '78-p394
SE-v43-Ap '79-p300
SLJ-v25-N '78-p73
They Came To Paris
BL-v72-N 15 '75-p444
BL-v72-N 15 '75-p452
BS-v35-N '75-p249
CCB-B-v29-F '76-p96
HB-v52-F '76-p62
KR-v43-S 15 '75-p1075
PW-v208-O 6 '75-p85
SLJ-v22-N '75-p89
SLJ-v22-D '75-p31
The Waters Of November
BL-v66-F 1 '70-p663
CCB-B-v23-F '70-p98
Comw-v91-N 21 '69-p263
LJ-v95-F 1 '70-p484
LJ-v95-F 15 '70-p787
PW-v196-Ag 25 '69-p284
SR-v52-N 8 '69-p72

* * *

GREENFIELD, Eloise
Africa Dream
BB-v6-My '78-p1
BL-v74-D 15 '77-p683
CCB-B-v31-F '78-p93
CE-v54-Ap '78-p305
Inter BC-v14-#7 '83-p27
LA-v55-Ap '78-p517
NHB-v41-Ja '78-p801
SLJ-v24-Mr '78-p118
Teacher-v96-O '78-p160
Alesia
BL-v78-F 1 '82-p706
CBRS-v10-F '82-p66
CCB-B-v35-Ja '82-p85
CLW-v53-Ap '82-p401
Hi Lo-v3-F '82-p6
Inter BC-v13-#4 '82-p7
SLJ-v28-Mr '82-p157
Bubbles
JNE-v43-Summer '74-p399
Childtimes
BL-v76-N 1 '79-p448
BW-v10-Ja 13 '80-p10
CBRS-v8-N '79-p27
HB-v55-D '79-p676
Inter BC-v11-My '80-p14
KR-v48-Ja 1 '80-p7
LA-v57-Ap '80-p437
PW-v216-N 19 '79-p78
SLJ-v26-D '79-p85
Darlene
BL-v77-Ja 1 '81-p624
BL-v78-N 1 '81-p396
CBRS-v9-Ja '81-p31
CCB-B-v34-Mr '81-p134
Inter BC-v12-#2 '81-p22
Inter BC-v14-#7 '83-p28
KR-v49-F 1 '81-p137
Daydreamers
BL-v78-S 15 '81-p105
CBRS-v9-Je '81-p92
CCB-B-v34-Je '81-p193
HB-v57-O '81-p547
Inter BC-v12-#6 '81-p18
KR-v49-Jl 15 '81-p869
PW-v219-Je 12 '81-p54
RT-v35-D '81-p364
SLJ-v28-S '81-p125
First Pink Light
BL-v73-D 1 '76-p540
BW-S 12 '76-pH4
CE-v60-My '84-p344
CLW-v48-F '77-p306
CSM-v68-N 3 '76-p22
HB-v53-Ap '77-p149
KR-v44-S 1 '76-p970
LA-v57-S '80-p657
RT-v31-O '77-p8
Good News
CCB-B-v31-O '77-p32

GREENFIELD, Eloise
(continued)
KR-v45-Je 1 '77-p573
LA-v57-S '80-p655
PW-v211-Je 13 '77-p108
SLJ-v24-D '77-p44
Grandmama's Joy
BL-v77-S 1 '80-p44
CCB-B-v34-O '80-p32
KR-v48-S 1 '80-p1158
SLJ-v27-O '80-p135
Honey, I Love
BB-v7-Ap '79-p2
BL-v74-Jl 15 '78-p1733
BL-v75-Mr 15 '79-p1165
BW-v11-My 10 '81-p14
CCB-B-v31-Jl '78-p177
CE-v55-N '78-p106
Inter BC-v14-#7 '83-p28
KR-v46-Mr 15 '78-p308
LA-v55-O '78-p866
LA-v59-Mr '82-p283
Ms-v11-D '82-p94
NYTBR-Ap 30 '78-p25
RT-v32-My '79-p977
RT-v36-Ja '83-p381
SLJ-v24-My '78-p55
I Can Do It By Myself
LA-v57-S '80-p657
Mary McLeod Bethune
BL-v73-My 15 '77-p1420
BW-My 1 '77-pE2
Bl S-v9-Ap '78-p57
CCB-B-v30-Je '77-p158
CE-v54-Mr '78-p260
HB-v53-O '77-p553
KR-v45-Mr 15 '77-p287
LA-v54-S '77-p689
LA-v57-S '80-p656
NHB-v41-S '78-p894
RT-v32-O '78-p40
SLJ-v24-S '77-p128
Me And Neesie
CCB-B-v29-F '76-p96
Choice-v14-N '77-p1178
Comw-v102-N 21 '75-p568
HB-v52-F '76-p44
KR-v43-Ag 15 '75-p910
LA-v57-S '80-p656
RT-v30-Ap '77-p824
SLJ-v22-N '75-p62
Paul Robeson
CCB-B-v29-Ja '76-p77
KR-v43-My 15 '75-p570
LA-v57-S '80-p656
PW-v207-Je 9 '75-p62
SLJ-v22-S '75-p82
Rosa Parks
BL-v70-Ja 1 '74-p488
CCB-B-v27-Je '74-p157
JNE-v43-Summer '74-p394
KR-v41-N 1 '73-p1206
KR-v41-D 15 '73-p1353
LJ-v99-Ap 15 '74-p1212
PT-v7-Ap '74-p4
Teacher-v92-N '74-p107
She Come Bringing Me That Little Baby Girl
BL-v71-O 15 '74-p242
BL-v71-Mr 15 '75-p766
BW-N 10 '74-p7
BW-D 8 '74-p7
CCB-B-v28-Mr '75-p113
CE-v51-Mr '75-p274
CLW-v47-D '75-p208
CLW-v47-My '76-p446
Choice-v12-N '75-p1132
Choice-v14-N '77-p1178
Comw-v101-N 22 '74-p192
HB-v51-Ap '75-p137
KR-v42-S 15 '74-p1004
NYTBR-N 3 '74-p48
PW-v206-S 30 '74-p60
RT-v36-Ap '83-p802
SLJ-v21-Ja '75-p39
Sister
BL-v71-S 1 '74-p41
CCB-B-v28-S '74-p8
CE-v51-Ap '75-p326
Choice-v14-N '77-p1178
HB-v50-O '74-p136
JNE-v43-Summer '74-p394
KR-v42-My 15 '74-p535
LA-v57-S '80-p656
LJ-v99-S 15 '74-p2268
NYTBR-My 5 '74-p16
NYTBR-N 3 '74-p53
Talk About A Family
BL-v74-Mr 1 '78-p1105
CE-v56-O '79-p44
Essence-v15-O '84-p142
Inter BC-v15-#4 '84-p10
KR-v46-Ap 15 '78-p436
LA-v56-Ja '79-p52
LA-v57-S '80-p658
SLJ-v24-My '78-p67

* * *

GREENFIELD, Jeff
Tiny Giant
BL-v72-Jl 15 '76-p1595
SLJ-v22-My '76-p80

* * *

GREENHOWE, Jean
Costumes For Nursery Tale Characters
AB-v58-N 8 '76-p2543
BL-v72-Ap 15 '76-p1185
HB-v52-Ag '76-p411
Making Miniature Toys And Dolls
BL-v74-Mr 15 '78-p1154
GP-v16-D '77-p3230
Stage Costumes For Girls
BL-v72-Je 15 '76-p1466
HB-v52-Ag '76-p411

* * *

GREENLEAF, Ann
No Room For Sarah
CCB-B-v37-My '84-p165
PW-v225-Ja 6 '84-p84
SLJ-v30-My '84-p66

* * *

GREENLEAF, Barbara Kaye
America Fever
BL-v67-O 1 '70-p139
BS-v30-O 15 '70-p298
CCB-B-v24-F '71-p92
KR-v38-Ap 1 '70-p393
LJ-v95-D 15 '70-p4361

* * *

GREENLEAF, Margery
Dirk
CCB-B-v25-D '71-p57
CSM-v63-Ag 7 '71-p17
LJ-v97-My 15 '72-p1922

* * *

GREENOAK, Francesca
Birds In Towns
JB-v43-D '79-p335
Sch Lib-v28-Mr '80-p45
TES-Ja 2 '81-p13
Trees
JB-v40-O '76-p269

* * *

GREENWALD, Sheila
All The Way To Wits' End
BL-v76-O 15 '79-p352
CCB-B-v33-D '79-p70
HB-v56-F '80-p55
KR-v47-D 15 '79-p1430
PW-v216-Jl 23 '79-p159
PW-v221-Ja 1 '82-p51
SLJ-v26-D '79-p85
The Atrocious Two
BB-v6-Ja '79-p2

GREENWALD, Sheila (continued)
BL-v74-Jl 1 '78-p1678
CCB-B-v32-S '78-p9
KR-v46-Mr 15 '78-p305
LA-v56-Ja '79-p51
RT-v32-Ja '79-p488
SLJ-v24-My '78-p84
Blissful Joy And The SATs
BL-v78-Mr 15 '82-p950
BW-v12-Ag 8 '82-p6
CBRS-v10-Ag '82-p138
CCB-B-v35-Ap '82-p148
CE-v59-Ja '83-p210
HB-v58-Ag '82-p412
J Read-v26-D '82-p277
KR-v50-Ap 15 '82-p494
PW-v221-Mr 19 '82-p71
SLJ-v28-Ap '82-p82
VOYA-v5-Je '82-p33
WLB-v57-Ja '83-p419
Give Us A Great Big Smile, Rosy Cole
BL-v77-Je 15 '81-p1345
BL-v78-F 15 '82-p762
CBRS-v9-Je '81-p97
CCB-B-v34-Je '81-p193
CE-v58-Ja '82-p180
HB-v57-Ag '81-p421
KR-v49-Jl 1 '81-p800
PW-v219-My 8 '81-p254
PW-v222-O 8 '82-p63
RT-v36-O '82-p76
SLJ-v28-S '81-p125
The Hot Day
CCB-B-v26-D '72-p56
KR-v40-Mr 15 '72-p320
LJ-v97-Je 15 '72-p2230
SR-v55-Ag 19 '72-p61
It All Began With Jane Eyre
BL-v76-My 1 '80-p1291
CBRS-v8-Jl '80-p126
CCB-B-v34-S '80-p10
CE-v57-Ja '81-p172
CSM-v72-O 14 '80-pB1
Emerg Lib-v9-Ja '82-p13
Emerg Lib-v9-My '82-p30
HB-v56-Ag '80-p407
KR-v48-Je 1 '80-p717
Kliatt-v16-Winter '82-p8
SLJ-v26-Ap '80-p124
The Mariah Delany Lending Library Disaster
BL-v74-N 15 '77-p550
CCB-B-v31-F '78-p93
HB-v54-F '78-p45
KR-v45-N 1 '77-p1144
RT-v32-O '78-p40
SLJ-v24-N '77-p56
SLJ-v27-Mr '81-p108
The Secret In Miranda's Closet
BL-v73-Ap 15 '77-p1266
CCB-B-v31-S '77-p15
KR-v45-Mr 1 '77-p223
LA-v54-N '77-p947
SLJ-v23-My '77-p61
The Secret Museum
BL-v70-Je 1 '74-p1104
CCB-B-v27-Jl '74-p177
CSM-v66-My 1 '74-pF3
KR-v42-Ap 15 '74-p424
LJ-v99-My 15 '74-p1473
PW-v205-Mr 25 '74-p56
Will The Real Gertrude Hollings Please Stand Up?
BL-v79-My 15 '83-p1216
CBRS-v11-Ag '83-p146
CCB-B-v37-D '83-p67
HB-v59-Ag '83-p443
KR-v51-My 15 '83-p579
PW-v223-F 25 '83-p89
SLJ-v29-Ag '83-p65
VOYA-v6-O '83-p202

* * *

GREENWAY, John
Gormless Tom
CCB-B-v22-S '68-p8
CE-v45-Ap '69-p462
LJ-v93-Jl '68-p2733

* * *

GREENWOOD, Angela
Numbers
GP-v18-Mr '80-p3663

* * *

GREENWOOD, Ann
A Pack Of Dreams
CBRS-v7-My '79-p92
CCB-B-v32-Jl '79-p192
SLJ-v26-S '79-p111

* * *

GREENWOOD, Ted
The Boy Who Saw God
GP-v22-Mr '84-p4207
Everlasting Circle
JB-v46-Ag '82-p132
TES-Je 11 '82-p37
Flora's Treasures
JB-v47-Ag '83-p171
Ginnie
JB-v43-O '79-p272
Marley And Friends
GP-My '84-p4265
JB-v48-Je '84-p127
TES-Ap 13 '84-p30
The Pochetto Coat
B&B-v25-Je '80-p45
JB-v44-O '80-p239
Terry's Brrrmmm
GP-v15-Jl '76-p2921

* * *

GREER, A
CSE Mathematics
TES-N 16 '79-p45

* * *

GREER, Gery
Max And Me And The Time Machine
BL-v79-Ag '83-p1465
CBRS-v12-O '83-p20
CCB-B-v37-O '83-p28
CE-v60-N '83-p137
CSM-v75-O 20 '83-p38
HB-v59-Ag '83-p443
KR-v51-Je 15 '83-p660
SF&FBR-O '83-p43
SLJ-v29-My '83-p32
SLJ-v29-My '83-p71
VOYA-v6-O '83-p214

* * *

GREET, W Cabell
Junior Thesaurus
BL-v66-My 1 '70-p1100
CCB-B-v24-D '70-p58
Comw-v92-My 22 '70-p254
Inst-v79-My '70-p104
KR-v37-D 15 '69-p1325
NYTBR-Jl 5 '70-p14
PW-v197-F 16 '70-p74
SR-v53-D 5 '70-p34
My First Picture Dictionary
CCB-B-v25-O '71-p25
CLW-v42-Ap '71-p519
Inst-v83-Ag '73-p186
LJ-v96-Ap 15 '71-p1493
My Pictionary
CCB-B-v24-Mr '71-p107
CLW-v42-Mr '71-p460
Inst-v83-Ag '73-p186
KR-v38-N 1 '70-p1197
LJ-v96-Ap 15 '71-p1493
Par-v46-Ap '71-p8
SR-v53-D 5 '70-p34

GREET, W Cabell (continued)
My Second Picture Dictionary
Inst-v83-Ag '73-p186
KR-v39-S 15 '71-p1017
LJ-v97-Jl '72-p2477

* * *

GREGG, Walter H
Physical Fitness Through Sports And Nutrition
ACSB-v9-Fall '76-p20
BL-v71-Jl 15 '75-p1190
BS-v35-S '75-p169
Inst-v85-F '76-p166
KR-v43-Je 1 '75-p615
SB-v11-Mr '76-p212
SLJ-v22-N '75-p68

* * *

GREGOR, Arthur
Animal Babies
Teacher-v94-Ja '77-p132
The Little Elephant
Teacher-v94-Ja '77-p132
One, Two, Three, Four, Five
CE-v61-S '84-p33
LJ-v96-Mr 15 '71-p1084

* * *

GREGOR, Arthur S
Adventure Of Man
BL-v63-F 15 '67-p620
CCB-B-v20-F '67-p89
CE-v43-F '67-p358
CLW-v38-N '66-p209
HB-v43-Ag '67-p493
KR-v34-Je 1 '66-p542
LJ-v91-O 15 '66-p5250
NH-v76-N '67-p29
SB-v2-Mr '67-p289
SR-v49-N 12 '66-p54
Amulets, Talismans, And Fetishes
BL-v72-Ja 15 '76-p678
BL-v72-Ja 15 '76-p684
CCB-B-v29-Je '76-p157
KR-v43-D 15 '75-p1385
SLJ-v22-Mr '76-p113
How The World's First Cities Began
CCB-B-v21-S '67-p6
Inst-v76-Je '67-p142
KR-v35-My 15 '67-p605
LJ-v92-Je 15 '67-p2450
SB-v3-D '67-p184
SR-v50-Jl 22 '67-p43
Man's Mark On The Land
ACSB-v8-Winter '75-p18
BL-v71-S 1 '74-p41
KR-v42-My 15 '74-p537
SB-v10-D '74-p246
SLJ-v21-Mr '75-p96

* * *

GREGOR, Hugh
Warships
GP-v19-N '80-p3784

* * *

GREGORIADOU SURELE, Galateia
O Mikros Bourlotieres
BL-v74-S 15 '77-p204
O Spurgites Me To Kokkino Gileko
BL-v72-Je 1 '76-p1411
Ta Dodeka Phengaria
BL-v72-Je 1 '76-p1412

* * *

GREGORIAN, Joyce Ballou
The Broken Citadel
BL-v72-O 1 '75-p235
CSM-v67-N 5 '75-pB2
HB-v52-Ap '76-p154
KR-v43-Jl 15 '75-p782
S Fict R-v12-F '83-p31
SLJ-v22-N '75-p90
Castledown
BL-v73-My 1 '77-p1352
CCB-B-v31-N '77-p47
KR-v45-Mr 15 '77-p290
SLJ-v23-My '77-p69

* * *

GREGORICH, Barbara
Beep, Beep
SLJ-v30-My '84-p96
The Fox On The Box
SLJ-v30-My '84-p96
The Gum On The Drum
CCB-B-v37-Ap '84-p147
SLJ-v30-My '84-p96
I Want A Pet
SLJ-v30-My '84-p96
Jog, Frog, Jog
SLJ-v30-My '84-p96
My Friend Goes Left
PW-v225-Mr 16 '84-p87
SLJ-v30-My '84-p96
Nine Men Chase A Hen
SLJ-v30-My '84-p96
Say Good Night
SLJ-v30-My '84-p96
Sue Likes Blue
SLJ-v30-My '84-p96
Up Went The Goat
SLJ-v30-My '84-p96

* * *

GREGOROWSKI, Christopher
Why A Donkey Was Chosen
Am-v135-D 11 '76-p427
CCB-B-v30-N '76-p42
GP-v14-D '75-p2774
HB-v53-F '77-p38
JB-v40-F '76-p14
SLJ-v23-O '76-p87

* * *

GREGORY, David
The Chappell Piano Book
JB-v47-D '83-p244
TES-N 11 '83-p25
The Chappell Recorder Book
JB-v46-Ag '82-p142
TES-Je 25 '82-p25

* * *

GREGORY, Diana
The Fog Burns Off By 11 O'Clock
BL-v78-S 1 '81-p44
CCB-B-v35-S '81-p9
PW-v219-Je 19 '81-p102
SLJ-v28-O '81-p150
VOYA-v4-D '81-p29
I'm Boo...That's Who!
KR-v47-D 1 '79-p1375
RT-v33-My '80-p974
SLJ-v26-D '79-p86
SLJ-v27-My '81-p27
There's A Caterpillar In My Lemonade
SLJ-v27-Ja '81-p61

* * *

GREGORY, G Robinson
Animals And Things
SLJ-v25-F '79-p42

* * *

GREGORY, Horace
The Silver Swan: Poems Of Mystery & Romance
BL-v63-Ja 1 '67-p484
BS-v26-D 1 '66-p339
CCB-B-v20-Ja '67-p74

GREGORY, Horace
(continued)
CLW-v38-Ja '67-p338
HB-v42-O '66-p578
KR-v34-My 15 '66-p518
KR-v34-O 15 '66-p1111
LJ-v91-Je 15 '66-p3266
NYTBR-v71-My 8 '66-p26
PW-v190-O 10 '66-p74
SR-v49-N 12 '66-p54

* * *

GREGORY, Lady Isabella Augusta Persse
Irish Legends For Children
CAY-v4-Fall '83-p17

* * *

GREGORY, Oliver
Oxford Introductory Maths Workbooks
TES-Mr 11 '83-p49
Oxford Junior English Workbooks
TES-Mr 7 '80-p40

* * *

GREGORY, Stephen
Bobsledding
BL-v72-Jl 15 '76-p1600
SLJ-v23-S '76-p107
Racing To Win
BL-v72-Jl 15 '76-p1600
SLJ-v23-S '76-p107
Tug-Of-War
JB-v43-O '79-p278

* * *

GREGSON, Bob
The Incredible Indoor Games Book
BL-v79-Ja 1 '83-p617
B Rpt-v2-N '83-p43
Cur R-v22-F '83-p21
The Outrageous Outdoor Games Book
Cur R-v24-N '84-p26

* * *

GREIG, Clarence
The Myceneans
GP-v17-My '78-p3336
TES-Mr 10 '78-p62

* * *

GRENDER, I
The Third 'Did I Ever Tell You...?' Book
JB-v44-Ag '80-p176

* * *

GRENDER, Iris
The Alphabet Bus
GP-v14-Mr '76-p2812
Did I Ever Tell You...?
GP-v16-Mr '78-p3274
JB-v42-F '78-p26
Did I Ever Tell You...About My Birthday Party?
JB-v47-Je '83-p124
TES-My 13 '83-p32
Measuring Things
SA-v235-D '76-p145
Very First Cook Book
GP-v14-Mr '76-p2826

* * *

GRENFELL, Joyce
George-Don't Do That
GP-v16-N '77-p3214
Lis-v98-S 1 '77-p274

* * *

GRENIER, Muriel
Blueberry Books
BIC-v10-Ap '81-p30
Can Child Lit-#25 '82-p67
Quill & Q-v47-O '81-p12

* * *

GRENZ, Margit
Katze, Hahn Und Mause Franz
BL-v72-Mr 1 '76-p985

* * *

GRETZ, Susanna
The Bears Who Stayed Indoors
B&B-v17-My '72-pR12
BW-v5-My 9 '71-p8
HB-v47-Ag '71-p374
LJ-v97-Ap 15 '72-p1596
NS-v80-N 6 '70-p612
NS-v83-Je 2 '72-p763
PW-v200-S 27 '71-p66
TLS-D 11 '70-p1455
The Bears Who Went To The Seaside
HB-v50-Ap '74-p140
KR-v41-D 15 '73-p1362
LJ-v99-My 15 '74-p1465
TLS-D 8 '72-p1498
Teddy Bears ABC
Inst-v85-N '75-p146
KR-v43-Ag 15 '75-p911
SLJ-v22-N '75-p62
Teacher-v93-F '76-p26
Teddy Bears And The Cold Cure
GP-v23-S '84-p4321
Obs-Ag 26 '84-p19
Teddy Bears Cookbook
SLJ-v25-N '78-p44
Teddy Bears Go Shopping
BL-v79-Ja 15 '83-p676
CBRS-v11-D '82-p32
GP-v21-N '82-p3991
JB-v47-F '83-p13
NS-v104-D 3 '82-p22
PW-v222-O 22 '82-p56
SLJ-v30-S '83-p106
TLS-S 17 '82-p1003
WLB-v57-F '83-p505
Teddy Bears' Moving Day
BL-v78-N 1 '81-p388
CBRS-v10-N '81-p22
GP-v20-S '81-p3936
KR-v49-N 1 '81-p1338
Obs-Jl 19 '81-p29
PW-v220-S 4 '81-p60
SLJ-v28-Ja '82-p64
Sch Lib-v30-Je '82-p120
TES-Je 5 '81-p36
Teddy Bears 1 To 10
CE-v61-S '84-p33
HB-v46-F '70-p32
LJ-v95-Mr 15 '70-p1186
LJ-v96-Mr 15 '71-p1086
PW-v196-S 15 '69-p61
TLS-O 16 '69-p1197
Ten Green Bottles
JB-v40-Ag '76-p189

* * *

GREY, Elizabeth
Behind The Scenes In A Film Studio
CCB-B-v22-Mr '69-p110
LJ-v93-Ap 15 '68-p1650
TLS-My 25 '67-p464
Behind The Scenes In The Theatre
AB-v44-D 22 '69-p2121
CCB-B-v23-Mr '70-p111
KR-v37-Ag 1 '69-p821
LJ-v95-Ap 15 '70-p1648
Winged Victory: The Story Of Amy Johnson
B&B-v11-Je '66-p58
CCB-B-v20-Ap '67-p121
CLW-v38-F '67-p394
KR-v34-S 15 '66-p990
LJ-v92-Ja 15 '67-p343
TLS-My 19 '66-p452

* * *

GREY, Sir George
Polynesian Mythology
RT-v34-Mr '81-p634

* * *

GREY, Jerry
The Facts Of Flight
LJ-v98-N 15 '73-p3464
Noise, Noise, Noise!
ACSB-v10-Winter '77-p20
KR-v44-F 1 '76-p141
SB-v12-S '76-p91
SLJ-v23-F '77-p72
The Race For Electric Power
BL-v69-My 1 '73-p855
CCB-B-v26-My '73-p138
LJ-v98-Mr 15 '73-p1012

* * *

GREY, John A
The Aesthetics Of The "Rougon-Macquart"
FR-v54-F '81-p473

* * *

GREY, Judith
Mud Pies
SLJ-v29-S '82-p102
What Time Is It?
CCB-B-v35-My '82-p170
SLJ-v29-S '82-p102
Yummy, Yummy
RT-v36-My '83-p929
SLJ-v29-S '82-p103

* * *

GREY, Vivian
The Chemist Who Lost His Head
ASBYP-v16-Fall '83-p30
BL-v79-Mr 1 '83-p906
B Rpt-v1-Mr '83-p42
CCB-B-v36-F '83-p108
KR-v50-D 1 '82-p1296
SB-v19-S '83-p28
SE-v47-Ap '83-p245
SLJ-v29-Mr '83-p176
Secret Of The Mysterious Rays
CCB-B-v20-Ap '67-p122
HB-v43-O '67-p610
LJ-v92-Ja 15 '67-p343
SB-v2-Mr '67-p269
Spec-v218-Je 2 '67-p656
TLS-N 30 '67-p1164

* * *

GREYDANUS, Rose
Animals At The Zoo
SLJ-v27-S '80-p59
Big Red Fire Engine
SLJ-v27-S '80-p59
Changing Seasons
ASBYP-v17-Spring '84-p54
SLJ-v30-D '83-p56
Double Trouble
RT-v36-My '83-p929
SLJ-v29-S '82-p103
Freddie The Frog
RT-v34-My '81-p953
SLJ-v27-S '80-p59
Hocus Pocus, Magic Show!
SLJ-v29-S '82-p103
Horses
ASBYP-v17-Spring '84-p54
SLJ-v30-D '83-p56
Let's Pretend
SLJ-v29-S '82-p103
Mike's New Bike
SLJ-v27-O '80-p135
My Secret Hiding Place
SLJ-v27-O '80-p135
Susie Goes Shopping
BL-v77-O 15 '80-p332
SLJ-v27-O '80-p135
Tree House Fun
BL-v77-O 15 '80-p332
SLJ-v27-O '80-p135
Trouble In Space
SLJ-v29-S '82-p103
Valentine's Day Grump
SLJ-v29-S '82-p103
Willie The Slowpoke
BL-v77-O 15 '80-p332
SLJ-v27-O '80-p135

* * *

GRIBBLE, D
Strange Things To Do And Make
JB-v43-Je '79-p157

* * *

GRIBBLE, Leonard
Famous Mysteries Of Modern Times
JB-v41-F '77-p50

* * *

GRIBBLE, McPhee
Bicycles
GP-v15-S '76-p2948
Creatures
Emerg Lib-v9-S '81-p28
GP-v20-My '81-p3896
Feasts For Special Or Greedy Days
Emerg Lib-v9-S '81-p28
Games
Emerg Lib-v9-S '81-p28
Things To Fly
Emerg Lib-v9-S '81-p29

* * *

GRICE, Frederick
The Black Hand Gang
TLS-Jl 2 '71-p775
TLS-Jl 15 '77-p866
Johnny-Head-In-Air
GP-v17-Jl '78-p3366
JB-v42-O '78-p267
Obs-Jl 23 '78-p21
TES-Je 16 '78-p47
TLS-Jl 7 '78-p765
The Moving Finger
GP-v14-O '75-p2730
Nine Days' Wonder
GP-v15-Mr '77-p3064
JB-v41-Ag '77-p221
TLS-D 10 '76-p1545
TLS-Jl 15 '77-p866

* * *

GRIDLEY, Marion E
Contemporary American Indian Leaders
BL-v69-Mr 1 '73-p643
CCB-B-v26-F '73-p91
KR-v40-N 1 '72-p1249
LJ-v98-Mr 15 '73-p1003
NYTBR, pt.2-N 5 '72-p20
SE-v37-D '73-p789
Maria Tallchief
BL-v70-D 1 '73-p386
KR-v41-Ag 1 '73-p815
LJ-v99-Mr 15 '74-p890
SE-v48-N '84-p556
SLJ-v24-D '77-p35

* * *

GRIEDER, Walter
The Great Feast
CCB-B-v22-F '69-p94
KR-v36-O 15 '68-p1157
LJ-v94-Ja 15 '69-p286

* * *

GRIESE, Arnold A
At The Mouth Of The Luckiest River
CCB-B-v27-S '73-p8
CE-v50-N '73-p97

GRIESE, Arnold A (continued)
CE-v57-Mr '81-p206
KR-v41-Je 1 '73-p599
LJ-v98-S 15 '73-p2650
NYTBR-Ag 5 '73-p8
RT-v34-F '81-p531
The Way Of Our People
BS-v35-D '75-p299
CCB-B-v29-F '76-p97
CE-v52-Ap '76-p318
HB-v52-F '76-p49
KR-v43-S 15 '75-p1066
SLJ-v22-N '75-p77
The Wind Is Not A River
BL-v75-D 15 '78-p685
CBRS-v7-Mr '79-p80
CCB-B-v32-Ap '79-p137
CSM-v70-O 23 '78-pB13
HB-v55-Ap '79-p194
KR-v47-Ja 1 '79-p5
SE-v43-Ap '79-p302
SLJ-v25-D '78-p52

* * *

GRIFALCONI, Ann
City Rhythms
BL-v62-Ap 1 '66-p775
BL-v69-My 1 '73-p836
CCB-B-v19-My '66-p149
CE-v46-Ap '70-p366
LJ-v91-My 15 '66-p2682
NYTBR-v71-Mr 27 '66-p34
The Matter With Lucy
CCB-B-v27-S '73-p9
Inst-v82-My '73-p76
KR-v41-Mr 1 '73-p250
LJ-v98-Jl '73-p2186
PW-v203-Mr 19 '73-p72
The Toy Trumpet
BL-v65-Ap 1 '69-p892
CCB-B-v22-Jl '69-p175
CE-v46-D '69-p168
CSM-v61-My 1 '69-pB2
LJ-v94-Mr 15 '69-p1318
PW-v194-S 16 '68-p71

* * *

GRIFFEN, Elizabeth
Dog's Book Of Bugs
CCB-B-v20-My '67-p140
KR-v35-F 1 '67-p128
LJ-v92-Mr 15 '67-p1310
NYTBR-v72-My 7 '67-p49
NYTBR-v72-N 5 '67-p66
PW-v191-F 27 '67-p103
SB-v3-My '67-p58
SR-v50-Ap 22 '67-p99
SR/W-v1-My 4 '74-p50
Teacher-v92-S '74-p131

* * *

GRIFFIN, A R
The Collier
TES-Ap 8 '83-p34

* * *

GRIFFIN, John
English Language
TES-D 31 '82-p25
Skulker Wheat And Other Stories
GP-v16-O '77-p3178
JB-v41-Je '77-p176

* * *

GRIFFIN, John Howard
A Time To Be Human
BL-v73-Mr 1 '77-p1013
CCB-B-v30-Jl '77-p175
CSM-v69-Ap 27 '77-p27
Cur R-v17-Ag '78-p176
HB-v53-Ag '77-p461
J Read-v22-F '79-p477
KR-v45-Ja 1 '77-p7
NYTBR-Ap 3 '77-p24
PW-v211-F 14 '77-p83
SB-v14-My '78-p7
SLJ-v23-F '77-p72

* * *

GRIFFIN, Judith Berry
The Magic Mirrors
BW-v5-My 9 '71-p17
CCB-B-v25-N '71-p43
Comw-v94-My 21 '71-p267
KR-v39-My 1 '71-p500
NYTBR, pt.2-My 2 '71-p43
PW-v199-My 31 '71-p135
Nat Turner
BL-v67-Ja 1 '71-p372
BW-v4-N 8 '70-p5
CCB-B-v24-Ja '71-p74
KR-v38-Je 15 '70-p641
LJ-v95-O 15 '70-p3627
Phoebe And The General
BL-v73-Je 1 '77-p1496
CCB-B-v30-Je '77-p158
CE-v54-Mr '78-p262
CLW-v49-D '77-p235
HB-v53-Ag '77-p459
KR-v45-Mr 1 '77-p224
NYTBR-Ap 3 '77-p24
SLJ-v24-S '77-p129

* * *

GRIFFIN-BEALE, Christopher
TV & Video
ASBYP-v16-Fall '83-p64
LATBR-Je 26 '83-p8
SLJ-v29-Ap '83-p123

* * *

GRIFFITH, Helen V
Alex And The Cat
BL-v78-Mr 15 '82-p965
CCB-B-v35-My '82-p170
HB-v58-Je '82-p284
KR-v50-Mr 1 '82-p273
PW-v221-Ap 30 '82-p59
SLJ-v28-My '82-p77
Alex Remembers
CBRS-v11-Jl '83-p130
CCB-B-v37-S '83-p8
KR-v51-Ap 15 '83-p457
NY-v59-D 5 '83-p204
RT-v37-N '83-p191
SLJ-v29-My '83-p61
Foxy
BL-v80-Jl '84-p1549
B Rpt-v3-S '84-p32
CCB-B-v37-Je '84-p186
KR-v52-My 1 '84-pJ38
LA-v61-O '84-p628
SLJ-v30-My '84-p80
VOYA-v7-Je '84-p95
Mine Will, Said John
BL-v76-Jl 15 '80-p1675
CBRS-v8-Ag '80-p132
CCB-B-v34-F '81-p111
HB-v56-O '80-p514
KR-v48-S 15 '80-p1228
PW-v218-N 7 '80-p62
RT-v35-O '81-p54
SLJ-v27-O '80-p135
More Alex And The Cat
CCB-B-v37-Mr '84-p127
CE-v60-Mr '84-p286
HB-v59-O '83-p568
KR-v51-S 1 '83-pJ149
RT-v37-F '84-p528
SLJ-v30-O '83-p149

* * *

GRIFFITH, Valeria W
A Ride For Jenny
CCB-B-v18-My '65-p129

* * *

GRIFFITH, William
Fantasies Two
SLJ-v27-D '80-p59

GRIGSON, Geoffrey
(continued)
BW-v4-My 17 '70-p29
CCB-B-v24-S '70-p9
CSM-v62-Je 20 '70-p13
Comw-v92-My 22 '70-p254
HB-v46-Ap '70-p175
KR-v37-D 1 '69-p1262
LJ-v95-Ap 15 '70-p1649
Lis-v82-N 6 '69-p643
NS-v79-My 15 '70-p707
Obs-D 7 '69-p31
PW-v196-D 8 '69-p47
Spec-v223-N 1 '69-p609
TLS-D 4 '69-p1398
Shapes And Stories: A Book About Pictures
BL-v62-Ja 15 '66-p487
CCB-B-v19-Ap '66-p129
CSM-v58-Mr 24 '66-p10
HB-v42-F '66-p75
KR-v33-S 15 '65-p982
LJ-v90-O 15 '65-p4629
NY-v41-D 4 '65-p246
NYTBR-v71-Ja 23 '66-p26
SR-v48-N 13 '65-p60

* * *

GRIGSON, Lionel
The Divided World
GP-v14-D '75-p2763

* * *

GRILLONE, Lisa
Small Worlds Close Up
ACSB-v12-Spring '79-p25
BL-v74-Jl 15 '78-p1734
BL-v80-O 15 '83-p369
CCB-B-v32-N '78-p44
CE-v55-Ja '79-p170
CE-v56-N '79-p114
CLW-v50-O '78-p110
CSM-v74-O 8 '82-pB6
Comw-v105-N 10 '78-p734
GP-v19-My '80-p3687
Inst-v88-Mr '79-p150
JB-v44-Ag '80-p176
KR-v46-Jl 15 '78-p755
LA-v55-O '78-p861
Lis-v104-N 6 '80-p626
PW-v213-Je 12 '78-p82
RT-v33-O '79-p51
SB-v15-S '79-p100
SLJ-v25-S '78-p158
TES-Ja 2 '81-p14
TLS-Mr 28 '80-p363

* * *

GRIMES, Brian
British Wild Animals
GP-v21-My '82-p3904
JB-v46-Je '82-p104

* * *

GRIMES, Nikki
Growin'
BW-Ja 8 '78-pE6
CCB-B-v31-Ap '78-p127
Inter BC-v9-Ag 80 '78-p17
Inter BC-v12-#4 '81-p21
KR-v45-D 1 '77-p1266
LA-v55-My '78-p620
PW-v212-N 14 '77-p67
RT-v32-D '78-p365
SLJ-v24-D '77-p49
Teacher-v95-My '78-p103
Something On My Mind
BB-v6-N '78-p2
BL-v74-Jl 15 '78-p1732
BL-v74-S 1 '78-p48
CCB-B-v32-O '78-p30
Comw-v107-F 29 '80-p115
KR-v46-Jl 15 '78-p747
PW-v213-My 29 '78-p51
RT-v33-My '80-p974
SLJ-v25-S '78-p137
SR-v5-My 27 '78-p66
Teacher-v96-N '78-p132

* * *

GRIMM, Jakob Ludwig Karl
About Wise Men And Simpletons
A Lib-v3-Ap '72-p420
BL-v68-F 1 '72-p466
BL-v68-Ap 1 '72-p669
CCB-B-v25-Ja '72-p74
CE-v48-Mr '72-p308
Comw-v95-N 19 '71-p187
HB-v47-D '71-p608
KR-v39-S 15 '71-p1011
LJ-v97-F 15 '72-p775
NCW-v216-Mr '73-p91
NS-v84-N 10 '72-p695
NY-v47-D 4 '71-p193
NYRB-v17-D 2 '71-p25
NYTBR-O 31 '71-p8
NYTBR-D 5 '71-p85
NYTBR, pt.2-N 7 '71-p28
SR-v54-D 11 '71-p46
Spec-v229-N 11 '72-p749
TLS-N 3 '72-p1332
TN-v28-Je '72-p434
The Bear And The Kingbird (Segal)
BW-v9-D 2 '79-p16
CBRS-v8-N '79-p24
CCB-B-v33-Ja '80-p95
KR-v47-S 15 '79-p1065
LA-v57-Mr '80-p321
NY-v55-D 3 '79-p200
NYTBR-N 11 '79-p64
PW-v216-S 10 '79-p74
SLJ-v26-D '79-p74
The Bearskinner (Hoffmann)
BL-v75-S 15 '78-p217
CCB-B-v32-F '79-p99
CLW-v51-S '79-p91
GP-v18-S '79-p3569
HB-v55-O '78-p507
JB-v43-Ag '79-p194
KR-v46-S 15 '78-p1015
LA-v56-Mr '79-p287
New R-v179-D 16 '78-p28
Obs-Ap 1 '79-p38
PW-v213-My 29 '78-p51
RT-v33-O '79-p38
RT-v34-N '80-p169
SLJ-v25-N '78-p62
Sch Lib-v27-D '79-p347
WLB-v53-Ja '79-p378
Beauty And The Beast
HB-v49-Ap '73-p137
NYTBR-Ja 14 '73-p8
The Best Of Grimm's Fairy Tales (Svend Otto S)
BL-v76-F 1 '80-p768
BW-v9-D 2 '79-p16
NYTBR-N 11 '79-p64
PW-v216-D 10 '79-p69
SLJ-v26-Ap '80-p90
Blanca Nieves Y Los Siete Enanos (Burkert)
BL-v79-Ag '83-p1459
The Blue Lamp (Fromm)
CR-v228-My '76-p280
JB-v40-Je '76-p143
NS-v91-My 21 '76-p689
Obs-Ap 11 '76-p33
The Brave Little Tailor
TLS-Jl 2 '71-p769
The Brave Little Tailor (Corcoran)
SLJ-v26-Mr '80-p117
The Brave Little Tailor (Svend Otto S)
BL-v76-F 1 '80-p770
CLW-v52-S '80-p91
HB-v56-Ap '80-p164

GRIMM, Jakob Ludwig Karl (continued)
NYTBR-N 11 '79-p64
SLJ-v26-Ap '80-p93
The Bremen Town Musicians
RT-v37-Ap '84-p705
The Bremen Town Musicians (Domanska)
BL-v77-O 15 '80-p326
BW-v10-D 14 '80-p11
CBRS-v9-N '80-p22
CE-v57-Mr '81-p236
GP-v20-S '81-p3947
HB-v56-O '80-p514
KR-v48-N 1 '80-p1391
LA-v58-My '81-p597
NYTBR-v85-N 9 '80-p64
PW-v218-O 31 '80-p86
RT-v34-Ap '81-p853
SLJ-v27-S '80-p59
TLS-Jl 24 '81-p840
The Bremen Town Musicians (Ford)
SLJ-v26-Ja '80-p53
The Brementown Musicians (Benvenuti)
SLJ-v26-Ja '80-p56
The Brothers Grimm: Popular Folk Tales (Alderson)
BB-v7-Mr '79-p3
B&B-v23-Je '78-p72
BL-v75-O 1 '78-p293
Brit Bk N C-Autumn '80-p3
CCB-B-v32-Ja '79-p81
Comw-v105-N 10 '78-p729
EJ-v68-O '79-p79
GP-v17-Jl '78-p3354
GP-v17-Mr '79-p3470
HB-v55-F '79-p74
ILN-v266-D '78-p127
JB-v42-D '78-p299
KR-v46-S 1 '78-p952
LA-v56-Mr '79-p293
RT-v32-My '79-p973
SLJ-v25-N '78-p62
Spec-v240-Ap 29 '78-p25
TES-My 5 '78-p20
TLS-Ap 7 '78-p387
Teacher-v96-My '79-p113
La Caperucita Roja (Bernadette)
BL-v76-Je 15 '80-p1546
The Cat And Mouse Who Shared A House (Hurlimann)
LJ-v99-Ap 15 '74-p1212
The Cat And Mouse Who Shared A House (Walck)
NY-v50-D 2 '74-p201
Cinderella (Bernadette)
GP-v18-S '79-p3569
Sch Lib-v27-D '79-p347
Cinderella (Elsasser)
LA-v57-N '80-p894
Cinderella (Svend Otto S)
BL-v75-Ja 15 '79-p809
CBRS-v7-F '79-p61
CCB-B-v32-My '79-p154
GP-v17-N '78-p3428
HB-v55-Ap '79-p182
JB-v43-F '79-p17
PW-v214-N 20 '78-p60
RT-v33-O '79-p93
SLJ-v25-Mr '79-p122
Cinderella (Watts)
JB-v43-Ag '79-p194
Clever Kate (Lobel)
CCB-B-v27-Ap '74-p129
LJ-v99-Ja 15 '74-p199
The Complete Grimm's Fairy Tales
TES-F 24 '84-p29
The Complete Grimm's Fairy Tales (Campbell)
NYTBR-N 3 '74-p23
The Complete Grimm's Fairy Tales (Scharl)
CCB-B-v28-My '75-p147
New R-v171-N 23 '74-p43
PT-v8-Mr '75-p96
TLS-S 19 '75-p1050
Time-v104-D 23 '74-p72
WSJ-v185-D 20 '74-p14
The Complete Grimm's Fairy Tales (Untermeyer)
NYTBR, pt.2-N 9 '69-p54
The Elves And The Shoemaker
GT-v89-F '72-p94
Obs-Ap 19 '70-p26
TLS-Ap 16 '70-p419
The Elves And The Shoemaker (Brandt)
LJ-v94-Ja 15 '69-p286
The Elves And The Shoemaker (Titleman)
SLJ-v29-O '82-p136
Fairy Tales
GP-v14-Ja '76-p2803
GP-v21-Ja '83-p3999
Sch Lib-v30-Mr '82-p32
Fairy Tales Of The Brothers Grimm (Nielsen)
BL-v76-D 1 '79-p563
BW-v9-D 2 '79-p16
Brit Bk N C-Autumn '80-p4
GP-v18-Ja '80-p3632
JB-v44-Ap '80-p59
KR-v48-Ja 15 '80-p69
Mac-v92-D 10 '79-p64
NW-v94-D 17 '79-p96
NY-v55-D 3 '79-p202
NYTBR-N 11 '79-p64
SLJ-v26-D '79-p86
Fairy Tales (Taylor)
GP-v17-Jl '78-p3354
TES-My 5 '78-p20
Favourite Tales From Grimm (Svend Otto S)
JB-v44-Je '80-p117
Sch Lib-v28-Mr '80-p25
The Fisherman And His Wife
LJ-v96-Mr 15 '71-p1108
NS-v79-My 15 '70-p707
PW-v198-D 7 '70-p50
TLS-Ap 16 '70-p419
The Fisherman And His Wife (Howe)
SLJ-v30-Ag '84-p68
The Fisherman And His Wife (Jarrell)
Art T-v10-Fall '80-p31
BL-v76-Je 1 '80-p1424
BW-v10-My 11 '80-p17
CBRS-v8-Je '80-p104
CCB-B-v34-S '80-p10
HB-v56-Ag '80-p397
KR-v48-Je 15 '80-p776
LA-v57-N '80-p894
NYTBR-v85-My 11 '80-p24
PW-v217-My 16 '80-p211
RT-v36-D '82-p287
SLJ-v26-My '80-p57
The Fisherman And His Wife (Laimgruber)
BL-v75-Je 15 '79-p1536
BW-v9-D 2 '79-p16
CBRS-v7-Spring '79-p114
JB-v43-F '79-p18
LA-v56-O '79-p820
NYTBR-S 23 '79-p26
SLJ-v26-S '79-p111
Sch Lib-v27-Mr '79-p27
TES-N 24 '78-p39
Fitcher's Bird
SLJ-v30-Ag '84-p68

GRIMM, Jakob Ludwig Karl (continued)
The Frog Prince (Baxter)
SLJ-v26-Ja '80-p53
The Frog Prince (Galdone)
KR-v43-Jl 1 '75-p708
Der Froschkonig (Brandt)
BL-v75-N 15 '78-p554
German Folk Tales (Magoun)
NYTBR-N 13 '77-p60
NYTBR, pt.2-N 9 '69-p54
The Golden Goose (Paterson)
SLJ-v29-O '82-p136
The Goose Girl
BW-v14-Jl 8 '84-p8
Grimm's Fairy Tales
Brit Bk N C-Spring '82-p6
Econ-v241-D 18 '71-p69
JB-v47-F '83-p25
LATBR-D 5 '82-p10
NYRB-v15-D 17 '70-p43
NYTBR-v87-N 14 '82-p49
NYTBR, pt.2-F 13 '72-p8
Punch-v281-D 2 '81-p1023
Punch-v286-Mr 21 '84-p17
Sch Lib-v31-Je '83-p135
TES-N 20 '81-p31
TES-Mr 18 '83-p33
TLS-N 20 '81-p1360
Grimm's Fairy Tales (Attwell)
NS-v93-My 20 '77-p684
TES-F 3 '78-p35
TLS-Mr 25 '77-p352
Grimm's Fairy Tales (Rackham)
BL-v70-Ja 1 '74-p488
BW-v7-D 9 '73-p6
CCB-B-v27-F '74-p95
Choice-v12-N '75-p1132
Inst-v83-My '74-p96
LJ-v99-Ja 15 '74-p209
NO-v12-D 8 '73-p23
NY-v49-D 3 '73-p208
NYTBR-Ja 13 '74-p8
New R-v170-F 16 '74-p34
Time-v102-D 10 '73-p101
Grimm's Fairy Tales (Scharl)
Brit Bk N C-Autumn '80-p3
Grimm's Fairy Tales (Schramm)
NYTBR-N 11 '79-p65
Grimm's Fairy Tales (Vredenburg)
TES-My 5 '78-p20
Grimm's Golden Goose (Mikolaycak)
LJ-v94-N 15 '69-p4278
Grimm's Household Tales
BSA-P-v64-O '70-p479
NYRB-v15-D 17 '70-p43
Grimm's Tales For Young And Old
BW-v13-S 11 '83-p16
Grimm's Tales For Young And Old (Manheim)
BL-v74-F 15 '78-p1014
Brit Bk N C-Autumn '80-p3
CCB-B-v31-F '78-p93
Choice-v15-Mr '78-p76
GP-v17-Mr '79-p3470
JAF-v93-Jl '80-p356
JB-v43-F '79-p36
KR-v45-O 15 '77-p1137
KR-v45-N 1 '77-p1153
LJ-v102-N 15 '77-p2348
Lis-v100-N 9 '78-p625
NW-v90-D 19 '77-p85
NY-v53-D 12 '77-p208
NYTBR-N 13 '77-p60
PW-v212-O 24 '77-p77
SE-v42-Ap '78-p320
SLJ-v24-N '77-p71
TES-N 24 '78-p39
Hans In Luck (Hoffmann)
BB-v3-Ag '75-p1
BL-v71-Mr 15 '75-p760
CCB-B-v28-Je '75-p161
CLW-v47-Ap '76-p397
GP-v14-My '75-p2647
HB-v51-Je '75-p260
JB-v39-Je '75-p175
KR-v43-Ap 15 '75-p444
NY-v51-D 1 '75-p174
SLJ-v22-S '75-p82
Hansel And Gretel
HB-v47-Ap '71-p161
KR-v39-F 15 '71-p173
KR-v39-Ag 15 '71-p870
LJ-v96-Ap 15 '71-p1522
NYTBR-Je 20 '71-p8
Spec-v225-D 5 '70-pR18
TLS-D 11 '70-p1448
Hansel And Gretel (Adams)
BB-v3-O '75-p2
BL-v71-Jl 15 '75-p1191
CCB-B-v29-Ja '76-p77
CE-v52-Mr '76-p270
Comw-v102-N 21 '75-p568
HB-v51-D '75-p585
KR-v43-Ag 15 '75-p911
LA-v53-F '76-p199
NW-v86-D 15 '75-p92
NYTBR-N 16 '75-p58
PW-v208-S 29 '75-p52
SLJ-v22-N '75-p62
SR-v3-N 29 '75-p32
Teacher-v93-N '75-p110
Hansel And Gretel (Bolliger-Savelli)
TES-N 20 '81-p31
TLS-N 20 '81-p1360
Hansel And Gretel (Browne)
BL-v78-Ag '82-p1525
CBRS-v10-Jl '82-p124
GP-v21-My '82-p3907
HB-v58-Je '82-p279
JB-v46-F '82-p17
RT-v36-O '82-p117
SLJ-v28-Ag '82-p98
Sch Lib-v29-D '81-p320
TES-N 20 '81-p31
TLS-N 20 '81-p1360
Hansel And Gretel (Galdone)
BL-v79-Ja 15 '83-p676
BW-v13-My 8 '83-p13
Hansel And Gretel (Jeffers)
BL-v77-O 15 '80-p326
BW-v10-D 14 '80-p11
CBRS-v9-O '80-p14
CCB-B-v34-F '81-p111
HB-v56-D '80-p634
Inst-v90-N '80-p51
JB-v45-Ag '81-p144
KR-v49-Ja 15 '81-p73
NYTBR-v86-Ja 4 '81-p25
PW-v218-S 12 '80-p66
RT-v35-O '81-p60
SLJ-v27-N '80-p62
SLJ-v28-Ag '82-p98
TLS-Mr 27 '81-p343
Hansel And Gretel (Svend Otto S)
BL-v79-Jl '83-p1400
BW-v13-My 8 '83-p13
CBRS-v11-Spring '83-p120
GP-v22-S '83-p4143
JB-v47-Ag '83-p153
TES-O 21 '83-p37
Hansel And Gretel (Watts)
JB-v39-F '75-p15
Hansel And Gretel (Zwerger)
BL-v76-Ap 1 '80-p1128
CBRS-v8-Ap '80-p84
CCB-B-v33-My '80-p173
CE-v60-My '84-p367
GP-v18-S '79-p3569

GRIMM, Jakob Ludwig Karl (continued)

I Musicanti Di Brema
BL-v70-O 1 '73-p167

The Musicians Of Bremen (Rogers)
PW-v206-O 14 '74-p57
SLJ-v22-S '75-p82
TLS-D 6 '74-p1382

The Musicians Of Bremen (Svend Otto S)
GP-v14-My '75-p2647
JB-v39-F '75-p21

The Musicians Of Bremen (Teissig)
B&B-v20-My '75-p81

A Pillo, Pillo Y Medio
BL-v79-Jl '83-p1406

Popular Folk Tales
GP-v17-Jl '78-p3354
TLS-Ap 7 '78-p387

The Queen Bee
BW-v14-Jl 8 '84-p8

Rapunzel (Ash)
JB-v46-Ag '82-p132

Rapunzel (Dodson)
SLJ-v26-Mr '80-p117

Rapunzel (Hague)
BW-v14-Jl 8 '84-p8

Rare Treasures From Grimm
BL-v78-D 15 '81-p548
CCB-B-v35-Ja '82-p85
HB-v58-Ap '82-p175
NYTBR-v87-F 7 '82-p26
PW-v220-D 4 '81-p50
SLJ-v28-F '82-p76

Red Riding Hood
BW-v6-My 7 '72-p6
CCB-B-v26-F '73-p91
CE-v49-O '72-p27
HB-v48-Je '72-p259
KR-v40-Ap 15 '72-p475
LJ-v97-Ap 15 '72-p1594
NYTBR, pt.2-My 7 '72-p38
PW-v201-Ja 31 '72-p247

Rumpelstiltskin
CSM-v63-Jl 3 '71-p17
KR-v39-My 15 '71-p549
NYTBR-Je 20 '71-p8
Spec-v225-D 5 '70-pR18
TLS-D 11 '70-p1448

Rumpelstiltskin (Hockerman)
SLJ-v26-Mr '80-p117

Rumpelstiltskin (Tarcov)
BW-S 19 '76-pH4

Rumpelstiltskin (Wallner)
BL-v80-Jl '84-p1549
Cur R-v24-N '84-p54
PW-v225-My 4 '84-p59
SLJ-v31-S '84-p103

Rumpelstilzchen (Gorey)
BL-v75-N 15 '78-p554

Schneewittchen (Svend Otto S)
BL-v75-N 15 '78-p554

Die Schonsten Kindermarchen
TLS-Ag 14 '70-p908

Selected Tales
NS-v105-Ja 14 '83-p24
TES-F 25 '83-p34
TLS-D 24 '82-p1409

The Seven Ravens (Zwerger)
AB-v70-N 15 '82-p3402
BL-v77-Ap 15 '81-p1153
BW-v11-My 10 '81-p18
CBRS-v9-Mr '81-p62
CE-v60-My '84-p367
Emerg Lib-v9-S '81-p26
GP-v20-S '81-p3948
HB-v57-Ag '81-p413
HB-v60-Je '84-p353
KR-v49-Ap 1 '81-p426
LATBR-D 11 '83-p10
NYTBR-v86-Ap 26 '81-p55
NYTBR-v88-N 20 '83-p47
PW-v219-My 29 '81-p42
PW-v224-N 4 '83-p65
SLJ-v27-Ap '81-p113
Sch Lib-v32-S '84-p234
TES-N 20 '81-p31
TES-O 12 '84-p33
Time-v118-D 21 '81-p76

The Shoemaker And The Elves (Adams)
CLW-v52-Ap '81-p389
PW-v219-Je 26 '81-p61

Six Against The World And Other Stories (Crouch)
TES-N 24 '78-p39

The Six Swans
TLS-Je 15 '73-p678

The Six Swans (Hospes)
KR-v42-N 1 '74-p1144
LJ-v99-D 15 '74-p3263

Sixty Fairy Tales Of The Brothers Grimm (Rackham)
BW-v9-D 2 '79-p4

The Sleeping Beauty
LJ-v95-S 15 '70-p3037
NYTBR-Je 21 '70-p22

The Sleeping Beauty (Moiseiwitsch)
TLS-D 6 '74-p1382

The Sleeping Beauty (Watts)
Sch Lib-v32-S '84-p234
TES-O 12 '84-p33

Snow-White And Rose-Red (Fromm)
JB-v48-F '84-p13

Snow-White And Rose Red (Topor)
BW-v14-Jl 8 '84-p8

Snow-White And Rose Red (Weren)
SLJ-v26-Ja '80-p53

Snow-White And The Seven Dwarfs
Am-v128-Ap 14 '73-p338
BL-v69-F 15 '73-p572
BW-v7-F 11 '73-p13
CCB-B-v26-Mr '73-p106
CE-v49-My '73-p421
CSM-v65-Ja 3 '73-p10
Comw-v99-N 23 '73-p214
HB-v49-Ap '73-p139
KR-v41-Ja 1 '73-p3
LJ-v98-Mr 15 '73-p993
Life-v73-D 8 '72-p23
NCW-v216-Mr '73-p91
NO-v12-Mr 17 '73-p23
NY-v48-D 2 '72-p195
NYTBR-D 3 '72-p82
NYTBR-N 4 '73-p54
NYTBR, pt.2-N 5 '72-p1
PW-v203-Ja 8 '73-p63
Par-v48-Ap '73-p67
SR-v55-O 14 '72-p82
SR-v1-Ja 13 '73-p60
SR-v1-Ap 14 '73-p86
Teacher-v90-Ap '73-p85
WSJ-v181-Je 25 '73-p10

Snow-White And The Seven Dwarfs (Burkert)
BL-v79-Je 1 '83-p1282
BL-v80-S 1 '83-p93
JB-v39-F '75-p15
RT-v34-Mr '81-p634
TES-N 21 '80-p36

Snow-White And The Seven Dwarfs (Gag)
ABC-v4-S '83-p42

Snow-White And The Seven Dwarfs (Heins)
BL-v71-Ja 1 '75-p460
BW-D 8 '74-p7
CCB-B-v28-My '75-p147

GRIMM, Jakob Ludwig Karl (continued)
Choice-v12-N '75-p1132
Comw-v102-N 21 '75-p568
HB-v51-F '75-p36
Inst-v84-My '75-p103
KR-v42-D 15 '74-p1302
NYTBR-F 23 '75-p8
PW-v206-D 16 '74-p52
Snow-White And The Seven Dwarfs (Jarrell)
GP-v13-Ja '75-p2552
KR-v41-D 15 '73-p1348
TLS-D 6 '74-p1382
Snow-White (Heins)
Inst-v89-Ja '80-p111
PW-v216-Jl 23 '79-p160
Snow-White (Hyman)
JB-v41-D '77-p329
NYTBR-S 23 '79-p43
Snow-White (Watts)
JB-v47-O '83-p196
PW-v223-Mr 25 '83-p51
SLJ-v30-S '83-p106
TES-O 21 '83-p37
The Story Of Snow-White And The Seven Dwarfs (Wegner)
B&B-v19-D '73-p104
LJ-v99-F 15 '74-p562
TLS-N 23 '73-p1431
The Table, The Donkey And The Stick (Galdone)
JB-v43-Ap '79-p95
Tales From Grimm
TLS-Ap 6 '73-p384
Tales From Grimm (Gag)
ABC-v4-S '83-p41
Thorn Rose (Le Cain)
BB-v6-F '78-p2
BL-v74-Ja 15 '78-p812
CCB-B-v31-Je '78-p159
Econ-v257-D 20 '75-p102
GP-v14-D '75-p2777
JB-v40-Ap '76-p81
KR-v45-N 15 '77-p1193
LA-v55-Ap '78-p519
Obs-N 30 '75-p27
RT-v32-O '78-p38
SLJ-v24-F '78-p57
Spec-v240-Ap 29 '78-p25
TES-O 31 '80-p24
TLS-D 5 '75-p1453
TLS-S 15 '78-p1021
Teacher-v96-O '78-p169
The Three Feathers
BW-v14-Jl 8 '84-p8
Three Gay Tales From Grimm
ABC-v4-S '83-p43
The Three Golden Hairs (Tresy)
JB-v48-F '84-p13
Three Grimms' Fairy Tales
KR-v49-N 15 '81-p1405
PW-v220-Jl 10 '81-p92
SLJ-v28-D '81-p52
WLB-v56-D '81-p291
Three Grimms' Fairy Tales (Watts)
TES-N 24 '78-p39
The Three Languages
BW-v14-Jl 8 '84-p8
Tom Thumb
GW-v108-Ap 7 '73-p26
HB-v49-Je '73-p264
KR-v41-Mr 15 '73-p311
LJ-v98-S 15 '73-p2640
NYTBR-N 4 '73-p61
PW-v203-My 21 '73-p49
TLS-Ap 6 '73-p384
Tom Thumb (Bell)
SLJ-v23-F '77-p64
Tom Thumb (Hoffmann)
BL-v69-Jl 1 '73-p1023
BL-v70-Mr 15 '74-p827
CCB-B-v27-D '73-p65
CE-v50-Ap '74-p335
Choice-v12-N '75-p1134
KR-v41-D 15 '73-p1348
LJ-v98-D 15 '73-p3690
NY-v49-D 3 '73-p203
Tom Thumb (Svend Otto S)
JB-v41-F '77-p14
Tom Thumb (Wiesner)
SR/W-v1-My 4 '74-p48
The Twelve Dancing Princesses (Hockerman)
SLJ-v26-Mr '80-p117
The Twelve Dancing Princesses (Le Cain)
BL-v75-N 1 '78-p478
CCB-B-v32-Ap '79-p137
GP-v17-Ja '79-p3448
HB-v55-F '79-p54
JB-v43-F '79-p18
KR-v47-Ja 15 '79-p61
PW-v214-O 2 '78-p133
SLJ-v25-Ja '79-p42
Wanda Gag's The Six Swans
KR-v50-N 15 '82-p1235
The Wolf And The Seven Little Kids (Craft)
SLJ-v26-Mr '80-p117
The Wolf And The Seven Little Kids (Hoffmann)
HB-v60-S '84-p621
The Wolf And The Seven Little Kids (Mathien)
GP-v23-Jl '84-p4293
The Wolf And The Seven Little Kids (Svend Otto S)
JB-v42-Ap '78-p80
NYTBR-N 13 '77-p31
SLJ-v24-Ap '78-p69

* * *

GRIMM, The Brothers
See Grimm, Jakob Ludwig Karl

* * *

GRIMM, William
Familiar Trees Of America
CSM-v70-S 25 '78-p15

* * *

GRIMM, William Carey
Indian Harvest
BL-v70-My 1 '74-p1001
CE-v51-Mr '75-p277
CSM-v67-Je 10 '75-p17
KR-v42-My 1 '74-p484
LJ-v99-Ap 15 '74-p1227
The Wondrous World Of Seedless Plants
BL-v70-D 1 '73-p381
BL-v70-D 1 '73-p386
HB-v50-Je '74-p302
KR-v41-Ag 1 '73-p822
LJ-v98-N 15 '73-p3464
SB-v9-Mr '74-p306

* * *

GRIMSHAW, Nigel
Bluntstone And The Wildkeepers
BL-v75-Mr 1 '79-p1090
TLS-Jl 5 '74-p721
The Wildkeepers' Guest
BL-v75-Mr 1 '79-p1090
GP-v16-My '77-p3120
JB-v41-Ap '77-p112
TLS-D 10 '76-p1547

* * *

GRINNELL, George B
The Whistling Skeleton
BL-v79-F 1 '83-p728
BL-v79-Mr 15 '83-p980

GRINNELL, George B (continued)
CBRS-v11-O '82-p19
CCB-B-v36-O '82-p26
CE-v59-Ja '83-p214
HB-v58-D '82-p663
Inst-v92-O '82-p24
KR-v50-Jl 15 '82-p799
LA-v60-Ap '83-p483
PW-v222-Ag 20 '82-p71
SLJ-v29-N '82-p84

* * *

GRIPARI, Pierre
Nanasse Et Gigantet
BL-v77-Mr 1 '81-p970
Pirlipipi, 2 Sirops, Une Sorciere
BL-v79-Je 15 '83-p1345
Tales Of The Rue Broca
BS-v29-F 1 '70-p422
CCB-B-v23-Ap '70-p128
KR-v37-O 15 '69-p1112
LJ-v95-My 15 '70-p1942
PW-v196-D 8 '69-p48
SR-v53-F 21 '70-p45

* * *

GRIPE, Maria
Elvis And His Friends
BB-v4-N '76-p2
BL-v72-My 1 '76-p1264
BS-v36-Ag '76-p149
CCB-B-v29-Jl '76-p174
GP-v17-N '78-p3414
HB-v52-Ag '76-p397
JB-v43-F '79-p31
KR-v44-Ap 15 '76-p469
Lis-v100-N 9 '78-p625
Obs-D 3 '78-p36
SLJ-v22-Ap '76-p74
TES-N 24 '78-p45
Elvis And His Secret
BB-v4-N '76-p2
B&B-v22-Je '77-p72
BL-v72-My 1 '76-p1264
BS-v36-Ag '76-p149
CCB-B-v29-Jl '76-p174
CLW-v51-My '80-p449
GP-v16-S '77-p3163
HB-v52-Ag '76-p397
JB-v41-D '77-p354
KR-v44-Ap 15 '76-p469
Obs-Je 12 '77-p25
PW-v209-My 17 '76-p56
SLJ-v22-Ap '76-p74
TES-O 14 '77-p20
TLS-Jl 15 '77-p865
The Glassblower's Children
BL-v70-O 1 '73-p170
BW-v7-N 11 '73-p2C
CCB-B-v27-S '73-p9
CLW-v51-My '80-p449
Choice-v12-N '75-p1132
GP-v13-Mr '75-p2568
JB-v39-F '75-p62
KR-v41-My 1 '73-p515
KR-v41-D 15 '73-p1350
LJ-v98-Jl '73-p2194
NY-v49-D 3 '73-p205
NYTBR-Je 10 '73-p40
NYTBR-S 2 '73-p20
NYTBR-N 4 '73-p54
NYTBR-S 8 '74-p37
Obs-D 1 '74-p35
TLS-Ap 4 '75-p365
TN-v30-Je '74-p434
The Green Coat
BB-v5-S '77-p4
BL-v73-Je 1 '77-p1496
BS-v37-Ag '77-p141
BW-D 11 '77-pE4
CCB-B-v31-S '77-p15
CLW-v49-O '77-p140
HB-v53-O '77-p539
KR-v45-My 1 '77-p493
PW-v211-Mr 21 '77-p94
SLJ-v24-S '77-p143
Hugo
CLW-v51-My '80-p449
CSM-v63-F 20 '71-p13
KR-v38-Jl 1 '70-p680
LJ-v95-N 15 '70-p4044
Lis-v86-N 11 '71-p662
NS-v82-N 12 '71-p663
Obs-Ag 1 '71-p25
TLS-O 22 '71-p1321
Hugo And Josephine
B&B-v16-Jl '71-p63
CCB-B-v23-Mr '70-p112
CLW-v51-My '80-p449
CSM-v61-N 6 '69-pB4
Comw-v91-N 21 '69-p254
KR-v37-S 1 '69-p929
LJ-v95-Ja 15 '70-p241
Lis-v86-N 11 '71-p662
NO-v8-D 29 '69-p17
NS-v81-Je 4 '71-p780
Obs-Ap 4 '71-p36
SR-v52-N 8 '69-p67
Spec-v226-My 29 '71-p758
TLS-Ap 2 '71-p391
In The Time Of The Bells
BL-v73-D 15 '76-p606
BS-v37-Ap '77-p30
CCB-B-v30-Ja '77-p76
CLW-v48-My '77-p443
HB-v53-F '77-p51
JB-v42-O '78-p268
KR-v44-S 1 '76-p982
SLJ-v23-Ja '77-p92
TES-Je 16 '78-p47
TLS-Jl 7 '78-p767
Josephine
CLW-v42-F '71-p382
CLW-v51-My '80-p449
CSM-v63-F 20 '71-p13
HB-v46-O '70-p478
KR-v38-Jl 1 '70-p680
LJ-v95-N 15 '70-p4044
Lis-v86-N 11 '71-p662
NS-v82-N 12 '71-p663
Obs-Ag 1 '71-p25
TLS-O 22 '71-p1321
Julia's House
BB-v3-S '75-p4
B&B-v21-D '75-p66
BL-v72-S 1 '75-p40
CCB-B-v28-Mr '75-p113
CE-v52-F '76-p206
CLW-v51-My '80-p449
GP-v14-Ja '76-p2797
HB-v51-O '75-p462
KR-v43-Je 1 '75-p603
LR-v25-Autumn '75-p164
Obs-D 7 '75-p32
PW-v207-Mr 31 '75-p49
SLJ-v21-My '75-p55
The Land Beyond
HB-v51-Ap '75-p152
KR-v42-S 1 '74-p949
LJ-v99-N 15 '74-p3045
LR-v25-Autumn '75-p149
NYTBR-O 6 '74-p8
PT-v8-F '75-p18
PW-v206-Ag 19 '74-p83
TLS-D 5 '75-p1457
The Night Daddy
BL-v67-Jl 15 '71-p954
BW-v5-My 9 '71-p15
CCB-B-v24-Jl '71-p170
CLW-v51-My '80-p449
EJ-v72-Ja '83-p26
HB-v47-Ag '71-p383
KR-v39-Ja 1 '71-p2
LJ-v96-Je 15 '71-p2131
Obs-Jl 22 '73-p32
PW-v199-Ap 19 '71-p48

GRIPE, Maria (continued)
SR-v54-My 15 '71-p47
TLS-Je 15 '73-p674
Pappa Pellerin's Daughter
B&B-v11-Je '66-p66
BS-v26-Ag 1 '66-p174
CCB-B-v20-S '66-p11
KR-v34-My 1 '66-p479
LJ-v91-O 15 '66-p5229
NYTBR-v71-S 18 '66-p30
Obs-Ap 10 '66-p20
PW-v189-Je 13 '66-p128
Punch-v250-Ap 20 '66-p594
SR-v49-Je 25 '66-p61
Spec-Je 3 '66-p706
TLS-My 19 '66-p430

* * *

GRISDALE, Alex
Wild Drums
Can Child Lit-#31 '83-p105

* * *

GRISE, Jeannette
Robert Benjamin And The Disappearing Act
SLJ-v27-Ag '81-p66
Robert Benjamin And The Great Blue Dog Joke
CBRS-v7-Winter '79-p57
SLJ-v25-Ja '79-p53

* * *

GRISSOM, Virgil
Gemini
BL-v65-S 15 '68-p90
CCB-B-v22-Ap '69-p126
KR-v36-Mr 1 '68-p303
KR-v36-Mr 15 '68-p351
LJ-v93-Je 1 '68-p2233
PW-v193-Mr 4 '68-p60
SB-v4-S '68-p150
TLS-Ap 17 '69-p421

* * *

GRITZNER, Charles F
Guyana In Pictures
SLJ-v22-S '75-p94

* * *

GROCH, Judith
Play The Bach, Dear!
BB-v6-Ag '78-p3
CCB-B-v31-Je '78-p159
CE-v55-Ja '79-p168
KR-v46-F 1 '78-p107
SLJ-v24-Ja '78-p89
WCRB-v4-Jl '78-p47

* * *

GROHSKOPF, Bernice
Blood & Roses
BB-v7-O '79-p1
BS-v39-S '79-p229
CBRS-v7-Ag '79-p137
CCB-B-v32-My '79-p154
Cur R-v19-Ap '80-p159
EJ-v68-N '79-p74
KR-v47-Mr 15 '79-p331
LA-v57-My '80-p558
PW-v215-F 5 '79-p95
SLJ-v25-Mr '79-p148
End Of Summer
BL-v78-Je 1 '82-p1307
BS-v42-O '82-p286
CCB-B-v35-My '82-p170
PW-v221-Ap 23 '82-p93
SLJ-v29-Ja '83-p84
Notes On The Hauter Experiment
KR-v43-Jl 15 '75-p776
PW-v208-Ag 11 '75-p117
SLJ-v22-Mr '76-p103
Shadow In The Sun
BL-v71-Mr 15 '75-p761
CCB-B-v29-N '75-p45
J Read-v19-F '76-p421
KR-v43-Mr 1 '75-p245
PW-v207-Ap 21 '75-p47
SLJ-v21-My '75-p64

* * *

GROL, Lini R
Leawala
Can Child Lit-#15 '80-p132
Magic Gifts
Can Child Lit-#15 '80-p132
Tales From The Niagara Peninsula
Can Child Lit-#15 '80-p132

* * *

GROLLMAN, Earl A
Talking About Death
CP-v22-Ag '77-p625
Inst-v88-Mr '79-p145
JMF-v36-F '74-p204
SB-v12-D '76-p156
Spectr-v47-Mr '71-p45
Talking About Divorce
PGJ-v55-O '76-p67
SB-v12-My '76-p37
Talking About Divorce And Separation
Par-v59-N '84-p198

* * *

GROLLMAN, Sharon Hya
More Time To Grow
Inst-v88-N '78-p113
SB-v14-S '78-p109

* * *

GROMAN, Gal
Gertie McMichaels And The Odd Body Mystery
KR-v43-Je 1 '75-p604
SLJ-v22-D '75-p66

* * *

GROMMER, Helmut
Das Lustige Spielebuch
BL-v73-Ap 15 '77-p1273

* * *

GRONOSET, Dagfinn
Anna
BL-v71-My 15 '75-p930
HB-v51-Ag '75-p402
KR-v43-Ja 1 '75-p51
KR-v43-F 1 '75-p132
LJ-v100-My 15 '75-p975
PW-v207-Ja 27 '75-p280
SLJ-v22-S '75-p134

* * *

GROSMAN, Ladislav
The Shop On Main Street
CCB-B-v23-My '70-p144
KR-v38-Ja 15 '70-p58
NYTBR-F 1 '70-p48

* * *

GROSS, Alan
Sometimes I Worry...
CBRS-v7-F '79-p61
Cur R-v18-F '79-p21
SLJ-v25-F '79-p42
Teacher-v96-Ja '79-p133
What If The Teacher Calls On Me?
SLJ-v27-Mr '81-p129

* * *

GROSS, David C
Pride Of Our People
BL-v76-N 1 '79-p449
SLJ-v26-F '80-p56

* * *

GROSS, Michael
The Fable Of The Fig Tree
BL-v72-S 1 '75-p40
HB-v51-O '75-p459
SLJ-v22-S '75-p82

* * *

GROSS, Ruth B
The Girl Who Wouldn't Get Married
BL-v80-N 15 '83-p497
CBRS-v12-N '83-p27
CCB-B-v37-D '83-p68
CE-v60-Ja '84-p208
Cur R-v24-N '84-p53
HB-v59-D '83-p700
KR-v51-S 1 '83-pJ149
PW-v224-Ag 19 '83-p78
SLJ-v30-N '83-p64
If You Were A Ballet Dancer
BL-v76-Ap 15 '80-p1204
BW-v10-My 11 '80-p18
CCB-B-v33-My '80-p173
Dance-v54-Ag '80-p92
Inst-v89-My '80-p92
KR-v48-Ap 1 '80-p441
RT-v34-D '80-p352
SLJ-v26-Ja '80-p70

* * *

GROSS, Ruth Belov
Alligators And Other Crocodilians
ACSB-v12-Spring '79-p25
BL-v74-Jl 15 '78-p1734
HB-v55-O '78-p541
KR-v46-Je 1 '78-p597
NYTBR-Ap 30 '78-p47
SB-v15-My '79-p41
A Book About Pandas
BL-v70-D 15 '73-p445
CCB-B-v27-Mr '74-p111
KR-v41-N 15 '73-p1268
LJ-v99-Mr 15 '74-p881
SB-v10-My '74-p73
A Book About Your Skeleton
ACSB-v13-Spring '80-p34
BL-v75-Jl 15 '79-p1626
CBRS-v7-Ag '79-p134
CCB-B-v33-D '79-p70
Cur R-v19-Ap '80-p124
SLJ-v26-F '80-p45
WCRB-v5-S '79-p84
The Bremen-Town Musicians
Teacher-v93-N '75-p115
Dangerous Adventure!
CCB-B-v31-Mr '78-p112
KR-v45-D 1 '77-p1263
SB-v14-D '78-p184
SLJ-v24-Mr '78-p128
The Emperor's New Clothes
BL-v74-N 15 '77-p545
CCB-B-v31-F '78-p89
KR-v45-Jl 15 '77-p723
SLJ-v24-S '77-p100
Money, Money, Money
BL-v69-Mr 1 '73-p647
KR-v40-Ag 15 '72-p943
LJ-v98-F 15 '73-p634
PW-v202-S 11 '72-p59
Teacher-v96-Ap '79-p26
Snakes
CCB-B-v29-S '75-p10
CE-v52-Ja '76-p158
Comw-v102-N 21 '75-p570
HB-v51-Ag '75-p394
KR-v43-Ap 15 '75-p461
NYTBR-My 4 '75-p41
PW-v207-Mr 31 '75-p50
SLJ-v22-S '75-p103
SR-v2-My 31 '75-p35
What Is That Alligator Saying?
ACSB-v13-Spring '80-p35
CCB-B-v26-O '72-p25
CE-v49-F '73-p260
Inst-v88-My '79-p114
LJ-v97-S 15 '72-p2934
PW-v203-Ja 8 '73-p65
SB-v8-S '72-p101

* * *

GROSS, Sarah Chokla
Every Child's Book Of Verse
CCB-B-v22-Jl '69-p175
KR-v36-S 1 '68-p981
LJ-v94-Ja 15 '69-p300
PW-v194-O 21 '68-p51

* * *

GROSSBART, Francine
A Big City
BL-v63-O 15 '66-p265
CC-v83-D 7 '66-p1509
CCB-B-v20-O '66-p25
CSM-v58-N 3 '66-pB2
KR-v34-Je 1 '66-p537
LJ-v91-Je 15 '66-p3250
NYTBR-v71-O 30 '66-p42
PW-v190-Ag 8 '66-p59
SR-v49-Ag 20 '66-p36

* * *

GROSSCUP, Clyde
Throw The Bomb
CCB-B-v21-Ap '68-p127

* * *

GROSSER, Morton
The Snake Horn
BL-v70-S 1 '73-p50
CCB-B-v26-Jl '73-p171
CE-v50-Ja '74-p166
KR-v41-F 1 '73-p114
LJ-v98-Ap 15 '73-p1387

* * *

GROSSET Starter Picture Dictionary
ARBA-v8-'77-p522
SLJ-v23-N '76-p47

* * *

GROSSET World Atlas
BL-v70-O 15 '73-p234
BL-v70-D 15 '73-p404
CCB-B-v27-Ja '74-p79
SB-v10-My '74-p65

* * *

GROSSMAN, Barney
Black Means...
BL-v69-My 1 '73-p836
CCB-B-v24-F '71-p92
CSM-v62-N 12 '70-pB6
KR-v38-S 15 '70-p1042
LJ-v96-Mr 15 '71-p1108
NYTBR-Ja 24 '71-p24
PW-v198-Ag 3 '70-p50
PW-v198-N 2 '70-p53

* * *

GROSSMAN, Mort
A Rage To Die
BS-v33-F 15 '74-p513
CCB-B-v27-D '73-p65
LJ-v99-F 15 '74-p580
PW-v204-O 8 '73-p96

* * *

GROSVENOR, Dave
Athletics
GP-My '84-p4268
Sch Lib-v32-Je '84-p170

* * *

GROSVENOR, Donna K
Pandas
BL-v70-F 15 '74-p656
SLJ-v30-Ag '84-p37
The Wild Ponies Of Assateague Island
ACSB-v9-Fall '76-p21
BL-v72-F 15 '76-p852
Zoo Babies
CCB-B-v32-My '79-p155
Cur R-v18-Ag '79-p176

GRYSKI, Camilla (continued)
SA-v251-D '84-p38
SLJ-v30-My '84-p80

* * *

GUARD, David
Hale-Mano
HB-v57-Ag '81-p441
SLJ-v28-D '81-p63

* * *

GUAY, Georgette
The Bling Said Hello. You'll Never Be The Same
Can Child Lit-#17 '80-p61

* * *

GUDE, Kathy
Holiday English
TES-Ag 8 '80-p18

* * *

GUERNSEY, JoAnn B
Five Summers
B Rpt-v2-S '83-p36
BS-v43-Je '83-p110
CBRS-v11-Spring '83-p124
KR-v51-Mr 15 '83-p309
PW-v223-Mr 18 '83-p70
SLJ-v29-My '83-p81
VOYA-v6-O '83-p202

* * *

GUEST, Elissa H
The Handsome Man
BL-v77-D 15 '80-p574
BS-v40-F '81-p415
CBRS-v9-F '81-p56
CCB-B-v34-Mr '81-p134
HB-v57-F '81-p58
KR-v49-F 1 '81-p145
SLJ-v27-S '80-p83
VOYA-v3-F '81-p30

* * *

GUGGENMOS, Josef
George The Dragon
JB-v42-Ap '78-p80
The Thumble Boy
NS-v90-N 28 '75-p688
Spec-v235-Jl 26 '75-p114
Wonder-Fish From The Sea
CCB-B-v25-N '71-p44
CLW-v43-N '71-p172
JLH-v199-My 17 '71-p63
LJ-v96-Jl '71-p2357

* * *

GUGLIOTTA, Bobette
Katzimo, Mysterious Mesa
CCB-B-v28-D '74-p62
KR-v42-Je 1 '74-p580
LJ-v99-S 15 '74-p2269

* * *

GUILCHER, Jean Michel
A Fern Is Born
BL-v68-Mr 1 '72-p563
CCB-B-v25-F '72-p92
CLW-v43-Ap '72-p479
Hort-v51-Ja '73-p12
Inst-v81-Je '72-p66
SR-v55-Ja 15 '72-p47
TLS-Jl 14 '72-p815
A Tree Grows Up
BL-v69-N 1 '72-p244
CCB-B-v26-Ja '73-p76
CLW-v44-F '73-p448
Hort-v51-Ap '73-p28
LJ-v97-D 15 '72-p4078
SB-v9-My '73-p74

* * *

GUILFOILE, Elizabeth
Nobody Listens To Andrew
CLW-v52-Ap '81-p389
Valentine's Day
BL-v62-O 1 '65-p160
CCB-B-v19-Ja '66-p82
CE-v42-O '65-p112
Comw-v82-My 28 '65-p334
LJ-v90-My 15 '65-p2394

* * *

GUILFOYLE, Ann
The Peaceable Kingdom
BL-v76-Ja 15 '80-p689
BOT-v2-D '79-p598
LJ-v104-D 15 '79-p2656
Punch-v281-N 11 '81-p870

* * *

GUILIANO, Edward
Lewis Carroll Observed
B&B-v23-Ja '78-p18
BL-v73-D 1 '76-p515
CSM-v69-D 17 '76-p27
Choice-v14-Mr '77-p63
Comw-v104-Jl 8 '77-p439
HB-v53-Ag '77-p462
KR-v44-Ag 1 '76-p879
LJ-v101-S 15 '76-p1857
NS-v94-D 23 '77-p902
NY-v52-D 20 '76-p119
PW-v210-Ag 23 '76-p62
Spec-v240-Ja 7 '78-p21
TLS-Ja 13 '78-p26
VQR-v53-Summer '77-p534

* * *

GUILLOT, Rene
The Castle Of The Crested Bird
CCB-B-v24-Jl '70-p178
LJ-v96-S 15 '71-p2905
Grishka And The Bear
RT-v35-N '81-p199
Grishka And The Wolves
LJ-v91-Je 15 '66-p3258
Imagenes Y Palabras
BL-v78-F 1 '82-p704
Master Of The Elephants
B&B-v15-N '69-p45
GP-v20-My '81-p3901
Sama
GP-v20-My '81-p3901
The Wild White Stallion
GP-v17-Jl '78-p3359

* * *

GUIRMA, Frederic
Princess Of The Full Moon
BL-v66-Je 15 '70-p1278
BW-v4-My 17 '70-p7
CCB-B-v24-O '70-p25
HB-v46-Je '70-p288
KR-v38-F 15 '70-p172
LJ-v95-D 15 '70-p4336
NYTBR-Ap 12 '70-p26
SR-v53-Jl 25 '70-p29
Tales Of Mogho
BW-v5-N 7 '71-p4
HB-v47-O '71-p478
KR-v39-Ag 1 '71-p810
LJ-v97-Mr 15 '72-p1170
PW-v200-O 18 '71-p51
SLJ-v26-N '79-p43

* * *

GULF Oil Corporation
An Eagle Eye On Energy
SLJ-v25-Ja '79-p19

* * *

GULIME, Alke
O Chrysaphenios Krinos
BL-v72-Je 1 '76-p1412

* * *

GULLETTE, Margaret M
The Lost Bellybutton
Lib Brow-v2-Spring '82-p5
SLJ-v23-Mr '77-p132

* * *

GUNAL, A
Typing For Children
JB-v47-Ag '83-p163

* * *

GUNDERSHEIMER, Karen
A B C Say With Me
CBRS-v13-S '84-p2
KR-v52-S 1 '84-pJ61
PW-v226-Ag 10 '84-p83
Happy Winter
BL-v79-S 1 '82-p42
CBRS-v11-S '82-p3
CCB-B-v36-F '83-p108
HB-v58-O '82-p511
NYTBR-v88-F 13 '83-p30
New Age-v8-D '82-p68
PW-v222-Jl 30 '82-p77
RT-v37-O '83-p58
SLJ-v28-Ag '82-p98
1 2 3 Play With Me
CBRS-v13-S '84-p2
KR-v52-S 1 '84-pJ61

* * *

GUNDREY, Elizabeth
Joining Things
JB-v42-F '78-p41
The Winter Book
GP-v16-Ap '78-p3300
JB-v42-F '78-p41
TES-O 21 '77-p22
250 More Things To Send Off For
TES-O 2 '81-p38
TES-N 27 '81-p23

* * *

GUNNING, Monica
The Two Georges/Los Dos Jorges
HB-v53-Ap '77-p191
SLJ-v23-Ap '77-p53

* * *

GUNNING, Thomas G
Amazing Escapes
B Rpt-v3-S '84-p40
CCB-B-v37-Jl '84-p204
RT-v38-D '84-p338
SLJ-v31-O '84-p157
VOYA-v7-O '84-p211
Unexplained Mysteries
CCB-B-v36-Jl '83-p210
SLJ-v29-Ag '83-p65
VOYA-v6-D '83-p286

* * *

GUNSTENSEN, Laura
How To Make Presents
GP-v17-S '78-p3391

* * *

GUNSTON, Bill
Coal
BL-v77-Jl 1 '81-p1394
JB-v45-O '81-p210
SLJ-v28-Ja '82-p74
Spotting Planes
Inst-v90-D '80-p36
SLJ-v27-Ja '81-p61
Transport
JB-v42-D '78-p300
TES-O 20 '78-p39
Water
BL-v79-Ja 15 '83-p674
Brit Bk N C-Spring '81-p29
Lis-v104-N 6 '80-p626
SB-v19-N '83-p77
SLJ-v29-Ap '83-p109
TES-Mr 6 '81-p38

* * *

GUNTER, Jack
The Gunter Papers
BL-v72-S 1 '75-p21
BL-v72-S 1 '75-p40
PW-v207-Je 2 '75-p56

* * *

GUNTHER, Louise
Anna's Snow Day
CBRS-v7-Je '79-p104
SLJ-v26-O '79-p140
A Tooth For The Tooth Fairy
CBRS-v7-Ja '79-p44
SLJ-v25-D '78-p66
Where Is Maria?
SLJ-v26-D '79-p97

* * *

GURDUS, Luba Krugman
The Death Train
HB-v55-Ag '79-p460
LJ-v104-Mr 1 '79-p623
PW-v215-Ja 15 '79-p122

* * *

GURKO, Leo
Ernest Hemingway And The Pursuit Of Heroism
AL-v41-Mr '69-p129
CCB-B-v22-My '69-p143
HB-v44-O '68-p569
KR-v36-Ag 15 '68-p911
LJ-v93-S 15 '68-p3316
Thomas Wolfe: Beyond The Romantic Ego
BL-v71-Je 15 '75-p1069
Choice-v12-N '75-p1164
HB-v51-O '75-p475
KR-v43-Je 1 '75-p615
SLJ-v22-My '76-p69
The Two Lives Of Joseph Conrad
Atl-v216-D '65-p158
BL-v62-D 1 '65-p357
CCB-B-v19-N '65-p44
HB-v42-Ap '66-p206
KR-v33-Ag 15 '65-p836
LJ-v90-S 15 '65-p3804
NYTBR-v70-N 7 '65-p24

* * *

GURKO, Miriam
Clarence Darrow
BL-v61-Jl 15 '65-p1060
BS-v25-My 15 '65-p98
CCB-B-v18-Je '65-p149
CSM-v57-My 6 '65-p8B
Comw-v82-My 28 '65-p330
KR-v33-Mr 15 '65-p327
LJ-v90-My 15 '65-p2418
NYTBR-v70-Jl 25 '65-p20
The Ladies Of Seneca Falls
BL-v71-Ja 15 '75-p501
BS-v34-Ja 15 '75-p474
BW-D 15 '74-p6
Choice-v12-Ap '75-p284
Cu H-v70-My '76-p228
HB-v50-O '74-p146
KR-v42-N 1 '74-p1164
KR-v43-Ja 1 '75-p13
LJ-v99-N 15 '74-p3053
LJ-v99-D 15 '74-p3247
PW-v206-S 16 '74-p60
Rp B Bk R-v22-O4 '77-p11

* * *

GURNEY, Eric
Pop-Up Book Of Cats
PW-v206-S 9 '74-p67
Pop-Up Book Of Dogs
CSM-v65-N 7 '73-pB4

* * *

GURNEY, Gene
The Launching Of Sputnik, October 4, 1957
CCB-B-v29-Mr '76-p110
KR-v43-Ag 15 '75-p925
SLJ-v22-Mr '76-p114
Space Technology Spinoffs
ACSB-v13-Spring '80-p35

GURNEY, Gene (continued)
SB-v15-Mr '80-p221
SLJ-v26-S '79-p157

* * *

GURNEY, Nancy
The King, The Mice And The Cheese
CCB-B-v19-F '66-p98
CSM-v57-N 4 '65-pB2
KR-v33-Jl 15 '65-p676
LJ-v90-O 15 '65-p4602
NS-v72-N 11 '66-p711
NYTBR-v70-N 7 '65-p56
Punch-v251-N 16 '66-p755

* * *

GUSTAFSON, Anita
Burrowing Birds
ASBYP-v16-Winter '83-p28
BW-v11-My 10 '81-p16
CCB-B-v35-O '81-p30
Inst-v91-Ap '82-p22
KR-v49-Jl 1 '81-p802
SLJ-v27-Ap '81-p127
Monster Rolling Skull And Other Native American Tales
CBRS-v8-My '80-p95
CCB-B-v34-S '80-p10
CE-v57-Ja '81-p175
LA-v57-N '80-p899
SLJ-v26-Ap '80-p109
Some Feet Have Noses
ASBYP-v17-Winter '84-p24
BL-v79-Jl '83-p1400
CCB-B-v37-O '83-p28
CE-v61-S '84-p68
HB-v59-O '83-p607
KR-v51-My 15 '83-p580
RT-v37-D '83-p309
SB-v19-Ja '84-p144
SLJ-v30-Ja '84-p76

* * *

GUSTAITIS, Rasa
Melissa Hayden: Ballerina
BS-v27-My 1 '67-p64
CCB-B-v21-S '67-p7
PW-v191-Je 5 '67-p176

* * *

GUSTKEY, Earl
Roman Gabriel
KR-v42-Jl 1 '74-p683
LJ-v99-D 15 '74-p3280

* * *

GUTHRIE, A B, Jr.
Arfive
Atl-v227-F '71-p127
BL-v67-F 15 '71-p476
BS-v30-Mr 1 '71-p526
BS-v33-O 1 '73-p310
BW-v7-N 11 '73-p20
CSM-v63-F 11 '71-p7
HB-v47-Je '71-p306
KR-v38-N 15 '70-p1263
KR-v39-Ja 1 '71-p11
LJ-v95-N 15 '70-p3926
LJ-v96-Ap 15 '71-p1528
LJ-v96-My 15 '71-p1783
Life-v70-F 12 '71-p7
Lis-v87-F 10 '72-p188
NO-v10-F 22 '71-p21
NS-v83-F 4 '72-p151
NYTBR-Ja 17 '71-p30
NYTBR-Je 6 '71-p3
NYTBR-D 5 '71-p82
Obs-F 20 '72-p28
PW-v198-N 9 '70-p58
SR-v54-Ja 23 '71-p73

* * *

GUTIERREZ, Josefina E
El Sapito No Se Cuantos
Hisp-v66-Mr '83-p91

* * *

GUTMAN, Bill
Dr. J
BL-v74-O 15 '77-p381
SLJ-v24-D '77-p65
Duke: The Musical Life Of Duke Ellington
BL-v73-Je 1 '77-p1490
BL-v73-Je 1 '77-p1496
CCB-B-v31-O '77-p32
EJ-v66-N '77-p81
KR-v45-My 1 '77-p494
SLJ-v24-S '77-p129
Football Superstars Of The '70s
BL-v72-D 15 '75-p578
EJ-v65-My '76-p91
KR-v43-Ag 15 '75-p926
NYTBR-N 16 '75-p48
SLJ-v22-D '75-p69
Great Sports Feats Of The '70's
SLJ-v26-D '79-p100
Hank Aaron
BL-v70-S 1 '73-p50
CCB-B-v27-N '73-p43
KR-v41-Mr 15 '73-p321
LJ-v98-My 15 '73-p1703
Jim Plunkett
KR-v41-Mr 15 '73-p321
LJ-v98-O 15 '73-p3145
Mark Fidrych
BL-v74-O 15 '77-p381
SLJ-v24-D '77-p65
Modern Baseball Superstars
Comw-v99-N 23 '73-p220
KR-v41-N 1 '73-p1210
LJ-v99-Ap 15 '74-p1219
Modern Basketball Superstars
SLJ-v22-D '75-p68
Modern Football Superstars
SLJ-v21-Ap '75-p52
Modern Hockey Superstars
CCB-B-v30-Ap '77-p124
Inst-v86-My '77-p121
SLJ-v23-D '76-p71
Modern Soccer Superstars
CCB-B-v33-Je '80-p190
Hi Lo-v1-Ap '80-p3
SLJ-v26-My '80-p88
Modern Women Superstars
BL-v74-Ja 15 '78-p809
BL-v74-Ja 15 '78-p817
CCB-B-v31-Je '78-p160
SLJ-v24-Mr '78-p128
More Modern Baseball Superstars
SLJ-v25-My '79-p83
Munson, Garvey, Brock, Carew
SLJ-v23-D '76-p70
"My Father, The Coach" And Other Sports Stories
KR-v44-Ap 1 '76-p406
SLJ-v22-My '76-p80
The Picture Life Of Reggie Jackson
BL-v74-Je 15 '78-p1621
SLJ-v25-S '78-p137
Teacher-v96-My '79-p124
Superstars Of The Sports World
RT-v33-O '79-p49
SLJ-v24-My '78-p86
Women Who Work With Animals
BL-v79-O 1 '82-p245
CCB-B-v35-Jl '82-p207
Hi Lo-v4-O '82-p6
SLJ-v29-N '82-p84
VOYA-v5-D '82-p42

* * *

GUTMAN, Nahum
Path Of The Orange Peels
BL-v76-Ja 15 '80-p720
CBRS-v8-F '80-p57
LA-v57-My '80-p556
SLJ-v26-F '80-p56

* * *

GUTNIK, Martin J
Energy
ACSB-v9-Fall '76-p21
BL-v72-Ja 1 '76-p626
SB-v12-My '76-p37
SLJ-v22-Mr '76-p103
Teacher-v93-F '76-p120
How Plants Are Made
BL-v72-Je 1 '76-p1406
Cur R-v16-O '77-p293
SB-v12-Mr '77-p210
SLJ-v23-O '76-p98
How Plants Make Food
BL-v72-Je 1 '76-p1406
Cur R-v16-O '77-p293
SB-v12-Mr '77-p210
SLJ-v23-O '76-p98
The Science Of Classification
BL-v77-F 1 '81-p752
SB-v17-N '81-p89
SLJ-v27-Ag '81-p66
What Plants Produce
BL-v72-Je 1 '76-p1406
Cur R-v16-O '77-p293
SB-v12-Mr '77-p210
SLJ-v23-O '76-p98

* * *

GUY, Rosa
The Disappearance
BL-v76-O 1 '79-p228
BOT-v2-D '79-p601
BW-v9-N 11 '79-p21
CBRS-v8-Ja '80-p46
CCB-B-v33-Ap '80-p153
CSM-v71-O 15 '79-pB4
EJ-v69-My '80-p91
GP-v19-S '80-p3757
HB-v56-F '80-p62
HM-v259-D '79-p77
Inst-v89-N '79-p59
JB-v44-Ag '80-p190
J Read-v24-O '80-p84
KR-v47-D 1 '79-p1380
NYTBR-N 25 '79-p22
NYTBR-D 2 '79-p40
NYTBR-v86-F 15 '81-p35
PW-v216-Ag 6 '79-p92
PW-v218-N 28 '80-p51
SLJ-v26-N '79-p88
SLJ-v27-N '80-p47
Sch Lib-v28-S '80-p289
TES-Je 6 '80-p27
TLS-Jl 18 '80-p807
WLB-v54-O '79-p122
Edith Jackson
BL-v74-Ap 15 '78-p1339
CCB-B-v32-Mr '79-p116
CSM-v70-O 23 '78-pB13
Comw-v107-F 29 '80-p112
Cur R-v22-F '83-p60
EJ-v69-S '80-p87
HB-v55-O '78-p524
JB-v43-Ag '79-p230
KR-v46-My 1 '78-p501
Kliatt-v16-Winter '82-p8
Lis-v102-N 8 '79-p643
NYTBR-Jl 2 '78-p11
NYTBR-v87-F 7 '82-p39
Obs-Ag 5 '79-p37
PW-v213-My 29 '78-p52
SLJ-v24-Ap '78-p93
SLJ-v28-Ap '82-p28
TES-Jl 15 '83-p18
TLS-D 14 '79-p124
WLB-v52-Ap '78-p639
The Friends
BL-v70-Ja 15 '74-p542
BS-v33-Mr 15 '74-p556
CCB-B-v27-Mr '74-p111
EJ-v63-Ap '74-p90
EJ-v64-D '75-p80
EJ-v69-S '80-p87
GP-v13-Ja '75-p2557
HB-v50-Ap '74-p152
JNE-v43-Summer '74-p397
J Read-v22-N '78-p127
KR-v41-O 1 '73-p1107
KR-v41-D 15 '73-p1356
LJ-v98-N 15 '73-p3464
LJ-v98-D 15 '73-p3690
NYTBR-N 4 '73-p26
NYTBR-N 4 '73-p52
NYTBR-D 2 '73-p79
NYTBR-S 8 '74-p37
PW-v204-D 10 '73-p36
TES-Jl 15 '83-p18
TLS-S 20 '74-p1006
Mirror Of Her Own
BS-v41-S '81-p238
Bl Bks B-v7-#3 '81-p67
CBRS-v9-My '81-p86
CCB-B-v34-My '81-p171
KR-v49-Je 1 '81-p682
PW-v219-Mr 27 '81-p52
SLJ-v27-My '81-p73
VOYA-v4-D '81-p30
Mother Crocodile
BL-v78-S 1 '81-p43
CBRS-v10-S '81-p2
CCB-B-v35-N '81-p44
HB-v57-D '81-p658
Inst-v90-My '81-p59
KR-v49-Ag 1 '81-p931
LA-v58-N '81-p951
NYTBR-v86-O 4 '81-p38
RT-v35-My '82-p976
SLJ-v28-S '81-p107
WLB-v56-O '81-p134
New Guys Around The Block
BL-v79-Mr 15 '83-p957
BS-v43-My '83-p73
CBRS-v11-Ap '83-p93
CCB-B-v36-Ap '83-p150
CLW-v55-D '83-p239
CLW-v55-Ap '84-p409
EJ-v72-O '83-p86
GP-v22-Jl '83-p4099
HB-v59-Je '83-p311
JB-v48-F '84-p32
J Read-v27-D '83-p281
KR-v51-Mr 15 '83-p309
NYTBR-v88-Ag 28 '83-p22
PW-v223-Mr 11 '83-p87
Punch-v285-Ag 17 '83-p51
SLJ-v29-Ap '83-p123
SLJ-v29-Ag '83-p27
Sch Lib-v31-S '83-p269
TES-Jl 15 '83-p18
VOYA-v6-O '83-p202
Ruby
BW-v9-O 7 '79-p15
CCB-B-v30-N '76-p42
HB-v52-D '76-p652
JB-v46-Ap '82-p76
LJ-v101-S 15 '76-p1882
PW-v209-Ap 19 '76-p80
SLJ-v22-My '76-p82
Sch Lib-v30-Mr '82-p51
TES-N 20 '81-p35

* * *

GUZZO, Sandra E
Fox And Heggie
BL-v80-F 15 '84-p856
CBRS-v12-Ap '84-p92
SLJ-v30-Mr '84-p144

* * *

GWYNDAF, R
A Farming Family In Wales
JB-v43-O '79-p272

* * *

GWYNDAF, Robin
A Farming Family In Wales
JB-v43-O '79-p272
Sch Lib-v28-Mr '80-p45

* * *

GWYNNE, Fred
A Chocolate Moose For Dinner
CCB-B-v30-Mr '77-p107
LA-v54-Mr '77-p325
RT-v31-O '77-p15
RT-v31-D '77-p331
RT-v32-D '78-p310
RT-v32-Ja '79-p444
RT-v38-D '84-p276
SLJ-v23-Mr '77-p132
Ick's ABC
CCB-B-v25-Mr '72-p107
LJ-v97-Ap 15 '72-p1597
NYTBR-Ja 2 '72-p8
SR-v55-F 19 '72-p75
The King Who Rained
KR-v38-N 15 '70-p1244
LJ-v96-Je 15 '71-p2125
RT-v32-N '78-p148
RT-v32-D '78-p310
RT-v32-Ja '79-p444
RT-v38-D '84-p276
The Sixteen Hand Horse
CCB-B-v34-O '80-p32

* * *

GYDAL, Monica
When Gemma's Parents Got Divorced
TLS-Ap 2 '76-p389
When Olly Had A Little Brother
TLS-Ap 2 '76-p389
When Olly Went To Hospital
TLS-Ap 2 '76-p389
When Olly's Grandad Died
JB-v40-Je '76-p150
TLS-Ap 2 '76-p389

H

HBJ Bookmark Reading Program
Inst-v93-Ag '83-p127

* * *

HBJ Health
Cur R-v22-D '83-p75

* * *

HBJ Language For Daily Use
Inst-v93-Ag '83-p127

* * *

HBJ Spelling Program
Inst-v93-Ag '83-p127

* * *

H.M. Queen Elizabeth The Queen Mother
TES-N 5 '82-p23

* * *

HAAR, Jaap Ter
Boris
BL-v67-F 15 '71-p493
CCB-B-v24-Mr '71-p115
Emerg Lib-v11-N '83-p21
GT-v89-F '72-p94
LJ-v96-Ja 15 '71-p279
LJ-v96-My 15 '71-p1782
NCW-v216-Mr '73-p93
NS-v78-O 31 '69-p622
Punch-v257-D 17 '69-p1016
SR-v53-N 14 '70-p36
TLS-D 4 '69-p1385
King Arthur
CLW-v49-D '77-p235
LA-v55-F '78-p214
SLJ-v24-S '77-p144

* * *

HAAS, Ben
Troubled Summer
BS-v26-Ja 1 '67-p368
CCB-B-v20-F '67-p89
CLW-v38-F '67-p395
KR-v34-O 1 '66-p1058
LJ-v91-D 15 '66-p6201
NYTBR-v72-Ja 22 '67-p26
PW-v193-Je 10 '68-p63

* * *

HAAS, Carolyn
Backyard Vacation
BL-v77-S 1 '80-p44
KR-v48-Ag 15 '80-p1082

* * *

HAAS, Dorothy
The Bears Upstairs
BL-v75-S 1 '78-p49
CBRS-v7-Mr '79-p76
CCB-B-v32-N '78-p44
CE-v55-Ap '79-p296
CLW-v50-O '78-p115
GP-v18-Mr '80-p3656
JB-v44-Je '80-p131
KR-v46-N 15 '78-p1248
PW-v214-Jl 31 '78-p99
PW-v219-Mr 27 '81-p52
SLJ-v25-O '78-p144
Sch Lib-v28-Je '80-p152
Poppy And The Outdoors Cat
BL-v77-Mr 15 '81-p1028
CCB-B-v34-Je '81-p193
SLJ-v27-My '81-p64
The Princess Book
PW-v206-O 21 '74-p51
Tink In A Tangle
BL-v80-Mr 15 '84-p1058
CBRS-v12-Je '84-p114
Learning-v12-Ap '84-p76
PW-v225-F 17 '84-p89
SLJ-v30-My '84-p80

* * *

HAAS, Irene
The Little Moon Theater
BL-v78-D 15 '81-p548
BW-v11-N 8 '81-p20
CBRS-v10-Winter '82-p54
CLW-v53-F '82-p301
CSM-v74-D 14 '81-pB12
KR-v49-O 15 '81-p1291
LA-v59-My '82-p483
NYTBR-v86-O 18 '81-p49
PW-v220-O 16 '81-p79
RT-v35-Ap '82-p868
SLJ-v28-O '81-p129
WCRB-v8-Ap '82-p48
The Little Moon Theatre
B&B-Jl '82-p37
JB-v46-Ag '82-p133
TES-S 21 '84-p37
The Maggie B
BL-v72-N 15 '75-p453
CCB-B-v29-My '76-p145
CE-v52-F '76-p206
Comw-v102-N 21 '75-p566
GP-v15-D '76-p3029
JB-v41-Ap '77-p77
KR-v43-O 15 '75-p1175
NW-v86-D 15 '75-p92
NYTBR-S 28 '75-p12
PW-v208-Ag 4 '75-p57
SLJ-v22-N '75-p62
Spec-v237-D 11 '76-p22

* * *

HAAS, Jessie
Keeping Barney
BL-v78-Je 1 '82-p1312
BS-v42-Je '82-p120
CBRS-v10-Spring '82-p116
CSM-v76-Jl 6 '84-pB5
HB-v58-Ag '82-p403
KR-v50-Ap 1 '82-p417
SLJ-v28-Ag '82-p116
SLJ-v29-Ap '83-p122
VOYA-v5-O '82-p42
Working Trot
B Rpt-v2-Mr '84-p32
CCB-B-v37-Ap '84-p147
KR-v51-S 1 '83-pJ161
SLJ-v30-Ja '84-p86
VOYA-v7-Ap '84-p30

* * *

HAAS, Victor E
The Magic Numerals Of Ali Khayyam
KR-v33-Ap 1 '65-p380
LJ-v90-Je 15 '65-p2884
SLJ-v26-O '79-p104

* * *

HABASHI, Labib
The Obelisks Of Egypt
Antiq J-v59-Ja 10 '79-p132
Choice-v15-Je '78-p595
SA-v237-D '77-p36

* * *

HABENSTREIT, Barbara
Men Against War
BL-v69-Je 15 '73-p984
BS-v33-Je 15 '73-p145
CCB-B-v26-My '73-p139
KR-v41-My 1 '73-p524
LJ-v98-O 15 '73-p3145
To My Brother Who Did A Crime
BL-v70-F 15 '74-p649
BS-v33-Mr 15 '74-p541
CCB-B-v27-My '74-p143
KR-v41-N 1 '73-p1216
KR-v41-D 15 '73-p1358
LJ-v99-Ja 15 '74-p217
PW-v204-D 3 '73-p40

* * *

HABER, Heinz
Our Friend The Atom
ABC-v4-Jl '83-p20
VV-v27-Je 15 '82-p53

* * *

HABER, Louis
Black Pioneers Of Science And Invention
BL-v67-S 15 '70-p107
CCB-B-v24-Ja '71-p74
Comw-v93-F 26 '71-p521
KR-v38-My 15 '70-p563
LJ-v95-D 15 '70-p4363
SB-v6-S '70-p97
Women Pioneers Of Science
ACSB-v13-Mr '80-p26
BL-v76-O 1 '79-p276
CCB-B-v33-Ap '80-p153
HB-v55-D '79-p677
Inter BC-v12-#1 '81-p16
KR-v47-N 15 '79-p1333
SB-v16-S '80-p30
SLJ-v26-F '80-p66
TES-N 7 '80-p24

* * *

HACKER, Carlotta
The Book Of Canadians
BIC-v13-Mr '84-p30
Quill & Q-v50-F '84-p16
Crowfoot
Can Child Lit-#23 '81-p86

* * *

HACKER, Jeffrey H
Carl Sandburg
BL-v80-Je 1 '84-p1397
CCB-B-v38-S '84-p5
SLJ-v31-S '84-p128
Franklin D. Roosevelt
BL-v79-Jl '83-p1401
CBRS-v11-Spring '83-p124
SLJ-v30-S '83-p134

* * *

HACKS, Peter
The Bear At The Hunters' Ball
BL-v73-Ja 1 '77-p666
KR-v44-S 1 '76-p970
NYTBR-N 14 '76-p26
PW-v210-Ag 2 '76-p115
SLJ-v23-O '76-p98
The Bear At The Huntsmen's Ball
GP-v14-O '75-p2712
LR-v25-Summer '75-p80
Meta Morfoss
BL-v72-Mr 1 '76-p985
TLS-Ap 2 '76-p390

* * *

HADAS, Moses
Imperial Rome
CW-v59-Ja '66-p163
SE-v43-N '79-p560
TLS-F 23 '67-p153

* * *

HADDAD, Helen R
Potato Printing
BL-v78-O 1 '81-p236
CBRS-v10-O '81-p14
CCB-B-v35-My '82-p171
CE-v58-My '82-p330
HB-v57-O '81-p551
Inst-v91-Ja '82-p145
KR-v49-O 15 '81-p1298
SLJ-v28-N '81-p92
Truck And Loader
BL-v78-Ap 15 '82-p1099
CCB-B-v36-S '82-p10
CLW-v54-D '82-p224
HB-v58-Ap '82-p162
SLJ-v28-My '82-p77

* * *

HADDELSEY, Vincent
Haddelsey's Horses
AB-v62-D 18 '78-p3820
BL-v75-S 1 '78-p13
BM-v121-F '79-p138
GP-v17-N '78-p3430
Lis-v100-D 14 '78-p794
PW-v213-Je 26 '78-p111

* * *

HADDON, Tessa
A Magic Book Of Birds
GP-v15-Ja '77-p3053
JB-v41-Ag '77-p221
TLS-D 10 '76-p1550

* * *

HADDRELL, Allan
A Day With A Footballer
TES-Mr 7 '80-p43
A Day With A Nurse
JB-v44-O '80-p239
TES-Mr 7 '80-p43

* * *

HADENIUS, Stig
How They Lived In A Medieval Monastery
JB-v42-D '78-p300
How They Lived In A Medieval Town
TLS-D 6 '74-p1385
How They Lived In A Viking Settlement
GP-v15-Ap '77-p3089
How They Lived In Ancient Egypt
TLS-D 6 '74-p1385
How They Lived In Ancient Greece
TLS-D 6 '74-p1385
How They Lived In Ancient Rome
TLS-D 6 '74-p1385
How They Lived In The Age Of Knights
JB-v41-Ap '77-p94
How They Lived In The Bronze Age
GP-v17-My '78-p3336
TES-Mr 10 '78-p62
How They Lived In The Iron Age
JB-v43-Je '79-p158

HADENIUS, Stig (continued)
How They Lived In The Stone Age
GP-v17-My '78-p3336
TES-Mr 10 '78-p62

* * *

HADER, Berta
The Big Snow
CSM-v70-Ja 30 '78-p15
Teacher-v92-D '74-p13

* * *

HADITHI, Mwenye
Greedy Zebra
BL-v81-S 15 '84-p127
GP-v23-Jl '84-p4293
PW-v226-S 28 '84-p112

* * *

HADLEY, Eric
Legends Of The Sun And Moon
CCB-B-v37-F '84-p108
JB-v47-O '83-p207
SLJ-v30-F '84-p71
Sch Lib-v32-Mr '84-p52
TES-O 21 '83-p37

* * *

HAGBRINK, Bodil
Children Of Lapland
BIC-v8-D '79-p13
BL-v76-F 15 '80-p833
GP-v18-Jl '79-p3549
HB-v56-Ap '80-p185
JB-v43-Ag '79-p195
SLJ-v26-My '80-p68
The Children Of Vernette
GP-v14-N '75-p2733
Obs-N 30 '75-p27

* * *

HAGELUND, W A
The Halibut Hunters
In Rev-v14-O '80-p29

* * *

HAGERMAN, Paul Stirling
It's A Mad, Mad World
SLJ-v25-O '78-p155
SLJ-v29-D '82-p32
It's An Odd World
Par-v52-N '77-p112
SLJ-v24-Mr '78-p128

* * *

HAGERSTROM, S
The Journey To Fleecy Mountain
JB-v45-Je '81-p114

* * *

HAGERUP, Inger
Helter Skelter
GP-v19-Jl '80-p3731
JB-v44-Je '80-p132
JB-v44-Ag '80-p176
SLJ-v28-O '81-p129

* * *

HAGGARD, Sir H Rider
King Solomon's Mines
TES-Jl 22 '83-p21
TES-D 2 '83-p25
TES-Ja 13 '84-p22

* * *

HAGON, Priscilla
Cruising To Danger
B&B-v13-Je '68-p43
BL-v63-O 1 '66-p182
CCB-B-v20-S '66-p11
KR-v34-Mr 1 '66-p249
LJ-v91-My 15 '66-p2717
NYTBR-v71-Je 5 '66-p42
Mystery At The Villa Bianca
CCB-B-v23-My '70-p144
KR-v37-S 1 '69-p938
LJ-v94-D 15 '69-p4619

* * *

HAGUE, Kathleen
Alphabears
BL-v80-Je 15 '84-p1483
CBRS-v12-Jl '84-p134
CCB-B-v38-S '84-p6
GP-v23-S '84-p4320
LA-v61-O '84-p629
NYTBR-v89-Jl 29 '84-p29
PW-v225-My 4 '84-p59
SLJ-v31-S '84-p103
East Of The Sun And West Of The Moon
BL-v77-N 1 '80-p404
BW-v10-D 14 '80-p11
CBRS-v9-D '80-p24
CCB-B-v34-D '80-p71
CSM-v73-Ja 12 '81-pB11
Cur R-v20-Ap '81-p171
HB-v57-Ap '81-p200
Inst-v90-Ja '81-p109
KR-v48-O 1 '80-p1301
LA-v58-My '81-p598
NW-v96-D 1 '80-p103
NYTBR-v86-Ja 4 '81-p25
PW-v218-S 19 '80-p161
RT-v34-Ap '81-p854
SLJ-v27-N '80-p75
The Man Who Kept House
BL-v77-Jl 1 '81-p1394
CBRS-v10-S '81-p3
KR-v49-My 15 '81-p631
LA-v59-Mr '82-p267
NW-v98-D 7 '81-p101
PW-v219-My 29 '81-p43
RT-v36-O '82-p72
RT-v37-O '83-p48
SLJ-v28-S '81-p107

* * *

HAGY, Jeannie
And Then Mom Joined The Army
CCB-B-v29-Jl '76-p174
KR-v44-Mr 1 '76-p256
SLJ-v23-O '76-p107

* * *

HAHN, Christine
Amusement Park Machines
ACSB-v13-Spring '80-p49
BL-v76-S 1 '79-p39
SLJ-v26-S '79-p106

* * *

HAHN, James
Babe! The Sports Career Of George Ruth
BL-v78-Ap 1 '82-p1023
SLJ-v28-F '82-p76
Bill Walton: Maverick Cager
BL-v75-Ap 1 '79-p1223
SLJ-v26-S '79-p138
Brown! The Sports Career Of James Brown
BL-v78-Ap 1 '82-p1023
SLJ-v28-F '82-p76
Chris! The Sports Career Of Chris Evert Lloyd
BL-v78-Ap 1 '82-p1023
SLJ-v28-F '82-p76
Environmental Careers
ACSB-v10-Winter '77-p20
BL-v72-Ap 1 '76-p1113
Cur R-v16-My '77-p95
KR-v44-Mr 15 '76-p333
SB-v12-D '76-p157
SLJ-v22-My '76-p69
Franz Beckenbauer: Soccer Superstar
SLJ-v26-S '79-p138

HAINING, Peter (continued)
KR-v44-F 1 '76-p159
TLS-My 7 '76-p561
WCRB-v3-N '77-p62
The Jules Verne Companion
CR-v233-D '78-p334
JB-v43-Ap '79-p121
The Leprechaun's Kingdom
B&B-v25-N '79-p50
JB-v44-Ap '80-p83
NYTBR-Mr 16 '80-p35
PW-v217-Ja 18 '80-p139
Punch-v277-D 12 '79-p1153

* * *

HAINSON, Margaret
Never Spread Like Marmalade
Brit Bk N C-Spring '81-p14
GP-v14-O '75-p2728
LR-v25-Autumn '75-p136
TLS-D 5 '75-p1457

* * *

HAIRSTON, William
World Of Carlos
BS-v27-F 1 '68-p430
CCB-B-v21-Mr '68-p109
KR-v35-D 1 '67-p1425
LJ-v93-Ja 15 '68-p304
YR-v4-Ap '68-p1

* * *

HAISLET, Barbara
Why Are Some People Left-Handed?
ASBYP-v15-Fall '82-p56
SLJ-v28-Ag '82-p92
HAISLIP, Barbara
Stars, Spells, Secrets And Sorcery
BL-v72-Je 15 '76-p1466
KR-v44-Mr 15 '76-p333
PW-v209-Mr 29 '76-p58
SLJ-v23-S '76-p134

HALACY, D S, Jr.
See Halacy, Daniel Stephen

HALACY, Daniel Stephen
Census
BL-v76-Ap 15 '80-p1194
CCB-B-v34-N '80-p53
LJ-v105-Ap 15 '80-p986
SLJ-v27-F '81-p75
Nine Roads To Tomorrow
CCB-B-v19-D '65-p63
Nuclear Energy
ACSB-v12-Fall '79-p28
BL-v80-Mr 15 '84-p1070
Radiation, Magnetism And Living Things
BS-v26-Ja 1 '67-p368
CCB-B-v20-Ap '67-p122
HB-v43-Ap '67-p224
LJ-v92-F 15 '67-p892
SB-v2-Mr '67-p267
The Robots Are Here!
BL-v62-Ja 1 '66-p450
CCB-B-v19-Ap '66-p130
CE-v42-F '66-p378
CSM-v57-N 4 '65-pB10
HB-v41-D '65-p647
KR-v33-Jl 1 '65-p636
LJ-v90-D 15 '65-p5526

* * *

HALACY, Daniel Stephen
Century 21
BL-v65-Ap 15 '69-p949
CCB-B-v22-Jl '69-p176
LJ-v94-Mr 15 '69-p1340
SB-v5-D '69-p210
Colonization Of The Moon
BL-v66-S 1 '69-p54
HB-v45-D '69-p695
KR-v36-Jl 15 '68-p761
KR-v36-N 1 '68-p1231
LJ-v93-S 15 '68-p3316
LJ-v94-My 15 '69-p2100
NYTBR-Ap 20 '69-p40
PW-v195-Je 2 '69-p136
SB-v5-S '69-p177
TN-v28-Ap '72-p290
The Energy Trap
ACSB-v9-Winter '76-p17
BL-v71-Mr 1 '75-p686
BS-v34-Mr 15 '75-p561
CCB-B-v28-My '75-p147
HB-v51-O '75-p490
KR-v43-Ja 1 '75-p26
SLJ-v21-Ap '75-p64
SLJ-v25-Ja '79-p20
Experiments With Solar Energy
BL-v66-My 15 '70-p1154
BS-v29-Ja 1 '70-p388
CCB-B-v23-Mr '70-p112
LJ-v95-O 15 '70-p3642
SB-v5-Mr '70-p340
How To Improve Your Memory
BL-v73-Je 1 '77-p1496
SLJ-v24-S '77-p144
Now Or Never
BL-v68-Mr 15 '72-p629
BS-v31-F 15 '72-p522
CCB-B-v25-Ap '72-p123
KR-v39-N 1 '71-p1165
LJ-v97-F 15 '72-p784
NYTBR-Ja 9 '72-p8
NYTBR, pt.2-N 7 '71-p28
SB-v8-My '72-p49
Nuclear Energy
ACSB-v12-Fall '79-p28
BL-v75-N 15 '78-p546
Cur R-v18-O '79-p301
SB-v15-S '79-p105
SLJ-v25-F '79-p56
On The Move
ACSB-v8-Fall '75-p14
BL-v71-S 1 '74-p35
KR-v42-Ap 1 '74-p374
LJ-v99-Ap 15 '74-p1227
SB-v10-D '74-p247
Return From Luna
CCB-B-v23-Ja '70-p81
KR-v37-F 1 '69-p106
LJ-v94-Mr 15 '69-p1340
PW-v195-Ap 7 '69-p56
The Sky Trap
KR-v43-Ag 15 '75-p924
SLJ-v22-N '75-p77
Survival In The World Of Work
BB-v3-Je '75-p4
BS-v35-Jl '75-p97
KR-v43-Mr 1 '75-p247
SLJ-v22-O '75-p106
With Wings As Eagles
BL-v72-D 15 '75-p572
BL-v72-D 15 '75-p578
LJ-v100-O 1 '75-p1841
PW-v208-S 15 '75-p48
SLJ-v22-F '76-p59

* * *

HALAM, Ann
The Alder Tree
GP-v21-My '82-p3894
JB-v46-Ag '82-p151
Punch-v283-S 1 '82-p328
Ally, Ally, Aster
GP-v20-S '81-p3944
JB-v45-O '81-p210
TES-Jl 24 '81-p27

* * *

HALD, Fibben
Matt's Grandfather
CLW-v47-Ap '76-p398

* * *

HALDANE, David
The Zoo Goes To France
Brit Bk N C-Autumn '82-p11

* * *

HALDANE, J B S
My Friend Mr. Leakey
JB-v48-Je '84-p111

* * *

HALDANE, Suzanne
Faces On Places
BL-v77-N 1 '80-p405
HB-v56-D '80-p653
Inst-v90-F '81-p24
KR-v48-N 1 '80-p1397
NYTBR-v85-N 9 '80-p68
SLJ-v27-D '80-p59
The See-Through Zoo
BL-v80-Ag '84-p1626
HB-v60-Ag '84-p485
KR-v52-My 1 '84-pJ45
SB-v20-N '84-p98
SLJ-v31-S '84-p118

* * *

HALE, Don
Railways
HT-v33-Mr '83-p52
Textiles
HT-v33-Mr '83-p52
TES-My 6 '83-p28

* * *

HALE, Irina
Brown Bear In A Brown Chair
BL-v79-Je 15 '83-p1338
JB-v47-O '83-p198
KR-v51-My 15 '83-p577
PW-v223-My 20 '83-p236
SLJ-v30-O '83-p149
TES-Ag 12 '83-p20
WLB-v58-F '84-p436
Chocolate Mouse And Sugar Pig
BB-v7-Ag '79-p3
BL-v75-Mr 15 '79-p1156
CBRS-v7-Spring '79-p112
GP-v17-Mr '79-p3477
JB-v43-Ap '79-p96
KR-v47-My 15 '79-p573
Obs-F 11 '79-p36
PW-v215-Mr 19 '79-p93
SLJ-v25-Ap '79-p43
WLB-v54-O '79-p120
Donkey's Dreadful Day
CBRS-v11-S '82-p3
CE-v60-S '83-p52
JB-v46-O '82-p181
PW-v221-Ja 22 '82-p64
SLJ-v28-My '82-p53
Sch Lib-v30-D '82-p318
WCRB-v8-S '82-p72
WLB-v57-N '82-p235

* * *

HALE, Janet Campbell
The Owl's Song
BL-v70-Jl 1 '74-p1194
BS-v34-My 15 '74-p101
CCB-B-v27-Jl '74-p178
EJ-v72-F '83-p47
KR-v42-Ap 1 '74-p372
LJ-v99-S 15 '74-p2290
NYTBR-Ag 25 '74-p8

* * *

HALE, Kathleen
A Camping Holiday
TES-D 1 '78-p24
Orlando And The Three Graces
Punch-v249-D 15 '65-p899
Punch-v286-Mr 21 '84-p16
Orlando And The Water Cats
Econ-v245-D 23 '72-p49
NS-v83-Je 2 '72-p762
SLJ-v26-Mr '80-p121
Spec-v228-Ap 22 '72-p624
TLS-Ap 28 '72-p482
Orlando Buys A Farm
SLJ-v26-Ag '80-p51
Orlando Goes To The Moon
GP-v18-My '79-p3533
Punch-v286-Mr 21 '84-p16
Orlando, The Frisky Housewife
Econ-v245-D 23 '72-p49
SLJ-v26-Mr '80-p121
Orlando The Judge
Punch-v286-Mr 21 '84-p16
Orlando, The Marmalade Cat
Obs-D 10 '78-p38

* * *

HALE, Nancy
The Night Of The Hurricane
CCB-B-v31-Jl '78-p177
HB-v54-Ag '78-p395
KR-v46-Ap 1 '78-p380
NYTBR-Ap 30 '78-p32
PW-v213-Ap 17 '78-p75
SLJ-v25-N '78-p63

* * *

HALE, Sara J
Mary Had A Little Lamb
BL-v80-Mr 15 '84-p1060
CBRS-v12-My '84-p101
Learning-v12-Ap '84-p72
PW-v225-My 18 '84-p153
SLJ-v30-Ap '84-p102
WLB-v58-Ap '84-p578

* * *

HALES, Richard
Help Your Child To Count
TES-N 16 '84-p41

* * *

HALEVY, Dominique
Historia De Las Armas Y De Los Soldados
BL-v72-My 15 '76-p1342

* * *

HALEY, Gail E
The Abominable Swamp Man
KR-v43-N 1 '75-p1229
SLJ-v22-Ja '76-p37
Costumes For Plays And Playing
GP-v16-D '77-p3229
JB-v41-D '77-p355
RT-v33-Ja '80-p482
SLJ-v26-Mr '80-p131
Go Away, Stay Away
CCB-B-v31-F '78-p94
JB-v42-F '78-p16
KR-v45-S 1 '77-p927
LA-v55-My '78-p617
NYTBR-O 16 '77-p47
Obs-S 25 '77-p25
PW-v212-S 5 '77-p72
SLJ-v24-N '77-p47
TLS-O 21 '77-p1245
The Green Man
BL-v76-Jl 1 '80-p1606
BW-v10-Jl 13 '80-p9

CBRS-v8-Ag '80-p132
CCB-B-v34-O '80-p32
CLW-v52-N '80-p185
Econ-v273-D 22 '79-p86
JB-v44-Ap '80-p62
KR-v48-Jl 15 '80-p906
LA-v57-N '80-p894
PW-v217-My 16 '80-p211
RT-v35-O '81-p66
SLJ-v27-S '80-p59
Sch Lib-v28-Je '80-p153
TES-N 23 '79-p31

Jack Jouett's Ride

BL-v70-N 15 '73-p339
BW-v7-N 11 '73-p5C
CCB-B-v27-F '74-p95
CE-v50-Mr '74-p293
CLW-v45-D '73-p242
CSM-v66-Ja 9 '74-pF4
Comw-v99-N 23 '73-p218
KR-v41-O 15 '73-p1153
LJ-v98-N 15 '73-p3440
NS-v88-N 8 '74-p664
PW-v204-N 12 '73-p37
SR/W-v1-D 4 '73-p29
TLS-S 20 '74-p1011
Teacher-v91-Ap '74-p86
Teacher-v93-Ap '76-p119

Noah's Ark

CCB-B-v25-S '71-p7
CE-v49-O '72-p27
CLW-v51-S '79-p56
Comw-v95-N 19 '71-p185
GT-v89-D '71-p83
HB-v47-O '71-p471
HB-v54-F '78-p29
LJ-v96-O 15 '71-p3458
NYTBR-S 19 '71-p8
TN-v40-Fall '83-p58

The Post Office Cat

Am-v135-D 11 '76-p428
BB-v5-Mr '77-p1
BL-v73-S 15 '76-p174
BW-Ag 8 '76-pF7
CLW-v48-F '77-p306
GP-v15-Jl '76-p2922
JB-v40-O '76-p263
KR-v44-Jl 1 '76-p726
Lis-v96-N 11 '76-p626
Obs-Jl 22 '79-p37
PW-v210-Ag 2 '76-p114
RT-v31-D '77-p331
SLJ-v23-S '76-p100

A Story, A Story

Am-v123-D 5 '70-p494
BL-v66-Je 1 '70-p1212
BL-v67-Ap 1 '71-p660
BL-v69-My 1 '73-p836
BW-v4-My 17 '70-p7
Brit Bk N C-Spring '81-p11
CCB-B-v24-D '70-p59
CE-v47-Ap '71-p378
CLW-v42-O '70-p133
Comw-v92-My 22 '70-p247
GT-v88-O '70-p20
HB-v46-Je '70-p289
KR-v38-Mr 1 '70-p241
LJ-v95-Je 15 '70-p2301
NYTBR-Ap 12 '70-p26
NYTBR, pt.2-N 8 '70-p42
PW-v197-Mr 16 '70-p56
SR-v53-S 19 '70-p34
TLS-Ap 6 '73-p384
TN-v27-N '70-p90
TN-v27-Ap '71-p243
Teacher-v94-O '76-p144

* * *

HALEY, Patrick

The Little Person

SLJ-v28-F '82-p67

* * *

HALEY-JAMES, Shirley

Houghton Mifflin English

Cur R-v22-Ag '83-p39

* * *

HALIBURTON, Gordon M

Clansmen Of Nova Scotia

Can Child Lit-#23 '81-p93

* * *

HALL, Amanda

The Gossipy Wife

BL-v80-Ap 1 '84-p1115
BW-v14-My 13 '84-p19
HB-v60-S '84-p580
JB-v46-Ap '82-p61
PW-v225-F 3 '84-p402
TLS-N 20 '81-p1358

* * *

HALL, Anna Gertrude

Cyrus Holt And The Civil War

CCB-B-v19-D '65-p63

* * *

HALL, Aylmer

Beware Of Moonlight

BL-v67-F 15 '71-p493
HB-v47-F '71-p55
KR-v38-S 15 '70-p1048
LJ-v96-Ja 15 '71-p275

HALL, Aylmer (continued)
NS-v78-O 31 '69-p624
Spec-v223-N 1 '69-p598
TLS-D 4 '69-p1385
Colonel Bull's Inheritance
BS-v29-Jl 1 '69-p149
HB-v45-Ag '69-p417
KR-v37-F 15 '69-p184
NS-v75-My 24 '68-p694
TLS-Je 6 '68-p580

* * *

HALL, Bill
A Year In The Forest
BL-v72-S 1 '75-p40
CCB-B-v29-O '75-p27
PW-v207-Ap 28 '75-p45
SLJ-v22-S '75-p83

* * *

HALL, Candace C
Shelley's Day
LJ-v106-Ja 15 '81-p131

* * *

HALL, Carol
I Been There
CCB-B-v31-O '77-p33
CE-v54-Mr '78-p258
KR-v45-Jl 15 '77-p723
SLJ-v24-N '77-p44
Super-Vroomer!
Inter BC-v10-F 1& '79-p25
Par-v54-F '79-p24
WCRB-v5-Ja '79-p55

* * *

HALL, Carolyn Vosburg
I Love Ice Cream
NYTBR-N 14 '76-p54
SLJ-v23-N '76-p58
I Love Popcorn
NYTBR-N 14 '76-p54
SLJ-v23-N '76-p58
SLJ-v23-Mr '77-p121

* * *

HALL, Derek
Exploring Nature
TES-D 1 '78-p25
My World Of Nature
GP-v14-Ap '76-p2854
Otter Swims
TES-N 16 '84-p37
Panda Climbs
TES-N 16 '84-p37
Prehistoric Mammals
BL-v80-Je 15 '84-p1483
GP-v22-Mr '84-p4224
GP-v23-Jl '84-p4275
Tiger Runs
TES-N 16 '84-p37

* * *

HALL, Donald
Ox-Cart Man
BL-v76-D 15 '79-p612
BOT-v2-D '79-p597
CCB-B-v33-F '80-p110
CE-v56-Ap '80-p304
GP-v19-N '80-p3791
HB-v56-F '80-p44
HB-v60-F '84-p82
HM-v259-D '79-p75
JB-v44-D '80-p283
KR-v47-D 1 '79-p1373
LA-v57-Ap '80-p434
NYTBR-N 11 '79-p51
NYTBR-N 25 '79-p26
NYTBR-v88-N 27 '83-p39
NYTBR-v89-Jl 22 '84-p24
Nat R-v31-D 21 '79-p1638
PW-v216-N 12 '79-p58
PW-v224-D 2 '83-p89
Parnassus-v8-#2 '80-p64
RT-v33-My '80-p971
RT-v34-Ap '81-p838
RT-v35-Ap '82-p792
SE-v44-O '80-p481
SLJ-v26-O '79-p140
TLS-S 19 '80-p1029
Time-v114-D 3 '79-p98
WLB-v54-My '80-p583
Riddle Rat
BL-v73-Jl 15 '77-p1728
PW-v211-Je 13 '77-p108
SLJ-v24-S '77-p108
SR-v5-N 26 '77-p42
Teacher-v95-Ja '78-p42

* * *

HALL, Douglas
Animal Nursery Rhymes
JB-v47-Ap '83-p75
Animal Tales From Listen With Mother
TES-Je 15 '84-p36

* * *

HALL, Elizabeth
From Pigeons To People
ACSB-v9-Spring '76-p22
BL-v72-Ja 15 '76-p684
CCB-B-v29-Ap '76-p124
CLW-v47-My '76-p452
KR-v43-O 15 '75-p1198
SB-v12-S '76-p66
SLJ-v22-D '75-p52
Phoebe Snow
CCB-B-v22-Mr '69-p111
HB-v45-F '69-p54
LJ-v94-Ja 15 '69-p300
Possible Impossibilities
BB-v6-Ap '78-p3
BL-v73-Jl 1 '77-p1645
BL-v73-Jl 1 '77-p1652
CLW-v49-N '77-p188
Cur R-v17-D '78-p385
EJ-v66-O '77-p77
HB-v53-Ag '77-p458
KR-v45-Ap 15 '77-p430
SB-v14-My '78-p2
SLJ-v23-My '77-p69
Stand Up, Lucy
BL-v67-Je 15 '71-p871
CCB-B-v24-Jl '71-p171
GT-v89-O '71-p93
KR-v39-Ap 15 '71-p433
LJ-v96-D 15 '71-p4184
PW-v199-Ap 19 '71-p47
Why We Do What We Do
BL-v70-Mr 1 '74-p735
CCB-B-v27-Je '74-p157
KR-v41-N 1 '73-p1217
LJ-v98-D 15 '73-p3711
PT-v7-D '73-p126
SB-v10-My '74-p3

* * *

HALL, Elvajean
Hong Kong
BL-v63-Je 15 '67-p1099
CCB-B-v21-S '67-p7
CSM-v59-My 4 '67-pB9
HB-v43-Je '67-p361
KR-v35-F 1 '67-p140
LJ-v92-Ap 15 '67-p1733
NYTBR-v72-My 7 '67-p4
Today In Old Boston
SLJ-v22-Mr '76-p103
Today In Old New York
SLJ-v22-Mr '76-p103
Today In Old Philadelphia
SLJ-v22-Mr '76-p103
The Volga: Lifeline Of Russia
BL-v62-S 1 '65-p56
CCB-B-v18-Je '65-p149
CE-v42-N '65-p184
CSM-v57-My 6 '65-p5B
GT-v83-N '65-p119
HB-v41-Je '65-p288
KR-v33-F 1 '65-p114
LJ-v90-Ap 15 '65-p2032
NYTBR-v70-My 9 '65-p21

* * *

HALL, Eva Litchfield
This I Cannot Forget
CCB-B-v18-Je '65-p149

* * *

HALL, Fergus
Groundsel
GP-v21-Ja '83-p4015
Lis-v108-N 4 '82-p27
SLJ-v30-S '83-p106
TLS-N 26 '82-p1305

* * *

HALL, J J
The Crystal Ball
GP-v21-Jl '82-p3921

* * *

HALL, James A
Reasons To Be Cheerful
Brit Bk N C-Autumn '82-p24
TES-My 28 '82-p30
TLS-Mr 26 '82-p352

* * *

HALL, Katy
Fishy Riddles
BL-v80-S 15 '83-p175
HB-v60-F '84-p48
PW-v224-Jl 22 '83-p133
SLJ-v30-D '83-p79
A Gallery Of Monsters
NYTBR-v86-Ap 26 '81-p51
SLJ-v28-Ap '82-p70
Nothing But Soup
BL-v73-F 15 '77-p896
SLJ-v23-Ja '77-p82

* * *

HALL, Lynn
The Boy In The Off-White Hat
KR-v52-S 1 '84-pJ70
Captain
SLJ-v23-F '77-p64
Careers For Dog Lovers
BB-v6-N '78-p2
BL-v74-My 15 '78-p1485
EJ-v67-O '78-p79
KR-v46-F 1 '78-p113
SLJ-v24-Mr '78-p129
WCRB-v4-Jl '78-p46
Danza!
BL-v78-N 15 '81-p438
CCB-B-v35-F '82-p107
Cur R-v21-O '82-p410
Inter BC-v14-#1 '83-p16
KR-v49-N 15 '81-p1408
SLJ-v28-N '81-p92
Denison's Daughter
BL-v80-S 15 '83-p170
BS-v43-D '83-p345
CBRS-v12-Ja '84-p52
CCB-B-v37-D '83-p68
HB-v59-O '83-p581
SLJ-v30-N '83-p92
VOYA-v7-Ap '84-p30
Dog Of The Bondi Castle
BL-v75-Mr 1 '79-p1091
CBRS-v7-Mr '79-p76
LA-v57-Ja '80-p83
SLJ-v25-My '79-p62
Dragon Defiant
BL-v73-My 15 '77-p1420
CE-v54-Ja '78-p138
CSM-v69-My 4 '77-pB8
LA-v55-Ja '78-p47
PW-v211-Ja 17 '77-p84
SLJ-v23-Mr '77-p145
Flowers Of Anger
BB-v5-Mr '77-p3
BL-v73-Ja 15 '77-p718
CCB-B-v30-Ap '77-p125
Kliatt-v12-Fall '78-p9
PW-v210-D 6 '76-p63
The Ghost Of The Great River Inn
SLJ-v27-D '80-p73
Half The Battle
BL-v78-My 1 '82-p1153
BS-v42-Ag '82-p202
CBRS-v10-Ag '82-p138
J Read-v26-Ja '83-p375
PW-v221-Mr 12 '82-p85
SE-v47-Ap '83-p251
SLJ-v28-Ag '82-p126
VOYA-v5-Ag '82-p31
The Haunting Of The Green Bird
BL-v77-Ap 15 '81-p1153
A Horse Called Dragon
BL-v68-D 15 '71-p367
CCB-B-v25-D '71-p57
LJ-v97-Mr 15 '72-p1170
PW-v200-S 20 '71-p49
The Horse Trader
BL-v77-Ap 1 '81-p1099
HB-v57-Ag '81-p422
J Read-v25-D '81-p285
KR-v49-Ap 15 '81-p507
LA-v58-O '81-p846
PW-v219-Mr 20 '81-p62
SLJ-v27-Ap '81-p139
VOYA-v4-O '81-p33
Kids And Dog Shows
BL-v71-Mr 1 '75-p692
CCB-B-v28-My '75-p148
Inst-v84-My '75-p100
LA-v53-My '76-p515
SLJ-v22-S '75-p103
The Leaving
BL-v77-O 1 '80-p206
CCB-B-v34-Ap '81-p151
EJ-v70-S '81-p77
SLJ-v27-D '80-p63
VOYA-v3-F '81-p30
Megan's Mare
BL-v79-Je 1 '83-p1276
CCB-B-v37-O '83-p28
SLJ-v30-O '83-p158
Mystery Of Plum Park Pony
SLJ-v27-D '80-p72
The Mystery Of Pony Hollow
BL-v75-D 15 '78-p686
BL-v77-O 1 '80-p261
CBRS-v7-Mr '79-p73
Cur R-v17-D '78-p389
SLJ-v25-D '78-p68
The Mystery Of Pony Hollow Panda
BL-v79-Je 1 '83-p1276
SLJ-v29-My '83-p92
The Mystery Of The Caramel Cat
BL-v78-N 15 '81-p438
BL-v79-Ap 1 '83-p1042
SLJ-v28-D '81-p82
The Mystery Of The Lost And Found Hound
SLJ-v26-D '79-p97
The Mystery Of The Schoolhouse Dog
CBRS-v7-Jl '79-p124
SLJ-v26-S '79-p111
Mystery Of The Stubborn Old Man
SLJ-v27-D '80-p72
New Day For Dragon
BL-v71-Jl 1 '75-p1127
CCB-B-v29-S '75-p10
KR-v43-My 1 '75-p512
LA-v53-My '76-p516
PW-v207-Je 2 '75-p54
SLJ-v21-Ja '75-p45
Owney, The Traveling Dog
BL-v74-Ja 15 '78-p818
Shadows
BL-v74-D 15 '77-p684
SLJ-v24-Ap '78-p84

HALL, Lynn (continued)
Shy Ones
BL-v64-F 15 '68-p699
CCB-B-v21-Mr '68-p110
KR-v35-O 1 '67-p1218
LJ-v93-Ja 15 '68-p304
The Siege Of Silent Henry
BL-v69-Ja 15 '73-p493
CCB-B-v26-F '73-p91
KR-v40-D 1 '72-p1358
LJ-v98-My 15 '73-p1688
NYTBR, pt.2-N 5 '72-p2
Sticks And Stones
BL-v68-Jl 1 '72-p939
CCB-B-v26-O '72-p25
Choice-v14-N '77-p1178
EJ-v62-Mr '73-p481
EJ-v62-D '73-p1300
LJ-v97-N 15 '72-p3813
NYTBR-My 28 '72-p8
NYTBR, pt.2-N 5 '72-p26
PW-v201-F 14 '72-p69
TN-v29-Ap '73-p257
TN-v30-Ja '74-p203
Stray
CCB-B-v28-F '75-p94
KR-v42-Ap 15 '74-p424
LJ-v99-S 15 '74-p2269
NYTBR-My 4 '75-p23
PW-v205-Je 17 '74-p69
Tin Can Tucker
BL-v79-S 1 '82-p36
CCB-B-v36-Mr '83-p127
HB-v58-O '82-p519
SLJ-v29-Ja '83-p84
VOYA-v6-Ap '83-p37
To Catch A Tartar
BL-v70-S 15 '73-p120
CCB-B-v27-O '73-p27
CSM-v65-My 2 '73-pB4
KR-v41-Ap 1 '73-p384
Too Near The Sun
CCB-B-v24-O '70-p26
CSM-v62-O 31 '70-p11
EJ-v61-S '72-p935
KR-v38-My 15 '70-p552
LJ-v95-My 15 '70-p1953
Troublemaker
NYTBR-My 4 '75-p23
SLJ-v21-Ja '75-p45
The Whispered Horse
BL-v76-Mr 1 '80-p982
BL-v77-O 1 '80-p261

* * *

HALL, Malcolm
And Then The Mouse...
CBRS-v8-Ap '80-p84
CCB-B-v33-Je '80-p190
KR-v48-Ap 1 '80-p435
LA-v57-N '80-p897
SLJ-v27-O '80-p136
Caricatures
BL-v75-S 15 '78-p228
Comw-v105-N 10 '78-p730
KR-v46-Ag 1 '78-p806
SLJ-v25-D '78-p65
Derek Koogar Was A Star
BL-v72-Ja 15 '76-p689
KR-v43-D 1 '75-p1334
SLJ-v22-Ja '76-p37
Edward, Benjamin & Butter
BL-v77-My 15 '81-p1258
KR-v49-Ap 1 '81-p429
RT-v36-O '82-p68
SLJ-v27-My '81-p80
The Electric Book
KR-v43-O 15 '75-p1183
PW-v208-D 1 '75-p66
SLJ-v22-My '76-p59
Forecast
BL-v74-N 15 '77-p559
CCB-B-v31-Mr '78-p112
CE-v54-Mr '78-p258
Comw-v104-N 11 '77-p729
GP-v18-Jl '79-p3542
KR-v45-O 1 '77-p1047
SLJ-v24-D '77-p60
The Friends Of Charlie Ant Bear
BL-v77-N 15 '80-p463
CCB-B-v34-Ja '81-p94
KR-v48-S 1 '80-p1161
SLJ-v27-D '80-p68
Headlines
BL-v70-Ja 15 '74-p542
JB-v39-Je '75-p184
KR-v41-S 15 '73-p1033
LJ-v99-F 15 '74-p563
NYTBR-N 4 '73-p59
SLJ-v25-N '78-p30
Teacher-v93-Ap '76-p124

* * *

HALL, Marjory
The April Ghost
CCB-B-v29-Ap '76-p124
KR-v43-Ag 15 '75-p917
SLJ-v22-Ja '76-p53
Clotheshorse
BS-v26-Je 1 '66-p100
CCB-B-v19-Jl '66-p179
KR-v34-Ap 1 '66-p377
LJ-v91-My 15 '66-p2706
Mystery At October House
BS-v37-O '77-p202
KR-v45-Ja 15 '77-p46
PW-v211-Je 6 '77-p82
SLJ-v23-My '77-p77
The Other Girl
CCB-B-v27-Jl '74-p178
KR-v42-Mr 15 '74-p299
LJ-v99-My 15 '74-p1482

* * *

HALL, Nancy C
Macmillan Fairy Tale Alphabet Book
CBRS-v11-Spring '83-p119
NYTBR-v88-O 9 '83-p39
PW-v224-Jl 1 '83-p102
RT-v37-Ja '84-p427

* * *

HALL, Pam
On The Edge Of The Eastern Ocean
Atl Pro Bk R-v10-N '83-p6
BIC-v11-D '82-p9
Quill & Q-v48-O '82-p32
SLJ-v30-S '83-p106

* * *

HALL, Richard
Explorers In Africa
NS-v90-N 7 '75-p585

* * *

HALL, Roger
Canada: A History In Photographs
BIC-v11-Ja '82-p29
In Rev-v16-Ap '82-p48
Captain Scrimshaw In Space
TES-Mr 12 '82-p35
How The Crab Got A Hard Back
TES-Mr 12 '82-p35

* * *

HALL, Rosalys
The Bright And Shining Breadboard
BL-v65-Je 15 '69-p1175
CCB-B-v22-My '69-p143
HB-v45-Ap '69-p165
KR-v37-F 1 '69-p94
LJ-v95-Mr 15 '70-p1186
NYTBR-Ap 6 '69-p18

HALL, Rosalys (continued)
Miranda's Dragon
CCB-B-v22-Ja '69-p78
KR-v36-S 15 '68-p1042
LJ-v93-N 15 '68-p4404
PW-v194-S 9 '68-p64
The Three Beggar Kings
CCB-B-v28-N '74-p42
HB-v50-D '74-p681
KR-v42-Jl 1 '74-p677
LJ-v99-O 15 '74-p2721
PW-v206-O 28 '74-p48
SR/W-v2-N 30 '74-p44

* * *

HALL, Susan
Street Smart
CCB-B-v26-N '72-p42
KR-v40-Ag 15 '72-p934
LJ-v98-F 15 '73-p634
SE-v37-D '73-p787

* * *

HALL, Terry
Kevin At The Launderette
GP-v17-My '78-p3332
Kevin Plays Leapfrog
GP-v17-My '78-p3332
Kevin's Dirty Shirt
GP-v17-My '78-p3332

* * *

HALL, Valerie
The Worzel Gummidge Cook Book
GP-v19-My '80-p3704

* * *

HALL, William N
Whatever Happens To Baby Horses?
CCB-B-v19-D '65-p63
Whatever Happens To Puppies?
CCB-B-v19-Jl '66-p179

* * *

HALL, Willis
The Incredible Kidnapping
GP-v14-Ap '76-p2849
JB-v40-Ap '76-p103
TLS-D 5 '75-p1460
The Last Vampire
JB-v47-F '83-p41
Sch Lib-v31-Mr '83-p34
The Summer Of The Dinosaur
JB-v41-O '77-p288

* * *

HALL-CLARKE, James
Fishes
Sch Lib-v31-S '83-p258

* * *

HALL-QUEST, Olga
From Colony To Nation
BL-v63-D 15 '66-p451
CCB-B-v20-D '66-p58
CSM-v58-N 3 '66-pB9
EL-v88-Ap '68-p349
KR-v34-Jl 1 '66-p632
LJ-v91-O 15 '66-p5251
NYTBR-Ja 1 '67-p16
SR-v49-N 12 '66-p52

* * *

HALLAMORE, Elisabeth
The Metric Book Of Amusing Things To Do
SLJ-v24-N '77-p31
TN-v34-Winter '78-p191

* * *

HALLARD, Peter
Boy On A White Giraffe
CCB-B-v23-Ap '70-p128
KR-v37-S 15 '69-p998
LJ-v95-Ja 15 '70-p241
Puppy Lost In Lapland
BL-v68-N 15 '71-p292
CCB-B-v25-Ja '72-p74
LJ-v96-O 15 '71-p3467
PW-v200-Ag 16 '71-p57
TN-v28-Je '72-p434

* * *

HALLER, Danita R
Not Just Any Ring
BL-v79-D 15 '82-p564
CBRS-v11-O '82-p14
CCB-B-v36-D '82-p68
CLW-v55-O '83-p140
Inter BC-v15-#3 '84-p16
RT-v36-Ja '83-p469
SE-v47-Ap '83-p251
SLJ-v29-Ja '83-p60
VV-v27-D 14 '82-p75

* * *

HALLER, David
You Can Swim
Brit Bk N C-Autumn '82-p26

* * *

HALLETT, P
Jumping Cats
JB-v42-F '78-p26

* * *

HALLETT, R
Cycling On
JB-v43-F '79-p31

* * *

HALLIBURTON, Warren J
The Picture Life Of Jesse Jackson
BL-v69-My 15 '73-p907
BL-v80-Ag '84-p1626
LJ-v98-F 15 '73-p634
SE-v37-D '73-p789
SLJ-v30-Ag '84-p73

* * *

HALLIDAY, E M
Russia In Revolution
BS-v27-F 1 '68-p430
CCB-B-v22-O '68-p29
KR-v35-D 1 '67-p1428
NYTBR-v73-Mr 10 '68-p22
TLS-O 3 '68-p1124

* * *

HALLIDAY, F E
Chaucer And His World
CCB-B-v23-N '69-p44
LJ-v94-Ap 15 '69-p1633
TLS-My 22 '69-p552

* * *

HALLINAN, P K
I'm Glad To Be Me
SLJ-v25-S '78-p116
I'm Thankful Each Day!
SLJ-v28-D '81-p52
Just Being Alone
SLJ-v23-D '76-p65
Just Open A Book
SLJ-v28-D '81-p52
That's What A Friend Is
CCB-B-v30-My '77-p142
SLJ-v23-My '77-p76
We're Very Good Friends, My Brother And I
CCB-B-v27-N '73-p43
LJ-v98-My 15 '73-p1696
PW-v204-Jl 2 '73-p80
Where's Michael?
SLJ-v25-N '78-p45

* * *

HALLMAN, Ruth
Breakaway
BL-v77-Mr 15 '81-p1024
CBRS-v9-My '81-p87
Hi Lo-v2-Je '81-p4
Inter BC-v13-#4 '82-p15

HALLMAN, Ruth (continued)
Kliatt-v17-Fall '83-p10
SLJ-v27-Ap '81-p139
Gimme Something, Mister
SLJ-v25-Ap '79-p56
Secrets Of A Silent Stranger
BL-v73-S 15 '76-p182
Cur R-v16-D '77-p360
KR-v44-Jl 15 '76-p794
SLJ-v23-D '76-p68

* * *

HALLSTEAD, William F
Broadcasting Careers For You
CCB-B-v37-N '83-p50
SLJ-v30-O '83-p168
VOYA-v7-Ap '84-p40
The Launching Of Linda Bell
BL-v78-D 15 '81-p546
CBRS-v10-F '82-p67
CCB-B-v35-Mr '82-p129
SLJ-v28-D '81-p71
VOYA-v5-Ap '82-p34
The Man Downstairs
BS-v39-S '79-p196
CBRS-v7-Jl '79-p127
CCB-B-v33-N '79-p48
KR-v47-Ag 1 '79-p860
NYTBR-My 13 '79-p27
PW-v215-F 19 '79-p107
SLJ-v25-My '79-p83

* * *

HALLWORTH, Grace
The Carnival Kite
Brit Bk N C-Spring '81-p11
Brit Bk N C-Spring '81-p20
GP-v19-N '80-p3798
JB-v45-Ap '81-p70
Sch Lib-v29-Je '81-p126
TLS-Mr 27 '81-p340
Listen To This Story
Brit Bk N C-Autumn '80-p3
Brit Bk N C-Spring '81-p11
GP-v16-Mr '78-p3259
JB-v42-Ap '78-p88
TES-Ja 9 '81-p24

* * *

HALM, Mary D
The Sara Summer
GP-v21-S '82-p3944

* * *

HALMI, Robert
Zoos Of The World
ACSB-v9-Fall '76-p23
BL-v72-Ja 1 '76-p626
CCB-B-v29-F '76-p97
Inst-v85-N '75-p162
KR-v43-Ag 15 '75-p922
SB-v12-My '76-p40
SLJ-v22-N '75-p77
Teacher-v93-F '76-p122

* * *

HALPERN, John
Early Birds
LJ-v106-Ja 15 '81-p160
PW-v218-N 28 '80-p41
SB-v17-N '81-p97

* * *

HALSELL, Grace
Getting To Know Guatemala, Honduras And British Honduras
Inter BC-v13-#2 '82-p9

* * *

HALSEY, William D
The Magic World Of Words
ARBA-v10-'79-p544
BL-v75-F 15 '79-p947
PW-v212-N 21 '77-p64
SLJ-v24-Ap '78-p70

* * *

HALSTEAD, Beverly
A Brontosaur
GP-v21-Mr '83-p4044
Nature-v300-D 9 '82-p547
TES-N 5 '82-p29
TES-N 11 '83-p24
TES-N 18 '83-p40
A Closer Look At Prehistoric Mammals
ACSB-v10-Fall '77-p20
B&B-v22-Je '77-p72
B&B-v23-Ja '78-p63
Cur R-v17-F '78-p3
JB-v40-Ag '76-p199
NS-v91-My 21 '76-p689
SB-v13-S '77-p95
SLJ-v23-Ap '77-p63
A Closer Look At Prehistoric Reptiles
ACSB-v12-Winter '79-p14
B&B-v23-Ja '78-p63
Cur R-v17-Ag '78-p157
Inst-v88-N '78-p133
JB-v41-O '77-p288
SB-v15-My '79-p40
SLJ-v25-S '78-p137
TES-O 21 '77-p18
TES-N 18 '77-p37
A Closer Look At The Dawn Of Life
ASBYP-v14-Winter '81-p29
Picture Book Of Dinosaurs
NS-v91-My 21 '76-p688
Terrible Claw
GP-v22-Mr '84-p4224
JB-v48-Ap '84-p70
TES-N 18 '83-p40

* * *

HALSTEAD, Bruce W
Tropical Fish
ARBA-v7-'76-p743
SLJ-v23-F '77-p64

* * *

HALSTEAD, L B
Dinosaurs
BL-v78-Ja 1 '82-p573
SA-v247-D '82-p34
SB-v16-My '81-p275
SB-v18-N '82-p75
SLJ-v27-Ja '81-p61
Sch Lib-v30-Mr '82-p67
The Evolution And Ecology Of The Dinosaurs
BL-v75-Ja 15 '79-p810
GP-v14-Ap '76-p2854
JB-v40-Ap '76-p103
The Evolution Of The Mammals
BOT-v4-S '81-p423
JB-v43-Ag '79-p219
LJ-v106-S 1 '81-p1639

* * *

HALTER, Jon C
Bill Bradley: One To Remember
BL-v71-Ap 1 '75-p816
KR-v43-Ja 15 '75-p73
LJ-v99-D 15 '74-p3279
Reggie Jackson: All-Star In Right
BL-v72-O 1 '75-p231
SLJ-v22-D '75-p68

* * *

HALY, George M
Samuel
WCRB-v8-S '82-p72

* * *

HAMALIAN, Leo
Rogues
BL-v75-Ap 1 '79-p1214
CCB-B-v33-O '79-p27
PW-v215-Ja 29 '79-p115

HAMALIAN, Leo (continued)
SLJ-v25-My '79-p72
TLS-Je 19 '81-p710

* * *

HAMANN, Bente
A Friendly ABC
JB-v40-Ag '76-p200
KR-v37-O 1 '69-p1067
LJ-v95-N 15 '70-p4034
LR-v25-Spring '76-p226
NYTBR-N 2 '69-p30
Obs-Jl 18 '76-p20
PW-v196-O 13 '69-p53

* * *

HAMBERGER, John
Birth Of A Pond
ACSB-v10-Winter '77-p21
BB-v4-Ag '76-p2
BL-v72-Mr 15 '76-p1045
KR-v44-Ja 15 '76-p75
PW-v209-Mr 22 '76-p45
SB-v12-Mr '77-p210
SLJ-v22-Ap '76-p74
The Lazy Dog
BL-v68-S 15 '71-p109
CCB-B-v24-Jl '71-p171
JLH-v199-My 17 '71-p63
LJ-v96-S 15 '71-p2906
A Sleepless Day
BW-v7-My 13 '73-p1
CCB-B-v27-D '73-p65
KR-v41-Ja 1 '73-p1
LJ-v98-Ap 15 '73-p1375
PW-v203-F 5 '73-p90

* * *

HAMBLIN, Dora Jane
Buried Cities And Ancient Treasures
BL-v70-F 15 '74-p650
CCB-B-v27-Ap '74-p130
LJ-v99-Mr 15 '74-p902
SB-v10-My '74-p57
TN-v30-Ap '74-p308
Pots And Robbers
BS-v30-Ap 1 '70-p17
CCB-B-v24-Jl '70-p178
NYTBR-Jl 5 '70-p14
SA-v223-D '70-p122
SB-v6-D '70-p265
SR-v53-Ap 18 '70-p37

* * *

HAMEL, Roland C
Trois Saisons Dans L'Enfance De Poney
In Rev-v14-D '80-p39

* * *

HAMER, Martyn
Cats
SLJ-v30-S '83-p123
The Night Sky
BL-v80-Ja 1 '84-p680
JB-v47-O '83-p208
SB-v20-N '84-p92
SLJ-v30-D '83-p66
TES-Mr 9 '84-p51
Trees
ASBYP-v17-Winter '84-p25
BL-v79-Ag '83-p1465
GP-v22-My '83-p4085
JB-v47-Ag '83-p163
SB-v19-Mr '84-p217
SLJ-v30-S '83-p123
Sch Lib-v31-S '83-p258

* * *

HAMER, Mick
Transport
ASBYP-v16-Winter '83-p62
BL-v78-Jl '82-p1444
JB-v46-O '82-p190
SLJ-v28-Ag '82-p116
TES-Ap 1 '83-p36

* * *

HAMERSTROM, Frances
Adventure Of The Stone Man
ABR-v1-D '78-p13
SA-v239-D '78-p28
SLJ-v25-S '78-p137
Walk When The Moon Is Full
ABR-v1-D '78-p13
BL-v72-Mr 1 '76-p977
KR-v44-Mr 15 '76-p322
PW-v209-My 3 '76-p65
SLJ-v22-My '76-p59

* * *

HAMEY, L A
The Roman Engineers
BL-v78-F 1 '82-p706
CCB-B-v35-Mr '82-p129
SLJ-v28-Ap '82-p80
TES-My 13 '83-p32

* * *

HAMILL, Dorothy
On And Off The Ice
BL-v80-Ja 15 '84-p754
B Rpt-v2-Mr '84-p42
BS-v43-Mr '84-p464
CCB-B-v37-F '84-p108
Cur R-v23-F '84-p100
KR-v51-N 1 '83-pJ212
PW-v224-D 9 '83-p50
SLJ-v30-Ja '84-p76
VOYA-v7-Ap '84-p46

* * *

HAMILTON, Alan
Paul McCartney
BL-v80-S 1 '83-p82
B Rpt-v2-Ja '84-p42
JB-v47-D '83-p257
SLJ-v30-O '83-p157
Prince Philip
TLS-O 19 '84-p1198
Queen Elizabeth II
BL-v79-My 15 '83-p1216
CCB-B-v36-Jl '83-p210
SLJ-v29-My '83-p71

* * *

HAMILTON, Ben
Houdini's Book Of Magic
Sch Lib-v30-Je '82-p148
TES-Ap 2 '82-p27

* * *

HAMILTON, Dorothy
Busboys At Big Bend
LJ-v99-D 15 '74-p3267
The Castle
SLJ-v22-F '76-p46
Cricket
SLJ-v22-S '75-p103
Daniel Forbes, A Pioneer Boy
SLJ-v28-D '81-p63
The Eagle
SLJ-v21-Ap '75-p53
Eric's Discovery
SLJ-v26-Ap '80-p110
Gina In-Between
SLJ-v28-My '82-p62
Holly's New Year
SLJ-v28-O '81-p157
Ken's Bright Room
SLJ-v29-Ag '83-p66
Ken's Hideout
SLJ-v26-S '79-p138
Last One Chosen
Inter BC-v14-#6 '83-p20
SLJ-v29-D '82-p85
Linda's Rain Tree
SLJ-v22-Ja '76-p46
Neva's Patchwork Pillow
SLJ-v22-S '75-p103

HAMILTON, Dorothy (continued)
Rosalie
SLJ-v24-O '77-p112
Scamp And The Blizzard Boys
SLJ-v26-My '80-p68
Straight Mark
SLJ-v23-Mr '77-p145
Winter Caboose
SLJ-v30-Ap '84-p115

* * *

HAMILTON, Franklin
1066
CCB-B-v18-My '65-p129

* * *

HAMILTON, Gail
A Candle To The Devil
Am-v133-D 6 '75-p403
BL-v72-S 15 '75-p164
KR-v43-Jl 15 '75-p777
PW-v207-Je 30 '75-p59
SLJ-v22-D '75-p67
Love Comes To Eunice K. O'Herlihy
BL-v74-O 1 '77-p294
CE-v54-F '78-p194
KR-v45-Ag 15 '77-p850
SLJ-v24-O '77-p112
Titania's Lodestone
BB-v3-O '75-p4
BL-v71-My 1 '75-p913
CCB-B-v29-N '75-p45
HB-v51-Ag '75-p387
J Read-v19-F '76-p421
KR-v43-Mr 1 '75-p238
SLJ-v22-S '75-p103

* * *

HAMILTON, Katie
Build It Together
LJ-v109-Je 1 '84-p1124
N Dir Wom-v13-N '84-p19
PW-v225-Ap 20 '84-p78

* * *

HAMILTON, Margaret
Spooks And Spirits
GP-v18-S '79-p3578
GP-v19-Ja '81-p3825
JB-v43-Ap '79-p116
Sch Lib-v27-Je '79-p157
TES-Ja 9 '81-p23

* * *

HAMILTON, Mary
The Sky Caribou
BIC-v9-D '80-p19
Can Child Lit-#29 '83-p69
In Rev-v14-D '80-p40
Quill & Q-v46-Ag '80-p29
SLJ-v27-My '81-p54
The Tin-Lined Trunk
BIC-v10-Ap '81-p29
Can Child Lit-#23 '81-p115
Emerg Lib-v9-My '82-p30
In Rev-v15-Ap '81-p39
Quill & Q-v47-My '81-p14
SLJ-v28-S '81-p125

* * *

HAMILTON, Morse
Big Sisters Are Bad Witches
CBRS-v9-Ap '81-p71
CCB-B-v34-Jl '81-p212
HB-v57-Ag '81-p414
KR-v49-Je 15 '81-p735
SLJ-v27-My '81-p55
How Do You Do, Mr. Birdsteps?
BL-v79-Je 15 '83-p1339
SLJ-v30-S '83-p106
My Name Is Emily
BL-v75-Mr 15 '79-p1158
CBRS-v7-Je '79-p102
KR-v47-F 15 '79-p192
PW-v215-Ap 9 '79-p110
SLJ-v25-Ap '79-p44
Who's Afraid Of The Dark?
BL-v79-Je 15 '83-p1339
SLJ-v30-S '83-p106

* * *

HAMILTON, Roger
Finding Fossils
GP-v16-Mr '78-p3271
JB-v41-D '77-p372
TES-F 10 '78-p25
TLS-Jl 15 '77-p867

* * *

HAMILTON, Virginia
Arilla Sun Down
BL-v72-Jl 15 '76-p1596
BW-N 7 '76-pG7
BW-Ap 8 '79-pL2
BW-v11-My 10 '81-p14
CCB-B-v30-N '76-p43
CE-v53-Mr '77-p257
CSM-v68-N 3 '76-p20
Choice-v14-N '77-p1178
GP-v16-Jl '77-p3145
HB-v52-D '76-p611
JB-v41-Je '77-p177
J Read-v20-My '77-p732
KR-v44-Jl 1 '76-p739
LA-v54-Ap '77-p441
Lis-v97-F 17 '77-p221
NO-v16-F 12 '77-p21
NYTBR-O 31 '76-p39
Obs-F 13 '77-p35
Obs-Je 26 '77-p29
RT-v31-My '78-p915
SE-v41-Ap '77-p350
SLJ-v23-O '76-p116
TLS-Mr 25 '77-p359
Teacher-v94-Ja '77-p131
Dustland
BS-v40-Je '80-p117
BW-v10-S 14 '80-p6
BW-v11-N 8 '81-p14
CBRS-v8-Ap '80-p87
CCB-B-v33-Mr '80-p134
CSM-v72-My 12 '80-pB9
HB-v56-Je '80-p305
JB-v45-Ap '81-p79
J Read-v24-D '80-p271
KR-v48-My 1 '80-p588
Kliatt-v16-Winter '82-p21
LA-v57-S '80-p651
NYTBR-v85-My 4 '80-p26
Obs-N 30 '80-p36
PW-v217-My 30 '80-p85
SLJ-v26-Mr '80-p140
Sch Lib-v29-Mr '81-p44
TLS-S 19 '80-p1024
The Gathering
BL-v77-Ap 1 '81-p1100
BW-v11-N 8 '81-p14
CBRS-v9-Ap '81-p77
CCB-B-v34-Mr '81-p134
CE-v58-Ja '82-p180
GP-v20-S '81-p3944
HB-v57-Ag '81-p432
JB-v46-Ap '82-p73
KR-v49-Je 1 '81-p682
Kliatt-v16-Winter '82-p21
LA-v58-S '81-p702
NYTBR-v86-S 27 '81-p36
PW-v219-My 22 '81-p76
SLJ-v27-Ap '81-p140
TLS-N 20 '81-p1362
VOYA-v4-O '81-p42
The House Of Dies Drear
BL-v65-N 1 '68-p311
BL-v65-Ap 1 '69-p900
BW-v2-N 3 '68-p12
Bl W-v20-Ag '71-p94
Comw-v91-F 27 '70-p584
EJ-v67-D '78-p83
HB-v44-O '68-p563
Inst-v78-F '69-p180

HAMILTON, Virginia
(continued)
KR-v36-Ag 1 '68-p818
NYTBR-v73-O 13 '68-p26
NYTBR-My 21 '78-p51
NYTBR, pt.2-N 8 '70-p30
NYTBR, pt.2-F 13 '72-p12
PW-v194-S 30 '68-p61
SE-v33-My '69-p555
SLJ-v24-F '78-p35
SR-v51-N 9 '68-p69
TN-v25-Ap '69-p310
Teacher-v86-Ap '69-p184
YR-v5-N '68-p14

Illusion And Reality
GP-v16-Jl '77-p3145

Jahdu
BL-v77-O 15 '80-p332
CCB-B-v34-N '80-p53
KR-v48-O 15 '80-p1354
PW-v218-N 21 '80-p58
SLJ-v27-D '80-p64

Justice And Her Brothers
BL-v75-O 1 '78-p294
BW-D 3 '78-pE4
BW-v11-N 8 '81-p14
CCB-B-v32-S '78-p9
CE-v55-Ap '79-p296
CSM-v71-Mr 12 '79-pB4
HB-v55-O '78-p517
JB-v43-Ag '79-p220
KR-v46-N 15 '78-p1253
Kliatt-v16-Winter '82-p21
LA-v56-Ap '79-p444
PW-v214-O 30 '78-p50
SLJ-v25-D '78-p60

A Little Love
BL-v80-Je 1 '84-p1392
CBRS-v13-S '84-p9
CCB-B-v38-S '84-p6
HB-v60-S '84-p597
N Dir Wom-v13-N '84-p19
PW-v226-Jl 13 '84-p51
SLJ-v31-O '84-p167

M.C. Higgins, The Great
BL-v71-S 1 '74-p41
BL-v71-Mr 15 '75-p747
BL-v71-Mr 15 '75-p766
BW-N 10 '74-p6
BW-D 15 '74-p6
CCB-B-v28-D '74-p63
CE-v51-Ja '75-p155
CSM-v69-N 2 '77-pB1
Choice-v12-N '75-p1132
EJ-v64-D '75-p80
GP-v14-S '75-p2690
HB-v50-O '74-p143
J Read-v25-My '82-p777
KR-v42-Jl 1 '74-p687
KR-v43-Ja 1 '75-p10
Kliatt-v11-Winter '77-p4
LA-v57-Ap '80-p420
LJ-v99-N 15 '74-p3054
LJ-v99-D 15 '74-p3247
Lis-v94-N 6 '75-p623
NYTBR-S 22 '74-p8
NYTBR-N 3 '74-p52
NYTBR-D 1 '74-p76
PW-v206-Ag 12 '74-p58
TLS-My 23 '75-p577
TLS-Jl 11 '75-p766
Teacher-v92-N '74-p109
Teacher-v92-My '75-p90
VV-v19-D 16 '74-p52

The Magical Adventures Of Pretty Pearl
BL-v79-Ap 1 '83-p1034
B Rpt-v2-N '83-p33
CBRS-v11-Ap '83-p93
CCB-B-v36-My '83-p167
CSM-v76-Ag 3 '84-pB5
HB-v59-Je '83-p312
Inter BC-v15-#5 '84-p17
KR-v51-Ap 1 '83-p380
LA-v61-Mr '84-p298
N Dir Wom-v13-N '84-p19
NYTBR-v88-S 4 '83-p14
New Age-v8-Je '83-p71
PW-v223-Mr 4 '83-p99
SE-v48-My '84-p376
SLJ-v29-Ap '83-p123
SLJ-v29-My '83-p32
SLJ-v30-Mr '84-p125
VOYA-v6-O '83-p215

Paul Robeson: The Life And Times Of A Free Black Man
BL-v71-S 1 '74-p35
BL-v71-Mr 15 '75-p766
BS-v34-Ja 15 '75-p474
BW-D 15 '74-p6
BW-Jl 8 '79-pE2
CCB-B-v28-Ap '75-p130
EJ-v69-F '80-p95
HB-v51-Ap '75-p159
HE-v39-Ag 25 '79-p10
KR-v42-N 15 '74-p1208
KR-v43-Ja 1 '75-p13
Kliatt-v13-Fall '79-p30
LJ-v99-N 15 '74-p3054
NYTBR-D 22 '74-p8
PW-v206-Jl 29 '74-p58
PW-v216-Jl 23 '79-p160

The Planet Of Junior Brown
A Lib-v3-Ap '72-p420
BL-v68-D 1 '71-p333
BL-v68-Ap 1 '72-p669
BL-v69-My 1 '73-p838
BL-v80-S 1 '83-p95
B Rpt-v1-Mr '83-p24
Bl W-v21-Mr '72-p70
CCB-B-v25-D '71-p57
CE-v48-Ja '72-p206
CSM-v63-N 11 '71-pB5
CSM-v64-My 2 '72-p4
Comw-v95-N 19 '71-p188
EJ-v63-Ja '74-p65
EJ-v67-My '78-p88
Emerg Lib-v11-Ja '84-p21
GT-v89-D '71-p84
GT-v89-My '72-p57
HB-v48-F '72-p81
KR-v39-S 1 '71-p954
LJ-v96-S 15 '71-p2928
LJ-v96-D 15 '71-p4159
NYRB-v18-Ap 20 '72-p13
NYTBR-Ag 24 '71-p8
NYTBR-Mr 10 '74-p35
NYTBR-My 21 '78-p51
PW-v200-Ag 23 '71-p81
SR-v54-N 13 '71-p61
TN-v28-Ap '72-p309

Sweet Whispers, Brother Rush
BL-v78-Ag '82-p1525
BS-v42-Ja '83-p405
BW-v12-N 7 '82-p14
BW-v13-O 9 '83-p13
CBRS-v10-Ag '82-p138
CCB-B-v35-Jl '82-p207
CSM-v76-Ag 3 '84-pB5
HB-v58-O '82-p505
Inter BC-v14-#1 '83-p32
J Read-v26-My '83-p742
KR-v50-Jl 15 '82-p801
LA-v60-My '83-p650
LA-v61-Ap '84-p423
N Dir Wom-v13-N '84-p19
NYT-v132-N 30 '82-p23
NYTBR-v87-N 14 '82-p41
NYTBR-v88-N 13 '83-p31
PW-v222-S 3 '82-p60
PW-v224-N 18 '83-p72
SE-v47-Ap '83-p252
SLJ-v29-S '82-p138
SLJ-v30-Ag '84-p38
SLJ-v31-O '84-p102
VOYA-v5-Ag '82-p31
VOYA-v5-F '83-p36
VV-v27-D 14 '82-p75

HAMILTON, Virginia (continued)
Time-Ago Lost
BL-v69-My 1 '73-p836
BL-v69-Je 15 '73-p988
CCB-B-v26-Ap '73-p124
CLW-v45-D '73-p242
CSM-v65-O 3 '73-p10
CSM-v66-D 5 '73-pB12
HB-v49-Je '73-p278
KR-v41-Ja 1 '73-p5
LJ-v98-Ap 15 '73-p1387
NO-v12-Ag 11 '73-p21
NYTBR-Ag 5 '73-p8
The Time-Ago Tales Of Jahdu
A Lib-v1-Ap '70-p385
BL-v66-N 15 '69-p408
CCB-B-v23-N '69-p45
CSM-v61-N 6 '69-pB6
Comw-v91-N 21 '69-p256
GT-v87-F '70-p145
HB-v46-F '70-p36
KR-v37-S 1 '69-p929
LJ-v94-D 15 '69-p4607
NYTBR-O 5 '69-p40
NYTBR-O 12 '69-p34
NYTBR, pt.2-N 9 '69-p62
PW-v196-Ag 25 '69-p284
SR-v52-N 8 '69-p65
W.E.B. Du Bois
BL-v69-O 1 '72-p148
BL-v69-My 1 '73-p837
BW-v6-Ag 13 '72-p6
CCB-B-v26-S '72-p8
CE-v49-D '72-p148
CSM-v64-My 4 '72-pB5
HB-v48-O '72-p476
KR-v40-My 15 '72-p591
LJ-v97-D 15 '72-p4078
PW-v202-Jl 31 '72-p71
Willie Bea And The Time The Martians Landed
BL-v80-N 1 '83-p408
B Rpt-v2-Mr '84-p32
CBRS-v12-D '83-p41
CCB-B-v37-N '83-p50
CE-v60-My '84-p362
CSM-v76-Mr 2 '84-pB7
CSM-v76-Ag 3 '84-pB5
HB-v60-F '84-p53
KR-v51-N 1 '83-pJ191
N Dir Wom-v13-N '84-p19
NYTBR-v89-Mr 18 '84-p31
PW-v224-D 9 '83-p50
SE-v48-My '84-p371
SLJ-v30-D '83-p67
VOYA-v7-Ag '84-p143
Zeely
BL-v63-Je 1 '67-p1045
BL-v69-My 1 '73-p837
CCB-B-v20-Jl '67-p170
CE-v46-Ap '70-p367
HB-v43-Ap '67-p205
KR-v34-D 1 '66-p1222
LJ-v92-My 15 '67-p2028
ND-v16-Ag '67-p93
NYTBR-My 21 '78-p51
PW-v191-Mr 13 '67-p61

* * *

HAMILTON, W R
The Life Of Prehistoric Animals
JB-v40-Ap '76-p103

* * *

HAMILTON-MERRITT, Jane
My First Days Of School
BL-v79-N 1 '82-p370
CCB-B-v36-D '82-p68
SLJ-v29-Ja '83-p60
Our New Baby
BL-v79-N 15 '82-p445

* * *

HAMILTON-PATERSON, James
Flight Underground
B&B-v15-D '69-p44
TES-S 22 '78-p23
Hostage!
BL-v76-Jl 1 '80-p1599
BS-v40-Je '80-p117
GP-v17-Jl '78-p3362
GP-v19-N '80-p3779
JB-v42-O '78-p268
Lis-v100-N 9 '78-p623
NYTBR-v85-O 5 '80-p30
SLJ-v26-Ag '80-p76
TES-Jl 14 '78-p21
TES-S 19 '80-p30
TLS-Ap 7 '78-p379
The House In The Waves
Am-v123-D 5 '70-p497
B&B-v15-Jl '70-p28
CCB-B-v24-S '70-p9
KR-v38-Ap 15 '70-p464
LJ-v95-Je 15 '70-p2313
NS-v79-My 15 '70-p704
Spec-v224-My 9 '70-p621
TLS-Jl 2 '70-p713
Mummies
B&B-v24-F '79-p54
BL-v76-S 15 '79-p109
CBRS-v8-Winter '80-p68
JB-v43-Ap '79-p121
PW-v215-Je 11 '79-p100
SB-v16-S '80-p28
SLJ-v26-S '79-p157
Sch Lib-v27-Mr '79-p81
TES-N 17 '78-p26

* * *

HAMISH Hamilton Book Of Other Worlds
GP-v15-Ja '77-p3052
JB-v41-F '77-p21
Spec-v237-D 11 '76-p25
TLS-D 10 '76-p1550

* * *

HAMLEY, Dennis
Landings
BL-v76-O 1 '79-p276
BS-v39-N '79-p290
GP-v18-S '79-p3566
JB-v43-O '79-p278
SLJ-v26-F '80-p66
Pageants Of Despair
Am-v131-D 7 '74-p374
BL-v71-F 15 '75-p618
BS-v34-D 15 '74-p422
KR-v42-O 1 '74-p1065
SLJ-v21-Ja '75-p54
TLS-Jl 5 '74-p717
Very Far From Here
GP-v15-Jl '76-p2904
GP-v18-S '79-p3566
JB-v40-D '76-p344
Obs-N 28 '76-p31
Spec-v237-Jl 17 '76-p24
TLS-Jl 16 '76-p884

* * *

HAMMER, Charles
Me, The Beef, And The Bum
BL-v80-Mr 15 '84-p1060
CCB-B-v37-Jl '84-p204
HB-v60-Ap '84-p201
KR-v52-Mr 1 '84-pJ14
SLJ-v30-Ap '84-p124
VOYA-v7-O '84-p196

* * *

HAMMOND, D
Plexers
Cur R-v22-O '83-p50

* * *

HAMMOND, Mildred
Square Dancing Is For Me
CCB-B-v36-My '83-p168

HAMMOND, Mildred (continued)
SLJ-v29-My '83-p95

* * *

HAMMOND, Nicholas
Looking At Wildlife
GP-v16-S '77-p3169
Obs-Ag 28 '77-p26

* * *

HAMMOND, Peter
The Tower Of London
TES-Ja 1 '82-p17

* * *

HAMMOND, Ray
Bobby Catches A Bug
Punch-v287-Ag 15 '84-p45
TES-N 11 '83-p26
Bobby Meets A Pirate
Obs-D 11 '83-p35
Punch-v287-Ag 15 '84-p45
TES-N 11 '83-p26
Computers And Your Child
BL-v80-Mr 1 '84-p942
Brit Bk N-S '84-p526
LJ-v109-Mr 1 '84-p502
TES-Ap 13 '84-p30

* * *

HAMMOND, Winifred G
Plants, Food And People
CCB-B-v18-F '65-p87
The Story Of Your Eye
KR-v43-Ag 15 '75-p922
SLJ-v22-N '75-p78

* * *

HAMMOND-INNES, Ralph
The Big Footprints
B&B-v22-My '77-p52
BL-v73-Ap 15 '77-p1239
BS-v37-Jl '77-p103
CSM-v69-My 11 '77-p27
GP-v15-Ap '77-p3096
KR-v45-F 1 '77-p114
Kliatt-v13-Winter '79-p10
LJ-v102-My 15 '77-p1209
Lis-v97-Ap 7 '77-p458
NYT-v126-My 26 '77-p28
NYTBR-My 15 '77-p14
Obs-F 20 '77-p31
PW-v211-Ja 31 '77-p64
PW-v214-Ag 7 '78-p81
Spec-v238-F 19 '77-p24
TLS-Mr 4 '77-p233
WLT-v53-Winter '79-p187
WSJ-v189-My 23 '77-p20
WSJ-v190-D 15 '77-p20

* * *

HAMMOND Reading Skills Series
RT-v32-Ja '79-p492
Teacher-v96-F '79-p122

* * *

HAMORI, Laszlo
Dangerous Journey
NYTBR-v71-Je 5 '66-p43
RT-v35-Ap '82-p823
Flight To The Promised Land
CLW-v43-F '72-p330
LJ-v95-F 15 '70-p742

* * *

HAMOY, Carol
What's Wrong? What's Wrong?
CCB-B-v18-Je '65-p149

* * *

HAMPDEN, John
The Gypsy Fiddle
BL-v66-Ap 15 '70-p1045
CLW-v41-My '70-p589
HB-v46-F '70-p38
KR-v37-N 1 '69-p1152

* * *

HAMPLE, Naomi
Hugging, Hitting And Other Family Matters
PW-v216-Ag 13 '79-p61
SLJ-v26-Ag '80-p64

* * *

HAMPLE, Stoo
Yet Another Big Fat Funny Silly Book
PW-v218-N 7 '80-p62
SLJ-v27-D '80-p44

* * *

HAMPLE, Stuart
Blood For Holly Warner
BS-v27-F 1 '68-p430
CCB-B-v21-F '68-p94
KR-v35-O 1 '67-p1218
LJ-v92-D 15 '67-p4622

* * *

HAMPLE, Stuart E
Stoo Hample's Silly Joke Book
BL-v75-Ja 15 '79-p810
BW-N 12 '78-pE2
KR-v47-F 1 '79-p128
SLJ-v25-Mr '79-p122
WCRB-v4-N '78-p82

* * *

HAMPSON, Brian
Make It Today 2. Pupil's Book
TES-Mr 12 '82-p37

* * *

HAMPSON, Sharon
Elephant Jam
BIC-v9-D '80-p19
Can Child Lit-#22 '81-p41
In Rev-v15-F '81-p47
M Ed J-v67-Mr '81-p73
Quill & Q-v47-F '81-p21

* * *

HAMPTON, David
We Work For The Council
TES-N 16 '84-p25

* * *

HAMPTON, Doris
Just For Manuel
BL-v68-Je 15 '72-p893
CCB-B-v25-Je '72-p155
LJ-v96-D 15 '71-p4197

* * *

HAMRE, Leif
Operation Arctic
KR-v41-N 15 '73-p1264
LJ-v99-F 15 '74-p573
SLJ-v28-N '81-p39
TLS-N 23 '73-p1434

* * *

HAMSA, Bobbie
Dirty Larry
SLJ-v30-Mr '84-p142
Fast Draw Freddie
BL-v80-Ag '84-p1632
SLJ-v30-Ag '84-p60
Your Pet Bear
RT-v34-D '80-p351
SLJ-v27-Mr '81-p132
Your Pet Beaver
SLJ-v27-Mr '81-p132
Your Pet Camel
SLJ-v27-Ap '81-p113
Your Pet Elephant
RT-v34-D '80-p351
SLJ-v27-Mr '81-p132
Your Pet Giraffe
SLJ-v29-O '82-p141
Your Pet Gorilla
CCB-B-v35-My '82-p171

HAMSA, Bobbie (continued)
Your Pet Kangaroo
SLJ-v27-Ap '81-p113
Your Pet Penguin
SLJ-v27-Ap '81-p113
Your Pet Sea Lion
SLJ-v29-O '82-p141

* * *

HAN, Ying
Duo-Duo Ai Qing Jie
BL-v80-S 1 '83-p96

* * *

HANAK, Mirko
Co Si Povidaji Zviratka V Noci
BL-v74-O 15 '77-p383

* * *

HANCKEL, Frances
A Way Of Love, A Way Of Life
BL-v76-O 1 '79-p229
BS-v39-D '79-p353
CBRS-v8-Winter '80-p68
Cur R-v19-Je '80-p233
HE-v39-Ag 25 '79-p10
KR-v47-O 15 '79-p1214
RSR-v12-Summer '84-p89
SLJ-v27-O '80-p155
TN-v36-Winter '80-p235

* * *

HANCOCK, Carla
Seven Founders Of American Literature
BL-v73-S 15 '76-p136
HB-v52-D '76-p632

* * *

HANCOCK, Gillian
Daring Dives Of Submarines And Submersibles
GP-v19-N '80-p3784
JB-v44-D '80-p306
The Great Volcanoes
GP-v21-N '82-p3980
TES-O 21 '83-p37

* * *

HANCOCK, Lyn
Love Affair With A Cougar
BIC-v9-Ag '80-p34
BS-v39-Ap '79-p13
KR-v46-S 15 '78-p1044
LJ-v103-N 15 '78-p2341
PW-v214-S 18 '78-p152

* * *

HANCOCK, Ralph
Mexico
CCB-B-v18-Ap '65-p117
Supermachines
ACSB-v13-Winter '80-p54
BL-v75-N 15 '78-p544
CBRS-v7-Winter '79-p56
SLJ-v25-N '78-p58

* * *

HANCOCK, Sibyl
An Ark And A Rainbow
SLJ-v23-D '76-p66
Bill Pickett: First Black Rodeo Star
Cur R-v17-Ag '78-p172
KR-v45-Ap 15 '77-p425
RT-v32-D '78-p363
SLJ-v23-My '77-p75
Teacher-v95-O '77-p163
The Blazing Hills
BL-v72-N 15 '75-p459
KR-v43-S 1 '75-p995
SLJ-v22-D '75-p64
Climbing Up To Nowhere
SLJ-v24-D '77-p59
Esteban And The Ghost
BL-v80-O 1 '83-p294
CBRS-v12-D '83-p34
CCB-B-v37-F '84-p108
CE-v61-S '84-p68
KR-v51-S 1 '83-pJ149
NYTBR-v89-Ja 22 '84-p24
PW-v224-S 23 '83-p73
RT-v37-My '84-p889
SLJ-v30-N '83-p78
Time-v122-D 19 '83-p77
Famous Firsts Of Black Americans
SLJ-v30-Ja '84-p76
Freaky Francie
CBRS-v8-F '80-p53
SLJ-v26-Ap '80-p93
The Grizzly Bear
LJ-v99-S 15 '74-p2248
SB-v10-Mr '75-p340
Old Blue
BL-v77-Ja 15 '81-p705
CLW-v52-Ap '81-p404
SLJ-v27-D '80-p65
SLJ-v28-F '82-p37
Theodore Roosevelt
BL-v74-Je 15 '78-p1617
CCB-B-v32-O '78-p30
CLW-v50-N '78-p179
KR-v46-Jl 1 '78-p692
LA-v56-My '79-p544
SLJ-v25-Ja '79-p54

* * *

HANCOCKS, David
Master Builders Of The Animal World
B&B-v18-S '73-p136
BW-v7-S 23 '73-p5
Choice-v11-Ap '74-p281
LJ-v98-N 1 '73-p3275
LJ-v99-Mr 1 '74-p618
LW-v37-Winter '74-p50
Nat-v219-O 5 '74-p313
SA-v231-D '74-p160
SB-v10-S '74-p125

* * *

HAND-BUILT Pottery (Beginning Crafts)
TES-F 3 '78-p43

* * *

HANDFUL Of Ghosts
B&B-v25-N '79-p56

* * *

HANDLING Language
TES-Jl 1 '83-p39

* * *

HANDMAN, Fran
The Upside-Down King Of Minnikin
BIC-v12-D '83-p13
Quill & Q-v49-N '83-p25

* * *

HANDWRITING Activities
TES-Jl 11 '80-p29

* * *

HANEY, Lynn
Chris Evert: The Young Champion
BL-v73-My 1 '77-p1352
CCB-B-v30-Ap '77-p125
KR-v44-D 1 '76-p1270
SLJ-v23-My '77-p80
The Flash Gordon Book
SLJ-v27-Ap '81-p113
I Am A Dancer
BL-v77-My 1 '81-p1197
BW-v11-Je 14 '81-p11
CBRS-v9-My '81-p87
CCB-B-v35-S '81-p9
Kliatt-v15-Spring '81-p50
NYTBR-v86-Ap 26 '81-p69
PW-v219-Mr 20 '81-p62
SLJ-v27-Ap '81-p127

HANEY, Lynn (continued)
Perfect Balance
BL-v75-Je 15 '79-p1536
CCB-B-v33-O '79-p27
KR-v47-Ag 1 '79-p856
NYTBR-Ap 29 '79-p45
PW-v215-Ap 16 '79-p75
SLJ-v26-Ja '80-p70
Ride 'Em Cowgirl!
BL-v72-O 1 '75-p235
CCB-B-v29-Ja '76-p78
KR-v43-Jl 15 '75-p780
PW-v208-Ag 11 '75-p118
SLJ-v22-D '75-p59
Skaters
CCB-B-v37-My '84-p165
SLJ-v30-D '83-p88
VOYA-v6-F '84-p346

* * *

HANFF, Helene
Butch Elects A Mayor
CCB-B-v23-Ap '70-p128
KR-v37-D 1 '69-p1250
LJ-v95-Ap 15 '70-p1627
The Duchess Of Bloomsbury Street
BL-v69-Jl 1 '73-p1006
BS-v33-My 15 '73-p77
CSM-v65-My 9 '73-p10
HB-v49-O '73-p491
KR-v41-Mr 1 '73-p288
LJ-v98-Ap 15 '73-p1275
PW-v203-Mr 5 '73-p77
PW-v209-Mr 1 '76-p97
TLS-My 10 '74-p508
Good Neighbors: The Peace Corps In Latin America
CCB-B-v20-Jl '67-p170
LJ-v91-Jl '66-p3534
The Movers And Shakers
BL-v67-S 15 '70-p96
CCB-B-v24-Ja '71-p74
KR-v38-Ap 1 '70-p394
LJ-v95-S 15 '70-p3056
NYTBR, pt.2-My 24 '70-p12
PW-v197-Je 1 '70-p68
Queen Of England
CCB-B-v23-S '69-p9
CE-v46-Ap '70-p380
CLW-v41-Ja '70-p317
KR-v37-Mr 15 '69-p321
LJ-v95-Ja 15 '70-p241
SE-v48-N '84-p563
Religious Freedom: The American Story
CCB-B-v19-Jl '66-p179
LJ-v91-Jl '66-p3534
Terrible Thomas
CCB-B-v18-Mr '65-p102
Underfoot In Show Business
CCB-B-v34-O '80-p33
GW-v124-Ja 11 '81-p22
Kliatt-v16-Winter '82-p36
Lis-v104-D 4 '80-p764
PW-v218-Jl 25 '80-p148
TES-Mr 12 '82-p25
TLS-D 19 '80-p1434

* * *

HANKO, Vanessa
The Secret Of The Missing Tintypes
WCRB-v9-S '83-p68

* * *

HANKS, Geoffrey
God's Special Army
TES-Ap 24 '81-p22
TES-My 8 '81-p27

* * *

HANLEY, Cliff
The Biggest Fish In The World
GP-v18-Jl '79-p3553

* * *

HANLEY, Hope
Fun With Needlepoint
AB-v50-D 4 '72-p1807
BL-v69-D 1 '72-p356
BS-v32-Ja 15 '73-p482
CCB-B-v26-My '73-p139
CSM-v64-N 8 '72-p8
KR-v40-Ag 15 '72-p952
PW-v202-Ag 21 '72-p80

* * *

HANLON, Emily
Circle Home
BL-v78-F 1 '82-p706
CBRS-v10-Ja '82-p47
CCB-B-v35-Mr '82-p130
KR-v50-F 15 '82-p208
LA-v59-My '82-p487
SLJ-v28-My '82-p70
TLS-Mr 30 '84-p336
VOYA-v5-Ap '82-p39
How A Horse Grew Hoarse On The Site Where He Sighted A Bare Bear
BL-v72-Je 15 '76-p1466
KR-v44-Ap 15 '76-p463
PW-v209-Mr 22 '76-p46
SLJ-v23-S '76-p100
It's Too Late For Sorry
BL-v75-O 15 '78-p368
CBRS-v7-Winter '79-p57
CCB-B-v32-F '79-p99
Comw-v107-F 29 '80-p114
Emerg Lib-v9-N '81-p32
HB-v54-D '78-p643
J Read-v24-Mr '81-p522
KR-v46-S 15 '78-p1020
Kliatt-v15-Spring '81-p8
RSR-v11-Fall '83-p27
SE-v43-Ap '79-p299
SLJ-v25-O '78-p145
TN-v36-Winter '80-p209
WLB-v53-Ja '79-p380
Love Is No Excuse
BL-v79-O 1 '82-p198
CBRS-v11-N '82-p28
CCB-B-v36-D '82-p68
J Read-v26-F '83-p468
KR-v50-Ag 15 '82-p940
SLJ-v29-Ja '83-p84
VOYA-v5-F '83-p36
The Swing
CBRS-v7-Je '79-p107
CCB-B-v33-S '79-p9
CLW-v51-D '79-p233
HB-v55-Ag '79-p414
Inter BC-v11-Ja 10 '80-p23
KR-v47-Jl 15 '79-p797
Kliatt-v16-Winter '82-p9
PW-v215-Ap 2 '79-p73
PW-v220-N 27 '81-p88
RT-v33-Ja '80-p481
SLJ-v26-S '79-p139
What If A Lion Eats Me And I Fall Into A Hippopotamus' Mud Hole?
BL-v72-D 1 '75-p515
CCB-B-v29-My '76-p145
KR-v43-O 15 '75-p1175
SLJ-v22-Ja '76-p37
WLB-v50-Ja '76-p405
The Wing And The Flame
BL-v77-O 1 '80-p206
CBRS-v9-D '80-p28
CCB-B-v34-N '80-p53
KR-v49-Ja 15 '81-p79
SLJ-v27-N '80-p86

* * *

HANN, Jacquie
Big Trouble
BB-v7-Mr '79-p1
KR-v46-S 15 '78-p1015
SLJ-v25-S '78-p116

HANN, Jacquie (continued)
Crybaby
CBRS-v7-Mr '79-p71
CCB-B-v32-My '79-p155
Inst-v88-My '79-p106
KR-v47-Mr 1 '79-p258
PW-v215-Mr 12 '79-p77
SLJ-v25-Ap '79-p44
Follow The Leader
BL-v79-S 15 '82-p114
CBRS-v10-Ag '82-p133
CCB-B-v36-N '82-p47
PW-v221-Je 18 '82-p74
SLJ-v29-N '82-p68
That Man Is Talking To His Toes
BL-v73-N 1 '76-p408
KR-v44-Ag 1 '76-p842
RT-v31-D '77-p331
Up Day, Down Day
HB-v54-Je '78-p265
KR-v46-F 15 '78-p174
PW-v212-D 26 '77-p67
SLJ-v24-Ap '78-p70
WCRB-v4-Mr '78-p42
Where's Mark?
BB-v5-O '77-p1
KR-v45-Mr 15 '77-p280
LA-v55-Mr '78-p365
PW-v211-Mr 14 '77-p94
RT-v32-O '78-p38
SLJ-v24-O '77-p102
WLB-v51-My '77-p770

* * *

HANN, Judith
The Family Scientist
JB-v44-Ap '80-p83
NS-v98-N 9 '79-p732
TES-Ja 11 '80-p26

* * *

HANN, Penelope
Edward The Elephant
CBRS-v10-Je '82-p101

* * *

HANNA, Ron
The Quest Of The Dragonslayer
JB-v47-Ag '83-p163

* * *

HANNAM, Charles
Almost An Englishman
BL-v76-N 1 '79-p439
BS-v39-N '79-p290
GW-v121-O 21 '79-p22
HB-v55-D '79-p677
JB-v43-D '79-p344
KR-v47-S 1 '79-p1005
SLJ-v26-O '79-p159
Sch Lib-v28-Mr '80-p92
A Boy In That Situation
BS-v38-Jl '78-p134
CCB-B-v31-Jl '78-p177
Comw-v105-N 10 '78-p733
HB-v54-Je '78-p287
J Read-v22-N '78-p183
KR-v46-Mr 1 '78-p249
Kliatt-v15-Winter '81-p3
NYTBR-Ap 30 '78-p30
PW-v213-Ap 17 '78-p75
SLJ-v24-My '78-p36
SLJ-v24-My '78-p76
A Boy In Your Situation
GP-v16-Jl '77-p3134
TLS-Mr 25 '77-p358

* * *

HANNAS, Linda
The Jigsaw Book
BW-v11-D 6 '81-p10
CC-v99-D 1 '82-p1236
GP-v20-N '81-p3984
TLS-N 13 '81-p1318
VV-v26-D 16 '81-p69

* * *

HANNAY, Allen
Love And Other Natural Disasters
BL-v78-Ap 15 '82-p1082
BS-v42-Ag '82-p171
CBRS-v10-Ag '82-p139
EJ-v72-D '83-p67
HB-v58-Ag '82-p412
J Read-v26-O '82-p88
KR-v50-Mr 15 '82-p360
LJ-v107-Ap 15 '82-p825
NY-v58-Je 14 '82-p134
PW-v221-Mr 26 '82-p67
SLJ-v28-My '82-p70
VOYA-v5-Je '82-p33

* * *

HANNELL, Christine
Across Canada
BIC-v9-Ag '80-p25
TES-Mr 13 '81-p28

* * *

HANNUM, Sara
Lean Out Of The Window
CCB-B-v20-D '66-p58
CE-v42-Ap '66-p505
CSM-v57-My 6 '65-p8B
GT-v83-N '65-p120
HB-v41-Ap '65-p181
HB-v42-F '66-p81
KR-v33-F 15 '65-p187
LJ-v90-Mr 15 '65-p1549
LJ-v90-My 15 '65-p2438
NYTBR-v70-My 9 '65-p37
Par-v41-D '66-p21
The Wind Is Round
BL-v67-N 15 '70-p263
CCB-B-v24-Ap '71-p124
CSM-v63-Ja 23 '71-p13
HB-v46-O '70-p485
KR-v38-Jl 15 '70-p750
LJ-v95-N 15 '70-p4054
NYTBR, pt.2-N 8 '70-p54
PW-v198-Ag 17 '70-p50

* * *

HANO, Arnold
Kareem! Basketball Great
BL-v71-Mr 15 '75-p761
KR-v43-Ja 15 '75-p73
LJ-v99-D 15 '74-p3278
Muhammad Ali: The Champion
BL-v74-O 1 '77-p303
KR-v45-My 15 '77-p544
NYTBR-Ap 30 '78-p56
SLJ-v24-S '77-p144
Sandy Koufax: Strikeout King
CCB-B-v19-S '65-p9

* * *

HANSEN, Carla
Barnaby Bear Builds A Boat
SLJ-v26-Ag '80-p51
Barnaby Bear Visits The Farm
SLJ-v26-Ag '80-p51

* * *

HANSEN, Caryl
I Think I'm Having A Baby
BL-v78-Je 1 '82-p1307
CCB-B-v36-S '82-p10
Kliatt-v16-Fall '82-p11
SLJ-v29-S '82-p138
VOYA-v5-Ag '82-p31

* * *

HANSEN, Elvig
In The Barn
Sch Lib-v32-S '84-p247
In The Chicken Run
TES-O 27 '78-p24
Life Around The Apple Tree
JB-v43-D '79-p336
Sch Lib-v28-Je '80-p165
Life In The Hedgerow
JB-v43-D '79-p336
Life In The Meadow
JB-v44-Je '80-p132

* * *

HANSEN, G
Life Among The Nettles
GP-v19-S '80-p3749
JB-v44-Je '80-p132

* * *

HANSEN, Jeff
Being A Fire Fighter Isn't Just Squirtin' Water
SLJ-v26-N '79-p65

* * *

HANSEN, Joyce
The Gift-Giver
BL-v77-Ja 1 '81-p624
CBRS-v7-Ag '79-p137
CBRS-v9-Ja '81-p37
CCB-B-v34-Ja '81-p94
HB-v56-D '80-p641
Inter BC-v12-#4 '81-p22
Inter BC-v15-#4 '84-p10
KR-v48-N 15 '80-p1464
PW-v218-O 24 '80-p49
RT-v35-O '81-p66
SLJ-v27-Mr '81-p144
Home Boy
BL-v79-O 15 '82-p304
B Rpt-v2-N '83-p33
BS-v42-F '83-p445
CBRS-v11-F '83-p70
CCB-B-v36-Ja '83-p89
CLW-v55-N '83-p188
Inter BC-v15-#4 '84-p10
KR-v50-N 1 '82-p1195
PW-v222-N 26 '82-p60
SLJ-v29-N '82-p100
VOYA-v5-F '83-p36

* * *

HANSEN, Keld
Salik And Arnaluk
BIC-v10-D '81-p8
Quill & Q-v48-Ap '82-p28
Salik And His Father
BIC-v10-D '81-p8
Quill & Q-v48-Ap '82-p28
Salik And The Big Ship
BIC-v10-D '81-p8
Quill & Q-v48-Ap '82-p28
Salik And The Summer Of The Song Duel
BIC-v10-D '81-p8
Quill & Q-v48-Ap '82-p28

* * *

HANSEN, Rosanna
The Fairy Tale Book Of Ballet
PW-v218-N 14 '80-p55
SLJ-v27-Ag '81-p66
Gymnastics
BL-v76-Jl 1 '80-p1613
PW-v217-Mr 28 '80-p50
SLJ-v26-My '80-p88
Wolves And Coyotes
BL-v78-F 1 '82-p706
SB-v18-S '82-p33

* * *

HANSER, Richard
The Glorious Hour Of Lt. Monroe
BB-v4-N '76-p3
BL-v72-Jl 1 '76-p1526
Comw-v103-N 19 '76-p758
KR-v44-F 1 '76-p141
NYTBR-My 2 '76-p34
SLJ-v22-Ap '76-p86

* * *

HANSON, Andrea
The Adventures Of Black Beauty
SLJ-v30-F '84-p71
Beauty And Vicky
SLJ-v31-S '84-p118

* * *

HANSON, Bernice
Laboratory Science Series
Cur R-v24-N '84-p80

* * *

HANSON, Harvey
Game Time
BL-v72-O 1 '75-p236
KR-v43-Jl 1 '75-p712
SLJ-v22-N '75-p90

* * *

HANSON, Joan
...I Won't Be Afraid
SLJ-v22-S '75-p83
Antonyms
BW-v6-N 5 '72-p3
CE-v49-My '73-p424
Inst-v83-Ja '74-p122
LJ-v98-Mr 15 '73-p994
British-American Synonyms
TES-Mr 12 '82-p35
Homographic Homophones
LJ-v99-S 15 '74-p2248
RT-v32-Ja '79-p444
Teacher-v91-Ap '74-p31
Homographs
BW-v6-N 5 '72-p3
CE-v49-My '73-p424
Inst-v83-Ja '74-p122
LJ-v98-Mr 15 '73-p994
RT-v32-Ja '79-p444
Homonyms
BW-v6-N 5 '72-p3
CE-v49-My '73-p424
Inst-v83-Ja '74-p122
LJ-v98-Mr 15 '73-p994
RT-v32-Ja '79-p444
I'm Going To Run Away
PW-v210-D 33 '76-p61
SLJ-v25-F '79-p42
More Antonyms
LJ-v99-S 15 '74-p2248
RT-v32-Ja '79-p444
Teacher-v91-Ap '74-p31
More Homonyms
LJ-v99-S 15 '74-p2248
RT-v32-Ja '79-p444
Teacher-v91-Ap '74-p31
More Similes
Cur R-v18-Ag '79-p175
Inst-v88-My '79-p114
SLJ-v26-O '79-p140
More Sound Words
Cur R-v18-Ag '79-p175
PW-v215-F 19 '79-p108
SLJ-v26-O '79-p140
TES-Mr 12 '82-p35
More Synonyms
LJ-v99-S 15 '74-p2248
RT-v32-Ja '79-p444
Teacher-v91-Ap '74-p31
Plurals
Cur R-v18-Ag '79-p175
SLJ-v26-O '79-p140
TES-Mr 12 '82-p35
Possessives
Cur R-v19-F '80-p49
LA-v57-F '80-p192
TES-Mr 12 '82-p35

HANSON, Joan (continued)
Similes
BL-v73-Mr 1 '77-p1013
SLJ-v23-Mr '77-p132
Sound Words
BL-v73-Mr 1 '77-p1014
SLJ-v23-Mr '77-p132
Still More Antonyms
BL-v73-Mr 1 '77-p1014
RT-v32-Ja '79-p444
SLJ-v23-Mr '77-p132
Still More Homonyms
BL-v73-Mr 1 '77-p1014
RT-v32-Ja '79-p444
SLJ-v23-Mr '77-p133
Synonyms
BW-v6-N 5 '72-p3
CE-v49-My '73-p424
Inst-v83-Ja '74-p122
LJ-v98-Mr 15 '73-p994
RT-v32-Ja '79-p444

* * *

HANSON, June Andrea
Summer Of The Stallion
BL-v75-Ap 15 '79-p1295
CBRS-v7-My '79-p97
KR-v47-Je 1 '79-p636
NYTBR-S 30 '79-p36
RT-v33-Ja '80-p483
SLJ-v25-Mr '79-p139
Winter Of The Owl
BL-v77-F 15 '81-p809
CBRS-v9-S '80-p7
CCB-B-v34-Je '81-p193
CE-v58-S '81-p48
HB-v57-F '81-p59
SLJ-v27-F '81-p66

* * *

HANSON, M J
The Boomerang Book
BL-v72-O 1 '75-p236
GP-v13-Mr '75-p2588
Inst-v85-N '75-p165
Obs-D 8 '74-p25
Teacher-v93-D '75-p87

* * *

HANSSON, Gunilla
A Surprise For Granny
JB-v47-D '83-p235

* * *

HAPGOOD, Miranda
Martha's Mad Day
CCB-B-v31-Ja '78-p78
HB-v53-D '77-p654
KR-v45-Jl 15 '77-p724
PW-v212-Jl 18 '77-p137
RT-v32-O '78-p35
SLJ-v24-D '77-p44

* * *

HARADA, Joyce
It's The ABC Book
SLJ-v28-Ap '82-p58

* * *

HARADA, Taiji
Tochan No Toneru
BL-v79-O 15 '82-p320

* * *

HARAYDA, Marel
Needlework Magic With Two Basic Stitches
BL-v74-Je 15 '78-p1617
SLJ-v25-S '78-p138

* * *

HARBISON, Peter
The Archaeology Of Ireland
Arch-v31-Jl '78-p67
Choice-v15-D '78-p1328
JB-v40-Ag '76-p228
LJ-v101-S 1 '76-p1774
SB-v13-My '77-p37
TLS-S 3 '76-p1073

* * *

HARDAWAY, B Touchstone
One Small Drum
SLJ-v29-My '83-p72

* * *

HARDCASTLE, M
The Gigantic Hit
JB-v46-Ag '82-p151

* * *

HARDCASTLE, Michael
Away From Home
GP-v13-Mr '75-p2579
Breakaway
GP-v15-Mr '77-p3059
Caught Out
JB-v48-Ap '84-p82
Sch Lib-v32-S '84-p238
The Demon Bowler
JB-v39-F '75-p63
Fast From The Gate
GP-My '84-p4265
JB-v47-Je '83-p124
TES-Mr 9 '84-p50
TES-Ap 27 '84-p27
The First Goal
GP-v15-Mr '77-p3059
Free Kick
GP-v13-Mr '75-p2579
Life Underground
JB-v40-F '76-p24
Roar To Victory
Brit Bk N C-Autumn '82-p19
JB-v46-Je '82-p105
TES-O 1 '82-p47
The Saturday Horse
B&B-v23-Ja '78-p64
GP-v16-O '77-p3190
JB-v42-Je '78-p154
Soccer Special
JB-v42-Ag '78-p203
Sch Lib-v27-Je '79-p136
TES-Jl 28 '78-p20
The Switch Horse
GP-v19-S '80-p3769
The Team That Wouldn't Give In
JB-v48-Je '84-p138
Top Of The League
JB-v44-Ap '80-p83
Top Soccer
Sch Lib-v27-D '79-p356
Where The Action Is
JB-v41-Ag '77-p234

* * *

HARDENDORFF, Jeanne B
The Bed Just So
BL-v72-Ap 15 '76-p1185
CE-v53-Mr '77-p257
CLW-v48-S '76-p90
Inst-v85-My '76-p120
KR-v44-Mr 1 '76-p250
PW-v209-Ap 26 '76-p59
SLJ-v22-My '76-p50
SR-v3-My 15 '76-p37
Just One More
BL-v65-Jl 1 '69-p1226
CCB-B-v23-N '69-p45
CSM-v61-My 8 '69-p13
LJ-v95-My 15 '70-p1942
PW-v195-Ap 21 '69-p66
Libraries And How To Use Them
CBRS-v7-My '79-p97
CCB-B-v33-S '79-p9
Cur R-v19-F '80-p27
SLJ-v26-S '79-p139
Sing Song Scuppernong
BL-v70-My 15 '74-p1055
CCB-B-v28-O '74-p28
Inst-v84-N '74-p133
KR-v42-My 1 '74-p485
LJ-v99-D 15 '74-p3263

HARDENDORFF, Jeanne B (continued)
PW-v205-My 27 '74-p65
Slip! Slop! Gobble!
BL-v67-Ja 15 '71-p420
HB-v47-Ap '71-p161
KR-v38-Ag 1 '70-p794
LJ-v95-D 15 '70-p4336
PW-v198-D 7 '70-p50
Tricky Peik And Other Picture Tales
BL-v63-My 1 '67-p948
CCB-B-v20-Jl '67-p170
CE-v44-F '68-p388
CLW-v39-O '67-p159
HB-v43-Ag '67-p463
KR-v35-F 15 '67-p203
LJ-v92-Ap 15 '67-p1734
NYTBR, pt.1-v72-My 7 '67-p44
PW-v191-Ap 10 '67-p82

* * *

HARDER, Janet D
Letters From Carrie
CSM-v73-Ag 10 '81-pB9

* * *

HARDING, Anthony
Car Facts & Feats
BL-v74-O 1 '77-p294
CLW-v50-My '79-p450
EJ-v67-N '78-p83
Kliatt-v12-Fall '78-p65

* * *

HARDING, Diana
Baboon Orphan
ASBYP-v15-Spring '82-p40
BL-v78-F 15 '82-p756
CCB-B-v35-Mr '82-p130
SB-v18-N '82-p92
SLJ-v28-Ap '82-p70

* * *

HARDING, Lee
The Fallen Spaceman
BOT-v4-F '81-p78
CBRS-v9-S '80-p8
CCB-B-v34-F '81-p111
Emerg Lib-v9-My '82-p28
Inst-v90-N '80-p158
KR-v48-N 15 '80-p1465
NYTBR-v85-N 9 '80-p58
NYTBR-v87-Mr 7 '82-p35
SLJ-v27-O '80-p146
Misplaced Persons
CBRS-v7-Jl '79-p127
CCB-B-v32-Je '79-p174
EJ-v68-N '79-p75
KR-v47-My 15 '79-p580
Kliatt-v17-Spring '83-p16
MFSF-v64-My '83-p42
NYTBR-Ag 19 '79-p20
NYTBR-v88-Ap 17 '83-p35
PW-v215-Ja 29 '79-p115
PW-v223-Ja 7 '83-p74
S Fict R-v12-F '83-p31

* * *

HARDING, Ron
Living In Moscow
Econ-v277-D 27 '80-p77
Moscow
TES-Mr 6 '81-p36

* * *

HARDING, Vincent
There Is A River
Am-v146-Mr 13 '82-p196
BL-v78-D 1 '81-p469
BS-v41-Ja '82-p390
BW-v11-D 20 '81-p9
CC-v99-Ja 20 '82-p67
CSM-v73-N 9 '81-pB3
Choice-v19-Ap '82-p1128
Comw-v111-F 24 '84-p120
Inter BC-v14-#7 '83-p29
J Am St-v17-Ap '83-p120
KR-v49-S 15 '81-p1203
Kliatt-v17-Spring '83-p32
LJ-v106-O 15 '81-p2025
NW-v99-Ja 4 '82-p59
NYTBR-v86-N 1 '81-p7
NYTBR-v88-Ja 23 '83-p27
Nat-v234-Mr 6 '82-p276
New R-v185-D 16 '81-p33
PW-v220-S 25 '81-p80
PW-v222-N 19 '82-p75
Phylon-v43-D '82-p386
Prog-v46-O '82-p56
SLJ-v29-Ja '83-p91
TT-v39-Jl '82-p210

* * *

HARDWICK, Mollie
Willowwood
KR-v48-Ag 15 '80-p1103
PW-v218-S 5 '80-p62
TES-Je 20 '80-p39

* * *

HARDWICK, Richard
Charles Richard Drew
BL-v64-Mr 15 '68-p868
BS-v27-F 1 '68-p430
CCB-B-v22-O '68-p28
KR-v35-O 15 '67-p1288
LJ-v93-Ja 15 '68-p291
NYTBR-v73-My 19 '68-p26
SB-v4-My '68-p53

* * *

HARDY, Aruna
Ravi Of India
JB-v45-Je '81-p115
TES-Ap 10 '81-p37

* * *

HARDY, David
Air And Weather
GP-v16-Ap '78-p3298
JB-v42-Je '78-p154
NS-v95-My 19 '78-p679
TES-F 10 '78-p25
Energy And The Future
Brit Bk N-Ap '80-p207
GP-v18-Mr '80-p3646
JB-v44-Ag '80-p190
Sch Lib-v28-S '80-p325
TES-Ap 11 '80-p24
Light And Sight
NS-v95-My 19 '78-p679
TES-Ap 21 '78-p22

* * *

HARDY, Thomas
Our Exploits At West Poley (Lawrence)
BL-v75-F 15 '79-p933
CCB-B-v32-My '79-p155
Econ-v269-D 23 '78-p99
GP-v17-Ja '79-p3439
HB-v55-Ap '79-p210
JB-v43-F '79-p52
KR-v47-F 1 '79-p125
Lis-v100-N 9 '78-p623
NS-v96-N 3 '78-p591
SLJ-v25-Ap '79-p68
TES-O 27 '78-p21
The Pinnacled Tower
BL-v71-Ap 15 '75-p861
CCB-B-v28-Jl '75-p177
CSM-v67-My 7 '75-pB5
KR-v43-Ap 15 '75-p470
PW-v207-Mr 17 '75-p56
SLJ-v21-My '75-p66
SR-v2-My 31 '75-p31

* * *

HARE, Barbara
Hoopla The Lamb
TES-Mr 7 '80-p47

HARGREAVES, Roger (continued)
Mr. Quiet
SLJ-v28-Mr '82-p132
Mr. Silly
LJ-v99-N 15 '74-p3038
SLJ-v27-Ja '81-p50
SR/W-v1-My 4 '74-p45
Mr. Skinny
SLJ-v28-Mr '82-p133
Mr. Small
SLJ-v28-Mr '82-p133
Mr. Sneeze
Obs-Ag 29 '71-p18
SLJ-v29-My '83-p62
Mr. Snow
SLJ-v29-My '83-p62
Mr. Stingy
SLJ-v29-My '83-p62
Mr. Tall
SLJ-v29-My '83-p62
Mr. Tickle
LJ-v99-N 15 '74-p3038
Obs-Ag 29 '71-p18
SLJ-v27-Ja '81-p50
SR/W-v1-My 4 '74-p45
Mr. Topsy-Turvy
LJ-v99-N 15 '74-p3038
SLJ-v29-My '83-p62
SR/W-v1-My 4 '74-p45
Mr. Worry
SLJ-v28-Mr '82-p133
Quack
Spec-v242-Je 30 '79-p26
Things
NS-v102-D 4 '81-p19

* * *

HARGROVE, James
Microcomputers At Work
BL-v81-S 1 '84-p64
SLJ-v31-O '84-p147

* * *

HARGROVE, Jim
Mountain Climbing
BL-v80-O 1 '83-p302
Cur R-v23-Ap '84-p58
GP-My '84-p4268
SLJ-v30-Ja '84-p74

* * *

HARKER, Ronald
Digging Up The Bible Lands
BL-v70-S 1 '73-p46
CCB-B-v27-O '73-p31
HB-v49-O '73-p477
KR-v41-Ap 1 '73-p401
LJ-v98-My 15 '73-p1581
LJ-v98-My 15 '73-p1655
LJ-v98-My 15 '73-p1689
NY-v49-D 3 '73-p219
Obs-Jl 16 '72-p31
PW-v203-Ap 2 '73-p65
SB-v9-Mr '74-p321
TLS-Jl 14 '72-p810

* * *

HARKINS, Philip
No Head For Soccer
CCB-B-v18-F '65-p87
HB-v41-Ap '65-p176

* * *

HARLAN, Jack R
Plant Scientists And What They Do
CCB-B-v19-O '65-p32

* * *

HARLAND, Sam
The How And Why Wonder Book Of Ships
TES-O 21 '77-p20

* * *

HARLER, Anne
Tracy Austin: Teenage Champion
CCB-B-v33-Jl '80-p213
SLJ-v26-My '80-p90

* * *

HARLEY, Ruth
Captain James Cook
SLJ-v26-Ja '80-p70
Ferdinand Magellan
SLJ-v26-Ja '80-p70
Henry Hudson
SLJ-v26-Ja '80-p70

* * *

HARLOW, Eve
Adventure Trail
GP-v19-N '80-p3796
JB-v43-Ag '79-p220
Sch Lib-v27-Mr '79-p89
TES-O 20 '78-p44
TES-S 19 '80-p30
No Time To Be Bored
JB-v41-F '77-p34

* * *

HARLOW, Joan H
Shadow Bear
CBRS-v9-Mr '81-p62
CCB-B-v34-My '81-p172
LA-v58-S '81-p699
NYTBR-v86-Ap 26 '81-p54
SLJ-v28-Ja '82-p64

* * *

HARMAN, Humphrey
Men Of Masaba
BL-v68-O 1 '71-p145
BS-v31-S 15 '71-p269
CCB-B-v25-O '71-p26
CLW-v43-F '72-p358
KR-v39-My 1 '71-p511
LJ-v96-S 15 '71-p2929
NYTBR, pt.2-My 2 '71-p43
SB-v7-D '71-p195
More Tales Told Near A Crocodile
B&B-v18-Jl '73-p140
TLS-Je 15 '73-p682
Tales Told Near A Crocodile
BL-v63-Je 15 '67-p1100
CCB-B-v21-My '68-p142
CE-v44-Mr '68-p444
CSM-v59-My 4 '67-pB10
HB-v43-Ag '67-p463
KR-v35-F 1 '67-p141
LJ-v92-Mr 15 '67-p1316
NYTBR-v72-Ap 2 '67-p30
Obs-O 3 '76-p22
PW-v191-Ap 10 '67-p81
Tales Told To An African King
GP-v17-Ja '79-p3458
JB-v43-Ap '79-p106
TES-N 10 '78-p24

* * *

HARMELING, Jean
The Incredible Will Of H.R. Heartman
CCB-B-v36-Jl '83-p210
NYTBR-v88-Je 12 '83-p49
PW-v223-Je 17 '83-p74
SLJ-v30-S '83-p123
TES-S 21 '84-p37
WCRB-v9-Jl '83-p38

* * *

HARMER, Mabel
The Circus
BL-v78-F 15 '82-p760
SLJ-v28-D '81-p78

* * *

HARMIN, Merrill
This Is Me
Cur R-v18-F '79-p17

* * *

HARMON, Margaret
The Engineering Medicine Man
ACSB-v10-Winter '77-p21
BL-v72-Ja 15 '76-p679
Cur R-v16-My '77-p93
PW-v209-Ap 5 '76-p101
SB-v12-D '76-p147
SLJ-v22-F '76-p52
Ms. Engineer
BL-v76-S 15 '79-p109
KR-v48-F 15 '80-p223
SLJ-v26-F '80-p56

* * *

HARMS, Valerie
Tryin' To Get To You
CBRS-v8-F '80-p57
SLJ-v26-Mr '80-p140

* * *

HARNAN, Terry
African Rhythm-American Dance
BL-v70-Je 1 '74-p1104
BS-v34-My 1 '74-p69
BW-My 19 '74-p4
CCB-B-v28-N '74-p43
Dance-v49-F '75-p27
KR-v42-Ap 15 '74-p436
LJ-v99-Ap 15 '74-p1228
NYTBR-Ag 4 '74-p8
PW-v205-Ap 22 '74-p74
SLJ-v24-D '77-p35
Gordon Parks
CCB-B-v25-Je '72-p156
LJ-v97-S 15 '72-p2950

* * *

HARNDEN, Ruth
Next Door
BW-v4-My 17 '70-p16
CCB-B-v24-D '70-p59
Comw-v92-My 22 '70-p248
KR-v38-Ap 15 '70-p453
LJ-v95-Jl '70-p2540

* * *

HARNETT, Cynthia
The Cargo Of The Madalena
Cur R-v24-N '84-p96
HB-v60-S '84-p616
Great House
BL-v64-Jl 1 '68-p1234
CCB-B-v21-Jl '68-p174
Cur R-v24-N '84-p96
HB-v44-Ag '68-p428
KR-v36-Ja 1 '68-p12
SE-v33-My '69-p555
The Merchant's Mark
Cur R-v24-N '84-p96
Ring Out Bow Bells!
B&B-v19-Ja '74-p94
GP-v18-My '79-p3525
The Sign Of The Green Falcon
Cur R-v24-N '84-p96
Stars Of Fortune
Cur R-v24-N '84-p96
TES-Jl 17 '81-p26
The Writing On The Hearth
B&B-v19-Mr '74-p99
BL-v69-Je 15 '73-p984
BL-v69-Je 15 '73-p988
CCB-B-v27-S '73-p9
Cur R-v24-N '84-p96
HB-v49-Je '73-p271
HT-v21-D '71-p887
KR-v41-Ap 15 '73-p463
LJ-v98-Jl '73-p2200
LR-v23-Spring '72-p205
PW-v204-Jl 16 '73-p111
TLS-D 3 '71-p1510
TN-v30-Je '74-p434

* * *

HARNISHFEGER, Lloyd
The Collector's Guide To American Indian Artifacts
LA-v54-Ap '77-p436

* * *

HARPER, Anita
Ella Climbs A Mountain
GP-v16-N '77-p3210
How We Feel
Brit Bk N C-Spring '81-p11
GP-v18-Mr '80-p3661
JB-v44-Je '80-p118
Obs-D 2 '79-p39
TLS-D 14 '79-p130
How We Live
BB-v6-F '78-p1
BL-v74-Ja 15 '78-p818
Brit Bk N C-Spring '81-p11
CCB-B-v31-F '78-p94
JB-v42-Je '78-p141
KR-v45-O 1 '77-p1043
Obs-N 27 '77-p29
SLJ-v24-D '77-p57
TES-N 4 '77-p24
TES-D 14 '79-p21
How We Play
Brit Bk N C-Spring '81-p11
JB-v44-Je '80-p133
Obs-D 2 '79-p39
TLS-D 14 '79-p130
How We Work
BB-v6-F '78-p1
BL-v74-Ja 15 '78-p818
Brit Bk N C-Spring '81-p11
CCB-B-v31-F '78-p94
KR-v45-O 1 '77-p1043
Obs-N 27 '77-p29
SLJ-v24-Ja '78-p78
TES-N 4 '77-p24
TES-D 14 '79-p21
TLS-O 21 '77-p1245

* * *

HARPER, Wilhelmina
Easter Chimes: Stories For Easter & The Spring
BL-v61-Ap 1 '65-p758
CCB-B-v18-Je '65-p149
HB-v41-Ap '65-p168
KR-v33-Ja 1 '65-p4
LJ-v90-F 15 '65-p961
Gunniwolf
Comw-v87-N 10 '67-p179
KR-v35-S 1 '67-p1040
LJ-v92-N 15 '67-p4244
NO-v6-N 27 '67-p21
NYTBR-v72-O 22 '67-p62
RT-v37-Ap '84-p702
SLJ-v25-N '78-p31

* * *

HARPER & Row English
Cur R-v22-My '83-p149

* * *

HARPER & Row Mathematics
Cur R-v21-My '82-p197

* * *

HARRAH, Michael
First Offender
BL-v76-Jl 15 '80-p1675
CBRS-v8-Je '80-p107
CCB-B-v33-Jl '80-p213
NYTBR-v85-O 5 '80-p30
SLJ-v26-Ag '80-p76

* * *

HARRANTH, Wolf
Michael Hat Einen Seemann
TLS-Mr 25 '77-p353
My Old Grandad
TES-Je 8 '84-p50
No Time For Claudia
JB-v45-F '81-p12

HARRANTH, Wolf (continued)
The Wonderful Meadow
GP-v19-Ja '81-p3818
JB-v45-Ap '81-p62
TES-N 21 '80-p30

* * *

HARRE, John
The Victors
TES-Ja 9 '81-p23

* * *

HARRELL, Sara Gordon
Cottage By The Sea
SLJ-v25-Ja '79-p51
John Ross
BL-v76-O 1 '79-p273
SLJ-v26-Mr '80-p129
Tomo-Chi-Chi: The Story Of An American Indian
SLJ-v24-Mr '78-p129
Teacher-v95-F '78-p139
Willowcat And The Chimney Sweep
SLJ-v27-Mr '81-p132

* * *

HARRIES, Ann
The Sound Of The Gora
GP-v19-S '80-p3757
JB-v44-O '80-p249
Sch Lib-v29-Mr '81-p50
Spec-v245-Ag 16 '80-p21
TES-F 13 '81-p25

* * *

HARRINGTON, Lyn
China And The Chinese
BL-v63-Mr 15 '67-p795
BS-v26-Ja 1 '67-p371
CCB-B-v20-Mr '67-p108
LJ-v92-Ja 15 '67-p343
NH-v76-N '67-p29
NYTBR, pt.1-v72-My 7 '67-p4
Pac A-v42-Spring '69-p83
SR-v50-Ap 22 '67-p100
Grand Canal Of China
CCB-B-v21-Mr '68-p110
KR-v35-N 1 '67-p1327
LJ-v93-Ja 15 '68-p304
Luck Of The La Verendryes
BS-v27-My 1 '67-p65
CCB-B-v21-D '67-p59
In Rev-v15-Ap '81-p16
KR-v35-F 1 '67-p141
LJ-v92-Jl '67-p2648
The Shaman's Evil Eye
Can Child Lit-#31 '83-p128
In Rev-v14-D '80-p40

* * *

HARRINGTON, Richard
The Inuit
BIC-v11-F '82-p30
CG-v102-F '82-p86
Can Child Lit-#31 '83-p126
In Rev-v16-F '82-p37
Mac-v94-D 14 '81-p66

* * *

HARRIOTT, T
Black Bear White Bear
JB-v44-Je '80-p118

* * *

HARRIS, Anthony B
Human Measurement
Choice-v16-N '79-p1194
TES-Ja 4 '80-p20

* * *

HARRIS, Aurand
The Arkansaw Bear
Dr-#2 '81-p56
Six Plays For Children
BL-v74-N 1 '77-p452
Choice-v15-Ap '78-p229
HB-v54-Ap '78-p179

* * *

HARRIS, Christie
Confessions Of A Toe-Hanger
BL-v64-S 1 '67-p54
CCB-B-v20-Jl '67-p170
CLW-v39-D '67-p292
CSM-v59-My 4 '67-pB10
HB-v43-Ap '67-p213
KR-v35-F 1 '67-p144
LJ-v92-Ap 15 '67-p1748
Trav-v24-N '67-p99
Figleafing Through History
BL-v68-S 1 '71-p53
CCB-B-v25-O '71-p26
Comw-v95-N 19 '71-p190
J Ho E-v65-O '73-p55
LJ-v96-S 15 '71-p2929
Forbidden Frontier
BL-v64-Je 15 '68-p1185
CCB-B-v21-Je '68-p159
CLW-v40-O '68-p148
HB-v44-Ap '68-p181
KR-v36-F 15 '68-p190
YR-v4-Je '68-p7
Let X Be Excitement
BL-v65-Je 15 '69-p1170
CCB-B-v22-Jl '69-p176
CLW-v41-O '69-p133
KR-v37-F 15 '69-p185
LJ-v94-S 15 '69-p3218
PW-v195-My 12 '69-p58
SR-v52-My 10 '69-p60
Mouse Woman And The Mischief-Makers
BB-v5-S '77-p3
BL-v74-S 15 '77-p193
BW-My 1 '77-pE2
CCB-B-v31-Ja '78-p78
CE-v54-Mr '78-p262
CE-v55-O '78-p42
Can Child Lit-#15 '80-p98
Cur R-v17-Ag '78-p182
GP-v17-Ja '79-p3459
HB-v53-Ag '77-p436
JB-v43-F '79-p31
KR-v45-My 1 '77-p489
LA-v55-F '78-p216
SLJ-v23-Ap '77-p67
Sch Lib-v27-Mr '79-p36
TN-v34-Winter '78-p189
Mouse Woman And The Muddleheads
BIC-v8-O '79-p28
BL-v75-Je 15 '79-p1536
Can Child Lit-#15 '80-p103
HB-v55-O '79-p542
JB-v45-Ap '81-p70
KR-v47-Jl 1 '79-p743
LA-v57-Mr '80-p324
Obs-N 30 '80-p36
RT-v33-Ja '80-p482
SA-v241-D '79-p48
SLJ-v26-S '79-p139
Sch Lib-v29-Mr '81-p30
TES-F 20 '81-p27
Mouse Woman And The Vanished Princesses
BB-v4-N '76-p2
BL-v72-My 15 '76-p1336
CCB-B-v30-N '76-p43
HB-v52-Je '76-p286
KR-v44-Ap 15 '76-p476
SE-v41-Ap '77-p349
SLJ-v22-Ap '76-p86
SLJ-v22-My '76-p34
Teacher-v94-N '76-p137
Mystery At The Edge Of Two Worlds
BB-v7-Ap '79-p4
CBRS-v7-F '79-p67
CCB-B-v32-D '78-p62
Can Child Lit-#15 '80-p29

HARRIS, Christie (continued)
Can Child Lit-#15 '80-p100
Cur R-v17-D '78-p389
KR-v46-O 15 '78-p1138
SLJ-v25-D '78-p68
Once More Upon A Totem
ABC-v24-Ja '74-p38
BL-v69-Je 15 '73-p989
CCB-B-v27-N '73-p43
CE-v50-O '73-p29
CSM-v65-Je 6 '73-p14
CSM-v66-D 5 '73-pB12
CSM-v67-Je 10 '75-p16
Comw-v99-N 23 '73-p214
HB-v49-Je '73-p266
KR-v41-Mr 1 '73-p257
LJ-v98-My 15 '73-p1681
SLJ-v26-N '79-p43
Once Upon A Totem
Atl Pro Bk R-v10-N '83-p2
SLJ-v26-N '79-p43
Raven's Cry
BL-v63-D 1 '66-p416
CCB-B-v20-D '66-p58
CLW-v38-Ja '67-p340
CSM-v59-D 8 '66-p13
HB-v42-O '66-p574
KR-v34-S 15 '66-p979
NH-v76-N '67-p28
NYTBR-v71-N 20 '66-p55
SA-v215-D '66-p144
SR-v49-N 12 '66-p53
Trav-v23-Ja '67-p195
Secret In The Stlalakum Wild
BL-v68-Je 15 '72-p908
CCB-B-v25-Jl '72-p169
CSM-v64-My 4 '72-pB4
Can Child Lit-#15 '80-p29
KR-v40-Ap 15 '72-p478
LJ-v97-My 15 '72-p1913
Quill & Q-v48-Je '82-p7
Sky Man On The Totem Pole?
BB-v3-N '75-p4
CCB-B-v29-D '75-p63
Can Child Lit-#15 '80-p29
HB-v51-Ag '75-p380
J Read-v19-Mr '76-p509
KR-v43-Mr 15 '75-p317
SLJ-v21-My '75-p55
The Trouble With Adventurers
BL-v78-Ag '82-p1525
BW-v12-My 9 '82-p21
Can Child Lit-#31 '83-p100
Cur R-v22-Ag '83-p89
HB-v58-Ag '82-p420
LA-v59-N '82-p869
Mac-v95-Je 28 '82-p57
Quill & Q-v48-Je '82-p36
SLJ-v28-Ag '82-p116
The Trouble With Princesses
BL-v76-Jl 15 '80-p1676
CCB-B-v33-Jl '80-p213
Can Child Lit-#20 '80-p42
HB-v56-Ag '80-p419
In Rev-v14-Ag '80-p50
LA-v57-N '80-p900
RT-v34-Ja '81-p485
West With The White Chiefs
BL-v62-N 1 '65-p272
CCB-B-v19-Ap '66-p130
HB-v41-Je '65-p279
KR-v33-Mr 1 '65-p242
LJ-v90-Ap 15 '65-p2033
NYTBR-v70-Ap 4 '65-p22

* * *

HARRIS, Colin
Fuzzbuzz. Level 3
TES-S 14 '84-p51

* * *

HARRIS, Dorothy Joan
Goodnight Jeffrey
PW-v224-S 9 '83-p65
SLJ-v30-D '83-p56
The House Mouse
B&B-v20-F '75-p79
CCB-B-v27-O '73-p27
Can Child Lit-#15 '80-p88
GP-v13-Ap '75-p2601
JB-v39-F '75-p39
KR-v41-My 15 '73-p559
LJ-v98-S 15 '73-p2640
PW-v203-My 21 '73-p49
The School Mouse
Can Child Lit-#15 '80-p88
PW-v211-My 2 '77-p70
SLJ-v24-O '77-p102
The School Mouse And The Hamster
Can Child Lit-#33 '84-p69
In Rev-v14-Ag '80-p50
KR-v48-F 1 '80-p121
PW-v216-D 3 '79-p52
RT-v34-O '80-p102
SLJ-v26-Mr '80-p121

* * *

HARRIS, Dwight
Computer Programming 1, 2, 3!
BL-v80-O 15 '83-p359
BL-v80-Ja 1 '84-p682
CBRS-v12-N '83-p30
SLJ-v30-N '83-p93
VOYA-v7-Je '84-p109

* * *

HARRIS, Geraldine
The Children Of The Wind
BL-v79-F 15 '83-p770
CBRS-v11-Mr '83-p82
CCB-B-v36-Ap '83-p150
GP-v21-Ja '83-p4007
HB-v59-Je '83-p312
JB-v47-F '83-p41
J Read-v27-O '83-p84
KR-v50-D 15 '82-p1335
RT-v37-N '83-p192
SF&FBR-Jl '83-p59
S Fict R-v12-My '83-p55
SLJ-v30-N '83-p93
TES-D 17 '82-p28
VOYA-v6-O '83-p215
The Dead Kingdom
BL-v80-N 1 '83-p403
B Rpt-v2-Mr '84-p32
CBRS-v12-Jl '84-p140
Fant R-v7-Ag '84-p47
HB-v60-F '84-p60
JB-v48-F '84-p32
RT-v37-N '83-p192
SLJ-v30-Ja '84-p86
Sch Lib-v31-S '83-p270
VOYA-v7-Ap '84-p38
Prince Of The Godborn
BL-v79-F 15 '83-p770
Brit Bk N C-Autumn '82-p24
CBRS-v11-Mr '83-p82
CCB-B-v36-Mr '83-p127
HB-v59-Je '83-p312
J Read-v27-O '83-p84
KR-v50-D 15 '82-p1335
Obs-Ap 11 '82-p31
RT-v37-N '83-p192
SF&FBR-Jl '83-p59
S Fict R-v12-My '83-p55
SLJ-v30-N '83-p93
TES-Ap 23 '82-p26
VOYA-v6-O '83-p215
The Seventh Gate
BL-v80-My 1 '84-p1234
B Rpt-v3-S '84-p33
CBRS-v12-Jl '84-p140
Fant R-v7-S '84-p40
GP-v22-Ja '84-p4192
HB-v60-Je '84-p336
JB-v48-Ap '84-p83
Obs-D 11 '83-p35
SLJ-v31-S '84-p128

HARRIS, Geraldine
(continued)
Sch Lib-v32-Je '84-p153
VOYA-v7-Ag '84-p147

* * *

HARRIS, Jacqueline L
Martin Luther King, Jr.
BL-v79-Je 15 '83-p1339
CBRS-v11-Spring '83-p124
SLJ-v29-My '83-p82

* * *

HARRIS, Janet
Black Pride
BL-v66-O 1 '69-p186
CCB-B-v23-D '69-p60
Comw-v90-My 23 '69-p299
Comw-v93-F 26 '71-p521
GT-v88-Ap '71-p89
Inst-v79-Ja '70-p152
KR-v37-Mr 1 '69-p249
LJ-v94-Je 15 '69-p2510
NYTBR, pt.2-My 4 '69-p20
NYTBR, pt.2-N 9 '69-p60
PW-v195-My 26 '69-p56
TN-v26-Ja '70-p207
Long Freedom Road
BL-v63-Je 1 '67-p1046
BS-v27-My 1 '67-p65
CCB-B-v21-S '67-p7
KR-v35-F 15 '67-p204
LJ-v92-My 15 '67-p2028
Lis-v79-My 16 '68-p643
NYTBR, pt.1-v72-My 7 '67-p5
PW-v191-Ap 10 '67-p82
TLS-Je 6 '68-p596
Teacher-v95-Ja '78-p45
Students In Revolt
BL-v67-S 1 '70-p52
CCB-B-v24-O '70-p26
KR-v38-F 15 '70-p182
LJ-v95-S 15 '70-p3056
NYTBR, pt.2-My 24 '70-p10
The Woman Who Created Frankenstein
BB-v7-O '79-p5
BL-v76-S 1 '79-p33
CBRS-v8-S '79-p8
CCB-B-v33-Ja '80-p96
HB-v55-D '79-p678
KR-v47-N 1 '79-p1269
SLJ-v26-S '79-p157

* * *

HARRIS, Joel Chandler
The Adventures Of Brer Rabbit
B&B-v17-My '72-pR10
BL-v77-Ap 1 '81-p1100
Brer Rabbit (Crouch)
GP-v16-Mr '78-p3259
JB-v42-F '78-p26
On The Plantation
Rp B Bk R-v25-#4 '80-p26

* * *

HARRIS, John
Endangered Predators
BL-v73-S 15 '76-p175
Cur R-v16-O '77-p256
KR-v44-My 15 '76-p596
SB-v12-Mr '77-p213
SLJ-v23-F '77-p65
The Interceptors
GP-v16-S '77-p3158
The Revolutionaries
GP-v17-Ja '79-p3454
JB-v43-Je '79-p167
The Tale Of A Tail
GP-v14-N '75-p2743

* * *

HARRIS, Jonathan
The New Terrorism
BL-v79-Mr 15 '83-p954
B Rpt-v2-N '83-p54
CCB-B-v37-S '83-p9
Cur R-v22-D '83-p97
KR-v51-F 15 '83-p188
SLJ-v29-Ag '83-p76

* * *

HARRIS, Leon
The Moscow Circus School
BL-v66-Jl 15 '70-p1407
CCB-B-v24-N '70-p42
Comw-v92-My 22 '70-p254
HB-v46-Je '70-p306
KR-v38-Mr 15 '70-p324
LJ-v95-My 15 '70-p1942
NYTBR-Mr 29 '70-p18
PW-v197-F 2 '70-p91
SR-v53-My 9 '70-p45
The Russian Ballet School
AB-v46-N 23 '70-p1570
BL-v67-N 1 '70-p227
BW-v4-N 8 '70-p25
CCB-B-v24-Mr '71-p107
CSM-v63-Ja 30 '71-p13
Comw-v93-N 20 '70-p206
Dance-v45-Ja '71-p80
Dance-v46-Jl '72-p90
GT-v88-Mr '71-p99
HB-v47-Je '71-p299
KR-v38-Jl 1 '70-p683
LJ-v95-S 15 '70-p3048
LJ-v98-O 15 '73-p3123
SR-v53-O 24 '70-p67
Yvette
BL-v67-Ja 1 '71-p372
BW-v4-N 8 '70-p25
CCB-B-v24-Mr '71-p107
CSM-v63-Ja 30 '71-p13
Dance-v46-Jl '72-p90
LJ-v96-F 15 '71-p714
LJ-v98-O 15 '73-p3123

* * *

HARRIS, Lorle
Biography Of A Mountain Gorilla
CCB-B-v35-Ap '82-p149
CLW-v54-D '82-p224
Inst-v91-My '82-p108
Biography Of A River Otter
ACSB-v13-Winter '80-p21
CLW-v51-Ap '80-p414
KR-v47-My 1 '79-p520
SB-v15-My '80-p278
The Biography Of A Whooping Crane
BB-v5-S '77-p3
BL-v73-Je 1 '77-p1497
KR-v45-Ap 1 '77-p355
LA-v55-Ja '78-p49
SB-v13-D '77-p166
SLJ-v24-S '77-p108

* * *

HARRIS, M A
A Negro History Tour Of Manhattan
CCB-B-v23-S '69-p10
LJ-v95-S 15 '70-p3062
NHB-v32-My '69-p23

* * *

HARRIS, Margaret
Sharks And Troubled Waters
CCB-B-v31-Jl '78-p177
Cur R-v17-Ag '78-p228
SLJ-v24-My '78-p63
Teacher-v96-N '78-p134

* * *

HARRIS, Marilyn
The Peppersalt Land
BW-v4-N 8 '70-p22
CCB-B-v24-My '71-p136

HARRIS, Marilyn (continued)
Comw-v94-My 21 '71-p268
Inst-v131-O '71-p146
LJ-v96-Ap 15 '71-p1504
NYTBR-Ja 31 '71-p26
The Runaway's Diary
BL-v68-F 1 '72-p463
BS-v31-N 15 '71-p386
CCB-B-v26-S '72-p8
KR-v39-O 15 '71-p1131
LJ-v97-Mr 15 '72-p1178
Teacher-v91-Ap '74-p89

* * *

HARRIS, Mark J
The Last Run
BL-v78-Ja 15 '82-p648
CBRS-v10-O '81-p18
CCB-B-v35-Ja '82-p86
CLW-v53-Ap '82-p401
KR-v50-F 15 '82-p208
SLJ-v28-N '81-p104
With A Wave Of The Wand
BL-v76-F 1 '80-p770
CBRS-v8-F '80-p58
KR-v48-Mr 15 '80-p365
RT-v35-O '81-p71
SLJ-v26-Mr '80-p132

* * *

HARRIS, Mary K
Bus Girls
CCB-B-v21-Mr '68-p110
KR-v36-Ja 15 '68-p57
SR-v51-My 11 '68-p41

* * *

HARRIS, Nathaniel
The Lawrences
GP-v14-Ap '76-p2836
JB-v40-Ag '76-p228
TLS-O 1 '76-p1250
The Nelsons
GP-v15-Ap '77-p3089
JB-v41-Ag '77-p235
NS-v93-My 20 '77-p686
TLS-Mr 25 '77-p347
The Shakespeares
GP-v14-Ap '76-p2836
JB-v40-Ag '76-p228
TLS-O 1 '76-p1250
The Shaws
B&B-v22-F '77-p58
JB-v41-D '77-p355
NS-v93-My 20 '77-p686
TLS-Mr 25 '77-p347

* * *

HARRIS, Pamela
Another Way Of Being
CF-v56-N '76-p50
Can Child Lit-#31 '83-p126

* * *

HARRIS, Paul
Oil
GP-v14-Ja '76-p2801
JB-v40-Ap '76-p92

* * *

HARRIS, Paula
Pisces
SLJ-v25-S '78-p138
Scorpio
SLJ-v25-S '78-p138

* * *

HARRIS, Peter
Monkey And The Three Wizards
Cur R-v17-Ag '78-p188
HB-v53-O '77-p529
JB-v41-Ap '77-p94
KR-v45-Mr 15 '77-p280
LA-v55-F '78-p216
PW-v211-My 23 '77-p247
SLJ-v24-N '77-p47

* * *

HARRIS, R
Tastes Good
TES-Ag 20 '82-p20

* * *

HARRIS, Robie H
Before You Were Three
BL-v74-S 15 '77-p193
KR-v45-My 1 '77-p489
LA-v55-Ap '78-p520
NYTBR-Je 12 '77-p31
SB-v14-My '78-p35
SLJ-v24-S '77-p129
Don't Forget To Come Back
BB-v7-Je '79-p1
BL-v75-O 15 '78-p381
CSM-v70-O 23 '78-pB11
KR-v46-N 15 '78-p1241
PW-v214-O 23 '78-p61
SLJ-v25-D '78-p44
I Hate Kisses
CBRS-v10-S '81-p3
CCB-B-v35-N '81-p46
KR-v49-O 15 '81-p1291
PW-v220-Jl 3 '81-p146
RT-v36-O '82-p70
SLJ-v28-Ja '82-p64
Rosie's Double Dare
CBRS-v8-Ag '80-p135
CLW-v52-Ap '81-p403
RT-v35-O '81-p67
SLJ-v27-D '80-p74
SLJ-v27-My '81-p27
Rosie's Razzle Dazzle Deal
BL-v78-Ap 1 '82-p1018
SLJ-v28-Ag '82-p116

* * *

HARRIS, Robin
Hello Kitty Sleeps Over
BL-v78-Ag '82-p1525
My Melody's New Bike
BL-v78-Ag '82-p1525

* * *

HARRIS, Rolf
Looking At Pictures With Rolf Harris
Brit Bk N C-Autumn '82-p10
GP-v18-My '79-p3511
JB-v43-F '79-p52
Obs-D 3 '78-p36
Spec-v241-D 9 '78-p35
TES-N 16 '79-p29
TES-N 16 '79-p30

* * *

HARRIS, Rosemary
Beauty And The Beast
BL-v76-My 1 '80-p1291
CE-v57-S '80-p46
JB-v44-F '80-p18
KR-v48-My 1 '80-p576
LA-v57-N '80-p894
NYTBR-v85-My 11 '80-p25
PW-v217-F 8 '80-p81
Punch-v281-D 2 '81-p1023
SLJ-v26-Ap '80-p110
Sch Lib-v28-Je '80-p141
TES-Je 20 '80-p42
TES-S 21 '84-p37
The Bright And Morning Star
BL-v68-Je 15 '72-p909
CCB-B-v25-Je '72-p156
CE-v49-Mr '73-p318
Comw-v97-N 17 '72-p158
HB-v48-Ap '72-p154
KR-v40-Mr 1 '72-p266
LJ-v97-Je 15 '72-p2243
NS-v83-Je 2 '72-p759
SLJ-v25-S '78-p43
SR-v55-My 20 '72-p82
Spec-v229-N 11 '72-p754
TLS-Jl 14 '72-p810
TN-v29-Ja '73-p167

HARRIS, Rosemary (continued)
The Child In The Bamboo Grove
B&B-v17-D '71-pR7
CCB-B-v26-Mr '73-p106
KR-v40-O 1 '72-p1144
Lis-v86-N 11 '71-p662
Obs-D 5 '71-p34
PW-v202-Ag 7 '72-p49
Spec-v227-N 13 '71-p690
TLS-O 22 '71-p1325
The Double Snare
B&B-v20-Ap '75-p77
BL-v72-S 15 '75-p117
GP-v14-Jl '75-p2675
Obs-Ja 19 '75-p29
TLS-Ja 17 '75-p49
The Enchanted Horse
Brit Bk N C-Autumn '81-p11
GP-v20-S '81-p3948
JB-v45-D '81-p242
The Flying Ship
GP-v13-Ap '75-p2612
JB-v39-Je '75-p175
Green Finger House
GP-v19-My '80-p3710
JB-v44-Ag '80-p168
Sch Lib-v28-D '80-p370
TLS-Jl 18 '80-p809
I Want To Be A Fish
Obs-Je 5 '77-p26
Janni's Stork
CCB-B-v37-Ap '84-p147
GP-v21-Mr '83-p4044
HB-v60-Je '84-p328
JB-v47-Ap '83-p67
PW-v225-Mr 2 '84-p93
SLJ-v30-Ag '84-p60
The King's White Elephant
NS-v93-My 20 '77-p683
TLS-N 23 '73-p1431
The Little Dog Of Fo
GP-v15-N '76-p2992
JB-v41-Ap '77-p78
The Moon In The Cloud
B&B-v17-D '71-pR7
BL-v66-Ap 1 '70-p982
BL-v67-Ap 1 '71-p660
BW-v4-My 10 '70-p5
CCB-B-v23-Je '70-p159
CSM-v61-My 1 '69-pB5
Comw-v92-My 22 '70-p246
GT-v89-D '71-p83
HB-v46-Ap '70-p167
KR-v38-Ja 1 '70-p7
LJ-v95-My 15 '70-p1911
LJ-v95-My 15 '70-p1953
LJ-v95-D 15 '70-p4325
NYTBR-Ap 12 '70-p26
PW-v197-F 2 '70-p91
SLJ-v25-S '78-p43
SR-v53-Mr 21 '70-p39
Spec-v238-Ap 16 '77-p27
TLS-Ap 28 '72-p486
A Quest For Orion
GP-v17-N '78-p3410
JB-v42-Ag '78-p203
NS-v96-N 3 '78-p594
Obs-D 3 '78-p36
Punch-v275-D 6 '78-p1024
Sch Lib-v27-Je '79-p158
TES-N 24 '78-p50
TES-Ap 2 '82-p27
TLS-S 29 '78-p1089
Sea Magic
BL-v70-Mr 15 '74-p819
CCB-B-v28-S '74-p9
CE-v51-N '74-p91
CSM-v66-My 1 '74-pF5
HB-v50-Ap '74-p145
KR-v42-F 15 '74-p192
LJ-v99-S 15 '74-p2290
The Seal-Singing
BL-v68-D 15 '71-p364
CCB-B-v25-D '71-p57
Comw-v95-N 19 '71-p180
GP-v16-Mr '78-p3280
HB-v48-F '72-p57
Inst-v131-D '71-p93
KR-v39-S 1 '71-p954
LA-v57-Ap '80-p405
LJ-v96-D 15 '71-p4190
NS-v82-N 12 '71-p661
NYTBR, pt.2-N 7 '71-p42
PW-v200-Ag 16 '71-p57
SR-v54-D 11 '71-p46
TLS-O 22 '71-p1318
The Shadow On The Sun
BL-v67-D 1 '70-p307
BW-v4-N 8 '70-p8
CCB-B-v24-Je '71-p157
HB-v46-O '70-p481
KR-v38-Ag 15 '70-p886
LJ-v95-N 15 '70-p4044
SLJ-v25-S '78-p43
Spec-v224-My 9 '70-p621
TLS-Jl 2 '70-p711
Tower Of The Stars
Brit Bk N C-Spring '81-p25
GP-v19-Mr '81-p3843
JB-v45-Ap '81-p80
Obs-N 30 '80-p36
Sch Lib-v29-Je '81-p152
TES-N 21 '80-p31
TLS-Mr 27 '81-p339
Zed
BL-v80-Jl '84-p1544
CCB-B-v38-S '84-p6
GP-v21-Mr '83-p4027
HB-v60-Ag '84-p475
JB-v46-D '82-p230
SLJ-v30-Ag '84-p83
Sch Lib-v31-Mr '83-p57
TES-N 19 '82-p35
TLS-N 26 '82-p1302

* * *

HARRIS, Stephen
The Harvest Mouse
Brit Bk N-O '80-p586
SLJ-v27-Ja '81-p58
Sch Lib-v28-S '80-p274

* * *

HARRIS, Susan
Boats And Ships
SLJ-v26-S '79-p111
Creatures That Look Alike
ACSB-v13-Winter '80-p21
SLJ-v26-S '79-p111
Creatures With Pockets
ASBYP-v14-Winter '81-p30
BL-v76-My 15 '80-p1364
SB-v16-Ja '81-p156
SLJ-v26-My '80-p82
Crocodiles And Alligators
ASBYP-v14-Winter '81-p31
SB-v16-N '80-p94
SLJ-v26-My '80-p83
Gems And Minerals
ASBYP-v14-Winter '81-p31
Cur R-v20-Ap '81-p196
SB-v16-N '80-p91
SLJ-v26-Ag '80-p52
Helicopters
BL-v76-N 15 '79-p504
Cur R-v19-Ap '80-p174
SB-v16-N '80-p97
SLJ-v26-Ap '80-p93
Odd Animals
Cur R-v16-O '77-p303
SLJ-v24-S '77-p108
Reptiles
ACSB-v12-Winter '79-p14
Cur R-v18-My '79-p146
HB-v54-Je '78-p306
SB-v14-Mr '79-p231
SLJ-v24-F '78-p47

HARRIS, Susan (continued)
SLJ-v30-Ag '84-p37
Space
ACSB-v13-Winter '80-p22
SB-v15-My '80-p275
SLJ-v26-S '79-p139
Swimming Mammals
CCB-B-v31-F '78-p95
CLW-v49-My '78-p454
SB-v14-D '78-p182
UFO's
ASBYP-v14-Winter '81-p31
SB-v16-Ja '81-p152
SLJ-v26-Ag '80-p52

Upside-Down Creatures
ACSB-v12-Winter '79-p15
SLJ-v24-My '78-p83
Volcanoes
SLJ-v26-F '80-p45
Whales
ASBYP-v14-Winter '81-p31
BL-v76-Mr 15 '80-p1056
SB-v16-Ja '81-p156
SLJ-v27-Mr '81-p132

* * *

HARRISON, C William
A Walk Through The Marsh
CCB-B-v26-Jl '73-p171
Hort-v52-Mr '74-p22
LJ-v98-Jl '73-p2186
Wildlife
BS-v30-D 15 '70-p414
CCB-B-v24-F '71-p92
KR-v38-O 1 '70-p1112
SB-v6-Mr '71-p321

* * *

HARRISON, David L
Detective Bob And The Great Ape Escape
CBRS-v9-Mr '81-p64
SLJ-v27-My '81-p79

* * *

HARRISON, George
The First Book Of Energy
BL-v62-S 1 '65-p56
CCB-B-v20-D '66-p59
HB-v41-Ag '65-p414
LJ-v90-Jl '65-p3132

* * *

HARRISON, Gregory
Daniel
JB-v42-D '78-p311
TLS-S 29 '78-p1088

* * *

HARRISON, Harry
The California Iceberg
BS-v35-N '75-p259
KR-v43-Jl 1 '75-p712
PW-v208-Ag 4 '75-p57
SLJ-v22-O '75-p99
The Men From P.I.G. And R.O.B.O.T.
BB-v7-Je '79-p3
BL-v74-Mr 15 '78-p1187
BL-v80-Ap 15 '84-p1200
CCB-B-v31-My '78-p142
CLW-v50-D '78-p235
HB-v54-Ag '78-p395
JB-v39-F '75-p63
KR-v46-Mr 15 '78-p311
LA-v56-Ap '79-p445
NYTBR-Ap 16 '78-p26
Obs-F 23 '75-p28
Obs-Jl 23 '78-p21
SLJ-v24-My '78-p68
Spec-v233-D 21 '74-p797
TES-S 22 '78-p23
TLS-Ap 4 '75-p360
WLB-v52-Ap '78-p639

* * *

HARRISON, Michael
The New Dragon Book Of Verse
GP-v17-Ja '79-p3451
JB-v42-D '78-p311
TES-N 24 '78-p42
TLS-S 29 '78-p1084
Noah's Ark
GP-v22-Ja '84-p4178
JB-v48-F '84-p23
SA-v251-D '84-p38
Sch Lib-v32-Mr '84-p61
TES-S 30 '83-p47

* * *

HARRISON, Molly
Home Inventions
ACSB-v13-Mr '80-p27
NS-v90-N 7 '75-p585
Homes In History
TES-N 11 '83-p28
In Georgian Times
TES-N 30 '84-p28
The Middle Ages
TES-N 30 '84-p28
The Nineteenth Century And After
TES-N 30 '84-p28
Tudor And Stuart Times
TES-N 30 '84-p28

* * *

HARRISON, Phyllis
The Home Children
BIC-v8-N '79-p26
In Rev-v14-F '80-p44
TLS-S 26 '80-p1066

* * *

HARRISON, Richard J
Deep Diving Animals
TES-Mr 28 '80-p40

* * *

HARRISON, Sarah
In Granny's Garden
Brit Bk N C-Spring '81-p15
CBRS-v9-O '80-p14
JB-v45-Je '81-p106
KR-v48-N 1 '80-p1391
LA-v58-Ap '81-p478
NY-v56-D 1 '80-p219
PW-v218-Jl 18 '80-p61
SLJ-v27-D '80-p44
Sch Arts-v80-My '81-p62
Sch Lib-v29-Mr '81-p34

* * *

HARRISON, Shirley
Who Is Father Christmas?
CAY-v4-Fall '83-p9
TES-N 20 '81-p33

* * *

HARRISON, Sidney
How To Appreciate Music
Brit Bk N-My '82-p313
TES-Jl 23 '82-p24

* * *

HARRISON, Stephen W
A Muslim Family In Britain
Sch Lib-v28-D '80-p384
TLS-Mr 28 '80-p364

* * *

HARRISON, Ted
Children Of The Yukon
CCB-B-v31-Ap '78-p127
A Northern Alphabet
Atl Pro Bk R-v10-N '83-p9
BIC-v11-D '82-p8
BL-v79-Ja 1 '83-p617
CBRS-v11-Ap '83-p89
Emerg Lib-v10-N '82-p35

HARRISON, Ted (continued)
Mac-v95-D 13 '82-p57
Quill & Q-v48-D '82-p25
RT-v36-My '83-p944
SLJ-v29-Ag '83-p51

* * *

HARRISSON, Tom
Living Through The Blitz
Econ-v260-Jl 31 '76-p80
GP-v15-N '76-p3008
GW-v115-Ag 8 '76-p20
Lis-v96-Ag 12 '76-p190
NS-v92-Jl 30 '76-p147
Obs-Ag 1 '76-p21
Punch-v274-Je 14 '78-p1026
TLS-N 5 '76-p1395

* * *

HARROP, Beatrice
Apusskidu
GP-v14-My '75-p2637
Obs-Jl 27 '75-p21
Okki-Tokki-Unga
Econ-v261-D 25 '76-p92
GP-v15-D '76-p3028
JB-v41-F '77-p21
Lis-v96-N 11 '76-p624
Obs-D 5 '76-p32
Sing Hey Diddle Diddle
GP-v22-N '83-p4174
JB-v48-Ap '84-p70
PW-v225-Ap 20 '84-p88
SLJ-v30-Ap '84-p102
Someone's Singing, Lord
JB-v41-Ag '77-p222

* * *

HARROP, Renny
Neat Eats
SLJ-v28-F '82-p76

* * *

HARROWVEN, Jean
Origins Of Festivals And Feasts
JB-v45-Ap '81-p81
Sch Lib-v29-Mr '81-p39

* * *

HARRY, P
Gone Children
JB-v43-F '79-p53

* * *

HARSHAW, Ruth
In What Book?
BL-v66-Je 15 '70-p1279
CCB-B-v24-N '70-p43
HB-v46-Je '70-p309
KR-v38-Ap 1 '70-p396

* * *

HART, Angela
Dogs
ASBYP-v16-Fall '83-p32
GP-v21-Mr '83-p4044
SB-v19-Ja '84-p158
SLJ-v29-Mr '83-p162
Farm Animals
ASBYP-v16-Fall '83-p32
GP-v21-Mr '83-p4044
SB-v19-Ja '84-p158
SLJ-v29-Mr '83-p162
Prehistoric Man
ASBYP-v17-Winter '84-p26
BL-v79-Ag '83-p1465
GP-v22-Jl '83-p4117
JB-v47-Ag '83-p163

* * *

HART, Carole
Delilah
BL-v70-D 15 '73-p445
CCB-B-v27-Ap '74-p130
CSM-v65-N 7 '73-pB7
KR-v41-O 1 '73-p1096
LJ-v99-Ja 15 '74-p199
VV-v18-D 20 '73-p31

* * *

HART, Jane
Sing A Song Of Sixpence
GP-v22-N '83-p4174
JB-v47-D '83-p236
Obs-D 11 '83-p35
Sch Lib-v32-Je '84-p125
Singing Bee!
BL-v79-Ja 15 '83-p679
BW-v13-Ja 9 '83-p13
CCB-B-v36-Mr '83-p127
CE-v59-My '83-p357
HB-v59-Ap '83-p178
Inst-v92-Mr '83-p19
KR-v50-N 1 '82-p1193
LA-v60-Ap '83-p486
PW-v222-N 19 '82-p77
SLJ-v29-D '82-p57

* * *

HART, Stephanie
Is There Any Way Out Of Sixth Grade?
CBRS-v7-Mr '79-p76
CCB-B-v32-Mr '79-p117
SLJ-v25-F '79-p56

* * *

HART, Tom
Fairies And Friends
JB-v45-O '81-p196

* * *

HART, Tony
Animals And Figures
GP-v22-Ja '84-p4198
SLJ-v31-S '84-p103
Anyone Can Draw
Brit Bk N C-Autumn '82-p10
Fun With Art
JB-v41-Ag '77-p222
Fun With Design
JB-v40-Ag '76-p200
Make It With Hart
JB-v44-Je '80-p133
Making Mosaics
JB-v40-D '76-p344
Making Treasure
GP-v22-Ja '84-p4198
SLJ-v31-S '84-p103
Printing And Patterns
GP-v22-Ja '84-p4198
SLJ-v31-S '84-p103
Puppets And Moving Toys
SLJ-v31-S '84-p103
Scrap Art
SLJ-v31-S '84-p103
The Tony Hart Art Factory
Brit Bk N C-Autumn '82-p10
TES-Mr 6 '81-p29
Wool 'N' Things
SLJ-v31-S '84-p103
Young Letterer: A How-it-is-Done Book Of Lettering
BL-v63-Mr 1 '67-p728
CCB-B-v21-O '67-p27
LJ-v91-D 15 '66-p6202

* * *

HARTE, Bret
The Outcasts Of Poker Flat
SLJ-v27-Ag '81-p52

* * *

HARTELIUS, Margaret A
The Birthday Trombone
RT-v32-O '78-p32
SLJ-v24-S '77-p108
The Chicken's Child
BL-v72-N 1 '75-p366
KR-v43-S 15 '75-p1061
NO-v14-S 27 '75-p21
SLJ-v22-N '75-p63
Time-v106-D 8 '75-p87

* * *

HARTER, Walter
Birds In Fact & Legend
SB-v16-S '80-p33
SLJ-v27-S '80-p83
Deadly Creatures Of The Sea
BL-v73-My 15 '77-p1420
SLJ-v24-S '77-p129
Osceola's Head
CCB-B-v28-S '74-p9
Inst-v84-N '74-p135
KR-v42-F 1 '74-p114
LJ-v99-Ap 15 '74-p1219
NYTBR-My 5 '74-p22
PW-v205-Mr 4 '74-p75
Osceola's Head And Other American Ghost Stories
BW-v10-Je 8 '80-p12
The Phantom Hand And Other American Hauntings
CE-v53-Ja '77-p154
KR-v44-My 15 '76-p596
SLJ-v23-N '76-p58
Steel
ASBYP-v14-Fall '81-p21
BL-v78-S 1 '81-p44
SB-v17-Mr '82-p218
SLJ-v28-F '82-p76

* * *

HARTH, Malcolm
The Nature Trail Book Of Birdwatching
TLS-Jl 16 '76-p887

* * *

HARTLEY, K
Topics And Questions In Textiles
TES-My 6 '83-p28

* * *

HARTLEY, Lucie
Maria Sanford: Pioneer Professor
SLJ-v24-O '77-p112
Pauline Johnson
Cur R-v18-O '79-p348
SLJ-v25-F '79-p52

* * *

HARTLEY, P
Better Squash Rackets
JB-v43-Je '79-p167

* * *

HARTLING, Peter
Granny
JB-v41-D '77-p333
TLS-D 2 '77-p1412
Oma
BL-v73-Ap 15 '77-p1273
BL-v74-F 1 '78-p925
CCB-B-v31-Mr '78-p113
CLW-v49-Mr '78-p356
Comw-v104-N 11 '77-p730
KR-v45-N 15 '77-p1197
LA-v55-My '78-p620
NYTBR-N 20 '77-p30
SE-v42-Ap '78-p319
SLJ-v24-S '77-p129
Teacher-v95-My '78-p103
Theo Runs Away
JB-v42-Ag '78-p204
TLS-Jl 7 '78-p771

* * *

HARTMAN, Arlene
The Calculator Game Book For Kids Of All Ages
Cur R-v17-O '78-p323

* * *

HARTMAN, Evert
War Without Friends
BL-v79-S 1 '82-p43
CBRS-v11-S '82-p8
CCB-B-v36-D '82-p69
GP-v22-My '83-p4073
HB-v58-D '82-p657
JB-v47-F '83-p42
KR-v50-Jl 15 '82-p801
LA-v60-F '83-p216
Lis-v108-N 4 '82-p24
NS-v104-D 3 '82-p21
RT-v36-D '82-p337
SE-v47-Ap '83-p252
SLJ-v29-O '82-p161
Sch Lib-v31-D '83-p378
Spec-v249-D 4 '82-p26
TLS-N 26 '82-p1302
VOYA-v5-D '82-p33
VOYA-v6-Je '83-p96

* * *

HARTMAN, Jane E
Animals That Live In Groups
ACSB-v13-Spring '80-p37
CCB-B-v33-O '79-p28
EJ-v68-N '79-p74
EJ-v70-Ja '81-p78
SLJ-v26-S '79-p158
Armadillos, Anteaters, And Sloths
ASBYP-v14-Winter '81-p32
BL-v76-Mr 15 '80-p1056
HB-v56-Je '80-p324
KR-v48-Jl 1 '80-p839
SB-v16-N '80-p78
SLJ-v27-S '80-p71
How Animals Care For Their Young
ASBYP-v14-Spring '81-p19
BL-v77-Ja 15 '81-p701
KR-v49-Ja 1 '81-p10
SB-v16-My '81-p263
SLJ-v27-Mr '81-p145
Living Together In Nature
BL-v74-N 15 '77-p550
CE-v54-Mr '78-p262
KR-v45-N 1 '77-p1145
SB-v14-S '78-p112
SLJ-v24-D '77-p49
Looking At Lizards
ACSB-v12-Fall '79-p30
BL-v75-S 15 '78-p220
Cur R-v18-My '79-p147
KR-v46-O 1 '78-p1074
SB-v15-S '79-p102
SLJ-v25-Ja '79-p61

* * *

HARTMAN, Lou
The Monstrous Leathern Man
BL-v67-D 15 '70-p341
CCB-B-v24-F '71-p93
CLW-v42-D '70-p258
CSM-v63-Ja 16 '71-pB11
KR-v38-Ag 1 '70-p799
LJ-v95-D 15 '70-p4375
NYTBR, pt.2-N 8 '70-p24
PW-v199-Ja 11 '71-p63

* * *

HARTMANN, Edward
American Immigration
BL-v76-D 1 '79-p558

* * *

HARTWICK, Harry
The Amazing Maze
CCB-B-v23-My '70-p144
Inst-v79-Ap '70-p144
KR-v37-D 1 '69-p1262
LJ-v95-Mr 15 '70-p1194

HARTWICK, Harry
(continued)
NYTBR-Ja 11 '70-p26
SA-v223-D '70-p132

* * *

HARVEY, Anne
A Present For Nellie
Brit Bk N C-Autumn '82-p20
JB-v46-Ag '82
Sch Lib-v30-D '82-p337
TES-Mr 19 '82-p28

* * *

HARVEY, Anthony
The World Of The Dinosaurs
CBRS-v8-Jl '80-p130
SB-v16-My '81-p275
SLJ-v27-S '80-p70

* * *

HARVEY, J
Fashion And Clothes
JB-v40-F '76-p24
LR-v25-Autumn '75-p136
History Of Entertainment
JB-v42-F '78-p41
NS-v94-N 4 '77-p629
TES-D 2 '77-p25

* * *

HARVEY, Jack
Gilbert And The Bicycle
JB-v47-Ap '83-p68
NS-v104-D 3 '82-p22

* * *

HARVEY, T
Railroads
CBRS-v8-Jl '80-p130
SLJ-v27-S '80-p70

* * *

HARVEY, Veronica
Stories Of The City
GP-v16-O '77-p3178
JB-v42-Je '78-p155
TES-F 3 '78-p46

* * *

HARWICK, B L
The Frog Prints
BL-v73-O 15 '76-p328
SLJ-v23-D '76-p65

* * *

HARWOOD, Alice
Merchant Of The Ruby
GP-v17-My '78-p3345

* * *

HARWOOD, David
Car Games
GP-v17-S '78-p3391

* * *

HARWOOD, Mark
Fun With Wood
PW-v208-Ag 11 '75-p118
SLJ-v22-N '75-p78

* * *

HARWOOD, Pearl
Mrs. Moon And Her Friends
CCB-B-v21-F '68-p95

* * *

HASEGAWA, Sam
The Coaches
SLJ-v22-S '75-p104
Jackie Stewart
BL-v72-O 15 '75-p307
SLJ-v22-D '75-p69
The Linebackers
SLJ-v22-S '75-p104
Mickey Mantle
SLJ-v22-S '75-p96
Peter Revson
SLJ-v22-D '75-p69
The Quarterbacks
SLJ-v22-S '75-p104
Stevie Wonder
SLJ-v22-S '75-p95
Terry Bradshaw
BL-v73-Je 15 '77-p1572
SLJ-v23-My '77-p81

* * *

HASELEY, Dennis
The Old Banjo
BL-v80-O 1 '83-p294
CBRS-v12-O '83-p16
LA-v60-O '83-p903
NYTBR-v88-S 18 '83-p39
PW-v224-O 14 '83-p54
SLJ-v30-N '83-p64
WCRB-v10-Mr '84-p47
The Pirate Who Tried To Capture The Moon
CBRS-v11-Ap '83-p86
KR-v51-F 1 '83-p117
NY-v59-D 5 '83-p204
RT-v37-O '83-p86
SLJ-v29-Ag '83-p51
The Scared One
CBRS-v12-F '84-p74
CCB-B-v37-Ja '84-p88
Inter BC-v15-Ja # '84-p36
PW-v224-S 16 '83-p125
SE-v48-My '84-p380
SLJ-v30-Ja '84-p77
The Soap Bandit
CBRS-v12-Spring '84-p126
NYTBR-v89-S 9 '84-p43
PW-v225-Je 22 '84-p99
SLJ-v30-Ap '84-p102

* * *

HASKELL, Helen E
Katrinka
RT-v35-Ja '82-p469

* * *

HASKINS, James
Adam Clayton Powell
BL-v71-S 15 '74-p100
BS-v34-S 15 '74-p285
BW-My 19 '74-p4
CCB-B-v28-D '74-p63
KR-v42-My 1 '74-p492
LJ-v99-S 15 '74-p2291
NYTBR-Ag 4 '74-p8
PW-v205-Ap 22 '74-p74
Always Movin' On
BL-v73-Ja 1 '77-p666
BS-v36-Ja '77-p323
Cur R-v17-Ag '78-p173
SLJ-v23-N '76-p69
Andrew Young: Man With A Mission
BB-v7-S '79-p4
BL-v75-Jl 15 '79-p1618
CBRS-v7-Ag '79-p137
HB-v55-O '79-p550
KR-v47-Je 15 '79-p692
NYTBR-S 23 '79-p26
PW-v215-Je 25 '79-p123
SLJ-v26-S '79-p158
Babe Ruth And Hank Aaron: The Home Run Kings
BL-v71-D 15 '74-p425
KR-v42-O 1 '74-p1063
LJ-v99-D 15 '74-p3278
Barbara Jordan: Speaking Out
BL-v74-D 1 '77-p607
BS-v38-Ap '78-p18
CCB-B-v31-F '78-p95
Cur R-v17-Ag '78-p176
EJ-v67-Ap '78-p91
KR-v45-D 1 '77-p1273
SLJ-v24-Ja '78-p94
Black Theater In America
BL-v79-Ja 1 '83-p604
B Rpt-v2-My '83-p51

HASKINS, James (continued)
BS-v42-Ja '83-p405
CBRS-v11-O '82-p19
CCB-B-v36-D '82-p69
CLW-v55-O '83-p137
HB-v59-F '83-p63
KR-v50-S 15 '82-p1062
SE-v47-Ap '83-p241
SLJ-v29-N '82-p100
Theat C-v17-Ap '83-p88
VOYA-v5-F '83-p50
Bob McAdoo: Superstar
BL-v75-Ja 1 '79-p753
SLJ-v25-D '78-p70
The Child Abuse Help Book
BL-v78-Ag '82-p1525
CBRS-v11-S '82-p8
SB-v18-Ja '83-p124
SLJ-v29-S '82-p139
VOYA-v5-F '83-p50
The Consumer Movement
BL-v71-Ap 15 '75-p861
BS-v35-Jl '75-p95
CCB-B-v28-Jl '75-p177
KR-v43-Ja 15 '75-p76
SLJ-v21-Ap '75-p64
The Creoles Of Color Of New Orleans
J Read-v19-Mr '76-p513
SLJ-v22-S '75-p104
Doctor J: A Biography Of Julius Erving
BL-v72-N 15 '75-p453
KR-v43-Jl 1 '75-p715
SLJ-v22-D '75-p68
Donna Summer: An Unauthorized Biography
BL-v79-Je 15 '83-p1331
CBRS-v11-Jl '83-p138
SLJ-v30-O '83-p168
VOYA-v6-Ag '83-p153
Fighting Shirley Chisholm
BL-v71-Mr 1 '75-p692
BS-v35-S '75-p167
CCB-B-v29-S '75-p10
KR-v43-My 15 '75-p578
PW-v207-Ja 20 '75-p77
SLJ-v22-S '75-p104
From Lew Alcindor To Kareem Abdul Jabbar
BL-v74-Jl 1 '78-p1683
CCB-B-v26-Ja '73-p76
CSM-v64-N 8 '72-pB5
EJ-v62-My '73-p825
KR-v40-Jl 15 '72-p805
KR-v46-Jl 15 '78-p752
LJ-v97-D 15 '72-p4089
SLJ-v25-S '78-p138
SLJ-v28-Ag '82-p113
The Guardian Angels
BL-v79-Je 15 '83-p1330
B Rpt-v2-Ja '84-p54
CBRS-v11-Jl '83-p138
CCB-B-v37-S '83-p9
CE-v60-Ja '84-p213
KR-v51-Je 15 '83-p667
LATBR-Jl 24 '83-p8
SLJ-v30-S '83-p134
I'm Gonna Make You Love Me
BL-v77-Ja 1 '81-p624
B Rpt-v2-S '83-p41
BS-v40-Mr '81-p448
CBRS-v9-N '80-p27
CCB-B-v34-O '80-p33
Emerg Lib-v10-N '82-p33
J Read-v25-O '81-p88
J Read-v27-Mr '84-p520
KR-v49-F 1 '81-p146
SLJ-v27-N '80-p86
VOYA-v4-Je '81-p43
James Van DerZee: The Picture-Takin' Man
BL-v75-Jl 15 '79-p1619
CBRS-v7-Jl '79-p127
CCB-B-v33-D '79-p71
KR-v47-Ag 1 '79-p862
NYTBR-O 7 '79-p34
PW-v215-Je 4 '79-p62
SLJ-v26-F '80-p66
Jobs In Business And Office
BL-v71-S 1 '74-p41
SLJ-v21-Ja '75-p45
Katherine Dunham
BL-v79-N 1 '82-p361
B Rpt-v2-S '83-p41
CBRS-v11-Ja '83-p49
CCB-B-v36-D '82-p69
Cur R-v23-F '84-p99
PW-v222-S 24 '82-p72
SLJ-v29-F '83-p88
Lena Horne
BL-v80-Ja 1 '84-p675
B Rpt-v3-My '84-p39
CBRS-v12-Ja '84-p52
CCB-B-v37-F '84-p109
KR-v51-N 1 '83-pJ212
RT-v37-My '84-p889
SLJ-v30-Mr '84-p172
VOYA-v7-Ap '84-p46
The Life And Death Of Martin Luther King, Jr.
BL-v74-O 1 '77-p294
BW-S 11 '77-pE6
CCB-B-v31-Ja '78-p78
CE-v55-N '78-p106
EJ-v66-N '77-p80
EJ-v67-Mr '78-p93
HB-v53-O '77-p553
KR-v45-Je 1 '77-p583
PW-v211-Je 13 '77-p107
SE-v42-Ap '78-p318
SLJ-v24-O '77-p112
The Long Struggle
BL-v73-Ap 1 '77-p1167
KR-v44-Ag 15 '76-p910
SLJ-v24-S '77-p144
The New Americans
BL-v79-Ja 15 '83-p676
B Rpt-v2-My '83-p48
CBRS-v9-D '80-p28
CBRS-v11-D '82-p36
CE-v57-My '81-p302
SLJ-v29-Mr '83-p192
VOYA-v3-F '81-p43
Pele: A Biography
BL-v73-D 15 '76-p608
CCB-B-v30-D '76-p57
Comw-v103-N 19 '76-p764
KR-v44-S 15 '76-p1041
SLJ-v23-D '76-p71
The Picture Life Of Malcolm X
KR-v43-Ja 15 '75-p73
SLJ-v21-Ap '75-p45
A Piece Of The Power
BL-v69-O 15 '72-p189
BL-v69-My 1 '73-p838
BS-v32-Jl 15 '72-p199
CCB-B-v26-Ja '73-p77
KR-v40-Je 1 '72-p631
LJ-v98-Ja 15 '73-p268
NYTBR, pt.2-My 7 '72-p30
PW-v201-Ap 10 '72-p58
SE-v37-D '73-p789
The Quiet Revolution
BL-v76-N 1 '79-p439
BL-v78-N 1 '81-p395
CBRS-v8-Ja '80-p47
CCB-B-v33-Ap '80-p153
Inter BC-v13-#4 '82-p16
KR-v47-D 15 '79-p1435
SB-v16-S '80-p8
SLJ-v26-Ja '80-p70
Religions
BL-v69-Jl 15 '73-p1069

HASKINS, James (continued)
CCB-B-v26-Je '73-p154
KR-v41-F 1 '73-p127
LJ-v98-O 15 '73-p3154
The Story Of Stevie Wonder
BL-v73-S 1 '76-p38
CCB-B-v30-Ap '77-p125
CLW-v48-Ap '77-p405
J Read-v27-Mr '84-p521
KR-v44-My 15 '76-p604
Kliatt-v13-Fall '79-p30
RT-v31-O '77-p22
SLJ-v23-Ja '77-p92
SLJ-v26-Ag '80-p39
Street Gangs Yesterday And Today
BL-v71-N 1 '74-p284
BS-v34-O 15 '74-p330
BW-N 10 '74-p8
CCB-B-v28-Ja '75-p78
CE-v51-Ap '75-p329
LJ-v99-N 15 '74-p3054
PW-v206-Ag 12 '74-p59
Werewolves
CBRS-v10-Ja '82-p47
SLJ-v28-Ja '82-p88
Who Are The Handicapped?
ACSB-v13-Winter '80-p22
BL-v75-S 1 '78-p38
BL-v78-N 1 '81-p397
CCB-B-v32-N '78-p44
CE-v55-Ja '79-p171
Cur R-v17-O '78-p275
Inter BC-v9-Ag 80 '78-p17
J Read-v22-My '79-p771
KR-v46-Jl 15 '78-p756
SB-v15-My '79-p11
SLJ-v25-N '78-p74
Your Rights, Past And Present
A Lib-v7-Ja '76-p59
BL-v72-O 15 '75-p302
CCB-B-v29-Mr '76-p111
Cur R-v16-F '77-p30
KR-v43-S 1 '75-p1007
SLJ-v22-Ja '76-p46
SMQ-v7-Winter '79-p124

* * *

HASKINS, Jim
Space Challenger
BL-v81-S 1 '84-p65
CBRS-v12-Ag '84-p150
SLJ-v31-O '84-p157

* * *

HASLER, Eveline
Martin Is Our Friend
CBRS-v10-O '81-p15
CCB-B-v35-D '81-p68
JB-v43-O '79-p266
SB-v18-N '82-p88
SLJ-v28-N '81-p76
Spec-v242-Je 30 '79-p26
Miranda's Magic
PW-v207-Ja 20 '75-p76
SLJ-v21-Ap '75-p45

* * *

HASS, E A
Come Quick, I'm Sick!
PW-v223-F 11 '83-p71
Incognito Mosquito, Private Insective
CBRS-v11-Winter '83-p54
CCB-B-v36-F '83-p108
KR-v50-O 1 '82-p1105
SLJ-v29-D '82-p82

* * *

HASS, Hans
The Human Animal
A Anth-v73-D '71-p1425
Atl-v226-S '70-p128
BS-v30-S 15 '70-p232
Choice-v8-S '71-p919
Econ-v239-My 1 '71-p55
HB-v47-Je '71-p306
KR-v38-Ap 15 '70-p491
LJ-v95-Je 15 '70-p2270
LJ-v96-Mr 1 '71-p787
NYT-v119-S 9 '70-p45
NYTBR-S 13 '70-p12
PW-v197-Ap 13 '70-p80

* * *

HASS, Patricia Cecil
Swampfire
GP-v15-My '76-p2899
JB-v40-Ag '76-p229
KR-v41-Jl 1 '73-p685
LJ-v98-O 15 '73-p3145
Windsong Summer
CSM-v70-S 18 '78-pB14
Inter BC-v10-F 1& '79-p28
KR-v46-Jl 15 '78-p749
PW-v214-Ag 28 '78-p394
SLJ-v25-O '78-p145

* * *

HASSLER, Jon
Four Miles To Pinecone
CCB-B-v31-O '77-p33
HB-v53-O '77-p531
NYTBR-My 15 '77-p40
PW-v211-Je 13 '77-p108
SLJ-v24-S '77-p144
Jemmy
BS-v40-Je '80-p117
CBRS-v8-My '80-p99
CCB-B-v34-O '80-p33
CE-v57-N '80-p112
HB-v56-Je '80-p305
Inter BC-v12-#7 '81-p24
J Read-v25-My '82-p777
KR-v48-My 1 '80-p588
NYTBR-v85-Ag 3 '80-p19
SLJ-v26-Ag '80-p76

* * *

HASTINGS, Paul
Medicine
BL-v71-N 1 '74-p284
JB-v39-F '75-p64
KR-v42-S 1 '74-p952
SB-v10-Mr '75-p313
SLJ-v21-Ja '75-p54

* * *

HASTINGS, Selina
Sir Gawain And The Green Knight
BL-v78-S 1 '81-p44
BL-v79-Je 1 '83-p1282
Brit Bk N C-Spring '82-p6
CBRS-v9-Ag '81-p124
GP-v20-Ja '82-p3996
HB-v57-D '81-p673
Inst-v91-F '82-p34
JB-v46-Je '82-p98
KR-v49-O 15 '81-p1298
NYTBR-v87-F 7 '82-p27
RT-v35-Ap '82-p869
SLJ-v28-O '81-p142
Sch Lib-v30-Je '82-p134
TLS-N 20 '81-p1360

* * *

HATCHER, C
Modern World Encyclopedia
JB-v40-Ap '76-p104

* * *

HATCHER, Charles
What Shape Is It?
CCB-B-v19-Ap '66-p130
SA-v215-D '66-p145
SB-v2-S '66-p96
What Size Is It?
CCB-B-v19-Ap '66-p130
KR-v33-D 1 '65-p1191

HATCHER, Charles
(continued)
SB-v2-S '66-p96

* * *

HATFIELD, John
Quintilian
GP-v20-S '81-p3957
Quintilian And The Curious Weather Shop
B&B-v15-D '69-p48
NS-v78-O 31 '69-p626
Obs-D 7 '69-p31
TLS-D 4 '69-p1386
Quintilian Meets Mr. Punch
GP-v14-My '75-p2654
Spec-v225-D 5 '70-pR15
TLS-O 30 '70-p1252

* * *

HATHAWAY, Nancy
Halloween Crafts And Cookbook
CBRS-v8-Ja '80-p44
SLJ-v27-O '80-p136
Thanksgiving Crafts And Cookbook
CBRS-v8-Ja '80-p44
SLJ-v27-O '80-p136

* * *

HATHAWAY, Polly
The Beginning Knowledge Book Of Backyard Flowers
CCB-B-v20-S '66-p12
CSM-v57-N 4 '65-pB9
LJ-v91-Ja 15 '66-p443
SB-v1-Mr '66-p224

* * *

HATHORN, Elizabeth
The Tram To Bondi Beach
Brit Bk N C-Autumn '82-p12
TLS-Jl 23 '82-p792

* * *

HATHORN, Libby
Lachlan's Walk
Brit Bk N C-Autumn '81-p13
JB-v45-Je '81-p107
Obs-My 10 '81-p33
Sch Lib-v29-S '81-p225
TES-Je 5 '81-p36
TLS-Jl 24 '81-p840

* * *

HATLEY, Jan
Killers In The Wild
Brit Bk N C-Spring '82-p16
GP-v20-N '81-p3977
JB-v46-Ag '82-p142
Lis-v106-N 5 '81-p547

* * *

HATMON, Paul W
Yesterday's Fire Engines
BL-v77-O 15 '80-p323
SLJ-v27-N '80-p70

* * *

HAUBENSAK-TELLENBACH, Margrit
The Story Of Noah's Ark
CBRS-v12-O '83-p16
PW-v224-N 18 '83-p71
SLJ-v30-Mr '84-p144

* * *

HAUCK, Philomena
Sourcebook On Canadian Women
ARBA-v12-'81-p357
Can Child Lit-#25 '82-p33
In Rev-v14-F '80-p43

* * *

HAUFF, Wilhelm
The Adventures Of Little Mouk
BB-v3-My '75-p1
B&B-v20-My '75-p70
BL-v71-Ap 15 '75-p866
CCB-B-v29-S '75-p10
CSM-v67-My 7 '75-pB6
HB-v51-Je '75-p257
JB-v39-F '75-p15
KR-v43-Ja 1 '75-p18
NYTBR-Mr 16 '75-p8
PW-v207-F 10 '75-p56
SLJ-v21-Ap '75-p53
Dwarf Long-Nose
GP-v18-My '79-p3507
JB-v43-Ag '79-p195
Obs-Ap 1 '79-p38
Sch Lib-v28-D '80-p378
Fairy Tales Of Wilhelm Hauff
BL-v66-Ap 15 '70-p1045
KR-v37-N 15 '69-p1199
LJ-v95-Ap 15 '70-p1638
NS-v78-O 31 '69-p631
PW-v196-D 8 '69-p47
TLS-Je 26 '69-p688

* * *

HAUGAARD, Erik C
The Princess And The Pea
TES-O 12 '84-p33

* * *

HAUGAARD, Erik Christian
A Boy's Will
CCB-B-v37-Ja '84-p88
HB-v59-D '83-p708
PW-v224-O 21 '83-p67
SLJ-v30-F '84-p71
Chase Me, Catch Nobody!
BL-v76-My 1 '80-p1291
CBRS-v8-Je '80-p107
CCB-B-v33-Je '80-p191
CE-v58-S '81-p48
GP-v22-S '83-p4137
HB-v56-Je '80-p296
KR-v48-Ag 1 '80-p984
NYTBR-v85-S 7 '80-p36
SLJ-v26-Ap '80-p124
Cromwell's Boy
BL-v75-D 1 '78-p616
BS-v38-Mr '79-p407
HB-v54-D '78-p644
KR-v46-D 15 '78-p1362
LA-v56-My '79-p547
SLJ-v25-D '78-p60
Leif The Unlucky
BL-v78-Ap 1 '82-p1018
CCB-B-v35-Jl '82-p207
CLW-v55-S '83-p87
HB-v58-Ag '82-p413
J Read-v26-N '82-p185
LA-v59-O '82-p752
SLJ-v28-Mr '82-p158
Little Fishes
BL-v63-Jl 1 '67-p1146
CCB-B-v20-Je '67-p152
CLW-v39-N '67-p240
HB-v43-Je '67-p352
Inst-v77-O '67-p175
Inter BC-v13-#6 '82-p19
KR-v35-My 1 '67-p565
LA-v58-Ap '81-p460
LJ-v92-My 15 '67-p2028
NYTBR-v72-N 5 '67-p64
NYTBR, pt.1-v72-My 7 '67-p14
Obs-Ap 14 '68-p27
PW-v191-Ap 24 '67-p95
Punch-v254-Mr 27 '68-p472
SR-v50-My 13 '67-p59
TLS-Mr 14 '68-p254
Trav-v24-N '67-p99
A Messenger For Parliament
BL-v73-O 15 '76-p322
CCB-B-v30-Ap '77-p125
HB-v53-F '77-p55
KR-v44-O 15 '76-p1145
SLJ-v23-N '76-p69

HAUGAARD, Erik Christian (continued)
The Rider And His Horse
B&B-v15-D '69-p44
BL-v65-F 15 '69-p656
BS-v28-F 1 '69-p447
BW-v3-Jl 13 '69-p16
CCB-B-v23-S '69-p10
LJ-v94-Ja 15 '69-p310
NS-v78-O 31 '69-p624
SE-v33-My '69-p557
TLS-O 16 '69-p1194
The Samurai's Tale
BL-v80-Ap 1 '84-p1115
BS-v44-Je '84-p116
CBRS-v13-S '84-p9
CCB-B-v37-Je '84-p186
HB-v60-Ap '84-p178
SLJ-v30-My '84-p89
A Slave's Tale
BL-v62-S 15 '65-p96
CCB-B-v19-Ap '66-p131
Comw-v82-My 28 '65-p329
HB-v41-Ag '65-p395
KR-v33-Ap 15 '65-p436
LJ-v90-Je 15 '65-p2894
NYTBR-v70-Ag 22 '65-p18
Obs-D 4 '66-p28
Punch-v251-N 16 '66-p754
Spec-N 11 '66-p625
TLS-N 24 '66-p1079
The Untold Tale
A Lib-v3-Ap '72-p420
BL-v68-S 15 '71-p109
BL-v68-Ap 1 '72-p669
CE-v48-D '71-p150
CLW-v43-N '71-p174
Comw-v95-N 19 '71-p187
HB-v47-Je '71-p292
KR-v39-Ap 15 '71-p442
LJ-v96-S 15 '71-p2929
LJ-v96-D 15 '71-p4159
NYTBR-My 9 '71-p8
NYTBR, pt.2-N 7 '71-p28
PW-v199-Je 28 '71-p63

* * *

HAUGAARD, Kay
China Boy
CCB-B-v25-S '71-p7
KR-v39-Je 1 '71-p592
LJ-v96-S 15 '71-p2930
Myeko's Gift
BL-v63-Ap 15 '67-p909
BL-v69-F 15 '73-p553
CCB-B-v20-Ap '67-p122
CLW-v39-N '67-p241
KR-v34-D 1 '66-p1221
LJ-v92-Mr 15 '67-p1316
NS-v73-My 26 '67-p732
Punch-v252-Ap 5 '67-p505
SR-v50-Mr 18 '67-p36
Spec-v218-Je 2 '67-p655
TLS-My 25 '67-p456

* * *

HAUGEN, Tormod
The Night Birds
BS-v42-F '83-p445
CBRS-v11-F '83-p70
CCB-B-v36-S '82-p10
KR-v50-S 1 '82-p998
PW-v222-Jl 2 '82-p56
RT-v36-Mr '83-p715
SLJ-v29-S '82-p108

* * *

HAUPTMANN, Tatjana
Adeline Schlime
CBRS-v9-F '81-p51
CSM-v73-Mr 16 '81-p23
KR-v49-F 1 '81-p138
RT-v34-My '81-p967
SLJ-v27-Ja '81-p50
TLS-Jl 24 '81-p840
A Day In The Life Of Petronella Pig
BW-v10-My 11 '80-p17
CBRS-v11-F '83-p64
GP-v18-N '79-p3610
JB-v43-D '79-p316
NYTBR-v85-Ap 27 '80-p49
Obs-D 2 '79-p39
PW-v222-S 17 '82-p114
RT-v37-O '83-p53
SLJ-v26-Ap '80-p94
Sch Lib-v27-D '79-p349
Hurray For Peregrine Pig
JB-v45-Ap '81-p62
Obs-D 7 '80-p31

* * *

HAUSER, Hillary
Women In Sports: Scuba Diving
SLJ-v23-S '76-p117

* * *

HAUSMAN, Gerald
Beth: The Little Girl Of Pine Knoll
PW-v206-O 21 '74-p51
SLJ-v21-Mr '75-p96
Sitting On The Blue-Eyed Bear
AIQ-v3-Winter '78-p364
BL-v72-My 1 '76-p1265
H Beh-v5-Jl '76-p76
PW-v208-N 10 '75-p50
SLJ-v23-N '76-p78
SLJ-v26-N '79-p43

* * *

HAUSMAN, Jim
Mystery At Sans Souci
BL-v74-Mr 15 '78-p1187
CCB-B-v31-Je '78-p160
KR-v46-Mr 1 '78-p244
SLJ-v24-My '78-p84

* * *

HAUTZIG, Deborah
The Christmas Story
CCB-B-v37-N '83-p43
PW-v224-O 14 '83-p57
The Handsomest Father
BL-v76-D 15 '79-p618
CCB-B-v33-O '79-p28
KR-v47-N 1 '79-p1260
RT-v33-Mr '80-p732
SLJ-v26-D '79-p94
Hey, Dollface
BL-v75-S 1 '78-p38
BS-v38-Ja '79-p330
CBRS-v7-Winter '79-p57
CCB-B-v32-O '78-p30
CLW-v50-O '78-p113
HB-v54-D '78-p644
Inter BC-v10-Je 60 '79-p16
JB-v43-Je '79-p168
KR-v46-Ag 1 '78-p811
Kliatt-v14-Fall '80-p7
Obs-Ap 8 '79-p38
PW-v214-Ag 21 '78-p60
PW-v218-O 24 '80-p50
SLJ-v25-D '78-p61
Second Star To The Right
CBRS-v9-Ag '81-p127
CCB-B-v35-S '81-p9
Econ-v281-D 26 '81-p107
GP-v20-Ja '82-p4011
HB-v57-D '81-p668
JB-v46-Je '82-p105
J Read-v25-F '82-p487
KR-v49-S 1 '81-p1086
Kliatt-v16-Fall '82-p11
LA-v59-Ap '82-p370
NYTBR-v87-Ja 17 '82-p30
PW-v220-Jl 31 '81-p58
SLJ-v27-Ag '81-p75

HAUTZIG, Deborah
(continued)
Sch Lib-v30-Je '82-p154
VOYA-v4-D '81-p30
The Wizard Of Oz
SLJ-v31-S '84-p114

* * *

HAUTZIG, Esther
Cool Cooking
BL-v70-N 1 '73-p292
CCB-B-v27-F '74-p95
KR-v41-Je 1 '73-p602
LJ-v98-N 15 '73-p3440
Endless Steppe
BS-v28-My 1 '68-p64
BW-v2-My 5 '68-p5
CCB-B-v21-My '68-p142
Comw-v88-My 24 '68-p302
The Endless Steppe
BL-v64-My 1 '68-p1043
BL-v65-Ap 1 '69-p900
EJ-v58-F '69-p293
Emerg Lib-v11-N '83-p21
HB-v44-Je '68-p311
KR-v36-Mr 15 '68-p343
LJ-v93-O 15 '68-p3982
LJ-v95-F 15 '70-p742
LR-v22-Summer '69-p95
NO-v7-O 7 '68-p23
NYTBR-v73-My 5 '68-p2
PW-v193-Mr 25 '68-p49
RT-v33-Ap '80-p810
SR-v51-My 11 '68-p42
Spec-v222-My 2 '69-p589
TLS-Ap 3 '69-p349
Trav-v25-N '68-p78
YR-v4-My '68-p11
A Gift For Mama
BL-v78-S 15 '81-p106
Brit Bk N C-Autumn '81-p20
CBRS-v10-Jl '81-p116
CCB-B-v35-S '81-p10
CSM-v73-Jl 1 '81-p18
HB-v57-Ag '81-p423
Inter BC-v13-#1 '82-p20
JB-v45-O '81-p196
KR-v49-Jl 15 '81-p872
LA-v58-O '81-p845
PW-v219-My 8 '81-p254
SLJ-v27-My '81-p64
Holiday Treats
BL-v80-Mr 1 '84-p967
CBRS-v12-N '83-p31
HB-v60-F '84-p74
SLJ-v30-F '84-p72
In School
BL-v66-D 15 '69-p516
CLW-v41-N '69-p202
HB-v45-D '69-p669
KR-v37-Ag 15 '69-p849
LJ-v94-D 15 '69-p4595
PW-v196-O 13 '69-p54
In The Park
BL-v64-Je 1 '68-p1140
CCB-B-v22-O '68-p28
CSM-v60-My '68-pB2
Comw-v88-My 24 '68-p309
KR-v36-F 15 '68-p178
LJ-v93-Jl '68-p2729
NYTBR-v73-My 5 '68-p51
PW-v193-Mr 11 '68-p49
SR-v51-S 21 '68-p36
Let's Make More Presents
BL-v70-D 15 '73-p445
CCB-B-v27-Je '74-p157
KR-v41-O 1 '73-p1105
LJ-v98-D 15 '73-p3690
LJ-v98-D 15 '73-p3707
NYTBR-N 4 '73-p62
PW-v204-O 1 '73-p81
Life With Working Parents
BL-v73-Ja 1 '77-p667
CCB-B-v30-Ap '77-p126
CLW-v48-Ap '77-p403
EJ-v67-Ap '78-p90
KR-v44-N 1 '76-p1171
PW-v211-Ja 3 '77-p69
SE-v41-Ap '77-p348
SLJ-v23-F '77-p65

* * *

HAVERSTOCK, Nathan A
Dominican Republic In Pictures
SLJ-v22-S '75-p120
El Salvador In Pictures
BL-v71-O 1 '74-p169
Inst-v84-N '74-p140
Inter BC-v13-#2 '82-p8
LJ-v99-N 15 '74-p3046
Nicaragua In Pictures
Inter BC-v13-#2 '82-p10
SLJ-v22-S '75-p94
Uruguay In Pictures
SLJ-v22-S '75-p120

* * *

HAVILAND, Virginia
Children And Literature
B&B-v21-Je '76-p64
CSM-v69-N 2 '77-pB1
Choice-v11-Mr '74-p80
Choice-v11-N '74-p1272
Choice-v12-N '75-p1122
HB-v50-F '74-p35
JB-v39-Je '75-p169
RSR-v2-Jl '74-p30
SLJ-v21-Ap '75-p37
Spec-v234-Ap 12 '75-p445
TLS-Ap 4 '75-p373
TN-v30-Ap '74-p316
TN-v31-Ap '75-p338
TN-v31-Je '75-p434
Children's Literature
ANQ-v5-Ap '67-p121
BL-v63-Je 1 '67-p1015
BSA-P-v61-Ap '67-p154
CE-v44-D '67-p268
Choice-v11-N '74-p1272
HB-v43-Ap '67-p218
LJ-v92-O 15 '67-p3825
LQ-v37-Jl '67-p322
LR-v21-Summer '67-p90
SR-v50-My 13 '67-p47
Trav-v24-N '67-p103
WLB-v41-My '67-p971
Children's Literature. 1st Suppl.
HB-v49-Ap '73-p155
LJ-v98-Mr 15 '73-p988
Children's Literature. 2nd Suppl.
AB-v62-N 13 '78-p2945
ARBA-v10-'79-p116
BL-v74-Jl 15 '78-p1739
Can Child Lit-#23 '81-p81
GP-v17-N '78-p3432
HB-v54-Ag '78-p416
JB-v42-O '78-p245
RSR-v8-Ja '80-p18
WLB-v53-S '78-p87
The Faber Book Of North American Legends
Brit Bk N C-Autumn '80-p3
GP-v18-Mr '80-p3647
JB-v43-O '79-p273
Sch Lib-v28-Mr '80-p35
TES-N 16 '79-p46
The Fairy Tale Treasury
BL-v69-D 1 '72-p356
CCB-B-v26-Ja '73-p77
CE-v49-F '73-p258
CSM-v64-N 8 '72-pB1
CSM-v67-Je 10 '75-p17
Comw-v99-N 23 '73-p214
HB-v48-D '72-p592
Inst-v90-Ja '81-p109
KR-v40-N 1 '72-p1236

HAVILAND, Virginia (continued)
LJ-v98-Ja 15 '73-p253
NS-v84-N 10 '72-p694
NYTBR, pt.2-N 5 '72-p28
PW-v202-N 20 '72-p65
Par-v48-Ja '73-p8
SLJ-v29-Ap '83-p31
Spec-v229-N 11 '72-p761
TLS-N 3 '72-p1332
TLS-D 6 '74-p1384
Favorite Fairy Tales Told In Czechoslovakia
BL-v62-F 15 '66-p585
CCB-B-v19-My '66-p150
CLW-v37-Ap '66-p547
HB-v42-Ap '66-p194
KR-v34-Ja 15 '66-p54
LJ-v91-Mr 15 '66-p1700
NYTBR-v71-My 8 '66-p41
PW-v189-My 9 '66-p79
RT-v33-Mr '80-p688
SR-v49-Mr 19 '66-p44
Spec-v224-My 9 '70-p624
TLS-Ap 16 '70-p420
Favorite Fairy Tales Told In Denmark
BL-v67-Ap 1 '71-p664
CCB-B-v24-Je '71-p157
CE-v48-My '72-p422
CSM-v63-Jl 3 '71-p17
Comw-v94-My 21 '71-p264
HB-v47-Je '71-p283
Inst-v130-Je '71-p75
KR-v39-Mr 1 '71-p239
LJ-v96-My 15 '71-p1827
NS-v82-N 12 '71-p668
PW-v199-My 3 '71-p57
SR-v54-Je 19 '71-p27
TLS-O 22 '71-p1316
Favorite Fairy Tales Told In England
TLS-Ap 3 '69-p353
Favorite Fairy Tales Told In France
TLS-N 30 '67-p1143
Favorite Fairy Tales Told In Germany
TLS-Ap 3 '69-p353
Favorite Fairy Tales Told In Greece
BL-v66-Ap 1 '70-p982
CLW-v42-O '70-p133
CSM-v62-My 7 '70-pB4
HB-v46-Je '70-p293
KR-v38-Mr 1 '70-p247
LJ-v95-My 15 '70-p1968
NS-v82-N 12 '71-p668
TLS-O 22 '71-p1316
Favorite Fairy Tales Told In India
BL-v70-O 15 '73-p234
CCB-B-v27-D '73-p66
CE-v50-F '74-p227
CSM-v65-Je 6 '73-p14
Choice-v12-N '75-p1132
Comw-v99-N 23 '73-p214
HB-v49-O '73-p462
Inst-v83-N '73-p124
KR-v41-Je 1 '73-p603
LJ-v99-Ja 15 '74-p210
PW-v203-Je 11 '73-p154
TLS-S 20 '74-p1007
Favorite Fairy Tales Told In Ireland
TLS-N 30 '67-p1143
Favorite Fairy Tales Told In Italy
BL-v62-S 1 '65-p56
CCB-B-v19-N '65-p45
CSM-v57-N 4 '65-pB5
GT-v83-Ja '66-p20
HB-v41-O '65-p499
KR-v33-Ag 15 '65-p818
LJ-v90-O 15 '65-p4640
NYTBR-v70-N 7 '65-p60
Spec-N 11 '66-p625
TLS-N 24 '66-p1089
Favorite Fairy Tales Told In Japan
BL-v64-D 1 '67-p446
CCB-B-v21-F '68-p95
HB-v44-Ap '68-p173
LJ-v92-D 15 '67-p4612
TLS-Ap 3 '69-p353
Favorite Fairy Tales Told In Poland
RT-v33-Ap '80-p810
TLS-N 24 '66-p1089
Favorite Fairy Tales Told In Russia
RT-v35-D '81-p339
TLS-N 30 '67-p1143
Favorite Fairy Tales Told In Scotland
Spec-N 11 '66-p625
TLS-N 24 '66-p1089
Favorite Fairy Tales Told In Spain
Spec-N 11 '66-p625
TLS-N 24 '66-p1089
Favorite Fairy Tales Told In Sweden
BL-v63-O 15 '66-p266
CCB-B-v20-Ja '67-p74
CE-v44-F '68-p386
CLW-v38-N '66-p216
CSM-v58-N 3 '66-pB2
HB-v43-F '67-p64
Inst-v76-D '66-p13
LJ-v92-Ja 15 '67-p334
SR-v49-N 12 '66-p49
TLS-Ap 3 '69-p353
Favourite Fairy Tales Told In France
Obs-D 3 '67-p26
Favourite Fairy Tales Told In Ireland
Obs-D 3 '67-p26
Favourite Fairy Tales Told In Japan
Comw-v87-N 10 '67-p182
KR-v35-Ag 1 '67-p883
Favourite Fairy Tales Told In Norway
Obs-D 3 '67-p26
Favourite Fairy Tales Told In Russia
Obs-D 3 '67-p26
North American Legends
BL-v76-S 1 '79-p45
BW-v9-Ag 12 '79-p8
CBRS-v8-S '79-p8
CE-v56-Ja '80-p172
CSM-v71-O 15 '79-pB3
HB-v55-Ag '79-p428
KR-v47-Je 15 '79-p687
RT-v33-Ap '80-p863
RT-v34-O '80-p50
SLJ-v26-N '79-p77
The Wide World Of Children's Books
BL-v69-Jl 15 '73-p1075
HB-v48-O '72-p481
William Penn: Founder And Friend
RT-v32-My '79-p920
Yankee Doodle's Literary Sampler Of Prose, Poetry, And Pictures
BL-v71-Mr 1 '75-p659
BW-Ja 12 '75-p4
CE-v51-Ap '75-p326
CSM-v67-F 7 '75-p10
Choice-v11-N '74-p1272
HB-v51-Je '75-p285
Inst-v84-My '75-p96

HAVILAND, Virginia
(continued)
KR-v43-Ja 1 '75-p27
NY-v51-D 1 '75-p162
SLJ-v21-Mr '75-p81
TN-v32-Je '76-p377
WLB-v49-My '75-p618

* * *

HAVIS, Allan
Albert The Astronomer
BB-v7-Ja '80-p4
CBRS-v8-S '79-p8
CCB-B-v33-D '79-p71
KR-v47-O 15 '79-p1210
SLJ-v26-O '79-p150

* * *

HAVREVOLD, Finn
Undertow
CCB-B-v21-Jl '68-p174
EJ-v72-Ja '83-p26
HB-v44-Ag '68-p428
KR-v36-Mr 1 '68-p271
LJ-v93-Ap 15 '68-p1811
SE-v33-My '69-p557
SR-v51-Jl 20 '68-p31

* * *

HAWES, Chris
A Valley Full Of Thieves
Brit Bk N C-Autumn '80-p24
JB-v44-O '80-p249
TES-Mr 21 '80-p30

* * *

HAWES, Colette
Good Food And A Simple Cure
TES-S 21 '84-p35

* * *

HAWES, Hugh
Accidents
TES-S 21 '84-p35

* * *

HAWES, Judy
Bees And Beelines
CCB-B-v18-Mr '65-p102
TLS-D 4 '69-p1401
Fireflies In The Night
Teacher-v94-Ja '77-p133
The Goats Who Killed The Leopard
HB-v46-D '70-p609
KR-v38-Jl 15 '70-p743
Ladybug, Ladybug, Fly Away Home
BL-v64-N 15 '67-p387
BW-v2-Ja 7 '68-p10
CCB-B-v21-Ja '68-p78
CSM-v60-D 21 '67-p11
CSM-v67-Je 10 '75-p17
HB-v44-F '68-p78
KR-v35-S 15 '67-p1139
LJ-v92-D 15 '67-p4603
NYTBR-v72-N 5 '67-p57
SB-v3-Mr '68-p320
SR-v50-D 16 '67-p35
TLS-O 30 '70-p1271
Teacher-v91-F '74-p99
Spring Peepers
ACSB-v8-Fall '75-p15
BL-v71-Mr 15 '75-p761
CCB-B-v29-S '75-p11
KR-v43-F 15 '75-p183
SA-v233-D '75-p128
SLJ-v21-My '75-p46
SR-v2-My 31 '75-p35
What I Like About Toads
BL-v66-N 15 '69-p410
CCB-B-v23-Ja '70-p81
Inst-v82-My '73-p77
KR-v37-S 1 '69-p933
LJ-v95-Ja 15 '70-p233
NY-v45-D 13 '69-p210
TLS-O 30 '70-p1271

* * *

HAWKE, Kathleen
I Love Butterflies
Sch Lib-v29-S '81-p229
I Love Chairs That Are Big And Soft
Sch Lib-v29-S '81-p229
I Love Going To The Beach
Sch Lib-v29-S '81-p229
I Love Running When I Take Off My Shoes
Sch Lib-v29-S '81-p229

* * *

HAWKER, Frances
Children Of The Meo Hill Tribes
TES-Ap 1 '83-p32
Festival Of The Full Moon In Bali
TES-Ap 1 '83-p32
My Home Is A Monastery In Nepal
TES-Ap 1 '83-p32
Search For A Magic Carpet In Kashmir
TES-Ap 1 '83-p32

* * *

HAWKES, Ann
Rose Kennedy
BL-v71-Ap 1 '75-p816
KR-v43-F 1 '75-p120
SLJ-v21-My '75-p68

* * *

HAWKES, Jacquetta
The Atlas Of Early Man
A Anth-v80-Mr '78-p192
ARBA-v9-'78-p177
Arch-v31-Ja '78-p63
BL-v73-F 1 '77-p801
BL-v73-F 1 '77-p833
CC-v93-D 15 '76-p1131
CLW-v48-Mr '77-p356
Choice-v14-Mr '77-p43
GW-v115-N 14 '76-p21
LJ-v102-Ap 15 '77-p916
NO-v15-D 4 '76-p22
NYTBR-D 12 '76-p21
Obs-D 5 '76-p31
RS-D 16 '76-p103
RSR-v5-O '77-p50
SLJ-v23-Mr '77-p156
TES-D 23 '77-p14
TLS-Ap 8 '77-p426
Time-v109-Ja 3 '77-p82
WLB-v51-F '77-p541

* * *

HAWKES, Nigel
Computers
ASBYP-v17-Spring '84-p23
BL-v80-Ja 1 '84-p682
BL-v80-F 1 '84-p813
CBRS-v12-Ap '84-p96
SLJ-v30-D '83-p67
Sch Lib-v31-D '83-p367
TES-N 11 '83-p26
Computers In Action
BL-v80-My 15 '84-p1343
JB-v48-F '84-p23
RT-v38-N '84-p227
SLJ-v31-O '84-p157
TES-Mr 9 '84-p53
Computers In The Home
JB-v48-Je '84-p127
SLJ-v30-Ag '84-p73
TES-Mr 9 '84-p53
The Electronic Revolution
SB-v20-S '84-p31

HAWKES, Nigel (continued)
Food And Farming
ASBYP-v16-Winter '83-p62
BL-v78-Jl '82-p1444
SB-v19-S '83-p36
SLJ-v28-Ag '82-p116
Nuclear
BL-v77-Jl 1 '81-p1394
JB-v46-Ap '82-p73
SLJ-v28-Ja '82-p74
Space Shuttle
ASBYP-v17-Winter '84-p27
BL-v79-Ag '83-p1465
Cur R-v24-N '84-p79
JB-v47-Ap '83-p75
Lis-v108-N 4 '82-p26
Nature-v300-D 9 '82-p548
SB-v19-Ja '84-p154
SLJ-v29-Ag '83-p66
TES-N 11 '83-p27

* * *

HAWKESWORTH, Eric
Paper Cutting
BB-v6-F '78-p3
CE-v54-Ja '78-p140
JB-v40-D '76-p345
LA-v55-My '78-p650
PW-v211-My 2 '77-p70
SLJ-v24-S '77-p129
Pleated Paper Folding
JB-v40-F '76-p43
Practical Lessons In Magic
BL-v65-Ap 15 '69-p961
CSM-v60-N 7 '68-pB8
LJ-v94-Ja 15 '69-p310
PW-v194-N 4 '68-p51
SLJ-v25-O '78-p121

* * *

HAWKESWORTH, Jenny
A Handbook Of Family Monsters
JB-v45-Ap '81-p71
The Lonely Skyscraper
Brit Bk N C-Autumn '80-p11
CBRS-v9-Ap '81-p71
KR-v48-O 1 '80-p1293
SLJ-v27-N '80-p63
TLS-S 19 '80-p1028

* * *

HAWKEY, Ron
Rice
JB-v44-D '80-p307
Sch Lib-v29-Mr '81-p39

* * *

HAWKIN, Terry
An Italian Fun Book
TES-Ap 20 '84-p24
TES-O 26 '84-p32
Italian Puzzles
TES-O 26 '84-p32

* * *

HAWKINS, Colin
Adding Animals
BL-v80-S 1 '83-p85
CBRS-v12-S '83-p3
CCB-B-v37-O '83-p28
PW-v224-Jl 8 '83-p66
SLJ-v30-O '83-p125
WLB-v58-D '83-p291
Boo! Who?
BL-v80-My 1 '84-p1246
NYTBR-v89-Mr 25 '84-p31
PW-v225-F 3 '84-p402
SLJ-v31-S '84-p103
WCRB-v10-My '84-p46
How To Look After Your Dog
TES-N 5 '82-p33
Mig The Pig
CBRS-v12-My '84-p101
GP-My '84-p4270
PW-v225-Mr 16 '84-p87
SLJ-v30-Ag '84-p60
Pat The Cat
BL-v79-Ag '83-p1465
CBRS-v11-Jl '83-p133
PW-v223-My 27 '83-p68
Punch-v285-N 16 '83-p60
SLJ-v30-O '83-p149
Spooks
JB-v48-Ap '84-p70
Vampires
JB-v46-D '82-p224
What Time Is It
JB-v48-Ap '84-p60
What Time Is It, Mr. Wolf?
BL-v80-Ja 15 '84-p748
CBRS-v12-F '84-p67
PW-v224-N 18 '83-p71
SLJ-v30-Ap '84-p102
What's The Time, Mr. Wolf?
Sch Lib-v31-D '83-p343
Witches
BL-v78-N 1 '81-p388
JB-v46-F '82-p16

* * *

HAWKINS, Jim W
Baton Twirling Is For Me
BL-v79-O 1 '82-p251
Cur R-v21-D '82-p474
RT-v36-Mr '83-p699
SLJ-v29-D '82-p85
Cheerleading Is For Me
BL-v78-F 1 '82-p709
SLJ-v28-F '82-p64

* * *

HAWKINS, Mark
A Lion Under Her Bed
BB-v7-Je '79-p1
CCB-B-v32-Je '79-p175
KR-v47-F 1 '79-p120
SLJ-v25-Mr '79-p122
WCRB-v5-Mr '79-p56

* * *

HAWKINS, Quail
Androcles And The Lion
BL-v67-Ap 1 '71-p664
HB-v47-F '71-p47
KR-v38-S 15 '70-p1029
LJ-v95-N 15 '70-p4035
PW-v198-D 7 '70-p50

* * *

HAWKINS, Robert
The Christmas Tree Farm
BL-v78-D 1 '81-p498
CCB-B-v35-D '81-p68
KR-v49-O 1 '81-p1237
SLJ-v28-O '81-p157

* * *

HAWKINSON, John
A Ball Of Clay
BL-v70-Ap 1 '74-p873
CCB-B-v27-Je '74-p157
LJ-v99-S 15 '74-p2248
Collect, Print And Paint From Nature
CCB-B-v19-O '65-p33
Let Me Take You On A Trail
BL-v69-Je 15 '73-p989
CCB-B-v26-Ap '73-p124
SB-v9-My '73-p74
Little Boy Who Lives Up High
BL-v64-Ap 1 '68-p930
CCB-B-v21-F '68-p95
KR-v35-N 1 '67-p1313
LJ-v92-D 15 '67-p4630
YR-v4-Mr '68-p5
Music And Instruments For Children To Make
BL-v66-O 1 '69-p208
CCB-B-v23-N '69-p45
CE-v47-N '70-p88
HB-v45-D '69-p684

HAWKINSON, John (continued)
LJ-v95-Je 15 '70-p2302
SLJ-v28-D '81-p80
Teacher-v94-Mr '77-p20
Our Wonderful Wayside
BL-v63-Ap 1 '67-p857
CCB-B-v21-D '67-p60
LJ-v91-O 15 '66-p5229
Pastels Are Great!
BL-v64-Jl 15 '68-p1285
KR-v36-Je 1 '68-p598
LJ-v93-S 15 '68-p3304
SR-v51-N 9 '68-p65
YR-v5-N '68-p13
Pat, Swish, Twist And The Story Of Patty Swish
Cur R-v18-O '79-p309
PW-v214-Jl 31 '78-p99
Rhythms, Music, And Instruments To Make
BL-v67-S 1 '70-p57
Teacher-v94-Mr '77-p20

* * *

HAWKINSON, Lucy
Dance, Dance, Amy-Chan!
CCB-B-v20-O '66-p25

* * *

HAWLEY, Newton
Key To Geometry
Cur R-v19-Ap '80-p163

* * *

HAWTIN, J C
Codes And Ciphers
TES-Mr 9 '84-p47

* * *

HAY, Alex
The Young Golfer
JB-v45-F '81-p28

* * *

HAY, Dean
Look At Me
JB-v45-O '81-p187
On The Farm
GP-v16-Ja '78-p3242
JB-v42-Je '78-p135
What Shape Is It?
GP-v13-Ap '75-p2594
JB-v39-F '75-p21
What Size Is It?
GP-v13-Ap '75-p2594

* * *

HAY, George M
Samuel George Washington Jones Snake
SLJ-v28-S '81-p108

* * *

HAYCRAFT, John
Action
MLJ-v64-Autumn '80-p403
TES-Ag 11 '78-p19

* * *

HAYDEN, Robert
Kaleidoscope
BL-v64-Mr 1 '68-p773
CCB-B-v21-Ap '68-p127
Comw-v87-N 10 '67-p184
HB-v44-Ap '68-p207
LJ-v93-Ja 15 '68-p305
ND-v17-Ja '68-p51
NYTBR-v72-N 5 '67-p38
PW-v192-O 2 '67-p56
SR-v51-My 11 '68-p85

* * *

HAYDEN, Robert C
Nine Black American Doctors
CLW-v48-Mr '77-p357
SB-v13-S '77-p86
SE-v41-Ap '77-p347

* * *

HAYDN Richards Junior English
TES-O 1 '82-p46

* * *

HAYES, Barbara
Before I Go To Sleep
B&B-v24-N '78-p58

* * *

HAYES, David
Human Rights
Brit Bk N C-Spring '81-p30
JB-v45-Ap '81-p81
Sch Lib-v29-Je '81-p164
Terrorists And Freedom Fighters
Brit Bk N C-Autumn '80-p29
Sch Lib-v28-S '80-p311
TES-Je 20 '80-p43

* * *

HAYES, Florence
Boy In The Roof-Top School
CCB-B-v21-S '67-p7
KR-v35-Mr 15 '67-p341
LJ-v92-Ap 15 '67-p1724

* * *

HAYES, Geoffrey
The Alligator And His Uncle Tooth
BL-v73-My 15 '77-p1420
BL-v77-Je 15 '81-p1352
BL-v78-F 15 '82-p762
CCB-B-v31-O '77-p33
CSM-v69-My 4 '77-pB8
HB-v53-Ag '77-p441
JB-v42-Ap '78-p88
KR-v45-Ap 1 '77-p350
NYTBR-My 1 '77-p47
RT-v31-D '77-p331
SLJ-v24-S '77-p109
TES-Mr 10 '78-p60
TLS-D 2 '77-p1414
Bear By Himself
BL-v73-S 1 '76-p38
CE-v53-F '77-p213
CLW-v49-D '77-p230
CSM-v68-N 3 '76-p28
GP-v16-Ja '78-p3250
KR-v44-Je 15 '76-p680
NYT-v126-D 20 '76-pC21
NYTBR-N 14 '76-p26
PW-v223-Ja 21 '83-p85
RT-v31-O '77-p10
SLJ-v23-O '76-p98
TES-F 3 '78-p45
Elroy And The Witch's Child
CBRS-v11-S '82-p3
KR-v50-Jl 15 '82-p795
New Age-v8-D '82-p68
PW-v222-S 10 '82-p76
SLJ-v29-S '82-p108
Patrick And Ted
BL-v80-Je 15 '84-p1483
CBRS-v12-Spring '84-p122
PW-v225-Mr 16 '84-p87
SLJ-v31-O '84-p147
Patrick Comes To Puttyville
GP-v18-S '79-p3583
TES-Jl 11 '80-p28
Patrick Comes To Puttyville And Other Stories
BL-v75-N 15 '78-p546
CBRS-v7-Winter '79-p54
CCB-B-v32-Mr '79-p117
KR-v46-D 15 '78-p1357
SLJ-v25-O '78-p145
The Secret Inside
KR-v48-My 15 '80-p642
PW-v217-My 2 '80-p76
SLJ-v26-My '80-p58

* * *

HAYES, John
A Land Divided
Can Child Lit-#23 '81-p58
In Rev-v15-F '81-p26

* * *

HAYES, Phyllis
Food Fun
CBRS-v10-D '81-p34
SLJ-v28-D '81-p80
Musical Instruments You Can Make
SLJ-v28-D '81-p80

* * *

HAYES, Richard
The Forbidden Teachers
GP-v17-My '78-p3325
JB-v42-Ag '78-p204
TES-F 3 '78-p36
TLS-Ap 7 '78-p382
Into The Fire
JB-v43-D '79-p336
The Secret Army
CBRS-v7-Spring '79-p118
CCB-B-v32-Ap '79-p137
GP-v16-S '77-p3163
JB-v41-O '77-p301
KR-v47-Je 1 '79-p637
PW-v215-F 19 '79-p107
Punch-v272-Je 15 '77-p152
SLJ-v25-Mr '79-p140
SLJ-v27-N '80-p47
TLS-Jl 15 '77-p864

* * *

HAYES, Sheila
The Carousel Horse
BL-v75-N 15 '78-p546
CBRS-v7-Winter '79-p57
CCB-B-v32-Je '79-p175
HB-v55-Ap '79-p194
KR-v47-Ja 15 '79-p66
PW-v214-N 6 '78-p78
RT-v33-O '79-p95
SLJ-v25-N '78-p63
Me And My Mona Lisa Smile
BL-v77-Je 15 '81-p1345
BS-v41-S '81-p238
CBRS-v9-Ap '81-p77
CCB-B-v34-Jl '81-p212
HB-v57-Ag '81-p424
SLJ-v27-Mr '81-p156
VOYA-v4-O '81-p33
Speaking Of Snapdragons
BL-v79-F 1 '83-p724
CBRS-v11-O '82-p19
CCB-B-v36-F '83-p109
SLJ-v29-N '82-p85

* * *

HAYES, William D
How The True Facts Started In Simpsonville
HB-v49-F '73-p48
KR-v40-Jl 15 '72-p803
LJ-v97-D 15 '72-p4072
PW-v202-Ag 14 '72-p46
Johnny And The Tool Chest
CCB-B-v18-Jl '65-p162

* * *

HAYHURST, Brian
Gymnastics
SLJ-v28-S '81-p119

* * *

HAYLES, Brian
The Moon Stallion
GP-v17-Mr '79-p3489
JB-v43-Ap '79-p117

* * *

HAYMAN, LeRoy
Thirteen Who Vanished
CCB-B-v32-Je '79-p175
KR-v47-Ap 1 '79-p394
SLJ-v25-My '79-p82
Up, Up, And Away
ASBYP-v14-Winter '81-p32
BL-v76-Jl 1 '80-p1608
CCB-B-v34-D '80-p71

* * *

HAYNES, Betsy
The Against Taffy Sinclair Club
CCB-B-v30-Mr '77-p107
Inst-v86-My '77-p119
KR-v44-O 15 '76-p1136
RT-v31-O '77-p14
SLJ-v23-O '76-p107
Cowslip
A Lib-v5-My '74-p236
BS-v33-My 15 '73-p98
CCB-B-v27-Ja '74-p79
KR-v41-Mr 15 '73-p316
NYTBR-S 16 '73-p12
SLMQ-v11-Spring '83-p192
The Ghost Of The Gravestone Hearth
BL-v74-S 1 '77-p41
CCB-B-v31-D '77-p60
KR-v45-Ap 1 '77-p351
PW-v212-Ag 1 '77-p116
SLJ-v23-My '77-p77
The Shadows Of Jeremy Pimm
BL-v77-Ap 1 '81-p1104
BS-v41-S '81-p238
CBRS-v9-Je '81-p97
SLJ-v27-My '81-p64
VOYA-v4-O '81-p33
Spies On The Devil's Belt
CCB-B-v29-S '75-p11
KR-v42-Ag 15 '74-p877
LJ-v99-O 15 '74-p2746
NYTBR-N 3 '74-p26
Taffy Sinclair Strikes Again
SLJ-v30-My '84-p80

* * *

HAYNES, Henry L
Squarehead And Me
CCB-B-v34-S '80-p11
SLJ-v26-My '80-p68

* * *

HAYNES, Mary
Pot Belly Tales
BL-v78-My 15 '82-p1257
CBRS-v10-My '82-p94
CCB-B-v35-My '82-p171
PW-v221-Mr 19 '82-p71
SLJ-v29-S '82-p122
Wordchanger
BL-v80-O 1 '83-p294
B Rpt-v2-Mr '84-p33
CCB-B-v37-O '83-p29
CE-v60-My '84-p362
Fant R-v7-Ag '84-p47
HB-v59-O '83-p573
J Read-v27-Ap '84-p662
SLJ-v30-S '83-p134
VOYA-v7-Ap '84-p30

* * *

HAYS, Anna Jane
See No Evil, Hear No Evil, Smell No Evil
SR-v3-N 29 '75-p33

* * *

HAYS, H R
Charley Sang A Song
CCB-B-v18-Ap '65-p117

* * *

HAYS, James D
Our Changing Climate
BL-v74-F 15 '78-p1004
CCB-B-v31-Ap '78-p128
EJ-v67-O '78-p79
KR-v45-N 15 '77-p1208
Par-v53-Ja '78-p80

HAYS, James D (continued)
SB-v14-S '78-p88
SLJ-v24-Ja '78-p89

* * *

HAYS, Wilma P
Goose That Was A Watchdog
CCB-B-v21-Ap '68-p127

* * *

HAYS, Wilma Pitchford
Little Yellow Fur
BL-v70-F 15 '74-p656
CCB-B-v27-Je '74-p157
Inst-v83-N '73-p125
KR-v41-S 1 '73-p964
LJ-v98-D 15 '73-p3716
The Long Blond Wig
CCB-B-v24-Jl '71-p171
KR-v39-Mr 15 '71-p288
LJ-v96-My 15 '71-p1820
PW-v199-Je 7 '71-p56
The Open Gate
BL-v67-F 1 '71-p450
CCB-B-v24-Mr '71-p107
KR-v38-S 15 '70-p1037
LJ-v96-F 15 '71-p714
Pilgrims To The Rescue
CCB-B-v25-Jl '72-p169
LJ-v97-S 15 '72-p2950
Pontiac: Lion In The Forest
CCB-B-v19-My '66-p150
GT-v88-O '70-p146
LJ-v90-Je 15 '65-p2883
Siege!
BB-v5-My '77-p4
KR-v44-Ap 15 '76-p469
SE-v41-Ap '77-p347
SLJ-v23-F '77-p65
Yellow Fur And Little Hawk
BL-v76-Je 15 '80-p1532
CCB-B-v33-Je '80-p191
KR-v48-My 1 '80-p582
SLJ-v26-My '80-p82

* * *

HAYTON, Hilary
Bedtime With Doris
GP-v21-S '82-p3950
Crystal Tipps And Alistair: Bread
TLS-D 6 '74-p1384
Crystal Tipps And Alistair: Monster
TLS-D 6 '74-p1384
Crystal Tipps And Alistair: Party Piece
TLS-D 6 '74-p1384
Crystal Tipps And Alistair: Tee For Two
TLS-D 6 '74-p1384
Eating With Doris
GP-v21-S '82-p3950
Keep Fit With Doris
GP-v21-S '82-p3950
Shopping With Doris
GP-v21-S '82-p3950

* * *

HAYWARD, Linda
Letters, Sounds, And Words
JB-v39-Ap '75-p104
LJ-v98-D 15 '73-p3700
PW-v203-Je 25 '73-p74
The Sesame Street Dictionary
ARBA-v12-'81-p520
BW-v10-N 9 '80-p17
CBRS-v9-Ja '81-p34
CCB-B-v34-Mr '81-p135
NYTBR-v85-N 9 '80-p56
PW-v218-N 21 '80-p59
SLJ-v27-D '80-p18
SLJ-v27-D '80-p44
SLJ-v28-My '82-p21

* * *

HAYWOOD, Carolyn
Away Went The Balloons
BL-v70-S 1 '73-p51
CCB-B-v26-My '73-p139
CSM-v65-My 2 '73-pB5
Inst-v82-My '73-p74
KR-v41-F 1 '73-p114
PW-v203-Ap 16 '73-p55
B Is For Betsy
BL-v80-F 15 '84-p868
Betsy And Mr. Kilpatrick
BL-v64-N 15 '67-p387
CCB-B-v21-Mr '68-p110
CSM-v59-N 2 '67-pB6
KR-v35-S 1 '67-p1047
LJ-v92-D 15 '67-p4612
Par-v43-My '68-p68
Betsy And The Boys
Teacher-v96-O '78-p173
Betsy And The Circus
Inst-v92-O '82-p24
PW-v221-My 21 '82-p77
Betsy's Play School
BB-v6-F '78-p3
BL-v74-O 1 '77-p295
CCB-B-v31-Ja '78-p78
CLW-v49-D '77-p235
KR-v45-Ag 1 '77-p784
LA-v55-Ap '78-p521
PW-v212-O 10 '77-p70
RT-v32-F '79-p609
SLJ-v24-N '77-p48
C Is For Cupcake
BL-v70-My 1 '74-p1002
CCB-B-v27-Jl '74-p178
CLW-v46-S '74-p89
CSM-v66-My 1 '74-pF3
KR-v42-F 15 '74-p185
LJ-v99-My 15 '74-p1465
A Christmas Fantasy
CCB-B-v26-O '72-p26
CLW-v44-Mr '73-p512
KR-v40-Jl 15 '72-p799
LJ-v97-O 15 '72-p3470
PW-v202-N 6 '72-p57
Eddie's Menagerie
BL-v75-S 15 '78-p220
CCB-B-v32-Ja '79-p81
KR-v46-S 1 '78-p950
PW-v214-Jl 17 '78-p169
SLJ-v25-O '78-p132
Eddie's Valuable Property
CCB-B-v29-O '75-p27
KR-v43-Mr 15 '75-p307
PW-v207-Mr 3 '75-p70
RT-v29-F '76-p511
SLJ-v21-My '75-p55
Ever-Ready Eddie
BL-v65-N 1 '68-p311
CCB-B-v22-Mr '69-p111
KR-v36-O 1 '68-p1114
LJ-v93-N 15 '68-p4394
PW-v194-O 14 '68-p65
Halloween Treats
BL-v78-S 15 '81-p106
CCB-B-v35-O '81-p30
CE-v59-S '82-p64
KR-v49-S 15 '81-p1159
SLJ-v28-O '81-p142
Happy Birthday From Carolyn Haywood
BL-v80-Je 15 '84-p1484
CCB-B-v37-Jl '84-p205
RT-v38-D '84-p339
SLJ-v30-Ag '84-p60
The King's Monster
BL-v76-My 15 '80-p1364
CBRS-v8-Mr '80-p72
CCB-B-v34-S '80-p11
CE-v57-Mr '81-p233
HB-v56-Je '80-p287
KR-v48-Je 15 '80-p776
LA-v58-Ja '81-p80
PW-v217-F 29 '80-p135
SLJ-v26-My '80-p58

HAYWOOD, Carolyn (continued)
Make A Joyful Noise!
SLJ-v31-S '84-p118
Merry Christmas From Betsy
BL-v67-O 1 '70-p145
BW-v4-D 20 '70-p8
CCB-B-v24-N '70-p43
Comw-v93-N 20 '70-p198
KR-v38-Ag 1 '70-p799
LJ-v95-O 15 '70-p3647
PW-v198-Ag 24 '70-p63
SR-v53-D 19 '70-p31
Santa Claus Forever!
CBRS-v12-N '83-p24
CCB-B-v37-O '83-p29
KR-v51-N 1 '83-pJ185
NYTBR-v88-D 4 '83-p79
PW-v224-S 2 '83-p80
SLJ-v30-O '83-p176
A Valentine Fantasy
BL-v72-Ap 1 '76-p1113
CE-v53-Ja '77-p147
KR-v44-Mr 15 '76-p316
SLJ-v22-Ap '76-p60

* * *

HAYWOOD, M
Rose Red
JB-v41-Ap '77-p124

* * *

HAYWOOD, Marion
Spud And The Jokers
GP-v19-Ja '81-p3808
JB-v45-Ap '81-p81

* * *

HAZARD, David
The Peaceable Kingdom
SLJ-v30-N '83-p64

* * *

HAZARD, Eleanor
Monkey
PW-v217-Ja 25 '80-p340
SLJ-v26-Ag '80-p67

* * *

HAZEL Pearson Handicrafts
Macrame
Cr Crafts-v7-Ap '80-p4

* * *

HAZELTON, Elizabeth Baldwin
Sammy, The Crow Who Remembered
CCB-B-v23-Mr '70-p112
CSM-v61-N 6 '69-pB10
KR-v37-O 1 '69-p1057
LJ-v95-Ja 15 '70-p233
PW-v196-N 17 '69-p82

* * *

HAZELTON, Nika
Raggedy Ann And Andy's Cookbook
NYTBR-N 16 '75-p34
PW-v208-Jl 21 '75-p69
SLJ-v22-D '75-p52

* * *

HAZEN, Barbara Shook
Amelia's Flying Machine
CCB-B-v31-S '77-p16
KR-v45-Ag 15 '77-p851
PW-v212-Jl 25 '77-p71
SLJ-v24-N '77-p48
Animal Manners
SLJ-v21-My '75-p47
Davy Crockett, Indian Fighter
SLJ-v22-Mr '76-p101
Even If I Did Something Awful
CBRS-v10-Ja '82-p41
CCB-B-v35-Ja '82-p86
CE-v58-My '82-p325
KR-v49-O 15 '81-p1292
New Age-v7-D '81-p78
PW-v220-Ag 21 '81-p55
SLJ-v28-N '81-p76
Frere Jacques
CE-v50-Ja '74-p166
CSM-v65-My 2 '73-pB3
KR-v41-F 15 '73-p182
LA-v56-Ap '79-p404
LJ-v98-Jl '73-p2186
PW-v203-F 5 '73-p89
The Golden Happy Birthday Book
SR-v3-My 15 '76-p38
Teacher-v96-S '78-p38
The Gorilla Did It
BL-v70-Mr 1 '74-p741
CCB-B-v27-Jl '74-p178
CE-v51-O '74-p33
CLW-v46-F '75-p315
JB-v40-D '76-p314
KR-v42-F 15 '74-p182
LJ-v99-My 15 '74-p1465
PT-v8-N '74-p30
PW-v205-F 4 '74-p73
SLJ-v26-Mr '80-p105
SR/W-v1-My 4 '74-p45
Teacher-v95-O '77-p162
Gorilla Wants To Be The Baby
BL-v75-O 1 '78-p294
KR-v46-D 15 '78-p1352
SLJ-v25-Ja '79-p42
Happy, Sad, Silly, Mad
CCB-B-v26-O '72-p26
If It Weren't For Benjamin (I'd Always Get To Lick The Icing Spoon)
Inter BC-v12-#2 '81-p19
SB-v16-S '80-p30
SLJ-v26-Ap '80-p94
It's A Shame About The Rain
CCB-B-v37-S '83-p9
SLJ-v29-Ag '83-p52
Last, First, Middle And Nick
BL-v76-N 15 '79-p504
Cur R-v19-Ap '80-p152
SLJ-v26-F '80-p56
The Me I See
CLW-v50-F '79-p301
Cur R-v18-F '79-p21
KR-v46-F 15 '78-p174
SLJ-v24-My '78-p55
SR-v5-My 27 '78-p66
WCRB-v4-Mr '78-p42
Peter Pan
SLJ-v23-N '76-p47
Please Pass The P's And Q's
LJ-v92-N 15 '67-p4251
Step On It, Andrew
CBRS-v9-Ja '81-p31
HB-v57-F '81-p42
KR-v48-N 1 '80-p1391
SLJ-v27-Ja '81-p50
Tight Times
BL-v76-O 1 '79-p276
CBRS-v8-D '79-p32
CCB-B-v33-F '80-p110
KR-v47-O 15 '79-p1207
PW-v224-S 23 '83-p73
To Be Me
SLJ-v22-Mr '76-p92
Two Homes To Live In
Ms-v12-N '83-p76
Par-v59-N '84-p198
SB-v15-My '79-p39
The Ups And Downs Of Marvin
BB-v5-Ap '77-p1
KR-v44-S 15 '76-p1035
SLJ-v23-N '76-p47
Very Shy
CCB-B-v36-My '83-p168
SLJ-v29-My '83-p62

HAZEN, Barbara Shook (continued)
Where Do Bears Sleep?
BL-v66-My 15 '70-p1160
BW-v4-My 17 '70-p7
CCB-B-v24-Jl '70-p178
Comw-v92-My 22 '70-p252
JB-v41-O '77-p277
LJ-v95-Je 15 '70-p2302
PW-v197-Mr 2 '70-p82
SR-v53-Ap 18 '70-p36
Why Couldn't I Be An Only Kid Like You, Wigger
BL-v72-S 15 '75-p165
HB-v51-D '75-p585
KR-v43-O 15 '75-p1176
SLJ-v22-O '75-p91
WLB-v50-N '75-p248
World, World, What Can I Do?
BB-v4-O '76-p1
CCB-B-v30-S '76-p10
KR-v44-Mr 1 '76-p250

* * *

HAZZARD, Russell
It Scares Me But I Like It
Can Child Lit-#18 '80-p135

* * *

HE, Zi
Tang Shi You Du
BL-v80-S 1 '83-p96

* * *

HEAD, Bessie
When Rain Clouds Gather
BL-v65-Ap 15 '69-p943
BS-v28-Mr 15 '69-p505
HB-v45-Ap '69-p193
KR-v37-Ja 1 '69-p24
LJ-v94-Mr 15 '69-p1161
LJ-v94-Ap 15 '69-p1803
NS-v77-My 16 '69-p696
Obs-Ag 10 '69-p24
PW-v195-Mr 3 '69-p50
Spec-v222-My 23 '69-p687
TLS-My 29 '69-p575
TN-v26-N '69-p86

* * *

HEADINGTON, Christopher
Orchestra And Its Instruments
BL-v64-Ap 1 '68-p930
BS-v27-F 1 '68-p430
CCB-B-v21-Ap '68-p127
LJ-v93-S 15 '68-p3316
The Performing World Of The Musician
Brit Bk N C-Autumn '81-p29
CCB-B-v35-Ap '82-p149
GP-v20-Ja '82-p4003
SLJ-v28-Ja '82-p83

* * *

HEADLINES
TES-Ja 1 '82-p17

* * *

HEADSTROM, Richard
Adventures With Insects
SB-v20-S '84-p35
Your Insect Pet
ACSB-v8-Winter '75-p19
BL-v70-Mr 1 '74-p741
KR-v41-O 15 '73-p1172
LJ-v99-F 15 '74-p580
SB-v10-My '74-p74

* * *

HEADWAY Program
Cur R-v18-D '79-p374
Inst-v89-Mr '80-p155
RT-v33-Mr '80-p736

* * *

HEADY, Eleanor B
High Meadow
BL-v67-D 1 '70-p307
BW-v4-N 8 '74-p4
CCB-B-v24-Mr '71-p108
CE-v47-My '71-p438
CSM-v62-N 12 '70-pB5
KR-v38-S 15 '70-p1053
LJ-v95-D 15 '70-p4350
SB-v6-Mr '71-p312
SR-v53-N 14 '70-p38
Plants On The Go
ACSB-v8-Fall '75-p15
BB-v3-S '75-p3
KR-v43-Ap 1 '75-p380
SLJ-v22-S '75-p76
Safiri The Singer
BL-v69-Jl 15 '73-p1073
CCB-B-v26-Ja '73-p77
LJ-v98-F 15 '73-p644
PW-v203-Ja 1 '73-p57
The Soil That Feeds Us
BL-v69-F 1 '73-p529
CCB-B-v25-Je '72-p156
KR-v40-My 1 '72-p539
LJ-v98-Mr 15 '73-p994
SB-v8-D '72-p227
Trees Are Forever
BL-v74-My 15 '78-p1494
SB-v14-Mr '79-p231
SLJ-v25-S '78-p116
Teacher-v96-N '78-p136
When The Stones Were Soft
BL-v64-Je 15 '68-p1186
CCB-B-v22-S '68-p8
HB-v44-Ag '68-p415
LJ-v93-Ap 15 '68-p1799
NYTBR-v73-My 5 '68-p30
PW-v193-Je 3 '68-p128
SA-v221-D '69-p136
SE-v33-My '69-p559
SR-v51-S 21 '68-p37

* * *

HEALEY, Larry
The Claw Of The Bear
BB-v6-Ag '78-p3
Cur R-v17-D '78-p389
JB-v42-D '78-p312
SLJ-v24-My '78-p86
The Hoard Of The Himalayas
BL-v78-S 15 '81-p98
BS-v41-O '81-p277
CBRS-v10-O '81-p18
CSM-v74-D 14 '81-pB10
SLJ-v28-D '81-p85
The Town Is On Fire
BL-v76-F 15 '80-p829
CBRS-v8-N '79-p27
SLJ-v26-D '79-p99
SLJ-v27-N '80-p47

* * *

HEALEY, Tim
Disasters
Lis-v100-N 9 '78-p624
TES-O 20 '78-p38
Secret Armies
BL-v78-Je 1 '82-p1312
CCB-B-v36-S '82-p11
SLJ-v29-N '82-p100

* * *

HEALTH Explorer
BL-v79-F 1 '83-p729

* * *

HEALTHFUL Living Program
Cur R-v19-Ap '80-p119

* * *

HEAPS, Willard A
Psychic Phenomena
BL-v71-F 15 '75-p612
BS-v35-Jl '75-p97
CCB-B-v29-O '75-p27
KR-v43-Ja 1 '75-p26

HEAPS, Willard A (continued)
PW-v207-Ja 6 '75-p58
SLJ-v21-Ap '75-p65
Riots, U.S.A. 1765-1965
BL-v62-Jl 1 '66-p1040
CCB-B-v20-F '67-p90
LJ-v92-F 15 '67-p893
NYTBR-v71-Jl 3 '66-p14
SS-v58-N '67-p271
Wandering Workers
BL-v65-F 1 '69-p582
BS-v28-Ja 1 '69-p421
CCB-B-v22-Ap '69-p126
NYTBR, pt.1-F 16 '69-p34

* * *

HEARN, Emily
Mighty Mites In Dinosaur Land
BIC-v10-D '81-p8
Can Child Lit-#29 '83-p58
In Rev-v16-F '82-p38
Quill & Q-v48-F '82-p36
Ring Around Duffy
SLJ-v21-Mr '75-p84
TV Kangaroo
SLJ-v22-D '75-p65
Whoosh! I Hear A Sound
BIC-v12-D '83-p14
Quill & Q-v49-N '83-p23

* * *

HEARN, John
The Young Collector
BIC-v13-Ja '84-p27

* * *

HEARN, Michael P
Breakfast, Books & Dreams
BL-v77-Jl 1 '81-p1393
BW-v11-Je 14 '81-p11
HB-v57-Ag '81-p442
Inst-v90-My '81-p58
KR-v49-Jl 15 '81-p874
LA-v58-N '81-p952
RT-v35-D '81-p364
SLJ-v28-S '81-p126
VV-v26-D 9 '81-p58
WLB-v56-O '81-p134
The Chocolate Book
BL-v80-N 1 '83-p406
SLJ-v30-Ja '84-p77
WCRB-v10-Ja '84-p54
A Day In Verse
PW-v219-Je 5 '81-p83

* * *

HEARNE, Betsy
Celebrating Children's Books
AB-v68-N 16 '81-p3445
BL-v78-O 1 '81-p241
BS-v41-N '81-p311
BW-v11-N 8 '81-p18
CBRS-v10-O '81-p19
CE-v58-My '82-p332
Choice-v19-D '81-p504
HB-v58-Ap '82-p185
PW-v220-Ag 21 '81-p47
Rp B Bk R-v27-#1 '82-p16
SLJ-v28-N '81-p41
TN-v38-Spring '82-p257
Choosing Books For Children
CBRS-v9-My '81-p87
HB-v57-Ag '81-p447
Inst-v91-N '81-p81
KR-v49-Je 1 '81-p684
LJ-v106-My 1 '81-p975
LQ-v52-Jl '82-p284
Ms-v9-D '80-p36
PW-v219-Mr 27 '81-p48
RT-v36-Ja '83-p474
SLJ-v27-My '81-p29
SLMQ-v10-Summer '82-p309
TN-v38-Summer '82-p335
TN-v39-Spring '83-p291

* * *

HEARNE, Betsy Gould
Home
BL-v75-Ap 15 '79-p1295
CBRS-v7-Spring '79-p118
CCB-B-v32-Je '79-p175
HB-v55-Je '79-p301
KR-v47-Ap 1 '79-p388
PW-v216-Jl 2 '79-p106
RT-v33-D '79-p360
SLJ-v25-My '79-p62
South Star
BL-v74-O 15 '77-p375
CCB-B-v31-Ja '78-p78
HB-v53-D '77-p662
KR-v45-S 15 '77-p990
LA-v55-Mr '78-p371
PW-v212-S 19 '77-p146
SLJ-v24-O '77-p112

* * *

HEARNE, Tina
Care For Your Guinea-Pig
GP-v20-Ja '82-p4007
Care For Your Pony
GP-v20-Ja '82-p4007
JB-v46-F '82-p25
The Observer's Book Of Pets
JB-v42-D '78-p312
TES-O 20 '78-p37
RSPCA Care For Your Dog
JB-v44-Ag '80-p191
Sch Lib-v28-S '80-p275

* * *

HEASLIP, Peter
Birthdays
Brit Bk N C-Spring '81-p12
The Clinic
Brit Bk N C-Spring '81-p12
A Hole In The Road
Brit Bk N C-Spring '81-p12
Jobs
Brit Bk N C-Spring '81-p12
The Launderette
Brit Bk N C-Spring '81-p12
The Market
Brit Bk N C-Spring '81-p12
Me
Brit Bk N C-Spring '81-p12
My Aunty
Brit Bk N C-Spring '81-p12
My Dad
Brit Bk N C-Spring '81-p12
TES-O 29 '82-p35
My Home
Brit Bk N C-Spring '81-p12
My Mum
Brit Bk N C-Spring '81-p12
TES-O 29 '82-p35
My School
Brit Bk N C-Spring '81-p12
The New Baby
Brit Bk N C-Spring '81-p12
TES-O 29 '82-p35
Our House
Brit Bk N C-Spring '81-p12
TES-O 29 '82-p35
School Dinners
Brit Bk N C-Spring '81-p12
The Supermarket
Brit Bk N C-Spring '81-p12
Terraced House Books
TES-Jl 8 '83-p22
Terraced House Books. Set D
TES-O 2 '81-p20
Terraced House Books. Sets C-D
Sch Lib-v29-Mr '81-p23
TES-Mr 6 '81-p31
TES-My 6 '83-p54
Terraced House Books. Sets E-F
Sch Lib-v31-D '83-p349

HEASLIP, Peter (continued)
TES-Mr 9 '84-p52

* * *

HEAT, Electricity, And Electromagnetism
TES-Ap 1 '83-p36

* * *

HEATH, Edward
Carols
GP-v16-Ja '78-p3248
NS-v94-D 16 '77-p853

* * *

HEATH, Jane
A Closer Look At Minoans
TES-Je 20 '80-p41
Plains Indians
SLJ-v28-S '81-p113
Sch Lib-v29-Mr '81-p39

* * *

HEATH, Mary L
What I Really Meant To Say
Cur R-v22-Ag '83-p22

* * *

HEATH, Veronica
Riding For Beginners
JB-v43-Ag '79-p205
So You Want To Be A Show Jumper
B&B-v20-My '75-p81

* * *

HEATH, W L
The Earthquake Man
CBRS-v9-F '81-p56
KR-v49-F 15 '81-p213
LA-v58-S '81-p702
RT-v35-O '81-p113
SLJ-v27-Ja '81-p61
Max The Great
CCB-B-v31-N '77-p47
PW-v211-Je 20 '77-p72
SLJ-v24-O '77-p113

* * *

HEATH English
Inst-v93-Ag '83-p126

* * *

HEATH-STUBBS, John
A Parliament Of Birds
B&B-v21-D '75-p62
GP-v14-D '75-p2780
TES-Ap 23 '82-p21
TLS-D 5 '75-p1452

* * *

HEATON, Peter
Songs Under Sail
Inst-v84-Ja '75-p116

* * *

HEAVILIN, Jay
Fast Ball Pitcher
CCB-B-v19-S '65-p9
Fear Rides High
CCB-B-v21-My '68-p142
The Nonsense Book Of Nonsense
LA-v55-N '78-p960

* * *

HEBERT, Marie-Francine
Abecedaire
BL-v80-Ja 15 '84-p758
In Rev-v14-Ag '80-p52
Ce Tellement "Cute" Des Enfants
Can Child Lit-#25 '82-p60

* * *

HECK, Bessie Holland
Cave-In At Mason's Mine
BL-v77-Mr 1 '81-p963
CBRS-v9-Mr '81-p64
CCB-B-v34-Je '81-p194
SLJ-v27-My '81-p64
Golden Arrow
CCB-B-v35-O '81-p30
SLJ-v28-N '81-p104
The Hopeful Years
CCB-B-v18-Ja '65-p75
Year At Boggy
CCB-B-v20-Ap '67-p122
KR-v34-Ag 15 '66-p837
LJ-v91-O 15 '66-p5230

* * *

HECK, Joseph
Dinosaur Riddles
PW-v222-D 24 '82-p65
TES-D 23 '83-p23

* * *

HECKART, Barbara H
Edmond Halley: The Man And His Comet
BL-v81-S 15 '84-p128
SLJ-v31-O '84-p157

* * *

HEDDERWICK, Mairi
Katie Morag Delivers The Mail
HB-v60-S '84-p580
Obs-Ap 22 '84-p23
SLJ-v31-O '84-p147
Sch Lib-v32-Je '84-p125
TES-Mr 9 '84-p47

* * *

HEDIGER, Heini
Born In The Zoo
CCB-B-v22-F '69-p95
TLS-F 13 '69-p166
Time-v92-N 29 '68-pE7

* * *

HEDLUND, Irene
Mighty Mountain And The Three Strong Women
Sch Lib-v32-S '84-p234

* * *

HEEKS, Peggy
Ways Of Knowing
GP-v21-Mr '83-p4052
JB-v47-Ag '83-p151
Sch Lib-v31-Je '83-p193
TES-N 11 '83-p28

* * *

HEERING, Philippine
The Grebe
SLJ-v27-F '81-p57
The Jay
CCB-B-v33-D '79-p71
RT-v33-Ja '80-p483
SB-v16-N '80-p94

* * *

HEFFNER, Richard
Picture Dictionary
TES-Jl 7 '78-p30

* * *

HEFFRON, Dorris
Crusty Crossed
TLS-D 10 '76-p1552
A Nice Fire And Some Moonpennies
CCB-B-v26-O '72-p26
HB-v48-Je '72-p275
KR-v40-F 1 '72-p143
LJ-v97-Ap 15 '72-p1616
NS-v82-N 12 '71-p660
Obs-N 28 '71-p35
TLS-O 22 '71-p1318
Rain And I
Brit Bk N C-Autumn '82-p24
JB-v46-Ag '82-p152
Obs-N 28 '82-p31
TES-Ja 21 '83-p34

* * *

HEFTER, Richard
An Animal Alphabet
LJ-v99-S 15 '74-p2248
NYTBR-S 8 '74-p8
Teacher-v95-My '78-p104
Una Blanca Sonrisa De Cocodrilo
BL-v79-Jl '83-p1406
The Great Big Alphabet Picture Book
NYTBR-S 8 '74-p8
Teacher-v92-F '75-p116
Hippo Jogs For Health
SLJ-v25-O '78-p132
Lion Is Down In The Dumps
SLJ-v24-Mr '78-p119
Moody Moose Buttons
SLJ-v24-Mr '78-p119
No Kicks For Dog
SLJ-v26-S '79-p111
A Noise In The Closet
PW-v206-O 21 '74-p52
SLJ-v21-My '75-p47
Pig Thinks Pink
SLJ-v26-S '79-p112
The Strawberry Book Of Colors
NYTBR-N 16 '75-p58
SLJ-v22-Ap '76-p61
The Strawberry Book Of Shapes
BL-v73-F 15 '77-p897
Cur R-v16-O '77-p279
RT-v31-F '78-p575
SLJ-v23-Mr '77-p133
The Strawberry Picture Dictionary
SLJ-v22-S '75-p83
The Strawberry Word Book
LJ-v99-N 15 '74-p3038
NYTBR-S 8 '74-p8
Teacher-v95-My '78-p104
Things That Go
SLJ-v22-Ap '76-p61
Turtle Throws A Tantrum
SLJ-v25-My '79-p51
Xerus Won't Allow It
SLJ-v25-Ja '79-p43
Yakety Yak Yak Yak
SLJ-v24-Mr '78-p119
Yes And No
BL-v72-N 1 '75-p366
SLJ-v22-Ap '76-p61

* * *

HEGWOOD, Mamie
My Friend Fish
BL-v72-Mr 1 '76-p978
CLW-v47-My '76-p444
KR-v43-N 15 '75-p1284
LA-v53-My '76-p509
SLJ-v23-O '76-p98

* * *

HEIDE, Florence P
The Adventures Of Treehorn
NYTBR-v88-O 23 '83-p43
Banana Blitz
BL-v79-Jl '83-p1401
CBRS-v11-Je '83-p114
KR-v51-Je 1 '83-p619
PW-v223-Ap 29 '83-p51
SLJ-v29-Ag '83-p66
Banana Twist
BL-v75-N 1 '78-p479
BL-v78-F 15 '82-p762
CBRS-v7-Winter '79-p57
CCB-B-v32-Ap '79-p137
CE-v56-O '79-p44
HB-v55-F '79-p61
KR-v46-D 1 '78-p1307
PW-v214-O 30 '78-p50
SLJ-v25-N '78-p74
WCRB-v5-Ja '79-p54
Benjamin Budge And Barnaby Ball
CCB-B-v21-My '68-p142
LJ-v93-Ap 15 '68-p1788
Body In The Brillstone Garage
SLJ-v26-My '80-p86
SLJ-v27-N '80-p47
Brillstone Break-In
SLJ-v24-S '77-p130
Fables You Shouldn't Pay Any Attention To
BL-v74-Ap 1 '78-p1254
CCB-B-v31-Jl '78-p178
HB-v54-Je '78-p271
KR-v46-F 15 '78-p177
NW-v92-D 18 '78-p100
NYTBR-Ap 30 '78-p46
PW-v213-Ja 30 '78-p129
SLJ-v25-F '79-p56
SR-v5-My 27 '78-p60
Face At The Brillstone Window
BL-v75-My 15 '79-p1445
CCB-B-v32-Je '79-p176
SLJ-v25-My '79-p81
Fear At Brillstone
CCB-B-v32-Ja '79-p81
SLJ-v25-D '78-p68
God And Me
SLJ-v22-S '75-p83
Growing Anyway Up
BB-v4-Ja '77-p3
BL-v72-Ap 1 '76-p1113
CCB-B-v30-S '76-p10
HB-v52-Je '76-p288
KR-v44-My 1 '76-p535
Kliatt-v13-Winter '79-p8
PW-v209-Ja 19 '76-p102
SLJ-v22-F '76-p53
Maximilian
BW-v1-D 31 '67-p10
CCB-B-v21-Ap '68-p128
KR-v35-S 1 '67-p1040
LJ-v92-O 15 '67-p3840
NYTBR-v72-N 5 '67-p63
Maximilian Becomes Famous
CCB-B-v24-Jl '70-p178
A Monster Is Coming! A Monster Is Coming!
BL-v77-F 15 '81-p813
My Castle
BW-v6-N 5 '72-p2
CCB-B-v26-Ja '73-p77
KR-v40-Ag 15 '72-p935
LJ-v97-D 15 '72-p4066
Mystery At Keyhole Carnival
SLJ-v23-My '77-p77
Mystery At Southport Cinema
SLJ-v25-D '78-p68
Mystery Of The Bewitched Bookmobile
SLJ-v22-D '75-p66
Mystery Of The Forgotten Island
BL-v76-Je 15 '80-p1540
SLJ-v27-S '80-p72
Mystery Of The Lonely Lantern
SLJ-v23-F '77-p65
Mystery Of The Melting Snowman
LJ-v99-D 15 '74-p3277
Mystery Of The Midnight Message
BL-v74-F 15 '78-p1013
CCB-B-v31-Ap '78-p128
SLJ-v24-Ap '78-p84
Mystery Of The Mummy's Mask
BL-v76-O 15 '79-p359
SLJ-v26-D '79-p98

* * *

HEIN, Lucille E
From Sea To Shining Sea
SLJ-v22-Ja '76-p38
My Very Special Friend
CCB-B-v28-Mr '75-p114
CE-v54-Ja '78-p124
RT-v35-My '82-p901
SE-v44-N '80-p603
SLJ-v21-Mr '75-p88
A Tree I Can Call My Own
ACSB-v8-Winter '75-p19
LJ-v99-S 15 '74-p2248

* * *

HEINE, Helme
Elefanteneinmaleins
TLS-Mr 25 '77-p353
Friends
BL-v79-Ja 1 '83-p617
CBRS-v11-My '83-p97
CE-v60-S '83-p52
JB-v46-O '82-p181
KR-v50-O 15 '82-p1151
NS-v104-D 3 '82-p22
NYTBR-v87-N 28 '82-p24
Obs-D 5 '82-p33
PW-v222-N 19 '82-p76
SLJ-v29-F '83-p66
TES-N 19 '82-p32
TLS-S 17 '82-p1003
TLS-S 7 '84-p1006
WLB-v57-My '83-p771
Imagine If...
GP-v18-Ja '80-p3640
JB-v44-Je '80-p118
King Bounce The 1st
B&B-Jl '82-p36
RT-v36-My '83-p944
SLJ-v29-Ja '83-p60
WLB-v57-S '82-p59
Merry-Go-Round
BL-v77-O 1 '80-p252
NS-v100-N 21 '80-p19
SLJ-v27-N '80-p63
Mr. Miller The Dog
CBRS-v9-Winter '81-p43
HB-v57-F '81-p42
KR-v48-N 1 '80-p1392
NYTBR-v85-D 7 '80-p42
PW-v218-Ag 1 '80-p50
RT-v35-O '81-p54
SLJ-v27-F '81-p57
TLS-Mr 27 '81-p342
The Most Wonderful Egg In The World
BL-v80-N 1 '83-p408
CBRS-v12-Mr '84-p78
CCB-B-v37-Ap '84-p148
GP-v22-S '83-p4144
HB-v60-F '84-p43
KR-v51-N 1 '83-pJ185
LA-v61-Mr '84-p295
NS-v106-D 2 '83-p24
NW-v102-D 5 '83-p112
NYT-v133-N 30 '83-p19
NYTBR-v88-N 13 '83-p55
PW-v224-Ag 5 '83-p91
SLJ-v30-Ja '84-p65
Sch Lib-v31-D '83-p344
Time-v122-D 19 '83-p77
WLB-v58-F '84-p436
The Pigs' Wedding
BL-v75-Mr 1 '79-p1091
BOT-v2-D '79-p597
CBRS-v7-Spring '79-p112
CSM-v71-My 14 '79-pB6
GP-v17-Ja '79-p3449
JB-v43-Ap '79-p96
KR-v47-Mr 1 '79-p258
LA-v57-Ja '80-p80
NW-v94-D 17 '79-p94
NYTBR-Ap 29 '79-p29
NYTBR-N 25 '79-p26
PW-v215-F 12 '79-p126
SLJ-v25-Mr '79-p122
Sch Lib-v27-Mr '79-p29
Superconejo
BL-v78-Jl '82-p1438
SLJ-v30-My '84-p36
Superhare
SLJ-v26-Ap '80-p94

* * *

HEINE, Marc E
The Poles
BL-v72-Ap 15 '76-p1178
BL-v72-Ap 15 '76-p1185
Choice-v13-S '76-p877
LJ-v101-My 1 '76-p1133
SS-v68-My '77-p134

* * *

HEINER, Carl W
People Create Technology
Cur R-v20-S '81-p398

* * *

HEINS, Paul
Crosscurrents Of Criticism
AB-v62-N 13 '78-p2944
BL-v74-Ap 15 '78-p1359
GP-v17-Jl '78-p3372
JB-v42-O '78-p245
LQ-v48-O '78-p557
PW-v212-N 14 '77-p67
TLS-Ap 7 '78-p381

* * *

HEINTZE, Carl
The Biosphere
BL-v74-O 1 '77-p295
BS-v37-O '77-p203
LJ-v102-Mr 15 '77-p719
PW-v211-F 21 '77-p72
SB-v14-S '78-p88
SLJ-v24-D '77-p49
The Bottom Of The Sea And Beyond
ACSB-v9-Spring '76-p23
CLW-v47-N '75-p187
KR-v43-Ap 15 '75-p469
LJ-v100-Mr 15 '75-p593
SLJ-v22-D '75-p59
Genetic Engineering
ACSB-v8-Fall '75-p16
BL-v71-O 1 '74-p157
KR-v42-Ap 15 '74-p436
LJ-v99-Je 1 '74-p1556
LJ-v99-N 15 '74-p3054
Summit Lake
BL-v73-Ja 15 '77-p719
J Read-v21-F '78-p472
KR-v44-My 1 '76-p544
LJ-v101-Je 1 '76-p1299
NYTBR-Ag 1 '76-p16
SB-v13-D '77-p136
SLJ-v23-S '76-p134

* * *

HEISERMAN, David L
Build Your Own Working Robot
SA-v235-D '76-p143

* * *

HELBERG, Kristin
Cowboys
SLJ-v29-N '82-p85
The Elegant Dollhouse Book
BksW-v1-F '78-p37
PW-v210-N 22 '76-p52

* * *

HELD, Jacqueline
The Baobab Car
New R-v180-Je 23 '79-p40
Fabian, The Fish-Boy
KR-v44-F 15 '76-p193
LA-v53-S '76-p696
Mais Ou Est Donc Arsinoe?
BL-v77-Mr 1 '81-p970

HELD, Jacqueline (continued)
Le Pommier Des Perloupette Et Deux Autres Contes
BL-v77-Mr 1 '81-p970

* * *

HELENA, Ann
The Lie
BL-v74-D 15 '77-p687

* * *

HELFER, Andrew
Superman
SLJ-v30-N '83-p78

* * *

HELFMAN, Elizabeth S
Apples, Apples, Apples
ACSB-v12-Winter '79-p16
BL-v74-Mr 1 '78-p1107
Comw-v105-N 10 '78-p734
KR-v46-F 15 '78-p185
SB-v15-S '79-p97
SLJ-v24-N '77-p56
Blissymbolics
BL-v77-D 1 '80-p509
CBRS-v10-Je '82-p107
SLJ-v28-My '82-p70
Celebrating Nature
BL-v66-D 1 '69-p458
BS-v29-D 1 '69-p353
CLW-v41-F '70-p384
Comw-v92-My 22 '70-p246
HB-v45-O '69-p544
KR-v37-S 15 '69-p1014
LJ-v95-Ja 15 '70-p253
PW-v196-D 15 '69-p36
Spectr-v48-My '72-p31
Signs And Symbols Around The World
BL-v64-F 15 '68-p699
BS-v27-Ja 1 '68-p393
CCB-B-v21-F '68-p95
CE-v45-S '68-p40
KR-v35-N 15 '67-p1373
LJ-v93-F 15 '68-p882
NYTBR-v73-My 5 '68-p40
PW-v192-N 13 '67-p80
SB-v3-Mr '68-p282
YR-v4-Mr '68-p5
Signs And Symbols Of The Sun
ACSB-v8-Spring '75-p21
BL-v71-Mr 1 '75-p692
Comw-v102-N 21 '75-p572
KR-v42-D 15 '74-p1308
SLJ-v21-Ja '75-p45

* * *

HELFMAN, Harry
Creating Things That Move
BL-v72-O 1 '75-p236
KR-v43-Jl 15 '75-p780
PW-v208-O 27 '75-p53
SLJ-v22-N '75-p78
Making Pictures Move
BL-v65-Jl 1 '69-p1226
CC-v86-Jl 30 '69-p1020
CCB-B-v23-O '69-p25
KR-v37-Mr 15 '69-p310
LJ-v94-O 15 '69-p3821
NYTBR-Jl 13 '69-p26
Making Pictures Without Paint
CCB-B-v27-N '73-p44
GP-v14-S '75-p2696
JB-v39-Je '75-p184
KR-v41-F 1 '73-p120
LJ-v98-Jl '73-p2194
PW-v203-Ap 2 '73-p66

* * *

HELGESEN, C
Mary Alice In The Palace
CCB-B-v21-S '67-p8
NYTBR-v72-My 7 '67-p45

* * *

HELITZER, Morrie
The Cold War
CCB-B-v31-F '78-p95
Cur R-v18-F '79-p76
SLJ-v24-D '77-p54

* * *

HELLBERG, Hans-Eric
Ben's Lucky Hat
BL-v79-O 1 '82-p245
CBRS-v11-N '82-p25
CCB-B-v36-Ja '83-p89
JB-v45-F '81-p19
KR-v50-Jl 15 '82-p798
LA-v60-Mr '83-p360
NS-v100-N 14 '80-p21
RT-v36-D '82-p338
SLJ-v29-Mr '83-p177
TES-D 26 '80-p17
TES-Je 8 '84-p50
Grandpa's Maria
CCB-B-v28-My '75-p148
KR-v42-O 15 '74-p1103
LJ-v99-N 15 '74-p3046
PW-v206-D 30 '74-p101
SE-v41-O '77-p532
I Am Maria
JB-v42-D '78-p312
TLS-Jl 7 '78-p771
Maria
JB-v39-F '75-p64
TLS-D 6 '74-p1372
Maria And Martin
GP-v14-My '75-p2640
TLS-Jl 11 '75-p763
The One-Eyed Bandits
JB-v42-Ag '78-p204

* * *

HELLEGERS, Louisa B
Family Book Of Crafts
CCB-B-v27-F '74-p96
LJ-v99-Ja 15 '74-p128
LJ-v99-Ja 15 '74-p217

* * *

HELLER, Julek
Giants
A Art-v43-N '79-p22
PW-v216-S 10 '79-p70

* * *

HELLER, Linda
Alexis And The Golden Ring
BL-v76-My 1 '80-p1292
CBRS-v8-Je '80-p104
CCB-B-v34-N '80-p54
KR-v48-Je 1 '80-p710
LA-v58-Ja '81-p79
NYTBR-v85-Ap 27 '80-p58
PW-v217-My 16 '80-p212
RT-v34-Ja '81-p479
RT-v35-D '81-p333
SLJ-v26-My '80-p58
The Castle On Hester Street
BL-v79-N 15 '82-p445
CBRS-v11-N '82-p25
PW-v222-Jl 2 '82-p55
SLJ-v29-F '83-p66
Horace Morris
CBRS-v9-Ja '81-p32
KR-v49-Ja 15 '81-p73
PW-v218-O 10 '80-p74
SLJ-v27-D '80-p44
Lily At The Table
BL-v76-S 15 '79-p120
CBRS-v7-Ag '79-p132
CCB-B-v33-Ja '80-p96
KR-v47-S 1 '79-p998
PW-v216-Jl 23 '79-p159
RT-v34-Ja '81-p419
SLJ-v26-O '79-p140
Trouble At Goodewoode Manor
CBRS-v10-O '81-p12
KR-v49-Ag 1 '81-p932

HELLER, Linda (continued)
PW-v219-My 8 '81-p255
SLJ-v28-O '81-p129

* * *

HELLER, Mark
The Young Skier
Econ-v273-D 22 '79-p86

* * *

HELLER, Rachelle
ALEF BASIC
SLJ-v31-O '84-p158

* * *

HELLER, Ruth
Animals Born Alive And Well
ASBYP-v16-Fall '83-p33
CBRS-v11-N '82-p22
CCB-B-v36-Ja '83-p90
LATBR-O 17 '82-p6
SB-v19-N '83-p97
SLJ-v29-F '83-p66
Sierra-v69-N '84-p94
Chickens Aren't The Only Ones
BL-v78-D 1 '81-p498
CBRS-v10-D '81-p32
CCB-B-v35-F '82-p108
NW-v98-D 7 '81-p99
NY-v57-D 7 '81-p227
PW-v220-O 16 '81-p79
SA-v247-D '82-p39
SB-v17-My '82-p271
The Reason For A Flower
LATBR-S 18 '83-p5
PW-v224-S 23 '83-p72
SLJ-v30-Mr '84-p144

* * *

HELLER, Wendy
Clementine And The Cage
CCB-B-v34-N '80-p54
SLJ-v27-S '80-p60
My Name Is Nabil
SLJ-v28-F '82-p67

* * *

HELLMAN, Charles S
8-Wheel Drive
SLJ-v26-My '80-p89

* * *

HELLMAN, Hal
Computer Basics
BL-v80-S 15 '83-p170
BL-v80-Ja 1 '84-p682
BW-v13-O 2 '83-p8
CBRS-v11-Ag '83-p147
SLJ-v30-O '83-p158

* * *

HELLMAN, Harold
Biology In The World Of The Future
BL-v68-S 1 '71-p53
BS-v30-Ap 1 '71-p4
CCB-B-v24-Jl '71-p171
SB-v7-S '71-p139
SR-v54-Je 19 '71-p27
Deadly Bugs And Killer Insects
ACSB-v12-Fall '79-p30
BL-v75-D 1 '78-p608
CBRS-v7-Winter '79-p57
SB-v15-S '79-p89
SLJ-v25-Mr '79-p140
Teacher-v96-Ap '79-p97
Defense Mechanisms
BL-v66-Ja 1 '70-p564
CCB-B-v23-N '69-p45
LJ-v95-F 15 '70-p788
SB-v5-D '69-p253
SR-v52-O 18 '69-p57
Energy And Inertia
HB-v47-D '71-p626
LJ-v96-My 15 '71-p1827
SB-v7-My '71-p32
Energy In The World Of The Future
BB-v3-Mr '75-p3
BS-v33-D 15 '73-p414
CCB-B-v27-Je '74-p158
KR-v42-F 1 '74-p122
SB-v10-S '74-p147
Feeding The World Of The Future
BL-v69-S 15 '72-p86
BL-v69-O 1 '72-p148
HB-v49-O '73-p490
LJ-v98-Mr 15 '73-p1013
SB-v8-D '72-p265
High Energy Physics
BL-v64-Je 1 '68-p1134
BS-v28-Jl 15 '68-p172
HB-v45-Ag '69-p432
KR-v36-Mr 15 '68-p347
LJ-v93-O 15 '68-p3982
The Lever And The Pulley
CCB-B-v26-O '72-p27
HB-v49-F '73-p73
KR-v39-D 1 '71-p1259
LJ-v97-Ap 15 '72-p1605
SB-v8-My '72-p29
Transportation In The World Of The Future
BB-v3-Mr '75-p3
BL-v65-Ja 15 '69-p542
BL-v70-Jl 15 '74-p1249
CCB-B-v22-Mr '69-p111
KR-v42-Je 1 '74-p592
LJ-v94-Jl '69-p2682
SB-v4-Mr '69-p265
SB-v10-D '74-p200

* * *

HELLMAN, Lillian
Pentimento
Am-v129-N 17 '73-p379
Am-v129-D 29 '73-p508
Atl-v240-N '77-p96
BL-v70-O 15 '73-p204
BS-v33-O 1 '73-p3036
BW-v7-S 16 '73-p1
BW-v7-D 9 '73-p2
BW-O 20 '74-p4
BW-D 22 '74-p3
CSM-v65-N 14 '73-p19
Choice-v10-Ja '74-p1718
Comt-v57-F '74-p88
Econ-v251-My 25 '74-p143
GW-v110-My 11 '74-p22
HB-v50-F '74-p76
HR-v26-Winter '74-p743
KR-v41-Jl 15 '73-p792
LJ-v98-Jl '73-p2157
LJ-v98-N 15 '73-p3369
Lis-v91-Ap 25 '74-p535
Ms-v2-Ja '74-p31
NBR-v5-Ag '80-p5
NO-v12-O 13 '73-p19
NS-v87-Ap 26 '74-p587
NW-v82-O 1 '73-p95
NYT-v122-S 17 '73-p31
NYTBR-S 23 '73-p1
NYTBR-D 2 '73-p2
NYTBR-O 13 '74-p46
New R-v169-O 20 '73-p27
Obs-Ap 28 '74-p36
PW-v204-Jl 16 '73-p106
SR-v2-Ag 28 '73-p39
TLS-Ap 26 '74-p440
Time-v102-O 1 '73-p114

* * *

HELLNER, Katarina
Joan Is Angry
Sch Lib-v28-S '80-p259
Joan Is Happy
Sch Lib-v28-S '80-p259

HELLNER, Katarina (continued)
Joan Is Sad
Sch Lib-v28-S '80-p259
Joan Is Scared
Sch Lib-v28-S '80-p259

* * *

HELLSING, Lennart
The Wonderful Pumpkin
BL-v73-N 15 '76-p472
CCB-B-v31-N '77-p48
CSM-v69-N 2 '77-pB8
HB-v53-F '77-p38
KR-v44-O 1 '76-p1089
SLJ-v23-O '76-p99

* * *

HELMERING, Doris Wild
I Have Two Families
BL-v77-Mr 15 '81-p1028
CBRS-v9-Mr '81-p65
CE-v58-Mr '82-p257
SLJ-v28-S '81-p108
We're Going To Have A Baby
Cur R-v18-F '79-p21
Inst-v87-My '78-p118
KR-v46-F 15 '78-p174
PW-v213-Ja 2 '78-p64
SE-v44-Mr '80-p246
SLJ-v25-S '78-p116

* * *

HELWEG, Hans
Farm Animals
Inst-v90-Ja '81-p116

* * *

HEMBLEN, Katie
The Night Sky/Ciel De Nuit
BIC-v9-D '80-p19
The Night Sky/Le Ciel De Nuit
Can Child Lit-#25 '82-p75

* * *

HEMINGWAY, Ernest
The Faithful Bull
JB-v45-Je '81-p107
El Toro Fiel
BL-v80-N 1 '83-p425

* * *

HEMMING, James
Sex And Love
ACSB-v8-Spring '75-p22
BL-v70-My 1 '74-p994
LJ-v99-My 15 '74-p1495
SLJ-v21-Mr '75-p105

* * *

HEMMING, Roy
Discovering Music
CC-v91-N 20 '74-p1103
CCB-B-v28-Mr '75-p114
CLW-v46-Ap '75-p405
KR-v42-N 1 '74-p1164

* * *

HEMPHILL, Charles F, Jr.
Famous Phrases From History
ARBA-v14-'83-p39
WLB-v57-N '82-p251

* * *

HEMPHILL, E
Your First Book Of Herb Gardening
JB-v45-Je '81-p115
TLS-N 21 '80-p1332

* * *

HENBEST, Nigel
Astronomy
JB-v47-Ag '83-p160
Physics
B Rpt-v3-My '84-p49
Cur R-v24-N '84-p79
JB-v47-Ag '83-p164
SLJ-v30-F '84-p72
TES-Ja 20 '84-p30
Physics Matter
CBRS-v12-Ap '84-p96

* * *

HENDERSON, Bruce
We Live In U.S.A.
TES-Mr 12 '82-p33

* * *

HENDERSON, Edmund H
Houghton Mifflin Spelling 1-6
Cur R-v21-Ag '82-p290

* * *

HENDERSON, Gordon
Sandy MacKenzie, Why Look So Glum?
Can Child Lit-#23 '81-p108
In Rev-v14-Ap '80-p44

* * *

HENDERSON, Jennifer
The Snowman
GP-v16-My '77-p3120
JB-v41-Je '77-p177
TLS-Mr 25 '77-p361

* * *

HENDERSON, John
Colour Book One
GP-v20-N '81-p3982
JB-v46-Ap '82-p61
TES-Ja 15 '82-p34
TLS-N 20 '81-p1360
Number Book One
GP-v20-N '81-p3982
JB-v46-Ap '82-p61
TES-Ja 15 '82-p34
TLS-N 20 '81-p1360
Picture Book One
GP-v20-N '81-p3982
JB-v46-Ap '82-p61
TES-Ja 15 '82-p34
TLS-N 20 '81-p1360

* * *

HENDERSON, Nancy
Celebrate America
SLJ-v25-Ap '79-p56
Janet Climbs
SLJ-v25-Ja '79-p51
Walk Together
CCB-B-v26-Mr '73-p106
KR-v40-Ag 15 '72-p952
LJ-v98-Ja 15 '73-p260
Teacher-v90-My '73-p64

* * *

HENDERSON, Nancy Wallace
Circle Of Life
BL-v71-N 1 '74-p290
KR-v42-S 15 '74-p1009
SLJ-v21-Ja '75-p45

* * *

HENDERSON, W F
Looking At Australia
BL-v73-My 1 '77-p1349
GP-v15-Ap '77-p3090
JB-v41-Ag '77-p222
SLJ-v24-D '77-p48
SLJ-v24-Ja '78-p26
TES-Ja 27 '78-p26

* * *

HENDRA, Judith
The Illustrated Treasury Of Humor For Children
NY-v56-D 1 '80-p220
PW-v218-D 5 '80-p53
The Illustrated Treasury Of Humour For Children
GP-v20-Mr '82-p4042
JB-v46-Ap '82-p67

HENDRA, Judith (continued)
TES-D 4 '81-p31

* * *

HENDRICH, Paula
The Girl Who Slipped Through Time
KR-v46-Ap 1 '78-p375
SLJ-v24-Mr '78-p129
Who Says So?
CCB-B-v26-D '72-p56
KR-v40-Mr 1 '72-p259
LJ-v98-F 15 '73-p644

* * *

HENDRICKSON, Walter B, Jr.
Manned Spacecraft To Mars And Venus
ACSB-v9-Spring '76-p23
HB-v51-Ag '75-p398
KR-v43-F 15 '75-p183
SB-v12-My '76-p32
SLJ-v21-Ap '75-p65
Who Really Invented The Rocket?
ACSB-v8-Winter '75-p20
BL-v71-S 1 '74-p41
KR-v42-Ap 15 '74-p429
LJ-v99-D 15 '74-p3272
SB-v10-D '74-p239

* * *

HENDRIX, Sue
Dwight Eisenhower: Planner, Leader, And President
SLJ-v22-S '75-p95

* * *

HENDRY, Diana
Midnight Pirate
GP-My '84-p4265
Sch Lib-v32-Je '84-p133
TLS-Mr 30 '84-p337

* * *

HENDRY, P G
Vintage And Veteran Cars
CCB-B-v28-S '74-p9
LJ-v99-S 15 '74-p2291

* * *

HENEGHAN, James
Puffin Rock
Atl Pro Bk R-v10-N '83-p6
BIC-v9-F '80-p23
Can Child Lit-#17 '80-p77
In Rev-v14-Je '80-p41

* * *

HENKEL, Cathy
Mary Decker: America's Nike
BL-v80-Ag '84-p1631

* * *

HENKES, Kevin
All Alone
CBRS-v10-Ja '82-p41
KR-v49-D 15 '81-p1517
NY-v57-D 7 '81-p228
PW-v220-D 18 '81-p70
RT-v35-Ja '82-p496
SLJ-v28-S '81-p108
Clean Enough
CBRS-v10-Ap '82-p82
JB-v47-D '83-p236
SLJ-v29-O '82-p141
TES-D 9 '83-p35
Margaret & Taylor
CCB-B-v37-Mr '84-p127
KR-v51-S 1 '83-pJ162
PW-v224-N 11 '83-p47
SLJ-v30-F '84-p72
Return To Sender
BL-v80-Je 1 '84-p1398
CBRS-v12-Jl '84-p138
CCB-B-v38-S '84-p7
KR-v52-My 1 '84-pJ39
SLJ-v31-S '84-p118

* * *

HENLEY, Alix
The Seven Of Us
JB-v42-O '78-p254
Sch Lib-v27-Mr '79-p64
TES-Je 23 '78-p19
TLS-Jl 7 '78-p774

* * *

HENLEY, Karyn
Hatch!
ASBYP-v14-Winter '81-p33
BL-v76-My 15 '80-p1370
Inst-v92-Ap '83-p20
SB-v16-N '80-p94
SLJ-v26-My '80-p83

* * *

HENNELL, Thomas
Lady Filmy Fern
BM-v123-Ja '81-p62
Brit Bk N C-Autumn '80-p11
Lis-v104-N 6 '80-p627
Obs-D 7 '80-p31
Punch-v279-S 24 '80-p520
SLJ-v27-My '81-p65
TES-Ja 16 '81-p27

* * *

HENNINGS, George
Keep Earth Clean, Blue And Green
Inst-v86-Ja '77-p143
SB-v13-My '77-p39

* * *

HENNY Penny (Byer)
SLJ-v29-O '82-p136

* * *

HENRIE, Fiona
Cats
JB-v44-D '80-p291
SLJ-v28-S '81-p108
TES-Ja 16 '81-p27
Dogs
JB-v45-F '81-p19
SLJ-v28-S '81-p108
TES-Ja 16 '81-p27
Fish
BL-v77-Ap 15 '81-p1153
Sch Lib-v29-Je '81-p146
Gerbils
SLJ-v28-S '81-p108
Sch Lib-v29-Mr '81-p39
Guinea Pigs
BL-v77-My 1 '81-p1197
SLJ-v28-O '81-p130
Hamsters
BL-v77-My 1 '81-p1197
JB-v45-Je '81-p115
Mice And Rats
BL-v77-My 1 '81-p1197
SLJ-v28-O '81-p130
Rabbits
SLJ-v28-S '81-p108

* * *

HENRIE, Jacqueline
Leonardo Da Vinci
GP-v16-Mr '78-p3272
Marie Curie
GP-v17-My '78-p3337

* * *

HENRIOD, Lorraine
Ancestor Hunting
SLJ-v26-F '80-p56
Grandma's Wheelchair
CBRS-v10-Ap '82-p85
CT-v11-Jl '82-p36
Inter BC-v13-#4 '82-p6
SB-v18-N '82-p89
SLJ-v28-My '82-p53
I Know A Grocer
KR-v37-D 15 '69-p1318

HENSTRA, Friso (continued)
KR-v46-O 1 '78-p1066
PW-v214-N 20 '78-p60
SLJ-v25-N '78-p45

* * *

HENTOFF, Nat
The Day They Came To Arrest The Book
AB-v70-N 15 '82-p3408
BL-v79-S 15 '82-p105
BS-v42-Ja '83-p406
BW-v12-N 7 '82-p18
CBRS-v11-D '82-p36
CCB-B-v36-S '82-p11
HB-v58-D '82-p657
Inter BC-v14-#6 '83-p18
KR-v50-S 15 '82-p1060
Kliatt-v18-Winter '84-p12
NYTBR-v88-Mr 6 '83-p30
NYTBR-v88-S 25 '83-p39
PW-v222-S 10 '82-p76
PW-v224-Ag 26 '83-p386
SE-v47-Ap '83-p249
SLJ-v29-O '82-p161
TES-N 2 '84-p24
VOYA-v5-F '83-p36
Does This School Have Capital Punishment?
BL-v77-Ap 15 '81-p1147
BS-v41-S '81-p239
BW-v11-Ag 9 '81-p8
BW-v13-Je 12 '83-p12
CBRS-v9-Ap '81-p77
CCB-B-v35-S '81-p10
CSM-v73-Jl 1 '81-p18
HB-v57-Ag '81-p432
J Read-v25-F '82-p486
KR-v49-Ap 1 '81-p437
Kliatt-v17-Fall '83-p11
LATBR-Ag 7 '83-p6
NYTBR-v86-Jl 26 '81-p13
PW-v219-F 13 '81-p94
PW-v223-Je 3 '83-p73
SLJ-v27-My '81-p74
TN-v38-Summer '82-p364
WLB-v55-Mr '81-p530
I'm Really Dragged But Nothing Gets Me Down
BS-v28-O 1 '68-p277
CCB-B-v22-Ja '69-p78
EJ-v58-My '69-p776
KR-v36-S 15 '68-p1059
LJ-v93-N 15 '68-p4414
LJ-v96-Ja 15 '71-p282
NYTBR-v73-N 3 '68-p2
NYTBR, pt.2-F 15 '70-p22
PW-v194-S 2 '68-p59
PW-v196-S 29 '69-p60
SR-v51-S 7 '68-p34
SR-v51-N 9 '68-p71
Time-v92-O 11 '68-pE8
In The Country Of Ourselves
BL-v68-Ja 1 '72-p391
BL-v68-Ja 1 '72-p393
CCB-B-v25-Ja '72-p74
CLW-v43-Ap '72-p469
KR-v39-O 1 '71-p1080
LJ-v96-D 15 '71-p4190
NYTBR, pt.2-N 7 '71-p3
PW-v200-N 1 '71-p55
SR-v55-Ja 15 '72-p47
Jazz Country
AB-v40-S 25 '67-p1096
BL-v61-Jl 1 '65-p1025
BS-v25-My 15 '65-p98
CCB-B-v18-Je '65-p150
CSM-v57-Je 24 '65-p7
Comw-v82-My 28 '65-p330
HB-v41-O '65-p517
KR-v33-Mr 1 '65-p252
LJ-v90-My 15 '65-p2418
LJ-v96-Ja 15 '71-p282
ND-v14-Je '65-p52
NO-v4-Jl 12 '65-p21
NYTBR-v70-My 9 '65-p3
NYTBR-v72-N 5 '67-p54
NYTBR-v73-F 25 '68-p20
Obs-Ag 7 '66-p21
PW-v192-Jl 10 '67-p188
SR-v50-Ja 28 '67-p45
Spec-Je 3 '66-p705
TLS-My 19 '66-p442
TN-v38-Summer '82-p364
This School Is Driving Me Crazy
BL-v72-O 15 '75-p302
CCB-B-v29-Ja '76-p78
Inst-v85-My '76-p124
JB-v42-Je '78-p155
KR-v43-N 15 '75-p1296
Kliatt-v12-Fall '78-p9
NO-v15-F 28 '76-p21
Obs-D 11 '77-p31
PW-v209-Ja 5 '76-p65
SLJ-v22-F '76-p53
TES-Ja 20 '78-p23
TLS-Ap 7 '78-p382

* * *

HENWOOD, Kay
Baron Battleaxe And The Magic Carpet
B&B-v22-D '76-p78
GP-v20-Ja '82-p4017
JB-v41-Ag '77-p211
The Magic Carpet Adventure
GP-v20-Ja '82-p4017
TLS-D 5 '75-p1453

* * *

HERBERT, Don
Mr. Wizard's Supermarket Science
ASBYP-v14-Spring '81-p20
BL-v77-F 1 '81-p752
BL-v80-O 15 '83-p369
CBRS-v9-Ja '81-p37
Cur R-v20-Ap '81-p192
SB-v17-S '81-p31

* * *

HERBERT, Ivor
Longacre
GP-v17-Ja '79-p3440

* * *

HERBERT, Mike
Mike Schmidt: The Human Vacuum Cleaner
BL-v80-Ja 15 '84-p754
SLJ-v30-F '84-p72

* * *

HERBERT, S
Diamonds
JB-v45-F '81-p28
TES-Mr 6 '81-p37

* * *

HERBERT, Wally
Eskimos
BL-v74-S 15 '77-p155
BL-v74-S 15 '77-p194
Cur R-v17-Ag '78-p185
GP-v15-Ap '77-p3090
JB-v41-Je '77-p178
SE-v42-Ap '78-p319
SLJ-v24-S '77-p144

* * *

HERBST, Judith
Sky Above And Worlds Beyond
BL-v80-N 15 '83-p497
BW-v14-My 13 '84-p16
CCB-B-v37-Mr '84-p128
KR-v51-Je 1 '83-p623
Learning-v12-Ap '84-p77
NY-v59-D 5 '83-p207
SB-v19-Mr '84-p216
SLJ-v30-S '83-p135

HERMES, Patricia (continued)
KR-v51-Je 15 '83-p660
SE-v48-My '84-p381
SLJ-v30-O '83-p158
You Shouldn't Have To Say Good-Bye
BL-v79-N 15 '82-p445
CBRS-v11-Ap '83-p94
CCB-B-v36-Mr '83-p127
Inst-v92-N '82-p151
J Read-v26-My '83-p742
KR-v50-N 1 '82-p1192
NYTBR-v89-My 20 '84-p29
PW-v225-Je 8 '84-p64
SE-v47-Ap '83-p252
SLJ-v29-F '83-p76
VOYA-v6-O '83-p203

* * *

HERODOTUS
Stories From Herodotus
BL-v62-N 1 '65-p272
CCB-B-v19-Ap '66-p128
CSM-v57-My 6 '65-p9B
CW-v59-N '65-p77
HB-v41-Je '65-p288
KR-v33-F 1 '65-p119
LJ-v90-F 15 '65-p960
NYTBR-v70-My 9 '65-p36

* * *

HEROLD, Ann B
The Helping Day
BL-v77-S 1 '80-p44
CBRS-v9-S '80-p2
CCB-B-v34-D '80-p72
KR-v48-S 1 '80-p1158
PW-v218-Jl 11 '80-p91
SLJ-v27-Mr '81-p132

* * *

HEROLD, J Christopher
Battle Of Waterloo
BL-v63-Jl 1 '67-p1147
BS-v27-Je 1 '67-p106
CCB-B-v21-Je '68-p160
HB-v43-Ag '67-p488
KR-v35-Ap 15 '67-p511
LJ-v92-Je 15 '67-p2460
NS-v73-My 26 '67-p730
NYTBR-v72-My 21 '67-p30
NYTBR-v72-N 5 '67-p64
PW-v191-Je 5 '67-p177
TLS-My 25 '67-p462

* * *

HERON, Ann
One Teenager In Ten
BL-v80-S 1 '83-p36
Inter BC-v14-#7 '83-p35
Ms-v12-Jl '83-p101
PW-v223-Ap 15 '83-p45
SLJ-v30-O '83-p168
VOYA-v6-Je '83-p77
VOYA-v6-O '83-p227

* * *

HERRICK, Robert
Poems
CCB-B-v21-My '68-p143

* * *

HERRIOT, James
Moses The Kitten
B&B-N '84-p23
CBRS-v13-S '84-p9
CSM-v76-S 7 '84-pB5
PW-v226-Jl 20 '84-p81

* * *

HERRMANN, Frank
The Giant Alexander
CCB-B-v19-O '65-p33
CE-v42-F '66-p374
HB-v41-O '65-p498
Inst-v75-N '65-p94
KR-v33-Jl 1 '65-p620
LJ-v90-S 15 '65-p3780
SR-v48-S 18 '65-p111
The Giant Alexander And Hannibal The Elephant
CCB-B-v26-N '72-p42
KR-v40-Mr 1 '72-p255
LJ-v97-S 15 '72-p2934
NS-v83-Je 2 '72-p762
PW-v201-Mr 6 '72-p62
TLS-D 3 '71-p1520
Giant Alexander And The Circus
CCB-B-v20-F '67-p90
CE-v43-My '67-p537
HB-v43-F '67-p57
KR-v34-N 1 '66-p1134
LJ-v92-F 15 '67-p872
PW-v190-O 24 '66-p51
Punch-v251-N 16 '66-p755
TLS-N 24 '66-p1088
The Giant Alexander In America
BL-v65-My 1 '69-p1016
BW-v3-Je 22 '69-p12
CCB-B-v23-O '69-p25
NS-v77-My 16 '69-p703
NYTBR-v73-N 3 '68-p67
SR-v52-F 22 '69-p46

* * *

HERRMANNS, Ralph
Children Of The North Pole
CCB-B-v18-Mr '65-p103
En Busca Del Abominable Hombre De Las Nieves
BL-v72-My 15 '76-p1343
River Boy: Adventure On The Amazon
CCB-B-v19-F '66-p99
CSM-v57-N 11 '65-p13
HB-v42-F '66-p75
LJ-v90-O 15 '65-p4615
NYTBR-v70-D 12 '65-p26
SR-v48-N 13 '65-p59

* * *

HERSCHELL, William
Crispin
GP-v14-Mr '76-p2830
TLS-D 5 '75-p1455

* * *

HERSON, Kathleen
Johnny Oswaldtwistle
JB-v42-F '78-p26
TLS-D 2 '77-p1412
Maybe It's A Tiger
Brit Bk N C-Spring '82-p2
JB-v46-F '82-p16
Sch Lib-v29-D '81-p319
TES-D 18 '81-p18
TES-Mr 12 '82-p38
TES-Jl 22 '83-p21
The Spitting Image
GP-v21-Ja '83-p4007
JB-v47-F '83-p42
Sch Lib-v30-D '82-p359

* * *

HERSTEIN, Rosaline
Time Out For Art
Cur R-v17-O '78-p294

* * *

HERTER, Jonina
88 Kisses
SLJ-v25-F '79-p42

* * *

HERTZ, Grete Janus
Hi, Daddy, Here I Am
CCB-B-v19-N '65-p45
LJ-v90-F 15 '65-p953
The Yellow House
Quill & Q-v49-F '83-p36

* * *

HERTZ, Ole
Tobias Catches Trout
BL-v80-Ag '84-p1626
CBRS-v12-Ag '84-p145
CCB-B-v38-S '84-p7
SLJ-v31-S '84-p104
Tobias Goes Ice Fishing
BL-v80-Ag '84-p1626
CBRS-v12-Ag '84-p145
SLJ-v31-S '84-p104
Tobias Goes Seal Hunting
BL-v80-Ag '84-p1626
CBRS-v12-Ag '84-p145
LA-v61-O '84-p629
SLJ-v31-S '84-p104
Tobias Has A Birthday
BL-v80-Ag '84-p1626
CBRS-v12-Ag '84-p145
LA-v61-O '84-p629
SLJ-v31-S '84-p104

* * *

HERTZER, Linda
Traditional Crafts
GP-v19-N '80-p3796

* * *

HERVE, Alain
Animal-Man
LA-v54-My '77-p578

* * *

HERZ, Grete J
Flowerpot Gardening
GP-v19-My '80-p3705

* * *

HERZ, Irene
Hey! Don't Do That!
BB-v7-Je '79-p2
BL-v75-F 1 '79-p866
CBRS-v7-F '79-p62
Inst-v88-My '79-p106
KR-v47-F 1 '79-p121
SLJ-v25-Ap '79-p44

* * *

HERZ, Peggy
The Mork And Mindy Story
CLW-v53-D '81-p228
TV Talk
SLJ-v23-O '76-p107
TV Talk 2
SLJ-v23-My '77-p62
TV Talk 3
CLW-v53-D '81-p228
TV Time '79
CLW-v53-D '81-p228
Inst-v88-My '79-p114
TV's Fabulous Faces
CLW-v53-D '81-p228
The Truth About Fonzie
SLJ-v24-S '77-p130

* * *

HERZIG, Alison
A Word To The Wise
CCB-B-v32-Mr '79-p118
KR-v47-Ja 1 '79-p5
SLJ-v25-S '78-p138

* * *

HERZIG, Alison C
Oh, Boy! Babies!
BL-v77-N 15 '80-p459
BW-v11-My 10 '81-p10
CCB-B-v34-F '81-p112
CE-v58-S '81-p50
CSM-v73-D 22 '80-p14
Cha Ti-v36-Je '82-p60
Inter BC-v13-#2 '82-p35
KR-v49-F 15 '81-p217
NYTBR-v85-D 14 '80-p36
SLJ-v27-D '80-p59
VOYA-v4-Je '81-p43
A Season Of Secrets
BL-v79-O 15 '82-p312
CBRS-v11-F '83-p70
CCB-B-v36-D '82-p70
Inter BC-v15-#5 '84-p16
KR-v50-Ag 1 '82-p871
PW-v222-D 24 '82-p64
SE-v47-Ap '83-p251
SLJ-v29-N '82-p85
VOYA-v6-Ap '83-p37

* * *

HERZKA, Heinz
Robin In Red Boots
CCB-B-v24-Jl '70-p179
CSM-v62-My 7 '70-pB3
KR-v38-F 15 '70-p169
LJ-v95-My 15 '70-p1929
NYTBR, pt.2-My 24 '70-p46

* * *

HERZOG, Barbara
My Mother Goose Menagerie
RT-v37-My '84-p889
The 3 Bears And I
RT-v37-My '84-p890

* * *

HESKETH, Phoebe
A Song Of Sunlight
LR-v24-Summer '74-p274
Lis-v92-N 7 '74-p617
NS-v87-My 24 '74-p742
Obs-Je 2 '74-p33
TLS-Jl 5 '74-p717

* * *

HESKY, Olga
The Sequin Syndicate
BS-v29-Ap 15 '69-p32
HB-v45-Je '69-p328
LJ-v94-Ap 1 '69-p1526
LJ-v95-F 15 '70-p742
NYTBR, pt.1-My 4 '69-p32
Obs-Ap 13 '69-p28
PW-v195-F 3 '69-p59
Punch-v256-Ap 16 '69-p583

* * *

HESLEWOOD, Juliet
Tales Of Sea And Shore
JB-v48-Ap '84-p84
Sch Lib-v32-Mr '84-p46
TES-D 30 '83-p22

* * *

HESS, Lilo
The Amazing Earthworm
ACSB-v12-Fall '79-p31
BL-v75-Ap 15 '79-p1295
CCB-B-v32-Je '79-p176
CE-v56-Ap '80-p308
Cur R-v19-Je '80-p267
HB-v55-Je '79-p337
KR-v47-Mr 1 '79-p265
LA-v56-N '79-p929
RT-v33-D '79-p359
SB-v15-My '80-p279
SLJ-v26-N '79-p65
Bird Companions
ASBYP-v15-Fall '82-p25
BL-v78-S 1 '81-p46
CCB-B-v35-N '81-p46
HB-v57-O '81-p552
Inst-v91-Ap '82-p22
SLJ-v28-N '81-p92
A Cat's Nine Lives
BL-v80-Je 1 '84-p1398
CCB-B-v37-My '84-p165
HB-v60-Je '84-p349
KR-v52-My 1 '84-pJ45
PW-v225-Ap 13 '84-p71
SLJ-v30-Ag '84-p74
The Curious Raccoons
CE-v46-N '69-p98
HB-v45-F '69-p68
KR-v36-S 1 '68-p981
LJ-v93-N 15 '68-p4394
NYTBR-v73-N 3 '68-p53
SB-v4-Mr '69-p302

HESS, Lilo (continued)
Diary Of A Rabbit
ASBYP-v16-Winter '83-p31
BL-v78-My 15 '82-p1257
HB-v58-Je '82-p307
SB-v18-N '82-p92
A Dog By Your Side
BL-v74-S 1 '77-p41
KR-v45-Je 1 '77-p578
RT-v32-D '78-p364
SLJ-v24-N '77-p57
Life Begins For Puppies
BL-v74-Je 15 '78-p1617
CCB-B-v32-N '78-p44
HB-v55-O '78-p541
Inst-v88-N '78-p133
KR-v46-Je 1 '78-p597
SLJ-v25-Ja '79-p43
Listen To Your Kitten Purr
BL-v76-Ap 1 '80-p1128
CLW-v52-O '80-p133
HB-v56-Je '80-p312
KR-v48-Ap 15 '80-p515
PW-v217-Mr 7 '80-p90
SLJ-v27-O '80-p146
Making Friends With Guinea Pigs
BL-v79-Ag '83-p1465
SB-v19-Ja '84-p161
SLJ-v30-S '83-p123
Monkeys And Apes Without Trees
HB-v49-O '73-p479
KR-v41-F 1 '73-p120
LJ-v98-O 15 '73-p3146
NYTBR-My 27 '73-p8
Mouse And Company
CCB-B-v26-S '72-p8
CE-v49-Ap '73-p378
KR-v40-Mr 15 '72-p329
LJ-v97-My 15 '72-p1913
SA-v227-D '72-p112
SB-v8-S '72-p156
TLS-Ap 6 '73-p390
A Pony To Love
BL-v71-Jl 1 '75-p1127
CCB-B-v29-N '75-p46
KR-v43-My 15 '75-p571
PW-v207-My 26 '75-p60
SLJ-v22-S '75-p104
Teacher-v95-My '78-p21
A Puppy For You
BB-v5-Mr '77-p1
BL-v73-N 15 '76-p472
KR-v44-S 1 '76-p977
SLJ-v23-N '76-p59
Teacher-v95-My '78-p20
Remarkable Chameleon
BL-v64-Je 1 '68-p1142
CCB-B-v21-Je '68-p159
Inst-v78-Ag '68-p190
KR-v36-My 1 '68-p514
LJ-v93-Je 15 '68-p2539
NYTBR-v73-My 5 '68-p50
SR-v51-My 11 '68-p39
TLS-N 3 '72-p1336
Sea Horses
BL-v62-Jl 15 '66-p1087
CCB-B-v21-N '67-p43
CLW-v38-N '66-p212
HB-v42-Ag '66-p451
KR-v34-Ap 1 '66-p374
LJ-v91-Jl '66-p3535
NYTBR-v71-My 8 '66-p43
PW-v189-My 30 '66-p89
SA-v215-D '66-p142
SB-v2-S '66-p130
SR-v49-My 14 '66-p41
TLS-Jl 2 '71-p778
Small Habitats
ACSB-v10-Winter '77-p22
BL-v72-Jl 1 '76-p1526
CCB-B-v30-N '76-p43
KR-v44-Ap 15 '76-p476
RT-v31-O '77-p22
SLJ-v23-S '76-p117
A Snail's Pace
ACSB-v8-Spring '75-p23
BL-v70-Mr 1 '74-p741
CCB-B-v27-Je '74-p158
CSM-v66-My 1 '74-pF5
CSM-v67-Je 10 '75-p17
Inst-v83-My '74-p91
KR-v42-Ja 15 '74-p56
LJ-v99-My 15 '74-p1473
PW-v205-F 18 '74-p74
SA-v231-D '74-p158
SB-v10-D '74-p257

* * *

HESSE, Hermann
If The War Goes On
B&B-v17-S '72-p97
BL-v68-O 15 '71-p177
BL-v68-N 1 '71-p240
BS-v31-Je 1 '71-p107
GW-v107-Ag 5 '72-p19
HB-v48-Ag '72-p393
KR-v39-Ap 1 '71-p426
LJ-v96-Je 15 '71-p2090
Obs-Jl 16 '72-p30
PW-v199-Ap 12 '71-p84
TLS-Ag 31 '73-p990
Knulp
B&B-v18-O '72-p36
BL-v68-N 1 '71-p231
CSM-v64-Ja 6 '72-p13
GW-v107-Ag 5 '72-p19
HB-v48-Ag '72-p393
LJ-v96-N 1 '71-p3638
Obs-Je 18 '72-p32
PW-v199-Je 28 '71-p61
PW-v200-O 25 '71-p51
TLS-Ag 31 '73-p990
Strange News From Another Star
Ant R-v32-Je '73-p498
BS-v32-Jl 15 '72-p193
Choice-v9-Ja '73-p1452
HB-v48-Ag '72-p393
KR-v40-Ap 15 '72-p501
LJ-v97-Ag '72-p2643
LJ-v98-F 15 '73-p660
Nat R-v24-Je 23 '72-p701
PW-v201-My 8 '72-p46
TLS-Ag 31 '73-p990
Wandering
B&B-v18-F '73-p101
BS-v31-Mr 1 '72-p538
CSM-v64-My 4 '72-pB6
HB-v48-Ag '72-p393
KR-v40-F 1 '72-p190
LJ-v97-Ap 15 '72-p1437
NS-v84-N 17 '72-p732
PW-v201-Ja 31 '72-p238
TLS-Ag 31 '73-p990
VQR-v48-Summer '72-pR106

* * *

HESSE, K A
Basic Arithmetic Practice 5
TES-Mr 9 '84-p46
The Four Rules Of Number
TES-Mr 11 '83-p49
Hesse Graded Workbook. No. 6
TES-Mr 10 '78-p54
An Introduction To Decimals
TES-Mr 10 '78-p54
An Introduction To First Problems
TES-Mr 11 '83-p49

* * *

HESSELBERG, Erik
Kon-Tiki And I
BL-v67-O 15 '70-p198
CCB-B-v24-N '70-p43
NYTBR-S 13 '70-p42
NYTBR, pt.2-N 8 '70-p38

HESSELBERG, Erik (continued)
PW-v198-Jl 20 '70-p70

* * *

HEST, Amy
The Crack-Of-Dawn Walkers
BL-v80-Ap 15 '84-p1190
CBRS-v12-My '84-p101
CCB-B-v37-Ap '84-p148
HB-v60-Je '84-p319
NYTBR-v89-My 13 '84-p20
PW-v225-F 24 '84-p140
Par-v59-N '84-p53
SLJ-v30-Ag '84-p60
Maybe Next Year...
BL-v79-S 1 '82-p43
CBRS-v11-F '83-p70
CCB-B-v36-F '83-p109
HB-v58-D '82-p649
PW-v222-N 5 '82-p70
SLJ-v29-N '82-p86

* * *

HESTWOOD, Diana L
Word Problems
Cur R-v21-O '82-p419

* * *

HETZER, Linda
Designer Crafts
SLJ-v25-N '78-p63
Hobby Crafts
SLJ-v25-N '78-p63
Playtime Crafts
SLJ-v25-N '78-p63
Workshop Crafts
SLJ-v25-N '78-p63
Yarn Crafts
Inst-v88-Ja '79-p135
SLJ-v25-N '78-p63

* * *

HEUCK, Sigrid
The Pony, The Bear And The Parrot
GP-v23-S '84-p4319
TES-Je 8 '84-p51
The Pony, The Bear And The Stolen Apples
GP-v16-Ap '78-p3295
JB-v42-F '78-p17
Spec-v239-D 10 '77-p24
TES-N 18 '77-p39
The Stolen Apples
BL-v75-My 15 '79-p1439

* * *

HEUMAN, William
The Goofer Pitch
CCB-B-v22-Je '69-p159
KR-v37-Mr 1 '69-p237
LJ-v94-My 15 '69-p2125
PW-v195-Ap 21 '69-p66
SR-v52-Je 28 '69-p38
Home Run Henri
CCB-B-v24-O '70-p26
KR-v38-My 15 '70-p552
LJ-v95-My 15 '70-p1963
Little League Hotshots
Inter BC-v14-#1 '83-p16
LJ-v97-My 15 '72-p1929

* * *

HEUSER, Edith
This Is How My Body Works
BW-v12-My 9 '82-p12

* * *

HEWARD, Constance
Ameliaranne And The Green Umbrella
TLS-D 6 '74-p1384

* * *

HEWES, Jeremy Joan
Build Your Own Playground
BL-v71-F 1 '75-p540
BL-v72-D 15 '75-p562
BW-Jl 13 '75-p4
Inst-v85-Ag '75-p206

* * *

HEWETT, Anita
The Anita Hewett Animal Story Book
TLS-D 8 '72-p1499
TLS-D 6 '74-p1384

* * *

HEWETT, Hilda
Harriet And The Cherry Pie
CCB-B-v18-Mr '65-p103
CLW-v36-F '65-p413

* * *

HEWETT, Joan
Fly Away Free
ACSB-v15-Winter '82-p29
SLJ-v28-N '81-p76
The Mouse And The Elephant
HB-v53-D '77-p654
KR-v45-S 15 '77-p985
SLJ-v24-N '77-p48
Watching Them Grow
ACSB-v13-Mr '80-p27
BL-v76-N 15 '79-p504
BOT-v2-D '79-p599
CCB-B-v33-F '80-p110
CLW-v51-My '80-p460
HB-v56-F '80-p85
KR-v48-F 1 '80-p130
PW-v216-D 10 '79-p69
SB-v16-S '80-p35
SLJ-v26-D '79-p86

* * *

HEWISH, Mark
The Young Scientist Book Of Jets
ACSB-v13-Spring '80-p38
SLJ-v25-Ap '79-p56

* * *

HEWITT, Garnet
Ytek And The Arctic Orchid
BL-v78-Mr 1 '82-p897
In Rev-v16-F '82-p39
PW-v220-N 27 '81-p88
Quill & Q-v48-Mr '82-p66
SLJ-v28-Ag '82-p117

* * *

HEWITT, James
What Makes A Camera Work?
GP-v16-N '77-p3212
JB-v42-F '78-p27

* * *

HEWITT, Kathryn
Two By Two
BL-v81-S 1 '84-p65

* * *

HEWITT, Marsha
One Proud Summer
Atl Pro Bk R-v10-N '83-p2
BIC-v10-D '81-p5
Can Child Lit-#29 '83-p45
In Rev-v16-F '82-p39

* * *

HEWITT, Philip
Looking At Russia
BL-v74-My 1 '78-p1431
NS-v94-N 4 '77-p629
SLJ-v24-Ap '78-p84

* * *

HEY, Nigel
How We Will Explore The Outer Planets
HB-v49-Je '73-p295
KR-v41-Ap 1 '73-p401
LJ-v98-S 15 '73-p2665

* * *

HEYDUCK-HUTH, Hilde
In The Forest
CSM-v67-S 22 '75-p22
Comw-v94-My 21 '71-p266
HB-v47-Je '71-p279
LJ-v96-S 15 '71-p2906
PW-v199-Mr 29 '71-p52
In The Meadow
JB-v41-Ap '77-p78
In The Village
CSM-v67-S 22 '75-p22
Comw-v94-My 21 '71-p266
HB-v47-Je '71-p279
LJ-v96-S 15 '71-p2906
PW-v199-Mr 29 '71-p52
The Red Spot
BL-v77-O 15 '80-p326
CBRS-v9-S '80-p2
JB-v44-Je '80-p119
SLJ-v27-D '80-p69
The Three Birds
CSM-v67-S 22 '75-p22
HB-v47-Je '71-p279
LJ-v96-S 15 '71-p2906
PW-v199-Mr 29 '71-p52
Wenn Die Sonne Scheint
BL-v75-N 15 '78-p554
When The Sun Shines
CSM-v67-S 22 '75-p22
HB-v47-Je '71-p279
LJ-v96-S 15 '71-p2906
PW-v199-Mr 29 '71-p52

* * *

HEYMAN, Anita
Exit From Home
BL-v73-Jl 1 '77-p1652
BS-v37-Ag '77-p142
CCB-B-v30-Je '77-p159
CE-v54-Ap '78-p305
Comw-v104-N 11 '77-p732
HB-v53-O '77-p540
J Read-v22-N '78-p183
J Read-v25-Ja '82-p354
KR-v45-My 15 '77-p543
LA-v54-N '77-p947
NYTBR-O 9 '77-p30
PW-v211-Je 27 '77-p111
Par-v52-S '77-p95
SLJ-v23-Ap '77-p76
Final Grades
BL-v80-O 1 '83-p233
B Rpt-v2-Ja '84-p34
BS-v43-D '83-p346
CBRS-v12-Ja '84-p52
CCB-B-v37-Ja '84-p89
J Read-v27-F '84-p467
KR-v51-N 1 '83-pJ203
SLJ-v30-N '83-p93
VOYA-v7-Ap '84-p32

* * *

HEYMANS, Annemie
The Fantastic Pillow
GP-v15-Jl '76-p2922
JB-v40-O '76-p263

* * *

HEYMANS, Margriet
Cats And Dolls
BB-v4-O '76-p1
BL-v72-Ap 15 '76-p1185
GP-v14-N '75-p2733
JB-v40-F '76-p13
KR-v44-Mr 1 '76-p251
NO-v15-Ag 21 '76-p16
NS-v90-N 28 '75-p688
NYTBR-My 2 '76-p48
New R-v175-N 27 '76-p31
Obs-O 12 '75-p31
PW-v209-Mr 15 '76-p57
SLJ-v22-My '76-p50
TLS-S 19 '75-p1054

* * *

HEYN, Jean
The Tessie C. Price
SLJ-v26-Ag '80-p64

* * *

HEYWARD, Du Bose
The Country Bunny And The Little Gold Shoes
RT-v36-Mr '83-p714

* * *

HIBBERT, Christopher
The Illustrated London News Social History Of Victorian Britain
GP-v14-D '75-p2763
The Search For King Arthur
B&B-v15-My '70-p40
BL-v66-My 1 '70-p1100
BS-v29-Mr 1 '70-p454
BW-v4-My 17 '70-p26
CCB-B-v24-Jl '70-p180
CSM-v62-My 2 '70-p17
LJ-v95-Jl '70-p2540
NS-v79-My 15 '70-p706
NYTBR-Mr 15 '70-p49
Obs-Jl 26 '70-p24
PW-v197-Ja 26 '70-p278
SR-v53-My 9 '70-p70
Spec-v224-My 9 '70-p622
TLS-Ap 16 '70-p424

* * *

HIBBERT, Margaret
Take A Walk, Johnny
Cur R-v21-F '82-p64

* * *

HIBOU
In Rev-v14-O '80-p44

* * *

HICHENS, Phoebe
All About Royal Food
GP-v21-Ja '83-p4021
All About Royal Palaces
GP-v21-Ja '83-p4021
All About Royal Travel
GP-v21-Ja '83-p4021

* * *

HICKMAN, Janet
The Stones
BL-v73-D 15 '76-p608
BS-v36-Mr '77-p386
CCB-B-v30-Mr '77-p107
HB-v53-F '77-p51
KR-v44-Jl 15 '76-p794
PW-v210-S 20 '76-p85
SLJ-v23-O '76-p107
The Thunder-Pup
BL-v78-N 15 '81-p438
CBRS-v10-O '81-p19
CCB-B-v35-D '81-p69
CE-v60-S '83-p52
CLW-v53-Ap '82-p402
HB-v58-F '82-p43
KR-v49-D 15 '81-p1519
SLJ-v28-N '81-p92
The Valley Of The Shadow
BL-v70-Jl 15 '74-p1253
HB-v50-Je '74-p286
KR-v42-My 1 '74-p489
Zoar Blue
BL-v75-N 1 '78-p479
CCB-B-v32-D '78-p62
CE-v56-O '79-p44
KR-v46-S 15 '78-p1021
Par-v53-O '78-p40
SLJ-v25-O '78-p155

* * *

HICKMAN, Martha W
I'm Moving
BB-v3-Ag '75-p2
BL-v71-Ap 1 '75-p817
BW-Jl 13 '75-p4
CE-v58-S '81-p37
SLJ-v21-Ap '75-p45

HICKMAN, Martha W (continued)
SR-v2-My 31 '75-p35
WLB-v50-S '75-p67
My Friend William Moved Away
BB-v7-N '79-p3
BL-v75-Ap 1 '79-p1218
CBRS-v7-Ap '79-p84
CCB-B-v32-Je '79-p176
CE-v58-S '81-p39
CLW-v51-F '80-p310
SLJ-v26-S '79-p112
The Reason I'm Not Quite Finished Tying My Shoes
CBRS-v9-Mr '81-p62
LA-v58-S '81-p699
PW-v219-Ja 16 '81-p80
SLJ-v28-O '81-p130
When Can Daddy Come Home?
Inter BC-v15-#3 '84-p19
SLJ-v30-S '83-p107

* * *

HICKS, Clifford B
Alvin Fernald, Foreign Trader
BL-v63-S 1 '66-p55
CCB-B-v20-O '66-p26
CSM-v58-S 1 '66-p13
Inst-v82-N '72-p136
KR-v34-Ap 1 '66-p371
LJ-v91-Je 15 '66-p3258
Alvin Fernald, Mayor For A Day
BL-v66-My 1 '70-p1102
CE-v47-Ja '71-p211
Comw-v92-My 22 '70-p247
GP-v14-O '75-p2721
GT-v89-F '72-p94
KR-v37-D 15 '69-p1316
LJ-v95-Je 15 '70-p2308
Lis-v94-N 6 '75-p625
NS-v90-N 7 '75-p587
PW-v197-Ja 19 '70-p81
TLS-S 19 '75-p1060
Alvin Fernald, Superweasel
KR-v42-Ap 15 '74-p425
LJ-v99-S 15 '74-p2269
Teacher-v95-My '78-p107
Alvin Fernald, TV Anchorman
BL-v77-N 15 '80-p459
KR-v48-N 1 '80-p1395
SLJ-v27-Mr '81-p145
Alvin's Secret Code
SLJ-v24-F '78-p35
Alvin's Swap Shop
BL-v73-F 15 '77-p897
BL-v76-Je 15 '80-p1544
CLW-v48-My '77-p443
GP-v17-Mr '79-p3468
KR-v44-N 15 '76-p1221
RT-v31-O '77-p18
RT-v31-Ap '78-p841
SLJ-v23-Ja '77-p92
Peter Potts
BL-v68-Mr 1 '72-p564
KR-v39-N 1 '71-p1155
LJ-v97-Ap 15 '72-p1605
PW-v200-D 13 '71-p43
PW-v215-Mr 26 '79-p82
The Wacky World Of Alvin Fernald
BL-v78-N 1 '81-p388
HB-v60-Je '84-p355
SLJ-v28-D '81-p64

* * *

HICKS, J L
A Closer Look At Arctic Lands
BL-v73-Je 15 '77-p1575
Cur R-v17-F '78-p3
SB-v14-My '78-p36
SLJ-v24-S '77-p130
A Closer Look At Birds
ACSB-v10-Spring '77-p23
B&B-v23-Ja '78-p63
Cur R-v17-F '78-p3
GP-v15-O '76-p2969
JB-v40-Ag '76-p200
SLJ-v23-Ap '77-p63
TLS-Jl 16 '76-p887

* * *

HICKSON, Joan
The Seven Sparrows And The Motor Car Picnic
GP-v20-Mr '82-p4037
JB-v46-Je '82-p93
SLJ-v29-Mr '83-p162
TLS-Mr 26 '82-p347

* * *

HICKSON, Joanna
Rebellion At Orford Castle
GP-v18-My '79-p3525
JB-v43-Ag '79-p220

* * *

HIEATT, Constance
The Castle Of Ladies
BL-v70-S 1 '73-p51
CCB-B-v27-N '73-p44
HB-v49-Ag '73-p375
KR-v41-Mr 15 '73-p321
LJ-v98-Jl '73-p2194
PW-v203-Ap 16 '73-p55
TN-v30-Ap '74-p308
The Joy Of The Court
BL-v67-Mr 15 '71-p619
CCB-B-v24-My '71-p136
HB-v47-Ap '71-p165
KR-v39-Ja 15 '71-p54
LJ-v96-Ap 15 '71-p1504
PW-v199-F 8 '71-p81
The Knight Of The Cart
BL-v66-D 15 '69-p516
CCB-B-v23-Ap '70-p129
Comw-v91-N 21 '69-p256
HB-v45-D '69-p671
KR-v37-O 1 '69-p1067
LJ-v95-Ja 15 '70-p242
NY-v45-D 13 '69-p198
The Knight Of The Lion
BL-v65-Ja 1 '69-p496
HB-v45-F '69-p49
KR-v36-S 15 '68-p1054
LJ-v93-N 15 '68-p4404
NYTBR-v73-O 20 '68-p38
SE-v33-My '69-p559
The Minstrel Knight
CCB-B-v28-D '74-p63
CE-v51-F '75-p216
HB-v50-Je '74-p276
KR-v42-Ja 15 '74-p56
LJ-v99-My 15 '74-p1473
PW-v206-D 9 '74-p68
Sir Gawain And The Green Knight
CCB-B-v21-My '68-p143
CE-v44-Mr '68-p444
HB-v43-Ag '67-p463
KR-v35-Ap 1 '67-p420
LJ-v92-Ap 15 '67-p1734
NYTBR-v72-Ap 16 '67-p22
NYTBR-v72-N 5 '67-p66
Trav-v24-Ja '68-p223
The Sword And The Grail
BL-v68-My 1 '72-p771
BW-v6-My 7 '72-p6
CCB-B-v26-S '72-p9
CE-v49-N '72-p85
HB-v48-Je '72-p266
KR-v40-Ja 15 '72-p71
LJ-v97-Ap 15 '72-p1605
NYTBR-Ag 20 '72-p8
NYTBR, pt.2-N 5 '72-p29

* * *

HIEBERT, Paul
For The Birds
In Rev-v15-Je '81-p37

* * *

HIGDON, Hal
Champions Of The Tennis Court
CCB-B-v25-My '72-p140
CSM-v63-N 11 '71-pB4
KR-v39-S 1 '71-p949
LJ-v96-D 15 '71-p4204
The Electronic Olympics
BL-v68-Ap 1 '72-p660
BL-v68-Ap 1 '72-p675
CCB-B-v25-F '72-p92
KR-v39-N 1 '71-p1155
LJ-v96-D 15 '71-p4200
SR-v55-Ap 22 '72-p86
Hitting, Pitching And Fielding
BB-v7-Mr '79-p3
SLJ-v25-D '78-p69
Johnny Rutherford
SLJ-v26-My '80-p88
The Last Series
BL-v71-D 15 '74-p425
CCB-B-v28-Ap '75-p131
KR-v42-O 1 '74-p1060
LJ-v99-D 15 '74-p3278
Showdown At Daytona
BL-v72-Jl 1 '76-p1527
KR-v44-My 15 '76-p596
SLJ-v23-S '76-p117
SLJ-v24-Mr '78-p107
Six Seconds To Glory
BL-v71-Jl 15 '75-p1191
KR-v43-My 1 '75-p517
SLJ-v22-S '75-p104
The Team That Played In The Space Bowl
CBRS-v10-Mr '82-p77
SLJ-v28-Mr '82-p148

* * *

HIGGINS, Don
I Am A Boy
CCB-B-v20-S '66-p12
I Am A Girl
CCB-B-v20-S '66-p12

* * *

HIGGINS, Dorothy
Ring Of Hades
CCB-B-v23-My '70-p145
KR-v37-D 1 '69-p1256
LJ-v95-Ap 15 '70-p1638

* * *

HIGGINS, James
Terribly Tough Tongue Twisters
LA-v55-N '78-p961
Tongue Twisters
LA-v55-N '78-p961

* * *

HIGGINS, Judith H
Energy
ACSB-v12-Fall '79-p32
ARBA-v11-'80-p647
BL-v75-Ap 15 '79-p1303
Cur R-v18-O '79-p291
SB-v15-D '79-p157
SLJ-v27-D '80-p22
WLB-v53-My '79-p653

* * *

HIGGINS, Muriel
Elementary Grammar
TES-N 18 '83-p39

* * *

HIGGINS, Reynold
The Archaeology Of Minoan Crete
B&B-v19-D '73-p96
BL-v70-N 15 '73-p334
CW-v69-S '75-p69
HB-v49-D '73-p602
Inst-v83-N '73-p129
KR-v41-Ag 1 '73-p822
LJ-v98-D 15 '73-p3712
Lis-v90-N 8 '73-p640
NY-v49-D 3 '73-p219
TLS-S 28 '73-p1119

* * *

HIGGINS, Stephanie
One, Two, Three
PW-v223-Ap 15 '83-p51

* * *

HIGGINS, Sydney
Tales Of Terror
Sch Lib-v29-Je '81-p127

* * *

HIGHAM, Charles
Life In The Old Stone Age
CCB-B-v31-My '78-p142
Cur R-v17-F '78-p4
SLJ-v24-Ap '78-p82
TLS-Jl 2 '71-p778

* * *

HIGHLIGHTS Book Of Nursery Rhymes
CE-v52-Ja '76-p154

* * *

HIGHLIGHTS For Children
BL-v79-F 1 '83-p730
CE-v59-My '83-p370
Mag Lib- '82-p216

* * *

HIGHTOWER, Florence
Dreamwold Castle
Am-v139-D 9 '78-p441
BL-v75-O 15 '78-p381
CBRS-v7-F '79-p67
CCB-B-v32-Mr '79-p118
HB-v54-D '78-p645
KR-v47-Ja 1 '79-p6
SLJ-v25-O '78-p146
Fayerweather Forecast
B&B-v13-Jl '68-p42
CCB-B-v21-S '67-p8
HB-v43-Ag '67-p470
KR-v35-My 1 '67-p561
LJ-v92-Je 15 '67-p2450
SLJ-v24-F '78-p35
The Secret Of The Crazy Quilt
BL-v69-O 1 '72-p148
CCB-B-v25-Jl '72-p170
HB-v48-Je '72-p275
KR-v40-Ap 15 '72-p485
KR-v40-D 15 '72-p1419
LJ-v98-Mr 15 '73-p1003
NY-v48-D 2 '72-p209
NYTBR-Je 18 '72-p8
SR-v55-My 20 '72-p81

* * *

HIGHWATER, Jamake
Anpao
BL-v74-N 15 '77-p542
BW-F 12 '78-pG4
BW-D 10 '78-pE5
CCB-B-v31-Mr '78-p113
CE-v55-O '78-p38
CLW-v49-D '77-p235
CLW-v50-O '78-p109
EJ-v72-F '83-p47
HB-v54-F '78-p55
J Read-v22-N '78-p184
KR-v45-O 1 '77-p1053
Kliatt-v14-Fall '80-p7
LA-v55-F '78-p213
LA-v60-O '83-p906
NYTBR-F 5 '78-p26

HIGHWATER, Jamake (continued)
SLJ-v24-O '77-p124
SLJ-v26-N '79-p43
Teacher-v95-My '78-p100
Legend Days
BL-v80-Jl '84-p1549
B Rpt-v3-S '84-p33
BS-v44-Je '84-p116
CBRS-v12-My '84-p108
CCB-B-v37-Je '84-p186
EJ-v73-S '84-p103
HB-v60-Je '84-p336
NYTBR-v89-S 9 '84-p43
PW-v225-Je 22 '84-p100
SLJ-v30-Ag '84-p84
VOYA-v7-Ag '84-p144
Many Smokes, Many Moons
ARBA-v11-'80-p205
BB-v6-O '78-p4
BL-v75-S 1 '78-p38
CCB-B-v32-O '78-p30
CE-v55-F '79-p226
CSM-v70-O 23 '78-pB6
HB-v55-O '78-p530
J Read-v22-Mr '79-p564
KR-v46-Ag 1 '78-p813
LA-v56-F '79-p188
NYTBR-Ap 30 '78-p42
PW-v214-Jl 3 '78-p65
SE-v43-Ap '79-p301
SLJ-v25-O '78-p155
Moonsong Lullaby
CBRS-v10-S '81-p3
CCB-B-v35-O '81-p31
Inter BC-v13-#2 '82-p35
KR-v50-Ja 1 '82-p2
LA-v59-Ap '82-p368
PW-v220-S 25 '81-p88
RT-v35-F '82-p623
SLJ-v28-S '81-p109

* * *

HIGONNET-SCHNOPPER, Janet
Tales From Atop A Russian Stove
BL-v70-S 1 '73-p51
Inst-v83-N '73-p123
LJ-v98-N 15 '73-p3441
RT-v35-D '81-p340

* * *

HILBERT, Peter Paul
Zoo On The First Floor
CCB-B-v21-O '67-p27
KR-v35-Ap 15 '67-p499
LJ-v92-Jl '67-p2655
Punch-v251-N 16 '66-p756
TLS-N 24 '66-p1091

* * *

HILDEBRANDT, Tim
How Do They Build It?
NYTBR-S 8 '74-p8
SLJ-v21-Ja '75-p39

* * *

HILDEBRANDTS, The
Animals!
SLJ-v26-S '79-p100
Here Come The Builders!
SLJ-v26-S '79-p100
Who Runs The City?
SLJ-v26-S '79-p100

* * *

HILDICK, E W
The Active-Enzyme Lemon-Freshened Junior High School Witch
BL-v75-O 1 '78-p305
CCB-B-v26-Je '73-p155
KR-v41-F 15 '73-p187
LJ-v98-N 15 '73-p3452
PW-v203-Mr 5 '73-p83
Birdy Jones
AB-v44-O 20 '69-p1181
Brit Bk N C-Spring '81-p14
CCB-B-v23-Mr '70-p113
HB-v46-F '70-p46
LJ-v95-Ap 15 '70-p1650
The Case Of The Bashful Bank Robber
BL-v77-My 1 '81-p1197
KR-v49-My 1 '81-p570
NYTBR-v86-Ap 26 '81-p62
SLJ-v27-My '81-p85
The Case Of The Condemned Cat
CCB-B-v29-My '76-p145
HB-v52-Ap '76-p155
JB-v40-F '76-p24
KR-v43-O 15 '75-p1184
SLJ-v22-D '75-p66
TLS-D 5 '75-p1448
The Case Of The Felon's Fiddle
BL-v79-Ja 1 '83-p617
CLW-v55-D '83-p231
KR-v50-O 15 '82-p1154
SLJ-v29-D '82-p82
The Case Of The Four Flying Fingers
BL-v78-O 1 '81-p236
KR-v49-O 1 '81-p1236
SLJ-v28-D '81-p82
WCRB-v8-F '82-p62
The Case Of The Invisible Dog
BL-v74-O 1 '77-p296
BL-v76-Je 15 '80-p1544
GP-v16-Mr '78-p3274
JB-v42-Je '78-p143
KR-v45-S 1 '77-p933
RT-v32-F '79-p607
SLJ-v24-D '77-p61
TES-F 10 '78-p24
TES-F 27 '81-p39
The Case Of The Nervous Newsboy
BL-v72-Jl 15 '76-p1596
GP-v15-N '76-p3006
JB-v40-Ag '76-p201
KR-v44-Ja 15 '76-p70
RT-v31-O '77-p15
SLJ-v22-My '76-p77
SLJ-v25-D '78-p33
Spec-v237-Jl 17 '76-p24
TES-My 2 '80-p24
The Case Of The Phantom Frog
BL-v75-Mr 1 '79-p1092
BW-My 13 '79-pK3
CCB-B-v33-N '79-p48
GP-v18-Ja '80-p3624
KR-v47-My 15 '79-p576
LA-v56-O '79-p818
SLJ-v25-My '79-p81
TES-Ja 18 '80-p43
The Case Of The Secret Scribbler
CCB-B-v32-D '78-p63
JB-v43-F '79-p31
SLJ-v25-D '78-p69
TES-N 24 '78-p50
TES-F 27 '81-p39
The Case Of The Slingshot Sniper
BL-v79-Je 15 '83-p1339
KR-v51-Ap 15 '83-p458
SLJ-v29-My '83-p92
The Case Of The Snowbound Spy
BL-v77-O 15 '80-p327
BL-v79-Ap 1 '83-p1042
KR-v48-Ag 15 '80-p1081
SLJ-v27-D '80-p73
The Case Of The Treetop Treasure
BL-v76-F 15 '80-p834

HILDICK, E W (continued)
GP-v19-Ja '81-p3808
JB-v45-F '81-p19
KR-v48-Mr 1 '80-p288
LA-v57-S '80-p648
SLJ-v26-My '80-p86
SLJ-v27-N '80-p47
A Cat Called Amnesia
BL-v73-S 15 '76-p175
GP-v16-S '77-p3171
JB-v41-O '77-p302
KR-v44-My 15 '76-p592
Lis-v98-N 10 '77-p624
SLJ-v22-My '76-p77
TLS-Jl 15 '77-p865
Teacher-v95-My '78-p109
Children & Fiction
AB-v48-S 6 '71-p514
B&B-v16-D '70-p60
BL-v68-N 1 '71-p227
CLW-v43-D '71-p223
CLW-v44-N '72-p242
Econ-v237-D 26 '70-p38
HB-v48-F '72-p67
KR-v39-Ag 1 '71-p821
LR-v23-Spring '71-p51
NS-v80-N 6 '70-p607
NYRB-v17-D 2 '71-p25
NYT-v121-D 20 '71-p33
PW-v200-S 6 '71-p50
TLS-D 11 '70-p1452
Deadline For McGurk
BL-v71-Je 1 '75-p1012
BL-v73-D 15 '76-p615
CCB-B-v28-Jl '75-p177
CLW-v47-N '75-p188
HB-v51-O '75-p464
KR-v43-Ap 1 '75-p374
LA-v53-My '76-p515
RT-v29-Ap '76-p721
SLJ-v21-My '75-p70
The Doughnut Dropout
CCB-B-v26-S '72-p9
KR-v40-My 1 '72-p537
LJ-v97-S 15 '72-p2950
The Ghost Squad Breaks Through
BL-v80-Je 1 '84-p1398
CBRS-v12-Ag '84-p151
SLJ-v30-My '84-p101
The Great Rabbit Rip-Off
BL-v73-Je 1 '77-p1497
SLJ-v23-My '77-p77
The Great Rabbit Robbery
JB-v41-Ag '77-p223
Here Comes Parren
B&B-v14-Mr '69-p52
CCB-B-v26-N '72-p42
LJ-v97-S 15 '72-p2936
NS-v77-My 16 '69-p702
Jim Starling And The Colonel
BL-v65-My 1 '69-p1016
GP-v21-S '82-p3969
KR-v36-Ag 1 '68-p818
LJ-v93-O 15 '68-p3982
Kids Commune
CCB-B-v27-N '73-p44
KR-v40-N 15 '72-p1304
PW-v202-O 16 '72-p50
Lemon Kelly
BW-v2-O 6 '68-p20
CCB-B-v22-O '68-p28
KR-v36-Je 1 '68-p596
LJ-v93-Je 15 '68-p2539
NS-v75-My 24 '68-p696
TLS-Je 6 '68-p583
Lemon Kelly Digs Deep
TES-S 30 '77-p24
Louie's Lot
BW-v2-O 13 '68-p14
CCB-B-v22-O '68-p29
CSM-v57-N 4 '65-pB6
HB-v45-Ap '69-p177
KR-v36-My 1 '68-p517
LJ-v93-My 15 '68-p2113
NYTBR-v73-Ag 4 '68-p20
Obs-My 26 '68-p27
SE-v33-My '69-p558
SR-v51-Ag 24 '68-p43
TES-D 14 '79-p21
TLS-D 9 '65-p1142
TLS-Mr 14 '68-p258
YR-v5-O '68-p7
Louie's Ransom
BL-v74-My 1 '78-p1432
CCB-B-v31-Je '78-p160
JB-v43-O '79-p278
KR-v46-Mr 15 '78-p306
NS-v98-N 9 '79-p729
NYTBR-Ap 30 '78-p44
SLJ-v24-My '78-p86
Sch Lib-v27-D '79-p387
Louie's Snowstorm
BL-v71-O 15 '74-p244
CCB-B-v28-N '74-p43
JB-v40-Je '76-p162
KR-v42-N 1 '74-p1151
KR-v43-Ja 1 '75-p10
LJ-v99-O 15 '74-p2721
NS-v91-My 21 '76-p690
PW-v206-N 11 '74-p49
Spec-v235-D 6 '75-p733
TLS-D 5 '75-p1449
Louie's SOS
BW-v4-N 8 '70-p21
CCB-B-v24-Ja '71-p74
CSM-v62-N 12 '70-pB2
HB-v47-F '71-p51
KR-v38-O 1 '70-p1096
LJ-v95-D 15 '70-p4351
PW-v198-N 30 '70-p41
Lucky Les
B&B-v20-F '75-p77
TLS-N 30 '67-p1153
TLS-D 6 '74-p1372
Manhattan Is Missing
B&B-v18-Ja '73-p123
BL-v65-Ap 1 '69-p894
BS-v28-Mr 1 '69-p490
BW-v3-My 4 '69-p30
CCB-B-v22-Ap '69-p127
HB-v45-Je '69-p306
KR-v37-Ja 15 '69-p54
LJ-v94-My 15 '69-p2073
LJ-v94-My 15 '69-p2100
LJ-v94-D 15 '69-p4582
Lis-v88-N 9 '72-p644
PW-v195-F 3 '69-p65
PW-v198-Ag 3 '70-p62
SLJ-v24-F '78-p35
SR-v52-Mr 22 '69-p63
Spec-v229-N 11 '72-p750
TLS-D 8 '72-p1490
McGurk Gets Good And Mad
BL-v79-O 1 '82-p245
KR-v50-My 1 '82-p555
SLJ-v28-My '82-p84
The Menaced Midget
TLS-S 19 '75-p1058
My Kid Sister
CCB-B-v25-N '71-p44
LJ-v96-O 15 '71-p3459
NS-v85-My 25 '73-p779
TLS-Je 15 '73-p682
The Nose Knows
HB-v49-O '73-p465
KR-v41-F 1 '73-p115
LJ-v98-O 15 '73-p3146
The Questers
BL-v67-D 15 '70-p342
CCB-B-v24-D '70-p60
LJ-v95-O 15 '70-p3627
NS-v72-N 11 '66-p710
Punch-v251-Ag 10 '66-p235
TLS-N 24 '66-p1074
The Secret Scribbler
BL-v74-Jl 1 '78-p1678

HILDICK, E W (continued)
KR-v46-S 1 '78-p951
The Secret Spenders
BS-v31-Ag 15 '71-p234
LJ-v96-My 15 '71-p1804
PW-v199-My 31 '71-p135
The Secret Winners
BW-v4-My 17 '70-p20
CCB-B-v24-N '70-p43
KR-v38-My 1 '70-p506
LJ-v95-My 15 '70-p1943
PW-v197-Je 1 '70-p67
Time Explorers, Inc.
BS-v36-O '76-p239
KR-v44-My 15 '76-p592
SLJ-v22-Ap '76-p89
WCRB-v3-S '77-p57
Top Boy At Twisters Creek
CCB-B-v23-Ap '70-p129
KR-v37-N 15 '69-p1195
SR-v53-F 21 '70-p45
The Top-Flight Fully-Automated Junior High School Girl Detective
CCB-B-v31-D '77-p60
HB-v53-D '77-p663
KR-v45-Ag 1 '77-p785
Kliatt-v13-Fall '79-p8
SLJ-v23-My '77-p78

* * *

HILGARTNER, Beth
Great Gorilla Grins
KR-v47-Mr 15 '79-p322
PW-v215-Mr 26 '79-p81
SLJ-v26-O '79-p140

* * *

HILL, Archie
Dark Pastures
Brit Bk N C-Autumn '81-p24
GP-v20-N '81-p3964
JB-v45-O '81-p211
Obs-N 29 '81-p27

* * *

HILL, Barbara W
Cooking The English Way
BL-v79-D 15 '82-p561
CBRS-v11-Ja '83-p49
NYTBR-v88-F 20 '83-p25
SLJ-v29-My '83-p69

* * *

HILL, Barry
Pepper Stories
Sch Lib-v31-Mr '83-p31

* * *

HILL, C W
Collecting Coins
JB-v45-Ap '81-p81
Flying Start Treasure Hunting
B&B-v24-Je '79-p58

* * *

HILL, Denise
The Birthday Surprise
JB-v42-D '78-p300
TLS-S 29 '78-p1085
No Friends For Simon
TES-Ap 7 '78-p20
TLS-Ap 7 '78-p378
The Witch At Lundy Cottage
JB-v40-F '76-p25
TLS-S 19 '75-p1058
The Wrong Side Of The Bed
TES-Je 12 '81-p27

* * *

HILL, Donna
Eerie Animals
CCB-B-v37-O '83
HB-v59-Ag '83
Inst-v92-My '83
SLJ-v30-S '83
Mr. Peeknuff's Tiny People
BL-v77-My 1 '81-p1197
CBRS-v9-Ag '81-p121
KR-v49-Jl 15 '81-p870
PW-v219-F 13 '81-p93
SLJ-v27-My '81-p55
Ms. Glee Was Waiting
Am-v139-D 9 '78-p439
CLW-v50-F '79-p312
KR-v46-F 15 '78-p175
NYTBR-Ap 30 '78-p29
PW-v213-F 13 '78-p127
RT-v32-Ja '79-p487
RT-v33-O '79-p46
RT-v37-Ap '84-p703
SLJ-v24-Ap '78-p70

* * *

HILL, Douglas
Alien Citadel
BL-v80-My 15 '84-p1339
BS-v44-Je '84-p116
GP-v23-S '84-p4308
SLJ-v30-My '84-p89
TES-Je 8 '84-p46
VOYA-v7-Ag '84-p147
Alien Worlds
Brit Bk N C-Spring '81-p25
Can Child Lit-#26 '82-p64
JB-v45-Ag '81-p159
Day Of The Starwind
BL-v78-O 1 '81-p188
BL-v80-Ap 15 '84-p1200
Brit Bk N C-Spring '81-p23
CBRS-v10-Winter '82-p58
GP-v19-Ja '81-p3816
JB-v45-Ap '81-p81
Obs-N 30 '80-p36
Quill & Q-v47-Ap '81-p35
SLJ-v28-N '81-p104
Sch Lib-v29-Mr '81-p51
TLS-N 20 '81-p1361
Deathwing Over Veynaa
BL-v77-Mr 15 '81-p1023
Brit Bk N C-Autumn '80-p24
CBRS-v9-Je '81-p97
CCB-B-v34-Je '81-p194
GP-v18-Mr '80-p3653
JB-v44-Ag '80-p191
SLJ-v27-Ag '81-p75
Sch Lib-v28-S '80-p290
TLS-N 20 '81-p1361
Exiles Of ColSec
GP-v22-Ja '84-p4192
JB-v48-Je '84-p139
Sch Lib-v32-Je '84-p153
TES-Je 8 '84-p46
TLS-Ap 13 '84-p414
Galactic Warlord
BL-v76-Ap 1 '80-p1116
BS-v40-My '80-p78
Brit Bk N C-Spring '80-p17
CBRS-v8-Jl '80-p127
CCB-B-v34-N '80-p54
GP-v18-N '79-p3614
HB-v56-Je '80-p306
In Rev-v14-F '80-p43
JB-v44-F '80-p27
LA-v58-Ja '81-p83
SLJ-v26-Ap '80-p125
TLS-N 20 '81-p1361
VOYA-v3-F '81-p38
The Huntsman
Can Child Lit-#33 '84-p81
GP-v21-S '82-p3953
JB-v46-O '82-p198
J Read-v26-F '83-p468
SLJ-v29-F '83-p89
Planet Of The Warlord
BL-v78-Mr 1 '82-p855
Brit Bk N C-Spring '82-p13
CLW-v54-D '82-p225
CSM-v74-My 14 '82-pB6
Can Child Lit-#26 '82-p64
GP-v20-S '81-p3945

HILL, Douglas (continued)
HB-v58-Ag '82-p413
In Rev-v16-Ap '82-p49
JB-v45-D '81-p249
Obs-N 29 '81-p27
Quill & Q-v48-Mr '82-p69
SF&FBR-Jl '82-p40
SLJ-v28-Ag '82-p126
Sch Lib-v29-D '81-p344
TES-Ap 23 '82-p26
TLS-N 20 '81-p1361
VOYA-v5-Je '82-p39
Warriors Of The Wasteland
BL-v79-Ap 1 '83-p1020
CBRS-v11-Je '83-p114
CSM-v75-My 13 '83-pB6
GP-v22-My '83-p4077
JB-v47-Je '83-p125
J Read-v27-O '83-p84
SLJ-v29-Mr '83-p192
TES-Mr 25 '83-p31
Young Legionary
BL-v80-S 15 '83-p158
BS-v43-N '83-p311
Fant R-v7-Ag '84-p47
GP-v21-Ja '83-p4007
HB-v59-O '83-p582
JB-v47-F '83-p43
Obs-N 28 '82-p31
SLJ-v30-D '83-p74

* * *

HILL, Elizabeth Starr
Evan's Corner
BL-v63-Mr 15 '67-p796
BL-v69-My 1 '73-p836
CCB-B-v20-Mr '67-p108
CE-v44-D '67-p258
CLW-v41-Ja '70-p321
EL-v88-F '68-p279
GT-v89-S '71-p158
HB-v43-Ap '67-p198
LJ-v92-D 15 '67-p4603
LJ-v96-O 15 '71-p3437
SR-v50-F 18 '67-p41
Trav-v24-N '67-p99
Ever-After Island
BL-v73-Je 1 '77-p1497
CCB-B-v31-O '77-p34
CSM-v69-N 2 '77-p15
KR-v45-Je 1 '77-p575
PW-v211-My 23 '77-p247
RT-v32-F '79-p608
SLJ-v24-S '77-p130
The Window Tulip
CCB-B-v18-Mr '65-p103

* * *

HILL, Eric
Animals
Brit Bk N C-Autumn '82-p5
Quill & Q-v49-F '83-p17
RT-v37-My '84-p857
At Home
CBRS-v11-My '83-p97
CCB-B-v36-My '83-p169
SLJ-v29-My '83-p62
TLS-N 26 '82-p1304
Baby Bear's Bedtime
GP-v23-Jl '84-p4293
SLJ-v31-S '84-p104
El Cumpleanos De Spot
BL-v80-Mr 1 '84-p999
WLB-v58-Ap '84-p578
Donde Esta Spot?
SLJ-v30-Ag '84-p88
WLB-v58-Ap '84-p578
Good Morning, Baby Bear
GP-v23-Jl '84-p4293
PW-v225-Ap 13 '84-p71
SLJ-v31-S '84-p104
My Pets
CBRS-v11-My '83-p97
CCB-B-v36-My '83-p169
SLJ-v29-My '83-p62
TLS-N 26 '82-p1304
Nursery Rhymes
Brit Bk N C-Autumn '82-p5
Quill & Q-v49-F '83-p17
RT-v37-My '84-p857
Opposites
Brit Bk N C-Autumn '82-p5
Quill & Q-v49-F '83-p17
RT-v37-My '84-p857
SLJ-v30-O '83-p125
The Park
CBRS-v11-My '83-p97
CCB-B-v36-My '83-p169
SLJ-v29-My '83-p62
TLS-N 26 '82-p1304
La Primera Navidad De Spot
BL-v80-Mr 1 '84-p999
SLJ-v30-Ag '84-p88
WLB-v58-Ap '84-p578
Puppy Love
PW-v222-N 12 '82-p66
Spot Learns To Count
TES-My 25 '84-p27
Spot Tells The Time
TES-My 25 '84-p27
Spot's Alphabet
TES-My 25 '84-p27
Spot's Birthday Party
GP-v22-My '83-p4081
JB-v47-Je '83-p108
RT-v37-My '84-p857
SLJ-v29-Ap '83-p102
SLJ-v30-O '83-p125
Sch Lib-v31-S '83-p232
Spot's Busy Year
TES-My 25 '84-p27
Spot's First Christmas
CBRS-v12-Ja '84-p46
JB-v48-Ap '84-p60
Lis-v110-N 3 '83-p27
NYTBR-v88-N 13 '83-p44
Obs-D 11 '83-p35
PW-v224-N 25 '83-p65
SLJ-v30-O '83-p176
Sch Lib-v32-Mr '84-p37
TES-D 16 '83-p20
Spot's First Walk
BL-v78-Ja 1 '82-p600
Brit Bk N C-Spring '82-p3
CBRS-v10-Winter '82-p51
CCB-B-v35-Ap '82-p149
JB-v46-Je '82-p93
KR-v49-N 15 '81-p1405
NW-v98-D 7 '81-p99
PW-v220-S 11 '81-p72
RT-v37-My '84-p857
SLJ-v29-N '82-p69
SLJ-v30-O '83-p125
TES-D 23 '83-p23
TLS-N 20 '81-p1360
Up There
CBRS-v11-My '83-p97
CCB-B-v36-My '83-p169
PW-v223-Mr 18 '83-p70
SLJ-v29-My '83-p62
TLS-N 26 '82-p1304
Where's Spot?
BL-v78-Ja 1 '82-p600
BL-v80-S 1 '83-p93
Brit Bk N-D '80-p714
CBRS-v9-D '80-p22
Emerg Lib-v11-Ja '84-p19
GP-v19-Ja '81-p3821
NS-v100-N 21 '80-p19
NYTBR-v85-D 7 '80-p41
PW-v218-D 12 '80-p47
Punch-v280-Ap 29 '81-p680
RT-v37-My '84-p857
SLJ-v27-Mr '81-p132
SLJ-v30-O '83-p125
Sch Lib-v29-Je '81-p122
TES-D 23 '83-p23
TLS-N 21 '80-p1328

HILLARY, Sir Edmund (continued)
GW-v112-Ap 5 '75-p21
HB-v52-Ap '76-p184
KR-v43-Mr 1 '75-p280
LJ-v100-Ap 15 '75-p753
Lis-v93-Ap 10 '75-p484
NS-v89-My 2 '75-p596
NYTBR-Ag 17 '75-p6
Obs-Mr 30 '75-p23
PW-v207-Mr 17 '75-p56
Spec-v234-Mr 29 '75-p374

* * *

HILLCOURT, William
Outdoor Things To Do
SLJ-v22-N '75-p78
SR-v2-My 31 '75-p34

* * *

HILLER, Carl E
Babylon To Brasilia
BL-v69-O 15 '72-p203
BS-v32-My 15 '72-p97
CCB-B-v26-Mr '73-p107
KR-v40-Ap 15 '72-p489
LJ-v97-O 15 '72-p3461
LJ-v97-D 15 '72-p4056
SE-v37-D '73-p787
Caves To Cathedrals
BL-v71-F 15 '75-p619
BS-v34-F 15 '75-p518
CCB-B-v28-Je '75-p161
Comw-v101-N 22 '74-p193
Inst-v84-My '75-p96
KR-v43-Ja 1 '75-p20
SLJ-v21-Mr '75-p106

* * *

HILLER, Catherine
Abracatabby
BL-v77-Je 15 '81-p1350
KR-v49-Jl 1 '81-p799
SLJ-v28-N '81-p77
Argentaybee And The Boonie
CBRS-v7-Jl '79-p122
KR-v47-My 1 '79-p513
SLJ-v26-S '79-p112

* * *

HILLER, Doris
Black Beach
BL-v74-Ja 15 '78-p809
BL-v75-O 15 '78-p357
Little Big Top
SLJ-v26-D '79-p98

* * *

HILLER, Ilo
Young Naturalist
BL-v80-Mr 1 '84-p967
CBRS-v12-Mr '84-p84
SLJ-v30-Mr '84-p160

* * *

HILLERICH, Robert L
Reading Fundamentals For Preschool And Primary Children
LA-v55-Ja '78-p57
RT-v31-F '78-p581

* * *

HILLERMAN, Tony
The Boy Who Made Dragonfly
BL-v69-Mr 1 '73-p647
CCB-B-v26-F '73-p92
CE-v49-My '73-p422
KR-v40-N 15 '72-p1305
LJ-v98-Ap 15 '73-p1387
SLJ-v26-N '79-p43

* * *

HILLERT, Margaret
Away Go The Boats
SLJ-v27-D '80-p70
Circus Fun
LJ-v95-My 15 '70-p1960
City Fun
SLJ-v27-D '80-p70
Come Play With Me
SLJ-v22-F '76-p36
The Cookie House
Cur R-v19-F '80-p50
SLJ-v25-S '78-p116
Four Good Friends
SLJ-v27-D '80-p70
The Golden Goose
Cur R-v19-F '80-p50
SLJ-v25-S '78-p116
Happy Birthday, Dear Dragon
SLJ-v25-D '78-p44
Happy Easter, Dear Dragon
CCB-B-v34-S '80-p12
SLJ-v27-D '80-p70
I Love You, Dear Dragon
SLJ-v27-D '80-p70
It's Halloween, Dear Dragon
SLJ-v27-D '80-p70
Let's Go, Dear Dragon
SLJ-v27-D '80-p70
Little Cookie
SLJ-v27-D '80-p70
The Little Cowboy And The Big Cowboy
SLJ-v27-D '80-p68
The Magic Nutcracker
SLJ-v27-O '80-p161
Merry Christmas, Dear Dragon
SLJ-v27-O '80-p161
Not I, Not I
SLJ-v27-D '80-p70
Play Ball
Cur R-v19-F '80-p50
SLJ-v25-S '78-p116
The Purple Pussycat
SLJ-v27-D '80-p70
Run To The Rainbow
PW-v217-Ap 25 '80-p81
SLJ-v27-D '80-p70
The Sleepytime Book
RT-v37-My '84-p857
What Am I?
SLJ-v27-D '80-p70
What Is It?
Cur R-v19-F '80-p50
PW-v213-Je 19 '78-p101
SLJ-v25-S '78-p116
Who Goes To School?
SLJ-v27-D '80-p70

* * *

HILLMAN, Priscilla
Book Of Opposites
SLJ-v29-Ag '83-p52
Book Of Toys
SLJ-v29-Ag '83-p52
Counting And Colors Book
SLJ-v29-Ag '83-p52
A Merry-Mouse Book Of Favorite Poems
LA-v58-N '81-p954
SLJ-v28-N '81-p77
A Merry-Mouse Book Of Months
PW-v217-Je 20 '80-p87
SLJ-v27-Ja '81-p51
The Merry-Mouse Book Of Prayers And Graces
PW-v224-S 16 '83-p125
SLJ-v30-Ja '84-p67
A Merry-Mouse Christmas ABC
CCB-B-v34-N '80-p55
PW-v217-Je 20 '80-p87
SLJ-v27-Ja '81-p51
TES-D 25 '81-p17

HILLMAN, Priscilla (continued)
The Merry-Mouse Schoolhouse
SLJ-v29-S '82-p108

* * *

HILLS, C A R
The Seine
BL-v78-S 1 '81-p40
SLJ-v28-N '81-p87
TES-Mr 6 '81-p36

* * *

HILTON, Irene
Enemy In The Sky
CCB-B-v18-Ap '65-p118

* * *

HILTON, Suzanne
Beat It, Burn It, And Drown It
BL-v70-Jl 1 '74-p1200
CCB-B-v28-D '74-p63
KR-v42-Ap 1 '74-p375
SB-v10-D '74-p253
Getting There
BL-v77-S 1 '80-p45
SLJ-v26-Ap '80-p110
Here Today And Gone Tomorrow
BB-v7-Ag '79-p4
BL-v75-O 15 '78-p368
PW-v214-D 4 '78-p66
SLJ-v25-Ap '79-p57
It's A Model World
CCB-B-v26-Mr '73
Inst-v82-N '72
KR-v40-N 1 '72
The Way It Was-1876
BL-v71-Je 15 '75-p1070
CCB-B-v29-N '75-p46
CLW-v47-D '75-p234
HB-v51-O '75-p482
KR-v43-Je 1 '75-p608
NYTBR-Ag 17 '75-p8
NYTBR-N 16 '75-p55
PW-v207-My 19 '75-p176
SE-v44-O '80-p479
SLJ-v21-My '75-p64
SLJ-v22-D '75-p31
Who Do You Think You Are?
BB-v5-F '77-p3
BL-v72-Mr 1 '76-p968
BL-v72-Mr 1 '76-p978
KR-v44-My 1 '76-p545
Kliatt-v12-Spring '78-p46
RT-v32-Ja '79-p444
SE-v41-Ap '77-p351
SLJ-v22-Mr '76-p114

* * *

HIMLER, Ann
Waiting For Cherries
BB-v4-Ap '76-p3
CSM-v68-My 12 '76-p23
GP-v16-Ja '78-p3238
KR-v44-Mr 1 '76-p251
SLJ-v22-Mr '76-p92

* * *

HIMLER, Ronald
The Girl On The Yellow Giraffe
BL-v73-O 1 '76-p252
CE-v60-My '84-p344
Inst-v86-N '76-p145
JB-v43-F '79-p18
KR-v44-Ag 1 '76-p842
RT-v31-O '77-p11
Little Owl, Keeper Of The Trees
BL-v71-F 1 '75-p570
CCB-B-v28-My '75-p148
KR-v42-O 15 '74-p1103
NYTBR-N 3 '74-p50
PW-v206-S 30 '74-p60
PW-v206-O 7 '74-p63
SLJ-v21-Ja '75-p39
Wake Up, Jeremiah
BL-v76-S 15 '79-p120
BL-v80-N 1 '83-p423
CBRS-v8-O '79-p12
CCB-B-v33-F '80-p111
CSM-v71-O 15 '79-pB6
Inst-v89-N '79-p138
KR-v47-O 15 '79-p1207
LA-v57-F '80-p187
NYTBR-O 28 '79-p18
PW-v216-Jl 23 '79-p159
RT-v36-D '82-p272
SLJ-v26-D '79-p74

* * *

HIMMELMAN, John
Talester The Lizard
BL-v78-Ag '82-p1525
CBRS-v10-Ap '82-p83
CCB-B-v35-Je '82-p188
HB-v58-Ag '82-p391
KR-v50-Ap 15 '82-p485
PW-v221-F 5 '82-p387
SLJ-v28-My '82-p53
WCRB-v8-S '82-p71

* * *

HINCHMAN, Jane
A Talent For Trouble
CCB-B-v20-S '66-p12
KR-v34-Ap 15 '66-p427
LJ-v91-Jl '66-p3543
NYTBR-v71-Jl 24 '66-p23

* * *

HIND, Dolores
The Animals Walk
In Rev-v14-Ag '80-p52

* * *

HINDE, Cecilia
The First Men On Earth
SB-v14-S '78-p111
SLJ-v24-Ap '78-p70
Floury Fingers
Punch-v276-Ap 18 '79-p688
Life In Prehistoric Times
SLJ-v25-S '78-p116
Prehistoric Mammals
SLJ-v25-S '78-p116
Your Book Of Breadmaking
JB-v42-F '78-p42
Lis-v98-N 10 '77-p626
Obs-N 27 '77-p29
TES-N 18 '77-p37

* * *

HINDEY Il Nahat, Arirat Al Dafadeh
BL-v75-O 15 '78-p393

* * *

HINDLE, Roy
Oh, No Dear!
TLS-N 26 '82-p1309

* * *

HINDLEY, Geoffrey
Secret Agents
TLS-N 21 '80-p1330
Under Siege
Brit Bk N-Je '80-p331
GP-v19-N '80-p3784
JB-v44-D '80-p307
Sch Lib-v28-S '80-p302
TES-Je 20 '80-p41

* * *

HINDLEY, Judy
Book Of Knights And Castles
NS-v92-N 5 '76-p642
The Counting Book
GP-v18-Mr '80-p3663
Fakes And Forgeries
TES-Ja 11 '80-p26

HINDLEY, Judy (continued)
How Your Body Works
GP-v15-S '76-p2947
The Time Traveler Book Of Knights And Castles
Inst-v90-N '80-p160

* * *

HINDS, L
Crockery
JB-v40-O '76-p269
Eggs
GP-v14-S '75-p2699
A First Look At Linen
JB-v40-F '76-p25

* * *

HINE, Al
A Letter To Anywhere
CCB-B-v19-F '66-p99
GT-v83-N '65-p123
HB-v41-Je '65-p288
KR-v33-F 15 '65-p172
LJ-v90-My 15 '65-p2396
SR-v48-My 15 '65-p44
This Land Is Mine: An Anthology Of American Verse
AL-v38-My '66-p273
BL-v62-Ja 1 '66-p444
CCB-B-v19-Ap '66-p131
CE-v42-Ap '66-p505
GT-v83-F '66-p24
HB-v42-F '66-p75
KR-v33-Ag 15 '65-p838
LJ-v91-Ja 15 '66-p435
NYTBR-v70-N 7 '65-p6

* * *

HINE, H G
The House That Jack Built
JB-v43-Ap '79-p97
The Life And Death Of An Apple Pie
JB-v43-Ap '79-p97

* * *

HINE, Lewis W
Men At Work
Choice-v14-Ja '78-p1487
M Photo-v42-F '78-p76
NBR-v4-D '78-p23
SA-v237-D '77-p36

* * *

HINES, Anna G
Come To The Meadow
BL-v80-My 1 '84-p1246
CBRS-v12-My '84-p101
PW-v225-Mr 30 '84-p56
SLJ-v30-Ag '84-p60
Maybe A Band-Aid Will Help
PW-v226-Jl 27 '84-p144
Taste The Raindrops
BL-v79-Ap 1 '83-p1035
CBRS-v11-Mr '83-p75
KR-v50-D 1 '82-p1291
SLJ-v29-Ag '83-p52

* * *

HINES, Barry
Kestrel For A Knave
B&B-v13-F '68-p31
GP-v16-O '77-p3196
Obs-My 12 '68-p28

* * *

HINOJOSA, Francisco
The Old Lady Who Ate People
CBRS-v13-S '84-p5
SLJ-v31-S '84-p98
La Vieja Que Comia Gente
BL-v79-F 15 '83-p783
BL-v81-O 1 '84-p256

* * *

HINTON, Nigel
Beaver Towers
Brit Bk N C-Spring '81-p23
JB-v45-F '81-p20
Buddy
Brit Bk N C-Autumn '82-p8
GP-v21-Jl '82-p3924
JB-v46-O '82-p204
NS-v104-D 3 '82-p21
Sch Lib-v31-Mr '83-p58
TES-Jl 13 '84-p25
Collision Course
BL-v74-S 15 '77-p194
BS-v37-O '77-p203
EJ-v67-F '78-p79
GP-v15-Ap '77-p3086
JB-v41-Ag '77-p235
KR-v45-My 15 '77-p543
NYTBR-O 9 '77-p28
Obs-N 28 '76-p31
SLJ-v24-S '77-p144
TES-My 2 '80-p24
TES-Jl 1 '83-p27
TLS-D 10 '76-p1544
Getting Free
BS-v39-Ag '79-p168
CCB-B-v32-Je '79-p176
GP-v17-Mr '79-p3485
HB-v55-Je '79-p308
JB-v43-Ap '79-p122
J Read-v23-D '79-p279
KR-v47-F 1 '79-p132
NS-v96-N 3 '78-p595
Obs-D 3 '78-p36
SLJ-v25-N '78-p74
Sch Lib-v27-Mr '79-p57
TES-N 24 '78-p48
TES-Jl 9 '82-p32

* * *

HINTON, S E
The Outsiders
Atl-v220-D '67-p136
BL-v64-O 1 '67-p176
BS-v27-Jl 1 '67-p144
CCB-B-v20-Jl '67-p171
CLW-v39-D '67-p292
EJ-v58-F '69-p295
EJ-v67-My '78-p88
EJ-v69-D '80-p56
HB-v43-Ag '67-p475
Hi Lo-v2-Ja '81-p4
J Read-v22-N '78-p126
KR-v35-Ap 15 '67-p506
LJ-v92-My 15 '67-p2028
NO-v6-Jl 17 '67-p19
NYTBR, pt.1-v72-My 7 '67-p10
NYTBR, pt.2-F 16 '69-p22
NYTBR, pt.2-My 4 '69-p6
PW-v191-My 22 '67-p64
SR-v50-My 13 '67-p59
SR-v51-Ja 27 '68-p34
TLS-O 30 '70-p1258
Rumble Fish
BL-v72-S 1 '75-p41
B Rpt-v2-S '83-p24
BS-v35-F '76-p362
CCB-B-v29-D '75-p63
EJ-v65-My '76-p91
GP-v15-My '76-p2891
HB-v51-D '75-p601
Inst-v85-N '75-p155
JB-v40-Ag '76-p229
J Read-v22-N '78-p127
J Read-v25-My '82-p777
KR-v43-O 15 '75-p1193
NS-v91-My 21 '76-p690
NYT-v125-D 20 '75-p25
NYTBR-D 14 '75-p8
Obs-N 28 '76-p31
PW-v208-Jl 28 '75-p122
SLJ-v22-O '75-p106
SLJ-v22-D '75-p31
SLJ-v28-Ap '82-p28
TLS-Ap 2 '76-p388
TN-v32-Ap '76-p284
Tex
BL-v76-O 15 '79-p353
BS-v39-Mr '80-p465

HINTON, S E (continued)
CBRS-v8-O '79-p17
CCB-B-v33-D '79-p71
EJ-v69-My '80-p74
EJ-v70-Ap '81-p76
GP-v19-My '80-p3686
HB-v55-D '79-p668
Hi Lo-v2-Ja '81-p4
JB-v44-D '80-p307
J Read-v24-O '80-p83
J Read-v25-My '82-p777
KR-v48-Ja 1 '80-p9
NYTBR-D 16 '79-p23
SLJ-v26-N '79-p88
Sch Lib-v28-Je '80-p177
TLS-Mr 28 '80-p356
WLB-v54-O '79-p122
That Was Then, This Is Now
BL-v67-Jl 15 '71-p951
BL-v68-Ap 1 '72-p664
BS-v31-Ag 15 '71-p235
BW-v5-My 9 '71-p5
CCB-B-v25-S '71-p8
EJ-v67-My '78-p88
HB-v47-Ag '71-p388
Hi Lo-v2-Ja '81-p4
J Read-v22-N '78-p126
KR-v39-Ap 15 '71-p442
LJ-v96-Je 15 '71-p2138
NYTBR-Ag 8 '71-p8
Obs-N 28 '71-p35
PW-v199-My 31 '71-p135
SLJ-v29-N '82-p35
SR-v54-Je 19 '71-p27
TLS-O 22 '71-p1318
TN-v28-Ap '72-p312

* * *

HINTZ, Martin
Circus Workin's
BL-v77-F 1 '81-p752
Finland
BL-v79-Ag '83-p1464
SLJ-v30-S '83-p122
Norway
BL-v79-Ap 1 '83-p1031
SLJ-v29-Ap '83-p111
Tons Of Fun
BL-v79-S 1 '82-p44
SLJ-v30-O '83-p158
West Germany
BL-v79-Ag '83-p1464
SLJ-v30-S '83-p122

* * *

HINTZ, Sandy
Computers In Our World
BL-v80-N 15 '83-p490
BL-v80-Ja 1 '84-p682
Brit Bk N-S '84-p526
CBRS-v12-D '83-p40
SLJ-v30-Ja '84-p70

* * *

HINZ, Bob
Baltimore Orioles
SLJ-v29-Mr '83-p170
Houston Astros
SLJ-v29-Mr '83-p170
Minnesota Twins
SLJ-v29-Mr '83-p170
Philadelphia Phillies
SLJ-v29-Mr '83-p170
San Diego Padres
SLJ-v29-Mr '83-p170
Seattle Mariners
SLJ-v29-Mr '83-p170

* * *

HIRIART-URDANIVIA, B
Los Titeres
BL-v79-F 15 '83-p783

* * *

HIRNSCHALL, Helmut
The Song Of Creation
In Rev-v14-O '80-p44

* * *

HIROSHIMA A-Bombed Teachers Association
Let's Cry For Peace
Inter BC-v13-#6 '82-p35

* * *

HIRSCH, Karen
Becky
CBRS-v10-F '82-p62
Ms-v13-O '84-p131
PW-v221-Ja 8 '82-p83
SLJ-v28-Mr '82-p133
My Sister
BL-v74-Mr 1 '78-p1107
CCB-B-v31-Je '78-p160
Cur R-v17-O '78-p269
Ms-v13-O '84-p131

* * *

HIRSCH, Linda
The Sick Story
BB-v5-N '77-p2
CCB-B-v31-S '77-p16
LA-v55-Ja '78-p46
PW-v211-F 21 '77-p78
SLJ-v23-My '77-p51
You're Going Out There A Kid, But You're Coming Back A Star
BL-v79-S 1 '82-p44
CBRS-v11-S '82-p9
CCB-B-v36-N '82-p48
SLJ-v29-O '82-p152

* * *

HIRSCH, S Carl
Famous American Revolutionary War Heroes
CCB-B-v28-Je '75-p161
Par-v50-Ja '75-p48
SLJ-v21-Mr '75-p97
Guardians Of Tomorrow
BL-v67-Jl 15 '71-p954
BW-v5-My 9 '71-p14
CCB-B-v24-Jl '71-p172
LJ-v96-Jl '71-p2364
PW-v199-My 10 '71-p44
SB-v7-S '71-p143
He And She
ACSB-v9-Spring '76-p24
BL-v72-N 15 '75-p453
CCB-B-v29-Mr '76-p111
KR-v43-S 15 '75-p1076
SB-v12-My '76-p25
SLJ-v22-N '75-p90
The Living Community: A Venture Into Ecology
BL-v62-Je 15 '66-p1000
BS-v26-My 1 '66-p58
CCB-B-v19-Je '66-p164
KR-v34-Mr 15 '66-p310
NH-v75-N '66-p62
SB-v2-S '66-p124
Meter Means Measure
BL-v70-F 1 '74-p600
BL-v71-O 15 '74-p225
CCB-B-v27-My '74-p144
CLW-v45-Ap '74-p457
CSM-v68-Mr 4 '76-p20
HB-v50-O '74-p155
KR-v41-O 15 '73-p1173
LJ-v99-Ja 15 '74-p210
NYTBR-My 5 '74-p34
SB-v10-My '74-p20
TN-v30-Ap '74-p308
On Course!
BL-v64-Ja 15 '68-p593
CCB-B-v21-Ap '68-p128
KR-v35-O 15 '67-p1289
LJ-v92-N 15 '67-p4251
SB-v3-Mr '68-p297

HIRSCH, S Carl (continued)
Printing From A Stone: The Story Of Lithography
AB-v40-Ag 7 '67-p414
BL-v64-S 1 '67-p65
BS-v27-Jl 1 '67-p145
CCB-B-v21-S '67-p8
HB-v43-Je '67-p358
KR-v35-Ap 15 '67-p511
LJ-v92-Mr 15 '67-p1325
NYTBR, pt.1-v72-My 7 '67-p24
SB-v3-S '67-p168
SR-v50-Je 17 '67-p36
The Riddle Of Racism
BL-v69-Ja 1 '73-p445
CCB-B-v26-D '72-p56
KR-v40-S 1 '72-p1038
LJ-v98-Mr 15 '73-p1013
PW-v202-S 11 '72-p59
SE-v37-D '73-p786
Stilts
BL-v69-Mr 1 '73-p648
CCB-B-v26-Jl '73-p171
CLW-v44-Mr '73-p509
CSM-v64-N 8 '72-pB4
KR-v40-O 1 '72-p1147
LJ-v98-F 15 '73-p644
Theater Of The Night
ACSB-v10-Fall '77-p20
BL-v73-F 15 '77-p897
CCB-B-v30-Je '77-p159
Par-v52-Mr '77-p30
SB-v13-S '77-p63
SLJ-v23-F '77-p72
This Is Automation
CCB-B-v19-O '65-p33

* * *

HIRSCHFELD, Burt
Spanish Armada: The Story Of A Glorious Defeat
BS-v26-D 1 '66-p340
CCB-B-v20-Ap '67-p123
KR-v34-S 15 '66-p986
LJ-v91-D 15 '66-p6202
NYTBR-v72-F 5 '67-p32

* * *

HIRSCHMANN, Linda
In A Lick Of A Flick Of A Tongue
ASBYP-v14-Winter '81-p34
BL-v77-S 1 '80-p45
Inst-v90-N '80-p158
KR-v48-S 15 '80-p1233
SB-v17-S '81-p33
SLJ-v27-N '80-p63

* * *

HIRSH, Marilyn
Ben Goes Into Business
CCB-B-v27-O '73-p28
KR-v41-Ap 1 '73-p380
LJ-v98-O 15 '73-p3138
PW-v203-Ap 30 '73-p55
Captain Jiri And Rabbi Jacob
BL-v73-O 15 '76-p322
CLW-v48-Ap '77-p404
Cur R-v17-Ag '78-p186
HB-v52-D '76-p617
KR-v44-S 1 '76-p971
NYTBR-N 28 '76-p41
PW-v210-D 27 '76-p60
SLJ-v23-N '76-p47
Could Anything Be Worse?
BL-v70-My 1 '74-p1003
CCB-B-v28-S '74-p9
CE-v51-O '74-p33
KR-v42-My 1 '74-p475
LJ-v99-S 15 '74-p2249
PW-v205-My 13 '74-p59
Teacher-v92-Ap '75-p107
Deborah The Dybbuk
BL-v74-My 1 '78-p1432
CE-v55-Ja '79-p168
CLW-v50-F '79-p312
KR-v46-Mr 15 '78-p299
LA-v55-O '78-p860
PW-v213-F 27 '78-p157
RT-v32-D '78-p365
RT-v35-Ap '82-p823
SE-v43-Ap '79-p300
SLJ-v24-My '78-p56
The Elephants And The Mice
JB-v47-Ap '83-p62
Hannibal And His 37 Elephants
BB-v6-Mr '78-p3
CCB-B-v31-F '78-p95
HB-v53-D '77-p654
KR-v45-O 1 '77-p1043
PW-v212-Jl 18 '77-p138
SLJ-v24-N '77-p48
The Hanukkah Story
HB-v54-Ap '78-p159
KR-v45-D 15 '77-p1319
SLJ-v24-O '77-p88
How The World Got Its Color
BW-v6-N 5 '72-p3
CCB-B-v26-D '72-p57
KR-v40-Ag 15 '72-p935
LJ-v97-N 15 '72-p3797
PW-v202-S 18 '72-p73
I Love Hanukkah
BL-v81-O 1 '84-p248
SLJ-v31-O '84-p173
Leela And The Watermelon
CLW-v43-Mr '72-p431
CSM-v63-Jl 3 '71-p17
HB-v47-Je '71-p279
KR-v39-Ap 15 '71-p428
LJ-v96-O 15 '71-p3459
One Little Goat
BL-v75-Jl 15 '79-p1626
CBRS-v7-Mr '79-p71
KR-v47-Ap 15 '79-p448
NYTBR-Je 24 '79-p34
SLJ-v25-My '79-p52
Potato Pancakes All Around
BL-v75-N 1 '78-p479
BW-D 10 '78-pE5
CBRS-v7-Mr '79-p71
CCB-B-v32-Ap '79-p138
KR-v47-F 1 '79-p121
LA-v55-N '78-p984
RT-v33-O '79-p42
SLJ-v25-O '78-p112
The Rabbi And The Twenty-Nine Witches
BB-v4-Ag '76-p3
BL-v72-Mr 15 '76-p1046
BW-My 2 '76-pL3
CE-v53-F '77-p213
HB-v52-Ag '76-p390
KR-v44-Mr 15 '76-p316
NYTBR-My 2 '76-p47
SE-v41-Ap '77-p349
SLJ-v22-Ap '76-p61
Teacher-v94-N '76-p137
WLB-v50-Ap '76-p642
The Secret Dinosaur
CBRS-v8-O '79-p16
CCB-B-v33-Ja '80-p96
KR-v48-F 1 '80-p121
PW-v216-S 10 '79-p75
SLJ-v26-D '79-p96
The Tower Of Babel
BL-v77-My 1 '81-p1197
CBRS-v9-Ap '81-p74
KR-v49-Jl 15 '81-p870
LA-v58-N '81-p952

* * *

HIRSHBERG, Albert
Bobby Orr: Fire On Ice
BL-v72-O 1 '75-p231
KR-v43-Je 15 '75-p664
SLJ-v22-D '75-p69

HIRSHBERG, Albert (continued)
The Greatest American Leaguers
BS-v30-Ap 1 '70-p18
CCB-B-v24-S '70-p9
KR-v38-F 1 '70-p107
LJ-v95-My 15 '70-p1964
SR-v53-Je 27 '70-p38
The Up-To-Date Biography Of Henry Aaron
BL-v71-O 1 '74-p173
LJ-v99-D 15 '74-p3279
NYTBR-N 3 '74-p30

* * *

HIRST, John
Victorians
JB-v42-O '78-p246

* * *

HIRST, Stephen
Life In A Narrow Place
AW-v14-S '77-p62
BL-v73-S 15 '76-p113
HB-v52-O '76-p509
KR-v44-My 1 '76-p545
SLJ-v22-Ap '76-p89

* * *

HISER, Iona
The Seals
ACSB-v8-Fall '75-p17
SLJ-v22-S '75-p83

* * *

HISLOP, Marion E
Dolls In Canada
Emerg Lib-v10-N '82-p31

* * *

HISPANO, Mariano
Cuentos De Siempre
EJ-v66-Mr '77-p51

* * *

HISS, Anthony
The Giant Panda Book
CCB-B-v27-Mr '74-p111
LJ-v99-Ap 15 '74-p1220
NY-v49-D 3 '73-p216
SB-v10-My '74-p74
SR/W-v1-D 4 '73-p28

* * *

HISTORICAL Catastrophe
SLJ-v29-Ap '83-p113

* * *

HISTORY Around Us
TES-N 5 '82-p22

* * *

HISTORY In Pictures
Brit Bk N C-Autumn '80-p4

* * *

HISTORY Of Entertainment (Macdonald Reference Library)
TES-D 2 '77-p25

* * *

HISTORY Of Little King Pippin
Brit Bk N C-Spring '80-p17

* * *

HITCHCOCK, Alfred
Alfred Hitchcock Presents: Suspenso Especial
BL-v72-My 15 '76-p1343
Alfred Hitchcock's Monster Museum
KR-v33-S 1 '65-p910
LJ-v91-Mr 15 '66-p1719
NYTBR-v70-N 7 '65-p51
SLJ-v28-My '82-p84
Alfred Hitchcock's Supernatural Tales Of Terror And Suspense
BL-v70-Ja 15 '74-p542
GP-v14-O '75-p2728
JB-v39-Je '75-p197
KR-v41-S 15 '73-p1036
LJ-v98-D 15 '73-p3720
NYTBR-F 24 '74-p10
Alfred Hitchcock's Witch's Brew
BB-v5-O '77-p4
JB-v43-Je '79-p168
PW-v212-O 24 '77-p77
SLJ-v24-Ja '78-p94
VOYA-v6-F '84-p352
Witch's Brew
TES-Ja 9 '81-p23

* * *

HITCHCOCK, Gordon
Let Joybells Ring
CCB-B-v29-F '76-p97

* * *

HITCHCOCK, Patricia
King Who Rides A Tiger And Other Folk Tales
BL-v63-F 1 '67-p582
CCB-B-v20-Je '67-p152
CE-v44-F '68-p386
HB-v43-F '67-p64
KR-v34-D 1 '66-p1224
LJ-v92-F 15 '67-p880
TLS-N 30 '67-p1142

* * *

HITTE, Kathryn
Boy, Was I Mad!
CCB-B-v24-Jl '70-p179
KR-v37-S 15 '69-p991
LJ-v94-D 15 '69-p4595
NYTBR, pt.2-N 9 '69-p68
SR-v52-O 18 '69-p56
TLS-Ap 2 '76-p395
Mexicali Soup
BL-v68-Je 15 '72-p893
BW-v4-N 8 '70-p27
CCB-B-v24-Jl '71-p172
CSM-v62-N 12 '70-pB6
LJ-v95-N 15 '70-p4035
Par-v46-Ap '71-p8
What Can You Do Without A Place To Play
BL-v68-My 1 '72-p771
CCB-B-v25-Ja '72-p75
KR-v39-D 1 '71-p1255
LJ-v97-Ap 15 '72-p1598
When Noodlehead Went To The Fair
HB-v45-Ap '69-p162
LJ-v93-N 15 '68-p4395

* * *

HITZ, Demi
The Adventures Of Marco Polo
BW-v12-My 9 '82-p19
CBRS-v10-Je '82-p103
CCB-B-v35-Je '82-p186
LA-v60-F '83-p212
NYTBR-v87-Ap 25 '82-p33
PW-v221-Ja 29 '82-p66
RT-v36-F '83-p594
SLJ-v28-Ap '82-p57
WCRB-v8-Jl '82-p47
Follow The Line
CBRS-v10-O '81-p12
KR-v49-N 15 '81-p1403
The Leaky Umbrella
CBRS-v9-Ja '81-p31
PW-v218-N 28 '80-p50
Liang And The Magic Paintbrush
BL-v77-S 15 '80-p113
CBRS-v9-O '80-p14

HITZ, Demi (continued)
KR-v48-N 15 '80-p1459
LA-v58-My '81-p592
NW-v96-D 1 '80-p103
PW-v217-Je 27 '80-p88
SLJ-v27-S '80-p68
WLB-v55-Ja '81-p371
Lu Pan: The Carpenter's Apprentice
BB-v7-F '79-p2
BL-v74-Jl 15 '78-p1734
CCB-B-v32-S '78-p10
KR-v46-Jl 1 '78-p687
SLJ-v25-S '78-p117
Three Little Elephants
CBRS-v10-N '81-p22
CCB-B-v35-Mr '82-p125
Under The Shade Of The Mulberry Tree
BL-v76-S 15 '79-p117
CBRS-v8-D '79-p32
HB-v55-D '79-p652
KR-v47-S 15 '79-p1064
NYTBR-Ap 29 '79-p31
PW-v216-N 19 '79-p78
SLJ-v26-N '79-p63
Where Is It?
BL-v76-Ap 15 '80-p1202
CBRS-v8-Ap '80-p83
CCB-B-v34-S '80-p6
CE-v57-Mr '81-p236
Cur R-v19-S '80-p328
NYTBR-v85-Ap 20 '80-p20
PW-v217-Mr 7 '80-p90
SLJ-v27-S '80-p58
TN-v37-Fall '80-p45
Where Is Willie Worm?
BL-v78-Ja 1 '82-p600
CBRS-v10-N '81-p22
CCB-B-v35-Mr '82-p125

* * *

HIWAY Series
Cur R-v16-D '77-p360

* * *

HLIBOK, Bruce
Silent Dancer
BL-v78-Mr 15 '82-p957
CCB-B-v35-My '82-p172
Inter BC-v13-#4 '82-p13
PW-v221-Mr 26 '82-p75
SLJ-v28-Ap '82-p70

* * *

HO, Minfong
Sing To The Dawn
CCB-B-v29-N '75-p46
Inst-v85-N '75-p154
KR-v43-Je 1 '75-p604
SLJ-v22-Mr '76-p104

* * *

HOAG, Edwin
American Houses: Colonial, Classic, And Contemporary
BL-v61-F 1 '65-p256
CCB-B-v18-Jl '65-p162
CLW-v36-Ja '65-p336
LJ-v90-Ja 15 '65-p388

* * *

HOARE, Penny
Jamaican Day
Sch Lib-v30-D '82-p327
TES-N 18 '83-p35

* * *

HOARE, Robert J
At The Bottom Of The Deep Blue Sea
JB-v39-Ap '75-p105
A Dictionary Of People
GP-v15-Ap '77-p3090
Gold
GP-v14-Ja '76-p2801
JB-v40-F '76-p25
Turn Of The Century
NS-v90-N 7 '75-p585
TLS-Jl 11 '75-p775
When The West Was Wild
JB-v40-Ag '76-p201

* * *

HOARE, Stephen
Bikes
TES-N 16 '84-p26

* * *

HOBAN, Brom
Jason And The Bees
ACSB-v13-Mr '80-p28
BL-v76-Mr 15 '80-p1065
BOT-v3-Jl '80-p303
CCB-B-v33-Jl '80-p214
KR-v48-Mr 15 '80-p363
SB-v16-N '80-p94
SLJ-v26-My '80-p83
The October Fort
CBRS-v10-Winter '82-p54
SLJ-v28-F '82-p76
Skunk Lane
CBRS-v11-Mr '83-p79
KR-v51-F 1 '83-p117
NY-v59-D 5 '83-p205
SLJ-v29-My '83-p87

* * *

HOBAN, Lillian
Arthur's Christmas Cookies
BL-v69-Mr 1 '73-p648
CCB-B-v26-D '72-p57
HB-v48-D '72-p581
KR-v40-N 1 '72-p1237
LJ-v97-O 15 '72-p3470
NYTBR-D 3 '72-p8
PW-v202-N 6 '72-p58
TLS-Mr 29 '74-p330
Teacher-v90-D '72-p72
Teacher-v92-D '74-p14
Arthur's Funny Money
BL-v78-N 15 '81-p446
BW-v14-Jl 8 '84-p12
CCB-B-v35-D '81-p69
CE-v59-S '82-p64
CSM-v74-D 14 '81-pB12
HB-v57-O '81-p531
KR-v49-N 1 '81-p1343
PW-v220-O 30 '81-p63
RT-v36-O '82-p61
SLJ-v28-D '81-p74
Arthur's Halloween Costume
CCB-B-v38-S '84-p7
HB-v60-S '84-p588
KR-v52-S 1 '84-pJ68
Arthur's Honey Bear
BL-v70-Jl 15 '74-p1253
BL-v73-Mr 15 '77-p1101
CCB-B-v28-S '74-p9
CSM-v66-Jl 3 '74-p7
Choice-v12-N '75-p1132
HB-v50-Ag '74-p371
KR-v42-My 15 '74-p533
LA-v52-O '75-p992
LJ-v99-S 15 '74-p2249
LJ-v99-D 15 '74-p3247
NYTBR-S 8 '74-p8
NYTBR-N 3 '74-p55
NYTBR-v87-N 14 '82-p35
PW-v205-My 27 '74-p65
PW-v222-O 22 '82-p56
Teacher-v92-S '74-p128
Arthur's Pen Pal
BB-v4-N '76-p1
BL-v72-Je 15 '76-p1470
CCB-B-v30-S '76-p11
CE-v53-F '77-p213
CLW-v48-S '76-p90
HB-v52-Ag '76-p392
KR-v44-My 1 '76-p533
RT-v31-O '77-p8
SLJ-v23-S '76-p100
Sch Lib-v29-Je '81-p124

HOBAN, Russell (continued)
CE-v46-F '70-p263
CSM-v61-N 6 '69-pB4
Comw-v91-N 21 '69-p253
HB-v45-O '69-p526
KR-v37-Jl 1 '69-p670
LJ-v94-O 15 '69-p3810
NCW-v216-Mr '73-p89
PW-v196-Ag 4 '69-p49
SR-v52-Ag 16 '69-p26
Spec-v227-N 13 '71-p699
TES-F 24 '84-p29
TLS-Jl 2 '71-p771
Big John Turkle
BW-v14-My 13 '84-p19
CBRS-v12-Jl '84-p134
SLJ-v30-Ag '84-p60
Birthday For Frances
BL-v65-N 1 '68-p312
BW-v2-S 29 '68-p18
CCB-B-v22-Ja '69-p79
CE-v45-F '69-p338
HB-v44-O '68-p552
KR-v36-Je 15 '68-p641
LJ-v93-S 15 '68-p3290
NCW-v222-Mr '79-p92
NS-v79-My 15 '70-p708
PW-v194-Jl 22 '68-p63
SR-v51-N 9 '68-p46
Spec-v224-My 9 '70-p620
TLS-Ap 16 '70-p418
Bread And Jam For Frances
CE-v41-F '65-p314
NCW-v216-Mr '73-p89
NYTBR-v70-Ja 17 '65-p38
TES-Jl 23 '82-p24
TLS-N 24 '66-p1083
Charlie Meadows
BW-v14-S 9 '84-p11
CBRS-v13-O '84-p14
Sch Lib-v32-S '84-p230
TLS-N 9 '84-p1294
Charlie The Tramp
LJ-v92-My 15 '67-p2014
NYTBR, pt.1-v72-My 7 '67-p51
Crocodile & Pierrot
CCB-B-v31-O '77-p34
KR-v45-My 15 '77-p538
SLJ-v24-S '77-p109
The Dancing Tigers
GP-v18-Jl '79-p3553
JB-v43-Ag '79-p196
KR-v49-Ap 15 '81-p499
Lis-v102-N 8 '79-p646
NYTBR-v86-Ap 26 '81-p54
Obs-Ap 1 '79-p38
PW-v219-F 27 '81-p149
SLJ-v27-Ag '81-p56
TLS-D 14 '79-p126
Dinner At Alberta's
BL-v72-O 15 '75-p302
CCB-B-v29-F '76-p98
CLW-v47-F '76-p309
CSM-v67-N 5 '75-pB4
GP-v16-Jl '77-p3151
HB-v52-F '76-p46
JB-v41-O '77-p288
KR-v43-S 1 '75-p993
NY-v51-D 1 '75-p181
PW-v208-O 6 '75-p86
SLJ-v22-D '75-p31
SLJ-v22-D '75-p64
SR-v3-N 29 '75-p31
TES-S 19 '80-p30
TES-Mr 9 '84-p50
Teacher-v94-N '76-p137
Egg Thoughts And Other Frances Songs
BL-v68-Je 1 '72-p860
CCB-B-v25-Ap '72-p123
GW-v108-Ap 7 '73-p26
KR-v40-Ap 1 '72-p396
LJ-v97-My 15 '72-p1885
LJ-v97-My 15 '72-p1900
LJ-v97-D 15 '72-p4056
NS-v85-My 25 '73-p780
NYTBR-Je 25 '72-p8
PW-v201-F 28 '72-p73
Spec-v230-Ap 14 '73-p462
TLS-Ap 6 '73-p384
Teacher-v92-F '75-p40
Emmet Otter's Jug-Band Christmas
BL-v68-D 1 '71-p333
CCB-B-v25-N '71-p44
CLW-v43-My '72-p536
CLW-v45-N '73-p172
Comw-v95-N 19 '71-p185
KR-v39-S 15 '71-p1013
LJ-v96-O 15 '71-p3487
LJ-v96-D 15 '71-p4159
NYTBR-D 5 '71-p90
PW-v200-N 8 '71-p48
SR-v54-D 11 '71-p45
TLS-N 23 '73-p1437
Flat Cat
BL-v77-Ap 15 '81-p1159
Brit Bk N C-Spring '81-p16
KR-v49-F 15 '81-p209
NS-v100-N 21 '80-p19
PW-v219-Ja 9 '81-p73
SLJ-v27-D '80-p44
TES-N 21 '80-p29
The Flight Of Bembel Rudzuk
BW-v12-N 7 '82-p13
CCB-B-v36-Ja '83-p90
GP-v21-Ja '83-p4015
JB-v46-D '82-p220
NS-v104-D 3 '82-p22
SLJ-v29-Ja '83-p60
Goodnight
CCB-B-v19-Ap '66-p131
KR-v34-Ja 15 '66-p53
LJ-v91-Ap 15 '66-p2198
TLS-O 16 '69-p1201
The Great Fruit Gum Robbery
Brit Bk N C-Spring '82-p2
Obs-D 6 '81-p28
Sch Lib-v30-Je '82-p120
TES-D 18 '81-p18
TLS-N 20 '81-p1357
The Great Gum Drop Robbery
BL-v78-Ap 1 '82-p1018
BW-v12-N 7 '82-p13
CBRS-v10-My '82-p92
CCB-B-v35-Mr '82-p130
LA-v60-F '83-p213
SLJ-v28-My '82-p54
Harvey's Hideout
BL-v65-Je 15 '69-p1175
CCB-B-v22-My '69-p143
CSM-v61-My 1 '69-pB2
HB-v45-Je '69-p295
Inst-v79-Ag '69-p191
KR-v37-Ap 15 '69-p434
LJ-v94-Ap 15 '69-p1768
PW-v195-F 24 '69-p65
SR-v52-Mr 22 '69-p62
TLS-N 23 '73-p1437
Henry And The Monstrous Din
Am-v115-Jl 2 '66-p15
KR-v34-Ap 15 '66-p417
LJ-v91-My 15 '66-p2682
TLS-My 25 '67-p452
Herman The Loser
TLS-Jl 14 '72-p808
How Tom Beat Captain Najork And His Hired Sportsmen
B&B-v20-Ja '75-p77
BL-v71-S 1 '74-p41
BL-v71-Mr 15 '75-p766
BW-D 8 '74-p7
CCB-B-v28-Ja '75-p78
CSM-v66-N 6 '74-p11
CSM-v70-S 18 '78-pB14
Choice-v12-N '75-p1132

HOBAN, Russell (continued)
HB-v51-Ap '75-p138
KR-v42-D 15 '74-p1299
KR-v43-Ja 1 '75-p2
LJ-v99-O 15 '74-p2733
Lis-v92-N 7 '74-p617
NS-v87-My 24 '74-p741
NY-v50-D 2 '74-p200
NYTBR-N 3 '74-p55
NYTBR-Ja 21 '79-p37
Obs-Je 2 '74-p33
PW-v206-S 9 '74-p67
SLJ-v27-O '80-p119
TLS-Jl 5 '74-p718
Teacher-v92-My '75-p91
Jim Frog
BW-v14-My 13 '84-p19
JB-v48-F '84-p23
PW-v225-My 4 '84-p59
SLJ-v30-Ag '84-p60
La Corona And The Tin Frog
B&B-v25-N '79-p54
CCB-B-v34-Je '81-p194
GP-v18-Ja '80-p3638
JB-v44-Ap '80-p62
KR-v49-Ap 1 '81-p432
NS-v98-N 9 '79-p732
Punch-v277-D 12 '79-p1153
SLJ-v27-Ag '81-p56
Sch Lib-v28-Mr '80-p36
TES-N 23 '79-p31
TLS-D 14 '79-p126
Lavinia Bat
BW-v14-S 9 '84-p11
CBRS-v13-O '84-p14
PW-v226-Ag 24 '84-p80
Sch Lib-v32-S '84-p230
TLS-N 9 '84-p1294
Letitia Rabbit's String Song
CCB-B-v27-S '73-p9
Comw-v99-N 23 '73-p212
KR-v41-Ap 15 '73-p454
LJ-v98-Jl '73-p2187
NYTBR-Ap 15 '73-p8
PW-v203-Ap 9 '73-p66
The Little Brute Family
BL-v63-N 1 '66-p324
CSM-v58-S 22 '66-p10
GT-v84-D '66-p122
Inst-v76-D '66-p13
KR-v34-Jl 1 '66-p621
LJ-v91-Jl '66-p3528
PW-v219-Ja 23 '81-p126
The Mole Family's Christmas
BL-v66-F 1 '70-p670
BW-v3-D 21 '69-p8
CCB-B-v23-D '69-p60
Econ-v249-D 29 '73-p60
KR-v37-D 1 '69-p1250
LJ-v94-O 15 '69-p3851
PW-v196-S 22 '69-p85
SR-v52-D 20 '69-p29
The Mouse And His Child
BL-v64-Ja 15 '68-p593
CCB-B-v21-My '68-p143
CE-v44-My '68-p562
CSM-v66-My 1 '74-pF5
Cres-v42-Je '79-p28
Emerg Lib-v11-S '83-p40
HB-v54-Ap '78-p198
KR-v35-S 15 '67-p1134
LJ-v92-D 15 '67-p4612
Lis-v82-N 6 '69-p640
Lis-v89-Mr 8 '73-p312
NS-v77-My 16 '69-p701
NS-v83-Je 2 '72-p763
NYTBR-v73-F 4 '68-p26
NYTBR-F 10 '74-p30
NYTBR-v87-Ag 22 '82-p31
Obs-Ap 6 '69-p26
Obs-Jl 11 '76-p23
Par-v52-My '77-p31
SR-v51-Ap 20 '68-p41
Spec-v222-My 16 '69-p654
TES-D 9 '77-p21
TES-S 19 '80-p30
TLS-Ap 3 '69-p357
TLS-Ap 28 '72-p486
YR-v4-Mr '68-p1
A Near Thing For Captain Najork
BL-v72-Ap 1 '76-p1114
CCB-B-v29-Jl '76-p175
CE-v53-N '76-p96
CLW-v48-S '76-p90
GP-v14-Ap '76-p2858
JB-v40-F '76-p15
KR-v44-Ap 1 '76-p385
NS-v90-N 28 '75-p688
Obs-N 30 '75-p27
PW-v209-Ap 12 '76-p66
SLJ-v22-F '76-p39
Spec-v235-D 6 '75-p734
TLS-D 5 '75-p1453
Nothing To Do
BL-v61-Ja 15 '65-p482
HB-v41-Ap '65-p163
NYTBR-v70-Ja 17 '65-p38
Owl At Home
BL-v73-Mr 15 '77-p1101
Pedaling Man
BL-v64-Jl 1 '68-p1234
KR-v36-My 1 '68-p515
LJ-v93-Jl '68-p2733
NYTBR-v73-My 5 '68-p44
TLS-Ap 16 '70-p414
Save My Place
KR-v35-Je 1 '67-p641
LJ-v92-S 15 '67-p3178
PW-v191-Mr 6 '67-p75
PW-v192-Ag 14 '67-p50
The Sea-Thing Child
CCB-B-v26-F '73-p92
CE-v49-My '73-p422
CSM-v64-N 8 '72-pB1
GW-v107-D 16 '72-p24
KR-v40-O 15 '72-p1188
KR-v40-D 15 '72-p1412
LJ-v98-F 15 '73-p644
NS-v84-N 10 '72-p698
NY-v48-D 2 '72-p202
PW-v202-N 13 '72-p45
TLS-N 3 '72-p1323
The Serpent Tower
Brit Bk N C-Autumn '81-p12
JB-v45-O '81-p197
Lis-v106-N 5 '81-p548
The Sorely Trying Day
GP-v17-Mr '79-p3477
Stone Doll Of Sister Brute
KR-v36-Ja 1 '68-p2
LJ-v93-Mr 15 '68-p1302
PW-v193-Ja 29 '68-p97
The Stone Doll Of Sister Brute
Emerg Lib-v9-N '81-p35
The Story Of Hester Mouse
CCB-B-v19-S '65-p10
Inst-v75-N '65-p95
KR-v33-Ag 15 '65-p819
LJ-v90-S 15 '65-p3791
NYTBR-v70-N 7 '65-p55
Ten What?
BB-v3-S '75-p2
B&B-v20-My '75-p72
BL-v72-S 1 '75-p41
CCB-B-v29-N '75-p46
HB-v51-Ag '75-p368
KR-v43-My 15 '75-p563
Lis-v92-N 7 '74-p617
Obs-D 8 '74-p30
PW-v207-Je 2 '75-p54
SLJ-v22-S '75-p83
SLJ-v26-O '79-p104
They Came From Aargh!
BW-v12-N 7 '82-p13
Brit Bk N C-Spring '82-p2
CBRS-v10-Ja '82-p42

HOBAN, Russell (continued)
CCB-B-v35-Ja '82-p86
HB-v58-F '82-p33
KR-v50-F 15 '82-p200
Obs-D 6 '81-p28
PW-v220-D 11 '81-p63
SLJ-v28-Ja '82-p65
TES-D 18 '81-p18
TLS-N 20 '81-p1357
Tom And The Two Handles
CCB-B-v18-My '65-p129
CSM-v57-My 6 '65-p2B
Comw-v82-My 28 '65-p327
KR-v33-Ap 1 '65-p376
LJ-v90-My 15 '65-p2394
NYRB-v7-D 15 '66-p27
NYTBR-v70-My 9 '65-p28
Turtle Diary
Atl-v238-Ag '76-p83
BL-v72-F 1 '76-p755
CSM-v68-Ap 7 '76-p27
Choice-v13-Je '76-p519
GP-v14-Jl '75-p2675
KR-v43-D 15 '75-p1394
LJ-v101-Ap 1 '76-p924
Lis-v93-Mr 27 '75-p421
NL-v59-Mr 15 '76-p17
NO-v15-Mr 27 '76-p19
NS-v89-Ap 11 '75-p489
NW-v87-Mr 1 '76-p76
NY-v52-Mr 22 '76-p130
NYTBR-Mr 21 '76-p6
Obs-Mr 23 '75-p30
Obs-F 27 '77-p29
PW-v208-D 15 '75-p47
PW-v214-O 30 '78-p49
SR-v3-My 1 '76-p36
Spec-v234-Ap 5 '75-p411
TLS-Mr 21 '75-p293
Time-v107-F 16 '76-p72
VLS-O '81-p22
The Twenty Elephant Restaurant
BL-v74-My 15 '78-p1494
Brit Bk N-D '80-p714
CCB-B-v32-S '78-p10
JB-v44-O '80-p239
KR-v46-Mr 15 '78-p299
Lis-v104-N 6 '80-p627
NS-v100-N 21 '80-p19
SLJ-v24-My '78-p56
Sch Lib-v29-Mr '81-p33
TES-N 21 '80-p29
TES-Mr 9 '84-p50
Time-v112-D 4 '78-p103
Ugly Bird
CSM-v61-N 6 '69-pB4
KR-v37-Jl 1 '69-p670
LJ-v94-N 15 '69-p4277
PW-v196-Ag 4 '69-p49
What Happened When Jack And Daisy Tried To Fool The Tooth Fairies
CCB-B-v20-N '66-p42
Wo Ist Meine Puppe?
BL-v75-N 15 '78-p555

* * *

HOBAN, Tana
A, B, See!
BL-v78-Mr 15 '82-p957
CBRS-v10-Mr '82-p72
CCB-B-v35-F '82-p108
CE-v59-Ja '83-p213
HB-v58-Je '82-p279
Inst-v92-S '82-p20
KR-v50-Mr 1 '82-p271
NYTBR-v87-Ap 25 '82-p38
PW-v221-Ja 8 '82-p83
SLJ-v28-Mr '82-p134
VLS-My '82-p12
Big Ones, Little Ones
ACSB-v10-Winter '77-p23
BB-v4-My '76-p2
BL-v72-Je 1 '76-p1406
CCB-B-v29-Jl '76-p175
CLW-v48-D '76-p234
HB-v52-O '76-p491
KR-v44-My 15 '76-p588
SA-v235-D '76-p145
SLJ-v23-S '76-p101
WLB-v50-Je '76-p802
Circles, Triangles And Squares
CCB-B-v28-Ja '75-p79
HB-v50-D '74-p683
KR-v42-Jl 15 '74-p736
LA-v52-S '75-p853
LJ-v99-O 15 '74-p2733
SA-v231-D '74-p150
Sch Arts-v80-Ja '81-p39
Count And See
B&B-v18-Jl '73-p140
BL-v68-Jl 1 '72-p942
CCB-B-v25-Jl '72-p170
CE-v49-O '72-p32
CLW-v52-Ap '81-p388
HB-v48-Ag '72-p361
KR-v40-Ap 15 '72-p472
LJ-v97-My 15 '72-p1885
LJ-v97-My 15 '72-p1900
NYTBR-Ag 11 '74-p23
PW-v201-My 1 '72-p50
SA-v227-D '72-p115
SLJ-v26-O '79-p104
SR-v55-Je 17 '72-p72
TLS-Je 15 '73-p687
Teacher-v90-O '72-p115
Teacher-v92-Ja '75-p111
Teacher-v96-F '79-p30
Dig, Drill, Dump, Fill
BL-v72-N 1 '75-p366
CCB-B-v29-Ap '76-p125
CE-v52-Mr '76-p272
KR-v43-O 15 '75-p1176
SLJ-v22-N '75-p63
I Read Signs
BL-v80-O 15 '83-p359
CBRS-v12-N '83-p25
CCB-B-v37-D '83-p68
CSM-v76-D 2 '83-pB10
HB-v59-D '83-p700
KR-v51-N 1 '83-pJ186
RT-v37-My '84-p889
SLJ-v30-N '83-p64
I Read Symbols
BL-v80-O 15 '83-p359
CBRS-v12-N '83-p25
CCB-B-v37-D '83-p68
CE-v60-My '84-p367
CSM-v76-D 2 '83-pB10
HB-v59-D '83-p700
KR-v51-N 1 '83-pJ186
PW-v224-O 21 '83-p68
RT-v37-My '84-p889
SLJ-v30-N '83-p64
I Walk And Read
BL-v80-My 15 '84-p1343
CBRS-v12-My '84-p102
CCB-B-v37-Jl '84-p205
HB-v60-Ag '84-p457
KR-v52-Mr 1 '84-pJ4
LA-v61-O '84-p629
NYTBR-v89-Ap 8 '84-p29
SLJ-v31-O '84-p147
Is It Red? Is It Yellow? Is It Blue?
BB-v6-Ja '79-p1
BL-v75-Ja 1 '79-p750
BL-v75-Mr 15 '79-p1164
CBRS-v7-Winter '79-p51
CCB-B-v32-Ja '79-p82
CE-v56-O '79-p48
CLW-v52-Ap '81-p388
CSM-v71-Ap 9 '79-pB10
Comw-v105-N 10 '78-p729
HB-v55-O '78-p508
KR-v47-Ja 1 '79-p3

HOBAN, Tana (continued)
Par-v58-Ag '83-p126
RT-v33-O '79-p35
RT-v35-My '82-p933
SLJ-v25-D '78-p44
Teacher-v96-F '79-p30
Teacher-v96-My '79-p108
Is It Rough? Is It Smooth? Is It Shiny?
BL-v81-O 1 '84-p248
CBRS-v13-O '84-p14
HB-v60-S '84-p581
KR-v52-S 1 '84-pJ61
SA-v251-D '84-p38
Look Again
ACSB-v13-Winter '80-p3
A Lib-v3-Ap '72-p420
BL-v67-Je 1 '71-p834
BL-v68-Ap 1 '72-p669
BW-v5-My 9 '71-p14
CCB-B-v24-Jl '71-p172
CE-v48-O '71-p29
CE-v60-S '83-p27
CSM-v63-My 6 '71-pB5
HB-v47-Ag '71-p396
KR-v39-F 15 '71-p168
LJ-v96-My 15 '71-p1781
LJ-v96-My 15 '71-p1796
LJ-v98-O 15 '73-p3162
NYTBR, pt.2-My 2 '71-p38
NYTBR, pt.2-N 7 '71-p4
NYTBR, pt.2-N 7 '71-p32
PW-v199-My 3 '71-p55
RT-v32-My '79-p944
RT-v35-Ap '82-p788
SA-v227-D '72-p117
SR-v54-Jl 17 '71-p36
TLS-Ap 28 '72-p490
Teacher-v96-F '79-p30
More Than One
CBRS-v9-Ag '81-p121
CCB-B-v35-O '81-p31
HB-v57-O '81-p527
KR-v49-S 15 '81-p1156
LA-v59-Mr '82-p267
SA-v245-D '81-p47
SLJ-v28-S '81-p109
One Little Kitten
CBRS-v8-N '79-p22
CCB-B-v33-N '79-p49
CE-v60-My '84-p344
HB-v55-O '79-p524
KR-v47-S 15 '79-p1065
PW-v216-O 8 '79-p70
RT-v34-O '80-p41
SLJ-v26-S '79-p112
Over, Under & Through
BL-v69-My 15 '73-p907
BW-v7-Jl 8 '73-p13
CCB-B-v26-My '73-p139
KR-v41-F 1 '73-p109
PW-v203-My 28 '73-p40
Over, Under And Through And Other Spatial Concepts
RT-v32-My '79-p943
Push-Pull Empty-Full
BL-v69-Ja 1 '73-p449
CCB-B-v26-N '72-p43
CE-v49-Ja '73-p206
CLW-v52-Ap '81-p388
KR-v40-S 1 '72-p1021
LJ-v97-N 15 '72-p3797
PW-v202-Jl 24 '72-p75
Par-v58-Ag '83-p126
RT-v32-N '78-p148
TES-N 13 '81-p24
TLS-Jl 5 '74-p718
Teacher-v90-Ja '73-p92
Round And Round And Round
BL-v79-Ap 15 '83-p1094
CBRS-v11-Je '83-p108
CE-v60-N '83-p138
HB-v59-Je '83-p290
KR-v51-Mr 15 '83-p304
LA-v60-O '83-p897
PW-v223-My 6 '83-p98
RT-v37-D '83-p309
SLJ-v29-Ap '83-p102
Shapes And Things
BL-v67-O 15 '70-p192
CCB-B-v24-F '71-p93
CLW-v42-D '70-p257
HB-v46-O '70-p492
Inst-v80-O '70-p142
KR-v38-Je 15 '70-p637
LJ-v95-D 15 '70-p4337
PW-v198-Jl 20 '70-p70
RT-v35-My '82-p933
SR-v53-N 14 '70-p34
Take Another Look
BL-v77-Mr 1 '81-p964
CBRS-v9-F '81-p51
CCB-B-v34-Je '81-p194
CE-v58-N '81-p112
HB-v57-Je '81-p292
Inst-v90-My '81-p62
KR-v49-Mr 1 '81-p279
RT-v35-My '82-p933
SLJ-v27-Mr '81-p132
Where Is It?
BL-v70-My 1 '74-p1003
CCB-B-v28-S '74-p10
CE-v51-F '75-p216
CE-v51-Mr '75-p274
HB-v50-Je '74-p273
Inst-v83-My '74-p94
KR-v42-Ja 15 '74-p51
LJ-v99-Mr 15 '74-p882
NYTBR-My 5 '74-p46
PW-v205-F 4 '74-p73
Teacher-v96-My '79-p116

* * *

HOBBS, Laura
Cars
BL-v73-My 1 '77-p1352
SLJ-v23-Ap '77-p55

* * *

HOBBY, Janice H
Staying Back
CSM-v75-My 23 '83-p15
SLJ-v29-Ap '83-p102

* * *

HOBDEN, E
Fun With Weaving
JB-v43-O '79-p279
LJ-v106-Mr 1 '81-p549

* * *

HOBERMAN, Mary Ann
Bugs
CCB-B-v30-My '77-p142
KR-v44-O 1 '76-p1098
LA-v54-My '77-p579
RT-v31-F '78-p576
SLJ-v23-Ja '77-p82
WCRB-v3-Mr '77-p48
WLB-v51-F '77-p488
The Cozy Book
CCB-B-v36-Mr '83-p128
Inst-v92-N '82-p150
KR-v50-Ag 1 '82-p864
PW-v222-D 3 '82-p60
SLJ-v29-Ja '83-p60
A House Is A House For Me
BL-v75-D 1 '78-p616
CCB-B-v32-My '79-p155
Econ-v269-D 23 '78-p102
GP-v18-S '79-p3580
Inst-v92-N '82-p152
KR-v46-O 1 '78-p1067
LA-v56-S '79-p684
LATBR-Je 13 '82-p8
Ms-v11-D '82-p94
PW-v214-Ag 28 '78-p395
RT-v33-O '79-p52
SLJ-v25-O '78-p133

HOBERMAN, Mary Ann (continued)
Spec-v241-D 16 '78-p23
TES-D 10 '82-p34
WCRB-v5-Mr '79-p56
I Like Old Clothes
BB-v4-O '76-p1
CCB-B-v29-Jl '76-p175
HB-v52-Ag '76-p386
KR-v44-Ap 1 '76-p385
New R-v175-N 27 '76-p32
PW-v209-Ap 5 '76-p102
SLJ-v23-S '76-p101
SR-v3-My 15 '76-p38
A Little Book Of Little Beasts
CCB-B-v26-Jl '73-p171
CE-v50-O '73-p29
CSM-v65-My 2 '73-pB2
KR-v41-Mr 1 '73-p251
PW-v203-Mr 19 '73-p72
The Looking Book
CCB-B-v27-F '74-p96
KR-v41-Ag 1 '73-p809
LJ-v98-N 15 '73-p3441
PW-v204-S 3 '73-p53
Not Enough Beds For The Babies
CCB-B-v18-Ap '65-p118
KR-v33-Mr 1 '65-p232
Nuts To You & Nuts To Me
CCB-B-v28-D '74-p64
HB-v51-Ap '75-p162
KR-v42-Je 15 '74-p631
LJ-v99-O 15 '74-p2733
PW-v206-Jl 29 '74-p57
SR/W-v2-N 30 '74-p44
Teacher-v92-Ap '75-p29
WLB-v49-F '75-p426
The Raucous Auk
BW-v7-N 11 '73-p2C
CCB-B-v27-Ap '74-p130
CE-v50-Ap '74-p338
CLW-v45-Ap '74-p457
Choice-v12-N '75-p1132
HB-v50-F '74-p59
KR-v41-O 15 '73-p1157
KR-v41-D 15 '73-p1353
LJ-v99-F 15 '74-p563
NY-v50-D 2 '74-p203
PW-v204-D 31 '73-p27
RT-v32-N '78-p148
TN-v30-Je '74-p434
Yellow Butter, Purple Jelly, Red Jam, Black Bread
BL-v77-Jl 15 '81-p1447
CCB-B-v35-S '81-p10
KR-v49-Ag 15 '81-p1009
LA-v58-N '81-p956
PW-v219-My 15 '81-p63

* * *

HOBLEY, L F
Christians And Christianity
Brit Bk N C-Spring '80-p20
JB-v44-Je '80-p142
Jews And Judaism
Brit Bk N C-Spring '80-p20
JB-v44-Je '80-p142
Moslems And Islam
Brit Bk N C-Spring '80-p20
JB-v44-Je '80-p142
Steps In History. Bk. 1
TES-N 5 '82-p31

* * *

HOBSON, Alan
Full Circle
B&B-v17-Mr '72-p45
CR-v222-Ap '73-p224
Choice-v9-N '72-p1130
Enc-v41-Jl '73-p69
LJ-v97-Jl '72-p2399
RES-v23-N '72-p484
TLS-Mr 10 '72-p270

* * *

HOBSON, Andrew
Film Animation As A Hobby
BL-v72-F 15 '76-p856
Des-v77-Summer '76-p33
Hob-v81-D '76-p139
SLJ-v22-Mr '76-p114

* * *

HOBSON, Laura Z
I'm Going To Have A Baby
CCB-B-v21-O '67-p27
CLW-v39-O '67-p159
CLW-v42-Ap '71-p501
KR-v35-Je 1 '67-p641
LJ-v92-My 15 '67-p2043
PW-v192-Jl 24 '67-p56
TLS-My 25 '67-p465

* * *

HOBSON, Polly
The Mystery House
CCB-B-v18-Mr '65-p103
HB-v41-Ap '65-p171
LJ-v90-Ja 15 '65-p379

* * *

HOBSON, Sam B
The Lion Of The Kalahari
CSM-v68-N 3 '76-p20
KR-v44-S 1 '76-p973

* * *

HOBZEK, Mildred
We Came A-Marching.... 1, 2, 3
BW-N 12 '78-pE2
CBRS-v7-F '79-p62
CCB-B-v32-Mr '79-p118
PW-v215-Ja 15 '79-p131
Par-v54-Ap '79-p24
SLJ-v25-Mr '79-p122

* * *

HOCH, Edward D
The Monkey's Clue/The Stolen Sapphire
SLJ-v25-F '79-p57
Mysteries For Crime-Busters
SLJ-v25-Mr '79-p134

* * *

HOCHMAN, Stan
Mike Schmidt: Baseball's King Of Swing
BL-v80-Ja 15 '84-p754
B Rpt-v3-My '84-p54
SLJ-v30-D '83-p87

* * *

HOCKEN, Sheila
Emma's Story
GP-v20-Mr '82-p4039
JB-v46-F '82-p25
Sch Lib-v30-Je '82-p148
TES-Ag 20 '82-p19

* * *

HOCKING, Anthony
Ontario And Quebec
CG-v97-D '78-p75
Prince Edward Island
CG-v97-D '78-p77
SLJ-v25-My '79-p62

* * *

HODDER-WILLIAMS, Christopher
The Main Experiment
BS-v24-Mr 15 '65-p486
CCB-B-v18-Ap '65-p118
LJ-v90-F 15 '65-p896
MFSF-v29-N '65-p22
NYTBR-v70-Mr 7 '65-p38
PW-v189-F 14 '66-p146
SR-v48-Mr 27 '65-p31

* * *

HODEIR, Andre
Warwick's 3 Bottles
CCB-B-v20-F '67-p91
KR-v34-O 15 '66-p1095
LJ-v91-N 15 '66-p5740
NO-v6-Je 19 '67-p19
NYRB-v7-D 15 '66-p28
NYTBR-v71-N 6 '66-p70
NYTBR-v71-D 4 '66-p66

* * *

HODES, Barbara T
Puzzling Canada
BIC-v9-Mr '80-p23
Can Child Lit-#23 '81-p108
Emerg Lib-v10-My '83-p30
In Rev-v14-Je '80-p43

* * *

HODGE, Ben
Football
BL-v74-Ja 1 '78-p751
SLJ-v24-D '77-p64

* * *

HODGES, C Walter
The Battlement Garden
BL-v76-Mr 15 '80-p1058
Brit Bk N C-Spring '80-p21
CCB-B-v33-Jl '80-p214
GP-v18-Ja '80-p3642
HB-v56-Ap '80-p185
HT-v30-Mr '80-p47
JB-v44-Je '80-p143
KR-v48-Mr 15 '80-p372
Lis-v102-N 8 '79-p645
SLJ-v26-Ag '80-p76
Sch Lib-v28-Mr '80-p73
TLS-D 14 '79-p130
The Emperor's Elephant
JB-v40-Ap '76-p82
Obs-N 30 '75-p27
TLS-Ap 2 '76-p381
Magna Carta
BL-v63-Mr 1 '67-p728
CCB-B-v20-Je '67-p152
LR-v21-Spring '67-p31
TLS-N 24 '66-p1094
Marsh King
BL-v64-S 15 '67-p130
BS-v27-Je 1 '67-p106
CCB-B-v20-Jl '67-p171
HB-v43-Je '67-p353
KR-v35-Mr 15 '67-p349
LJ-v92-My 15 '67-p2029
LR-v21-Autumn '67-p154
NYTBR, pt.1-v72-My 7 '67-p14
Obs-S 27 '70-p26
PW-v191-My 29 '67-p64
SR-v50-My 13 '67-p60
TLS-N 30 '67-p1139
The Namesake
CCB-B-v18-Jl '65-p162
Lis-v77-My 18 '67-p661
NYTBR-v70-Ja 24 '65-p26
Obs-Ag 1 '76-p18
Spec-Je 4 '65-p729
TLS-My 25 '67-p447
TLS-D 4 '69-p1384
Norman Conquest
BL-v63-Mr 1 '67-p728
CCB-B-v20-Je '67-p153
HB-v43-F '67-p83
KR-v34-D 1 '66-p1223
LR-v20-Autumn '66-p500
TLS-My 19 '66-p445
The Overland Launch
B&B-v17-My '72-pR14
BL-v66-Jl 15 '70-p1407
BL-v67-Ap 1 '71-p660
BS-v30-Jl 1 '70-p145
CCB-B-v24-O '70-p26
HB-v46-Ag '70-p393
KR-v38-Je 1 '70-p604
LJ-v95-O 15 '70-p3638
NS-v78-O 31 '69-p623
Obs-N 30 '69-p35
PW-v197-Je 1 '70-p68
SR-v53-Ag 22 '70-p53
Spec-v223-N 1 '69-p598
TLS-D 4 '69-p1400
Plain Lane Christmas
BB-v6-D '78-p3
CCB-B-v32-D '78-p63
JB-v42-D '78-p292
KR-v46-D 15 '78-p1357
PW-v214-O 16 '78-p122
SLJ-v25-O '78-p112
Spec-v241-D 16 '78-p23
TES-N 17 '78-p26
Playhouse Tales
BL-v71-Mr 1 '75-p692
CCB-B-v28-Je '75-p162
CE-v52-N '75-p90
GP-v13-Ja '75-p2544
HB-v51-Je '75-p274
HT-v24-D '74-p879
JB-v39-F '75-p65
KR-v43-Ja 1 '75-p24
LR-v24-Winter '75-p366
NYTBR-Mr 9 '75-p8
SLJ-v21-Mr '75-p106
TLS-Ap 4 '75-p369
The Puritan Revolution
CCB-B-v26-F '73-p92
KR-v40-Mr 15 '72-p329
LJ-v98-Mr 15 '73-p1003
Spanish Armada
BL-v64-Mr 15 '68-p868
CCB-B-v21-Mr '68-p111
CLW-v39-Ap '68-p608
CSM-v60-My 2 '68-pB9
KR-v36-Ja 1 '68-p9
LJ-v93-Ap 15 '68-p1811
NS-v74-N 3 '67-p604
Obs-D 3 '67-p26
SE-v33-My '69-p563
SR-v51-Mr 16 '68-p39
TLS-N 30 '67-p1159

* * *

HODGES, Charles Du Bois
In Search Of Young Beauty
LJ-v90-F 15 '65-p861

* * *

HODGES, Elizabeth D
Books For Elementary School Libraries
BL-v66-N 15 '69-p353
CLW-v41-N '69-p189
HB-v46-Je '70-p310
LJ-v95-Ja 15 '70-p220
Sch L-v19-Spring '70-p34
WLB-v44-O '69-p205

* * *

HODGES, Elizabeth Jamison
Free As A Frog
CCB-B-v23-Je '70-p159
LJ-v95-Mr 15 '70-p1187
PW-v198-Ag 3 '70-p60
A Song For Gilgamesh
CLW-v43-N '71-p171
CSM-v63-My 29 '71-p15
HB-v47-Ap '71-p168
KR-v39-Mr 1 '71-p242
LJ-v96-S 15 '71-p2917

* * *

HODGES, Glen A
Lost Bear
ACSB-v9-Winter '76-p18
BL-v72-S 1 '75-p41
KR-v43-Je 1 '75-p604
SLJ-v21-My '75-p56

* * *

HODGES, Margaret
The Avenger
BL-v79-F 1 '83-p724
CCB-B-v36-F '83-p109

HODGES, Margaret
(continued)
KR-v50-O 1 '82-p1109
PW-v222-N 26 '82-p60
SLJ-v29-N '82-p100
The Fire Bringer
Am-v127-D 2 '72-p480
BL-v69-Ja 15 '73-p493
CCB-B-v26-Ap '73-p124
CE-v49-Mr '73-p320
HB-v49-F '73-p44
KR-v40-N 1 '72-p1233
LJ-v97-D 15 '72-p4056
LJ-v97-D 15 '72-p4067
NYTBR, pt.2-N 5 '72-p20
PW-v203-Ja 8 '73-p64
SE-v37-D '73-p789
SLJ-v26-N '79-p43
TN-v29-Je '73-p356
Teacher-v90-Mr '73-p80
The Freewheeling Of Joshua Cobb
CCB-B-v28-Mr '75-p114
HB-v50-O '74-p137
KR-v42-D 1 '74-p1259
KR-v43-Ja 1 '75-p10
LA-v52-O '75-p995
LJ-v99-S 15 '74-p2270
Teacher-v92-Mr '75-p112
The Gorgon's Head
BW-v6-My 7 '72-p6
CCB-B-v26-Mr '73-p107
KR-v40-Ja 15 '72-p71
LJ-v97-S 15 '72-p2950
NYTBR-Ag 27 '72-p24
Hatching Of Joshua Cobb
BL-v64-N 15 '67-p388
CCB-B-v21-N '67-p43
HB-v43-O '67-p594
KR-v35-Je 1 '67-p645
LJ-v92-S 15 '67-p3186
SR-v50-S 16 '67-p49
Teacher-v86-My '69-p132
The High Riders
BL-v76-My 15 '80-p1365
CCB-B-v34-S '80-p12
CE-v57-N '80-p112
HB-v56-Ag '80-p413
KR-v48-Ag 15 '80-p1084
SLJ-v26-My '80-p75
Hopkins Of The Mayflower
BL-v69-F 1 '73-p525
HB-v49-F '73-p61
KR-v40-N 15 '72-p1316
NY-v48-D 2 '72-p212
Knight Prisoner
BL-v73-F 1 '77-p833
CCB-B-v30-Ap '77-p126
HB-v52-D '76-p632
KR-v44-O 1 '76-p1105
LA-v54-Ap '77-p444
SLJ-v23-D '76-p60
Teacher-v94-Ja '77-p131
Lady Queen Anne
BL-v66-O 15 '69-p266
BW-v3-S 21 '69-p14
CLW-v41-Ja '70-p317
CLW-v41-F '70-p385
GT-v87-Ja '70-p140
HB-v45-Je '69-p315
KR-v37-My 1 '69-p518
LJ-v94-S 15 '69-p3218
PW-v195-My 19 '69-p71
TN-v26-Ja '70-p207
The Little Humpbacked Horse
BL-v77-D 1 '80-p513
BW-v10-D 14 '80-p13
CBRS-v9-Ja '81-p35
CCB-B-v34-My '81-p172
CE-v57-Mr '81-p236
CSM-v73-Mr 16 '81-p23
HB-v57-F '81-p61
Inst-v90-Mr '81-p26
KR-v48-N 15 '80-p1461
PW-v218-N 14 '80-p55
RT-v35-D '81-p333
SLJ-v27-D '80-p44
Sch Arts-v80-My '81-p61
The Making Of Joshua Cobb
BL-v67-Je 1 '71-p834
CCB-B-v25-N '71-p44
CLW-v43-Mr '72-p429
GT-v89-O '71-p94
HB-v47-Je '71-p287
KR-v39-F 1 '71-p105
LJ-v96-Ap 15 '71-p1504
NYT-v121-D 16 '71-p67
NYTBR, pt.2-My 2 '71-p34
NYTBR, pt.2-N 7 '71-p30
PW-v199-Mr 22 '71-p53
The Other World
BL-v70-S 15 '73-p120
Comw-v99-N 23 '73-p214
HB-v49-Je '73-p267
KR-v41-My 15 '73-p570
LJ-v98-Jl '73-p2194
PW-v203-Je 18 '73-p70
Persephone And The Springtime
CCB-B-v27-O '73-p28
KR-v41-Ap 15 '73-p455
LJ-v99-My 15 '74-p1466

* * *

HODGETTS, Blake Christopher
Dream Of The Dinosaurs
CCB-B-v32-Ja '79-p82
CSM-v71-Ja 8 '79-pB6
KR-v46-O 15 '78-p1133
PW-v214-O 9 '78-p77
SLJ-v25-N '78-p45

* * *

HODGKIN, E C
The Arabs
GP-v14-D '75-p2763

* * *

HODGKINS, Sylvia
A Cat Called Hamlet Cat
B&B-v20-F '75-p77

* * *

HODGMAN, Ann
Skystars
ASBYP-v15-Spring '82-p42
BL-v78-N 1 '81-p376
CCB-B-v35-D '81-p69
Cur R-v21-My '82-p224
HB-v57-D '81-p677
SB-v17-Mr '82-p218
SLJ-v28-D '81-p64
VOYA-v4-F '82-p41

* * *

HODGSON, Louise
Breathing Backwards
CCB-B-v21-S '67-p8
SB-v3-S '67-p130

* * *

HODGSON, Mary Anne
Fast And Easy Needlepoint
BB-v6-My '78-p2
BL-v74-Mr 15 '78-p1188
CCB-B-v31-Je '78-p161
Inst-v87-My '78-p113
KR-v46-Ja 15 '78-p49
PW-v213-Ja 23 '78-p373
SLJ-v24-My '78-p68

* * *

HODGSON, Miriam
A Touch Of Gold
GP-v22-N '83-p4156
Sch Lib-v32-Mr '84-p52

HOFF, Syd (continued)
Teacher-v96-O '78-p170
The Man Who Loved Animals
CCB-B-v35-Jl '82-p208
SE-v47-Ap '83-p245
SLJ-v28-My '82-p78
Merry Christmas, Henrietta!
CCB-B-v34-N '80-p55
SLJ-v27-D '80-p68
Pete's Pup
KR-v43-My 15 '75-p563
SLJ-v22-S '75-p84
Roberto And The Bull
BW-v3-Ag 31 '69-p10
CCB-B-v22-Je '69-p159
CLW-v42-O '70-p137
KR-v37-Ap 15 '69-p434
LJ-v94-My 15 '69-p2089
SR-v52-My 10 '69-p54
TLS-O 22 '71-p1343
Sammy The Seal
BW-v11-F 8 '81-p8
SLMQ-v12-Summer '84-p326
Santa's Moose
CCB-B-v33-O '79-p28
KR-v48-Ja 1 '80-p5
PW-v216-Jl 30 '79-p62
SLJ-v26-O '79-p119
Scarface Al And His Uncle Sam
CCB-B-v34-Ja '81-p95
KR-v48-Ag 15 '80-p1081
SLJ-v27-D '80-p70
Slugger Sal's Slump
PW-v216-N 12 '79-p58
SLJ-v26-D '79-p96
Soft Skull Sam
CCB-B-v34-Je '81-p195
KR-v49-Ap 1 '81-p429
LA-v59-Mr '82-p270
PW-v219-Mr 20 '81-p63
RT-v36-O '82-p65
SLJ-v27-My '81-p86
Syd Hoff's Best Jokes Ever
KR-v46-Jl 15 '78-p752
SLJ-v25-S '78-p117
Syd Hoff's How To Draw Dinosaurs
SLJ-v28-N '81-p77
A Walk Past Ellen's House
CCB-B-v27-My '74-p144
Inst-v83-N '73-p120
LJ-v98-D 15 '73-p3716
PW-v204-S 24 '73-p187
Sch Lib-v28-S '80-p253
Walpole
CCB-B-v31-N '77-p48
HB-v53-O '77-p528
KR-v45-Ap 1 '77-p349
PW-v211-Je 6 '77-p82
SLJ-v24-O '77-p103
Wanda's Wand
CCB-B-v22-S '68-p8
When Will It Snow
CCB-B-v25-Mr '72-p107
CE-v49-N '72-p88
Comw-v95-N 19 '71-p186
HB-v47-D '71-p600
KR-v39-S 15 '71-p1009
LJ-v96-O 15 '71-p3487
SR-v54-D 11 '71-p45
The Witch, The Cat, And The Baseball Bat
CCB-B-v21-Jl '68-p175
LJ-v94-My 15 '69-p2090
PW-v193-Je 10 '68-p61
The Young Cartoonist
CCB-B-v36-Jl '83-p211
HB-v59-Je '83-p321

* * *

HOFFER, Alice
Gretchen's World
CBRS-v10-O '81-p12
RT-v36-O '82-p70

* * *

HOFFMAN, Alice
Property Of
BL-v74-S 1 '77-p23
CR-v233-Jl '78-p45
EJ-v68-Ja '79-p57
HB-v53-O '77-p561
KR-v45-Mr 15 '77-p302
Kliatt-v12-Fall '78-p10
LJ-v102-My 15 '77-p1209
NS-v95-Ap 7 '78-p471
NW-v89-My 23 '77-p88
NYT-v126-Jl 14 '77-p16
NYTBR-Jl 10 '77-p10
NYTBR-Je 25 '78-p53
Obs-Ap 2 '78-p25
Obs-Jl 23 '78-p21
PW-v211-Mr 21 '77-p78
PW-v213-Ap 10 '78-p71
SLJ-v24-O '77-p128
TLS-Ap 21 '78-p432
YR-v67-D '77-p260

* * *

HOFFMAN, Beth Greiner
Red Is For Apples
CCB-B-v20-Je '67-p153
KR-v34-O 15 '66-p1095
LJ-v91-D 15 '66-p6184

* * *

HOFFMAN, Betsy
Haunted Places
BL-v78-My 1 '82-p1160

* * *

HOFFMAN, Edwin D
Pathways To Freedom
CCB-B-v18-Jl '65-p162

* * *

HOFFMAN, Elizabeth P
Here A Ghost, There A Ghost
Cur R-v17-D '78-p384
RT-v33-O '79-p50
This House Is Haunted!
SLJ-v25-N '78-p55
Visions Of The Future
SLJ-v25-N '78-p55

* * *

HOFFMAN, Hans
Children's Life Of Jesus
RR-v26-My '67-p575

* * *

HOFFMAN, Judy
Joseph And Me In The Days Of The Holocaust
SLJ-v27-F '81-p66

* * *

HOFFMAN, Mary
Animals In The Wild: Tiger
PW-v226-Ag 17 '84-p60
Elephant
JB-v47-Ag '83-p164
Sch Lib-v31-S '83-p239
TES-N 11 '83-p24
TES-N 11 '83-p26
TES-Mr 9 '84-p54
Monkey
Sch Lib-v31-S '83-p239
TES-N 11 '83-p24
TES-N 11 '83-p26
Panda
Sch Lib-v31-S '83-p239
TES-N 11 '83-p24
TES-N 11 '83-p26
Tiger
Sch Lib-v31-S '83-p239
TES-N 11 '83-p24
TES-N 11 '83-p26

* * *

HOFFMAN, Nancy
Women Working
BW-Ag 5 '79-pE2
CT-v10-Mr '81-p16
Cur R-v21-My '82-p222
HER-v50-F '80-p121
Inter BC-v11-#7 '80-p20
Kliatt-v13-Spring '79-p48
LJ-v104-D 1 '79-p2573
PW-v215-Mr 26 '79-p78
SLJ-v26-S '79-p171

* * *

HOFFMAN, Phyllis
Happy Halloween!
BL-v79-O 15 '82-p312
SLJ-v29-F '83-p66
Play Ball With The Yankees
PW-v224-Ag 12 '83-p67
Steffie And Me
BL-v67-Ja 1 '71-p372
BW-v4-N 8 '70-p3
CCB-B-v24-Ap '71-p124
KR-v38-Ag 1 '70-p795
Spectr-v47-Mr '71-p46

* * *

HOFFMAN, Rosekrans
Anna Banana
Comw-v102-N 21 '75-p566
KR-v43-Ag 1 '75-p843
SLJ-v22-F '76-p39
Sister Sweet Ella
BL-v78-Mr 15 '82-p959
CBRS-v10-Ap '82-p83
PW-v221-Ap 16 '82-p71
SLJ-v28-Mr '82-p134

* * *

HOFFMANN, E T A
Nutcracker (Sendak)
B&B-N '84-p20
BL-v81-O 1 '84-p146
KR-v52-S 1 '84-pJ75
PW-v226-S 7 '84-p79
Par-v59-N '84-p65

* * *

HOFFMANN, Felix
Boy Went Out To Gather Pears
Atl-v218-D '66-p156
BL-v63-D 15 '66-p450
CCB-B-v20-Je '67-p153
HB-v42-D '66-p703
KR-v34-S 1 '66-p895
LJ-v91-S 15 '66-p4311
NYTBR-v71-N 6 '66-p68
PW-v190-S 5 '66-p67
Punch-v251-N 16 '66-p755
TLS-N 24 '66-p1077
Hans In Luck
PW-v207-Je 9 '75-p63
Joggeli Wott Go Birli Schuttle
BL-v75-D 1 '78-p622
The Story Of Christmas
Am-v133-D 6 '75-p401
BB-v3-D '75-p4
BL-v72-S 15 '75-p165
CCB-B-v29-N '75-p40
CE-v53-N '76-p100
CSM-v67-N 5 '75-pB8
Comw-v102-N 21 '75-p572
HB-v51-D '75-p582
JB-v41-F '77-p14
KR-v43-O 1 '75-p1121
LA-v53-My '76-p510
NYTBR-D 7 '75-p8
PW-v208-S 15 '75-p59
SLJ-v22-O '75-p81
SLJ-v22-D '75-p31
Teacher-v93-N '75-p112

* * *

HOFFMANN, Heinrich
Struwwelpeter
BL-v75-N 15 '78-p554
Punch-v286-Mr 21 '84-p17

* * *

HOFFMANN, Hilde
Green Grass Grows All Around
BL-v64-My 1 '68-p1043
BW-v2-Ag 11 '68-p12
CCB-B-v21-Je '68-p159
KR-v36-Ja 15 '68-p47
LJ-v93-Mr 15 '68-p1302
NYTBR-v73-Mr 17 '68-p30
RR-v86-Mr '69-p174
SR-v51-My 11 '68-p36

* * *

HOFMANN, Ginnie
Who Wants An Old Teddy Bear?
PW-v218-S 26 '80-p122

* * *

HOFMANN, Melita
A Trip To The Pond: An Adventure In Nature
CCB-B-v20-O '66-p26
CSM-v58-N 3 '66-pB11
KR-v34-My 15 '66-p511
LJ-v91-Jl '66-p3535
SB-v2-S '66-p124

* * *

HOFSINDE, Robert
Indian Arts
BL-v67-Ap 15 '71-p701
CCB-B-v25-Mr '72-p107
CSM-v63-Jl 10 '71-p15
KR-v39-Ap 1 '71-p373
LJ-v96-N 15 '71-p3900
The Indian Medicine Man
BL-v62-Ap 15 '66-p832
CCB-B-v20-N '66-p42
GT-v84-O '66-p62
HB-v42-Je '66-p323
LJ-v91-Ap 15 '66-p2210
NYTBR-v71-Ap 3 '66-p26
SB-v2-My '66-p50
Indian Music Makers
BL-v63-Je 1 '67-p1046
CCB-B-v22-S '68-p8
CSM-v59-Je 22 '67-p7
KR-v35-Mr 1 '67-p274
LJ-v92-My 15 '67-p2021
SA-v217-D '67-p148
SB-v3-My '67-p44
Indians At Home
CCB-B-v18-Ap '65-p118
Indians On The Move
BL-v66-Ap 15 '70-p1046
CCB-B-v24-N '70-p44
KR-v38-F 15 '70-p176
LJ-v95-S 15 '70-p3048
SB-v6-S '70-p91

* * *

HOFSTEIN, Sadie
The Human Story
CCB-B-v23-Ja '70-p81
CLW-v42-My '71-p568
KR-v37-My 1 '69-p509
LJ-v94-S 15 '69-p3218
NYTBR-Ag 2 '70-p18
SB-v5-S '69-p167

* * *

HOFSTRAND, Mary
Albion Pig
PW-v226-S 28 '84-p113

* * *

HOGAN, Bernice
My Grandmother Died But I Won't Forget Her
SLJ-v30-D '83-p56

* * *

HOGAN, Paula Z
The Beaver
ACSB-v13-Mr '80-p28
The Black Swan
ACSB-v13-Spring '80-p38
BL-v76-S 1 '79-p43
SB-v15-Mr '80-p228
SLJ-v26-S '79-p112
The Butterfly
ACSB-v13-Spring '80-p38
BL-v76-S 1 '79-p43
CE-v56-Ja '80-p172
SB-v15-My '80-p277
SLJ-v26-S '79-p112
The Compass
ASBYP-v16-Spring '83-p26
BL-v79-Mr 1 '83-p905
KR-v50-N 15 '82-p1238
SB-v18-My '83-p275
SLJ-v29-Ja '83-p75
The Dandelion
ACSB-v13-Spring '80-p38
BL-v76-S 1 '79-p43
SB-v15-My '80-p276
SLJ-v26-S '79-p112
The Frog
ACSB-v13-Spring '80-p38
BL-v76-S 1 '79-p43
SB-v15-My '80-p277
SLJ-v26-S '79-p112
Sch Lib-v28-Mr '80-p45
The Honeybee
ACSB-v13-Spring '80-p38
BL-v76-S 1 '79-p43
SB-v15-My '80-p279
SLJ-v26-S '79-p112
The Hospital Scares Me
CCB-B-v34-Ja '81-p95
SLJ-v27-F '81-p56
I Hate Boys/I Hate Girls
SLJ-v27-F '81-p56
Life Cycles
Cur R-v19-Je '80-p264
Mum, Will Dad Ever Come Back Home ?
TES-Ap 30 '82-p29
The Oak Tree
ACSB-v13-Spring '80-p38
BL-v76-S 1 '79-p43
SB-v15-My '80-p276
SLJ-v26-S '79-p112
The Penguin
ACSB-v13-Spring '80-p38
BL-v76-S 1 '79-p43
SB-v15-My '80-p277
SLJ-v26-F '80-p46
The Salmon
ACSB-v13-Spring '80-p38
BL-v76-S 1 '79-p43
SLJ-v26-S '79-p112
Sometimes I Don't Like School
SLJ-v27-F '81-p56
Sometimes I Get So Mad
SLJ-v27-F '81-p56
Will Dad Ever Move Back Home?
SLJ-v27-F '81-p56

* * *

HOGARTH, Elizabeth
Wigwams, Igloos And Bungalows
TES-O 21 '77-p22

* * *

HOGARTH, Grace
The Funny Guy
B&B-v20-My '75-p77
Obs-Jl 27 '75-p21
A Sister For Helen
B&B-v22-D '76-p78
GP-v15-Ap '77-p3086
JB-v41-Ap '77-p106
TLS-D 10 '76-p1552

* * *

HOGBEN, Lancelot
Astronomer Priest And Ancient Mariner
ACSB-v8-Winter '75-p21
BS-v34-Jl 15 '74-p201
KR-v41-D 15 '73-p1372
PW-v204-O 1 '73-p82
TLS-N 3 '72-p1336
Beginnings And Blunders
B&B-v16-N '70-p59
BL-v68-S 1 '71-p58
CCB-B-v25-S '71-p8
LJ-v96-Je 15 '71-p2138
SR-v54-My 15 '71-p48
TLS-O 30 '70-p1271
Columbus, The Cannon Ball And The Common Pump
JB-v39-Je '75-p197
Maps, Mirrors And Mechanics
ACSB-v8-Winter '75-p22
B&B-v19-O '73-p126
BS-v34-Jl 15 '74-p201
Obs-N 25 '73-p39
Spec-v231-O 20 '73-pR18
TLS-S 28 '73-p1128
El Maravilloso Mundo De Las Matematicas
BL-v72-My 15 '76-p1342
The Wonderful World Of Mathematics
BS-v28-Ja 1 '69-p424
HB-v45-F '69-p75
KR-v36-N 1 '68-p1236
LJ-v94-My 15 '69-p2113
SB-v5-My '69-p18
SLJ-v26-O '79-p104
TLS-O 3 '68-p1127

* * *

HOGEWEG, Martin
The Green Frog
RT-v34-N '80-p236
SLJ-v26-Ap '80-p110
The Weasel
SB-v16-N '80-p94

* * *

HOGG, Gordon
Twists
TES-Mr 12 '82-p35

* * *

HOGG, Helen Sawyer
The Stars Belong To Everyone
CGJ-v94-Ap '77-p76
SA-v235-D '76-p141
S&T-v52-D '76-p464
SB-v13-My '77-p15

* * *

HOGG, Maria C
Patterns And Sequences
TES-N 18 '83-p39

* * *

HOGNER, Dorothy Childs
Endangered Plants
HB-v54-F '78-p73
KR-v45-N 1 '77-p1146
SB-v14-Mr '79-p231
Good Bugs And Bad Bugs In Your Garden
ACSB-v8-Winter '75-p22
BL-v71-D 1 '74-p379
CCB-B-v28-Mr '75-p115
KR-v42-N 15 '74-p1204
SB-v11-My '75-p39
SLJ-v21-Mr '75-p97
Moths
CCB-B-v19-O '65-p33
HB-v41-F '65-p68
Sea Mammals
ACSB-v13-Mr '80-p29
BL-v76-Ja 1 '80-p667

HOGNER, Dorothy Childs
(continued)
KR-v48-Ja 1 '80-p7
SB-v16-N '80-p94
SLJ-v26-Ja '80-p71
Water Plants
ACSB-v12-Winter '79-p17
BL-v74-F 15 '78-p1004
KR-v45-N 1 '77-p1146
SLJ-v24-F '78-p58

* * *

HOGROGIAN, Nonny
Apples
BL-v69-O 1 '72-p148
CCB-B-v26-O '72-p27
HB-v48-O '72-p457
KR-v40-My 15 '72-p574
LJ-v97-S 15 '72-p2936
NYTBR, pt.2-My 7 '72-p39
Carrot Cake
BL-v74-S 1 '77-p42
BW-N 13 '77-pE2
CCB-B-v31-Ja '78-p79
CLW-v49-D '77-p230
CLW-v49-Ap '78-p403
HB-v53-O '77-p524
KR-v45-Jl 1 '77-p666
Obs-D 10 '78-p38
PW-v212-S 12 '77-p133
RT-v32-O '78-p32
SLJ-v24-O '77-p103
Cinderella
BL-v77-Mr 15 '81-p1028
BW-v11-My 10 '81-p18
CBRS-v9-Ap '81-p71
CCB-B-v34-Jl '81-p212
HB-v57-Je '81-p292
KR-v49-Je 15 '81-p735
LA-v58-N '81-p950
NYTBR-v86-Ap 26 '81-p66
PW-v219-Mr 13 '81-p89
SLJ-v27-Ap '81-p113
The Contest
BL-v73-O 1 '76-p252
BW-N 7 '76-pG6
BW-D 5 '76-pH6
CCB-B-v30-Ap '77-p126
HB-v52-D '76-p618
JB-v41-Je '77-p155
KR-v44-S 1 '76-p971
PW-v210-Ag 16 '76-p123
RT-v35-N '81-p199
SLJ-v23-N '76-p48
TLS-Mr 25 '77-p355
Teacher-v94-My '77-p106
The Devil With The Three Golden Hairs
AB-v72-N 14 '83-p3340
BL-v79-Je 1 '83-p1282
BW-v13-My 8 '83-p13
CBRS-v11-Mr '83-p79
CCB-B-v36-Ap '83-p150
CE-v60-S '83-p56
CE-v60-Mr '84-p290
Cur R-v24-N '84-p53
HB-v59-Ag '83-p431
KR-v51-F 15 '83-p180
LA-v61-Ja '84-p66
NYT-v133-D 1 '83-p23
NYTBR-v88-Mr 20 '83-p30
PW-v223-Ap 22 '83-p104
SLJ-v29-Mr '83-p162
SLJ-v29-My '83-p32
Handmade Secret Hiding Places
BL-v72-S 15 '75-p165
CCB-B-v29-D '75-p64
KR-v43-Jl 15 '75-p774
LA-v53-My '76-p504
PW-v207-Je 30 '75-p57
SLJ-v22-N '75-p78
SR-v3-N 29 '75-p33
Teacher-v94-My '77-p21
WLB-v50-D '75-p290
One Fine Day
A Lib-v3-Ap '72-p420
Am-v125-D 4 '71-p486
BL-v68-O 1 '71-p150
BL-v68-Ap 1 '72-p669
BL-v80-S 1 '83-p93
CCB-B-v25-N '71-p44
CE-v48-Ja '72-p206
CSM-v63-N 11 '71-pB2
CSM-v64-Ap 4 '72-p6
Comw-v95-N 19 '71-p187
Emerg Lib-v11-Ja '84-p19
GT-v89-My '72-p56
HB-v47-D '71-p604
KR-v39-Jl 15 '71-p735
LJ-v96-N 15 '71-p3892
NS-v84-N 10 '72-p697
NYTBR-S 19 '71-p8
NYTBR-Ag 11 '74-p23
Obs-N 26 '72-p37
PW-v200-S 27 '71-p67
Par-v47-Ja '72-p83
RT-v32-My '79-p943
RT-v35-N '81-p199
SR-v54-O 16 '71-p56
Spec-v229-N 11 '72-p762
TLS-D 8 '72-p1498
TN-v28-Ja '72-p203
Renowned History Of Little Red Riding-Hood
BL-v64-F 1 '68-p642
BW-v1-N 5 '67-p1
CCB-B-v21-Ap '68-p128
CSM-v60-N 30 '67-pB5
HB-v43-D '67-p742
KR-v35-S 1 '67-p1040
LJ-v92-D 15 '67-p4605
NO-v6-N 27 '67-p21
PW-v192-Jl 31 '67-p55
Rooster Brother
BL-v70-Ap 15 '74-p941
BW-My 19 '74-p4
CE-v51-N '74-p91
Comw-v101-N 22 '74-p193
GP-v14-My '75-p2647
JB-v39-Ap '75-p96
KR-v42-Ap 1 '74-p360
LJ-v99-My 15 '74-p1466
PW-v205-Ap 22 '74-p75
RT-v35-N '81-p200

* * *

HOGUET, Susan R
I Unpacked My Grandmother's Trunk
BL-v80-Ja 15 '84-p749
CBRS-v12-N '83-p25
CCB-B-v37-Mr '84-p128
CE-v60-Mr '84-p288
HB-v60-Ap '84-p182
LATBR-O 30 '83-p9
NYTBR-v88-O 9 '83-p39
PW-v224-Ag 12 '83-p67
SLJ-v30-N '83-p64

* * *

HOHLER, Franz
The Little Scottish Ghost
JB-v44-D '80-p284

* * *

HOKE, Helen
Ants
BL-v67-O 15 '70-p193
SB-v6-D '70-p240
Arctic Mammals
BL-v66-My 15 '70-p1160
SB-v6-S '70-p149
The Big Book Of Jokes
LJ-v97-Jl '72-p2484
NY-v47-D 4 '71-p190
A Chilling Collection
CE-v57-Ja '81-p171
GP-v19-Jl '80-p3731
JB-v44-Ag '80-p191

HOKE, Helen (continued)
PW-v217-F 29 '80-p136
SLJ-v26-N '79-p78
Sch Lib-v29-S '81-p253
TLS-Ja 2 '81-p19
Creepies, Creepies, Creepies
BL-v74-N 15 '77-p549
Cur R-v17-My '78-p127
JB-v42-Ag '78-p205
NYTBR-N 13 '77-p46
SLJ-v24-N '77-p71
TES-Je 16 '78-p48
Demonic, Dangerous & Deadly
BL-v79-Ap 15 '83-p1084
GP-v22-Jl '83-p4095
JB-v47-Je '83-p125
SF&FBR-N '83-p47
SLJ-v29-My '83-p82
Devils, Devils, Devils
BL-v72-Ap 15 '76-p1184
GP-v14-O '75-p2728
SLJ-v23-S '76-p117
Dolls
TLS-O 22 '71-p1344
Dragons, Dragons, Dragons
BL-v69-S 15 '72-p100
LJ-v98-F 15 '73-p644
Eerie, Weird And Wicked
GP-v16-O '77-p3178
JB-v41-D '77-p355
NYTBR-N 13 '77-p46
SLJ-v24-F '78-p65
Etiquette
BL-v66-My 15 '70-p1160
LJ-v95-My 15 '70-p1943
Fear! Fear! Fear!
SLJ-v27-Ag '81-p67
Fleas
CLW-v46-S '74-p89
KR-v42-F 1 '74-p114
LJ-v99-S 15 '74-p2270
SA-v231-D '74-p158
Ghastly, Ghoulish, Gripping Tales
CCB-B-v36-Ap '83-p151
SLJ-v29-Ap '83-p124
Ghostly, Grim And Gruesome
BB-v6-Mr '78-p4
B&B-v22-D '76-p76
BL-v73-Je 15 '77-p1569
BL-v73-Je 15 '77-p1575
EJ-v66-S '77-p77
JB-v41-Ag '77-p236
NYTBR-N 13 '77-p46
Obs-N 28 '76-p31
PW-v211-My 9 '77-p92
SLJ-v24-O '77-p124
Ghosts And Ghastlies
BL-v73-Ja 1 '77-p666
JB-v40-Je '76-p163
SLJ-v23-N '76-p59
Giants! Giants! Giants!
JB-v44-Ag '80-p191
SLJ-v27-Ag '81-p56
Hoke's Jokes, Cartoons & Funny Things
KR-v43-F 15 '75-p183
SLJ-v21-My '75-p47
Horrors, Horrors, Horrors
BL-v75-O 1 '78-p284
GP-v17-N '78-p3421
JB-v42-D '78-p313
SLJ-v25-D '78-p61
The Horse That Takes The Milk Around
TLS-O 16 '69-p1201
Jokes And Fun
BL-v70-O 1 '73-p172
LJ-v98-S 15 '73-p2651
PW-v203-Ap 23 '73-p73
Jokes, Fun And Folly With Hoke And Ollie
PW-v212-D 26 '77-p67
Jokes, Fun And Folly With Hoke And Olly
JB-v40-F '76-p26
Jokes, Giggles & Guffaws
BB-v3-N '75-p2
KR-v43-S 1 '75-p1000
PW-v208-S 1 '75-p70
SLJ-v22-S '75-p104
Jokes, Jokes, Jokes
LA-v55-N '78-p961
The Little Riddle Book
Obs-D 8 '74-p30
Monsters, Monsters, Monsters
BL-v72-S 1 '75-p41
BS-v35-F '76-p363
CLW-v47-D '75-p233
KR-v43-O 15 '75-p1184
SLJ-v22-N '75-p90
More Jokes, Jokes, Jokes
CC-v82-Jl 21 '65-p918
LJ-v90-S 15 '65-p3805
More Riddles, Riddles, Riddles
BL-v73-N 15 '76-p476
Inst-v86-N '76-p153
SLJ-v23-N '76-p59
Mysterious, Menacing & Macabre
BL-v78-O 1 '81-p188
JB-v46-Je '82-p105
PW-v220-Jl 31 '81-p59
SLJ-v28-D '81-p83
TES-N 20 '81-p34
VOYA-v4-D '81-p33
Owls
BL-v71-Jl 15 '75-p1191
CCB-B-v29-D '75-p64
CE-v52-Ap '76-p322
JB-v39-F '75-p65
KR-v43-My 1 '75-p517
NYTBR-My 4 '75-p22
SLJ-v22-S '75-p104
Riddle Giggles
B&B-v20-My '75-p79
KR-v43-S 15 '75-p1071
Obs-Jl 27 '75-p21
SLJ-v22-Ja '76-p38
Riddles, Riddles And More Riddles
JB-v40-Ap '76-p104
Sinister, Strange And Supernatural
BL-v77-D 1 '80-p512
CCB-B-v34-Je '81-p195
JB-v45-D '81-p251
LA-v58-O '81-p848
PW-v219-Ja 16 '81-p77
SLJ-v27-Ja '81-p62
TLS-Je 5 '81-p627
VOYA-v4-D '81-p34
Spectres, Spooks And Shuddery Shades
GP-v16-O '77-p3178
JB-v41-O '77-p303
Spooks, Spooks, Spooks
BL-v63-Mr 15 '67-p796
LJ-v92-Ja 15 '67-p335
Tales Of Fear And Frightening Phenomena
BL-v78-Ag '82-p1519
JB-v46-D '82-p230
PW-v222-Ag 27 '82-p357
SLJ-v29-S '82-p139
Terrors, Torments And Traumas
BL-v74-My 1 '78-p1425
CCB-B-v32-N '78-p45
JB-v42-D '78-p313
KR-v46-Ag 15 '78-p881
PW-v213-F 27 '78-p157
SLJ-v25-D '78-p61

HOKE, Helen (continued)
Thrillers, Chillers And Killers
BL-v75-Je 1 '79-p1487
EJ-v68-D '79-p66
JB-v44-Ag '80-p191
J Read-v23-Ap '80-p662
PW-v216-Jl 9 '79-p106
SLJ-v26-F '80-p67
TES-Ja 18 '80-p38
Toys
TLS-O 22 '71-p1344
Uncanny Tales Of Unearthly And Unexpected Horrors
CCB-B-v37-Mr '84-p128
Fant R-v7-Ag '84-p47
PW-v224-S 23 '83-p72
SLJ-v30-N '83-p94
VOYA-v7-Je '84-p98
Weirdies, Weirdies, Weirdies
BL-v71-My 1 '75-p914
SLJ-v21-Mr '75-p106
Whales
BL-v77-My 15 '81-p1253
KR-v41-Ag 15 '73-p885
LJ-v98-N 15 '73-p3453
PW-v204-S 10 '73-p53
SB-v9-Mr '74-p308
SLJ-v27-Ag '81-p67
Witches, Witches, Witches
JB-v42-F '78-p42
TES-D 16 '77-p21

* * *

HOKE, John
Aquariums
ACSB-v9-Winter '76-p19
BL-v71-Ap 15 '75-p866
CLW-v47-N '75-p188
JB-v42-Ag '78-p204
KR-v43-F 1 '75-p125
SLJ-v21-Ap '75-p53
Discovering The World Of The Three-Toed Sloth
BL-v73-D 1 '76-p540
HB-v53-F '77-p77
NYTBR-N 14 '76-p46
SA-v237-D '77-p26
SLJ-v23-N '76-p59
Solar Energy
ACSB-v13-Winter '80-p24
BL-v64-Jl 15 '68-p1286
BL-v75-Ja 1 '79-p750
CSM-v60-My 2 '68-pB10
Cur R-v18-O '79-p295
KR-v36-Je 1 '68-p598
S&T-v36-Ag '68-p112
S&T-v57-Mr '79-p290
SB-v4-My '68-p59
SB-v15-S '79-p96
SLJ-v25-N '78-p75
Terrariums
BL-v69-D 15 '72-p405
CE-v49-Ap '73-p378
Hort-v52-Mr '74-p23
JB-v39-F '75-p66
LJ-v98-F 15 '73-p644
PW-v202-O 30 '72-p57
SA-v227-D '72-p115
SB-v8-D '72-p243

* * *

HOLABIRD, Katharine
Angelina Ballerina
BL-v80-Ja 15 '84-p747
CBRS-v12-F '84-p67
CCB-B-v37-Mr '84-p128
GP-v22-Ja '84-p4201
KR-v51-N 1 '83-pJ186
LA-v61-Ap '84-p394
NW-v102-D 5 '83-p111
NY-v59-D 5 '83-p204
PW-v224-D 9 '83-p50
SLJ-v30-F '84-p58
TES-Ja 13 '84-p44
WLB-v58-Je '84-p739
The Little Mouse ABC
NYTBR-v88-O 9 '83-p38
PW-v224-S 2 '83-p80
SLJ-v30-My '84-p66

* * *

HOLBERG, Ruth L
Michael And The Captain
RT-v33-F '80-p561

* * *

HOLBROOK, John
A Closer Look At Elephants
B&B-v23-Ja '78-p63
BL-v73-Je 15 '77-p1575
Cur R-v17-F '78-p3
SB-v14-My '78-p36
SLJ-v24-S '77-p125
SR-v4-My 28 '77-p31
TES-My 26 '78-p51

* * *

HOLBROOK, Sabra
American Virgin Islanders On St. Croix, St. John And St. Thomas
KR-v42-N 1 '74-p1154
SE-v39-Mr '75-p175
SLJ-v21-Mr '75-p97
Canada's Kids
BL-v80-Ja 15 '84-p749
CCB-B-v37-My '84-p166
SE-v48-My '84-p371
SLJ-v30-D '83-p67
The French Founders Of North America And Their Heritage
BL-v72-Mr 15 '76-p1033
Comw-v103-N 19 '76-p763
HB-v52-Ag '76-p414
KR-v44-F 1 '76-p141
RR-v35-S '76-p787
SLJ-v22-Ap '76-p89
The Goat That Made A Boy Grow Big
CCB-B-v18-My '65-p130
KR-v33-F 1 '65-p108
LJ-v90-Ap 15 '65-p2021
Growing Up In France
BL-v76-Je 15 '80-p1532
CCB-B-v34-O '80-p33
KR-v48-Jl 1 '80-p839
SLJ-v26-My '80-p75
A Stranger In My Land
BL-v68-Jl 15 '72-p998
CCB-B-v26-D '72-p57
KR-v40-My 15 '72-p591
LJ-v97-My 15 '72-p1885
LJ-v97-My 15 '72-p1922

* * *

HOLDEN, A J
No Trains At The Bay
JB-v41-Ag '77-p236
TLS-D 10 '76-p1548

* * *

HOLDEN, Barbara
A Child's Guide To San Francisco
NYTBR, pt.2-My 4 '69-p45

* * *

HOLDEN, Edith
The Hedgehog Feast
B&B-v23-Jl '78-p58
CSM-v70-S 18 '78-pB14
JB-v42-O '78-p253
LA-v56-Mr '79-p288
PW-v214-Ag 7 '78-p82
SLJ-v25-D '78-p47
Time-v112-D 4 '78-p101

* * *

HOLDEN, Edward
The Earth And Sky
ASBYP-v15-Spring '82-p14

* * *

HOLDEN, P
Fawn
JB-v41-Ag '77-p236

* * *

HOLDEN, Peter
A First Book Of Birds
TES-N 16 '84-p24

* * *

HOLDEN, Philip
Stag
GP-v19-N '80-p3775
JB-v45-Je '81-p123
TES-N 21 '80-p34
White Patch
GP-v21-N '82-p3988

* * *

HOLDER, Glenn
Talking Totem Poles
BL-v70-My 1 '74-p1003
CCB-B-v27-My '74-p144
KR-v41-D 15 '73-p1366
LJ-v99-Ap 15 '74-p1220

* * *

HOLDER, Meg
Papa Panov's Special Day
TES-D 14 '79-p21

* * *

HOLDER, William G
Saturn V
BL-v66-N 1 '69-p347
BL-v67-N 15 '70-p271
BS-v29-My 1 '69-p57
BS-v30-O 15 '70-p298
HB-v45-D '69-p694
LJ-v94-Jl '69-p2682
LJ-v96-F 15 '71-p742
SB-v5-S '69-p177
TN-v28-Ap '72-p291
Skylab, Pioneer Space Station
BB-v2-Ja '75-p3

* * *

HOLDING, James
The Three Wishes Of Hu
CCB-B-v18-Mr '65-p104
KR-v33-Ja 1 '65-p3
LJ-v90-Mr 15 '65-p1542

* * *

HOLDSWORTH, William C
The Little Red Hen
HB-v45-D '69-p668
KR-v37-Ag 1 '69-p772
LJ-v94-N 15 '69-p4277

* * *

HOLGUIN JIMENEZ, Emma
Para Chiquitines
SLJ-v29-Mr '83-p91

* * *

HOLIDAY, Ensor
Altair Design
NYTBR-N 4 '73-p62
SA-v229-D '73-p131
Altair Design 4
Inst-v88-N '78-p133

* * *

HOLIDAY, Jane
Biddy's Talking Pineapple
Brit Bk N C-Autumn '80-p17
JB-v44-O '80-p240
Sch Lib-v28-D '80-p378
Chun's Chinese Dragon
JB-v45-O '81-p197
Sch Lib-v29-S '81-p234
TES-Je 12 '81-p27
Merman In Maids Moreton
TES-My 22 '81-p26
Peacock In Paradise Street
JB-v40-Ag '76-p230
TLS-Jl 16 '76-p882
Victor The Vulture
JB-v43-Je '79-p158

* * *

HOLIDAY (Catland Series)
TES-N 17 '78-p26

* * *

HOLL, Adelaide
The ABC Of Cars, Trucks And Machines
CCB-B-v24-S '70-p9
Inst-v79-Je '70-p105
LJ-v95-N 15 '70-p4035
PW-v197-Mr 16 '70-p56
Bedtime For Bears
LJ-v98-D 15 '73-p3716
Bright, Bright Morning
CSM-v61-My 1 '69-pB2
KR-v37-F 1 '69-p94
LJ-v95-F 15 '70-p771
PW-v195-F 10 '69-p74
Gus Gets The Message
SLJ-v21-Mr '75-p84
Have You Seen My Puppy
TLS-O 22 '71-p1329
Hide-And-Seek ABC
NY-v47-D 4 '71-p188
PW-v199-Je 14 '71-p53
If We Could Make Wishes
RT-v32-O '78-p91
SLJ-v24-S '77-p105
Let's Count
GP-v15-Ja '77-p3050
Inst-v85-My '76-p119
JB-v41-Ap '77-p79
KR-v44-F 15 '76-p193
PW-v209-Mr 8 '76-p66
WLB-v50-Mr '76-p549
The Little Viking
KR-v43-Jl 1 '75-p709
PW-v208-S 22 '75-p132
SLJ-v22-N '75-p63
The Long Birthday
SLJ-v21-Mr '75-p84
The Man Who Had No Dream
BW-v4-My 17 '70-p7
Minnikin, Midgie, And Moppet
BL-v74-D 15 '77-p684
PW-v211-Je 27 '77-p110
Mrs. McGarrity's Peppermint Sweater
KR-v34-Ja 15 '66-p54
LJ-v91-Ap 15 '66-p2198
NYTBR-v71-My 22 '66-p26
PW-v189-Ap 4 '66-p62
SR-v49-My 14 '66-p37
Moon Mouse
CCB-B-v22-Jl '69-p176
CSM-v61-My 1 '69-pB4
KR-v37-Ap 1 '69-p369
LJ-v94-S 15 '69-p3196
TN-v28-Ap '72-p297
A Mouse Story
SLJ-v24-Ap '78-p71
My Father And I
BL-v69-Je 15 '73-p989
BW-v7-My 13 '73-p2
LJ-v98-S 15 '73-p2640
PW-v203-Ap 30 '73-p55
One Kitten For Kim
BL-v66-N 1 '69-p347
CCB-B-v23-F '70-p98
GT-v87-Ja '70-p141
LJ-v95-F 15 '70-p771
PW-v196-Ag 18 '69-p74
The Parade
BL-v71-My 1 '75-p916
CCB-B-v29-N '75-p46
KR-v43-Mr 1 '75-p235
SLJ-v21-My '75-p48
The Rain Puddle
BL-v62-O 1 '65-p161

HOLLAND, Isabelle (continued)
CSM-v62-My 7 '70-pB6
HB-v46-Je '70-p297
KR-v38-F 15 '70-p173
LJ-v96-Mr 15 '71-p1116
NYTBR-My 3 '70-p23
PW-v197-My 18 '70-p38
SR-v53-My 9 '70-p69
Dinah And The Green Fat Kingdom
BL-v75-D 15 '78-p687
BS-v39-Je '79-p111
BW-F 11 '79-pF4
CCB-B-v32-Ap '79-p138
CLW-v54-O '82-p117
HB-v55-Ap '79-p194
J Read-v23-D '79-p280
KR-v47-F 1 '79-p125
Kliatt-v15-Spring '81-p8
PW-v214-D 4 '78-p67
SLJ-v25-Ja '79-p61
The Empty House
CBRS-v12-D '83-p42
CCB-B-v37-D '83-p69
PW-v224-D 2 '83-p86
SLJ-v30-D '83-p84
VOYA-v7-Ap '84-p30
God, Mrs. Muskrat And Aunt Dot
HB-v59-O '83-p574
NY-v59-D 5 '83-p206
PW-v224-Jl 1 '83-p102
SLJ-v30-O '83-p158
Green Andrew Green
CBRS-v13-O '84-p17
PW-v226-Jl 27 '84-p143
SLJ-v31-S '84-p119
Heads You Win, Tails I Lose
A Lib-v5-My '74-p235
BL-v70-O 15 '73-p234
BS-v33-S 15 '73-p280
CCB-B-v27-Ja '74-p80
EJ-v63-My '74-p91
HB-v50-F '74-p56
KR-v41-Jl 15 '73-p759
LJ-v98-O 15 '73-p3155
NO-v12-D 29 '73-p15
NYTBR-N 25 '73-p10
PW-v204-S 17 '73-p57
TN-v30-N '73-p81
Hitchhike
CCB-B-v31-Ja '78-p79
EJ-v67-F '78-p99
HB-v53-D '77-p668
KR-v45-Ag 1 '77-p789
Kliatt-v14-Winter '80-p8
NYTBR-O 30 '77-p34
PW-v212-S 12 '77-p133
SLJ-v24-S '77-p145
A Horse Named Peaceable
BL-v79-O 15 '82-p312
CBRS-v11-N '82-p28
CCB-B-v36-N '82-p48
CLW-v55-D '83-p231
SLJ-v29-Ja '83-p76
VOYA-v6-Ap '83-p37
Journey For Three
CCB-B-v29-S '75-p11
CE-v52-O '75-p32
CSM-v67-Je 10 '75-p16
HB-v51-Ag '75-p381
KR-v43-F 15 '75-p182
NYTBR-Ap 20 '75-p8
SLJ-v22-S '75-p104
Kevin's Hat
CBRS-v12-Jl '84-p134
Kilgaren
BS-v34-Je 1 '74-p111
CCB-B-v28-N '74-p43
CSM-v66-Je 12 '74-pF5
KR-v42-F 15 '74-p204
LJ-v99-My 1 '74-p1330
LJ-v99-S 15 '74-p2304
LJ-v99-D 15 '74-p3249
PW-v205-Mr 11 '74-p44
The Man Without A Face
BL-v68-My 15 '72-p816
BS-v32-Ap 15 '72-p46
BW-v6-Ag 6 '72-p2
CCB-B-v25-Jl '72-p170
Choice-v14-N '77-p1178
Comw-v97-N 17 '72-p157
EJ-v62-D '73-p1300
HB-v48-Ag '72-p375
KR-v40-Ja 15 '72-p73
LJ-v97-Jl '72-p2489
NW-v83-Mr 4 '74-p83
NYTBR-Ap 9 '72-p8
NYTBR, pt.2-N 5 '72-p26
Nat R-v24-Jl 7 '72-p754
PW-v201-Ap 17 '72-p59
TN-v29-Ap '73-p257
TN-v30-Ja '74-p203
Now Is Not Too Late
BL-v76-Ja 1 '80-p667
CBRS-v8-Mr '80-p76
CCB-B-v33-Mr '80-p135
CE-v57-N '80-p112
HB-v56-Je '80-p296
RT-v34-D '80-p353
SLJ-v26-Mr '80-p132
Of Love And Death And Other Journeys
BB-v3-My '75-p3
BL-v71-F 15 '75-p612
BS-v35-My '75-p33
CCB-B-v28-Jl '75-p178
CE-v52-Ja '76-p154
EJ-v65-Ja '76-p97
EJ-v67-My '78-p89
HB-v51-Je '75-p274
KR-v43-Ap 1 '75-p383
LA-v52-N '75-p1168
PW-v207-My 12 '75-p66
SLJ-v22-S '75-p120
TN-v32-Ap '76-p284
Perdita
BL-v79-Ap 15 '83-p1084
BW-v13-My 8 '83-p18
CBRS-v12-S '83-p8
CCB-B-v37-O '83-p30
HB-v59-O '83-p582
KR-v51-Je 15 '83-p663
Kliatt-v18-Fall '84-p12
PW-v223-Je 10 '83-p64
SLJ-v30-O '83-p168

* * *

HOLLAND, John
Come To France
GP-v18-Jl '79-p3549
JB-v44-Ag '80-p177
SLJ-v26-D '79-p86
The Way It Is
BW-v3-S 21 '69-p14
CCB-B-v23-Ap '70-p129
Choice-v6-N '69-p1310
Comw-v93-F 26 '71-p523
HB-v45-Ag '69-p427
KR-v37-Ap 1 '69-p389
LJ-v94-My 15 '69-p2102
NYTBR, pt.2-My 4 '69-p32
PW-v195-My 26 '69-p55
RR-v28-Jl '69-p698
SR-v52-My 10 '69-p57

* * *

HOLLAND, Ruth
A Bad Day
CCB-B-v18-Mr '65-p104
Mill Child
BL-v66-My 15 '70-p1161
BL-v70-O 15 '73-p225
BW-v4-My 17 '70-p31
CCB-B-v24-S '70-p10
KR-v38-F 15 '70-p182
LJ-v95-My 15 '70-p1954
NYTBR-Mr 8 '70-p22

HOLLAND, Ruth (continued)
NYTBR, pt.2-N 8 '70-p36
TN-v27-Je '71-p432
TN-v41-Fall '84-p97

* * *

HOLLAND, Viki
We Are Having A Baby
BL-v68-Je 15 '72-p909
BW-v6-My 7 '72-p4
CCB-B-v25-My '72-p140
CE-v49-O '72-p34
CSM-v64-My 4 '72-pB2
HB-v48-Ag '72-p362
KR-v40-F 1 '72-p139
KR-v40-D 15 '72-p1416
LJ-v98-Ja 15 '73-p253
NYTBR, pt.2-My 7 '72-p32
Par-v58-O '83-p70

* * *

HOLLANDER, John
The Immense Parade On Supererogation Day And What Happened To It
BW-v6-N 5 '72-p3
CCB-B-v26-Je '73-p155
KR-v40-N 1 '72-p1233
LJ-v98-My 15 '73-p1682
NYTBR, pt.2-N 5 '72-p47
PW-v202-D 11 '72-p35

* * *

HOLLANDER, Neil
The Chocolate Feast
Brit Bk N C-Autumn '82-p12
GP-v21-N '82-p3994
The Great Zoo Break
JB-v47-F '83-p14
TES-N 19 '82-p32
Penguin Voyages
JB-v43-D '79-p326
TES-D 7 '79-p25

* * *

HOLLANDER, Phyllis
Dan Fouts, Ken Anderson, Joe Theismann And Other All-Time Great Quarterbacks
BL-v80-Ja 15 '84-p754
B Rpt-v2-Ja '84-p56
SLJ-v30-D '83-p87
Touchdown!
BL-v79-Ja 1 '83-p622
B Rpt-v1-Mr '83-p54
SLJ-v29-D '82-p85
100 Greatest Women In Sports
BL-v73-F 1 '77-p834
CSM-v68-O 18 '76-p22
RT-v31-O '77-p21
SLJ-v23-D '76-p72

* * *

HOLLANDER, Zander
The Baseball Book
ARBA-v14-'83-p306
BL-v78-Jl '82-p1450
B Rpt-v2-My '83-p51
SLJ-v29-D '82-p85
VOYA-v5-O '82-p52
Home Run
BL-v80-Jl '84-p1553
Roller Hockey
BL-v72-N 1 '75-p366
Comw-v102-N 21 '75-p571
LJ-v100-O 15 '75-p1944
SLJ-v22-D '75-p70

* * *

HOLLEBONE, Sarah
Screen Printing
JB-v45-Je '81-p123
TES-N 7 '80-p21

* * *

HOLLING, Holling C
Minn Of The Mississippi
BW-N 12 '78-pE2
CLW-v38-Mr '67-p472
Paddle-To-The-Sea
HB-v59-O '83-p551
Inst-v89-My '80-p94
Inst-v90-Ja '81-p110
NH-v87-Ag '78-p135
NYTBR-v85-Mr 23 '80-p39
SA-v243-D '80-p50
Tree In The Trail
HB-v59-O '83-p551

* * *

HOLLINGS, Jill
African Nationalism
Africa T-v27-#3 '80-p34
BL-v68-Je 1 '72-p860
CE-v49-F '73-p260
KR-v40-Mr 15 '72-p339
TLS-D 3 '71-p1521

* * *

HOLLINGSWORTH, A C
I'd Like The Goo-Gen-Heim
CCB-B-v23-My '70-p145
KR-v38-Mr 1 '70-p239
LJ-v95-O 15 '70-p3620
PW-v197-Ja 19 '70-p81

* * *

HOLLMAN, Eckhard
Looking At Landscapes
GP-v15-Mr '77-p3070
Sch Arts-v81-F '82-p43

* * *

HOLLOWAY, Judith
Jimmy, The Ghost-Catcher
TES-Mr 12 '82-p35

* * *

HOLLY Hobbie Books
Cur R-v18-O '79-p309

* * *

HOLLY Hobbie's Answer Book
SLJ-v25-D '78-p44

* * *

HOLLY Hobbie's Around The House Book
SLJ-v25-D '78-p44

* * *

HOLLY Hobbie's Book About Time
SLJ-v25-D '78-p44

* * *

HOLLY Hobbie's Book Of ABC's
SLJ-v25-D '78-p44

* * *

HOLLY Hobbie's Cookbook
CLW-v52-S '80-p91
SLJ-v27-O '80-p146
SLJ-v30-F '84-p72

* * *

HOLLY Hobbie's Happy Day Book
SLJ-v25-D '78-p44

* * *

HOLLY Hobbie's Special Days
SLJ-v26-S '79-p113

* * *

HOLLY Hobbie's Through The Year Book
SLJ-v25-D '78-p44

* * *

HOLLYER, Belinda
Daniel In The Lion's Den
TES-D 16 '83-p26
David And Goliath
TES-D 16 '83-p26
How Why When Where
JB-v47-F '83-p26
TES-N 5 '82-p28
Jonah And The Great Fish
TES-D 16 '83-p26
Noah And The Ark
TES-D 16 '83-p26
The Prehistoric World
GP-v14-Ap '76-p2854

* * *

HOLM, Anne
The Hostage
EJ-v72-Ja '83-p26
GP-v19-N '80-p3781
JB-v45-Ap '81-p82
TLS-Mr 27 '81-p339
North To Freedom
BL-v62-S 1 '65-p56
BS-v25-Je 15 '65-p145
CCB-B-v19-S '65-p10
EJ-v72-Ja '83-p26
GT-v83-S '65-p16
HB-v41-Ag '65-p380
KR-v33-Mr 1 '65-p243
LJ-v90-My 15 '65-p2420
NYTBR-v70-Jl 4 '65-p12
SLJ-v28-N '81-p39
SR-v48-My 15 '65-p46
TCR-v68-F '67-p451
Teacher-v92-D '74-p79

* * *

HOLM, Jens K
Kim And The Buried Treasure
TLS-D 5 '75-p1448
Kim The Detective
LR-v25-Autumn '75-p136
TLS-D 5 '75-p1448

* * *

HOLM, Mayling Mack
A Forest Christmas
BB-v5-D '77-p2
BL-v74-N 15 '77-p550
CCB-B-v31-F '78-p96
Comw-v104-N 11 '77-p728
KR-v45-N 15 '77-p1193
NYTBR-D 11 '77-p26
PW-v212-N 28 '77-p50
SLJ-v24-O '77-p88

* * *

HOLMAN, D
The Royal George Of Arcady
JB-v43-Ag '79-p220

* * *

HOLMAN, Felice
At The Top Of My Voice And Other Poems
BL-v72-My 15 '76-p1336
BW-v4-My 17 '70-p22
CCB-B-v24-O '70-p27
CSM-v68-My 12 '76-p27
HB-v52-Ag '76-p417
KR-v38-Mr 15 '70-p324
LA-v53-S '76-p703
LJ-v95-S 15 '70-p3039
NYTBR-My 2 '76-p42
NYTBR, pt.2-My 24 '70-p42
PW-v197-Mr 16 '70-p56
SR-v53-Ap 18 '70-p37
Blackmail Machine
BL-v64-Ap 15 '68-p995
BW-v2-My 5 '68-p20
CCB-B-v21-Ap '68-p129
CE-v45-O '68-p87
HB-v44-Ap '68-p173
Inst-v82-My '73-p78
KR-v35-D 15 '67-p1472
LJ-v93-F 15 '68-p870
PW-v193-F 5 '68-p66
Punch-v255-S 4 '68-p347
TLS-O 3 '68-p1112
YR-v4-Ap '68-p11
Cricket Winter
BL-v64-Mr 1 '68-p784
BS-v27-Ja 1 '68-p393
BW-v2-F 4 '68-p22
CCB-B-v21-Mr '68-p111
LJ-v92-O 15 '67-p3849
NYTBR-v72-N 5 '67-p42
NYTBR-v72-N 5 '67-p66
PW-v192-N 27 '67-p43
SR-v50-N 11 '67-p45
YR-v5-O '68-p1
The Drac
BL-v72-O 15 '75-p303
BS-v35-D '75-p298
CCB-B-v29-Je '76-p157
CE-v53-O '76-p33
HB-v51-D '75-p590
KR-v43-Ag 15 '75-p918
LA-v53-My '76-p512
NYT-v125-D 20 '75-p25
NYTBR-N 16 '75-p29
NYTBR-N 16 '75-p56
NYTBR-D 7 '75-p66
PW-v208-N 3 '75-p72
SLJ-v22-Ja '76-p53
Elisabeth And The Marsh Mystery
BL-v63-N 1 '66-p325
CCB-B-v19-Jl '66-p179
KR-v34-Mr 1 '66-p244
LJ-v91-Jl '66-p3528
PW-v190-Jl 18 '66-p77
SR-v49-Je 25 '66-p60
Teacher-v92-N '74-p111
The Escape Of The Giant Hogstalk
BL-v73-My 15 '77-p1426
CCB-B-v28-O '74-p28
CE-v51-N '74-p91
HB-v50-Je '74-p283
KR-v42-Ap 1 '74-p363
LJ-v99-S 15 '74-p2270
PW-v205-Ap 15 '74-p52
The Escape Of The Giant Hogweed
JB-v42-O '78-p255
Obs-D 10 '78-p38
TES-Ag 11 '78-p18
The Future Of Hooper Toote
BL-v69-F 1 '73-p529
CCB-B-v25-Jl '72-p171
KR-v40-Mr 1 '72-p259
LJ-v97-S 15 '72-p2951
NYTBR-Jl 16 '72-p8
SR-v55-My 20 '72-p81
I Hear You Smiling
BL-v70-D 15 '73-p445
CCB-B-v27-F '74-p96
HB-v50-F '74-p60
KR-v41-O 15 '73-p1166
LJ-v99-Ja 15 '74-p210
PW-v204-S 10 '73-p53
RT-v36-Ja '83-p381
The Murderer
BL-v75-D 15 '78-p687
BS-v38-Mr '79-p408
CBRS-v7-F '79-p67
CE-v56-N '79-p111
CSM-v71-F 12 '79-pB10
EJ-v70-F '81-p61
HB-v55-F '79-p61
Inter BC-v10-Je 60 '79-p19
KR-v46-D 15 '78-p1362
NYTBR-Ja 21 '79-p31

HOLME, Bryan (continued)
TES-F 3 '78-p35
TLS-Ap 7 '78-p387

* * *

HOLMES, Anita
Cactus
ASBYP-v16-Winter '83-p31
BL-v78-Ag '82-p1516
CCB-B-v36-N '82-p49
CE-v59-My '83-p357
HB-v59-F '83-p83
KR-v50-Je 15 '82-p683
RT-v36-My '83-p944
SB-v18-N '82-p91
SLJ-v28-Ag '82-p126
Pierced & Pretty
BL-v81-S 15 '84-p119
CCB-B-v38-S '84-p7
The 100-Year-Old Cactus
ASBYP-v17-Winter '84-p27
BL-v80-O 1 '83-p295
BW-v13-Ag 14 '83-p6
CE-v60-Ja '84-p213
HB-v60-F '84-p88
KR-v51-S 1 '83-pJ169
SB-v19-Ja '84-p156
SLJ-v30-N '83-p64

* * *

HOLMES, Burnham
Early Morning Rounds
ACSB-v15-Winter '82-p30
BL-v78-S 1 '81-p46
CCB-B-v35-S '81-p11
CLW-v53-Ap '82-p402
KR-v49-Jl 15 '81-p877
SLJ-v27-My '81-p65
Nefertiti: The Mystery Queen
Cur R-v17-Ag '78-p228
SLJ-v25-N '78-p64

* * *

HOLMES, Edward
Great Men Of Science
ACSB-v13-Mr '80-p30
CBRS-v8-O '79-p18
SB-v16-S '80-p11
SLJ-v27-S '80-p83
Horse And Pony Care In Pictures
SLJ-v25-Ap '79-p57
SR-v5-My 27 '78-p58
Know About Horses
GP-v14-Jl '75-p2669
Know About The World
BW-v6-My 7 '72-p12
SB-v8-D '72-p220

* * *

HOLMES, Efner Tudor
Amy's Goose
BB-v6-Ap '78-p2
BL-v74-Ja 1 '78-p747
LA-v55-My '78-p617
SLJ-v24-F '78-p48
Carrie's Gift
BL-v75-D 1 '78-p616
CBRS-v7-F '79-p64
Ms-v9-Ag '80-p92
SLJ-v25-Ja '79-p43
VV-v23-N 13 '78-p121
The Christmas Cat
BW-D 5 '76-pH5
CCB-B-v30-D '76-p58
Comw-v103-N 19 '76-p759
KR-v44-O 1 '76-p1090
PW-v210-N 15 '76-p75
SLJ-v23-O '76-p87

* * *

HOLMES, Neal J
Gateways To Science
Cur R-v18-Ag '79-p235
Cur R-v22-Ag '83-p71

* * *

HOLMES, Peggy
It Could Have Been Worse
BIC-v9-Je '80-p25
Can Child Lit-#23 '81-p125
In Rev-v15-Ag '81-p42

* * *

HOLMGREN, Virginia C
The Pheasant
BL-v79-Ag '83-p1460
SLJ-v30-S '83-p114
Swallows Come Home
CCB-B-v24-Jl '70-p179
CSM-v61-N 6 '69-pB7
LJ-v95-Je 15 '70-p2302

* * *

HOLSAERT, Eunice
Dinosaurs
BW-v9-Ag 12 '79-p8
Inst-v89-Ja '80-p114

* * *

HOLST, Barbara J S
The Little Girl And The Lonely Teddy
Sch Lib-v31-Mr '83-p27

* * *

HOLST, Imogen
Bach
BL-v62-F 15 '66-p585
CCB-B-v19-F '66-p99
HB-v42-Ap '66-p206
LJ-v91-Ja 15 '66-p426
NYTBR-v71-Ja 9 '66-p26
Spec-Je 4 '65-p731
TLS-Je 17 '65-p515
Britten
CCB-B-v20-N '66-p43
SLJ-v27-Ja '81-p70
Holst
B&B-v19-Jl '74-p85
GP-v20-Ja '82-p4004
TLS-D 27 '74-p1465

* * *

HOLT, Deloris L
The ABC's Of Black History
CCB-B-v25-O '71-p26
LJ-v96-S 15 '71-p2906
PW-v199-My 10 '71-p43

* * *

HOLT, Elizabeth
Customs And Ceremonies
JB-v45-Ap '81-p81
Historic Transport
JB-v44-Je '80-p133
NS-v98-N 9 '79-p733
TES-Mr 7 '80-p45
Hobbies
JB-v44-Je '80-p133
NS-v98-N 9 '79-p733
TES-Mr 7 '80-p45
Industrial Archaeology
GP-v19-S '80-p3761
JB-v44-D '80-p308
Kids' Historic London
B&B-v21-Je '76-p64
JB-v40-Ag '76-p230
LR-v25-Spring '76-p226
Obs-Jl 18 '76-p20
TLS-Jl 16 '76-p886
Sport
JB-v44-Je '80-p133
NS-v98-N 9 '79-p733
Sch Lib-v28-Mr '80-p73
TES-Mr 7 '80-p45
Wildlife
JB-v44-Ap '80-p68
NS-v98-N 9 '79-p733

* * *

HOLT, Lindle Jarvis
How To Be A Better Athlete
Teacher-v92-Mr '75-p41

* * *

HOLT, Michael
Basic Arithmetic Puzzles
TES-Mr 9 '84-p46
Doctor Who's Quiz Book Of Dinosaurs
TES-D 10 '82-p34
First Maths
TES-O 28 '83-p26
Maps, Tracks, And The Bridges Of Konigsberg
ACSB-v9-Fall '76-p23
BL-v72-D 15 '75-p582
HB-v52-Ap '76-p181
KR-v43-N 15 '75-p1291
SB-v12-S '76-p101
SLJ-v22-F '76-p39

* * *

HOLT Basic Reading System
Cur R-v17-F '78-p32

* * *

HOLT Elementary Science
Cur R-v19-S '80-p350

* * *

HOLT School Mathematics, K-8
Cur R-v16-D '77-p324

* * *

HOLTON, Jean Laity
Algebra
BL-v65-Ja 15 '69-p546
HB-v45-F '69-p75
KR-v36-Jl 1 '68-p701
LJ-v94-F 15 '69-p884

* * *

HOLYER, Ernie M
The Southern Sea Otter
ACSB-v9-Winter '76-p19
SLJ-v22-O '75-p99

* * *

HOLZ, Loretta
The Christmas Spider
BL-v77-D 15 '80-p574
CCB-B-v34-D '80-p72
SLJ-v27-O '80-p165
Foster Child
BL-v80-Je 15 '84-p1484
KR-v52-My 1 '84-pJ45
SLJ-v31-S '84-p119
Jumping Jacks
GP-v17-S '78-p3391
Make It And Sell It
BL-v75-S 15 '78-p220
CCB-B-v32-D '78-p63
KR-v46-Jl 1 '78-p697
Mobiles You Can Make
BB-v4-F '76-p2
BL-v72-D 1 '75-p515
CCB-B-v29-Mr '76-p112
Comw-v102-N 21 '75-p571
KR-v43-N 1 '75-p1234
SLJ-v22-Ja '76-p46
Teach Yourself Embroidery
JB-v41-Ag '77-p223
TES-D 9 '77-p21

* * *

HOLZENTHALER, Jean
My Feet Do
BL-v75-Je 15 '79-p1541
CE-v56-Ja '80-p172
CLW-v51-F '80-p310
HM-v259-D '79-p77
RT-v33-Ja '80-p482
SLJ-v26-S '79-p113
My Hands Can
BL-v75-Ja 1 '79-p750
CBRS-v7-Ja '79-p42
KR-v47-Ja 1 '79-p3
SLJ-v25-F '79-p43

* * *

HOM, Jesper
For Kids Only
CCB-B-v30-Je '77-p160
KR-v45-F 1 '77-p96
RT-v31-D '77-p332
WCRB-v3-S '77-p55

* * *

HOMAN, Dianne
Christina's Toolbox
Inter BC-v14-#7 '83-p28
In Christina's Toolbox
Inter BC-v13-#6 '82-p40
Lib Brow-v2-Spring '82-p9

* * *

HOME Activity Series
NYTBR-v86-Ja 25 '81-p32

* * *

HOMER, David
Australian Tales
TES-Ap 29 '83-p53

* * *

HOMER, Larona
Blackbeard The Pirate And Other Stories Of The Pine Barrens
SLJ-v26-N '79-p78

* * *

HOMERUS
Demeter And Persephone
BL-v69-Ja 1 '73-p450
BW-v6-N 5 '72-p4
CCB-B-v26-N '72-p47
CE-v49-Ja '73-p202
HB-v48-D '72-p588
KR-v40-S 1 '72-p1022
PW-v202-S 18 '72-p74
Dionysos And The Pirates
HB-v46-O '70-p473
HB-v60-S '84-p621
PW-v198-S 21 '70-p59

* * *

HOMME, Bob
The Friendly Giant's Birthday
BIC-v10-D '81-p3
Can Child Lit-#27 '82-p196
In Rev-v15-O '81-p37
Quill & Q-v48-Ja '82-p35
The Friendly Giant's Book Of Fire Engines
BIC-v10-D '81-p3
Can Child Lit-#27 '82-p196
In Rev-v15-O '81-p37
Quill & Q-v48-Ja '82-p35

* * *

HOMOLA, Priscilla
The Willow Whistle
B Rpt-v2-Ja '84-p34
CCB-B-v37-Ja '84-p89
PW-v224-Jl 29 '83-p70
SLJ-v30-D '83-p67

* * *

HOMZE, Alma
Willy Brandt: A Biography
BL-v71-N 1 '74-p284
BL-v71-N 1 '74-p290
KR-v42-Ap 1 '74-p375
LJ-v99-N 15 '74-p3055

* * *

HONEYMAN, Arthur
Sam And His Cart
Inter BC-v13-#4 '82-p12

* * *

HONEYSETT, Martin
Animal Nonsense Rhymes
TES-Je 8 '84-p50

* * *

HONIG, Donald
Breaking In
BL-v71-O 15 '74-p244
LJ-v99-D 15 '74-p3279
Coming Back
BL-v71-O 15 '74-p244
Inst-v84-N '74-p140
LJ-v99-D 15 '74-p3280
Fury On Skates
BL-v71-D 15 '74-p425
CSM-v67-F 5 '75-p8
KR-v42-S 1 '74-p950
LJ-v99-D 15 '74-p3280
Going The Distance
BL-v72-Jl 15 '76-p1601
BS-v36-O '76-p239
JB-v41-Ap '77-p112
SLJ-v22-My '76-p80
Hurry Home
CCB-B-v29-Je '76-p157
KR-v44-F 15 '76-p194
SLJ-v22-My '76-p80
Johnny Lee
CCB-B-v25-S '71-p8
CLW-v42-My '71-p581
Comw-v94-My 21 '71-p268
KR-v39-Mr 1 '71-p236
LJ-v96-My 15 '71-p1823
SR-v54-Jl 17 '71-p36
Playing For Keeps
BL-v71-O 15 '74-p244
LJ-v99-D 15 '74-p3280
The Professional
BL-v71-O 15 '74-p244
LJ-v99-D 15 '74-p3278
Running Harder
BL-v72-Jl 15 '76-p1601
BS-v36-O '76-p239
JB-v41-Ag '77-p237
SLJ-v22-My '76-p80
Up From The Minor Leagues
Am-v123-D 5 '70-p498
CCB-B-v25-S '71-p9
CSM-v62-My 7 '70-pB7
KR-v38-Ap 1 '70-p395
LJ-v95-My 15 '70-p1964
PW-v197-Je 15 '70-p65
SR-v54-Jl 17 '71-p36
Way To Go, Teddy
BL-v69-Je 15 '73-p989
CCB-B-v26-Jl '73-p171
LJ-v98-My 15 '73-p1703
SLJ-v24-My '78-p39
Winter Always Comes
BL-v73-Je 1 '77-p1490
BL-v73-Je 1 '77-p1498
BS-v37-Ag '77-p142
CCB-B-v31-S '77-p16
KR-v45-Ap 1 '77-p351
NYTBR-My 1 '77-p41
SLJ-v23-My '77-p79

* * *

HONNESS, Elizabeth
The Etruscans
BL-v69-D 1 '72-p356
CCB-B-v26-D '72-p57
CLW-v44-Mr '73-p510
KR-v40-S 15 '72-p1108
LJ-v98-Mr 15 '73-p1004
PW-v203-Ja 15 '73-p65
The Spy At Tory Hole
KR-v44-My 15 '76-p592
SLJ-v23-S '76-p117

* * *

HONOUR, Alan
Tormented Genius
BL-v64-Mr 1 '68-p774
BS-v27-D 1 '67-p361
CCB-B-v21-Ja '68-p78
Comw-v87-N 10 '67-p183
EJ-v57-My '68-p756
HB-v43-D '67-p764
KR-v35-S 15 '67-p1150
LJ-v92-O 15 '67-p3864
NYTBR-v73-Ja 14 '68-p26
PW-v192-D 25 '67-p60
YR-v5-N '68-p9
Treasures Under The Sand
B&B-v14-F '69-p50
BL-v64-Ja 15 '68-p593
BS-v27-F 1 '68-p431
BW-v2-Je 23 '68-p11
CCB-B-v21-F '68-p95
KR-v35-O 1 '67-p1223
LJ-v92-N 15 '67-p4261
PW-v192-D 25 '67-p60
SB-v3-Mr '68-p309
SR-v50-N 11 '67-p49

* * *

HOOBLER, Dorothy
An Album Of World War I
BL-v72-My 15 '76-p1336
SLJ-v23-S '76-p117
Teacher-v94-O '76-p153
An Album Of World War II
BL-v74-Ja 1 '78-p747
GP-v17-My '78-p3337
SE-v42-My '78-p383
SLJ-v24-D '77-p54
Teacher-v95-F '78-p137
Photographing History
BB-v6-O '78-p4
BL-v74-Ja 15 '78-p806
CE-v55-O '78-p42
KR-v45-O 1 '77-p1055
PW-v212-S 19 '77-p146
SLJ-v24-F '78-p65
Teacher-v96-My '79-p26
Photographing The Frontier
BL-v76-Ap 1 '80-p1117
CCB-B-v33-Je '80-p192
PW-v217-Ap 25 '80-p80
SLJ-v26-Ag '80-p77
The Trenches
BL-v75-D 15 '78-p687
HB-v55-F '79-p77
SLJ-v25-D '78-p62

* * *

HOOD, Flora
One Luminaria For Antonio
BL-v68-Je 15 '72-p893
CCB-B-v20-My '67-p140
KR-v34-D 1 '66-p1221
LJ-v92-My 15 '67-p2043
The Turquoise Horse
BL-v69-Ap 15 '73-p812
CCB-B-v26-Mr '73-p107
KR-v40-S 15 '72-p1102
LJ-v97-D 15 '72-p4072
NYTBR, pt.2-N 5 '72-p7

* * *

HOOD, Flora Mae
Pink Puppy
CCB-B-v20-Je '67-p153
KR-v35-F 1 '67-p131
LJ-v92-Mr 15 '67-p1310

* * *

HOOD, Jasper
Contact With Maldonia
JB-v47-Ap '83-p81
SLJ-v30-Mr '84-p160
Sch Lib-v31-Mr '83-p37
TES-N 26 '82-p28

* * *

HOOD, Robert
Let's Go To A Baseball Game
CCB-B-v26-Je '73-p155
KR-v41-Mr 15 '73-p321
LJ-v98-My 15 '73-p1704

HOOD, Robert (continued)
Let's Go To A Basketball Game
KR-v44-N 1 '76-p1172
SLJ-v23-D '76-p71
Let's Go To A Football Game
KR-v43-S 1 '75-p1000
SLJ-v22-D '75-p69
Let's Go To A Stock Car Race
KR-v42-Jl 15 '74-p745
KR-v42-Ag 1 '74-p806

* * *

HOOD, Thomas
Hood Winked
JB-v46-D '82-p231
Sch Lib-v31-Je '83-p155
TES-N 19 '82-p31
In Summer When I Go To Bed
TES-Mr 9 '84-p50

* * *

HOOD, Tom
Petsetilla's Posy
Rp B Bk R-v23-O1 '78-p29

* * *

HOOK, Richard
Elizabethan Costume Dolls
GP-v14-Mr '76-p2826
Napoleonic Uniform Dolls
GP-v14-Mr '76-p2826

* * *

HOOKE, Nina W
A Donkey Called Paloma
Brit Bk N C-Autumn '81-p19
TES-Jl 10 '81-p26
TLS-Mr 27 '81-p340
Little Dog Lost
NS-v106-D 2 '83-p25
The Moon On The Water
Brit Bk N C-Autumn '82-p19
GP-v14-Ja '76-p2785
The Seal Summer
BL-v61-Je 1 '65-p942
BS-v24-Mr 15 '65-p489
CCB-B-v19-S '65-p11
CLW-v36-My '65-p627
KR-v33-Ja 1 '65-p35
LJ-v90-F 15 '65-p886
TLS-F 18 '65-p133
The Snow Kitten
GP-v17-Mr '79-p3474

* * *

HOOKER, Janet
Start Here
TES-F 11 '83-p32

* * *

HOOKER, Ruth
Kennaquhair
BB-v5-My '77-p4
Cur R-v18-F '79-p71
SLJ-v23-Ja '77-p93
The Kidnapping Of Anna
SLJ-v26-D '79-p98
The Pelican Mystery
SLJ-v24-D '77-p61

* * *

HOOKER, Y
One Green Frog
JB-v45-O '81-p187

* * *

HOOKS, William H
Circle Of Fire
BL-v79-S 1 '82-p44
BS-v42-D '82-p365
CBRS-v11-F '83-p70
CCB-B-v36-O '82-p27
CSM-v74-O 8 '82-pB12
HB-v58-O '82-p517
Inter BC-v14-#5 '83-p25
J Read-v26-Mr '83-p565
KR-v50-Ag 1 '82-p867
PW-v222-Jl 16 '82-p79
RT-v36-Ja '83-p469
SE-v47-Ap '83-p241
SLJ-v29-O '82-p168
VOYA-v5-F '83-p37
Crossing The Line
BL-v75-N 1 '78-p479
BS-v38-Mr '79-p407
CCB-B-v32-Ap '79-p138
EJ-v68-N '79-p77
HB-v54-D '78-p640
Inter BC-v10-My 50 '79-p17
KR-v47-Ja 1 '79-p6
NYTBR-Ap 1 '79-p26
SLJ-v25-N '78-p75
Doug Meets The Nutcracker
BL-v74-F 1 '78-p925
RT-v32-O '78-p93
SLJ-v24-O '77-p88
SLJ-v24-D '77-p35
Maria's Cave
CCB-B-v31-S '77-p16
CE-v55-Ap '79-p263
KR-v45-My 1 '77-p489
PW-v211-Ap 18 '77-p62
SLJ-v24-S '77-p130
Mean Jake And The Devils
BL-v78-F 15 '82-p756
CBRS-v10-F '82-p63
CCB-B-v35-My '82-p172
HB-v58-Ap '82-p164
KR-v50-F 15 '82-p202
NYTBR-v86-N 29 '81-p42
PW-v220-S 11 '81-p76
SLJ-v28-Ja '82-p77
The Mystery On Bleeker Street
BL-v77-O 15 '80-p327
CLW-v52-Ap '81-p403
SLJ-v27-D '80-p73
The Mystery On Liberty Street
BL-v79-D 15 '82-p565
CBRS-v11-O '82-p19
KR-v50-Jl 15 '82-p799
PW-v222-S 3 '82-p60
SLJ-v29-D '82-p82
The Seventeen Gerbils Of Class 4-A
BW-D 5 '76-pH5
HB-v52-O '76-p525
KR-v44-Je 1 '76-p633
PW-v209-My 31 '76-p198
RT-v31-O '77-p17
SLJ-v23-S '76-p101
Three Rounds With Rabbit
CBRS-v12-Jl '84-p134
CCB-B-v37-My '84-p166
PW-v225-F 3 '84-p402
SLJ-v30-Ag '84-p61

* * *

HOOPER, J K
Kaspar And The Iron Poodle
GP-v21-Mr '83-p4033
JB-v47-F '83-p26
TES-N 19 '82-p37

* * *

HOOPER, Meredith
Everyday Inventions
BL-v73-S 15 '76-p137
BL-v73-S 15 '76-p175
LJ-v101-O 15 '76-p2186
LJ-v102-Mr 1 '77-p553
Obs-Mr 23 '75-p27
Obs-Jl 18 '76-p20
PW-v210-Jl 19 '76-p133
TLS-D 8 '72-p1500
TLS-D 6 '74-p1385
More Everyday Inventions
B&B-v22-Ja '77-p61

HOOPER, Meredith
(continued)
JB-v41-Ap '77-p113
NS-v93-My 20 '77-p685
Obs-D 5 '76-p32
The Story Of Australia
NS-v93-My 20 '77-p686
SLJ-v24-F '78-p58

* * *

HOOPES, Lyn L
Daddy's Coming Home!
CBRS-v13-O '84-p14
Nana
CBRS-v10-S '81-p3
KR-v49-O 15 '81-p1292
RT-v36-O '82-p73
SLJ-v28-N '81-p77
When I Was Little
CBRS-v11-Je '83-p108
HB-v59-Je '83-p291
KR-v51-F 15 '83-p181
PW-v223-Ap 29 '83-p52
SLJ-v29-Ag '83-p52

* * *

HOOPES, Roy
What A Baseball Manager Does
BL-v67-O 15 '70-p180
CCB-B-v24-F '71-p93
CLW-v42-O '70-p135
KR-v38-Jl 1 '70-p684
LJ-v95-D 15 '70-p4379
NYTBR-S 13 '70-p42
NYTBR, pt.2-N 8 '70-p40
What A Pro Football Coach Does
KR-v40-S 15 '72-p1102
LJ-v97-D 15 '72-p4090
NYTBR-Ja 7 '73-p8
PW-v202-O 2 '72-p54
What A State Governor Does
BL-v70-S 1 '73-p51
CCB-B-v26-My '73-p140
KR-v41-Mr 15 '73-p321
What A United States Congressman Does
KR-v40-Je 1 '72-p625
LJ-v98-Mr 15 '73-p1004
What A United States Senator Does
BS-v29-Mr 1 '70-p454
CLW-v41-Ap '70-p528
CLW-v42-O '70-p133
Comw-v92-My 22 '70-p251
KR-v38-F 1 '70-p107
LJ-v95-Je 15 '70-p2313
SLJ-v22-My '76-p60
What The President Of The United States Does
KR-v42-D 1 '74-p1256

* * *

HOOPLE, Cheryl G
As I Saw It
BB-v7-My '79-p4
BL-v75-D 1 '78-p613
BW-O 8 '78-pE8
CBRS-v7-Winter '79-p58
CCB-B-v32-Mr '79-p119
CLW-v50-My '79-p448
EJ-v68-N '79-p76
HB-v55-Ap '79-p206
Inst-v88-My '79-p114
KR-v46-D 1 '78-p1313
PW-v214-O 9 '78-p77
SE-v43-Ap '79-p298
SLJ-v25-D '78-p62
The Heritage Sampler
AB-v58-D 20 '76-p3374
BB-v3-D '75-p2
BL-v72-N 15 '75-p454
CC-v92-N 26 '75-p1092
CCB-B-v29-Mr '76-p112
CE-v52-Mr '76-p272
Comw-v102-N 21 '75-p570
KR-v43-O 1 '75-p1135
PW-v208-Ag 25 '75-p294
SLJ-v22-D '75-p52

* * *

HOOVER, H M
Another Heaven, Another Earth
BL-v78-O 15 '81-p296
CBRS-v10-F '82-p67
CCB-B-v35-My '82-p172
HB-v57-D '81-p668
JB-v48-F '84-p33
J Read-v25-Ap '82-p709
LA-v59-Ap '82-p372
SF&FBR-Ap '82-p14
SLJ-v28-D '81-p71
TES-S 16 '83-p24
The Bell Tree
BL-v79-O 15 '82-p312
BS-v42-D '82-p365
BW-v13-Ja 9 '83-p11
CBRS-v11-Winter '83-p57
CCB-B-v36-Ja '83-p90
HB-v58-D '82-p658
J Read-v26-D '82-p277
LA-v60-Mr '83-p363
SLJ-v29-N '82-p100
VOYA-v5-F '83-p44
Children Of Morrow
BL-v69-Je 1 '73-p944
BL-v69-Je 1 '73-p947
CCB-B-v27-O '73-p28
CE-v50-N '73-p98
GP-v14-Mr '76-p2820
KR-v41-Ja 1 '73-p5
LJ-v98-Mr 15 '73-p1004
Obs-Jl 13 '75-p23
TLS-Jl 11 '75-p767
TN-v34-Spring '78-p265
The Delikon
BL-v73-Ap 1 '77-p1168
BS-v37-Ag '77-p142
HB-v53-Ag '77-p449
KR-v45-Ap 15 '77-p435
LA-v54-O '77-p806
SLJ-v23-Ap '77-p68
TES-Ag 18 '78-p17
TLS-S 29 '78-p1089
TN-v39-Fall '82-p71
The Lion's Cub
BL-v71-N 1 '74-p290
CCB-B-v28-Ja '75-p79
J Read-v25-Ja '82-p354
KR-v42-N 15 '74-p1201
LJ-v99-D 15 '74-p3267
The Lost Star
BL-v75-Ap 15 '79-p1295
CBRS-v7-Ap '79-p88
CCB-B-v32-Mr '79-p119
CE-v56-Ja '80-p169
CLW-v51-N '79-p183
GP-v19-Ja '81-p3816
HB-v55-Ap '79-p199
JB-v45-Ap '81-p82
KR-v47-Je 1 '79-p642
Kliatt-v14-Fall '80-p14
LA-v57-F '80-p190
SLJ-v25-Mr '79-p148
TLS-N 20 '81-p1361
The Rains Of Eridan
BL-v74-N 1 '77-p477
BS-v37-D '77-p265
CCB-B-v31-F '78-p96
CE-v54-Ap '78-p306
EJ-v67-S '78-p90
HB-v54-Ap '78-p169
KR-v45-Ag 15 '77-p855
Kliatt-v13-Spring '79-p18
SLJ-v24-N '77-p57
TN-v39-Fall '82-p71
Return To Earth
BL-v76-My 1 '80-p1292

HOOVER, H M (continued)
CBRS-v8-Spring '80-p117
CCB-B-v33-My '80-p173
EJ-v69-My '80-p91
HB-v56-Je '80-p306
Inst-v89-My '80-p92
JB-v45-O '81-p211
Kliatt-v15-Fall '81-p22
LA-v58-Ja '81-p84
Obs-N 29 '81-p27
SLJ-v26-Mr '80-p141
Sch Lib-v30-Mr '82-p51
TES-Je 5 '81-p41
TLS-N 20 '81-p1361
The Shepherd Moon
BL-v80-My 1 '84-p1246
B Rpt-v3-S '84-p33
BS-v44-S '84-p232
CBRS-v12-Ap '84-p96
CCB-B-v37-My '84-p166
Fant R-v7-S '84-p40
HB-v60-Je '84-p337
RT-v38-D '84-p339
S Fict R-v13-N '84-p18
SLJ-v30-My '84-p90
This Time Of Darkness
BL-v77-N 15 '80-p459
CCB-B-v34-Ap '81-p152
GP-v21-S '82-p3953
HB-v56-D '80-p641
Inst-v90-N '80-p158
KR-v48-D 15 '80-p1573
S Fict R-v10-N '81-p59
SLJ-v27-O '80-p147
TLS-Jl 23 '82-p791
VOYA-v4-Ap '81-p40
Treasures Of Morrow
BB-v5-F '77-p4
BL-v72-Je 1 '76-p1406
CCB-B-v29-Jl '76-p175
KR-v44-Mr 1 '76-p256
LA-v54-Ja '77-p81
SLJ-v22-Ap '76-p74

* * *

HOPCRAFT, Jan
What's Cooking?
GP-v15-Ja '77-p3048
JB-v41-F '77-p35
Lis-v96-N 11 '76-p624
TLS-O 1 '76-p1250

* * *

HOPE, Anthony
The Prisoner Of Zenda
GP-v14-N '75-p2754
PW-v192-S 4 '67-p59

* * *

HOPE, C E G
The Horseman's Manual
LJ-v99-F 1 '74-p372
RSR-v2-Jl '74-p42
Riding
GP-v14-Jl '75-p2669

* * *

HOPE, Laura L
The Blue Poodle Mystery
BW-v10-Ag 17 '80-p12
CCB-B-v34-O '80-p33
SLJ-v26-My '80-p86
The Camp Fire Mystery
CSM-v74-O 8 '82-pB8
The Dune Buggy Mystery
NYTBR-v86-Ap 26 '81-p63
SLJ-v28-O '81-p130
The Missing Pony Mystery
NYTBR-v86-Ap 26 '81-p63
SLJ-v27-My '81-p85
The Rose Parade Mystery
SLJ-v28-D '81-p82
Secret In The Pirate's Cave
SLJ-v27-D '80-p73

* * *

HOPE, Laura Lee
The Mystery At Cherry Corners
CCB-B-v25-N '71-p45

* * *

HOPE, Robert
Cities
TES-My 18 '84-p37

* * *

HOPE-SIMPSON, Jacynth
Black Madonna
BB-v6-Mr '78-p4
BL-v73-N 1 '76-p401
CCB-B-v30-My '77-p142
GP-v14-Ap '76-p2844
GP-v16-N '77-p3216
JB-v40-Je '76-p163
KR-v44-O 15 '76-p1137
RT-v33-F '80-p562
SLJ-v23-N '76-p69
TLS-Ap 2 '76-p388
The Hijacked Hovercraft
Spec-v235-Jl 26 '75-p114
TLS-Jl 11 '75-p770
The Making Of The Machine Age
GP-v17-Mr '79-p3480
JB-v43-Je '79-p168
Sch Lib-v27-Je '79-p183
Save Tarranmoor!
B&B-v20-Ja '75-p76
NS-v87-My 24 '74-p738
Obs-Ag 4 '74-p28
TLS-Jl 5 '74-p716
The Unknown Island
CCB-B-v23-Mr '70-p113
KR-v37-O 15 '69-p1123
LJ-v94-Jl '69-p2682
NY-v45-D 13 '69-p200
TLS-Je 6 '68-p581
Vote For Victoria
JB-v41-F '77-p35
Who Knows?
JB-v39-Ap '75-p118
KR-v44-Ap 15 '76-p477

* * *

HOPF, Alice L
Animal And Plant Life Spans
ACSB-v12-Winter '79-p18
BL-v74-Je 1 '78-p1545
CLW-v50-Ap '79-p399
EJ-v67-O '78-p80
HB-v55-O '78-p543
KR-v46-Je 1 '78-p601
SB-v14-Mr '79-p230
Animals That Eat Nectar And Honey
ACSB-v13-Winter '80-p25
BL-v75-My 1 '79-p1363
CCB-B-v33-O '79-p29
CE-v56-Ja '80-p172
EJ-v70-Ja '81-p78
SLJ-v26-S '79-p140
Biography Of A Giraffe
ACSB-v13-Winter '80-p26
BL-v75-D 15 '78-p687
CCB-B-v32-Mr '79-p119
KR-v47-F 1 '79-p128
SB-v15-D '79-p166
SLJ-v25-Ja '79-p54
Biography Of A Komodo Dragon
ACSB-v15-Winter '82-p31
BL-v77-Je 1 '81-p1299
KR-v49-Ap 15 '81-p506
SLJ-v28-O '81-p142
Biography Of A Rhino
BL-v69-Mr 15 '73-p715
CCB-B-v26-D '72-p58
KR-v40-Ag 1 '72-p862
LJ-v98-F 15 '73-p636
SB-v8-Mr '73-p340
Biography Of A Snowy Owl
ACSB-v12-Fall '79-p33

HOPF, Alice L (continued)
BL-v75-Ap 15 '79-p1295
CCB-B-v32-Jl '79-p192
KR-v47-Mr 1 '79-p265
SB-v15-D '79-p166
SLJ-v26-S '79-p140
Biography Of An American Reindeer
ACSB-v10-Spring '77-p24
BB-v5-Mr '77-p2
BL-v73-D 1 '76-p542
KR-v44-Jl 15 '76-p797
SB-v13-S '77-p98
SLJ-v23-N '76-p48
Biography Of An Ant
ACSB-v9-Winter '76-p20
BL-v70-Ap 1 '74-p874
CCB-B-v27-Jl '74-p178
Inst-v83-My '74-p91
KR-v42-F 1 '74-p114
LJ-v99-S 15 '74-p2270
SB-v10-S '74-p169
Biography Of An Armadillo
ACSB-v10-Winter '77-p23
BL-v73-N 1 '76-p408
CCB-B-v30-N '76-p43
HB-v53-F '77-p77
KR-v44-Jl 15 '76-p797
NYTBR-N 14 '76-p46
SB-v13-My '77-p43
SLJ-v23-O '76-p99
Biography Of An Octopus
BL-v68-Ja 1 '72-p393
CCB-B-v25-Mr '72-p108
GT-v89-Mr '72-p110
KR-v39-N 1 '71-p1161
LJ-v97-Jl '72-p2477
SB-v8-My '72-p58
Biography Of An Ostrich
BL-v71-Mr 15 '75-p761
CCB-B-v29-S '75-p11
KR-v43-F 1 '75-p125
NYTBR-My 4 '75-p22
SLJ-v21-My '75-p56
WLB-v49-Ap '75-p585
Bugs-Big And Little
ASBYP-v14-Spring '81-p21
BL-v77-F 1 '81-p753
SB-v17-S '81-p33
Hyenas
BL-v80-N 1 '83-p417
CSM-v76-Ap 6 '84-pB6
SB-v19-Mr '84-p217
SLJ-v30-F '84-p66
Misplaced Animals And Other Living Creatures
BL-v72-My 1 '76-p1265
CCB-B-v29-My '76-p145
KR-v44-Ja 15 '76-p81
SB-v12-S '76-p103
SLJ-v22-Ap '76-p89
Nature's Pretenders
ACSB-v13-Winter '80-p27
BL-v76-S 15 '79-p120
CCB-B-v33-D '79-p72
KR-v47-S 1 '79-p1003
SB-v15-Mr '80-p228
SLJ-v26-Ja '80-p79
Pigs Wild And Tame
ACSB-v13-Mr '80-p30
BL-v76-N 1 '79-p449
EJ-v69-My '80-p76
KR-v48-F 1 '80-p130
SB-v15-My '80-p277
SLJ-v26-Ja '80-p79
Whose House Is It?
ASBYP-v14-Spring '81-p21
BL-v77-Ja 15 '81-p702
KR-v48-D 15 '80-p1571
PW-v218-S 26 '80-p121
SB-v17-S '81-p33
SLJ-v27-Ja '81-p51
Wild Cousins Of The Cat
ACSB-v9-Fall '76-p24
KR-v43-Je 1 '75-p609
SB-v11-Mr '76-p196
SLJ-v22-S '75-p120
Wild Cousins Of The Dog
BL-v69-Ap 15 '73-p812
KR-v41-F 1 '73-p121
LJ-v98-Jl '73-p2201
Wild Cousins Of The Horse
BB-v6-N '78-p4
BL-v74-Mr 1 '78-p1108
KR-v45-O 1 '77-p1056
SLJ-v24-Ja '78-p95

* * *

HOPKE, Stephen L
Elementary And Junior High School Wrestling
Ath J-v58-D '77-p52
BL-v74-Ja 1 '78-p751

* * *

HOPKINS, Elisabeth M
The Painted Cougar
Can Child Lit-#15 '80-p119

HOPKINS, Lee B
Ahaunting We Will Go
BL-v73-My 1 '77-p1343
CCB-B-v30-Jl '77-p175
Cur R-v17-My '78-p127
SLJ-v23-My '77-p78
And God Bless Me
BL-v78-My 15 '82-p1253
CCB-B-v36-S '82-p12
PW-v221-Mr 12 '82-p84
SLJ-v29-S '82-p108
Beat The Drum, Independence Day Has Come
BL-v73-My 15 '77-p1416
KR-v45-Ap 15 '77-p431
PW-v211-Ap 18 '77-p62
SLJ-v23-Mr '77-p133
A Book Of Poems
Par-v52-Ja '77-p70
Books Are By People
AB-v45-Ja 26 '70-p254
CLW-v41-Mr '70-p483
GT-v88-S '70-p163
HB-v46-Ap '70-p180
LJ-v95-F 15 '70-p752
Teacher-v91-N '73-p50
WLB-v44-Ap '70-p871
By Myself
BL-v77-Ja 1 '81-p622
KR-v48-N 15 '80-p1467
NYTBR-v85-N 9 '80-p62
RT-v34-Ap '81-p853
SLJ-v27-Mr '81-p146
Charlie's World
CCB-B-v26-Mr '73-p107
KR-v40-D 1 '72-p1349
LJ-v98-Mr 15 '73-p995
Circus! Circus!
BL-v79-O 1 '82-p242
CCB-B-v36-O '82-p28
Inst-v92-O '82-p24
Inst-v92-N '82-p150
SLJ-v29-Ja '83-p61
The City Spreads Its Wings
BL-v67-Mr 1 '71-p559
CCB-B-v25-S '71-p9
CE-v47-My '71-p437
CLW-v42-Mr '71-p460
LJ-v96-Ap 15 '71-p1494
NYTBR-N 15 '70-p44
City Talk
BL-v67-S 15 '70-p107
BW-v4-My 17 '70-p22
CCB-B-v24-Ap '71-p124
CSM-v62-My 7 '70-pB5
Comw-v93-N 20 '70-p205

HOPKINS, Lee B (continued)
A Song In Stone
CCB-B-v37-N '83-p51
HB-v59-O '83-p588
Inst-v93-N '83-p147
LA-v60-N '83-p1019
PW-v224-Jl 8 '83-p65
SLJ-v30-Ja '84-p77
SLMQ-v12-Spring '84-p188
Surprises
BL-v81-S 15 '84-p137
Take Hold!
BL-v71-Ap 15 '75-p862
BS-v35-My '75-p49
KR-v42-Ag 15 '74-p883
NYTBR-D 29 '74-p8
PW-v206-Jl 29 '74-p58
SLJ-v21-My '75-p56
Thread One To A Star
BB-v4-O '76-p3
BL-v72-Je 15 '76-p1468
KR-v44-Ap 1 '76-p398
SLJ-v23-D '76-p54
To Look At Anything
BL-v74-My 1 '78-p1439
Cur R-v18-F '79-p44
KR-v46-My 15 '78-p549
LA-v55-O '78-p861
SLJ-v25-N '78-p64
Witching Time
BL-v74-S 1 '77-p46
PW-v211-Je 27 '77-p111
SLJ-v24-F '78-p58
Wonder Wheels
BL-v75-Mr 15 '79-p1145
BS-v39-Ag '79-p168
CBRS-v7-Ap '79-p89
CCB-B-v32-Je '79-p177
Hi Lo-v1-Mr '80-p3
KR-v47-Ap 1 '79-p392
NYTBR-Ap 8 '79-p32
RT-v34-O '80-p54
SLJ-v25-My '79-p86

* * *

HOPKINS, Linda
Storylines No. 7
GP-v16-S '77-p3175

* * *

HOPKINS, Margo
Honey Rabbit
PW-v221-F 12 '82-p99

* * *

HOPKINS, T
On Target
JB-v41-Je '77-p178

* * *

HOPKINS, Tim
Jimmy Swift
GP-v18-Jl '79-p3559
JB-v43-Ag '79-p221

* * *

HOPPE, Joanne
April Spell
CBRS-v7-Spring '79-p118
EJ-v68-N '79-p75
KR-v47-Jl 15 '79-p797
PW-v215-Je 11 '79-p103
SLJ-v26-O '79-p159
The Lesson Is Murder
BB-v6-Je '78-p5
CCB-B-v31-S '77-p17
KR-v45-Ap 15 '77-p436
NYTBR-Je 12 '77-p31
PW-v211-F 28 '77-p123
SLJ-v23-My '77-p78
SLJ-v27-N '80-p47

* * *

HOPPEL, Joe
The Sporting News Baseball Trivia Book
SLJ-v30-My '84-p27

* * *

HOPPER, Nancy J
Ape Ears And Beaky
PW-v226-S 21 '84-p96
Hang On, Harvey!
CBRS-v11-Jl '83-p138
CCB-B-v37-S '83-p10
CE-v60-Ja '84-p208
HB-v59-Ag '83-p445
KR-v51-Ap 15 '83-p459
SLJ-v29-Ap '83-p114
Just Vernon
BS-v42-D '82-p365
CBRS-v11-Winter '83-p57
Inter BC-v15-#3 '84-p16
KR-v50-S 15 '82-p1060
PW-v222-N 5 '82-p70
SLJ-v29-Ja '83-p84
Lies
BL-v80-Je 1 '84-p1392
CBRS-v12-Spring '84-p128
CCB-B-v37-Ap '84-p148
HB-v60-Ag '84-p476
SLJ-v31-S '84-p119
Secrets
CBRS-v8-S '79-p8
KR-v47-Ag 1 '79-p860
PW-v215-Ap 9 '79-p107
SLJ-v25-My '79-p72
The Seven 1/2 Sins Of Stacey Kendall
BL-v78-Jl '82-p1445
CBRS-v10-My '82-p97
KR-v50-Ap 1 '82-p418
SLJ-v28-My '82-p63

* * *

HOPSCOTCH Books
TES-O 1 '82-p47

* * *

HORAI, Wence
Magician's Musical Pie
BIC-v9-D '80-p19
In Rev-v15-Je '81-p38
Miller's Helper
Atl Pro Bk R-v10-N '83-p4
BIC-v12-D '83-p13

* * *

HORAK, Wenceslaus
Grey Feathers
Can Child Lit-#31 '83-p105

* * *

HORDER, Mervyn
On Christmas Day
B&B-v15-N '69-p45
BL-v66-D 1 '69-p458
BW-v3-D 21 '69-p8
CCB-B-v23-N '69-p46
Comw-v91-N 21 '69-p252
KR-v37-S 15 '69-p1005
Obs-D 7 '69-p31
PW-v196-S 1 '69-p52
SR-v52-D 20 '69-p28
TLS-O 16 '69-p1200

* * *

HORENSTEIN, Sidney
The Big Strawberry Book Of Dinosaurs And Other Prehistoric Animals
CLW-v50-Ap '79-p403

HORNE, Richard Henry (continued)
Obs-S 10 '67-p23
Spec-v219-N 3 '67-p543
TLS-N 30 '67-p1143

* * *

HORNER, Althea J
Little Big Girl
SLJ-v30-O '83-p150

* * *

HORNER, Deborah
Masks Of The World
PW-v213-Ja 16 '78-p100

* * *

HORNER, Deborah R
The Great Disguise Book
NYTBR-v85-O 26 '80-p27

* * *

HORNSBY, Jeremy
The Story Of Inventions
Lis-v98-N 10 '77-p626

* * *

HORNSBY, Ken
Wet Behind The Ears
JB-v45-Ag '81-p159
Punch-v280-Ap 29 '81-p680
TES-Ap 10 '81-p24
TLS-Mr 27 '81-p339

* * *

HOROWITZ, Anthony
The Devil's Door-Bell
BL-v80-F 1 '84-p814
BL-v80-Mr 15 '84-p1070
CBRS-v12-My '84-p108
JB-v47-D '83-p257
KR-v52-Mr 1 '84-pJ15
Learning-v12-Ap '84-p77
SLJ-v30-Ap '84-p124
Sch Lib-v32-Mr '84-p68
TES-O 28 '83-p25
The Sinister Secret Of Frederick K. Bower
B&B-v25-Je '80-p48

* * *

HOROWITZ, Susan
Hansel And Gretel With Benjy And Bubbles
SLJ-v25-O '78-p133
Jack And The Beanstalk With Benjy And Bubbles
SLJ-v25-O '78-p133
Little Red Riding Hood With Benjy And Bubbles
SLJ-v26-S '79-p113
Rumpelstiltskin With Benjy And Bubbles
SLJ-v26-N '79-p65

* * *

HORSBURGH, Peg
Living Light
ACSB-v12-Spring '79-p26
BL-v75-S 1 '78-p50
Cur R-v18-F '79-p62
KR-v46-Ag 1 '78-p810
SB-v15-S '79-p101

* * *

HORSE, Harry
The Ogopogo
TES-Mr 9 '84-p33

* * *

HORSES And Ponies (Granada Guides)
TES-Ap 16 '82-p24

* * *

HORSES (Discoveries)
TES-Mr 6 '81-p37

* * *

HORSFORD, Marisa
Poems
Sch Lib-v30-S '82-p262

* * *

HORTON, Adey
The Child Jesus
CC-v92-N 26 '75-p1093
CLW-v47-F '76-p307
CR-v228-Mr '76-p164
HB-v51-D '75-p617

* * *

HORTON, C
A Closer Look At Grasslands
JB-v43-D '79-p326
TES-N 16 '79-p30

* * *

HORTON, Casey
Animals
ASBYP-v15-Fall '82-p54
SLJ-v27-Ag '81-p67
Fish
Cur R-v24-N '84-p79
JB-v47-D '83-p244
SB-v20-S '84-p34
SLJ-v30-F '84-p73
TES-Mr 9 '84-p54
Insects
ASBYP-v15-Fall '82-p54
BL-v80-Je 15 '84-p1484
SLJ-v27-Ag '81-p67
TES-N 11 '83-p26
Machines
ASBYP-v15-Fall '82-p54
SLJ-v27-Ag '81-p67
Mammals
JB-v47-Ag '83-p165

* * *

HORTON, Louise
Careers In Theatre, Music, And Dance
BL-v73-O 15 '76-p314
BL-v73-O 15 '76-p323
CCB-B-v30-F '77-p91
Cur R-v16-My '77-p95
Cur R-v17-F '78-p82
SLJ-v23-F '77-p72
SLJ-v24-D '77-p35

* * *

HORVATH, Betty
Be Nice To Josephine
BL-v67-D 1 '70-p308
CCB-B-v24-Ja '71-p75
CLW-v42-Ap '71-p519
SR-v53-O 24 '70-p66
The Cheerful Quiet
BL-v66-Ap 15 '70-p1046
CCB-B-v24-S '70-p10
LJ-v95-Je 15 '70-p2302
Hooray For Jasper
CCB-B-v20-O '66-p27
KR-v34-Je 1 '66-p538
LJ-v91-S 15 '66-p4314
Jasper And The Hero Business
BW-N 12 '78-pE2
Inter BC-v9-Ag 80 '78-p18
SLJ-v24-D '77-p60
Jasper Makes Music
CCB-B-v20-Mr '67-p109
LJ-v92-My 15 '67-p2015
Not Enough Indians
GT-v89-Ap '72-p84
KR-v39-F 15 '71-p175
LJ-v96-Ap 15 '71-p1495
PW-v199-Mr 8 '71-p71

* * *

HORVATH, Joan
Film Making For Beginners
A Lib-v6-N '75-p619
BL-v71-O 1 '74-p173
CCB-B-v28-Ap '75-p131
KR-v42-My 1 '74-p493

HORVATH, Joan (continued)
LJ-v99-Ap 15 '74-p1228
PW-v206-N 11 '74-p48
TN-v31-Ap '75-p336

* * *

HORWITZ, Eleanor
Ways Of Wildlife
Cha Ti-v31-D '77-p35
Cur R-v16-O '77-p257
SB-v14-D '78-p165
Teacher-v95-Ja '78-p131

* * *

HORWITZ, Elinor L
How To Wreck A Building
BL-v78-My 15 '82-p1257
CCB-B-v35-Jl '82-p208
HB-v58-Je '82-p307
KR-v50-Mr 15 '82-p348
NYTBR-v87-Ap 25 '82-p33
SLJ-v28-My '82-p54
On The Land
BL-v76-Jl 1 '80-p1600
CCB-B-v34-N '80-p55
KR-v48-Je 15 '80-p785
SB-v16-Ja '81-p149
SLJ-v27-O '80-p155
Sometimes It Happens
BL-v77-Je 1 '81-p1299
CBRS-v9-My '81-p84
CCB-B-v35-O '81-p31
Inter BC-v14-#1 '83-p35
KR-v49-Je 15 '81-p739
PW-v219-Je 19 '81-p102
SLJ-v28-Ap '82-p58

* * *

HORWITZ, Elinor Lander
The Bird, The Banner, And Uncle Sam
A Art-v40-D '76-p29
BB-v5-F '77-p4
BF-v2-Fall '76-p527
BL-v73-D 15 '76-p600
BL-v73-D 15 '76-p608
JAF-v91-Ja '78-p613
KR-v44-O 1 '76-p1105
LJ-v102-F 15 '77-p479
SLJ-v23-N '76-p70
A Child's Garden Of Sculpture
BL-v73-F 15 '77-p897
BS-v36-O '76-p240
CT-v6-My '77-p30
Cur R-v16-F '77-p15
SLJ-v23-F '77-p65
A Child's Garden Sculpture
Sch Arts-v80-Ja '81-p39
Contemporary American Folk Artists
BL-v72-N 15 '75-p444
BL-v72-N 15 '75-p454
CCB-B-v29-Ap '76-p125
Choice-v13-My '76-p356
Cur R-v17-F '78-p80
Des-v77-MW '76-p32
HB-v52-Ap '76-p178
KR-v43-O 1 '75-p1141
SLJ-v22-D '75-p59
Madness, Magic, And Medicine
BL-v73-Jl 1 '77-p1646
BL-v73-Jl 1 '77-p1653
CCB-B-v31-O '77-p34
Comw-v104-N 11 '77-p733
HB-v53-Ag '77-p457
KR-v45-My 1 '77-p494
SB-v14-My '78-p10
SLJ-v23-My '77-p36
SLJ-v23-My '77-p70
Mountain People, Mountain Crafts
A Arch-v38-Ja '75-p63
A Art-v38-N '74-p85
BL-v70-Jl 15 '74-p1249
BW-My 19 '74-p5
Cr H-v34-O '74-p17
HB-v50-O '74-p150
KR-v42-My 15 '74-p543
KR-v43-Ja 1 '75-p13
LJ-v99-Jl '74-p1798
LJ-v99-S 15 '74-p2291
LJ-v99-D 15 '74-p3247
NYTBR-Je 2 '74-p8
NYTBR-Je 2 '74-p38
NYTBR-N 3 '74-p54
The Strange Story Of The Frog Who Became A Prince
CSM-v63-My 6 '71-pB5
HB-v47-Je '71-p282
JLH-v199-My 17 '71-p63
KR-v39-Ap 15 '71-p428
LJ-v96-S 15 '71-p2906
NYTBR, pt.2-My 2 '71-p8
When The Sky Is Like Lace
BL-v72-O 15 '75-p303
CCB-B-v29-Ja '76-p78
CLW-v47-F '76-p309
CSM-v67-N 5 '75-pB6
HB-v51-D '75-p585
JB-v41-O '77-p278
KR-v43-Ag 1 '75-p843
NYTBR-S 14 '75-p8
NYTBR-N 16 '75-p56
NYTBR-D 7 '75-p68
PW-v208-Jl 21 '75-p70
RT-v31-Ja '78-p26
RT-v31-Ja '78-p426
SLJ-v22-Mr '76-p92
SLJ-v25-N '78-p31
Teacher-v93-Ap '76-p34
WLB-v50-O '75-p173

* * *

HORWITZ, Joshua
Doll Hospital
BL-v79-Je 15 '83-p1339
CCB-B-v37-O '83-p30
CE-v60-N '83-p140
HB-v59-O '83-p591
KR-v51-Je 1 '83-p620
SE-v48-My '84-p370
SLJ-v30-S '83-p124
Night Markets
BL-v80-My 1 '84-p1246
CCB-B-v37-My '84-p166
CE-v61-S '84-p68
Inst-v93-My '84-p104
KR-v52-Mr 1 '84-pJ19
Learning-v12-Ap '84-p77
NYTBR-v89-Ap 8 '84-p29
PW-v225-Je 8 '84-p64
RT-v38-N '84-p227
SLJ-v30-My '84-p80

* * *

HORWITZ, Sylvia L
Francisco Goya: Painter Of Kings And Demons
BL-v71-Ja 15 '75-p502
HB-v51-F '75-p60
KR-v42-O 15 '74-p1114
SLJ-v21-Ja '75-p54
Toulouse-Lautrec
BL-v70-Mr 1 '74-p736
BS-v33-D 15 '73-p429
Choice-v12-N '75-p1133
Comw-v99-N 23 '73-p220
KR-v41-D 1 '73-p1315
LJ-v99-Ap 15 '74-p1228

* * *

HORWOOD, Harold
Tales Of The Labrador Indians
Can Child Lit-#31 '83-p134

* * *

HORYCH-TSMOTS, Bohdonna
Hosti
BL-v77-Ja 15 '81-p706
Mushka Motrushka
BL-v77-Ja 15 '81-p706
Zajchyk Natalchyk
BL-v77-Ja 15 '81-p706

* * *

HOSFORD, Jessie
You Bet Your Boots I Can
B&B-v18-My '73-pR13
B&B-v20-My '75-p66
BL-v69-S 15 '72-p100
BS-v32-Ag 15 '72-p243
CCB-B-v26-S '72-p9
CE-v49-O '72-p28
CLW-v45-O '73-p136
EJ-v61-S '72-p937
KR-v40-Ja 1 '72-p8
KR-v40-D 15 '72-p1419
LJ-v97-S 15 '72-p2962
TLS-Ap 6 '73-p378

* * *

HOSSENT, Harry
The Beaver Book Of Bikes
Obs-Jl 19 '81-p29
Sch Lib-v29-Je '81-p164
TES-F 27 '81-p39

* * *

HOSTETLER, Marian
African Adventure
SLJ-v23-Ja '77-p93
Fear In Algeria
SLJ-v26-Ap '80-p111
Journey To Jerusalem
SLJ-v25-S '78-p139

* * *

HOT Dog!
BL-v79-F 1 '83-p731
Cha Ti-v37-Ag '83-p47

* * *

HOTTON, Nicholas, III
The Evidence Of Evolution
CCB-B-v23-S '69-p10
Choice-v5-F '69-p1600
LJ-v93-O 1 '68-p3572
NH-v78-D '69-p73
Teacher-v86-F '69-p184

* * *

HOUCK, Carter
The Big Bag Book
BL-v74-F 15 '78-p969
HB-v55-O '78-p547
PW-v212-Ag 15 '77-p68
Warm As Wool, Cool As Cotton
BL-v71-Jl 15 '75-p1191
KR-v43-My 15 '75-p571
SLJ-v22-S '75-p105

* * *

HOUGH, Charlotte
Bad Cat
GP-v14-Jl '75-p2671
Obs-Je 29 '75-p21
TLS-S 19 '75-p1054
Charlotte Hough's Holiday Book
GP-v14-Ap '76-p2856
JB-v40-F '76-p26
Obs-F 15 '76-p26
Spec-v235-D 6 '75-p732
The Mixture As Before
JB-v41-Ap '77-p95
TES-S 22 '78-p23
Pink Pig
GP-v14-Jl '75-p2671
Obs-Je 29 '75-p21
TLS-S 19 '75-p1054
Red Biddy
CCB-B-v22-S '68-p8
Verse And Various
Brit Bk N C-Spring '80-p11
Sch Lib-v28-S '80-p276
TES-Ja 18 '80-p39
Wonky Donkey
GP-v14-Jl '75-p2671
Obs-Je 29 '75-p21

* * *

HOUGH, Henry Beetle
Tuesday Will Be Different
BL-v68-Ja 1 '72-p377
BS-v31-D 15 '71-p414
HB-v48-F '72-p78
KR-v39-Ag 15 '71-p912
LJ-v96-S 15 '71-p2763
NYTBR-O 31 '71-p32
New R-v165-N 6 '71-p28
PW-v200-S 6 '71-p46

* * *

HOUGH, Richard
Captain Bligh & Mr. Christian
B&B-v18-Ja '73-p116
BL-v69-My 1 '73-p822
BS-v32-F 1 '73-p494
BW-v7-Ja 28 '73-p3
Choice-v10-My '73-p509
Econ-v245-O 7 '72-p69
GW-v107-D 9 '72-p23
HB-v50-Ap '74-p172
KR-v40-N 15 '72-p1335
LJ-v98-Mr 15 '73-p866
NY-v48-F 10 '73-p115
NYTBR-S 23 '73-p26
Nat R-v24-N 24 '72-p1306
Nat R-v25-My 25 '73-p593
Obs-O 1 '72-p41
PQ-v52-Jl '73-p354
PW-v202-D 11 '72-p31
TLS-Ja 26 '73-p101
Galapagos
BL-v72-N 15 '75-p454
CLW-v48-O '76-p135
GP-v14-S '75-p2699
Obs-N 9 '75-p27
SB-v12-My '76-p40
SLJ-v22-F '76-p46
Teacher-v93-F '76-p125
Razor Eyes
BL-v80-O 1 '83-p233
BS-v43-Mr '84-p464
Brit Bk N C-Spring '82-p13
CCB-B-v37-Ap '84-p148
Emerg Lib-v11-N '83-p20
GP-v20-Mr '82-p4031
HB-v60-F '84-p61
JB-v46-F '82-p33
KR-v52-Mr 1 '84-pJ21
Obs-N 29 '81-p27
SLJ-v30-Ja '84-p86
Sch Lib-v29-D '81-p344
VOYA-v7-Je '84-p95

* * *

HOUGHTON, Eric
A Giant Can Do Anything
JB-v40-F '76-p15
TLS-D 5 '75-p1453
The Mouse And The Magician
GP-v15-O '76-p2974
JB-v41-F '77-p15
LJ-v96-Mr 15 '71-p1108
Obs-Ag 22 '76-p21
SLJ-v26-Mr '80-p121
Spec-v237-D 11 '76-p22
TLS-D 11 '70-p1462
Steps Out Of Time
BL-v77-N 1 '80-p405
CBRS-v9-Ja '81-p37
CCB-B-v34-S '80-p12

HOUGHTON, Eric (continued)
SLJ-v27-S '80-p72
Sch Lib-v27-D '79-p388
VOYA-v3-F '81-p38

* * *

HOUGHTON Mifflin Mathematics
Cur R-v22-O '83-p57

* * *

HOUGHTON Mifflin Reading Program 1981
Cur R-v19-N '80-p404

* * *

HOUGHTON Mifflin Reading Series
Cur R-v15-D '76-p298
Cur R-v18-F '79-p3
RT-v30-F '77-p558

* * *

HOUGHTON Mifflin Reading Series 1976
Inst-v85-F '76-p164
Teacher-v94-S '76-p158

* * *

HOUGHTON Mifflin Science
Cur R-v19-F '80-p76

* * *

HOUGHTON Mifflin Social Studies
Cur R-v20-Ja '81-p76

* * *

HOULDSWORTH, P B
Allons En France. Pt. 4
TES-Ap 22 '83-p29

* * *

HOULE, Denise
Contes Quebecois
In Rev-v15-Ag '81-p42

* * *

HOURIHANE, Ursula
Stumpy Goes To The Fair
SLJ-v24-Mr '78-p114

* * *

HOUSBY, Trevor
Sea Angling
TES-Je 16 '78-p52

* * *

HOUSE, Charles
The Friendly Woods
CCB-B-v27-My '74-p144
KR-v41-D 15 '73-p1364
LJ-v99-Ap 15 '74-p1212
PW-v205-Ja 7 '74-p54

* * *

HOUSE That Jack Built (Benvenuti)
SLJ-v26-Ja '80-p56

* * *

HOUSEHOLD, Geoffrey
The Cats To Come
B&B-v23-N '77-p80
Escape Into Daylight
Am-v135-D 11 '76-p429
BL-v73-D 15 '76-p608
BS-v36-Ja '77-p324
CCB-B-v30-F '77-p91
CSM-v68-N 3 '76-p20
GP-v14-Ap '76-p2844
JB-v40-Ag '76-p230
KR-v44-S 1 '76-p974
Kliatt-v12-Winter '78-p8
SLJ-v23-D '76-p68
Spec-v236-Ap 10 '76-p25
TLS-Ap 2 '76-p388
Teacher-v95-My '78-p109
Prisoner Of The Indies
BL-v64-My 1 '68-p1044
BS-v28-Je 1 '68-p113
BW-v2-My 5 '68-p28
CCB-B-v21-Jl '68-p175
Comw-v88-My 24 '68-p302
HB-v44-Ag '68-p429
HT-v17-D '67-p862
KR-v36-Mr 15 '68-p344
LJ-v93-Ap 15 '68-p1799
NO-v7-Ag 19 '68-p17
NYTBR-v73-Jl 28 '68-p24
Obs-N 26 '67-p28
PW-v193-F 19 '68-p101
SE-v33-My '69-p558
TLS-N 30 '67-p1138
YR-v4-My '68-p14

* * *

HOUSER, Norman W
Drugs
BL-v66-N 1 '69-p347
BL-v66-N 15 '69-p366
BS-v29-S 1 '69-p211
CC-v86-D 10 '69-p1585
CLW-v41-O '69-p134
CLW-v41-My '70-p577
HB-v45-D '69-p687
KR-v37-Je 15 '69-p636
LJ-v94-O 15 '69-p3845
NYTBR-S 21 '69-p30
NYTBR, pt.2-N 9 '69-p60
SB-v5-D '69-p267

* * *

HOUSMAN, Laurence
Cotton-Wooleena
BL-v70-My 15 '74-p1056
CE-v51-N '74-p92
KR-v42-Ap 15 '74-p425
LJ-v99-S 15 '74-p2270
Moonlight And Fairyland
GP-v17-Ja '79-p3459
ILN-v266-D '78-p127
JB-v43-F '79-p13
TLS-D 1 '78-p1398
The Rat-Catcher's Daughter
BL-v70-Ap 1 '74-p874
CSM-v66-My 1 '74-pF5
HB-v50-Ag '74-p379
Inst-v84-N '74-p134
KR-v42-Mr 1 '74-p244
LJ-v99-My 15 '74-p1451
LJ-v99-My 15 '74-p1473
NY-v50-D 2 '74-p197
NYTBR-My 5 '74-p17
NYTBR-N 3 '74-p53
PW-v205-Mr 25 '74-p57
The Story Of The Seven Young Goslings
GP-v14-O '75-p2711

* * *

HOUSTON, James
Akavak
BL-v65-Ap 1 '69-p901
BL-v69-O 15 '72-p177
CCB-B-v22-Ap '69-p127
HB-v45-F '69-p54
NO-v8-Ap 7 '69-p19
SE-v33-My '69-p556
TN-v25-Ap '69-p310
Teacher-v86-My '69-p132
Black Diamonds
Atl Pro Bk R-v10-N '83-p2
BIC-v11-Je '82-p32
BL-v78-My 1 '82-p1160
CCB-B-v35-Jl '82-p209
CLW-v54-O '82-p134
Cur R-v22-O '83-p49
Emerg Lib-v11-N '83-p37
HB-v58-Je '82-p298
LA-v59-O '82-p751
Mac-v95-Je 28 '82-p56
Quill & Q-v48-Je '82-p35
RT-v36-D '82-p338
SLJ-v29-D '82-p72
VOYA-v5-Ag '82-p32

HOUSTON, James (continued)
Eagle Mask: A West Coast Indian Tale
BL-v63-D 1 '66-p418
CCB-B-v20-Ja '67-p74
HB-v42-D '66-p716
Inst-v76-D '66-p13
KR-v34-Je 15 '66-p577
LJ-v91-S 15 '66-p4336
NYTBR-v71-N 6 '66-p40
SR-v49-N 12 '66-p50
Frozen Fire
BB-v6-Ap '78-p4
BL-v74-F 15 '78-p1009
BS-v37-Ja '78-p335
CCB-B-v31-Mr '78-p113
CE-v54-Mr '78-p258
CE-v55-Ap '79-p263
Cur R-v17-Ag '78-p184
GP-v19-My '80-p3698
HB-v54-F '78-p47
J Read-v22-F '79-p477
KR-v45-N 15 '77-p1197
LA-v55-Mr '78-p367
RT-v32-O '78-p43
RT-v35-N '81-p238
SE-v42-Ap '78-p321
SLJ-v24-N '77-p57
Ghost Fox
CF-v57-Je '77-p49
HB-v53-D '77-p697
KR-v44-N 1 '76-p1183
LJ-v102-Ja 1 '77-p127
Obs-O 30 '77-p29
SLJ-v23-Ap '77-p81
SLJ-v23-My '77-p37
SN-v92-My '77-p72
WLB-v52-S '77-p77
WSJ-v189-Mr 3 '77-p14
Ghost Paddle
BL-v69-Ja 15 '73-p493
CCB-B-v26-N '72-p43
HB-v49-F '73-p48
Inst-v82-N '72-p126
KR-v40-S 1 '72-p1027
LJ-v98-Ja 15 '73-p261
NYTBR, pt.2-N 5 '72-p14
PW-v202-O 9 '72-p113
SLJ-v27-S '80-p43
SN-v88-Ja '73-p34
Kiviok's Magic Journey
Atl Pro Bk R-v10-N '83-p2
CCB-B-v27-Ap '74-p130
CLW-v45-Mr '74-p398
CSM-v66-My 1 '74-pF5
HB-v50-Ap '74-p146
KR-v41-O 15 '73-p1166
LJ-v98-D 15 '73-p3700
PW-v204-N 19 '73-p61
RT-v36-D '82-p336
Long Claws
BIC-v10-O '81-p33
BL-v78-O 1 '81-p236
CCB-B-v35-Mr '82-p130
In Rev-v15-O '81-p38
KR-v49-D 15 '81-p1519
LA-v59-Ap '82-p369
Mac-v94-D 21 '81-p44
PW-v220-S 18 '81-p155
Quill & Q-v47-N '81-p25
SLJ-v28-F '82-p76
River Runners
Atl Pro Bk R-v10-N '83-p2
BL-v76-F 15 '80-p834
CBRS-v8-F '80-p58
CCB-B-v33-Ap '80-p153
CE-v56-Ap '80-p304
Can Child Lit-#20 '80-p84
HB-v56-Ap '80-p176
In Rev-v14-F '80-p44
SLJ-v26-F '80-p67
Songs Of The Dream People
BL-v69-Ja 15 '73-p493
CCB-B-v26-Ap '73-p125
Comw-v99-N 23 '73-p220
HB-v49-Ap '73-p149
KR-v40-N 15 '72-p1309
KR-v40-D 15 '72-p1416
LJ-v98-Mr 15 '73-p1004
NYTBR, pt.2-N 5 '72-p7
TN-v29-Je '73-p356
Tikta' Liktak
CCB-B-v20-D '66-p59
CE-v43-D '66-p234
LA-v60-Ap '83-p438
SLJ-v27-S '80-p43
TN-v34-Winter '78-p189
Tikta'Liktak
BL-v62-Ja 1 '66-p450
HB-v41-D '65-p633
KR-v33-Je 15 '65-p575
LJ-v90-N 15 '65-p5077
The White Archer
BL-v64-O 1 '67-p198
BW-v1-N 5 '67-p22
BW-v10-Ap 13 '80-p13
CCB-B-v21-O '67-p28
HB-v43-O '67-p588
KR-v35-Je 15 '67-p694
LJ-v92-S 15 '67-p3187
LJ-v95-O 15 '70-p3603
NYTBR-v72-O 8 '67-p38
PW-v192-N 20 '67-p56
Par-v43-S '68-p84
SLJ-v27-S '80-p43
White Archer: An Eskimo Legend
SR-v50-S 16 '67-p49
Wolf Run
BL-v67-Ap 15 '71-p701
CCB-B-v25-S '71-p9
CE-v48-My '72-p422
CSM-v63-Jl 10 '71-p15
HB-v47-Je '71-p287
KR-v39-Ap 1 '71-p365
LJ-v96-Je 15 '71-p2131
PW-v199-Mr 8 '71-p71
SR-v54-Ag 21 '71-p27

* * *

HOUSTON, John
A Mouse In My House
CCB-B-v26-N '72-p43
KR-v40-Mr 1 '72-p255
LJ-v98-F 15 '73-p636

* * *

HOVER, M
Here Comes Santa Claus
SLJ-v29-O '82-p168

* * *

HOVEY, Tamara
John Reed: Witness To Revolution
BL-v72-O 1 '75-p227
BS-v35-O '75-p228
CCB-B-v29-Ja '76-p79
Comw-v102-N 21 '75-p570
HB-v52-Ap '76-p179
KR-v43-Jl 15 '75-p785
NO-v14-O 18 '75-p21
PW-v208-Ag 18 '75-p67
PW-v221-F 12 '82-p97
SLJ-v22-N '75-p91
A Mind Of Her Own
BL-v74-S 15 '77-p155
BL-v74-S 15 '77-p194
CCB-B-v31-Ja '78-p79
Comw-v104-N 11 '77-p732
EJ-v67-F '78-p80
HB-v54-Ag '78-p428
KR-v45-N 15 '77-p1209
SE-v42-Ap '78-p321

* * *

HOW It Works
ACSB-v12-Fall '79-p29
ARBA-v9-'78-p617

* * *

HOW The Tiger Got Its Stripes
Sch Lib-v27-D '79-p365

* * *

HOW To Catch A Dragon
TES-Jl 16 '82-p22

* * *

HOW To Make Magic
Obs-N 9 '75-p27

* * *

HOW To Re-Cycle Your Rubbish
Obs-N 9 '75-p27

* * *

HOWARD, Alan
Nativity Stories
NYTBR-v85-D 14 '80-p37
SLJ-v27-D '80-p53

* * *

HOWARD, C
Mom And Me
CCB-B-v29-Mr '76-p112

* * *

HOWARD, Coralie
What Do You Want To Know?
CCB-B-v23-N '69-p47
LJ-v94-F 15 '69-p874
SB-v5-My '69-p13

* * *

HOWARD, Elizabeth
Out Of Step With The Dancers
BB-v6-Ag '78-p4
BL-v74-Ap 1 '78-p1255
CCB-B-v32-S '78-p10
KR-v46-My 1 '78-p501
SLJ-v24-Ap '78-p94
Verity's Voyage
CCB-B-v18-Ja '65-p75
GT-v82-F '65-p108

* * *

HOWARD, Ellen
Circle Of Giving
BL-v80-My 15 '84-p1343
CBRS-v12-Spring '84-p128
CCB-B-v37-Ap '84-p148
SLJ-v30-Ag '84-p74

* * *

HOWARD, Jean G
Of Mice And Men
SLJ-v25-F '79-p43

* * *

HOWARD, Joanna
How A Town Works
JB-v42-Ap '78-p88
NS-v94-N 4 '77-p629
TES-D 2 '77-p25
The Human Body
TES-O 20 '78-p42

* * *

HOWARD, Katherine
I Can Count To 100...Can You?
SLJ-v26-Ja '80-p56

* * *

HOWARD, Max
People Papers
CCB-B-v28-My '75-p148
KR-v42-N 1 '74-p1145
SLJ-v21-Ja '75-p46

* * *

HOWARD, Moses L
The Human Mandolin
BL-v71-Ja 15 '75-p507
Inst-v84-My '75-p104
KR-v43-Ja 1 '75-p18
SLJ-v22-S '75-p84
WLB-v49-Mr '75-p522
The Ostrich Chase
CCB-B-v28-O '74-p29
KR-v42-My 1 '74-p479
LA-v52-S '75-p856
LJ-v99-S 15 '74-p2270
PW-v205-My 27 '74-p65

* * *

HOWARD, Sam
Communications Machines
ASBYP-v14-Fall '81-p29
JB-v45-O '81-p197
SB-v17-S '81-p34
SLJ-v27-F '81-p53

* * *

HOWARD, Ted
Who Should Play God?
BL-v74-F 1 '78-p883
CC-v95-Ap 12 '78-p403
Choice-v15-Mr '78-p94
Choice-v18-Jl '81-p1522
HB-v54-Ag '78-p429
KR-v45-N 15 '77-p1242
LJ-v102-D 1 '77-p2419
PW-v212-O 24 '77-p71
SB-v14-S '78-p92

* * *

HOWARD, Vanessa
A Screaming Whisper
ANQ-v11-O '72-p26
BL-v69-N 1 '72-p239
BL-v69-N 1 '72-p244
BS-v32-O 15 '72-p339
CCB-B-v26-D '72-p58
CLW-v44-F '73-p449
CT-v10-My '81-p10
EJ-v62-My '73-p829
KR-v40-Ag 15 '72-p953
LJ-v97-D 15 '72-p4056
LJ-v97-D 15 '72-p4078
NYTBR, pt.2-N 5 '72-p32

* * *

HOWARD, Vernon
Pantomimes, Charades And Skits
Inst-v84-My '75-p96
SLJ-v21-Ap '75-p53

* * *

HOWARTH, David
Great Britons
B&B-v24-Ja '79-p60
JB-v42-D '78-p313

* * *

HOWARTH, Mary
Could Dracula Live In Woodford?
BIC-v13-Mr '84-p29
Quill & Q-v49-N '83-p24
SLJ-v30-My '84-p81

* * *

HOWE, A
I Can't Make Head Or Tail Of It
TES-F 4 '83-p28

* * *

HOWE, Caroline W
Counting Penguins
CBRS-v12-O '83-p13
PW-v224-Jl 8 '83-p66
RT-v37-Mr '84-p646
SLJ-v30-D '83-p56
Teddy Bear's Bird And Beast Band
CBRS-v8-My '80-p92
KR-v48-Jl 1 '80-p834
SLJ-v27-S '80-p60

* * *

HOWE, Deborah
Bunnicula
BL-v75-My 15 '79-p1439
BL-v79-Ap 1 '83-p1042
BW-My 13 '79-pK3
BW-v11-O 11 '81-p12
CBRS-v7-Ag '79-p137
CCB-B-v32-Jl '79-p192
KR-v47-Jl 1 '79-p741
NY-v55-D 3 '79-p208
NYTBR-S 30 '79-p36
PW-v215-Mr 19 '79-p94
PW-v218-D 19 '80-p51
RT-v34-O '80-p48
SLJ-v25-My '79-p81
Teddy Bear's Scrapbook
BL-v76-Je 1 '80-p1424
CBRS-v9-O '80-p15
CCB-B-v34-S '80-p13
KR-v48-Jl 15 '80-p911
PW-v217-My 30 '80-p85
PW-v220-Ag 28 '81-p395
SLJ-v27-S '80-p60

* * *

HOWE, Fanny
Radio City
BL-v80-My 15 '84-p1344
CCB-B-v37-Jl '84-p205
SLJ-v31-S '84-p128
VOYA-v7-Je '84-p95

* * *

HOWE, Irving
Yiddish Stories, Old And New
BL-v71-O 15 '74-p244
HB-v51-Ap '75-p155
KR-v42-N 1 '74-p1155
PW-v206-S 2 '74-p70
SLJ-v21-Mr '75-p106

* * *

HOWE, James
The Case Of The Missing Mother
SLJ-v30-N '83-p65
The Celery Stalks At Midnight
BL-v80-O 1 '83-p295
CCB-B-v37-O '83-p30
HB-v59-D '83-p709
NYTBR-v88-N 6 '83-p43
PW-v224-S 9 '83-p64
SLJ-v30-S '83-p124
The Day The Teacher Went Bananas
CBRS-v13-O '84-p14
PW-v226-Ag 3 '84-p67
The Hospital Book
ASBYP-v14-Fall '81-p22
BL-v77-My 15 '81-p1253
CBRS-v9-Je '81-p94
CCB-B-v34-Je '81-p195
CE-v58-N '81-p113
HB-v57-O '81-p553
Inst-v90-Ja '81-p116
Inter BC-v13-#6 '82-p42
KR-v49-Je 1 '81-p681
NYTBR-v86-Ap 26 '81-p56
PW-v219-Ap 17 '81-p63
Par-v57-O '82-p140
RT-v36-Ap '83-p802
SLJ-v27-My '81-p56
How The Ewoks Saved The Trees
SLJ-v31-S '84-p104
Howliday Inn
BL-v78-My 15 '82-p1257
CBRS-v10-Spring '82-p117
CCB-B-v36-S '82-p12
LA-v60-Mr '83-p362
PW-v221-Mr 19 '82-p71
SLJ-v28-Ag '82-p117
Morgan's Zoo
SLJ-v31-S '84-p119
A Night Without Stars
BL-v79-Ap 1 '83-p1035
CBRS-v11-Spring '83-p125
HB-v59-Ap '83-p166
KR-v51-F 15 '83-p184
PW-v223-Ap 29 '83-p51
SLJ-v29-Ap '83-p124

* * *

HOWE, Norma
God, The Universe, And Hot Fudge Sundaes
BL-v80-Ap 15 '84-p1161
BS-v44-Je '84-p116
CBRS-v12-Ag '84-p151
CCB-B-v37-Jl '84-p205
HB-v60-Je '84-p337
SLJ-v30-Ag '84-p84
VOYA-v7-O '84-p196

* * *

HOWE, Raymond
Hannibal And The Pet Show
GP-v17-Ja '79-p3444
Hannibal Goes To School
GP-v17-Ja '79-p3444
Hannibal On Holiday
GP-v15-Mr '77-p3073
Hannibal On The Farm
GP-v15-Mr '77-p3073
Hannibal On The Nature Trail
GP-v17-Ja '79-p3444
Hannibal Runs Away
GP-v15-Mr '77-p3073

* * *

HOWELL, Arnold
Mathematics For Schools. Level 2
TES-O 3 '80-p27

* * *

HOWELL, F Clark
Early Man
A Anth-v68-D '66-p1581
BL-v62-O 1 '65-p135
Inst-v92-N '82-p96

* * *

HOWELL, Michael
The Elephant Man
CCB-B-v37-Ap '84-p149
JB-v48-Ap '84-p84
KR-v52-Mr 1 '84-pJ20
Lis-v110-N 3 '83-p30
SLJ-v30-Mr '84-p160
Sch Lib-v32-Je '84-p134

* * *

HOWELL, Ruth R
Everything Changes
ACSB-v13-Winter '80-p3
BL-v64-Je 1 '68-p1142
CSM-v60-My 2 '68-pB8
Comw-v88-My 24 '68-p302
KR-v36-F 1 '68-p119
LJ-v93-Mr 15 '68-p1303
NYTBR-v73-My 5 '68-p50
PW-v193-Ap 15 '68-p98
SB-v4-My '68-p41

* * *

HOWELL, Ruth Rea
A Crack In The Pavement
BL-v67-S 1 '70-p57
CCB-B-v24-O '70-p27
CE-v48-Ja '72-p208
CLW-v42-O '70-p133
CSM-v62-My 7 '70-pB5
Comw-v92-My 22 '70-p252
KR-v38-Mr 15 '70-p325
LJ-v95-N 15 '70-p4036
SB-v6-D '70-p221
The Dome People
BL-v70-Jl 1 '74-p1200
CCB-B-v28-O '74-p29

HOWELL, Ruth Rea
(continued)
CLW-v46-My '75-p453
KR-v42-My 15 '74-p544
LJ-v99-S 15 '74-p2270
SA-v231-D '74-p145
Splash And Flow
BL-v70-N 15 '73-p339
CCB-B-v27-Ja '74-p80
CLW-v45-D '73-p242
Inst-v83-N '73-p126
KR-v41-Jl 1 '73-p688
LJ-v98-O 15 '73-p3139
SA-v229-D '73-p132

* * *

HOWELLS, Mildred
The Woman Who Lived In Holland
BL-v70-S 1 '73-p51
CCB-B-v26-Je '73-p156
KR-v41-Mr 1 '73-p251
LJ-v98-Jl '73-p2187
PW-v203-Mr 19 '73-p71

* * *

HOWKER, Janni
Badger On The Barge
TES-Jl 20 '84-p21

* * *

HOY, Linda
The Damned
GP-v22-Ja '84-p4186
JB-v47-O '83-p216
Sch Lib-v32-Mr '84-p68
Sch Lib-v32-S '84-p212
TES-S 30 '83-p48
Your Friend, Rebecca
Brit Bk N C-Autumn '81-p24
GP-v20-My '81-p3883
JB-v45-O '81-p222
Sch Lib-v29-D '81-p344
TES-Je 5 '81-p41
TES-Jl 3 '81-p25
TES-N 11 '83-p25
TES-Je 29 '84-p32
TLS-S 18 '81-p1065

* * *

HOYLAND, John
The Ivy Garland
CCB-B-v36-Jl '83-p211
JB-v46-D '82-p231
SLJ-v30-Mr '84-p160
TES-N 19 '82-p34

* * *

HOYLE, D J
Drums At Buntale
BL-v73-Jl 15 '77-p1734

* * *

HOYLE, Fred
The Planet Of Death
Nature-v300-D 9 '82-p548

* * *

HOYLE, Geoffrey
Disaster
GP-v13-Mr '75-p2576
JB-v39-Ap '75-p105

* * *

HOYT, Edwin P
Arab Science
CCB-B-v29-Ja '76-p79
KR-v43-My 1 '75-p525
LJ-v100-My 15 '75-p995
SB-v12-My '76-p15
Horatio's Boys
AB-v54-N 11 '74-p2053
BHR-v49-Spring '75-p110
BL-v71-S 1 '74-p14
BS-v34-D 15 '74-p410
Choice-v12-Ap '75-p220
LJ-v99-Ag '74-p1937
PW-v205-Jl 22 '74-p68
VLS-Mr '84-p18
James Knox Polk
BL-v62-Mr 1 '66-p665
BS-v25-N 1 '65-p312
CCB-B-v19-D '65-p64
CSM-v57-N 4 '65-pB8
LJ-v91-F 15 '66-p1072

* * *

HOYT, Marie A
Kitchen Chemistry And Front Porch Physics
N Dir Wom-v13-My '84-p16

* * *

HOYT, Olga
The Bedouins
CCB-B-v23-S '69-p11
KR-v37-Ap 15 '69-p462
LJ-v94-S 15 '69-p3206
Demons, Devils And Djinn
KR-v42-My 1 '74-p485
LJ-v99-S 15 '74-p2292
NYTBR-My 5 '74-p22
PW-v205-Ap 22 '74-p74
Teacher-v92-F '75-p38

* * *

HRUBIN, Frantisek
Svit Slunicko, Svit
BL-v74-O 15 '77-p383

* * *

HSIAO, Ellen
A Chinese Year
BL-v67-Ap 1 '71-p664
BL-v69-F 15 '73-p553
CCB-B-v24-Ap '71-p125
PW-v199-Ja 11 '71-p63
SR-v54-F 20 '71-p31

* * *

HSIAO, Pia
Games You Make And Play
JB-v40-F '76-p44
Superbook Of Things To Make
GP-v13-Mr '75-p2588
Lis-v92-N 7 '74-p615
TLS-D 6 '74-p1385

* * *

HSIAO, Yen
I Chih Huo Yeh Tu Ts'e
BL-v77-Ja 1 '81-p629

* * *

HSU, Chin-Yeh
Erh Tung Pe K'o Chung Shu
BL-v73-F 1 '77-p839
Ka Tung Ku Shih Chi
BL-v73-F 1 '77-p839
Shi Chieh Wei Jen Ku Shih
BL-v73-F 1 '77-p839

* * *

HUANG, Paul C
The Illustrated Step-By-Step Beginner's Cookbook
KR-v48-My 15 '80-p647
PW-v218-Jl 4 '80-p90
SLJ-v27-S '80-p72

* * *

HUBBARD, D L
Dragon Comes To Admela
CCB-B-v22-O '68-p29
KR-v35-S 1 '67-p1047
LJ-v92-O 15 '67-p3850

* * *

HUBBARD, Dexter
The Young Privateersmen
Can Child Lit-#26 '82-p80

* * *

HUBBARD, Guy
Art: Choosing And Expressing
Cur R-v17-O '78-p291
Art: Discovering And Creating
Cur R-v17-O '78-p291
Art: Meaning, Method, And Media
Cur R-v17-O '78-p291

* * *

HUBBELL, Patricia
The Apple Vendor's Fair
Teacher-v92-F '75-p40
Catch Me A Wind
CCB-B-v23-S '69-p11
CLW-v40-O '68-p146
CSM-v60-My 2 '68-pB6
KR-v36-F 15 '68-p187
LJ-v93-Ap 15 '68-p1788
NYTBR-v73-My 5 '68-p44
Teacher-v96-N '78-p90

* * *

HUBER, Frederick C
Light
ACSB-v12-Winter '79-p18
Cur R-v18-F '79-p61
SLJ-v25-S '78-p139
Teacher-v96-N '78-p135

* * *

HUBLEY, Faith
The Hat
KR-v42-D 15 '74-p1299
PW-v206-N 4 '74-p69

* * *

HUBLEY, John
Jamaican Village
Brit Bk N C-Autumn '82-p28
JB-v46-O '82-p190
SLJ-v30-S '83-p105
Sch Lib-v30-D '82-p350
TES-N 5 '82-p31

* * *

HUBNER, Carol K
The Tattered Tallis
PW-v217-Ap 4 '80-p75
SLJ-v26-My '80-p86
The Whispering Mezuzah
SLJ-v26-My '80-p86

* * *

HUBNER, Carol Korb
The Haunted Shul And Other Devora Doresh Mysteries
SLJ-v26-S '79-p140

* * *

HUDDY, Delia
Blow-Up!
GP-v17-N '78-p3423
Creaky-Knees
JB-v43-Ap '79-p106
Gatecrashers
GP-v17-N '78-p3423
The Humboldt Effect
BS-v42-Ja '83-p406
CCB-B-v36-D '82-p70
GP-v21-S '82-p3953
HB-v59-F '83-p52
JB-v46-D '82-p231
KR-v50-O 15 '82-p1158
Obs-S 26 '82-p35
SLJ-v29-Ja '83-p85
TLS-S 17 '82-p1001
Hush-A-Bye-Baby
GP-v17-N '78-p3423
My Kind Of Cake
JB-v42-Ag '78-p205
No Ladder For Tom Bates
GP-v17-N '78-p3423
No Place Like Trickett's Green
GP-My '84-p4273
NS-v77-My 16 '69-p699
Sch Lib-v27-D '79-p367
Sandwich Street Blue
TLS-Jl 5 '74-p722
Sandwich Street Safari
JB-v41-D '77-p333
The Tale Of The Crooked Crab
Brit Bk N C-Spring '81-p17
CBRS-v9-Je '81-p93
JB-v45-Ag '81-p150
Sch Lib-v29-D '81-p326
TES-Mr 6 '81-p29
TLS-Mr 27 '81-p340
Tea-On-Friday Tigger
TLS-Jl 11 '75-p770
Time Piper
CBRS-v7-Ag '79-p138
CCB-B-v33-O '79-p29
CE-v56-Ap '80-p304
GP-v15-D '76-p3011
GP-v16-Ap '78-p3304
HB-v55-Je '79-p309
JB-v41-Ap '77-p113
KR-v47-My 15 '79-p580
LA-v57-My '80-p559
Obs-N 28 '76-p31
SLJ-v25-Mr '79-p140
TLS-D 10 '76-p1547

* * *

HUDLOW, Jean
Eric Plants A Garden
CCB-B-v25-N '71-p44
KR-v39-Jl 15 '71-p742
LJ-v96-D 15 '71-p4196
SR-v54-S 18 '71-p48

* * *

HUDSON, Eleanor
The Care Bears Help Out
SLJ-v30-S '83-p107
A Whale Of A Rescue
PW-v223-Ap 15 '83-p51
SLJ-v30-N '83-p62

* * *

HUDSON, Joyce R
Long Man's Song
CLW-v47-O '75-p132

* * *

HUDSON, Kenneth
The Archaeology Of Industry
Arch-v30-S '77-p356
GP-v15-Jl '76-p2925
JB-v41-F '77-p35
MN-v55-Mr '77-p66
SLJ-v23-S '76-p146
Behind The High Street
GP-v21-S '82-p3961
JB-v46-O '82-p190
TES-N 5 '82-p23
TES-Mr 11 '83-p48
Churchyards And Cemeteries
GP-v23-S '84-p4317
RT-v38-N '84-p227
TES-N 16 '84-p26
Clues To Yesterday's Transport
GP-v23-S '84-p4317
TES-N 16 '84-p26
Farm Furniture
GP-v19-My '80-p3687
JB-v44-O '80-p240
Sch Lib-v28-S '80-p276
TES-Jl 4 '80-p22
A Pocket Book For Industrial Archaeologists
BHR-v51-Winter '77-p536
JB-v41-F '77-p36

HUDSON, Kenneth
(continued)
Street Furniture
GP-v18-Ja '80-p3642
JB-v44-Ap '80-p68
Sch Lib-v28-Je '80-p165
Waterside Furniture
JB-v46-O '82-p190
TES-N 5 '82-p23
TES-Mr 11 '83-p48

* * *

HUDSON, Robert G
Nature's Nursery
BL-v65-My 15 '69-p1076
BL-v67-Mr 15 '71-p619
CCB-B-v22-Jl '69-p176
KR-v38-O 1 '70-p1099
LJ-v94-Mr 15 '69-p1328
SB-v7-My '71-p61

* * *

HUFF, Vivian
Let's Make Paper Dolls
CCB-B-v31-Jl '78-p178
KR-v46-F 15 '78-p180
SLJ-v25-S '78-p117
Teacher-v96-O '78-p169

* * *

HUGGETT, F E
Slaves And Slavery
JB-v40-F '76-p44

* * *

HUGGETT, Frank E
Netherlands
Lis-v96-N 11 '76-p624
The Past, Present And Future Of Life And Work At Sea
GP-v14-S '75-p2680

* * *

HUGGINS, Alice M
Spend Your Heart
BS-v25-Ap 15 '65-p52
CCB-B-v18-Mr '65-p104
KR-v33-F 15 '65-p186

* * *

HUGGINS, Edward
Blue And Green Wonders And Other Latvian Tales
CCB-B-v25-Ap '72-p123
KR-v39-O 15 '71-p1127
LJ-v97-Mr 15 '72-p1170

* * *

HUGH-JONES, Stephen
A Closer Look At Amazonian Indians
JB-v43-Ap '79-p107
TES-N 16 '79-p30

* * *

HUGHES, Carolyn
First Steps With Your Spectrum
TES-S 2 '83-p26

* * *

HUGHES, D
English Seven To Twelve
TES-Mr 7 '80-p32

* * *

HUGHES, Dean
Honestly, Myron
BL-v78-Je 1 '82-p1312
CBRS-v10-Ag '82-p135
Cur R-v22-O '83-p49
KR-v50-Ap 15 '82-p489
New Age-v7-Je '82-p70
SLJ-v28-Ag '82-p117
Millie Willenheimer And The Chestnut Corporation
BL-v79-Ap 15 '83-p1095
CBRS-v11-Spring '83-p125
CCB-B-v37-S '83-p10
KR-v51-Ap 1 '83-p377
RT-v37-N '83-p193
SLJ-v29-My '83-p72
Nutty For President
BL-v77-My 15 '81-p1254
BL-v78-F 15 '82-p762
CBRS-v10-Jl '81-p117
CE-v58-Mr '82-p257
HB-v57-Je '81-p302
KR-v49-My 1 '81-p570
PW-v219-Ap 10 '81-p71
SLJ-v28-F '82-p77
Switching Tracks
BL-v79-S 15 '82-p116
CBRS-v11-Winter '83-p58
CLW-v55-D '83-p231
J Read-v26-Ap '83-p653
KR-v50-Jl 15 '82-p802
SE-v47-Ap '83-p252
SLJ-v29-S '82-p139
VOYA-v5-F '83-p37

* * *

HUGHES, Gerald
Introducing The Bible
TES-Ag 21 '81-p19

* * *

HUGHES, J
A Monkey About The Place
JB-v43-F '79-p32

* * *

HUGHES, Janie
A Little Pandemonium
Obs-O 7 '79-p39

* * *

HUGHES, Jill
Aztecs
SLJ-v27-Ag '81-p67
TN-v41-Fall '84-p64
A Closer Look At Aborigines
TES-Je 20 '80-p41
A Closer Look At Apes
B&B-v23-Ja '78-p63
Cur R-v17-F '78-p3
A Closer Look At Aztecs
JB-v43-D '79-p326
A Closer Look At Bees And Wasps
BL-v73-Je 15 '77-p1576
Cur R-v17-F '78-p3
JB-v41-F '77-p37
SLJ-v24-S '77-p125
A Closer Look At Eskimos
B&B-v22-Je '77-p72
JB-v41-D '77-p334
TES-O 21 '77-p18
TES-N 18 '77-p37
Eskimos
Cur R-v17-O '78-p346
Inter BC-v10-Je 60 '79-p17
SLJ-v25-N '78-p56
Plains Indians
BL-v81-S 1 '84-p65
SLJ-v31-O '84-p158
Vikings
BL-v81-S 1 '84-p65
SLJ-v31-O '84-p158

* * *

HUGHES, Judy
A Bird In The Hand And A Bear In The Bush
LJ-v101-My 15 '76-p1219
PW-v209-Mr 29 '76-p56
SB-v12-Mr '77-p212

* * *

HUGHES, Langston
Black Misery
Atl-v224-Ag '69-p103
CCB-B-v24-Jl '70-p180
CE-v46-My '70-p431

HUGHES, Langston
(continued)
Comw-v91-N 21 '69-p259
LJ-v94-Jl '69-p2687
PW-v195-Mr 10 '69-p67
SR-v52-Ag 16 '69-p27
Don't You Turn Back
A Lib-v1-Ap '70-p385
ASR-v87-Ap '70-p108
BL-v66-Mr 1 '70-p847
BL-v69-My 1 '73-p838
BS-v29-Ja 1 '70-p389
CCB-B-v24-S '70-p10
KR-v37-D 1 '69-p1270
LJ-v95-Jl '70-p2533
PW-v196-D 8 '69-p47
SR-v53-My 9 '70-p47
The First Book Of Jazz
BL-v73-N 15 '76-p474
SLJ-v23-O '76-p107

* * *

HUGHES, Linda Ann
America's Favorite Poems
BL-v72-Je 1 '76-p1406

* * *

HUGHES, Margaret
Reading And How A
Quill & Q-v50-F '84-p11

* * *

HUGHES, Mary Vivian
A London Child Of The 1870s
Obs-D 24 '78-p23
Rp B Bk R-v22-4 '77-p40
Spec-v238-Ap 23 '77-p23
A London Girl Of The 1880s
Obs-D 24 '78-p23
A London Home In The 1890s
NY-v54-F 5 '79-p129

* * *

HUGHES, Molly
The Anne Of Green Gables Picture Book
Can Child Lit-#30 '83-p61

* * *

HUGHES, Monica
Beckoning Lights
BIC-v11-D '82-p11
HB-v60-S '84-p663
Quill & Q-v49-F '83-p39
Beyond The Dark River
BL-v77-My 1 '81-p1197
BS-v41-My '81-p77
CBRS-v9-Spring '81-p107
CCB-B-v34-Je '81-p195
CLW-v53-S '81-p92
Can Child Lit-#17 '80-p25
GP-v18-N '79-p3615
HB-v57-Je '81-p308
In Rev-v14-Ap '80-p46
JB-v44-Je '80-p144
J Read-v25-N '81-p180
KR-v49-Je 15 '81-p744
Obs-D 2 '79-p39
SLJ-v27-Mr '81-p146
TES-F 15 '80-p28
TLS-D 14 '79-p122
TLS-Mr 28 '80-p357
VOYA-v4-Ag '81-p31
Crisis On Conshelf Ten
Atl Pro Bk R-v10-N '83-p2
BL-v73-Ap 15 '77-p1266
CCB-B-v30-Je '77-p160
Can Child Lit-#17 '80-p21
GP-v14-Mr '76-p2820
HB-v60-S '84-p663
KR-v45-F 1 '77-p98
SLJ-v23-My '77-p62
TLS-S 19 '75-p1052
Earthdark
GP-v16-S '77-p3173
JB-v41-Je '77-p179
The Ghost Dance Caper
JB-v42-D '78-p313
RT-v35-N '81-p237
The Guardian Of Isis
Atl Pro Bk R-v10-N '83-p2
BL-v78-Ap 15 '82-p1084
Brit Bk N C-Spring '82-p14
CBRS-v10-Ag '82-p139
CCB-B-v35-Ap '82-p150
HB-v58-Je '82-p298
HB-v60-S '84-p661
JB-v45-O '81-p212
SF&FBR-Jl '82-p41
SLJ-v29-F '83-p77
TES-Je 5 '81-p41
TES-My 21 '82-p31
TLS-S 18 '81-p1069
VOYA-v5-Ag '82-p39
Hunter In The Dark
BIC-v11-Je '82-p32
BL-v79-Mr 15 '83-p958
B Rpt-v2-S '83-p37
CBRS-v11-Je '83-p114
CCB-B-v36-Jl '83-p211
Emerg Lib-v10-My '83-p35
HB-v59-Je '83-p313
In Rev-v16-Ap '82-p50
KR-v51-F 15 '83-p187
Kliatt-v18-Spring '84-p10
Mac-v95-Je 28 '82-p56
Quill & Q-v48-Ap '82-p32
SE-v48-My '84-p379
SLJ-v29-My '83-p82
SLJ-v30-Mr '84-p125
VOYA-v6-O '83-p203
The Isis Pedlar
BIC-v12-F '83-p33
BL-v80-S 1 '83-p38
BS-v43-D '83-p346
CBRS-v12-Ja '84-p52
GP-v21-Ja '83-p4007
HB-v59-O '83-p583
HB-v60-S '84-p661
JB-v47-F '83-p43
LA-v61-Ja '84-p73
Quill & Q-v49-Mr '83-p67
SLJ-v30-O '83-p169
Sch Lib-v31-Je '83-p165
TES-N 19 '82-p34
The Keeper Of The Isis Light
BL-v78-S 15 '81-p98
BS-v41-Ja '82-p402
CBRS-v10-F '82-p67
CCB-B-v35-Ap '82-p150
CE-v58-My '82-p325
Can Child Lit-#17 '80-p26
Can Child Lit-#33 '84-p40
EJ-v72-Ja '83-p79
HB-v57-O '81-p541
HB-v60-S '84-p661
JB-v44-O '80-p250
LA-v59-My '82-p487
SF&FBR-Mr '82-p21
SLJ-v28-Ap '82-p70
Sch Lib-v28-S '80-p290
TES-O 9 '81-p29
VOYA-v5-Ap '82-p39
Ring-Rise Ring-Set
GP-v21-S '82-p3953
HB-v60-S '84-p663
JB-v46-Ag '82-p152
Quill & Q-v48-Jl '82-p67
Sch Lib-v30-S '82-p253
Sch Lib-v31-Je '83-p100
TES-N 11 '83-p25
TLS-Jl 23 '82-p791
Space Trap
BIC-v12-D '83-p16
CBRS-v12-Jl '84-p141
GP-v22-Ja '84-p4192
HB-v60-S '84-p663
JB-v47-D '83-p258
Quill & Q-v49-N '83-p24
Sch Lib-v31-D '83-p378
TES-Je 8 '84-p46

HUGHES, Monica (continued)
The Tomorrow City
GP-v17-N '78-p3410
JB-v42-O '78-p269
Obs-D 3 '78-p36
TES-Ag 18 '78-p17
TLS-S 29 '78-p1089

* * *

HUGHES, Richard
Gertrude's Child
CCB-B-v20-Ap '67-p123
KR-v43-My 1 '75-p512
LJ-v91-N 15 '66-p5740
NY-v44-D 14 '68-p219
NY-v51-D 1 '75-p178
NYRB-v7-D 15 '66-p28
NYTBR-v71-N 6 '66-p60
NYTBR-Jl 27 '75-p8
SLJ-v22-S '75-p84
TLS-D 14 '67-p1225
The Wonder-Dog
JB-v41-D '77-p334
KR-v45-N 15 '77-p1197
Lis-v98-N 10 '77-p624
NS-v94-N 4 '77-p626
Punch-v273-N 23 '77-p1018
SLJ-v24-Ap '78-p84
SR-v5-N 26 '77-p40
TES-D 16 '77-p21
TES-S 19 '80-p30
TLS-O 28 '77-p1273

* * *

HUGHES, Roy E
Sentence Combining Rock Groups
EJ-v73-S '84-p97

* * *

HUGHES, Shirley
Alfie Gets In First
BL-v78-Ap 15 '82-p1096
Brit Bk N C-Spring '82-p2
CBRS-v10-Je '82-p102
CCB-B-v35-Je '82-p189
CE-v59-N '82-p133
GP-v20-Mr '82-p4037
HB-v58-Ap '82-p155
JB-v46-F '82-p16
KR-v50-Mr 1 '82-p272
Punch-v281-D 2 '81-p1023
RT-v36-O '82-p116
SLJ-v28-Mr '82-p134
Sch Lib-v30-Mr '82-p26
TES-D 18 '81-p18
TLS-N 20 '81-p1359
Alfie Gives A Hand
BL-v80-My 15 '84-p1344
CCB-B-v37-My '84-p167
HB-v60-Je '84-p320
JB-v48-F '84-p13
KR-v52-Mr 1 '84-pJ5
NYTBR-v89-Je 24 '84-p33
PW-v225-Mr 30 '84-p56
SLJ-v30-Ag '84-p61
Sch Lib-v32-Je '84-p125
Alfie's Feet
BL-v79-Ap 1 '83-p1035
BW-v13-My 8 '83-p16
Brit Bk N C-Autumn '82-p12
CBRS-v11-Ap '83-p87
CCB-B-v36-Mr '83-p128
CE-v60-Ja '84-p209
GP-v21-Ja '83-p4015
HB-v59-Ap '83-p160
JB-v47-F '83-p7
KR-v51-Ja 15 '83-p60
LA-v61-Ap '84-p395
RT-v37-N '83-p193
SLJ-v29-Mr '83-p162
TLS-S 17 '82-p1003
TLS-S 7 '84-p1006
Charlie Moon And The Big Bonanza Bust-Up
Brit Bk N C-Autumn '82-p20
JB-v47-Ap '83-p76
Sch Lib-v31-Mr '83-p37
TES-N 19 '82-p37
TLS-S 17 '82-p1002
David And Dog
BB-v7-Mr '79-p1
BL-v75-D 1 '78-p617
BW-N 12 '78-pE3
BW-D 3 '78-pE4
BW-v11-My 10 '81-p10
CCB-B-v32-Ja '79-p82
CE-v55-F '79-p223
HB-v54-D '78-p632
HB-v59-O '83-p552
KR-v46-O 1 '78-p1067
PW-v214-Jl 3 '78-p65
PW-v219-Je 26 '81-p61
SLJ-v25-Ja '79-p43
Dogger
GP-v16-Ja '78-p3250
JB-v42-F '78-p16
TES-N 18 '77-p32
TES-D 14 '79-p21
TLS-D 2 '77-p1411
An Evening At Alfie's
TES-O 5 '84-p29
George The Babysitter
BL-v74-My 1 '78-p1432
BW-Ap 9 '78-pE4
BW-D 3 '78-pE4
CCB-B-v31-Jl '78-p178
CE-v55-F '79-p223
KR-v46-F 15 '78-p175
PW-v213-My 8 '78-p74
PW-v218-N 28 '80-p51
RT-v33-O '79-p39
SLJ-v24-My '78-p56
Haunted House
CCB-B-v32-N '78-p45
CE-v55-F '79-p223
Cur R-v17-D '78-p388
KR-v46-Jl 1 '78-p689
SLJ-v25-S '78-p118
Helpers
Econ-v257-D 20 '75-p100
GP-v14-N '75-p2733
JB-v40-F '76-p16
TES-Mr 12 '82-p38
TLS-D 5 '75-p1453
Here Comes Charlie Moon
Brit Bk N-D '80-p714
Econ-v277-D 27 '80-p77
GP-v19-Mr '81-p3853
JB-v45-Ap '81-p71
Sch Lib-v29-Je '81-p133
TES-N 28 '80-p25
TLS-N 21 '80-p1330
It's Too Frightening For Me!
JB-v42-Ap '78-p88
TES-N 18 '77-p32
Lucy And Tom At The Seaside
GP-v15-D '76-p3030
JB-v40-O '76-p263
TLS-O 1 '76-p1244
Lucy And Tom Go To School
TES-Jl 17 '81-p26
TLS-N 23 '73-p1437
Lucy And Tom's ABC
TES-Je 8 '84-p52
TLS-Je 15 '84-p677
Lucy And Tom's Christmas
GP-v20-N '81-p3972
JB-v46-F '82-p16
Punch-v281-D 2 '81-p1023
Sch Lib-v30-Mr '82-p26
TES-N 20 '81-p33
TLS-N 20 '81-p1358
Moving Molly
BB-v7-Ag '79-p1
BL-v75-Jl 1 '79-p1579
BW-Mr 11 '79-pF5
CBRS-v7-Ap '79-p84

HUGHES, Shirley (continued)
CCB-B-v32-Je '79-p177
CE-v56-Ja '80-p169
CE-v58-S '81-p37
GP-v17-Ja '79-p3449
HB-v55-Je '79-p293
JB-v43-F '79-p18
KR-v47-F 15 '79-p193
PW-v215-F 26 '79-p183
PW-v222-Jl 9 '82-p49
SLJ-v26-N '79-p65
Sch Lib-v27-Mr '79-p27
TLS-Mr 27 '81-p346
Over The Moon
Brit Bk N-D '80-p715
CCB-B-v34-Ap '81-p152
JB-v45-Je '81-p115
SLJ-v27-Mr '81-p146
Sch Lib-v29-Je '81-p146
TLS-S 19 '80-p1025
Sally's Secret
B&B-v18-S '73-p137
BL-v77-Ja 1 '81-p624
Obs-N 7 '76-p23
SLJ-v27-Ag '81-p56
TLS-S 28 '73-p1120
Up And Up
BL-v76-Mr 15 '80-p1058
Brit Bk N C-Spring '80-p8
CCB-B-v33-Je '80-p192
CLW-v52-N '80-p185
GP-v18-Ja '80-p3640
JB-v44-F '80-p15
Lis-v102-N 8 '79-p646
Obs-D 2 '79-p39
PW-v217-Mr 7 '80-p90
SLJ-v26-Ap '80-p94
SLJ-v27-O '80-p119
TES-N 23 '79-p30
TLS-D 14 '79-p127

* * *

HUGHES, Ted
Meet My Folks
CSM-v65-N 7 '73-pB2
GP-v17-My '78-p3340
KR-v41-Ag 1 '73-p815
LJ-v98-S 15 '73-p2651
Obs-Ag 28 '77-p26
Obs-O 2 '77-p25
PW-v204-O 22 '73-p111
SR/W-v1-D 4 '73-p29
Moon-Whales And Other Moon Poems
BL-v73-Ja 1 '77-p667
BW-N 7 '76-pG5
CCB-B-v30-My '77-p143
Choice-v14-Je '77-p532
HB-v53-Ap '77-p181
HR-v30-Summer '77-p290
KR-v44-O 15 '76-p1148
LA-v54-N '77-p950
NYTBR-Ja 9 '77-p10
PW-v210-D 13 '76-p61
Poet-v132-Ap '78-p31
SLJ-v23-D '76-p60
Nessie The Monster
BL-v70-Ap 1 '74-p874
BW-My 19 '74-p4
CSM-v66-My 1 '74-pF5
KR-v42-F 1 '74-p105
LJ-v99-S 15 '74-p2270
Teacher-v92-F '75-p40
Poetry Is
BL-v67-D 15 '70-p336
BW-v4-N 8 '70-p5
CCB-B-v24-Ja '71-p75
Choice-v16-Je '79-p496
EJ-v60-Mr '71-p406
HB-v47-F '71-p57
HB-v57-Je '81-p349
KR-v38-O 1 '70-p1112
LJ-v95-D 15 '70-p4364
NY-v46-D 5 '70-p219
NYTBR, pt.2-N 8 '70-p55
NYTBR, pt.2-N 7 '71-p47
PW-v198-N 16 '70-p77
SR-v53-N 14 '70-p38
SR-v54-Ag 21 '71-p26
The Rattle Bag
Econ-v285-D 25 '82-p105
HB-v59-Ap '83-p218
Lis-v108-N 4 '82-p27
Lon R Bks-v4-D 30 '82-p3
NS-v104-D 17 '82-p39
Obs-N 28 '82-p31
Obs-D 5 '82-p34
Sch Lib-v31-Je '83-p187
TES-N 19 '82-p31
TLS-N 26 '82-p1308
Season Songs
BL-v72-D 15 '75-p578
CCB-B-v29-F '76-p98
Choice-v12-F '76-p1572
GP-v15-O '76-p2958
GW-v116-Ja 2 '77-p15
HB-v52-Ap '76-p172
JB-v40-Ag '76-p231
KR-v43-O 15 '75-p1198
Lis-v95-My 20 '76-p651
NYTBR-D 21 '75-p8
Obs-Jl 4 '76-p22
PW-v208-O 6 '75-p85
SLJ-v22-D '75-p52
SR-v3-N 29 '75-p30
Sew R-v84-Jl '76-pR93
Spec-v237-Jl 17 '76-p25
TLS-Jl 16 '76-p882
The Tiger's Bones And Other Plays For Children
BL-v70-Ap 1 '74-p874
HB-v50-Ap '74-p155
KR-v42-Ja 1 '74-p7
LJ-v99-Mr 15 '74-p902
PW-v205-Mr 11 '74-p49
Teacher-v92-My '75-p28
Under The North Star
Atl-v247-My '81-p84
BL-v77-My 15 '81-p1254
Brit Bk N C-Autumn '81-p16
CSM-v74-D 14 '81-pB11
Econ-v281-D 26 '81-p105
GP-v20-S '81-p3952
JB-v45-Ag '81-p159
KR-v49-Je 15 '81-p747
LA-v58-N '81-p954
LJ-v106-Ap 1 '81-p799
Lis-v106-N 5 '81-p548
NS-v101-Je 26 '81-p18
NYRB-v29-Je 10 '82-p38
PW-v219-F 6 '81-p365
Punch-v280-Je 24 '81-p1024
RT-v35-D '81-p365
Sch Lib-v29-D '81-p367
TES-Je 5 '81-p35
TLS-Jl 24 '81-p849
What Is The Truth?
TES-N 2 '84-p26
TLS-Jl 13 '84-p794

* * *

HUGHES, Thomas
The Scouring Of The White Horse
GP-v17-Mr '79-p3489
Tom Brown's Schooldays
B&B-v22-N '76-p71
Obs-N 21 '71-p26
Tom Brown's Schooldays (Dent)
Punch-v286-Mr 21 '84-p17
Tom Brown's Schooldays (Puffin)
CSM-v76-Jl 6 '84-pB4
Punch-v286-Mr 21 '84-p16

* * *

HUGHES, W Howard
Alexander Fleming And Penicillin
ACSB-v12-Spring '79-p26

* * *

HUGHES-STANTON, Penelope
See Inside An Ancient Chinese Town
GP-v18-Ja '80-p3643
JB-v43-D '79-p326
SLJ-v26-Ja '80-p71

* * *

HUGHEY, Pat
Scavengers And Decomposers
BL-v80-Je 15 '84-p1484
HB-v60-Ag '84-p485
Inst-v93-My '84-p104
RT-v38-N '84-p227
SLJ-v30-Ag '84-p74

* * *

HUGHS, Dean
Honestly, Myron
RT-v36-N '82-p242

* * *

HUGO, Victor
Belles Histoires
BL-v74-N 1 '77-p487

* * *

HULBERT, J
Think About It
TES-Mr 9 '84-p46

* * *

HULBERT, John
All About Navigating And Route Finding
Obs-F 9 '75-p25
TLS-Ap 2 '76-p395

* * *

HULL, Anne
Maestro Spinetti's Music Shop
CCB-B-v25-O '71-p26
KR-v39-Jl 15 '71-p736
LJ-v96-O 15 '71-p3459

* * *

HULL, Eleanor
Alice With Golden Hair
BL-v78-O 1 '81-p188
BS-v41-N '81-p318
CBRS-v10-F '82-p68
CCB-B-v35-Mr '82-p131
Cur R-v21-F '82-p34
Inter BC-v13-#4 '82-p14
Kliatt-v17-Winter '83-p8
PW-v220-Jl 17 '81-p95
RSR-v11-Fall '83-p27
RT-v37-F '84-p508
SLJ-v28-N '81-p105
VOYA-v4-F '82-p33
VOYA-v5-Ap '82-p34
The Summer People
CBRS-v12-Ag '84-p151
CCB-B-v37-Ap '84-p149
HB-v60-Je '84-p338
SLJ-v30-Ap '84-p124
VOYA-v7-O '84-p196
Trainful Of Strangers
BL-v65-N 1 '68-p312
CCB-B-v22-Ja '69-p79
CSM-v60-N 7 '68-pB6
HB-v45-F '69-p54
KR-v36-Ag 15 '68-p899
LJ-v94-Ja 15 '69-p301
NYTBR-v73-O 13 '68-p26
RR-v28-Ja '69-p169
YR-v5-N '68-p6

* * *

HULL, Katherine
The Far-Distant Oxus
BL-v65-Ap 1 '69-p899
CCB-B-v22-Jl '69-p177
GP-v17-Ja '79-p3440
KR-v37-F 1 '69-p100
LJ-v94-S 15 '69-p3206
SR-v52-My 10 '69-p53

* * *

HULL, Rod
Emu's ABC
GP-v23-S '84-p4303
Emu's Opposites
GP-v23-S '84-p4303
The Reluctant Pote
JB-v48-F '84-p23
Sch Lib-v32-Mr '84-p62

* * *

HULME-BEAMAN, S G
The Showing Up Of Larry The Lamb
TES-Ja 9 '81-p23

* * *

HULSE, Larry
Just The Right Amount Of Wrong
BS-v42-Ag '82-p203
CBRS-v10-My '82-p98
HB-v58-Ag '82-p414
KR-v50-Ap 15 '82-p495
NYTBR-v87-My 16 '82-p28
SLJ-v28-Ap '82-p82
VOYA-v5-Ag '82-p32

* * *

HULSHOF, Paul
The Quest For The Missing Queen
NS-v90-N 7 '75-p586
Spec-v235-Jl 26 '75-p114

* * *

HUMAN Rights (World Topics)
NS-v96-N 3 '78-p595

* * *

HUMBERSTONE, Eliot
Things At Home
GP-v20-Jl '81-p3917
TES-Mr 12 '82-p39
Things Outdoors
TES-Mr 12 '82-p39
Things That Go
GP-v20-Jl '81-p3917
TES-Mr 12 '82-p39

* * *

HUME, Pat
Dick Whittington And His Amazing Cat
Dr-#2 '81-p56

* * *

HUME, Ruth
Great Women Of Medicine
CCB-B-v18-Ja '65-p75
LJ-v90-Ja 15 '65-p388
King Of Song: The Story Of John McCormack
BS-v24-F 15 '65-p454
CCB-B-v18-Ap '65-p118
CLW-v36-Ap '65-p572
NO-v4-Mr 8 '65-p19
NYTBR-v70-F 7 '65-p26
The Lion Of Poland
RT-v33-Ap '80-p810

* * *

HUMMINGBIRD Books
TES-Mr 10 '78-p52

* * *

HUMMINGBIRDS
TES-Jl 1 '83-p39

* * *

HUMPHREY, Henry
The Farm
ACSB-v12-Spring '79-p27
CCB-B-v31-My '78-p142
Inst-v87-My '78-p112
KR-v46-F 15 '78-p180
SB-v15-My '79-p40
SLJ-v25-S '78-p118
Sailing The High Seas
SLJ-v26-F '80-p56
What Is It For
BL-v66-Ap 1 '70-p983
CCB-B-v24-S '70-p11
KR-v37-Ag 15 '69-p850
LJ-v95-My 15 '70-p1929
SR-v52-O 18 '69-p57
What's Inside
CCB-B-v25-F '72-p92
LJ-v97-My 15 '72-p1903
SR-v54-N 13 '71-p60
When Is Now?
BL-v78-S 15 '81-p106
CBRS-v9-Spring '81-p107
SLJ-v28-F '82-p77

* * *

HUMPHREY, James H
Sports Skills For Boys And Girls
SLJ-v27-D '80-p77

* * *

HUMPHREY, Judith
Trip To Paris
TES-Ap 21 '78-p23

* * *

HUMPHREY, Margo
The River That Gave Gifts
Inter BC-v14-#7 '83-p28

* * *

HUMPTY-DUMPTY
BW-My 1 '77-pE4
Ser R-v6-O '80-p5

* * *

HUMPTY Dumpty And Other First Rhymes
SLJ-v27-Ag '81-p56

* * *

HUMPTY Dumpty Magazine
Little Songs For Little People
LJ-v93-Jl '68-p2730
Wishing Penny & Other Fantasy Stories
CLW-v39-O '67-p158
KR-v35-Mr 15 '67-p342
LJ-v92-My 15 '67-p2022
NYTBR, pt.1-v72-My 7 '67-p51

* * *

HUMPTY Dumpty's Holiday Stories
CCB-B-v26-Jl '73-p172
KR-v41-Ap 1 '73-p394
LJ-v98-S 15 '73-p2645

* * *

HUMPTY Dumpty's Magazine
BL-v79-F 1 '83-p729
CE-v59-My '83-p370
Cha Ti-v37-Ag '83-p47
Mag Lib- '82-p216

* * *

HUMPTY Dumpty's Magazine
Humpty Dumpty's Storybook
LJ-v91-O 15 '66-p5216

* * *

HUNG, Chien-Chuan
Hung Chien-Chuan Erh Tung Wo Hsueh Chiung Tso Chiang
BL-v73-F 1 '77-p839

* * *

HUNIA, Fran
Ananse And The Sky God
Sch Lib-v28-S '80-p259
The Enormous Turnip
Sch Lib-v28-S '80-p259
Rapunzel
Sch Lib-v28-S '80-p259
The Wizard Of Oz
Sch Lib-v28-S '80-p259

* * *

HUNIG, Klaus
Astro-Dome
WCRB-v10-Ja '84-p54

* * *

HUNN, David
Gymnastics
JB-v45-F '81-p20
Skateboarding
Lis-v98-N 10 '77-p626
TES-F 3 '78-p41

* * *

HUNT, Abby C
The World Of Books For Children
ARBA-v12-'81-p563
LA-v60-Ap '83-p520
SLJ-v26-N '79-p47

* * *

HUNT, Bernice Kohn
Apples
BL-v72-Je 1 '76-p1407
Communications Satellites
BL-v71-Jl 15 '75-p1191
Dams
BL-v73-Jl 15 '77-p1728
SB-v13-D '77-p168
SLJ-v24-O '77-p114
Great Bread!
BL-v74-S 1 '77-p32
BL-v74-S 1 '77-p42
Comw-v104-N 11 '77-p734
PW-v211-Je 27 '77-p111
SLJ-v24-S '77-p145
Marriage
BL-v72-My 1 '76-p1252
BS-v36-S '76-p201
KR-v44-My 15 '76-p605
SB-v13-My '77-p8
SLJ-v22-My '76-p70
Pigeons
KR-v41-Ag 1 '73-p816
LJ-v98-D 15 '73-p3700
SB-v9-Mr '74-p332
Prime Time
BL-v71-My 1 '75-p885
KR-v42-D 1 '74-p1283
LJ-v100-F 15 '75-p399
NYTBR-Ap 13 '75-p6
PW-v207-Ja 6 '75-p56
Skunks
CCB-B-v27-Ja '74-p80
KR-v41-S 15 '73-p1040
LJ-v98-D 15 '73-p3701
What A Funny Thing To Say!
BL-v70-Je 1 '74-p1104
The Whatchamacallit Book
BL-v73-F 15 '77-p897
KR-v44-N 1 '76-p1172
SLJ-v24-O '77-p114
SLJ-v25-N '78-p31
Your Ant Is A Which
BL-v72-My 15 '76-p1340
KR-v44-Mr 15 '76-p319
PW-v209-My 3 '76-p65
RT-v32-Ja '79-p444
SLJ-v22-Ap '76-p58
SLJ-v25-N '78-p31
SR-v3-My 15 '76-p38
Teacher-v94-Ja '77-p134

HUNT, Patricia (continued)
Bible Stories From The Old Testament
TES-N 18 '83-p34
Gibbons
ASBYP-v17-Winter '84-p28
BL-v80-N 15 '83-p497
SB-v19-My '84-p299
SLJ-v30-F '84-p66
Koalas
ASBYP-v14-Winter '81-p34
BL-v77-N 1 '80-p405
CCB-B-v34-D '80-p72
HB-v57-F '81-p78
Inst-v90-N '80-p158
SB-v16-My '81-p277
SLJ-v27-F '81-p62
Snowy Owls
ASBYP-v16-Winter '83-p33
BL-v79-D 1 '82-p499
SB-v18-Mr '83-p211
SLJ-v29-Ap '83-p114
Tigers
ACSB-v15-Winter '82-p32
BL-v77-Jl 1 '81-p1394
KR-v49-Je 15 '81-p742
SB-v17-N '81-p94
SLJ-v28-Ja '82-p78

* * *

HUNT, Pauline
Red Pepper
JB-v47-O '83-p213
TES-F 24 '84-p29

* * *

HUNT, Peter
The Maps Of Time
GP-v22-My '83-p4077
JB-v47-Je '83-p125
Punch-v284-Je 8 '83-p57
Sch Lib-v31-D '83-p378
TES-Ja 14 '83-p31

* * *

HUNT, Rod
Hoaxers And Swindlers
Sch Lib-v27-Je '79-p131
Jokers And Conmen
TES-D 12 '80-p23

* * *

HUNT, Roderick
Chutney And The Fossil
GP-v16-S '77-p3171
Chutney At The Circus
GP-v16-S '77-p3171
Ghosts, Witches And Things Like That
TES-O 26 '84-p27
The Oxford Christmas Book For Children
CCB-B-v37-N '83-p51
Oxford Junior Readers
Sch Lib-v27-D '79-p358

* * *

HUNTER, Bernice T
That Scatterbrain Booky
BIC-v10-D '81-p6
Can Child Lit-#29 '83-p63
Emerg Lib-v9-My '82-p28
In Rev-v16-F '82-p40
Quill & Q-v48-Ja '82-p35
With Love From Booky
BIC-v12-D '83-p16
Quill & Q-v49-N '83-p24

* * *

HUNTER, Deirdre
We The Chinese
BL-v69-S 1 '72-p41
CCB-B-v25-My '72-p140
KR-v39-My 1 '71-p512
LJ-v96-Je 15 '71-p2138
NYTBR-My 14 '72-p10
SS-v63-D '72-p345

* * *

HUNTER, Edith
Sue Ellen
CE-v46-My '70-p431
CLW-v41-F '70-p382
LJ-v95-Mr 15 '70-p1195
Ms-v3-D '74-p79

* * *

HUNTER, Edith F
Child Of The Silent Night
CLW-v55-F '84-p288
GT-v89-S '71-p160
Punch-v250-Ap 20 '66-p595
RT-v31-Ap '78-p804
Spec-Je 3 '66-p704
TLS-My 19 '66-p452
Children Of The Silent Night
Inter BC-v11-Ja 10 '80-p21

* * *

HUNTER, Eileen
Tales Of Waybeyond
JB-v43-D '79-p327
SLJ-v26-Ap '80-p94

* * *

HUNTER, Evan
Me And Mr. Stenner
B&B-v22-Ag '77-p54
BL-v73-S 15 '76-p175
CCB-B-v30-F '77-p91
CE-v60-My '84-p308
JB-v41-Je '77-p179
KR-v44-Jl 15 '76-p795
Kliatt-v12-Fall '78-p10
LA-v54-Ap '77-p442
PW-v210-O 4 '76-p74
SE-v41-Ap '77-p348
SLJ-v23-O '76-p117
TLS-Mr 25 '77-p359
Teacher-v96-O '78-p177

* * *

HUNTER, Ilene
Simple Folk Instruments To Make And Play
BL-v73-Jl 15 '77-p1692
BL-v73-Jl 15 '77-p1728
Choice-v14-N '77-p1227
KR-v45-My 1 '77-p536
KR-v45-Je 1 '77-p585
LJ-v102-Je 15 '77-p1368

* * *

HUNTER, Jim
The Sun In The Morning
JB-v40-F '76-p45

* * *

HUNTER, Kristin
Boss Cat
BL-v68-F 15 '72-p506
CCB-B-v25-My '72-p140
CE-v49-O '72-p28
Choice-v14-N '77-p1178
KR-v39-N 15 '71-p1212
LJ-v97-Jl '72-p2484
PW-v200-D 13 '71-p43
Teacher-v92-My '75-p92
Guests In The Promised Land
BL-v69-Je 1 '73-p947
BS-v33-Ap 15 '73-p45
Bl W-v23-S '74-p91
CCB-B-v26-Je '73-p156
CE-v50-O '73-p29
Choice-v14-N '77-p1178
Comw-v99-N 23 '73-p216
HB-v49-Ag '73-p386
KR-v41-My 15 '73-p567
LJ-v98-S 15 '73-p2651
NO-v12-Ag 11 '73-p21
PW-v203-My 28 '73-p40
Teacher-v92-S '74-p130

HUNTER, Kristin (continued)
Teacher-v94-O '76-p151
Lou In The Limelight
BL-v78-N 15 '81-p435
CBRS-v10-Ja '82-p48
CCB-B-v35-F '82-p108
HB-v58-Ap '82-p172
KR-v50-F 1 '82-p140
NYTBR-v87-F 21 '82-p35
SLJ-v28-N '81-p105
TN-v38-Summer '82-p364
VOYA-v4-F '82-p33
The Soul Brothers And Sister Lou
BL-v65-N 1 '68-p312
BL-v65-Ap 1 '69-p901
BL-v69-My 1 '73-p838
BS-v28-O 1 '68-p277
BW-v2-N 3 '68-p20
CE-v46-Ap '70-p368
Choice-v14-N '77-p1178
Comw-v91-F 27 '70-p585
EJ-v64-D '75-p80
EL-v31-Ap '74-p593
HB-v45-Ap '69-p177
KR-v36-Jl 15 '68-p765
LJ-v93-N 15 '68-p4419
NS-v81-Mr 5 '71-p312
NYTBR-Ja 26 '69-p26
NYTBR, pt.2-F 15 '70-p22
PW-v194-S 30 '68-p61
PW-v196-S 29 '69-p60
SE-v33-My '69-p558
SR-v51-O 19 '68-p37
TN-v38-Summer '82-p364
Teacher-v96-Ja '79-p64
YR-v5-N '68-p11

* * *

HUNTER, Mel
How Fishes Began
CCB-B-v26-Ap '73-p125

* * *

HUNTER, Mollie
The Dragonfly Years
GP-v22-Jl '83-p4099
JB-v47-O '83-p213
Sch Lib-v31-S '83-p275
TES-Je 17 '83-p28
TES-Ja 13 '84-p39
Hold On To Love
BL-v80-My 1 '84-p1248
B Rpt-v3-My '84-p33
BS-v44-Ap '84-p40
CBRS-v12-Ap '84-p96
CCB-B-v37-Mr '84-p129
CSM-v76-Mr 2 '84-pB6
HB-v60-Je '84-p338
KR-v52-Mr 1 '84-pJ21
NYTBR-v89-Je 10 '84-p35
PW-v225-Mr 16 '84-p86
SLJ-v30-My '84-p90
VOYA-v7-Je '84-p96
Kelpie's Pearls
BL-v63-D 15 '66-p451
CCB-B-v20-Mr '67-p109
HB-v42-D '66-p710
KR-v34-Jl 15 '66-p688
LJ-v91-O 15 '66-p5231
NYTBR-v72-F 5 '67-p32
PW-v190-O 31 '66-p85
SR-v49-D 10 '66-p57
TES-Ja 13 '84-p39
TES-Jl 13 '84-p25
The Knight Of The Golden Plain
BL-v80-S 1 '83-p86
CBRS-v12-S '83-p5
CCB-B-v37-N '83-p51
GP-v22-N '83-p4156
HB-v60-F '84-p54
JB-v47-O '83-p208
KR-v51-S 1 '83-pJ162
NY-v59-D 5 '83-p205
NYTBR-v88-N 6 '83-p43
PW-v224-Jl 22 '83-p132
SLJ-v30-S '83-p108
Sch Lib-v32-Je '84-p134
TES-Ja 13 '84-p39
Spanish Letters
BL-v63-Je 1 '67-p1048
BS-v27-Ag 1 '67-p183
CCB-B-v21-S '67-p9
HB-v43-Ag '67-p471
KR-v35-F 15 '67-p208
LJ-v92-S 15 '67-p3199
PW-v191-My 22 '67-p64
SR-v50-My 13 '67-p57
Thomas And The Warlock
BL-v64-D 1 '67-p450
BW-v2-F 11 '68-p15
CCB-B-v21-D '67-p60
HB-v43-D '67-p749
KR-v35-Jl 15 '67-p808
LJ-v92-O 15 '67-p3850
LR-v21-Summer '67-p94
Lis-v77-My 18 '67-p660
PW-v192-Ag 21 '67-p75
SR-v50-O 21 '67-p43
TLS-My 25 '67-p451

HUNTER, Mollie
See Also McIlwraith, Maureen Mollie Hunter McVeigh
HUNTER, Norman
The Best Of Branestawm
GP-v20-My '81-p3875
Punch-v286-Mr 21 '84-p16
SLJ-v28-Ja '82-p78
Book Of Magic
JB-v39-F '75-p40
Count Bakwerdz On The Carpet And Other Incredible Stories
JB-v43-Ag '79-p205
SLJ-v28-Ja '82-p78
Dust-Up At The Royal Disco
JB-v40-F '76-p26
TLS-D 5 '75-p1460
The Incredible Adventures Of Professor Branestawm
BL-v76-D 1 '79-p558
SLJ-v26-Ag '80-p64
SLJ-v28-Ja '82-p33
Spec-v245-D 6 '80-p26
Professor Branestawm And The Wild Letters
GP-v20-My '81-p3875
Professor Branestawm Round The Bend
GP-v17-Jl '78-p3347
JB-v42-F '78-p42
Professor Branestawm's Building Bust-Up
SLJ-v29-Mr '83-p162
Sch Lib-v31-Mr '83-p37
Professor Branestawm's Compendium
TES-F 24 '78-p30
Professor Branestawm's Crunchy Crockery
JB-v48-F '84-p23
Sch Lib-v32-Je '84-p134
Professor Branestawm's Dictionary
TLS-Je 15 '73-p687
Professor Branestawm's Do-It-Yourself Handbook
GP-v15-Ja '77-p3048
JB-v41-Ap '77-p114
Professor Branestawm's Great Revolution
JB-v39-Ap '75-p105
Professor Branestawm's Hair-Raising Idea
JB-v48-Ap '84-p71
Professor Branestawm's Mouse War
JB-v46-O '82-p190

HUNTER, Norman (continued)
Professor Branestawm's Perilous Pudding
JB-v44-Je '80-p133
TES-Mr 4 '83-p32
Professor Branestawm's Pocket Motor Car
GP-v20-My '81-p3875
Sch Lib-v29-Je '81-p134
TES-D 10 '82-p34
Professor Branestawm's Treasure Hunt
Obs-O 2 '66-p22
PW-v190-O 10 '66-p79
The Puffin Book Of Magic
PW-v195-Ja 20 '69-p272
TLS-D 24 '76-p1598
Sneeze And Be Slain
JB-v44-D '80-p292
Sch Lib-v29-S '81-p237
Vanishing Ladies And Other Magic
TLS-D 1 '78-p1399
The Wizard Book Of Magic
SLJ-v25-O '78-p146
Wizards Are A Nuisance
TLS-Je 15 '73-p687

* * *

HUNTER, Rob
Chris Bonington
JB-v48-Ap '84-p71
SLJ-v31-S '84-p128
TES-N 25 '83-p29

* * *

HUNTER, W F
Learning Basic Arithmetic
Cur R-v19-S '80-p341

* * *

HUNTINGTON, Harriet E
Let's Go To The Woods
BL-v65-O 1 '68-p187
CCB-B-v22-F '69-p95
KR-v36-Ag 15 '68-p903
LJ-v93-N 15 '68-p4395
SB-v5-My '69-p46
Let's Look At Cats
ASBYP-v15-Fall '82-p26
HB-v58-F '82-p65
SB-v18-S '82-p33
Let's Look At Dogs
ACSB-v13-Mr '80-p31
SLJ-v26-Mr '80-p132
WCRB-v6-Ja '80-p21
Let's Look At Flowers
BL-v66-N 1 '69-p348
CCB-B-v23-N '69-p47
LJ-v94-O 15 '69-p3821
SB-v5-S '69-p150

* * *

HUNTINGTON, Lee P
Maybe A Miracle
BL-v81-O 1 '84-p249
CBRS-v12-Ag '84-p151
CCB-B-v37-Jl '84-p206
HB-v60-S '84-p591
SLJ-v31-O '84-p158
Simple Shelters
ACSB-v13-Spring '80-p39
BL-v76-Ja 1 '80-p667
HB-v56-F '80-p74
KR-v48-F 15 '80-p218
SLJ-v26-F '80-p56

* * *

HUNTINGTON, Lee Pennock
The Arctic And The Antarctic
BL-v72-D 1 '75-p515
KR-v43-Ag 1 '75-p853
SB-v12-S '76-p108
SLJ-v22-N '75-p64
Brothers In Arms
SLJ-v23-D '76-p54
Simple Shelters
BL-v76-Ja 1 '80-p667
SLJ-v26-F '80-p56

* * *

HUNTLEY, Accabre
At School Today
Brit Bk N C-Spring '81-p11

* * *

HUNTLEY, Dennis
Modelling & Sculpture
BL-v74-Ja 1 '78-p772

* * *

HUNTSBERRY, William E
The Big Hang-Up
Am-v123-D 5 '70-p497
BS-v30-My 1 '70-p61
CCB-B-v24-D '70-p60
Comw-v92-My 22 '70-p248
KR-v38-F 15 '70-p178
Big Wheels
Am-v117-N 4 '67-p518
BL-v64-Ap 15 '68-p983
BS-v27-O 1 '67-p263
BW-v1-N 19 '67-p24
CCB-B-v21-D '67-p60
CSM-v59-N 2 '67-pB12
HB-v43-O '67-p601
KR-v35-Jl 15 '67-p816
LJ-v93-F 15 '68-p882
NYTBR-v72-O 8 '67-p38
SR-v50-N 11 '67-p50

* * *

HURD, Edith Thacher
The Black Dog Who Went Into The Woods
BL-v76-Mr 15 '80-p1058
CBRS-v8-16 '80-p65
CCB-B-v33-Jl '80-p215
KR-v48-My 1 '80-p576
NYTBR-v85-Jl 27 '80-p22
SLJ-v26-Ap '80-p95
Catfish
BW-v4-My 17 '70-p4
CCB-B-v24-S '70-p11
Comw-v92-My 22 '70-p246
HB-v46-Je '70-p291
KR-v38-F 15 '70-p169
LJ-v95-Je 15 '70-p2302
PW-v197-Mr 23 '70-p67
SR-v53-Jl 25 '70-p28
TLS-D 3 '71-p1517
Catfish And The Kidnapped Cat
CCB-B-v28-S '74-p10
KR-v42-Mr 15 '74-p293
LJ-v99-S 15 '74-p2249
PW-v205-Ap 22 '74-p75
Come With Me To Nursery School
BL-v67-S 1 '70-p57
CCB-B-v24-O '70-p27
KR-v38-Je 15 '70-p637
LJ-v95-S 15 '70-p3039
The Day The Sun Danced
CCB-B-v20-Mr '67-p109
CE-v43-S '66-p44
Inst-v75-Ap '66-p109
KR-v34-F 1 '66-p104
LJ-v91-Mr 15 '66-p1690
NYTBR-v71-Mr 13 '66-p26
PW-v189-F 14 '66-p144
SR-v49-Mr 19 '66-p44
Dinosaur My Darling
CCB-B-v32-Ja '79-p82
CSM-v71-Ja 8 '79-pB6
Comw-v105-N 10 '78-p729
Inst-v88-N '78-p142
KR-v46-N 1 '78-p1185
PW-v214-Jl 24 '78-p100
SLJ-v25-O '78-p134
I Dance In My Red Pajamas
BL-v78-Ap 1 '82-p1019
CBRS-v10-Ap '82-p83
HB-v58-Ap '82-p156

HURD, Edith Thacher
(continued)
LA-v60-Mr '83-p359
PW-v221-Ap 9 '82-p51
Par-v57-N '82-p59
RT-v37-O '83-p58
SE-v47-Ap '83-p251
SLJ-v28-Ap '82-p59
Johnny Lion's Bad Day
BL-v66-Jl 1 '70-p1341
CCB-B-v24-O '70-p28
GT-v88-Ap '71-p24
KR-v38-Ap 15 '70-p450
LJ-v95-D 15 '70-p4370
NYTBR, pt.2-My 24 '70-p43
PW-v197-My 4 '70-p64
TLS-O 22 '71-p1329
Johnny Lion's Book
BL-v62-D 1 '65-p363
CCB-B-v19-Ja '66-p82
HB-v41-D '65-p625
KR-v33-S 1 '65-p901
LJ-v90-O 15 '65-p4602
NYTBR-v70-N 7 '65-p56
SR-v48-N 13 '65-p54
Johnny Lion's Rubber Boots
BL-v68-Jl 1 '72-p942
CCB-B-v25-My '72-p141
CE-v49-N '72-p90
KR-v40-Ap 1 '72-p397
LJ-v97-My 15 '72-p1926
TLS-N 23 '73-p1439
Little Dog, Dreaming
HB-v43-Je '67-p336
KR-v35-Ap 1 '67-p407
LJ-v92-My 15 '67-p2015
PW-v191-Ap 17 '67-p58
Look For A Bird
CCB-B-v31-Ja '78-p79
Comw-v104-N 11 '77-p727
KR-v45-Ag 1 '77-p783
SB-v14-S '78-p113
SLJ-v24-D '77-p59
The Mother Beaver
BL-v67-Je 15 '71-p871
KR-v39-Ap 15 '71-p439
LJ-v96-Jl '71-p2358
NYTBR-My 16 '71-p8
PW-v199-Je 21 '71-p71
SB-v7-S '71-p155
The Mother Chimpanzee
ACSB-v12-Spring '79-p27
BL-v74-F 15 '78-p1009
CCB-B-v31-My '78-p143
Inst-v87-My '78-p112
KR-v46-Mr 15 '78-p309
PW-v213-F 6 '78-p101
SLJ-v24-Mr '78-p119
The Mother Deer
BL-v69-Mr 1 '73-p648
Inst-v82-N '72-p128
KR-v40-S 15 '72-p1093
LJ-v98-F 15 '73-p636
PW-v202-O 30 '72-p57
The Mother Kangaroo
BL-v73-S 15 '76-p175
CSM-v68-N 3 '76-p24
HB-v52-O '76-p515
KR-v44-Je 15 '76-p688
PW-v209-Je 14 '76-p114
SB-v13-S '77-p98
SLJ-v23-O '76-p99
The Mother Owl
BL-v71-Ja 1 '75-p461
CCB-B-v28-Ap '75-p132
Inst-v84-N '74-p137
KR-v42-D 1 '74-p1256
SLJ-v21-Mr '75-p88
The Mother Whale
BL-v70-D 15 '73-p445
CCB-B-v27-Mr '74-p111
CSM-v66-My 1 '74-pF5
Comw-v99-N 23 '73-p219
KR-v41-O 15 '73-p1169
LJ-v99-Ja 15 '74-p199
PW-v204-O 22 '73-p111
SB-v10-My '74-p74
WLB-v48-Ja '74-p381
Rain And The Valley
KR-v36-Ap 1 '68-p399
LJ-v93-My 15 '68-p2106
SB-v4-S '68-p82
The So-So Cat
BL-v62-O 1 '65-p161
CSM-v57-O 28 '65-p5
GT-v83-O '65-p32
HB-v41-O '65-p491
KR-v33-Ag 1 '65-p748
LJ-v90-S 15 '65-p3812
Song Of The Sea Otter
CSM-v75-N 21 '83-p55
HB-v60-Ap '84-p209
KR-v51-N 1 '83-pJ196
SB-v19-My '84-p299
SLJ-v30-Mr '84-p160
This Is The Forest
Comw-v92-My 22 '70-p252
KR-v37-O 1 '69-p1068
LJ-v95-Ap 15 '70-p1628
Under The Lemon Tree
CBRS-v8-Jl '80-p123
HB-v56-Je '80-p287
KR-v48-Ap 1 '80-p435
SLJ-v26-My '80-p58
What Whale? Where?
BL-v63-Ja 15 '67-p537
CCB-B-v20-My '67-p141
CE-v44-N '67-p197
CSM-v58-N 3 '66-pB3
KR-v34-O 1 '66-p1043
LJ-v91-O 15 '66-p5217
PW-v190-S 5 '66-p67
The White Horse
BL-v67-S 1 '70-p58
CCB-B-v24-N '70-p44
KR-v38-My 1 '70-p503
LJ-v95-My 15 '70-p1958
PW-v197-My 25 '70-p57
SR-v53-S 19 '70-p34
Who Will Be Mine?
CE-v43-D '66-p234
KR-v34-Mr 1 '66-p241
LJ-v91-My 15 '66-p2684
NYTBR-v71-My 8 '66-p43
SR-v49-Jl 23 '66-p57
Wilkie's World
Obs-Jl 15 '73-p33
TLS-Je 15 '73-p686
Wilson's World
BW-v5-N 7 '71-p2
KR-v39-Ag 1 '71-p803
LJ-v96-O 15 '71-p3459
NYTBR-Ja 2 '72-p8
PW-v200-O 4 '71-p59

* * *

HURD, Michael
Mendelssohn
BL-v68-S 15 '71-p100
HB-v47-O '71-p492
Inst-v131-O '71-p146
KR-v39-Je 15 '71-p646
LJ-v96-S 15 '71-p2930
Obs-Jl 26 '70-p24
TLS-O 30 '70-p1268
The Oxford Junior Companion To Music
ARBA-v12-'81-p459
BL-v76-F 1 '80-p770
BW-v10-N 9 '80-p17
CCB-B-v33-Ap '80-p154
SLJ-v27-D '80-p19
TES-N 23 '79-p36
TLS-D 14 '79-p130
Vaughan Williams
BL-v67-N 15 '70-p264
HB-v46-O '70-p487
KR-v38-Jl 1 '70-p691
LJ-v95-N 15 '70-p4062

HURD, Michael (continued)
TLS-Jl 2 '70-p719
Young Person's Guide To Opera
CCB-B-v20-O '66-p27
KR-v34-F 1 '66-p119
LJ-v91-Jl '66-p3543

* * *

HURD, Thacher
Axle The Freeway Cat
BL-v78-O 15 '81-p304
CBRS-v10-N '81-p23
KR-v49-D 15 '81-p1517
SLJ-v28-O '81-p130
WCRB-v8-F '82-p61
Hobo Dog
SLJ-v28-N '81-p78
Mama Don't Allow
BL-v81-O 1 '84-p249
CBRS-v13-O '84-p14
KR-v52-S 1 '84-pJ62
PW-v226-Ag 17 '84-p59
SLJ-v31-O '84-p148
WLB-v59-O '84-p129
Mystery On The Docks
BL-v79-Mr 15 '83-p970
CBRS-v11-Ap '83-p87
CCB-B-v37-S '83-p10
HB-v59-Je '83-p291
KR-v51-Ja 15 '83-p60
PW-v223-Mr 11 '83-p86
PW-v226-Ag 10 '84-p83
SLJ-v29-My '83-p91
The Old Chair
BB-v6-O '78-p1
KR-v46-F 1 '78-p103
PW-v213-Ja 30 '78-p129
SLJ-v24-F '78-p48
The Quiet Evening
BL-v75-S 15 '78-p220
CBRS-v7-Ja '79-p42
HB-v55-F '79-p54
KR-v46-D 15 '78-p1353
SLJ-v25-O '78-p134
SLJ-v26-Mr '80-p105

* * *

HURFORD, John
The Dormouse
JB-v39-F '75-p22
TLS-S 20 '74-p1011
Fredgehog
Brit Bk N C-Autumn '81-p11
JB-v45-Je '81-p107
TLS-Mr 27 '81-p342
Spec-v235-D 6 '75-p735
TLS-S 19 '75-p1054

* * *

HURLEY, L
Shamus And The Green Cat
JB-v41-Ap '77-p95

* * *

HURLEY, Linda
ZX81/TS1000 Programing For Young Programmers
BW-v13-O 2 '83-p9

* * *

HURLIMANN, Bettina
Barry
BL-v64-Jl 1 '68-p1234
BW-v2-S 8 '68-p24
CCB-B-v21-Jl '68-p175
CE-v46-D '69-p167
HB-v44-Ag '68-p412
HB-v56-Je '80-p278
KR-v36-My 1 '68-p507
LJ-v93-My 15 '68-p2106
Lis-v79-My 16 '68-p641
NYTBR-v73-My 5 '68-p46
PW-v193-Mr 4 '68-p63
SR-v51-My 11 '68-p37
TLS-Je 6 '68-p586
Picture-Book World
BL-v66-D 15 '69-p484
CLW-v41-D '69-p262
Comw-v91-N 21 '69-p263
HB-v45-Ag '69-p426
TLS-Je 6 '68-p587
Seven Houses
BL-v74-S 15 '77-p202
GP-v15-D '76-p3031
HB-v54-F '78-p63
JB-v40-O '76-p257
KR-v45-Jl 1 '77-p674
LA-v55-My '78-p652
William Tell And His Son
BL-v63-Jl 15 '67-p1193
CCB-B-v21-O '67-p28
HB-v43-Je '67-p340
HB-v56-Je '80-p278
KR-v35-Mr 1 '67-p264
LJ-v92-Ap 15 '67-p1734
NYTBR, pt.1-v72-My 7 '67-p50
Obs-D 7 '69-p31
PW-v191-Mr 27 '67-p61

* * *

HURLIMANN, Ruth
The Cat And Mouse Who Shared A House
B&B-v20-Mr '75-p81
BL-v70-Mr 15 '74-p819
BW-My 19 '74-p4
CCB-B-v27-Jl '74-p177
Choice-v12-N '75-p1133
HB-v50-Je '74-p277
HB-v56-Je '80-p280
KR-v42-Ja 15 '74-p51
KR-v43-Ja 1 '75-p3
NS-v87-My 24 '74-p739
Obs-My 2 '76-p27
PW-v205-F 4 '74-p72
SR/W-v1-My 4 '74-p45
TLS-Jl 5 '74-p718
TN-v30-Je '74-p434
WLB-v48-My '74-p716
The Mouse With The Daisy Hat
HB-v56-Je '80-p280
KR-v39-Mr 1 '71-p230
LJ-v96-S 15 '71-p2906
NS-v81-Je 4 '71-p781
TLS-Jl 2 '71-p771
TLS-D 6 '74-p1384
The Proud White Cat
BL-v73-Ap 1 '77-p1168
CCB-B-v30-Je '77-p161
CLW-v49-D '77-p235
CSM-v69-My 4 '77-pB5
GP-v16-O '77-p3193
HB-v53-Je '77-p299
HB-v56-Je '80-p280
JB-v41-O '77-p276
KR-v45-F 1 '77-p90
NYTBR-S 11 '77-p30
PW-v211-F 7 '77-p95
SLJ-v24-S '77-p109

* * *

HURMENCE, Belinda
A Girl Called Boy
BL-v78-Jl '82-p1445
CBRS-v10-Spring '82-p117
CCB-B-v36-S '82-p12
CE-v59-N '82-p133
HB-v58-Ag '82-p404
KR-v50-Ap 15 '82-p490
LA-v60-Ap '83-p506
RT-v36-N '82-p242
SLJ-v28-My '82-p63
Tancy
BL-v80-My 15 '84-p1339
B Rpt-v3-S '84-p34
BS-v44-S '84-p232
CBRS-v12-Jl '84-p141
CCB-B-v37-Je '84-p187
EJ-v73-S '84-p103
PW-v225-Mr 30 '84-p57

HURMENCE, Belinda
(continued)
SLJ-v31-S '84-p128
VOYA-v7-O '84-p196
Tough Tiffany
BL-v76-F 15 '80-p834
CBRS-v8-Ap '80-p87
CCB-B-v33-Mr '80-p135
CE-v58-S '81-p49
HB-v56-Je '80-p297
KR-v48-Mr 1 '80-p289
LA-v58-My '81-p593
PW-v217-Mr 14 '80-p74
SLJ-v26-F '80-p56

* * *

HURRELL, Elaine
The Common Dormouse
Brit Bk N-O '80-p586
SLJ-v27-Ja '81-p58

* * *

HURT, Roger
Addition
TES-N 5 '82-p22
Division
TES-N 5 '82-p22
Multiplication
TES-N 5 '82-p22
Subtraction
TES-N 5 '82-p22

* * *

HURWITZ, Abraham B
More Number Games
KR-v44-O 15 '76-p1157
SB-v13-D '77-p169
Number Games To Improve Your Child's Arithmetic
LJ-v100-Mr 1 '75-p476
SB-v11-Mr '76-p208

* * *

HURWITZ, Johanna
Aldo Applesauce
BL-v76-O 1 '79-p276
CBRS-v8-N '79-p24
CCB-B-v33-Ja '80-p96
CSM-v71-O 15 '79-pB4
HB-v55-D '79-p663
KR-v47-S 15 '79-p1068
PW-v216-S 10 '79-p75
RT-v34-O '80-p47
SLJ-v26-N '79-p78
Aldo Ice Cream
BL-v77-Mr 1 '81-p964
BL-v78-F 15 '82-p762
CCB-B-v34-Ap '81-p152
KR-v49-My 1 '81-p571
LA-v58-O '81-p845
PW-v219-Ja 30 '81-p75
PW-v222-S 10 '82-p76
RT-v35-N '81-p238
SLJ-v28-F '82-p67
All About Aldo
PW-v219-My 22 '81-p77
Baseball Fever
BL-v78-Ja 1 '82-p597
CBRS-v10-N '81-p28
CCB-B-v35-N '81-p47
CLW-v53-Ap '82-p402
HB-v57-D '81-p664
Inst-v91-Ap '82-p22
KR-v50-Ja 15 '82-p68
LA-v59-My '82-p484
SLJ-v28-D '81-p85
Busybody Nora
BL-v72-Mr 15 '76-p1046
CCB-B-v29-Je '76-p158
HB-v52-Je '76-p284
KR-v44-F 15 '76-p200
PW-v209-F 2 '76-p99
SLJ-v22-My '76-p50
Teacher-v95-My '78-p106
The Hot And Cold Summer
BL-v80-My 1 '84-p1248
CBRS-v12-Spring '84-p126
CCB-B-v37-My '84-p167
KR-v52-My 1 '84-pJ39
PW-v225-Je 29 '84-p104
SLJ-v30-My '84-p81
The Law Of Gravity
BB-v6-S '78-p3
BL-v74-Je 1 '78-p1552
BL-v75-Jl 15 '79-p1635
CCB-B-v31-Ap '78-p129
CE-v55-Ja '79-p168
KR-v46-Mr 1 '78-p245
PW-v213-Ja 16 '78-p99
SLJ-v24-Mr '78-p129
Much Ado About Aldo
BL-v75-S 15 '78-p221
Comw-v105-N 10 '78-p731
HB-v54-D '78-p641
Inst-v88-N '78-p146
KR-v46-S 1 '78-p951
LA-v56-Mr '79-p289
PW-v214-S 4 '78-p114
SLJ-v25-O '78-p134
New Neighbors For Nora
BL-v75-My 15 '79-p1439
CBRS-v7-Spring '79-p115
KR-v47-Ap 1 '79-p388
PW-v215-Ap 2 '79-p73
RT-v33-D '79-p358
SLJ-v26-S '79-p113
Nora And Mrs. Mind-Your-Own-Business
BB-v6-Mr '78-p3
BL-v73-My 1 '77-p1353
Emerg Lib-v9-N '81-p35
KR-v45-F 15 '77-p166
LA-v54-N '77-p946
PW-v211-My 9 '77-p92
SLJ-v24-S '77-p109
Once I Was A Plum Tree
BL-v76-Ja 1 '80-p667
CBRS-v8-Mr '80-p76
CCB-B-v33-Je '80-p192
Inter BC-v12-#1 '81-p18
KR-v48-Ap 1 '80-p439
PW-v217-My 23 '80-p77
SLJ-v26-F '80-p57
The Rabbi's Girls
BL-v78-Je 15 '82-p1368
CBRS-v10-Je '82-p107
CCB-B-v35-Ap '82-p150
HB-v58-Je '82-p288
KR-v50-Ap 1 '82-p418
LA-v59-O '82-p750
PW-v221-F 19 '82-p65
SLJ-v29-Ja '83-p76
Rip-Roaring Russell
BL-v80-S 1 '83-p86
CBRS-v12-S '83-p3
CCB-B-v37-Ja '84-p89
HB-v59-D '83-p710
KR-v51-S 1 '83-pJ163
PW-v224-S 2 '83-p81
SLJ-v30-O '83-p150
Superduper Teddy
BL-v77-S 1 '80-p45
CBRS-v8-Ag '80-p135
CCB-B-v34-D '80-p72
CE-v57-My '81-p300
KR-v48-Ag 15 '80-p1081
PW-v218-Ag 8 '80-p83
SLJ-v27-D '80-p53
Tough-Luck Karen
BL-v79-O 1 '82-p246
CBRS-v11-N '82-p28
CE-v59-Mr '83-p278
CSM-v76-Jl 6 '84-pB4
HB-v58-O '82-p517
KR-v50-Ag 1 '82-p868
PW-v222-N 26 '82-p60
PW-v225-My 11 '84-p273
SLJ-v29-O '82-p152

HURWITZ, Johanna (continued)
What Goes Up Must Come Down
PW-v224-N 4 '83-p66

* * *

HUSS, Sally Moore
How To Play Power Tennis With Ease
LA-v56-N '79-p933
SLJ-v26-S '79-p158

* * *

HUSSEY, Lois J
Collecting For The City Naturalist
BL-v71-Jl 15 '75-p1191
CCB-B-v29-S '75-p11
KR-v43-My 1 '75-p517
SLJ-v22-Mr '76-p115

* * *

HUSTON, Anne
Ollie's Go-Kart
CCB-B-v25-O '71-p27
CLW-v43-Mr '72-p430
KR-v39-Ap 15 '71-p433
LJ-v96-S 15 '71-p2917
Trust A City Kid
BL-v63-Ja 15 '67-p537
CC-v83-D 7 '66-p1510
CCB-B-v20-My '67-p141
CE-v44-D '67-p260
HB-v43-Ap '67-p206
KR-v34-S 15 '66-p978
LJ-v92-Ja 15 '67-p336
NYTBR-v72-Ja 22 '67-p26
TLS-N 30 '67-p1157

* * *

HUTCHESON, G
The Flower Book
JB-v43-O '79-p273

* * *

HUTCHINGS, Carolyn
The Story Of Our Canals
GP-v14-Ja '76-p2801

* * *

HUTCHINGS, Margaret
Nature's Toyshop
GP-v14-Mr '76-p2826
JB-v40-F '76-p45
Sculpting In Burlap
BL-v72-S 15 '75-p110
HB-v51-O '75-p473
LJ-v100-My 15 '75-p974
Toys From The Tales Of Beatrix Potter
BL-v70-My 1 '74-p971
HB-v50-O '74-p150
LJ-v99-Je 1 '74-p1537
TLS-N 23 '73-p1456

* * *

HUTCHINGS, Monica
Brocky
GP-v15-O '76-p2965

* * *

HUTCHINS, Carleen Maley
Moon Moth
CCB-B-v19-F '66-p99
Comw-v83-N 5 '65-p163
HB-v41-Ag '65-p402
KR-v33-Ap 1 '65-p378
LJ-v90-My 15 '65-p2406
Who Will Drown The Sound
CCB-B-v26-Je '73-p156
KR-v40-D 1 '72-p1356
LJ-v98-Mr 15 '73-p995

* * *

HUTCHINS, H J
The Three And Many Wishes Of Jason Reid
BIC-v12-D '83-p16
Quill & Q-v50-F '84-p39

* * *

HUTCHINS, Pat
The Best Train Set Ever
BB-v6-D '78-p2
BW-My 14 '78-pG2
CCB-B-v31-Jl '78-p179
Comw-v105-N 10 '78-p730
GP-v17-Mr '79-p3477
HB-v54-Je '78-p272
JB-v43-Ap '79-p107
KR-v46-Mr 15 '78-p303
PW-v213-F 27 '78-p156
SLJ-v24-My '78-p81
WLB-v53-Je '79-p709
Changes, Changes
A Lib-v3-Ap '72-p420
BL-v67-My 1 '71-p748
BL-v68-Ap 1 '72-p669
BW-v5-My 9 '71-p4
CCB-B-v24-Je '71-p158
CE-v48-O '71-p32
Comw-v94-My 21 '71-p266
GT-v89-S '71-p156
HB-v47-Ap '71-p158
KR-v39-F 15 '71-p168
LJ-v96-My 15 '71-p1796
LJ-v98-O 15 '73-p3162
Life-v71-D 17 '71-p44
NCW-v216-Mr '73-p90
NS-v81-Je 4 '71-p781
NYTBR-Mr 7 '71-p30
NYTBR, pt.2-N 7 '71-p4
NYTBR, pt.2-N 7 '71-p32
Obs-My 13 '73-p33
PW-v199-Mr 29 '71-p52
RT-v35-My '82-p933
SR-v54-My 15 '71-p46
TLS-Ap 2 '71-p387
TN-v28-N '71-p73
Teacher-v96-F '79-p30
Teacher-v96-Mr '79-p112
Clocks And More Clocks
BL-v67-O 1 '70-p145
BW-v4-N 8 '70-p2
CCB-B-v24-D '70-p60
CLW-v42-F '71-p380
HB-v46-O '70-p470
Inst-v80-O '70-p143
Inst-v82-My '73-p77
KR-v38-Jl 1 '70-p677
LJ-v95-S 15 '70-p3039
NS-v81-Mr 5 '71-p314
Obs-N 29 '70-p31
PW-v198-Jl 27 '70-p74
SR-v53-S 19 '70-p34
Spec-v225-D 5 '70-pR15
TLS-D 11 '70-p1455
Teacher-v91-N '73-p131
The Curse Of The Egyptian Mummy
BL-v80-Mr 1 '84-p967
CBRS-v12-F '84-p69
CE-v60-My '84-p362
GP-My '84-p4265
JB-v48-F '84-p24
KR-v51-N 1 '83-pJ192
RT-v37-My '84-p889
SLJ-v30-D '83-p82
Don't Forget The Bacon!
BB-v4-O '76-p1
BL-v72-F 1 '76-p787
CCB-B-v30-S '76-p11
CE-v60-My '84-p344
Comw-v103-N 19 '76-p760
JB-v40-Ag '76-p191
KR-v44-Ja 15 '76-p68
NO-v15-Ag 21 '76-p16
PW-v209-Ja 12 '76-p51
RT-v31-O '77-p11
SLJ-v22-F '76-p39
Spec-v245-D 6 '80-p26
TES-O 31 '80-p24

HUTCHINS, Pat (continued)
PW-v200-O 25 '71-p49
RT-v32-My '79-p943
Spec-v228-Ap 22 '72-p624
TLS-Ap 28 '72-p483
Tom And Sam
BL-v65-F 15 '69-p656
HB-v45-Ap '69-p162
Inst-v78-Ap '69-p144
KR-v36-O 15 '68-p1157
LJ-v94-Mr 15 '69-p1319
LJ-v95-O 15 '70-p3602
Spec-v223-N 1 '69-p606
The Wind Blew
B&B-v20-My '75-p81
BL-v70-My 1 '74-p1003
CCB-B-v27-Je '74-p158
CE-v51-O '74-p33
HB-v50-Ap '74-p140
KR-v42-Ja 1 '74-p3
KR-v43-Ja 1 '75-p3
LJ-v99-Ap 15 '74-p1212
Spec-v245-D 6 '80-p26
TES-O 31 '80-p24
TLS-Jl 5 '74-p718
Teacher-v92-S '74-p128
You'll Soon Grow Into Them, Titch
BL-v79-F 15 '83-p777
CBRS-v11-Mr '83-p75
CCB-B-v36-Mr '83-p128
HB-v59-Je '83-p291
JB-v47-Ag '83-p154
KR-v50-D 1 '82-p1291
SLJ-v29-Mr '83-p162
WCRB-v9-Mr '83-p56
1 Hunter
TES-N 5 '82-p27
TES-S 21 '84-p37
TLS-S 7 '84-p1006

* * *

HUTCHINS, Robert M
The Learning Society
AE-v20-Summer '70-p233
BL-v64-Jl 15 '68-p1248
Enc-v32-My '69-p82
KR-v36-F 1 '68-p160
LJ-v93-F 15 '68-p749
NYTBR-v73-My 19 '68-p40
PW-v193-Ja 29 '68-p94
SR-v51-Jl 20 '68-p52
TLS-Ja 16 '69-p58

* * *

HUTCHINS, Ross E
The Ant Realm
SB-v3-Mr '68-p320
Adelbert The Penguin
LJ-v94-N 15 '69-p4277
PW-v195-Je 30 '69-p63
SB-v5-S '69-p159
The Amazing Seeds
BL-v62-N 1 '65-p272
CSM-v57-N 4 '65-pB9
Comw-v83-N 5 '65-p163
HB-v42-F '66-p79
LJ-v90-O 15 '65-p4630
NH-v75-N '66-p62
The Ant Realm
Aud-v71-Ja '69-p86
BL-v64-Ja 1 '68-p545
BS-v27-N 1 '67-p314
CCB-B-v21-My '68-p144
CLW-v39-F '68-p442
CSM-v60-D 21 '67-p11
HB-v44-F '68-p79
KR-v35-Ag 15 '67-p974
LJ-v92-O 15 '67-p3865
NYTBR-v72-N 5 '67-p56
PW-v192-N 13 '67-p79
The Bug Clan
BL-v70-N 1 '73-p292
CCB-B-v27-N '73-p44
KR-v41-Jl 1 '73-p688
LJ-v98-D 15 '73-p3712
SA-v229-D '73-p137
SB-v9-Mr '74-p331
Caddis Insects: Nature's Carpenters And Stonemasons
BL-v62-Ap 15 '66-p832
CCB-B-v19-Jl '66-p180
HB-v42-Ag '66-p452
Inst-v75-My '66-p119
LJ-v91-My 15 '66-p2692
SA-v215-D '66-p142
SB-v2-My '66-p44
The Carpenter Bee
CCB-B-v26-N '72-p43
KR-v40-Mr 15 '72-p330
LJ-v97-O 15 '72-p3448
SB-v8-D '72-p248
The Cicada
BL-v68-O 1 '71-p152
SB-v8-My '72-p59
Galls And Gall Insects
BL-v66-F 1 '70-p670
Choice-v7-Mr '70-p106
LJ-v95-S 15 '70-p3072
SA-v223-D '70-p133
SB-v6-My '70-p48
Grasshoppers And Their Kin
BL-v69-N 15 '72-p301
KR-v40-My 1 '72-p544
SA-v227-D '72-p114
SB-v8-D '72-p248
Hop, Skim, Fly
SB-v6-D '70-p241
Spectr-v47-Mr '71-p44
How Animals Survive
BL-v71-N 1 '74-p292
Inst-v84-My '75-p98
SB-v11-My '75-p35
SLJ-v21-Mr '75-p98
Insects
BL-v62-My 15 '66-p898
Choice-v3-S '66-p540
KR-v34-F 1 '66-p169
KR-v34-Mr 1 '66-p256
LJ-v91-Ap 1 '66-p1915
LJ-v91-Jl '66-p3557
NH-v75-N '66-p68
PW-v189-Ja 31 '66-p98
SA-v215-D '66-p142
SB-v2-D '66-p211
SR-v49-N 19 '66-p62
Time-v87-Ap 15 '66-pE5
WSJ-v46-Je 20 '66-p10
Insects And Their Young
ACSB-v9-Winter '76-p20
BL-v71-My 1 '75-p914
HB-v51-Ag '75-p397
KR-v43-Mr 1 '75-p247
NYTBR-My 4 '75-p36
SLJ-v21-My '75-p56
Insects In Armor
BL-v69-O 1 '72-p148
KR-v40-Mr 15 '72-p330
LJ-v98-F 15 '73-p645
SB-v8-S '72-p152
Island Of Adventure
Aud-v71-Mr '69-p92
BL-v65-Mr 15 '69-p794
LJ-v94-Mr 1 '69-p1008
LJ-v94-Mr 15 '69-p1348
NYTBR, pt.1-v73-N 3 '68-p40
PW-v194-Ag 5 '68-p48
SB-v4-Mr '69-p291
Last Trumpeters
BL-v64-Ja 1 '68-p545
BW-v2-Ja 7 '68-p10
CCB-B-v21-Mr '68-p111
CSM-v59-N 2 '67-pB11
EL-v88-Ap '68-p338
KR-v35-Jl 1 '67-p743
LJ-v92-N 15 '67-p4252

HUTTNER, Doralies
(continued)
TLS-D 2 '77-p1412

* * *

HUTTON, Darryl
Ventriloquism
BL-v72-F 15 '76-p856
SLJ-v22-Mr '76-p115

* * *

HUTTON, Warwick
Jonah And The Great Fish
BL-v80-My 1 '84-p1248
CAY-v5-Summer '84-p7
CCB-B-v37-Ap '84-p143
HB-v60-Ag '84-p458
Inst-v93-My '84-p87
KR-v52-My 1 '84-pJ30
NY-v60-D 3 '84-p187
NYTBR-v89-Ap 22 '84-p25
PW-v225-Ap 20 '84-p87
SLJ-v31-S '84-p104
Noah And The Great Flood
Am-v137-D 3 '77-p404
BB-v6-Mr '78-p1
BL-v74-O 1 '77-p296
CCB-B-v31-Ap '78-p122
Comw-v104-N 11 '77-p728
GP-v16-Ap '78-p3293
HB-v53-D '77-p655
JB-v42-Je '78-p135
KR-v45-N 1 '77-p1141
LA-v55-Mr '78-p365
NYTBR-N 13 '77-p36
PW-v212-S 5 '77-p72
SLJ-v24-O '77-p103
SR-v5-N 26 '77-p41
TLS-Ap 7 '78-p385
TN-v35-Summer '79-p401
TN-v36-Winter '80-p220
TN-v40-Fall '83-p57
The Nose Tree
BL-v78-S 1 '81-p46
CBRS-v10-Winter '82-p55
HB-v58-F '82-p34
Inst-v91-Ja '82-p144
JB-v46-Ap '82-p62
KR-v49-N 1 '81-p1339
LA-v59-S '82-p603
NYTBR-v86-N 29 '81-p42
PW-v220-N 27 '81-p87
RT-v35-Ap '82-p868
SLJ-v28-N '81-p78
TLS-Mr 26 '82-p347
Time-v118-D 21 '81-p76
The Sleeping Beauty
BL-v75-Mr 15 '79-p1156
BW-v9-D 2 '79-p16
GP-v18-S '79-p3569
HB-v55-Je '79-p293
JB-v43-Ag '79-p192
KR-v47-Jl 1 '79-p737
LA-v57-Mr '80-p325
NYTBR-Ap 22 '79-p25
PW-v215-Ja 15 '79-p132
SLJ-v25-Mr '79-p123
Sch Lib-v27-D '79-p355

* * *

HUXLEY, Aldous
Crows Of Pearblossom
B&B-v14-Ja '69-p36
BW-v2-Ja 21 '68-p12
CCB-B-v21-F '68-p96
CSM-v60-N 30 '67-pB5
Comw-v87-N 10 '67-p179
KR-v35-O 1 '67-p1207
LJ-v92-D 15 '67-p4603
NS-v92-N 5 '76-p647
NY-v43-D 16 '67-p181
NYTBR, pt.2-v72-N 5 '67-p63
NYTBR, pt.2-v72-N 5 '67-p66
Obs-N 21 '76-p31
PW-v192-O 16 '67-p58
SR-v50-N 11 '67-p41
YR-v4-Mr '68-p15
Die Krahen Von Birnblute
BL-v75-N 15 '78-p555

* * *

HUYGEN, Wil
Gnomes
A Art-v42-Je '78-p14
Analog-v98-Ap '78-p172
Atl-v241-Ja '78-p94
BL-v74-Ja 1 '78-p720
BW-D 11 '77-pE4
CSM-v71-D 4 '78-pB3
Cha Ti-v33-Ap '79-p37
EJ-v68-Ja '79-p59
NW-v90-D 19 '77-p81
NYRB-v26-Mr 8 '79-p16
NYTBR-F 4 '79-p41
PW-v212-O 24 '77-p73
Time-v110-N 21 '77-p66
Time-v111-Ap 3 '78-p55
WSJ-v190-D 19 '77-p14
Secrets Of The Gnomes
LATBR-D 12 '82-p8
LJ-v107-N 15 '82-p2186
NY-v58-D 6 '82-p187
PW-v222-S 17 '82-p105
WCRB-v8-N '82-p24

* * *

HUYK, Helen
The Baby Streetcar
Can Child Lit-#15 '80-p108

* * *

HUYNH, Quang N
The Land I Lost
BL-v78-Je 15 '82-p1368
B Rpt-v1-Ja '83-p40
BW-v12-Jl 11 '82-p11
CBRS-v10-Je '82-p109
CCB-B-v36-O '82-p28
CLW-v54-Ap '83-p380
HB-v58-Je '82-p308
KR-v50-Ap 1 '82-p420
LA-v60-Ap '83-p504
PW-v221-Mr 5 '82-p71
SE-v47-Ap '83-p243
SLJ-v29-N '82-p88

* * *

HYAMS, Edward
The Changing Face Of England
B&B-v20-Mr '75-p34
JB-v39-Ap '75-p143
Working For Man
GP-v14-D '75-p2779

* * *

HYDE, Dayton O
Island Of The Loons
PW-v226-Jl 13 '84-p51

* * *

HYDE, Laurence
Captain Deadlock
BW-v2-O 6 '68-p20
CCB-B-v22-Mr '69-p112
HB-v44-Ag '68-p429
KR-v36-My 1 '68-p517
LJ-v93-Jl '68-p2733

* * *

HYDE, Margaret
Atoms Today And Tomorrow
ABC-v4-Jl '83-p19

* * *

HYDE, Margaret O
Alcohol
BL-v70-Jl 1 '74-p1194
CCB-B-v28-N '74-p44
LJ-v99-S 15 '74-p2271
SB-v10-D '74-p233

HYMAN, Jane (continued)
SLJ-v28-D '81-p64

* * *

HYMAN, R
Peter's Magic Hide-And-Seek
JB-v47-F '83-p14

* * *

HYMAN, Robin
Casper And The Rainbow Bird
SLJ-v26-O '79-p141
The Magical Fish
JB-v39-F '75-p22
The Treasure Box
JB-v45-Ap '81-p63

* * *

HYMAN, Trina S
The Enchanted Forest
PW-v225-Je 8 '84-p64
How Six Found Christmas
BL-v66-D 1 '69-p458
BW-v3-D 21 '69-p8
CCB-B-v23-N '69-p47
CE-v46-Ap '70-p380
HB-v45-D '69-p662
Inst-v79-D '69-p114
KR-v37-O 15 '69-p1110
LJ-v94-O 15 '69-p3851
PW-v196-S 1 '69-p52
PW-v216-N 26 '79-p53
A Little Alphabet
BL-v77-O 1 '80-p252
KR-v48-O 15 '80-p1351
LA-v58-Ap '81-p475
NYTBR-v85-D 7 '80-p41
PW-v218-Ag 22 '80-p50
SLJ-v27-O '80-p136
Little Red Riding Hood
BL-v79-Mr 1 '83-p905
BL-v80-S 1 '83-p93
CBRS-v11-Ap '83-p86
CCB-B-v36-Mr '83-p126
CE-v60-Mr '84-p290
CSM-v76-Ja 23 '84-p22
Emerg Lib-v11-Ja '84-p19
HB-v59-Ap '83-p159
Inst-v92-My '83-p92
KR-v51-F 15 '83-p181
LA-v60-S '83-p777
LATBR-My 15 '83-p7
NYTBR-v88-My 1 '83-p30
PW-v223-Ja 21 '83-p85
RT-v37-Ja '84-p427
SLJ-v29-Mr '83-p162
TES-O 12 '84-p33
Self-Portrait
BL-v78-D 1 '81-p498
BL-v79-Je 1 '83-p1282
CBRS-v10-D '81-p38
CCB-B-v35-Mr '82-p131
HB-v58-F '82-p65
NYTBR-v87-Ja 31 '82-p27
RT-v35-F '82-p621
SLJ-v28-D '81-p65
The Sleeping Beauty
AB-v60-N 14 '77-p2821
BL-v74-S 15 '77-p194
BW-N 13 '77-pE2
CCB-B-v31-F '78-p93
Comw-v104-N 11 '77-p730
GP-v18-S '79-p3570
HB-v53-D '77-p659
Inst-v92-My '83-p93
JB-v43-Ag '79-p192
KR-v45-N 15 '77-p1193
NYTBR-N 13 '77-p31
NYTBR-v88-Ap 10 '83-p43
PW-v212-Ag 15 '77-p69
RT-v32-O '78-p42
SLJ-v24-Mr '78-p119
Teacher-v95-My '78-p102

* * *

HYMEN, R
The Greatest Explorers In The World
JB-v43-F '79-p19

* * *

HYMES, Lucia
Hooray For Chocolate And Other Easy-To-Read Jingles
LA-v55-N '78-p961

* * *

HYMNS And Songs
TES-Ap 4 '80-p30

* * *

HYNARD, Julia
Percival's Party
SLJ-v30-S '83-p104
TES-F 12 '82-p29

* * *

HYNARD, Stephen
Snowy The Rabbit
SLJ-v30-S '83-p104

* * *

HYNDMAN, Jane Andrews Lee
The Winter Child
BL-v67-O 1 '70-p145
CCB-B-v24-Ja '71-p84
CLW-v42-D '70-p257
Comw-v93-N 20 '70-p199
KR-v38-Je 1 '70-p598
LJ-v95-D 15 '70-p4344

* * *

HYNDMAN, M
People Before History. Book 1
LR-v24-Autumn '74-p320

* * *

HYNDMAN, Robert Utley
Tales The People Tell In China
BL-v68-N 15 '71-p295
CCB-B-v24-Je '71-p164
Comw-v95-N 19 '71-p187
HB-v47-Ap '71-p167
HB-v47-D '71-p609
KR-v39-Ag 1 '71-p813
PW-v200-O 18 '71-p51

* * *

HYNDS, Marie
Christmas Candles
GP-v15-S '76-p2953
The Fire Bell
GP-v14-Ja '76-p2809
The Green Bubble Bath
GP-v15-S '76-p2953
The House Of The Future
GP-v17-My '78-p3332
The Mint Market
GP-v17-My '78-p3332
The Monster Lucky Bag
TLS-D 5 '75-p1446
The Mother Of Pearl Box
GP-v14-Ja '76-p2809
The Roman Eagle
GP-v15-S '76-p2953
Sparks Bookshelf Level 3
TES-Jl 14 '78-p21
The Wishing Bottle
TLS-D 5 '75-p1446

I

I Am An Owl
TES-N 13 '81-p24

* * *

I And The Others Writers' Collective
It's Scary Sometimes
Cur R-v18-F '79-p21
SB-v15-S '79-p99
SLJ-v26-O '79-p141

* * *

I Can Jump Puddles (Structural Readers)
TES-Ja 1 '82-p17

* * *

I Can Read
TES-Ja 14 '83-p34

* * *

I See What You Mean
TES-Jl 1 '83-p39
TES-Jl 8 '83-p27

* * *

I Want To Be A Pilot
TES-Ap 6 '84-p29

* * *

I Was Walking Down The Road
Edu D-v12-Ja '80-p4

* * *

IBBOTSON, Christine
Daniel's Shed
GP-v22-S '83-p4149

* * *

IBBOTSON, Eva
The Great Ghost Rescue
BB-v3-N '75-p3
Cur R-v16-My '77-p126
GP-v13-Ap '75-p2597
HB-v51-D '75-p593
KR-v43-Je 1 '75-p605
NS-v89-My 23 '75-p695
NYTBR-Jl 27 '75-p8
PW-v208-O 13 '75-p111
SLJ-v21-My '75-p70
Which Witch?
GP-v18-N '79-p3597
JB-v43-O '79-p279
Sch Lib-v28-S '80-p266
TES-Je 13 '80-p25
The Worm And The Toffee-Nosed Princess And Other Stories Of Monsters
Lis-v110-N 3 '83-p29
TES-Ag 19 '83-p19

* * *

IBONGIA, John M
The Magic Stone
BL-v73-Jl 15 '77-p1734

* * *

ICE Hockey (Macdonald Educational)
TES-Mr 6 '81-p29

* * *

ICENHOWER, Joseph B
Submarines
TES-O 20 '78-p39

* * *

ICHIKAWA, Satomi
A Child's Book Of Seasons
BB-v4-Ap '76-p1
BL-v72-Ap 1 '76-p1114
CCB-B-v29-Jl '76-p176
CE-v53-N '76-p96
CSM-v68-My 12 '76-p23
HB-v52-Je '76-p280
JB-v40-Je '76-p143
KR-v44-F 1 '76-p130
NS-v91-My 21 '76-p689
NYTBR-Ap 25 '76-p14
PW-v209-F 23 '76-p120
SE-v41-Ap '77-p349
Spec-v236-Ap 10 '76-p24
TLS-Ap 2 '76-p381
Friends
BB-v5-S '77-p1
BL-v73-Jl 1 '77-p1653
CCB-B-v30-My '77-p143
CSM-v69-My 4 '77-pB4
Comw-v104-N 11 '77-p728
GP-v15-D '76-p3030
JB-v41-F '77-p14
KR-v45-F 15 '77-p161
NYTBR-Je 5 '77-p22
Obs-N 21 '76-p31
Par-v52-My '77-p31
RT-v31-D '77-p331
Let's Play
BL-v78-Ja 1 '82-p598
BL-v80-N 1 '83-p423
CBRS-v10-Ja '82-p42
GP-v20-S '81-p3936
JB-v45-O '81-p187
KR-v50-F 15 '82-p201
PW-v220-N 13 '81-p88
TES-D 18 '81-p18
TLS-S 18 '81-p1066
Sun Through Small Leaves
BL-v76-Jl 1 '80-p1612
NYTBR-v85-Ap 27 '80-p61
SLJ-v26-Ag '80-p52
Suzanne And Nicholas And The Four Seasons
GP-v18-S '79-p3584
JB-v43-Ap '79-p97
Obs-F 11 '79-p36
Suzanne And Nicholas At The Market
GP-v16-Ja '78-p3252
JB-v42-Ap '78-p89
Suzanne And Nicholas In The Garden
GP-v16-Ja '78-p3252

* * *

ICKIS, Marguerite
Book Of Religious Holidays And Celebrations
BL-v63-Ap 15 '67-p881
CCB-B-v21-S '67-p9
LJ-v92-F 1 '67-p584
LJ-v92-Jl '67-p2663
SR-v50-My 20 '67-p60

* * *

IFE, Elaine
The Childhood Of Jesus
SLJ-v30-Ap '84-p103
Moses In The Bulrushes
SLJ-v30-Ap '84-p103
Noah And The Ark
SLJ-v30-Ap '84-p103
Stories Jesus Told
SLJ-v30-Ap '84-p103

* * *

IFKOVIC, Edward
The Yugoslavs In America
BL-v74-My 1 '78-p1428
CE-v55-O '78-p40
SLJ-v25-S '78-p129

* * *

IGER, Eve Marie
Weather On The Move
BL-v67-F 1 '71-p452
HB-v47-Ap '71-p188
LJ-v96-Ja 15 '71-p276

* * *

IGER, Martin
Building A Skyscraper
CCB-B-v21-O '67-p29
HB-v43-Ag '67-p489
KR-v35-Ap 15 '67-p503
LJ-v92-Jl '67-p2655
NYTBR, pt.1-v72-My 7 '67-p43
SA-v217-D '67-p148
SB-v3-S '67-p167

* * *

IGGULDEN, M
Sam On Radio 321
TES-Ag 13 '82-p21

* * *

IGLEHART, Anne
Radio Dog
SLJ-v26-Mr '80-p122

* * *

IGUCHI, Bunshu
Convent Cat
GP-v14-Mr '76-p2829
Inst-v86-N '76-p145
JB-v40-F '76-p11
PW-v210-S 13 '76-p99
Par-v52-F '77-p67
SLJ-v23-N '76-p52
Spec-v235-D 6 '75-p734
TLS-D 5 '75-p1453
A Donkey's Tale
JB-v43-D '79-p317
An Elephant's Tale
TES-Ja 1 '82-p17
The Shepherd Boy's Christmas
SLJ-v25-O '78-p112
WCRB-v4-S '78-p43

* * *

IKE, Jane H
A Japanese Fairy Tale
BL-v78-Ag '82-p1526
CCB-B-v36-S '82-p12
CE-v59-N '82-p133
PW-v221-Ap 16 '82-p70
RT-v36-O '82-p117
SLJ-v29-F '83-p67

* * *

ILLING, Walter
Drachenschiff Vor Amerika
ANQ-v16-Mr '78-p112

* * *

ILLUSTRATED Disney Song Book
BL-v76-Mr 1 '80-p983
CCB-B-v33-Ap '80-p149
WSJ-v194-D 13 '79-p26

* * *

ILLUSTRATED Family Guide To Life, Love And Sex
SR/W-v2-N 30 '74-p27

* * *

ILLUSTRATED Space Encyclopedia
CCB-B-v20-S '66-p3
LJ-v91-F 15 '66-p1069
SB-v1-Mr '66-p237

* * *

ILLUSTRATED World Encyclopedia
BL-v65-Mr 15 '69-p778
BL-v69-My 15 '73-p865
BL-v74-Ja 15 '78-p836
BL-v75-D 1 '78-p635

* * *

ILLYES, Gyula
Hetvenhet Magyar Nepmese
BL-v62-F 1 '66-p521
BL-v78-S 15 '81-p115
Ludas Matyi
BL-v78-S 15 '81-p115
Matt The Gooseherd
BW-Ap 8 '79-pL2
RT-v35-Ap '82-p823
SLJ-v26-S '79-p103
Once Upon A Time
ANQ-v9-Mr '71-p107
RT-v35-Ap '82-p824
TLS-Jl 2 '70-p714

* * *

ILOWITE, Sheldon A
Hockey Defenseman
CCB-B-v25-Ap '72-p124
On The Wing
BL-v73-Ja 1 '77-p667

* * *

IMAM, A B
Ruwam Bagaja, The Water Of Cure
J Read-v25-Mr '82-p519

* * *

IMMERZEEL, George
Problem Solving Workbooks
Cur R-v20-Je '81-p232

* * *

IMPERATO, Helen C
Science And Reading
Cur R-v20-N '81-p519

* * *

IMRIE, J
Using The Microscope
JB-v40-D '76-p358
Wild Flowers Of Verges And Waste Land
JB-v42-F '78-p42
TES-O 21 '77-p23
Woodland In Autumn And Winter
JB-v46-Je '82-p98
Woodland In Spring And Summer
JB-v46-Je '82-p98

* * *

IN The Beginning
Sch Lib-v28-D '80-p379

* * *

IN Town
TES-O 24 '80-p21

* * *

INCREASING Comprehension (Skillboosters)
RT-v31-Ja '78-p444

* * *

INDIAN (Macdonald Educational)
TES-Je 20 '80-p41

* * *

INDIVIDUAL Corrective English
Teacher-v95-F '78-p135

* * *

INDUSTRY And Resources (Place And People)
TES-N 25 '77-p25

* * *

INGALLS, Robert P
Point Of Order
BL-v78-Ja 15 '82-p649
CCB-B-v35-F '82-p109
NYTBR-v86-N 15 '81-p55
Perspec-v11-My '82-p78
SLJ-v28-Mr '82-p159

* * *

INGAWA, A
The Adventures Of Iliya Dam Markarfi
J Read-v25-Mr '82-p519

* * *

INGERSOLL, Daniel
Experimental Archaeology
Choice-v15-S '78-p928
Earth S-v31-Mr '78-p90
RA-v7-Spring '80-p177
SB-v14-D '78-p177

* * *

INGLE, Annie
The Big City Book
NYT-v125-D 5 '75-p37
NYTBR-F 8 '76-p16
SLJ-v22-Ja '76-p38
The Big Farm Book
SLJ-v23-F '77-p56

* * *

INGLIS, Fred
The Promise Of Happiness
B Rpt-v1-Mr '83-p45
Brit Bk N-Ag '81-p502
Brit Bk N-D '82-p719
Brit Bk N C-Autumn '81-p4
Can Child Lit-#27 '82-p171
Emerg Lib-v10-N '82-p25
Emerg Lib-v11-N '83-p19
SLJ-v29-Ap '83-p30
Socio R-v30-F '82-p162
TES-Je 5 '81-p22
TES-O 15 '82-p41
TLS-Jl 24 '81-p837

* * *

INGMAN, Nicholas
The Story Of Music
BL-v73-Ja 15 '77-p719
CSM-v69-My 4 '77-pB8
Inst-v89-Ap '80-p122
PW-v210-Ag 16 '76-p123
TLS-Ap 6 '73-p386
What Instrument Shall I Play?
BL-v73-Ja 15 '77-p719
CSM-v69-My 4 '77-pB8
JB-v40-F '76-p46
Obs-N 9 '75-p27
PW-v210-Ag 16 '76-p123

* * *

INGOLFSRUD, Elizabeth
All About Ontario Desks
In Rev-v14-Je '80-p44

* * *

INGRAM, Anne Bower
Shudders And Shakes
TLS-D 6 '74-p1384
Too True
GP-v14-O '75-p2729

* * *

INGRAM, Tom
The Night Rider
BB-v3-Ja '76-p3
BL-v71-Jl 1 '75-p1128
CCB-B-v29-N '75-p47
GP-v15-S '76-p2932
JB-v40-Ag '76-p231
KR-v43-My 1 '75-p521
PW-v207-Je 2 '75-p52
SLJ-v22-S '75-p105
The Outcasts
JB-v42-Ap '78-p103
NS-v94-N 4 '77-p630
TES-F 3 '78-p40

* * *

INGRAMS, Doreen
Mosques And Minarets
BL-v71-Ap 15 '75-p866
Inst-v84-My '75-p99
SLJ-v22-S '75-p105
New Ways For Ancient Lands
BL-v71-Ap 15 '75-p866
Inst-v84-My '75-p99
SLJ-v22-S '75-p105
Tents To City Sidewalks
BL-v71-Ap 15 '75-p866
Inst-v84-My '75-p99
SLJ-v22-S '75-p105

* * *

INGRHAM, Leonard W
An Album Of Colonial America
GP-v17-S '78-p3376

* * *

INGVES, Gunilla
The Dandelion
GP-v21-Mr '83-p4045
TES-Mr 11 '83-p42
The Fly
GP-v21-Mr '83-p4045
Sch Lib-v31-S '83-p232
TES-Mr 11 '83-p42
The Grasshopper
GP-v21-Mr '83-p4045
Sch Lib-v31-S '83-p232
TES-Mr 11 '83-p42
The Ladybird
GP-v21-Mr '83-p4045
TES-Mr 11 '83-p42
The Mushroom
GP-v21-Mr '83-p4045
TES-Mr 11 '83-p42
Pigs
SLJ-v30-F '84-p59
TES-Mr 9 '84-p54
Sheep
SLJ-v30-F '84-p59
TES-Mr 9 '84-p54
The Snail
GP-v21-Mr '83-p4045
TES-Mr 11 '83-p42

* * *

INKIOW, Dimiter
Me And Clara And Baldwin The Pony
SLJ-v26-Ag '80-p52
Me And Clara And Casimir The Cat
CBRS-v8-O '79-p16
CSM-v71-O 15 '79-pB8
HB-v56-Ap '80-p173
KR-v47-D 1 '79-p1375
SLJ-v26-Mr '80-p122

IPCAR, Dahlov (continued)
The Land Of Flowers
BL-v70-Mr 15 '74-p820
CCB-B-v28-S '74-p11
KR-v42-F 15 '74-p182
LJ-v99-My 15 '74-p1466
PW-v205-F 25 '74-p113
Lost And Found
CBRS-v9-Mr '81-p63
Inst-v90-My '81-p59
LA-v58-S '81-p698
PW-v219-Ja 16 '81-p80
SLJ-v27-My '81-p56
The Queen Of Spells
BL-v70-S 1 '73-p51
CCB-B-v27-N '73-p45
KR-v41-Ap 1 '73-p396
LJ-v98-S 15 '73-p2665
PW-v203-My 28 '73-p40

* * *

IPSEN, D C
What Does A Bee See
BL-v67-Je 15 '71-p871
CSM-v63-My 6 '71-pB3
HB-v48-F '72-p77
LJ-v96-N 15 '71-p3901
SB-v7-My '71-p59

* * *

IRELAND, K
The Werewolf Mask
JB-v47-Je '83-p126

* * *

IRELAND, Karin
Helicopters At Work
SLJ-v30-Ap '84-p115
Hollywood Stuntpeople
BL-v77-D 1 '80-p513
CCB-B-v34-Ap '81-p152
SLJ-v27-F '81-p66

* * *

IRELAND, Kenneth
The Cove
GP-v18-Jl '79-p3559
JB-v43-O '79-p279
The Fogou
JB-v42-Ap '78-p103
Obs-D 11 '77-p31
TES-Ja 13 '78-p22
The Quail Message
Brit Bk N C-Autumn '80-p20
JB-v44-O '80-p250
The Werewolf Mask
GP-v22-Jl '83-p4095
Sch Lib-v31-D '83-p379
TES-O 28 '83-p25

* * *

IRELAND, Robert J
Ernie
Can Child Lit-#14 '79-p85

* * *

IRELAND, Timothy
Catherine Loves
Brit Bk N C-Autumn '80-p25
GP-v19-S '80-p3757
JB-v45-F '81-p33
Sch Lib-v28-D '80-p393
TES-S 26 '80-p24
TLS-Jl 18 '80-p807
To Be Looked For
Brit Bk N C-Spring '82-p14
JB-v46-Je '82-p111
Sch Lib-v30-Je '82-p155
TES-S 10 '82-p33

* * *

IRESON, Barbara
The Bike
GP-v18-Mr '80-p3664
Sch Lib-v27-D '79-p358
A Bright Red Lorry And Other Rhymes
GP-v14-D '75-p2780
Fantasy Tales
GP-v16-D '77-p3232
JB-v42-F '78-p42
Obs-D 11 '77-p31
TES-N 27 '81-p23
The Gingerbread Man
GP-v19-Ja '81-p3829
KR-v33-F 15 '65-p169
LJ-v90-Mr 15 '65-p1542
Obs-Ap 21 '68-p27
Haunting Tales
B&B-v19-Ja '74-p94
BL-v71-F 1 '75-p570
HB-v50-D '74-p697
KR-v42-N 1 '74-p1161
Obs-N 25 '73-p39
PW-v206-O 14 '74-p57
Moving Along
GP-v17-My '78-p3340
JB-v42-Ap '78-p104
TES-F 3 '78-p44
One-Eyed Jack And Other Rhymes
GP-v14-D '75-p2780
Obs-Jl 27 '75-p21
SLJ-v24-Mr '78-p114
Out Of The Dark
GP-v18-Mr '80-p3664
Sch Lib-v27-D '79-p358
Over And Over Again
GP-v23-S '84-p4323
TES-Je 16 '78-p47
Rhyme Time
GP-v16-My '77-p3127
JB-v42-Ap '78-p89
TES-D 16 '77-p21
Rhyme Time 2
Sch Lib-v32-Je '84-p146
Spooky Stories 1 And 2
GP-v18-S '79-p3578
The Story Of The Pied Piper
GP-v16-Ap '78-p3304
Tales Out Of Time
BL-v77-Je 15 '81-p1342
Brit Bk N C-Spring '80-p17
CCB-B-v35-S '81-p11
JB-v44-F '80-p28
NS-v98-N 9 '79-p729
Obs-D 2 '79-p38
SLJ-v28-S '81-p136
Sch Lib-v28-Mr '80-p94
Spec-v243-D 15 '79-p24
TES-Ja 18 '80-p38
TLS-D 14 '79-p122
Tumbling Jack And Other Rhymes
SLJ-v24-Mr '78-p114

* * *

IRION, Ruth Hershey
The Christmas Cookie Tree
CCB-B-v30-F '77-p91
HB-v52-D '76-p613
KR-v44-S 1 '76-p974
NYTBR-N 14 '76-p54
PW-v210-Ag 9 '76-p79
SLJ-v23-O '76-p87

* * *

IRVINE, Georgeanne
Alberta The Gorilla
SB-v19-S '83-p33
Bo The Orangutan
SLJ-v30-Mr '84-p144
Elmer The Elephant
SLJ-v30-Mr '84-p144
Georgie The Giraffe
SLJ-v30-Mr '84-p144
Lindi The Leopard
SLJ-v30-Mr '84-p144
Nanuck The Polar Bear
SB-v19-S '83-p33
SLJ-v29-My '83-p62
The Nursery Babies
SLJ-v30-Mr '84-p144

IRVINE, Georgeanne (continued)
Sasha The Cheetah
SB-v19-S '83-p33
SLJ-v29-Ap '83-p102
Sydney The Koala
SB-v19-S '83-p33
Tully The Tree Kangaroo
SLJ-v30-Mr '84-p144
Wilbur And Orville The Otter Twins
CCB-B-v36-F '83-p110
SB-v19-S '83-p33
Zelda The Zebra
SB-v19-S '83-p33
Zoo Babies
Cur R-v22-Ag '83-p73

* * *

IRVINE, Mat
TV And Video
BL-v80-My 15 '84-p1345
JB-v48-F '84-p24
RT-v38-N '84-p228
SLJ-v31-O '84-p157

* * *

IRVING, Washington
Rip Van Winkle, The Legend Of Sleepy Hollow
AB-v58-N 8 '76-p2540
AB-v66-N 17 '80-p3314
BL-v71-Mr 1 '75-p694
Rp B Bk R-v24-Ap 40 '79-p18
SR-v2-My 31 '75-p34
Rip Van Winkle, The Legend Of Sleepy Hollow (Boughton)
BL-v77-O 15 '80-p327
Brit Bk N C-Autumn '80-p11

* * *

IRWIN, Constance
Strange Footprints On The Land
Arch-v34-S '81-p73
BL-v76-Jl 15 '80-p1676
BOT-v3-Jl '80-p304
CCB-B-v33-Je '80-p193
HB-v56-Je '80-p313
J Read-v24-Mr '81-p549
KR-v48-Je 15 '80-p785
LA-v58-Mr '81-p345
NY-v56-D 1 '80-p222
NYTBR-v85-Ap 27 '80-p50
SLJ-v26-Ap '80-p125

* * *

IRWIN, Hadley
Bring To A Boil And Separate
BL-v76-Ap 1 '80-p1128
CBRS-v8-Je '80-p107
CCB-B-v33-Jl '80-p215
KR-v48-Ap 1 '80-p440
RT-v34-Ja '81-p483
SLJ-v26-Ap '80-p111
I Be Somebody
CCB-B-v38-S '84-p7
KR-v52-S 1 '84-pJ70
PW-v226-Ag 31 '84-p436
The Lilith Summer
BL-v76-O 1 '79-p278
BW-v9-S 9 '79-p10
HB-v56-Ap '80-p174
Inter BC-v11-Ja 10 '80-p25
NYTBR-Ja 27 '80-p24
PW-v216-Ag 13 '79-p65
Par-v54-D '79-p66
SLJ-v26-N '79-p78
TN-v38-Winter '82-p121
We Are Mesquakie, We Are One
Inter BC-v12-#7 '81-p22
SLJ-v27-Ja '81-p62
TES-Ag 3 '84-p23
TN-v38-Winter '82-p121
VOYA-v4-F '82-p33
What About Grandma?
BL-v78-Ap 15 '82-p1084
CBRS-v10-Spring '82-p117
CCB-B-v35-Jl '82-p209
Inter BC-v15-#3 '84-p17
J Read-v26-N '82-p185
SE-v47-Ap '83-p252
SLJ-v29-S '82-p140
VOYA-v5-Ag '82-p32

* * *

IRWIN, Keith Gordon
Romance Of Physics
BL-v63-Mr 15 '67-p796
BS-v26-Ja 1 '67-p368
CCB-B-v21-N '67-p43
CLW-v38-Mr '67-p478
CLW-v39-O '67-p153
KR-v35-Ja 1 '67-p14
LJ-v92-F 15 '67-p894
PW-v191-Ap 10 '67-p82
SB-v2-Mr '67-p264

* * *

ISAAC, Joanne
Amanda
CCB-B-v22-F '69-p95

* * *

ISAAC, Peter
Which Pet?
GP-v21-Mr '83-p4050
Sch Lib-v31-S '83-p258

* * *

ISADORA, Rachel
Ben's Trumpet
BL-v75-F 15 '79-p934
BL-v79-Je 1 '83-p1282
BL-v80-S 1 '83-p93
CBRS-v7-My '79-p92
CCB-B-v32-Jl '79-p192
CLW-v52-Ap '81-p389
CSM-v71-Jl 9 '79-pB6
Emerg Lib-v11-Ja '84-p19
HB-v55-Je '79-p293
Inst-v88-My '79-p107
JB-v45-Ap '81-p63
KR-v47-Mr 15 '79-p323
NYTBR-Ap 29 '79-p47
PW-v215-Ja 15 '79-p131
RT-v33-My '80-p971
RT-v37-Ap '84-p704
SLJ-v25-F '79-p43
SLJ-v25-My '79-p35
TES-Ja 9 '81-p25
WLB-v53-Je '79-p710
City Seen From A To Z
BL-v79-My 15 '83-p1216
BW-v13-My 8 '83-p16
CBRS-v11-Je '83-p108
CCB-B-v36-Ap '83-p151
CE-v60-Ja '84-p209
HB-v59-Je '83-p292
Inter BC-v14-#7 '83-p28
KR-v51-F 15 '83-p181
LA-v60-O '83-p897
NYTBR-v88-My 22 '83-p39
PW-v223-Ja 28 '83-p85
RT-v37-D '83-p308
SE-v48-My '84-p378
SLJ-v29-Ag '83-p52
Jesse & Abe
BL-v77-Mr 1 '81-p964
CBRS-v9-F '81-p52
CCB-B-v34-Je '81-p196
KR-v49-Mr 1 '81-p280
LA-v58-S '81-p697
NYTBR-v86-Mr 1 '81-p24
SLJ-v27-Mr '81-p132
Max
BL-v73-S 15 '76-p176
BL-v73-Mr 15 '77-p1101
CCB-B-v30-F '77-p92
CE-v60-My '84-p344

ISADORA, Rachel (continued)
CSM-v68-N 3 '76-p28
KR-v44-Jl 15 '76-p791
PW-v210-Ag 2 '76-p114
RT-v31-O '77-p12
RT-v31-D '77-p331
SE-v41-Ap '77-p351
SLJ-v23-D '76-p70
SLJ-v24-D '77-p35
Teacher-v94-My '77-p108
My Ballet Class
BL-v76-Ja 15 '80-p720
BW-v10-My 11 '80-p18
CBRS-v8-F '80-p53
CCB-B-v33-F '80-p111
Dance-v54-S '80-p112
Dance-v54-N '80-p90
GP-v20-Ja '82-p4004
HB-v56-Ap '80-p164
Inst-v89-My '80-p91
KR-v48-Mr 1 '80-p283
PW-v217-Ja 25 '80-p341
SLJ-v26-F '80-p46
Sch Lib-v29-D '81-p330
No, Agatha!
BL-v77-O 1 '80-p253
BW-v10-N 9 '80-p14
CBRS-v9-S '80-p2
CCB-B-v34-N '80-p55
Inst-v90-N '80-p156
KR-v48-N 1 '80-p1392
LA-v58-Ap '81-p475
PW-v218-S 19 '80-p160
RT-v34-Mr '81-p734
SLJ-v27-S '80-p60
The Nutcracker
BL-v78-O 15 '81-p304
BW-v11-D 13 '81-p8
CBRS-v10-O '81-p12
KR-v49-O 15 '81-p1292
NYTBR-v86-D 27 '81-p17
PW-v220-O 9 '81-p67
RT-v35-F '82-p621
SLJ-v28-O '81-p155
VV-v26-D 9 '81-p58
Opening Night
BL-v81-S 1 '84-p66
CBRS-v13-S '84-p3
HB-v60-S '84-p581
KR-v52-S 1 '84-pJ62
NY-v60-D 3 '84-p191
The Potters' Kitchen
BL-v73-Ap 15 '77-p1266
CCB-B-v31-S '77-p17
CE-v58-S '81-p37
KR-v45-F 15 '77-p162
SLJ-v24-S '77-p110
Willaby
BL-v74-S 15 '77-p195
CLW-v52-Ap '81-p389
CSM-v69-N 2 '77-pB2
HB-v54-F '78-p35
Inst-v87-N '77-p153
KR-v45-Jl 1 '77-p667
LA-v55-My '78-p619
PW-v211-Je 27 '77-p110
RT-v32-O '78-p39
RT-v35-Ap '82-p793
SLJ-v24-O '77-p104
Teacher-v95-My '78-p101

* * *

ISEBORG, Harry
John And The Big Dog
GP-v15-S '76-p2953
John Sails His Boat
GP-v16-N '77-p3210

* * *

ISELE, Elizabeth
The Frog Princess
BL-v80-Ap 1 '84-p1116
CBRS-v12-Je '84-p114
CCB-B-v37-Ap '84-p149
CSM-v76-My 4 '84-pB4
KR-v52-Mr 1 '84-pJ5
PW-v225-Mr 23 '84-p71
SLJ-v31-S '84-p104
Pooks
CBRS-v11-My '83-p98
CCB-B-v36-Ap '83-p152
KR-v51-Ja 15 '83-p61
PW-v223-F 25 '83-p88
SLJ-v30-O '83-p150

* * *

ISENBART, Hans-Heinrich
Baby Animals On The Farm
BL-v81-S 15 '84-p128
CCB-B-v37-Jl '84-p206
SLJ-v31-O '84-p148
Birth Of A Duckling
JB-v44-D '80-p292
Sch Lib-v29-Je '81-p146
TES-O 24 '80-p20
TES-Jl 31 '81-p19
A Duckling Is Born
ASBYP-v16-Spring '83-p26
BL-v78-Ja 15 '82-p649
BL-v80-O 15 '83-p369
CCB-B-v35-Ja '82-p87
SB-v17-My '82-p271
SLJ-v28-Mr '82-p135
A Foal Is Born
ACSB-v10-Spring '77-p24
BB-v5-Ap '77-p1
BL-v72-Jl 15 '76-p1596
BL-v77-O 1 '80-p262
GP-v16-My '77-p3125
KR-v44-Je 1 '76-p637
NYTBR-N 14 '76-p46
SB-v12-Mr '77-p213
SLJ-v24-S '77-p110
SR-v4-N 27 '76-p36

* * *

ISENBERG, Barbara
The Adventures Of Albert, The Running Bear
BL-v79-S 1 '82-p44
CBRS-v11-F '83-p64
CCB-B-v36-F '83-p110
CLW-v55-O '83-p140
LA-v61-F '84-p199
PW-v222-Ag 20 '82-p72
SLJ-v29-F '83-p67
Albert The Running Bear's Exercise Book
PW-v226-S 7 '84-p79

* * *

ISH-KISHOR, S
A Boy Of Old Prague
HT-v16-D '66-p867
Obs-D 4 '66-p28
RT-v33-Mr '80-p688
Spec-N 11 '66-p625
TLS-N 24 '66-p1079

* * *

ISH-KISHOR, Sulamith
Drusilla
HB-v46-Ag '70-p393
KR-v38-My 1 '70-p506
LJ-v95-Jl '70-p2540
The Master Of Miracle
A Lib-v3-Ap '72-p420
BL-v68-Ja 1 '72-p394
BL-v68-Ap 1 '72-p669
CLW-v43-Ap '72-p481
HB-v47-D '71-p611
KR-v39-O 15 '71-p1120
LJ-v96-N 15 '71-p3902
NYT-v121-D 16 '71-p67
NYTBR-D 5 '71-p86
NYTBR, pt.2-N 7 '71-p7
NYTBR, pt.2-N 7 '71-p30
PW-v200-N 1 '71-p55
TN-v28-Ap '72-p310
Our Eddie
A Lib-v1-Ap '70-p385

ISH-KISHOR, Sulamith (continued)
BL-v65-My 15 '69-p1076
BS-v29-F 1 '70-p423
BW-v3-My 4 '69-p36
CCB-B-v23-O '69-p25
CSM-v61-My 1 '69-pB6
HB-v45-Ag '69-p417
Inst-v79-Ag '69-p191
KR-v37-Mr 15 '69-p315
LJ-v94-My 15 '69-p2114
NYTBR-Jl 20 '69-p22
PW-v195-Je 9 '69-p63
SR-v52-My 10 '69-p60

* * *

ISHAM, Charlotte H
Freddie's Discoveries
SLJ-v22-S '75-p84

* * *

ISHERWOOD, Christopher
People One Ought To Know
BL-v79-O 1 '82-p184
BW-v12-S 12 '82-p6
JB-v46-D '82-p224
LA-v60-Ap '83-p485
Lis-v108-N 25 '82-p26
NS-v104-D 3 '82-p24
NW-v100-D 6 '82-p132
NYT-v131-Ag 4 '82-p18
Quill & Q-v48-D '82-p30
SLJ-v29-D '82-p64
SLMQ-v11-Spring '83-p174
TES-N 19 '82-p31

* * *

ISHERWOOD, Shirley
Is That You, Mrs. Pinkerton-Trunks?
GP-v23-S '84-p4323

* * *

ISHII, Momoko
The Dolls' Day For Yoshiko
CCB-B-v20-N '66-p43
HB-v42-Ag '66-p427
KR-v34-F 15 '66-p180
LJ-v91-My 15 '66-p2692
PW-v189-My 30 '66-p88
Issun Boshi, The Inchling
BL-v64-F 15 '68-p700
BL-v79-O 15 '82-p320
Comw-v87-N 10 '67-p182
HB-v44-F '68-p55
KR-v35-N 1 '67-p1313
LJ-v92-D 15 '67-p4604
NYTBR-v72-N 5 '67-p71
PW-v192-D 11 '67-p46
SR-v51-Ap 20 '68-p40

* * *

ISRAEL, Abby
A Boy And A Boa
CBRS-v10-D '81-p34
CSM-v73-O 13 '81-pB7
PW-v220-Ag 7 '81-p78
SLJ-v28-O '81-p143

* * *

ISRAEL, Elaine
The Great Energy Search
ACSB-v8-Fall '75-p18
KR-v42-N 1 '74-p1155
SB-v11-My '75-p32
SLJ-v21-Ja '75-p46
SLJ-v25-Ja '79-p19
The Hungry World
KR-v45-O 15 '77-p1100
SB-v14-D '78-p179
SLJ-v24-F '78-p58

* * *

ISRAEL (Macdonald Countries Series)
NS-v94-N 4 '77-p629

* * *

ISSLER, Anne Roller
Young Red Flicker
BS-v28-My 1 '68-p65
CCB-B-v21-Je '68-p160
KR-v36-Ap 1 '68-p403
LJ-v93-My 15 '68-p2122

* * *

ITALIANO, Carlo
Sleighs
BW-D 10 '78-pE5
CCB-B-v32-Mr '79-p120
HB-v55-F '79-p78
SLJ-v25-Ap '79-p57
The Sleighs Of My Childhood
BL-v71-Ja 15 '75-p507
BL-v72-S 15 '75-p173
NYTBR-D 1 '74-p8
The Sleighs Of My Childhood/Les Traineaux De Mon Enfance
TN-v34-Winter '78-p191
The Sleighs Of Old Montreal
JB-v43-F '79-p19

* * *

ITANI, Frances
Linger By The Sea
BIC-v8-D '79-p13
In Rev-v14-F '80-p47

* * *

ITARD, Jean-Gaspard
L'Enfant Sauvage
TCR-v84-Summer '83-p934

* * *

ITAYEMI, Phoebean
The Torn Veil And Other Stories
J Read-v25-Mr '82-p522

* * *

ITER Gallicum
NS-v95-My 19 '78-p681

* * *

ITERSON, S R Van
The Curse Of Laguna Grande
BL-v69-My 15 '73-p902
HB-v49-Ag '73-p383
KR-v41-Mr 1 '73-p259
KR-v41-D 15 '73-p1358
LJ-v98-S 15 '73-p2669
LJ-v98-D 15 '73-p3691
PW-v204-Jl 16 '73-p111
In The Spell Of The Past
HB-v51-Ag '75-p389
KR-v43-Mr 1 '75-p246
PW-v207-Je 9 '75-p63
SLJ-v21-My '75-p71
Pulga
A Lib-v3-Ap '72-p420
Am-v125-D 4 '71-p490
BL-v67-Je 15 '71-p873
BL-v68-Ap 1 '72-p669
CCB-B-v24-Je '71-p163
CE-v48-Ap '72-p377
CLW-v43-N '71-p174
CSM-v63-My 6 '71-pB6
EJ-v60-S '71-p828
HB-v48-Ap '72-p150
Inst-v130-Je '71-p75
KR-v39-Mr 15 '71-p293
NYTBR, pt.2-My 2 '71-p20
PW-v199-Ap 12 '71-p83
SR-v54-My 15 '71-p47
The Smugglers Of Buenaventura
BL-v70-Je 15 '74-p1154
CCB-B-v28-S '74-p18
KR-v42-Ap 1 '74-p374
LJ-v99-My 15 '74-p1487
Village Of Outcasts
BL-v68-Je 15 '72-p903
CCB-B-v25-Jl '72-p178
HB-v48-Je '72-p277

ITERSON, S R Van
(continued)
KR-v40-Mr 1 '72-p267
KR-v40-D 15 '72-p1422
LJ-v97-My 15 '72-p1924
PW-v201-My 1 '72-p50
SR-v55-My 20 '72-p82

* * *

ITERSON, S R Van
The Spirits Of Chocamata
BL-v73-Je 1 '77-p1499
CCB-B-v31-N '77-p56
KR-v45-My 15 '77-p540
LA-v54-N '77-p948
SLJ-v24-S '77-p138

* * *

IT'S Easy To Have A Caterpillar To Stay
GP-v19-S '80-p3749
Sch Lib-v29-Mr '81-p23
TES-Je 20 '80-p25
TES-O 24 '80-p20
TLS-S 19 '80-p1035

* * *

IT'S Easy To Have A Caterpillar Visit You
ASBYP-v14-Spring '81-p30
BL-v77-S 15 '80-p115
CBRS-v8-Ag '80-p133
Inst-v90-N '80-p158
KR-v48-S 1 '80-p1159
SB-v16-Mr '81-p221
SLJ-v27-O '80-p138

* * *

IT'S Easy To Have A Ladybird To Stay
Brit Bk N C-Autumn '81-p28
GP-v20-N '81-p3977
Sch Lib-v30-Mr '82-p42

* * *

IT'S Easy To Have A Snail To Stay
GP-v19-S '80-p3749
JB-v44-D '80-p295
Sch Lib-v28-S '80-p283
TES-Je 20 '80-p25
TES-O 24 '80-p20
TLS-S 19 '80-p1035

* * *

IT'S Easy To Have A Snail Visit You
ASBYP-v14-Spring '81-p30
BL-v77-S 15 '80-p115
CBRS-v8-Ag '80-p133
Inst-v90-N '80-p158
KR-v48-S 1 '80-p1159
SB-v16-Mr '81-p221
SLJ-v27-O '80-p138

* * *

IT'S Easy To Have A Worm To Stay
GP-v19-S '80-p3749
Lis-v104-N 6 '80-p626
Sch Lib-v29-Mr '81-p23
TES-Je 20 '80-p25
TLS-S 19 '80-p1035

* * *

IT'S Easy To Have A Worm Visit You
ASBYP-v14-Spring '81-p30
BL-v77-S 15 '80-p115
CBRS-v8-Ag '80-p133
Inst-v90-N '80-p158
KR-v48-S 1 '80-p1159
SB-v16-Mr '81-p221
SLJ-v27-O '80-p138

* * *

IT'S Easy To Have Ants To Stay
Brit Bk N C-Autumn '81-p28
GP-v20-N '81-p3977

* * *

IT'S Easy To Have Woodlice To Stay
Brit Bk N C-Autumn '81-p28
GP-v20-N '81-p3977

* * *

IVENBAUM, Elliott
Drawing People
SLJ-v27-S '80-p72

* * *

IVERSON, Genie
I Want To Be Big
CBRS-v7-Je '79-p102
CCB-B-v33-O '79-p30
CSM-v71-My 14 '79-pB7
KR-v47-Je 1 '79-p634
LA-v57-Ap '80-p434
RT-v33-Ja '80-p482
SLJ-v26-S '79-p114
WCRB-v5-Jl '79-p62
Jacques Cousteau
BB-v4-Ag '76-p3
BL-v73-S 1 '76-p38
KR-v44-Mr 15 '76-p319
RT-v31-O '77-p21
SB-v12-Mr '77-p210
SLJ-v22-My '76-p76
SLJ-v25-D '78-p33
Louis Armstrong
BL-v73-Ap 15 '77-p1267
KR-v44-N 15 '76-p1224
PW-v210-D 13 '76-p61
SLJ-v23-Mr '77-p146
Margaret Bourke-White: News Photographer
BL-v77-F 1 '81-p753
BL-v80-Ja 15 '84-p719
SLJ-v27-Ag '81-p68

* * *

IVES, Burl
Albad The Oaf
CCB-B-v19-Ap '66-p131
KR-v33-D 1 '65-p1187
LJ-v91-Ja 15 '66-p426
NO-v5-Ja 10 '66-p27
PW-v189-Ja 10 '66-p89

* * *

IVIMEY, John W
Complete Version Of Ye Three Blind Mice
BL-v76-D 15 '79-p613
GP-v18-S '79-p3584
Inter BC-v11-Mr 30 '80-p24
LA-v57-My '80-p553
PW-v216-N 12 '79-p58
Punch-v277-D 12 '79-p1153
SLJ-v26-Mr '80-p122

* * *

IVORY, Lesley Anne
At The Airport
GP-v17-N '78-p3423
At The Fair
GP-v17-N '78-p3423
JB-v43-Ag '79-p196
A Day In London
CBRS-v11-F '83-p65
CCB-B-v36-Ap '83-p152
SLJ-v29-Mr '83-p162
Sch Lib-v31-Mr '83-p33
TES-Mr 11 '83-p40
A Day In New York
SLJ-v29-Mr '83-p162
Sch Lib-v31-Mr '83-p33
TES-Mr 11 '83-p40
How Do We Go?
GP-v17-N '78-p3423
In Hospital
GP-v17-N '78-p3423
JB-v42-D '78-p300

* * *

IWAMURA, Kazuo
Nat's Braces
JB-v46-O '82-p184
Sch Lib-v30-S '82-p226
Nat's Hat
Sch Lib-v30-S '82-p226
Tan Tan's Hat
CBRS-v12-O '83-p17
PW-v224-Jl 22 '83-p133
SLJ-v30-Mr '84-p145
Tan Tan's Suspenders
BL-v80-Ja 15 '84-p749
CBRS-v12-O '83-p17
SLJ-v30-Mr '84-p145
WCRB-v9-N '83-p68
Ton And Pon: Big And Little
BL-v80-Ag '84-p1626
CBRS-v12-Jl '84-p135
CCB-B-v37-Jl '84-p206
PW-v225-My 25 '84-p60
SLJ-v31-S '84-p105
Ton And Pon: Two Good Friends
BL-v80-Ag '84-p1626
CBRS-v12-Jl '84-p135
CCB-B-v37-Jl '84-p206
SLJ-v31-S '84-p105

* * *

IWASAKI, Chihiro
The Birthday Wish
BB-v2-Ja '75-p1
KR-v42-Je 15 '74-p631
LJ-v99-O 15 '74-p2733
PW-v206-Jl 15 '74-p114
WLB-v49-S '74-p84
Momoko And The Pretty Bird
Brit Bk N C-Spring '81-p11
Obs-Jl 30 '72-p32
TES-Je 20 '80-p38
Momoko's Birthday
Brit Bk N C-Spring '81-p11
TES-Je 20 '80-p38
What's Fun Without A Friend?
BB-v3-S '75-p2
CCB-B-v29-D '75-p64
KR-v43-Jl 1 '75-p709
LA-v53-My '76-p497
NO-v14-S 27 '75-p21
PW-v207-Je 30 '75-p57

* * *

IZAWA, Tadasu
My First Book
CCB-B-v37-D '83-p69
SLJ-v30-F '84-p62

* * *

IZENBERG, Jerry
Great Latin Sports Figures
BL-v73-S 1 '76-p38
Comw-v103-N 19 '76-p764
KR-v44-My 15 '76-p596
RT-v31-Mr '78-p708
The Proud People
SLJ-v22-My '76-p78

J

J.A.M.
In Rev-v14-D '80-p42
NMR-v2-N '80-p7

* * *

JABBERWOCKY
Can Child Lit-#14 '79-p41

* * *

JABER, William
Exploring The Sun
ASBYP-v14-Winter '81-p35
Cur R-v20-S '81-p400
SB-v16-Mr '81-p218
Whatever Happened To The Dinosaurs?
ACSB-v12-Spring '79-p29
KR-v46-D 1 '78-p1313
SB-v15-D '79-p147
SLJ-v25-N '78-p64

* * *

JABLOW, Alta
Gassire's Lute
A Lib-v3-Ap '72-p420
BL-v68-S 1 '71-p58
BL-v68-Ap 1 '72-p669
CCB-B-v25-D '71-p58
CLW-v43-N '71-p171
HB-v47-O '71-p478
LJ-v96-S 15 '71-p2918
TN-v28-N '71-p73

* * *

JACK, Adrienne
Witches And Witchcraft
SLJ-v27-Ag '81-p68

* * *

JACK And Jill
BL-v79-F 1 '83-p729
BW-My 1 '77-pE4
CE-v59-My '83-p370
Mag Lib- '82-p216
Ser R-v6-O '80-p5
Ser R-v7-O '81-p15

* * *

JACK And The Beanstalk (Francois)
SLJ-v30-Ag '84-p68

* * *

JACK And The Beanstalk (Herring)
TLS-Mr 29 '74-p331

* * *

JACK And The Beanstalk (Parker)
SLJ-v26-Mr '80-p117

* * *

JACK And The Beanstalk (Shepherd)
JB-v42-F '78-p12

* * *

JACKANORY Stories
B&B-v23-N '77-p80
JB-v42-Ap '78-p89
Lis-v98-N 10 '77-p624
Obs-D 11 '77-p31
Spec-v239-D 10 '77-p24
Spec-v240-Ap 29 '78-p25
TES-D 9 '77-p21

* * *

JACKER, Corinne
The Biological Revolution
BL-v68-F 15 '72-p502
BL-v68-F 15 '72-p506
CCB-B-v25-F '72-p92
KR-v39-N 15 '71-p1220
LJ-v98-Mr 1 '73-p697
SB-v8-My '72-p44
SR-v55-Ja 15 '72-p47
Window On The Unknown: A History Of The Microscope
BL-v63-My 1 '67-p949
CCB-B-v21-N '67-p43
CLW-v39-Ja '68-p373
KR-v34-S 15 '66-p992
LJ-v91-D 15 '66-p6202
NH-v76-N '67-p74
SB-v3-My '67-p52

* * *

JACKMAN, Leslie
The Beach
GP-v14-My '75-p2650
Exploring The Garden
TES-O 21 '77-p18

* * *

JACKSON, C
The Eye Of Elba
JB-v40-Ag '76-p232

* * *

JACKSON, C Paul
How To Play Better Basketball
HB-v45-F '69-p70
How To Play Better Soccer
BL-v74-Jl 1 '78-p1683
CCB-B-v32-S '78-p11
NYTBR-Je 11 '78-p30
SLJ-v25-S '78-p139
Rookie Catcher With The Atlanta Braves
BS-v26-My 1 '66-p58
CCB-B-v19-Jl '66-p180
KR-v34-Ja 1 '66-p10
LJ-v91-Jl '66-p3550
NYTBR-v71-My 8 '66-p47

* * *

JACKSON, Caroline
Dawn Daring
BW-v13-Ja 9 '83-p10

* * *

JACKSON, David
The Orange Storyhouse
Sch Lib-v28-Mr '80-p31
Sch Lib-v30-Mr '82-p36
The Way To The Zoo
JB-v48-Ap '84-p71
NYTBR-v89-Mr 11 '84-p23
Sch Lib-v32-Mr '84-p62

JACKSON, David (continued)
TES-Ja 13 '84-p39
Ways Of Talking
TES-N 24 '78-p42

* * *

JACKSON, Ellen B
The Bear In The Bathtub
CBRS-v10-Jl '81-p112
CSM-v73-Jl 1 '81-p18
KR-v49-Je 1 '81-p677
PW-v219-Ap 17 '81-p62
SLJ-v28-S '81-p109
The Grumpus Under The Rug
BL-v78-D 15 '81-p553
Cur R-v21-F '82-p64

* * *

JACKSON, Gordon
Rum Old Tales For Children And Other Lively Folk
TES-Ag 31 '84-p21

* * *

JACKSON, Gregory
Getting Into Broadcast Journalism
BL-v71-Ja 15 '75-p502
CCB-B-v28-Mr '75-p115
KR-v42-D 15 '74-p1313
PW-v206-D 9 '74-p68

* * *

JACKSON, Jacqueline
Chicken Ten Thousand
BW-v2-O 6 '68-p20
CCB-B-v22-S '68-p9
CSM-v60-N 7 '68-pB3
HB-v44-O '68-p553
KR-v36-Jl 1 '68-p687
LJ-v93-S 15 '68-p3290
PW-v194-Jl 22 '68-p63
SR-v51-Ag 24 '68-p42
YR-v5-N '68-p10
The Endless Pavement
Am-v129-D 1 '73-p427
CCB-B-v27-F '74-p96
KR-v41-O 1 '73-p1096
LJ-v98-N 15 '73-p3453
NYTBR-Ja 13 '74-p10
PW-v204-S 17 '73-p56
The Ghost Boat
BW-v3-My 4 '69-p30
HB-v45-Je '69-p307
KR-v37-Ap 15 '69-p441
LJ-v94-My 15 '69-p2122
PW-v195-My 5 '69-p52
Missing Melinda
Am-v117-N 4 '67-p516
CCB-B-v21-Ja '68-p79
CSM-v59-N 2 '67-pB15
HB-v44-Ap '68-p177
KR-v35-Ag 1 '67-p878
LJ-v92-N 15 '67-p4269
PW-v193-Ja 8 '68-p67
Par-v43-Ag '68-p76
SLJ-v24-F '78-p35
The Orchestra Mice
CCB-B-v24-Jl '70-p180
KR-v38-F 1 '70-p100
LJ-v95-My 15 '70-p1943
M Ed J-v58-S '71-p79
SR-v53-My 9 '70-p43
Spring Song
CCB-B-v23-Ap '70-p129
NO-v8-N 3 '69-p21
The Taste Of Spruce Gum
BL-v63-N 1 '66-p325
CCB-B-v20-D '66-p59
CLW-v39-O '67-p157
HB-v42-D '66-p716
KR-v34-Jl 15 '66-p688
LJ-v91-O 15 '66-p5252
SR-v49-O 22 '66-p61

* * *

JACKSON, Jesse
Black In America
CCB-B-v27-Ap '74-p130
KR-v41-N 1 '73-p1207
LJ-v99-Ap 15 '74-p1220
Make A Joyful Noise Unto The Lord!
BW-My 19 '74-p4
CCB-B-v28-N '74-p44
Comw-v101-N 22 '74-p195
HB-v50-D '74-p700
KR-v42-Je 1 '74-p590
NYTBR-Je 16 '74-p8
PW-v205-My 13 '74-p58
SLJ-v21-Ja '75-p43
The Sickest Don't Always Die The Quickest
CCB-B-v25-S '71-p9
EJ-v60-My '71-p665
KR-v38-D 1 '70-p1292
LJ-v96-My 15 '71-p1813
NYTBR-F 14 '71-p20
PW-v199-F 8 '71-p81
Tessie
BL-v65-S 15 '68-p122
BS-v28-Jl 1 '68-p154
BW-v2-My 5 '68-p34
CCB-B-v22-S '68-p9
CSM-v60-Je 13 '68-p5
Comw-v88-My 24 '68-p306
HB-v44-Ag '68-p430
KR-v36-My 1 '68-p518
LJ-v93-O 15 '68-p3983
NYTBR-v73-My 26 '68-p30
PW-v196-Jl 14 '69-p177
SR-v51-Je 15 '68-p33
TN-v25-Ja '69-p205

* * *

JACKSON, June
Papercraft
TES-F 3 '78-p43

* * *

JACKSON, Karen
Health
ASBYP-v15-Spring '82-p53

* * *

JACKSON, Kathryn
Around The World With Koa Koala
PW-v205-Je 10 '74-p41
SLJ-v22-S '75-p84
The Story Of Christmas
CCB-B-v27-Ap '74-p123
LJ-v98-O 15 '73-p3127

* * *

JACKSON, Lionel
Fit For Heroes
GP-v14-D '75-p2763

* * *

JACKSON, Louise A
Grandpa Had A Windmill, Grandma Had A Churn
BB-v6-F '78-p3
BL-v74-O 15 '77-p375
CCB-B-v31-Ja '78-p80
CE-v54-F '78-p198
Inst-v89-O '79-p88
KR-v45-S 1 '77-p928
LA-v55-Mr '78-p365
PW-v212-S 5 '77-p72
Par-v52-N '77-p112
RT-v35-My '82-p901
SE-v42-My '78-p382
SLJ-v24-N '77-p48
Over On The River
LA-v58-Ja '81-p80
NYTBR-v85-Ap 20 '80-p20
PW-v217-Ja 18 '80-p140
SLJ-v26-My '80-p59

* * *

JACKSON, Noel
Effective Horsemanship For Dressage, Three-Day Event, Jumping, And Polo
HB-v45-F '69-p70
LJ-v97-N 15 '72-p3725

* * *

JACKSON, Reggie
Reggie Jackson's Scrapbook
CCB-B-v32-O '78-p31
Comw-v105-N 10 '78-p735
KR-v46-My 15 '78-p549
NYTBR-Ap 23 '78-p31
PW-v213-My 1 '78-p84
SLJ-v25-O '78-p141
Teacher-v96-O '78-p177

* * *

JACKSON, Robert B
Antique Cars
BL-v72-D 15 '75-p578
PW-v208-O 27 '75-p52
SLJ-v22-N '75-p78
Bicycle Racing
BL-v72-Je 1 '76-p1407
KR-v44-My 1 '76-p538
SLJ-v23-S '76-p118
Earl The Pearl
Inst-v81-F '72-p139
Inst-v84-My '75-p100
KR-v37-D 1 '69-p1262
LJ-v95-My 15 '70-p1965
Fisk Of Fenway Park
BL-v72-Jl 15 '76-p1596
KR-v44-My 15 '76-p597
SLJ-v23-S '76-p118
The Gasoline Buggy Of The Duryea Brothers
CCB-B-v22-Jl '69-p177
KR-v36-Ag 15 '68-p904
PW-v194-O 28 '68-p60
SB-v4-Mr '69-p316
Joe Namath, Superstar
CCB-B-v22-Mr '69-p112
CSM-v60-N 7 '68-pB12
KR-v36-S 1 '68-p982
PW-v194-O 7 '68-p55
Quarter-Mile Combat
BL-v72-D 1 '75-p516
KR-v43-S 15 '75-p1071
SLJ-v22-O '75-p99
Remarkable Ride Of The Abernathy Boys
BW-v1-O 22 '67-p14
CCB-B-v21-Mr '68-p112
CE-v44-Ja '68-p326
HB-v43-D '67-p764
KR-v35-S 15 '67-p1139
LJ-v92-O 15 '67-p3850
NYTBR-v72-S 24 '67-p34
PW-v192-Jl 24 '67-p56
SA-v217-D '67-p152
Road Race Round The World
EL-v86-My '66-p573
SLJ-v24-S '77-p130
Robert B. Jackson's Big Book Of Old Cars
BL-v75-F 1 '79-p866
PW-v214-O 2 '78-p133
SLJ-v25-Ja '79-p54
Soccer
SLJ-v26-O '79-p151
The Steam Cars Of The Stanley Twins
CCB-B-v24-S '70-p12
KR-v37-S 15 '69-p1015
LJ-v95-S 15 '70-p3074
SA-v221-D '69-p144
SB-v5-D '69-p273
Swift Sport
BL-v74-Jl 1 '78-p1683
SLJ-v25-S '78-p139
Waves, Wheels And Wings
BL-v71-S 1 '74-p43
KR-v42-Jl 1 '74-p683
LJ-v99-D 15 '74-p3267
PW-v206-Jl 15 '74-p114

* * *

JACKSON, Rosalind
City Summer
NS-v100-N 14 '80-p20
City Summer And Other Stories
Brit Bk N C-Spring '81-p22
GP-v19-Ja '81-p3825
JB-v45-F '81-p28
TES-D 5 '80-p23
TES-Ja 9 '81-p24

* * *

JACKSON, Sarah
A Child's History Of Texas Coloring Book
AB-v67-Ja 26 '81-p591

* * *

JACKSON, Shirley
Famous Sally
CCB-B-v20-F '67-p91
LJ-v92-F 15 '67-p872
NYRB-v7-D 15 '66-p28
PW-v190-D 26 '66-p99
TLS-Jl 2 '70-p716

* * *

JACKSON, Steve
Fighting Fantasy
TES-S 21 '84-p37
The Warlock Of Firetop Mountain
Fant R-v7-Ag '84-p48
TES-O 1 '82-p31
TES-Ja 13 '84-p38

* * *

JACKSON, Sylvia
Change
TES-Ap 1 '83-p36
Electricity
TES-Ap 1 '83-p36
Energy
TES-Mr 6 '81-p38
Heat
TES-Ap 1 '83-p36
Introducing Science
TES-O 1 '82-p44
Light
TES-Mr 6 '81-p38
Living, Dead Or Never Alive
TES-Mr 6 '81-p38
Our Environment
TES-Ap 1 '83-p36
Solids, Liquids And Gases
TES-Mr 6 '81-p38
Structure And Function
TES-Ap 1 '83-p36

* * *

JACKSON Family Series
Spec-v241-D 16 '78-p22

* * *

JACOB, Helen Pierce
The Diary Of The Strawbridge Place
BL-v74-Ap 15 '78-p1350
CCB-B-v32-S '78-p10
CE-v55-N '78-p102
KR-v46-Ap 1 '78-p375
SE-v43-Ap '79-p298
SLJ-v24-Ap '78-p85
A Garland For Gandhi
HB-v45-F '69-p47
LJ-v94-My 15 '69-p2102
The Secret Of The Strawbridge Place
Am-v135-D 11 '76-p429
BL-v72-My 15 '76-p1337
BL-v73-D 15 '76-p615
BS-v36-Ag '76-p150

JACOB, Helen Pierce
(continued)
KR-v44-Ap 15 '76-p470
SLJ-v22-My '76-p77
SLJ-v24-F '78-p35

* * *

JACOBS, Allan D
Sports And Games In Verse And Rhyme
SLJ-v22-Ja '76-p38

* * *

JACOBS, Anita
Where Has Deedie Wooster Been All These Years?
BL-v78-D 15 '81-p548
BS-v41-F '82-p441
CBRS-v10-D '81-p38
CCB-B-v35-Mr '82-p131
Kliatt-v17-Spring '83-p8
SLJ-v28-O '81-p151
VOYA-v5-Ap '82-p36

* * *

JACOBS, David
Beethoven
BL-v66-Je 1 '70-p1214
BS-v30-Ap 1 '70-p18
CCB-B-v24-Jl '70-p180
CSM-v62-My 7 '70-pB7
KR-v38-F 1 '70-p115
LJ-v96-Jl '71-p2373
PW-v197-Mr 30 '70-p65
SR-v53-My 9 '70-p70
TLS-O 30 '70-p1268
Chaplin, The Movies, & Charlie
BL-v72-N 15 '75-p444
BL-v72-N 15 '75-p454
CCB-B-v29-My '76-p146
HB-v51-O '75-p476
Inst-v85-N '75-p158
KR-v43-Jl 15 '75-p785
PW-v208-Jl 28 '75-p124
SLJ-v22-F '76-p53
Disney's America On Parade
SLJ-v22-Mr '76-p104

* * *

JACOBS, Dee
Laura's Gift
SLJ-v28-D '81-p65

* * *

JACOBS, Flora G
The Haunted Birdhouse
CCB-B-v24-O '70-p28
KR-v38-My 15 '70-p553
LJ-v95-D 15 '70-p4375
A World Of Doll Houses
BL-v61-Jl 15 '65-p1064
CCB-B-v19-S '65-p11
HB-v41-Ag '65-p403
KR-v33-Ap 1 '65-p386
LJ-v90-Je 15 '65-p2895

* * *

JACOBS, Francine
Africa's Flamingo Lake
ASBYP-v14-Winter '81-p36
BL-v76-O 15 '79-p353
CCB-B-v33-Ja '80-p97
CLW-v51-My '80-p460
KR-v47-S 15 '79-p1070
RT-v33-Mr '80-p734
SB-v15-My '80-p263
SLJ-v26-Ap '80-p111
Barracuda
ACSB-v15-Winter '82-p32
BL-v78-O 15 '81-p306
CE-v59-S '82-p60
KR-v49-N 15 '81-p1412
SB-v17-Mr '82-p216
SLJ-v28-N '81-p78
Bermuda Petrel
BL-v77-My 1 '81-p1197
BW-v11-My 10 '81-p16
CSM-v73-Mr 16 '81-p23
HB-v57-Ap '81-p203
Inst-v91-Ap '82-p22
KR-v49-Ap 1 '81-p434
RT-v35-F '82-p620
SLJ-v27-Mr '81-p146
Coral
ASBYP-v14-Winter '81-p37
BL-v77-O 15 '80-p332
KR-v48-O 1 '80-p1297
SB-v16-Mr '81-p219
SLJ-v27-D '80-p70
Cosmic Countdown
BL-v79-Je 15 '83-p1331
CBRS-v12-S '83-p9
SLJ-v30-O '83-p169
Fire Snake
BL-v77-O 1 '80-p253
BOT-v4-F '81-p79
CE-v57-N '80-p114
HB-v56-O '80-p535
KR-v48-S 1 '80-p1168
NYTBR-v86-Ja 18 '81-p31
The Freshwater Eel
BL-v70-N 15 '73-p340
CLW-v45-Mr '74-p398
CSM-v65-N 7 '73-pB5
HB-v49-D '73-p613
KR-v41-Jl 1 '73-p688
LJ-v99-Ap 15 '74-p1220
PW-v204-S 10 '73-p52
SB-v10-My '74-p75
The Legs Of The Moon
CCB-B-v24-Jl '71-p172
CSM-v63-Jl 3 '71-p17
KR-v39-My 1 '71-p498
LJ-v96-O 15 '71-p3459
NYTBR-Je 20 '71-p8
Nature's Light
BL-v71-S 15 '74-p100
KR-v42-Jl 15 '74-p746
SB-v11-My '75-p34
The Red Sea
ACSB-v12-Fall '79-p34
BL-v75-N 1 '78-p479
KR-v46-O 1 '78-p1074
SLJ-v25-D '78-p53
The Sargasso Sea
BL-v72-N 15 '75-p454
KR-v43-Jl 15 '75-p780
SLJ-v22-Mr '76-p93
A Secret Language Of Animals
ACSB-v10-Spring '77-p25
BL-v73-F 15 '77-p897
CLW-v48-Ap '77-p406
KR-v44-O 15 '76-p1142
SB-v13-S '77-p97
SLJ-v23-F '77-p72
Sewer Sam
ACSB-v13-Mr '80-p31
KR-v48-F 1 '80-p131
SB-v16-N '80-p94
SLJ-v26-F '80-p46
Sounds In The Sea
BB-v6-My '78-p4
BL-v74-F 1 '78-p925
KR-v45-N 15 '77-p1201
SB-v14-D '78-p182
SLJ-v24-Mr '78-p130
Teacher-v96-Mr '79-p32
Supersaurus
BL-v79-S 15 '82-p122
CCB-B-v36-D '82-p70
HB-v59-F '83-p81
KR-v50-Je 15 '82-p677
SA-v247-D '82-p34
SB-v18-Ja '83-p146
SLJ-v29-F '83-p67
The Wisher's Handbook
CCB-B-v23-O '69-p26
LJ-v94-Mr 15 '69-p1319

*   *   *

JACOBS, Frank
Alvin Steadfast On Vernacular Island
BW-Jl 8 '79-pE2
CCB-B-v19-Ja '66-p83
LJ-v91-Ja 15 '66-p426
NYRB-v5-D 9 '65-p39
NYTBR-v70-N 21 '65-p60
Nat R-v17-D 14 '65-p1165
Mad Goes Wild
SLJ-v28-O '81-p140
VOYA-v4-O '81-p48

*   *   *

JACOBS, Helen Hull
Courage To Conquer
BS-v27-Ja 1 '68-p393
CCB-B-v21-My '68-p144
KR-v35-N 1 '67-p1318
LJ-v92-D 15 '67-p4623
NO-v7-Ja 15 '68-p20
Famous Modern American Women Athletes
KR-v43-N 1 '75-p1234
SLJ-v22-D '75-p69
SLJ-v22-My '76-p80
The Tennis Machine
BS-v31-Mr 15 '72-p566
CCB-B-v25-My '72-p141
KR-v40-F 15 '72-p202
LJ-v97-My 15 '72-p1931

*   *   *

JACOBS, Joseph
Celtic Fairy Tales
Choice-v15-D '78-p1328
LJ-v97-Ja 15 '72-p282
PW-v193-F 26 '68-p179
PW-v199-My 3 '71-p57
Spec-v224-My 9 '70-p624
TLS-Ap 16 '70-p420
Coo-My-Dove, My Dear
BL-v73-N 1 '76-p409
HB-v52-O '76-p492
KR-v44-Jl 1 '76-p726
LA-v54-Mr '77-p329
SLJ-v23-O '76-p108
English Fairy Tales
B&B-v16-F '71-p54
BL-v76-Je 15 '80-p1541
Brit Bk N-Ag '84-p455
Brit Bk N C-Autumn '80-p3
NYTBR, pt.2-F 13 '72-p8
Obs-Ja 10 '71-p23
SLJ-v27-S '80-p60
TES-Ag 31 '84-p21
TLS-Je 6 '68-p585
TLS-Ag 10 '84-p902
Henny-Penny
HB-v46-Ag '70-p379
TN-v27-N '70-p90
Hudden And Dudden And Donald O'Neary
BL-v64-Jl 15 '68-p1286
CCB-B-v22-O '68-p30
KR-v36-My 1 '68-p508
LJ-v93-Je 15 '68-p2532
SR-v51-S 21 '68-p36
Jack And The Beanstalk
BL-v72-S 1 '75-p41
HB-v43-F '67-p59
KR-v43-Je 15 '75-p657
NYTBR-v71-N 6 '66-p68
PW-v208-Jl 7 '75-p86
SLJ-v22-S '75-p84
TLS-Ap 4 '75-p366
Master Of All Masters
BL-v69-Ap 15 '73-p812
HB-v49-F '73-p41
KR-v40-S 15 '72-p1093
LJ-v98-Ja 15 '73-p253
NYTBR-D 17 '72-p8
Mr. Miacca: An English Folk Tale
Am-v117-N 4 '67-p514
BL-v64-S 15 '67-p130
CCB-B-v21-S '67-p9
HB-v43-Ag '67-p456
KR-v35-Je 15 '67-p692
LJ-v92-Jl '67-p2644
NYTBR-v72-Jl 9 '67-p34
SR-v50-S 16 '67-p48
Trav-v24-Ja '68-p224
Munachar & Manachar
BL-v67-Ja 15 '71-p421
CCB-B-v24-My '71-p136
HB-v47-F '71-p48
KR-v38-O 1 '70-p1092
LJ-v95-N 15 '70-p4036
PW-v198-D 7 '70-p50
Old Mother Wiggle-Waggle
GP-v14-O '75-p2712
SLJ-v27-F '81-p57
The Stars In The Sky
BL-v76-D 15 '79-p613
CCB-B-v33-Mr '80-p135
KR-v48-F 1 '80-p121
PW-v217-Ja 18 '80-p141
SLJ-v26-F '80-p57

*   *   *

JACOBS, Karen F
The Story Of A Young Gymnast Tracee Talavera
Inter BC-v12-#3 '81-p17
SLJ-v27-D '80-p76

*   *   *

JACOBS, Karen Folger
Girl Sports
Inter BC-v12-#1 '81-p13
LJ-v103-My 15 '78-p1075
SLJ-v24-My '78-p86
WLB-v52-Ap '78-p639

*   *   *

JACOBS, Leland B
Funny Bone Ticklers In Verse And Rhyme
LJ-v99-F 15 '74-p563
RT-v32-N '78-p148
Is Somewhere Always Far Away?
BW-v1-D 24 '67-p10
CCB-B-v21-Ja '68-p79
CE-v44-My '68-p561
KR-v35-Jl 15 '67-p805
LJ-v92-O 15 '67-p3840
Poetry For Bird Watchers
CCB-B-v24-My '71-p137
CLW-v42-Ap '71-p519
Inst-v130-Ap '71-p135
LJ-v95-D 15 '70-p4371
Teeny-Tiny
SLJ-v23-S '76-p101

*   *   *

JACOBS, Linda
Annemarie Proell: Queen Of The Mountain
BL-v71-Jl 15 '75-p1191
CLW-v48-F '77-p287
Inst-v85-N '75-p158
SLJ-v22-S '75-p105
Arthur Ashe: Alone In The Crowd
BL-v72-Jl 1 '76-p1527
SLJ-v23-S '76-p118
Barbara Jordan: Keeping Faith
SLJ-v26-S '79-p140
Cathy Rigby: On The Beam
SLJ-v21-My '75-p72
Cher: Simply Cher
SLJ-v22-D '75-p52
Cindy Nelson: North Country Skier
BL-v73-S 15 '76-p176

JACOBS, William Jay (continued)
NYTBR-v88-N 13 '83-p41
PW-v224-N 18 '83-p72
SLJ-v30-F '84-p74
Mother, Aunt Susan And Me
BL-v76-S 15 '79-p120
CBRS-v8-S '79-p9
CCB-B-v33-Ja '80-p97
Inter BC-v11-My '80-p15
Inter BC-v13-#1 '82-p5
KR-v47-S 15 '79-p1070
Robert Cavelier De La Salle
BL-v72-D 1 '75-p516
BS-v35-D '75-p296
KR-v43-N 1 '75-p1234
SLJ-v22-N '75-p78
Roger Williams
BL-v71-My 15 '75-p965
CCB-B-v29-S '75-p12
KR-v43-Ja 15 '75-p73
SLJ-v21-Mr '75-p98
Samuel De Champlain
BL-v70-Je 1 '74-p1105
CE-v51-Ja '75-p159
KR-v42-Mr 1 '74-p249
William Bradford Of Plymouth Colony
BL-v71-Ja 1 '75-p461
KR-v42-S 1 '74-p947
SLJ-v21-Ja '75-p46

* * *

JACOBSEN, Karen
Computers
BL-v78-Je 15 '82-p1365
SB-v18-Ja '83-p144
SLJ-v29-O '82-p137
Farm Animals
ASBYP-v15-Spring '82-p53
BL-v78-F 15 '82-p760
SB-v18-S '82-p33
SLJ-v28-D '81-p78
Health
SLJ-v28-D '81-p78
Japan
BL-v79-Mr 1 '83-p902
SLJ-v30-S '83-p108
SLJ-v30-N '83-p39
Mexico
BL-v79-Mr 1 '83-p902
SLJ-v30-S '83-p108
Stamps
BL-v80-F 15 '84-p854
SLJ-v30-Ap '84-p101
Television
ASBYP-v16-Fall '83-p66
BL-v79-Mr 1 '83-p902
CCB-B-v36-Ap '83-p152
Zoos
ASBYP-v16-Fall '83-p66
BL-v79-Mr 1 '83-p902
SB-v19-N '83-p98
SLJ-v29-Ag '83-p52

* * *

JACOBSEN, Peter O
A Family In France
TES-Mr 9 '84-p53
A Family In Mexico
TES-Mr 9 '84-p53

* * *

JACOBSON, Daniel
The Fishermen
KR-v43-S 15 '75-p1071
SB-v12-S '76-p108
The Gatherers
BL-v74-S 1 '77-p42
CCB-B-v30-Ap '77-p127
Cur R-v17-Ag '78-p180
Inst-v86-My '77-p126
SLJ-v23-Ap '77-p77
The North Central States
BL-v80-Ap 15 '84-p1186
SLJ-v30-Ag '84-p74

* * *

JACOBSON, Jane
City, Sing For Me
SLJ-v25-O '78-p134

* * *

JACOBSON, Morris K
Wonders Of Corals And Coral Reefs
ACSB-v13-Spring '80-p41
BL-v75-Jl 15 '79-p1627
CCB-B-v33-D '79-p72
SB-v15-Mr '80-p226
Wonders Of Jellyfish
ACSB-v12-Spring '79-p29
BL-v75-S 1 '78-p50
KR-v46-Ag 1 '78-p810
SB-v15-S '79-p102
SLJ-v25-N '78-p76
Wonders Of Sponges
ACSB-v10-Winter '77-p24
BL-v73-S 1 '76-p39
KR-v44-Je 1 '76-p638
SB-v12-Mr '77-p212
SLJ-v23-S '76-p134
Wonders Of Starfish
BL-v74-S 15 '77-p195
CCB-B-v31-N '77-p49
HB-v54-Je '78-p306
KR-v45-Jl 1 '77-p670
SB-v14-S '78-p113
SLJ-v24-D '77-p54
Teacher-v95-Mr '78-p116
Wonders Of The World Of Shells
CCB-B-v25-N '71-p45
KR-v39-My 15 '71-p557
LJ-v96-S 15 '71-p2918
SB-v7-D '71-p242

* * *

JACOBSON, Willard J
Science Activities For Children
BL-v79-Mr 15 '83-p934
Cur R-v22-O '83-p74
Inst-v93-S '83-p192
SB-v18-My '83-p272

* * *

JACQUEMIER, S
Spotter's Guide To Woodland Life
JB-v43-D '79-p327

* * *

JAFFE, Charlotte S
On The Road To Creativity
Cur R-v24-N '84-p24

* * *

JAFFE, Ivan
Illustrated Ballet Dictionary
SLJ-v26-Ap '80-p111

* * *

JAFFEE, Al
Ghastly Jokes
NYTBR-My 1 '77-p34
SLJ-v24-S '77-p110

* * *

JAGENDORF, M A
The Magic Boat And Other Chinese Folk Stories
CBRS-v9-Winter '81-p48
CCB-B-v34-F '81-p113
LJ-v105-N 15 '80-p2427
SLJ-v27-My '81-p65

* * *

JAGENDORF, Moritz A
The Ghost Of Peg-Leg Peter
BL-v62-Ap 1 '66-p775
CCB-B-v21-D '67-p60
HB-v42-Je '66-p306
KR-v33-S 1 '65-p900
LJ-v91-Mr 15 '66-p1701

JAMES, T G H (continued)
LJ-v98-My 15 '73-p1689
NY-v49-D 3 '73-p219
Obs-Jl 16 '72-p31
PW-v203-Ap 2 '73-p65
SLJ-v25-S '78-p43
TLS-Jl 14 '72-p810

* * *

JAMES Madison: The Detailed True-Life Story Of The Man Who Helped Frame The U.S. Constitution
SLJ-v23-Ap '77-p59

* * *

JAMESON, Cynthia
Catofy The Clever
CCB-B-v26-D '72-p58
CLW-v43-Ap '72-p478
KR-v40-F 1 '72-p131
LJ-v97-D 15 '72-p4067
The Clay Pot Boy
BL-v69-Je 1 '73-p948
BW-My 4 '75-p4
CCB-B-v26-Je '73-p156
CE-v50-N '73-p98
GP-v14-Jl '75-p2671
JB-v39-F '75-p22
KR-v41-Ja 1 '73-p3
LJ-v98-My 15 '73-p1696
NYTBR-Ap 22 '73-p8
NYTBR-N 4 '73-p57
PW-v203-F 26 '73-p124
RT-v35-D '81-p333
SLJ-v28-F '82-p37
TLS-D 6 '74-p1378
Teacher-v92-Ap '75-p112
A Day With Whisker Wickles
KR-v43-My 15 '75-p563
NYTBR-My 4 '75-p43
PW-v207-Je 2 '75-p54
SLJ-v22-S '75-p84
The Flying Shoes
BL-v70-S 15 '73-p120
CCB-B-v27-N '73-p45
CE-v50-Mr '74-p293
LJ-v98-S 15 '73-p2640
The House Of Five Bears
CBRS-v7-Winter '79-p54
CCB-B-v32-F '79-p100
KR-v46-N 15 '78-p1241
SLJ-v25-D '78-p65
Mr. Wolf Gets Ready For Supper
CCB-B-v28-Jl '75-p178
KR-v43-Mr 15 '75-p304
LA-v53-My '76-p507
SLJ-v21-My '75-p68
The Secret Of The Royal Mounds
BL-v77-N 15 '80-p459
CCB-B-v34-Ja '81-p96
KR-v48-D 1 '80-p1520
SLJ-v27-Mr '81-p146
Tales From The Steppes
BL-v72-F 1 '76-p787
CE-v53-O '76-p34
HB-v52-Ap '76-p151
KR-v43-D 1 '75-p1335
RT-v35-N '81-p200
SLJ-v22-F '76-p46
Winter Hut
CE-v50-N '73-p98
KR-v41-Je 15 '73-p639
LJ-v98-D 15 '73-p3716
RT-v35-D '81-p333

* * *

JAMESON, Jon
Monsters Of The Mountains
ASBYP-v14-Winter '81-p39
SLJ-v26-My '80-p83
Sch Lib-v28-S '80-p276
The Picture Life Of O.J. Simpson
Comw-v104-N 11 '77-p734
SLJ-v23-My '77-p80
Teacher-v96-O '78-p174

* * *

JAMESON, Kenneth
Art And The Young Child
Choice-v6-Jl '69-p688
HB-v45-Ag '69-p427
LJ-v94-F 15 '69-p752
RR-v86-Mr '69-p177

* * *

JAMIESON, Alan
Cars, Boats, Trains And Planes
TES-Jl 17 '81-p26
Castles, Churches And Houses
TES-Jl 17 '81-p26
Find Out For Yourself
TES-Mr 6 '81-p37
TES-Mr 13 '81-p28
Letter Writing
TES-F 3 '84-p31
The Spelling And Writing Word Book
TES-My 19 '78-p32
Spelling Problems And Puzzles
TES-Jl 11 '80-p30

* * *

JAMIESON, David
Mary Chipperfield's Circus Book
GP-v18-N '79-p3603

* * *

JAMPOLSKY, Gerald G
Children As Teachers Of Peace
Cur R-v22-My '83-p139
New Age-v8-O '82-p64

* * *

JANECZKO, Paul
Don't Forget To Fly
BL-v78-Mr 1 '82-p853
CBRS-v10-F '82-p68
CCB-B-v35-Mr '82-p131
EJ-v71-S '82-p87
HB-v58-Je '82-p303
PW-v220-O 16 '81-p78
SLJ-v28-D '81-p71
VOYA-v5-Ap '82-p46

* * *

JANECZKO, Paul B
Poetspeak
BL-v79-Jl '83-p1396
B Rpt-v2-Ja '84-p39
CBRS-v11-Jl '83-p138
EJ-v73-Ja '84-p89
HB-v59-D '83-p721
PW-v223-Je 10 '83-p64
SLJ-v30-S '83-p135
SLJ-v30-Ag '84-p39
SLMQ-v12-Spring '84-p189
VOYA-v6-F '84-p348
Postcard Poems
BL-v76-N 1 '79-p441
CCB-B-v33-Ap '80-p154
EJ-v69-Ap '80-p85
HB-v56-F '80-p69
NYTBR-v85-Ap 27 '80-p61
SLJ-v26-My '80-p76
Strings
BL-v80-Jl '84-p1543
B Rpt-v3-S '84-p40
CBRS-v12-Ag '84-p151
CCB-B-v37-Je '84-p187
HB-v60-Ag '84-p482
SLJ-v31-S '84-p129

JANSSON, Tove (continued)
KR-v43-F 15 '75-p194
PW-v207-Mr 17 '75-p48
PW-v209-My 24 '76-p59
SLJ-v21-Ap '75-p66
TLS-D 5 '75-p1460
WSJ-v185-Je 20 '75-p8
Tales From Moominvalley
Par-v52-My '77-p31
Who Will Comfort Toffle?
CCB-B-v23-My '70-p145
CSM-v62-Ja 15 '70-p5
KR-v37-O 1 '69-p3757

* * *

JANULEWICZ, Mike
Plants
BL-v80-Je 15 '84-p1484
TES-N 11 '83-p26

* * *

JANVIER, Jeannine
Fabulous Birds You Can Make
SLJ-v23-Ap '77-p66
Fantastic Fish You Can Make
BL-v73-Mr 1 '77-p1013
SLJ-v23-Ap '77-p66

* * *

JAPUONJO, Roeland
Mzee Nyachote
BL-v73-Jl 15 '77-p1734

* * *

JAQUES, Edna
Prairie Born, Prairie Bred
In Rev-v14-F '80-p48

* * *

JAQUES, Faith
Kidnap In Willowbank Wood
JB-v47-F '83-p14
Sch Lib-v31-Mr '83-p25
Little Grey Rabbit's House
JB-v47-Ap '83-p76
Our Village Shop
GP-v22-Ja '84-p4198
PW-v225-Mr 2 '84-p94
Tilly's House
BL-v76-S 1 '79-p44
CBRS-v8-Winter '80-p66
CE-v56-Ap '80-p304
GP-v18-Ja '80-p3618
JB-v43-D '79-p317
KR-v47-D 15 '79-p1428
LA-v57-My '80-p554
NYTBR-D 30 '79-p19
Obs-O 7 '79-p39
PW-v216-Jl 16 '79-p70
RT-v34-N '80-p235
SLJ-v26-F '80-p46
TES-N 23 '79-p31
TLS-D 14 '79-p127
Tilly's Rescue
BL-v77-Ap 1 '81-p1104
BW-v11-D 13 '81-p13
Brit Bk N C-Spring '81-p20
CBRS-v10-S '81-p4
CCB-B-v35-S '81-p11
CE-v58-N '81-p109
GP-v20-S '81-p3936
HB-v57-Je '81-p293
JB-v45-Je '81-p107
KR-v49-My 15 '81-p631
PW-v219-Ja 9 '81-p73
RT-v35-D '81-p366
SLJ-v28-O '81-p155
TES-D 26 '80-p17

* * *

JAQUITH, Priscilla
Bo Rabbit Smart For True
BL-v78-S 15 '81-p106
BW-v11-O 11 '81-p10
CBRS-v10-Jl '81-p113
CCB-B-v35-S '81-p11
HB-v57-D '81-p674
KR-v49-S 15 '81-p1163
RT-v35-My '82-p975
SA-v245-D '81-p41
SLJ-v28-S '81-p109
VV-v26-D 9 '81-p58
WLB-v56-Je '82-p771

* * *

JARMAN, J
Junior Soccer
JB-v40-Ag '76-p220

* * *

JARMAN, Rosemary Hawley
We Speak No Treason
A Lib-v2-O '71-p1010
Atl-v229-Ja '72-p96
BS-v31-S 1 '71-p251
CSM-v63-N 4 '71-p11
HB-v48-Ap '72-p170
KR-v39-Jl 15 '71-p765
KR-v39-Ag 1 '71-p822
LJ-v96-O 1 '71-p3159
Life-v71-S 10 '71-p14
Obs-Ap 4 '71-p37
PW-v200-Jl 5 '71-p48
TLS-My 14 '71-p571
Time-v99-Ja 3 '72-p68

* * *

JARNER, Bo
My New Sister
JB-v41-O '77-p278
TES-Mr 10 '78-p57

* * *

JAROCH, F A
The Adventures Of The Sneeky Sneekers
SLJ-v24-Ap '78-p85
The Ghost Of Gleason Mansion
SLJ-v25-S '78-p140
Washout At Liberty Valley
CBRS-v7-Winter '79-p55
SLJ-v25-Mr '79-p124

* * *

JARRELL, Mary
The Knee-Baby
CCB-B-v27-My '74-p145
CE-v50-Ap '74-p336
KR-v41-N 15 '73-p1258
LJ-v99-F 15 '74-p563
PW-v204-N 26 '73-p38

* * *

JARRELL, Randall
Animal Family
Lis-v78-N 16 '67-p643
The Animal Family
BL-v62-Ja 15 '66-p487
CCB-B-v19-F '66-p100
CE-v43-S '66-p44
CM-v8-Winter '67-p123
GT-v83-My '66-p33
HB-v42-F '66-p45
HM-v232-Mr '66-p152
Inst-v81-F '72-p139
JB-v40-Ag '76-p232
LJ-v90-D 15 '65-p5516
NO-v5-Mr 14 '66-p20
NYTBR-v70-N 21 '65-p56
NYTBR, pt.2-N 7 '71-p46
NYTBR, pt.2-F 13 '72-p12
Par-v41-Je '66-p76
Par-v41-Ag '66-p70
SR-v48-D 11 '65-p44
TCR-v67-My '66-p640
TLS-Ap 2 '76-p392
The Animal Farm
A Lib-v8-My '77-p270
A Bat Is Born
Am-v139-D 9 '78-p440
BB-v6-N '78-p2
CCB-B-v31-Mr '78-p113
Cur R-v17-My '78-p140

JARRELL, Randall (continued)
KR-v46-Ja 15 '78-p45
LA-v55-S '78-p742
NYTBR-Mr 19 '78-p30
PW-v213-Ja 2 '78-p64
RT-v32-O '78-p92
SB-v14-D '78-p182
SLJ-v24-Mr '78-p119
Sierra-v63-S '78-p47
The Bat-Poet
BW-Jl 10 '77-pH10
HB-v57-Ag '81-p453
JB-v42-Je '78-p141
NYTBR-Ap 3 '77-p52
Obs-D 11 '77-p31
SLMQ-v11-Spring '83-p192
SR-v4-My 28 '77-p33
TES-F 3 '78-p44
TLS-D 2 '77-p1413
Fly By Night
B&B-v23-Ja '78-p64
BL-v73-N 15 '76-p474
BW-Ja 9 '77-pK4
CCB-B-v30-F '77-p92
HB-v53-F '77-p52
JB-v42-F '78-p27
KR-v44-O 15 '76-p1137
LA-v54-My '77-p583
NO-v15-D 25 '76-p15
NYTBR-N 14 '76-p25
New R-v176-Ja 1 '77-p30
Obs-D 11 '77-p31
SLJ-v23-N '76-p59
TES-N 18 '77-p31
TLS-D 2 '77-p1413
Snow White And The Seven Dwarfs
Emerg Lib-v11-Ja '84-p19

* * *

JARUNKOVA, Klara
Don't Cry For Me
BL-v65-O 15 '68-p234
BS-v28-Ag 1 '68-p195
CCB-B-v22-O '68-p30
EJ-v58-F '69-p295
LJ-v93-My 15 '68-p2123
NYTBR-v73-S 22 '68-p28
RT-v33-Mr '80-p688
YR-v5-O '68-p1
O Tomazu, Ki Se Ni Bal Teme
BL-v80-Je 1 '84-p1402

* * *

JARVEY, Paulette S
You Can Dough It!
LJ-v106-Ap 1 '81-p786

* * *

JARVIS, Sally Melcher
Fried Onions & Marshmallows And Other Little Plays For Little People
CCB-B-v22-Mr '69-p112
LJ-v94-Mr 15 '69-p1319

* * *

JASPERSOHN, William
The Ballpark
BL-v76-Jl 1 '80-p1613
BOT-v4-F '81-p80
BW-v10-Jl 20 '80-p6
CCB-B-v33-My '80-p173
CE-v57-Ja '81-p175
HB-v56-Je '80-p313
Inst-v89-My '80-p92
KR-v48-Je 15 '80-p781
NYTBR-v85-Ap 27 '80-p47
SLJ-v26-My '80-p88
A Day In The Life Of A Marine Biologist
ASBYP-v16-Winter '83-p34
BL-v78-Je 1 '82-p1313
BL-v80-O 15 '83-p369
B Rpt-v2-N '83-p51
CCB-B-v35-Jl '82-p209
HB-v58-O '82-p551
KR-v50-Ap 15 '82-p492
PW-v221-My 14 '82-p216
SB-v18-N '82-p76
SLJ-v29-Ja '83-p85
A Day In The Life Of A Television News Reporter
BL-v77-My 15 '81-p1254
CCB-B-v34-Jl '81-p213
KR-v49-Jl 1 '81-p803
PW-v219-My 8 '81-p255
SLJ-v28-N '81-p92
A Day In The Life Of A Veterinarian
BL-v75-D 15 '78-p687
CCB-B-v32-Ap '79-p139
CLW-v50-My '79-p448
Inst-v88-My '79-p115
KR-v47-F 1 '79-p129
SB-v15-Mr '80-p231
SLJ-v25-Ja '79-p54
How The Forest Grew
ACSB-v13-Mr '80-p32
BL-v76-Mr 15 '80-p1065
BL-v80-O 15 '83-p369
CE-v58-S '81-p50
CLW-v52-O '80-p133
HB-v56-O '80-p535
Inst-v89-My '80-p92
KR-v48-Ap 15 '80-p512
RT-v34-D '80-p352
SB-v16-Ja '81-p154
SLJ-v26-My '80-p83
Magazine
BL-v79-Je 15 '83-p1339
BW-v13-Je 12 '83-p9
EJ-v73-F '84-p105
HB-v59-Je '83-p322
J Read-v27-D '83-p281
KR-v51-Mr 15 '83-p312
LA-v61-F '84-p187
NYTBR-v88-Je 5 '83-p34
PW-v223-My 13 '83-p56
SE-v48-My '84-p370
SLJ-v29-Ag '83-p76

* * *

JASSEM, Kate
Chief Joseph: Leader Of Destiny
SLJ-v26-Ag '80-p63
Pocahontas: Girl Of Jamestown
SLJ-v26-Ag '80-p63
Sacajawea: Wilderness Guide
CCB-B-v33-N '79-p49
Inter BC-v11-My '80-p15
SLJ-v26-Ag '80-p63
Squanto: The Pilgrim Adventure
SLJ-v26-Ag '80-p63

* * *

JATAKAS. Selections
Jataka Tales (DeRoin)
BL-v71-Je 1 '75-p1013

* * *

JAUREGUI, A L
400 Adivinanzas Infantiles
BL-v81-O 1 '84-p256

* * *

JAUREGUIBERRY, Martine
The Wonderful Rainy Week
BL-v79-My 15 '83-p1218
CBRS-v11-Je '83-p111

* * *

JAY, Michael
Airports
JB-v46-Je '82-p98
SLJ-v29-Ja '83-p61
Cars
SLJ-v30-S '83-p108

JAY, Michael (continued)
The Moon
ASBYP-v16-Winter '83-p34
BL-v79-S 1 '82-p45
CE-v60-S '83-p56
JB-v46-Je '82-p98
SLJ-v29-Ja '83-p61
TES-N 5 '82-p28
Space Shuttle
BL-v80-Je 15 '84-p1483
JB-v48-Je '84-p128
SLJ-v31-S '84-p119
Spacecraft
ASBYP-v17-Winter '84-p28
CBRS-v11-Je '83-p115
JB-v47-Je '83-p115
SB-v19-Ja '84-p154
SLJ-v30-S '83-p124
Sch Lib-v31-Je '83-p155

* * *

JAYNES, Ruth
Los Cuatro Sombreros De Benny
SLJ-v30-My '84-p35

* * *

JEFFERDS, Vincent
Disney's Elegant ABC Book
NYTBR-v88-O 9 '83-p9
SLJ-v30-Ja '84-p65

* * *

JEFFERIES, Lawrence
Air, Air, Air
ASBYP-v17-Spring '84-p55
SB-v20-N '84-p93
SLJ-v30-F '84-p55
All About Stars
ASBYP-v17-Spring '84-p55
SB-v19-Ja '84-p154
SLJ-v30-F '84-p55
Amazing World Of Animals
ASBYP-v17-Spring '84-p55
SB-v19-Ja '84-p158

* * *

JEFFERIES, Richard
Bevis
B&B-v20-Jl '75-p62
TES-My 1 '81-p25

* * *

JEFFERIS, David
Robots
JB-v47-F '83-p27
SLJ-v30-S '83-p102
Trailbikes
BL-v80-Je 15 '84-p1483
GP-My '84-p4267
JB-v48-Je '84-p128
SLJ-v31-S '84-p119

* * *

JEFFERS, Susan
All The Pretty Horses
BL-v71-S 15 '74-p100
CCB-B-v28-Ja '75-p79
CLW-v46-Ap '75-p406
HB-v51-F '75-p44
KR-v42-O 1 '74-p1058
LJ-v99-N 15 '74-p3038
NYTBR-F 2 '75-p8
PT-v8-D '74-p131
PW-v206-Ag 26 '74-p307
Teacher-v92-Ja '75-p109
VV-v19-D 16 '74-p51
Three Jovial Huntsmen
A Art-v41-D '77-p34
B&B-Jl '82-p35
BL-v70-D 15 '73-p446
BW-F 10 '74-p4
CE-v50-Mr '74-p294
CLW-v55-O '83-p131
CSM-v66-My 1 '74-pF2
CSM-v69-N 2 '77-pB1
Choice-v12-N '75-p1133
HB-v50-F '74-p37
KR-v41-N 15 '73-p1258
KR-v41-D 15 '73-p1348
LJ-v98-D 15 '73-p3701
NYTBR-N 4 '73-p61
TES-N 5 '82-p27
TLS-Jl 5 '74-p718
TN-v30-Ap '74-p247
Teacher-v91-F '74-p100
Teacher-v91-My '74-p78
Wild Robin
BL-v73-Ja 15 '77-p719
CE-v60-My '84-p344
HB-v53-Ap '77-p150
Inst-v86-My '77-p118
KR-v44-D 1 '76-p1261
LA-v54-Mr '77-p328
PW-v210-D 6 '76-p62
RT-v31-O '77-p14
SLJ-v23-Ja '77-p82
Teacher-v94-My '77-p107

* * *

JEFFERSON, Thomas
Thomas Jefferson; A Biography In His Own Words
BL-v71-N 15 '74-p337
BW-S 15 '74-p4
Choice-v12-Mr '75-p136
HB-v51-Ap '75-p173

* * *

JEFFERY, G
Erinord
GP-v15-O '76-p2960
JB-v41-Ap '77-p114
TLS-O 1 '76-p1242

* * *

JEFFRIES, R
Peril At Sea
JB-v47-D '83-p258

* * *

JEFFRIES, Richard
Bevis (Puffin)
BW-v14-O 14 '84-p11

* * *

JEFFRIES, Roderic
Against Time!
Inst-v89-Ja '80-p114
NYTBR-v85-Jl 6 '80-p19
SLJ-v24-F '78-p35
The Boy Who Knew Too Much
GP-v16-S '77-p3163
JB-v41-O '77-p303
TLS-Jl 15 '77-p861
Dick Knox At Le Mans
KR-v42-Je 15 '74-p639
LJ-v99-D 15 '74-p3281
Eighteen Desperate Hours
GP-v18-Jl '79-p3546
JB-v44-F '80-p28
Grand Prix Monaco
CCB-B-v22-Jl '69-p170
The Missing Man
Brit Bk N C-Autumn '80-p22
JB-v45-F '81-p28
TES-O 1 '82-p31
Patrol Car
BL-v63-Jl 15 '67-p1193
CCB-B-v21-S '67-p10
HB-v43-Je '67-p354
KR-v35-F 1 '67-p138
LJ-v92-My 15 '67-p2039
PW-v191-Je 12 '67-p59
Police Dog
Am-v113-N 20 '65-p640
BL-v62-O 1 '65-p161
CCB-B-v19-Ja '66-p83
HB-v41-O '65-p505
KR-v33-Jl 1 '65-p629
LJ-v90-N 15 '65-p5103
NYTBR-v70-N 7 '65-p42
TLS-Je 17 '65-p518

JEFFRIES, Roderic (continued)
Teacher-v95-O '77-p168
The Riddle In The Parchment
JB-v40-Ap '76-p90
TLS-Ap 2 '76-p388
Trapped
Am-v127-D 2 '72-p477
B&B-v18-Je '73-p136
CCB-B-v25-Ap '72-p124
HB-v48-Je '72-p269
KR-v40-F 1 '72-p136
LJ-v97-Je 15 '72-p2243
Voyage Into Danger
Brit Bk N C-Spring '82-p11

* * *

JEFIMENKO, Oleg D
How To Entertain With Your Pocket Calculator
Cur R-v16-Ag '77-p213
Inst-v85-Mr '76-p132

* * *

JELINEK, Henry, Jr.
On Thin Ice
BL-v62-O 15 '65-p190
CCB-B-v19-O '65-p34
KR-v33-Je 15 '65-p599
KR-v33-Jl 1 '65-p640
LJ-v90-S 15 '65-p3598

* * *

JELKS, Peggy A
Much Ado About Math
Cur R-v21-Ag '82-p311

* * *

JELLINEK, Joanna
Georgina And The Dragon
JB-v41-O '77-p279
Obs-N 27 '77-p29
Raviola Sneezes
Brit Bk N-D '80-p714

* * *

JENKINS, A J
Earth Our Planet
TES-My 8 '81-p45

* * *

JENKINS, Alan C
Aslak The Hunter
JB-v40-Ag '76-p204
TLS-Ap 2 '76-p376
The Ghost Elephant
Brit Bk N C-Spring '82-p5
The Golden Band
BL-v65-My 1 '69-p1004
CCB-B-v22-My '69-p143
LJ-v94-S 15 '69-p3220
Spec-v218-Je 2 '67-p656
TLS-My 25 '67-p464
Great Discoveries
JB-v40-Ap '76-p92
Ice At Midsummer
GP-v17-Ja '79-p3461
HT-v21-D '71-p887
TLS-Ap 2 '71-p381
Kingdom Of The Elephants
BL-v63-S 1 '66-p55
GP-v20-My '81-p3901
KR-v34-My 1 '66-p474
LJ-v91-Je 15 '66-p3267
The Prodigal Earth
GP-v15-Ap '77-p3093
JB-v41-Ap '77-p114
The Struggle For The North And South Poles
GP-v14-Ja '76-p2793
The Winter Sleeper
JB-v41-Je '77-p162
TLS-Mr 25 '77-p360
The World Of Ghosts
CCB-B-v32-Ap '79-p139
JB-v41-F '77-p37

* * *

JENKINS, Elizabeth
The Princes In The Tower
Atl-v243-Ja '79-p98
BL-v75-Ja 1 '79-p733
BS-v38-Mr '79-p397
Choice-v16-Mr '79-p134
GP-v17-Mr '79-p3480
KR-v46-S 15 '78-p1048
LJ-v103-N 15 '78-p2329
Man-v6-N '79-p46
PW-v214-O 16 '78-p111
WCRB-v5-Ja '79-p38

* * *

JENKINS, Geoffrey
A Grue Of Ice
GP-v16-Ja '78-p3256
Spec-v231-N 17 '73-p643

* * *

JENKINS, Gerald
Mathematical Curiosities 3
BW-v13-Mr 13 '83-p12

* * *

JENKINS, Jordan
Learning About Love
Inst-v88-My '79-p107
SLJ-v26-S '79-p101

* * *

JENKINS, Marie M
Animals Without Parents
BL-v67-D 1 '70-p308
BW-v4-N 8 '70-p4
HB-v47-F '71-p70
Inst-v80-O '70-p142
LJ-v95-N 15 '70-p4054
SB-v6-Mr '71-p321
TN-v27-Ap '71-p306
Deer, Moose, Elk, And Their Family
ACSB-v13-Mr '80-p33
BL-v76-N 1 '79-p449
EJ-v70-Ja '81-p78
KR-v48-F 1 '80-p131
SLJ-v26-F '80-p67
Embryos And How They Develop
ACSB-v9-Spring '76-p25
BL-v71-My 15 '75-p958
CCB-B-v29-O '75-p28
KR-v43-My 15 '75-p578
SB-v11-Mr '76-p196
SLJ-v22-S '75-p121
Goats, Sheep, And How They Live
ACSB-v12-Winter '79-p19
BL-v74-Jl 1 '78-p1678
Cur R-v18-My '79-p149
KR-v46-Ap 1 '78-p381
SB-v14-Mr '79-p231
SLJ-v25-S '78-p140
Kangaroos, Opossums, And Other Marsupials
ACSB-v9-Spring '76-p25
BL-v72-Ja 15 '76-p684
KR-v43-O 15 '75-p1199
SB-v12-S '76-p106
SLJ-v22-Ja '76-p46

* * *

JENKINS, William A
My First Picture Dictionary
ARBA-v9-'78-p528
Inst-v87-N '77-p154
SLJ-v24-S '77-p110
SR-v53-D 5 '70-p34
My Second Picture Dictionary
RSR-v8-Ja '80-p10

* * *

JENNER, Bruce
The Olympics And Me
CCB-B-v33-My '80-p174
SLJ-v26-My '80-p90

* * *

JENNESS, Aylette
Along The Niger River
BL-v71-S 1 '74-p43
CCB-B-v28-D '74-p64
CLW-v47-O '75-p129
Choice-v12-N '75-p1133
HB-v50-O '74-p148
KR-v42-Jl 1 '74-p683
KR-v43-Ja 1 '75-p7
PW-v206-Jl 8 '74-p75
SLJ-v28-S '81-p41
The Bakery Factory
BB-v6-N '78-p2
BL-v74-Ap 1 '78-p1255
CCB-B-v31-Jl '78-p179
HB-v54-Je '78-p295
KR-v46-Mr 1 '78-p246
NYTBR-Ap 30 '78-p46
SE-v43-Ap '79-p302
SE-v44-Mr '80-p246
SLJ-v24-My '78-p68
Dwellers Of The Tundra
BL-v66-Je 15 '70-p1272
BW-v4-My 17 '70-p5
CCB-B-v24-S '70-p12
CSM-v62-My 7 '70-pB4
HB-v46-Je '70-p307
KR-v38-F 1 '70-p115
LJ-v95-My 15 '70-p1912
LJ-v95-My 15 '70-p1944
NYTBR-Mr 8 '70-p22
NYTBR, pt.2-N 8 '70-p36
PW-v197-Mr 30 '70-p65
SA-v223-D '70-p122
SR-v53-Je 27 '70-p39
A Life Of Their Own
BL-v72-Mr 1 '76-p978
CCB-B-v29-My '76-p146
KR-v43-D 15 '75-p1382
SA-v235-D '76-p141
SLJ-v22-Mr '76-p104
SLJ-v24-Ja '78-p26
SLJ-v28-S '81-p41

* * *

JENNINGS, Coleman A
Plays Children Love
BL-v78-Mr 1 '82-p900
CBRS-v10-F '82-p67
CCB-B-v35-Mr '82-p132
HB-v58-Ap '82-p179
RT-v37-Ap '84-p714
SLJ-v29-F '83-p77

* * *

JENNINGS, Elizabeth
After The Ark
JB-v43-F '79-p32
TES-N 24 '78-p42

* * *

JENNINGS, Eve
The Mine Kid Kidnap
B&B-v23-Ja '78-p64
JB-v41-D '77-p356
TES-Ja 13 '78-p22
TLS-D 2 '77-p1412

* * *

JENNINGS, Gary
Black Magic, White Magic
BL-v61-Jl 1 '65-p1029
BS-v24-F 15 '65-p454
CCB-B-v19-Ap '66-p131
CE-v42-O '65-p112
CLW-v36-My '65-p640
CLW-v37-O '65-p143
GT-v83-N '65-p123
HB-v41-Ag '65-p400
LJ-v90-Ap 15 '65-p2034
NYTBR-v70-Mr 14 '65-p30
SA-v213-D '65-p116
The Earth Book
KR-v42-N 15 '74-p1204
NYTBR-D 22 '74-p8
SE-v39-Mr '75-p174
SLJ-v21-Ja '75-p46
Parades!
BL-v63-Mr 1 '67-p728
CCB-B-v20-F '67-p91
HB-v43-F '67-p88
KR-v34-Ag 15 '66-p838
LJ-v92-Ja 15 '67-p344
NYTBR-v71-N 6 '66-p50
The Rope In The Jungle
BB-v5-F '77-p4
HB-v53-F '77-p56
KR-v44-Ag 15 '76-p909
NYTBR-S 26 '76-p14
SLJ-v23-O '76-p117
The Shrinking Outdoors
BL-v68-Ap 15 '72-p724
BW-v6-My 7 '72-p12
BW-v6-N 12 '72-p13
CCB-B-v25-Ap '72-p124
CLW-v44-O '72-p191
KR-v40-Ja 15 '72-p76
KR-v40-D 15 '72-p1424
NYTBR, pt.2-My 7 '72-p8
SB-v8-S '72-p138
SE-v37-D '73-p790
SR-v55-Je 17 '72-p76
The Teenager's Realistic Guide To Astrology
CCB-B-v25-Ap '72-p124
LJ-v96-S 15 '71-p2941
PW-v200-Jl 5 '71-p50

* * *

JENNINGS, Gordon
Minibikes
KR-v42-D 15 '74-p1310

* * *

JENNINGS, L
The Dandelion Dreamer
JB-v47-O '83-p202

* * *

JENNINGS, Linda
The Musicians Of Bremen
TES-O 12 '84-p33
The Nutcracker
Econ-v285-D 25 '82-p103
GP-v21-Ja '83-p4013
JB-v47-F '83-p14

* * *

JENNINGS, Linda M
The Christmas Tomten
BL-v78-O 15 '81-p310
BW-v11-D 13 '81-p13
CBRS-v10-N '81-p24
CCB-B-v35-N '81-p56
CLW-v53-Mr '82-p357
GP-v20-N '81-p3974
HB-v57-D '81-p655
KR-v49-O 1 '81-p1232
PW-v220-S 4 '81-p60
SLJ-v28-O '81-p155
The Prince And The Firebird
TLS-S 17 '82-p1003

* * *

JENNINGS, Michael
The Bears Who Came To Breakfix
SLJ-v25-S '78-p118
Mattie Fritts And The Cuckoo Caper
KR-v44-S 1 '76-p974
SLJ-v23-Ja '77-p93
Mattie Fritts And The Flying Mushroom
JB-v39-F '75-p40
KR-v41-Je 1 '73-p600
LJ-v98-N 15 '73-p3453
PW-v203-Je 18 '73-p70

JENNINGS, Michael (continued)
Robin Goodfellow And The Giant Dwarf
BL-v78-O 15 '81-p306
CBRS-v10-F '82-p61
PW-v220-O 30 '81-p63
SLJ-v28-My '82-p54

* * *

JENNINGS, Paul
Great Jelly Of London
Obs-N 26 '67-p28
Punch-v253-N 29 '67-p834
TLS-N 30 '67-p1137
TLS-Ap 2 '76-p395
The Train To Yesterday
JB-v39-Ap '75-p108
LR-v24-Winter '75-p366
Spec-v234-Ap 12 '75-p445
TLS-Ap 4 '75-p365

* * *

JENNINGS, Richard W
The Tragic Tale Of The Dog Who Killed Himself
CBRS-v8-Spring '80-p117
PW-v217-Mr 28 '80-p50
SLJ-v27-S '80-p72

* * *

JENNINGS, Ruth
In The Bin
GP-v18-N '79-p3607
JB-v44-Ap '80-p63
NS-v98-N 9 '79-p732
Sch Lib-v28-Je '80-p142
Spec-v243-D 15 '79-p23
TES-Ap 25 '80-p25
TLS-D 14 '79-p127

* * *

JENNINGS, Terry
Conservation Today
GP-v17-My '78-p3320
JB-v42-Ag '78-p205
TES-O 6 '78-p30
Mammals In Britain And Ireland
GP-v16-S '77-p3169
TLS-D 2 '77-p1417
Small Garden Animals
GP-v20-N '81-p3978
Studying Birds In The Garden
LR-v25-Summer '75-p81
The Wild Life In Your Home
TES-N 16 '84-p38
The World Of A Hedge
ACSB-v13-Winter '80-p29
GP-v17-S '78-p3383
JB-v42-O '78-p255
TLS-S 29 '78-p1091
The Young Scientist Investigates
TES-O 1 '82-p44
The Young Scientist Investigates Air
TES-Ap 15 '83-p33
The Young Scientist Investigates Electricity And Magnetism
TES-Ap 15 '83-p33
The Young Scientist Investigates Heat
TES-Ap 15 '83-p33
The Young Scientist Investigates Light And Colour
TES-N 5 '82-p22
TES-Ap 15 '83-p33
The Young Scientist Investigates Rocks And Soil
GP-v21-N '82-p3980
TES-Ap 15 '83-p33
The Young Scientist Investigates Trees
Sch Lib-v30-Mr '82-p43
The Young Scientist Investigates Water
TES-Ap 15 '83-p33
Your Book Of Prehistoric Animals
ASBYP-v14-Winter '81-p39
Brit Bk N C-Autumn '80-p29
JB-v44-Ag '80-p192
SB-v16-N '80-p92
SLJ-v27-O '80-p147

* * *

JENSEN, Ann
Time Of Rosie
CCB-B-v21-S '67-p10
Inst-v76-Je '67-p144
LJ-v92-Ap 15 '67-p1735

* * *

JENSEN, Helen
Games For Home, Travel, And Parties
SLJ-v22-D '75-p42

* * *

JENSEN, Malcolm C
Francisco Coronado
BL-v70-My 1 '74-p1003
CE-v51-F '75-p218
CE-v51-Mr '75-p278
KR-v42-F 1 '74-p115
KR-v43-Ja 1 '75-p7

* * *

JENSEN, Morgens
Micro-Life In Rubbish
GP-v21-My '82-p3904

* * *

JENSEN, Niels
Days Of Courage
BL-v70-Ja 15 '74-p542
CCB-B-v27-F '74-p96
KR-v41-N 15 '73-p1265
LJ-v98-N 15 '73-p3466

* * *

JENSEN, Pauline L
Out Of House And Home
CCB-B-v19-Ja '66-p83
KR-v33-My 15 '65-p501
Thicker Than Water
CCB-B-v21-S '67-p10
CE-v44-N '67-p196
KR-v34-O 1 '66-p1047
LJ-v91-D 15 '66-p6192

* * *

JENSEN, Virginia A
Catching
BL-v80-Je 1 '84-p1399
CBRS-v12-Je '84-p112
CCB-B-v37-My '84-p167
GP-My '84-p4270
HB-v60-Ag '84-p458
JB-v48-Je '84-p129
SLJ-v31-S '84-p105
TLS-Mr 30 '84-p339
WCRB-v10-Mr '84-p48
Red Thread Riddles
BL-v77-Ja 1 '81-p624
Brit Bk N C-Spring '81-p2
CBRS-v9-D '80-p28
JB-v44-O '80-p240
Ms-v13-O '84-p131
SLJ-v27-Ja '81-p51
TES-O 23 '81-p33

* * *

JENSEN, Virginia Allen
The Nisse From Timsgaard
GP-v13-Ap '75-p2612
KR-v40-N 15 '72-p1305
Sara And The Door
CCB-B-v30-My '77-p143
CSM-v69-My 19 '77-p26
Inst-v86-My '77-p117
PW-v211-Ja 24 '77-p333

JENSEN, Virginia Allen (continued)
RT-v32-O '78-p37
SLJ-v24-O '77-p104
WCRB-v3-My '77-p39
WLB-v51-Mr '77-p595
What's That?
BL-v75-Ap 15 '79-p1295
Brit Bk N C-Spring '81-p2
CBRS-v7-Ap '79-p82
CCB-B-v32-My '79-p156
CE-v57-Mr '81-p205
NYTBR-Ap 29 '79-p45
PW-v215-F 26 '79-p184
SLJ-v26-N '79-p66
Sch Lib-v28-Mr '80-p26
TES-O 23 '81-p33

* * *

JEREMIAH, David
The Computer Revolution
Sch Lib-v31-D '83-p367

* * *

JERMIESON, Allan
The House With No Windows
GP-v16-My '77-p3119
TES-D 2 '77-p24
TLS-Jl 15 '77-p864

* * *

JEROME, Jerome K
My Uncle Podger
JB-v41-Ag '77-p211
KR-v43-Jl 15 '75-p774
SLJ-v22-S '75-p84

* * *

JEROME, Judson
I Never Saw...
BL-v70-Je 1 '74-p1105
CCB-B-v28-O '74-p30
LJ-v99-My 15 '74-p1466
PW-v205-My 6 '74-p69
Teacher-v92-Ap '75-p29

* * *

JESCHKE, Susan
Angela And Bear
BL-v75-Je 15 '79-p1537
CBRS-v8-O '79-p12
CLW-v51-F '80-p310
KR-v47-Jl 15 '79-p791
New R-v180-Je 23 '79-p38
PW-v215-Je 4 '79-p62
RT-v33-Ap '80-p861
SLJ-v26-S '79-p114
The Devil Did It
BL-v72-N 1 '75-p368
CCB-B-v29-My '76-p146
HB-v52-Ap '76-p149
KR-v43-S 1 '75-p994
PW-v208-S 29 '75-p50
SLJ-v22-D '75-p47
Firerose
BL-v70-Ap 1 '74-p875
BL-v71-Mr 15 '75-p767
CCB-B-v27-Jl '74-p179
CE-v60-My '84-p344
Choice-v12-N '75-p1133
KR-v42-F 15 '74-p183
LJ-v99-My 15 '74-p1466
NY-v50-D 2 '74-p200
PW-v205-Ap 22 '74-p74
SR/W-v1-My 4 '74-p45
Teacher-v92-O '74-p112
Mia, Grandma And The Genie
BB-v6-Ap '78-p2
BL-v74-F 1 '78-p926
KR-v46-Ja 15 '78-p45
PW-v212-O 17 '77-p84
RT-v35-My '82-p901
SLJ-v24-F '78-p48
Perfect The Pig
BL-v77-My 15 '81-p1254
BW-v11-My 10 '81-p18
CBRS-v10-Jl '81-p112
CCB-B-v34-Je '81-p196
KR-v49-Je 15 '81-p736
LA-v59-Ja '82-p54
NYTBR-v86-My 10 '81-p38
PW-v219-Mr 6 '81-p95
SLJ-v27-My '81-p56
Rima And Zeppo
BL-v73-D 15 '76-p608
CCB-B-v30-F '77-p92
CLW-v48-F '77-p306
PW-v210-N 15 '76-p75
SLJ-v23-Ja '77-p83
Sidney
BW-v9-Ag 12 '79-p8
CCB-B-v29-O '75-p28
CLW-v47-My '76-p444
HB-v51-Ag '75-p368
KR-v43-Ap 1 '75-p368
PW-v207-Mr 24 '75-p48
PW-v216-S 24 '79-p106
SLJ-v21-My '75-p48
Teacher-v93-N '75-p111
Tamar And The Tiger
CBRS-v8-Ag '80-p132
CCB-B-v34-O '80-p34
KR-v48-Ag 1 '80-p978
LA-v58-Ja '81-p81
PW-v217-My 2 '80-p76
RT-v34-Mr '81-p734
SLJ-v27-N '80-p64
Victoria's Adventure
CE-v54-N '77-p86
CLW-v48-F '77-p306
NYTBR-N 14 '76-p26
SLJ-v23-O '76-p99
WCRB-v3-Mr '77-p48

* * *

JESPERSEN, James
Mercury's Web
ASBYP-v16-Winter '83-p35
BL-v78-D 15 '81-p544
CCB-B-v35-F '82-p110
HB-v58-Ap '82-p195
Inst-v91-Ap '82-p22
SB-v17-My '82-p243
Time & Clocks For The Space Age
ACSB-v13-Mr '80-p33
BL-v76-D 15 '79-p605
BOT-v2-D '79-p599
CCB-B-v33-Ap '80-p154
HB-v56-Ap '80-p193
KR-v48-F 1 '80-p138
S&T-v61-Ja '81-p59
SB-v16-Ja '81-p132
SLJ-v26-F '80-p67

* * *

JESSEL, Camilla
Away For The Night
Brit Bk N C-Autumn '81-p12
JB-v45-O '81-p187
Sch Lib-v30-Mr '82-p28
TLS-S 18 '81-p1066
Going To Hospital
JB-v47-D '83-p244
Going To The Doctor
Brit Bk N C-Autumn '81-p12
JB-v45-O '81-p188
TLS-S 18 '81-p1066
The Joy Of Birth
ASBYP-v17-Winter '84-p29
BL-v79-Je 15 '83-p1340
JB-v47-F '83-p27
TES-N 5 '82-p33
TES-N 11 '83-p24
VOYA-v6-D '83-p292
Learner Bird
GP-v22-S '83-p4127
JB-v48-F '84-p24
Punch-v285-Ag 17 '83-p52
TES-N 11 '83-p24
TES-Mr 9 '84-p54

JESSEL, Camilla (continued)
Life At The Royal Ballet School
BL-v76-S 15 '79-p122
BW-v10-My 11 '80-p18
Brit Bk N C-Spring '80-p18
CCB-B-v33-Ja '80-p97
CLW-v51-My '80-p460
Dance-v54-Mr '80-p121
GP-v18-N '79-p3603
HB-v56-Ap '80-p185
JB-v44-Ap '80-p84
NS-v98-N 9 '79-p733
NYTBR-F 17 '80-p24
RT-v33-My '80-p975
SLJ-v26-Ja '80-p72
Sch Lib-v27-D '79-p381
TES-N 16 '79-p28
TES-D 21 '79-p20
Lost And Found
JB-v47-D '83-p244
Mark's Wheelchair Adventures
Brit Bk N C-Spring '81-p2
NS-v89-My 23 '75-p698
Spec-v235-Jl 26 '75-p114
Moving House
Brit Bk N C-Autumn '81-p12
JB-v45-O '81-p188
Sch Lib-v30-Mr '82-p28
TLS-S 18 '81-p1066
The New Baby
Brit Bk N C-Autumn '81-p12
JB-v45-O '81-p188
TLS-S 18 '81-p1066
The Puppy Book
BL-v77-D 1 '80-p514
CBRS-v9-D '80-p28
NY-v57-D 7 '81-p228
SB-v17-S '81-p33
TES-Ja 16 '81-p27
GP-v18-Jl '79-p3553
KR-v46-Mr 1 '78-p238
LA-v55-S '78-p735
PW-v213-F 6 '78-p101
RT-v33-O '79-p38
SLJ-v24-My '78-p56
Cheer Up, Pig!
HB-v51-Ag '75-p374
KR-v43-Ap 15 '75-p445
PW-v207-Mr 24 '75-p48
SLJ-v22-S '75-p85
The Family Under The Moon
CCB-B-v30-Ap '77-p127
KR-v44-S 15 '76-p1035
NYTBR-O 17 '76-p41
SLJ-v23-N '76-p48
Time For Uncle Joe
CBRS-v9-Mr '81-p65
CCB-B-v34-My '81-p172
KR-v49-Ap 15 '81-p499
SLJ-v27-Ap '81-p114

* * *

JEWELL, Nancy
ABC Cat
CBRS-v12-S '83-p4
CCB-B-v37-F '84-p109
CSM-v76-Ja 6 '84-pB5
Inst-v93-N '83-p146
NYTBR-v88-O 9 '83-p38
PW-v224-Jl 29 '83-p70
SLJ-v30-D '83-p56
Bus Ride
BB-v6-S '78-p1
BL-v74-Mr 15 '78-p1190
CCB-B-v31-My '78-p143
CE-v55-N '78-p102

* * *

JEWETT, Eleanore M
Big John's Secret
GP-v14-Ja '76-p2810
Which Was Witch?
EJ-v69-Ap '80-p100

* * *

JEWETT, Frances L
Wilderness Treasure
CCB-B-v18-Ap '65-p119

* * *

JEZARD, Alison
Albert Goes Treasure-Hunting
GP-v17-N '78-p3403
JB-v42-Ag '78-p191
TLS-Jl 7 '78-p771
Albert Goes Trekking
JB-v40-Ap '76-p74
Albert On The Farm
JB-v43-Ag '79-p205
TES-O 9 '81-p29
Albert, Police Bear
TLS-Jl 11 '75-p770
Albert's Christmas
GP-v17-N '78-p3403
Albert's Circus
JB-v41-O '77-p289
TLS-O 21 '77-p1248

* * *

JHABVALA, Ruth Prawer
Travelers
Atl-v232-Jl '73-p104
BL-v70-S 1 '73-p31
CSM-v65-Jl 18 '73-p9
Choice-v10-O '73-p1204
Comt-v56-N '73-p80
HB-v49-D '73-p614
KR-v41-Ap 1 '73-p408
Kliatt-v12-Fall '78-p10
LJ-v98-Ag '73-p2334
LJ-v98-S 15 '73-p2680
NL-v57-F 18 '74-p19
NO-v12-Jl 14 '73-p23
NY-v49-Je 16 '73-p106
NYT-v122-Ag 30 '73-p31
NYTBR-Jl 8 '73-p6
NYTBR-D 2 '73-p78
PW-v203-My 7 '73-p59
SR-v2-Je 5 '73-p66
Sew R-v82-Ja '74-pR13

* * *

JI Er Di Shi Shi
BL-v80-S 1 '83-p97

* * *

JILER, John
Wild Berry Moon
BL-v79-Ja 1 '83-p617
CBRS-v11-Winter '83-p58
KR-v50-Ag 15 '82-p938
SLJ-v29-Ja '83-p76

* * *

JILES, Paulette
The Golden Hawks
Can Child Lit-#18 '80-p130

* * *

JIM Hunter Books
J Read-v23-Mr '80-p564

* * *

JIM-JAM
Pun Strips
NS-v95-My 19 '78-p680

* * *

JIMENEZ HERNANDEZ, Miguel
Max En La Ciudad Triste
BL-v78-My 1 '82-p1154

* * *

JIMENEZ-LANDI MARTINEZ, Antonio
La Familia
BL-v73-D 1 '76-p546

* * *

JOBB, Jamie
My Garden Companion
BL-v74-O 1 '77-p296

JOBB, Jamie (continued)
BW-Je 4 '78-pE4
CCB-B-v31-O '77-p34
Comw-v104-N 11 '77-p727
HB-v53-Ag '77-p456
Inst-v87-S '77-p247
KR-v45-Je 1 '77-p579
NYTBR-Ag 7 '77-p24
SB-v14-My '78-p42
SLJ-v24-S '77-p130
Teacher-v95-D '77-p91
The Night Sky Book
BL-v74-Mr 15 '78-p1190
CSM-v70-My 3 '78-pB9
HB-v54-Ap '78-p188
KR-v45-D 1 '77-p1268
SB-v14-D '78-p180
SLJ-v24-F '78-p58
WCRB-v4-Mr '78-p41

* * *

JOBE, Frank W
The Official Little League Fitness Guide
BL-v80-My 1 '84-p1219
SLJ-v30-My '84-p105

* * *

JOBIN, A
Games For Indoors And Out
JB-v46-O '82-p191

* * *

JOCHNOWITZ, Carol
Careers In Medicine For The New Woman
ACSB-v13-Winter '80-p29
BL-v74-Ap 15 '78-p1339
CCB-B-v32-S '78-p11
CLW-v50-Ap '79-p402
Cur R-v17-My '78-p111
SB-v14-Mr '79-p221

* * *

JOERNS, Consuelo
The Foggy Rescue
BL-v77-D 1 '80-p514
CBRS-v9-S '80-p2
CCB-B-v34-N '80-p56
CSM-v72-N 10 '80-pB10
KR-v48-O 1 '80-p1294
PW-v218-O 31 '80-p85
SLJ-v27-D '80-p53
The Forgotten Bear
BB-v7-Ag '79-p1
CCB-B-v32-N '78-p45
GP-v17-Mr '79-p3477
KR-v46-O 1 '78-p1067
PW-v214-N 27 '78-p61
SLJ-v25-O '78-p135
The Lost & Found House
BL-v76-S 1 '79-p44
CBRS-v8-S '79-p5
HB-v55-D '79-p655
KR-v47-O 1 '79-p1141
NYTBR-D 30 '79-p19
PW-v216-D 24 '79-p58
SLJ-v26-Ja '80-p56
The Midnight Castle
CCB-B-v37-F '84-p109
HB-v59-D '83-p704
SLJ-v30-Ja '84-p65
Oliver's Escape
BL-v78-O 15 '81-p306
CBRS-v10-D '81-p32
CCB-B-v35-O '81-p31
Inst-v91-Ja '82-p144
KR-v49-N 1 '81-p1339
PW-v220-S 4 '81-p60
SLJ-v28-Ja '82-p65

* * *

JOFFO, Joseph
A Bag Of Marbles
BL-v71-N 1 '74-p264
CSM-v66-O 2 '74-p13
GP-v14-Jl '75-p2676
KR-v42-Ag 1 '74-p851
KR-v42-Ag 15 '74-p886
LJ-v99-Ag '74-p1937
NO-v13-N 2 '74-p23
PW-v206-Ag 5 '74-p57

* * *

JOHANNESSON, Olaf
Tale Of The Big Computer
BL-v64-Ap 15 '68-p974
CCB-B-v21-Ap '68-p129
LJ-v93-Ja 1 '68-p96
MFSF-v34-Je '68-p52
NYTBR-v73-Mr 3 '68-p41
YR-v4-Ap '68-p7

* * *

JOHANSEN, Mary Lee
Word Problems In Math
Cur R-v17-My '78-p128

* * *

JOHANSSON I BACKE, Kerstin
Sveket
BL-v81-S 1 '84-p75

* * *

JOHN, Mary
Blue Stones
GP-v22-My '83-p4073
JB-v47-Je '83-p126

* * *

JOHN, Naomi
Roadrunner
BL-v77-D 1 '80-p514
CBRS-v9-D '80-p24
HB-v57-F '81-p43
KR-v49-Ja 1 '81-p2
RT-v34-Ap '81-p856
SLJ-v27-F '81-p58

* * *

JOHN, Sue
Bread Basket
TES-N 5 '82-p23
The Breadbasket Cookbook
CBRS-v10-Ag '82-p139
SLJ-v29-Mr '83-p178
The How-To Cookbook
CBRS-v11-Winter '83-p58
Kitchencraft
JB-v46-D '82-p224
TES-N 12 '82-p26
Special Days
JB-v47-F '83-p27
The Special Days Cookbook
CBRS-v10-Ag '82-p139
PW-v221-Je 18 '82-p75
SLJ-v29-Mr '83-p178
Time To Eat
TES-N 12 '82-p26
The Time To Eat Cookbook
CBRS-v11-Winter '83-p58

* * *

JOHN, Timothy
The Great Song Book
BL-v75-O 15 '78-p380
BW-D 10 '78-pE5
CBRS-v7-Winter '79-p60
CCB-B-v32-Ja '79-p83
CSM-v71-D 4 '78-pB20
Comw-v105-N 10 '78-p729
GP-v17-N '78-p3422
HB-v54-D '78-p649
ILN-v266-D '78-p127
JB-v43-F '79-p32
KR-v46-D 1 '78-p1308
LA-v56-S '79-p686
PW-v214-S 25 '78-p140
Par-v54-F '79-p24
Par-v58-O '83-p158
RT-v33-O '79-p95

JOHN, Timothy (continued)
SLJ-v25-D '78-p44
SR-v5-N 25 '78-p44
TES-O 20 '78-p43
TLS-D 1 '78-p1399
Teacher-v96-Mr '79-p118

* * *

JOHN Adams: The Stimulating True-Life Story Of The Patriot Who Helped America Win Freedom
SLJ-v23-Ap '77-p59

* * *

JOHN PAUL II , Pope
Beloved Young People
JB-v46-Je '82-p108

* * *

JOHNNY Morris Looks At The Zoo
TES-O 21 '77-p23

* * *

JOHNSEN, Jan
Gardening Without Soil
ACSB-v13-Mr '80-p34
BL-v76-F 15 '80-p834
SLJ-v26-Ap '80-p112

* * *

JOHNSON, A E
A Blues I Can Whistle
BL-v66-Ja 15 '70-p616
BS-v29-D 1 '69-p353
CCB-B-v23-F '70-p98
EJ-v59-Mr '70-p435
LJ-v95-Ja 15 '70-p254
NYTBR, pt.2-N 9 '69-p2

* * *

JOHNSON, Ann Donegan
Helen Keller
BS-v36-Ag '76-p150
NO-v15-Ag 21 '76-p17
The Value Of Adventure
CCB-B-v34-Jl '81-p213
SLJ-v28-Ja '82-p65
The Value Of Caring
SE-v48-N '84-p543
SLJ-v24-N '77-p58
The Value Of Determination
SLJ-v24-N '77-p58
The Value Of Giving
SLJ-v26-D '79-p87
The Value Of Love
SLJ-v26-D '79-p87
The Value Of Respect
CCB-B-v31-Je '78-p161
SLJ-v25-S '78-p118
The Value Of Truth And Trust
SLJ-v24-N '77-p58

* * *

JOHNSON, Annabel
An Alien Music
BL-v79-D 15 '82-p560
CBRS-v11-Winter '83-p58
CCB-B-v36-Ja '83-p90
J Read-v26-F '83-p468
SLJ-v29-Ap '83-p124
VOYA-v6-Ap '83-p45
Burning Glass
BL-v63-D 1 '66-p418
BS-v26-N 1 '66-p294
CCB-B-v20-D '66-p60
CLW-v38-Ja '67-p340
CSM-v58-N 3 '66-pB11
HB-v42-D '66-p719
KR-v34-S 1 '66-p913
LJ-v91-N 15 '66-p5760
Count Me Gone
BL-v64-Jl 15 '68-p1281
BS-v30-F 1 '71-p484
BW-v2-O 13 '68-p14
CCB-B-v21-Jl '68-p176
CSM-v60-Je 13 '68-p5
EJ-v58-F '69-p295
HB-v44-Ag '68-p431
LJ-v93-O 15 '68-p3983
LJ-v96-Ja 15 '71-p283
NYTBR-v73-My 5 '68-p8
YR-v4-Je '68-p9
The Danger Quotient
BL-v80-Je 1 '84-p1392
B Rpt-v3-S '84-p34
BS-v44-S '84-p233
CBRS-v12-Spring '84-p129
CCB-B-v37-Jl '84-p206
HB-v60-Ap '84-p201
SLJ-v30-Ag '84-p84
VOYA-v7-O '84-p206
Finders, Keepers
BL-v78-S 1 '81-p46
BS-v41-O '81-p278
CBRS-v10-Jl '81-p117
KR-v49-Ag 1 '81-p939
SLJ-v28-S '81-p137
VOYA-v5-Je '82-p34
A Peculiar Magic
BL-v62-D 1 '65-p364
CCB-B-v19-Ja '66-p84
CLW-v37-Ja '66-p336
HB-v41-D '65-p633
KR-v33-S 1 '65-p908
LJ-v90-O 15 '65-p4630

* * *

JOHNSON, Bob
Hockey
BL-v65-Je 1 '69-p1103
CCB-B-v22-My '69-p143
LJ-v94-My 1 '69-p1895
LJ-v94-My 15 '69-p2125

* * *

JOHNSON, Celia
The Lamp-Post Marauders
JB-v48-F '84-p24
Spec-v251-D 10 '83-p30
TES-Ag 17 '84-p22

* * *

JOHNSON, Corinne Benson
Love And Sex And Growing Up
BW-F 11 '79-pF2
Ms-v9-Je '81-p70
SB-v14-D '78-p178
SLJ-v24-Mr '78-p130

* * *

JOHNSON, Crockett
Castles In The Sand
CCB-B-v18-Jl '65-p163
CE-v42-Ja '66-p314
KR-v33-F 15 '65-p171
LJ-v90-My 15 '65-p2396
NYTBR-v70-My 9 '65-p4
SR-v48-My 15 '65-p44
TLS-N 30 '67-p1137
Ellen's Lion
HB-v60-Ag '84-p492
PW-v225-Ap 6 '84-p75
Gordy And The Pirate
CCB-B-v20-S '66-p13
KR-v33-N 1 '65-p1116
Harold And The Purple Crayon
PW-v219-My 22 '81-p77
Par-v58-O '83-p158
RT-v31-Ja '78-p426
TLS-D 8 '72-p1498
Upside Down
CCB-B-v23-S '69-p11
HB-v45-D '69-p663
KR-v37-Je 15 '69-p629
LJ-v95-My 15 '70-p1929
We Wonder What Will Walter Be?
CCB-B-v18-My '65-p130
HB-v41-F '65-p41

JOHNSON, Crockett
(continued)
LJ-v90-Ja 15 '65-p376

* * *

JOHNSON, D William
Jack And The Beanstalk
CCB-B-v30-F '77-p92
KR-v44-O 15 '76-p1133
NYTBR-N 14 '76-p50
SLJ-v23-D '76-p54
WLB-v51-Ja '77-p434
The Willow Flute
BL-v71-Jl 1 '75-p1128
CCB-B-v29-Ja '76-p80
SLJ-v22-S '75-p85

* * *

JOHNSON, Donna Kay
Brighteyes
SLJ-v25-F '79-p43

* * *

JOHNSON, Doris
Su An
EJ-v69-Ap '80-p100
LJ-v94-Ja 15 '69-p301

* * *

JOHNSON, Dorothy M
All The Buffalo Returning
BL-v75-Ap 15 '79-p1296
BS-v39-Ag '79-p169
HB-v55-Ag '79-p422
LJ-v104-Je 15 '79-p1357
SLJ-v25-Ap '79-p68
Buffalo Woman
BL-v73-Jl 1 '77-p1653
BS-v37-Ag '77-p142
CCB-B-v31-S '77-p17
SLJ-v23-Mr '77-p152

* * *

JOHNSON, Elizabeth
Break A Magic Circle
BL-v68-S 15 '71-p109
CCB-B-v25-O '71-p27
GT-v89-N '71-p93
HB-v47-O '71-p482
KR-v39-Jl 1 '71-p676
SR-v54-Jl 17 '71-p37
No Magic, Thank You
CCB-B-v18-Ap '65-p119

* * *

JOHNSON, Emily R
Spring And The Shadow Man
BL-v81-S 1 '84-p66
HB-v60-S '84-p592
PW-v225-Je 29 '84-p104
SLJ-v31-S '84-p120

* * *

JOHNSON, Enid
Rails Across The Continent
CCB-B-v20-O '66-p27
GT-v83-N '65-p122
KR-v33-Mr 15 '65-p329
LJ-v90-My 15 '65-p2420

* * *

JOHNSON, Eric W
Love And Sex And Growing Up
BL-v67-N 15 '70-p269
HB-v47-F '71-p65
KR-v38-Ag 15 '70-p880
LJ-v95-S 15 '70-p3049
SB-v6-D '70-p250
Sex
BL-v67-D 1 '70-p303
BL-v75-Je 1 '79-p1492
Comw-v93-N 20 '70-p205
KR-v38-N 15 '70-p1257
NYTBR, pt.2-N 7 '71-p47
Par-v46-F '71-p42
SB-v6-Mr '71-p331
SB-v15-My '80-p274
TN-v30-Ja '74-p193
The Stolen Ruler
CCB-B-v24-D '70-p60
CLW-v42-D '70-p259
KR-v38-Ag 1 '70-p800
LJ-v95-D 15 '70-p4351
Spectr-v47-Mr '71-p43
V.D.
BL-v70-O 15 '73-p222
BL-v75-D 1 '78-p608
BL-v76-D 1 '79-p549
CCB-B-v27-Ap '74-p131
CCB-B-v32-F '79-p100
CE-v50-Mr '74-p298
EJ-v68-N '79-p72
HB-v55-D '79-p686
KR-v41-Ag 15 '73-p890
LJ-v98-N 15 '73-p3466
LJ-v98-D 15 '73-p3690
SB-v10-My '74-p47
SLJ-v25-Ja '79-p54
WLB-v53-Je '79-p712

* * *

JOHNSON, Evelyne
The Cow In The Kitchen
SLJ-v30-O '83-p150
The Elephant's Ball
PW-v211-Je 13 '77-p107
RT-v32-O '78-p33
SLJ-v24-O '77-p104

* * *

JOHNSON, Fred
The Big Bears
CCB-B-v27-Ap '74-p131
SB-v10-My '74-p73

* * *

JOHNSON, Fridolf
Mythical Beasts Coloring Book
A Art-v40-D '76-p30

* * *

JOHNSON, Gerald W
The Cabinet
BL-v62-My 1 '66-p876
CCB-B-v19-Je '66-p164
GT-v84-O '66-p62
HB-v42-Je '66-p323
KR-v34-Mr 1 '66-p251
LJ-v91-Je 15 '66-p3259
NY-v42-D 17 '66-p227
NYTBR-v71-Jl 3 '66-p14
SR-v49-O 22 '66-p62
Franklin D. Roosevelt: Portrait Of A Great Man
BL-v63-Jl 15 '67-p1194
BS-v27-Jl 1 '67-p145
CCB-B-v20-Jl '67-p171
CE-v44-Ja '68-p324
EJ-v56-N '67-p1221
Inst-v76-Je '67-p142
KR-v35-Mr 15 '67-p346
LJ-v92-S 15 '67-p3200
NO-v6-Je 19 '67-p19
NY-v43-D 16 '67-p182
NYTBR-v72-My 7 '67-p36
NYTBR-v72-N 5 '67-p65
PW-v191-Ap 10 '67-p82
SR-v50-My 13 '67-p56

* * *

JOHNSON, Hannah Lyons
From Apple Seed To Applesauce
BB-v5-N '77-p2
BL-v73-Jl 1 '77-p1653
CCB-B-v31-N '77-p49
Inst-v87-N '77-p157
KR-v45-My 1 '77-p490
SB-v14-S '78-p115
SLJ-v24-S '77-p130
From Seed To Jack-O'-Lantern
ACSB-v8-Spring '75-p24

JOHNSON, Hannah Lyons
(continued)
BL-v71-N 15 '74-p344
KR-v42-Ag 1 '74-p807
LJ-v99-N 15 '74-p3038
NYTBR-O 27 '74-p8
PW-v206-O 14 '74-p57
SA-v231-D '74-p158
From Seed To Salad
ACSB-v12-Spring '79-p30
BL-v74-Jl 15 '78-p1734
CLW-v50-My '79-p448
KR-v46-Jl 1 '78-p692
SB-v15-S '79-p105
SLJ-v25-S '78-p118
Let's Bake Bread
BL-v69-Je 15 '73-p989
CCB-B-v27-N '73-p45
CE-v50-O '73-p32
CSM-v65-My 17 '73-pB2
KR-v41-Ap 1 '73-p390
LJ-v98-Jl '73-p2187
NYTBR-N 4 '73-p32
Let's Make Jam
BB-v4-Ap '76-p2
BL-v71-Ap 1 '75-p817
CE-v52-F '76-p208
KR-v43-Mr 15 '75-p313
NYTBR-N 16 '75-p34
SLJ-v21-My '75-p57
Let's Make Soup
BL-v72-F 15 '76-p856
CE-v53-O '76-p37
KR-v44-Ap 1 '76-p398
PW-v209-Mr 22 '76-p46
SLJ-v22-Mr '76-p104
Picture The Past 1900-1915
BL-v71-Jl 1 '75-p1128
CCB-B-v29-N '75-p47
KR-v43-My 15 '75-p571
SLJ-v22-S '75-p105

* * *

JOHNSON, Jacqueline
Global Issues In The Intermediate Classroom
Cur R-v21-My '82-p227

* * *

JOHNSON, James
Lasers
ACSB-v15-Winter '82-p39
SLJ-v27-Ag '81-p63
Sch Lib-v30-Mr '82-p68
TES-Mr 12 '82-p39

* * *

JOHNSON, James Ralph
Anyone Can Backpack In Comfort
BL-v62-Ja 1 '66-p426
CCB-B-v19-S '65-p11
HB-v42-Ap '66-p201
KR-v33-Jl 15 '65-p693
LJ-v90-N 15 '65-p5096
Zoos Of Today
BL-v68-My 1 '72-p772
CCB-B-v26-O '72-p27
KR-v39-S 1 '71-p956
LJ-v97-F 15 '72-p786

* * *

JOHNSON, James Weldon
Lift Every Voice And Sing
BL-v67-D 15 '70-p342
BL-v67-Ap 1 '71-p660
BL-v69-My 1 '73-p837
BW-v4-N 8 '70-p5
CCB-B-v24-My '71-p137
CSM-v62-N 12 '70-pB2
GT-v89-N '71-p90
Inst-v80-D '70-p98
LJ-v95-D 15 '70-p4338
NYTBR-Ja 24 '71-p24
PW-v198-N 23 '70-p39
TN-v27-Ja '71-p209

* * *

JOHNSON, Jane
Bertie On The Beach
GP-v20-Mr '82-p4037
JB-v46-Ap '82-p62
KR-v49-D 15 '81-p1517
SLJ-v28-Ja '82-p66
TES-Ja 15 '82-p35
TLS-S 18 '81-p1067
Sybil And The Blue Rabbit
BL-v77-D 15 '80-p574
BOT-v4-F '81-p77
Brit Bk N C-Spring '80-p8
CBRS-v9-Ap '81-p72
JB-v44-Je '80-p119
LA-v58-My '81-p593
PW-v218-S 12 '80-p66
SLJ-v27-D '80-p53
Sch Lib-v28-Je '80-p141

* * *

JOHNSON, Jim
A Look Inside Lasers
SB-v17-N '81-p97

* * *

JOHNSON, John
The Me Book
SLJ-v29-Mr '83-p121

* * *

JOHNSON, John E
My First Book Of Things
CCB-B-v32-Jl '79-p193
SLJ-v26-S '79-p114

* * *

JOHNSON, Kate
The Complete Book Of Treasure Hunting
TES-Je 20 '80-p43

* * *

JOHNSON, Laura R
The Teddy Bear ABC
PW-v222-S 17 '82-p115

* * *

JOHNSON, Linton K
Dread, Beat And Blood
Brit Bk N C-Spring '81-p11
NS-v100-N 21 '80-p17

* * *

JOHNSON, Lois S
Christmas Stories Round The World
CC-v87-D 16 '70-p1516
CCB-B-v24-N '70-p44
CSM-v63-D 12 '70-p17
Comw-v93-N 20 '70-p198
LJ-v95-O 15 '70-p3647
SR-v53-D 19 '70-p31
Spec-N 12 '65-p631
Happy New Year Round The World
B&B-v18-D '72-p124
BL-v63-D 15 '66-p451
CCB-B-v20-F '67-p91
CE-v43-F '67-p354
HB-v42-D '66-p701
Inst-v76-N '66-p51
LJ-v92-Ja 15 '67-p336

* * *

JOHNSON, Louise
Malunda
ASBYP-v15-Fall '82-p26
SB-v18-N '82-p92
SLJ-v28-My '82-p78

* * *

JOHNSON, Marjorie Seddon
American Book Reading Program
Cur R-v17-D '78-p373

* * *

JOHNSON, Mary
Chemistry Experiments
TES-Mr 12 '82-p36

* * *

JOHNSON, Mildred D
Wait, Skates
BL-v79-Ag '83-p1470
SLJ-v30-N '83-p63

* * *

JOHNSON, Natalie
Jenny
CCB-B-v35-Ap '82-p150
Kliatt-v16-Spring '82-p8
VOYA-v5-O '82-p43

* * *

JOHNSON, Philip
The Great Canadian Alphabet
Quill & Q-v47-O '81-p13
The Great Canadian Alphabet Book
Can Child Lit-#29 '83-p49
In Rev-v15-O '81-p39
Mac-v94-D 21 '81-p46

* * *

JOHNSON, Raymond
The Rio Grande
BL-v78-S 1 '81-p40
SB-v17-Mr '82-p211
SLJ-v28-N '81-p87
TES-Mr 6 '81-p36

* * *

JOHNSON, Robert Proctor
Chief Joseph
BL-v71-D 15 '74-p426

* * *

JOHNSON, Ruth
What To Do Till The Garbageman Arrives
BL-v73-Jl 15 '77-p1697
BL-v73-Jl 15 '77-p1728

* * *

JOHNSON, S Lawrence
Captain Ducky And Other Children's Sermons
S Liv-v13-Mr '78-p231
Cats And Dogs Together And Other Children's Sermons
S Liv-v13-Mr '78-p231
The Squirrel's Bank Account
S Liv-v13-Mr '78-p231

* * *

JOHNSON, Samuel
The Fountains
Punch-v274-Mr 29 '78-p544
Sch Lib-v27-Je '79-p136

* * *

JOHNSON, Spencer
Elizabeth Fry
BS-v36-Ag '76-p150
NO-v15-Ag 21 '76-p17
Louis Pasteur
BS-v36-Ag '76-p150
NO-v15-Ag 21 '76-p17
The Value Of Believing In Yourself
SB-v14-S '78-p110
SLJ-v24-N '77-p58
The Value Of Courage
SLJ-v24-N '77-p58
The Value Of Curiosity
CCB-B-v31-Je '78-p161
SLJ-v25-S '78-p118
The Value Of Honesty
SLJ-v26-D '79-p87
The Value Of Humor
SLJ-v24-N '77-p58
The Value Of Kindness
SLJ-v24-N '77-p58
The Value Of Patience
SB-v14-S '78-p110
SLJ-v24-N '77-p58
The Value Of Understanding
SLJ-v26-D '79-p87
The Wright Brothers
BS-v36-Ag '76-p150
NO-v15-Ag 21 '76-p17

* * *

JOHNSON, Sylvia A
Animals Of The Deserts
ACSB-v10-Winter '77-p24
BB-v4-O '76-p2
BL-v73-S 1 '76-p39
CCB-B-v30-D '76-p58
SB-v12-Mr '77-p212
SLJ-v23-S '76-p118
Animals Of The Grasslands
ACSB-v10-Winter '77-p25
BB-v4-O '76-p2
BL-v73-S 1 '76-p39
SB-v12-Mr '77-p212
SLJ-v23-S '76-p118
Animals Of The Mountains
ACSB-v10-Spring '77-p26
BB-v4-O '76-p2
BL-v73-S 1 '76-p39
SB-v12-Mr '77-p212
SLJ-v23-S '76-p118
Animals Of The Polar Regions
ACSB-v10-Spring '77-p26
BB-v4-O '76-p2
BL-v73-S 1 '76-p39
SB-v12-Mr '77-p212
SLJ-v23-S '76-p118
Animals Of The Temperate Forests
ACSB-v10-Spring '77-p27
BB-v4-O '76-p2
BL-v73-S 1 '76-p39
SB-v12-Mr '77-p212
SLJ-v23-S '76-p118
Animals Of The Tropical Forests
ACSB-v10-Winter '77-p26
BB-v4-O '76-p2
BL-v73-S 1 '76-p39
SB-v12-Mr '77-p212
SLJ-v23-S '76-p118
Apple Trees
ASBYP-v17-Spring '84-p52
BL-v80-Mr 1 '84-p967
JB-v48-Je '84-p129
SLJ-v30-Ap '84-p115
Beetles
ASBYP-v16-Winter '83-p65
BL-v79-N 1 '82-p371
CLW-v54-My '83-p425
SB-v19-S '83-p33
SLJ-v29-N '82-p80
Coral Reefs
BL-v81-S 15 '84-p129
Crabs
ASBYP-v16-Winter '83-p65
BL-v79-F 15 '83-p777
CCB-B-v36-Ja '83-p91
SB-v19-S '83-p34
Downy The Duckling
ACSB-v10-Spring '77-p7
SLJ-v23-Ap '77-p60
Elephants Around The World
SB-v14-My '78-p39
Inside An Egg
ASBYP-v16-Winter '83-p64
BL-v79-S 1 '82-p40
Inst-v92-Ap '83-p20
SB-v18-Mr '83-p211

JOHNSON, Sylvia A
(continued)
SLJ-v29-Ja '83-p74
Ladybugs
ASBYP-v17-Spring '84-p52
BL-v80-Mr 1 '84-p967
CE-v61-S '84-p68
HB-v60-Je '84-p368
SA-v251-D '84-p34
SLJ-v30-Ap '84-p115
Lerner Wildlife Library
Cur R-v16-O '77-p303
The Lions Of Africa
SB-v14-My '78-p39
Mantises
BL-v80-Je 1 '84-p1399
SLJ-v31-S '84-p120
Mosses
ASBYP-v17-Spring '84-p52
BL-v80-Mr 1 '84-p967
CE-v61-S '84-p68
HB-v60-Je '84-p370
JB-v48-Je '84-p129
SB-v20-S '84-p19
SLJ-v30-Ap '84-p115
Mushrooms
BL-v79-Ja 1 '83-p617
SB-v18-Mr '83-p209
SLJ-v29-Ja '83-p74
Penelope The Tortoise
ACSB-v10-Spring '77-p7
SLJ-v23-Ap '77-p60
Penguins
ACSB-v15-Winter '82-p38
BL-v78-S 1 '81-p43
CBRS-v10-Jl '81-p116
CLW-v53-Ap '82-p402
PW-v219-My 22 '81-p76
SLJ-v28-S '81-p122
Penny And Pete The Lambs
SLJ-v23-Ap '77-p60
Potatoes
BL-v81-S 15 '84-p129
Silkworms
BL-v79-N 1 '82-p371
GP-v22-Jl '83-p4105
SA-v247-D '82-p36
SB-v19-S '83-p36
SLJ-v29-N '82-p80
Snails
ASBYP-v16-Winter '83-p65
BL-v79-F 15 '83-p777
SB-v18-My '83-p274
Wasps
BL-v80-Je 15 '84-p1484
SLJ-v31-S '84-p120

* * *

JOHNSON, Virginia Weisel
The Cedars Of Charlo
CCB-B-v23-Ja '70-p82
KR-v37-S 15 '69-p1008
PW-v196-D 29 '69-p68
SR-v52-N 8 '69-p70

* * *

JOHNSON, Vivienne
What Makes Arith-Me-Tick?
Cur R-v22-O '83-p60

* * *

JOHNSTON, Basil
How The Birds Got Their Colours
Can Child Lit-#20 '80-p57

* * *

JOHNSTON, Basil H
Tales The Elders Told
BIC-v10-O '81-p33
CG-v101-D '81-p84
In Rev-v15-O '81-p39
Quill & Q-v47-O '81-p36

* * *

JOHNSTON, Brenda A
Between The Devil And The Sea
BL-v71-Ja 1 '75-p461
CCB-B-v28-My '75-p148
KR-v42-N 15 '74-p1208
PW-v206-S 9 '74-p68
SLJ-v21-Ja '75-p46

* * *

JOHNSTON, Catherine D
I Hear The Day
Inter BC-v11-Ja 10 '80-p19

* * *

JOHNSTON, H A S
The Donkey, The Hyena, And Other Stories
J Read-v25-Mr '82-p519

* * *

JOHNSTON, J M
Computers: Beeps, Whirs And Blinking Lights
SB-v19-My '84-p259
Computers: Menus, Loops And Mice
SB-v19-My '84-p259
Computers: Sizes, Shapes And Flavors
CSM-v75-N 10 '83-p42
SB-v19-My '84-p260

* * *

JOHNSTON, Jean
Rob And The Rebels 1837
BIC-v11-Mr '82-p26

* * *

JOHNSTON, Johanna
A Birthday For General Washington
SLJ-v23-S '76-p101
The Fabulous Fox
ACSB-v13-Winter '80-p30
BL-v75-Je 15 '79-p1534
KR-v47-Ap 1 '79-p390
LA-v57-Mr '80-p322
SLJ-v26-O '79-p159
Frederick Law Olmstead, Partner With Nature
BL-v71-Je 15 '75-p1075
BW-Ap 20 '75-p2
KR-v43-F 1 '75-p130
SLJ-v23-O '76-p108
Harriet And The Runaway Book
Am-v137-D 3 '77-p407
BW-My 1 '77-pE2
CCB-B-v30-Jl '77-p175
CE-v54-O '77-p31
HB-v53-Ag '77-p459
KR-v45-Mr 1 '77-p226
LA-v54-S '77-p689
NYTBR-Jl 24 '77-p18
RT-v32-O '78-p40
SE-v42-Ap '78-p318
The Indians And The Strangers
BL-v69-Mr 1 '73-p648
CCB-B-v26-Ja '73-p78
KR-v40-S 15 '72-p1102
LJ-v98-Ap 15 '73-p1387
NYTBR, pt.2-N 5 '72-p22
PW-v203-Ja 29 '73-p260
Speak Up, Edie!
CCB-B-v27-Jl '74-p179
CE-v51-O '74-p33
KR-v42-Mr 15 '74-p294
LJ-v99-O 15 '74-p2733
Special Bravery
BL-v64-F 1 '68-p638
CCB-B-v21-Je '68-p160
CLW-v40-Mr '69-p458
Comw-v89-F 21 '69-p647
KR-v35-S 15 '67-p1140
LJ-v92-N 15 '67-p4252
NYTBR-v73-Ja 14 '68-p26
PW-v192-D 25 '67-p60
PW-v198-Jl 13 '70-p166

JOHNSTON, Johanna
(continued)
Sugarplum & Snowball
CLW-v40-O '68-p150
GP-v15-Mr '77-p3076
JB-v41-Je '77-p151
KR-v36-Je 1 '68-p593
LJ-v93-Jl '68-p2729
PW-v193-Ap 22 '68-p52
That's Right, Edie
BL-v63-My 15 '67-p996
CCB-B-v20-Ap '67-p124
CE-v44-D '67-p262
Inst-v76-My '67-p132
KR-v34-D 15 '66-p1284
LJ-v92-F 15 '67-p872
SR-v50-Ja 28 '67-p45
Together In America: Two Races And One Nation
BL-v62-S 1 '65-p56
BS-v25-Ap 15 '65-p52
CC-v82-Je 30 '65-p838
CCB-B-v18-Ap '65-p119
CLW-v36-My '65-p639
Comw-v82-My 28 '65-p331
KR-v33-F 1 '65-p113
LJ-v90-F 15 '65-p972

* * *

JOHNSTON, Mary Anne
Sing Me A Song
SLJ-v24-Ja '78-p78

* * *

JOHNSTON, Norma
The Crucible Year
BB-v7-Ja '80-p4
BL-v75-Mr 15 '79-p1142
CBRS-v7-Jl '79-p128
CCB-B-v32-Je '79-p177
HB-v55-Ap '79-p200
KR-v47-Ap 15 '79-p456
SLJ-v25-Mr '79-p148
Gabriel's Girl
BL-v80-S 1 '83-p75
BS-v43-D '83-p347
CBRS-v12-Ap '84-p97
HB-v59-O '83-p583
SLJ-v30-D '83-p85
Glory In The Flower
BL-v70-Mr 15 '74-p820
CCB-B-v27-Jl '74-p179
KR-v42-F 15 '74-p192
Kliatt-v16-Winter '82-p12
LJ-v99-Mr 15 '74-p902
PT-v8-S '74-p132
If You Love Me, Let Me Go
BB-v7-Je '79-p4
BL-v75-S 1 '78-p39
CCB-B-v32-D '78-p63
KR-v46-D 1 '78-p1309
SLJ-v25-O '78-p156
The Keeping Days
BL-v70-D 15 '73-p441
BL-v70-D 15 '73-p446
BL-v75-F 15 '79-p928
CLW-v45-Ap '74-p457
HB-v49-D '73-p591
KR-v41-N 1 '73-p1211
LJ-v98-O 15 '73-p3156
VOYA-v5-Ap '82-p58
A Mustard Seed Of Magic
BL-v74-O 1 '77-p298
BS-v37-D '77-p294
CCB-B-v31-F '78-p97
KR-v45-O 1 '77-p1054
SLJ-v24-O '77-p124
VOYA-v6-Ag '83-p158
Myself And I
BL-v77-Ap 1 '81-p1105
CCB-B-v34-Ap '81-p153
CLW-v53-S '81-p92
KR-v49-O 1 '81-p1240
SLJ-v28-N '81-p106
A Nice Girl Like You
BL-v76-Mr 15 '80-p1058
BS-v40-Je '80-p118
CBRS-v8-Spring '80-p118
CCB-B-v33-Jl '80-p215
HB-v56-Je '80-p306
KR-v48-My 15 '80-p650
Kliatt-v16-Fall '82-p12
SLJ-v26-My '80-p76
Of Time And Seasons
BB-v3-Ja '76-p3
BL-v72-N 1 '75-p368
BS-v35-D '75-p296
CLW-v47-F '76-p308
KR-v43-O 15 '75-p1193
SLJ-v22-N '75-p91
The Sanctuary Tree
BL-v73-Ap 15 '77-p1267
CCB-B-v31-S '77-p18
KR-v45-F 1 '77-p98
Kliatt-v16-Spring '82-p12
SLJ-v24-S '77-p145
VOYA-v6-Ag '83-p158
Strangers Dark And Gold
BL-v71-Je 15 '75-p1070
BS-v35-Je '75-p60
CCB-B-v29-S '75-p12
KR-v43-Mr 1 '75-p245
NYTBR-My 11 '75-p8
SLJ-v21-Ap '75-p66
A Striving After Wind
BB-v4-Ja '77-p2
BL-v73-S 15 '76-p176
CCB-B-v30-Mr '77-p108
KR-v44-S 1 '76-p982
SLJ-v23-S '76-p134
The Swallow's Song
BB-v6-Ja '79-p3
BL-v74-Ap 1 '78-p1249
BS-v38-Jl '78-p135
CCB-B-v32-S '78-p11
EJ-v67-S '78-p90
KR-v46-Je 1 '78-p599
SLJ-v24-My '78-p77
Timewarp Summer
BL-v79-Mr 1 '83-p870
CCB-B-v36-Ap '83-p152
HB-v59-Ap '83-p171
KR-v51-Ja 1 '83-p6
SLJ-v30-S '83-p135
VOYA-v6-O '83-p203

* * *

JOHNSTON, R J
The New Zealanders
BL-v72-Jl 1 '76-p1522
BL-v72-Jl 1 '76-p1527
LJ-v101-Jl '76-p1545
SLJ-v23-S '76-p149

* * *

JOHNSTON, Ted
Science Magic With Chemistry And Biology
ACSB-v9-Winter '76-p21
Inst-v85-N '75-p164
SLJ-v22-S '75-p105

* * *

JOHNSTON, Tony
The Adventures Of Mole And Troll
CLW-v44-Mr '73-p512
JB-v39-Ap '75-p98
KR-v40-Ag 15 '72-p938
LJ-v97-D 15 '72-p4085
NYTBR-O 8 '72-p8
Fig Tale
BB-v2-Ja '75-p2
BL-v71-O 15 '74-p244
KR-v42-S 1 '74-p939
LJ-v99-D 15 '74-p3263
Five Little Foxes And The Snow
BL-v74-F 1 '78-p926
JB-v43-D '79-p327

JONES, Adrienne (continued)
PW-v200-N 22 '71-p41
The Beckoner
BL-v76-Jl 15 '80-p1671
BS-v40-My '80-p79
CBRS-v8-Mr '80-p77
HB-v56-Ap '80-p177
KR-v48-Ag 15 '80-p1085
NYTBR-v85-Jl 27 '80-p22
PW-v217-Mr 28 '80-p49
SLJ-v26-Mr '80-p141
The Hawks Of Chelney
BL-v74-Mr 1 '78-p1108
BS-v38-Ag '78-p155
BW-My 14 '78-pG4
CCB-B-v32-N '78-p45
CE-v55-Ja '79-p168
CLW-v50-O '78-p115
CLW-v50-D '78-p235
EJ-v68-F '79-p102
HB-v54-Je '78-p283
JB-v43-Ap '79-p117
J Read-v22-Mr '79-p561
KR-v46-Je 15 '78-p640
SLJ-v24-Ap '78-p94
Sch Lib-v27-Je '79-p158
TLS-D 14 '79-p122
A Matter Of Spunk
BL-v79-Ag '83-p1457
B Rpt-v3-My '84-p34
BS-v43-D '83-p347
CBRS-v12-N '83-p31
CCB-B-v37-D '83-p70
HB-v59-O '83-p584
J Read-v27-F '84-p467
KR-v51-S 1 '83-pJ175
N Dir Wom-v13-Jl '84-p12
SLJ-v30-S '83-p136
VOYA-v6-F '84-p338
The Mural Master
CCB-B-v28-N '74-p44
CE-v51-N '74-p92
HB-v50-Je '74-p283
KR-v42-Je 1 '74-p581
LJ-v99-S 15 '74-p2271
PT-v8-S '74-p131
PW-v205-Je 17 '74-p69
Sail, Calypso
BL-v65-O 15 '68-p248
BW-v2-N 3 '68-p22
CCB-B-v22-Je '69-p159
HB-v44-O '68-p561
KR-v36-Jl 15 '68-p762
LJ-v93-O 15 '68-p3971
So, Nothing Is Forever
KR-v42-N 15 '74-p1206
RT-v31-My '78-p915
SLJ-v21-Ja '75-p54
Whistle Down A Dark Lane
BL-v79-S 15 '82-p105
B Rpt-v2-My '83-p37
BS-v42-D '82-p366
CBRS-v11-Ja '83-p49
CCB-B-v36-N '82-p49
J Read-v26-F '83-p468
KR-v50-Ag 1 '82-p872
SLJ-v29-O '82-p162
VOYA-v6-Ap '83-p38

* * *

JONES, Aubrey B, Jr.
I Speak BASIC To My VIC
BW-v13-O 2 '83-p10
SB-v19-My '84-p251

* * *

JONES, Beryl
The Enchanted Harp
KR-v45-My 15 '77-p539

* * *

JONES, Betty M
King Solomon's Mines
SLJ-v29-F '83-p76
Wonder Women Of Sports
BL-v77-Ap 15 '81-p1159
CE-v58-Ja '82-p183
Cur R-v21-My '82-p225
Inter BC-v13-#6 '82-p41
SLJ-v27-My '81-p88

* * *

JONES, Brian
The Spitfire On The Northern Line
B&B-v21-D '75-p62
GP-v14-D '75-p2780
LR-v25-Autumn '75-p137
TLS-D 5 '75-p1452

* * *

JONES, Carol
The Painted Boats
GP-v18-Ja '80-p3619
JB-v44-Ap '80-p84
Sch Lib-v28-Je '80-p178
TLS-D 14 '79-p123

* * *

JONES, Claire
Sailboat Racing
BL-v77-Mr 15 '81-p1028
SLJ-v27-My '81-p88

* * *

JONES, Clarence Medlycott
Starting Tennis
LJ-v101-D 1 '76-p2506
LR-v25-Summer '75-p81

* * *

JONES, Cordelia
British Children's Authors
A Lib-v8-Je '77-p348
ARBA-v8-'77-p594
BL-v73-F 15 '77-p901
HB-v53-Ag '77-p463
LQ-v47-O '77-p520
LR-v26-Autumn '77-p270
SMQ-v5-Summer '77-p293
TN-v34-Fall '77-p98
Nobody's Garden
BL-v62-Jl 15 '66-p1087
CCB-B-v21-N '67-p44
CLW-v38-N '66-p214
HB-v42-Je '66-p312
KR-v34-Mr 1 '66-p249
LJ-v91-My 15 '66-p2692
PW-v189-Ap 25 '66-p122
SR-v49-Ag 20 '66-p37
The View From The Window
GP-v17-Mr '79-p3485
JB-v43-Ap '79-p122
Obs-D 3 '78-p36
Sch Lib-v27-Mr '79-p57

* * *

JONES, David
Your Book Of Abbeys
GP-v17-Mr '79-p3481
JB-v43-Ag '79-p206
Your Book Of Anglo-Saxon England
CCB-B-v32-My '79-p156
GP-v15-Jl '76-p2926
JB-v40-O '76-p274

* * *

JONES, David P
Geography In A Changing World. Bk. 1
TES-My 8 '81-p45
Geography In A Changing World. Bk. 3
TES-Ap 1 '83-p26

* * *

JONES, Diana W
Archer's Goon
BL-v80-Mr 15 '84-p1060
BS-v44-Je '84-p117
BW-v14-My 13 '84-p18

JONES, Diana W (continued)
CBRS-v12-Spring '84-p129
CCB-B-v37-My '84-p167
HB-v60-Ap '84-p202
PW-v225-Je 29 '84-p104
SLJ-v30-Mr '84-p160
TLS-O 19 '84-p1198
VOYA-v7-Je '84-p101
The Four Grannies
JB-v45-F '81-p21
TES-N 21 '80-p30
TES-F 5 '82-p28
TLS-S 19 '80-p1026
The Homeward Bounders
BL-v78-S 15 '81-p98
CBRS-v9-Ag '81-p127
CCB-B-v35-S '81-p12
CE-v59-S '82-p56
GP-v20-My '81-p3880
HB-v57-O '81-p542
JB-v45-O '81-p212
KR-v49-S 15 '81-p1164
SLJ-v28-S '81-p137
Sch Lib-v29-S '81-p254
TES-Je 5 '81-p37
TES-F 24 '84-p29
TLS-Mr 27 '81-p339
TLS-N 20 '81-p1361
The Magicians Of Caprona
BL-v76-Jl 15 '80-p1676
Brit Bk N C-Autumn '80-p9
CBRS-v8-Jl '80-p127
CCB-B-v33-Jl '80-p216
CE-v57-N '80-p112
HB-v56-Ag '80-p407
JB-v44-Ag '80-p192
KR-v48-S 1 '80-p1163
Obs-N 30 '80-p36
S Fict R-v10-Ag '81-p47
SLJ-v27-O '80-p147
TES-Ap 18 '80-p25
TLS-Mr 28 '80-p360
The Time Of The Ghost
Brit Bk N C-Spring '82-p7
Brit Bk N C-Autumn '82-p8
GP-v20-Ja '82-p3991
JB-v46-F '82-p33
NS-v102-D 4 '81-p20
Obs-N 29 '81-p27
Sch Lib-v30-Mr '82-p52
TES-N 20 '81-p35
TLS-N 20 '81-p1354
Warlock At The Wheel And Other Stories
TLS-O 19 '84-p1198
Witch Week
B&B-Jl '82-p33
BL-v79-O 1 '82-p246
BS-v42-N '82-p325
Brit Bk N C-Autumn '82-p8
Brit Bk N C-Autumn '82-p20
CBRS-v11-S '82-p9
CCB-B-v36-N '82-p49
CLW-v55-S '83-p88
GP-v21-N '82-p3983
HB-v59-F '83-p44
JB-v46-D '82-p231
KR-v50-Ag 15 '82-p938
Lis-v108-N 4 '82-p24
Obs-Ag 1 '82-p30
PW-v222-Ag 27 '82-p357
RT-v36-F '83-p594
SLJ-v29-N '82-p86
Sch Lib-v30-D '82-p359
TES-Je 11 '82-p41
TLS-Jl 23 '82-p794
VOYA-v6-Ap '83-p38

* * *

JONES, Diana Wynne
Cart And Cwidder
BL-v73-Mr 1 '77-p1014
CCB-B-v30-Je '77-p161
CE-v54-Ja '78-p138
CLW-v49-N '77-p188
EJ-v66-N '77-p82
GP-v14-O '75-p2708
HB-v53-Ag '77-p443
KR-v45-Mr 1 '77-p224
SLJ-v23-My '77-p70
TES-Jl 7 '78-p30
TLS-Jl 11 '75-p764
Charmed Life
Am-v139-D 9 '78-p442
BL-v74-F 15 '78-p1009
CCB-B-v31-Mr '78-p113
CE-v56-N '79-p111
GW-v120-Ja 1 '79-p15
HB-v54-Ag '78-p396
JB-v41-O '77-p303
KR-v46-F 15 '78-p177
LA-v55-S '78-p740
NS-v93-My 20 '77-p686
PW-v213-My 1 '78-p85
SLJ-v24-Ap '78-p94
TES-D 14 '79-p21
TLS-Mr 25 '77-p348
Dogsbody
BL-v73-My 15 '77-p1421
BL-v80-Ap 15 '84-p1200
CCB-B-v30-Jl '77-p176
CE-v54-O '77-p28
GP-v14-D '75-p2769
HB-v53-Je '77-p319
JB-v40-F '76-p46
KR-v45-F 1 '77-p95
LA-v54-O '77-p807
Obs-N 30 '75-p27
PW-v211-Mr 14 '77-p93
SLJ-v23-My '77-p62
TLS-Ap 2 '76-p383
Drowned Ammet
BL-v74-Ap 1 '78-p1255
CCB-B-v31-Je '78-p161
GP-v16-Mr '78-p3279
HB-v54-Ag '78-p403
JB-v42-Je '78-p156
KR-v46-F 15 '78-p177
LA-v55-N '78-p988
SLJ-v24-Ap '78-p85
TES-N 18 '77-p40
TLS-Ap 7 '78-p377
Eight Days Of Luke
GP-v13-Ap '75-p2597
JB-v39-Je '75-p198
Obs-Ag 28 '77-p26
TES-O 7 '77-p22
TLS-Ap 4 '75-p365
The Ogre Downstairs
B&B-v19-My '74-p106
BL-v71-Je 15 '75-p1075
Brit Bk N C-Spring '81-p14
CCB-B-v28-Jl '75-p179
HB-v51-O '75-p464
KR-v43-Ap 15 '75-p453
NS-v87-My 24 '74-p738
Obs-F 6 '77-p27
SLJ-v22-S '75-p105
TLS-Jl 5 '74-p714
Power Of Three
BL-v74-O 1 '77-p298
CSM-v70-My 3 '78-pB2
GP-v15-S '76-p2932
HB-v54-F '78-p47
JB-v40-O '76-p275
KR-v45-Ag 1 '77-p790
SLJ-v24-N '77-p58
Spec-v242-Je 30 '79-p28
TLS-Ap 2 '76-p383
The Spellcoats
B&B-v25-N '79-p58
CCB-B-v33-F '80-p111
Emerg Lib-v9-Ja '82-p14
GP-v18-S '79-p3562
HB-v55-D '79-p669
JB-v43-Ag '79-p221
KR-v47-S 15 '79-p1072
Kliatt-v15-Winter '81-p12

JONES, Diana Wynne
(continued)
SLJ-v26-N '79-p89
Sch Lib-v27-D '79-p386
TES-N 30 '79-p25
VOYA-v4-Ap '81-p53
Who Got Rid Of Angus Flint?
Brit Bk N C-Spring '81-p14
JB-v43-F '79-p33
TES-D 1 '78-p24

* * *

JONES, E Willis
The Santa Claus Book
A Art-v40-N '76-p30
BL-v73-Mr 1 '77-p1014
VV-v21-D 13 '76-p78

* * *

JONES, Elwyn
Dick Barton, Special Agent
NS-v93-F 11 '77-p195
TLS-Mr 25 '77-p351

* * *

JONES, Eurfron Gwynne
Television Magic
ACSB-v13-Winter '80-p54
BL-v75-N 15 '78-p544
CBRS-v7-Winter '79-p56
RT-v33-O '79-p51
SLJ-v25-N '78-p58

* * *

JONES, G
Learning To Think In Science Lessons
TES-F 4 '83-p28

* * *

JONES, G A
The Influence Of Ironwood
JB-v43-Ag '79-p222

* * *

JONES, Gareth L
Valley With A Bright Cloud
Brit Bk N C-Spring '81-p26
Econ-v277-D 27 '80-p73
GP-v19-Mr '81-p3842
JB-v45-Je '81-p124
NS-v100-N 28 '80-p30
Obs-N 30 '80-p36

* * *

JONES, Gareth Lovett
Tricks Of The Light
GP-v17-Ja '79-p3441
JB-v43-Ap '79-p123

* * *

JONES, Gwyn
Welsh Legends And Folk-Tales
Brit Bk N C-Autumn '80-p3

* * *

JONES, Gwyneth A
Water In The Air
GP-v16-Mr '78-p3278
JB-v42-Ap '78-p104
TLS-D 2 '77-p1409

* * *

JONES, H W
The Flying Sorcerer
JB-v40-Ag '76-p205

* * *

JONES, Harold
A Happy Christmas
GP-v22-Mr '84-p4219
JB-v48-F '84-p14
Spec-v251-D 3 '83-p27
TES-D 16 '83-p20
Silver Bells And Cockle-Shells
B&B-v25-N '79-p59
GP-v18-S '79-p3584
JB-v43-Ag '79-p196
Tales From Aesop
BL-v78-Je 1 '82-p1313
Brit Bk N C-Spring '82-p6
CBRS-v10-Spring '82-p113
GP-v20-Ja '82-p4001
HB-v58-Je '82-p302
JB-v46-F '82-p16
Punch-v281-D 2 '81-p1023
SLJ-v28-My '82-p54
Sch Lib-v29-D '81-p320
TES-N 20 '81-p32
TLS-N 20 '81-p1360
There & Back Again
BB-v7-Mr '79-p1
GP-v17-N '78-p3403
HB-v53-D '77-p655
JB-v42-Ap '78-p80
KR-v45-N 1 '77-p1142
NYTBR-N 13 '77-p56
Obs-N 27 '77-p29
PW-v212-Jl 11 '77-p81
SLJ-v24-O '77-p104
TES-Mr 10 '78-p60
TLS-D 2 '77-p1411

* * *

JONES, Harold Kenneth
Sweetie Feetie
KR-v43-Jl 1 '75-p709
PW-v207-Je 9 '75-p63
Par-v50-O '75-p69
SLJ-v22-S '75-p85

* * *

JONES, Helen H
Over The Mormon Trail
SLJ-v27-F '81-p66

* * *

JONES, Hettie
Big Star Fallin' Mama
BL-v70-Mr 1 '74-p741
BS-v34-Ap 15 '74-p53
Bl W-v24-Jl '75-p62
CCB-B-v27-My '74-p145
Inst-v83-N '73-p125
KR-v41-O 15 '73-p1173
KR-v41-D 15 '73-p1359
LJ-v99-My 15 '74-p1483
NYTBR-D 30 '73-p10
PW-v205-Ja 28 '74-p301
Coyote Tales
BL-v71-N 1 '74-p292
CCB-B-v28-My '75-p149
KR-v42-O 1 '74-p1063
SLJ-v21-Ap '75-p53
How To Eat Your ABC's
ACSB-v10-Winter '77-p26
BL-v73-S 15 '76-p177
CCB-B-v30-N '76-p44
KR-v44-My 15 '76-p597
SB-v12-Mr '77-p215
SLJ-v23-S '76-p119
I Hate To Talk About Your Mother
CBRS-v8-Je '80-p108
CCB-B-v33-My '80-p174
KR-v48-My 1 '80-p589
SLJ-v26-My '80-p76
WLB-v54-My '80-p585
Longhouse Winter
BL-v69-My 1 '73-p856
CCB-B-v26-Je '73-p157
CE-v50-O '73-p29
HB-v48-O '72-p462
KR-v40-Jl 15 '72-p805
LJ-v98-F 15 '73-p645
NYTBR, pt.2-N 5 '72-p20
Mustang Country
BL-v72-Je 1 '76-p1394
BL-v72-Je 1 '76-p1407

JONES, Hettie (continued)
The Trees Stand Shining
A Lib-v3-Ap '72-p420
Am-v125-D 4 '71-p491
BL-v67-Jl 1 '71-p908
BL-v68-Ap 1 '72-p669
BL-v69-O 15 '72-p177
CCB-B-v25-O '71-p27
CE-v48-N '71-p104
Comw-v94-My 21 '71-p264
HB-v47-O '71-p480
KR-v39-My 1 '71-p504
LJ-v96-My 15 '71-p1781
LJ-v96-My 15 '71-p1804
LJ-v96-D 15 '71-p4159
NYTBR-Je 27 '71-p8
PW-v199-Ap 5 '71-p55
SR-v54-My 15 '71-p47
TN-v28-Je '72-p434
Teacher-v92-Mr '75-p39

* * *

JONES, Howard
The Cave Under The Water
JB-v39-Ap '75-p118

* * *

JONES, Iris Sanderson
Early North American Dollmaking
BL-v73-Mr 15 '77-p1064
BL-v73-Mr 15 '77-p1092
CSM-v70-Ag 24 '78-pB4
Cr Crafts-v6-Je '78-p11
Hob-v83-N '78-p133

* * *

JONES, J
How To Record Graveyards
TES-Ap 11 '80-p34

* * *

JONES, James M
Prejudice And Racism
Inter BC-v14-#7 '83-p28

* * *

JONES, Jennifer
Benji And Carlos
TES-My 11 '84-p30

* * *

JONES, John
Let's Eat Out!
CCB-B-v19-F '66-p100

* * *

JONES, Judith
Knead It, Punch It, Bake It!
BL-v78-Ja 1 '82-p598
BW-v11-N 8 '81-p23
CLW-v53-My '82-p448
CSM-v74-D 14 '81-pB10
Cha Ti-v36-N '82-p66
KR-v50-Ja 1 '82-p9
NYTBR-v86-D 6 '81-p82
SLJ-v28-Ja '82-p78

* * *

JONES, Llewelyn
Schoolin's Log
TES-Jl 18 '80-p21

* * *

JONES, Madeline
Stuart People
NS-v95-My 19 '78-p680

* * *

JONES, Mary F
La Patrie Quebecoise Au Debut De La Confederation
FR-v56-O '82-p192
In Rev-v15-Ap '81-p40

* * *

JONES, McClure
Cast Down The Stars
BL-v75-S 15 '78-p178
CBRS-v7-F '79-p68
CCB-B-v32-F '79-p100
HB-v55-F '79-p68
LA-v56-Ap '79-p444
SLJ-v25-D '78-p53

* * *

JONES, Olive
A Little Box Of Fairy Tales
PW-v224-Jl 15 '83-p52
A Treasure Box Of Fairy Tales
PW-v226-Ag 24 '84-p80

* * *

JONES, P
Turning The Beer Brown
TES-F 4 '83-p28

* * *

JONES, Penelope
Holding Together
BL-v78-S 15 '81-p108
CBRS-v10-Jl '81-p114
CCB-B-v35-N '81-p47
CLW-v53-Ap '82-p402
PW-v219-Je 12 '81-p54
SLJ-v28-O '81-p143
I Didn't Want To Be Nice
BB-v6-Ap '78-p1
CCB-B-v31-Jl '78-p179
CLW-v49-Ap '78-p403
KR-v45-D 15 '77-p1319
SLJ-v24-Mr '78-p120
I'm Not Moving!
CBRS-v8-Ag '80-p132
CCB-B-v34-N '80-p56
PW-v217-Je 27 '80-p88
SLJ-v27-D '80-p54
The Stealing Thing
BL-v79-Je 15 '83-p1340
CBRS-v11-Je '83-p115
CCB-B-v36-My '83-p169
HB-v59-O '83-p574
SLJ-v30-S '83-p124

* * *

JONES, Philip
The Forces Of Nature
SB-v19-S '83-p31
SLJ-v29-S '82-p122
Sch Lib-v29-D '81-p356

* * *

JONES, Rachael
Emergency
TES-N 12 '82-p26
First Aid
TES-N 12 '82-p26

* * *

JONES, Ray
The Mouse That Roared And Other Animal Fables
Brit Bk N C-Spring '80-p11
GP-v18-Mr '80-p3647
JB-v44-Je '80-p134
Sch Lib-v28-Je '80-p153

* * *

JONES, Rebecca C
Angie And Me
BL-v78-O 15 '81-p306
BS-v41-Mr '82-p475
CBRS-v10-D '81-p39
CCB-B-v35-D '81-p70
CLW-v53-My '82-p448
HB-v58-Ap '82-p164
Inter BC-v14-#6 '83-p17
KR-v50-Ja 15 '82-p68
PW-v220-Jl 31 '81-p59
SLJ-v28-N '81-p92
The Biggest, Meanest, Ugliest Dog In The Whole Wide World
BL-v79-D 1 '82-p499
CBRS-v11-D '82-p32
CCB-B-v36-F '83-p110
CE-v59-Mr '83-p278

JONES, Rebecca C (continued)
HB-v59-Ap '83-p161
KR-v50-O 15 '82-p1152
PW-v222-O 8 '82-p62
RT-v37-O '83-p56
SLJ-v29-F '83-p67
Madeline And The Great (Old) Escape Artist
BL-v80-F 1 '84-p814
CBRS-v12-F '84-p74
CCB-B-v37-D '83-p70
SLJ-v30-Ja '84-p77

* * *

JONES, Rhodri
Facing Up To The World
TES-S 26 '80-p25
My World
TES-S 26 '80-p25
Other Places, Other Worlds
TES-S 26 '80-p25
The World Ahead
TES-S 26 '80-p25
The World Around Us
TES-S 26 '80-p25

* * *

JONES, Ron
The Acorn People
BL-v73-My 1 '77-p1331
BksW-v1-Ap '77-p38
CE-v57-Mr '81-p208
Cur R-v17-O '78-p272
Inst-v88-F '79-p188
Inter BC-v13-#4 '82-p7
Kliatt-v12-Winter '78-p23
Teacher-v95-My '78-p109

* * *

JONES, Sandra
Blunderkin And The Reality Machines
In Rev-v14-Ag '80-p53

* * *

JONES, Sandy
Learning For Little Kids
BL-v75-Ap 15 '79-p1264
BW-F 4 '79-pE2
Inter BC-v10-My 50 '79-p21
KR-v47-Ja 1 '79-p59
LJ-v104-Mr 15 '79-p725

* * *

JONES, Sanford W
Great Recitations
Teacher-v94-Ja '77-p135

* * *

JONES, T F G
Black Sun
GP-v19-Jl '80-p3720
JB-v44-Ag '80-p193
Sch Lib-v28-D '80-p394
TES-Je 13 '80-p25

* * *

JONES, Terry
Fairy Tales
Brit Bk N C-Spring '82-p6
CCB-B-v36-My '83-p169
Econ-v289-N 26 '83-p96
GP-v20-Ja '82-p3996
ILN-v269-D '81-p75
JB-v46-F '82-p26
LATBR-D 5 '82-p10
NS-v102-D 4 '81-p18
NS-v106-D 2 '83-p25
NS-v106-D 16 '83-p39
NY-v58-D 6 '82-p187
NYTBR-v88-Ja 16 '83-p22
New Age-v8-Je '83-p70
Sch Lib-v30-S '82-p235
Spec-v247-D 19 '81-p33
TES-Ja 15 '82-p36
TES-N 11 '83-p25
TLS-N 20 '81-p1360
VV-v27-D 14 '82-p75
The Saga Of Erik The Viking
CCB-B-v37-Ap '84-p149
Econ-v289-N 26 '83-p96
GP-My '84-p4247
LATBR-D 4 '83-p8
NS-v106-D 2 '83-p25
NW-v102-D 5 '83-p112
NY-v59-D 5 '83-p205
NYTBR-v88-O 30 '83-p26
Nat R-v35-D 23 '83-p1628
PW-v224-O 21 '83-p67
SLJ-v30-Ja '84-p78
TES-N 4 '83-p24

* * *

JONES, Toeckey
Go Well, Stay Well
B&B-v25-F '80-p66
BL-v76-My 1 '80-p1268
CBRS-v8-Mr '80-p77
CCB-B-v33-Je '80-p193
GP-v19-S '80-p3758
HB-v56-Je '80-p307
JB-v44-Ap '80-p84
KR-v48-My 15 '80-p650
LA-v57-S '80-p649
SLJ-v26-Mr '80-p133
Sch Lib-v28-Je '80-p178
TES-Ja 18 '80-p39
TES-Mr 26 '82-p29
TES-Jl 23 '82-p24
TES-Jl 15 '83-p18
TLS-D 14 '79-p124

* * *

JONES, Weyman
The Talking Leaf
CCB-B-v19-Ap '66-p132
CLW-v37-Ja '66-p334
GT-v83-F '66-p22
KR-v33-O 15 '65-p1081
LJ-v91-F 15 '66-p1064
NYTBR-v70-N 7 '65-p40

* * *

JONES, Wilmer L
Learning To Compute
Cur R-v20-Ja '81-p60

* * *

JONG, Erica
Megan's Book Of Divorce
LATBR-Je 24 '84-p12
NYTBR-v89-Jl 1 '84-p23
SLJ-v31-O '84-p148

* * *

JONSEN, George
Favorite Tales Of Monsters And Trolls
PW-v211-My 30 '77-p45
SLJ-v24-Mr '78-p117

* * *

JONSON, Marian
A Troubled Grandeur
HB-v49-F '73-p61
KR-v40-O 15 '72-p1206
LJ-v98-Mr 15 '73-p1013
PW-v203-Ja 15 '73-p65

* * *

JONSON, Wilfred
Magic Tricks And Card Tricks
TES-F 24 '78-p30

* * *

JONSSON, Runer
Viki Viking
BL-v64-My 15 '68-p1094
CCB-B-v21-Ap '68-p129
HB-v44-Je '68-p324
KR-v35-D 15 '67-p1473
LJ-v93-My 15 '68-p2114
YR-v4-Je '68-p4

* * *

JOODE, Ton De
The Backyard Bestiary
BL-v79-F 15 '83-p751
LATBR-D 19 '82-p8
NYTBR-v87-D 5 '82-p64
VV-v27-D 14 '82-p74
WSJ-v200-D 13 '82-p30

* * *

JOOSSE, Barbara M
Spiders In The Fruit Cellar
BL-v79-Mr 15 '83-p970
CBRS-v11-My '83-p98
KR-v51-F 15 '83-p181
LA-v60-N '83-p1020
PW-v223-F 18 '83-p129
SLJ-v29-Ag '83-p52
The Thinking Place
CBRS-v10-Mr '82-p72
CLW-v54-N '82-p181
LA-v59-O '82-p747
PW-v221-Mr 19 '82-p70
Par-v57-N '82-p59
SLJ-v28-Ap '82-p59

* * *

JORDAN, Hope Dahle
The Fortune Cake
BL-v68-Jl 1 '72-p942
HB-v48-O '72-p467
KR-v40-Ja 15 '72-p68
LJ-v97-Ap 15 '72-p1606
Haunted Summer
CCB-B-v21-S '67-p10
HB-v43-Ag '67-p475
KR-v35-My 15 '67-p608
LJ-v92-S 15 '67-p3200
NYTBR-v72-N 5 '67-p64
NYTBR, pt.1-v72-My 7 '67-p12
Trav-v24-N '67-p99
Stranger In Their Midst
KR-v42-Jl 15 '74-p749
LJ-v99-D 15 '74-p3276
Supermarket Sleuth
BS-v29-D 1 '69-p353
CCB-B-v23-My '70-p145
LJ-v94-D 15 '69-p4619
Talk About The Tarchers
BL-v64-Jl 1 '68-p1229
BS-v28-Je 1 '68-p113
CCB-B-v22-Ja '69-p79
CSM-v60-Je 13 '68-p5
KR-v36-Ap 15 '68-p467
LJ-v93-Jl '68-p2738

* * *

JORDAN, June
Dry Victories
BL-v69-Ja 1 '73-p449
CCB-B-v26-Ap '73-p125
EJ-v63-Ja '74-p67
KR-v40-Jl 15 '72-p809
KR-v40-D 15 '72-p1424
LJ-v97-N 15 '72-p3806
NYTBR, pt.1-F 11 '73-p8
SE-v37-D '73-p785
Teacher-v93-Ap '76-p122
Fannie Lou Hamer
BL-v69-Ap 15 '73-p813
CCB-B-v26-Ap '73-p125
CE-v50-Ja '74-p168
CSM-v65-F 7 '73-p14
HB-v49-Ap '73-p151
KR-v40-D 1 '72-p1356
LJ-v98-Ap 15 '73-p1387
NHB-v36-D '73-p185
NYTBR-Ap 29 '73-p8
Teacher-v91-D '73-p72
His Own Where
BL-v68-Ja 1 '72-p391
BL-v68-Ja 1 '72-p394
BL-v68-Ap 1 '72-p664
BL-v80-O 15 '82-p352
CCB-B-v25-D '71-p58
CSM-v63-N 11 '71-pB6
CSM-v64-F 24 '72-p7
Comw-v95-N 19 '71-p188
EJ-v63-Ja '74-p65
EJ-v67-My '78-p88
HB-v47-D '71-p620
KR-v39-S 15 '71-p1021
LJ-v96-D 15 '71-p4159
LJ-v96-D 15 '71-p4190
NYRB-v18-Ap 20 '72-p13
NYT-v121-D 16 '71-p67
NYTBR, pt.2-N 7 '71-p6
NYTBR, pt.2-N 7 '71-p28
NYTBR, pt.2-My 6 '73-p28
PW-v200-O 18 '71-p50
TN-v28-Ap '72-p312
Kimako's Story
CBRS-v10-D '81-p35
CCB-B-v35-Mr '82-p132
CE-v58-Mr '82-p258
Essence-v15-O '84-p142
KR-v49-D 1 '81-p1465
NYTBR-v87-Ap 18 '82-p38
PW-v220-D 11 '81-p63
SLJ-v28-S '81-p110
New Life: New Room
BL-v71-Je 15 '75-p1075
CCB-B-v29-N '75-p47
Choice-v14-N '77-p1178
KR-v43-Ap 15 '75-p454
LA-v53-F '76-p200
PW-v207-My 19 '75-p175
RT-v30-Ap '77-p824
SLJ-v21-My '75-p48
The Voice Of The Children
BL-v67-F 15 '71-p490
CCB-B-v24-My '71-p137
CE-v48-N '71-p106
EJ-v60-My '71-p669
KR-v38-O 15 '70-p1169
LJ-v96-Mr 15 '71-p964
LJ-v96-My 15 '71-p1813
LJ-v97-My 15 '72-p1883
NYTBR-Ja 24 '71-p24
PW-v198-N 16 '70-p77
SR-v54-Mr 20 '71-p55
SR-v54-Ap 17 '71-p45
SR-v54-Ag 21 '71-p26
TCR-v73-S '71-p150
Who Look At Me
A Lib-v1-Ap '70-p386
BL-v66-D 15 '69-p510
BL-v69-My 1 '73-p838
CCB-B-v23-N '69-p47
Comw-v91-N 21 '69-p262
EJ-v58-N '69-p1267
HB-v46-F '70-p47
Inst-v79-D '69-p114
KR-v37-Ag 15 '69-p863
LJ-v95-F 15 '70-p789
ND-v19-F '70-p91
NO-v8-N 24 '69-p25
NYTBR-N 16 '69-p52
PW-v196-O 6 '69-p51
SR-v52-S 13 '69-p37
TN-v26-Ap '70-p307
WHR-v24-Spring '70-p202

* * *

JORDAN, Mildred
Proud To Be Amish
CCB-B-v23-N '69-p48
CLW-v42-Ap '71-p523
CLW-v43-F '72-p330
KR-v36-O 15 '68-p1162
LJ-v94-Ja 15 '69-p301

* * *

JORDANA, Jose L
Cuando Los Animales Hablaban
BL-v81-O 1 '84-p256
Leyendas Amazonicas
BL-v81-O 1 '84-p256

* * *

JORGENSEN, Bent
Wildlife Of The World
NS-v98-N 9 '79-p732

* * *

JOSEPH, Joan
Black African Empires
BL-v70-Je 1 '74-p1105
CCB-B-v28-N '74-p45
KR-v42-Mr 15 '74-p306
LJ-v99-S 15 '74-p2292
Folk Toys Around The World
BL-v69-Ja 15 '73-p493
CCB-B-v26-F '73-p92
KR-v40-N 1 '72-p1251
KR-v40-D 15 '72-p1424
LJ-v98-Ap 15 '73-p1387
NYTBR, pt.2-N 5 '72-p38
PW-v202-O 30 '72-p56
Henry Hudson
BL-v70-Je 15 '74-p1154
CE-v51-F '75-p218
CE-v51-Mr '75-p278
KR-v42-F 15 '74-p188
LJ-v99-S 15 '74-p2271
Pet Birds
BL-v72-N 1 '75-p368
CCB-B-v29-Ap '76-p125
KR-v43-D 15 '75-p1383
SB-v12-S '76-p107
SLJ-v22-Mr '76-p115
Teacher-v93-F '76-p125

* * *

JOSEPHS, Rebecca
Early Disorder
BL-v76-My 15 '80-p1357
BOT-v3-Jl '80-p311
B Rpt-v1-Mr '83-p24
CBRS-v8-Jl '80-p127
Emerg Lib-v10-N '82-p33
HB-v56-O '80-p526
KR-v48-F 15 '80-p239
KR-v48-Mr 15 '80-p374
Kliatt-v14-Fall '80-p65
LJ-v105-Ap 1 '80-p878
NYTBR-v85-Ag 17 '80-p18
PW-v217-Mr 14 '80-p70
SLJ-v26-Mr '80-p141
VOYA-v3-F '81-p30
VOYA-v4-D '81-p58

* * *

JOSLIN, S
Spaghetti For Breakfast: Phrases In Italian And English
BL-v61-Ap 15 '65-p802
CCB-B-v19-N '65-p45
CSM-v57-My 6 '65-p6B
Comw-v82-My 28 '65-p334
HB-v41-Je '65-p271
KR-v33-Mr 1 '65-p240
LJ-v90-Ap 15 '65-p2022

* * *

JOSLIN, Sesyle
Baby Elephant's Baby Book
CCB-B-v18-Ja '65-p75
The Gentle Savages
BL-v76-S 15 '79-p122
CBRS-v8-F '80-p58
KR-v48-Ja 1 '80-p9
NYTBR-Mr 2 '80-p20
SLJ-v26-S '79-p158
La Petite Famille
B&B-v11-D '65-p71
CCB-B-v18-Jl '65-p163
Spec-N 12 '65-p627
TLS-D 9 '65-p1154
Please Share That Peanut!
CCB-B-v19-N '65-p45
GT-v83-N '65-p107
KR-v33-Jl 1 '65-p621
LJ-v90-O 15 '65-p4616
The Spy Lady And The Muffin Man
BL-v67-Je 1 '71-p834
CCB-B-v24-Jl '71-p173
KR-v39-Mr 15 '71-p288
LJ-v96-My 15 '71-p1804
PW-v199-Ap 12 '71-p83
TLS-Jl 11 '75-p763
There Is A Bull On My Balcony
BL-v62-Ap 1 '66-p775
CCB-B-v19-Je '66-p164
HB-v42-Ag '66-p426
KR-v34-Ja 1 '66-p7
LJ-v91-Mr 15 '66-p1702
NYTBR-v71-Mr 27 '66-p34
PW-v189-Ap 4 '66-p62
SLJ-v27-Ja '81-p33
What Do You Say, Dear?
BW-v10-My 11 '80-p11
NYTBR-v85-My 11 '80-p47
PW-v217-Ap 25 '80-p81
Par-v58-S '83-p58

* * *

JOURDAN, Eveline
Butterflies And Moths Around The World
ACSB-v15-Winter '82-p33
BL-v77-Mr 15 '81-p1028
CBRS-v9-Ap '81-p78
SB-v17-N '81-p95
SLJ-v28-F '82-p77

* * *

JOUTSEN, Britta-Lisa
Lingonberries In The Snow
CCB-B-v22-My '69-p144
KR-v35-D 15 '67-p1473

* * *

JOVER, Maria L
El Gran Juego De Los Colores
SLJ-v30-My '84-p36

* * *

JOY, Charles R
Getting To Know Costa Rica, El Salvador And Nicaragua
Inter BC-v13-#2 '82-p9

* * *

JOY, Margaret
Gran's Dragon
Brit Bk N C-Autumn '80-p17
JB-v44-Ag '80-p177
SLJ-v26-Ag '80-p64
Sch Lib-v29-Je '81-p134
TES-Mr 7 '80-p47
Hairy And Slug
JB-v47-O '83-p208
SLJ-v30-F '84-p74
TES-S 30 '83-p46
Highdays And Holidays
GP-v20-Ja '82-p4005
JB-v46-F '82-p34
SLJ-v29-O '82-p153
Sch Lib-v30-Je '82-p178
Monday Magic
CCB-B-v36-Ap '83-p153
JB-v46-D '82-p224
SLJ-v29-Mr '83-p163
Sch Lib-v31-Je '83-p143
Tales From Allotment Lane School
SLJ-v30-Mr '84-p146
Sch Lib-v31-S '83-p248
TES-Ag 26 '83-p20

* * *

JOYCE, James
The Cat And The Devil
HB-v41-F '65-p46

* * *

JUNIOR Ladybird Books
TES-N 5 '82-p23

* * *

JUNIOR Pears Encyclopedia
ACSB-v12-Winter '79-p6
ARBA-v10-'79-p34
Econ-v285-D 25 '82-p104
GP-v21-Ja '83-p4018
Sch Lib-v31-Je '83-p196
TES-N 5 '82-p28
TES-N 16 '84-p25

* * *

JUNIOR Scholastic
BL-v79-F 1 '83-p731
BL-v80-Je 15 '84-p1479
Mag YA- '84-p155

* * *

JUNNE, I K
Floating Clouds, Floating Dreams
BL-v70-Jl 15 '74-p1254
BW-S 8 '74-p2
CE-v51-Ja '75-p158
KR-v42-Je 15 '74-p635
LJ-v99-S 15 '74-p2272
PW-v205-Je 24 '74-p60

* * *

JUPO, Frank
Atu, The Silent One
CCB-B-v21-My '68-p144
KR-v35-O 15 '67-p1265
LJ-v93-Ap 15 '68-p1789
Christmas Here, There, And Everywhere
KR-v45-N 1 '77-p1146
SLJ-v24-O '77-p88
Count Carrot
CCB-B-v19-Je '66-p165
KR-v34-Ap 15 '66-p419
LJ-v91-Je 15 '66-p3250
NYTBR-v71-My 8 '66-p39
No Place Too Far
CCB-B-v21-My '68-p144
KR-v35-Je 1 '67-p646
LJ-v92-Jl '67-p2655
A Place To Stay
CCB-B-v28-O '74-p30
LJ-v99-S 15 '74-p2272
PW-v205-My 13 '74-p59
SB-v10-D '74-p245
The Thanksgiving Book
CCB-B-v34-O '80-p34
KR-v48-S 1 '80-p1165
SLJ-v27-N '80-p76
To Carry And To Keep
BL-v72-My 15 '76-p1337
CCB-B-v30-N '76-p44
KR-v44-Mr 15 '76-p327
SB-v12-Mr '77-p214
SLJ-v23-S '76-p119
Walls, Gates, And Avenues
CCB-B-v18-Ap '65-p119

* * *

JURCA, Branka
Anca Pomaranca
BL-v80-Je 1 '84-p1402

* * *

JURICA, Joyce
The Greedy Dragon
GP-v14-Jl '75-p2672

* * *

JURICH, Jeff
Guess How High I Jumped To Kiss The Laughing Moon's Nose
PW-v225-Je 1 '84-p65

* * *

JURY, Mark
Gramp
BL-v72-My 1 '76-p1241
BL-v73-Ap 1 '77-p1152
CLW-v48-Ap '77-p404
Choice-v16-Ap '79-p188
Comw-v103-Ap 9 '76-p253
Comw-v103-Je 4 '76-p376
EJ-v67-Ja '78-p94
H Beh-v5-Je '76-p75
LJ-v101-Ap 1 '76-p878
NO-v15-Mr 6 '76-p19
NW-v87-Mr 22 '76-p81
NYT-v125-Mr 3 '76-p35
PW-v209-F 16 '76-p90
RS-Ap 22 '76-p87
SE-v41-O '77-p533
SLJ-v23-S '76-p146

* * *

JUST How Stories
Econ-v281-D 26 '81-p106
JB-v46-F '82-p27
NS-v102-D 4 '81-p17
SLJ-v28-Ag '82-p99
TLS-N 20 '81-p1358

* * *

JUST William's Cookin' Book
Punch-v276-Ap 18 '79-p688

* * *

JUSTER, Norton
Alberic The Wise And Other Journeys
CCB-B-v19-My '66-p150
HB-v42-F '66-p54
LJ-v91-F 15 '66-p1064
NY-v41-D 4 '65-p236
NYRB-v5-D 9 '65-p38
Obs-N 27 '66-p28
SR-v49-Ja 22 '66-p45
TLS-N 24 '66-p1089
Otter Nonsense
CLW-v55-D '83-p231
JB-v48-Ap '84-p60
NYTBR-v87-N 14 '82-p43
SLJ-v29-Mr '83-p178
The Phantom Tollbooth
NYTBR, pt.2-N 7 '71-p47
NYTBR, pt.2-F 13 '72-p12
Obs-Jl 4 '65-p18
Obs-Je 26 '77-p29

* * *

JUSTICE, Jennifer
Archaeology
Comw-v104-N 11 '77-p732
Cur R-v16-Ag '77-p233
Let's Look At Horses And Ponies
TES-O 20 '78-p26
The Tiger
BL-v76-N 1 '79-p449
SLJ-v26-F '80-p46
TES-D 28 '79-p19

* * *

JUSTICE, Jennifer L
War And Weapons
SLJ-v28-Ag '82-p117

* * *

JUSTNE, Kery H
Zengo ABC
BL-v78-S 15 '81-p115

* * *

JUSTUS, May
Gabby Gaffer
Inst-v85-N '75-p154
SLJ-v22-N '75-p64
Jumping Jack
LJ-v99-D 15 '74-p3263
New Home For Billy
CCB-B-v20-Mr '67-p110
LJ-v92-Ja 15 '67-p336

K

K-POWER
BL-v80-Je 15 '84-p1476
Mag YA- '84-p155
SLJ-v30-My '84-p39

* * *

KAATZ, Evelyn
Motorcycle Road Racer
KR-v45-D 1 '77-p1268
SLJ-v24-F '78-p59
Race Car Driver
CCB-B-v33-Mr '80-p136
SLJ-v26-Ja '80-p72
Soccer!
BL-v77-Jl 15 '81-p1451
SLJ-v28-Ja '82-p78
SLJ-v28-F '82-p77

* * *

KADESCH, Robert R
Math Menagerie
BL-v67-F 15 '71-p490
BL-v67-Ap 1 '71-p660
BS-v30-Ja 15 '71-p452
CCB-B-v24-Jl '71-p173
Comw-v93-N 20 '70-p205
KR-v38-O 15 '70-p1169
LJ-v96-Ja 15 '71-p277
NY-v46-D 5 '70-p208
SB-v6-Mr '71-p293

* * *

KAFF, F
Monster For A Day
CBRS-v8-16 '80-p62

* * *

KAFKA, Sherry
Big Enough
CCB-B-v24-O '70-p28
KR-v38-Jl 1 '70-p678
LJ-v95-D 15 '70-p4373
I Need A Friend
BL-v68-S 15 '71-p109
CCB-B-v25-N '71-p45
CLW-v47-Ap '76-p398
KR-v39-Ap 15 '71-p428
LJ-v96-Jl '71-p2358
PW-v199-Je 14 '71-p54

* * *

KAHL, M P
Wonders Of Storks
BL-v75-D 15 '78-p687
KR-v46-D 15 '78-p1359
SB-v15-D '79-p168
SLJ-v25-Ja '79-p55

* * *

KAHL, Virginia
The Duchess Bakes A Cake
BW-Ap 8 '79-pL2
GT-v89-Ja '72-p91
SLMQ-v12-Summer '84-p326
Giants, Indeed!
CCB-B-v27-Jl '74-p179
KR-v42-F 1 '74-p105
LJ-v99-My 15 '74-p1466
PW-v205-F 4 '74-p73
WLB-v48-My '74-p716
Gunhilde And The Halloween Spell
BB-v3-O '75-p2
HB-v51-O '75-p453
KR-v43-Ag 1 '75-p844
SLJ-v22-O '75-p91
Gunhilde's Christmas Booke
BL-v69-Mr 15 '73-p715
CCB-B-v26-N '72-p44
KR-v40-O 15 '72-p1185
LJ-v97-O 15 '72-p3470
PW-v202-N 6 '72-p58
How Do You Hide A Monster
BL-v67-Je 15 '71-p871
HB-v47-Ag '71-p375
KR-v39-Ap 1 '71-p356
LJ-v96-Je 15 '71-p2125
How Many Dragons Are Behind The Door?
KR-v45-Ap 1 '77-p348
NYTBR-My 1 '77-p28
PW-v211-Ap 18 '77-p61
SLJ-v24-S '77-p110
Whose Cat Is That?
BB-v7-Ag '79-p1
BL-v75-Jl 1 '79-p1580
BW-Jl 8 '79-pE5
CCB-B-v33-O '79-p30
KR-v47-Mr 15 '79-p323
LA-v56-O '79-p819
PW-v215-Mr 19 '79-p93
RT-v33-D '79-p357
SLJ-v26-O '79-p141
WLB-v54-O '79-p120

* * *

KAHN, Ely Jacques
A Building Goes Up
BL-v65-Je 15 '69-p1176
CCB-B-v22-Je '69-p160
KR-v37-Mr 15 '69-p310
LJ-v95-My 15 '70-p1944
SB-v5-My '69-p84
SR-v52-My 10 '69-p59

* * *

KAHN, Joan
Hi, Jock, Run Around The Block
CCB-B-v32-O '78-p31
KR-v46-Mr 1 '78-p239
PW-v213-F 27 '78-p156
SLJ-v25-Ja '79-p43
Seesaw
CCB-B-v18-Ja '65-p75
Some Things Dark And Dangerous
BL-v67-D 1 '70-p303
BS-v31-Ap 15 '71-p47
CCB-B-v24-Ja '71-p75
KR-v38-S 15 '70-p1054
LJ-v95-D 15 '70-p4376
MFSF-v41-Jl '71-p73
NS-v81-Je 4 '71-p782
NYTBR, pt.2-N 8 '70-p24
NYTBR, pt.2-N 8 '70-p36

KAHN, Joan (continued)
PW-v198-O 5 '70-p63
VOYA-v6-Ap '83-p59
WLB-v57-My '83-p773
Some Things Fierce And Fatal
BL-v68-N 1 '71-p242
BS-v31-N 15 '71-p386
BW-v5-N 7 '71-p11
CCB-B-v25-D '71-p58
CE-v49-N '72-p85
CLW-v43-F '72-p361
KR-v39-Ag 15 '71-p886
LJ-v96-D 15 '71-p4200
NY-v47-D 4 '71-p199
NYTBR, pt.1-F 13 '72-p8
PW-v200-O 18 '71-p51
TLS-Ap 28 '72-p484
WLB-v57-My '83-p773
Some Things Weird And Wicked
BL-v72-My 15 '76-p1331
BL-v72-My 15 '76-p1339
HB-v52-Ag '76-p411
PW-v209-Ap 5 '76-p102
SLJ-v22-My '76-p78
You Can't Catch Me
CCB-B-v30-My '77-p144
CLW-v48-F '77-p306
KR-v44-O 15 '76-p1133
SLJ-v23-F '77-p56
SR-v4-N 27 '76-p36

* * *

KAHN, Michele
Crafts Around The World
TES-Ag 4 '78-p19
The Earth And Sky
Nature-v300-D 9 '82-p547
My Everyday French Word Book
BL-v78-Ja 15 '82-p649
CCB-B-v35-Ap '82-p151
CE-v59-S '82-p60
HE-v40-Je 21 '80-p17
HE-v40-S 6 '80-p16
SLJ-v29-F '83-p68
TES-Mr 12 '82-p37
My Everyday Spanish Word Book
BL-v79-N 15 '82-p446
SLJ-v29-Mr '83-p163
Tell Me About Things At Home
TLS-N 26 '82-p1309
Wild Animals
JB-v47-D '83-p250
TES-Ap 1 '83-p36

* * *

KAHN, Peggy
The Care Bears And The New Baby
SLJ-v30-S '83-p107
The Care Bears' Book Of ABC's
PW-v223-My 27 '83-p68
The Handy Girls Can Fix It!
N Dir Wom-v13-Jl '84-p12

* * *

KAHN, Roger
The Boys Of Summer
Am-v126-Ap 15 '72-p411
Am-v127-N 18 '72-p426
Atl-v229-Ap '72-p124
BL-v68-My 15 '72-p787
BL-v68-Je 1 '72-p857
BS-v31-Mr 15 '72-p554
BW-v6-F 27 '72-p4
BW-v7-Ap 1 '73-p14
CLW-v44-O '72-p187
CM-v13-Fall '73-p90
CSM-v64-F 24 '72-p7
Comw-v96-Jl 14 '72-p387
HB-v48-D '72-p613
JAH-v66-S '79-p351
KR-v40-Ja 15 '72-p112
LJ-v97-F 15 '72-p696
LJ-v97-S 15 '72-p2972
Life-v72-Mr 3 '72-p16
Life-v73-D 29 '72-p24
NBR-v5-N '80-p23
NW-v79-Mr 13 '72-p94
NYT-v121-F 25 '72-p37
NYTBR-Mr 5 '72-p32
NYTBR-Je 4 '72-p20
NYTBR-D 3 '72-p68
NYTBR, pt.2-F 11 '73-p20
PW-v201-Ja 24 '72-p63
PW-v203-Ja 8 '73-p66
SR-v55-Mr 11 '72-p67
SR-v55-D 2 '72-p90
Sports Ill-v52-Je 9 '80-p6
TLS-F 27 '81-p217
Time-v99-Mr 13 '72-p84
VLS-O '83-p18
WLB-v46-Ap '72-p706
WSJ-v180-Jl 24 '72-p8
How The Weather Was
Am-v129-N 17 '73-p385
BL-v70-N 1 '73-p269
BL-v70-N 15 '73-p334
Choice-v10-F '74-p1860
HB-v50-Ap '74-p173
KR-v41-Ag 1 '73-p859
LJ-v98-S 1 '73-p2460
NO-v12-O 13 '73-p19
NYTBR-Ja 6 '74-p10
PW-v204-Ag 27 '73-p276
SR/W-v1-D 18 '73-p32

* * *

KAILER, Claude
Animal Adventures
Econ-v281-D 26 '81-p106

* * *

KALAN, Robert
Blue Sea
CBRS-v7-Jl '79-p122
KR-v47-F 15 '79-p193
LA-v57-Ap '80-p433
PW-v215-F 19 '79-p108
SLJ-v25-Mr '79-p124
Jump, Frog, Jump!
BL-v78-Ja 1 '82-p598
CBRS-v10-D '81-p32
EJ-v73-F '84-p104
HB-v58-Ap '82-p156
JB-v46-O '82-p181
KR-v50-Ja 1 '82-p3
LA-v59-Ap '82-p368
RT-v36-O '82-p71
SLJ-v28-N '81-p78
WLB-v56-Mr '82-p530
Rain
BB-v7-Mr '79-p2
KR-v46-Ag 15 '78-p876
RT-v33-O '79-p94
SLJ-v25-O '78-p131
SLJ-v26-O '79-p122
WLB-v53-Ap '79-p576

* * *

KALASHNIKOFF, Nicholas
The Defender
CLW-v38-Mr '67-p472
J Read-v25-F '82-p460
My Friend Yakub
J Read-v25-F '82-p460

* * *

KALB, Jonah
The Easy Baseball Book
BL-v72-Jl 15 '76-p1602
CLW-v48-D '76-p234
KR-v44-My 1 '76-p538
SLJ-v22-My '76-p75
The Easy Hockey Book
BL-v74-N 15 '77-p560
CCB-B-v31-Mr '78-p114
Comw-v104-N 11 '77-p734
KR-v45-N 15 '77-p1201

KALB, Jonah (continued)
RT-v32-O '78-p45
SLJ-v24-D '77-p64
The Easy Ice Skating Book
HB-v58-F '82-p66
SLJ-v28-D '81-p85
The Goof That Won The Pennant
BL-v73-F 1 '77-p834
CCB-B-v30-F '77-p93
HB-v53-Ap '77-p159
KR-v44-O 15 '76-p1137
RT-v31-O '77-p16
SLJ-v23-D '76-p70
SLJ-v24-My '78-p39
SLJ-v25-D '78-p33
The Kids' Candidate
CLW-v47-Ap '76-p410
KR-v43-O 15 '75-p1184
SLJ-v22-Ja '76-p47
What Every Kid Should Know
BL-v73-S 1 '76-p39
BS-v36-Ag '76-p150
CLW-v48-S '76-p84
Comw-v103-N 19 '76-p764
KR-v44-Ap 15 '76-p477
SLJ-v22-My '76-p70

* * *

KALCHMAN, Lois
Safety On Ice
Can Child Lit-#20 '80-p50
In Rev-v14-Ap '80-p48

* * *

KALEIDESCOPE: English For Juniors. Stage 3
TES-My 19 '78-p32

* * *

KALEIDOSCOPE
A Lib-v13-S '82-p550
LJ-v103-Ja 15 '78-p149
LJ-v108-Mr 1 '83-p481
TES-Jl 1 '83-p39
WLB-v57-Je '83-p892

* * *

KALINA, Sigmund
Air, The Invisible Ocean
BL-v70-S 1 '73-p51
CCB-B-v27-N '73-p45
KR-v41-F 1 '73-p121
LJ-v98-Jl '73-p2194
PW-v203-Je 25 '73-p74
How To Make A Dinosaur
BB-v4-Ja '77-p2
BL-v73-N 1 '76-p409
KR-v44-S 1 '76-p977
SLJ-v23-N '76-p60
How To Sharpen Your Study Skills
BL-v72-Ja 1 '76-p626
CCB-B-v29-Mr '76-p112
KR-v43-N 1 '75-p1234
SB-v12-My '76-p11
SLJ-v22-F '76-p53
Three Drops Of Water
ACSB-v8-Spring '75-p24
BL-v70-Ap 15 '74-p942
CCB-B-v28-O '74-p30
KR-v42-F 15 '74-p189
LJ-v99-S 15 '74-p2249
Learning-v12-Ap '84-p88
SB-v10-D '74-p247
Your Blood And Its Cargo
ACSB-v8-Spring '75-p25
KR-v42-Jl 15 '74-p746
SLJ-v21-Ja '75-p39

* * *

KALIOTSOS, Panteles
Ta Xylina Spathia
BL-v74-S 15 '77-p204

* * *

KALISH, Betty McKelvey
Eleven!
BL-v66-Je 15 '70-p1279
BW-v4-My 17 '70-p18
HB-v46-Ap '70-p160
KR-v38-F 1 '70-p104
LJ-v95-Je 15 '70-p2308
PW-v197-My 18 '70-p38

* * *

KALMAN, Benjamin
Animals In Danger
ASBYP-v16-Spring '83-p27
LA-v60-Ap '83-p484
SLJ-v29-F '83-p68

* * *

KALMAN, Bobbie
Early Christmas
In Rev-v15-Ag '81-p44
Early Stores And Markets
In Rev-v15-Ag '81-p44
Early Travel
In Rev-v16-Ap '82-p50

* * *

KALMAN, Y
Sparkles
JB-v47-D '83-p258

* * *

KALNAY, Francis
It Happened In Chichipica
BL-v68-O 15 '71-p204
CCB-B-v25-D '71-p58
HB-v47-O '71-p483
KR-v39-Ag 1 '71-p807
LJ-v96-O 15 '71-p3467
SR-v54-O 16 '71-p57

* * *

KAMEN, Gloria
Charlie Chaplin
BL-v79-Mr 15 '83-p970
BW-v13-F 13 '83-p9
KR-v50-O 15 '82-p1157
SLJ-v29-Mr '83-p178
Fiorello: His Honor, The Little Flower
BL-v78-N 15 '81-p439
CCB-B-v35-Ja '82-p87
KR-v49-O 1 '81-p1237
SLJ-v28-F '82-p77

* * *

KAMERMAN, Sylvia E
Christmas Play Favorites For Young People
BL-v79-D 15 '82-p562
SLJ-v29-Ag '83-p66
Dramatized Folk Tales Of The World
CCB-B-v25-O '71-p27
LJ-v97-F 15 '72-p775
Fifty Plays For Holidays
CCB-B-v23-D '69-p61
LJ-v95-F 15 '70-p779
Holiday Plays Round The Year
BL-v80-Ja 1 '84-p682
SLJ-v30-F '84-p74
On Stage For Christmas
BL-v75-D 15 '78-p688
CCB-B-v32-D '78-p64
SLJ-v25-Mr '79-p140
Space And Science Fiction Plays For Young People
BL-v78-F 1 '82-p709
LA-v60-F '83-p254
SF&FBR-Ja '82-p23
SLJ-v29-F '83-p89

* * *

KAMIEN, Janet
What If You Couldn't...?
ACSB-v13-Spring '80-p41
BL-v75-Ap 1 '79-p1218
BL-v78-N 1 '81-p397

KAMIEN, Janet (continued)
BW-Mr 11 '79-pF5
CCB-B-v32-Je '79-p178
CE-v57-Mr '81-p208
HB-v55-Ag '79-p435
Inter BC-v13-#4 '82-p14
KR-v47-F 1 '79-p129
MN-v58-N '79-p84
RT-v37-F '84-p506
SLJ-v26-S '79-p141
SLJ-v28-D '81-p29
Teacher-v96-Ja '79-p32

* * *

KAMIKAMICA, Esiteri
Come To My Place
SLJ-v29-S '82-p122

* * *

KAMM, A
Choosing Books For Younger Children
JB-v42-Je '78-p132
The Story Of Islam
JB-v40-Ag '76-p205

* * *

KAMM, Josephine
Hebrew People
BL-v64-My 15 '68-p1088
BS-v28-My 1 '68-p65
CCB-B-v22-Ja '69-p80
KR-v36-Mr 15 '68-p347
LJ-v93-Ap 15 '68-p1812
PW-v193-My 6 '68-p46
SE-v33-My '69-p563
TLS-Ja 25 '68-p94
Kings, Prophets & History: New Look At Old Testament
BL-v63-S 1 '66-p39
CCB-B-v20-S '66-p13
KR-v34-Ap 15 '66-p429
NYTBR-v71-My 1 '66-p30
TLS-D 9 '65-p1155
Runaways
JB-v42-D '78-p314
Obs-D 3 '78-p36
TES-O 13 '78-p25
TLS-S 29 '78-p1083
The Starting Point
B&B-v20-Jl '75-p64
GP-v14-My '75-p2654
TLS-Ap 4 '75-p361
Young Mother
CCB-B-v19-F '66-p100
KR-v33-Ag 1 '65-p762
LJ-v90-O 15 '65-p4631
NYTBR-v70-N 7 '65-p16
Sch Lib-v32-S '84-p207
Spec-Je 4 '65-p729
TLS-Je 17 '65-p504

* * *

KAN, Lai P
The Ancient Chinese
BL-v78-N 15 '81-p439
SLJ-v28-Ag '82-p118

* * *

KANBE, J
The Lonely Hare
JB-v40-Je '76-p143

* * *

KANDELL, Alice
Sikkim
CCB-B-v25-Je '72-p157
Cr H-v31-D '71-p66
KR-v39-Ag 1 '71-p810
LJ-v96-O 15 '71-p3468
PW-v200-N 15 '71-p72

* * *

KANE, Betty
Medicine
CCB-B-v28-Mr '75-p115
CE-v51-F '75-p218
SLJ-v21-Mr '75-p106

* * *

KANE, George Francis
What's The Next Move?
BL-v71-F 15 '75-p619
NYTBR-D 8 '74-p16
SLJ-v22-S '75-p106

* * *

KANE, Henry B
Four Seasons In The Woods
Aud-v71-Mr '69-p109
BL-v65-My 15 '69-p1077
CCB-B-v22-Mr '69-p113
CSM-v61-Jl 31 '69-p7
Inst-v79-Ja '70-p154
SR-v52-F 22 '69-p47
Wings, Legs Or Fins
CCB-B-v20-O '66-p28
CSM-v57-N 4 '65-pB9
NYTBR-v71-F 6 '66-p26
SB-v1-Mr '66-p226
SR-v49-My 14 '66-p41

* * *

KANE, Joseph Nathan
Facts About The Presidents
ARBA-v8-'77-p254
ARBA-v13-'82-p273
BL-v71-Ja 1 '75-p469
BL-v72-Jl 1 '76-p1527
BL-v78-D 1 '81-p481
BL-v78-Je 15 '82-p1385
Choice-v15-Ap '78-p197
Choice-v19-D '81-p488
RSR-v3-Ja '75-p19
RSR-v10-Jl '82-p68
WLB-v43-O '68-p177
WLB-v47-S '72-p21
WLB-v49-N '74-p249

* * *

KANER, Peter
Integrated Mathematics Scheme IMS L1
TES-O 14 '83-p38

* * *

KANETZKE, Howard W
Airplanes And Balloons
ACSB-v12-Fall '79-p48
BL-v75-Je 1 '79-p1488
SLJ-v25-My '79-p48
The Story Of Cars
ACSB-v12-Fall '79-p48
BL-v75-Je 1 '79-p1488
SLJ-v25-My '79-p48
Trains And Railroads
ACSB-v12-Fall '79-p48
BL-v75-Je 1 '79-p1488
CCB-B-v32-Je '79-p178
SLJ-v25-My '79-p48

* * *

KANTROWITZ, Mildred
Good-Bye, Kitchen
CCB-B-v25-Je '72-p157
CE-v58-S '81-p39
KR-v40-Mr 1 '72-p255
LJ-v97-S 15 '72-p2936
PW-v201-My 1 '72-p50
I Wonder If Herbie's Home Yet
CCB-B-v24-My '71-p137
LJ-v96-Je 15 '71-p2125
SR-v54-Ap 17 '71-p44
Maxie
BL-v67-O 1 '70-p145
CCB-B-v24-Je '71-p158
LJ-v95-N 15 '70-p4036
LJ-v95-D 15 '70-p4326
NYTBR, pt.2-My 24 '70-p46
TLS-Ap 28 '72-p483
When Violet Died
CCB-B-v27-Je '74-p158
CLW-v49-O '77-p103
Inst-v84-Ag '74-p178
JB-v39-F '75-p41

KANTROWITZ, Mildred
(continued)
KR-v41-N 1 '73-p1195
LJ-v98-N 15 '73-p3441
Par-v49-Ja '74-p26
TLS-S 20 '74-p1013
Willy Bear
BB-v4-Ja '77-p1
BL-v73-O 1 '76-p252
CSM-v68-N 3 '76-p25
Inst-v86-N '76-p145
JB-v42-Je '78-p135
KR-v44-S 15 '76-p1036
NYTBR-N 14 '76-p26
Par-v51-N '76-p29
SLJ-v23-Ja '77-p83
Teacher-v96-O '78-p169

* * *

KANZAWA, Toshiko
Ahiru No Baba-Chan
BL-v75-Jl 15 '79-p1636
Baba-Chan No Omimai
BL-v75-Jl 15 '79-p1636
Baba-Chan To Tondekita Boshi
BL-v75-Jl 15 '79-p1636

* * *

KAO, George
Chinese Wit And Humor
SLJ-v22-Ja '76-p25

* * *

KAPLAN, Bess
The Empty Chair
BL-v74-My 1 '78-p1432
BS-v38-S '78-p179
CCB-B-v31-Je '78-p162
Comw-v105-N 10 '78-p732
EJ-v67-S '78-p90
HB-v54-Je '78-p284
KR-v46-Je 1 '78-p599
SLJ-v24-My '78-p68

* * *

KAPLAN, Helen S
Making Sense Of Sex
ACSB-v13-Mr '80-p35
BW-v9-N 11 '79-p18
Cur R-v19-Je '80-p233
KR-v47-O 1 '79-p1187
KR-v47-O 15 '79-p1217
LJ-v105-Ja 1 '80-p109
SLJ-v27-S '80-p84
WLB-v54-Ja '80-p327

* * *

KAPLAN, Rhoda
The Apple That Wanted To Be Famous
BksW-v1-F '78-p37

* * *

KAPLAN, Sandra
The Big Book Of Collections
Teacher-v93-My '76-p93
The Big Book Of People And Words
Teacher-v95-D '77-p89
The Big Book Of Writing Games And Activities
Inst-v86-Mr '77-p152
LA-v54-F '77-p215
Teacher-v93-My '76-p92

* * *

KAPLOW, Robert
Two In The City
BS-v39-Ag '79-p169
CBRS-v7-Jl '79-p128
CCB-B-v33-O '79-p30
CLW-v51-D '79-p234
HB-v55-Je '79-p309
J Read-v23-D '79-p279
KR-v47-Jl 1 '79-p744
NYTBR-Ap 29 '79-p38
SLJ-v25-Ap '79-p69

* * *

KARAVASIL, Josephine
Houses And Homes Around The World
TES-N 18 '83-p35

* * *

KARAVASIL, Josie
Blood And Thunder
GP-v23-S '84-p4317
School's OK
GP-v21-Mr '83-p4027
JB-v47-F '83-p43
TES-Ja 14 '83-p30
Tricks And Treats
GP-v23-S '84-p4317

* * *

KARDISH, Laurence
Reel Plastic Magic
AB-10 '72-p17
BL-v69-O 15 '72-p190
BS-v32-O 15 '72-p319
BS-v34-Ap 1 '74-p23
CLW-v44-My '73-p608
EJ-v61-D '72-p1382
FQ-v26-Summer '73-p34
HB-v48-O '72-p478
KR-v40-Je 15 '72-p680
LJ-v97-Ag '72-p2638
LJ-v98-Mr 15 '73-p1024

* * *

KAREN, Ruth
Kingdom Of The Sun
BL-v72-Ja 15 '76-p679
BL-v72-Ja 15 '76-p685
BS-v36-Ap '76-p16
CCB-B-v29-Je '76-p158
CE-v53-O '76-p38
Comw-v103-N 19 '76-p763
HB-v52-Ap '76-p171
KR-v43-O 15 '75-p1199
NYTBR-N 16 '75-p55
NYTBR-Mr 14 '76-p12
SB-v12-S '76-p98
SLJ-v22-Ja '76-p53
The Land And People Of Central America
BL-v62-N 1 '65-p272
BS-v25-Je 15 '65-p145
Inter BC-v13-#2 '82-p10
LJ-v90-S 15 '65-p3813
Song Of The Quail
BL-v69-Mr 1 '73-p644
BW-v7-Ja 7 '73-p15
CCB-B-v26-Ap '73-p126
CLW-v45-N '73-p185
Comw-v99-N 23 '73-p217
HB-v49-Ap '73-p152
Inst-v82-My '73-p72
KR-v40-D 15 '72-p1433
LJ-v98-S 15 '73-p2652
PW-v203-Ja 29 '73-p260
SE-v37-D '73-p792

* * *

KARGER, Delmar W
How To Choose A Career
CBRS-v7-Ja '79-p46
Cur R-v18-Ag '79-p195

* * *

KARKAVITSAS, Andreas
Logia Tes Plores
BL-v72-Ap 15 '76-p1175
BL-v74-S 15 '77-p204

* * *

KARL, Frederick R
The Naked I
PW-v199-Ja 11 '71-p64

* * *

KARL, Jean
From Childhood To Childhood
BL-v67-O 15 '70-p155
CLW-v42-O '70-p139
Comw-v93-N 20 '70-p207
GT-v88-D '70-p84
HB-v46-O '70-p491
KR-v38-Ap 1 '70-p425
KR-v38-Ap 15 '70-p473
NYTBR, pt.2-My 2 '71-p2
PW-v197-Ap 20 '70-p60
PW-v197-My 18 '70-p38
SR-v54-Ap 17 '71-p44
TN-v27-Ja '71-p213
WLB-v45-Ja '71-p499

* * *

KARL, Jean E
Beloved Benjamin Is Waiting
BL-v74-My 1 '78-p1434
CCB-B-v32-S '78-p11
CE-v55-F '79-p223
Comw-v105-N 10 '78-p732
HB-v54-Je '78-p277
KR-v46-Ap 15 '78-p437
LA-v56-Ap '79-p441
NYTBR-My 21 '78-p25
PW-v213-F 20 '78-p127
PW-v217-F 1 '80-p110
SLJ-v24-Ap '78-p85
SLJ-v24-My '78-p36
Teacher-v96-O '78-p162
But We Are Not Of Earth
BL-v77-Je 1 '81-p1299
CBRS-v9-My '81-p87
CCB-B-v35-S '81-p12
CLW-v53-S '81-p92
HB-v57-Je '81-p309
J Read-v25-N '81-p179
KR-v49-Jl 15 '81-p872
NYTBR-v86-Ap 26 '81-p60
PW-v219-F 13 '81-p94
PW-v225-Je 1 '84-p65
RT-v35-O '81-p113
SLJ-v27-My '81-p66
The Turning Place
BB-v4-Ja '77-p4
BL-v72-Ap 15 '76-p1186
CCB-B-v29-Jl '76-p176
CLW-v48-O '76-p138
HB-v52-Je '76-p295
KR-v44-Mr 15 '76-p322
Kliatt-v13-Spring '79-p26
LA-v53-S '76-p702
NYTBR-Ap 25 '76-p16
PW-v209-F 2 '76-p100
RT-v31-O '77-p20
SLJ-v22-Ap '76-p90
SLJ-v22-My '76-p34
Teacher-v94-N '76-p139

* * *

KARLIN, Nurit
The Blue Frog
CBRS-v11-My '83-p98
SLJ-v30-S '83-p108
A Train For The King
CBRS-v11-My '83-p98
PW-v223-F 18 '83-p129
SLJ-v30-S '83-p108

* * *

KARLOWICH, Robert A
Young Defector
BL-v79-F 15 '83-p777
SLJ-v29-Ag '83-p67

* * *

KARLSTROM, Bjorn
Biggles And The Golden Bird
TLS-S 29 '78-p1090
Biggles And The Saragasso Triangle
TLS-S 29 '78-p1090
Biggles And The Tiger
TES-O 9 '81-p29

* * *

KARNES, Merle B
Creative Games For Learning
Inst-v89-Ap '80-p121

* * *

KARP, Naomi J
The Turning Point
BL-v73-D 15 '76-p608
CCB-B-v30-Ja '77-p76
GP-v16-S '77-p3163
KR-v44-Jl 1 '76-p732
SLJ-v23-S '76-p119

* * *

KARRAS, Alex
Alex Karras: My Life In Football, Television, And Movies
NYTBR-Jl 8 '79-p31
SLJ-v25-My '79-p84

* * *

KARSTAD, Aleta
Wild Habitats
ACSB-v13-Mr '80-p35
EJ-v70-Ja '81-p76
KR-v47-Ag 1 '79-p912
NY-v55-S 3 '79-p107
PW-v216-Jl 9 '79-p96
SA-v241-D '79-p36
SB-v15-My '80-p263
SLJ-v26-F '80-p76

* * *

KASE, Judith B
The Emperor's New Clothes
Dr-Ap '80-p68

* * *

KASPER, Vancy
Always Ask For A Transfer
BIC-v13-Ag '84-p32
Quill & Q-v50-Je '84-p35

* * *

KASSIL, Lev
Brother Of The Hero
BL-v64-Je 1 '68-p1142
BW-v2-My 5 '68-p33
CCB-B-v21-Je '68-p161
HB-v44-Ag '68-p420
J Read-v25-F '82-p461
KR-v36-Ap 15 '68-p460
LJ-v93-My 15 '68-p2114
NYTBR-v73-My 5 '68-p42
PW-v193-Je 3 '68-p129
YR-v4-My '68-p4
Once In A Lifetime
BL-v67-O 1 '70-p145
CCB-B-v24-O '70-p28
HB-v46-Ag '70-p394
J Read-v25-F '82-p461
KR-v38-My 15 '70-p559
SR-v53-Jl 25 '70-p29

* * *

KASSIRER, Norma
Magic Elizabeth
CCB-B-v20-N '66-p44
CE-v43-Ap '67-p476
KR-v34-Mr 15 '66-p304
LJ-v91-Jl '66-p3535
Par-v41-N '66-p14

* * *

KASTNER, Erich
Emil And The Detectives
GT-v82-Ap '65-p112
SLJ-v24-F '78-p35
Lisa And Lottie
BL-v65-Jl 1 '69-p1229
CCB-B-v24-Jl '70-p181
GT-v89-S '71-p155
KR-v37-Ap 15 '69-p443
LJ-v94-S 15 '69-p3206

KASTNER, Erich (continued)
The Little Man
BL-v63-Mr 1 '67-p728
CCB-B-v20-Ap '67-p124
KR-v34-O 15 '66-p1101
LJ-v91-D 15 '66-p6192
NYRB-v7-D 15 '66-p29
NYTBR-v71-N 6 '66-p40
NYTBR-v71-D 4 '66-p66
NYTBR-v85-D 28 '80-p19
PW-v190-N 21 '66-p76
Spec-N 11 '66-p626
TLS-N 24 '66-p1077
The Little Man And The Big Thief
BL-v66-Jl 15 '70-p1408
BW-v4-My 17 '70-p5
HB-v46-Ag '70-p388
KR-v38-Mr 15 '70-p322
LJ-v95-Jl '70-p2534
NYTBR, pt.2-My 24 '70-p4
PW-v197-Ap 13 '70-p85
TN-v27-N '70-p90

* * *

KASTNER, John
SuperDan And The Dinosaurs
CBRS-v9-D '80-p24
CCB-B-v34-Ja '81-p96
KR-v48-O 1 '80-p1294
SLJ-v27-N '80-p64

* * *

KASTNER, Jonathan
Sleep
BL-v64-Jl 1 '68-p1236
BS-v28-Jl 15 '68-p173
CCB-B-v23-S '69-p11
KR-v36-My 1 '68-p522
LJ-v93-O 15 '68-p3971
NYTBR-v73-My 5 '68-p18
Teacher-v86-Ja '69-p143
YR-v5-S '68-p3

* * *

KASUYA, Masahiro
St. Francis And The Wolf
JB-v47-Je '83-p109
The Tiniest Christmas Star
SLJ-v26-O '79-p116

* * *

KATAN, Norma J
Hieroglyphs
BL-v77-Jl 15 '81-p1448
CBRS-v9-Ag '81-p127
CLW-v53-N '81-p190
KR-v49-Jl 15 '81-p874
LA-v59-F '82-p156
SA-v245-D '81-p47
SLJ-v28-Ja '82-p78

* * *

KATAOKA, Barbara Slavin
Pictures And Pollution
SB-v13-Mr '78-p219
SLJ-v24-S '77-p118

* * *

KATER, John
The Letter Of John To James
SLJ-v28-Mr '82-p135

* * *

KATI See ReKai, Kati

* * *

KATTERER, Lisbeth
Bauz, Der Tupfelkater
BL-v77-O 1 '80-p263

* * *

KATZ, Bobbi
The Manifesto And Me-Meg
CCB-B-v28-Ja '75-p79
Choice-v14-N '77-p1178
KR-v42-Ag 1 '74-p804
LJ-v99-N 15 '74-p3047
Rod-And-Reel Trouble
CCB-B-v28-N '74-p45
LJ-v99-D 15 '74-p3282
Snow Bunny
BL-v72-Jl 15 '76-p1602
CCB-B-v30-O '76-p26
SLJ-v23-S '76-p119
Volleyball Jinx
BL-v74-F 15 '78-p1013
CCB-B-v31-My '78-p143
SLJ-v24-Ap '78-p86
1,001 Words
CCB-B-v29-Ja '76-p80
Cur R-v16-My '77-p126
KR-v43-Ag 1 '75-p848
SLJ-v22-Ap '76-p74

* * *

KATZ, Herbert
Museum Adventures
BL-v66-Ap 1 '70-p983
BS-v29-N 1 '69-p306
CCB-B-v23-Ap '70-p130
Comw-v91-N 21 '69-p263
KR-v37-O 1 '69-p1077
LJ-v95-My 15 '70-p1944
PW-v196-O 27 '69-p60
SR-v53-Mr 21 '70-p39

* * *

KATZ, Jane
Let Me Be A Free Man
BL-v72-Ja 15 '76-p685
Comw-v102-N 21 '75-p570
J Read-v20-My '77-p732
KR-v43-O 15 '75-p1201
SLJ-v22-Ja '76-p54
This Song Remembers
AIQ-v5-N '79-p375
BL-v77-D 1 '80-p510
CBRS-v9-Winter '81-p48
CCB-B-v34-Ap '81-p153
Choice-v18-Mr '81-p991
HB-v57-Ap '81-p203
Inst-v91-S '81-p30
Inter BC-v12-#7 '81-p25
KR-v49-Ja 1 '81-p14
RT-v35-O '81-p113
SE-v46-O '82-p456
SLJ-v27-Ja '81-p70
VOYA-v4-Ap '81-p44
We Rode The Wind
BL-v72-Ja 15 '76-p685
Comw-v102-N 21 '75-p570
J Read-v20-My '77-p732
KR-v43-O 15 '75-p1201
SB-v12-S '76-p99
SLJ-v22-Ja '76-p54

* * *

KATZ, Judy H
White Awareness
BL-v75-D 1 '78-p584
Inter BC-v11-Mr 30 '80-p15
Inter BC-v14-#7 '83-p28

* * *

KATZ, Marjorie P
Fingerprint Owls And Other Fantasies
B&B-v20-My '75-p79
BL-v69-Ja 15 '73-p494
BW-v7-N 11 '73-p4C
CCB-B-v26-F '73-p93
CE-v49-Mr '73-p323
GP-v13-Mr '75-p2588
KR-v40-D 1 '72-p1350
PW-v202-O 30 '72-p56

* * *

KATZ, Ruth J
Make It And Wear It
BL-v78-F 1 '82-p701
CBRS-v10-F '82-p68
CCB-B-v35-Mr '82-p132
SLJ-v28-Ap '82-p70
VOYA-v5-Ap '82-p46

KATZ, Ruth J (continued)
WCRB-v8-F '82-p61
Pumpkin Personalities
BB-v7-O '79-p6
CBRS-v8-S '79-p5

* * *

KATZ, Susan
Erik Estrada Scrapbook
SLJ-v27-Ag '81-p68
WLB-v55-Ap '81-p613
Kristy And Jimmy
SLJ-v25-Mr '79-p140

* * *

KATZ, Welwyn
The Prophesy Of Tau Ridoo
BIC-v12-D '83-p16

* * *

KATZ, William Loren
An Album Of Reconstruction
BL-v71-D 1 '74-p379
KR-v42-S 15 '74-p1009
An Album Of The Civil War
BL-v70-Je 1 '74-p1099
BL-v70-Je 1 '74-p1105
KR-v42-F 15 '74-p189
LJ-v99-S 15 '74-p2272
SS-v66-Ja '75-p41
TES-O 21 '77-p22
An Album Of The Great Depression
BL-v75-D 1 '78-p617
CCB-B-v32-Mr '79-p120
CLW-v50-My '79-p448
SE-v43-Ap '79-p298
SLJ-v25-F '79-p57
Black People Who Made The Old West
BB-v6-Ap '78-p3
BL-v74-D 15 '77-p684
CE-v54-Ap '78-p308
KR-v45-S 15 '77-p997
PW-v212-Ag 29 '77-p366
SLJ-v24-Mr '78-p137
Making Our Way
BL-v72-Ja 15 '76-p686
CE-v53-O '76-p38
CLW-v47-Mr '76-p355
KR-v43-N 1 '75-p1243
LJ-v101-Mr 15 '76-p812
PW-v208-Ag 11 '75-p118
SLJ-v22-Ja '76-p54

* * *

KATZMAN, Susan Manlin
For Kids Who Cook
BL-v74-O 15 '77-p376
KR-v45-Je 15 '77-p627
PW-v211-Je 6 '77-p82
SLJ-v24-S '77-p146

* * *

KAUFMAN, Charles
The Frog And The Beanpole
BL-v76-Jl 1 '80-p1608
CBRS-v8-Mr '80-p77
CCB-B-v33-My '80-p174
KR-v48-Jl 1 '80-p836
LA-v57-S '80-p650
NYTBR-v85-Ap 27 '80-p64
RT-v34-Ja '81-p484
SLJ-v26-Ag '80-p65

* * *

KAUFMAN, Fredrick
African Roots Of Jazz
Inst-v91-F '82-p173

* * *

KAUFMAN, Joe
About The Big Sky, About The High Hills, About The Rich Earth...And The Deep Sea
ACSB-v12-Fall '79-p35
PW-v213-Je 12 '78-p82
SLJ-v25-Mr '79-p124
Big And Little
CCB-B-v20-My '67-p141
CLW-v39-Ja '68-p374
How We Are Born, How We Grow, How Our Bodies Work...And How We Learn
CCB-B-v29-Ap '76-p126
Teacher-v94-N '76-p32
Joe Kaufman's Book About Busy People And How They Do Their Work
CCB-B-v27-Mr '74-p111
Inst-v83-N '73-p128
PW-v204-Jl 2 '73-p80
Wings Paws Hoofs And Flippers
ASBYP-v15-Fall '82-p27
PW-v220-D 4 '81-p50
Words
BW-My 2 '76-pL2

* * *

KAUFMAN, Mervyn
Fiorello La Guardia
CC-v89-N 29 '72-p1218
CCB-B-v26-S '72-p10
KR-v40-Je 1 '72-p626
SR-v55-My 20 '72-p81
Teacher-v90-O '72-p115
Jesse Owens
BL-v70-O 1 '73-p172
CCB-B-v27-O '73-p28
KR-v41-My 15 '73-p563
LJ-v98-D 15 '73-p3724

* * *

KAUFMAN, Michael
Rooftops & Alleys
BL-v70-O 1 '73-p172
BW-v7-My 13 '73-p1
CCB-B-v27-D '73-p66
CE-v50-F '74-p232
KR-v41-My 15 '73-p564
KR-v41-D 15 '73-p1353
LJ-v98-N 15 '73-p3453

* * *

KAUFMAN, William I
UNICEF Book Of Children's Prayers
SLJ-v29-Ap '83-p100

* * *

KAUFMANN, Alicia
No Room For Nicky
CCB-B-v23-My '70-p146

* * *

KAUFMANN, Helen L
Anvil Chorus
BS-v24-F 15 '65-p454
CCB-B-v18-Je '65-p151
CLW-v36-Mr '65-p478
Comw-v82-My 28 '65-p334
LJ-v90-F 15 '65-p962
NYTBR-v70-F 7 '65-p26
TLS-Je 6 '68-p594
The Story Of Sergei Prokofiev
CCB-B-v25-N '71-p46
LJ-v96-O 15 '71-p3468
M Ed J-v58-D '71-p14

* * *

KAUFMANN, John
Bats In The Dark
BL-v68-My 15 '72-p821
CCB-B-v25-Je '72-p157
HB-v48-Je '72-p263
KR-v40-F 15 '72-p198
SB-v8-S '72-p156

KAUFMANN, John (continued)
TLS-Ap 6 '73-p390
Birds Are Flying
ACSB-v13-Mr '80-p36
BL-v76-D 1 '79-p558
KR-v47-D 15 '79-p1432
SB-v16-S '80-p33
SLJ-v26-Ja '80-p57
TES-Mr 6 '81-p38
Birds In Flight
BL-v66-Jl 1 '70-p1342
KR-v38-Mr 15 '70-p333
SB-v6-My '70-p50
TLS-Jl 14 '72-p815
Chimney Swift
BL-v67-Ap 15 '71-p702
CSM-v63-My 6 '71-pB3
KR-v39-Ja 1 '71-p5
LJ-v96-My 15 '71-p1797
NYTBR-My 16 '71-p8
SB-v7-My '71-p61
Falcons Return
ACSB-v9-Winter '76-p22
BL-v71-Je 1 '75-p1006
CCB-B-v29-N '75-p47
HB-v51-O '75-p478
KR-v43-My 1 '75-p518
SLJ-v22-S '75-p121
Fish Hawk
BL-v64-Ja 15 '68-p594
KR-v35-Jl 15 '67-p811
LJ-v92-N 15 '67-p4252
SB-v3-D '67-p243
Fly It!
CBRS-v8-Ag '80-p135
CE-v57-N '80-p114
HB-v56-O '80-p537
SLJ-v27-S '80-p72
Flying Giants Of Long Ago
BL-v80-My 1 '84-p1248
CCB-B-v37-Je '84-p188
HB-v60-Ag '84-p486
SLJ-v30-My '84-p66
Flying Hand-Launched Gliders
BL-v70-Je 15 '74-p1154
BW-My 19 '74-p5
KR-v42-Ap 1 '74-p369
LJ-v99-S 15 '74-p2272
NYTBR-My 5 '74-p44
Flying Reptiles
ACSB-v10-Spring '77-p28
BL-v73-S 15 '76-p177
KR-v44-Je 15 '76-p688
PW-v209-Je 28 '76-p99
SB-v12-Mr '77-p210
SLJ-v23-D '76-p66
Insect Travelers
BL-v69-Ja 1 '73-p449
KR-v40-O 15 '72-p1207
LJ-v98-My 15 '73-p1690
SB-v9-My '73-p76
Little Dinosaurs And Early Birds
ACSB-v10-Fall '77-p21
BL-v73-Mr 15 '77-p1092
CCB-B-v30-My '77-p144
Comw-v104-N 11 '77-p733
HB-v53-O '77-p557
KR-v45-Ja 15 '77-p47
SLJ-v23-Ap '77-p55
TES-Je 6 '80-p27
TLS-Mr 28 '80-p363
Robins Fly North, Robins Fly South
BL-v67-N 15 '70-p269
CCB-B-v24-Mr '71-p108
KR-v38-S 15 '70-p1043
LJ-v96-Ja 15 '71-p258
SB-v6-Mr '71-p324
SR-v53-N 14 '70-p35
Streamlined
ACSB-v8-Spring '75-p25
BL-v71-N 15 '74-p344
CCB-B-v28-Ap '75-p132
KR-v42-O 1 '74-p1064
SB-v11-My '75-p33
TLS-Mr 28 '80-p363
Winds And Weather
KR-v39-Ag 15 '71-p878
LJ-v96-N 15 '71-p3902
SB-v7-D '71-p228
TLS-Je 15 '73-p689
Wings, Sun, And Stars
A Lib-v1-Ap '70-p386
BL-v65-Je 1 '69-p1124
CSM-v61-My 1 '69-pB5
HB-v45-O '69-p550
KR-v37-F 1 '69-p112
LJ-v94-Ap 15 '69-p1796
PW-v195-Mr 3 '69-p59
SB-v5-My '69-p57

* * *

KAULA, Edna Mason
Bantu Africans
BL-v64-Ap 15 '68-p996
KR-v36-Mr 1 '68-p264
LJ-v93-Ap 15 '68-p1812
SLJ-v28-S '81-p41
The Land And People Of New Zealand
CCB-B-v19-D '65-p64
Leaders Of The New Africa
BL-v62-Jl 15 '66-p1088
CCB-B-v21-S '67-p11
Inst-v76-Mr '67-p170
LJ-v91-D 15 '66-p6202
NYTBR-v71-N 6 '66-p2
PW-v189-My 30 '66-p88
SR-v49-Je 25 '66-p61

* * *

KAVALER, Lucy
Dangerous Air
BL-v64-N 15 '67-p388
CCB-B-v21-O '67-p29
KR-v35-Jl 1 '67-p750
LJ-v92-D 15 '67-p4613
SB-v3-D '67-p254
SR-v50-O 21 '67-p44
The Dangers Of Noise
ACSB-v12-Spring '79-p31
BL-v75-N 15 '78-p547
CCB-B-v32-D '78-p64
Comw-v105-N 10 '78-p735
HB-v54-D '78-p665
KR-v46-O 1 '78-p1075
SB-v15-D '79-p155
SLJ-v25-S '78-p140
Green Magic
ASBYP-v17-Winter '84-p30
BL-v80-S 1 '83-p86
BW-v13-Ag 14 '83-p7
CCB-B-v37-S '83-p10
Cur R-v24-N '84-p62
HB-v59-Je '83-p333
KR-v51-Mr 15 '83-p308
SB-v19-Ja '84-p156
SLJ-v30-O '83-p159
Life Battles Cold
BL-v70-F 15 '74-p657
CCB-B-v27-My '74-p145
KR-v41-O 1 '73-p1112
LJ-v99-Ja 15 '74-p210
SB-v10-My '74-p39
TLS-Jl 5 '74-p724
A Matter Of Degree
BL-v77-Jl 1 '81-p1376
BOT-v4-O '81-p456
CCB-B-v35-O '81-p32
KR-v49-My 15 '81-p664
LJ-v106-Jl '81-p1434
NYTBR-v86-Ag 2 '81-p12
PW-v219-Je 5 '81-p74
SB-v17-Mr '82-p200

KAVALER, Lucy (continued)
Mushrooms, Molds, And Miracles
BL-v62-S 1 '65-p19
BS-v25-Jl 1 '65-p163
CCB-B-v19-S '65-p11
Choice-v3-Je '66-p329
KR-v33-Mr 1 '65-p290
LJ-v90-My 15 '65-p2275
NYTBR-v70-Jl 11 '65-p16
PW-v190-Ag 29 '66-p346
SB-v2-Mr '67-p292
TLS-N 9 '67-p1070
Time-v85-Je 25 '65-p106

* * *

KAVANAGH, P J
Rebel For Good
Brit Bk N C-Spring '81-p26
GP-v19-Mr '81-p3832
JB-v45-Je '81-p124
Obs-N 30 '80-p36
Sch Lib-v29-Mr '81-p51
TES-N 7 '80-p24
TLS-N 21 '80-p1324
Scarf Jack
B&B-v23-Je '78-p72
GP-v17-Jl '78-p3367
HT-v30-D '80-p62
NS-v95-My 19 '78-p683
TES-Je 30 '78-p19
TES-My 15 '81-p29
TLS-Jl 7 '78-p766

* * *

KAVANAUGH, Dorriet
Listen To Us!
BL-v75-Ja 15 '79-p780
BW-Mr 4 '79-pF3
CCB-B-v32-My '79-p156
KR-v46-D 15 '78-p1366
Kliatt-v13-Spring '79-p29
PW-v215-Ja 22 '79-p370
Par-v54-Je '79-p14
SLJ-v25-Ap '79-p69
SR-v6-My 26 '79-p62
TN-v37-Fall '80-p51

* * *

KAVCIC, Vladimir
The Golden Bird
BL-v66-S 1 '69-p56
BW-v3-Ag 17 '69-p12
LJ-v94-Jl '69-p2676
NS-v80-N 6 '70-p616
RT-v33-F '80-p564
TLS-O 30 '70-p1255

* * *

KAY, Christain
English Through Pictures
TES-Ag 8 '80-p20

* * *

KAY, Eleanor
The Clinic
CCB-B-v25-Mr '72-p109
LJ-v96-Jl '71-p2374
LJ-v98-Mr 15 '73-p1020
The Emergency Room
BL-v67-Ja 15 '71-p421
CCB-B-v24-Ap '71-p125
LJ-v96-Mr 15 '71-p1116
NYTBR-O 11 '70-p30
The Operating Room
BL-v67-S 15 '70-p108
CCB-B-v24-S '70-p12
LJ-v95-S 15 '70-p3049
LJ-v98-Mr 15 '73-p1020
Sex And The Young Teen-Ager
CCB-B-v27-My '74-p146
JB-v42-Ag '78-p208
KR-v41-O 1 '73-p1113
LJ-v98-D 15 '73-p3712
SB-v10-D '74-p230
TES-My 19 '78-p32

* * *

KAY, George
Stewpot's Travel Fun Book
TES-S 22 '78-p23

* * *

KAY, Helen
A Day In The Life Of A Baby Gibbon
CCB-B-v26-Ja '73-p78
KR-v40-My 1 '72-p539
LJ-v97-O 15 '72-p3448
SB-v8-D '72-p250
TLS-N 3 '72-p1336
An Egg Is For Wishing
BL-v62-Jl 1 '66-p1048
CLW-v38-N '66-p217
HB-v42-Je '66-p303
KR-v34-Mr 1 '66-p237
LJ-v91-My 15 '66-p2684
NYTBR-v71-Ap 10 '66-p20
RT-v35-Mr '82-p720
SR-v49-My 14 '66-p36
TLS-N 24 '66-p1083
Henri's Hands For Pablo Picasso
CCB-B-v19-Je '66-p165
HB-v42-F '66-p50
KR-v33-O 15 '65-p1076
LJ-v90-D 15 '65-p5517
NYTBR-v70-N 7 '65-p55
Obs-Ap 10 '66-p20
TLS-My 19 '66-p430
A Stocking For A Kitten
CCB-B-v20-S '66-p13
CSM-v57-My 6 '65-p3B
Comw-v82-My 28 '65-p327
HB-v41-Je '65-p273
KR-v33-Mr 1 '65-p233
LJ-v90-My 15 '65-p2396

* * *

KAY, Mara
A House Full Of Echoes
BL-v77-Je 1 '81-p1299
CBRS-v10-Jl '81-p117
CCB-B-v35-O '81-p32
RT-v35-N '81-p239
SLJ-v28-S '81-p137
VOYA-v4-O '81-p40
In Face Of Danger
Am-v137-D 3 '77-p406
BB-v5-Ja '78-p4
BL-v74-S 15 '77-p195
BS-v37-D '77-p294
CE-v55-Ap '79-p263
Cur R-v17-O '78-p343
HB-v54-F '78-p53
KR-v45-S 1 '77-p933
LA-v55-Mr '78-p368
NYTBR-N 13 '77-p39
PW-v212-O 17 '77-p84
SLJ-v24-N '77-p73
In Place Of Katia
J Read-v25-Ja '82-p355
TLS-D 9 '65-p1147
Lolo
Brit Bk N C-Spring '82-p14
HT-v31-D '81-p53
JB-v46-F '82-p34
Sch Lib-v30-Mr '82-p52
TLS-N 20 '81-p1355
Masha
BL-v65-Ja 15 '69-p546
BS-v28-Ja 1 '69-p422
BW-v2-N 3 '68-p30
CCB-B-v22-Mr '69-p113
CLW-v41-O '69-p140
J Read-v25-Ja '82-p355
KR-v36-N 1 '68-p1225
NS-v75-My 24 '68-p694
Obs-Ap 14 '68-p27
SE-v33-My '69-p558
SR-v51-N 9 '68-p69
TLS-Je 6 '68-p579

KAY, Mara (continued)
One Small Clue
BL-v78-Jl '82-p1445
BS-v42-O '82-p287
CBRS-v10-Spring '82-p117
CCB-B-v35-Jl '82-p210
CSM-v74-O 8 '82-pB12
Cur R-v21-O '82-p409
KR-v50-My 15 '82-p608
SLJ-v28-Ag '82-p126
VOYA-v5-D '82-p33
Restless Shadows
JB-v44-D '80-p308
Sch Lib-v28-D '80-p394
Storm Warning
Emerg Lib-v11-N '83-p21
GP-v15-Jl '76-p2904
JB-v40-Je '76-p164
Obs-Ap 11 '76-p33
TLS-Ap 2 '76-p377

* * *

KAY, Ronald
Something On My Mind
TES-Je 15 '84-p36

* * *

KAY, Shirley
Digging Into The Past
Indexer-v12-Ap '80-p30
NS-v88-N 8 '74-p668
SB-v11-My '75-p40
TLS-D 6 '74-p1385

* * *

KAYANO, Shigeru
Kaze No Kami To Okikurumi
BL-v79-O 15 '82-p320

* * *

KAYE, Geraldine
The Beautiful Take-Away Palace
Brit Bk N C-Autumn '80-p22
GP-v19-N '80-p3794
Sch Lib-v29-Je '81-p134
Billy-Boy
JB-v39-Ap '75-p119
TLS-Ap 4 '75-p364
Children Of The Turnpike
JB-v40-Ap '76-p105
The Day After Yesterday
CCB-B-v35-Ap '82-p151
GP-v20-N '81-p3967
JB-v45-O '81-p198
SLJ-v29-S '82-p123
Sch Lib-v30-Je '82-p130
TES-Ag 14 '81-p29
TLS-S 18 '81-p1068
A Different Sort Of Christmas
GP-v15-N '76-p3006
JB-v40-O '76-p270
The Donkey Strike
GP-My '84-p4266
Frangipani Summer
JB-v46-D '82-p232
Good-Bye Ruby Red
BL-v72-Je 15 '76-p1470
SLJ-v23-S '76-p97
Joanna All Alone
BS-v36-Ap '76-p30
CCB-B-v29-My '76-p147
GP-v13-Ja '75-p2557
JB-v39-Ap '75-p108
KR-v43-Ag 15 '75-p918
SLJ-v22-O '75-p99
TLS-D 6 '74-p1373
King Of The Knockdown Gingers
Brit Bk N C-Spring '80-p11
Kofi And The Eagle
Obs-Jl 13 '80-p29
TLS-Ap 6 '73-p387
A Nail, A Stick And A Lid
BL-v72-Je 15 '76-p1470
SLJ-v23-S '76-p97
Penny Black
B&B-v22-Je '77-p74
GP-v15-My '76-p2890
JB-v40-Je '76-p170
Spec-v236-Ap 10 '76-p25
TLS-Ap 2 '76-p377
The Plum Tree Party
GP-v21-S '82-p3962
JB-v46-O '82-p191
The Rotten Old Car
SLJ-v23-S '76-p97
TLS-S 28 '73-p1127
The Sky-Blue Dragon
JB-v47-D '83-p245
Sch Lib-v31-S '83-p248
TES-Je 3 '83-p38
Tim And The Red Indian Headdress
SLJ-v23-S '76-p97
Where Is Fred?
SLJ-v23-My '77-p77
The Yellow Pom-Pom Hat
BL-v72-Je 15 '76-p1470
SLJ-v23-S '76-p97

* * *

KAYE, M M
The Ordinary Princess
BW-v14-N 11 '84-p14
CBRS-v13-O '84-p17
CCB-B-v38-S '84-p8
Econ-v277-D 27 '80-p73
GP-v19-Mr '81-p3857
JB-v45-Ap '81-p71
NS-v100-N 14 '80-p20
PW-v226-Ag 31 '84-p436
Par-v59-N '84-p56
TLS-N 21 '80-p1326
Thistledown
Econ-v281-D 26 '81-p106
TLS-Mr 26 '82-p347

* * *

KAYE Geraldine
The Plum Tree Party
JB-v46-Ag '82-p143

* * *

KAZAKOV, Yuri
Arcturus The Hunting Hound
BL-v65-S 1 '68-p64
BS-v28-Je 1 '68-p114
BW-v2-My 5 '68-p33
CCB-B-v21-Jl '68-p176
HB-v44-Je '68-p324
KR-v36-My 15 '68-p555
LJ-v93-O 15 '68-p3983
NYTBR-v73-My 5 '68-p42
PW-v193-Je 3 '68-p129

* * *

KAZANTZAKIS, Nikos
Alexander The Great: A Novel
BS-v42-Jl '82-p130
LJ-v106-D 15 '81-p2407

* * *

KAZIMIROFF, Theodore L
The Last Algonquin
A Anth-v85-Mr '83-p206
BL-v78-Jl '82-p1418
B Rpt-v1-Ja '83-p44
BS-v42-Jl '82-p144
Inter BC-v14-#7 '83-p31
J Read-v26-Ja '83-p375
Kliatt-v18-Winter '84-p37
LJ-v107-Jl '82-p1318
NYT-v131-Jl 30 '82-p24
New Age-v8-N '82-p75
PW-v221-Mr 19 '82-p63
SLJ-v29-D '82-p89
VOYA-v5-D '82-p43

* * *

KEAREY, Charles
Last Plane From Uli
Africa T-v27-#3 '80-p36
Fly-v91-S '72-p22
KR-v40-Jl 1 '72-p745
LJ-v97-N 1 '72-p3618
NYTBR-O 1 '72-p42
PW-v202-Jl 31 '72-p69
Trav-v139-Je '73-p10

* * *

KEARNS, Doris
Lyndon Johnson And The American Dream
AHR-v82-Je '77-p776
APSR-v72-Mr '78-p268
Am-v135-S 25 '76-p176
Am-v135-N 13 '76-p328
BL-v72-Jl 1 '76-p1504
BS-v36-S '76-p197
BW-My 30 '76-pF7
BW-Je 6 '76-pH1
BW-D 12 '76-pH9
Choice-v13-O '76-p1045
Comt-v62-Ag '76-p75
Enc-v48-Ja '77-p82
GW-v116-Ja 16 '77-p22
HB-v52-D '76-p652
KR-v44-Ap 1 '76-p442
Kliatt-v12-Winter '78-p23
LJ-v101-Je 1 '76-p1293
NCR-v67-Jl '78-p346
NL-v59-My 24 '76-p5
NO-v15-Je 19 '76-p21
NS-v92-O 8 '76-p484
NW-v87-My 31 '76-p69
NY-v52-Je 7 '76-p136
NYRB-v23-Je 24 '76-p8
NYT-v125-My 7 '76-pC17
NYT-v125-Jl 30 '76-pC19
NYTBR-Je 6 '76-p1
NYTBR-Ag 7 '77-p33
Nat R-v28-Ag 20 '76-p905
New R-v175-Ag 7 '76-p27
PAR-v38-Ja '78-p93
PSQ-v91-Winter '77-p699
PT-v10-S '76-p88
PW-v209-Ap 12 '76-p65
PW-v211-Je 13 '77-p106
Prog-v40-Jl '76-p40
RAH-v5-Mr '77-p130
SR-v3-Je 12 '76-p25
Spec-v237-O 16 '76-p20
TLS-D 10 '76-p1536
VQR-v53-Summer '77-p90
VV-v21-Mr 29 '76-p42
VV-v21-Ag 23 '76-p36
WP-v32-Ap '80-p406
WSJ-v187-Je 4 '76-p10
WSJ-v188-D 8 '76-p24
Wil Q-v6-Summer '82-p150

* * *

KEARY, A
The Heroes Of Asgard
TLS-D 14 '79-p131

* * *

KEARY, Eliza
At Home Again
JB-v44-D '80-p292

* * *

KEATING, Bern
Chaka, King Of The Zulus
Africa T-v27-#3 '80-p33
CSM-v60-My 2 '68-pB6
KR-v36-Ja 15 '68-p60
LJ-v93-My 15 '68-p2123

* * *

KEATING, Norma
Mr. Chu
CCB-B-v19-F '66-p100
LJ-v90-N 15 '65-p5072
NYTBR-v70-My 9 '65-p24
SR-v48-My 15 '65-p45
TLS-Mr 14 '68-p260

* * *

KEATS, Ezra J
Clementina's Cactus
BL-v79-O 15 '82-p313
CBRS-v11-Ja '83-p42
CCB-B-v36-O '82-p28
CE-v59-My '83-p354
HB-v58-D '82-p641
JB-v47-Ag '83-p155
KR-v50-Jl 15 '82-p795
LA-v60-My '83-p645
New Age-v8-D '82-p68
PW-v222-O 29 '82-p45
RT-v36-F '83-p594
SLJ-v29-N '82-p69

* * *

KEATS, Ezra Jack
Apt. 3
CCB-B-v25-D '71-p58
CE-v60-S '83-p27
Comw-v95-N 19 '71-p187
HB-v47-D '71-p601
KR-v39-Jl 15 '71-p736
LJ-v96-O 15 '71-p3460
LJ-v96-D 15 '71-p4159
NS-v84-N 10 '72-p697
NYTBR-S 19 '71-p8
Obs-S 24 '72-p37
PW-v200-Ag 9 '71-p47
SR-v54-N 13 '71-p59
Spec-v229-N 11 '72-p759
TN-v28-Ja '72-p203
Dreams
BB-v3-F '75-p1
B&B-v21-Mr '76-p66
BL-v71-N 1 '74-p292
BW-N 10 '74-p5
CCB-B-v28-Ja '75-p80
CE-v51-Mr '75-p274
HB-v50-D '74-p684
Inst-v84-N '74-p130
JB-v39-Ap '75-p97
KR-v42-S 1 '74-p939
KR-v43-Ja 1 '75-p3
LJ-v99-S 15 '74-p2249
PT-v8-Mr '75-p94
PW-v206-Ag 26 '74-p307
Spec-v233-D 7 '74-p739
Teacher-v92-Ja '75-p109
Goggles!
A Lib-v1-Ap '70-p386
BL-v66-D 1 '69-p459
BL-v69-My 1 '73-p836
CCB-B-v23-D '69-p61
CE-v46-My '70-p432
CLW-v41-N '69-p201
CSM-v61-N 6 '69-pB1
Comw-v91-N 21 '69-p253
GT-v87-Ja '70-p140
GT-v89-Ja '72-p92
HB-v45-O '69-p526
KR-v37-S 1 '69-p925
LJ-v94-D 15 '69-p4596
NYTBR, pt.2-N 9 '69-p68
Par-v45-Ap '70-p28
SR-v52-O 18 '69-p56
TLS-O 30 '70-p1260
Hi, Cat!
BL-v67-O 15 '70-p193
BW-v4-N 8 '74-p2
Bl W-v20-Ja '71-p90
Brit Bk N C-Spring '81-p11
CCB-B-v24-Ja '71-p75
CLW-v42-F '71-p380
GT-v88-D '70-p82
HB-v46-D '70-p606
KR-v38-Jl 1 '70-p678
LJ-v95-O 15 '70-p3620
NS-v81-Je 4 '71-p781
NYTBR, pt.2-N 5 '72-p42
PW-v198-Ag 3 '70-p60

KEATS, Ezra Jack (continued)
SR-v53-N 14 '70-p34
Spectr-v47-Mr '71-p45
TES-Je 20 '80-p38
TLS-Jl 2 '71-p769
TLS-S 29 '78-p1087
TN-v27-Ja '71-p209
Time-v96-D 21 '70-p72
Jennie's Hat
BL-v62-Je 1 '66-p960
CCB-B-v19-Je '66-p165
HB-v42-Je '66-p299
LJ-v91-My 15 '66-p2684
NYTBR-v71-Ap 3 '66-p26
SR-v49-Ap 16 '66-p49
TES-Jl 7 '78-p30
John Henry: An American Legend
BL-v62-N 1 '65-p272
CC-v82-Je 30 '65-p838
CCB-B-v18-Jl '65-p163
CE-v42-O '65-p112
CLW-v37-O '65-p146
CLW-v52-Ap '81-p389
CSM-v57-My 6 '65-p7B
Comw-v82-My 28 '65-p334
GT-v83-N '65-p120
GT-v83-Ap '66-p24
HB-v41-Ag '65-p383
LJ-v90-Je 15 '65-p2881
NO-v4-Jl 12 '65-p21
NYTBR-v70-Ap 25 '65-p26
Par-v41-Ja '66-p20
SE-v44-O '80-p481
SR-v48-Je 19 '65-p41
Kitten For A Day
BB-v3-Ap '75-p1
BL-v78-My 1 '82-p1161
CCB-B-v28-Ap '75-p132
CE-v51-Ap '75-p328
CLW-v54-N '82-p181
KR-v42-D 15 '74-p1299
LA-v60-F '83-p213
PT-v8-Ap '75-p108
PW-v206-N 25 '74-p44
SLJ-v21-Mr '75-p88
WLB-v49-F '75-p426
Letter To Amy
BL-v65-N 1 '68-p313
BW-v2-N 3 '68-p5
KR-v36-O 1 '68-p1106
PW-v194-O 14 '68-p64
A Letter To Amy
CCB-B-v22-F '69-p96
CE-v45-My '69-p532
CE-v46-Ap '70-p365
HB-v45-F '69-p41
NYTBR-F 2 '69-p26
SR-v52-Ja 18 '69-p40
TLS-O 16 '69-p1201
The Little Drummer Boy
CLW-v41-O '69-p141
CLW-v52-Ap '81-p388
CSM-v60-N 7 '68-pB2
KR-v36-S 15 '68-p1042
LA-v56-Ap '79-p401
LJ-v93-O 15 '68-p3990
NYTBR-v73-D 1 '68-p74
TN-v25-Ap '69-p310
Teacher-v92-D '74-p13
Louie
BL-v80-Ja 1 '84-p682
CCB-B-v29-Ja '76-p80
CLW-v47-F '76-p309
CSM-v67-N 5 '75-pB6
GP-v15-Jl '76-p2922
HB-v51-O '75-p454
KR-v43-Jl 15 '75-p774
NW-v86-D 15 '75-p89
Obs-Jl 18 '76-p20
PW-v208-Jl 14 '75-p60
PW-v215-Mr 26 '79-p82
RT-v37-F '84-p506
SLJ-v22-O '75-p91
Louie And The Trip
Inst-v89-Ja '80-p111
Louie's Search
BW-v10-N 9 '80-p15
CBRS-v9-O '80-p12
CCB-B-v34-D '80-p73
CSM-v73-Mr 16 '81-p23
JB-v45-Ap '81-p63
KR-v48-O 1 '80-p1294
LA-v58-F '81-p182
NYTBR-v85-N 9 '80-p64
PW-v218-S 5 '80-p68
SLJ-v27-N '80-p64
TLS-N 21 '80-p1328
Maggie And The Pirate
BL-v76-S 15 '79-p124
CBRS-v7-Jl '79-p122
HB-v55-O '79-p525
KR-v47-Jl 1 '79-p738
LA-v57-Ja '80-p80
NYTBR-N 11 '79-p51
PW-v216-Ag 20 '79-p81
SLJ-v26-N '79-p66
Maggie And The Pirates
CCB-B-v33-My '80-p174
LA-v57-Ja '80-p80
SLJ-v26-N '79-p66
SLJ-v30-Mr '84-p119
My Dog Is Lost
BL-v69-Ja 15 '73-p477
CLW-v52-Ap '81-p390
Night
CCB-B-v23-Ja '70-p82
CLW-v41-D '69-p262
EJ-v59-Mr '70-p437
KR-v37-O 15 '69-p1126
LJ-v94-N 15 '69-p4131
LJ-v94-D 15 '69-p4607
Over In The Meadow
CCB-B-v25-Jl '72-p171
CE-v49-Ap '73-p374
CSM-v64-My 4 '72-pB2
HB-v48-Ag '72-p362
KR-v40-My 15 '72-p575
KR-v40-D 15 '72-p1409
LA-v56-Ap '79-p402
LJ-v97-S 15 '72-p2936
SR-v55-My 20 '72-p80
Spec-v230-Ap 14 '73-p465
TLS-Je 15 '73-p686
Pet Show
Am-v127-D 2 '72-p475
BL-v68-Jl 15 '72-p1004
CCB-B-v26-S '72-p10
CE-v49-D '72-p145
Comw-v97-F 23 '73-p474
HB-v48-Ag '72-p363
KR-v40-Ap 15 '72-p473
LJ-v97-Je 15 '72-p2231
NS-v84-N 10 '72-p697
NYT-v121-Ag 4 '72-p29
Spec-v229-N 11 '72-p759
TLS-N 3 '72-p1326
Peter's Chair
BL-v63-Jl 15 '67-p1194
Brit Bk N C-Spring '81-p11
CCB-B-v21-S '67-p11
CE-v44-Ja '68-p322
CE-v46-Ap '70-p365
CLW-v39-O '67-p158
CSM-v59-Ag 31 '67-p5
GP-v19-My '80-p3710
HB-v43-O '67-p582
Inst-v77-Ag '67-p207
KR-v35-Mr 1 '67-p265
LJ-v92-F 15 '67-p872
NYTBR-v72-Je 18 '67-p30
NYTBR-v88-Ag 28 '83-p23
PW-v191-My 22 '67-p64
SR-v50-Je 17 '67-p35
TES-Mr 28 '80-p28
TES-Je 20 '80-p38
Pssst, Doggie
CCB-B-v27-N '73-p46

KEENE, Carolyn (continued)
The Haunted Carousel
SLJ-v30-D '83-p81
The Haunted Lagoon
CSM-v65-My 2 '73-pB4
NS-v104-D 3 '82-p24
The Kachina Doll Mystery
SLJ-v28-D '81-p81
Mountain-Peak Mystery
SLJ-v24-My '78-p84
Mystery Of The Lost Dogs
SLJ-v24-My '78-p83
Nancy Drew And The Hardy Boys Super Sleuths!
SLJ-v28-My '82-p84
The Nancy Drew Cookbook
RT-v34-F '81-p585
The Nancy Drew Sleuth Book
BW-Mr 11 '79-pF5
CCB-B-v32-Jl '79-p193
SLJ-v25-My '79-p81
The Secret In The Old Lace
Inst-v90-Ja '81-p115
SLJ-v27-D '80-p73
The Secret Of The Forgotten City
CCB-B-v29-D '75-p64
The Secret Of The Swiss Chalet
CSM-v65-My 2 '73-pB4
NS-v104-D 3 '82-p24
TES-O 1 '82-p31
The Secret Of The Twin Puppets
CCB-B-v31-Je '78-p162
The Silver Cobweb
SLJ-v30-D '83-p81
The Sinister Omen
CSM-v74-O 8 '82-pB8
SLJ-v29-D '82-p82
The Sky Phantom
CCB-B-v29-Je '76-p158
The Swami's Ring
SLJ-v28-D '81-p81
The Twin Dilemma
SLJ-v28-D '81-p81

* * *

KEENEY, Mary Jane
Your Wonderful Brain
CCB-B-v25-Ja '72-p75
SB-v8-My '72-p70

* * *

KEEP, David
History Through Stamps
Inst-v85-O '75-p189
LJ-v100-Ap 15 '75-p778
NYTBR-My 2 '76-p45
TLS-Ap 25 '75-p465

* * *

KEEPING, Charles
Alfie Finds "The Other Side Of The World"
CCB-B-v22-Mr '69-p113
CSM-v61-N 29 '68-pB9
SR-v51-N 9 '68-p46
YR-v5-N '68-p2
Black Dolly
GP-v22-My '83-p4081
LR-v21-Spring '67-p32
Spec-N 11 '66-p627
TES-My 27 '83-p29
TLS-N 24 '66-p1083
Charley, Charlotte And The Golden Canary
CCB-B-v21-Jl '68-p176
CCB-B-v22-S '68-p9
Inst-v77-Ap '68-p154
KR-v36-Ja 1 '68-p2
LJ-v93-Ja 15 '68-p283
Obs-S 10 '67-p23
PW-v193-Ja 22 '68-p274
SR-v51-Jl 20 '00-p30
TLS-N 30 '67-p1149
YR-v4-Ap '68-p8
The Christmas Story
BW-v3-D 21 '69-p8
CCB-B-v23-O '69-p26
KR-v37-Ja 1 '69-p1
LJ-v94-O 15 '69-p3851
PW-v196-S 1 '69-p52
SR-v52-D 20 '69-p28
Cockney Ding Dong
Econ-v257-D 20 '75-p103
TLS-D 5 '75-p1456
Inter-City
GP-v16-O '77-p3193
JB-v41-O '77-p279
Lis-v98-N 10 '77-p626
TLS-Jl 15 '77-p862
Joseph's Yard
B&B-v15-Mr '70-p36
CCB-B-v24-Jl '70-p181
GP-My '84-p4273
LJ-v95-Jl '70-p2528
TLS-D 4 '69-p1393
Miss Emily And The Bird Of Make-Believe
GP-v17-Ja '79-p3449
JB-v43-F '79-p15
NS-v96-N 3 '78-p593
Molly O' The Moors: The Story Of A Pony
CCB-B-v20-Ap '67-p124
LJ-v92-Mr 15 '67-p1311
NYTBR-v72-My 7 '67-p52
PW-v191-F 27 '67-p103
The Nanny Goat And The Fierce Dog
BL-v71-S 1 '74-p43
CCB-B-v28-Ja '75-p80
KR-v42-Jl 15 '74-p736
LR-v24-Autumn '73-p127
PW-v205-Jl 1 '74-p83
SLJ-v21-Ja '75-p39
Spec-v231-O 20 '73-pR22
TLS-S 28 '73-p1126
WLB-v49-S '74-p85
Railway Passage
GP-v13-Mr '75-p2582
River
GP-v17-Jl '78-p3370
JB-v42-O '78-p250
Lis-v100-N 9 '78-p626
NS-v95-My 19 '78-p682
Sch Lib-v27-Mr '79-p30
TES-O 6 '78-p28
TLS-Jl 7 '78-p763
Shaun And The Cart-Horse
CCB-B-v20-Jl '67-p171
LJ-v92-F 15 '67-p873
TLS-N 24 '66-p1083
Through The Window
B&B-v16-N '70-p56
CCB-B-v24-My '71-p138
CLW-v42-Mr '71-p458
NS-v80-N 6 '70-p612
PW-v198-N 23 '70-p39
Spec-v225-D 5 '70-pR12
TLS-O 30 '70-p1260
Wasteground Circus
GP-v14-Ap '76-p2858
JB-v40-Ap '76-p82
LR-v25-Autumn '75-p137
TLS-D 5 '75-p1453
Willie's Fire-Engine
CCB-B-v34-Ap '81-p153
GP-v19-N '80-p3794
HB-v57-Ap '81-p181
JB-v44-D '80-p284
PW-v218-O 10 '80-p74
SLJ-v27-Ja '81-p51
Sch Lib-v29-Je '81-p122
TLS-S 19 '80-p1028

* * *

KEESING, James
Gardening
GP-v14-N '75-p2746

* * *

KEESING, Marie M
Hidden Valleys And Unknown Shores
SLJ-v24-Ap '78-p86

* * *

KEESING, N
The Golden Dream
JB-v39-F '75-p66

* * *

KEETON, Betty
Esmeralda
BS-v30-Ap 1 '70-p18
BW-v4-My 17 '70-p16
CCB-B-v24-D '70-p61
CSM-v62-My 7 '70-pB5
KR-v38-Mr 1 '70-p243

* * *

KEETON, Elizabeth B
Friday Nights And Robert
BS-v33-Ag 15 '73-p234
CCB-B-v26-Ap '73-p126
Comw-v99-N 23 '73-p215
KR-v41-Ja 15 '73-p61
LJ-v98-S 15 '73-p2652
PW-v203-F 12 '73-p68

* * *

KEHLE, Roberta
Escape!
TES-S 21 '84-p37

* * *

KEHOE, Michael
The Puzzle Of Books
BL-v78-Ag '82-p1526
CCB-B-v36-S '82-p13
Inter BC-v15-#4 '84-p17
SA-v247-D '82-p40
SLJ-v29-S '82-p109
SLMQ-v12-Summer '84-p263
Road Closed
BL-v79-D 1 '82-p500
CCB-B-v36-Ja '83-p91
NYTBR-v87-N 14 '82-p63
SLJ-v29-Ja '83-p61
The Rock Quarry Book
ASBYP-v14-Fall '81-p23
BL-v77-Je 1 '81-p1299
CCB-B-v35-S '81-p12
LA-v59-F '82-p155
PW-v219-Ap 3 '81-p74
SB-v17-N '81-p97
SLJ-v28-Ja '82-p66

* * *

KEIDEL, Eudene
African Fables That Teach About God
SLJ-v28-S '81-p110

* * *

KEIGHTLEY, Moy
Investigating Art
BL-v73-D 15 '76-p600
BL-v73-D 15 '76-p608
Cur R-v16-F '77-p15

* * *

KEITH, Eros
Bedita's Bad Day
CCB-B-v25-Ja '72-p75
CLW-v43-My '72-p537
GT-v89-Mr '72-p88
KR-v39-O 15 '71-p1114
LJ-v97-Je 15 '72-p2231
PW-v200-O 25 '71-p50
Nancy's Backyard
BL-v69-Ap 15 '73-p813
CCB-B-v26-Jl '73-p172
KR-v41-F 15 '73-p183
LJ-v98-Ap 15 '73-p1376
Rrra-Ah
BL-v66-Ap 1 '70-p983
CCB-B-v23-Je '70-p160
CSM-v62-My 7 '70-pB1
GT-v88-S '70-p161
KR-v37-D 15 '69-p1313
LJ-v95-Ap 15 '70-p1628
PW-v197-Ja 19 '70-p81
SR-v53-Mr 21 '70-p39
A Small Lot
CCB-B-v22-F '69-p96
HB-v45-F '69-p41
KR-v36-O 15 '68-p1158
LJ-v94-Ap 15 '69-p1770
NYTBR-v73-N 3 '68-p71

* * *

KEITH, Harold
Komantcia
BL-v62-Ja 15 '66-p482
CCB-B-v19-Ap '66-p132
GT-v83-Mr '66-p32
HB-v42-F '66-p65
HT-v16-D '66-p863
KR-v33-S 1 '65-p913
LJ-v90-N 15 '65-p5096
NO-v4-D 13 '65-p21
NYTBR-v70-N 7 '65-p8
Obs-D 4 '66-p28
TLS-N 24 '66-p1078
The Obstinate Land
BB-v6-Ap '78-p3
BL-v74-N 15 '77-p551
CE-v54-Mr '78-p258
CLW-v49-Mr '78-p357
J Read-v22-F '79-p477
KR-v45-S 1 '77-p937
LA-v55-Ap '78-p524
LA-v58-Ap '81-p459
NYTBR-N 13 '77-p63
SLJ-v24-F '78-p59
Rifles For Watie
Inter BC-v13-#6 '82-p19
Sports And Games
BL-v66-Ja 15 '70-p623
BL-v73-Mr 1 '77-p1015
LJ-v95-Ja 15 '70-p262
LJ-v95-My 15 '70-p1967
PW-v196-N 3 '69-p49
SLJ-v23-D '76-p72
Teacher-v95-Ap '78-p30
Susy's Scoundrel
CCB-B-v28-F '75-p95
Kliatt-v11-Winter '77-p5
NYTBR-D 1 '74-p8
SLJ-v21-Mr '75-p98

* * *

KELEN, Emery
Fantastic Tales, Strange Animals, Riddles, Jests, And Prophecies Of Leonardo Da Vinci
HB-v47-D '71-p622
Mr. Nonsense
CCB-B-v27-D '73-p66
GP-v13-Ja '75-p2545
JB-v39-Ap '75-p119
KR-v41-Mr 1 '73-p262
PW-v204-Jl 23 '73-p70
Spec-v233-O 26 '74-p542
Stamps Tell The Story Of Space Travel
CLW-v44-F '73-p446
LJ-v98-Mr 15 '73-p1004
NYTBR-My 2 '76-p45
SS-v64-Ap '73-p188

* * *

KELLEHER, Victor
The Hunting Of Shadroth
Brit Bk N C-Spring '81-p26
Brit Bk N C-Autumn '82-p8
GP-v19-Mr '81-p3843

KELLEHER, Victor (continued)
JB-v45-Je '81-p125
Obs-Mr 1 '81-p33
Sch Lib-v29-Je '81-p154
TES-Je 5 '81-p37
TLS-Mr 27 '81-p341
Master Of The Grove
Brit Bk N C-Autumn '82-p8
Brit Bk N C-Autumn '82-p25
Fant R-v7-Ag '84-p48
JB-v46-Je '82-p105
Sch Lib-v30-Je '82-p155
TES-Ap 23 '82-p26
TLS-Mr 26 '82-p344
Papio
GP-v22-Mr '84-p4212
JB-v48-Je '84-p139
TLS-Mr 9 '84-p253

* * *

KELLER, Beverly
The Bee Sneeze
BL-v79-O 15 '82-p317
CCB-B-v36-Ja '83-p91
SLJ-v29-D '82-p77
The Beetle Bush
BL-v72-Jl 15 '76-p1602
CCB-B-v30-O '76-p26
Comw-v103-N 19 '76-p760
KR-v44-Je 1 '76-p633
SLJ-v23-D '76-p64
Teacher-v96-O '78-p170
Don't Throw Another One, Dover!
CCB-B-v30-My '77-p144
KR-v44-D 1 '76-p1263
RT-v35-My '82-p901
SLJ-v23-Mr '77-p133
Fiona's Bee
BL-v72-D 15 '75-p582
CCB-B-v29-Ap '76-p126
HB-v52-Ap '76-p151
KR-v43-O 1 '75-p1128
SLJ-v22-D '75-p31
SLJ-v22-D '75-p62
SLJ-v28-F '82-p37
Teacher-v95-O '77-p163
Fiona's Flea
CCB-B-v34-Je '81-p196
KR-v49-Mr 1 '81-p283
SLJ-v27-My '81-p82
The Genuine, Ingenious, Thrift Shop Genie, Clarissa Mae Bean & Me
BB-v7-Mr '79-p3
CCB-B-v31-My '78-p143
KR-v46-Ja 1 '78-p3
SLJ-v24-Mr '78-p130
My Awful Cousin Norbert
CCB-B-v35-Je '82-p190
PW-v221-Je 4 '82-p67
SLJ-v28-Ag '82-p98
No Beasts! No Children!
BL-v80-S 1 '83-p87
CBRS-v11-My '83-p102
CCB-B-v36-Ap '83-p153
KR-v51-F 1 '83-p121
SLJ-v29-My '83-p32
SLJ-v29-My '83-p72
Pimm's Place
KR-v47-F 15 '79-p195
SLJ-v25-F '79-p43
The Sea Watch
CBRS-v10-Jl '81-p117
CLW-v53-Ap '82-p402
KR-v49-Ag 1 '81-p939
RT-v35-O '81-p113
SLJ-v28-N '81-p106
A Small, Elderly Dragon
BL-v80-My 1 '84-p1248
BW-v14-My 13 '84-p15
CBRS-v12-Spring '84-p129
CCB-B-v37-Je '84-p188
CE-v61-S '84-p65
HB-v60-Ag '84-p466
SLJ-v30-My '84-p81
VOYA-v7-Ag '84-p147
When Mother Got The Flu
CCB-B-v37-Jl '84-p207
SLJ-v31-O '84-p148

* * *

KELLER, Charles
Alexander The Grape
CCB-B-v36-S '82-p13
PW-v221-Ap 2 '82-p79
SLJ-v28-Ag '82-p118
Daffynitions
BL-v73-S 1 '76-p39
Inst-v86-N '76-p152
KR-v44-Je 1 '76-p638
SLJ-v23-S '76-p119
Teacher-v95-Ja '78-p42
Giggle Puss
BL-v73-Jl 15 '77-p1728
KR-v45-Ap 15 '77-p431
NYTBR-My 1 '77-p34
SLJ-v24-F '78-p47
Glory, Glory, How Peculiar
BL-v73-Mr 1 '77-p1012
CCB-B-v30-Ap '77-p127
KR-v44-N 15 '76-p1224
SLJ-v23-F '77-p56
TN-v36-Winter '80-p205
Going Bananas
BL-v71-Jl 15 '75-p1191
KR-v43-Ap 1 '75-p380
LA-v53-My '76-p514
SLJ-v22-S '75-p85
SR-v2-My 31 '75-p31
Grime Doesn't Pay
BL-v80-My 15 '84-p1345
SLJ-v30-Ag '84-p74
Growing Up Laughing
CCB-B-v35-Ja '82-p87
VOYA-v5-Je '82-p34
Laughing
BL-v74-N 15 '77-p543
CCB-B-v31-Ja '78-p80
KR-v45-O 1 '77-p1051
NYTBR-N 13 '77-p34
PW-v212-S 12 '77-p132
SLJ-v24-D '77-p66
Llama Beans
BL-v76-S 15 '79-p124
SLJ-v26-N '79-p60
More Ballpoint Bananas
BL-v74-F 15 '78-p1010
KR-v45-D 15 '77-p1323
SLJ-v25-S '78-p140
News Breaks
NYTBR-v86-Ap 26 '81-p51
SLJ-v28-S '81-p126
Norma Lee I Don't Knock On Doors
BL-v79-Ag '83-p1467
SLJ-v30-O '83-p159
The Nutty Joke Book
BL-v74-Jl 15 '78-p1736
SLJ-v25-S '78-p118
Oh, Brother!
BL-v79-S 1 '82-p45
Ohm On The Range
BL-v79-F 15 '83-p778
SLJ-v29-Mr '83-p179
Punch Lines
BL-v72-D 15 '75-p579
PW-v208-D 1 '75-p65
SLJ-v22-Ja '76-p47
Remember The A La Mode!
BL-v80-F 15 '84-p858
SLJ-v30-Mr '84-p160
School Daze
BL-v75-Mr 15 '79-p1160
CCB-B-v32-Jl '79-p193
PW-v220-S 25 '81-p92
SLJ-v25-Mr '79-p124
The Silly Song Book
BW-v10-Je 8 '80-p12

KELLER, Charles (continued)
Smokey The Shark And Other Fishy Tales
CLW-v53-N '81-p190
RT-v36-O '82-p79
SLJ-v28-S '81-p124
The Star-Spangled Banana
BL-v71-S 1 '74-p43
HB-v50-O '74-p151
HER-v46-Ag '76-p474
KR-v42-O 1 '74-p1064
LA-v53-My '76-p513
LJ-v99-O 15 '74-p2740
NYTBR-N 3 '74-p38
PW-v206-Ag 5 '74-p59
Teacher-v92-Mr '75-p112
Still Going Bananas
BL-v76-Je 15 '80-p1532
SLJ-v26-Ag '80-p65
What's The Score?
SLJ-v28-D '81-p85

* * *

KELLER, Helen
Story Of My Life
Inter BC-v11-Ja 10 '80-p22
RR-v86-Mr '69-p169

* * *

KELLER, Holly
Cromwell's Glasses
BL-v78-My 1 '82-p1161
CBRS-v10-Je '82-p102
PW-v221-F 26 '82-p147
SLJ-v28-Mr '82-p136
Geraldine's Blanket
BL-v80-Je 15 '84-p1484
CBRS-v12-Ag '84-p145
KR-v52-Mr 1 '84-pJ5
PW-v225-Je 1 '84-p64
Par-v59-N '84-p48
SLJ-v30-Ag '84-p62
Ten Sleepy Sheep
BL-v80-O 1 '83-p296
CBRS-v12-O '83-p13
GP-v22-Mr '84-p4220
JB-v48-Je '84-p118
KR-v51-S 1 '83-pJ150
PW-v224-O 7 '83-p94
SLJ-v30-F '84-p59
Too Big
BL-v79-Ap 15 '83-p1095
CBRS-v11-Ag '83-p140
HB-v60-F '84-p43
KR-v51-F 1 '83-p118
PW-v224-Jl 8 '83-p66
SLJ-v29-Ag '83-p53

* * *

KELLER, Irene
Kenny The Kitty
SLJ-v30-S '83-p103
The Thingumajig Book Of Manners
SLJ-v28-D '81-p53

* * *

KELLER, John G
Krispin's Fair
BL-v72-Jl 1 '76-p1527
CCB-B-v30-S '76-p11
KR-v44-My 15 '76-p589
PW-v209-Ap 26 '76-p59
SLJ-v23-S '76-p101

* * *

KELLER, Keith
The Mickey Mouse Club Scrapbook
SLJ-v22-Ap '76-p75
WLB-v50-My '76-p676

* * *

KELLER, Mollie
Marie Curie
ASBYP-v16-Spring '83-p28
BL-v79-D 15 '82-p565
CBRS-v11-Ja '83-p50
SB-v18-My '83-p270
SE-v47-Ap '83-p245
SLJ-v29-N '82-p101

* * *

KELLER, Victor
The Scary Woods
CCB-B-v25-O '71-p28
KR-v39-Ap 15 '71-p429
SR-v54-Ag 21 '71-p26

* * *

KELLER, W Phillip
A Child's Look At The Twenty Third Psalm
SLJ-v28-F '82-p77

* * *

KELLERHALS-STEWART, Heather
Muktu, The Backward Muskox
SN-v91-N '76-p73

* * *

KELLETT, Robert
Tightrope To Terror
GP-My '84-p4252

* * *

KELLEY, Alberta
Lenses, Spectacles, Eyeglasses, And Contacts
ACSB-v13-Spring '80-p42
BL-v75-Mr 15 '79-p1143
CCB-B-v32-Je '79-p178
PW-v214-N 6 '78-p78
SLJ-v25-Ja '79-p55

* * *

KELLEY, Emily
April Fools' Day
BL-v80-F 15 '84-p858
SLJ-v30-Mr '84-p146
Happy New Year!
SLJ-v31-O '84-p173

* * *

KELLEY, Leo P
Dead Moon
BL-v75-Jl 15 '79-p1632
SLJ-v27-F '81-p67
Good-Bye To Earth
BL-v75-Jl 15 '79-p1632
CCB-B-v34-Mr '81-p135
SLJ-v27-F '81-p67
King Of The Stars
BL-v75-Jl 15 '79-p1632
SLJ-v27-F '81-p67
Night Of Fire And Blood
SLJ-v26-D '79-p82
On The Red World
BL-v75-Jl 15 '79-p1632
SLJ-v27-F '81-p67
Star Gold
BL-v76-Ap 15 '80-p1184
SLJ-v26-D '79-p82
Vacation In Space
BL-v75-Jl 15 '79-p1632
SLJ-v27-F '81-p67
Where No Sun Shines
BL-v75-Jl 15 '79-p1633
SLJ-v27-F '81-p67

* * *

KELLEY, Sally
Trouble With Explosives
CCB-B-v30-O '76-p26
KR-v44-Ap 15 '76-p470
PW-v209-Mr 1 '76-p95
SLJ-v22-Ap '76-p75

* * *

KELLEY, Sandra
Spotlight On Writing
Cur R-v18-D '79-p407

* * *

KELLEY, True

Buggly Bear's Hiccup Cure

CBRS-v11-N '82-p25
JB-v47-O '83-p209
SLJ-v29-D '82-p77
WCRB-v9-Ja '83-p46

The Mouses' Terrible Christmas

BB-v6-D '78-p2
BL-v75-N 15 '78-p552
CCB-B-v32-D '78-p64
KR-v46-N 1 '78-p1187
PW-v215-Ja 15 '79-p131
SLJ-v25-O '78-p112

The Mouses' Terrible Halloween

BL-v77-O 15 '80-p333
BW-v10-O 12 '80-p8
CBRS-v8-Ag '80-p135
CCB-B-v34-N '80-p57
KR-v48-S 1 '80-p1162
NYTBR-v85-O 26 '80-p26
PW-v218-Jl 25 '80-p157
SLJ-v27-D '80-p65
SLJ-v28-D '81-p78

A Valentine For Fuzzboom

BL-v77-Mr 15 '81-p1028
CBRS-v9-Ap '81-p72
KR-v49-Mr 1 '81-p280
PW-v219-F 6 '81-p373
RT-v36-O '82-p75
SLJ-v27-Ap '81-p114

* * *

KELLNER, Esther

Animals Come To My House

ACSB-v10-Spring '77-p28
BL-v73-S 15 '76-p177
HB-v53-Ap '77-p169
KR-v44-Je 15 '76-p688
SB-v13-S '77-p97
SLJ-v23-O '76-p108

* * *

KELLOGG, Jean

Hans And The Winged Horse

CCB-B-v18-My '65-p130

* * *

KELLOGG, Marjorie

Like The Lion's Tooth

Atl-v230-N '72-p129
B&B-v19-O '73-p107
BW-v6-O 1 '72-p15
BW-F 24 '74-p4
EJ-v62-Ja '73-p145
EJ-v62-D '73-p1299
HB-v49-F '73-p75
KR-v40-Ag 1 '72-p876
LJ-v97-N 1 '72-p3616
LJ-v97-N 15 '72-p3819
LJ-v97-D 15 '72-p4058
NS-v85-My 11 '73-p702
NW-v80-O 16 '72-p112
NYT-v122-O 18 '72-p45
NYTBR, pt.1-N 5 '72-p4
PW-v202-Ag 28 '72-p262
SR-v55-O 14 '72-p83
TLS-My 11 '73-p535

* * *

KELLOGG, Steven

Can I Keep Him

Am-v125-D 4 '71-p486
BL-v67-Jl 15 '71-p955
BW-v5-My 9 '71-p8
CCB-B-v25-D '71-p59
CE-v48-O '71-p32
KR-v39-My 1 '71-p498
LJ-v96-My 15 '71-p1781
LJ-v96-My 15 '71-p1797
LJ-v96-D 15 '71-p4159
NO-v15-Ag 21 '76-p16
NY-v47-D 4 '71-p188
PW-v199-Mr 1 '71-p58
SR-v54-Je 19 '71-p26
Teacher-v94-O '76-p144

The Island Of The Skog

A Lib-v5-S '74-p423
BL-v70-Mr 15 '74-p821
BL-v80-S 1 '83-p93
BW-S 19 '76-pH4
CCB-B-v27-My '74-p146
Emerg Lib-v11-Ja '84-p19
JB-v42-F '78-p17
KR-v41-N 1 '73-p1196
LJ-v99-F 15 '74-p564
PW-v205-Ja 14 '74-p94
WLB-v48-Ap '74-p633

Much Bigger Than Martin

BL-v73-S 1 '76-p39
CCB-B-v30-D '76-p58
Comw-v103-N 19 '76-p760
HB-v52-O '76-p492
JB-v42-Ap '78-p80
KR-v44-Jl 15 '76-p791
PW-v210-Ag 2 '76-p114
SLJ-v23-N '76-p48

The Mysterious Tadpole

BL-v74-D 1 '77-p613
BW-v9-Ag 12 '79-p8
CCB-B-v31-Mr '78-p114
CE-v55-O '78-p38
CLW-v49-Ap '78-p403
CSM-v70-My 3 '78-pB3
Comw-v104-N 11 '77-p729
EJ-v73-F '84-p104
GP-v18-N '79-p3610
HB-v54-F '78-p36
Inst-v87-My '78-p119
Inst-v89-Ja '80-p111
JB-v44-Je '80-p116
KR-v45-O 15 '77-p1095
NS-v98-N 9 '79-p732
PW-v212-O 31 '77-p58
RT-v32-O '78-p36
SLJ-v24-Ja '78-p78
TES-N 23 '79-p30

The Mystery Beast Of Ostergeest

JB-v41-O '77-p280
KR-v39-O 15 '71-p1114
LJ-v97-F 15 '72-p764
PW-v200-O 25 '71-p50

The Mystery Of The Flying Orange Pumpkin

BL-v77-S 1 '80-p45
BW-v10-O 12 '80-p8
CBRS-v9-S '80-p2
CCB-B-v34-O '80-p35
HB-v56-O '80-p508
KR-v48-O 15 '80-p1352
NYTBR-v85-O 26 '80-p26
PW-v218-Jl 11 '80-p91
PW-v224-Ag 12 '83-p67
RT-v35-O '81-p54
SLJ-v27-D '80-p72

The Mystery Of The Magic Green Ball

BL-v75-O 1 '78-p294
KR-v46-S 15 '78-p1015
PW-v214-Ag 7 '78-p82
SLJ-v25-N '78-p46
TES-Jl 11 '80-p38
TLS-Jl 18 '80-p809

The Mystery Of The Missing Red Mitten

BL-v70-Ap 1 '74-p875
CCB-B-v28-S '74-p11
Choice-v12-N '75-p1133
HB-v50-Ag '74-p368
JB-v45-F '81-p12
KR-v42-Ap 15 '74-p419
LA-v52-S '75-p852
LJ-v99-My 15 '74-p1466
PW-v205-Mr 18 '74-p52
SR/W-v1-My 4 '74-p45
Sch Lib-v28-S '80-p255
TES-Jl 11 '80-p38
TLS-Jl 18 '80-p809

KELLOGG, Steven (continued)
Teacher-v92-D '74-p77
The Mystery Of The Stolen Blue Paint
BL-v78-Jl '82-p1445
BW-v12-Ap 11 '82-p11
CCB-B-v35-Je '82-p190
KR-v50-Ap 15 '82-p485
PW-v221-Ap 16 '82-p71
SLJ-v29-Ja '83-p61
The Orchard Cat
CCB-B-v26-S '72-p10
KR-v40-My 15 '72-p575
LJ-v97-My 15 '72-p1903
PW-v201-Je 26 '72-p63
PW-v223-Mr 4 '83-p100
Paul Bunyan
PW-v226-O 19 '84-p48
Par-v59-N '84-p65
Pinkerton, Behave!
BL-v76-N 15 '79-p506
CBRS-v8-Ja '80-p42
CCB-B-v33-Ap '80-p155
GP-v20-N '81-p3959
HB-v56-F '80-p46
JB-v45-D '81-p244
KR-v48-F 15 '80-p211
NW-v94-D 17 '79-p94
PW-v216-N 26 '79-p52
SLJ-v26-Ja '80-p57
Ralph's Secret Weapon
BL-v80-O 1 '83-p296
CBRS-v12-O '83-p13
CCB-B-v37-N '83-p51
HB-v59-O '83-p562
JB-v48-Ap '84-p60
KR-v51-S 1 '83-pJ150
LATBR-O 30 '83-p9
PW-v224-Ag 5 '83-p91
SLJ-v30-O '83-p150
A Rose For Pinkerton
BL-v78-D 15 '81-p548
CBRS-v10-Ja '82-p42
CCB-B-v35-Mr '82-p132
CLW-v53-F '82-p301
HB-v58-F '82-p34
HB-v60-Ag '84-p492
JB-v46-Ag '82-p133
NW-v98-D 7 '81-p99
PW-v220-N 13 '81-p88
PW-v225-Mr 2 '84-p94
RT-v35-Mr '82-p751
SLJ-v28-Ja '82-p66
WCRB-v8-F '82-p61
WLB-v56-Ap '82-p610
Tallyho, Pinkerton!
BL-v79-D 1 '82-p497
CBRS-v11-Ja '83-p42
CLW-v55-O '83-p140
GP-v22-My '83-p4082
JB-v47-Je '83-p109
PW-v222-N 26 '82-p59
SLJ-v29-My '83-p63
There Was An Old Woman
BL-v70-My 15 '74-p1056
BW-My 19 '74-p4
JB-v42-O '78-p251
KR-v42-Ap 1 '74-p360
LA-v56-Ap '79-p402
LJ-v99-S 15 '74-p2249
PW-v205-Ap 8 '74-p83
RT-v32-N '78-p148
TLS-Jl 7 '78-p763
VV-v19-D 16 '74-p51
Won't Somebody Play With Me
BL-v69-Ap 1 '73-p764
CCB-B-v26-Jl '73-p172
JB-v42-F '78-p17
KR-v40-O 1 '72-p1140
LJ-v98-Ja 15 '73-p254
NYTBR, pt.2-N 5 '72-p44
PW-v202-S 18 '72-p73

* * *

KELLY, Brendan
Math Clues
Cur R-v21-O '82-p417
Quill & Q-v46-O '80-p16

* * *

KELLY, Eric P
In Clean Hay
RT-v33-Ap '80-p811

* * *

KELLY, Gerard W
Metric System Simplified
Inst-v83-Ja '74-p123
LJ-v98-D 15 '73-p3713
SB-v13-My '77-p11
SLJ-v23-O '76-p108
SLJ-v24-N '77-p31
Teacher-v91-N '73-p70

* * *

KELLY, James E
The Dam Builders
BL-v74-Ap 15 '78-p1351
CCB-B-v31-Jl '78-p180
NYTBR-Ap 30 '78-p46
SLJ-v24-My '78-p56
SR-v5-My 27 '78-p59
The Tunnel Builders
BL-v72-Mr 15 '76-p1046
CE-v53-N '76-p99
Inst-v85-My '76-p115
KR-v44-Mr 15 '76-p328
SB-v12-D '76-p162
SLJ-v22-My '76-p50

* * *

KELLY, Jim
Star Flower
CCB-B-v28-My '75-p149

* * *

KELLY, Karen
Tilda's Treat
SLJ-v22-Mr '76-p104

* * *

KELLY, Marty
The House On Deer-Track Trail
BS-v36-My '76-p62
KR-v44-Mr 15 '76-p322
PW-v209-My 3 '76-p64
SLJ-v23-S '76-p102

* * *

KELLY, Mary
The Puffin Book Of Gardening
GP-v16-Ap '78-p3300
Obs-Ag 28 '77-p26
TES-O 21 '77-p18

* * *

KELLY, Owen
Tales Out Of School
Punch-v280-Ap 29 '81-p680
TES-Ja 16 '81-p34
TLS-O 31 '80-p1240

* * *

KELLY, Patricia M
The Mighty Human Cell
HB-v46-O '70-p498
KR-v35-N 15 '67-p1374
LJ-v92-D 15 '67-p4613
SB-v4-My '68-p40
TLS-Ap 16 '70-p427

* * *

KELLY, Regina Z
Miss Jefferson In Paris
CCB-B-v25-F '72-p93
KR-v39-O 1 '71-p1076

KELLY, Regina Z (continued)
LJ-v96-D 15 '71-p4184

* * *

KELLY, Rosalie
Addie's Year
BL-v78-S 15 '81-p108
CBRS-v9-Spring '81-p107
HB-v57-D '81-p664
SLJ-v28-Ja '82-p88
The Great Toozy Takeover
BL-v71-Jl 1 '75-p1128
CCB-B-v29-O '75-p28
KR-v43-Ap 15 '75-p454
NYTBR-Jl 20 '75-p8
PW-v207-Je 2 '75-p53
SLJ-v22-S '75-p106

* * *

KELLY, Walt
Pogo Even Better
BW-v14-Jl 1 '84-p12
LATBR-Ag 12 '84-p8
Pogo's Double Sundae
BW-Jl 23 '78-pF2
Walt Kelly's Pogo Romances Recaptured
SR-v3-N 29 '75-p30

* * *

KELSALL, Freda
How We Used To Live In Victorian Times
Lis-v100-N 9 '78-p624
How We Used To Live 1900-1945
JB-v41-F '77-p38
How We Used To Live 1908-1918
GP-v14-D '75-p2763

* * *

KELSEY, Alice
Once The Hodja
RT-v34-Mr '81-p634

* * *

KELSEY, Alice G
Thirty Gilt Pennies
CCB-B-v22-Ja '69-p80
KR-v36-Jl 1 '68-p695
LJ-v93-O 15 '68-p3971
PW-v194-S 23 '68-p96

* * *

KELSEY, Edward
Max-The Muddleville Millionaire
TES-Mr 12 '82-p41
Mrs. Witchitt Works It Out
TES-Mr 12 '82-p41
Muddleville Olympics
TES-Mr 12 '82-p41
Pirate Gold
TES-Mr 12 '82-p41
The See For Yourself Science Book
TES-N 18 '83-p27

* * *

KELTON, Nancy
The Finger Game Miracle
Cur R-v16-D '77-p363
Inter BC-v13-#4 '82-p6
SLJ-v24-S '77-p130
Harry Four Eyes
Cur R-v16-D '77-p363
SLJ-v24-S '77-p130
Rebel Slave
Cur R-v16-D '77-p363
SLJ-v24-S '77-p131
The Sled The Brothers Made
Cur R-v16-D '77-p363
SLJ-v24-S '77-p130

* * *

KEMP, David
A Child Growing Up
Can Child Lit-#18 '80-p135
In Rev-v14-Ap '80-p39
SLJ-v27-Ja '81-p70

* * *

KEMP, Gene
Charlie Lewis Plays For Time
CCB-B-v38-S '84-p8
GP-v23-Jl '84-p4284
Obs-Ag 26 '84-p19
TES-Je 8 '84-p49
TLS-Je 29 '84-p737
Christmas With Tamworth Pig
CCB-B-v33-D '79-p72
GP-v16-Ap '78-p3289
JB-v42-Je '78-p142
SLJ-v26-O '79-p118
TLS-Ap 7 '78-p378
The Clock Tower Ghost
CCB-B-v35-My '82-p173
JB-v46-F '82-p26
Sch Lib-v30-Je '82-p130
TES-Ja 29 '82-p30
TES-Ap 27 '84-p27
TLS-S 7 '84-p1006
Dog Days And Cat Naps
CCB-B-v34-Je '81-p197
GP-v19-Ja '81-p3826
JB-v45-Je '81-p116
SLJ-v28-S '81-p138
Sch Lib-v29-Je '81-p137
TES-N 21 '80-p33
Ducks And Dragons
Brit Bk N C-Spring '80-p2
GP-v19-Jl '80-p3731
JB-v44-Ag '80-p177
SLJ-v27-Ap '81-p128
Sch Lib-v29-Mr '81-p40
TES-Mr 7 '80-p46
TES-N 11 '83-p25
Gowie Corby Plays Chicken
Brit Bk N C-Spring '80-p14
Brit Bk N C-Autumn '81-p3
CCB-B-v34-N '80-p56
GP-v18-Ja '80-p3264
JB-v44-Ap '80-p85
Obs-O 7 '79-p39
RT-v34-D '80-p353
SLJ-v26-Ag '80-p65
Sch Lib-v27-D '79-p383
TES-Ja 18 '80-p39
TES-N 27 '81-p23
TES-Je 29 '84-p32
TLS-D 14 '79-p124
No Place Like
CCB-B-v37-Mr '84-p129
GP-v22-Ja '84-p4186
JB-v48-Ap '84-p85
Lis-v110-N 3 '83-p28
Obs-D 4 '83-p32
SLJ-v30-D '83-p75
TES-S 30 '83-p46
The Prime Of Tamworth Pig
GP-v18-Jl '79-p3542
TLS-Jl 14 '72-p805
Tamworth Pig And The Litter
GP-v14-Ja '76-p2785
TLS-D 5 '75-p1446
Tamworth Pig Saves The Trees
B&B-v18-Ag '73-p136
SLJ-v27-My '81-p66
TLS-Je 15 '73-p687
The Turbulent Term Of Tyke Tiler
CCB-B-v33-Je '80-p193
GP-v15-Ap '77-p3085
JB-v41-O '77-p304
NS-v100-N 21 '80-p18
SLJ-v26-Mr '80-p133
TES-S 30 '83-p41
TES-Je 29 '84-p32
TLS-Mr 25 '77-p361
TLS-Jl 15 '77-p866

KENEALLY, Thomas (continued)
PW-v213-Ja 16 '78-p95
Spec-v239-S 3 '77-p19
TLS-O 14 '77-p1185
WCRB-v4-Jl '78-p38
WLT-v52-Autumn '78-p690

* * *

KENEALY, James P
Better Camping For Boys
BL-v70-Mr 15 '74-p821
CCB-B-v27-Je '74-p159
CLW-v45-My '74-p503
KR-v42-Ja 15 '74-p57
LJ-v99-Ap 15 '74-p1220
NYTBR-My 5 '74-p44
Better Fishing For Boys
LJ-v94-My 15 '69-p2125

* * *

KENG
The Stuck-Up Kitty
SLJ-v26-Ag '80-p52

* * *

KENNAWAY, Eric
The Rubber Band Book
GP-v16-Jl '77-p3152
TES-O 21 '77-p24

* * *

KENNEDY, Jean
The Nunga Punga & The Booch
KR-v43-Je 15 '75-p660
PW-v207-Je 30 '75-p58
SLJ-v22-S '75-p106

* * *

KENNEDY, Jimmy
The Teddy Bears' Picnic
BL-v80-N 15 '83-p497
NW-v102-D 5 '83-p111
NYTBR-v89-Ja 8 '84-p20
PW-v224-O 14 '83-p57
SLJ-v30-Ag '84-p62

* * *

KENNEDY, Joe
Kaleidoscope Math
Cur R-v18-O '79-p332
A Tangle Of Mathematical Yarns
Cur R-v19-Je '80-p257

* * *

KENNEDY, Mary
Wings
SLJ-v27-Ja '81-p51

* * *

KENNEDY, Paul E
Audubon's Birds Of America Coloring Book
AB-v54-N 11 '74-p2053

* * *

KENNEDY, Richard
The Blue Stone
BL-v73-O 15 '76-p323
CCB-B-v30-Ap '77-p127
CE-v53-Ap '77-p314
KR-v44-O 1 '76-p1094
NYTBR-O 31 '76-p39
PW-v210-O 18 '76-p64
SLJ-v23-N '76-p60
Teacher-v95-O '77-p158
The Boxcar At The Center Of The Universe
BL-v78-Je 1 '82-p1307
BS-v42-Ag '82-p203
CBRS-v10-Ap '82-p88
CCB-B-v36-D '82-p70
J Read-v26-N '82-p184
KR-v50-Ap 15 '82-p496
LA-v59-N '82-p867
NYTBR-v87-Ag 5 '82-p22
PW-v221-My 28 '82-p72
SLJ-v28-Ag '82-p126
VOYA-v5-Ag '82-p33
Come Again In The Spring
BB-v5-Mr '77-p2
BL-v73-O 1 '76-p253
CCB-B-v30-D '76-p59
HB-v53-Ap '77-p154
Inst-v86-N '76-p150
Inst-v89-O '79-p100
JB-v43-F '79-p18
KR-v44-Ag 15 '76-p904
NYTBR-S 26 '76-p16
NYTBR-N 14 '76-p53
NYTBR-v85-N 9 '80-p51
PW-v210-Ag 9 '76-p79
SLJ-v23-F '77-p56
Teacher-v94-Ja '77-p126
The Contests At Cowlick
Am-v133-D 6 '75-p402
BL-v71-Jl 15 '75-p1192
KR-v43-Je 1 '75-p601
LA-v53-My '76-p507
NYTBR-My 4 '75-p44
NYTBR-v85-N 9 '80-p51
PW-v207-Je 2 '75-p54
SLJ-v22-S '75-p85
SR-v3-N 29 '75-p32
Crazy In Love
BL-v77-Ja 1 '81-p625
BW-v11-Ja 11 '81-p7
HB-v57-F '81-p51
KR-v49-Ja 1 '81-p7
LA-v58-My '81-p595
NYTBR-v85-N 9 '80-p51
PW-v218-O 17 '80-p66
RT-v35-O '81-p66
SLJ-v27-Ja '81-p62
The Dark Princess
HB-v54-D '78-p641
KR-v46-O 15 '78-p1137
PW-v214-S 11 '78-p90
SLJ-v25-D '78-p53
SLJ-v25-Ap '79-p29
Delta Baby & Two Sea Songs
KR-v47-Ap 15 '79-p454
PW-v215-F 19 '79-p108
SLJ-v25-My '79-p63
Inside My Feet
BB-v7-O '79-p2
BL-v76-N 1 '79-p449
BOT-v2-D '79-p600
CBRS-v8-S '79-p9
CCB-B-v33-Ap '80-p155
CE-v57-S '80-p43
KR-v47-O 15 '79-p1210
LA-v57-My '80-p558
NYTBR-N 11 '79-p58
NYTBR-N 25 '79-p22
NYTBR-v85-N 9 '80-p51
PW-v216-D 3 '79-p52
SLJ-v26-S '79-p141
The Leprechaun's Story
BL-v76-N 15 '79-p506
CBRS-v8-N '79-p22
CE-v56-Ap '80-p305
HB-v56-F '80-p47
KR-v47-O 1 '79-p1141
LA-v57-Mr '80-p324
RT-v33-Mr '80-p732
SLJ-v26-D '79-p75
The Lost Kingdom Of Karnica
BL-v76-S 1 '79-p44
BL-v79-Je 1 '83-p1282
CBRS-v8-N '79-p24
CCB-B-v33-Ap '80-p155
HB-v55-D '79-p656
KR-v47-S 1 '79-p998
LA-v57-F '80-p187
NYTBR-O 7 '79-p34
NYTBR-v85-N 9 '80-p51
PW-v216-O 8 '79-p71
RT-v33-My '80-p972
SLJ-v26-O '79-p142
Time-v114-D 3 '79-p99
WLB-v54-Ap '80-p518

KENNEDY, Richard (continued)
The Mouse God
BL-v75-My 15 '79-p1440
HB-v55-Ag '79-p407
KR-v47-Ap 1 '79-p385
NYTBR-Ap 29 '79-p26
PW-v215-Ap 2 '79-p73
SLJ-v25-My '79-p52
Oliver Hyde's Dishcloth Concert
BL-v73-Ap 1 '77-p1169
CCB-B-v31-S '77-p18
HB-v53-Je '77-p308
Inst-v86-My '77-p118
KR-v45-F 1 '77-p93
NW-v90-Jl 18 '77-p92
NYTBR-Je 5 '77-p22
NYTBR-N 13 '77-p54
NYTBR-v85-N 9 '80-p51
PW-v211-F 28 '77-p123
RT-v32-O '78-p41
SLJ-v23-Ap '77-p55
WCRB-v3-My '77-p39
The Parrot And The Thief
BL-v71-D 1 '74-p379
KR-v42-N 1 '74-p1148
KR-v43-Ja 1 '75-p3
LJ-v99-D 15 '74-p3263
PW-v206-D 9 '74-p68
The Porcelain Man
Am-v135-D 11 '76-p428
BL-v72-Jl 15 '76-p1596
HB-v53-F '77-p39
ILN-v265-D '77-p109
JB-v42-F '78-p18
KR-v44-My 15 '76-p589
NYTBR-S 12 '76-p26
NYTBR-v85-N 9 '80-p51
PW-v209-Je 14 '76-p114
SLJ-v24-S '77-p110
TES-N 18 '77-p39
Teacher-v94-N '76-p137
The Rise And Fall Of Ben Gizzard
BL-v75-Ap 1 '79-p1218
BL-v78-F 15 '82-p762
HB-v55-F '79-p62
KR-v46-D 1 '78-p1305
NYTBR-F 25 '79-p30
NYTBR-v85-N 9 '80-p51
PW-v214-S 18 '78-p167
SLJ-v25-D '78-p53
Song Of The Horse
BL-v78-Ja 15 '82-p649
BL-v79-Je 1 '83-p1282
CBRS-v10-Winter '82-p55
HB-v58-Ap '82-p157
LA-v59-S '82-p603
LA-v60-Ap '83-p505
NYTBR-v87-Ja 31 '82-p27
PW-v221-Mr 12 '82-p84
RT-v35-Ap '82-p869
SLJ-v28-Mr '82-p136

* * *

KENNEDY, X J
Did Adam Name The Vinegarroon?
BL-v79-N 15 '82-p446
BW-v12-S 12 '82-p6
HB-v58-D '82-p664
KR-v50-Ag 1 '82-p870
LATBR-S 5 '82-p7
NYTBR-v87-N 14 '82-p45
PW-v222-Ag 27 '82-p358
SLJ-v29-N '82-p86
SLMQ-v11-Spring '83-p174
Knock At A Star
BL-v79-Ja 1 '83-p617
CCB-B-v36-F '83-p110
CE-v59-My '83-p357
CLW-v55-D '83-p231
CSM-v75-Je 29 '83-p9
Cur R-v22-D '83-p46
HB-v58-D '82-p664
Inst-v92-F '83-p20
KR-v50-Jl 1 '82-p735
LA-v60-Ap '83-p485
LA-v60-S '83-p780
LA-v61-Ap '84-p421
SLJ-v29-D '82-p65
SLMQ-v11-Spring '83-p174
One Winter Night In August
CE-v52-Ja '76-p158
HB-v52-F '76-p67
KR-v43-Ap 1 '75-p380
NY-v51-D 1 '75-p184
NYTBR-My 4 '75-p24
NYTBR-Je 1 '75-p29
NYTBR-N 16 '75-p56
NYTBR-D 7 '75-p68
RT-v36-Ja '83-p381
SLJ-v22-N '75-p79
SR-v2-My 31 '75-p31
Time-v106-D 8 '75-p87
The Owlstone Crown
BL-v80-Mr 1 '84-p992
BW-v14-F 12 '84-p10
CBRS-v12-F '84-p74
Fant R-v7-Ag '84-p48
KR-v51-N 1 '83-pJ192
NYTBR-v89-Ja 22 '84-p24
PW-v224-D 9 '83-p50
SLJ-v30-Ja '84-p78
The Phantom Ice Cream Man
Cur R-v18-Ag '79-p211
HB-v55-Ag '79-p433
KR-v47-My 15 '79-p577
NYTBR-Ap 29 '79-p25
Parnassus-v8-#2 '80-p63
SLJ-v25-My '79-p63
SR-v6-My 26 '79-p63

* * *

KENNEMORE, Tim
The Fortunate Few
Brit Bk N C-Spring '82-p14
Brit Bk N C-Autumn '82-p8
CBRS-v11-N '82-p29
Emerg Lib-v11-S '83-p42
GP-v20-N '81-p3968
HB-v59-F '83-p52
JB-v46-Je '82-p106
J Read-v26-Ap '83-p653
Lis-v106-N 5 '81-p545
RT-v37-O '83-p65
SLJ-v29-D '82-p86
Sch Lib-v29-D '81-p345
TES-My 27 '83-p29
VOYA-v5-F '83-p44
Here Tomorrow, Gone Today
GP-v22-Jl '83-p4099
JB-v47-Je '83-p127
SLJ-v30-Ap '84-p116
Sch Lib-v32-Mr '84-p68
TES-My 13 '83-p32
The Middle Of The Sandwich
GP-v20-Jl '81-p3902
JB-v45-O '81-p213
SLJ-v28-N '81-p93
Sch Lib-v29-D '81-p345
TES-Ag 14 '81-p29
TES-Jl 22 '83-p21
TLS-Jl 24 '81-p838
Wall Of Words
B&B-Jl '82-p33
BL-v79-My 15 '83-p1218
Brit Bk N C-Autumn '82-p19
CCB-B-v36-Jl '83-p212
GP-v21-Jl '82-p3924
HB-v59-O '83-p575
JB-v46-Ag '82-p153
Obs-N 28 '82-p31
SLJ-v29-Ag '83-p67
TES-O 8 '82-p31
TES-Jl 13 '84-p25
TLS-Jl 23 '82-p789

* * *

KENNER, Hugh
Bucky
BL-v69-My 1 '73-p827
BL-v69-My 15 '73-p902
BW-Jl 13 '75-p2
CC-v90-Ag 29 '73-p835
CSM-v65-F 21 '73-p11
Choice-v10-Je '73-p604
Comt-v56-O '73-p59
Esq-v79-Je '73-p96
HB-v50-Ap '74-p173
KR-v40-D 1 '72-p1390
LJ-v98-Ja 15 '73-p160
LJ-v98-My 15 '73-p1713
NY-v49-F 24 '73-p130
NYRB-v21-F 7 '74-p29
NYT-v122-F 19 '73-p21
NYTBR-Mr 11 '73-p5
NYTBR-Je 10 '73-p38
NYTBR-D 2 '73-p68
NYTBR-Ap 14 '74-p23
Nat R-v24-D 22 '72-p1415
Nat R-v25-Ag 31 '73-p953
New R-v168-Mr 3 '73-p25
PW-v202-D 4 '72-p59
SB-v10-My '74-p21
Time-v101-F 19 '73-p87
Geodesic Math And How To Use It
Choice-v14-My '77-p408
Nat R-v28-N 26 '76-p1296
SA-v235-D '76-p144
SB-v13-D '77-p138

* * *

KENNET, Frances
A Child's Guide To Looking At Paintings
Brit Bk N C-Autumn '82-p10
Looking At Paintings
BL-v76-S 1 '79-p44
CE-v57-S '80-p46
Inst-v89-O '79-p193
SLJ-v26-S '79-p141

* * *

KENNEWAY, Eric
Folding Faces
NS-v95-My 19 '78-p680

* * *

KENNY, Kathryn
Trixie Belden And The Mystery At Mead's Mountain
SLJ-v25-Mr '79-p140
Trixie Belden And The Mystery Of The Castaway Children
SLJ-v25-Mr '79-p140
Trixie Belden And The Mystery Off Old Telegraph Road
SLJ-v25-Mr '79-p140

* * *

KENNY, Kevin
Sometimes My Mom Drinks Too Much
CCB-B-v34-Ja '81-p96
SB-v16-My '81-p273
SLJ-v27-F '81-p56
Sometimes My Mum Drinks Too Much
TES-Ap 30 '82-p29

* * *

KENT, Alexander
Midshipman Bolitho And The Avenger
JB-v42-Ag '78-p205
KR-v46-D 15 '78-p1363
SLJ-v25-Ja '79-p61
Richard Bolitho, Midshipman
KR-v44-Je 1 '76-p633
NYTBR-Jl 18 '76-p28
SLJ-v23-S '76-p134

* * *

KENT, B
Better Skiing
JB-v41-Je '77-p180

* * *

KENT, David
The Desert People
SLJ-v28-Ap '82-p70
Escape From Egypt
SLJ-v28-Ap '82-p70
Kings Of Israel
SLJ-v28-Ap '82-p70
The Last Journey
SLJ-v28-Ap '82-p70
Miracles And Parables
SLJ-v28-Ap '82-p70
The Time Of The Prophets
SLJ-v28-Ap '82-p70

* * *

KENT, Deborah
Belonging
CCB-B-v31-Je '78-p162
CLW-v50-O '78-p109
Comw-v105-N 10 '78-p733
HB-v55-O '78-p524
KR-v46-My 15 '78-p551
Kliatt-v14-Spring '80-p6
SLJ-v24-My '78-p77
TN-v36-Summer '80-p367

* * *

KENT, Graeme
English Everywhere
TES-Mr 7 '80-p40
Fighting Sports
Brit Bk N C-Spring '82-p16
TES-N 5 '82-p23

* * *

KENT, Howarth
Yoga
TES-Mr 6 '81-p29

* * *

KENT, Jack
The Biggest Shadow In The Zoo
BL-v78-Ja 15 '82-p658
CBRS-v10-D '81-p35
CCB-B-v35-Ja '82-p87
LA-v59-Mr '82-p268
PW-v220-S 18 '81-p154
SLJ-v28-D '81-p77
The Blah
B&B-v20-My '75-p81
KR-v38-Ap 1 '70-p376
Obs-D 1 '74-p35
TLS-S 20 '74-p1011
The Caterpillar And The Polliwog
CBRS-v11-N '82-p22
CCB-B-v36-Ja '83-p91
HB-v58-D '82-p641
PW-v222-S 17 '82-p114
SLJ-v29-Ja '83-p62
The Christmas Pinata
BB-v3-D '75-p4
CCB-B-v29-N '75-p48
JB-v41-Ap '77-p79
KR-v43-O 1 '75-p1121
NYTBR-D 7 '75-p8
SLJ-v22-O '75-p81
SR-v3-N 29 '75-p32
Clotilda
BB-v7-F '79-p1
CCB-B-v23-S '69-p11
KR-v37-F 15 '69-p170
LJ-v94-S 15 '69-p3196
PW-v214-Jl 31 '78-p98
RT-v33-N '79-p217
SLJ-v25-N '78-p46
Clotilda's Magic
Obs-F 1 '81-p29

KENT, Jack (continued)
Sch Lib-v29-Je '81-p122
The Egg Book
BB-v3-Mr '75-p2
CCB-B-v29-S '75-p13
CLW-v47-S '75-p93
HB-v51-Ag '75-p369
Inst-v84-My '75-p102
KR-v43-F 1 '75-p117
LA-v53-F '76-p197
RT-v29-My '76-p829
SLJ-v21-Ap '75-p46
SR-v2-My 31 '75-p36
The Fat Cat
BL-v67-Jl 15 '71-p954
CCB-B-v25-S '71-p10
CSM-v63-My 6 '71-pB4
LJ-v96-Je 15 '71-p2126
NS-v83-Je 2 '72-p762
RT-v32-My '79-p944
SLMQ-v12-Summer '84-p326
Spec-v228-Ap 22 '72-p625
Floyd, The Tiniest Elephant
KR-v47-S 15 '79-p1065
PW-v215-My 28 '79-p57
SLJ-v26-N '79-p66
The Funny Book
SLJ-v24-Ap '78-p71
SR-v5-N 26 '77-p42
The Grown-Up Day
CCB-B-v24-Jl '70-p181
KR-v37-O 15 '69-p1107
Hoddy Doddy
BL-v75-Ap 15 '79-p1301
HB-v55-Ag '79-p407
KR-v47-Ap 1 '79-p386
SLJ-v25-My '79-p78
Jack Kent's Happy-Ever-After Book
CCB-B-v30-D '76-p59
CE-v53-Mr '77-p258
KR-v44-Jl 1 '76-p726
NYTBR-N 14 '76-p50
NYTBR-N 14 '76-p53
PW-v210-Jl 5 '76-p91
SLJ-v23-O '76-p99
SR-v4-N 27 '76-p36
Jack Kent's Hokus Pokus Bedtime Book
CBRS-v8-S '79-p5
PW-v216-S 3 '79-p96
SLJ-v26-F '80-p46
Jack Kent's Hop, Skip, And Jump Book
SLJ-v21-Ja '75-p39
Jack Kent's Twelve Days Of Christmas
CCB-B-v27-N '73-p46
CSM-v66-D 12 '73-p14
Comw-v99-N 23 '73-p212
Econ-v249-D 29 '73-p60
GP-v15-D '76-p3033
KR-v41-S 15 '73-p1031
LA-v56-Ap '79-p401
LJ-v98-O 15 '73-p3127
PW-v204-N 5 '73-p57
SR/W-v1-D 4 '73-p29
TLS-N 23 '73-p1437
Teacher-v91-D '73-p72
Jim, Jimmy, And James
BL-v80-My 1 '84-p1248
CBRS-v12-Mr '84-p78
HB-v60-Ap '84-p183
KR-v52-Mr 1 '84-pJ6
SLJ-v30-My '84-p66
Joey
PW-v226-Ag 31 '84-p437
Just Only John
LJ-v93-S 15 '68-p3291
NO-v7-N 4 '68-p23
YR-v5-O '68-p10
Knee-High Nina
CBRS-v9-F '81-p52
CCB-B-v34-My '81-p172
HB-v57-Je '81-p293
SLJ-v27-Mr '81-p133
Little Peep
BL-v77-Je 15 '81-p1346
CBRS-v9-Spring '81-p101
HB-v57-O '81-p528
HB-v60-Je '84-p354
KR-v49-Ag 1 '81-p932
PW-v219-Ap 10 '81-p70
PW-v224-N 11 '83-p48
SLJ-v28-S '81-p110
Mr. Elephant's Birthday Party
KR-v37-F 15 '69-p170
LJ-v94-S 15 '69-p3230
PW-v195-Ap 28 '69-p88
Mr. Meebles
CLW-v42-Ap '71-p520
CSM-v62-N 12 '70-pB3
KR-v38-S 15 '70-p1029
NS-v83-Je 2 '72-p762
Obs-Ag 1 '76-p18
Spec-v228-Ap 22 '72-p625
TLS-Ap 28 '72-p482
Mrs. Mooley
CCB-B-v27-O '73-p29
LJ-v98-Jl '73-p2187
PW-v203-Ap 9 '73-p67
More Fables Of Aesop
BL-v70-Ap 15 '74-p942
CCB-B-v27-My '74-p137
CE-v51-N '74-p92
CSM-v66-My 1 '74-pF2
KR-v42-Mr 15 '74-p294
PW-v205-Mr 4 '74-p76
Par-v49-Je '74-p50
The Once-Upon-A-Time Dragon
CBRS-v11-F '83-p64
CCB-B-v36-Ja '83-p92
NYTBR-v87-N 14 '82-p43
PW-v222-N 26 '82-p59
RT-v36-My '83-p944
SLJ-v29-N '82-p69
Piggy Bank Gonzales
CBRS-v8-D '79-p33
SLJ-v26-Mr '80-p122
Round Robin
CBRS-v10-My '82-p92
HB-v58-Je '82-p279
PW-v221-Ap 16 '82-p71
RT-v37-O '83-p61
SLJ-v28-My '82-p55
The Scribble Monster
CBRS-v10-N '81-p23
RT-v35-Mr '82-p739
SLJ-v28-N '81-p79
Silly Goose
CBRS-v11-Je '83-p108
PW-v223-Je 10 '83-p65
RT-v37-O '83-p86
SLJ-v30-S '83-p108
Socks For Supper
PW-v214-N 6 '78-p78
RT-v33-O '79-p42
RT-v33-O '79-p94
SLJ-v25-Ja '79-p43
There's No Such Thing As A Dragon
BB-v3-Ag '75-p1
CCB-B-v29-Je '76-p158
CSM-v67-My 7 '75-pB4
JB-v42-Je '78-p136
SLJ-v22-N '75-p64

* * *

KENT, Sherman
A Boy And A Pig, But Mostly Horses
BL-v71-Mr 1 '75-p694
KR-v42-Jl 1 '74-p681
SLJ-v21-Ja '75-p46

* * *

KENTNER, Louis
Piano
ARG-v40-Mr '77-p61
BL-v73-O 1 '76-p229
Choice-v13-D '76-p1306
GP-v15-My '76-p2878
JB-v40-O '76-p295
TLS-Jl 16 '76-p886

* * *

KENTZER, M
Collins Young Scientist's Book Of Power
JB-v43-O '79-p279
TES-Ja 11 '80-p26
Collins Young Scientist's Book Of Space
TES-Ja 11 '80-p26
Collins Young Scientist's Book Of Strength
TES-Mr 10 '78-p59
Collins Young Scientist's Book Of Waves
JB-v42-Je '78-p154
SLJ-v27-S '80-p80
TES-Mr 10 '78-p59
Space
GP-v18-N '79-p3613
JB-v43-Ag '79-p206
Young Scientist's Book Of Cold
JB-v41-Je '77-p163

* * *

KENWARD, Jean
Clutterby Hogg
Econ-v277-D 27 '80-p77
GP-v19-N '80-p3789
Ragdolly Anna Stories
GP-v19-My '80-p3694
JB-v44-F '80-p20
PW-v217-Ja 25 '80-p341
SLJ-v27-O '80-p164

* * *

KENWORTHY, Leonard S
Camels And Their Cousins
ACSB-v9-Fall '76-p25
SB-v12-S '76-p106
SLJ-v22-Mr '76-p104
Hats, Caps, And Crowns
KR-v45-N 15 '77-p1202
SLJ-v24-Ap '78-p71
Soybeans
ACSB-v10-Spring '77-p29
BL-v72-Je 15 '76-p1466
Cur R-v16-O '77-p293
SE-v41-Ap '77-p349
SLJ-v23-S '76-p119
Teacher-v94-Ap '77-p103
The Story Of Rice
ACSB-v13-Spring '80-p43
BL-v76-N 1 '79-p449
SB-v16-S '80-p30
SLJ-v26-F '80-p57

* * *

KENYON, Michael
Brainbox And Bull
GP-v14-Ap '76-p2844
JB-v40-O '76-p275

* * *

KENYON, Nicholas
Mozart The Young Musician
GP-v18-My '79-p3512

* * *

KEOGH, David B
Earthquakes
TES-O 21 '83-p37
Volcanoes
TES-O 21 '83-p37

* * *

KEPES, Juliet
Cock-A-Doodle-Doo
BB-v6-S '78-p1
KR-v46-F 1 '78-p103
LA-v56-Ja '79-p47
NYTBR-Ap 30 '78-p29
PW-v213-Mr 27 '78-p72
SLJ-v24-Ap '78-p72
SR-v5-My 27 '78-p59
Five Little Monkey Business
BL-v61-Je 1 '65-p958
CCB-B-v18-Je '65-p151
CSM-v57-Ap 22 '65-p7
HB-v41-Ap '65-p163
KR-v33-F 1 '65-p106
LJ-v90-Ap 15 '65-p2012
NYTBR-v70-My 9 '65-p5
SR-v48-My 15 '65-p43
Five Little Monkeys
CSM-v70-O 23 '78-pB9
Teacher-v96-O '78-p169
Run, Little Monkeys! Run, Run, Run!
BL-v70-My 1 '74-p1004
HB-v50-Je '74-p274
KR-v42-F 1 '74-p106
LJ-v99-S 15 '74-p2250
PW-v205-F 25 '74-p112
SR/W-v1-My 4 '74-p46
Teacher-v92-F '75-p111
The Story Of A Bragging Duck
CBRS-v11-Spring '83-p119
HB-v59-Je '83-p292
KR-v51-Ja 1 '83-p1
PW-v223-Ap 1 '83-p60
SLJ-v29-Mr '83-p163

* * *

KERBER, Linda K
Women's America
BL-v78-Ja 1 '82-p573
HER-v53-My '83-p237
HRNB-v10-Ag '82-p221
Inter BC-v14-#7 '83-p38
J Am St-v18-Ap '84-p151
JEH-v42-D '82-p948
LATBR-Je 6 '82-p8
LJ-v107-F 1 '82-p258
SLJ-v29-S '82-p152

* * *

KERBO, Ronal C
Caves
ASBYP-v15-Spring '82-p43
BL-v78-Mr 1 '82-p898
Cur R-v22-Ag '83-p49
SB-v18-S '82-p32

* * *

KERMAN, Gertrude
Cabeza De Vaca, Defender Of The Indians
KR-v42-D 1 '74-p1256
SE-v39-Mr '75-p172

* * *

KERR, Betty
Check Up Tests In English Comprehension
TES-Mr 6 '81-p34
First Check Up Test In English Comprehension
TES-N 18 '83-p39
Intermediate Check Up Test In English Comprehension
TES-N 18 '83-p39

* * *

KERR, Helen V
Helga's Magic
CCB-B-v25-S '71-p10
KR-v38-Ag 15 '70-p874
LJ-v96-Ap 15 '71-p1505
PW-v199-Ja 11 '71-p63

* * *

KERR, Jessica
Shakespeare's Flowers
Aud-v72-My '70-p98
BW-v13-F 13 '83-p12
Hort-v49-D '71-p10
KR-v37-S 15 '69-p1016
LJ-v95-Mr 15 '70-p1196
LR-v22-Winter '69-p213
NY-v46-Mr 28 '70-p121
NYTBR, pt.2-N 9 '69-p53
PW-v196-D 15 '69-p36
TLS-O 2 '69-p1137

* * *

KERR, Judith
Mog And The Baby
JB-v45-F '81-p12
Obs-S 28 '80-p33
Sch Lib-v29-Je '81-p137
TES-N 21 '80-p30
Mog In The Dark
GP-v22-N '83-p4169
JB-v48-Ap '84-p61
TES-S 30 '83-p42
Mog The Forgetful Cat
CLW-v44-N '72-p249
Econ-v237-D 26 '70-p39
KR-v40-F 15 '72-p192
LJ-v97-My 15 '72-p1903
NS-v81-Mr 5 '71-p314
Obs-N 29 '70-p31
Obs-F 9 '75-p25
PW-v201-Mr 20 '72-p69
TLS-D 11 '70-p1455
Mog's Christmas
JB-v41-Je '77-p155
LR-v25-Autumn '76-p279
NYTBR-D 11 '77-p26
PW-v212-Jl 18 '77-p138
SLJ-v24-O '77-p88
TLS-D 10 '76-p1551
The Other Way Round
BL-v72-S 1 '75-p34
BW-Ap 8 '79-pL2
CCB-B-v29-D '75-p65
CE-v52-Ap '76-p318
EJ-v69-O '80-p14
Emerg Lib-v11-N '83-p20
GP-v14-My '75-p2632
HB-v51-O '75-p470
JB-v39-Je '75-p198
KR-v43-Jl 1 '75-p717
NS-v89-My 23 '75-p698
NYTBR-D 28 '75-p10
Obs-Mr 30 '75-p24
Obs-Ag 28 '77-p26
PW-v207-Je 30 '75-p58
SLJ-v22-S '75-p106
SLJ-v22-D '75-p31
TLS-Ap 4 '75-p361
A Small Person Far Away
BL-v75-Mr 1 '79-p1048
CCB-B-v32-Je '79-p178
HB-v55-Je '79-p310
JB-v43-F '79-p67
KR-v47-F 15 '79-p200
Obs-O 22 '78-p35
PW-v215-Mr 19 '79-p94
SLJ-v25-Mr '79-p152
Sch Lib-v27-Mr '79-p57
Tiger Who Came To Tea
KR-v36-S 15 '68-p1042
LJ-v93-N 15 '68-p4395
Lis-v110-N 3 '83-p27
TLS-O 3 '68-p1116
When Hitler Stole Pink Rabbit
B&B-v17-Ja '72-p78
BL-v68-Ap 15 '72-p724
BW-v6-My 7 '72-p5
CCB-B-v25-Je '72-p158
CSM-v66-My 1 '74-pF5
EJ-v69-O '80-p14
Econ-v241-D 18 '71-p69
Emerg Lib-v10-S '82-p29
Emerg Lib-v11-N '83-p21
HB-v48-Ag '72-p371
KR-v40-F 1 '72-p136
KR-v40-D 15 '72-p1413
LJ-v97-My 15 '72-p1885
LJ-v97-My 15 '72-p1914
LJ-v97-D 15 '72-p4056
NY-v48-D 2 '72-p209
NYTBR, pt.2-N 5 '72-p3
Obs-D 8 '74-p25
SR-v55-Mr 25 '72-p110
TLS-O 22 '71-p1331
Teacher-v90-N '72-p69
When Willy Went To The Wedding
CCB-B-v26-Je '73-p157
KR-v41-Mr 15 '73-p312
LJ-v98-Jl '73-p2187
Sch Lib-v30-S '82-p224
Spec-v229-N 11 '72-p765
TLS-N 3 '72-p1333

* * *

KERR, Laura
Louisa: The Life Of Mrs. John Quincy Adams
CCB-B-v18-Ap '65-p120

* * *

KERR, M E
Dinky Hocker Shoots Smack
BL-v69-D 1 '72-p351
BL-v69-D 1 '72-p357
BS-v32-O 15 '72-p339
BS-v33-N 1 '73-p355
CCB-B-v26-D '72-p59
CLW-v49-D '77-p211
EJ-v62-D '73-p1298
EJ-v63-My '74-p91
EJ-v68-O '79-p102
Econ-v249-D 29 '73-p59
HB-v49-F '73-p56
J Read-v26-O '82-p65
KR-v40-O 1 '72-p1152
KR-v40-D 15 '72-p1420
LJ-v97-D 15 '72-p4056
LJ-v97-D 15 '72-p4079
NS-v86-N 9 '73-p700
NY-v48-D 2 '72-p190
NYTBR, pt.1-F 11 '73-p8
PW-v203-Ja 1 '73-p57
Spec-v231-O 20 '73-pR10
TLS-N 23 '73-p1433
TN-v29-Ap '73-p253
TN-v30-Ja '74-p203
Teacher-v90-Mr '73-p80
Gentlehands
BB-v6-Ja '79-p3
BL-v74-Mr 15 '78-p1175
BS-v38-S '78-p180
BW-Jl 9 '78-pE4
CCB-B-v31-Ap '78-p129
CLW-v50-O '78-p110
CLW-v50-O '78-p116
CLW-v50-D '78-p235
Comw-v105-N 10 '78-p733
EJ-v67-S '78-p90
EJ-v68-D '79-p78
Econ-v269-D 23 '78-p102
GP-v17-Mr '79-p3486
HB-v54-Je '78-p284
Inter BC-v9-Ag 80 '78-p18
J Read-v22-N '78-p183
KR-v46-F 15 '78-p183
NYTBR-Ap 30 '78-p30
NYTBR-My 6 '79-p41
PW-v213-Ja 9 '78-p81
PW-v215-Ap 23 '79-p80
SLJ-v24-Mr '78-p138
SLJ-v24-My '78-p36
SLJ-v29-N '82-p35
Sch Lib-v27-Mr '79-p58
TLS-D 1 '78-p1395
TN-v37-Fall '80-p60

KERR, M E (continued)
Him She Loves?
BL-v80-Ap 15 '84-p1161
BS-v44-S '84-p233
CBRS-v12-My '84-p108
CCB-B-v37-Ap '84-p150
HB-v60-Je '84-p339
KR-v52-My 1 '84-pJ48
NYTBR-v89-Jl 1 '84-p23
PW-v225-F 24 '84-p140
Par-v59-N '84-p62
SLJ-v30-Ag '84-p84
VOYA-v7-Ag '84-p144
If I Love You, Am I Trapped Forever
BL-v69-Je 15 '73-p984
BS-v33-My 15 '73-p98
CCB-B-v26-Je '73-p157
CSM-v65-My 5 '73-p10
EJ-v66-O '77-p57
EJ-v67-My '78-p89
EJ-v68-O '79-p102
HB-v49-Je '73-p276
KR-v41-F 1 '73-p123
LJ-v98-Ap 15 '73-p1395
NYTBR-S 16 '73-p8
NYTBR-N 4 '73-p52
NYTBR-My 12 '74-p39
PT-v7-D '73-p126
PW-v203-F 12 '73-p68
TN-v37-Fall '80-p60
I'll Love You When You're More Like Me
BB-v5-Ja '78-p3
BL-v74-S 1 '77-p32
BL-v74-S 1 '77-p42
BS-v37-D '77-p294
CCB-B-v31-S '77-p18
EJ-v67-F '78-p99
HB-v53-D '77-p668
KR-v45-Jl 1 '77-p673
Kliatt-v13-Spring '79-p9
NYTBR-N 13 '77-p50
PW-v211-Je 27 '77-p111
SLJ-v24-O '77-p124
TN-v37-Fall '80-p60
WCRB-v3-N '77-p48
Is That You, Miss Blue?
BB-v3-My '75-p3
BL-v71-F 15 '75-p613
BS-v35-My '75-p49
BW-Ag 10 '75-p4
CCB-B-v28-Jl '75-p179
CLW-v47-F '76-p308
Comw-v102-N 21 '75-p570
EJ-v65-Ja '76-p97
HB-v51-Ag '75-p365
HB-v53-Je '77-p290
Inter BC-v11-Ja 10 '80-p22
KR-v43-Ap 1 '75-p384
NYT-v125-D 20 '75-p25
NYTBR-Ap 13 '75-p8
NYTBR-Je 1 '75-p28
NYTBR-N 16 '75-p54
NYTBR-D 7 '75-p68
PT-v9-Ag '75-p25
PW-v207-Ja 20 '75-p77
SLJ-v21-Ap '75-p66
SLJ-v28-Ap '82-p28
TN-v32-Ap '76-p284
Little Little
BL-v77-Ap 1 '81-p1085
B Rpt-v1-Mr '83-p24
BW-v11-My 10 '81-p15
BW-v13-Ja 9 '83-p12
CBRS-v9-My '81-p87
CCB-B-v34-Ap '81-p153
CLW-v55-S '83-p80
EJ-v70-S '81-p77
HB-v57-Je '81-p309
Inter BC-v13-#4 '82-p15
J Read-v25-O '81-p88
J Read-v26-O '82-p65
KR-v49-Mr 15 '81-p360
NYTBR-v86-My 17 '81-p38
PW-v219-Ap 24 '81-p75
RT-v35-N '81-p238
SLJ-v27-F '81-p76
VOYA-v4-Ag '81-p26
WLB-v55-Mr '81-p530
Love Is A Missing Person
BB-v3-O '75-p4
BL-v72-S 1 '75-p34
BS-v35-D '75-p299
CCB-B-v29-N '75-p48
EJ-v65-Mr '76-p90
EJ-v68-O '79-p102
J Read-v20-O '76-p79
J Read-v26-F '83-p411
KR-v43-Jl 1 '75-p717
Kliatt-v11-Spring '77-p6
NYTBR-O 19 '75-p10
PW-v207-Je 30 '75-p58
SLJ-v22-N '75-p92
Me, Me, Me, Me, Me
BL-v79-Je 1 '83-p1266
B Rpt-v2-S '83-p41
BS-v43-Je '83-p110
CBRS-v11-Je '83-p115
CCB-B-v36-Jl '83-p212
EJ-v72-O '83-p85
HB-v59-Ag '83-p462
KR-v51-F 15 '83-p189
NYT-v133-D 1 '83-p23
NYTBR-v88-My 22 '83-p39
PW-v223-Ap 15 '83-p51
SLJ-v29-Ag '83-p77
VOYA-v6-Je '83-p104
WLB-v57-Ap '83-p693
The Son Of Someone Famous
BL-v70-Ap 1 '74-p869
BS-v34-Ap 15 '74-p54
BW-My 19 '74-p5
CCB-B-v27-My '74-p146
Choice-v14-N '77-p1178
EJ-v64-Ja '75-p112
EJ-v68-O '79-p102
HB-v50-Ag '74-p384
HB-v53-Je '77-p289
KR-v42-F 1 '74-p120
KR-v43-Ja 1 '75-p10
LJ-v99-Mr 15 '74-p902
LJ-v99-My 15 '74-p1451
LJ-v99-D 15 '74-p3247
NS-v90-N 7 '75-p584
NY-v50-D 2 '74-p187
NYTBR-Ap 7 '74-p8
PW-v205-Mr 25 '74-p56
TLS-S 19 '75-p1051
What I Really Think Of You
BL-v78-Ap 15 '82-p1086
BS-v42-Ag '82-p203
BW-v12-Jl 11 '82-p11
BW-v13-Ap 10 '83-p12
CBRS-v10-My '82-p98
CCB-B-v35-Je '82-p190
KR-v50-Mr 15 '82-p349
NYTBR-v87-S 12 '82-p49
NYTBR-v88-Je 5 '83-p39
PW-v221-F 12 '82-p98
SLJ-v28-My '82-p71
VOYA-v5-F '83-p37

* * *

KERR, Nigel
A Guide To Anglo-Saxon Sites
ILN-v271-Jl '83-p69
TES-O 14 '83-p31

* * *

KERROD, Robin
Boats And Ships
JB-v42-D '78-p300
Cars
JB-v39-Ap '75-p109
JB-v47-Je '83-p115
The Challenge Of Space
CBRS-v8-Jl '80-p129

KERROD, Robin (continued)
SB-v16-Ja '81-p158
SLJ-v27-S '80-p70
Coal Mining
Indexer-v12-Ap '80-p32
Mission Outer Space
CBRS-v8-Jl '80-p129
SLJ-v27-S '80-p70
The Mysterious Universe
CBRS-v8-Jl '80-p129
SLJ-v27-S '80-p70
The Question And Answer Book Of Space
JB-v43-Je '79-p158
Race For The Moon
CBRS-v8-Jl '80-p129
SB-v16-Ja '81-p158
SLJ-v27-S '80-p70
Rocks And Minerals
ACSB-v12-Winter '79-p20
BL-v74-My 1 '78-p1434
SB-v14-Mr '79-p230
SLJ-v25-S '78-p140
See Inside A Space Station
BL-v76-N 15 '79-p506
JB-v42-D '78-p315
SB-v15-My '80-p280
SLJ-v26-Mr '80-p133
Space
TES-D 7 '79-p25
Tools
JB-v42-Ap '78-p89
The Universe
ACSB-v10-Fall '77-p22
BL-v73-F 1 '77-p835
Comw-v103-N 19 '76-p764
Cur R-v17-My '78-p141
S&T-v53-F '77-p135
SB-v13-D '77-p141
SLJ-v23-Ja '77-p101
The Way It Works
LJ-v105-S 15 '80-p1872
NYTBR-v85-Ag 31 '80-p19
SB-v16-My '81-p277
The World Of Tomorrow
BL-v77-Mr 1 '81-p965

* * *

KERSHAW, Andrew
Guide To Airlines
GP-v18-My '79-p3528

* * *

KERVEN, Rosalind
Mysteries Of The Seals
Brit Bk N C-Autumn '81-p20
JB-v45-O '81-p213
Obs-My 10 '81-p33
Sch Lib-v29-S '81-p237
The Reindeer And The Drum
Brit Bk N C-Autumn '80-p22
GP-v19-Jl '80-p3737
JB-v44-Ag '80-p178
Treasure On Bird Island
GP-v22-My '83-p4077
JB-v47-D '83-p259

* * *

KESSEL, Joyce K
Careers In Dental Care
BL-v81-O 1 '84-p246
Halloween
BL-v77-Ja 15 '81-p705
CBRS-v9-O '80-p15
CCB-B-v34-O '80-p35
NYTBR-v85-O 26 '80-p27
PW-v218-Ag 22 '80-p50
RT-v35-O '81-p71
SLJ-v27-Mr '81-p133
St. Patrick's Day
BL-v79-Ja 15 '83-p681
Inst-v92-Mr '83-p19
Squanto And The First Thanksgiving
BL-v79-Mr 15 '83-p974
CE-v60-S '83-p56
SE-v48-My '84-p375
SLJ-v29-Ap '83-p102
Valentine's Day
BL-v78-Ap 15 '82-p1099
CCB-B-v35-F '82-p110
Inst-v91-F '82-p34

* * *

KESSELMAN, Judi R
I Can Use Tools
Inter BC-v13-#6 '82-p41
LA-v59-F '82-p154
SLJ-v28-Ja '82-p67
Vans
SLJ-v26-S '79-p114

* * *

KESSELMAN, Wendy
Angelita
BL-v67-Ap 1 '71-p664
BL-v69-Ja 15 '73-p478
Choice-v14-N '77-p1178
LJ-v96-Mr 15 '71-p1109
NYTBR-Ja 3 '71-p12
Emma
BL-v77-F 1 '81-p753
BW-v10-N 9 '80-p14
CBRS-v9-O '80-p12
CE-v57-Mr '81-p234
KR-v48-S 15 '80-p1229
PW-v218-Jl 11 '80-p91
RT-v34-Ap '81-p855
SLJ-v27-Ja '81-p52
Sch Arts-v80-My '81-p62
Flick
B Rpt-v2-Ja '84-p34
CBRS-v11-Je '83-p115
CCB-B-v36-My '83-p170
KR-v51-Ja 15 '83-p65
SLJ-v30-O '83-p170
VOYA-v6-Ag '83-p145
Joey
CCB-B-v26-Mr '73-p108
LJ-v98-Jl '73-p2194
There's A Train Going By My Window
BL-v78-My 15 '82-p1257
CBRS-v10-Spring '82-p111
GP-v22-N '83-p4169
JB-v48-F '84-p14
LA-v59-N '82-p866
NY-v58-D 6 '82-p182
PW-v221-My 7 '82-p79
Par-v57-N '82-p56
RT-v36-Ap '83-p852
SLJ-v28-Ag '82-p98
VV-v27-D 14 '82-p76
Time For Jody
BB-v4-F '76-p2
BL-v72-D 15 '75-p579
CCB-B-v29-Ap '76-p126
KR-v43-N 15 '75-p1284
LA-v53-My '76-p499
NY-v51-D 1 '75-p182
SLJ-v22-Mr '76-p93
SR-v3-N 29 '75-p31
WLB-v50-D '75-p316

* * *

KESSLER, Deirdre
A Child's Anne
Atl Pro Bk R-v10-N '83-p5
Can Child Lit-#30 '83-p61
Quill & Q-v49-N '83-p22
The Private Adventures Of Brupp
Atl Pro Bk R-v10-N '83-p19
BIC-v12-D '83-p14

* * *

KESSLER, Ethel
All For Fall
KR-v42-S 15 '74-p1005
LA-v52-S '75-p853
LJ-v99-D 15 '74-p3263
NYTBR-N 3 '74-p56

KESSLER, Ethel (continued)
SB-v10-Mr '75-p335
Baby-Sitter, Duck
SLJ-v28-D '81-p77
The Big Fight
SLJ-v28-D '81-p77
The Day Daddy Stayed Home
GT-v89-Ja '72-p92
Do Baby Bears Sit In Chairs?
SLJ-v25-My '79-p38
Grandpa Witch And The Magic Doobelator
BL-v78-Mr 15 '82-p965
CE-v59-S '82-p64
KR-v50-F 1 '82-p135
SLJ-v28-D '81-p76
Night Story
CCB-B-v34-My '81-p173
CE-v58-My '82-p326
KR-v49-Ap 1 '81-p429
LA-v59-Mr '82-p269
NYTBR-v86-Ap 26 '81-p71
PW-v219-F 6 '81-p373
SLJ-v27-My '81-p83
Our Tooth Story
CCB-B-v26-F '73-p93
KR-v40-Mr 15 '72-p330
SB-v8-D '72-p260
Pig's New Hat
BL-v78-N 15 '81-p446
SLJ-v28-D '81-p77
Pig's Orange House
BL-v78-N 15 '81-p446
SLJ-v28-D '81-p77
Slush, Slush
CCB-B-v27-F '74-p97
KR-v41-O 15 '73-p1153
LJ-v99-Ja 15 '74-p200
Splish Splash
KR-v41-Ap 15 '73-p452
LJ-v98-D 15 '73-p3701
Two, Four, Six, Eight
CBRS-v9-O '80-p12
KR-v48-S 15 '80-p1229
PW-v218-Ag 8 '80-p83
SLJ-v27-O '80-p136
What Do You Play On A Summer Day?
CCB-B-v30-Jl '77-p176
KR-v45-F 15 '77-p162
PW-v211-Mr 14 '77-p94
SLJ-v24-F '78-p48
What's Inside The Box?
JB-v42-O '78-p256
KR-v44-Jl 1 '76-p727
RT-v31-O '77-p9
SLJ-v23-D '76-p65

* * *

KESSLER, Leonard
Aqui Viene El Ponchado
HB-v55-Je '79-p330
LJ-v95-S 15 '70-p3037
SLJ-v29-Mr '83-p91
The Big Mile Race
CCB-B-v36-My '83-p170
HB-v59-Je '83-p297
KR-v51-F 15 '83-p183
SLJ-v29-My '83-p88
Did You Ever Hear A Klunk Say Please?
CCB-B-v20-Je '67-p154
KR-v35-F 1 '67-p126
LJ-v92-F 15 '67-p873
NY-v43-D 16 '67-p157
Do You Have Any Carrots?
CBRS-v7-Spring '79-p115
Cur R-v19-F '80-p50
SLJ-v26-S '79-p114
The Forgetful Pirate
SLJ-v21-Mr '75-p84
Here Comes The Strikeout
BL-v61-Je 1 '65-p958
CCB-B-v18-Je '65-p151
CSM-v57-My 6 '65-p2B
CSM-v68-D 22 '75-p18
KR-v33-Ap 1 '65-p376
LJ-v90-My 15 '65-p2394
NYTBR-v70-My 9 '65-p28
PW-v215-F 26 '79-p183
SR-v48-Je 19 '65-p40
Hey Diddle Diddle
BL-v77-D 15 '80-p577
SLJ-v27-D '80-p70
Hickory Dickory Dock
SLJ-v27-D '80-p71
Kick, Pass, And Run
CCB-B-v20-Ja '67-p75
CSM-v58-N 3 '66-pB5
KR-v34-S 15 '66-p974
LJ-v91-N 15 '66-p5768
PW-v190-O 3 '66-p84
SR-v49-N 12 '66-p47
Teacher-v93-S '75-p50
Mr. Pine's Purple House
NYTBR-v70-My 9 '65-p28
Mr. Pine's Storybook
CBRS-v11-D '82-p32
WCRB-v9-Mr '83-p56
Mrs. Pine Takes A Trip
LJ-v91-Jl '66-p3528
NYTBR-v71-My 8 '66-p35
Mixed-Up Mother Goose
SLJ-v27-D '80-p71
The Mother Goose Game
SLJ-v27-D '80-p71
Old Turtle's Baseball Stories
BL-v78-Ag '82-p1530
CCB-B-v35-My '82-p173
RT-v37-O '83-p60
SLJ-v28-My '82-p86
Old Turtle's Winter Games
BL-v80-O 15 '83-p367
CCB-B-v37-Ja '84-p90
KR-v51-S 1 '83-pJ157
SLJ-v30-D '83-p79
The Pirates' Adventure On Spooky Island
CBRS-v7-Spring '79-p115
SLJ-v26-S '79-p112
Riddles That Rhyme For Halloween Time
SLJ-v25-S '78-p117
The Silly Mother Hubbard
SLJ-v27-D '80-p71
Super Bowl
CCB-B-v34-Ja '81-p97
KR-v48-O 15 '80-p1355
RT-v35-O '81-p56
SLJ-v27-D '80-p74
Tricks For Treats On Halloween
CBRS-v7-Spring '79-p115
Cur R-v19-F '80-p50
SLJ-v26-S '79-p114
Who Tossed That Bat
CCB-B-v26-My '73-p140
Inst-v82-My '73-p68
KR-v41-Ja 1 '73-p2
LJ-v98-My 15 '73-p1706

* * *

KESTER, Ellen Skinner
The Climbing Rope
SLJ-v25-Ja '79-p51

* * *

KESTEVEN, G R
The Awakening Water
B&B-v25-N '79-p58
CBRS-v7-Ap '79-p89
CCB-B-v32-Jl '79-p193
GP-v16-D '77-p3225
HB-v55-Ag '79-p414
JB-v42-F '78-p43
SLJ-v25-Ap '79-p69
TES-N 18 '77-p33
TLS-O 21 '77-p1246

KEY, Alexander (continued)
Return From Witch Mountain
KR-v46-Ap 15 '78-p437
SLJ-v25-S '78-p140
The Sword Of Aradel
BL-v73-Jl 15 '77-p1728
CCB-B-v31-O '77-p35
EJ-v66-N '77-p82
SLJ-v24-S '77-p146

* * *

KEY, Francis Scott
The Star-Spangled Banner
CE-v43-F '67-p356
CE-v50-Ap '74-p338
Choice-v12-N '75-p1133
LJ-v91-O 15 '66-p5231
LJ-v99-F 15 '74-p564

* * *

KEY Phonics
TES-Jl 11 '80-p29

* * *

KEYS, Donald
Earth At Omega
CSM-v75-D 3 '82-pB10
New Age-v8-O '82-p64

* * *

KEYS To Reading
Cur R-v18-D '79-p378

* * *

KEYSER, Marcia
Roger On His Own
CBRS-v11-N '82-p22
PW-v222-O 15 '82-p65
RT-v36-Mr '83-p716
RT-v37-O '83-p61
SLJ-v29-F '83-p68

* * *

KEYSER, William R
The Days Of The Week
BB-v5-F '77-p2
SLJ-v23-S '76-p102

* * *

KEYSTONES
TES-Jl 11 '80-p30

* * *

KEYSTROKES
Cur R-v19-Ap '80-p161

* * *

KEYTEXT
Cur R-v18-Ag '79-p205
Cur R-v21-D '82-p476

* * *

KHA, Dang Manh
In The Land Of Small Dragon
BL-v75-My 1 '79-p1363
CBRS-v7-Spring '79-p114
KR-v47-My 15 '79-p572
LA-v56-O '79-p821
NY-v55-D 3 '79-p202
NYTBR-Je 10 '79-p51
PW-v215-Ap 9 '79-p107
SLJ-v25-My '79-p59

* * *

KHALSA, Dayal K
The Baabee Books
BIC-v12-D '83-p14
Quill & Q-v49-My '83-p12

* * *

KHAN, Hassina
Aqiqa And The Crocus
TES-Je 3 '83-p38
TES-Jl 8 '83-p22
Tariq Learns To Swim
CCB-B-v37-Mr '84-p129
GP-v22-S '83-p4144
JB-v48-F '84-p14
SLJ-v30-F '84-p59

* * *

KHERDIAN, David
The Animal
PW-v226-S 7 '84-p78
Country Cat, City Cat
BL-v74-Mr 15 '78-p1190
HB-v54-Je '78-p293
Inst-v87-My '78-p119
KR-v46-Mr 1 '78-p239
LA-v55-O '78-p866
NYTBR-Ap 30 '78-p25
PW-v213-Ja 23 '78-p373
SLJ-v24-My '78-p56
The Dog Writes On The Window With His Nose
BL-v73-Ap 1 '77-p1165
BW-My 1 '77-pE3
CCB-B-v30-Je '77-p161
CSM-v69-My 4 '77-pB4
Comw-v104-N 11 '77-p734
KR-v45-F 15 '77-p167
NYTBR-My 1 '77-p33
PW-v211-Ja 24 '77-p333
SLJ-v24-S '77-p110
Finding Home
BL-v77-F 15 '81-p805
BW-v11-My 10 '81-p19
CBRS-v9-Mr '81-p68
CCB-B-v34-My '81-p173
CLW-v53-N '81-p190
HB-v57-Je '81-p318
KR-v49-Jl 15 '81-p877
LA-v58-S '81-p701
SLJ-v27-My '81-p74
VOYA-v4-O '81-p34
I Sing The Song Of Myself
BL-v75-N 15 '78-p537
KR-v47-Ja 1 '79-p14
LA-v56-S '79-p686
SLJ-v25-N '78-p76
If Dragon Flies Made Honey
BW-N 13 '77-pE4
KR-v45-O 1 '77-p1044
NYTBR-N 13 '77-p47
SLJ-v24-N '77-p48
SLJ-v25-N '78-p31
It Started With Old Man Bean
BL-v76-Ja 1 '80-p668
CBRS-v8-F '80-p58
CCB-B-v34-S '80-p13
KR-v48-Mr 15 '80-p365
NYTBR-v85-Ap 27 '80-p63
SLJ-v26-Ja '80-p79
The Mystery Of The Diamond In The Wood
BL-v80-O 1 '83-p297
B Rpt-v2-Mr '84-p33
BW-v13-N 6 '83-p16
CBRS-v12-N '83-p31
CCB-B-v37-Ja '84-p90
PW-v224-D 23 '83-p59
SLJ-v30-D '83-p83
Poems Here And Now
BL-v72-Mr 15 '76-p1049
CCB-B-v30-S '76-p11
KR-v44-Mr 15 '76-p333
PW-v209-Mr 8 '76-p66
SLJ-v22-My '76-p70
WLB-v51-Ja '77-p385
Right Now
BL-v80-Ja 1 '84-p682
CBRS-v12-O '83-p13
CCB-B-v37-Ja '84-p90
KR-v51-N 1 '83-pJ186
LA-v60-N '83-p1020
PW-v224-S 23 '83-p73
SLJ-v30-Ja '84-p65
WCRB-v10-My '84-p46
The Road From Home
BB-v7-N '79-p4
BL-v75-Mr 1 '79-p1049
CCB-B-v33-Ja '80-p97
CE-v56-N '79-p115

KHERDIAN, David
(continued)
CLW-v51-N '79-p183
HB-v55-Je '79-p318
JB-v44-O '80-p251
KR-v47-Je 1 '79-p644
Kliatt-v15-Winter '81-p3
LA-v57-Ap '80-p438
NY-v55-D 3 '79-p212
SLJ-v25-Ap '79-p69
SLJ-v25-My '79-p35
SLJ-v30-Ja '84-p43
Sch Lib-v29-Mr '81-p53
TES-F 13 '81-p25
Settling America
BB-v3-F '75-p4
BL-v71-N 15 '74-p338
KR-v42-N 1 '74-p1165
KR-v43-Ja 1 '75-p13
NYTBR-D 29 '74-p8
The Song In The Walnut Grove
CBRS-v11-Winter '83-p59
Inst-v92-N '82-p151
KR-v50-O 1 '82-p1106
NYTBR-v87-D 19 '82-p26
PW-v222-D 17 '82-p75
SLJ-v29-N '82-p86
Traveling America With Today's Poets
EJ-v66-O '77-p77
J Read-v22-My '79-p774
KR-v45-Ja 1 '77-p7
NYTBR-My 1 '77-p33
SLJ-v23-My '77-p70

* * *

KHIDDU-MAKUBUYA
The Newcomer
BL-v73-Jl 15 '77-p1734

* * *

KHOWANO, Il Shojaah
BL-v75-O 15 '78-p393

* * *

KIBBE, Pat
The Hocus-Pocus Dilemma
BL-v75-Mr 15 '79-p1159
BL-v75-Jl 15 '79-p1635
BL-v76-Je 15 '80-p1544
CBRS-v7-Mr '79-p74
CCB-B-v33-S '79-p9
CLW-v51-N '79-p183
KR-v47-Ap 1 '79-p389
SLJ-v25-Mr '79-p141
Mrs. Kiddy And The Moonblooms
CBRS-v12-F '84-p69
SLJ-v30-Ap '84-p116
My Mother The Mayor, Maybe
BL-v78-O 1 '81-p237
BL-v81-S 15 '84-p138
BS-v41-F '82-p442
CBRS-v10-O '81-p19
CCB-B-v35-D '81-p70
CSM-v74-My 14 '82-pB9
KR-v49-N 15 '81-p1409
SLJ-v28-S '81-p126

* * *

KIDD, Bruce
Hockey Showdown
BIC-v8-D '79-p12
In Rev-v14-D '80-p44
Tom Longboat
Can Child Lit-#23 '81-p86
In Rev-v15-Je '81-p39
Who's A Soccer Player?
In Rev-v14-Ag '80-p54

* * *

KIDD, Margaret
Ashok's Kite
Inst-v89-D '79-p59

* * *

KIDD, Ronald
Dunker
BS-v42-Ag '82-p204
CBRS-v10-Je '82-p107
SLJ-v28-My '82-p86
SLJ-v29-D '82-p29
VOYA-v5-O '82-p43
Sizzle And Splat
BL-v80-N 15 '83-p498
CBRS-v12-Mr '84-p84
CCB-B-v37-Mr '84-p130
KR-v51-N 1 '83-pJ204
SLJ-v30-D '83-p85
That's What Friends Are For
BS-v39-My '79-p71
CCB-B-v32-My '79-p157
J Read-v23-D '79-p280
KR-v47-F 1 '79-p126
PW-v214-D 25 '78-p60
SLJ-v25-N '78-p76
Who Is Felix The Great?
BL-v79-Ag '83-p1465
BS-v43-Je '83-p110
CBRS-v11-Mr '83-p82
CCB-B-v36-Jl '83-p212
HB-v59-Ap '83-p171
KR-v51-Ja 1 '83-p7
SLJ-v30-S '83-p136

* * *

KIDD, Virginia
Millennial Women
BL-v74-Je 1 '78-p1545
CCB-B-v32-N '78-p46
CSM-v71-Mr 15 '79-p18
EJ-v68-F '79-p103
EJ-v68-D '79-p74
KR-v46-My 1 '78-p516
LJ-v103-Je 15 '78-p1294
Ms-v7-Jl '78-p35
PW-v213-Je 19 '78-p96
SLJ-v25-D '78-p72

* * *

KIDDELL, John
A Community Of Men
BL-v66-Mr 15 '70-p911
CCB-B-v23-F '70-p99
CLW-v41-F '70-p389
KR-v37-N 15 '69-p1202
LJ-v95-Mr 15 '70-p1203
SR-v52-D 20 '69-p30
Euloowirree Walkabout
BL-v64-Jl 1 '68-p1230
BW-v2-My 5 '68-p28
CCB-B-v22-S '68-p9
KR-v36-F 15 '68-p190

* * *

KIDDER, Harvey
Illustrated Chess For Children
B&B-v19-O '73-p124
BL-v67-Mr 1 '71-p560
CCB-B-v24-Ap '71-p125
GT-v89-Ap '72-p86
Inst-v80-F '71-p137
LJ-v96-O 15 '71-p3468
NY-v46-D 5 '70-p209
SR-v54-Mr 20 '71-p31
TLS-S 28 '73-p1128

* * *

KIDS Cooking Contest Cookbook 1978
SLJ-v26-Ja '80-p45

* * *

KIDS For Nature Yearbook 1983
PW-v222-Jl 23 '82-p132

* * *

KIDS For Nature Yearbook 1984
PW-v224-N 25 '83-p65

* * *

KIDS Like Us
TES-Ja 9 '81-p25

* * *

KIDS Of The World
Sch Lib-v28-S '80-p279

* * *

KIDS Plays
Quill & Q-v47-F '81-p19

* * *

KIEDY Ty Spisz
BL-v73-S 15 '76-p184

* * *

KIEFER, Irene
Energy For America
ACSB-v13-Mr '80-p37
BL-v76-Ja 1 '80-p661
BW-v10-N 9 '80-p18
CBRS-v8-F '80-p59
Cur R-v20-S '81-p400
HB-v56-Ap '80-p193
KR-v48-Ja 1 '80-p11
SB-v16-S '80-p7
SLJ-v26-Mr '80-p141
Global Jigsaw Puzzle
ACSB-v12-Spring '79-p32
BL-v74-Jl 1 '78-p1679
CE-v56-O '79-p48
HB-v54-D '78-p666
KR-v46-Je 15 '78-p642
LA-v56-F '79-p188
S&T-v96-S '78-p247
SB-v15-S '79-p84
SLJ-v25-N '78-p76
Nuclear Energy At The Crossroads
BL-v79-D 15 '82-p559
CBRS-v11-Winter '83-p59
CCB-B-v36-Ap '83-p153
Cur R-v22-O '83-p21
HB-v59-Ap '83-p202
KR-v50-O 1 '82-p1110
SLJ-v29-Ag '83-p78
VOYA-v6-Je '83-p104
Poisoned Land
ACSB-v15-Winter '82-p35
BL-v78-S 1 '81-p47
BL-v80-O 15 '83-p369
BL-v80-My 15 '84-p1352
CBRS-v9-Ag '81-p128
CCB-B-v35-N '81-p47
CE-v59-S '82-p60
HB-v57-D '81-p688
KR-v49-My 15 '81-p637
SLJ-v28-O '81-p151
Underground Furnaces
BL-v73-F 1 '77-p835
CLW-v48-My '77-p440
HB-v53-Ap '77-p196
KR-v44-O 1 '76-p1098
SB-v13-S '77-p99
SLJ-v23-F '77-p66

* * *

KIESEL, Stanley
Skinny Malinky Leads The War For Kidness
B Rpt-v3-S '84-p34
BS-v44-S '84-p233
CBRS-v12-My '84-p109
CCB-B-v37-My '84-p168
The War Between The Pitiful Teachers And The Splendid Kids
BOT-v4-F '81-p79
BS-v41-My '81-p79
CBRS-v9-F '81-p57
KR-v49-F 15 '81-p214
NYTBR-v86-Ja 11 '81-p28
NYTBR-v87-Ja 17 '82-p35
PW-v218-D 26 '80-p59
PW-v221-Mr 26 '82-p75
SLJ-v27-F '81-p67
VOYA-v5-Ap '82-p39

* * *

KIESZAK, Kenneth
Look It Up
Cur R-v21-Ag '82-p271

* * *

KIFT, Roy
Stronger Than Superman
Dr-Spring '83-p24
TES-F 12 '82-p29

* * *

KILBOURNE, Frances
Overnight Adventure
Can Child Lit-#25 '82-p37
The Recyclers
BIC-v8-D '79-p12
Can Child Lit-#25 '82-p37
In Rev-v14-F '80-p49
Quill & Q-v48-Je '82-p3

* * *

KILBURN, Christopher
Stars And Planets
TES-S 12 '80-p25

* * *

KILEY, Denise
Biggest Machines
ASBYP-v14-Fall '81-p29
SB-v17-S '81-p34

* * *

KILGORE, Kathleen
The Ghost-Maker
BL-v80-Je 15 '84-p1484
BS-v44-Je '84-p117
CBRS-v12-Ag '84-p152
HB-v60-Je '84-p339
KR-v52-Mr 1 '84-pJ22
PW-v225-My 25 '84-p59
SLJ-v30-My '84-p103
The Wolfman Of Beacon Hill
BL-v79-D 15 '82-p565
BS-v42-F '83-p445
CBRS-v11-Winter '83-p59
CCB-B-v36-D '82-p71
HB-v58-D '82-p658
KR-v50-Ag 1 '82-p872
PW-v222-N 5 '82-p70
SLJ-v29-S '82-p140
VOYA-v5-O '82-p44

* * *

KILIAN, Crawford
Wonders, Inc.
BL-v65-F 1 '69-p593
BW-v3-Ap 20 '69-p12
CCB-B-v22-Ja '69-p80
EJ-v73-F '84-p104
HB-v45-F '69-p48
LJ-v94-Jl '69-p2676
NYTBR-F 23 '69-p22
PW-v194-Ag 19 '68-p78
PW-v218-Jl 25 '80-p158
SR-v51-N 9 '68-p64

* * *

KILLENS, John Oliver
Great Gittin' Up Morning
BL-v68-Je 1 '72-p862
BL-v69-My 1 '73-p838
BS-v31-Mr 15 '72-p566
CCB-B-v26-Mr '73-p108
CSM-v64-My 4 '72-pB5
KR-v40-Ja 1 '72-p11
LJ-v97-S 15 '72-p2962
NYRB-v18-Ap 20 '72-p39
NYTBR-Ap 30 '72-p8

KILLENS, John Oliver (continued)
PW-v201-Ap 10 '72-p58
SE-v37-D '73-p789

* * *

KILLIP, Kathleen
Saint Bridget's Night
B&B-v21-N '75-p64
GP-v14-Ja '76-p2804
Obs-D 7 '75-p32
TLS-D 5 '75-p1456
A Stork On The Roof
GP-v15-O '76-p2960
JB-v40-D '76-p319
Twisting The Rope
Brit Bk N C-Autumn '80-p3
GP-v19-S '80-p3765
JB-v44-O '80-p251
TES-Je 20 '80-p41
TLS-S 19 '80-p1027

* * *

KILNER, Geoffrey
Joe Burkinshaw's Progress
GP-v18-Ja '80-p3619
HT-v29-D '79-p846
Sch Lib-v28-Mr '80-p36
TES-N 23 '79-p34
Kingfisher
GP-v19-Ja '81-p3819
JB-v45-Ap '81-p82

* * *

KILPATRICK, C
Hidden Animals
JB-v42-Ap '78-p90
Kirkmouse
SLJ-v26-O '79-p117
Let's Look At Animal Homes
TES-O 21 '77-p24
Nature Trails
JB-v40-Ap '76-p93

* * *

KILPATRICK, Cathy
Creepy Crawlies
ASBYP-v16-Spring '83-p60
LATBR-Je 26 '83-p8
TES-Mr 11 '83-p42
Giraffes
ASBYP-v14-Spring '81-p23
Brit Bk N C-Autumn '80-p30
SB-v17-S '81-p33
SLJ-v27-Ap '81-p110
Leopards
JB-v45-Ag '81-p151
TES-Mr 6 '81-p37
Tigers
ASBYP-v14-Fall '81-p23
Brit Bk N C-Autumn '80-p30
SB-v17-S '81-p34
SLJ-v27-Ap '81-p110

* * *

KILROY, Sally
Animal Noises
CBRS-v12-F '84-p68
SLJ-v30-Ap '84-p103
Babies' Bodies
CBRS-v12-F '84-p68
CCB-B-v37-Mr '84-p130
PW-v224-N 25 '83-p64
SLJ-v30-Ap '84-p103
Baby Colors
CBRS-v12-F '84-p68
SLJ-v30-Ap '84-p103
Copycat Drawing Book
BL-v78-D 1 '81-p499
CBRS-v10-N '81-p25
Inst-v91-Ja '82-p145
KR-v49-N 1 '81-p1340
PW-v220-Jl 24 '81-p149
SLJ-v28-D '81-p53
Noisy Homes
CBRS-v12-F '84-p68
SLJ-v30-Ap '84-p103
The Young Puffin Quiz Book
TES-O 1 '82-p31

* * *

KILVERT, Francis
Ardizzone's Kilvert
B&B-v22-N '76-p78
B&B-v22-Ja '77-p61
GW-v115-D 5 '76-p22
JB-v41-F '77-p43
TLS-O 1 '76-p1246

* * *

KIM, Joy
Come On Up!
SLJ-v29-S '82-p103
Rainbows And Frogs
SLJ-v29-S '82-p103

* * *

KIM, Scott
Inversions
Choice-v19-Ja '82-p615
NYTBR-v86-O 18 '81-p47
Sch Arts-v82-O '82-p36

* * *

KIM, Yong Ik
Love In Winter
BL-v66-Ja 15 '70-p616
CCB-B-v23-Mr '70-p113
EJ-v69-Ap '80-p101
PW-v196-O 20 '69-p60
The Shoes From Yang San Valley
BL-v67-Ja 1 '71-p373
BS-v30-O 15 '70-p298
EJ-v69-Ap '80-p101
HB-v46-O '70-p481
LJ-v96-Ja 15 '71-p269

* * *

KIMBALL, Gwen
The Cardiff Giant
CCB-B-v20-Ap '67-p124
KR-v34-My 1 '66-p477
LJ-v91-Jl '66-p3544
SLJ-v30-F '84-p84
SR-v49-Jl 23 '66-p57

* * *

KIMBALL, Kathleen
Big Foot, Little Foot
SLJ-v27-O '80-p136

* * *

KIMBROUGH, Richard
Cross-Country Courage
CCB-B-v26-F '73-p93
EJ-v62-Ap '73-p648
KR-v40-O 15 '72-p1201
LJ-v97-D 15 '72-p4091

* * *

KIMISHIMA, Hisako
Hoshi Ni Natta Ryu No Kiba
BL-v75-Jl 15 '79-p1636
The Magic Brush
GP-v14-Ja '76-p2804
JB-v40-Ap '76-p82
The Princess Of The Rice Fields
CE-v47-D '70-p159
CLW-v42-O '70-p133
HB-v46-Ap '70-p155
KR-v38-F 15 '70-p170
LJ-v95-My 15 '70-p1930
NYTBR, pt.2-My 24 '70-p47
Ushi-Kai To Orihime
BL-v75-Jl 15 '79-p1636

* * *

KIMMEL, Eric
Why Worry?
BB-v7-N '79-p1

* * *

KIMMEL, Eric A
Hershel Of Ostropol
BL-v78-Je 15 '82-p1368
Mishka, Pishka & Fishka And Other Galician Tales
BL-v73-S 1 '76-p40
CE-v53-Ja '77-p147
HB-v52-O '76-p497
KR-v44-Je 1 '76-p634
NYTBR-Ag 8 '76-p18
RT-v35-D '81-p340
SLJ-v23-S '76-p119
Nicanor's Gate
CBRS-v8-Spring '80-p113
PW-v217-My 16 '80-p211
The Tartar's Sword
BL-v70-Mr 1 '74-p742
CE-v51-O '74-p33
HB-v50-Ag '74-p385
KR-v42-Ja 15 '74-p61
LJ-v99-S 15 '74-p2292
NYTBR-Ag 25 '74-p10
PW-v205-Je 10 '74-p41
Why Worry?
BB-v7-N '79-p1
CBRS-v7-My '79-p95
NYTBR-Je 24 '79-p34
SLJ-v26-S '79-p114

* * *

KIMMEL, Margaret M
For Reading Out Loud!
A Lib-v14-Ap '83-p234
BL-v79-Ja 15 '83-p683
BW-v14-F 12 '84-p12
CBRS-v11-Ja '83-p50
CE-v59-My '83-p360
Choice-v20-Ap '83-p1185
Emerg Lib-v10-My '83-p25
HB-v59-F '83-p67
KR-v50-D 1 '82-p1297
LJ-v108-F 1 '83-p204
Learning-v12-Ap '84-p72
SLJ-v29-Ap '83-p32
TN-v39-Spring '83-p292

* * *

KIMMEL, Margaret Mary
Magic In The Mist
BL-v71-Ap 15 '75-p867
CCB-B-v29-O '75-p28
CE-v52-F '76-p206
CE-v55-Ap '79-p261
CLW-v47-S '75-p93
HB-v51-Ap '75-p139
KR-v43-F 1 '75-p119
PW-v207-Ap 14 '75-p54
SLJ-v21-Ap '75-p46
Time-v106-D 8 '75-p87
WLB-v49-Je '75-p704

* * *

KIMPTON, Laurence
Geography In A Changing World. Bk. 2
TES-Ap 1 '83-p26

* * *

KIMURA, Yasuko
Fergus And The Sea Monster
CSM-v70-My 3 '78-pB6
PW-v213-Ap 24 '78-p84
SLJ-v23-My '77-p51
SLJ-v24-My '78-p57
WLB-v52-Je '78-p802
Fergus And The Snow Deer
SLJ-v26-Ap '80-p95

* * *

KINCAID, Doug
Ears And Hearing
SLJ-v30-My '84-p67
TES-Mr 12 '82-p39
Eyes And Looking
SLJ-v30-My '84-p67
TES-Mr 12 '82-p39
The Read And Do Series
TES-O 1 '82-p44
Science In A Topic: Food
TES-Ap 21 '78-p22
Taste And Smell
SLJ-v30-My '84-p67
TES-Mr 12 '82-p39
Touch And Feel
SLJ-v30-My '84-p67
TES-Mr 12 '82-p39

* * *

KINCAID, Eric
Cuentos De Magos Y Encantadores
SLJ-v30-My '84-p36

* * *

KINCAID, Lucy
Chicken Licken
SLJ-v30-Ap '84-p104
Cinderella
SLJ-v30-Mr '84-p146
The Elves And The Shoemaker
SLJ-v30-Mr '84-p146
Foolish Jack
SLJ-v30-Ap '84-p104
Goldilocks And The Three Bears
SLJ-v30-Ap '84-p104
Jack And The Beanstalk
SLJ-v30-Mr '84-p146
Little Red Hen
SLJ-v30-Ap '84-p104
Little Red Riding Hood
SLJ-v30-Ap '84-p104
Puss In Boots
SLJ-v30-Ap '84-p104
Rapunzel
SLJ-v30-Ap '84-p104
Rumpelstiltskin
SLJ-v30-Mr '84-p146
Sleeping Beauty
SLJ-v30-Ap '84-p104
Snow White And The Seven Dwarfs
SLJ-v30-Mr '84-p146
Three Little Pigs
SLJ-v30-Ap '84-p104
The Ugly Duckling
SLJ-v30-Ap '84-p104

* * *

KINCL, Kay Owens
Mandy's Laughing Book
SLJ-v25-My '79-p52

* * *

KIND
BL-v79-F 1 '83-p730
Ser R-v7-O '81-p16

* * *

KINDRED, Wendy
Hank And Fred
KR-v44-Mr 1 '76-p251
PW-v209-Ja 19 '76-p102
SLJ-v23-S '76-p120
Ida's Idea
HB-v49-Ap '73-p131
KR-v40-Ag 15 '72-p935
LJ-v97-D 15 '72-p4067
PW-v202-S 18 '72-p72
Negatu In The Garden
CCB-B-v25-Ap '72-p125
LJ-v97-F 15 '72-p765

* * *

KING, Alexander
Memoirs Of A Certain Mouse
CCB-B-v20-Ap '67-p125
HB-v42-D '66-p710
KR-v34-O 1 '66-p1048

KING, Alexander (continued)
LJ-v92-F 15 '67-p881
NYTBR-v71-N 6 '66-p42
PW-v190-O 17 '66-p63

* * *

KING, Billie Jean
Billie Jean
BL-v78-Je 15 '82-p1338
BS-v34-Ag 15 '74-p234
BW-D 8 '74-p4
CSM-v66-Ag 28 '74-p10
Choice-v11-Ja '75-p1667
Inter BC-v10-Ap 40 '07-p910
Inter BC-v12-#1 '81-p13
KR-v42-My 15 '74-p564
LJ-v99-Jl '74-p1842
LJ-v99-N 15 '74-p3064
NS-v90-Jl 4 '75-p28
NYT-v123-Je 20 '74-p37
New R-v170-Je 8 '74-p28
PW-v205-My 20 '74-p60
PW-v207-My 19 '75-p178
TLS-Jl 1 '77-p790
WSJ-v184-Jl 5 '74-p4

* * *

KING, C Richard
A Birthday In Texas
SLJ-v28-Mr '82-p148

* * *

KING, Charles
People At Work: Catering
JB-v40-D '76-p346
People At Work: Coal
GP-v14-S '75-p2701
JB-v39-Je '75-p198

* * *

KING, Clive
Accident
GP-v15-Mr '77-p3073
Birds
TES-Mr 7 '80-p43
The Birds From Africa
Sch Lib-v28-Je '80-p145
TES-Mr 7 '80-p43
The Devil's Cut
GP-v17-Ja '79-p3455
JB-v42-D '78-p301
First Day Out
GP-v15-Mr '77-p3073
Highjacks Low Jacks
GP-v15-Mr '77-p3073
Me And My Million
BL-v76-D 15 '79-p613
BL-v78-F 15 '82-p762
BS-v39-F '80-p408
Brit Bk N C-Spring '81-p14
CBRS-v8-N '79-p28
CCB-B-v33-F '80-p111
GP-v14-Ap '76-p2844
HB-v56-F '80-p56
JB-v40-Je '76-p164
KR-v47-N 1 '79-p1267
NS-v91-My 21 '76-p690
NW-v94-D 17 '79-p96
SLJ-v26-O '79-p151
TLS-Ap 2 '76-p388
The Night The Water Came
B&B-v18-Je '73-p136
BL-v78-Jl '82-p1445
CCB-B-v35-Jl '82-p210
HB-v58-Je '82-p288
Inst-v91-My '82-p105
KR-v50-Ap 1 '82-p418
NS-v85-My 25 '73-p778
Obs-D 12 '76-p23
SLJ-v28-My '82-p64
Spec-v230-Ap 14 '73-p461
TLS-Je 15 '73-p674
VOYA-v5-Je '82-p34
Ninny's Boat
BL-v78-Ja 1 '82-p598
BS-v41-Mr '82-p475
Brit Bk N C-Autumn '80-p22
CBRS-v10-N '81-p28
CCB-B-v35-D '81-p70
CE-v59-S '82-p57
Cur R-v22-F '83-p59
HB-v58-Ap '82-p165
HT-v30-D '80-p62
JB-v44-O '80-p251
Lis-v104-N 6 '80-p624
NS-v100-N 21 '80-p18
NYTBR-v87-Mr 28 '82-p28
Obs-Ag 24 '80-p27
SLJ-v28-N '81-p93
Sch Lib-v29-Mr '81-p53
TES-N 7 '80-p24
TES-F 24 '84-p29
TLS-S 19 '80-p1024
The Secret
GP-v15-Mr '77-p3073
Snakes And Snakes
GP-v14-O '75-p2721
Stig Of The Dump
HT-v30-D '80-p62
TES-N 27 '81-p23
Teacher-v96-O '78-p175
The 22 Letters
B&B-v11-Je '66-p66
BS-v27-Jl 1 '67-p145
CCB-B-v21-D '67-p61
KR-v35-Ap 1 '67-p423
LJ-v92-S 15 '67-p3200
LR-v20-Autumn '66-p500
Obs-Ap 10 '66-p20
Punch-v250-My 4 '66-p667
Spec-Je 3 '66-p702
TLS-My 19 '66-p435

* * *

KING, Coretta Scott
My Life With Martin Luther King, Jr.
Am-v121-N 8 '69-p426
Am-v121-N 29 '69-p530
B&B-v15-Mr '70-p20
BL-v66-D 15 '69-p479
BS-v30-Ag 15 '70-p196
BW-v3-S 28 '69-p5
BW-v3-D 7 '69-p8
Bl W-v20-Ag '71-p97
CC-v87-Ja 14 '70-p53
CE-v46-F '70-p289
CLW-v41-Mr '70-p477
CR-v216-Mr '70-p165
CSM-v61-S 25 '69-p15
Comw-v91-D 5 '69-p317
HB-v46-Je '70-p316
KR-v37-S 1 '69-p972
KR-v37-S 15 '69-p1021
LJ-v94-O 15 '69-p3636
LJ-v94-N 15 '69-p4310
Lis-v83-F 5 '70-p189
NS-v79-Ja 23 '70-p118
NYT-v119-S 29 '69-p45
Obs-Ja 18 '70-p33
PW-v196-Ag 18 '69-p56
PW-v198-Jl 27 '70-p76
SR-v52-O 11 '69-p33
Spec-v224-Ja 24 '70-p114
TLS-Je 11 '70-p640
TN-v26-Ap '70-p310
Time-v94-O 3 '69-p100
WSJ-v174-O 1 '69-p18

* * *

KING, Cynthia
In The Morning Of Time
BL-v67-O 1 '70-p146
BS-v30-Je 1 '70-p105
HB-v46-Ag '70-p383
KR-v38-F 1 '70-p111
LJ-v95-My 15 '70-p1954
Sailing Home
BS-v42-Ag '82-p204
CBRS-v10-Je '82-p107
KR-v50-Ap 1 '82-p421

KING, Cynthia (continued)
NYTBR-v87-Ap 25 '82-p44
SLJ-v28-My '82-p72
VOYA-v5-O '82-p44
The Year Of Mr. Nobody
BB-v6-O '78-p2
CCB-B-v32-S '78-p12
KR-v46-Ap 15 '78-p437
PW-v213-F 13 '78-p127
SLJ-v24-My '78-p57

* * *

KING, Deborah
Rook
Econ-v277-D 27 '80-p74
GP-v19-Mr '81-p3850
Obs-S 28 '80-p33
Punch-v279-S 24 '80-p520
SLJ-v28-Ag '82-p118
TES-N 21 '80-p30
TLS-N 21 '80-p1327
Sirius And Saba
Brit Bk N C-Autumn '81-p11
GP-v20-N '81-p3959
JB-v45-Ag '81-p145
SLJ-v28-Ag '82-p99
TES-Je 5 '81-p36

* * *

KING, Dennis
The Grey Nuns And The Red River Settlement
Can Child Lit-#23 '81-p103
In Rev-v14-D '80-p45

* * *

KING, Frederick M
Understanding The Social Sciences
Cur R-v18-O '79-p334

* * *

KING, Gerald M
Alice Through The Pillar-Box And What She Found There
B&B-v24-F '79-p64

* * *

KING, Helen H
Willy
BW-v5-N 7 '71-p10
CCB-B-v25-N '71-p46
KR-v39-S 1 '71-p935
LJ-v97-Mr 15 '72-p1170

* * *

KING, Jean Callan
Miss Mehitable's Monster
CCB-B-v25-Mr '72-p109
KR-v39-N 15 '71-p1210
LJ-v97-My 15 '72-p1904

* * *

KING, Kay
Melanie In England
GP-v15-Jl '76-p2909

* * *

KING, L
Computers And You
JB-v42-Ag '78-p213

* * *

KING, Marian
Mary Baker Eddy
CCB-B-v22-F '69-p96
CSM-v60-My 2 '68-pB10
KR-v36-My 15 '68-p561
LJ-v93-S 15 '68-p3317
PW-v193-My 13 '68-p60

* * *

KING, Mary Louise
History Of Western Architecture
BL-v64-S 15 '67-p114
BS-v27-Jl 1 '67-p145
CC-v84-D 13 '67-p1602
CCB-B-v21-D '67-p61
CE-v44-Mr '68-p452
CLW-v39-N '67-p236
HB-v43-Ag '67-p489
KR-v34-D 15 '66-p1292
LJ-v92-Jl '67-p2659
PW-v191-Ap 10 '67-p81
SB-v3-D '67-p267

* * *

KING, Susan
Horses Galore
GP-v18-N '79-p3605
JB-v44-F '80-p29

* * *

KING, Tony
Butterflies
Nature-v300-D 9 '82-p547
TES-Ja 7 '83-p24
Frogs
JB-v46-D '82-p226
Nature-v300-D 9 '82-p547
Obs-D 5 '82-p33
TES-Ja 7 '83-p24
The Moving Alphabet Book
CBRS-v10-Ag '82-p133
GP-v21-N '82-p3972
GP-v22-Jl '83-p4109
NYTBR-v87-S 26 '82-p31
PW-v222-Jl 23 '82-p132
WLB-v57-Mr '83-p591
The Moving Animal Book
CCB-B-v37-Ja '84-p91
JB-v47-Je '83-p109

* * *

KING FooFoo
TES-Mr 7 '80-p46

* * *

KING-SMITH, Dick
Daggie Dogfoot
Brit Bk N C-Autumn '80-p22
GP-v19-N '80-p3775
JB-v44-D '80-p292
Obs-N 30 '80-p36
Punch-v280-Ap 29 '81-p680
TES-My 21 '82-p31
The Fox Busters
GP-v17-Jl '78-p3347
JB-v42-D '78-p301
Sch Lib-v27-Mr '79-p39
TLS-Jl 7 '78-p770
Magnus Powermouse
BL-v80-Ap 15 '84-p1191
CBRS-v12-Jl '84-p141
CCB-B-v37-Jl '84-p207
GP-v21-N '82-p3988
HB-v60-Je '84-p329
JB-v46-D '82-p224
KR-v52-My 1 '84-pJ40
RT-v38-D '84-p339
SLJ-v30-Ag '84-p74
Sch Lib-v31-Mr '83-p37
TES-S 21 '84-p37
The Mouse Butcher
BL-v78-Ag '82-p1526
Brit Bk N C-Autumn '81-p20
CBRS-v10-Ag '82-p139
CCB-B-v36-D '82-p71
GP-v19-Mr '81-p3839
HB-v58-Ag '82-p404
JB-v45-O '81-p198
KR-v50-My 15 '82-p605
LA-v60-Mr '83-p363
SLJ-v28-Ap '82-p71
Sch Lib-v29-D '81-p326
TES-O 16 '81-p33
TES-D 23 '83-p23
Pigs Might Fly
BL-v78-Je 15 '82-p1368
CBRS-v10-Ag '82-p139
CCB-B-v36-O '82-p29
CE-v59-N '82-p133
HB-v58-Ag '82-p405
KR-v50-Ap 1 '82-p419

KING-SMITH, Dick (continued)
PW-v221-Mr 5 '82-p71
SLJ-v28-Ag '82-p99
The Queen's Nose
GP-v21-Mr '83-p4033
JB-v47-Ag '83-p165
Sch Lib-v31-Je '83-p144
The Sheep-Pig
JB-v48-Ap '84-p72
Obs-D 11 '83-p35
Punch-v287-Ag 15 '84-p45

* * *

KINGCUP Cottage
Spec-v241-D 16 '78-p22

* * *

KINGDOM Of Stone (Langridge)
TLS-D 6 '74-p1382

* * *

KINGDON, Jill
The ABC Dinosaur Book
ASBYP-v16-Winter '83-p36
CBRS-v11-Mr '83-p76
SLJ-v29-My '83-p63

* * *

KINGMAN, Lee
Break A Leg, Betsy Maybe!
BL-v73-N 15 '76-p466
BL-v73-N 15 '76-p474
CCB-B-v30-My '77-p144
EJ-v69-Ja '80-p78
HB-v53-F '77-p56
KR-v44-O 1 '76-p1101
SLJ-v23-O '76-p118
Escape From The Evil Prophecy
BL-v70-D 1 '73-p381
BL-v70-D 1 '73-p387
HB-v49-O '73-p465
KR-v41-Ag 1 '73-p812
LJ-v98-O 15 '73-p3156
PW-v204-D 10 '73-p37
Georgina And The Dragon
BL-v69-N 15 '72-p302
CLW-v44-N '72-p249
HB-v48-Ag '72-p372
KR-v40-Ap 15 '72-p478
LJ-v97-S 15 '72-p2951
NYTBR, pt.2-My 7 '72-p24
RT-v34-Ap '81-p794
Head Over Wheels
BL-v75-D 15 '78-p679
BS-v38-Mr '79-p408
CCB-B-v32-Mr '79-p120
EJ-v68-N '79-p76
EJ-v68-D '79-p78
Emerg Lib-v9-N '81-p32
HB-v55-F '79-p69
Inter BC-v12-#7 '81-p19
JB-v44-F '80-p29
J Read-v23-O '79-p88
KR-v47-Ja 1 '79-p12
Kliatt-v15-Spring '81-p9
RSR-v11-Fall '83-p27
SLJ-v25-O '78-p156
Sch Lib-v28-Je '80-p181
TN-v36-Summer '80-p364
The Illustrator's Notebook
AB-v62-N 13 '78-p2944
BL-v75-N 1 '78-p485
GP-v17-N '78-p3432
JB-v42-O '78-p246
KR-v46-My 15 '78-p554
TLS-Jl 7 '78-p768
Illustrators Of Children's Books 1967-1976
AB-v64-N 12 '79-p3247
ARBA-v10-'79-p438
BL-v75-F 1 '79-p871
Choice-v16-Je '79-p524
JB-v43-Je '79-p153
KR-v47-F 1 '79-p134
TN-v35-Summer '79-p424
WLB-v53-Mr '79-p522
The Meeting Post
BL-v69-Mr 1 '73-p648
CCB-B-v26-D '72-p59
CE-v49-F '73-p258
HB-v49-F '73-p48
LJ-v98-Ja 15 '73-p261
SE-v37-D '73-p791
Newbery And Caldecott Medal Books 1966-1975
A Art-v40-D '76-p26
ARBA-v8-'77-p578
Choice-v13-Jl '76-p656
GP-v15-Jl '76-p2927
HB-v52-Je '76-p276
JB-v40-Ag '76-p188
SLJ-v22-Ap '76-p46
TLS-Jl 16 '76-p888
The Peter Pan Bag
BL-v67-S 15 '70-p96
CCB-B-v24-O '70-p29
CSM-v62-My 7 '70-pB6
Comw-v92-My 22 '70-p250
HB-v46-Ag '70-p394
KR-v38-Ap 15 '70-p465
LJ-v96-Ap 15 '71-p1516
NYTBR-Jl 12 '70-p26
NYTBR, pt.2-N 7 '71-p47
SR-v53-Je 27 '70-p56
The Refiner's Fire
BL-v78-S 1 '81-p47
BS-v41-N '81-p318
CBRS-v10-D '81-p39
CCB-B-v35-Ja '82-p87
CLW-v53-Ap '82-p402
HB-v57-O '81-p542
J Read-v25-Ap '82-p710
SLJ-v28-N '81-p106
VOYA-v4-F '82-p35
Year Of The Raccoon
BL-v63-Ja 15 '67-p538
CCB-B-v20-Ap '67-p125
CLW-v38-Ja '67-p340
CLW-v49-D '77-p211
HB-v42-D '66-p719
HB-v54-F '78-p74
Inst-v84-N '74-p142
KR-v34-O 1 '66-p1053
LJ-v92-Ja 15 '67-p344
Teacher-v92-N '74-p110

* * *

KINGSLEY, Charles
The Heroes
BL-v77-O 15 '80-p327
Brit Bk N C-Autumn '80-p10
LJ-v95-N 15 '70-p4044
TLS-Jl 18 '80-p797
The Water-Babies
NY-v56-D 1 '80-p214
Rp B Bk R-v25-F '80-p19
Spec-v231-D 22 '73-p823
TES-N 20 '81-p31
VLS-N '82-p18
The Water-Babies (Fry)
B&B-v22-N '76-p71

* * *

KINGSLEY, Emily P
Cookie Monster's Storybook
SLJ-v26-D '79-p75
Farley Goes To The Doctor
Par-v57-O '82-p140
The Sesame Street Book Of Fairy Tales
SLJ-v22-Mr '76-p94

* * *

KINGSTON, Jeremy
The Bird Who Saved The Jungle
Obs-Ap 3 '77-p24
Spec-v231-D 22 '73-p823
TLS-Mr 29 '74-p330

KINGSTON, Jeremy (continued)
The Dustbin Who Wanted To Be A General
GP-v17-S '78-p3401
Spec-v226-My 29 '71-p758
TLS-Ap 2 '71-p386

* * *

KINMONTH, Patrick
Mr. Potter's Pigeon
JB-v44-Ap '80-p69
Obs-D 2 '79-p39
Sch Lib-v28-Mr '80-p26
TES-S 30 '83-p42

* * *

KINNELL, Galway
How The Alligator Missed Breakfast
BW-v12-N 7 '82-p17
CBRS-v11-Winter '83-p53
KR-v50-Jl 15 '82-p795
NYTBR-v88-F 13 '83-p30
PW-v222-Jl 9 '82-p48
SLJ-v29-O '82-p142

* * *

KINNEY, Jean
What Does The Tide Do?
CCB-B-v20-Ap '67-p125
KR-v34-N 1 '66-p1135
LJ-v91-S 15 '66-p4314
SA-v217-D '67-p142
SB-v2-Mr '67-p276
21 Kinds Of American Folk Art And How To Make Each One
BL-v69-O 1 '72-p149
CLW-v44-N '72-p248
HB-v48-Ag '72-p387
NYTBR-Jl 2 '72-p8
NYTBR, pt.2-N 5 '72-p28
23 Varieties Of Ethnic Art And How To Make Each One
BB-v5-Mr '77-p3
Cur R-v16-F '77-p65
KR-v44-S 15 '76-p1046
SE-v41-Ap '77-p348
SLJ-v23-Ja '77-p101
Teacher-v95-N '77-p39

* * *

KINSER, Charleen
Outdoor Art For Kids
BL-v72-S 1 '75-p41
KR-v43-Jl 1 '75-p716
PW-v208-Jl 7 '75-p86
SLJ-v22-O '75-p100

* * *

KINSLER, Doris
Computers
CSM-v60-N 7 '68-pB8
HB-v45-F '69-p74
LJ-v94-F 15 '69-p874
SB-v4-Mr '69-p271
Teacher-v86-Ja '69-p138

* * *

KIPLING, John L
A Kipling ABC
GP-v18-Mr '80-p3663
JB-v44-Ag '80-p169
TES-F 8 '80-p28

* * *

KIPLING, Rudyard
The Beginning Of The Armadilloes (Keeping)
BL-v80-F 15 '84-p859
CBRS-v12-Ap '84-p92
GP-v21-Ja '83-p4000
HB-v58-O '82-p568
HB-v60-Je '84-p357
JB-v47-F '83-p14
SLJ-v30-F '84-p60
TES-O 29 '82-p25
The Beginning Of The Armadillos (Maestro)
CLW-v42-O '70-p137
CSM-v62-My 7 '70-pB7
KR-v38-Ap 15 '70-p445
LJ-v96-S 15 '71-p2935
NS-v80-N 6 '70-p612
NY-v46-D 5 '70-p214
NYTBR-Je 21 '70-p22
Obs-N 29 '70-p31
PW-v197-My 25 '70-p57
TLS-D 11 '70-p1462
The Butterfly That Stamped
BL-v80-F 15 '84-p859
CBRS-v12-Ap '84-p92
GP-v21-Ja '83-p4000
HB-v58-O '82-p568
JB-v47-F '83-p14
PW-v224-S 30 '83-p116
SLJ-v30-F '84-p60
TES-O 29 '82-p25
The Cat That Walked By Himself
BL-v80-F 15 '84-p859
CBRS-v12-Ap '84-p92
GP-v21-Ja '83-p4000
HB-v58-O '82-p568
JB-v47-F '83-p14
KR-v38-Je 1 '70-p598
LJ-v95-S 15 '70-p3049
SLJ-v30-F '84-p60
TES-O 29 '82-p25
The Crab That Played With The Sea
BL-v80-F 15 '84-p859
CBRS-v12-Ap '84-p92
GP-v21-Ja '83-p4000
HB-v58-O '82-p568
HB-v60-Je '84-p358
JB-v47-F '83-p14
SLJ-v30-F '84-p60
TES-O 29 '82-p25
The Elephant's Child
BL-v80-S 1 '83-p87
CBRS-v12-D '83-p38
CC-v86-D 10 '69-p1584
CCB-B-v37-Mr '84-p130
CE-v47-N '70-p87
CLW-v41-F '70-p384
KR-v38-N 15 '70-p1245
LJ-v95-Mr 15 '70-p1188
LJ-v96-Ja 15 '71-p258
NY-v45-D 13 '69-p192
PW-v198-D 7 '70-p50
SLJ-v27-O '80-p118
SLJ-v30-O '83-p150
How The Alphabet Was Made
JB-v48-F '84-p15
How The Leopard Got His Spots
B&B-v18-F '73-p120
BL-v69-Je 1 '73-p948
CSM-v65-My 2 '73-pB3
Inst-v83-N '73-p124
KR-v41-Ap 1 '73-p381
LJ-v98-O 15 '73-p3139
NY-v50-D 2 '74-p200
NYTBR-Ja 14 '73-p8
PW-v203-Ap 9 '73-p66
TLS-N 3 '72-p1333
How The Rhinoceros Got His Skin (Weisgard)
BL-v70-Je 15 '74-p1154
CCB-B-v28-N '74-p45
Econ-v249-D 29 '73-p62
LJ-v99-S 15 '74-p2250
Spec-v231-D 22 '73-p823
TLS-N 23 '73-p1431
How The Whale Got His Throat
JB-v48-F '84-p15
KR-v39-N 1 '71-p1154
The Jungle Book
BW-v11-N 8 '81-p14

KIPLING, Rudyard
(continued)
HB-v58-O '82-p544
PW-v192-N 20 '67-p60
The Jungle Book (Wilson)
GP-v22-Ja '84-p4190
JB-v48-F '84-p25
Just So Stories
BL-v79-F 15 '83-p778
BW-v6-N 5 '72-p1
CCB-B-v26-F '73-p93
CSM-v68-D 22 '75-p18
GP-v22-S '83-p4126
HB-v58-O '82-p565
HB-v59-Je '83-p271
KR-v40-Ag 15 '72-p940
KR-v40-D 15 '72-p1413
LJ-v98-My 15 '73-p1682
NYTBR-Ja 14 '73-p6
PW-v202-N 20 '72-p65
TES-Je 10 '83-p32
Just So Stories For Little Children
BL-v77-O 15 '80-p327
NY-v56-D 1 '80-p214
Rp B Bk R-v26-#2 '81-p17
Il Piccolo Elefante
TLS-Ap 2 '76-p378
Rikki-Tikki-Tavi
Time-v120-D 20 '82-p79
The Second Jungle Book
GP-v23-Jl '84-p4280
Stalky And Co.
GP-v21-My '82-p3888
HB-v58-O '82-p567
PW-v193-Ap 8 '68-p53
The White Seal
SLJ-v29-Mr '83-p164
Time-v120-D 20 '82-p79

* * *

KIPNIS, Lynne
You Can't Catch Diabetes From A Friend
BL-v75-My 15 '79-p1440
CCB-B-v33-N '79-p49
Cur R-v19-Ap '80-p125
KR-v47-My 15 '79-p577
SB-v15-Mr '80-p231
SLJ-v26-S '79-p114

* * *

KIPPING, John
Nature's Pets
Inst-v87-N '77-p158
SLJ-v22-Ja '76-p47
Teacher-v93-My '76-p22

* * *

KIRBY, Susan E
Ike And Porker
CCB-B-v37-F '84-p109
HB-v59-D '83-p710
SLJ-v30-F '84-p74

* * *

KIRCHBERG, Ursula
Fridolin
BL-v75-N 15 '78-p555

* * *

KIRK, Barbara
Grandpa, Me And Our House In The Tree
BL-v75-Ja 15 '79-p810
CBRS-v7-Winter '79-p55
CCB-B-v32-My '79-p157
Inst-v88-My '79-p107
Ms-v9-Ag '80-p92
SE-v44-N '80-p603
SLJ-v25-F '79-p43
Teacher-v96-My '79-p108
WCRB-v4-N '78-p81

* * *

KIRK, Helen
Double-Quick Gardens
GP-v15-Jl '76-p2916
JB-v40-Ag '76-p205

* * *

KIRK, Ruth
David, Young Chief Of The Quileutes
BL-v63-My 15 '67-p996
CCB-B-v21-S '67-p11
HB-v43-Je '67-p362
Inst-v76-My '67-p132
KR-v35-F 15 '67-p204
LJ-v92-Ap 15 '67-p1735
SR-v50-My 13 '67-p52
Desert Life
BW-v4-My 17 '70-p30
CCB-B-v24-D '70-p61
KR-v38-Ap 15 '70-p460
LJ-v95-S 15 '70-p3040
NY-v46-D 5 '70-p205
NYTBR-My 3 '70-p22
SB-v6-S '70-p134
Hunters Of The Whale
A Lib-v6-Mr '75-p167
BB-v3-Ap '75-p4
BL-v70-My 15 '74-p1052
BL-v70-My 15 '74-p1056
CCB-B-v28-O '74-p30
Choice-v12-N '75-p1133
KR-v42-Ap 1 '74-p375
LJ-v99-S 15 '74-p2273
PW-v206-Jl 29 '74-p58
SA-v231-D '74-p150
The Oldest Man In America
CCB-B-v25-S '71-p10
CLW-v42-My '71-p579
KR-v38-N 1 '70-p1205
LJ-v96-My 15 '71-p1804
SB-v6-Mr '71-p345
Yellowstone
ACSB-v8-Winter '75-p23
BL-v71-O 15 '74-p244
CLW-v46-My '75-p453
KR-v42-S 1 '74-p953
SB-v11-My '75-p9
SLJ-v21-Ja '75-p46

* * *

KIRKEGAARD, Ole Lund
Otto Is A Rhino
KR-v44-Jl 15 '76-p795
PW-v210-Ag 23 '76-p75
SLJ-v23-O '76-p108

* * *

KIRKLAND, Jessica
The Story Of Giovanni Fideli
CCB-B-v24-My '71-p138
CSM-v63-Jl 3 '71-p17
KR-v39-Mr 1 '71-p233
LJ-v96-My 15 '71-p1797

* * *

KIRKPATRICK, Doris
Honey In The Rock
CBRS-v7-Je '79-p107
CCB-B-v33-N '79-p49
J Read-v23-F '80-p471
KR-v47-Jl 15 '79-p797
SE-v44-O '80-p480
SLJ-v25-My '79-p73

* * *

KIRKPATRICK, Penny
The World Of The Microscope
NS-v90-N 7 '75-p585

* * *

KIRKPATRICK, Rena K
Look At Flowers
SLJ-v26-S '79-p115
Look At Insects
SLJ-v26-S '79-p115
Look At Leaves
BL-v75-Ap 15 '79-p1301
SLJ-v26-S '79-p115

KIRKPATRICK, Rena K (continued)
Look At Magnets
BL-v75-Ap 15 '79-p1302
SLJ-v26-S '79-p115
Look At Pond Life
BL-v75-Ap 15 '79-p1302
SLJ-v26-S '79-p115
Look At Rainbow Colors
SLJ-v26-S '79-p115
Look At Seeds And Weeds
SLJ-v26-S '79-p115
Look At Shore Life
BL-v75-Ap 15 '79-p1302
SLJ-v26-S '79-p115
Look At Trees
BL-v75-Ap 15 '79-p1302
SLJ-v26-S '79-p115
Look At Weather
SLJ-v26-S '79-p115

* * *

KIRKUP, James
Insect Summer
CE-v48-F '72-p257
HB-v47-O '71-p483
KR-v39-Ag 15 '71-p874
LJ-v97-F 15 '72-p775
The Magic Drum
BL-v70-Ja 1 '74-p488
HB-v50-F '74-p50
Inst-v83-My '74-p95
KR-v41-Ag 1 '73-p812
LJ-v98-D 15 '73-p3707

* * *

KIRKUS, Virginia
The First Book Of Gardening
BL-v73-S 15 '76-p177
SLJ-v23-S '76-p120

* * *

KIRKWOOD, Ken
Search For The Rare Plumador
JB-v47-D '83-p236
PW-v224-S 30 '83-p116
Punch-v285-N 16 '83-p60

* * *

KIRN, Ann
Never Run Scared
BL-v71-D 1 '74-p380
Inst-v84-My '75-p102
KR-v42-N 1 '74-p1145
LA-v52-S '75-p854
LJ-v99-D 15 '74-p3263
PW-v206-N 18 '74-p53
The Peacock And The Crow
CCB-B-v23-F '70-p99
HB-v46-Ap '70-p155
LJ-v94-D 15 '69-p4596

* * *

KIRST, Werner
Ants
Obs-Ap 4 '76-p27
Money
GP-v19-My '80-p3687
Sch Lib-v28-Je '80-p166
TES-F 1 '80-p43

* * *

KISHI, Nami
Oni No Yomesan
BL-v79-O 15 '82-p320

* * *

KISHI, Takeo
Kumauchi No Hi Made
BL-v79-O 15 '82-p320

* * *

KISHIDA, Eriko
E. Humperdinck's Hansel And Gretel
B&B-v22-D '76-p81
JB-v40-D '76-p326
The Hippo Boat
BW-v2-N 3 '68-p4
CCB-B-v22-My '69-p144
HB-v45-F '69-p42
KR-v36-Ag 15 '68-p891
LJ-v93-N 15 '68-p4395
NYTBR-v73-O 27 '68-p42
PW-v194-Jl 29 '68-p65
The Lion And The Bird's Nest
BL-v69-Mr 15 '73-p716
CCB-B-v26-Je '73-p157
HB-v49-Je '73-p258
KR-v41-Ja 15 '73-p59
LJ-v98-Ap 15 '73-p1376
PW-v203-F 5 '73-p89
TLS-N 3 '72-p1327
Swan Lake
GP-v14-My '75-p2637

* * *

KITADA, Taxi
The Night Express
GP-v21-Mr '83-p4048
JB-v47-Je '83-p111
Sch Lib-v31-Je '83-p129
TES-Ag 12 '83-p20

* * *

KITCHEN, Bert
Animal Alphabet
BL-v80-Ag '84-p1626
CCB-B-v37-My '84-p168
HB-v60-Ag '84-p458
KR-v52-My 1 '84-pJ31
NYTBR-v89-My 6 '84-p23
Obs-Ag 26 '84-p19
PW-v225-Ap 13 '84-p71
Par-v59-N '84-p65
SLJ-v30-Ag '84-p62
Sch Lib-v32-S '84-p224
TES-Ap 13 '84-p30

* * *

KITT, Tamara
Special Birthday Party For Someone Very Special
CCB-B-v20-Je '67-p154
KR-v34-O 15 '66-p1096
LJ-v91-N 15 '66-p5741
PW-v190-S 12 '66-p89

* * *

KITZHABER, Albert R
Spectrum Of English
Cur R-v17-O '78-p305
Inst-v88-F '79-p189

* * *

KIVELOWITZ, Terri
Diabetes
BL-v78-S 1 '81-p11
SB-v17-Mr '82-p217

* * *

KJELGAARD, Jim
Haunt Fox
BW-v11-N 8 '81-p14
Irish Red
GP-v19-N '80-p3775
Par-v52-My '77-p31
Lion Hound
GP-v20-Mr '82-p4039
Stormy
GP-v19-Mr '81-p3850
TES-F 27 '81-p39

* * *

KLAGER, Max
Letters, Types And Pictures
Cur R-v16-F '77-p15
Inst-v85-Ja '76-p123
RT-v29-F '76-p510

* * *

KLAGSBRUN, Francine
Read About The Librarian
CCB-B-v24-Ja '71-p76
LJ-v95-S 15 '70-p3050
Read About The Parkman
CCB-B-v24-Jl '71-p173
GT-v89-Mr '72-p108
KR-v39-F 1 '71-p109
LJ-v96-Ap 15 '71-p1523
The Story Of Moses
CCB-B-v22-Mr '69-p113
LJ-v94-F 15 '69-p886

* * *

KLAITS, Barrie
When You Find A Rock
ACSB-v10-Spring '77-p31
ARBA-v8-'77-p694
BL-v72-My 1 '76-p1266
CE-v53-N '76-p99
KR-v44-Mr 15 '76-p328
SB-v12-D '76-p159
SLJ-v22-My '76-p60

* * *

KLAPERMAN, Libby M
A Different Girl
CCB-B-v23-Je '70-p160
Inst-v79-Ap '70-p144
LJ-v95-Ap 15 '70-p1639

* * *

KLASS, Sheila S
Alive And Starting Over
BS-v43-Ja '84-p388
CBRS-v12-Mr '84-p84
CCB-B-v37-F '84-p110
NYTBR-v88-D 11 '83-p44
SLJ-v30-D '83-p75
VOYA-v7-Je '84-p96
Nobody Knows Me In Miami
BL-v78-S 1 '81-p47
CBRS-v9-Ag '81-p128
CCB-B-v35-N '81-p47
KR-v49-Ag 1 '81-p935
RT-v35-Ja '82-p499
SLJ-v28-Ap '82-p71
To See My Mother Dance
BL-v78-D 1 '81-p499
BS-v42-My '82-p77
CBRS-v10-Ap '82-p89
CCB-B-v35-My '82-p173
Cur R-v21-F '82-p35
Kliatt-v17-Fall '83-p16
PW-v220-D 18 '81-p71
SLJ-v28-Ja '82-p88

* * *

KLAVENESS, Jan O'D
The Griffin Legacy
BL-v80-O 1 '83-p297
CBRS-v12-O '83-p20
CCB-B-v37-F '84-p110
HB-v60-F '84-p61
J Read-v27-Ap '84-p661
LA-v61-Mr '84-p295
PW-v224-D 23 '83-p59
SLJ-v30-D '83-p85
VOYA-v7-Ap '84-p32

* * *

KLAYER, Connie
Circus Time!
BB-v7-S '79-p2
BL-v75-Jl 1 '79-p1580
KR-v47-Je 15 '79-p688
SLJ-v26-S '79-p115

* * *

KLEBERGER, Ilse
Traveling With Oma
BL-v66-Jl 1 '70-p1342
HB-v46-Ag '70-p389
KR-v38-Mr 1 '70-p243
LJ-v95-My 15 '70-p1944

* * *

KLEEBERG, Irene Cumming
Bicycle Touring
BL-v72-N 1 '75-p368
SLJ-v22-D '75-p60
Teacher-v94-My '77-p20
Christianity
BL-v72-Je 1 '76-p1407
KR-v44-Mr 15 '76-p328
SLJ-v23-S '76-p120
Teacher-v94-O '76-p153
Going To Camp
SLJ-v25-Ap '79-p57

* * *

KLEIN, Aaron E
Beyond Time And Matter
BL-v70-Ja 1 '74-p484
CCB-B-v27-F '74-p97
KR-v41-O 1 '73-p1112
LJ-v99-Ja 15 '74-p218
The Electron Microscope
BL-v70-Jl 15 '74-p1249
CCB-B-v28-D '74-p64
HB-v50-D '74-p708
LJ-v99-N 15 '74-p3055
SB-v10-D '74-p204
Mind Trips
BL-v76-O 1 '79-p278
CCB-B-v33-F '80-p112
KR-v47-N 15 '79-p1333
SLJ-v26-F '80-p67
The Parasites We Humans Harbor
BL-v77-Ap 1 '81-p1068
CCB-B-v34-My '81-p173
SB-v17-N '81-p83
Threads Of Life
BL-v67-D 1 '70-p304
BS-v30-O 15 '70-p298
CCB-B-v24-F '71-p93
HB-v47-F '71-p70
LJ-v95-N 15 '70-p4055
SB-v6-D '70-p229
Trial By Fury
BL-v69-Ap 1 '73-p758
BS-v32-F 15 '73-p530
CCB-B-v26-My '73-p140
Choice-v10-Jl '73-p792
KR-v40-S 1 '72-p1070
KR-v40-D 1 '72-p1362
LJ-v97-O 1 '72-p3170
PW-v202-S 18 '72-p70
PW-v203-Ja 29 '73-p260
SB-v9-My '73-p53
You And Your Body
RT-v32-D '78-p364
SB-v14-My '78-p41
SLJ-v24-F '78-p65

* * *

KLEIN, Dave
Great Infielders Of The Major Leagues
CCB-B-v25-Je '72-p158
KR-v40-Ap 15 '72-p481
LJ-v97-D 15 '72-p4088
On The Way Up
BL-v74-O 1 '77-p303
KR-v45-S 1 '77-p940
SLJ-v24-D '77-p63

* * *

KLEIN, Gerda W
Promise Of A New Spring
PW-v221-Mr 26 '82-p74

* * *

KLEIN, Gillian
The Fancy Dress Party
Sch Lib-v30-S '82-p227
TES-Mr 12 '82-p36
Scrapbooks
TES-N 16 '84-p44

* * *

KLEIN, H Arthur
Bioluminescence
BL-v62-S 15 '65-p97
BS-v25-Jl 15 '65-p181
CCB-B-v19-Ja '66-p84
HB-v41-Ag '65-p413
LJ-v90-Jl '65-p3133
SA-v213-D '65-p115
Great Structures Of The World
BS-v28-S 1 '68-p227
CCB-B-v25-Mr '72-p109
KR-v39-N 15 '71-p1222
LJ-v93-Ap 15 '68-p1812
YR-v5-N '68-p7
Holography
BL-v67-F 1 '71-p447
HB-v47-Ag '71-p405
LJ-v96-Je 15 '71-p2138
SB-v6-Mr '71-p300
The New Gravitation
HB-v48-F '72-p77
KR-v39-S 1 '71-p957
LJ-v97-F 15 '72-p786
SB-v7-Mr '72-p296
Peter Bruegel The Elder
BL-v65-Mr 15 '69-p808
BS-v29-O 1 '69-p255
BW-v2-N 3 '68-p6
CCB-B-v23-O '69-p26
KR-v36-O 1 '68-p1180
PW-v194-N 4 '68-p50

* * *

KLEIN, Kenneth
Getting Better
BL-v77-My 1 '81-p1179
BS-v41-Jl '81-p153
CCB-B-v34-My '81-p173
CHE-v22-My 18 '81-p19
Kliatt-v16-Fall '82-p35
LJ-v106-Mr 15 '81-p657
SLJ-v27-Ag '81-p84
VOYA-v4-Ag '81-p38
VOYA-v5-D '82-p51
WLB-v55-Je '81-p773

* * *

KLEIN, Larry
Jim Brown: The Running Back
CCB-B-v19-N '65-p46
KR-v33-Jl 1 '65-p632
LJ-v90-O 15 '65-p4638

* * *

KLEIN, Leonore
D Is For Rover
CCB-B-v24-My '71-p138
LJ-v96-My 15 '71-p1797
How Old Is Old ?
CCB-B-v21-F '68-p96
LJ-v92-Jl '67-p2644
Just Like You
CCB-B-v21-Ap '68-p129
LJ-v93-Ap 15 '68-p1789
Old, Older, Oldest
BL-v79-Ag '83-p1466
CCB-B-v37-O '83-p31
SLJ-v30-N '83-p65
WCRB-v10-Ja '84-p54
Picnics And Parades
KR-v44-Jl 1 '76-p727
What Is An Inch?
CCB-B-v20-F '67-p92
LJ-v91-Jl '66-p3529
LJ-v96-Mr 15 '71-p1088
SB-v2-Mr '67-p250

* * *

KLEIN, Mina C
Hitler's Hang-Ups
BL-v73-Mr 1 '77-p1015
CCB-B-v30-My '77-p145
SLJ-v23-Mr '77-p152
Israel, Land Of The Jews
BS-v32-Je 15 '72-p135
CCB-B-v25-Jl '72-p171
KR-v40-Mr 1 '72-p269
LJ-v97-O 15 '72-p3461
NYTBR-O 15 '72-p8
SE-v37-D '73-p791
Kathe Kollwitz
A Art-v37-Ja '73-p15
BL-v68-Jl 1 '72-p924
BL-v68-Jl 1 '72-p940
BW-v6-Ag 13 '72-p6
CCB-B-v26-S '72-p11
KR-v40-F 15 '72-p206
LJ-v97-Je 15 '72-p2243
LJ-v97-D 15 '72-p4056
Nat-v221-D 13 '75-p630
PW-v202-N 27 '72-p41
TLS-Ap 16 '76-p452
The Kremlin
BL-v69-Jl 15 '73-p1070
CCB-B-v27-D '73-p67
KR-v41-F 15 '73-p198
LJ-v98-N 15 '73-p3467

* * *

KLEIN, Monica
Backyard Basketball Superstar
BL-v78-D 15 '81-p553
CBRS-v10-S '81-p5
CCB-B-v35-N '81-p48
KR-v49-N 1 '81-p1343
RT-v36-O '82-p66
SLJ-v28-D '81-p85

* * *

KLEIN, Norma
Angel Face
BS-v44-S '84-p234
CBRS-v12-My '84-p109
CCB-B-v38-S '84-p8
KR-v52-My 1 '84-pJ48
NYTBR-v89-Je 17 '84-p24
PW-v225-Mr 16 '84-p86
SLJ-v30-My '84-p90
Baryshnikov's Nutcracker
SLJ-v30-F '84-p72
Bizou
BL-v80-O 15 '83-p360
B Rpt-v2-Ja '84-p35
BS-v43-D '83-p347
CBRS-v12-D '83-p42
CCB-B-v37-N '83-p52
HB-v60-F '84-p62
KR-v51-N 1 '83-pJ204
PW-v224-S 2 '83-p81
SLJ-v30-N '83-p94
Blue Trees, Red Sky
BL-v72-D 1 '75-p516
CCB-B-v29-Mr '76-p113
KR-v43-O 1 '75-p1130
LA-v53-F '76-p200
NYTBR-F 8 '76-p14
SLJ-v22-N '75-p64
Breaking Up
BL-v77-S 15 '80-p110
BS-v40-N '80-p301
CBRS-v9-D '80-p29
CCB-B-v34-N '80-p56
Emerg Lib-v9-Ja '82-p33
Inter BC-v12-#3 '81-p19
J Read-v24-Ap '81-p647
KR-v49-Ja 1 '81-p12
SLJ-v27-O '80-p156
VOYA-v4-Je '81-p28
WLB-v55-D '80-p293
Confessions Of An Only Child
BL-v70-Ap 1 '74-p876
BW-My 19 '74-p3
CCB-B-v27-Je '74-p159

KLEIN, Norma (continued)
CLW-v47-N '75-p164
Choice-v14-N '77-p1178
KR-v42-F 1 '74-p110
LJ-v99-Ap 15 '74-p1220
NYTBR-My 5 '74-p16
PW-v205-Mr 4 '74-p76
Dinosaur's Housewarming Party
BL-v71-O 15 '74-p245
CCB-B-v28-My '75-p149
KR-v42-O 15 '74-p1099
NYTBR-D 1 '74-p8
SLJ-v21-Ja '75-p40
Teacher-v92-F '75-p37
Girls Can Be Anything
BL-v69-My 1 '73-p856
BW-v7-My 13 '73-p2
CCB-B-v26-Ap '73-p126
Inst-v82-My '73-p74
KR-v41-F 1 '73-p109
LJ-v98-My 15 '73-p1674
NYTBR-Jl 15 '73-p8
PW-v203-My 21 '73-p50
Teacher-v93-Ap '76-p124
Hiding
BL-v73-N 1 '76-p402
CCB-B-v30-Ap '77-p128
HB-v52-D '76-p629
KR-v44-S 15 '76-p1044
Kliatt-v12-Winter '78-p9
PW-v210-N 8 '76-p49
SLJ-v23-N '76-p66
WCRB-v3-Mr '77-p58
A Honey Of A Chimp
BL-v76-My 1 '80-p1294
CBRS-v8-Mr '80-p77
CCB-B-v33-Jl '80-p216
KR-v48-My 15 '80-p645
LA-v57-O '80-p791
NYTBR-v85-Jl 13 '80-p22
SLJ-v26-Ap '80-p112
If I Had My Way
BL-v70-Ap 15 '74-p942
CCB-B-v28-S '74-p11
KR-v42-F 1 '74-p106
LJ-v99-My 15 '74-p1466
NYTBR-My 5 '74-p47
PW-v205-Ap 8 '74-p83
It's Not What You Expect
BL-v70-S 15 '73-p122
BS-v33-My 15 '73-p98
BS-v34-Je 1 '74-p127
BW-v7-My 13 '73-p7
CCB-B-v26-Jl '73-p172
Choice-v14-N '77-p1178
KR-v41-F 15 '73-p194
NYTBR-Je 3 '73-p8
PW-v203-Mr 5 '73-p82
TN-v30-Ja '74-p199
Mom, The Wolf Man, And Me
BL-v69-Ja 1 '73-p449
BL-v80-S 1 '83-p95
CCB-B-v26-F '73-p93
Comw-v97-N 17 '72-p158
Emerg Lib-v11-Ja '84-p21
HB-v49-F '73-p56
KR-v40-S 1 '72-p1027
LJ-v97-D 15 '72-p4057
LJ-v97-D 15 '72-p4072
NW-v83-Mr 4 '74-p83
NYTBR-S 24 '72-p8
NYTBR-F 10 '74-p30
NYTBR, pt.2-N 5 '72-p28
PW-v202-N 13 '72-p46
TN-v30-Ja '74-p203
Teacher-v90-Ja '73-p92
Naomi In The Middle
CCB-B-v28-Mr '75-p116
KR-v42-N 1 '74-p1151
LJ-v99-N 15 '74-p3047
Ms-v3-D '74-p78
NYTBR-N 3 '74-p48
Robbie And The Leap Year Blues
BL-v78-D 1 '81-p499
CBRS-v10-O '81-p19
HB-v58-Ap '82-p165
PW-v220-S 4 '81-p56
SLJ-v28-O '81-p143
Taking Sides
BL-v70-Jl 15 '74-p1254
CCB-B-v28-N '74-p46
KR-v42-Jl 1 '74-p688
LJ-v99-O 15 '74-p2747
NYTBR-S 29 '74-p8
PW-v205-Jl 22 '74-p70
Tomboy
BL-v75-O 15 '78-p382
CCB-B-v32-F '79-p100
KR-v46-S 15 '78-p1017
LA-v56-Mr '79-p290
SLJ-v25-S '78-p140
A Train For Jane
Choice-v14-N '77-p1178
KR-v42-D 15 '74-p1299
PW-v206-N 25 '74-p44
Visiting Pamela
BL-v75-My 15 '79-p1440
CBRS-v7-My '79-p92
CCB-B-v33-N '79-p50
KR-v47-My 1 '79-p513
RT-v33-Ap '80-p861
SLJ-v25-My '79-p53
What It's All About
BL-v72-N 1 '75-p369
CCB-B-v29-Ap '76-p126
KR-v43-S 15 '75-p1067
LA-v53-My '76-p519
NYTBR-N 16 '75-p50
RT-v31-My '78-p915
SLJ-v22-N '75-p79

* * *

KLEIN, Robin
The Giraffe In Pepperell Street
GP-v17-N '78-p3426
JB-v43-Ag '79-p196
Hating Alison Ashley
TES-S 21 '84-p37
Junk Castle
GP-My '84-p4266
JB-v48-Je '84-p129
PW-v225-Mr 23 '84-p71
Sch Lib-v32-S '84-p238
Penny Pollard's Diary
CCB-B-v38-S '84-p9
JB-v48-Je '84-p129
Thing
BL-v79-Jl '83-p1402
Brit Bk N C-Autumn '82-p12
CCB-B-v37-N '83-p52
JB-v46-O '82-p182
Obs-Jl 4 '82-p28
SLJ-v30-Mr '84-p146
Sch Lib-v30-D '82-p321
TES-Ap 27 '84-p27

* * *

KLEIN, Stanley
The Final Mystery
BL-v70-Jl 1 '74-p1200
CCB-B-v28-Ja '75-p80
CP-v20-O '75-p839
KR-v42-O 15 '74-p1108
SB-v11-My '75-p31

* * *

KLEIN, Suzanne
An Elephant In My Bed
BB-v3-Mr '75-p2

* * *

KLEINBARD, Gitel
Oh, Zalmy
BL-v73-Ap 1 '77-p1176

* * *

KLEINER, Art
Robots
ACSB-v15-Winter '82-p39
BL-v77-Je 15 '81-p1344
SLJ-v27-Ag '81-p63
TES-Mr 12 '82-p39

* * *

KLEVER, Anita
Women In Television
BB-v4-Ap '76-p4
CCB-B-v29-My '76-p147
Cur R-v16-O '77-p315
JQ-v53-Summer '76-p366
KR-v43-N 1 '75-p1244
SLJ-v22-N '75-p92

* * *

KLEVIN, Jill R
The Turtle Street Trading Co.
BL-v79-N 1 '82-p371
CBRS-v11-N '82-p29
CCB-B-v36-S '82-p13
KR-v50-O 15 '82-p1154
SLJ-v29-N '82-p86
Turtles Together Forever!
BL-v79-N 1 '82-p371
CBRS-v11-N '82-p29
KR-v50-O 15 '82-p1154
SLJ-v29-N '82-p86

* * *

KLIKA, Thom
Rainbows
SLJ-v26-N '79-p78

* * *

KLIMA, Pappy
The Almost Anything You Might Ask Almanac
NYTBR-N 21 '76-p63

* * *

KLIMENKO, Galina
Russia In Pictures
CCB-B-v21-Jl '68-p176

* * *

KLIMO, Kate
Heroic Horses And Their Riders
SLJ-v21-Ja '75-p47

* * *

KLIMOWICZ, Barbara
Fred, Fred, Use Your Head
CCB-B-v20-My '67-p141
LJ-v91-S 15 '66-p4314
Ha, Ha, Ha, Henrietta
KR-v43-Je 15 '75-p657
SLJ-v22-S '75-p85
When Shoes Eat Socks
CCB-B-v25-N '71-p46
CLW-v43-Mr '72-p431

* * *

KLING, J B, Jr.
Cajun Night Before Christmas
NYTBR-D 12 '76-p35
RT-v36-D '82-p266
SLJ-v25-N '78-p31
SR/W-v2-N 30 '74-p29

* * *

KLINGBERG, Gote
Children's Books In Translation
JB-v43-Ap '79-p89
TN-v35-Spring '79-p328

* * *

KLINGE, Paul E
Discovering Natural Science
CLW-v43-D '71-p223
HB-v48-F '72-p77

* * *

KLINGER, Gene
The Spectaculars
CCB-B-v25-Ap '72-p125
KR-v39-O 1 '71-p1083
LJ-v96-D 15 '71-p4185

* * *

KLINK, J L
Bible For Children
TN-v35-Summer '79-p399
Bible For Children. Vol. 2
CC-v86-Jl 30 '69-p1020
LJ-v94-N 15 '69-p4287
NYTBR-Mr 30 '69-p26
NYTBR, pt.2-N 9 '69-p62
The New Testament With Songs And Plays
TN-v35-Summer '79-p399

* * *

KLINKOWITZ, Jerome
Vonnegut In America
BL-v74-O 1 '77-p263
CHE-v15-D 5 '77-p13
Choice-v14-F '78-p1650
HB-v54-Je '78-p314
KR-v45-Jl 17 '77-p10
LJ-v102-S 15 '77-p1854
PW-v212-Jl 25 '77-p62

* * *

KLOPFER, Peter H
On Behavior
BS-v33-S 15 '73-p280
HB-v49-D '73-p613
KR-v41-S 1 '73-p975
LJ-v99-Mr 15 '74-p902
SA-v229-D '73-p141
SB-v10-My '74-p5

* * *

KLUGE, Gisela
Dibujar, Pintar, Imprimir
BL-v72-My 15 '76-p1342
Drawing, Painting, Printing
GP-v15-Jl '76-p2917
JB-v40-O '76-p275

* * *

KLUGER, Phyllis
A Needlepoint Gallery Of Patterns From The Past
BL-v72-F 15 '76-p835
CSM-v68-Mr 16 '76-p22
JB-v40-Je '76-p170
LJ-v101-Mr 15 '76-p804
NYTBR-D 7 '75-p74
Time-v106-D 22 '75-p68

* * *

KLUSHANTSEV, Pave
All About The Telescope
ASBYP-v15-Fall '82-p27

* * *

KNAB, Linda Z
The Day Is Waiting
BL-v76-Mr 1 '80-p983
CBRS-v8-Je '80-p102
HB-v56-Je '80-p287
KR-v48-My 1 '80-p577
LA-v57-O '80-p789
NW-v96-D 1 '80-p103
PW-v217-Ap 4 '80-p75
SLJ-v26-Ap '80-p95

* * *

KNAPP, Caroline
Shimon, Leah And Benjamin
Brit Bk N C-Spring '81-p12
JB-v44-Je '80-p134
Sch Lib-v28-Je '80-p166
TES-O 24 '80-p20

* * *

KNAPP, Chris
Tea-Time
CBRS-v12-Jl '84-p135
JB-v48-F '84-p15

* * *

KNAPP, John, II
A Pillar Of Pepper And Other Bible Nursery Rhymes
SLJ-v29-N '82-p70

* * *

KNAPP, Ron
From Prison To The Major Leagues
BL-v77-Ja 1 '81-p627
RT-v35-O '81-p68
SLJ-v27-D '80-p75
Tutankhamun And The Mysteries Of Ancient Egypt
SB-v16-S '80-p36
SLJ-v26-F '80-p57

* * *

KNAPPERT, Jan
Fables From Africa
Brit Bk N-D '80-p715
JB-v45-Ap '81-p71
Sch Lib-v29-Je '81-p137
TES-N 21 '80-p31

* * *

KNAUTH, Percy
The Metalsmiths
A Anth-v78-Mr '76-p186
SB-v10-D '74-p244

* * *

KNIGGE, Robert
Silver Spurs
CCB-B-v29-D '75-p65
NYTBR-D 7 '75-p8

* * *

KNIGHT, D
Let's Find Out About Sound
JB-v41-O '77-p289

* * *

KNIGHT, Damon
Beyond Tomorrow
BS-v25-S 15 '65-p252
CCB-B-v19-D '65-p64
CSM-v57-N 4 '65-pB8
HB-v42-Ap '66-p216
KR-v33-Jl 1 '65-p655
KR-v33-Jl 15 '65-p694
LJ-v90-S 15 '65-p3806
LJ-v90-O 1 '65-p4109
MFSF-v30-Ap '66-p39
NYTBR-v70-N 14 '65-p66
TLS-Je 6 '68-p588
Tomorrow And Tomorrow
BL-v70-N 15 '73-p334
CCB-B-v27-Mr '74-p112
KR-v41-O 1 '73-p1108
LJ-v99-S 15 '74-p2293
TLS-S 20 '74-p1006
Toward Infinity
BL-v65-Mr 1 '69-p744
CCB-B-v22-Ap '69-p128
KR-v36-S 1 '68-p991
SR-v52-Mr 22 '69-p63
Worlds To Come
BL-v64-O 15 '67-p249
CCB-B-v21-S '67-p11
CLW-v39-N '67-p236
EL-v88-Ap '68-p356
KR-v35-F 1 '67-p144
LJ-v92-Ap 15 '67-p1749
LR-v22-Summer '69-p95
Obs-F 16 '69-p29
PW-v191-Ap 10 '67-p82
PW-v193-Je 10 '68-p63

* * *

KNIGHT, David
All About Sound
ASBYP-v17-Spring '84-p55
SB-v19-My '84-p296
Vasco Da Gamma
SLJ-v26-Ja '80-p70

* * *

KNIGHT, David C
American Astronauts And Spacecraft
ACSB-v9-Spring '76-p26
BL-v67-Mr 1 '71-p556
BL-v69-D 15 '72-p407
BS-v32-Jl 15 '72-p199
CCB-B-v24-My '71-p139
CCB-B-v25-Jl '72-p171
LJ-v96-Ap 15 '71-p1505
NYTBR-Ja 17 '71-p14
S&T-v41-Ap '71-p242
S&T-v44-Jl '72-p44
S&T-v51-Ja '76-p51
SB-v7-My '71-p80
SB-v8-S '72-p174
SB-v12-S '76-p93
SLJ-v22-Ja '76-p47
TN-v28-Ap '72-p301
The Battle Of The Dinosaurs
HE-v42-S 4 '82-p17
PW-v223-Ja 21 '83-p84
SLJ-v29-Mr '83-p179
Bees Can't Fly, But They Do
ACSB-v10-Spring '77-p32
CE-v53-Ap '77-p316
KR-v44-Jl 15 '76-p797
PW-v210-Jl 26 '76-p79
RT-v31-O '77-p20
SB-v13-D '77-p161
SLJ-v23-O '76-p108
SR-v4-N 27 '76-p34
Colonies In Orbit
Am-v137-D 3 '77-p408
BB-v5-S '77-p4
BL-v73-Jl 15 '77-p1728
CE-v54-F '78-p198
HB-v53-D '77-p691
KR-v45-My 15 '77-p542
SB-v14-My '78-p41
SLJ-v24-F '78-p65
Comets
CSM-v60-N 14 '68-p14
HB-v45-Ap '69-p190
KR-v36-Je 1 '68-p608
LJ-v93-N 15 '68-p4420
Dinosaur Days
BL-v74-Ja 1 '78-p748
CE-v54-Mr '78-p262
PW-v212-O 17 '77-p84
SLJ-v24-Ja '78-p78
Eavesdropping On Space
ACSB-v9-Winter '76-p23
HB-v51-Ag '75-p398
KR-v43-My 1 '75-p525
SLJ-v22-D '75-p60
First Book Of The Sun
BL-v64-My 1 '68-p1045
CCB-B-v23-N '69-p48
KR-v36-Ja 1 '68-p15
LJ-v93-Ap 15 '68-p1812
Harnessing The Sun
ACSB-v10-Winter '77-p27
BL-v72-Je 1 '76-p1407
KR-v44-My 15 '76-p605
SB-v12-D '76-p133
SLJ-v23-S '76-p134
The Haunted Souvenir Warehouse
Cur R-v17-D '78-p389
KR-v46-F 1 '78-p108
SLJ-v24-F '78-p66
High Sounds, Low Sounds
SLJ-v21-My '75-p68
Let's Find Out About Earth
ACSB-v9-Winter '76-p23
KR-v36-Ja 1 '68-p11
SB-v3-Mr '68-p294
SLJ-v21-My '75-p68
Let's Find Out About Magnets
CCB-B-v20-Ap '67-p125
HB-v43-Je '67-p366

KNIGHT, David C (continued)
KR-v34-D 15 '66-p1286
LJ-v92-F 15 '67-p874
SB-v2-Mr '67-p267
Let's Find Out About Sound
ACSB-v9-Winter '76-p24
SLJ-v21-My '75-p68
Let's Find Out About Telephones
CCB-B-v20-Je '67-p155
KR-v34-D 15 '66-p1287
LJ-v92-F 15 '67-p873
SB-v2-Mr '67-p309
Meteors And Meteorites
EJ-v58-My '69-p776
HB-v45-D '69-p696
KR-v37-F 1 '69-p113
LJ-v94-Ap 15 '69-p1797
SB-v5-My '69-p24
The Moving Coffins
BL-v80-Ja 1 '84-p675
CBRS-v12-Mr '84-p84
SLJ-v30-Mr '84-p172
Poltergeists
B&B-v23-D '77-p62
BL-v69-Mr 1 '73-p649
CE-v50-O '73-p32
JB-v42-Ap '78-p104
KR-v40-O 15 '72-p1207
SR-v55-N 11 '72-p78
TES-F 3 '78-p39
Robotics
ASBYP-v17-Winter '84-p31
BL-v80-S 1 '83-p87
BW-v13-Je 12 '83-p9
CBRS-v11-Ag '83-p147
CCB-B-v37-S '83-p11
CE-v60-S '83-p56
HB-v59-Ag '83-p482
J Read-v27-O '83-p84
KR-v51-Je 1 '83-p621
SB-v19-Ja '84-p150
SLJ-v30-O '83-p170
VOYA-v6-D '83-p287
Silent Sound
ASBYP-v14-Spring '81-p23
BL-v77-D 1 '80-p514
HB-v57-Ap '81-p213
SB-v16-Mr '81-p197
SLJ-v28-N '81-p106
Sounds All About
SLJ-v21-My '75-p68
Thirty-Two Moons
ACSB-v8-Spring '75-p26
BL-v70-Je 15 '74-p1154
CLW-v46-S '74-p89
HB-v51-F '75-p74
KR-v42-Mr 1 '74-p249
LJ-v99-Ap 15 '74-p1229
SB-v10-D '74-p252
Those Mysterious UFO's
ACSB-v9-Fall '76-p26
BL-v72-D 15 '75-p579
CLW-v47-My '76-p452
EJ-v65-My '76-p91
SB-v12-My '76-p36
SLJ-v22-F '76-p46
The Tiny Planets
BL-v70-O 1 '73-p172
HB-v49-Je '73-p295
KR-v41-Ap 1 '73-p391
LJ-v98-Jl '73-p2194
UFOs
ACSB-v13-Mr '80-p37
LJ-v105-F 1 '80-p415
PW-v216-N 5 '79-p67
SLJ-v26-F '80-p76
Viruses
ASBYP-v15-Fall '82-p28
BL-v78-F 1 '82-p707
CCB-B-v35-Mr '82-p133
KR-v49-N 1 '81-p1347
SB-v18-N '82-p81
SLJ-v28-Ag '82-p118
Your Body's Defenses
BL-v71-Mr 1 '75-p694
CCB-B-v28-My '75-p149
Cur R-v16-O '77-p302
SB-v11-My '75-p38
SLJ-v21-Ap '75-p54

* * *

KNIGHT, Eric
Lassie Come-Home
BL-v68-F 1 '72-p468
BL-v74-Jl 15 '78-p1734
GP-v19-Mr '81-p3851
LJ-v97-Ap 15 '72-p1606
NYTBR, pt.2-F 13 '72-p12
PW-v200-N 22 '71-p41
Teacher-v90-F '73-p125

* * *

KNIGHT, Frank
The Golden Age Of The Galleon
JB-v40-O '76-p276
TLS-Ap 2 '76-p394

* * *

KNIGHT, Hilary
The Circus Is Coming
KR-v47-F 1 '79-p121
PW-v215-F 5 '79-p95
SLJ-v26-S '79-p115
Hilary Knight's Cinderella
PW-v222-Jl 30 '82-p77
Hilary Knight's The Owl And The Pussy-Cat
BL-v80-F 1 '84-p814
CBRS-v12-Ja '84-p47
CCB-B-v37-Ap '84-p150
Learning-v12-Ap '84-p72
NW-v102-D 5 '83-p113
NYTBR-v89-Ja 29 '84-p20
PW-v224-D 9 '83-p50
SLJ-v30-Mr '84-p146
Hilary Knight's The Twelve Days Of Christmas
BL-v78-O 1 '81-p236
BW-v11-D 13 '81-p8
CBRS-v10-N '81-p23
CCB-B-v35-N '81-p48
CE-v59-S '82-p64
CSM-v74-D 14 '81-pB10
KR-v49-O 1 '81-p1231
PW-v220-S 11 '81-p76
SLJ-v28-O '81-p155
Where's Wallace?
CLW-v36-F '65-p414
CLW-v55-O '83-p131
HB-v41-F '65-p42

* * *

KNIGHT, Jan
A-Z Of Ghosts And The Supernatural
JB-v45-Ap '81-p83
TES-O 24 '80-p24
TLS-N 21 '80-p1330

* * *

KNIGHT, Mary
The Fox That Wanted Nine Golden Tails
B&B-v16-N '70-p54
CCB-B-v22-Ap '69-p128
CLW-v40-Ap '69-p527
KR-v37-Ja 15 '69-p56
LJ-v94-Mr 15 '69-p1328
NYTBR-Mr 9 '69-p26
NYTBR, pt.2-N 9 '69-p63
PW-v195-F 3 '69-p65
SR-v52-Mr 22 '69-p63
Spec-v225-D 5 '70-pR16
TLS-D 11 '70-p1462

* * *

KNIGHT, Michael
Evans Graded Verse 1-3
TES-Ag 11 '78-p19

KNIGHT, Michael (continued)
Evans Graded Verse 1-3: Teacher's Guide
TES-Ag 11 '78-p19

* * *

KNIGHT, Vick, Jr.
Earle The Squirrel
PW-v207-Ja 27 '75-p285

* * *

KNIGHTLEY, Phillip
Lawrence Of Arabia
BB-v5-Je '77-p3
B&B-v21-Jl '76-p40
BS-v37-Jl '77-p126
CE-v54-Ja '78-p142
GP-v14-Ap '76-p2836
KR-v44-S 15 '76-p1041
LJ-v94-D 15 '69-p4520
SLJ-v23-D '76-p55

* * *

KNIGHTS And Castles (Time Traveller)
Obs-D 11 '77-p31

* * *

KNIGHTS At War (Battlegame Books)
Obs-D 11 '77-p31

* * *

KNOBLER, Susan
The Black Ant
JB-v42-F '78-p27
TLS-D 2 '77-p1417
The Tadpole And The Frog
SLJ-v22-S '75-p85
TLS-S 20 '74-p1014

* * *

KNOEPFLE, John
Dogs And Cats And Things Like That
CCB-B-v25-My '72-p141
LJ-v97-Jl '72-p2478

* * *

KNOOP, Faith Yingling
Sitting Bull
SLJ-v21-Ap '75-p54

* * *

KNOPF, Howard H
Creative Writing Fun
Cur R-v22-F '83-p24

* * *

KNOPF, Mildred O
Around America
BL-v66-F 1 '70-p671
BS-v29-N 1 '69-p306
BW-v4-F 15 '70-p3
CCB-B-v24-Jl '70-p182
Comw-v91-N 21 '69-p261
Inst-v79-N '69-p140
KR-v37-S 1 '69-p942
LJ-v95-F 15 '70-p790
NYTBR, pt.2-N 9 '69-p42
PW-v196-O 27 '69-p60

* * *

KNOTTS, Howard
Follow The Brook
BL-v71-Je 15 '75-p1076
CCB-B-v29-O '75-p29
KR-v43-Ap 15 '75-p445
SLJ-v22-S '75-p85
Great-Grandfather, The Baby And Me
BL-v75-S 15 '78-p221
CCB-B-v32-Mr '79-p121
CE-v55-Ap '79-p262
CE-v56-N '79-p111
CSM-v70-O 23 '78-pB12
Cur R-v18-F '79-p21
Inter BC-v10-My 50 '79-p18
KR-v46-D 15 '78-p1353
RT-v35-My '82-p901
SLJ-v25-O '78-p135
Teacher-v96-My '79-p108
The Lost Christmas
BL-v75-N 15 '78-p552
CBRS-v7-Ja '79-p44
CCB-B-v32-N '78-p46
KR-v46-N 1 '78-p1187
PW-v214-Jl 24 '78-p100
SLJ-v25-O '78-p112
The Summer Cat
BL-v77-Mr 15 '81-p1030
CE-v58-N '81-p109
HB-v57-Ap '81-p181
KR-v49-Ap 15 '81-p499
LA-v59-My '82-p484
PW-v219-Mr 13 '81-p89
SLJ-v27-Ag '81-p56
The Winter Cat
BL-v69-F 15 '73-p573
CCB-B-v26-Ap '73-p126
CE-v49-My '73-p422
GP-v13-Mr '75-p2582
KR-v40-S 15 '72-p1094
LJ-v98-F 15 '73-p637
NYTBR-F 18 '73-p8
Obs-Ap 6 '75-p30
PW-v202-S 18 '72-p73
TLS-Ap 4 '75-p366
Teacher-v90-My '73-p73
Teacher-v92-D '74-p13

* * *

KNOW How Book Of Experiments
TES-O 1 '82-p44

* * *

KNOW Your World
Ser R-v7-O '81-p16

* * *

KNOW Your World Extra
BL-v79-F 1 '83-p731
BL-v80-Je 15 '84-p1479
Mag YA- '84-p158

* * *

KNOWLES, A
Sea Change
JB-v44-F '80-p29

* * *

KNOWLES, Andrew
The Crossroad Children's Bible
CC-v99-F 24 '82-p219
Fount Children's Bible
Sch Lib-v30-Mr '82-p43
TES-D 25 '81-p17

* * *

KNOWLES, Anne
Flag
GP-v15-N '76-p3007
JB-v41-F '77-p38
TLS-O 1 '76-p1240
The Halcyon Island
BL-v77-Je 1 '81-p1300
CCB-B-v34-Jl '81-p213
HB-v57-Je '81-p302
J Read-v25-N '81-p180
KR-v49-My 1 '81-p571
Obs-S 28 '80-p33
SLJ-v27-Ap '81-p128
TES-Jl 13 '84-p25
VOYA-v4-Je '81-p28
Under The Shadow
BL-v80-S 15 '83-p171
CCB-B-v37-D '83-p70
Inter BC-v15-#5 '84-p18
SLJ-v30-N '83-p78

* * *

KNOWLES, Tony
The Book Mice
Econ-v277-D 27 '80-p74
JB-v45-Ap '81-p72

* * *

KNOWLTON, Bill
Classroom Chuckles
LA-v55-N '78-p961

* * *

KNOWLTON, Derrick
Central Southern England
GP-v18-Jl '79-p3549
JB-v43-Ag '79-p206

* * *

KNOX, Albert
Cloth
BL-v73-N 1 '76-p409
SB-v13-S '77-p100
SLJ-v23-D '76-p67

* * *

KNOX, Charlotte
The Seal
SLJ-v30-Mr '84-p144
The Turtle
SLJ-v30-Mr '84-p144

* * *

KNOX, Margaret
Betsey's Bee Tree
SLJ-v27-Ag '81-p56

* * *

KNOX-JOHNSTON, Robin
Sailing
JB-v42-F '78-p43
Par-v53-D '78-p26
SLJ-v24-Ja '78-p95
A World Of My Own
BL-v66-Je 1 '70-p1192
BL-v66-Je 1 '70-p1207
BS-v30-Mr 1 '71-p530
BW-v4-F 22 '70-p12
GJ-v136-Mr '70-p148
HB-v46-Je '70-p316
KR-v37-N 1 '69-p1184
LJ-v95-F 15 '70-p797
LJ-v95-My 1 '70-p1741
Lis-v82-D 25 '69-p895
NYTBR-Jl 12 '70-p42
Obs-O 12 '69-p34
PW-v196-D 1 '69-p35
TLS-Ja 15 '70-p65
Yacht-v127-F '70-p94

* * *

KNOX-WAGNER, Elaine
My Grandpa Retired Today
BL-v79-S 1 '82-p45
CBRS-v11-S '82-p6
CCB-B-v36-S '82-p13
PW-v221-Je 25 '82-p118
SLJ-v29-F '83-p68
The Oldest Kid
CBRS-v10-S '81-p5
CCB-B-v35-D '81-p71
SLJ-v28-O '81-p130

* * *

KNUDSEN, Per Holm
The True Story Of How Babies Are Made
CCB-B-v27-My '74-p147
PW-v204-Ag 13 '73-p55
TN-v34-Winter '78-p160

* * *

KNUDSON, R R
Fox Running
BL-v72-S 15 '75-p166
BS-v36-Ap '76-p30
CCB-B-v29-My '76-p147
HB-v52-F '76-p56
KR-v43-N 1 '75-p1239
SLJ-v22-D '75-p69
Jesus Song
CCB-B-v27-S '73-p10
CLW-v46-S '74-p92
KR-v41-My 1 '73-p521
LJ-v98-Jl '73-p2201
PW-v203-Ap 16 '73-p55
Muscles!
BL-v80-O 1 '83-p303
SLJ-v29-My '83-p95
Punch!
BL-v80-O 1 '83-p303
SLJ-v29-My '83-p95
Rinehart Lifts
BL-v77-S 1 '80-p45
CBRS-v9-S '80-p8
CCB-B-v34-O '80-p35
CE-v58-S '81-p49
Emerg Lib-v9-My '82-p28
Inter BC-v12-#1 '81-p19
KR-v48-S 15 '80-p1232
LA-v58-F '81-p186
SLJ-v26-My '80-p88
SLJ-v27-My '81-p27
Zanballer
BL-v69-Ap 1 '73-p764
CCB-B-v26-Ap '73-p127
EJ-v62-Ap '73-p649
EJ-v64-S '75-p80
KR-v40-O 15 '72-p1201
LJ-v97-D 15 '72-p4089
SLJ-v24-My '78-p39
Zanbanger
BS-v37-Ag '77-p142
BS-v38-Mr '79-p408
CCB-B-v30-My '77-p145
EJ-v66-S '77-p84
KR-v45-Mr 15 '77-p290
Kliatt-v13-Fall '79-p8
SLJ-v23-My '77-p79
SLJ-v27-My '81-p27

* * *

KNUDSON, Richard L
Classic Sports Cars
BL-v76-N 15 '79-p506
SLJ-v26-F '80-p57
Fabulous Cars Of The 1920s And 1930s
BL-v78-Mr 15 '82-p959
PW-v220-N 20 '81-p54
SLJ-v28-F '82-p74
Land Speed Record-Breakers
BL-v77-Mr 15 '81-p1028
SLJ-v27-My '81-p88
Model Cars
BL-v77-Mr 15 '81-p1028
SLJ-v27-Ag '81-p68
Rallying
BL-v77-Mr 15 '81-p1028
SLJ-v27-My '81-p88

* * *

K'O, Chien-Hsin
Han Hsin
BL-v74-Mr 1 '78-p1112

* * *

K'O, Wen-Yang
Wo Men Te Hai Yang
BL-v77-Ja 1 '81-p629
Yu Ch'u Ti Shu
BL-v77-Ja 1 '81-p629

* * *

KOBAYASHI, Fusae
Living In Tokyo
Brit Bk N C-Autumn '80-p7
Brit Bk N C-Autumn '80-p28
JB-v44-D '80-p309
Sch Lib-v28-S '80-p305

* * *

KOBAYASHI, Issa
A Few Flies And I
BL-v66-S 15 '69-p137
BL-v69-F 15 '73-p553

KOBAYASHI, Issa (continued)
BW-v3-S 21 '69-p14
CCB-B-v23-D '69-p60
KR-v37-Ap 15 '69-p446
LJ-v94-Jl '69-p2682
NYTBR, pt.2-My 4 '69-p46
NYTBR, pt.2-N 9 '69-p63
PW-v195-My 26 '69-p55
SR-v52-N 8 '69-p66
Teacher-v94-Ap '77-p36
VQR-v47-Spring '71-pR80
VV-v17-My 18 '72-p16

* * *

KOBS, Betty
Magic
BL-v73-D 15 '76-p608
SLJ-v23-Ja '77-p84

* * *

KOCH, Charlotte
Florence Nightingale
CBRS-v7-Je '79-p104
SLJ-v26-S '79-p115

* * *

KOCH, Dorothy
Up The Big Mountain
CCB-B-v18-Jl '65-p163
HB-v41-F '65-p46

* * *

KOCH, H
Stickybeak
JB-v44-F '80-p18

* * *

KOCH, John R
Where Did You Come From?
CCB-B-v22-My '69-p144

* * *

KOCH, Kenneth
Wishes, Lies, And Dreams
BL-v67-F 15 '71-p470
BW-v5-O 31 '71-p12
CE-v48-O '71-p35
CE-v61-S '84-p42
Choice-v16-Je '79-p496
EJ-v61-S '72-p931
Inst-v80-F '71-p138
KR-v38-Jl 15 '70-p752
KR-v38-S 15 '70-p1075
LJ-v95-N 15 '70-p3904
LJ-v97-My 15 '72-p1883
NL-v54-Ja 25 '71-p21
NYTBR-D 23 '73-p1
PW-v197-Je 8 '70-p180
PW-v198-Jl 6 '70-p53
PW-v200-Ag 9 '71-p49
SR-v54-Mr 20 '71-p55

* * *

KOCI, Marta
Blackard
GP-v20-My '81-p3893
Blackie And Marie
CBRS-v9-Ap '81-p72
Inst-v90-My '81-p58
KR-v49-Mr 1 '81-p280
PW-v219-F 6 '81-p373
SLJ-v27-My '81-p56
VV-v26-D 9 '81-p56
Ivan, Divan, And Zariman
BL-v73-Ap 1 '77-p1169
KR-v45-Ja 15 '77-p42
LA-v55-Ja '78-p44
PW-v211-F 14 '77-p83
RT-v32-O '78-p35
SLJ-v24-O '77-p104
Katie's Kitten
CBRS-v11-F '83-p65
GP-v17-Mr '79-p3478
JB-v43-Ap '79-p97
NW-v100-D 6 '82-p131
Obs-D 10 '78-p38
PW-v222-D 24 '82-p64
SLJ-v29-Ag '83-p53
The Wind Men Are Coming!
GP-v17-Ja '79-p3449
JB-v43-Ap '79-p97

* * *

KODICEK, Susan
Black Theatre For Children
GP-v16-D '77-p3229
JB-v42-F '78-p43

* * *

KOEBNER, Linda
Forgotten Animals
BL-v80-Je 1 '84-p1399
CCB-B-v38-S '84-p9
KR-v52-My 1 '84-pJ55
SLJ-v30-Ap '84-p125
From Cage To Freedom
ASBYP-v15-Spring '82-p43
BL-v78-F 1 '82-p707
CBRS-v10-Mr '82-p78
CE-v59-S '82-p60
HB-v58-F '82-p75
SB-v18-S '82-p19
SLJ-v28-O '81-p143

* * *

KOEHLER, George
My Family
CCB-B-v22-F '69-p96
CSM-v60-N 7 '68-pB8
LJ-v94-Ap 15 '69-p1797

* * *

KOEHN, Ilse
Mischling, Second Degree
BB-v5-Ja '78-p4
BL-v74-D 1 '77-p595
BL-v74-D 1 '77-p613
BL-v81-O 1 '84-p213
BS-v37-Ja '78-p317
CCB-B-v31-Ja '78-p80
CE-v54-Mr '78-p262
CE-v55-Ap '79-p264
CLW-v49-My '78-p455
CLW-v50-O '78-p111
Comw-v105-N 10 '78-p731
EJ-v67-Mr '78-p80
EJ-v69-O '80-p15
Econ-v267-My 6 '78-p129
HB-v53-D '77-p671
JB-v42-Ag '78-p206
J Read-v22-F '79-p477
KR-v45-N 1 '77-p1151
Kliatt-v13-Winter '79-p31
LA-v58-Ap '81-p460
NY-v54-My 1 '78-p142
Obs-Je 4 '78-p30
PW-v212-Ag 15 '77-p69
SLJ-v24-N '77-p73
TES-Je 16 '78-p49
TES-Je 5 '81-p42
TES-Mr 18 '83-p35
TLS-Jl 7 '78-p772
Teacher-v95-My '78-p102
Tilla
BL-v78-O 1 '81-p188
BS-v41-Ja '82-p402
CBRS-v10-Ja '82-p48
CCB-B-v35-N '81-p48
EJ-v72-Ja '83-p78
KR-v50-Ja 15 '82-p71
SLJ-v28-O '81-p151
VOYA-v4-F '82-p34

* * *

KOELLING, Caryl
Animal Mix And Match
CBRS-v8-My '80-p92
CLW-v55-O '83-p131
SLJ-v26-Ag '80-p52

KOELLING, Caryl (continued)
Mad Monsters Mix And Match
CBRS-v8-My '80-p92
SLJ-v26-Ag '80-p52
Molly Mouse Goes Shopping
RT-v37-My '84-p857
Silly Stories Mix And Match
CBRS-v8-My '80-p92
SLJ-v26-Ag '80-p52
Whose House Is This?
RT-v37-My '84-p857

* * *

KOENIG, Alma J
Gudrun
BL-v76-Ja 1 '80-p668
CCB-B-v33-Ap '80-p156
CE-v56-Ap '80-p305
GP-v18-Jl '79-p3536
HB-v56-F '80-p66
JB-v43-Ag '79-p223
J Read-v23-My '80-p761
KR-v47-D 1 '79-p1380
LA-v57-Mr '80-p322
SLJ-v26-O '79-p159

* * *

KOENIG, Marion
The Tale Of Fancy Nancy
GP-v16-Ja '78-p3253
JB-v42-F '78-p18
NW-v94-D 17 '79-p94
NYTBR-Ap 29 '79-p26
SLJ-v26-My '80-p59
TES-N 18 '77-p31

* * *

KOENIG, Teresa
Careers With A Petroleum Company
BL-v80-Mr 1 '84-p992
SLJ-v30-F '84-p74

* * *

KOENNER, Alfred
Be Quite Quiet Beside The Lake
SLJ-v28-F '82-p67
High Flies The Ball
SLJ-v31-S '84-p106

* * *

KOFF, Richard M
Christopher
CCB-B-v35-F '82-p110
Kliatt-v18-Fall '84-p28
SLJ-v28-F '82-p78
VOYA-v4-F '82-p34

* * *

KOFFLER, Camilla
Two Little Bears
Teacher-v94-Ja '77-p133

* * *

KOGAN, Marilyn H
Organizing The School Library
A Lib-v12-Ja '81-p50
Can Child Lit-#30 '83-p77
In Rev-v14-D '80-p33

* * *

KOGER, Earl
Jocko
BW-Je 13 '76-pM2
Cur R-v17-Ag '78-p172
KR-v44-My 15 '76-p593
SE-v41-Ap '77-p347
SLJ-v23-S '76-p120

* * *

KOHEN, Deborah A
Beauty And The Beast
CBRS-v9-N '80-p25
SLJ-v27-Ja '81-p62

* * *

KOHL, Herbert
A Book Of Puzzlements
CC-v98-D 16 '81-p1319
CCB-B-v35-Mr '82-p133
HB-v58-Ap '82-p180
Inst-v91-Ap '82-p121
LJ-v107-Ja 15 '82-p173
SLJ-v28-Mr '82-p148

* * *

KOHLER, Charles
Granpa Tell Us A Story
TES-Je 15 '84-p36

* * *

KOHN, Bernice
Apples
ACSB-v10-Fall '77-p23
Cur R-v16-O '77-p294
HB-v52-O '76-p526
SB-v12-D '76-p163
SLJ-v23-N '76-p48
The Bat Book
ACSB-v13-Winter '80-p32
KR-v35-F 15 '67-p205
LJ-v93-Ja 15 '68-p292
SLJ-v26-N '79-p78
TLS-Ap 3 '69-p365
The Beachcomber's Book
BL-v66-Je 1 '70-p1214
BW-v4-My 17 '70-p30
CCB-B-v24-S '70-p13
Comw-v92-My 22 '70-p252
GT-v88-Ja '71-p109
GT-v89-Mr '72-p100
HB-v46-O '70-p492
KR-v38-F 15 '70-p176
LJ-v95-My 15 '70-p1944
NYTBR-Je 7 '70-p32
PW-v197-Je 15 '70-p66
SR-v53-My 9 '70-p46
The Busy Honeybee
BL-v69-Je 1 '73-p948
CCB-B-v26-D '72-p59
KR-v40-S 15 '72-p1103
LJ-v98-Ap 15 '73-p1376
PW-v202-Ag 21 '72-p80
SB-v8-Mr '73-p336
Chipmunks
BL-v67-Mr 15 '71-p620
BW-Mr 11 '79-pF2
CCB-B-v24-Ap '71-p125
KR-v38-D 15 '70-p1345
LJ-v96-Mr 15 '71-p1133
PW-v215-Mr 26 '79-p81
SB-v7-My '71-p64
Communications Satellites
ACSB-v9-Winter '76-p25
CCB-B-v29-S '75-p13
HB-v51-Ag '75-p398
KR-v43-My 1 '75-p518
SA-v233-D '75-p134
SLJ-v22-S '75-p121
Easy Gourmet Cooking
BL-v70-Ja 15 '74-p543
CCB-B-v27-Mr '74-p112
KR-v41-D 1 '73-p1315
LJ-v99-Mr 15 '74-p902
NYTBR-N 4 '73-p32
Echoes
ACSB-v13-Winter '80-p32
CCB-B-v33-N '79-p50
CLW-v37-Ja '66-p337
LJ-v90-D 15 '65-p5502
NYTBR-v70-N 7 '65-p56
Light
ACSB-v13-Winter '80-p33
KR-v33-Mr 1 '65-p234
LJ-v90-My 15 '65-p2407
NYTBR-v70-F 28 '65-p30
SLJ-v26-N '79-p78
TLS-My 25 '67-p465
One Day It Rained Cats And Dogs
CCB-B-v20-S '66-p13
CE-v42-Ap '66-p506

KOHN, Bernice (continued)
HB-v41-O '65-p493
KR-v33-Je 15 '65-p571
LJ-v90-Jl '65-p3126
NYTBR-v70-O 31 '65-p56
One Sad Day
CCB-B-v25-Jl '72-p171
KR-v40-Mr 15 '72-p320
LJ-v97-S 15 '72-p2936
NYT-v121-Ag 4 '72-p29
The Organic Living Book
BL-v69-Ap 1 '73-p764
BW-v6-N 12 '72-p13
CCB-B-v26-N '72-p44
HB-v48-O '72-p483
KR-v40-My 1 '72-p544
LJ-v97-S 15 '72-p2951
NYTBR, pt.2-My 7 '72-p8
NYTBR, pt.2-My 6 '73-p28
SB-v8-S '72-p135
Teacher-v90-My '73-p78
WLB-v47-My '73-p740
Telephones
ACSB-v13-Winter '80-p33
BL-v64-F 15 '68-p701
KR-v35-Jl 15 '67-p811
LJ-v92-O 15 '67-p3841
SB-v4-My '68-p57
SLJ-v26-N '79-p78
What A Funny Thing To Say
BW-My 19 '74-p5
CCB-B-v28-N '74-p46
EJ-v67-D '78-p64
HB-v50-O '74-p153
KR-v42-Ja 15 '74-p57
LJ-v99-Mr 15 '74-p891
Par-v49-Ag '74-p57
RT-v32-N '78-p148

* * *

KOHN, Michael
The Dandelion Book Of Nursery Games
CBRS-v7-My '79-p93
The Dandelion Book Of Nursery Songs
CBRS-v7-My '79-p93

* * *

KOIDE, Tan
May We Sleep Here Tonight?
BL-v80-S 15 '83-p171
BL-v80-N 1 '83-p423
CBRS-v12-Ja '84-p47
CSM-v76-Ja 6 '84-pB5
GP-v23-S '84-p4320
KR-v51-S 1 '83-pJ150
Obs-Ag 26 '84-p19
PW-v225-Ja 13 '84-p69
RT-v37-Ap '84-p778
SLJ-v30-D '83-p57
TLS-S 28 '84-p1106

* * *

KOJIMA, Naomi
The Flying Grandmother
BL-v78-N 15 '81-p439
CBRS-v10-N '81-p23
CCB-B-v35-D '81-p71
KR-v49-N 1 '81-p1340
PW-v220-Ag 28 '81-p394
SLJ-v28-Ja '82-p67
Mr. And Mrs. Thief
CBRS-v8-Ap '80-p81
CCB-B-v33-Jl '80-p217
KR-v48-My 15 '80-p642
LA-v58-F '81-p183
SLJ-v26-My '80-p85

* * *

KOLA, Pamela
East African How Stories
BL-v73-Jl 15 '77-p1734
East African When Stories
BL-v73-Jl 15 '77-p1734
East African Why Stories
BL-v73-Jl 15 '77-p1734

* * *

KOLKMEYER, Alexandra
The Clear Red Stone
SLJ-v29-O '82-p153

* * *

KOLLANDER, Kathy
TM Is For Kids, Too!
WLB-v51-My '77-p709

* * *

KOLPAS, Norman
Abraham Lincoln
BL-v78-N 15 '81-p439
GP-v21-My '82-p3901
SLJ-v28-Mr '82-p159

* * *

KOLTZ, Tony
Vampire Express
SLJ-v31-S '84-p139
VOYA-v7-O '84-p199

* * *

KOMAROFF, Katherine
Sky Gods
BL-v71-S 1 '74-p43
CSM-v67-F 5 '75-p8
KR-v42-D 15 '74-p1308
Kliatt-v11-Winter '77-p37

* * *

KOMISAR, Lucy
The New Feminism
BL-v68-S 1 '71-p53
BL-v69-Ja 1 '73-p435
BS-v31-My 15 '71-p90
CCB-B-v25-S '71-p10
Comw-v94-My 21 '71-p263
EJ-v63-Ap '74-p91
KR-v39-F 15 '71-p183
LJ-v96-Je 15 '71-p2138
NYTBR-Mr 28 '71-p28
PW-v199-My 10 '71-p43
PW-v201-Je 5 '72-p141
TLS-F 4 '72-p138

* * *

KOMODA, Beverly
The Lake Mess Monster
CBRS-v9-My '81-p84
PW-v219-F 6 '81-p373
SLJ-v27-My '81-p80
Simon's Soup
BL-v74-My 1 '78-p1434
PW-v213-Mr 13 '78-p110
Par-v53-N '78-p28
SLJ-v25-S '78-p118

* * *

KOMORI, Atsuhi
Animal Mothers
JB-v44-F '80-p20

* * *

KOMORI, Atsushi
Animal Mothers
BL-v80-Ja 1 '84-p683
CCB-B-v37-F '84-p110
HB-v60-Ap '84-p183
SLJ-v30-Mr '84-p146

* * *

KONANTZ, Gail
Manitobans In Profile: Edith Rogers
Can Child Lit-#23 '81-p121
In Rev-v15-Ag '81-p45

* * *

KONDO, Herbert
Adventures In Space And Time: Story Of Relativity
BL-v63-My 1 '67-p949
CCB-B-v20-Mr '67-p110
HB-v43-F '67-p91
LJ-v91-D 15 '66-p6203
SB-v2-Mr '67-p269

KONDO, Herbert (continued)
The Moon
LJ-v96-O 15 '71-p3477
SB-v7-D '71-p216
TES-Ap 21 '78-p22

* * *

KONDO, Riki H
Instant Nature Guide: Birds
NYTBR-Ap 29 '79-p44
Instant Nature Guide: Insects
SB-v15-My '80-p275
Instant Nature Guide: Reptiles And Amphibians
SB-v15-My '80-p275
Instant Nature Guide: Rocks And Minerals
SB-v15-My '80-p276
Instant Nature Guide: Trees
SB-v15-My '80-p276

* * *

KONDO, Yumiko
Moontoo The Cat
PW-v215-F 12 '79-p126
SLJ-v26-O '79-p142
WLB-v54-D '79-p247

* * *

KONIGSBURG, E L
About The B'nai Bagels
BL-v65-Je 15 '69-p1176
CCB-B-v23-S '69-p12
CE-v46-F '70-p263
CLW-v41-D '69-p262
CLW-v41-Ja '70-p318
CLW-v43-F '72-p330
CLW-v48-F '77-p281
Comw-v90-My 23 '69-p297
Comw-v91-N 21 '69-p256
HB-v45-Je '69-p307
HB-v49-Ap '73-p173
KR-v37-F 15 '69-p179
LJ-v94-Mr 15 '69-p1329
LJ-v95-F 15 '70-p742
NCW-v216-Mr '73-p93
NO-v8-S 1 '69-p17
NYTBR-Mr 30 '69-p28
NYTBR-Je 8 '69-p44
NYTBR, pt.2-N 9 '69-p61
PW-v195-Mr 31 '69-p57
RR-v28-Jl '69-p700
SLJ-v24-My '78-p39
SR-v52-Mr 22 '69-p63
Altogether, One At A Time
BL-v67-Jl 1 '71-p908
CCB-B-v25-S '71-p10
Comw-v95-N 19 '71-p187
GT-v89-S '71-p153
HB-v47-Ag '71-p384
KR-v39-Ap 15 '71-p433
LJ-v96-My 15 '71-p1782
LJ-v96-My 15 '71-p1805
LJ-v96-D 15 '71-p4159
NYTBR-My 30 '71-p8
PW-v199-F 15 '71-p79
SR-v54-Ap 17 '71-p45
TN-v28-N '71-p74
Teacher-v93-N '75-p116
Benjamin Dickinson Carr And His George
Obs-F 9 '75-p25
The Dragon In The Ghetto Caper
BL-v71-S 1 '74-p43
Comw-v101-N 22 '74-p194
GP-v18-Jl '79-p3539
HB-v50-D '74-p692
JB-v43-O '79-p280
KR-v42-Jl 15 '74-p742
LJ-v99-S 15 '74-p2273
NYTBR-O 20 '74-p10
PT-v8-Ap '75-p16
PW-v206-S 2 '74-p70
Sch Lib-v27-D '79-p387
Father's Arcane Daughter
BB-v4-D '76-p4
BL-v73-S 15 '76-p177
B Rpt-v1-Mr '83-p24
CCB-B-v30-S '76-p12
Comw-v103-N 19 '76-p762
GP-v16-Jl '77-p3145
HB-v52-O '76-p504
JB-v41-Je '77-p180
J Read-v24-Mr '81-p522
KR-v44-Jl 15 '76-p795
NO-v15-D 25 '76-p15
NS-v93-My 20 '77-p686
NYTBR-N 7 '76-p44
Obs-F 13 '77-p35
PW-v210-Jl 19 '76-p132
PW-v215-Ap 23 '79-p80
RT-v31-O '77-p19
SLJ-v23-S '76-p134
SMQ-v8-Fall '79-p27
TLS-Mr 25 '77-p359
TN-v36-Summer '80-p365
Teacher-v94-Ja '77-p132
From The Mixed-Up Files Of Mrs. Basil E. Frankweiler
Am-v117-N 4 '67-p516
B&B-v14-Jl '69-p36
BL-v64-O 1 '67-p199
BL-v80-S 1 '83-p95
BW-v1-N 5 '67-p20
BW-v11-My 10 '81-p14
CCB-B-v21-Mr '68-p112
CLW-v39-Ja '68-p371
CLW-v39-F '68-p438
CSM-v59-N 2 '67-pB10
Emerg Lib-v11-Ja '84-p21
GP-v22-N '83-p4177
HB-v43-O '67-p595
KR-v35-Jl 1 '67-p740
LJ-v92-O 15 '67-p3851
Lis-v82-N 6 '69-p638
NO-v7-F 26 '68-p21
NYTBR-v72-N 5 '67-p44
NYTBR, pt.2-N 5 '72-p42
Obs-Ap 6 '69-p26
Obs-Je 2 '74-p29
PW-v192-Ag 7 '67-p54
Par-v43-Je '68-p68
SR-v50-O 21 '67-p43
Spec-v222-My 16 '69-p657
TLS-Ap 3 '69-p355
Teacher-v90-Ja '73-p90
Trav-v24-Ja '68-p223
(George)
BL-v67-N 15 '70-p269
BW-v4-N 8 '70-p18
CCB-B-v24-F '71-p94
Comw-v93-N 20 '70-p200
GT-v88-F '71-p137
HB-v46-D '70-p619
KR-v38-O 15 '70-p1148
LJ-v95-D 15 '70-p4351
NO-v10-Ja 4 '71-p19
NS-v81-Je 4 '71-p779
NYTBR, pt.2-N 8 '70-p12
PW-v198-S 28 '70-p78
SR-v53-N 14 '70-p37
TLS-Jl 2 '71-p765
TN-v27-Ap '71-p306
Jennifer, Hecate, Macbeth, William McKinley, And Me, Elizabet h
BL-v63-Je 1 '67-p1048
CCB-B-v20-Je '67-p155
CLW-v39-N '67-p241
HB-v43-Ap '67-p206
Inst-v76-My '67-p132
KR-v35-F 1 '67-p131
LJ-v92-My 15 '67-p2022
PW-v191-Ap 10 '67-p80
Par-v43-Je '68-p68
SR-v50-Ap 22 '67-p100
TLS-O 3 '68-p1112
Trav-v24-N '67-p99

KORAL, April (continued)
SLJ-v28-N '81-p93

* * *

KORALEK, Jenny
Badgers Three
GP-v22-Mr '84-p4220
John Logan's Rooster
Sch Lib-v29-S '81-p237
TES-Je 12 '81-p27
The Song Of Roland Smith
GP-v22-N '83-p4161
JB-v47-D '83-p259
TES-Ap 13 '84-p30

* * *

KOREN, Edward
Behind The Wheel
BL-v68-Jl 1 '72-p942
BW-v6-My 7 '72-p6
CCB-B-v25-Jl '72-p172
CE-v49-N '72-p88
HB-v49-Ap '73-p132
KR-v40-Mr 15 '72-p320
KR-v40-D 15 '72-p1409
LJ-v97-S 15 '72-p2936
NYTBR-Ap 9 '72-p8
NYTBR-N 13 '77-p40
NYTBR, pt.2-N 5 '72-p30
SR-v55-Je 17 '72-p72
Don't Talk To Strange Bears
CCB-B-v22-Jl '69-p177
Comw-v90-My 23 '69-p294
KR-v37-F 1 '69-p95
NYTBR-Ap 6 '69-p18

* * *

KORINETZ, Yuri
In The Middle Of The World
GP-v16-S '77-p3158
JB-v41-O '77-p289
TES-D 30 '77-p13
The River And The Forest
GP-v17-Jl '78-p3346
JB-v42-O '78-p269
Obs-Mr 26 '78-p25
TES-My 19 '78-p32
There, Far Beyond The River
B&B-v19-O '73-p124
BL-v70-F 15 '74-p657
CCB-B-v27-Jl '74-p180
CSM-v66-My 1 '74-pF5
GP-v17-Ja '79-p3461
HB-v50-Ap '74-p148
J Read-v25-F '82-p462
KR-v41-N 1 '73-p1212
KR-v41-D 15 '73-p1350
LJ-v99-Ap 15 '74-p1229
Lis-v90-N 8 '73-p642
Obs-N 25 '73-p39
TLS-S 28 '73-p1113
TN-v30-Je '74-p434

* * *

KORMAN, Gordon
Go Jump In The Pool!
BL-v79-F 15 '83-p778
Can Child Lit-#20 '80-p39
In Rev-v14-Je '80-p46
Kliatt-v17-Winter '83-p10
I Want To Go Home!
Atl Pro Bk R-v10-N '83-p2
Atl Pro Bk R-v10-N '83-p13
CSM-v76-Jl 6 '84-pB5
Emerg Lib-v9-S '81-p29
In Rev-v15-Ag '81-p46
In Rev-v16-F '82-p41
Quill & Q-v47-Je '81-p33
The War With Mr. Wizzle
BIC-v11-D '82-p10
BL-v79-F 15 '83-p778
Kliatt-v17-Winter '83-p10
Quill & Q-v49-Ja '83-p34
SLJ-v30-S '83-p136

* * *

KORN, Ellen
Teach Yourself Calligraphy
CE-v59-My '83-p357
PW-v222-O 22 '82-p56
SLJ-v29-Mr '83-p179

* * *

KORNER, Wolfgang
The Green Frontier
BB-v6-Je '78-p5
BL-v74-D 1 '77-p613
CE-v55-Ap '79-p264
EJ-v67-Ap '78-p91
HB-v54-Ap '78-p169
J Read-v22-F '79-p477
KR-v45-O 15 '77-p1103
NYTBR-N 13 '77-p39
SLJ-v24-D '77-p54

* * *

KORR, David
The Day The Count Stopped Counting
SLJ-v24-Ap '78-p72

* * *

KORSCHUNOW, Irina
The Foundling Fox
KR-v52-S 1 '84-pJ62
Johnny's Dragon
GP-v21-S '82-p3965
Sch Lib-v30-Je '82-p133
A Night In Distant Motion
BL-v80-O 15 '83-p337
BS-v43-N '83-p311
CCB-B-v37-Ja '84-p91
HB-v59-D '83-p717
KR-v51-S 1 '83-pJ175
NW-v102-D 5 '83-p113
PW-v224-Jl 29 '83-p70
SLJ-v30-D '83-p75
VOYA-v6-F '84-p339
Who Killed Christopher?
BL-v77-S 15 '80-p111
CBRS-v9-S '80-p8
CCB-B-v34-D '80-p73
HB-v57-F '81-p59
KR-v48-O 1 '80-p1302
NYTBR-v86-F 1 '81-p28
SLJ-v27-N '80-p86

* * *

KORSHAK, Jack
Strange Story Of Oliver Jones
CCB-B-v20-F '67-p92
KR-v34-Ag 15 '66-p827
LJ-v91-Ag 15 '66-p4321

* * *

KORSHOLM, Pia
Ants
TES-Mr 11 '83-p42
Bees
TES-Mr 11 '83-p42
Social Insects
TES-Mr 11 '83-p42
Wasps
TES-Mr 11 '83-p42

* * *

KORTUM, Jeanie
Ghost Vision
BL-v80-F 1 '84-p814
CBRS-v12-Mr '84-p85
CCB-B-v37-F '84-p110
EJ-v73-S '84-p104
Inst-v93-N '83-p147
SE-v48-My '84-p371
SLJ-v30-Ja '84-p78

* * *

KORTY, Carol
Plays From African Folktales
RT-v37-Ap '84-p714
VOYA-v6-Ag '83-p143
Plays From African Folktales With Ideas For Acting, Dance, Costumes And Music
BL-v72-S 1 '75-p42

KORTY, Carol (continued)
CCB-B-v29-Ja '76-p81
HB-v52-Ap '76-p173
KR-v43-Je 15 '75-p665
LA-v53-Mr '76-p338
SLJ-v22-F '76-p46
Silly Soup
BL-v74-F 1 '78-p926
CE-v55-O '78-p42
CLW-v49-Mr '78-p357
KR-v45-N 15 '77-p1202
SLJ-v24-F '78-p59

* * *

KOSTERINA, Nina
The Diary Of Nina Kosterina
BL-v65-F 15 '69-p647
CCB-B-v22-Ap '69-p128
GT-v88-F '71-p152
HB-v45-F '69-p77
J Read-v25-Ja '82-p355
KR-v36-O 1 '68-p1180

* * *

KOSTICH, Dragos D
George Morrison
BL-v73-S 15 '76-p177
KR-v44-Je 1 '76-p641
SLJ-v23-N '76-p70

* * *

KOSTMAN, Samuel
Twentieth Century Women Of Achievement
BL-v72-Jl 1 '76-p1522
BL-v72-Jl 1 '76-p1527
Cur R-v16-O '77-p316

* * *

KOTKER, Norman
Holy Land In The Time Of Jesus
B&B-v13-Ag '68-p23
BL-v63-Ap 15 '67-p910
CCB-B-v20-Je '67-p154
CLW-v39-N '67-p239
HB-v43-Je '67-p362
KR-v35-F 1 '67-p143
LJ-v92-Mr 15 '67-p1325
NS-v75-My 24 '68-p699
NYTBR-v72-Mr 26 '67-p23
PW-v191-Mr 6 '67-p75
SR-v50-My 13 '67-p60
TLS-Je 6 '68-p581

* * *

KOTOWSKA, Monika
The Bridge To The Other Side
BL-v67-Ja 15 '71-p417
BS-v30-N 15 '70-p362
CLW-v42-F '71-p382
Comw-v93-N 20 '70-p202
HB-v46-O '70-p482
KR-v38-Ag 1 '70-p805
KR-v38-Ag 1 '70-p822
LJ-v95-N 15 '70-p4055
LJ-v95-D 15 '70-p4326
NYTBR-O 11 '70-p42
PW-v198-Ag 31 '70-p279

* * *

KOTTLER, Dorothy
I Really Like Myself
SB-v10-D '74-p245
SLJ-v21-Ja '75-p40
I Wonder Where I Came From
ACSB-v8-Winter '75-p24
SB-v10-D '74-p261

* * *

KOTTMEYER, William
Basic Goals In Spelling
Cur R-v19-Ap '80-p158
Inst-v82-O '72-p183
LA-v55-Mr '78-p406
Teacher-v94-S '76-p146

* * *

KOTZWINKLE, William
The Ants Who Took Away Time
BW-D 3 '78-pE4
KR-v46-N 15 '78-p1248
LA-v56-Ap '79-p441
RT-v33-O '79-p95
SLJ-v25-Ja '79-p43
Dream Of Dark Harbor
CCB-B-v32-Jl '79-p194
Cur R-v19-S '80-p336
KR-v47-F 15 '79-p197
PW-v215-F 19 '79-p107
SLJ-v25-Ap '79-p58
E.T.: El Extraterrestre
BL-v79-Ag '83-p1459
E.T.: The Extra-Terrestrial Storybook
B Rpt-v2-My '83-p37
CCB-B-v36-Ja '83-p92
Inst-v92-Mr '83-p33
SF&FBR-S '82-p36
S Fict R-v12-Ag '83-p33
TLS-Ja 7 '83-p13
Elephant Boy
CE-v47-Ja '71-p211
HB-v46-Je '70-p286
KR-v38-Mr 15 '70-p316
LJ-v95-My 15 '70-p1930
PW-v197-Ap 6 '70-p61
The Firemen
HB-v45-Ag '69-p397
LJ-v94-N 15 '69-p4277
The Leopard's Tooth
BB-v4-Ag '76-p4
CCB-B-v30-S '76-p12
KR-v44-Ap 1 '76-p390
Kliatt-v17-Spring '83-p16
SLJ-v22-My '76-p60
The Nap Master
CBRS-v7-Je '79-p102
KR-v47-Mr 15 '79-p323
PW-v215-F 12 '79-p126
SLJ-v25-Ap '79-p44
The Oldest Man
CCB-B-v26-O '72-p27
KR-v39-S 15 '71-p1013
LJ-v97-My 15 '72-p1914
PW-v200-O 18 '71-p51
The Ship That Came Down The Gutter
BL-v67-Mr 15 '71-p620
GP-v15-Jl '76-p2922
JB-v40-Je '76-p146
LJ-v96-My 15 '71-p1797
Obs-Ap 11 '76-p33
PW-v198-S 7 '70-p61
The Supreme, Superb, Exalted And Delightful, One And Only Magic Building
BL-v70-S 1 '73-p52
CCB-B-v27-O '73-p29
KR-v41-Ap 15 '73-p452
LJ-v98-S 15 '73-p2641
NYTBR-Ja 13 '74-p10
PW-v203-Ap 30 '73-p55
Trouble In Bugland
AB-v73-Ap 16 '84-p2922
BL-v80-N 15 '83-p469
B Rpt-v3-My '84-p34
BW-v13-N 6 '83-p16
CSM-v76-D 2 '83-pB7
Fant R-v7-My '84-p33
HB-v60-Ap '84-p196
KR-v51-S 15 '83-p1022
LATBR-Ja 22 '84-p8
NYTBR-v89-Ja 1 '84-p23
PW-v224-D 2 '83-p86
SLJ-v30-F '84-p74
Up The Alley With Jack And Joe
CCB-B-v28-Ja '75-p80
KR-v42-Ag 1 '74-p801
LJ-v99-D 15 '74-p3275

KOTZWINKLE, William
(continued)
SR/W-v2-N 30 '74-p27
KR-v44-F 1 '76-p171
PW-v209-F 9 '76-p89

* * *

KOUHI, Elizabeth
North Country Spring
In Rev-v15-O '81-p40
The Story Of Philip
BIC-v11-D '82-p8

* * *

KOUZEL, Daisy
The Cuckoo's Reward/El Premio Del Cuco
HB-v53-Ap '77-p191
KR-v45-F 15 '77-p162
LA-v55-F '78-p210
SLJ-v23-My '77-p52

* * *

KOVACS, Freda B
Selected Hungarian Legends
RT-v35-Ap '82-p824

* * *

KOVACS, Klara
Kirandulas Az Abece-Hegyre
BL-v78-S 15 '81-p115

* * *

KOVAL, Yuri
A Pig In A Poke
GP-v14-Ap '76-p2849
JB-v40-Je '76-p153
LR-v25-Autumn '75-p137

* * *

KOVALIK, Tibor
From Tale To Tale
BIC-v8-D '79-p13
Can Child Lit-#18 '80-p104
In Rev-v14-F '80-p50

* * *

KOVASH, Emily
How To Have Fun Making Cards
SLJ-v22-S '75-p97

* * *

KOVIC, Kajetan
Maj Prijatelj Piki Jakob
BL-v80-Je 1 '84-p1402

* * *

KOWET, Don
Pele
BL-v72-My 15 '76-p1330
BL-v72-My 15 '76-p1337
CCB-B-v30-O '76-p26

* * *

KOZIAKIN, Vladimir
Mighty Marvel Mazes
CSM-v70-D 19 '77-p23
Son Of Mighty Marvel Mazes
CSM-v70-D 19 '77-p23

* * *

KOZIKOWSKI, Renate
Sophie's Hideaway
CBRS-v12-N '83-p25
CCB-B-v37-D '83-p71
JB-v48-F '84-p15
PW-v224-Ag 26 '83-p386
SLJ-v30-O '83-p125
Titus Bear Goes To Bed
GP-v23-Jl '84-p4294
SLJ-v31-O '84-p148
TES-My 25 '84-p27
Titus Bear Goes To School
GP-v23-Jl '84-p4294
JB-v48-Je '84-p118
SLJ-v31-O '84-p148
TES-My 25 '84-p27
Titus Bear Goes To The Beach
GP-v23-Jl '84-p4294
SLJ-v31-O '84-p148
TES-My 25 '84-p27
Titus Bear Goes To Town
GP-v23-Jl '84-p4294
PW-v224-Ja 20 '84-p88
SLJ-v31-O '84-p148
TES-My 25 '84-p27

* * *

KOZOL, Jonathan
Children Of The Revolution
BL-v75-D 1 '78-p584
BW-N 19 '78-pE1
CSM-v71-Ja 29 '79-p27
Choice-v16-Mr '79-p126
Cng-v10-D '78-p77
EJ-v68-Mr '79-p84
ES-v10-Fall '79-p286
HB-v55-Ag '79-p460
KR-v46-S 1 '78-p990
Kliatt-v14-Spring '80-p29
LJ-v103-D 15 '78-p2503
Nat-v227-O 28 '78-p448
PW-v214-Ag 21 '78-p49
PW-v216-N 5 '79-p66

* * *

KOZUKI, Russell
Competing In Karate
BL-v71-F 1 '75-p557
SLJ-v21-Mr '75-p98
Junior Karate
LJ-v96-D 15 '71-p4204
Teacher-v95-My '78-p106
Karate For Young People
BL-v70-Je 1 '74-p1100
LJ-v99-D 15 '74-p3282
PW-v205-Jl 1 '74-p83

* * *

KOZUSZEK, Jane E
Hygiene
BL-v74-Jl 15 '78-p1734
Cur R-v18-Ag '79-p242
Inst-v87-My '78-p115
SB-v15-My '79-p43
SLJ-v25-S '78-p141

* * *

KRAFT, Betsy H
Coal
ASBYP-v16-Spring '83-p29
BL-v73-O 15 '76-p323
BL-v79-F 15 '83-p778
CLW-v54-My '83-p425
Cur R-v22-O '83-p76
SB-v13-D '77-p164
SLJ-v23-N '76-p60
SLJ-v29-F '83-p77
Oil And Natural Gas
ACSB-v12-Winter '79-p21
ASBYP-v16-Fall '83-p34
BL-v74-Jl 1 '78-p1679
BL-v79-F 15 '83-p778
Cur R-v18-O '79-p301
Cur R-v22-O '83-p76
SB-v14-Mr '79-p230
SB-v18-My '83-p269
SLJ-v25-S '78-p141
SLJ-v29-F '83-p77

* * *

KRAFT, Eric
Do Clams Bite?
Choice-v20-My '83-p1290
My Mother Takes A Tumble
Choice-v20-My '83-p1290

* * *

KRAHN, Fernando
April Fools
BL-v70-My 15 '74-p1057
CCB-B-v28-S '74-p11
J Read-v27-N '83-p121

KRAHN, Fernando (continued)
KR-v42-Ap 15 '74-p419
LJ-v99-S 15 '74-p2250
PW-v205-My 6 '74-p69
Teacher-v92-Ap '75-p107
Arthur's Adventure In The Abandoned House
BL-v77-Je 15 '81-p1346
CBRS-v9-Spring '81-p101
HB-v57-Ag '81-p414
KR-v49-Ap 15 '81-p500
PW-v219-My 22 '81-p76
RT-v35-D '81-p366
SLJ-v27-Ap '81-p114
The Biggest Christmas Tree On Earth
BB-v6-D '78-p2
BL-v75-S 15 '78-p221
BW-D 10 '78-pE5
CCB-B-v32-D '78-p65
KR-v46-D 15 '78-p1353
PW-v214-Jl 3 '78-p65
SLJ-v25-O '78-p112
Teacher-v96-F '79-p30
Catch That Cat!
BL-v74-My 1 '78-p1434
HB-v54-Je '78-p265
KR-v46-Mr 1 '78-p239
RT-v32-O '78-p91
SLJ-v24-My '78-p57
The Creepy Thing
KR-v50-Ap 15 '82-p485
PW-v221-Mr 5 '82-p70
SLJ-v28-Ag '82-p99
The Family Minus
BL-v73-Ap 1 '77-p1169
CCB-B-v30-Je '77-p161
Inst-v86-My '77-p117
KR-v45-F 1 '77-p91
PW-v211-Ja 31 '77-p75
Par-v52-Ag '77-p61
RT-v32-O '78-p33
SLJ-v23-Ap '77-p55
WCRB-v3-My '77-p39
A Flying Saucer Full Of Spaghetti
BW-v4-N 8 '70-p3
CLW-v43-O '71-p115
LJ-v95-N 15 '70-p4036
PW-v198-Ag 17 '70-p50
A Funny Friend From Heaven
BL-v74-S 15 '77-p195
HB-v54-F '78-p36
KR-v45-S 15 '77-p985
SLJ-v24-O '77-p105
SR-v5-N 26 '77-p42
The Great Ape
J Read-v27-N '83-p121
KR-v46-S 15 '78-p1015
PW-v214-Ag 14 '78-p69
SLJ-v25-D '78-p45
Here Comes Alex Pumpernickel!
BL-v77-Ap 15 '81-p1154
CBRS-v9-Je '81-p92
KR-v49-Ap 15 '81-p500
PW-v219-F 13 '81-p93
RT-v35-F '82-p622
Hilderita Y Maximiliano
BL-v78-S 1 '81-p39
How Santa Claus Had A Long And Difficult Journey Delivering His Presents
BW-v4-D 20 '70-p8
GT-v88-D '70-p82
KR-v38-S 15 '70-p1029
LJ-v95-O 15 '70-p3645
PW-v198-N 9 '70-p60
PW-v212-N 21 '77-p64
SR-v53-D 19 '70-p31
Teacher-v95-My '78-p104
Little Love Story
BB-v5-F '77-p2
BL-v73-S 15 '76-p178
CCB-B-v30-F '77-p93
CLW-v48-F '77-p306
KR-v44-Jl 1 '76-p727
PW-v209-Je 28 '76-p99
RT-v31-O '77-p12
SLJ-v23-O '76-p99
Teacher-v96-F '79-p30
Mr. Top
CBRS-v12-S '83-p4
HB-v59-D '83-p701
KR-v51-S 1 '83-pJ151
PW-v224-Jl 29 '83-p70
SLJ-v30-O '83-p159
The Mystery Of The Giant Footprints
HB-v53-Ag '77-p430
KR-v45-Ap 15 '77-p422
LA-v54-O '77-p804
PW-v211-My 16 '77-p63
RT-v32-O '78-p36
RT-v34-Ja '81-p419
SLJ-v24-O '77-p105
WLB-v51-Je '77-p808
Robot-Bot-Bot
BB-v7-S '79-p1
CCB-B-v33-S '79-p10
KR-v47-Mr 1 '79-p259
PW-v215-F 26 '79-p183
RT-v34-O '80-p46
SLJ-v25-My '79-p53
Sebastian And The Mushroom
BB-v4-My '76-p2
BL-v72-Je 15 '76-p1466
J Read-v27-N '83-p121
KR-v44-Ap 15 '76-p463
PW-v209-My 24 '76-p60
SLJ-v23-S '76-p102
The Secret In The Dungeon
CE-v60-Mr '84-p288
KR-v51-Mr 1 '83-p242
PW-v223-Ja 7 '83-p74
RT-v37-N '83-p191
SLJ-v29-Ag '83-p53
The Self-Made Snowman
BB-v2-Ja '75-p1
BL-v71-S 1 '74-p44
CCB-B-v28-N '74-p46
KR-v42-Jl 15 '74-p736
LJ-v99-O 15 '74-p2721
PW-v206-Ag 26 '74-p307
Teacher-v92-D '74-p77
Teacher-v96-F '79-p30
Sleep Tight, Alex Pumpernickel
BL-v78-Je 1 '82-p1314
RT-v36-O '82-p117
SLJ-v29-O '82-p142
Who's Seen The Scissors?
BL-v71-My 15 '75-p965
CCB-B-v28-Jl '75-p179
CLW-v47-S '75-p93
HB-v51-Ag '75-p369
KR-v43-Ap 15 '75-p445
LA-v53-F '76-p197
RT-v34-Ja '81-p420
SLJ-v22-S '75-p85

* * *

KRAILING, Tessa
A Dinosaur Called Minerva
TLS-Mr 27 '81-p346
Washington And The Marrow Raiders
Brit Bk N C-Spring '82-p9

* * *

KRAL, Brian
O. Henry's The Ransom Of Red Chief
Dr-#2 '81-p56
Special Class
Dr-Spring '83-p24

* * *

KRAMER, George
Kid Battery
CCB-B-v22-S '68-p10
CSM-v60-N 7 '68-pB12
KR-v36-F 1 '68-p115
LJ-v93-My 15 '68-p2129
PW-v193-Je 10 '68-p61

* * *

KRAMER, Jack
Plant Hobbies
ACSB-v12-Spring '79-p32
KR-v46-S 1 '78-p952
Teacher-v96-Ja '79-p132
Plant Sculptures
ACSB-v12-Spring '79-p34
BL-v74-Jl 15 '78-p1735
HB-v55-O '78-p531
SLJ-v25-S '78-p141
Queen's Tears And Elephant's Ears
BL-v74-D 1 '77-p613
CCB-B-v31-Mr '78-p114
HB-v54-F '78-p60
KR-v45-O 15 '77-p1100
SLJ-v24-F '78-p59

* * *

KRAMON, Florence
Eugene And The New Baby
CCB-B-v21-Ap '68-p130
KR-v35-N 1 '67-p1314
LJ-v93-Ap 15 '68-p1789
Eugene And The Policeman
CCB-B-v22-S '68-p10
KR-v35-N 1 '67-p1314
LJ-v93-Je 15 '68-p2533
Eugene, Pack A Grip
KR-v35-N 1 '67-p1314
Hippolito And Eugene
KR-v35-N 1 '67-p1314
LJ-v93-Je 15 '68-p1790
Nobody Looks At Eugene
KR-v35-N 1 '67-p1314
LJ-v93-Je 15 '68-p2533
Wallpaper For Eugene's Room
KR-v35-N 1 '67-p1314
LJ-v93-Je 15 '68-p2533

* * *

KRAMP, Harry
Swimming For Boys And Girls
LJ-v92-Ja 15 '67-p351

* * *

KRANE, Louis
Phonics Is Fun
Cur R-v19-F '80-p41

* * *

KRANTZ, Hazel Newman
The Secret Raft
BL-v62-Mr 15 '66-p717
CCB-B-v19-Jl '66-p180
HB-v42-F '66-p58
KR-v33-Je 15 '65-p578
LJ-v90-Jl '65-p3126

* * *

KRAPESH, Patricia
A Tale Of Two Cities
SLJ-v27-F '81-p64

* * *

KRASILOVSKY, Jessica
The Boy Who Spoke Chinese
CCB-B-v26-N '72-p44
KR-v40-My 15 '72-p575
LJ-v97-S 15 '72-p2937
NYTBR-My 21 '72-p8

* * *

KRASILOVSKY, Phyllis
Benny's Flag
BL-v69-O 15 '72-p177
The Cow Who Fell Into The Canal
Obs-N 22 '70-p27
The First Tulips In Holland
BL-v78-My 15 '82-p1258
CBRS-v10-Je '82-p102
CCB-B-v35-Je '82-p190
CSM-v74-My 14 '82-pB12
NYT-v132-N 29 '82-p17
NYTBR-v87-Ap 25 '82-p38
PW-v221-Ap 23 '82-p92
SLJ-v28-Mr '82-p136
WCRB-v8-S '82-p72
The Girl Who Was A Cowboy
CCB-B-v18-F '65-p87
Inst-v74-My '65-p30
LJ-v90-F 15 '65-p954
NYTBR-v70-Mr 14 '65-p30
TES-S 30 '77-p24
L.C. Is The Greatest
BL-v72-S 1 '75-p42
KR-v43-My 1 '75-p521
PW-v208-Jl 7 '75-p86
SLJ-v21-Ap '75-p66
The Man Who Cooked For Himself
CBRS-v10-My '82-p94
SLJ-v28-My '82-p80
The Man Who Didn't Wash His Dishes
BW-N 12 '78-pE2
The Man Who Entered A Contest
BL-v77-Ja 15 '81-p705
CCB-B-v34-Ap '81-p154
HB-v57-Ap '81-p186
NYTBR-v86-Mr 8 '81-p30
PW-v218-N 21 '80-p58
SLJ-v27-Mr '81-p133
The Man Who Tried To Save Time
BL-v76-O 15 '79-p360
CBRS-v8-O '79-p15
CCB-B-v33-D '79-p73
Cur R-v19-F '80-p51
HB-v55-O '79-p529
KR-v47-S 15 '79-p1066
PW-v216-N 12 '79-p59
SLJ-v26-D '79-p93
The Popular Girls Club
JB-v39-F '75-p41
KR-v40-Ag 15 '72-p940
LJ-v98-Ja 15 '73-p261
NYTBR, pt.2-N 5 '72-p16
PW-v202-O 16 '72-p50
The Shy Little Girl
CSM-v62-My 7 '70-pB3
Comw-v92-My 22 '70-p246
KR-v38-Ap 15 '70-p445
LJ-v95-Jl '70-p2528
Obs-D 5 '71-p34
SR-v53-My 9 '70-p42
TLS-Ap 28 '72-p483
The Very Little Boy
GT-v89-F '72-p94
The Very Little Girl
GT-v89-F '72-p94
Inst-v74-Ja '65-p38
The Very Tall Little Girl
CCB-B-v23-Ja '70-p82
KR-v37-O 1 '69-p1058
LJ-v95-F 15 '70-p772
SR-v52-N 8 '69-p62
Spectr-v47-Mr '71-p43

* * *

KRASKA, Edie
Toys And Tales From Grandmother's Attic
BB-v7-D '79-p4
BW-v9-N 11 '79-p13
CCB-B-v33-Ap '80-p156
HB-v55-D '79-p678
PW-v216-Jl 9 '79-p106

KRASKA, Edie (continued)
SLJ-v26-D '79-p87

* * *

KRASKE, Robert
Daredevils Do Amazing Things
SLJ-v25-S '78-p119
Is There Life In Outer Space?
ACSB-v10-Winter '77-p27
BB-v4-N '76-p3
BL-v73-S 1 '76-p40
Inst-v85-My '76-p116
KR-v44-My 1 '76-p545
PW-v209-F 23 '76-p119
SB-v13-My '77-p42
SLJ-v23-S '76-p134
Magicians Do Amazing Things
BB-v7-O '79-p4
BL-v75-Jl 15 '79-p1633
RT-v33-D '79-p358
SLJ-v26-Mr '80-p122
SR-v6-My 26 '79-p63
Riddles Of The Stars
ACSB-v13-Mr '80-p38
CBRS-v8-Ja '80-p47
SB-v16-S '80-p31
SLJ-v26-D '79-p87
TES-Ja 8 '82-p26
The Sea Robbers
BL-v74-O 1 '77-p298
RT-v32-F '79-p606
SLJ-v24-D '77-p49
The Story Of The Dictionary
BL-v71-Je 1 '75-p1013
CCB-B-v29-N '75-p48
CE-v52-N '75-p94
CSM-v67-My 7 '75-pB5
HB-v51-O '75-p482
Inst-v84-My '75-p99
KR-v43-F 1 '75-p125
SLJ-v21-Ap '75-p54
SLJ-v22-D '75-p31
SR-v2-My 31 '75-p31
The Twelve Million Dollar Note
KR-v45-O 1 '77-p1056
SA-v239-D '78-p34
SLJ-v24-S '77-p131

* * *

KRASNOFF, Barbara
Robots
BL-v78-My 15 '82-p1233
CCB-B-v35-Ap '82-p151
HB-v58-Ag '82-p442
LJ-v107-Ja 1 '82-p103
LJ-v108-Mr 1 '83-p445
SB-v18-N '82-p84

* * *

KRATZ, Marilyn
Whose Garden?
SLJ-v23-F '77-p57

* * *

KRAUS, Joanna H
The Dragon Hammer And The Tale Of Oniroku
SLJ-v26-Ja '80-p72

* * *

KRAUS, Pamela
A Treasury Of Windmill Books
CCB-B-v35-My '82-p174
SLJ-v28-My '82-p55

* * *

KRAUS, Robert
Amanda Remembers
CCB-B-v19-N '65-p46
KR-v33-Ag 15 '65-p817
LJ-v90-S 15 '65-p3780
NYTBR-v70-O 24 '65-p34
Another Mouse To Feed
CBRS-v8-Je '80-p102
KR-v48-Jl 1 '80-p834
NYTBR-v85-Ap 27 '80-p49
PW-v217-My 23 '80-p76
SLJ-v27-S '80-p60
WLB-v55-N '80-p213
Big Brother
CCB-B-v27-O '73-p29
CLW-v45-N '73-p190
KR-v41-My 1 '73-p511
LJ-v98-S 15 '73-p2641
PW-v203-My 21 '73-p49
Boris Bad Enough
BW-v10-My 25 '80-p13
CCB-B-v30-F '77-p93
HB-v53-Ap '77-p151
JB-v47-O '83-p199
SLJ-v23-Ja '77-p84
The Bunny's Nutshell Library
CLW-v36-Ap '65-p576
KR-v33-Mr 1 '65-p231
LJ-v90-Ap 15 '65-p2012
NYTBR-v70-Ap 11 '65-p26
SR-v48-Mr 27 '65-p33
Bunya The Witch
BW-v5-My 9 '71-p8
KR-v39-My 15 '71-p549
LJ-v96-S 15 '71-p2906
NYTBR, pt.2-My 2 '71-p8
The Children Who Got Married
KR-v37-Ag 15 '69-p851
Daddy Long Ears
HB-v46-Je '70-p286
LJ-v95-Jl '70-p2528
NY-v49-D 3 '73-p198
The Detective Of London
BL-v74-My 15 '78-p1495
GP-v18-Jl '79-p3554
JB-v43-Ag '79-p200
KR-v46-Ap 15 '78-p432
SLJ-v25-O '78-p135
The First Robin
CCB-B-v19-F '66-p101
The Gondolier Of Venice
BB-v4-N '76-p1
GP-v16-Ap '78-p3296
JB-v42-F '78-p18
KR-v44-Ap 1 '76-p386
LA-v54-Ja '77-p78
SLJ-v23-O '76-p99
TES-D 16 '77-p50
The Good Mousekeeper
CCB-B-v31-N '77-p49
PW-v211-Je 6 '77-p82
PW-v221-F 26 '82-p148
SLJ-v24-N '77-p48
Good Night Little ABC
CCB-B-v27-S '73-p11
KR-v40-D 1 '72-p1350
NYTBR-N 12 '72-p8
Good Night Little One
CCB-B-v27-S '73-p11
KR-v40-D 1 '72-p1350
NYTBR-N 12 '72-p8
Good Night Richard Rabbit
CCB-B-v27-S '73-p11
KR-v40-D 1 '72-p1350
NYTBR-N 12 '72-p8
Hello Hippopotamus
CCB-B-v23-O '69-p26
CSM-v61-My 1 '69-pB4
KR-v37-Mr 15 '69-p299
LJ-v94-S 15 '69-p3195
NYTBR-My 11 '69-p26
Herman The Helper
Am-v131-D 7 '74-p370
CCB-B-v28-D '74-p65
CSM-v66-Jl 3 '74-p7
GP-v15-Ap '77-p3083
HB-v50-O '74-p129
Inst-v84-N '74-p132
JB-v41-Je '77-p156
KR-v42-Ag 1 '74-p799

KRAUS, Robert (continued)
LJ-v99-N 15 '74-p3038
NYTBR-S 22 '74-p8
NYTBR-S 4 '77-p23
Obs-Ap 10 '77-p21
PW-v206-Jl 29 '74-p57
RT-v32-My '79-p943
WLB-v49-O '74-p138
How Spider Saved Christmas
CCB-B-v24-My '71-p139
CLW-v42-Ap '71-p520
KR-v38-O 15 '70-p1140
LJ-v95-O 15 '70-p3644
NY-v49-D 3 '73-p198
SR-v53-D 19 '70-p31
How Spider Saved Halloween
KR-v41-S 15 '73-p1031
LJ-v99-Ja 15 '74-p200
PW-v204-O 15 '73-p62
SLMQ-v12-Summer '84-p327
I, Mouse
RT-v32-Ja '79-p487
Teacher-v96-O '78-p169
I'm A Monkey
BB-v4-Mr '76-p1
CCB-B-v29-Je '76-p159
KR-v43-O 1 '75-p1121
SLJ-v22-D '75-p65
Jose El Gran Ayudante
HB-v53-D '77-p686
SLJ-v27-Ja '81-p33
Jose El Gran Ayudante/ Herman The Helper
BL-v78-S 1 '81-p54
Junior The Spoiled Cat
NY-v49-D 3 '73-p198
The King's Trousers
BW-v11-O 11 '81-p10
KR-v49-Ag 1 '81-p932
NY-v57-D 7 '81-p230
PW-v219-Je 12 '81-p54
RT-v35-My '82-p976
SLJ-v28-N '81-p79
Kittens For Nothing
BB-v4-Jl '76-p1
BL-v72-Ap 15 '76-p1186
KR-v44-Mr 1 '76-p251
LA-v53-S '76-p698
PW-v209-Mr 15 '76-p57
RT-v31-O '77-p12
SLJ-v23-S '76-p102
Ladybug, Ladybug
SR-v5-N 26 '77-p42
Leo El Capullo Tardio
HB-v53-D '77-p687
SLJ-v27-Ja '81-p33
Leo El Capullo Tardio/Leo The Late Bloomer
BL-v78-S 1 '81-p54
Leo The Late Bloomer
BL-v68-Mr 1 '72-p565
CCB-B-v25-Ja '72-p75
CSM-v64-My 4 '72-pB3
CSM-v65-D 4 '72-p19
CSM-v68-D 22 '75-p18
HB-v48-F '72-p41
Inst-v84-My '75-p107
KR-v40-Ja 1 '72-p1
LJ-v97-Ap 15 '72-p1598
LJ-v97-My 15 '72-p1885
NYTBR-Ja 16 '72-p8
Obs-Ap 22 '73-p33
Obs-Mr 23 '75-p27
PW-v200-D 6 '71-p53
SLJ-v25-My '79-p39
SR-v54-D 11 '71-p45
TLS-Ap 6 '73-p385
TLS-Ap 2 '76-p395
Lillian, Morgan And Teddy
KR-v39-My 15 '71-p550
LJ-v96-O 15 '71-p3460
Little Giant
KR-v35-Ap 1 '67-p407
LJ-v92-Mr 15 '67-p1311
NO-v6-Jl 17 '67-p19
NYTBR, pt.1-v72-My 7 '67-p53
Teacher-v95-My '78-p106
Ludwig The Dog Who Snored Symphonies
CCB-B-v25-Ja '72-p75
KR-v40-Ja 1 '72-p2
Mert The Blurt
CCB-B-v34-My '81-p174
HB-v57-Je '81-p293
PW-v219-F 13 '81-p93
SLJ-v27-My '81-p56
Milton El Madrugador
HB-v53-D '77-p687
SLJ-v27-Ja '81-p33
Milton El Madrugador/ Milton The Early Riser
BL-v78-S 1 '81-p54
Milton The Early Riser
BL-v69-Ja 15 '73-p494
BW-v6-N 5 '72-p2
CCB-B-v26-My '73-p140
CE-v50-O '73-p30
CSM-v64-N 8 '72-pB2
HB-v49-F '73-p38
KR-v40-O 15 '72-p1186
LJ-v98-Ja 15 '73-p254
NYT-v122-D 11 '72-p37
NYTBR-N 12 '72-p8
NYTBR-D 3 '72-p82
NYTBR-S 4 '77-p23
NYTBR, pt.2-N 5 '72-p30
Obs-D 1 '74-p35
PW-v202-N 20 '72-p66
TN-v29-Je '73-p357
Milton The Early Riser Takes A Trip
PW-v221-Ja 1 '82-p50
My Son The Mouse
KR-v34-Ag 15 '66-p826
LJ-v91-O 15 '66-p5217
NYTBR-v71-S 25 '66-p34
The Night-Lite Storybook
KR-v43-My 1 '75-p509
PW-v207-My 12 '75-p66
PW-v221-Ja 1 '82-p51
Noel The Coward
CCB-B-v31-Mr '78-p115
CLW-v49-Ap '78-p403
KR-v45-N 15 '77-p1193
LA-v55-My '78-p618
PW-v212-O 24 '77-p76
SLJ-v24-Ja '78-p79
The Old Fashioned Raggedy Ann & Andy ABC Book
NW-v98-D 7 '81-p99
PW-v220-O 9 '81-p66
Owliver
BL-v71-Ja 1 '75-p461
BL-v71-Mr 15 '75-p767
CCB-B-v28-Ap '75-p132
CLW-v47-Ap '76-p397
CLW-v49-D '77-p211
Choice-v12-N '75-p1133
GP-v15-O '76-p2975
Inst-v84-My '75-p102
JB-v41-F '77-p15
KR-v42-N 15 '74-p1200
NYTBR-N 3 '74-p55
NYTBR-N 3 '74-p57
NYTBR-S 4 '77-p23
Obs-Ag 22 '76-p21
PW-v206-D 9 '74-p67
SR-v2-My 31 '75-p36
TLS-O 1 '76-p1244
Teacher-v92-F '75-p111
WLB-v49-F '75-p427
Palmer Cox's A Box Of Brownies
SLJ-v27-Mr '81-p133
Pinchpenny Mouse
B&B-v22-D '76-p78
CCB-B-v28-My '75-p150
CSM-v71-D 4 '78-pB19

* * *

KREDENSER, Gail

ABC Of Bumptious Beasts

NYTBR-v71-N 6 '66-p6

One Dancing Drum

CCB-B-v25-Ap '72-p125
CSM-v63-N 11 '71-pB2
GT-v89-D '71-p82
LJ-v97-Jl '72-p2478
PW-v200-N 15 '71-p71
LJ-v91-N 15 '66-p5749

* * *

KREIDOLF, Ernst

Dream Garden

CBRS-v8-Spring '80-p118
HB-v56-Je '80-p276
SLJ-v26-Ag '80-p52

Flower Fairy Tales

CBRS-v8-Spring '80-p118
HB-v56-Je '80-p276
SLJ-v26-Ag '80-p52

Servants Of The Spring

CBRS-v8-Spring '80-p118
HB-v56-Je '80-p276
SLJ-v26-Ag '80-p52

* * *

KREMENTZ, Jill

How It Feels To Be Adopted

BL-v79-F 1 '83-p724
BW-v13-Ja 9 '83-p10
CBRS-v11-F '83-p71
CCB-B-v36-F '83-p111
J Read-v26-Ap '83-p653
KR-v50-N 15 '82-p1239
LATBR-D 5 '82-p10
LJ-v108-Ja 1 '83-p60
Ms-v12-D '83-p70
PW-v222-N 5 '82-p70
SLJ-v29-D '82-p65
VOYA-v6-Ap '83-p50

How It Feels When A Parent Dies

BL-v78-S 1 '81-p48
BOT-v4-S '81-p403
BS-v41-Ag '81-p197
CBRS-v10-Jl '81-p117
CCB-B-v35-D '81-p72
CLW-v53-D '81-p231
Cur R-v21-F '82-p31
HB-v57-O '81-p553
JB-v47-Je '83-p127
J Read-v25-Ja '82-p390
KR-v49-Ag 1 '81-p937
NYTBR-v86-Jl 19 '81-p8
PW-v219-Ap 17 '81-p63
SLJ-v28-S '81-p127
SLJ-v30-Ja '84-p42
TES-Je 17 '83-p28
VOYA-v5-Je '82-p45

How It Feels When Parents Divorce

BW-v14-N 11 '84-p17

Sweet Pea

CCB-B-v24-Jl '70-p182
LJ-v95-Jl '70-p2534
NYTBR, pt.2-N 9 '69-p50
PW-v196-D 8 '69-p48
SR-v53-My 9 '70-p44

A Very Young Circus Flyer

BL-v75-Je 1 '79-p1492
CBRS-v7-My '79-p98
CCB-B-v32-Jl '79-p194
CLW-v51-D '79-p234
HB-v55-Ag '79-p436
KR-v47-Ap 15 '79-p454
PW-v215-Ap 2 '79-p73
RT-v34-O '80-p47
SLJ-v25-My '79-p35
SLJ-v25-My '79-p63
SLJ-v28-D '81-p78

A Very Young Dancer

BL-v73-Ja 15 '77-p719
BW-N 7 '76-pG7
CCB-B-v30-Ap '77-p128
CSM-v68-N 24 '76-pB7
DN-v62-Ja '77-p16
Esq-v87-F '77-p18
GP-v18-N '79-p3604
HB-v53-Ap '77-p173
KR-v44-N 1 '76-p1172
NYT-v126-Ja 14 '77-pC19
NYTBR-D 26 '76-p11
PW-v210-O 18 '76-p63
SLJ-v23-D '76-p49
SLJ-v24-D '77-p35
SR-v4-N 27 '76-p34
Sch Lib-v27-D '79-p381
Teacher-v94-My '77-p108
Teacher-v95-D '77-p29
Teacher-v95-Ja '78-p44
VV-v21-D 13 '76-p70
WLB-v51-Ja '77-p388

A Very Young Gymnast

BL-v75-D 15 '78-p688
CCB-B-v32-F '79-p101
CSM-v71-D 4 '78-pB19
Econ-v273-D 22 '79-p86
HB-v55-F '79-p78
JB-v44-Ap '80-p69
KR-v46-D 15 '78-p1360
PW-v214-O 16 '78-p122
RT-v33-O '79-p47
SLJ-v25-D '78-p71
Teacher-v96-My '79-p115

A Very Young Rider

BL-v74-N 15 '77-p551
BL-v77-O 1 '80-p262
BS-v37-Ja '78-p335
BW-D 11 '77-pE4
CCB-B-v31-My '78-p144
Comw-v104-N 11 '77-p734
HB-v54-F '78-p65
KR-v45-N 15 '77-p1202
NYTBR-D 11 '77-p16
New R-v177-D 3 '77-p28
PW-v212-S 12 '77-p132
RT-v32-O '78-p42
SLJ-v24-D '77-p49
SR-v5-N 26 '77-p40
Teacher-v95-My '78-p21

A Very Young Skater

BL-v76-D 15 '79-p613
CCB-B-v33-F '80-p112
HB-v56-F '80-p72
KR-v48-Ja 15 '80-p69
SLJ-v26-D '79-p101

* * *

KRENSKY, Stephen

A Big Day For Scepters

BB-v5-Je '77-p4
BL-v73-Je 15 '77-p1576
CLW-v49-F '78-p313
EJ-v66-N '77-p82
KR-v45-Ap 1 '77-p352
LA-v55-My '78-p623
NYTBR-Je 19 '77-p28
SLJ-v23-Ap '77-p68

Castles In The Air And Other Tales

CCB-B-v33-N '79-p50
Cur R-v19-Ap '80-p152
KR-v47-Je 1 '79-p637
LA-v57-My '80-p557
SLJ-v26-S '79-p142

Conqueror And Hero

BL-v78-O 1 '81-p237
CCB-B-v35-Ja '82-p88
HB-v57-D '81-p677
KR-v49-O 15 '81-p1298
PW-v220-Jl 10 '81-p92
SLJ-v28-N '81-p106
TES-S 24 '82-p35

The Dragon Circle

B&B-v25-Je '80-p50
BL-v74-N 1 '77-p477
CCB-B-v31-F '78-p97
KR-v45-Jl 15 '77-p728

KRENSKY, Stephen (continued)
RT-v32-F '79-p609
SLJ-v24-O '77-p115
A Ghostly Business
PW-v226-Jl 27 '84-p143
The Lion Upstairs
CBRS-v11-Spring '83-p119
CSM-v75-My 13 '83-pB4
KR-v51-Mr 15 '83-p305
PW-v223-My 27 '83-p67
SLJ-v29-Ag '83-p53
The Perils Of Putney
BL-v75-N 1 '78-p480
CBRS-v7-F '79-p68
CE-v55-F '79-p223
KR-v46-N 1 '78-p1189
SLJ-v25-O '78-p146
A Troll In Passing
BL-v76-Je 1 '80-p1424
CBRS-v8-Jl '80-p127
CCB-B-v33-My '80-p175
CE-v57-Ja '81-p172
KR-v48-Ap 1 '80-p440
LA-v57-S '80-p650
PW-v217-Je 13 '80-p73
RT-v34-D '80-p354
SLJ-v26-My '80-p68
The Wilder Plot
BL-v79-S 1 '82-p45
CBRS-v11-F '83-p71
CCB-B-v36-O '82-p29
CE-v60-S '83-p52
KR-v50-Ag 1 '82-p868
SLJ-v29-Ja '83-p77
The Witching Hour
BL-v78-N 1 '81-p390
CBRS-v10-Ja '82-p48
SF&FBR-Ap '82-p10
SLJ-v28-D '81-p65
Woodland Crossings
KR-v46-My 1 '78-p497
LA-v56-Ap '79-p443
NYTBR-Ap 30 '78-p46
SLJ-v24-My '78-p69

* * *

KREUSCH-JACOB, Dorothee
Music Workshop
JB-v45-D '81-p247

* * *

KREYE, Walter
Ein Bauer Und Viele Rauber
BL-v77-O 1 '80-p263
The Ragamuffin King
JB-v43-F '79-p19
Sch Lib-v27-Mr '79-p29
Rat Trickery
GP-v18-Jl '79-p3554
JB-v43-Ag '79-p191
Sch Lib-v27-D '79-p348
Spec-v242-Je 30 '79-p26

* * *

KRIPKE, Dorothy K
Let's Talk About Loving
SLJ-v28-O '81-p143
Let's Talk About The Jewish Holidays
LJ-v96-My 15 '71-p1797

* * *

KRISHEF, Robert K
Introducing Country Music
M Ed J-v66-F '80-p29
SLJ-v26-Ap '80-p112
More New Breed Stars
SLJ-v26-Ap '80-p112

* * *

KRISHNAMURTI, G
The Adventures Of Rama
JB-v40-F '76-p46

* * *

KRISTOF, Jane
Steal Away Home
Am-v121-D 13 '69-p594
CCB-B-v23-Je '70-p160
CE-v46-Mr '70-p319
CSM-v61-N 6 '69-pB5
Comw-v93-F 26 '71-p523
GT-v88-Ap '71-p85
KR-v37-Jl 1 '69-p674
LJ-v95-Mr 15 '70-p1196
NO-v8-N 3 '69-p21
NYTBR, pt.2-N 9 '69-p38

* * *

KRISTOS, Kyle
Voodoo
BL-v73-D 15 '76-p606
KR-v44-S 1 '76-p977
SLJ-v23-D '76-p61

* * *

KRIVIN, Felix
Greatgrandmother Universe
SLJ-v30-D '83-p57

* * *

KROEBER, Theodora
Carrousel
CCB-B-v31-F '78-p97
HB-v53-D '77-p664
KR-v45-N 15 '77-p1198
LA-v55-Mr '78-p370
SLJ-v24-N '77-p49
WCRB-v3-N '77-p48
A Green Christmas
BL-v64-D 15 '67-p502
BW-v1-D 10 '67-p502
CCB-B-v21-D '67-p61
HB-v43-D '67-p739
HB-v59-D '83-p752
KR-v35-N 1 '67-p1314
LJ-v92-D 15 '67-p4604
NYTBR-v72-D 3 '67-p68
The Inland Whale
EJ-v63-Ja '74-p71
GP-v15-O '76-p2960
JB-v41-F '77-p39
Obs-D 5 '76-p32
SLJ-v26-N '79-p43
Ishi, Last Of His Tribe
BL-v69-O 15 '72-p178
LJ-v90-Mr 15 '65-p1560
Obs-O 3 '76-p22
TLS-D 6 '74-p1376

* * *

KROG, Inge
Fourteen Days Overdue
B&B-v20-Jl '75-p64
GP-v14-My '75-p2642
Obs-Mr 30 '75-p24
TLS-Ap 4 '75-p361

* * *

KROLL, Steven
Amanda And The Giggling Ghost
BL-v77-O 15 '80-p328
CBRS-v9-O '80-p12
KR-v49-Ja 15 '81-p73
RT-v35-O '81-p57
SLJ-v27-Ja '81-p52
Are You Pirates?
CBRS-v11-Ja '83-p42
KR-v50-O 1 '82-p1103
PW-v222-O 15 '82-p66
SLJ-v29-F '83-p68
Banana Bits
Emerg Lib-v9-My '82-p28
SLJ-v28-My '82-p81
Bathrooms
Emerg Lib-v9-My '82-p28
SLJ-v28-My '82-p80
The Big Bunny And The Easter Eggs
BL-v78-Ap 15 '82-p1096

KROLL, Steven (continued)
CBRS-v10-My '82-p92
CCB-B-v35-Ap '82-p152
Inst-v92-Ap '83-p20
KR-v50-Ap 15 '82-p486
RT-v36-Mr '83-p715
SLJ-v29-Mr '83-p164
The Biggest Pumpkin Ever
BL-v81-S 15 '84-p129
CBRS-v13-O '84-p15
The Candy Witch
BL-v76-N 1 '79-p450
CBRS-v8-N '79-p24
KR-v48-Ja 15 '80-p63
PW-v216-S 17 '79-p145
SLJ-v26-Ja '80-p57
Dirty Feet
CBRS-v9-My '81-p81
CE-v58-My '82-p326
SLJ-v27-My '81-p80
Fat Magic
KR-v46-D 15 '78-p1353
SLJ-v25-N '78-p46
Friday The 13th
BL-v78-Ja 15 '82-p650
CBRS-v10-O '81-p15
KR-v50-F 1 '82-p132
PW-v220-D 11 '81-p63
SLJ-v28-D '81-p85
Giant Journey
CBRS-v9-Ap '81-p74
KR-v49-Jl 1 '81-p797
PW-v219-Je 12 '81-p54
SLJ-v28-O '81-p131
The Goat Parade
CBRS-v11-Ap '83-p89
SLJ-v29-My '83-p89
Gobbledygook
CCB-B-v30-Je '77-p162
KR-v45-Mr 15 '77-p281
PW-v211-My 30 '77-p45
SLJ-v23-My '77-p52
SLJ-v25-N '78-p31
The Hand-Me-Down Doll
CBRS-v12-O '83-p13
CCB-B-v37-D '83-p71
PW-v224-Jl 22 '83-p133
RT-v37-Ap '84-p779
SLJ-v30-Ja '84-p65
If I Could Be My Grandmother
BB-v5-N '77-p2
BL-v74-N 15 '77-p552
CCB-B-v31-My '78-p144
KR-v45-S 15 '77-p986
PW-v212-Ag 22 '77-p66
RT-v32-O '78-p35
SLJ-v24-Ap '78-p72
Is Milton Missing?
BB-v4-Mr '76-p2
BL-v72-O 1 '75-p237
CCB-B-v29-Ja '76-p81
Inst-v85-N '75-p149
JB-v43-Ag '79-p196
KR-v43-Ag 1 '75-p844
PW-v208-Ag 11 '75-p116
SLJ-v22-N '75-p64
Loose Tooth
BL-v80-My 1 '84-p1250
CBRS-v12-Je '84-p112
CCB-B-v37-Jl '84-p207
SLJ-v31-S '84-p106
Monster Birthday
CBRS-v8-Ap '80-p84
CCB-B-v33-Je '80-p194
KR-v48-Jl 15 '80-p907
PW-v217-My 23 '80-p76
SLJ-v26-My '80-p59
One Tough Turkey
BL-v79-O 15 '82-p313
CBRS-v11-O '82-p15
CCB-B-v36-D '82-p71
KR-v50-S 15 '82-p1055
PW-v222-N 12 '82-p66
SLJ-v29-O '82-p142
Otto
CBRS-v11-Ag '83-p143
SLJ-v30-N '83-p65
Pigs In The House
NYTBR-v88-N 13 '83-p51
SLJ-v30-Ap '84-p104
Santa's Crash-Bang Christmas
BB-v5-D '77-p3
BL-v74-S 15 '77-p195
CCB-B-v31-N '77-p49
CE-v54-N '77-p86
HB-v53-D '77-p650
Inst-v87-N '77-p152
KR-v45-S 15 '77-p986
NYTBR-D 11 '77-p26
PW-v212-O 10 '77-p71
SLJ-v24-O '77-p88
SR-v5-N 26 '77-p42
Sleepy Ida And Other Nonsense Poems
CCB-B-v31-O '77-p35
LA-v54-N '77-p951
NYTBR-My 1 '77-p31
SLJ-v24-S '77-p131
SR-v4-My 28 '77-p33
Space Cats
BL-v75-Ap 15 '79-p1296
CBRS-v7-Ap '79-p84
Emerg Lib-v9-S '81-p28
KR-v47-Mr 15 '79-p328
SLJ-v25-Ap '79-p58
T.J. Folger, Thief
KR-v46-Mr 15 '78-p306
LA-v55-S '78-p738
PW-v213-F 13 '78-p127
SLJ-v24-Ap '78-p86
Take It Easy!
B Rpt-v2-Ja '84-p35
BS-v43-My '83-p74
CBRS-v11-Je '83-p116
CCB-B-v37-S '83-p11
KR-v51-F 1 '83-p124
SLJ-v29-Ag '83-p78
VOYA-v6-O '83-p204
That Makes Me Mad!
KR-v44-Ap 15 '76-p463
SB-v12-D '76-p156
SLJ-v22-My '76-p51
Toot! Toot!
BL-v79-My 15 '83-p1218
CBRS-v11-My '83-p98
CCB-B-v37-O '83-p31
Inst-v92-My '83-p92
KR-v51-Mr 15 '83-p305
SLJ-v29-Ag '83-p54
The Tyrannosaurus Game
BL-v72-Mr 15 '76-p1046
CE-v60-My '84-p344
CLW-v48-S '76-p90
HB-v52-Je '76-p281
KR-v44-F 15 '76-p194
NYTBR-My 2 '76-p48
PW-v209-Ap 12 '76-p66
RT-v31-O '77-p14
SLJ-v22-Ap '76-p61
SR-v3-My 15 '76-p37
Woof, Woof!
CBRS-v11-My '83-p100
KR-v51-Mr 1 '83-p243
PW-v223-F 11 '83-p70
SLJ-v30-S '83-p108
WLB-v58-S '83-p51

* * *

KRONENWETTER, Michael
Are You A Liberal? Are You A Conservative?
BL-v80-Jl '84-p1549
CCB-B-v37-Je '84-p188
SLJ-v30-Ag '84-p85

KRUSS, James (continued)
KR-v33-Je 15 '65-p571
LJ-v90-Jl '65-p3121
LJ-v96-Mr 15 '71-p1084
TLS-Je 17 '65-p506
Das U-Boat Fritz
TLS-Mr 25 '77-p353
3 X 3 An Einem Tag
BL-v77-O 1 '80-p263

* * *

KRUUSE, M
Scatty Ricky
JB-v40-F '76-p47

* * *

KRYLOV, Alexei
From The Bonfire To The Reactor
RT-v38-D '84-p338

* * *

KRYLOV, Ivan A
Fifteen Fables Of Krylov
CSM-v57-N 4 '65-pB5
HB-v42-F '66-p55
KR-v33-Jl 15 '65-p673
RT-v35-D '81-p340
Krylov's Fables
RT-v35-D '81-p340

* * *

KUBALKA, Margarete
Abracadabra
GP-v22-S '83-p4144
JB-v47-O '83-p197
TES-Je 3 '83-p44

* * *

KUBIE, Nora Benjamin
Israel
BL-v65-F 1 '69-p597
BL-v71-Je 15 '75-p1076
BL-v75-N 1 '78-p473
CCB-B-v23-O '69-p27
CLW-v41-Ja '70-p322
KR-v36-O 1 '68-p1118
LJ-v94-My 15 '69-p2114
SLJ-v22-S '75-p106
SLJ-v25-D '78-p54

* * *

KUBLER, Arthur
Peter And The Rabbits
CCB-B-v24-Jl '70-p182
CLW-v41-My '70-p593
KR-v37-N 1 '69-p1145
PW-v196-N 3 '69-p49
TLS-Ap 16 '70-p419
Tomaya
CCB-B-v25-N '71-p46
LJ-v96-Je 15 '71-p2126
NS-v81-Mr 5 '71-p314
TLS-Ap 2 '71-p387
TN-v28-N '71-p74

* * *

KUBLER, Suzanne
The Three Friends
GP-v23-Jl '84-p4294

* * *

KUBLER-ROSS, Elisabeth
Remember The Secret
CCB-B-v35-Je '82-p191
New Age-v7-Ap '82-p68
New Age-v7-Je '82-p71
PW-v221-Mr 5 '82-p71
SLJ-v29-F '83-p68

* * *

KUBLY, Herbert
Switzerland
CCB-B-v19-O '65-p35

* * *

KUCHALLA, Susan
All About Seeds
ASBYP-v15-Fall '82-p57
BL-v78-Je 1 '82-p1311
SB-v18-S '82-p33
SLJ-v28-Ag '82-p95
Baby Animals
ASBYP-v15-Fall '82-p57
SB-v18-Ja '83-p146
SLJ-v28-Ag '82-p95
Bears
ASBYP-v15-Fall '82-p57
BL-v78-Je 1 '82-p1311
SB-v18-N '82-p92
SLJ-v28-Ag '82-p95
Birds
ASBYP-v15-Fall '82-p57
BL-v78-Je 1 '82-p1311
SLJ-v28-Ag '82-p95
Now I Know Bears
SLJ-v30-Ag '84-p37
What Is A Reptile
ASBYP-v15-Fall '82-p57
SLJ-v28-Ag '82-p95

* * *

KUDRNA, C Imbior
Two-Way Words
Cur R-v20-Je '81-p244
SLJ-v27-Ag '81-p56

* * *

KUIJER, Guus
Daisy's New Head
Sch Lib-v29-Mr '81-p33
TES-N 28 '80-p25

* * *

KUJOTH, Jean Spealman
The Boys' And Girls' Book Of Clubs And Organizations
ARBA-v7-'76-p344
BL-v71-Jl 15 '75-p1192
SLJ-v22-S '75-p106

* * *

KUKLIN, Susan
Mine For A Year
BL-v81-S 1 '84-p67
CCB-B-v37-Jl '84-p207
HB-v60-S '84-p607
NYTBR-v89-Jl 1 '84-p23
SLJ-v31-O '84-p158

* * *

KULAS, Jim E
Puppy's 1-2-3 Book
CE-v61-S '84-p33

* * *

KULLMAN, Harry
The Battle Horse
BL-v77-Jl 15 '81-p1448
CBRS-v9-Je '81-p97
CCB-B-v35-O '81-p32
EJ-v72-Ja '83-p26
HB-v57-O '81-p543
KR-v49-Jl 1 '81-p805
SLJ-v27-My '81-p74
SLJ-v31-O '84-p109
VOYA-v4-O '81-p34
VOYA-v4-D '81-p32

* * *

KUMAR, Chandra
Mahatma Gandhi: His Life And Influence
B&B-F '83-p18
Brit Bk N-My '83-p334
HT-v33-Ap '83-p60
TES-D 10 '82-p22

* * *

KUMIN, Maxine
Joey And The Birthday Present
BL-v68-O 15 '71-p204
CCB-B-v25-O '71-p28
CE-v48-N '71-p100
GT-v89-F '72-p78

KUMIN, Maxine (continued)
HB-v47-D '71-p605
LJ-v96-O 15 '71-p3460
NY-v47-D 4 '71-p187
The Microscope
CBRS-v13-S '84-p5
PW-v226-S 7 '84-p78
Par-v59-N '84-p53
SLJ-v31-O '84-p149
What Color Is Caesar?
BL-v74-My 15 '78-p1495
CCB-B-v32-D '78-p65
NYTBR-Ap 23 '78-p32
PW-v213-Ap 17 '78-p76
SLJ-v25-S '78-p119
WCRB-v4-My '78-p54
WLB-v52-Je '78-p802
When Grand-mother Was Young
CCB-B-v23-F '70-p99
KR-v37-Je 15 '69-p629
LJ-v94-S 15 '69-p3206
When Great-Grandmother Was Young
KR-v39-F 1 '71-p102
LJ-v97-Ap 15 '72-p1598
RT-v35-My '82-p901
When Mother Was Young
CCB-B-v24-O '70-p29
KR-v38-F 1 '70-p100
SR-v53-My 9 '70-p43
The Wizard's Tears
BB-v3-N '75-p2
CCB-B-v29-F '76-p99
HB-v51-D '75-p587
KR-v43-Ag 15 '75-p911
LA-v53-My '76-p501
PW-v208-S 15 '75-p60
SLJ-v22-N '75-p64
SLJ-v22-D '75-p31
WLB-v50-Ap '76-p643
Wonderful Babies Of 1809
CCB-B-v22-S '68-p10
LJ-v93-O 15 '00-p3971

* * *

KUNHARDT, Dorothy Meserve
Kitty's New Doll
PW-v225-Je 15 '84-p82
Pat The Bunny
BW-My 14 '78-pG2
LATBR-O 21 '84-p6
New R-v177-D 3 '77-p26
RT-v37-My '84-p857
Pudding Is Nice
PW-v208-N 17 '75-p97
SR-v3-N 29 '75-p33

* * *

KUNHARDT, Edith
Pat The Cat
PW-v226-Jl 6 '84-p64

* * *

KUNNAS, Mauri
The Best Sports Book In The Whole World
CCB-B-v37-Jl '84-p208
SLJ-v31-S '84-p106
Santa Claus And His Elves
BL-v79-Mr 15 '83-p970
BW-v12-D 12 '82-p8
CBRS-v11-F '83-p66
JB-v47-F '83-p28

* * *

KUNZ, Virginia Brainard
Germans In America
CCB-B-v20-N '66-p44
LJ-v91-O 15 '66-p5250

* * *

KUO Yu Yueh Pao
Erh Tang K'o Hsieh Tu Wu Hsien Chi
BL-v74-Mr 1 '78-p1112

* * *

KUPERMAN, Larissa
The Story Of Plucky
In Rev-v15-Ap '81-p42

* * *

KUPFERBERG, Herbert
A Rainbow Of Sound
BL-v70-N 15 '73-p340
HB-v50-F '74-p61
Inst-v83-F '74-p152
KR-v41-O 15 '73-p1167
LJ-v98-D 15 '73-p3707
M Ed J-v61-Ja '75-p75
PW-v204-N 12 '73-p36

* * *

KUPPER, Mike
Driven To Win
SLJ-v22-Mr '76-p105

* * *

KURATOMI, Chizuko
Helpful Mr. Bear
KR-v36-Mr 1 '68-p255
LJ-v93-Ap 15 '68-p1790
Jamu Jamu Donkuma-San
BL-v79-O 15 '82-p320
Mr. Bear And Apple Jam
Lis-v90-N 8 '73-p644
TLS-N 23 '73-p1441
Mr. Bear And The Robbers
BB-v3-Ja '76-p2
BL-v71-N 15 '74-p344
BW-F 9 '75-p4
CCB-B-v28-Je '75-p162
CSM-v67-My 7 '75-pB6
HB-v51-Ag '75-p370
KR-v42-D 15 '74-p1300
LA-v52-N '75-p1164
PW-v206-D 2 '74-p63
SLJ-v21-Ja '75-p40
Spec-v227-N 13 '71-p700
TLS-O 22 '71-p1325
Teacher-v93-Ap '76-p114
WLB-v49-Mr '75-p522
Mr. Bear, Babyminder
Lis-v96-N 11 '76-p626
Mr. Bear, Baker
TLS-N 20 '81-p1359
Mr. Bear Goes To Sea
PW-v198-D 7 '70-p50
TES-Ap 27 '84-p27
TLS-O 3 '68-p1116
Mr. Bear In The Air
LJ-v96-O 15 '71-p3460
Spec-v223-N 1 '69-p606
TLS-D 4 '69-p1397
Mr. Bear, Postman
GP-v18-N '79-p3611
TES-Ap 25 '80-p25
Mr. Bear's Drawing
JB-v40-F '76-p16
Spec-v235-D 6 '75-p735
Mr. Bear's Journey
JB-v48-F '84-p15
Mr. Bear's Meal
NS-v96-N 3 '78-p593
Obs-D 10 '78-p38
Mr. Bear's Trumpet
LJ-v96-My 15 '71-p1797
PW-v198-D 7 '70-p50
Spectr-v47-Mr '71-p44
TLS-D 11 '70-p1462
Mr. Bear's Winter Sleep
GP-v21-Mr '83-p4047
Mr Bear, Station-Master
TLS-D 8 '72-p1495
Remember Mr. Bear
TLS-Je 6 '68-p586

* * *

KURELEK, William
Fields
BL-v72-Jl 15 '76-p1564
BL-v72-Jl 15 '76-p1596

KURELEK, William (continued)
The Last Of The Arctic
BL-v73-Ap 1 '77-p1150
SLJ-v27-S '80-p43
Lumberjack
BL-v71-S 1 '74-p44
BL-v71-Mr 15 '75-p767
BL-v72-S 15 '75-p173
CCB-B-v28-Ap '75-p132
Choice-v12-N '75-p1133
HB-v50-D '74-p684
Inst-v84-My '75-p105
JB-v42-F '78-p44
KR-v42-N 1 '74-p1155
KR-v43-Ja 1 '75-p7
LA-v53-My '76-p503
NYT-v124-D 12 '74-p45
NYTBR-N 3 '74-p29
NYTBR-N 3 '74-p54
NYTBR-D 1 '74-p76
PW-v206-O 7 '74-p63
SE-v43-O '79-p476
SLJ-v21-Ja '75-p47
SLJ-v27-S '80-p43
SN-v91-Je '76-p71
TLS-O 21 '77-p1245
Time-v104-D 23 '74-p73
A Northern Nativity
BL-v73-F 1 '77-p835
BW-D 5 '76-pH5
CCB-B-v30-F '77-p93
CE-v54-O '77-p31
Can Child Lit-#14 '79-p46
HB-v53-Ap '77-p151
KR-v44-N 15 '76-p1225
NYTBR-D 12 '76-p35
PW-v211-Ja 3 '77-p69
SE-v43-O '79-p476
SLJ-v23-O '76-p87
A Prairie Boy's Summer
BL-v71-Je 1 '75-p1014
CCB-B-v28-Jl '75-p179
CE-v52-O '75-p38
Comw-v102-N 21 '75-p570
HB-v51-Ag '75-p381
HB-v60-Je '84-p379
KR-v43-Ap 15 '75-p462
NYTBR-My 4 '75-p38
NYTBR-N 16 '75-p56
SE-v43-O '79-p476
SLJ-v22-S '75-p106
SLJ-v27-S '80-p43
SN-v91-Je '76-p71
SR-v2-My 31 '75-p34
TLS-Mr 25 '77-p355
A Prairie Boy's Winter
BL-v70-Ja 15 '74-p543
BL-v72-S 15 '75-p173
CCB-B-v27-Mr '74-p112
CE-v50-Ap '74-p340
CSM-v66-My 1 '74-pF2
GP-v15-D '76-p3030
HB-v49-O '73-p456
HB-v60-Je '84-p379
JB-v41-O '77-p280
KR-v41-O 15 '73-p1160
KR-v41-D 15 '73-p1350
LJ-v98-O 15 '73-p3147
NYT-v123-D 10 '73-p35
NYTBR-N 4 '73-p57
NYTBR-D 2 '73-p79
NYTBR-D 9 '73-p8
Obs-N 21 '76-p31
PW-v204-O 1 '73-p82
SE-v43-O '79-p476
SLJ-v27-S '80-p43
SLMQ-v11-Spring '83-p192
SN-v89-Ap '74-p42
SN-v91-Je '76-p71
TLS-Mr 25 '77-p355
TN-v30-Ap '74-p308
TN-v34-Winter '78-p189
Teacher-v91-F '74-p100
Teacher-v92-D '74-p13

* * *

KURTEN, Bjorn
The Cave Bear Story
BL-v73-N 15 '76-p440
Choice-v14-Mr '77-p87
LJ-v101-Je 1 '76-p1299
SA-v235-D '76-p136
SB-v13-My '77-p19
TLS-Ap 29 '77-p526

* * *

KURTH, H
Canals
JB-v41-Ap '77-p115
Echo-Location
JB-v40-D '76-p346
Glass
JB-v39-F '75-p42
Tides
JB-v39-Ap '75-p109

* * *

KURTH, Heinz
At The Airport
Inst-v86-N '76-p158
SB-v12-D '76-p157
Bridges
JB-v40-Ap '76-p93
Build A House
GP-v14-N '75-p2740
NS-v91-My 21 '76-p688
Computers
Brit Bk N C-Autumn '80-p7
JB-v45-F '81-p29
Sch Lib-v29-Mr '81-p40
TES-O 24 '80-p22
Down The River
NS-v91-My 21 '76-p688
SB-v12-D '76-p162
Food For Keeps
GP-v18-My '79-p3528
Houses And Homes
GP-v19-S '80-p3762
JB-v44-Ag '80-p178
Sch Lib-v28-S '80-p279
A Night In Town
GP-v17-S '78-p3397
Spec-v240-Ap 29 '78-p25
TES-N 3 '78-p23
Print A Book
NS-v91-My 21 '76-p688
Robots
GP-v22-N '83-p4165
Submarine
JB-v43-F '79-p33
TES-O 20 '78-p39
Textiles
GP-v16-N '77-p3212
JB-v41-D '77-p335
TES-N 11 '77-p23
Windpower
GP-v17-S '78-p3397
JB-v42-O '78-p256

* * *

KURTIS, Arlene Harris
Puerto Ricans, From Island To Mainland
BL-v66-S 15 '69-p138
BL-v69-Ja 15 '73-p479
CCB-B-v22-Je '69-p160
KR-v37-Ap 1 '69-p380
SR-v52-My 10 '69-p58

* * *

KURTYCZ, Marcos
De Tigres Y Tlacuaches
BL-v79-F 15 '83-p783
Tigers And Opossums
BL-v80-Ag '84-p1626
CBRS-v13-S '84-p5
SLJ-v31-S '84-p98

* * *

KURTZ, Carmen
Oscar En Africa
BL-v73-D 1 '76-p547
EJ-v66-Mr '77-p51
Oscar Y Corazon De Purpura
BL-v73-D 1 '76-p548

* * *

KURTZ, Henry Ira
Captain John Smith
BL-v72-Mr 1 '76-p978
Inst-v85-My '76-p113
KR-v44-Ja 15 '76-p76
SE-v41-Ap '77-p346
SLJ-v22-Ap '76-p75

* * *

KURTZ, Irma
The Children's Guide To Paris
GP-v23-Jl '84-p4288
TES-N 16 '84-p23
The Children's Guide To Rome
GP-v23-Jl '84-p4288
TES-N 16 '84-p23

* * *

KURUSA
El Burrito Y La Tuna
BL-v81-O 1 '84-p256
La Calle Es Libre
BL-v79-Ap 1 '83-p1024
BL-v79-Jl '83-p1407
Nowhere To Play
GP-v21-Ja '83-p4016
JB-v47-F '83-p27
Sch Lib-v31-Mr '83-p25
TES-F 4 '83-p28
El Rabipelado Burlado
BL-v81-O 1 '84-p256
El Tigre Y El Rayo
BL-v79-F 1 '83-p721
BL-v79-F 15 '83-p784

* * *

KUSAN, Ivan
The Mystery Of Green Hill
GT-v88-Ap '71-p85
RT-v33-F '80-p564
The Mystery Of The Stolen Painting
HB-v51-Ag '75-p381
KR-v43-Ap 15 '75-p454
SLJ-v21-My '75-p70

* * *

KUSE, James A
Bunny Tales
SLJ-v26-S '79-p104

* * *

KUSHNER, Donn
The Violin-Maker's Gift
BIC-v9-D '80-p19
BL-v78-Jl '82-p1445
BW-v12-My 9 '82-p23
CBRS-v10-Je '82-p107
CCB-B-v35-Je '82-p191
GP-v20-Jl '81-p3924
In Rev-v15-Ap '81-p43
JB-v45-Ag '81-p151
LA-v60-F '83-p217
PW-v221-Ap 9 '82-p51
Quill & Q-v47-My '81-p14
SLJ-v29-S '82-p123
WSJ-v200-D 7 '82-p32

* * *

KUSKIN, Karla
All Sizes Of Noises
LA-v56-N '79-p938
Any Me I Want To Be
BL-v69-F 15 '73-p573
CCB-B-v26-F '73-p94
CLW-v44-F '73-p449
CSM-v64-N 8 '72-pB2
KR-v40-S 15 '72-p1103
LA-v56-N '79-p939
LJ-v98-Ja 15 '73-p254
NYTBR, pt.2-N 5 '72-p32
SR-v55-O 14 '72-p82
A Boy Had A Mother Who Bought Him A Hat
BL-v73-D 1 '76-p542
CCB-B-v30-F '77-p94
CE-v53-Mr '77-p258
HB-v52-D '76-p635
KR-v44-Ag 15 '76-p904
NYTBR-F 27 '77-p12
PW-v210-D 27 '76-p60
SLJ-v23-D '76-p50
Dogs And Dragons, Trees And Dreams
BW-v11-Mr 8 '81-p10
CCB-B-v34-My '81-p174
CLW-v52-F '81-p309
Emerg Lib-v9-Mr '82-p33
HB-v57-F '81-p62
Inst-v90-N '80-p156
KR-v49-F 1 '81-p143
LA-v58-Ap '81-p478
NYTBR-v85-N 9 '80-p51
RT-v36-Ja '83-p381
Time-v116-D 29 '80-p65
Herbert Hated Being Small
BL-v76-O 1 '79-p279
CBRS-v8-Ja '80-p42
CCB-B-v33-Mr '80-p136
KR-v47-N 1 '79-p1257
SLJ-v26-O '79-p142
Time-v114-D 3 '79-p100
Near The Window Tree
BL-v72-S 1 '75-p42
CCB-B-v29-D '75-p65
CLW-v47-O '75-p132
CSM-v67-My 7 '75-pB8
KR-v43-Ap 15 '75-p462
LA-v56-N '79-p939
NYTBR-My 4 '75-p24
RSR-v3-Jl '75-p29
RT-v29-F '76-p515
SLJ-v22-N '75-p64
Teacher-v92-My '75-p31
Time-v106-D 8 '75-p87
Night Again
CCB-B-v34-My '81-p174
KR-v49-Ap 15 '81-p500
NYTBR-v86-Ap 26 '81-p71
PW-v219-Ap 10 '81-p70
SLJ-v27-My '81-p57
The Philharmonic Gets Dressed
BL-v79-Ja 1 '83-p618
CBRS-v11-S '82-p3
CCB-B-v36-S '82-p14
CE-v59-Mr '83-p278
HB-v58-O '82-p515
Inst-v92-Mr '83-p19
KR-v50-Jl 15 '82-p795
LA-v60-My '83-p645
LA-v61-Ap '84-p419
LATBR-O 17 '82-p6
NY-v58-D 6 '82-p185
NYT-v132-N 30 '82-p23
NYTBR-v87-O 17 '82-p37
PW-v222-Jl 23 '82-p132
RT-v36-Mr '83-p716
RT-v37-Ap '84-p705
SLJ-v28-Ag '82-p99
Time-v120-D 20 '82-p79
WCRB-v8-N '82-p67
WLB-v57-F '83-p505
Roar And More
NYTBR-O 16 '77-p55
RT-v32-N '78-p148
SLJ-v25-My '79-p39
Teacher-v95-My '78-p104

KUSKIN, Karla (continued)
Sand And Snow
KR-v33-O 1 '65-p1038
RT-v32-N '78-p148
A Space Story
ACSB-v13-Winter '80-p2
ASBYP-v15-Spring '82-p14
Am-v139-D 9 '78-p440
CCB-B-v32-Mr '79-p121
KR-v47-Ja 1 '79-p3
LA-v56-Ap '79-p441
PW-v214-O 9 '78-p76
SA-v241-D '79-p40
SB-v15-D '79-p164
SLJ-v25-D '78-p45
SLJ-v26-Mr '80-p105
Time-v112-D 4 '78-p101
Watson
CCB-B-v22-O '68-p30
KR-v36-My 1 '68-p508
LJ-v93-O 15 '68-p3956
PW-v193-Ap 8 '68-p51
YR-v4-Je '68-p11
Which Horse Is William?
CLW-v55-O '83-p131

* * *

KUSNICK, Barry A
The Boatman's Bible
HB-v54-Je '78-p315
SLJ-v24-N '77-p84
Yacht-v143-Ap '78-p154

* * *

KWASNIEWSKA, E
Czy To Pies, Czy To Bies?
BL-v73-S 15 '76-p184

* * *

KWITZ, Mary DeBall
Little Chick's Big Day
BL-v77-Mr 15 '81-p1037
CCB-B-v34-Je '81-p197
CLW-v53-O '81-p141
Inst-v90-My '81-p59
KR-v49-Ap 1 '81-p430
LA-v59-Mr '82-p269
SLJ-v27-My '81-p82
TES-Jl 1 '83-p26
Little Chick's Breakfast
KR-v51-S 1 '83-pJ157
PW-v224-N 18 '83-p71
SLJ-v30-D '83-p79
Little Chick's Story
BL-v74-My 15 '78-p1498
KR-v46-Mr 15 '78-p303
NYTBR-Ap 30 '78-p31
SLJ-v24-My '78-p81
Rabbits' Search For A Little House
KR-v45-N 1 '77-p1142
PW-v212-N 14 '77-p66
SLJ-v24-Ja '78-p79
The Secret World
CCB-B-v25-Ap '72-p125
LJ-v97-Jl '72-p2478
SB-v7-Mr '72-p311
When It Rains
CCB-B-v28-O '74-p31
CE-v51-N '74-p96
LJ-v99-S 15 '74-p2250
SB-v10-D '74-p257

* * *

KWOLEK, Constance
Loner
CCB-B-v24-Mr '71-p108
KR-v38-Jl 1 '70-p689
LJ-v95-O 15 '70-p3638

* * *

KYLE, Elisabeth
Duet
BL-v65-N 1 '68-p306
CCB-B-v22-Ap '69-p128
HB-v44-O '68-p570
KR-v36-S 15 '68-p1059
LJ-v93-N 15 '68-p4405
PW-v194-O 14 '68-p65
TLS-Mr 14 '68-p262
TN-v25-Ap '69-p310
YR-v5-N '68-p15
Great Ambitions
BL-v64-Ap 1 '68-p928
BS-v27-Mr 1 '68-p466
CCB-B-v21-Mr '68-p112
Comw-v88-My 24 '68-p302
HB-v44-Ap '68-p190
KR-v35-D 15 '67-p1480
NO-v7-Ag 26 '68-p17
NYTBR-v73-Je 23 '68-p22
The Key Of The Castle
JB-v41-Ap '77-p96
Princess Of Orange
BL-v63-S 1 '66-p54
CCB-B-v20-S '66-p14
CLW-v38-Ja '67-p340
Comw-v85-N 11 '66-p176
HB-v42-Ag '66-p442
KR-v34-Ap 1 '66-p379
LJ-v91-My 15 '66-p2708
NYTBR-v71-Jl 31 '66-p18
Song Of The Waterfall
CCB-B-v23-Je '70-p161
CLW-v41-Ap '70-p536
HB-v45-D '69-p683
KR-v37-D 1 '69-p1272
LJ-v95-Ap 15 '70-p1652
LR-v22-Autumn '70-p383
NS-v80-N 6 '70-p613

* * *

KYTE, Dennis
The Last Elegant Bear
NY-v60-D 3 '84-p187
PW-v223-My 27 '83-p47
PW-v224-N 11 '83-p48

* * *

KYTE, Kathy S
In Charge
B Rpt-v2-S '83-p44
CBRS-v11-Spring '83-p125
CCB-B-v36-Ap '83-p154
CE-v60-N '83-p140
HB-v59-Je '83-p322
Inst-v92-My '83-p93
J Read-v27-Mr '84-p563
KR-v51-My 15 '83-p581
RT-v37-D '83-p309
SLJ-v29-My '83-p72
VOYA-v6-Ag '83-p153
WCRB-v9-S '83-p67
Play It Safe
BL-v80-F 15 '84-p859
CBRS-v12-Mr '84-p85
PW-v224-N 11 '83-p48
SLJ-v30-Mr '84-p161
VOYA-v7-Je '84-p110

* * *

KYTLE, Calvin
Gandhi: Soldier Of Nonviolence
Am-v121-N 22 '69-p502
BL-v66-Ja 1 '70-p560
BL-v79-Je 1 '83-p1266
BS-v42-F '83-p446
BW-v13-F 6 '83-p4
CC-v86-D 10 '69-p1585
CC-v100-Ag 17 '83-p756
LATBR-Ja 16 '83-p3
LJ-v95-Ja 15 '70-p254
PW-v196-Jl 21 '69-p55
TN-v35-Summer '79-p403
WCRB-v9-Ja '83-p35

(Continued from front endsheets)

JLH	Journal of Library History, Philosophy, and Comparative Librarianship
JMF	Journal of Marriage and the Family
JNE	Journal of Negro Education
JNH	Journal of Negro History
JPC	Journal of Popular Culture (1976)
JPE	Journal of Political Economy
J Phil	Journal of Philosophy
J Pol	Journal of Politics
JQ	Journalism Quarterly (1976)
J Read	Journal of Reading (1976)
JSH	Journal of Southern History (1973)
Ken R	Kenyon Reivew
KR	Kirkus Reviews
Kliatt	Kliatt Young Adult Paperback Book Guide (1977)
LA	Language Arts (Formerly Elementary English)
LATBR	Los Angeles Times Book Review (1982)
LJ	Library Journal
LL	Lifelong Learning (1977)
LQ	Library Quarterly
LR	Library Review
LW	Living Wilderness
Learning	Learning: the Magazine for Creative Teaching (1984)
Lib	The Library
Lib Brow	Librarians' Browser (1981)
Life	Life
Lis	Listener
Lon R Bks	London Review of Books (1982)
MA	Modern Age
MEJ	Middle East Journal
M Ed J	Music Educators Journal
MFS	Modern Fiction Studies (1977)
MFSF	Magazine of Fantasy and Science Fiction
MLJ	Modern Language Journal
MLR	Modern Language Review
M Lab R	Monthly Labor Review (1975)
MN	Museum News
MP	Modern Philology
M Photo	Modern Photography (1977)
Mac	Maclean's (1978)
Mag Lib	Magazines for Libraries, 4th Ed.
Mag YA	Magazines for Young Adults (1984)
Man	Mankind (1978)
Money	Money (1972)
Ms	Ms. (1974)
NAR	North American Review (1976)
NASSP-B	National Association of Secondary School Principals. Bulletin
NBR	New Boston Review (1978)
NCR	National Civic Review
NCW	New Catholic World (Formerly Catholic World)
ND	Negro Digest
N Dir Wom	New Directions for Women (1984)
NEQ	New England Quarterly
NGSQ	National Genealogical Society Quarterly (1977)
NH	Natural History
NHB	Negro History Bulletin
NL	New Leader
NMR	New Magazine Review (1979)
NO	National Observer
NP	National Parks
NS	New Statesman
NT	New Times (1977)
NW	Newsweek
NY	New Yorker
NYRB	New York Review of Books
NYT	New York Times (Daily)
NYTBR	New York Times Book Review
NYTBR, pt. 1	New York Times Book Review, Pt. 1
NYTBR, pt. 2	New York Times Book Review, Pt. 2
Nat	Nation
Nat For	National Forum (1979)
Nat R	National Review
Nature	Nature (1982)
New Age	New Age Journal (1981)
New Pages	New Pages (1984)
New R	New Republic
Notes	Notes (Music Library Association)
ON	Opera News (1975)
Obs	Observer (London)
PAR	Public Administration Review
P&R	Parks and Recreation
PGJ	Personnel and Guidance Journal
PHR	Pacific Historical Review
PJ	Personnel Journal
PQ	Philological Quarterly
PR	Partisan Review
PS	Prairie Schooner
PSQ	Political Science Quarterly
PT	Psychology Today (1973)
PW	Publishers Weekly
Pac A	Pacific Affairs
Par	Parents Magazine
Parabola	Parabola: Myth and the Quest for Meaning (1983)
Parnassus	Parnassus: Poetry in Review (1979)
Perspec	Perspective (1981)
Pet PM	Petersen's Photographic Magazine (1978)
Phi D K	Phi Delta Kappan (1979)
Phylon	Phylon (1976)
Poet	Poetry
Prog	Progressive (1969)
Punch	Punch
QJS	Quarterly Journal of Speech
Quill & Q	Quill & Quire (Canada 1980)
RA	Reviews in Anthropology (1975)
RAH	Reviews in American History (1975)
RES	Review of English Studies
RM	Review of Metaphysics
RMR	Rocky Mountain Review (1981)
RQ	RQ
RR	Review for Religious
RS	Rolling Stone (1976)
RSR	Reference Services Review (1973)
RT	Reading Teacher (1976)
Refl	Reflections . . . The Wanderer Review of Literature, Culture, the Arts (1983)